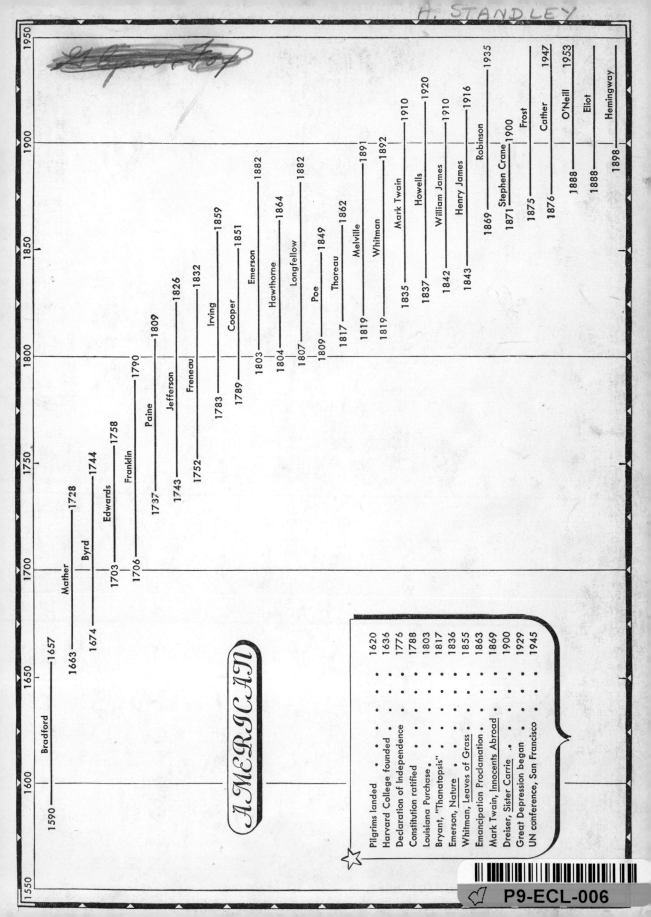

AMERICAN

Pilgrims landed	1620
Harvard College founded	1636
Declaration of Independence	1776
Constitution ratified	1788
Louisiana Purchase	1803
Bryant, "Thanatopsis"	1817
Emerson, Nature	1836
Whitman, Leaves of Grass	1855
Emancipation Proclamation	1863
Mark Twain, Innocents Abroad	1869
Dreiser, Sister Carrie	1900
Great Depression began	1929
UN conference, San Francisco	1945

Timeline (top axis): 1550 — 1600 — 1650 — 1700 — 1750 — 1800 — 1850 — 1900 — 1950

Authors and dates:
- Bradford 1590 – 1657
- Mather 1663 – 1728
- Byrd 1674 – 1744
- Edwards 1703 – 1758
- Franklin 1706 – 1790
- Paine 1737 – 1809
- Jefferson 1743 – 1826
- Freneau 1752 – 1832
- Irving 1783 – 1859
- Cooper 1789 – 1851
- Emerson 1803 – 1882
- Hawthorne 1804 – 1864
- Longfellow 1807 – 1882
- Poe 1809 – 1849
- Thoreau 1817 – 1862
- Melville 1819 – 1891
- Whitman 1819 – 1892
- Mark Twain 1835 – 1910
- Howells 1837 – 1920
- William James 1842 – 1910
- Henry James 1843 – 1916
- Robinson 1869 – 1935
- Stephen Crane 1871 – 1900
- Frost 1875 – 1947
- Cather 1876 – 1947
- O'Neill 1888 – 1953
- Eliot 1888 –
- Hemingway 1898 –

UNDER THE GENERAL EDITORSHIP OF

Robert Morss Lovett

Professor Emeritus of English, University of Chicago

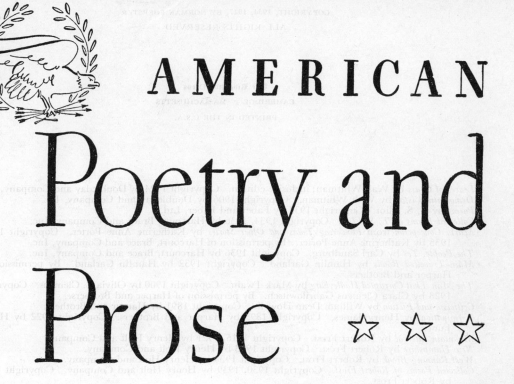

AMERICAN

Poetry and

Prose ☆☆☆

Edited by Norman Foerster

SHORTER EDITION, *prepared with supplementary notes*

by William Charvat, *Ohio State University*

HOUGHTON MIFFLIN COMPANY

Boston · New York · Chicago · Dallas · Atlanta · San Francisco

The Riverside Press Cambridge

The Riverside Press

CAMBRIDGE · MASSACHUSETTS

PRINTED IN THE U.S.A.

PREFACE TO THE SHORTER EDITION

★ ★

THE OBJECTIVES of this new edition of Norman Foerster's standard anthology are two: to provide a smaller text for use in short courses in American literature; and to offer further critical guidance to students in an entirely new section called "Supplementary Notes." The plan of these notes is described at the beginning of the section (page 877); but the policy I have followed in cutting authors and selections needs some explanation here.

It is assumed that, in a short course in American literature, teachers and students will wish to devote the time at their disposal to major authors and to works of acknowledged literary quality rather than to that marginal literature which is valuable chiefly as illustration of intellectual, social, and cultural trends. I have, therefore, deleted most of those authors and selections whose worth is mainly historical. For example, I have sacrificed Cotton Mather in order to give full representation to Jonathan Edwards; John Fiske in favor of Whitman; minor humorists in favor of Mark Twain. The loss is not too serious, for the great writer in any period sums up much of what his lesser contemporaries attempt to say. Occasionally, however, a minor writer expresses an idea or an ideal better than anyone else; for this reason I have retained such documents as Crèvecoeur's "What is an American?" and the *Federalist* papers. I have tried, further, to accord to major writers the relatively large representation which they are given in the full edition.

In accord with recent and increasing critical recognition of Edith Wharton and F. Scott Fitzgerald, I have added stories by these writers. I have also made some substitutions in the selections from Edward Taylor, Philip Freneau, and Wallace Stevens, and have added more lyrics by Emily Dickinson.

The sections have been somewhat reorganized. "Puritanism" and "Rationalism" have been brought together, as have "The Rise of Realism" and "Realism and Naturalism." "The Twentieth Century" writers now appear under that heading because the terms "Realism" and "Naturalism" begin less and less adequately to describe the diverse tendencies and tones of the literature of our time. The introductory essays for these sections have been revised, and some of the author headnotes, particularly in their bibliographical aspects, have been modified to bring them up to date.

WILLIAM CHARVAT

FROM THE PREFACE TO THE THIRD EDITION

* *

AMERICAN LITERATURE has become one of the leading national literatures of the modern world. In sober fact, without chauvinism, it may be said that Poe and Emerson, Hawthorne and Melville, Whitman and Mark Twain and Henry James were surpassed, in their century, in few countries, and that in the twentieth century, especially in the period between the wars, American writers showed a fresh creative impulse not equaled by those of England or perhaps any other land. We have, of course, no older classics, no Dante or Molière, no Chaucer or Shakespeare. Yet our literature clearly has a claim upon attention because of its value as literature — its evocation of imaginative forms, its varied and penetrating comment on human life. It also has a claim because of its revelation of the development of the American mind, of the enduring and changing aspects of our intellectual and spiritual condition.

These claims have been increasingly recognized in the curricula of our colleges and universities. Students and instructors alike have experienced a growing interest in American literature, both as literature and, even more, as a means to national self-knowledge. Between 1890 and 1918 American literature became the subject of an established course in a majority of our institutions. Today the course is offered in virtually all colleges, and more detailed courses are offered in many graduate schools.

Along with educational experience has come growth in scholarship. Great progress has been made since Barrett Wendell's *Literary History of America* and William P. Trent's *History of American Literature*, which appeared nearly half a century ago. The limits of interpretation in those days are suggested by the manner in which the subject was outlined. Wendell wrote on The Seventeenth Century, The Eighteenth Century, The Nineteenth Century, Literature in the Middle States from 1789 to 1857, The Renaissance of New England, and The Rest of the Story. His history, it has been said, is little more than an account of Harvard College in relation to American literature. Trent divided the subject into The Colonial Period, The Revolutionary Period, The Formative Period, and The Sectional Period. Though writing in 1903, he found it necessary to end at 1865; indeed, he even apologized for including 1830 to 1865, on the ground that this period forced him to treat "tentatively and to a certain extent in impressionist fashion authors who have seemed almost a part of our generation."

In the years since these works appeared, the field of American literature has been widely cultivated. We have had the valuable *Cambridge History of American Literature;* we have had Parrington's substantial survey of American thought; we have had no end of special studies of periods, authors, forms, ideas, etc. We have had such literary critics as W. C. Brownell, Paul E. More, H. S. Canby, Van Wyck Brooks (*America's Coming-of-Age*), Lewis Mumford (*The Golden Day*), and F. O. Matthiessen. We have had more and more historical specialists, we have had the American Literature Group of the Modern Language Association, we have had the learned journal *American Literature*, we are on the verge of securing a new collaborative literary history of the United States by our best scholars. Thanks to the development of criticism, scholarship, and instruction, we are now in a far better position to estimate the achievement of the United States in literature, and to understand the historical growth of that literature as a main feature of American civilization.

To register this progress in terms of a college textbook, and if possible to add something to it by a fresh effort to see essential meanings and values, is the object of the third edition of the present work. If the new edition is markedly different from the first and second, it is largely because scholars know more and understand better. Yet the governing intention is exactly that stated in the preface to the first edition, published in 1925: "To provide materials for a study of (1) the literary achievement of our writers, especially of the major writers of all periods, and (2) the historical development of our literature." . . . .

I have never omitted standard literature because it seemed hackneyed, and I have never included novelties because they seemed fresh and attractive. I have tried not to ride any hobbies, nor to allow my "personal estimate" to play a part. I have aimed only to be loyal to the subject, which is American literature, to the student who is to experience and understand it, and to the instructor who is to guide the student in experiencing and understanding it.

Headnotes, bibliography, and mechanics. In writing the headnotes on authors I have sought to be objective, not by giving biographical facts in a random and aimless manner, but by presenting them in a way that would suggest their significance — the kind of personality, mind, and achievement they point to. As an appendix I have included an "American Civilization" bibliography, selected and arranged in harmony with the aims and organization of the book.

As in previous editions, dates of publication below the titles are in ordinary type, dates of composition in italic type. Subtitles for which I am responsible are printed in italic type within brackets. Omissions from the text for which I am responsible are marked with asterisks; omissions made by editors of the standard texts are indicated by extra periods.

NORMAN FOERSTER

CONTENTS

* *

Puritanism and Rationalism

The Romantic Movement

Realism and Naturalism

The Twentieth Century

LIST OF ILLUSTRATIONS

Puritanism and Rationalism

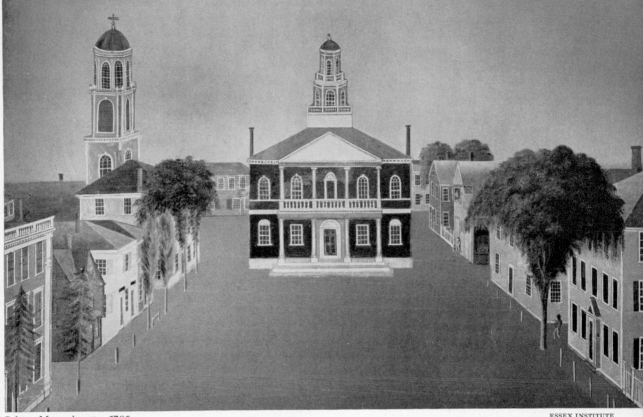

Salem, Massachusetts, 1785

Monticello, Virginia

The architecture of prosperous eighteenth-century Salem, like other aspects of the culture of the region, represents American adaptation of British forms.

In finding analogies between the new republic and the republics of antiquity, some Americans also found ways of escaping from the domination of British culture. Jefferson, who designed his own home, Monticello, turned away from English classicism in architecture, and studied original Greek and Roman designs and adaptations of these by the French.

The Atlantic Civilization is epitomized in the "Poor Richard" maxims. They probably originated in Europe; and after Franklin polished them up, Europe borrowed them back for publication in many languages. The illustration shown here was published in London in the late eighteenth century.

An English Illustration for "Poor Richard"

Historically, the most significant fact about this picture is that the "psalm" being sung is really a canon or round — a secular form of music usually associated with pleasure rather than devotion. The date of the engraving (by Paul Revere) is 1770 — the height of the Age of Reason. A hundred years earlier such a secularization of the hymn would have been unusual.

New England Psalm Singers

"The Court of Death," by Rembrandt Peale

(suggestive of mood as well as content)

In 1820, art in America, like literature, was an instrument of society rather than of the private ego. This picture, exhibited in a thirteen months' tour, was viewed by 32,000 people. In a promotional pamphlet, Peale described it as "pure and natural allegory," which was intended to "render useful the rational contemplation of death." As "literary" as most painting of the time, it was inspired by a poem on death by a Bishop Porteous — one of many "graveyard" poems that were popular in the transitional period between the Age of Reason and the Romantic Movement.

"The Tea Party," by Henry Sargent

The subordination of the individual to the social milieu is suggested in this "anecdote" picture, in which emphasis is given to the arrangement of the group as a whole rather than to differentiating characteristics of the individuals in the group. See the note on Franklin's prose, page 879.

"The Residence of David Twining, 1787," by Edward Hicks

This prosperous Pennsylvania Quaker farm represents the ideal of "subsistence" agriculture in pre-industrial America — the kind of New World life that Crèvecoeur celebrated in his *Letters*. Natural objects in the picture are idealized and stylized, as they were in pre-Romantic literature.

When work on the Erie Canal was begun in 1817, few could have predicted that new ventures in transportation and the opening of the West would radically change the spirit and forms of the American life that had evolved in the colonial and Federal periods.

"Looking Westward on the Erie Canal," by J. W. Hill

Puritanism and Rationalism

[handwritten marginalia: "centuries Facts", "Centuries & Politics"]

EUROPE IN AMERICA

EIGHTEEN MONTHS after the first colonists had anchored their boats in the James River, the first English book written in America was in print. That book — *A True Relation of such occurrences and accidents of noate as hath hapned in Virginia since the first planting of that Collony, which is now resident in the South part thereof, till the last returns from thence* — may be considered a piece of "American" literature only by straining the term. It is a piece of English literature written in America. Its very title is Elizabethan. The book has the true gusto of Elizabethan prose. It is just the kind of travel literature that Elizabethan sea-captains and explorers naturally sent home to advertise the new colonies. Moreover, Captain John Smith dispatched his manuscript to London to be printed, and had in mind English readers. But this book, with its long title and strange contents, was the opening chapter in the story of American literature, a story which has now covered about three and a half centuries.

When John Smith wrote *A True Relation*, the London stage was awaiting new plays by Shakespeare. The King James Bible was in preparation. Elizabeth had been dead only four years; Milton was not yet born. Colonial America at its foundation was merely an outpost of Elizabethan England. What a change a few centuries brought! In 1600 there was no such thing as English-speaking America. In 1700 twelve British colonies were strung along the Atlantic coast. In 1800 there was no British colony from Maine to the Gulf, and a federation of states was playing awkwardly with its new independence. In 1900 the United States of America was strong among the nations. In the mid-twentieth century it is one of the greatest powers of the world.

Against this background of political changes we are to consider the development of an American literature. American literature is an expression of the American mind. The American mind is a very elusive thing — is not quite the same in any two persons, and is vastly different in different periods of our national culture. As the history of American literature unfolds, we may discern certain periods or states of mind which can be isolated by drawing light chronological lines. The first hundred years gave us mainly an expression of the Puritan mind. Broadly speaking, it was a century of theology. The second hundred years — the eighteenth century — was the American "Age of Reason." Broadly speaking, this was a century of politics. Then came three quarters of a century which we may designate as the Romantic movement. And then another three quarters of a century when Realism rose, flourished, and passed into Naturalism. The bulk of American writing that we think of as "literature" — poetry, plays, novels, and the like — appeared after 1800. Yet a knowledge of what men thought and wrote in the first two cen-

1

turies is needed for an understanding of the important literature that came later.

To comprehend how American literature came to be, especially in the first two centuries, we shall do well to keep in mind the two great factors in its development: *America* and *Europe*, what America contributed and what Europe contributed. In the story of American literature, the action, what happened, has been shaped mainly by the setting, American geography, and by the characters, European people who brought their culture with them and kept importing it.

America furnished the geographical factor. Remoteness from the old world, especially in the days of sailing vessels, encouraged a sense of separate interests and made independent nationality more natural. When the early adventurers and settlers crossed the ocean they landed on what was then the frontier — the American frontier of Europe. The first frontier was the Atlantic coast and the first American book was frontier advertisement. Slowly, at the beginning, the frontier moved west. In the New England of the end of the seventeenth century, the General Court of Massachusetts named as frontier towns Haverhill, Groton, and Deerfield.

South of New England, when the first explorers pushed westward from the coast they traveled a few hundred miles on a low tidewater plain. Then abruptly the land changed and the plain became the higher, rockier Piedmont plateau. This was the "fall line," where the stream plunged from the rocks of the Piedmont to the soft soil of the tidewater plain. Rivers were navigable only as far as the fall line. It has often been remarked that the entire history of America would have been changed if a large navigable river had led west from the Atlantic. There was none; the Hudson was navigable, but it led north. Consequently, the early settlers proceeded across the Piedmont by foot and horse, and found, beyond it, the mountains.

The Appalachians loomed high and forbidding with few easy passes. Until Revolutionary days these mountains dammed up the tide of immigration. Once across them, however, the explorers found the broad valley drained by the Mississippi and its tributaries. Here the progress of civilization was easier, for streams led through the virgin forests. A settler of Fort Pitt could ship his possessions by water to New Orleans much more cheaply than he could return them by land to New England. Civilization spread rapidly through the valley and on to the great plains beyond the Mississippi. These plains, the scouts discovered, climbed higher and higher until, a mile high, they were terminated by the soaring Rockies. Beyond the Rocky Mountain barrier lay the desert, the coast ranges, and the western ocean. American history, American literature, the American mind and character have been profoundly shaped and colored by the westward-moving frontier.

To most colonists before the Revolution, however, the West was formidable, if not simply irrelevant. Like their fellow Britons across the Atlantic they thought of British expansion and enterprise in terms of commerce and sea power rather than in terms of agricultural exploitation of the interior of the continent. In the mid-eighteenth century Franklin was one of the very few whose vision embraced the whole of the West, and who argued that agricultural settlement would provide a great market for British manufactures.[1]

Europe sent people, and with the people came European traditions and ways of life, soon modified by fading memories and by the new milieu. The heaviest migration did not occur till the nineteenth century. After 1830 came great numbers of Irish and Germans and Scandinavians, who were followed by peoples from southern and eastern Europe: Slavs, Poles, Hungarians, Greeks, Italians, Russians, Lithuanians, Jews, and others.[2] But there was no such diversity in the early

[1] An enlightening and indispensable book on the subject of the West is by H. N. Smith, *Virgin Land: The American West as Symbol and Myth*, Cambridge, 1950.

[2] This is vividly emphasized by a map of European emigration in Morison and Commager, *The Growth of the American Republic*, II, 176.

periods of American history. At first the migration was almost entirely English: merchants, yeomen, laborers, artisans, scholars, including some twenty thousand Puritans. The English language which they spoke was destined to remain the language of America to this day, and the language of American literature. About the end of the seventeenth century, religious persecution and economic distress brought many Scotch-Irish and Germans, who also played an important rôle in the early development of the country.

Admirable in many ways were the aristocrats of the colonial South, whom Louis B. Wright has described as "a hard-working lot, intent upon the architecture of their fortunes, determined to procure the means to be landed gentlemen in the English manner. Many of them had come from simple origins, but land and the wealth that it brought enabled them to imitate the gentry of the mother country. Most significant of all, these planters carried over into Virginia not merely the outward forms of aristocracy but a remarkable sense of social responsibility." They produced a group of leaders and statesmen of extraordinary ability for the troubled days of the Revolution and the young nation. They also produced a prose literature of considerable interest. Though writing in Virginia was "the monopoly of the governing class" and was therefore "anti-democratic in value," it was often a vivid expression of the life it reported. It was a secular, non-theological literature. Its writers "see and touch and taste and smell; they themselves have travelled into the woods . . . interrogated Indians; watched the rattlesnake . . . heard the frenzied speeches of Governor Berkeley." By the same token it was a literature "lacking in introspection, in philosophic and moral meditation . . . without the play of general ideas." [1]

For these qualities we must turn to the writings of the Puritans of New England.

[1] H. M. Jones, *The Literature of Virginia in the Seventeenth Century*, Boston, 1946, pp. 46–47.

THE PURITANS AND WHAT THEY BELIEVED

In the present century the word "Puritan," or, with a small letter, "puritan," became a word of reproach. Especially in the "Jazz" decade after the first World War — the decade of "Flaming Youth" and the "Hard-boiled Virgin" — the word was used very frequently and very loosely. It was applied to a person too strict with himself, too conscientious. It was applied to a person too exacting and censorious toward others — a sort of nasty killjoy. Excess in these attitudes was often measured by a theory of self-expression, of "creative" living unhampered by conventions, a theory of bohemianism supposed to be supported by the Freudian psychology. Viewed in this light, a person could be called a puritan if he was much in earnest about anything. Used so indiscriminately and emotively, the word has made it hard for us today to see the early Puritans of New England as they really were.

While their faith was still vital, before it hardened into habitual forms, their lives displayed much that we can admire. Three words, it is said, were carved by a former occupant over the mantel of Nathaniel Ward's house, three words summing up the Puritan ethics: *Sobriety, Justice, Piety*, and to these Ward added a fourth: *Laughter*. The Puritans took pleasure in simple things, including bright-colored clothes, and smoking and drinking. To Increase Mather, for instance, drink was "a good creature of God, and to be received with thankfulness." Their emotions were strong, even if they did not wear their hearts on their sleeves. They knew the imperiousness of sex and referred to it frankly, calling a spade a spade. They showed a sense of beauty in making household objects such as pewter and furniture prized today by collectors, and, on a much higher plane, pursued the beauty of holiness. They were energetically intellectual, thinking with a strictness and continuity not surpassed, probably not equaled, by any later generation including our own. They were men of the Renaissance in their appreciation of classical literature despite the "pagan" or "heathen" nature of that literature. As Miller and Johnson remind us in their book *The Puritans*, the rich and powerful fusion of Puritanism and Hellenism achieved in England by John Milton "is unique only in his grandeur of expression; the same combination of religious dogma with the classics, of Protestant theology and ancient morality, was the aim of the curriculum at Harvard College, and it was sustained, though on a rudimentary or pedestrian level, in the sermons of Yankee parsons throughout the seventeenth century."

Hence it is anything but clear that the Puritans were "narrow," or at least that they were narrower than we (in our quite different way) or than men have been in most ages of history. Nor is it clear that they were less interested than we in "reality," though they had a different idea of reality, believed in it more earnestly, and would have thought ours superficial.

Puritanism may be defined as the way of thinking or set of values brought to New England by the early settlers. Because it varied in different groups, times, and places we cannot define it much more specifically without getting involved in the disagreements of historical scholars. Many of its most marked characteristics, besides, were not peculiar to it. Perhaps ninety per cent of its ideas, it has been said, were shared in common with other religious groups of the age, such as the Anglicans. Yet there was a difference, which has been clearly stated in *The Puritans:*

The difference between the Anglican and the Puritan was that the Puritan thought the Bible, the revealed word of God, was the word of God from one end to the other, a complete body of laws, an absolute code in everything it touched upon; the Anglican thought this a rigid, doctrinaire, and utterly unjustifiable extension of the authority of scripture. The Puritan held that the Bible was sufficiently plain and explicit so that men with the proper learning, following the proper rules of deduction and interpretation, could establish its meaning and intention on every subject, not only in theology, but in ethics, costume, diplomacy,

military tactics, inheritances, profits, marriages and judicial procedure.

Anglican and Puritan agreed that scripture should be found harmonious with human reason. To make this possible the Anglican sought to reduce the doctrines required by scripture to a bare minimum, while the Puritan, extending scripture to cover the whole of life, undertook to show that the entire content of scripture is reasonable.

While claiming the right of the individual to read and interpret the Bible for himself, the Puritan usually found himself in large agreement with John Calvin, the French Protestant reformer of Geneva. The five points of Calvinism may be stated as follows: (1) God elects individuals to be saved. (2) He designs complete redemption only for these elect. (3) Fallen man is of himself incapable of true faith and repentance. (4) God's grace is efficient for the salvation of the elect. (5) A soul once regenerated is never ultimately lost. When the Puritan of New England agreed with Calvin, he did so, not because Calvin was authoritative for him, but because Calvin seemed confirmed by the Bible and experience. And he conducted his argument in terms of his English tradition, constantly aware of the issues and shades of doctrine as they had appeared in the religious controversies of the mother country.

The Puritan faith made life anything but dull; indeed, it produced a high excitement. The world was the setting for a great drama, the drama of man in relation to God and Satan, to Heaven and Hell. It was a drama of individual man facing unspeakable bliss or unspeakable torment. It was also the drama of the Christian society. Having come to America as to a promised land, the Puritans soon developed the concept of a Holy Commonwealth, a theocracy, a social organization centering in the churches and their ministers. The more this corporate blessedness was subverted by Satan — acting through the Indians, the witches, and the internal conflicts of the churches — the more passionately was it believed in and propagated. But not even such strenuous leaders as Increase and Cotton Mather could save the Christian society, and in the failure of Jonathan Edwards and the Great Awakening, the whole Calvinistic structure was finally doomed. It was not disproved; it was merely abandoned.

For a new age was coming on, with new beliefs and interests, almost the opposite of those of the Puritans. By 1729, when Edwards assumed the pastorship at Northampton, the New England theology was already in a state of decline. In the seventeenth century a theology which posited God's absolute sovereignty over the destinies of man was "congenial to the minds of men who lived in a society wherein the distinctions of power and dignity, of authority and privilege, were well accepted facts." [1] But such a theology was to be increasingly uncongenial in a society which put a premium on the individual's enterprise, resourcefulness, and independence.

Yet today, in the mid-twentieth century, as Miller and Johnson venture to conclude, "we are terribly aware once more, thanks to the revelation of psychologists and the events of recent political history, that men are not perfect or essentially good. The Puritan description of them, we have been reluctantly compelled to admit, is closer to what we have witnessed than the description given in Jeffersonian democracy or in transcendentalism."

Instead of belaboring the Puritans for their shortcomings, which were as real as our own are, it may be more profitable to acknowledge our debt to them. Together with other religious groups, they assured the development of America as a Christian nation, established a tradition of reverence and high purposes and moral integrity which survives to this day despite the decay of formal creeds. They passed on the torch of classical learning to the neo-classical age of the colonies and the young republic, to transcendentalism and the romantic period generally, a heritage still a force in American culture. And the Puritans,

almost despite themselves, co-operated with the forces that developed the United States as a democracy. As H. S. Commager has said, commenting on R. B. Perry's work *Puritanism and Democracy* (1944):

What have Puritanism and democracy in common? Both respect the individual, "irrespective of his place in any ecclesiastical, political, social or other institution." Both recognize the ultimate authority of reason and, conversely, refuse to recognize as ultimate authority mere temporal rulers — kings, parliaments, armies. Both respect the dignity of man. Both are equalitarian and leveling, for to the Puritan salvation was dependent on merit or grace, not on wealth or class or talents, and to the democrat equality was part of common humanity. Both accepted the principle of contract or covenant as basic to religion and government, and to a large extent our constitutional government is derived from, and rests upon, this compact principle. Both emphasize the importance of education that men might attain to truth — spiritual or political. Both, finally, gave their allegiance to ideas or principles rather than to men or institutions, and both instinctively resisted the arrogant pretensions of tyrants.

THE AGE OF REASON

In the eighteenth century the faith of the Puritans subsided, despite the heroic efforts of Edwards as theologian and evangelist, and a new age arrived, a worldly age which came to bear such proud names as "The Enlightenment" and "The Age of Reason."

Calvinism and the new age were substantially opposite. Broadly speaking, the Bible gave way to the book of Nature. An omnipotent Providence intimately concerned with every human action became a pallid and remote Deity who created the universe and let it run undisturbed. The primal guilt of Adam inherited by all his sons — evil being in the heart of man — was supplanted by the nearer and more accessible guilt of kings and priests — evil being in arbitrary institutions. By no means depraved by nature and in need of regeneration through grace, men came into the world, it was now conceived, wholly malleable by experience, or even good and compassionate by nature. The proper study of mankind was no longer God but Man. The pilgrim's progress was now the progress of

[1] Joseph Haroutunian, *Piety Versus Moralism: The Passing of the New England Theology*, New York, 1932, p. xi.

society. In England, in France, in America, the Enlightenment resembled, it has been said, a new religion, of which Reason was God, Newton's *Principia* the Bible, and Voltaire the prophet.

Instead of Voltaire, the American colonies had Benjamin Franklin, a cosmopolitan *philosophe* notable alike for his simple wisdom, his wide curiosity, his cool rationality, his benevolent good humor, his gracious and lucid prose. We may look upon him as a symbol of the new age. As Carl Becker has said in the *Dictionary of American Biography*:

He was a true child of the Enlightenment.... He accepted without question and expressed without effort all the characteristic ideas and prepossessions of the century — its aversion to "superstition" and "enthusiasm" and mystery; its contempt for hocus-pocus and its dislike of dim perspectives; its passion for freedom and its humane sympathies; its preoccupation with the world that is evident to the senses; its profound faith in common sense and in the efficacy of Reason for the solution of human problems and the advancement of human welfare.

We may take to be symbolical, also, the fact that Franklin was born in Boston but removed to Philadelphia. For in the eighteenth century Pennsylvania became one of the leading provinces, having an ideal government in the eyes of European political philosophers, and Philadelphia became the largest town in the colonies and their chief cultural center. Here was an appropriate home for a progressive and optimistic spirit convinced of the efficacy of reason and its applicability to all human concerns.

We will not make the mistake of supposing that Franklin's age possessed a monopoly of reason, or even that it possessed greater powers of reason than the age of the Puritans. The Puritans had been close and energetic logicians, and it was Edwards who, while in the eighteenth century but not of it, had the most formidable intellect which America has produced. Furthermore, the Puritans believed man to be a rational creature and assigned a large and increasing rôle to his faculty of reason, so that they gradually drew closer to the rationalism of the new age and

prepared the way for Unitarianism. What distinguished the new age was its almost exclusive reliance upon reason, the belief of many of its intellectuals (not the masses of men) that unaided human reason can solve all questions rather easily, or at least all questions that need to be solved. It has been said of Thomas Jefferson, for instance, that "he found in reason a sufficient source of all we need to know, and beyond the limits of reason he had no desire to penetrate."

Reason was supreme. *Aimez donc la raison!* — this was the motto the new age inherited from the time of Descartes and Boileau. A recent scholar, Lovejoy, has stated a typical attitude of the eighteenth century by saying that the object was "not to proclaim to men truths which they had never known before, but to purge their minds of 'prejudices' and so to fix their attention upon the central, simple truths which they had really always known." In the words of the Declaration of Independence, "We hold these truths to be self-evident." Men in this neo-classical age also applied the test of clarity. Hostile to the vague, unformed, and mysterious, they found a signal virtue in clear conceptions: if an idea was really clear, it was probably true. The clarity they sought, especially in France, was not that of concrete facts, which they slighted, but rather that of abstractions, based not on historical but on mathematical principles. It was the clarity of truth naked, not clothed in the relativities of circumstance and fashion. The result was a prevalence of abstract systems of economics, of politics, of well-nigh anything, a tendency to discuss institutions, social contracts and forms, in a vacuum. By this abstract method they could conclude, to give one example, that all men are created equal.

The European thinker found most useful in the American age of reason, at least for political discussion preceding the War of Independence, was a seventeenth-century philosopher, John Locke. Locke had conceived that man is not born into the world with any ideas latent in him or any moral stigma from

Adam's sin, but with a mind clean and fresh like a blank page, on which will be written the experience of the senses from which he will derive all his ideas. On this basis it could be argued that men are created equal intellectually, morally, or politically, and that to reform men it is only necessary to reform the institutions of society which environ them. Suppose we go back, said Locke, to the time when man was still in a state of nature, subject only to the laws of Nature. Then each man had a right to punish the transgressor of that law. But since this would lead to no end of confusion, men formed a social contract, in return for their new advantages surrendering to the public, or commonwealth, their power of executing the law of Nature, yet retaining their inalienable rights. These rights were generally assumed in American discussions to be life, liberty, and property. The pursuit of happiness was also commonly viewed as a right and was accepted as such, apparently without debate, by the convention which voted the Declaration written by Jefferson. If a government flouted these natural rights and lost the consent of the governed, it was argued that the people had a right to alter or abolish it and to set up a new government. While Locke provided the immediate materials for such political reasoning, the idea of a law of Nature with which human institutions should harmonize may be traced back, through English Puritans, to Thomas Aquinas in the Middle Ages and ultimately to Cicero and Aristotle in the ancient world. At the same time it was implied in Newtonian science.

The age of reason was also an age of science. The preceding century, to be sure, had been scientific as well as religious. American Puritans had shown a strong interest in science — the adoption of inoculation for smallpox, for instance, was partly due to the efforts of Boston clergymen, Increase and Cotton Mather; and Jonathan Edwards understood Locke and Newton well enough to adapt their concepts to his own Calvinistic purposes. What Sir Isaac Newton, author of the *Prin-*

cipia, meant to the age of reason is suggested by Pope's lines:

Nature and Nature's laws lay hid in night:
God said, *Let Newton be!* and all was light.

Newton's discovery of the law of gravitation, his conception of the world-machine, a sort of perpetual-motion machine, a vast harmonious order completely submissive, from the planet to the blade of grass, to the physical law of Nature — this mathematical vision of the universe seemed to offer a formula usable as a pattern for thought in human law, in ethics and religion, indeed in any and every field. If today, as Sir James Jeans declares, this conception has failed dismally on both the scientific and philosophical sides, to the eighteenth century it meant a boundless hope for knowledge and for wise living. Encouraged by Bacon's break with the past, fortified by the ever-widening advances of science on many fronts, men came more and more to look forward instead of backward, to see perfection not in the past but in the future. The idea of progress took a commanding hold of the modern mind. Formulated and expanded in England and France, it crossed the ocean and blended easily with the optimism of a frontier land of opportunity. Naturally enough, as Charles A. Beard has remarked, "philosophers of progress in France, especially Saint-Simon, who fought under Washington in the American Revolution, looked upon the United States as the best possible theater in which to carry the new idea to full fruition." Europeans like Voltaire, Turgot, the Encyclopedists and Physiocrats, Condorcet, Godwin, etc., who embraced the new faith, had their counterparts in Americans like Franklin, Paine, Jefferson, Ethan Allen, and Joel Barlow.

In religion, the typical expression of the age of reason was deism. Newton's universe of harmonious law appeared to be self-sufficient, once God had established it. To the Puritans God had been both creator and ruler; to the deists he was only creator. The universe, as it seemed to the eye of reason, could be accounted for only on the assumption of a First Cause, a cause of all subsequent causes and effects. Furthermore, it seemed necessary to believe that the wonderful order and regularity of the universe was the work of a supreme intelligence. Through the argument of a First Cause and the argument from design, the deists considered reason adequate to prove the fact of a Creator. And they found reason competent to do more. In addition to a deity that made the universe, they were prepared to accept whatever else was universally held in the religions of the world, whatever was believed in at all times, all places, by all men. By separating these general elements of faith from the specific doctrines of specific religions such as Christianity, they tried to establish an abstract or "natural religion" conforming to the demands of reason alone. It is true that the earlier deists, while rejecting divine interference with the events of the world, accepted revealed religion as a necessary support for natural religion, and thus won many adherents who were unwilling to dispense with their Christian heritage. Later, however, radical deists like Ethan Allen and Thomas Paine placed themselves in sharp opposition to revealed religion. Irate orthodox Christians proceeded to accuse them, unjustly, of the sin of atheism. As a matter of fact, atheism appeared rather in France, where the spirit of skepticism found even deism untenable and passed on to a frank denial of God. In England and America, God was at least an "absentee landlord" who had established that vast and marvelous estate, the universe, where the law of Nature reigns.

In the field of ethics, we should expect the eighteenth century to have insisted on a morality based on reason, a morality in terms of abstract rational principles. But in fact an English deist, Lord Shaftesbury, early in the century shifted the whole discussion of ethics to a different realm. With him and many of his successors morality was made dependent on sentiment. Shaftesbury lent philosophic support to a movement already stirring for many years — the sentimental movement. As summed up by E. Bernbaum:

Its chief doctrines, rhapsodically promulgated by this amiable and original enthusiast, were that the universe and all its creatures constitute a perfect harmony; and that Man, owing to his innate moral and aesthetic sense, needs no supernatural revelation of religious or ethical truth, because if he will discard the prejudices of tradition, he will instinctively, when face to face with Nature, recognize the Spirit which dwells therein, — and, correspondingly, when in the presence of a good deed he will recognize its morality. In other words, God and Nature are one; and Man is instinctively good, his cardinal virtue being the love of humanity, his true religion the love of Nature. Be therefore of good cheer: evil merely appears to exist, sin is a figment of false psychology; lead mankind to return to the natural, and they will find happiness.

In America, the sentimental movement flourished less than in England and France. Another prince of sentimentalists like Rousseau was hardly to be looked for in a land deeply impregnated with the Puritan spirit, facing the practical necessities of frontier life, and engaging in a desperate war. But sentimentalism appeared, as we shall see, in our literature, and speculative thought took a new turn reminiscent of the British moralists of the period. Reacting against the Puritan view that man is naturally bad and depraved, the sentimentalist saw man as naturally good and benevolent. Thomas Paine, for example, declared in favor of the more flattering of these extremes when he said that "Man, where he is not corrupted by governments, is naturally the friend of man. . . . Human nature is not of itself vicious." From this time on, Americans were less and less impressed with the Fall of Man as the explanation of the terrible evils with which the record of history is strewn. As the secular spirit grew, as the idea of progress raised great hopes for the future, men more and more came to conceive that evil is not internal but external: not in the divided heart of man where good and evil clash, but in the environing political processes and social systems. Individually, men were good, as Rousseau affirmed, or at least entirely plastic, as Locke affirmed. Evil lay in the environment, in the prejudices of tradition and irrational institutions. We must not accuse the human heart.

Men cannot live by reason alone, even in an age of reason. The eighteenth century was also an age of feeling, of warm or delicate sensibility. If men are naturally good — all men, no matter how humble, unfortunate, or apparently evil — they merit a generous sympathy, their sad estate warrants the tribute of tears. Compassion was found to be enjoyable, and often led to little more than a mere indulgence in feeling.

In the last decades of the eighteenth century, "The Age of Reason became," says J. H. Randall, "the great age of humanitarianism." Rationalists who proclaimed that all men have equal rights to liberty and happiness, sentimentalists who sympathized with the miseries of men good by nature, Christian groups such as the Quakers and the Wesleyan evangelists who were concerned for the lowly, and scientific men who were turning knowledge into inventions for the relief of man's estate, all these played an important part in starting the modern movement known as humanitarianism. Historians have agreed that it is one of the major features of the age, but none has yet traced with care its genesis and growth. According to G. M. Trevelyan, "Humanitarianism was an eighteenth-century product, whereas the evils it sought to remedy were, with the exception of gin, as old as civilized man." Why, then, did the concerted effort to remove these evils begin in this century? Not because they were increasing, for it appears that they were actually diminishing. Nor because it was a religious age, for Christianity was fast losing ground; in France, indeed, humanitarianism flourished as a reaction against the Church. The very opposite answer has been suggested: because it was a secular age, an age materialistic in its aims, desiring worldly comfort and the avoidance of physical want and suffering. What was increasing was not suffering but the consciousness of it and hatred of it. The idea of the dignity of man, inherited from the classical and Christian traditions, was taken to imply, as a minimum, that unnecessary pain is intolerable. Men of good will now came to the rescue, as never before, of the oppressed and abused — slaves, criminals, the insane, animals — and undertook reforms that seemed long overdue. Here was a program that could bring together men as different as the practical rationalist Franklin and the Quaker mystic Woolman.

If the American colonial period, as the historian Curti has put it, "saw the development of virtually every aspect of the Enlightenment," the revolutionary period added something new: a new nation. The germ of American nationality, it has been suggested, may be found in the lines of an anonymous poem as far back as 1610, in which a governor of Virginia is represented as saying:

We hope to plant a nation
Where none before hath stood.

Though insubordination to the Crown began in that century, it was not till 1763, the end of the Seven Years' War, that the ties with England began seriously to weaken. In the debate that went on year after year, English opinion was divided, and so was American. Increasing crises and tensions drove men to more extreme positions and eventually forced a rupture. The result was a double revolution: class was arrayed against class, a section of the empire against imperial centralization. The cultural life of the colonies was profoundly disordered. Many intellectuals like Franklin and Jefferson were forced to neglect scientific and philosophic studies dear to them. A large proportion of the most cultivated colonists were Loyalists, many of whom fled to other lands, to our great loss. Science, education, and the churches were disrupted by the turmoil of the times. But in the end the war was won, the critical period following the war was surmounted, a remarkable constitution was framed and adopted, the United States of America were born. With political independence came a desire for intellectual and cultural independence — a desire, for one thing, for an *American* literature. At this juncture the impulse of the Romantic movement came from abroad, fanning the ardors of nationalism. In America as in Europe, the cosmopolitan eighteenth century was over; the nationalistic nineteenth century had arrived.

LITERATURE IN THE AGE OF REASON

The Age of Reason speaks through its literature. All of the motives, points of view, and ideas we have been glancing at are revealed in the American writers of the eighteenth century. Understandably, most of the writers were, as the Puritan divines and historians had been, primarily utilitarian authors rather than literary artists. It was largely an age of controversy, an age in which religious orthodoxy was assailed and defended, and in which the growing fact of economic and political independence was tallied with arguments in favor of and against sundry degrees of independence.

The most successful writing of the age might be called civic literature. It was possible for the elder William Pitt, speaking in the House of Lords in 1775, to say of the political papers coming from America: "For solidity of reasoning, force of sagacity, and wisdom of conclusion, no nation or body of men can stand in preference to the General Congress in Philadelphia." At a later time such praise was merited even more fully by the authors of the *Federalist* papers in support of the new Constitution. And over a long period of time Franklin, busy man of affairs though he was, composed a body of writings, in various forms, which deserve a significant place in our literature. In all such writing a new prose style was apparent — new in its perfection but long in the making. At the end of the seventeenth century the sermons of Cotton Mather were studded with capital letters, italics, Greek and Latin quotations, learned references and citations, and word-play. But ministers were discovering that if they were to be understood by the common man, and if they were to avoid the controversies they were tired of, they must strive for a "simple, lucid, and direct prose style." [1] This they did, and thus it was that orthodox and liberal Calvinists joined the Deists, scientists, and publicists in the movement toward a style suited to the age of prose and reason. What a recent scholar says of the new style abroad is true of it as well in America: "Gone were the involved sentences, the antithetical balance of sonorous clauses, the unwieldy parentheses, the luscious Latinized diction, the mass of corroborative quotations from books ancient and modern; the new style, in the words of Fontenelle, seemed to be 'written by the hand of a geometer.' " In America, as in England, writers in general sought to communicate thought with something like the plainness of science. A style proper to scientists would be, in the words of Sprat, the contemporary historian of the Royal Society, "a close, naked, natural way of speaking; positive expressions, clear senses, a native easiness; bringing all things as near the mathematical plainness as they can."

This intellectualistic bent appears not only in utilitarian works but also in the neo-classical essays of Franklin and Dennie. And it appears even in the poetry. It was an age, said Austin Dobson much later,

When Phoebus touched the Poet's trembling ear
With one supreme commandment, Be thou clear!

It was the age of neo-classical poetry, descriptive, didactic, satirical, commonly in heroic couplets. Pope, Young, Thomson, Gray, Goldsmith, and many others had their American imitators, unhappily on a plane rarely inspired, in forgotten writers of magazine verse and in the group of Connecticut wits: Trumbull, Dwight, Barlow, Humphreys, Hopkins, who were mostly conservatives in religion and politics, devoted to literature as an art and as an expression of the national spirit.

The emotional side of the century is illus-

[1] H. M. Jones, "American Prose Style: 1700–1770," in *Ideas in America*, Cambridge, 1944.

trated plainly, if feebly, in many sentimental novels, unreadable today, but consumed avidly at the time by young and old. They were imported from England, and had their American imitations in *The Power of Sympathy*, *Charlotte Temple*, and other productions described by H. R. Brown in the first part of his *Sentimental Novel in America, 1789–1860*. Jefferson was far from alone in regarding this sort of reading as a national menace. "When this passion infects the mind," he declared, "it destroys its tone and revolts it against wholesome reading. . . . The result is a bloated imagination, sickly judgments, and disgust towards all the real businesses of life." It is worth noting, however, that the first English novel printed in America was Franklin's edition of Richardson's *Pamela,* model of numerous sentimental novels in this country. Typically, our early novelists celebrated the natural goodness and benevolence of the human heart, and pictured characters interested in sensibility, seduction, and suicide. With them may be mentioned the first American novelist of any stature, Charles Brockden Brown, whose *Wieland* and *Edgar Huntley*, at the close of the century, were affected by the sentimental movement and the related school of "Gothic" horror.

Sentimentalism appears also in the essays ("letters") of Crèvecoeur, the American farmer of feeling; in Paine and Freneau, and in many another writer of prose or verse. In Freneau, it should be added, emotion is often fresh, true, richly imagined; when his language works free of the neo-classical conventions he attains a telling naturalness equal to that of the pre-romantic poets in England. At his rare best Freneau was capable of a haunting music that anticipates Coleridge and Poe.

It will be seen from the foregoing that America in the eighteenth century was not an isolated settlement but part of a culture that has been called the "Atlantic civilization" — a concept that once more, in the present state of world affairs, is attracting attention. It is sufficiently well known that British and Continental goods, books, and ideas flowed freely and abundantly across the water; but it is not fully realized that the Colonies contributed to Europe. As the historian of the concept says, "Europe was undergoing transformation resulting from New World influence. These economic, social, scientific, and psychological changes were in the direction of a more democratic society, and to this end North America lent its vigorous weight." [1]

[1] Michael Kraus, *The Atlantic Civilization: Eighteenth Century Origins*, Ithaca, 1949, p. vii.

MICHAEL WIGGLESWORTH (1631-1705)

The "poet laureate of New England Puritanism" was born in England and brought to America in 1638, when he was seven years old. He graduated from Harvard apparently with the intention of becoming a physician, but served for a time as tutor in the college, and then became pastor of the church at Malden, Mass., where he remained almost a half century.

Illness gave him leisure, part of which he devoted to a crude, earnest, horrible poem of "two hundred twenty-four stanzas of jigging octosyllabics" on *The Day of Doom, or a Description of the Great and Last Judgment, with a short discourse about Eternity. Eccles. 12. 14. For God shall bring every work into judgment with every secret thing, whether it be good, or whether it be evil.* Published in 1662, the first edition of eighteen hundred copies was exhausted within a year. Ten editions were required in the next century. Children committed it to memory along with the catechism. It was estimated that there was one copy for every thirty-five people in New England.

The Rev. Michael Wigglesworth, a "feeble, little shadow of a man" as Cotton Mather called him in his funeral sermon, rode to poetic fame on the currents of his time. His "blazing and sulphurous poem" largely expressed the temper of Calvinism as it existed in the leaders of the New England colonies — Winthrop, the Mathers, John Cotton. Furthermore, he wrote in a verse form that was easy to read and easy to learn. Many of the passages that inspired the Puritans merely entertain us today, but we have no other document that shows how real heaven and hell appeared to the Puritan, and how intensely dramatically he conceived everything in religion.

K. B. Murdock has edited *The Day of Doom*, 1929, with biographical material. J. W. Dean's *Memoir of Rev. Michael Wigglesworth*, 1871, is scarce. F. O. Matthiessen has written on "Michael Wigglesworth, a Puritan Artist," *New England Quarterly*, October, 1928.

From The Day of Doom

(1662)

[Men of Good Works]

XCII

Then were brought nigh a company
   of civil honest men,
That loved true dealing and hated stealing,
   ne'er wronged their bretheren,
Who pleaded thus: "Thou knowest us   5
   that we were blameless livers;
No whoremongers, no murderers,
   no quarrelers nor strivers.

XCIII

"Idolaters, adulterers,
   church-robbers we were none,   10
Nor false dealers, nor cozeners,
   but paid each man his own.

Our way was fair, our dealing square,
   we were no wasteful spenders,
No lewd toss-pots, no drunken sots,   15
   no scandalous offenders.

XCIV

"We hated vice and set great price,
   by virtuous conversation;
And by the same we got a name
   and no small commendation.   20
God's laws express that righteousness
   is that which He doth prize;
And to obey, as He doth say,
   is more than sacrifice.

XCV

"Thus to obey hath been our way;   25
   let our good deeds, we pray,
Find some regard and some reward
   with Thee, O Lord, this day.

And whereas we transgressors be,
  of Adam's race were none, 30
No, not the best, but have confessed
  themselves to have misdone."

XCVI

Then answerèd unto their dread,
  the Judge: "True piety
God doth desire and eke require, 35
  no less than honesty.
Justice demands at all your hands
  perfect obedience;
If but in part you have come short,
  that is a just offense. 40

XCVII

"On earth below, where men did owe
  a thousand pounds and more,
Could twenty pence it recompense?
  Could that have cleared the score?
Think you to buy felicity 45
  with part of what's due debt?
Or for desert of one small part,
  the whole should off be set?

XCVIII

"And yet that part whose great desert
  you think to reach so far, 50
For your excuse doth you accuse,
  and will your boasting mar.
However fair, however square
  your way and work hath been
Before men's eyes, yet God espies 55
  iniquity therein.

XCIX

"God looks upon th'affectiön
  and temper of the heart;
Not only on the actiön,
  and the external part. 60
Whatever end vain men pretend,
  God knows the verity,
And by the end which they intend
  their words and deeds doth try.

C

"Without true faith, the Scripture saith, 65
  God cannot take delight
In any deed that doth proceed
  from any sinful wight.
And without love all actions prove
  but barren empty things; 70

Dead works they be and vanity,
  the which vexation brings.

CI

"Nor from true faith, which quencheth
    wrath,
  hath your obedience flown;
Nor from true love, which wont to move 75
  believers, hath it grown.
Your argument shows your intent
  in all that you have done;
You thought to scale heav'n's lofty wall
  by ladders of your own. 80

CII

"Your blinded spirit hoping to merit
  by your own righteousness,
Needed no Saviour but your behavior,
  and blameless carriages.
You trusted to what you could do, 85
  and in no need you stood;
Your hearty pride laid Me aside,
  and trampled on My blood.

CIII

"All men have gone astray, and done
  that which God's laws condemn; 90
But My purchase and offered grace
  all men did not contemn.
The Ninevites and Sodomites
  had no such sin as this;
Yet as if all your sins were small, 95
  you say, 'All did amiss.'

CIV

"Again yon thought and mainly sought
  a name with men t' acquire;
Pride bare the bell that made you swell,
  and your own selves admire. 100
Mean fruit it is, and vile, I wis,
  that springs from such a root;
Virtue divine and genuine
  wonts not from pride to shoot.

CV

"Such deeds as your are worse than poor; 105
  they are but sins gilt over
With silver dross, whose glist'ring gloss
  can them no longer cover.
The best of them would you condemn,
  and ruin you alone, 110
Although you were from faults so clear,
  the other you had none.

CVI

"Your gold is brass, your silver dross,
    your righteousness is sin;
And think you by such honesty   115
    eternal life to win?
You much mistake, if for its sake
    you dream of acceptation;
Whereas the same deserveth shame
    and meriteth damnation.   120

[The Heathen and the Infants]

Then were brought near with trembling fear,
    a number numberless,
Of blind heathen, and brutish men that did
    God's law transgress;

CLVII

Whose wicked ways Christ open lays, and
    makes their sins appear,
They making pleas their case to ease, if not
    themselves to clear.
"Thy Written Word," say they, "good Lord,
    we never did enjoy;   5
We ne'er refus'd, nor it abus'd; Oh, do not
    us destroy!"

CLVIII

"You ne'er abus'd, nor yet refus'd my
    Written Word, you plead;
That's true," quoth he, "therefore shall ye
    the less be punishéd.
You shall not smart for any part of other
    men's offense,
But for your own transgressi-on receive due
    recompense."   10

CLIX

"But we were blind," say they, "in mind; too
    dim was Nature's light,
Our only guide, as hath been tried, to bring
    us to the sight
Of our estate degenerate, and curs'd by
    Adam's Fall;
How we were born and lay forlorn in bondage
    and in thrall.

CLX

"We did not know a Christ till now, nor how
    fall'n men be savéd,   15
Else would we not, right well we wot, have so
    ourselves behavéd.

We should have mourn'd, we should have
    turn'd from sin at thy Reproof,
And been more wise through thy advice, for
    our own soul's behoof.

CLXI

"But Nature's light shin'd not so bright, to
    teach us the right way:
We might have lov'd it and well improv'd it,
    and yet have gone astray."   20
The Judge most High makes this reply: "You
    ignorance pretend,
Dimness of sight, and want of light, your
    course Heav'nward to bend.

CLXII

"How came your mind to be so blind?   I
    once you knowledge gave,
Clearness of sight and judgment right: who
    did the same deprave?
If to your cost you have it lost, and quite
    defac'd the same,   25
Your own desert hath caus'd the smart; you
    ought not me to blame.

CLXIII

"Yourselves into a pit of woe, your own trans-
    gression led,
If I to none my Grace had shown, who had
    been injured?
If to a few, and not to you, I shew'd a way of
    life,
My Grace so free, you clearly see gives you
    no ground of strife.   30

CLXIV

"'Tis vain to tell, you wot full well, if you in
    time had known
Your misery and remedy, your actions had it
    shown:
You, sinful crew, have not been true unto
    the light of Nature,
Nor done the good you understood, nor
    ownéd your Creator.

CLXV

"He that the Light, because 'tis slight, hath
    uséd to despise,   35
Would not the Light shining more bright, be
    likely for to prize.

If you had lov'd, and well improv'd your
    knowledge and dim sight,
Herein your pain had not been vain, your
    plagues had been more light."

CLXVI

Then to the bar all they drew near who died
    in infancy,
And never had or good or bad effected
    pers'nally;   40
But from the womb unto the tomb were
    straightway carrièd,
(Or at the least ere they transgress'd) who
    thus began to plead:

CLXVII

"If for our own transgressi-on, or diso-
    bedience,
We here did stand at thy left hand, just were
    the recompense;
But Adam's guilt our souls hath split, his
    fault is charg'd upon us;   45
And that alone hath overthrown and utterly
    undone us.

CLXVIII

"Not we, but he ate of the Tree, whose fruit
    was interdicted;
Yet on us all of his sad Fall the punishment's
    inflicted.
How could we sin that had not been, or how
    is his sin our,
Without consent, which to prevent we never
    had the pow'r?   50

CLXIX

"O great Creator why was our Nature de-
    pravèd and forlorn?
Why so defil'd, and made so vil'd, whilst we
    were yet unborn?
If it be just, and needs we must transgressors
    reckon'd be,
Thy mercy, Lord, to us afford, which sinners
    hath set free.

CLXX

"Behold we see Adam set free, and sav'd
    from his trespass,   55
Whose sinful Fall hath split us all, and
    brought us to this pass.

Canst thou deny us once to try, or grace to
    us to tender,
When he finds grace before thy face, who
    was the chief offender?"

CLXXI

Then answerèd the Judge most dread: "God
    doth such doom forbid,
That men should die eternally for what they
    never did.   60
But what you call old Adam's Fall, and only
    his trespass,
You call amiss to call it his, both his and yours
    it was.

CLXXII

"He was design'd of all mankind to be a
    public head;
A common root, whence all should shoot, and
    stood in all their stead.
He stood and fell, did ill or well, not for
    himself alone,   65
But for you all, who now his Fall and trespass
    would disown.

CLXXIII

"If he had stood, then all his brood had been
    establishèd
In God's true love never to move, nor once
    awry to tread;
Then all his race my Father's grace should
    have enjoy'd for ever,
And wicked sprites by subtile sleights could
    them have harmèd never.   70

CLXXIV

"Would you have griev'd to have recciv'd
    through Adam so much good,
As had been your for evermore, if he at first
    had stood?
Would you have said, 'We ne'er obey'd nor
    did thy laws regard;
It ill befits with benefits, us, Lord, to so
    reward?'

CLXXV

"Since then to share in his welfare, you could
    have been content,   75
You may with reason share in his treason,
    and in the punishment.

Hence you were born in state forlorn, with
    natures so depravéd;
Death was your due because that you had
    thus yourselves behavéd.

CLXXVI

"You think 'If we had been as he, whom
    God did so betrust,
We to our cost would ne'er have lost all for
    a paltry lust.'   80
Had you been made in Adam's stead, you
    would like things have wrought,
And so into the self-same woe, yourselves and
    yours have brought.

CLXXVII

"I may deny you once to try, or grace to you
    to tender,
Though he finds grace before my face who
    was the chief offender;
Else should my grace cease to be grace, for it
    would not be free,   85
If to release whom I should please I have no
    liberty.

CLXXVIII

"If upon one what's due to none I frankly
    shall bestow,
And on the rest shall not think best com-
    passion's skirt to throw,
Whom injure I? will you envy and grudge
    at others' weal?
Or me accuse, who do refuse yourselves to
    help and heal?   90

CLXXIX

"Am I alone of what's my own, no Master
    or no Lord?

And if I am, how can you claim what I to
    some afford?
Will you demand grace at my hand, and
    challenge what is mine?
Will you teach me whom to set free, and thus
    my grace confine?

CLXXX

"You sinners are, and such a share as sinners,
    may expect;   95
Such you shall have, for I do save none but
    mine own Elect.
Yet to compare your sin with their who liv'd
    a longer time,
I do confess yours is much less, though every
    sin's a crime.

CLXXXI

"A crime it is, therefore in bliss you may not
    hope to dwell:
But unto you I shall allow the easiest room in
    Hell."   100
The glorious King thus answering, they cease,
    and plead no longer;
Their consciences must needs confess his
    reasons are the stronger.

CLXXXII

Thus all men's pleas the Judge with ease doth
    answer and confute,
Until that all, both great and small, are
    silencéd and mute.
Vain hopes are cropt, all mouths are stopt,
    sinners have naught to say,   105
But that 'tis just and equal most they should
    be damn'd for aye.

EDWARD TAYLOR (1645?-1729)

The best American poems of the seventeenth century were discovered only in the twentieth. As T. H. Johnson says, "It seems probable that had the poetry of Edward Taylor been published during his lifetime, he would long since have taken a place among the major figures of colonial American literature. It is startling at so late a period to run upon him. Edward Taylor was an orthodox Puritan minister, who lived nearly sixty years in the frontier village of Westfield, Massachusetts, writing poetry until 1725 in the mannered style of the pre-restoration sacred poets. Though no imitator, he was really in the tradition of Donne and the Anglo-Catholic conceitists. His sole inspiration was a glowing, passionate love for Christ, expressed in terms of his own unworthiness and wistful yearning. However much the substance of his imagination was erected within the frame of a special theology, his vitality as a prosodist and his evident delight in tone and color indicate how thoroughly he enjoyed poetry as an art."

Taylor had been born in England and emigrated to Boston in 1668. After graduating from Harvard he served as physician as well as pastor in Westfield. His grandson, President Stiles of Yale, described him as "a man of small stature, but firm; of quick passions, yet serious and grave. Exemplary in piety, and for a very sacred observance of the Lord's day."

Taylor requested his heirs not to publish any of his writings, and it was not till 1937 that a few of his poems were brought to light by Thomas H. Johnson, who has edited a generous selection from the poems, *The Poetical Works of Edward Taylor*. Interpretative essays have been written by Austin Warren, "Edward Taylor's Poetry: Colonial Baroque," *Kenyon Review*, Summer, 1941; W. C. Brown, "Edward Taylor: An American 'Metaphysical,'" *American Literature*, November, 1944; and R. H. Pearce, "Edward Taylor: The Poet as Puritan," *New England Quarterly*, March, 1950.

The Preface

Infinity, when all things it beheld,
In nothing, and of nothing all did build,
Upon what base was fixed the lath wherein
He turned this globe and riggaled it so trim?
Who blew the bellows of His furnace vast?   5
Or held the mould wherein the world was
    cast?
Who laid its corner-stone? Or whose command?
Where stand the pillars upon which it stands?
Who laced and filleted the earth so fine
With rivers like green ribbons smaragdine?   10
Who made the seas its selvedge, and it locks
Like a quilt ball within a silver box?
Who spread its canopy? Or curtains spun?
Who in this bowling alley bowled the sun?
Who made it always when it rises, set: 15
To go at once both down and up to get?
Who the curtain rods made for this tapestry?
Who hung the twinkling lanthorns in the sky?
Who? who did this? or who is he? Why,
    know
It's only Might Almighty this did do.   20
His hand hath made this noble work which
    stands
His glorious handiwork not made by hands.
Who spake all things from nothing; and with
    ease
Can speak all things to nothing, if He please.

Whose little finger at His pleasure can   25
Out mete ten thousand worlds with half a
    span.
Whose might almighty can by half a look
Root up the rocks and rock the hills by th'
    roots.
Can take this mighty world up in His hand
And shake it like a squitchen or a wand.   30
Whose single frown will make the heavens
    shake
Like as an aspen leaf the wind makes quake.
Oh! what a might is this! Whose single
    frown
Doth shake the world as it would shake it
    down?
Which all from nothing fet, from nothing
    all;   35
Hath all on nothing set, lets nothing fall.
Gave all to nothing man indeed, whereby
Through nothing man all might Him glorify.
In nothing is embossed the brightest gem   39
More precious than all preciousness in them.
But nothing man did throw down all by sin,
And darkened that lightsome gem in him,
    That now His brightest diamond is grown
    Darker by far than any coal-pit stone.

The Soul's Admiration

What, I such praises sing! How can it be?
    Shall I in heaven sing?

What, I, that scarce durst hope to see,
    Lord, such a thing?
    Though nothing is too hard for Thee,   5
One hope hereof seems hard to me.

What, can I ever tune those melodies,
    Who have no tune at all,
Not knowing where to stop nor rise,
        Nor when to fall?
    To sing Thy praise I am unfit;   10
I have not learned my gamut yet.

But should these praises on stringed instru-
        ments
    Be sweetly tuned? I find
I nonplussed am, for no consents   15
        I ever mind.
    My tongue is neither quill nor bow,
Nor can my fingers quavers show.

But was it otherwise, I have no kit; [1]
    Which though I had, I could   20
Not tune the strings, which soon would slip
        Though others should.
    But should they not, I cannot play,
But for an F should strike an A.

And should Thy praise upon wind instru-
        ments   25
    Sound all o'er heaven shrill?
My breath will hardly through such vents
        A whistle fill.
    Which though it should, it's past my spell
By stops and falls to sound it well.   30

How should I then join in such exercise?
    One sight of Thee'll entice
Mine eyes to heft, whose ecstasies
        Will stob [2] my voice.
    Hereby mine eyes will bind my tongue   35
Unless Thou, Lord, do cut the thong.

What use of useless me then there, poor
        snake?
    There saints and angels sing
Thy praise in full career, which make
    The heavens to ring.   40

    [1] Kit: miniature violin.
    [2] Stob: "The sense in which this rare word is here
used (and elsewhere in the poems) — to interrupt,
bring to a halt, or overpower — is not recorded in
the *New English Dictionary*, unless the word is to be
taken figuratively." [T. H. Johnson's note.]

Yet if Thou wilt, Thou canst me raise
With angels bright to sing Thy praise.

The Joy of Church Fellowship

In heaven soaring up I dropt an ear
    On earth, and, oh! sweet melody!
And listening found it was the saints who were
    Encoached for heaven that sang for joy.
For in Christ's coach they sweetly sing   5
As they to glory ride therein.

Oh, joyous hearts! Enfired with holy flame!
    Is speech thus tasselèd with praise?
Will not your inward fire of joy contain,
    That it in open flames doth blaze?   10
For in Christ's coach saints sweetly sing
As they to glory ride therein.

And if a string do slip by chance, they soon
    Do screw it up again, whereby
They set it in a more melodious tune   15
    And a diviner harmony.
For in Christ's coach they sweetly sing
As they to glory ride therein.

In all their acts public and private, nay
    And secret too, they praise impart;   20
But in their acts divine and worship, they
    With hymns do offer up their heart.
Thus in Christ's coach they sweetly sing
As they to glory ride therein.

Some few not in; and some, whose time and
        place   25
    Block up this coach's way, do go
As travellers afoot, and so do trace
    The road that gives them right thereto.
While in this coach these sweetly sing
As they to glory ride therein.   30

Housewifery

Make me, O Lord, Thy spinning-wheel com-
        plete.
    Thy holy Word my distaff make for me;
Make mine affections Thy swift flyers neat;
    And make my soul Thy holy spool to be;
My conversation make to be Thy reel,   5
    And reel the yarn thereon spun of Thy
        wheel.

Make me Thy loom then; knit therein this twine;
  And make Thy Holy Spirit, Lord, wind quills;
Then weave the web Thyself. The yarn is fine.
  Thine ordinances make my fulling mills. 10
Then dye the same in heavenly colors choice,
  All pinked with varnished flowers of paradise.

Then clothe therewith mine understanding, will,
  Affections, judgment, conscience, memory,
My words and actions, that their shine may fill 15
  My ways with glory and Thee glorify.
Then mine apparel shall display before Ye
That I am clothed in holy robes for glory.

The Ebb and Flow

When first Thou on me, Lord, wroughtest Thy sweet print,
  My heart was made Thy tinder box.
My 'ffections were Thy tinder in't,
  Where fell Thy sparks by drops.
These holy sparks of heavenly fire that came 5
Did ever catch and often out would flame.

But now my heart is made Thy censer trim,
  Full of Thy golden altar's fire,
To offer up sweet incense in
  Unto Thyself entire: 10
I find my tinder scarce Thy sparks can feel
That drop out from Thy holy flint and steel.

Hence doubts out-bud for fear Thy fire in me
  Is a mocking ignis fatuus;
Or lest Thine altar's fire out be 15
  It's hid in ashes thus.
Yet when the bellows of Thy spirit blow
Away mine ashes, then Thy fire doth glow.

The Reflection

Canticles II: 1: I am the rose of Sharon.

Lord, art Thou at the table-head above
  Meat, medicine, sweetness, sparkling beauties, to

Enamour souls with flaming flakes of love,
  And not my trencher nor my cup o'erflow?
Ben't I a bidden guest? Oh! sweat, mine eye, 5
  O'erflow with tears. Oh! draw thy fountains dry.

Shall I not smell Thy sweet, oh! Sharon's rose?
  Shall not mine eye salute Thy beauty? Why?
Shall Thy sweet leaves their beauteous sweets upclose?
  As half-ashamed my sight should on them lie? 10
Woe's me! For this my sighs shall be in grain,
Offered on sorrow's altar for the same.

Had not my soul's (Thy conduit) pipes stopped been
  With mud, what ravishment would'st Thou convey?
Let grace's golden spade dig till the spring 15
  Of tears arise, and clear this filth away.
Lord, let Thy spirit raise my sighings till
These pipes my soul do with Thy sweetness fill.

Earth once was paradise of heaven below,
  Till ink-faced sin had it with poison stocked, 20
And chased this paradise away into
  Heaven's upmost loft and it in glory locked.
But Thou, sweet Lord, hast with Thy golden key
Unlocked the door and made a golden day.

Once at Thy feast I saw Thee pearl-like stand 25
  'Tween heaven and earth, where heaven's bright glory all
In streams fell on Thee as a floodgate, and
  Like sun beams through Thee on the world to fall.
Oh! sugar-sweet then! My dear sweet Lord, I see
Saints' heaven-lost happiness restored by Thee. 30

Shall heaven and earth's bright glory all
   up-lie
     Like sun beams bundled in the sun in
       Thee?
Dost Thou sit rose at table-head, where I
     Do sit, and carv'st no morsel sweet for
       me?
       So much before, so little now! Sprindge,
        Lord,   35
       Thy rosy leaves, and me their glee afford.

Shall not Thy rose my garden fresh perfume?
     Shall not Thy beauty my dull heart
       assail?
Shall not Thy golden gleams run through
     this gloom?
     Shall my black velvet mask Thy fair
       face veil?   40
     Pass o'er my faults. Shine forth, bright
       sun: arise!
     Enthrone Thy rosy-self within mine eyes.

Meditation Seven

Psalm XLV: 2: *Grace is poured into thy lips.*

Thy human frame, my glorious Lord, I spy,
   A golden still with heavenly choice drugs
     filled:

Thy holy love, the glowing heat whereby
   The spirit of grace is graciously distilled.
   Thy mouth the neck through which these
     spirits still;   5
   My soul Thy vial make, and therewith
     fill.

Thy speech the liquour in Thy vessel stands,
   Well tinged with grace, a blessed tinc-
     ture, lo,
Thy words distilled grace in Thy lips poured,
   and
   Give grace's tincture in them where they
     go.   10
Thy words in grace's tincture stilled,
     Lord, may
   The tincture of Thy grace in me convey.

That golden mint of words Thy mouth divine
   Doth tip these words, which by my fall
     were spoiled;   14
And dub with gold dug out of grace's mine,
   That they Thine image might have in
     them foiled.
Grace in Thy lips poured out's as
     liquid gold:
   Thy bottle make my soul, Lord, it to
     hold.

JONATHAN EDWARDS (1703–1758)

Calvinism's last great champion in America was its greatest. Increase Mather had already lost the presidency of Harvard and Cotton Mather was beginning to wonder if his were not a lost cause, when, on October 5, 1703, Jonathan Edwards was born at Windsor, Connecticut, fifth of eleven children and the only son. For lack of schools he was taught at home, until he was ready to enter Yale in 1716. Before his college days the precocious youth had written a remarkable essay on the flying spider. In college he continued his scientific observation and speculation, but gave his mind more and more to philosophy and theology. As a sophomore, at the age of fourteen, he read Locke *On the Human Understanding* with a delight similar to Keats's on first reading Chapman's Homer. Before graduation he wrote his famous paper "Of Being," arriving at conclusions that suggest the influence of Berkeley but which he quite possibly attained alone.

After he was graduated from Yale in September of 1720, Edwards studied theology for two years in New Haven. He served eight months as a Presbyterian minister in New York and returned to Yale as a tutor, which position he resigned in 1726 to become the colleague of his grandfather, Solomon Stoddard, in his pastorate at Northampton, Massachusetts. "In his parish, with meager aid from books and limited bodily energy, Edwards lived the life which before the age of twenty he had vowed in his seventy 'Resolutions,' " says Francis A. Christie in *DAB*, "a life of stern discipline over the springs of impulse and of intense mental application; rising at 4:00 A.M., devoting thirteen hours of the day to study, finding recreation in solitary woodland rambles, during which he jotted down memoranda of his thoughts for later elaboration." During his days in New Haven he had known Sarah Pierrepont, and had written the description of her that appears in this volume when he was twenty and she thirteen. Four years later, in 1727, she became the bride of the new pastor at Northampton.

Stoddard died in 1729, and Edwards was left in sole charge of the church. He attained to a great reputation as a preacher. The intensity that always marked his delivery was not demonstrative, but was effectively restrained. He preached many kinds of sermons in addition to the kind for which he is, unfortunately, best remembered — the "revivalist" discourses such as the terrible Enfield sermon, *Sinners in the Hands of an Angry God*, which he delivered in 1741 during the Great Awakening. His success in revivals was astounding. There had been no important revivals in New England since the day of John Cotton, a century before. Then — "In December 1734 there were six sudden conversions and in the following spring they were counted as thirty a week. Since visitors from other towns flocked to Northampton, the revival spread through the country and many places in Connecticut. Religious themes absorbed the thought and talk of the whole population of Northampton, even at weddings. Children formed their own religious meetings. One notable conversion was that of Phoebe Bartlett, a child of four." (*DAB*) The revival ended in May after an epidemic of suicides among those who had been unable to be regenerated. A similar revival was held during the Great Awakening of the early 1740's.

In 1747, Edwards's parishioners began to rebel openly against the rigor of his doctrines. His relation with the church was finally dissolved in 1750, and he wrote in July 5 of that year: "I am now thrown upon the wide ocean of the world, and know not what will become of me, and my numerous and chargeable family." The following year he became missionary to the Indians of Stockbridge, Mass. Here he completed, in 1754, the work on which rests his fame, *The Freedom of the Will*, a treatise which has been said to be the only American contribution to abstract thought. It is a formulation and logical justification of Calvinism: the greatest philosophical monument of the religion appeared when the religion itself was nearly spent.

His end was not to be in his mission. In 1757 he was chosen president of the College of New Jersey (now Princeton). He was inaugurated in January of 1758, and died there on March 28 of the same year, of the smallpox. As he lay dying in Princeton, he sent the following message to his wife: "Tell her," he said, "that the uncommon union which has so long subsisted between us has been of such a nature as I trust is spiritual, and therefore will continue forever." Poet and mystic, he was still cautious logician to the end.

The best edition of Edwards is that of S. Austin, 1808 (also 1844 and often thereafter). The best life is by O. E. Winslow, 1940. H. W. Schneider, *A History of American Philosophy*, 1946, sets Edwards's thought in historical context, but all earlier discussions are superseded by Perry Miller, *Jonathan Edwards*, 1949. Miller has also edited Edwards's hitherto unpublished *Images or Shadows of Divine Things*, 1948. An excellent volume of selections, with introduction and bibliography, was edited for the *AWS* in 1935 by C. H. Faust and T. H. Johnson.

Personal Narrative

(ca. 1743)

I had a variety of concerns and exercises about my soul from my childhood; but had two more remarkable seasons of awakening, before I met with that change by which I was brought to those new dispositions, and that new sense of things, that I have since had. The first time was when I was a boy, some years before I went to college, at a time of remarkable awakening in my father's congregation. I was then very much affected for many months, and concerned about the things of religion, and my soul's salvation; and was abundant in duties. I used to pray five times a day in secret, and to spend much time in religious talk with other boys, and used to meet with them to pray together. I experienced I know not what kind of delight in religion. My mind was much engaged in it, and had much self-righteous pleasure; and it was my delight to abound in religious duties. I with some of my schoolmates joined together, and built a booth in a swamp, in a very retired spot, for a place of prayer. And besides, I had particular secret places of my own in the woods, where I used to retire by myself; and was from time to time much affected. My affections seemed to be lively and easily moved, and I seemed to be in my element when engaged in religious duties. And I am ready to think, many are deceived with such affections, and such a kind of delight as I then had in religion, and mistake it for grace.

But in process of time, my convictions and affections wore off; and I entirely lost all those affections and delights and left off secret prayer, at least as to any constant performance of it; and returned like a dog to his vomit, and went on in the ways of sin. Indeed I was at times very uneasy, especially towards the latter part of my time at college; when it pleased God, to seize me with the pleurisy; in which he brought me nigh to the grave, and shook me over the pit of hell. And yet, it was not long after my recovery, before

I fell again into my old ways of sin. But God would not suffer me to go on with my quietness; I had great and violent inward struggles, till, after many conflicts, with wicked inclinations, repeated resolutions, and bonds that I laid myself under by a kind of vows to God, I was brought wholly to break off all former wicked ways, and all ways of known outward sin; and to apply myself to seek salvation, and practice many religious duties; but without that kind of affection and delight which I had formerly experienced. My concern now wrought more by inward struggles and conflicts, and self-reflections. I made seeking my salvation the main business of my life. But yet, it seems to me, I sought after a miserable manner; which has made me sometimes since to question, whether ever it issued in that which was saving; being ready to doubt, whether such miserable seeking ever succeeded. I was indeed brought to seek salvation in a manner that I never was before; I felt a spirit to part with all things in the world, for an interest in Christ. — My concern continued and prevailed, with many exercising thoughts and inward struggles; but yet it never seemed to be proper to express that concern by the name of terror.

From my childhood up, my mind had been full of objections against the doctrine of God's sovereignty, in choosing whom he would to eternal life, and rejecting whom he pleased; leaving them eternally to perish, and be everlastingly tormented in hell. It used to appear like a horrible doctrine to me. But I remember the time very well, when I seemed to be convinced, and fully satisfied, as to this sovereignty of God, and his justice in thus eternally disposing of men, according to his sovereign pleasure. But never could give an account, how, or by what means, I was thus convinced, not in the least imagining at the time, nor a long time after, that there was any extraordinary influence of God's Spirit in it; but only that now I saw further, and my reason apprehended the justice and reasonableness of it. However, my mind rested in it; and it put an end to all those cavils and objections. And there has been a wonderful alteration in my mind, with respect to the doctrine of God's sovereignty, from that day to this; so that I scarce ever have found so much as the rising of an objection against it, in the most absolute sense, in God's shewing mercy to whom he will shew mercy, and hardening whom he will. God's absolute sovereignty and justice, with respect to salvation and damnation, is what my mind seems to rest assured of, as much as of any thing that I see with my eyes; at least it is so at times. But I have often, since that first conviction, had quite another kind of sense of God's sovereignty than I had then. I have often since had not only a conviction, but a delightful conviction. The doctrine has very often appeared exceeding pleasant, bright, and sweet.

Absolute sovereignty is what I love to ascribe to God. But my first conviction was not so.

The first instance that I remember of that sort of inward, sweet delight in God and divine things that I have lived much in since, was on reading those words, 1 Tim. i: 17. *Now unto the King eternal, immortal, invisible, the only wise God, be honor and glory forever and ever, Amen.* As I read the words, there came into my soul, and was as it were diffused through it, a sense of the glory of the Divine Being; a new sense, quite different from any thing I ever experienced before. Never any words of scripture seemed to me as these words did. I thought within myself, how excellent a being that was, and how happy I should be, if I might enjoy that God, and be wrapt up in heaven, and be as it were swallowed up in him forever! I kept saying, and as it were singing over these words of scripture to myself; and went to pray to God that I might enjoy him, and prayed in a manner quite different from what I used to do; with a new sort of affection. But it never came into my thought, that there was any thing spiritual, or of a saving nature in this.

From about that time, I began to have a new kind of apprehensions and ideas of Christ, and the work of redemption, and the glorious way of salvation by him. An inward, sweet sense of these things, at times, came into my heart; and my soul was led away in pleasant views and contemplations of them. And my mind was greatly engaged to spend my time in reading and meditating on Christ, on the beauty and excellency of his person, and the lovely way of salvation by free grace in him. I found no books so delightful to me, as those that treated of these subjects. Those words, Cant. ii: 1, used to be abundantly with me, *I am the Rose of Sharon, and the Lily of the valleys.* The words seemed to me, sweetly to represent the loveliness and beauty of Jesus Christ. The whole book of Canticles used to be pleasant to me, and I used to be much in reading it, about that time; and found, from time to time, an inward sweetness, that would carry me away, in my contemplations. This I know not how to express otherwise, than by a calm, sweet abstraction of soul from all the concerns of this world; and sometimes a kind of vision, or fixed ideas and imaginations, of being alone in the mountains, or some solitary wilderness, far from all mankind, sweetly conversing with Christ, and wrapt and swallowed up in God. The sense I had of divine things, would often of a sudden kindle up, as it were, a sweet burning in my heart; an ardor of soul, that I know not how to express.

Not long after I began to experience these things, I gave an account to my father of some things that had passed in my mind. I was pretty much affected by the discourse we had together; and when the discourse was ended, I walked abroad alone, in a solitary place in my father's pasture for contemplation. And as I was walking there and looking up on the sky and clouds, there came into my mind so sweet a sense of the glorious *majesty* and *grace* of God, that I know not how to express. I seemed to see them both in a sweet conjunction; majesty and meekness joined together; it was a gentle, and holy majesty; and also a majestic meekness; a high, great, and holy gentleness.

After this my sense of divine things gradually increased, and became more and more lively, and had more of that inward sweetness. The appearance of every thing was altered; there seemed to be, as it were, a calm, sweet cast, or appearance of divine glory, in almost every thing. God's excellence, his wisdom, his purity and love, seemed to appear in every thing; in the sun, moon, and stars; in the clouds, and blue sky; in the grass, flowers, trees; in the water, and all nature; which used greatly to fix my mind. I often used to sit and view the moon for continuance; and in the day, spent much time in viewing the clouds and sky, to behold the sweet glory of God in these things; in the mean time, singing forth, with a low voice; my contemplations of the Creator and Redeemer. And scarce any thing, among all the works of nature, was so delightful to me as thunder and lightning; formerly, nothing had been so terrible to me. Before, I used to be uncommonly terrified with thunder, and to be struck with terror when I saw a thunder storm rising; but now, on the contrary, it rejoiced me. I felt God, so to speak, at the first appearance of a thunder storm; and used to take the opportunity, at such times, to fix myself in order to view the clouds, and see the lightnings play, and hear the majestic and awful voice of God's thunder, which oftentimes was exceedingly entertaining, leading me to sweet contemplations of my great and glorious God. While thus engaged, it always seemed natural to me to sing, or chant for my meditations; or, to speak my thoughts in soliloquies with a singing voice.

I felt then great satisfaction, as to my good state; but that did not content me. I had vehement longings of soul after God and Christ, and after more holiness, wherewith my heart seemed to be full, and ready to break; which often brought to my mind the words of the Psalmist, Psal. cxix. 28: *My soul breaketh for the longing it hath.* I often felt a mourning and lamenting in my heart, that I had not turned to God sooner, that I might have had more time to grow in grace. My mind was greatly fixed on divine things; almost perpetually in the contemplation of them. I spent most of my time in thinking of divine things, year after year; often walking alone in the woods, and solitary places, for meditation, soliloquy, and prayer, and converse with God; and it was always my manner, at such times, to sing forth my contemplations. I was almost constantly in ejaculatory prayer, wherever I was. Prayer seemed to be natural to me, as the breath by which the inward burnings of my heart had vent. The delights which I now felt in the things of religion, were of an exceedingly dif-

ferent kind from those before mentioned, that I had when a boy; and what I then had no more notion of, than one born blind has of pleasant and beautiful colors. They were of a more inward, pure, soul-animating and refreshing nature. Those former delights never reached the heart; and did not arise from any sight of the divine excellency of the things of God; or any taste of the soul-satisfying and life-giving good there is in them.

My sense of divine things seemed gradually to increase, until I went to preach at New York, which was about a year and a half after they began; and while I was there, I felt them, very sensibly, in a higher degree than I had done before. My longings after God and holiness, were much increased. Pure and humble, holy and heavenly Christianity, appeared exceedingly amiable to me. I felt a burning desire to be in every thing a complete Christian; and conform to the blessed image of Christ; and that I might live, in all things, according to the pure and blessed rules of the gospel. I had an eager thirsting after progress in these things; which put me upon pursuing and pressing after them. It was my continual strife day and night, and constant inquiry, how I should *be* more holy, and *live* more holily, and more becoming a child of God, and a disciple of Christ. I now sought an increase of grace and holiness, and a holy life, with much more earnestness, than ever I sought grace before I had it. I used to be continually examining myself, and studying and contriving for likely ways and means, how I should live holily, with far greater diligence and earnestness, than ever I pursued any thing in my life; but yet with too great a dependence on my own strength; which afterwards proved a great damage to me. My experience had not then taught me, as it has done since, my extreme feebleness and impotence, every manner of way; and the bottomless depths of secret corruption and deceit there was in my heart. However, I went on with my eager pursuit after more holiness, and conformity to Christ.

The heaven I desired was a heaven of holiness; to be with God, and to spend my eternity in divine love, and holy communion with Christ. My mind was very much taken up with contemplations on heaven, and the enjoyments there, and living there in perfect holiness, humility and love. And it used at that time to appear a great part of the happiness of heaven, that there the saints could express their love to Christ. It appeared to me a great clog and burden, that what I felt within, I could not express as I desired. The inward ardor of my soul, seemed to be hindered and pent up, and could not freely flame out as it would. I used often to think, how in heaven this principle should freely and fully vent and express itself. Heaven appeared exceedingly delightful, as a world of love; and that all happiness consisted in living in pure, humble, heavenly, divine love.

I remember the thoughts I used then to have of holiness; and said sometimes to myself, "I do certainly know that I love holiness, such as the gospel prescribes." It appeared to me, that there was nothing in it but what was ravishingly lovely; the highest beauty and amiableness — a *divine* beauty; far purer than any thing here upon earth; and that every thing else was like mire and defilement, in comparison of it.

Holiness, as I then wrote down some of my contemplations on it, appeared to me to be of a sweet, pleasant, charming, serene, calm nature; which brought an inexpressible purity, brightness, peacefulness and ravishment to the soul. In other words, that it made the soul like a field or garden of God, with all manner of pleasant flowers; all pleasant, delightful, and undisturbed; enjoying a sweet calm, and the gently vivifying beams of the sun. The soul of a true Christian, as I then wrote my meditations, appeared like such a little white flower as we see in the spring of the year; low and humble on the ground, opening its bosom to receive the pleasant beams of the sun's glory; rejoicing as it were in a calm rapture; diffusing around a sweet fragrancy; standing peacefully and lovingly, in the midst of other flowers round about; all in like manner opening their bosoms, to drink in the light of the sun. There was no part of creature holiness, that I had so great a sense of its loveliness, as humility, brokenness of heart and poverty of spirit; and there was nothing that I so earnestly longed for. My heart panted after this, to lie low before God, as in the dust; that I might be nothing, and that God might be ALL, that I might become as a little child.

While at New York, I was sometimes much affected with reflections on my past life, considering how late it was before I began to be truly religious; and how wickedly I had lived till then; and once so as to weep abundantly, and for a considerable time together.

On *January* 12, 1723. I made a solemn dedication of myself to God, and wrote it down; giving up myself, and all that I had to God; to be for the future in no respect my own; to act as one that had no right to himself, in any respect. And solemnly vowed to take God for my whole portion and felicity; looking on nothing else as any part of my happiness, nor acting as if it were; and his law for the constant rule of my obedience; engaging to fight with all my might, against the world, the flesh and the devil, to the end of my life. But I have reason to be infinitely humbled, when I consider how much I have failed of answering my obligation.

I had then abundance of sweet religious conversation in the family where I lived, with Mr. John Smith and his pious mother. My heart was knit in affection to those in whom were appearances of true piety; and I could bear the thoughts of no other companions, but such as were holy, and the disciples of the blessed Jesus. I had great longings for the advancement of Christ's kingdom in the world; and my secret prayer used to be, in great part, taken up in praying for it. If I heard the least hint of any thing that happened, in any part of the world, that appeared, in some respect or other, to have a favorable aspect on the interest of Christ's kingdom, my soul eagerly catched at it; and it would much animate and refresh me. I used to be eager to read public news letters, mainly for that end; to see if I could not find some news favorable to the interest of religion in the world.

I very frequently used to retire into a solitary place, on the banks of Hudson's river, at some distance from the city, for contemplation on divine things, and secret converse with God; and had many sweet hours there. Sometimes Mr. Smith and I walked there together, to converse on the things of God; and our conversation used to turn much on the advancement of Christ's kingdom in the world, and the glorious things that God would accomplish for his church in the latter days. I had then, and at other times, the greatest delight in the holy scriptures, of any book whatsoever. Oftentimes in reading it, every word seemed to touch my heart. I felt a harmony between something in my heart, and those sweet and powerful words. I seemed often to see so much light exhibited by every sentence, and such a refreshing food communicated, that I could not get along in reading; often dwelling long on one sentence, to see the wonders contained in it; and yet almost every sentence seemed to be full of wonders.

I came away from New York in the month of April, 1723, and had a most bitter parting with Madam Smith and her son. My heart seemed to sink within me at leaving the family and city, where I had enjoyed so many sweet and pleasant days. I went from New York to Weathersfield, by water, and as I sailed away, I kept sight of the city as long as I could. However, that night, after this sorrowful parting, I was greatly comforted in God at Westchester, where we went ashore to lodge; and had a pleasant time of it all the voyage to Saybrook. It was sweet to me to think of meeting dear Christians in heaven, where we should never part more. At Saybrook we went ashore to lodge, on Saturday, and there kept the Sabbath; where I had a sweet and refreshing season, walking alone in the fields.

After I came home to Windsor, I remained much in a like frame of mind, as when at New York; only sometimes I felt my heart ready to sink with the thoughts of my friends at New York. My support was in contemplations on the heavenly state; as I find in my Diary of May 1, 1723. It was a comfort to think of that state, where there is fulness of joy; where reigns heavenly, calm, and delightful love, without alloy; where there are continually the dearest expressions of this love; where is the enjoyment of the persons loved, without ever parting; where those persons who appear so lovely in this world, will really be inexpressibly more lovely and full of love to us. And how sweetly will the mutual lovers join together to sing the praises of God and the Lamb! How will it fill us with joy to think, that this enjoyment, these sweet exercises will never cease, but will last to all eternity! I continued much in the same frame, in the general, as when at New York, till I went to New Haven as tutor to the college; particularly once at Bolton, on a journey from Boston, while walking out alone in the fields. After I went to New Haven I sunk in religion; my mind being diverted from my eager pursuits after holiness, by some affairs that greatly perplexed and distracted my thoughts.

In September, 1725, I was taken ill at New Haven, and while endeavoring to go home to Windsor, was so ill at the North Village, that I could go no further; where I lay sick for about a quarter of a year. In this sickness God was pleased to visit me again with the sweet influences of his Spirit. My mind was greatly engaged there in divine, pleasant contemplations, and longings of soul. I observed that those who watched with me, would often be looking out wishfully for the morning; which brought to my mind those words of the Psalmist, and which my soul with delight made its own language, *My soul waiteth for the Lord, more than they that watch for the morning, I say, more than they that watch for the morning;* and when the light of day came in at the windows, it refreshed my soul from one morning to another. It seemed to be some image of the light of God's glory.

I remember, about that time, I used greatly to long for the conversion of some that I was concerned with; I could gladly honor them, and with delight be a servant to them, and lie at their feet, if they were but truly holy. But, some time after this, I was again greatly diverted in my mind with some temporal concerns that exceedingly took up my thoughts, greatly to the wounding of my soul; and went on through various exercises, that it would be tedious to relate, which gave me much more experience of my own heart, than ever I had before.

Since I came to this town, I have often had sweet complacency in God, in views of his glorious perfections and the excellency of Jesus Christ. God has appeared to me a glorious and lovely being, chiefly on the account of his holiness. The holiness of God has always appeared to me the most lovely of all

expression for them, but I always think of myself, that I ought, and it is an expression that has long been natural for me to use in prayer, "to lie infinitely low before God." And it is affecting to think, how ignorant I was, when a young Christian, of the bottomless, infinite depths of wickedness, pride, hypocrisy and deceit, left in my heart.

I have a much greater sense of my universal, exceeding dependence on God's grace and strength, and mere good pleasure, of late, than I used formerly to have; and have experienced more of an abhorrence of my own righteousness. The very thought of any joy arising in me, on any consideration of my own amiableness, performances, or experiences or any goodness of heart or life, is nauseous and detestable to me. And yet I am greatly afflicted with a proud and selfrighteous spirit, much more sensibly than I used to be formerly. I see that serpent rising and putting forth its head continually, every where, all around me.

Though it seems to me, that, in some respects, I was a far better Christian, for two or three years after my first conversion, than I am now; and lived in a more constant delight and pleasure; yet, of late years, I have had a more full and constant sense of the absolute sovereignty of God, and a delight in that sovereignty; and have had more of a sense of the glory of Christ, as a Mediator revealed in the gospel. On one Saturday night, in particular, I had such a discovery of the excellency of the gospel above all other doctrines, that I could not but say to myself, "This is my chosen light, my chosen doctrine;" and of Christ, "This is my chosen Prophet." It appeared sweet, beyond all expression, to follow Christ, and to be taught, and enlightened, and instructed by him; to learn of him, and live to him. Another Saturday night, (January, 1739) I had such a sense, how sweet and blessed a thing it was to walk in the way of duty; to do that which was right and meet to be done, and agreeable to the holy mind of God; and it caused me to break forth into a kind of loud weeping, which held me some time, so that I was forced to shut myself up, and fasten the doors. I could not but, as it were, cry out, "How happy are they which do that which is right in the sight of God! They are blessed indeed, they are the happy ones!" I had, at the same time, a very affecting sense, how meet and suitable it was that God should govern the world, and order all things according to his own pleasure; and I rejoiced in it, that God reigned, and that his will was done.

Sarah Pierrepont

(1723)

Edwards married Miss Pierrepont four years after he wrote the following description of her. Some years after the marriage, they were visited at Northampton by the evangelist Whitefield, who thus recorded his impressions: "On the Sabbath felt wonderful satisfaction in being at the house of Mr. Edwards. He is a son himself and hath also a daughter of Abraham for his wife. A sweeter couple I have not seen. Their children were dressed, not in silks and satins, but plain, as becomes the children of those who in all things ought to be examples of Christian simplicity. She is a woman adorned with a meek and quiet spirit, and talked so feelingly and so solidly of the things of God, and seemed to be such an helpmeet to her husband, that she caused me to renew those prayers which for some months I have put up to God, that He would send me a daughter of Abraham to be my wife" (Allen, *Jonathan Edwards*, 48).

They say there is a young lady in [New Haven] who is beloved of that Great Being, who made and rules the world, and that there are certain seasons in which this Great Being, in some way or other invisible, comes to her and fills her mind with exceeding sweet delight, and that she hardly cares for anything, except to meditate on him — that she expects after a while to be received up where he is, to be raised up out of the world and caught up into heaven; being assured that he loves her too well to let her remain at a distance from him always. There she is to dwell with him, and to be ravished with his love and delight forever. Therefore, if you present all the world before her, with the richest of its treasures, she disregards it and cares not for it, and is unmindful of any pain or affliction. She has a strange sweetness in her mind, and singular purity in her affections; is most just and conscientious in all her conduct; and you could not persuade her to do any thing wrong or sinful, if you would give her all the world, lest she should offend this Great Being. She is of a wonderful sweetness, calmness and universal benevolence of mind; especially after this Great God has manifested himself to her mind. She will sometimes go about from place to place, singing sweetly; and seems to be always full of joy and pleasure; and no one knows for what. She loves to be alone, walking in the fields and groves, and seems to have some one invisible always conversing with her.

Nature

We have shown that the Son of God created the world for this very end, to communicate Himself in an image of His own excellency. He communicates Himself properly only to spirits, and they only are capable of being proper images of His excellency, for they only are properly *beings*, as we have shown. Yet He communicates a sort of a shadow or glimpse of His excellencies to bodies which, as we have shown, are but the shadows of beings and not real beings. He who, by His immediate influence, gives being every moment, and by His spirit actuates the world, because He inclines to communicate Himself and His excellencies, doth doubtless communicate His excellency to bodies, as far as there is any consent or analogy. And the beauty of face and sweet airs in men are not always the effect of the corresponding excellencies of mind; yet the beauties of nature are really emanations or shadows of the excellency of the Son of God.

So that, when we are delighted with flowery meadows and gentle breezes of wind, we may consider that we see only the emanations of the sweet benevolence of Jesus Christ. When we behold the fragrant rose and lily, we see His love and purity. So the green trees and fields, and singing of birds, are the emanations of His infinite joy and benignity. The easiness and naturalness of trees and vines are shadows of His beauty and loveliness. The crystal rivers and murmuring streams are the footsteps of His favor, grace, and beauty. When we behold the light and brightness of the sun, the golden edges of an evening cloud, or the beauteous bow, we behold the adumbrations of His glory and goodness; and in the blue sky, of his mildness and gentleness. There are also many things wherein we may behold His awful majesty: in the sun in his strength, in comets, in thunder, in the hovering thunder-clouds, in ragged rocks and the brows of mountains. That beauteous light with which the world is filled in a clear day is a lively shadow of His spotless holiness, and happiness and delight in communicating Himself. And doubtless this is a reason that Christ is compared so often to those things, and called by their names, as the Sun of Righteousness, the morning-star, the rose of Sharon, and lily of the valley, the apple-tree among trees of the wood, a bundle of myrrh, a roe, or a young hart. By this we may discover the beauty of many of those metaphors and similes which to an *unphilosophical person do seem so uncouth.*

In like manner, when we behold the beauty of man's body in its perfection, we still see like emanations of Christ's divine perfections, although they do not always flow from the mental excellencies of the person that has them. But we see the most proper image of the beauty of Christ when we see beauty in the human soul.

Sinners in the Hands of an Angry God
(1741)

"While the people in neighboring towns were in great distress for their souls, the inhabitants of that town (Enfield) were very secure, loose, and vain," writes Benjamin Trumbull in his *History of Connecticut.* "A lecture had been appointed at Enfield, and the neighboring people, the night before, were so affected at the thoughtlessness of the inhabitants, and in such fear that God would, in his righteous judgment, pass them by, while the divine showers were falling all around them, as to be prostrate before him a considerable part of it, supplicating mercy for their souls. When the time appointed for the lecture came, a number of the neighboring ministers attended, and some from a distance. When they went into the meetinghouse, the appearance of the assembly was thoughtless and vain. The people hardly conducted themselves with common decency. The Rev. Mr. Edwards, of Northampton, preached, and before the sermon was ended, the assembly appeared deeply impressed and bowed down, with an awful conviction of their sin and danger. There was such a breathing of distress and weeping, that the preacher was obliged to speak to the people and desire silence, that he might be heard. This was the beginning of the same great and prevailing concern in that place, with which the colony in general was visited." Trumbull heard this account from a minister, Mr. Wheelock, who was present when the sermon was preached.

Edwards's pupil Samuel Hopkins, thus describes his preaching:

"His appearance in the desk was with a good grace, and his delivery easy, natural and very solemn. He had not a strong, loud voice, but appeared with such gravity and solemnity, and spake with such distinctness, clearness and precision, his words were so full of ideas, set in such a plain and striking light, that few speakers have been so able to demand the attention of an audience as he. His words often discovered a great degree of inward fervor, without much noise or external emotion, and fell with great weight on the minds of his hearers. He made but little motion of his head or hands in the desk, but spake as to discover the motion of his own heart, which tended in the most natural and effectual manner to move and affect others."

Deuteronomy xxxii. 35. — Their foot shall slide in due time.

In this verse is threatened the vengeance of God on the wicked unbelieving Israelites, that were God's visible people, and lived under means of grace; and that notwithstanding all God's wonderful works that he had wrought towards that people, yet remained, as is expressed verse 28, void of counsel, having no understanding in them; and that, under all the cultivations of heaven, brought forth bitter and poisonous fruit; as in the two verses next preceding the text.

The expression that I have chosen for my text, *their foot shall slide in due time*, seems to imply the following things relating to the punishment and destruction that these wicked Israelites were exposed to.

1. That they were *always* exposed to destruction; as one that stands or walks in slippery places is always exposed to fall. This is implied in the manner of their destruction's coming upon them, being represented by their foot's sliding. The same is expressed, Psalm lxxiii. 18: "Surely thou didst set them in slippery places; thou castedst them down into destruction."

2. It implies that they were always exposed to *sudden*, unexpected destruction; as he that walks in slippery places is every moment liable to fall, he can't foresee one moment whether he shall stand or fall the next;

and when he does fall, he falls at once, without warning, which is also expressed in that Psalm lxxiii. 18, 19: "Surely thou didst set them in slippery places: thou castedst them down into destruction. How are they brought into desolation, as *in a moment!*"

3. Another thing implied is, that they are liable to fall of *themselves*, without being thrown down by the hand of another; as he that stands or walks on slippery ground needs nothing but his own weight to throw him down.

4. That the reason why they are not fallen already, and don't fall now, is only that God's appointed time is not come. For it is said that when that due time, or appointed time comes, *their foot shall slide*. Then they shall be left to fall, as they are inclined by their own weight. God won't hold them up in these slippery places any longer, but will let them go; and then, at that very instant, they shall fall to destruction; as he that stands in such slippery declining ground on the edge of a pit that he can't stand alone, when he is let go he immediately falls and is lost.

The observation from the words that I would now insist upon is this,

There is nothing that keeps wicked men at any one moment out of hell, but the mere pleasure of God.

By the mere pleasure of God, I mean his sovereign pleasure, his arbitrary will, restrained by no obligation, hindered by no manner of difficulty, any more than if nothing else but God's mere will had in the least degree or in any respect whatsoever any hand in the preservation of wicked men one moment.

The truth of this observation may appear by the following considerations.

1. There is no want of *power* in God to cast wicked men into hell at any moment. Men's hands can't be strong when God rises up: the strongest have no power to resist him, nor can any deliver out of his hands.

He is not only able to cast wicked men into hell, but he can most easily do it. Sometimes an earthly prince meets with a great deal of difficulty to subdue a rebel that has found means to fortify himself, and has made himself strong by the number of his followers. But it is not so with God. There is no fortress that is any defence against the power of God.

Though hand join in hand, and vast multitudes of God's enemies combine and associate themselves, they are easily broken in pieces: they are as great heaps of light chaff before the whirlwind; or large quantities of dry stubble before devouring flames. We find it easy to tread on and crush a worm that we see crawling on the earth; so 'tis easy for us to cut or singe a slender thread that any thing hangs by; thus easy is it for God, when he pleases, to cast his enemies down to hell. What are we, that we should think to stand before him, at whose rebuke the earth trembles, and before whom the rocks are thrown down!

2. They *deserve* to be cast into hell; so that divine justice never stands in the way, it makes no objection against God's using his power at any moment to destroy them. Yea, on the contrary, justice calls aloud for an infinite punishment of their sins. Divine justice says of the tree that brings forth such grapes of Sodom, "Cut it down, why cumbereth it the ground?" Luke xiii. 7. The sword of divine justice is every moment brandished over their heads, and 'tis nothing but the hand of arbitrary mercy, and God's mere will, that holds it back.

3. They are *already* under a sentence of condemnation to hell. They don't only justly deserve to be cast down thither, but the sentence of the law of God, that eternal and immutable rule of righteousness that God has fixed between him and mankind, is gone out against them, and stands against them; so that they are bound over already to hell: John iii. 18, "He that believeth not is condemned already." So that every unconverted man properly belongs to hell; that is his place; from thence he is: John viii. 23, "Ye are from beneath:" and thither he is bound; 'tis the place that justice, and God's word, and the sentence of his unchangeable law, assigns to him.

4. They are now the objects of that very *same* anger and wrath of God, that is expressed in the torments of hell: and the reason why they don't go down to hell at each moment is not because God, in whose power they are, is not then very angry with them; as angry as he is with many of those miserable creatures that he is now tormenting in hell,

and do there feel and bear the fierceness of his wrath. Yea, God is a great deal more angry with great numbers that are now on earth, yea, doubtless, with many that are now in this congregation, that, it may be, are at ease and quiet, than he is with many of those that are now in the flames of hell.

So that it is not because God is unmindful of their wickedness, and don't resent it, that he don't let loose his hand and cut them off. God is not altogether such a one as themselves, though they may imagine him to be so. The wrath of God burns against them; their damnation don't slumber; the pit is prepared; the fire is made ready; the furnace is now hot, ready to receive them; the flames do now rage and glow. The glittering sword is whet, and held over them, and the pit hath opened her mouth under them.

5. The *devil* stands ready to fall upon them, and seize them as his own, at what moment God shall permit him. They belong to him; he has their souls in his possession, and under his dominion. The Scripture represents them as his *goods*, Luke xi. 21. The devils watch them; they are ever by them, at their right hand; they stand waiting for them, like greedy hungry lions that see their prey, and expect to have it, but are for the present kept back; if God should withdraw his hand by which they are restrained, they would in one moment fly upon their poor souls. The old serpent is gaping for them; hell opens its mouth wide to receive them; and if God should permit it, they would be hastily swallowed up and lost.

6. There are in the souls of wicked men those hellish *principles* reigning, that would presently kindle and flame out into hell-fire, if it were not for God's restraints. There is laid in the very nature of carnal men a foundation for the torments of hell: there are those corrupt principles, in reigning power in them, and in full possession of them, that are seeds of hell-fire. These principles are active and powerful, exceeding violent in their nature, and if it were not for the restraining hand of God upon them, they would soon break out, they would flame out after the same manner as the same corruptions, the same enmity does in the heart of damned souls, and would beget the same torments in 'em as they do in

them. The souls of the wicked are in Scripture compared to the troubled sea, Isaiah lvii. 20. For the present God restrains their wickedness by his mighty power, as he does the raging waves of the troubled sea, saying, "Hitherto shalt thou come, and no further;" but if God should withdraw that restraining power, it would soon carry all afore it. Sin is the ruin and misery of the soul; it is destructive in its nature; and if God should leave it without restraint, there would need nothing else to make the soul perfectly miserable. The corruption of the heart of man is a thing that is immoderate and boundless in its fury; and while wicked men live here, it is like fire pent up by God's restraints, whenas if it were let loose, it would set on fire the course of nature; and as the heart is now a sink of sin, so, if sin was not restrained, it would immediately turn the soul into a fiery oven, or a furnace of fire and brimstone.

7. It is no security to wicked men for one moment, that there are no *visible means of death* at hand. 'Tis no security to a natural man, that he is now in health, and that he don't see which way he should now immediately go out of the world by any accident, and that there is no visible danger in any respect in his circumstances. The manifold and continual experience of the world in all ages shows that this is no evidence that a man is not on the very brink of eternity, and that the next step won't be into another world. The unseen, unthought of ways and means of persons' going suddenly out of the world are innumerable and inconceivable. Unconverted men walk over the pit of hell on a rotten covering, and there are innumerable places in this covering so weak that they won't bear their weight, and these places are not seen. The arrows of death fly unseen at noonday; the sharpest sight can't discern them. God has so many different, unsearchable ways of taking wicked men out of the world and sending 'em to hell, that there is nothing to make it appear that God had need to be at the expense of a miracle, or go out of the ordinary course of his providence, to destroy any wicked man, at any moment. All the means that there are of sinners' going out of the world are so in God's hands, and so absolutely subject to his power and determination, that it don't depend at all less on the mere will of God, whether sinners shall at any moment go to hell, than if means were never made use of, or at all concerned in the case.

8. Natural men's *prudence* and *care* to preserve their own *lives*, or the care of others to preserve them, don't secure 'em a moment. This, divine providence and universal experience does also bear testimony to. There is this clear evidence that men's own wisdom is no security to them from death; that if it were otherwise we should see some difference between the wise and politic men of the world and others, with regard to their liableness to early and unexpected death; but how is it in fact? Eccles. ii. 16, "How dieth the wise man? As the fool."

9. All wicked men's *pains* and *contrivance* they use to escape *hell*, while they continue to reject Christ, and so remain wicked men, don't secure 'em from hell one moment. Almost every natural man that hears of hell flatters himself that he shall escape it; he depends upon himself for his own security, he flatters himself in what he has done, in what he is now doing, or what he intends to do; every one lays out matters in his own mind how he shall avoid damnation, and flatters himself that he contrives well for himself, and that his schemes won't fail. They hear indeed that there are but few saved, and that the bigger part of men that have died heretofore are gone to hell; but each one imagines that he lays out matters better for his own escape than others have done: he don't intend to come to that place of torment; he says within himself, that he intends to take care that shall be effectual, and to order matters so for himself as not to fail.

But the foolish children of men do miserably delude themselves in their own schemes, and in their confidence in their own strength and wisdom; they trust to nothing but a shadow. The bigger part of those that heretofore have lived under the same means of grace, and are now dead, are undoubtedly gone to hell; and it was not because they were not as wise as those that are now alive; it was not because they did not lay out matters as well for themselves to secure their own escape. If it were so that we could come to speak with them, and could inquire of them, one by one, whether they expected, when alive, and when they used to hear about hell, ever to be subjects of that misery, we, doubtless, should hear one and another reply, "No, I never intended to come here: I had laid out matters otherwise in my mind; I thought I should contrive well for myself: I thought my scheme good: I intended to take effectual care; but it came upon me unexpected; I did not look for it at that time, and in that manner; it came as a thief: death outwitted me: God's wrath was too quick for me. O my cursed foolishness! I was flattering myself, and pleasing myself with vain dreams of what I would do hereafter; and when I was saying peace and safety, then sudden destruction came upon me."

10. God has laid himself under *no obligation*, by any promise, to keep any natural man out of hell one moment. God certainly has made no promises either of eternal life, or of any deliverance or preservation from eternal death, but what are contained in the covenant of grace, the promises that are given in Christ, in whom all the promises are yea and amen. But surely they have no interest in the promises of the covenant of grace that are not the children of the covenant, and that do not believe in any of the promises of the covenant, and have no interest in the Mediator of the Covenant.

So that, whatever some have imagined and pretended about promises made to natural men's earnest seeking and knocking, 'tis plain and manifest, that whatever pains a natural man takes in religion, whatever prayers he makes, till he believes in Christ, God is under no manner of obligation to keep him a moment from eternal destruction.

So that thus it is, that natural men are held in the hand of God over the pit of hell; they have deserved the fiery pit, and are already sentenced to it; and God is dreadfully provoked, his anger is as great towards them as to those that are actually suffering the executions of the fierceness of his wrath in hell, and they have done nothing in the least to appease or abate that anger, neither is God in the least bound by any promise to hold 'em up one moment; the devil is waiting for them, hell is gaping for them, the flames gather and flash about them, and would fain lay hold on them and swallow them up; the fire pent up

in their own hearts is struggling to break out; and they have no interest in any Mediator, there are no means within reach that can be any security to them. In short they have no refuge, nothing to take hold of; all that preserves them every moment is the mere arbitrary will, and uncovenanted, unobliged forbearance of an incensed God.

Application

The use may be of *awakening* to unconverted persons in this congregation. This that you have heard is the case of every one of you that are out of Christ. That world of misery, that lake of burning brimstone, is extended abroad under you. *There* is the dreadful pit of the glowing flames of the wrath of God; there is hell's wide gaping mouth open; and you have nothing to stand upon, nor any thing to take hold of. There is nothing between you and hell but the air; 'tis only the power and mere pleasure of God that holds you up.

You probably are not sensible of this; you find you are kept out of hell, but don't see the hand of God in it, but look at other things, as the good state of your bodily constitution, your care of your own life, and the means you use for your own preservation. But indeed these things are nothing; if God should withdraw his hand, they would avail no more to keep you from falling than the thin air to hold up a person that is suspended in it.

Your wickedness makes you as it were heavy as lead, and to tend downwards with great weight and pressure towards hell; and if God should let you go, you would immediately sink and swiftly descend and plunge into the bottomless gulf, and your healthy constitution, and your own care and prudence, and best contrivance, and all your righteousness, would have no more influence to uphold you and keep you out of hell than a spider's web would have to stop a falling rock. Were it not that so is the sovereign pleasure of God, the earth would not bear you one moment; for you are a burden to it; the creation groans with you; the creature is made subject to the bondage of your corruption, not willingly; the sun don't willingly shine upon you to give you light to serve sin and Satan; the earth don't willingly yield her increase to satisfy your lusts; nor is it willingly a stage for your wickedness to be acted upon; the air don't willingly serve you for breath to maintain the flame of life in your vitals, while you spend your life in the service of God's enemies. God's creatures are good, and were made for men to serve God with, and don't willingly subserve to any other purpose, and groan when they are abused to purposes so directly contrary to their nature and end. And the world would spew you out, were it not for the sovereign hand of him who hath subjected it in hope. There are the black clouds of God's wrath now hanging directly over your heads, full of the dreadful storm, and big with thunder; and were it not for the restraining hand of God, it would immediately burst forth upon you. The sovereign pleasure of God, for the present, stays his rough wind; otherwise it would come with fury, and your destruction would come like a whirlwind, and you would be like the chaff of the summer threshing floor.

The wrath of God is like great waters that are dammed for the present; they increase more and more, and rise higher and higher, till an outlet is given; and the longer the stream is stopped, the more rapid and mighty is its course, when once it is let loose. 'Tis true, that judgment against your evil work has not been executed hitherto; the floods of God's vengeance have been withheld; but your guilt in the mean time is constantly increasing, and you are every day treasuring up more wrath; the waters are continually rising, and waxing more and more mighty; and there is nothing but the mere pleasure of God that holds the waters back, that are unwilling to be stopped, and press hard to go forward. If God should only withdraw his hand from the floodgate, it would immediately fly open, and the fiery floods of the fierceness and wrath of God would rush forth with inconceivable fury, and would come upon you with omnipotent power; and if your strength were ten thousand times greater than it is, yea, ten thousand times greater than the strength of the stoutest, sturdiest devil in hell, it would be nothing to withstand or endure it.

The bow of God's wrath is bent, and the arrow made ready on the string, and justice bends the arrow at your heart, and strains the bow, and it is nothing but the mere pleasure of God, and that of an angry God, without any promise or obligation at all, that keeps the arrow one moment from being made drunk with your blood.

Thus are all you that never passed under a great change of heart by the mighty power of the Spirit of God upon your souls; all that were never born again, and made new creatures, and raised from being dead in sin to a state of new and before altogether unexperienced light and life, (however you may have reformed your life in many things, and may have had religious affections, and may keep up a form of religion in your families and closets, and in the house of God, and may be strict in it), you are thus in the hands of an angry God; 'tis nothing but his mere pleasure that keeps you from being this moment swallowed up in everlasting destruction.

However unconvinced you may now be of the truth of what you hear, by and by you will be fully convinced of it. Those that are gone from being in the like circumstances with you see that it was so with them; for destruction came suddenly upon most of them; when they expected nothing of it, and while they were saying, Peace and safety: now they see, that those things that they depended on for peace and safety were nothing but thin air and empty shadows.

The God that holds you over the pit of hell, much as one holds a spider or some loathsome insect over the fire, abhors you, and is dreadfully provoked; his wrath towards you burns like fire; he looks upon you as worthy of nothing else, but to be cast into the fire; he is of purer eyes than to bear to have you in his sight; you are ten thousand times so abominable in his eyes, as the most hateful and venomous serpent is in ours. You have offended him infinitely more than ever a stubborn rebel did his prince: and yet it is nothing but his hand that holds you from falling into the fire every moment. 'Tis ascribed to nothing else, that you did not go to hell the last night; that you was suffered to awake again in this world after you closed your eyes to sleep; and there is no other reason to be given why you have not dropped into hell since you arose in the morning, but that God's hand has held you up. There is no other reason to be given why you han't gone to hell since you have sat here in the house of God, provoking his pure eyes by your sinful wicked manner of attending his solemn worship. Yea, there is nothing else that is to be given as a reason why you don't this very moment drop down into hell.

O sinner! consider the fearful danger you are in. 'Tis a great furnace of wrath, a wide and bottomless pit, full of the fire of wrath, that you are held over in the hand of that God whose wrath is provoked and incensed as much against you as against many of the damned in hell. You hang by a slender thread, with the flames of divine wrath flashing about it, and ready every moment to singe it and burn it asunder; and you have no interest in any Mediator, and nothing to lay hold of to save yourself, nothing to keep off the flames of wrath, nothing of your own, nothing that you ever have done, nothing that you can do, to induce God to spare you one moment.

And consider here more particularly several things concerning that wrath that you are in such danger of.

1. *Whose* wrath it is. It is the wrath of the infinite God. If it were only the wrath of man, though it were of the most potent prince, it would be comparatively little to be regarded. The wrath of kings is very much dreaded, especially of absolute monarchs, that have the possessions and lives of their subjects wholly in their power, to be disposed of at their mere will. Prov. xx. 2, "The fear of a king is as the roaring of a lion: whoso provoketh him to anger sinneth against his own soul." The subject that very much enrages an arbitrary prince is liable to suffer the most extreme torments that human art can invent, or human power can inflict. But the greatest earthly potentates, in their greatest majesty and strength, and when clothed in their greatest terrors, are but feeble, despicable worms of the dust, in comparison of the great and almighty Creator and King of heaven and earth: it is but little that they can do when most enraged, and when they have exerted the utmost of their fury. All the kings of the earth before God are as grasshoppers; they are nothing, and less than nothing: both their love and their hatred is to be despised. The wrath of the great King of kings is as much more terrible than theirs, as his majesty is greater. Luke xii. 4, 5, "And I say unto you my friends, Be not afraid of them that kill the body, and after that have no more that they can do. But I will forewarn you whom you shall fear: Fear him, which after he hath killed hath power to cast into hell; yea, I say unto you, Fear him."

2. 'Tis the *fierceness* of his wrath that you are exposed to. We often read of the *fury* of God; as in Isaiah lix. 18: "According to their deeds, accordingly he will repay fury to his adversaries." So Isaiah lxvi. 15, "For, behold, the Lord will come with fire, and with his chariots like a whirlwind, to render his anger with fury, and his rebuke with flames of fire." And so in many other places. So we read of God's *fierceness*, Rev. xix. 15. There we read of "the wine-press of the fierceness and wrath of Almighty God." The words are exceeding terrible: if it had only been said, "the wrath of God," the words would have implied that which is infinitely dreadful: but 'tis not only said so, but "the fierceness and wrath of God." The fury of God! The fierceness of Jehovah! Oh, how dreadful must that be! Who can utter or conceive what such expressions carry in them! But it is not only said so, but "the fierceness and wrath of Almighty God." As though there would be a very great manifestation of his almighty power in what the fierceness of his wrath should inflict, as though omnipotence should be as it were enraged, and exerted, as men are wont to exert their strength in the fierceness of their wrath. Oh! then, what will be the consequence! What will become of the poor worm that shall suffer it! Whose hands can be strong! And whose heart endure! To what a dreadful, inexpressible, inconceivable depth of misery must the poor creature be sunk who shall be the subject of this!

Consider this, you that are here present, that yet remain in an unregenerate state. That God will execute the fierceness of his anger implies that he will inflict wrath without any pity. When God beholds the ineffable extremity of your case, and sees your torment so vastly disproportioned to your strength, and sees how your poor soul is crushed, and sinks down, as it were, into an infinite gloom; he will have no compassion upon you, he will not forbear the executions of his wrath, or in the least lighten his hand; there shall be no moderation or mercy, nor will God then at all stay his rough wind; he will have no regard to your welfare, nor be at all careful lest you should suffer too much in any other sense, than only that you should not suffer beyond what strict justice requires: nothing shall be withheld because it is so hard for you to bear. Ezek. viii. 18, "Therefore will I also deal in fury: mine eye shall not spare, neither will I have pity: and though they cry in mine ears with a loud voice, yet will I not hear them." Now God stands ready to pity you; this is a day of mercy; you may cry now with some encouragement of obtaining mercy: but when once the day of mercy is past, your most lamentable and dolorous cries and shrieks will be in vain; you will be wholly lost and thrown away of God, as to any regard to your welfare; God will have no other use to put you to, but only to suffer misery; you shall be continued in being to no other end; for you will be a vessel of wrath fitted to destruction; and there will be no other use of this vessel, but only to be filled full of wrath: God will be so far from pitying you when you cry to him, that 'tis said he will only "laugh and mock," Prov. i. 25, 26, &c.

How awful are those words, Isaiah lxiii. 3, which are the words of the great God: "I will tread them in mine anger, and trample them in my fury; and their blood shall be sprinkled upon my garments, and I will stain all my raiment." 'Tis perhaps impossible to conceive of words that carry in them greater manifestations of these three things, viz., contempt and hatred and fierceness of indignation. If you cry to God to pity you, he will be so far from pitying you in your doleful case, or showing you the least regard or favor, that instead of that he'll only tread you under foot: and though he will know that you can't bear the weight of omnipotence treading upon you, yet he won't regard that, but he will crush you under his feet without mercy; he'll crush out your blood, and make it fly, and it shall be sprinkled on his garments, so as to stain all his raiment. He will not only hate you, but he will have you in the utmost contempt; no place shall be thought fit for you but under

his feet, to be trodden down as the mire of the streets.

3. The misery you are exposed to is that which God will inflict to that end, that he might *show* what that *wrath of Jehovah* is God hath had it on his heart to show to angels and men, both how excellent his love is, and also how terrible his wrath is. Sometimes earthly kings have a mind to show how terrible their wrath is, by the extreme punishments they would execute on those that provoke 'em. Nebuchadnezzar, that mighty and haughty monarch of the Chaldean empire, was willing to show his wrath when enraged with Shadrach, Meshech, and Abednego; and accordingly gave order that the burning fiery furnace should be heated seven times hotter than it was before; doubtless, it was raised to the utmost degree of fierceness that human art could raise it; but the great God is also willing to show his wrath, and magnify his awful Majesty and mighty power in the extreme sufferings of his enemies. Rom. ix. 22, "What if God, willing to show his wrath, and to make his power known, endured with much long-suffering the vessels of wrath fitted to destruction?" And seeing this is his design, and what he has determined, to show how terrible the unmixed, unrestrained wrath, the fury and fierceness of Jehovah is, he will do it to effect. There will be something accomplished and brought to pass that will be dreadful with a witness. When the great and angry God hath risen up and executed his awful vengeance on the poor sinner, and the wretch is actually suffering the infinite weight and power of his indignation, then will God call upon the whole universe to behold that awful majesty and mighty power that is to be seen in it. Isa. xxxiii. 12, 13, 14, "And the people shall be as the burnings of lime, as thorns cut up shall they be burnt in the fire. Hear, ye that are far off, what I have done; and ye that are near, acknowledge my might. The sinners in Zion are afraid; fearfulness hath surprised the hypocrites," &c.

Thus it will be with you that are in an unconverted state, if you continue in it; the infinite might, and majesty, and terribleness, of the Omnipotent God shall be magnified upon you in the ineffable strength of your torments. You shall be tormented in the presence of the holy angels, and in the presence of the Lamb; and when you shall be in this state of suffering, the glorious inhabitants of heaven shall go forth and look on the awful spectacle, that they may see what the wrath and fierceness of the Almighty is; and when they have seen it, they will fall down and adore that great power and majesty. Isa. lxvi. 23, 24, "And it shall come to pass, that from one new moon to another, and from one sabbath to another, shall all flesh come to worship before me, saith the Lord. And they shall go forth, and look upon the carcasses of the men that have transgressed against me: for their worm shall not die, neither shall their fire be quenched; and they shall be an abhorring unto all flesh."

4. It is *everlasting* wrath. It would be dreadful to suffer this fierceness and wrath of Almighty God one moment; but you must suffer it to all eternity: there will be no end to this exquisite, horrible misery. When you look forward, you shall see a long forever, a boundless duration before you, which will swallow up your thoughts, and amaze your soul; and you will absolutely despair of ever having any deliverance, any end, any mitigation, any rest at all; you will know certainly that you must wear out long ages, millions of millions of ages, in wrestling and conflicting with this almighty, merciless vengeance; and then when you have so done, when so many ages have actually been spent by you in this manner, you will know that all is but a point to what remains. So that your punishment will indeed be infinite. Oh, who can express what the state of a soul in such circumstances is! All that we can possibly say about it gives but a very feeble, faint representation of it; it is inexpressible and inconceivable: for "who knows the power of God's anger?"

How dreadful is the state of those that are daily and hourly in danger of this great wrath and infinite misery! But this is the dismal case of every soul in this congregation that has not been born again, however moral and strict, sober and religious, they may otherwise be. Oh, that you would consider it, whether you be young or old! There is reason to think that there are many in this congregation now hearing this discourse, that will actually be the subjects of this very misery to all eternity. We know not who they are, or in what seats they sit, or what thoughts they now have. It may be they are now at ease, and hear all these things without much disturbance, and are now flattering themselves that they are not the persons, promising themselves that they shall escape. If we knew that there was one person, and but one, in the whole congregation, that was to be the subject of this misery, what an awful thing it would be to think of! If we knew who it was, what an awful sight would it be to see such a person! How might all the rest of the congregation lift up a lamentable and bitter cry over him! But alas! instead of one, how many is it likely will remember this discourse in hell! And it would be a wonder, if some that are now present should not be in hell in a very short time, before this year is out. And it would be no wonder if some persons that now sit here in some seats of this meeting-house in health, and quiet and secure, should be there before to-morrow morning. Those of you that finally continue in a natural condition, that shall keep out of hell longest, will be there in a little time! Your damnation don't slumber; it will come swiftly and, in all probability, very suddenly upon many of you. You have reason to wonder that you are not already in hell. 'Tis doubtless the case of some that heretofore you have seen and known, that never deserved hell more than you and that heretofore appeared as likely to have been now alive as you. Their case is past all hope; they are crying in extreme misery and perfect despair. But here you are in the land of the living and in the house of God, and have an opportunity to obtain salvation. What would not those poor, damned, hopeless souls give for one day's such opportunity as you now enjoy!

And now you have an extraordinary opportunity, a day wherein Christ has flung the door of mercy wide open, and stands in the door calling and crying with a loud voice to poor sinners; a day wherein many are flocking to him and pressing into the Kingdom of God. Many are daily coming from the east, west, north and south; many that were very likely in the same miserable condition that you are in are in now a happy state, with their hearts filled with love to him that has loved them and washed them from their sins in his own blood, and rejoicing in hope of the glory of God. How awful is it to be left behind at such a day! To see so many others feasting, while you are pining and perishing! To see so many rejoicing and singing for joy of heart, while you have cause to mourn for sorrow of heart and howl for vexation of spirit! How can you rest for one moment in such a condition? Are not your souls as precious as the souls of the people at Suffield, where they are flocking from day to day to Christ?

Are there not many here that have lived long in the world that are not to this day born again, and so are aliens from the commonwealth of Israel and have done nothing ever since they have lived but treasure up wrath against the day of wrath? Oh, sirs, your case in an especial manner is extremely dangerous; your guilt and hardness of heart is extremely great. Don't you see how generally persons of your years are passed over and left in the present remarkable and wonderful dispensation of God's mercy? You had need to consider yourselves and wake thoroughly out of sleep; you cannot bear the fierceness and the wrath of the infinite God.

And you that are young men and young women, will you neglect this precious season that you now enjoy, when so many others of your age are renouncing all youthful vanities and flocking to Christ? You especially have now an extraordinary opportunity; but if you neglect it, it will soon be with you as it is with those persons that spent away all the precious days of youth in sin and are now come to such a dreadful pass in blindness and hardness.

And you children that are unconverted, don't you know that you are going down to hell to bear the dreadful wrath of that God that is now angry with you every day and every night? Will you be content to be the children of the devil, when so many other children in the land are converted and are become the holy and happy children of the King of kings?

And let every one that is yet out of Christ and hanging over the pit of hell, whether they be old men and women or middle-aged or young people or little children, now hearken to the loud calls of God's word and providence. This acceptable year of the Lord that is a day of such great favor to some will doubtless be a day of as remarkable vengeance to others. Men's hearts harden and their guilt increases apace at such a day as this, if they neglect their souls. And never was there so great danger of such persons being given up to hardness of heart and blindness of mind. God seems now to be hastily gathering in his elect in all parts of the land; and probably the bigger part of adult persons that ever shall be saved will be brought in now in a little time, and that it will be as it was on that great outpouring of the Spirit upon the Jews in the Apostles' days, the election will obtain and the rest will be blinded. If this should be the case with you, you will eternally curse this day, and will curse the day that ever you was born to see such a season of the pouring out of God's Spirit, and will wish that you had died and gone to hell before you had seen it. Now undoubtedly it is as it was in the days of John the Baptist, the axe is in an extraordinary manner laid at the root of the trees, that every tree that bringeth not forth good fruit may be hewn down and cast into the fire.

Therefore let every one that is out of Christ now awake and fly from the wrath to come. The wrath of Almighty God is now undoubtedly hanging over great part of this congregation. Let every one fly out of Sodom. *"Haste and escape for your lives, look not behind you, escape to the mountain, lest ye be consumed."*

Conclusion to
The Freedom of the Will
(1754)

As it has been demonstrated that the futurity of all future events is established by previous necessity, either natural or moral; so it is manifest that the Sovereign Creator and Disposer of the world has ordered this necessity by ordering his own conduct, either in designedly acting or forbearing to act. For, as the being of the world is from God, so the circumstances in which it had its being at first, both negative and positive, must be ordered by him in one of these ways; and all the necessary consequences of these circumstances must be ordered by him. And God's active and positive interpositions, after the world was created, and the consequences of these inter-positions; also every instance of his forbearing to interpose, and the sure consequences of this forbearance, must all be determined accord-ing to his pleasure. And therefore every event, which is the consequence of any thing whatsoever, or that is connected with any foregoing thing or circumstance, either posi-tive or negative, as the ground or reason of its existence, must be ordered of God; either by a designed efficiency and interposition or a designed forbearing to operate or interpose. But, as has been proved, all events whatsoever are necessarily connected with something fore-going, either positive or negative, which is the ground of their existence. It follows, therefore, that the whole series of events is thus connected with something in the state of things, either positive or negative, which is original in the series; i.e., something which is connected with nothing preceding that, but God's own immediate conduct, either his acting or forbearing to act. From whence it follows, that as God designedly orders his own conduct, and its connected consequences, it must necessarily be that he designedly orders all things.

BENJAMIN FRANKLIN (1706–1790)

The one document which no student of Franklin's life can ignore is his *Autobiography*. Looking backward from patriarchal heights, Franklin traces in his narrative his first fifty years. Born in Boston, January 17, 1706, the son of a tallow chandler, he was apprenticed early in his brother's printing shop, but at the age of seventeen ran away to Philadelphia. The next year he sailed for England, bearing with him letters that proved worthless. He returned to Philadelphia in 1726, found his opportunity and husbanded it with shrewd Yankee genius. He was printer, publisher, and shop-keeper.

"In December, 1732," he says, "I first published my Almanack, under the name of *Richard Saunders*." The price was five pence. Within the month three editions were sold, and it was continued for twenty-five years thereafter with an average sale of 10,000 copies annually. "The publication ranks as one of the most influential in the world. . . . 'Poor Richard' was the revered and popular schoolmaster of a young na-tion during its period of tutelage." (Morse, *Benjamin Franklin*.) Nor was the influ-ence of the book confined to America. P. L. Ford wrote in 1899: "Seventy-five edi-tions of it have been printed in English, fifty-six in French, eleven in German, and nine in Italian. It has been translated into Spanish, Danish, Swedish, Welsh, Polish, Gaelic, Russian, Bohemian, Dutch, Catalan, Chinese, modern Greek, and phonetic writing."

When he had kept his shop so well that it kept him, Franklin felt that he had leisure to devote to Philadelphia public life. He became interested also in scientific experi-ment and in 1752 demonstrated the identity of lightning with electricity. He was deputy postmaster-general for the colonies for twenty-one years. In 1757, the year when Edwards was called to the presidency of the College of New Jersey, Franklin was sent to the British court as agent for Pennsylvania.

Here the *Autobiography* ends, just as Benjamin Franklin ended his period of provin-cialism and began to stand forth as the representative man of the eighteenth century. He remained in England, except for short periods, until 1775, representing other colonies as well as his own. He returned home when relations became desperate, signed the Declaration of Independence, and the same year went as ambassador to France. The revolution accomplished and peace concluded, he returned to America. He might have been excused for retiring to his study and finishing his *Autobiography*, but the end to his public career was not yet. He was at once elected president of Pennsylvania and sat in the constitutional convention of 1787.

As a scientist, Franklin left the world a wider knowledge of electricity, a map of the Gulf Stream, Franklin stoves, bi-focal glasses, lightning rods, and a progressive viewpoint. As a man of public affairs he left for his monuments the Philadelphia Public Library, the University of Pennsylvania, a postal system, a magazine, and — more important — the friendship of France and the respect of all Europe. He was the only American whose name is signed to the four principal political documents of revolutionary days: the Declaration of Independence, the treaty with France, the treaty of peace with England, and the Constitution of the United States. As a man of letters he is remembered for one book that is a masterpiece of its kind, the *Autobiography*, and for many slighter works written with a clear and urbane style that might have been approved by Joseph Addison and Dr. Johnson.

The achievement of Franklin has been summed up by Preserved Smith in *A History of Modern Culture*. "Self-educated and self-made, versatile, optimistic, practical, benevolent, and tireless, he became, in the eyes of Europe, the first embodiment of the American character. He was also typical of one large aspect of his age, of the popular, democratic, and utilitarian side of the Enlightenment. At a time when science was in the air, he contributed importantly to science. In the age when journals were beginning to absorb a large portion of the attention of the reading public, he was a brilliant journalist. In those great days of rationalism and humanitarianism he was the tireless preacher of reason, of prudence, and of kindness. In the first age of popular education, he did much to foster and to supply the demand for it. In the formative period of modern democracy, he was the typical democrat. In the adolescence of America, he was the representative American."

For Franklin's collected works, see the edition of A. H. Smyth, 1905. Among many reprints of the *Autobiography*, the student may find useful Max Farrand's edition of 1949, which is based on all authentic texts. A short life is by C. L. Becker in *DAB*. More extensive studies of much interest are P. L. Ford, *The Many-Sided Franklin*, 1899; W. C. Bruce, *Benjamin Franklin Self-Revealed*, 1918; B. Faÿ, *Franklin, the Apostle of Modern Times*, 1930; C. Van Doren, *Benjamin Franklin*, 1938. A copious volume of selections was edited by F. L. Mott and C. E. Jorgenson in the *AWS*, 1936.

From his Autobiography

(1771, 1784–89)

[Ancestry]

This obscure family of ours was early in the Reformation, and continued Protestants through the reign of Queen Mary, when they were sometimes in danger of trouble on account of their zeal against popery. They had got an English Bible, and to conceal and secure it, it was fastened open with tapes under and within the cover of a joint-stool. When my great-great-grandfather read it to his family, he turned up the joint-stool upon his knees, turning over the leaves then under the tapes. One of the children stood at the door to give notice if he saw the apparitor coming, who was an officer of the spiritual court. In that case the stool was turned down again upon its feet, when the Bible remained concealed under it as before. This anecdote I had from my uncle Benjamin. The family continued all of the Church of England till about the end of Charles the Second's reign, when some of the ministers that had been outed for non-conformity holding conventicles in Northamptonshire, Benjamin and Josiah adhered to them, and so continued all their lives: the rest of the family remained with the Episcopal Church.

Josiah, my father, married young, and carried his wife with three children into New England, about 1682. The conventicles having been forbidden by law, and frequently disturbed, induced some considerable men of his acquaintance to remove to that country, and he was prevailed with to accompany them thither, where they expected to enjoy their mode of religion with freedom. By the same wife he had four children more born there, and by a second wife ten more, in all seventeen; of which I remember thirteen sitting at one time at his table, who all grew up to be men and women, and married; I was the youngest son, and the youngest child but two, and was born in Boston, New England. My mother, the second wife, was Abiah Folger, daughter of Peter Folger, one of the first settlers of New England, of whom honorable mention is made by Cotton Mather, in his church history of that country, entitled Magnalia Christi Americana, as "*a godly, learned Englishman*," if I remember the words rightly. I have heard that he wrote sundry small occasional pieces, but only one of them was printed, which I saw now many years since. It was written in 1675, in the homespun verse of that time and people, and addressed to those then concerned in the government there. It was in favor of liberty of conscience, and in behalf of the Baptists, Quakers, and other sectaries that had been under persecution, ascribing the Indian wars, and other distresses that had befallen the country, to that persecution, as so many judgments of God to punish so heinous an offense, and exhorting a repeal of those uncharitable laws. The whole appeared to me as written with a good deal of decent plainness and manly freedom. The six concluding lines I remember, though I have forgotten the two first of the stanza; but the purport of them was, that his censures proceeded from good-will, and,

therefore, he would be known to be the author.

"Because to be a libeller (says he)
    I hate it with my heart;
From Sherburne town, where now I dwell
    My name I do put here;
Without offense your real friend,
    It is Peter Folgier."

[*Studies*]

My elder brothers were all put apprentices to different trades. I was put to the grammar-school at eight years of age, my father intending to devote me, as the tithe of his sons, to the service of the Church. My early readiness in learning to read (which must have been very early, as I do not remember when I could not read), and the opinion of all his friends, that I should certainly make a good scholar, encouraged him in this purpose of his. My uncle Benjamin, too, approved of it, and proposed to give me all his short-hand volumes of sermons, I suppose as a stock to set up with, if I would learn his character. I continued, however, at the grammar-school not quite one year, though in that time I had risen gradually from the middle of the class of that year to be the head of it, and farther was removed into the next class above it, in order to go with that into the third at the end of the year. But my father, in the meantime, from a view of the expense of a college education, which having so large a family he could not well afford, and the mean living many so educated were afterwards able to obtain — reasons that he gave to his friends in my hearing — altered his first intention, took me from the grammar-school, and sent me to a school for writing and arithmetic, kept by a then famous man, Mr. George Brownell, very successful in his profession generally, and that by mild, encouraging methods. Under him I acquired fair writing pretty soon, but I failed in the arithmetic, and made no progress in it. At ten years old I was taken home to assist my father in his business, which was that of a tallow-chandler and sope-boiler; a business he was not bred to, but had assumed on his arrival in New England, and on finding his dying trade would not maintain his family, being in little request. Accordingly, I was employed in cutting wick for the candles, filling the dipping mold and the molds for cast candles, attending the shop, going of errands, etc. * * *

From a child I was fond of reading, and all the little money that came into my hands was ever laid out in books. Pleased with the *Pilgrim's Progress*, my first collection was of John Bunyan's works in separate little volumes. I afterward sold them to enable me to buy R. Burton's *Historical Collections*; they were small chapmen's books, and cheap, 40 or 50 in all. My father's little library consisted chiefly of books in polemic divinity, most of which I read, and have since often regretted that, at a time when I had such a thirst for knowledge, more proper books had not fallen in my way, since it was now resolved I should not be a clergyman. Plutarch's *Lives* there was in which I read abundantly, and I still think that time spent to great advantage. There was also a book of De Foe's, called an *Essay on Projects*, and another of Dr. Mather's, called *Essays to do Good*, which perhaps gave me a turn of thinking that had an influence on some of the principal future events of my life.

This bookish inclination at length determined my father to make me a printer, though he had already one son (James) of that profession. In 1717 my brother James returned from England with a press and letters to set up his business in Boston. I liked it much better than that of my father, but still had a hankering for the sea. To prevent the apprehended effect of such an inclination, my father was impatient to have me bound to my brother. I stood out some time, but at last was persuaded, and signed the indentures when I was yet but twelve years old. I was to serve as an apprentice till I was twenty-one years of age, only I was to be allowed journeyman's wages during the last year. In a little time I made great proficiency in the business, and became a useful hand to my brother. I now had access to better books. An acquaintance with the apprentices of booksellers enabled me sometimes to borrow a small one, which I was careful to return soon and clean. Often I sat up in my room reading the greatest part of the night, when the book was borrowed in the evening and to be returned early in the morning, lest it should be missed or wanted.

And after some time an ingenious tradesman, Mr. Matthew Adams, who had a pretty collection of books, and who frequented our printing-house, took notice of me, invited me to his library, and very kindly lent me such books as I chose to read. I now took a fancy to poetry, and made some little pieces; my brother, thinking it might turn to account, encouraged me, and put me on composing occasional ballads. One was called *The Lighthouse Tragedy*, and contained an account of the drowning of Captain Worthilake, with his two daughters: the other was a sailor's song, on the taking of *Teach* (or blackbeard) the pirate. They were wretched stuff, in the Grub-street-ballad style; and when they were printed he sent me about the town to sell them. The first sold wonderfully; the event being recent, having made a great noise. This flattered my vanity; but my father discouraged me by ridiculing my performances, and telling me verse-makers were generally beggars. So I escaped being a poet, most probably a very bad one; but as prose writing has been of great use to me in the course of my life, and was a principal means of my advancement, I shall tell you how, in such a situation, I acquired what little ability I have in that way.

There was another bookish lad in the town, John Collins by name, with whom I was intimately acquainted. We sometimes disputed, and very fond we were of argument, and very desirous of confuting one another, which disputatious turn, by the way, is apt to become a very bad habit, making people often extremely disagreeable in company by the contradiction that is necessary to bring it into practice; and thence, besides souring and spoiling the conversation, is productive of disgusts and, perhaps, enmities where you may have occasion for friendship. I had caught it by reading my father's books of dispute about religion. Persons of good sense, I have since observed, seldom fall into it, except lawyers, university men, and men of all sorts that have been bred at Edinborough.

A question was once, somehow or other, started between Collins and me, of the propriety of educating the female sex in learning, and their abilities for study. He was of opinion that it was improper, and that they were naturally unequal to it. I took the contrary side, perhaps a little for dispute's sake. He was naturally more eloquent, had a ready plenty of words; and sometimes, as I thought, bore me down more by his fluency than by the strength of his reasons. As we parted without settling the point, and were not to see one another again for some time, I sat down to put my arguments in writing, which I copied fair and sent to him. He answered, and I replied. Three or four letters of a side had passed, when my father happened to find my papers and read them. Without entering into the discussion, he took occasion to talk to me about the manner of my writing; observed that, though I had the advantage of my antagonist in correct spelling and pointing (which I ow'd to the printing-house), I fell far short in elegance of expression, in method and in perspicuity, of which he convinced me by several instances. I saw the justice of his remarks, and thence grew more attentive to the manner in writing, and determined to endeavor at improvement.

About this time I met with an odd volume of the *Spectator*. It was the third. I had never before seen any of them. I bought it, read it over and over, and was much delighted with it. I thought the writing excellent, and wished, if possible, to imitate it. With this view I took some of the papers, and, making short hints of the sentiment in each sentence, laid them by a few days, and then, without looking at the book, try'd to compleat the papers again, by expressing each hinted sentiment at length, and as fully as it had been expressed before, in any suitable words that should come to hand. Then I compared my *Spectator* with the original, discovered some of my faults, and corrected them. But I found I wanted a stock of words, or a readiness in recollecting and using them, which I thought I should have acquired before that time if I had gone on making verses; since the continual occasion for words of the same import, but of different length, to suit the measure, or of different sound for the rhyme, would have laid me under a constant necessity of searching for variety, and also have tended to fix that variety in my mind, and make me master of it. Therefore I took some of the tales and turned them into verse; and, after a time,

when I had pretty well forgotten the prose, turned them back again. I also sometimes jumbled my collections of hints into confusion, and after some weeks endeavored to reduce them into the best order, before I began to form the full sentences and compleat the paper. This was to teach me method in the arrangement of thoughts. By comparing my work afterwards with the original, I discovered my faults and amended them; but I sometimes had the pleasure of fancying that, in certain particulars of small import, I had been lucky enough to improve the method or the language, and this encouraged me to think I might possibly in time come to be a tolerable English writer, of which I was extremely ambitious. My time for these exercises and for reading was at night, after work or before it began in the morning, or on Sundays, when I contrived to be in the printing-house alone, evading as much as I could the common attendance on public worship which my father used to exact on me when I was under his care, and which indeed I still thought a duty, though I could not, as it seemed to me, afford time to practise it.

When about 16 years of age I happened to meet with a book, written by one Tryon, recommending a vegetable diet. I determined to go into it. My brother, being yet unmarried, did not keep house, but boarded himself and his apprentices in another family. My refusing to eat flesh occasioned an inconveniency, and I was frequently chid for my singularity. I made myself acquainted with Tryon's manner of preparing some of his dishes, such as boiling potatoes or rice, making hasty pudding, and a few others, and then proposed to my brother, that if he would give me, weekly, half the money he paid for my board, I would board myself. He instantly agreed to it, and I presently found that I could save half what he paid me. This was an additional fund for buying books. But I had another advantage in it. My brother and the rest going from the printing-house to their meals, I remained there alone, and, despatching presently my light repast, which often was no more than a bisket or a slice of bread, a handful of raisins or a tart from the pastrycook's, and a glass of water, had the rest of the time till their return for study, in which I made the greater progress, from that greater clearness of head and quicker apprehension which usually attend temperance in eating and drinking.

And now it was that, being on some occasion made asham'd of my ignorance in figures, which I had twice failed in learning when at school, I took Cocker's book of Arithmetick, and went through the whole by myself with great ease. I also read Seller's and Shermy's books of Navigation, and became acquainted with the little geometry they contain; but never proceeded far in that science. And I read about this time Locke *On Human Understanding*, and the *Art of Thinking*, by Messrs. du Port Royal.

While I was intent on improving my language, I met with an English grammar (I think it was Greenwood's), at the end of which there were two little sketches of the arts of rhetoric and logic, the latter finishing with a specimen of a dispute in the Socratic method; and soon after I procur'd Xenophon's *Memorable Things of Socrates*, wherein there are many instances of the same method. I was charm'd with it, adopted it, dropt my abrupt contradiction and positive argumentation, and put on the humble inquirer and doubter. And being then, from reading Shaftesbury and Collins, become a real doubter in many points of our religious doctrine, I found this method safest for myself and very embarrassing to those against whom I used it; therefore I took a delight in it, practis'd it continually, and grew very artful and expert in drawing people, even of superior knowledge, into concessions, the consequences of which they did not foresee, entangling them in difficulties out of which they could not extricate themselves, and so obtaining victories that neither myself nor my cause always deserved. I continu'd this method some few years, but gradually left it, retaining only the habit of expressing myself in terms of modest diffidence; never using, when I advanced anything that may possibly be disputed, the words *certainly*, *undoubtedly*, or any others that give the air of positiveness to an opinion, but rather say, I conceive or apprehend a thing to be so and so; it appears to me, or *I should think it so or so*, for such and such reasons; or *I imagine it to be so;* or *it is so, if*

I am not mistaken. This habit, I believe, has been of great advantage to me when I have had occasion to inculcate my opinions, and persuade men into measures that I have been from time to time engag'd in promoting; and, as the chief ends of conversation are to *inform* or to be *informed*, to *please* or to *persuade*, I wish well-meaning, sensible men would not lessen their power of doing good by a positive, assuming manner, that seldom fails to disgust, tends to create opposition, and to defeat everyone of those purposes for which speech was given to us, to wit, giving or receiving information or pleasure. For, if you would inform, a positive and dogmatical manner in advancing your sentiments may provoke contradiction and prevent a candid attention. If you wish information and improvement from the knowledge of others, and yet at the same time express yourself as firmly fix'd in your present opinions, modest, sensible men, who do not love disputation, will probably leave you undisturbed in the possession of your error. And by such a manner, you can seldom hope to recommend yourself in *pleasing* your hearers, or to persuade those whose concurrence you desire. Pope says, judiciously:

> *"Men should be taught as if you taught them not,*
> *And things unknown propos'd as things forgot;"*

farther recommending to us

"To speak, tho' sure, with seeming diffidence."

And he might have coupled with this line that which he has coupled with another, I think, less properly,

"For want of modesty is want of sense."

If you ask, Why less properly? I must repeat the lines,

> "Immodest words admit of no defense,
> For want of modesty is want of sense."

Now, is not *want of sense* (where a man is so unfortunate as to want it) some apology for his *want of modesty?* and would not the lines stand more justly thus?

> "Immodest words admit *but* this defense,
> That want of modesty is want of sense."

This, however, I should submit to better judgments.

[Morals]

Before I enter upon my public appearance in business, it may be well to let you know the then state of my mind with regard to my principles and morals, that you may see how far those influenc'd the future events of my life. My parents had early given me religious impressions, and brought me through my childhood piously in the Dissenting way. But I was scarce fifteen, when, after doubting by turns of several points, as I found them disputed in the different books I read, I began to doubt of Revelation itself. Some books against Deism fell into my hands; they were said to be the substance of sermons preached at Boyle's Lectures. It happened that they wrought an effect on me quite contrary to what was intended by them; for the arguments of the Deists, which were quoted to be refuted, appeared to me much stronger than the refutations; in short, I soon became a thorough Deist. My arguments perverted some others, particularly Collins and Ralph; but, each of them having afterwards wrong'd me greatly without the least compunction, and recollecting Keith's conduct towards me (who was another freethinker), and my own towards Vernon and Miss Read, which at times gave me great trouble, I began to suspect that this doctrine, tho' it might be true, was not very useful. My London pamphlet, which had for its motto these lines of Dryden:

"Whatever is, is right. Though purblind man
    Sees but a part o' the chain, the nearest link:
    His eyes not carrying to the equal beam,
    That poises all above;"

and from the attributes of God, his infinite wisdom, goodness and power, concluded that nothing could possibly be wrong in the world, and that vice and virtue were empty distinctions, no such things existing, appear'd now not so clever a performance as I once thought it; and I doubted whether some error had not insinuated itself unperceiv'd into my argument, so as to infect all that follow'd, as is common in metaphysical reasonings.

I grew convinc'd that *truth, sincerity* and *integrity* in dealings between man and man were of the utmost importance to the felicity of life; and I form'd written resolutions, which

still remain in my journal book, to practice them ever while I lived. Revelation had indeed no weight with me, as such; but I entertain'd an opinion that, though certain actions might not be bad *because* they were forbidden by it, or good *because* it commanded them, yet probably these actions might be forbidden *because* they were bad for us, or commanded *because* they were beneficial to us, in their own natures, all the circumstances of things considered. And this persuasion, with the kind hand of Providence, or some guardian angel, or accidental favorable circumstances and situations, or all together, preserved me, thro' this dangerous time of youth, and the hazardous situations I was sometimes in among strangers, remote from the eye and advice of my father, without any willful gross immorality or injustice, that might have been expected from my want of religion. I say willful, because the instances I have mentioned had something of *necessity* in them, from my youth, inexperience, and the knavery of others. I had therefore a tolerable character to begin with; I valued it properly, and determined to preserve it. * * *

It was about this time [between 1731 and 1733] I conceiv'd the bold and arduous project of arriving at moral perfection. I wish'd to live without committing any fault at any time; I would conquer all that either natural inclination, custom, or company might lead me into. As I knew, or thought I knew, what was right and wrong, I did not see why I might not always do the one and avoid the other. But I soon found I had undertaken a task of more difficulty than I had imagined. While my care was employ'd in guarding against one fault, I was often surprised by another; habit took the advantage of inattention; inclination was sometimes too strong for reason. I concluded, at length, that the mere speculative conviction that it was our interest to be completely virtuous, was not sufficient to prevent our slipping; and that the contrary habits must be broken, and good ones acquired and established, before we can have any dependence on a steady, uniform rectitude of conduct. For this purpose I therefore contrived the following method.

In the various enumerations of the moral

virtues I had met with in my reading, I found the catalogue more or less numerous, as different writers included more or fewer ideas under the same name. Temperance, for example, was by some confined to eating and drinking, while by others it was extended to mean the moderating every other pleasure, appetite, inclination, or passion, bodily or mental, even to our avarice and ambition. I propos'd to myself, for the sake of clearness, to use rather more names, with fewer ideas annex'd to each, than a few names with more ideas; and I included under thirteen names of virtues all that at that time occurr'd to me as necessary or desirable, and annexed to each a short precept, which fully express'd the extent I gave to its meaning.

These names of virtue, with their precepts, were:

1. TEMPERANCE.

Eat not to dullness; drink not to elevation.

2. SILENCE.

Speak not but what may benefit others or yourself; avoid trifling conversation.

3. ORDER.

Let all your things have their places; let each part of your business have its time.

4. RESOLUTION.

Resolve to perform what you ought; perform without fail what you resolve.

5. FRUGALITY.

Make no expense but to do good to others or yourself; i.e., waste nothing.

6. INDUSTRY.

Lose no time; be always employ'd in something useful; cut off all unnecessary actions.

7. SINCERITY.

Use no hurtful deceit; think innocently and justly, and, if you speak, speak accordingly.

8. JUSTICE.

Wrong none by doing injuries, or omitting the benefits that are your duty.

9. MODERATION.

Avoid extreams; forbear resenting injuries so much as you think they deserve.

10. CLEANLINESS.

Tolerate no uncleanliness in body, cloaths, or habitation.

11. TRANQUILLITY.

Be not disturbed at trifles, or at accidents common or unavoidable.

12. CHASTITY.

Rarely use venery but for health or offspring, never to dulness, weakness, or the injury of your own or another's peace or reputation.

13. HUMILITY.

Imitate Jesus and Socrates.

My intention being to acquire the *habitude* of all these virtues, I judg'd it would be well not to distract my attention by attempting the whole at once, but to fix it on one of them at a time; and, when I should be master of that, then to proceed to another, and so on, till I should have gone thro' the thirteen; and, as the previous acquisition of some might facilitate the acquisition of certain others, I arrang'd them with that view, as they stand above. Temperance first, as it tends to procure that coolness and clearness of head, which is so necessary where constant vigilance was to be kept up, and guard maintained against the unremitting attraction of ancient habits, and the force of perpetual temptations. This being acquir'd and establish'd, Silence would be more easy; and my desire being to gain knowledge at the same time that I improv'd in virtue, and considering that in conversation it was obtain'd rather by the use of the ears than of the tongue, and therefore wishing to break a habit I was getting into of prattling, punning, and joking, which only made me acceptable to trifling company, I gave *Silence* the second place. This and the next, *Order*, I expected would allow me more time for attending to my project and my studies. *Resolution*, once become habitual, would keep me firm in my endeavors to obtain all the subsequent virtues; *Frugality* and Industry freeing me from my remaining debt, and producing affluence and independence, would make more easy the practice of Sincerity and Justice, etc., etc. Conceiving then, that, agreeably to the advice of Pythagoras in his Golden Verses, daily examination would be necessary, I contrived the following method for conducting that examination.

I made a little book, in which I allotted a page for each of the virtues. I rul'd each page with red ink, so as to have seven columns, one for each day of the week, marking each column with a letter for the day. I cross'd these columns with thirteen red lines, marking the beginning of each line with the first letter of one of the virtues, on which line, and in its proper column, I might mark, by a little black spot, every fault I found upon examination to have been committed respecting that virtue upon that day.

I determined to give a week's strict attention to each of the virtues successively. Thus, in the first week, my great guard was to avoid every the least offence against *Temperance*, leaving the other virtues to their ordinary chance, only marking every evening the faults of the day. Thus, if in the first week I could keep my first line, marked T, clear of spots, I suppos'd the habit of that virtue so much strengthen'd, and its opposite weaken'd, that I might venture extending my attention to include the next, and for the following week keep both lines clear of spots. Proceeding thus to the last, I could go thro' a course compleat in thirteen weeks, and four courses in a year. And like him who, having a garden to weed, does not attempt to eradicate all the bad herbs at once, which would exceed his reach and his strength, but works on one of the beds at a time, and, having accomplish'd the first, proceeds to a second, so I should have, I hoped, the encouraging pleasure of seeing on my pages the progress I made in virtue, by clearing successively my lines of their spots, till in the end, by a number of courses, I should be happy in viewing a clean book, after a thirteen weeks' daily examination.

Form of the pages.

	S.	M.	T.	W.	T.	F.	S.
TEMPERANCE.							
EAT NOT TO DULNESS; DRINK NOT TO ELEVATION.							
T.							
S.	*	*		*		*	
O.	* *	*	*		*	*	*
R.			*			*	
F.		*			*		
I.			*				
S.							
J.							
M.							
C.							
T.							
C.							
H.							

This my little book had for its motto these lines from Addison's *Cato:*

"Here will I hold. If there's a power above us
(And that there is, all nature cries aloud
Thro' all her works), He must delight in virtue;
And that which He delights in must be happy."

Another from Cicero,

"O vitæ Philosophia dux! O virtutum indagatrix expultrixque vitiorum! Unus dies, bene et ex præceptis tuis actus, peccanti immortalitati est anteponendus."

[O Philosophy, leader of life! O inducer of virtues and expeller of vices. One day well spent on account of your precepts ought to be preferred to a sinful immortality.]

Another from the Proverbs of Solomon, speaking of wisdom or virtue:

"Length of days is in her right hand, and in her left hand riches and honour. Her ways are ways of pleasantness, and all her paths are peace." iii. 16, 17.

And conceiving God to be the fountain of wisdom, I thought it right and necessary to solicit his assistance for obtaining it; to this end I formed the following little prayer, which was prefix'd to my tables of examination, for daily use:

"*O powerful Goodness! bountiful Father! merciful Guide! Increase in me that wisdom which discovers my truest interest. Strengthen my resolutions to perform what that wisdom dictates. Accept my kind offices to thy other children as the only return in my power for thy continual favours to me.*"

I used also sometimes a little prayer which I took from Thomson's Poems, viz.:

"Father of light and life, thou Good Supreme!
O teach me what is good; teach me Thyself!
Save me from folly, vanity, and vice,
From every low pursuit; and fill my soul
With knowledge, conscious peace, and virtue pure;
Sacred, substantial, never-fading bliss!"

The precept of *Order* requiring that *every part of my business should have its allotted time,* one page in my little book contain'd the following scheme of employment for the twenty-four hours of a natural day.

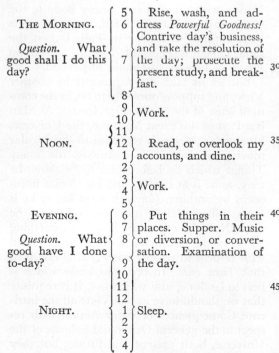

THE MORNING.	5 6 7	Rise, wash, and address *Powerful Goodness!* Contrive day's business, and take the resolution of the day; prosecute the present study, and breakfast.
Question. What good shall I do this day?		
	8 9 10 11	Work.
NOON.	12 1	Read, or overlook my accounts, and dine.
	2 3 4 5	Work.
EVENING.	6 7 8 9	Put things in their places. Supper. Music or diversion, or conversation. Examination of the day.
Question. What good have I done to-day?		
	10 11 12	
NIGHT.	1 2 3 4	Sleep.

I enter'd upon the execution of this plan for self-examination, and continu'd it with occasional intermissions for some time. I was surpris'd to find myself so much fuller of faults than I had imagined; but I had the satisfaction of seeing them diminish. To avoid the trouble of renewing now and then my little book, which, by scraping out the marks on the paper of old faults to make room for new ones in a new course, became full of holes, I transferr'd my tables and precepts to the ivory leaves of a memorandum book, on which the lines were drawn with red ink, that made a durable stain, and on those lines I mark'd my faults with a black-lead pencil, which marks I could easily wipe out with a wet sponge. After a while I went thro' one course only in a year, and afterward only one in several years, till at length I omitted them entirely, being employ'd in voyages and business abroad, with a multiplicity of affairs that interfered; but I always carried my little book with me.

My scheme of ORDER gave me the most trouble; and I found that, tho' it might be practicable where a man's business was such as to leave him the disposition of his time, that of a journeyman printer, for instance, it was not possible to be exactly observed by a master, who must mix with the world, and often receive people of business at their own hours. *Order,* too, with regard to places for things, papers, etc., I found extreamly difficult to acquire. I had not been early accustomed to it, and, having an exceeding good memory, I was not so sensible of the inconvenience attending want of method. This article, therefore, cost me so much painful attention, and my faults in it vexed me so much, and I made so little progress in amendment, and had such frequent relapses, that I was almost ready to give up the attempt, and content myself with a faulty character in that respect, like the man who, in buying an ax of a smith, my neighbour, desired to have the whole of its surface as bright as the edge. The smith consented to grind it bright for him if he would turn the wheel; he turn'd, while the smith press'd the broad face of the ax hard and heavily on the stone, which made the turning of it very fatiguing. The man came every now and then from the wheel to see how the work went on, and at length would take his ax as it was, without farther grinding. "No,"

said the smith, "turn on, turn on; we shall
have it bright by-and-by; as yet, it is only
speckled." "Yes," says the man, "*but I like
a speckled ax best.*" And I believe this may
have been the case with many, who, having,
for want of some such means as I employ'd,
found the difficulty of obtaining good and
breaking bad habits in other points of vice
and virtue, have given up the struggle, and
concluded that "*a speckled ax was best*"; for
something, that pretended to be reason, was
every now and then suggesting to me that
such extream nicety as I exacted of myself
might be a kind of foppery in morals, which,
if it were known, would make me ridiculous;
that a perfect character might be attended
with the inconvenience of being envied and
hated; and that a benevolent man should
allow a few faults in himself, to keep his
friends in countenance.

In truth, I found myself incorrigible with
respect to Order; and now I am grown old,
and my memory bad, I feel very sensibly the
want of it. But, on the whole, tho' I never
arrived at the perfection I had been so ambitious of obtaining, but fell far short of it, yet
I was, by the endeavour, a better and a happier man than I otherwise should have been
if I had not attempted it; as those who aim
at perfect writing by imitating the engraved
copies, tho' they never reach the wish'd-for
excellence of those copies, their hand is
mended by the endeavor, and is tolerable
while it continues fair and legible.

It may be well my posterity should be informed that to this little artifice, with the
blessing of God, their ancestor ow'd the constant felicity of his life, down to his 79th year,
in which this is written. What reverses may
attend the remainder is in the hand of Providence; but, if they arrive, the reflection on
past happiness enjoy'd ought to help his bearing them with more resignation. To Temperance he ascribes his long-continued health,
and what is still left to him of a good constitution; to Industry and Frugality, the early
easiness of his circumstances and acquisition
of his fortune, with all that knowledge that
enabled him to be a useful citizen, and obtained for him some degree of reputation
among the learned; to Sincerity and Justice,
the confidence of his country, and the honor-

able employs it conferred upon him; and to
the joint influence of the whole mass of the
virtues, even in the imperfect state he was
able to acquire them, all that evenness of
temper, and that cheerfulness in conversation, which makes his company still sought
for, and agreeable even to his younger acquaintance. I hope, therefore, that some of
my descendants may follow the example and
reap the benefit.

From On Liberty and Necessity

(1725)

[*Man in the Newtonian Universe*]

VII. *If the Creature is thus limited in his Actions, being able to do only such Things as God
would have him to do, and not being able to refuse
doing what God would have done; then he can have
no such Thing as Liberty, Free-will or Power to do
or refrain an Action.*

By *Liberty* is sometimes understood the Absence of Opposition; and in this Sense, indeed,
all our Actions may be said to be the Effects
of our Liberty: But it is a Liberty of the same
Nature with the Fall of a heavy Body to the
Ground; it has Liberty to fall, that is, it meets
with nothing to hinder its Fall, but at the
same Time it is necessitated to fall, and has no
Power or Liberty to remain suspended.

But let us take the Argument in another
View, and suppose ourselves to be, in the common sense of the Word, *Free Agents.* As Man
is a Part of this great Machine, the Universe,
his regular Acting is requisite to the regular
moving of the whole. Among the many
Things which lie before him to be done, he
may, as he is at Liberty and his Choice influenc'd by nothing, (for so it must be, or he is
not at Liberty) chuse any one, and refuse the
rest. Now there is every Moment something
best to be done, which is alone then *good,* and
with respect to which, every Thing else is at
that Time *evil.* In order to know which is
best to be done, and which not, it is requisite
that we should have at one View all the intricate Consequences of every Action with respect to the general Order and Scheme of the
Universe, both present and future; but they
are innumerable and incomprehensible by
any Thing but Omniscience. As we cannot
know these, we have but as one Chance to ten

thousand, to hit on the right Action; we should then be perpetually blundering about in the Dark, and putting the Scheme in Disorder; for every wrong Action of a Part, is a Defect or Blemish in the Order of the Whole. Is it not necessary then, that our Actions should be over-rul'd and govern'd by an all-wise Providence? — How exact and regular is every Thing in the *natural* World! How wisely in every Part contriv'd! We cannot here find the least Defect! Those who have study'd the mere animal and vegetable Creation, demonstrate that nothing can be more harmonious and beautiful! All the heavenly Bodies, the Stars and Planets, are regulated with the utmost Wisdom! And can we suppose less Care to be taken in the Order of the *moral* than in the *natural* System? It is as if an ingenious Artificer, having fram'd a curious Machine or Clock, and put its many intricate Wheels and Powers in such a Dependance on one another, but the whole might move in the most exact Order and Regularity, had nevertheless plac'd in it several other Wheels endu'd with an independent *Self-Motion*, but ignorant of the general Interest of the Clock; and these would every now and then be moving wrong, disordering the true Movement, and making continual Work for the Mender: which might better be prevented, by depriving them of that Power of Self-Motion, and placing them in a Dependance on the regular Part of the Clock.

VIII. *If there is no such Thing as Free-Will in Creatures, there can be neither Merit nor Demerit in Creatures.*

IX. *And therefore every Creature must be equally esteem'd by the Creator.*

These Propositions appear to be the necessary Consequences of the former. And certainly no Reason can be given, why the Creator should prefer in his Esteem one Part of His Works to another, if with equal Wisdom and Goodness he design'd and created them all, since all Ill or Defect, as contrary to his Nature, is excluded by his Power. We will sum up the Argument thus, When the Creator first design'd the Universe, either it was His Will and Intention that all Things should exist and be in the Manner they are at this Time; or it was his Will they should *be* otherwise, *i.e.* in a different Manner: To say it was

His Will Things should be otherwise than they are, is to say Somewhat hath contradicted His Will, and broken His Measures, which is impossible because inconsistent with his Power; therefore we must allow that all Things exist now in a Manner agreeable to His Will, and in consequence of that are all equally Good, and therefore equally esteem'd by Him.

A Proposal for Promoting Useful Knowledge

This is a circular letter which Franklin sent to his friends.

Philadelphia, May 14, 1743.

The English are possessed of a long tract of continent, from Nova Scotia to Georgia, extending north and south through different climates, having different soils, producing different plants, mines, and minerals, and capable of different improvements, manufactures, &c.

The first drudgery of settling new colonies, which confines the attention of people to mere necessaries, is now pretty well over; and there are many in every province in circumstances that set them at ease, and afford leisure to cultivate the finer arts and improve the common stock of knowledge. To such of these who are men of speculation, many hints must from time to time arise, many observations occur, which if well examined, pursued, and improved, might produce discoveries to the advantage of some or all of the British plantations, or to the benefit of mankind in general.

But as from the extent of the country such persons are widely separated, and seldom can see and converse or be acquainted with each other, so that many useful particulars remain uncommunicated, die with the discoverers, and are lost to mankind; it is, to remedy this inconvenience for the future, proposed,

That one society be formed of *virtuosi* or ingenious men, residing in the several colonies, to be called *The American Philosophical Society*, who are to maintain a constant correspondence.

That Philadelphia, being the city nearest the centre of the continent colonies, communi-

cating with all of them northward and southward by post, and with all the island by sea,
and having the advantage of a good growing
library, be the centre of the Society.

That at Philadelphia there be always at
least seven members, viz. a physician, a
botanist, a mathematician, a chemist, a mechanician, a geographer, and a general natural
philosopher, besides a president, treasurer,
and secretary.

That these members meet once a month,
or oftener, at their own expense, to communicate to each other their observations and
experiments, to receive, read, and consider
such letters, communications, or queries as
shall be sent from distant members; to direct
the dispersing of copies of such communications as are valuable, to other distant members, in order to procure their sentiments
thereupon.

That the subjects of the correspondence be:
all new-discovered plants, herbs, trees, roots,
their virtues, uses, &.; methods of propagat-
ing them, and making such as are useful,
but particular to some plantations, more
general; improvements of vegetable juices, as
ciders, wines, &c.; new methods of curing
or preventing diseases; all new-discovered
fossils in different countries, as mines, minerals, and quarries; new and useful improvements in any branch of mathematics; new
discoveries in chemistry, such as improvements in distillation, brewing, and assaying
of ores; new mechanical inventions for saving
labour, as mills and carriages, and for raising
and conveying of water, draining of meadows,
&c.; all new arts, trades, and manufactures,
that may be proposed or thought of; surveys,
maps, and charts of particular parts of the
sea-coasts or inland countries; course and
junction of rivers and great roads, situation
of lakes and mountains, nature of the soil and
productions; new methods of improving the
breed of useful animals; introducing other
sorts from foreign countries; new improvements in planting, gardening, and clearing
land; and all philosophical experiments that
let light into the nature of things, tend to increase the power of man over matter, and
multiply the conveniences or pleasures of life.

That a correspondence, already begun by
some intended members, shall be kept up by
this Society with the ROYAL SOCIETY of
London, and with the DUBLIN SOCIETY.

That every member shall have abstracts
sent him quarterly, of every thing valuable
communicated to the Society's Secretary at
Philadelphia; free of all charge except the
yearly payment hereafter mentioned.

That, by permission of the postmaster-
general, such communications pass between
the Secretary of the Society and the members,
postage-free.

That, for defraying the expense of such experiments as the Society shall judge proper
to cause to be made, and other contingent
charges for the common good, every member
send a piece of eight per annum to the treasurer, at Philadelphia, to form a common
stock, to be disbursed by order of the President with the consent of the majority of the
members that can conveniently be consulted
thereupon, to such persons and places where
and by whom the experiments are to be
made, and otherwise as there shall be occasion; of which disbursements an exact account
shall be kept, and communicated yearly to
every member.

That, at the first meetings of the members
at Philadelphia, such rules be formed for
regulating their meetings and transactions for
the general benefit, as shall be convenient
and necessary; to be afterwards changed and
improved as there shall be occasion, wherein
due regard is to be had to the advice of distant
members.

That, at the end of every year, collections
be made and printed, of such experiments,
discoveries, and improvements, as may be
thought of public advantage; and that every
member have a copy sent him.

That the business and duty of the Secretary
be to receive all letters intended for the Society, and lay them before the President and
members at their meetings; to abstract, correct, and methodize such papers as require
it, and as he shall be directed to do by the
President, after they have been considered,
debated, and digested in the Society; to enter
copies thereof in the Society's books, and
make out copies for distant members; to
answer their letters by direction of the President, and keep records of all material transactions of the Society.

Benjamin Franklin, the writer of this Proposal, offers himself to serve the Society as their secretary, till they shall be provided with one more capable.

The Way to Wealth
(1758)

This "speech of Father Abraham at an auction" was first published as a sort of preface to *Poor Richard's Almanac* for 1758.

COURTEOUS READER,

I have heard that nothing gives an Author so great Pleasure, as to find his Works respectfully quoted by other learned Authors. This Pleasure I have seldom enjoyed; for tho' I have been, if I may say it without Vanity, an *eminent Author* of Almanacks annually now a full Quarter of a Century, my Brother Authors in the same Way, for what Reason I know not, have ever been very sparing in their Applauses, and no other Author has taken the least Notice of me, so that did not my Writings produce me some solid *Pudding*, the great Deficiency of *Praise* would have quite discouraged me.

I concluded at length, that the People were the best Judges of my merit; for they buy my Works; and besides, in my Rambles, where I am not personally known, I have frequently heard one or other of my Adages repeated, with, *as Poor Richard says*, at the End on 't; this gave me some Satisfaction, as it showed not only that my Instructions were regarded, but discovered likewise some Respect for my Authority; and I own, that to encourage the Practice of remembering and repeating those wise Sentences, I have sometimes *quoted myself* with great Gravity.

Judge, then how much I must have been gratified by an Incident I am going to relate to you. I stopt my Horse lately where a great Number of People were collected at a Vendue of Merchant Goods. The Hour of Sale not being come, they were conversing on the Badness of the Times and one of the Company call'd to a plain clean old Man, with white Locks, "Pray, Father Abraham, what think you of the Times? Won't these heavy Taxes quite ruin the Country? How shall we be ever able to pay them? What would you advise us to?" Father *Abraham* stood up, and reply'd, "If you'd have my Advice, I'll give it you in short, for *A Word to the Wise is enough*, and *many Words won't fill a Bushel*, as *Poor Richard* says." They join'd in desiring him to speak his Mind, and gathering round him, he proceeded as follows;

"Friends," says he, "and Neighbours, the Taxes are indeed very heavy, and if those laid on by the Government were the only Ones we had to pay, we might more easily discharge them; but we have many others, and much more grievous to some of us. We are taxed twice as much by our *Idleness*, three times as much by our *Pride*, and four times as much by our *Folly;* and from these Taxes the Commissioners cannot ease or deliver us by allowing an Abatement. However let us hearken to good Advice, and something may be done for us; *God helps them that help themselves*, as *Poor Richard* says, in his Almanack of 1733.

It would be thought a hard Government that should tax its People one-tenth Part of their *Time*, to be employed in its Service. But *Idleness* taxes many of us much more, if we reckon all that is spent in absolute *Sloth*, or doing of nothing, with that which is spent in idle Employments or Amusements, that amount to nothing. *Sloth*, by bringing on Diseases, absolutely shortens Life. *Sloth, like Rust, consumes faster than Labour wears; while the used Key is always bright,* as *Poor Richard* says. *But dost thou love Life, then do not squander Time; for that's the stuff Life is made of,* as *Poor Richard* says. How much more than is necessary do we spend in sleep, forgetting that *The Sleeping Fox catches no Poultry*, and that *There will be sleeping enough in the Grave*, as *Poor Richard* says.

If Time be of all Things the most precious, wasting Time must be, as *Poor Richard* says, *the greatest Prodigality;* since, as he elsewhere tells us, *Lost Time is never found again; and what we call Time enough, always proves little enough:* Let us then up and be doing, and doing to the Purpose; so by Diligence shall we do more with less Perplexity. *Sloth makes all Things difficult, but Industry all easy,* as *Poor Richard* says; and *He that riseth late must trot all Day, and shall scarce overtake his Business at Night;* while *Laziness travels so slowly, that Poverty soon overtakes him,* as we read in *Poor Richard*, who adds, *Drive thy Business, let not that drive thee;* and *Early to Bed, and early to rise, makes a Man healthy, wealthy, and wise.*

So what signifies *wishing* and *hoping* for better Times. We may make these Times better, if we bestir ourselves. *Industry need not wish*, as *Poor Richard* says, *and he that lives upon Hope will die fasting. There are no Gains without Pains; then Help Hands, for I have no Lands*, or if I have, they are smartly taxed. And, as *Poor Richard* likewise observes, *He that hath a Trade hath an Estate; and he that hath a Calling, hath an Office of Profit and Honour;* but then the *Trade* must be worked at, and the *Calling* well followed, or neither the *Estate* nor the *Office* will enable us to pay our Taxes. If we are industrious we shall never starve; for, as *Poor Richard* says, *At the working Man's House Hunger looks in, but dares not enter.* Nor will the Bailiff or the Constable enter, for *Industry pays Debts, while Despair encreaseth them*, says *Poor Richard*. What though you have found no Treasure, nor has any rich Relation left you a Legacy, *Diligence is the Mother of Goodluck* as *Poor Richard* says *and God gives all Things to Industry. Then plough deep, while Sluggards sleep, and you shall have Corn to sell and to keep*, says *Poor Dick*. Work while it is called To-day, for you know not how much you may be hindered To-morrow, which makes *Poor Richard* say, *One to-day is worth two To-morrows*, and farther, *Have you somewhat to do To-morrow, do it To-day.* If you were a Servant, would you not be ashamed that a good Master should catch you idle? Are you then your own Master, *be ashamed to catch yourself idle*, as *Poor Dick* says. When there is so much to be done for yourself, your Family, your Country, and your gracious King, be up by Peep of Day; *Let not the Sun look down and say, Inglorious here he lies.* Handle your tools without Mittens; remember that *The Cat in Gloves catches no Mice*, as *Poor Richard* says. 'Tis true there is much to be done, and perhaps you are weak-handed, but stick to it steadily; and you will see great Effects, for *Constant Dropping wears away Stones*, and by *Diligence and Patience the Mouse ate in two the Cable;* and *Little Strokes fell great Oaks*, as *Poor*

Richard says in his Almanack, the Year I cannot just now remember.

Methinks I hear some of you say, *Must a Man afford himself no Leisure?* I will tell thee, my friend, what *Poor Richard* says, *Employ thy Time well, if thou meanest to gain Leisure; and, since thou art not sure of a Minute, throw not away an Hour.* Leisure, is Time for doing something useful; this Leisure the diligent Man will obtain, but the lazy Man never; so that, as *Poor Richard* says, *A Life of Leisure and a Life of Laziness are two Things.* Do you imagine that Sloth will afford you more Comfort than Labour? No, for as *Poor Richard* says, *Trouble springs from Idleness, and grievous Toil from needless Ease. Many without Labour, would live by their Wits only, but they break for want of Stock.* Whereas Industry gives Comfort, and Plenty, and Respect: *Fly Pleasures, and they'll follow you. The diligent Spinner has a large Shift; and now I have a Sheep and a Cow, everybody bids me good Morrow;* all which is well said by *Poor Richard*.

But with our Industry, we must likewise be *steady, settled*, and *careful*, and oversee our own Affairs *with our own Eyes*, and not trust too much to others; for, as *Poor Richard* says

I never saw an oft-removed Tree,
Nor yet an oft-removed Family,
That throve so well as those that settled be.

And again, *Three Removes is as bad as a Fire;* and again, *Keep thy Shop, and thy Shop will keep thee;* and again, *If you would have your Business done, go; if not, send.* And again

He that by the Plough would thrive,
Himself must either hold or drive.

And again, *The Eye of a Master will do more Work than both his Hands;* and again, *Want of Care does us more Damage than Want of Knowledge;* and again, *Not to oversee Workmen, is to leave them your Purse open.* Trusting too much to others' Care is the Ruin of many; for, as the Almanack says, *In the Affairs of this World, Men are saved, not by Faith, but by the Want of it;* but a Man's own Care is profitable; for, saith *Poor Dick, Learning is to the Studious*, and *Riches to the Careful*, as well as *Power to the Bold*, and *Heaven to the Virtuous*, and farther, *If you would have a faithful Servant, and one that you like, serve yourself.* And again, he adviseth to Circumspection and Care, even in the smallest Matters, because sometimes *A little Neglect may breed great Mischief;* adding, *for want of a Nail the Shoe was lost; for want of a Shoe the Horse was lost; and for want of a Horse the Rider was lost, being overtaken and slain by the Enemy; all for want of Care about a Horse-shoe Nail.*

So much for Industry, my Friends, and Attention to one's own Business; but to these we must add *Frugality,* if we would make our *Industry* more certainly successful. A Man may, if he knows not how to save as he gets, *keep his Nose all his Life to the Grindstone,* and die not worth a *Groat* at last. *A fat Kitchen makes a lean Will,* as *Poor Richard* says; and

> *Many Estates are spent in the Getting,*
> *Since Women for Tea forsook Spinning and Knitting,*
> *And Men for Punch forsook Hewing and Splitting.*

If you would be wealthy, says he, in another Almanack, *think of Saving as well as of Getting: The Indies have not made Spain rich, because her Outgoes are greater than her Incomes.*

Away then with your expensive Follies, and you will not then have so much Cause to complain of hard Times, heavy Taxes, and chargeable Families; for, as *Poor Dick* says,

> *Women and Wine, Game and Deceit,*
> *Make the Wealth small and the Wants great.*

And farther, *What maintains one Vice, would bring up two Children.* You may think perhaps, that a *little* Tea, or a *little* Punch now and then, Diet a *little* more costly, Clothes a *little* finer, and a *little* Entertainment now and then, can be no *great* Matter; but remember what *Poor Richard* says, *Many a Little makes a Mickle;* and farther, *Beware of little Expences; A small Leak will sink a great Ship;* and again, *Who Dainties love, shall Beggars prove;* and moreover, *Fools make Feasts, and wise Men eat them.*

Here you are all got together at this Vendue of *Fineries* and *Knicknacks.* You call them *Goods;* but if you do not take Care, they will prove *Evils* to some of you. You expect they will be sold *cheap,* and perhaps they may for less than they cost, but if you have no Occasion for them, they must be dear to you. Remember what *Poor Richard* says, *Buy what thou hast no Need of, and ere* long thou shalt sell thy Necessaries. And again, *At a great Pennyworth pause a while:* He means, that perhaps the Cheapness is *apparent only,* and not *Real;* or the bargain, by straitening thee in thy Business, may do thee more Harm than Good. For in another Place he says, *Many have been ruined by buying good Pennyworths.* Again, *Poor Richard* says, 'tis foolish to lay out *Money in a Purchase of Repentance;* and yet this Folly is practised every Day at Vendues, for want of minding the Almanack. *Wise Men,* as *Poor Dick* says, *learn by others Harms, Fools scarcely by their own; but felix quem faciunt aliena pericula cautum.* [Happy is he whom the mistakes of others makes cautious.] Many a one, for the Sake of Finery on the Back, have gone with a hungry Belly, and half-starved their Families. *Silks and Sattins, Scarlet and Velvets,* as *Poor Richard* says, *put out the Kitchen Fire.*

These are not the *Necessaries* of Life, they can scarcely be called the *Conveniences;* and yet only because they look pretty, how many *want* to *have* them! The *artificial* Wants of Mankind thus become more numerous than the *Natural;* and, as *Poor Dick* says, *for one poor Person, there are an hundred indigent.* By these, and other Extravagancies, the Genteel are reduced to poverty, and forced to borrow of those whom they formerly despised, but who through Industry and Frugality have maintained their Standing; in which Case it appears plainly, that *A Ploughman on his Legs is higher than a Gentleman on his Knees,* as *Poor Richard* says. Perhaps they have had a small Estate left them, which they knew not the Getting of, they think, 'tis Day, and will never be Night; that a little to be spent out of *so much,* is not worth minding; *a Child and a Fool,* as *Poor Richard* says, *imagine Twenty shillings and Twenty Years can never be spent* but, *always taking out of the Meal-tub, and never putting in, soon comes to the Bottom;* as *Poor Dick* says, *When the Well's dry, they know the Worth of Water.* But this they might have known before, if they had taken his Advice; *If you would know the Value of Money, go and try to borrow some; or, he that goes a borrowing goes a sorrowing;* and indeed so does he that lends to such People, when he goes *to get it in again.* *Poor Dick* farther advises, and says,

Fond Pride of Dress is sure a very Curse;
E'er Fancy you consult, consult your Purse.

And again, *Pride is as loud a Beggar as Want*
and a great deal more saucy. When you have
bought one fine Thing, you must buy ten
more, that your Appearance may be all of a
Piece; but *Poor Dick* says, *'Tis easier to sup-*
press the first Desire, than to satisfy all that follows
it. And 'tis as truly Folly for the Poor to
ape the Rich, as for the Frog to swell, in
order to equal the ox.

> *Great Estates may venture more,*
> *But little Boats should keep near Shore.*

'Tis, however, a Folly soon punished; for
Pride that dines on Vanity, sups on Contempt,
as *Poor Richard* says. And in another Place,
Pride breakfasted with Plenty, dined with Poverty,
and supped with Infamy. And after all, of
what Use is this *Pride of Appearance,* for which
so much is risked, so much is suffered? It
cannot promote Health, or ease Pain; it
makes no Increase of Merit in the Person,
it creates Envy, it hastens Misfortune.

> *What is a Butterfly? At best*
> *He's but a Caterpillar drest*
> *The gaudy Fop's his Picture just,*

as *Poor Richard* says.

But what Madness must it be to *run in*
Debt for these Superfluities! We are offered,
by the Terms of this Vendue, *Six Months'*
Credit; and that perhaps has induced some
of us to attend it, because we cannot spare
the ready Money, and hope now to be fine
without it. But, ah, think what you do
when you run in Debt; *you give to another*
Power over your Liberty. If you cannot pay
at the Time, you will be ashamed to see your
Creditor; you will be in Fear when you
speak to him; you will make poor pitiful
sneaking Excuses, and by Degrees come to
lose your Veracity, and sink into base down-
right lying; for, as *Poor Richard* says, *The*
second Vice is Lying, the first is running in Debt.
And again, to the same Purpose, *Lying rides*
upon Debt's Back. Whereas a free-born
Englishman ought not to be ashamed or afraid
to see or speak to any Man living. But
Poverty often deprives a Man of all Spirit

and Virtue: *'Tis hard for an empty Bag to*
stand upright, as *Poor Richard* truly says.

What would you think of that Prince, or
that Government, who should issue an Edict
forbidding you to dress like a Gentleman or a
Gentlewoman, on Pain of Imprisonment or
Servitude? Would you not say, that you
were free, have a Right to dress as you please,
and that such an Edict would be a Breach
of your Privileges, and such a Government
tyrannical? And yet you are about to put
yourself under that tyranny, when you run in
Debt for such Dress! Your Creditor has
Authority, at his Pleasure to deprive you of
your Liberty, by confining you in Gaol for
Life, or to sell you for a Servant, if you should
not be able to pay him! When you have got
your Bargain, you may, perhaps, think little
of Payment; but *Creditors, Poor Richard* tells
us, *have better Memories than Debtors;* and in
another Place says, *Creditors are a superstitious*
Sect, great Observers of set Days and Times.
The Day comes round before you are aware,
and the Demand is made before you are
prepared to satisfy it; or if you bear your
Debt in Mind, the Term which at first
seemed so long, will, as it lessens, appear
extreamly short. *Time* will seem to have
added Wings to his Heels as well as Shoulders. *Those have a short Lent,* saith *Poor*
Richard, who owe Money to be paid at Easter.
Then since, as he says, *The Borrower is a*
Slave to the Lender, and the Debtor to the Creditor,
disdain the Chain, preserve your Freedom;
and maintain your Independency: Be *In-*
dustrious and *free;* be *frugal* and *free.* At
present, perhaps, you may think yourself
in thriving Circumstances, and that you can
bear a little Extravagance without Injury;
but,

> *For Age and Want, save while you may;*
> *No Morning Sun lasts a whole Day,*

as *Poor Richard* says. Gain may be tempo-
rary and uncertain, but ever while you live,
Expence is constant and certain; and *'tis*
easier to build two Chimnies, than to keep one in
Fuel, as *Poor Richard* says. So, *Rather go to*
Bed supperless than rise in Debt.

> *Get what you can, and what you get hold;*
> *'Tis the Stone that will turn all your lead into Gold,*

as *Poor Richard* says. And when you have got the Philosopher's Stone, sure you will no longer complain of bad Times, or the Difficulty of paying Taxes.

This Doctrine, my Friends, is *Reason* and *Wisdom;* but after all, do not depend too much upon your own *Industry*, and *Frugality*, and Prudence, though excellent Things, for they may all be blasted without the Blessing of Heaven; and therefore, ask that Blessing humbly, and be not uncharitable to those that at present seem to want it, but comfort and help them. Remember, *Job* suffered, and was afterwards prosperous.

And now to conclude, *Experience keeps a dear School, but Fools will learn in no other, and scarce in that;* for it is true, *we may give Advice, but we cannot give Conduct*, as *Poor Richard* says: However, remember this, *They that won't be counselled, can't be helped*, as *Poor Richard* says: and farther, That, *if you will not hear Reason, she'll surely rap your Knuckles.*"

Thus the old Gentleman ended his Harangue. The People heard it, and approved the Doctrine, and immediately practised the contrary, just as if it had been a common Sermon; for the Vendue opened, and they began to buy extravagantly, notwithstanding his Cautions and their own Fear of Taxes. I found the good Man had thoroughly studied my Almanacks, and digested all I had dropt on these Topicks during the Course of Five and twenty Years. The frequent Mention he made of me must have tired any one else, but my Vanity was wonderfully delighted with it, though I was conscious that not a tenth Part of the Wisdom was my own, which he ascribed to me, but rather the *Gleanings* I had made of the Sense of all Ages and Nations. However, I resolved to be the better for the Echo of it; and though I had at first determined to buy Stuff for a new Coat, I went away resolved to wear my old One a little longer. *Reader*, if thou wilt do the same, thy Profit will be as great as mine. I am, *as ever, thine to serve thee.*

RICHARD SAUNDERS.

July 7, 1757

Letters

[*Future of Science*]

Passy, Feb. 8, 1780.

DEAR SIR,

Your kind Letter of September 27 came to hand but very lately, the Bearer having staied long in Holland. I always rejoice to hear of your being still employ'd in experimental Researches into Nature, and of the Success you meet with. The rapid Progress *true* Science now makes, occasions my regretting sometimes that I was born so soon. It is impossible to imagine the Height to which may be carried, in a thousand years, the Power of Man over Matter. We may perhaps learn to deprive large Masses of their Gravity, and give them absolute Levity, for the sake of easy Transport. Agriculture may diminish its Labour and double its Produce; all Diseases may by sure means be prevented or cured, not excepting even that of Old Age, and our Lives lengthened at pleasure even beyond the antediluvian Standard. O that moral Science were in as fair a way of Improvement, that Man would cease to be Wolves to one another, and that human Beings would at length learn what they now improperly call Humanity!

I am glad my little Paper on the *Aurora Borealis* pleased. If it should occasion further Enquiry, and so produce a better Hypothesis, it will not be wholly useless. I am ever, with the greatest and most sincere Esteem, dear Sir, yours very affectionately

B FRANKLIN

[To Joseph Priestley]

[*Cotton Mather*]

Written to Samuel, son of Cotton Mather, and pastor of the church formerly presided over by his father and grandfather.

Passy, May 12, 1784.

REV^D. SIR,

I received your kind letter, with your excellent advice to the people of the United States, which I read with great pleasure, and hope it will be duly regarded. Such writings, though they may be lightly passed over by many readers, yet, if they make a deep impression on one active mind in a hundred, the effects may be considerable. Permit me to mention one little instance, which, though it relates to myself, will not be quite uninteresting to you. When I was a boy, I met with a book, entitled "*Essays to do Good*," which I think was written by your father. It had been so little regarded by a former possessor, that several leaves of it were torn out; but the remainder gave me such a turn of thinking, as to have an influence on my conduct through life; for I have always set a greater value on the character of a *doer of good*, than on any other kind of reputation; and if I have been, as you seem to think, a useful citizen, the public owes the advantage of it to that book.

You mention your being in your 78th year; I am in my 79th; we are grown old together. It is now more than 60 years since I left Boston, but I remember well both your father and grandfather, having heard them both in the pulpit, and seen them in their houses. The last time I saw your father was in the beginning of 1724, when I visited him after my first trip to Pennsylvania. He received me in his library, and on my taking leave showed me a shorter way out of the house through a narrow passage, which was crossed by a beam over head. We were still talking as I withdrew, he accompanying me behind, and I turning partly towards him, when he said hastily, "*Stoop, stoop!*" I did not understand him, till I felt my head hit against the beam. He was a man that never missed any occasion of giving instruction, and upon this he said to me, "*You are young, and have the world before you;* STOOP *as you go through it, and you will miss many hard thumps.*" This advice, thus beat into my head, has frequently been of use to me; and I often think of it, when I see pride mortified, and misfortunes brought upon people by their carrying their heads too high.

I long much to see again my native place, and to lay my bones there. I left it in 1723; I visited it in 1733, 1743, 1753, and 1763. In 1773 I was in England; in 1775 I had a sight of it, but could not enter, it being in possession of the enemy. I did hope to have been there in 1783, but could not obtain my dismission from this employment here; and now I fear I shall never have that happiness. My best wishes however attend my dear country. *Esto perpetua.* It is now blest with an excellent constitution; may it last forever!

This powerful monarchy continues its friendship for the United States. It is a friendship of the utmost importance to our security, and should be carefully cultivated. Britain has not yet well digested the loss of its dominion over us, and has still at times some flattering hopes of recovering it. Accidents may increase those hopes, and encourage dangerous attempts. A breach between us and France would infallibly bring the English again upon our backs; and yet we have some wild heads among our countrymen, who are endeavouring to weaken that connexion! Let us preserve our reputation by performing our engagements; our credit by fulfilling our contracts; and friends by gratitude and kindness; for we know not how soon we may again have occasion for all of them. With great and sincere esteem, I have the honour to be, &c.

B. FRANKLIN.

[To Samuel Mather]

ST. JOHN DE CRÈVECOEUR (1735–1813)

Michel-Guillaume Jean de Crèvecoeur (he called himself J. Hector St. John de Crèvecoeur merely because he liked the name) was born of a noble family near Caen, in Normandy. He emigrated, served under Montcalm in the last of the French and Indian wars, and explored the region between the Great Lakes and the Ohio River. He took out naturalization papers in 1765, married four years later, and settled in Orange County, New York. There he spent idyllic years until the American Revolution brought anxiety and trouble. In 1780 he sailed for England, where he sold his *Letters* to a publisher, and in 1781 was back in France. Through Franklin, he secured nomination as French consul in New York. From 1783 to 1790 he lived in America, and from 1790 to his death in 1813 lived in France once more — witnessing, from retirement, a second and greater revolution.

Crèvecoeur was a Rousseauistic "man of feeling," that complement of the eighteenth-century man of good sense typified in America by Franklin. His *Letters from an American Farmer*, published in London, give an Arcadian description of America as a land of promise "providentially intended," as he put it, "for the general asylum of the world," a land for happy farmers "possessing freedom of action, freedom of thoughts, ruled by a mode of government which requires but little from us."

As a "farmer of feelings" — the phrase appears in his *Letters* — Crèvecoeur was not a speculative thinker, but he belongs with the Physiocrats both in his agrarian emphasis and his ardent humanitarianism. When the Revolution brought the horrors of civil war, this humanitarian pacifist kept apart from the struggle, lamenting the evils of the time with a sentimentalism as melancholy as it had previously been rosy.

Letters from an American Farmer was republished in 1904 with a preface by W. P. Trent, and also in a convenient edition in Everyman's Library. *Sketches of Eighteenth Century America* is a collection of newly discovered Crèvecoeur writings edited by H. L. Bourdin, R. H. Gabriel, and S. T. Williams, 1925. There are biographies by J. P. Mitchell, 1916, and H. C. Rice (in French), 1933, and an article in *DAB* by S. T. Williams.

From
Letters from an American Farmer
(1782)
What is an American?

I wish I could be acquainted with the feelings and thoughts which must agitate the heart and present themselves to the mind of an enlightened Englishman, when he first lands on this continent. He must greatly rejoice that he lived at a time to see this fair country discovered and settled; he must necessarily feel a share of national pride, when he views the chain of settlements which embellishes these extended shores. When he says to himself, this is the work of my countrymen, who, when convulsed by factions, afflicted by a variety of miseries and wants, restless and impatient, took refuge here. They brought along with them their national genius, to which they principally owe what liberty they enjoy, and what substance they possess. Here he sees the industry of his native country displayed in a new manner, and traces in their works the embryos of all the arts, sciences, and ingenuity which flourish in Europe. Here he beholds fair cities, substantial villages, extensive fields, an immense country filled with decent houses, good roads, orchards, meadows, and bridges, where an hundred years ago all was wild, woody, and uncultivated! What a train of pleasing ideas this fair spectacle must suggest; it is a prospect which must inspire a good citizen with the most heartfelt pleasure. The difficulty consists in the manner of viewing so extensive a scene. He is arrived on a new continent; a modern society offers itself to his contemplation, different from what he had hitherto seen. It is not composed, as in Europe, of great lords who possess everything, and of a herd of people who have nothing. Here are no aristocratical families, no courts, no kings, no bishops, no ecclesiastical dominion, no invisible power giving to a few a very visible one; no great manufacturers employing thousands, no great refinements of luxury. The rich and the poor are not so far removed from each other as they are in Europe. Some few towns excepted, we are all tillers of the earth, from Nova Scotia to West Florida.

We are a people of cultivators, scattered over an immense territory, communicating with each other by means of good roads and navigable rivers, united by the silken bands of mild government, all respecting the laws, without dreading their power, because they are equitable. We are all animated with the spirit of an industry which is unfettered and unrestrained, because each person works for himself. If he travels through our rural districts he views not the hostile castle, and the haughty mansion, contrasted with the clay-built hut and miserable cabin, where cattle and men help to keep each other warm, and dwell in meanness, smoke, and indigence. A pleasing uniformity of decent competence appears throughout our habitations. The meanest of our log-houses is a dry and comfortable habitation. Lawyer or merchant are the fairest titles our towns afford; that of a farmer is the only appellation of the rural inhabitants of our country. It must take some time ere he can reconcile himself to our dictionary, which is but short in words of dignity, and names of honour. There, on a Sunday, he sees a congregation of respectable farmers and their wives, all clad in neat homespun, well mounted, or riding in their own humble waggons. There is not among them an esquire, saving the unlettered magistrate. There he sees a parson as simple as his flock, a farmer who does not riot on the labour of others. We have no princes, for whom we toil, starve, and bleed: we are the most perfect society now existing in the world. Here man is free as he ought to be; nor is this pleasing equality so transitory as many others are. Many ages will not see the shores of our great lakes replenished with inland nations. nor the unknown bounds of North America entirely peopled. Who can tell how far it extends? Who can tell the millions of men whom it will feed and contain? for no European foot has as yet travelled half the extent of this mighty continent!

The next wish of this traveller will be to know whence came all these people? they are a mixture of English, Scotch, Irish, French, Dutch, Germans, and Swedes. From this promiscuous breed, that race now called Americans have arisen. The eastern provinces must indeed be excepted, as being the unmixed descendants of Englishmen. I have heard many wish that they had been more intermixed also: for my part, I am no wisher, and think it much better as it has happened. They exhibit a more conspicuous figure in this great and variegated picture; they too enter for a great share in the pleasing perspective displayed in these thirteen provinces. I know it is fashionable to reflect on them, but I respect them for what they have done; for the accuracy and wisdom with which they have settled their territory; for the decency of their manners; for their early love of letters; their ancient college, the first in this hemisphere; for their industry; which to me who am but a farmer, is the criterion of everything. There never was a people, situated as they are, who with so ungrateful a soil have done more in so short a time. Do you think that the monarchical ingredients which are more prevalent in other governments, have purged them from all foul stains? Their histories assert the contrary.

In this great American asylum, the poor of Europe have by some means met together, and in consequence of various causes; to what purpose should they ask one another what countrymen they are? Alas, two thirds of them had no country. Can a wretch who wanders about, who works and starves, whose life is a continual scene of sore affliction or pinching penury; can that man call England or any other kingdom his country? A country that had no bread for him, whose fields procured him no harvest, who met with nothing but the frowns of the rich, the severity of the laws, with jails and punishments; who owned not a single foot of the extensive surface of this planet? No! urged by a variety of motives, here they came. Every thing has tended to regenerate them; new laws, a new mode of living, a new social system; here they are become men: in Europe they were as so many useless plants, wanting vegetative mould, and refreshing showers; they withered, and were mowed down by want, hunger, and war; but now by the power of transplantation, like all other plants they have taken root and flourished! Formerly they were not numbered in any civil lists of their country, except in those of the poor; here they rank as citizens. By what invisible power has this surprising metamorphosis been performed? By that of the laws and that of their industry. The laws, the indulgent laws, protect them as they arrive, stamping on them the symbol of adoption; they receive ample rewards for their labours; these accumulated rewards procure them lands; those lands confer on them the title of freemen, and to that title every benefit is affixed which men can possibly require. This is the great operation daily performed by our laws. From whence proceed these laws? From our government. Whence the government? It is derived from the original genius and strong desire of the people ratified and confirmed by the crown. This is the great chain which links us all, this is the picture which every province exhibits, Nova Scotia excepted. There the crown has done all; either there were no people who had genius, or it was not much attended to: the consequence is, that the province is very thinly inhabited indeed; the power of the crown in conjunction with the musketos has prevented men from settling there. Yet some parts of it flourished once, and it contained a mild harmless set of people. But for the fault of a few leaders, the whole were banished. The greatest political error the crown ever committed in America, was to cut off men from a country which wanted nothing but men!

What attachment can a poor European emigrant have for a country where he had nothing? The knowledge of the language, the love of a few kindred as poor as himself, were the only cords that tied him: his country is now that which gives him land, bread, protection, and consequence. *Ubi panis ibi patria*, [Where bread is, there is a fatherland] is the motto of all emigrants. What then is the American, this new man? He is either an European, or the descendant of an European, hence that strange mixture of blood, which you will find in no other country. I could point out to you a family whose grandfather was an Englishman, whose wife was Dutch, whose son married a French woman, and whose present four sons have now four wives

of different nations. *He* is an American, who, leaving behind him all his ancient prejudices and manners, receives new ones from the new mode of life he has embraced, the new government he obeys, and the new rank he holds. He becomes an American by being received in the broad lap of our great *Alma Mater*. Here individuals of all nations are melted into a new race of men, whose labours and posterity will one day cause great changes in the world. Americans are the western pilgrims, who are carrying along with them that great mass of arts, sciences, vigour, and industry which began long since in the east; they will finish the great circle. The Americans were once scattered all over Europe; here they are incorporated into one of the finest systems of population which has ever appeared, and which will hereafter become distinct by the power of the different climates they inhabit. The American ought therefore to love this country much better than that wherein either he or his forefathers were born. Here the rewards of his industry follow with equal steps the progress of his labour; his labour is founded on the basis of nature, *self-interest;* can it want a stronger allurement? Wives and children, who before in vain demanded of him a morsel of bread, now, fat and frolicsome, gladly help their father to clear those fields whence exuberant crops are to arise to feed and to clothe them all; without any part being claimed, either by a despotic prince, a rich abbot, or a mighty lord. Here religion demands but little of him; a small voluntary salary to the minister, and gratitude to God; can he refuse these? The American is a new man, who acts upon new principles; he must therefore entertain new ideas, and form new opinions. From involuntary idleness, servile dependence, penury, and useless labour, he has passed to toils of a very different nature, rewarded by ample subsistence. — This is an American.

British America is divided into many provinces, forming a large association, scattered along a coast 1500 miles extent and about 200 wide. This society I would fain examine, at least such as it appears in the middle provinces; if it does not afford that variety of tinges and gradations which may be observed in Europe, we have colours peculiar to ourselves. For instance, it is natural to conceive that those who live near the sea, must be very different from those who live in the woods; the intermediate space will afford a separate and distinct class.

Men are like plants; the goodness and flavour of the fruit proceeds from the peculiar soil and exposition in which they grow. We are nothing but what we derive from the air we breathe, the climate we inhabit, the government we obey, the system of religion we profess, and the nature of our employment. Here you will find but few crimes; these have acquired as yet no root among us. I wish I was able to trace all my ideas; if my ignorance prevents me from describing them properly, I hope I shall be able to delineate a few of the outlines, which are all I propose.

Those who live near the sea, feed more on fish than on flesh, and often encounter that boisterous element. This renders them more bold and enterprising; this leads them to neglect the confined occupations of the land. They see and converse with a variety of people; their intercourse with mankind becomes extensive. The sea inspires them with a love of traffic, a desire of transporting produce from one place to another; and leads them to a variety of resources which supply the place of labour. Those who inhabit the middle settlements, by far the most numerous, must be very different; the simple cultivation of the earth purifies them, but the indulgences of the government, the soft remonstrances of religion, the rank of independent freeholders, must necessarily inspire them with sentiments, very little known in Europe among people of the same class. What do I say? Europe has no such class of men; the early knowledge they acquire, the early bargains they make, give them a great degree of sagacity. As freemen they will be litigious; pride and obstinacy are often the cause of law suits; the nature of our laws and governments may be another. As citizens it is easy to imagine, that they will carefully read the newspapers, enter into every political disquisition, freely blame or censure governors and others. As farmers they will be careful and anxious to get as much as they can, because what they get is their own. As

northern men they will love the cheerful cup. As Christians, religion curbs them not in their opinions; the general indulgence leaves every one to think for themselves in spiritual matters; the laws inspect our actions, our thoughts are left to God. Industry, good living, selfishness, litigiousness, country politics, the pride of freemen, religious indifference, are their characteristics. If you recede still farther from the sea, you will come into more modern settlements; they exhibit the same strong lineaments, in a ruder appearance. Religion seems to have still less influence, and their manners are less improved.

Now we arrive near the great woods, near the last inhabited districts; there men seem to be placed still farther beyond the reach of government, which in some measure leaves them to themselves. How can it pervade every corner; as they were driven there by misfortunes, necessity of beginnings, desire of acquiring large tracts of land, idleness, frequent want of economy, ancient debts; the re-union of such people does not afford a very pleasing spectacle. When discord, want of unity and friendship; when either drunkenness or idleness prevail in such remote districts; contention, inactivity, and wretchedness must ensue. There are not the same remedies to these evils as in a long established community. The few magistrates they have, are in general little better than the rest; they are often in a perfect state of war; that of man against man, sometimes decided by blows, sometimes by means of the law; that of man against every wild inhabitant of these venerable woods, of which they are come to dispossess them. These men appear to be no better than carnivorous animals of a superior rank, living on the flesh of wild animals when they can catch them, and when they are not able, they subsist on grain. He who would wish to see America in its proper light, and have a true idea of its feeble beginnings and barbarous rudiments, must visit our extended line of frontiers where the last settlers dwell, and where he may see the first labours of settlement, the mode of clearing the earth, in all their different appearances; where men are wholly left dependent on their native tempers, and on the spur of uncertain industry, which often fails when not sanctified by the efficacy of a few moral rules. There, remote from the power of example and check of shame, many families exhibit the most hideous parts of our society. They are a kind of forlorn hope, preceding by ten or twelve years the most respectable army of veterans which come after them. In that space, prosperity will polish some, vice and the law will drive off the rest, who uniting again with others like themselves will recede still farther; making room for more industrious people, who will finish their improvements, convert the loghouse into a convenient habitation, and rejoicing that the first heavy labours are finished, will change in a few years that hitherto barbarous country into a fine fertile, well regulated district. Such is our progress, such is the march of the Europeans toward the interior parts of this continent. In all societies there are off-casts; this impure part serves as our precursors or pioneers; my father himself was one of that class, but he came upon honest principles, and was therefore one of the few who held fast; by good conduct and temperance, he transmitted to me his fair inheritance, when not above one in fourteen of his contemporaries had the same good fortune.

Forty years ago this smiling country was thus inhabited; it is now purged, a general decency of manners prevails throughout, and such has been the fate of our best countries.

Exclusive of those general characteristics, each province has its own, founded on the government, climate, mode of husbandry, customs, and peculiarity of circumstances. Europeans submit insensibly to these great powers, and become, in the course of a few generations, not only Americans in general, but either Pennsylvanians, Virginians, or provincials under some other name. Whoever traverses the continent must easily observe those strong differences, which will grow more evident in time. The inhabitants of Canada, Massachusetts, the middle provinces, the southern ones will be as different as their climates; their only points of unity will be those of religion and language.

As I have endeavoured to show you how Europeans become Americans; it may not be disagreeable to show you likewise how the various Christian sects introduced, wear out, and how religious indifference becomes prevalent. When any considerable number of a particular sect happen to dwell contiguous to each other, they immediately erect a temple, and there worship the Divinity agreeably to their own peculiar ideas. Nobody disturbs them. If any new sect springs up in Europe it may happen that many of its professors will come and settle in America. As they bring their zeal with them, they are at liberty to make proselytes if they can, and to build a meeting and to follow the dictates of their consciences; for neither the government nor any other power interferes. If they are peaceable subjects, and are industrious, what is it to their neighbours how and in what manner they think fit to address their prayers to the Supreme Being? But if the sectaries are not settled close together, if they are mixed with other denominations, their zeal will cool for want of fuel, and will be extinguished in a little time. Then the Americans become as to religion, what they are as to country, allied to all. In them the name of Englishman, Frenchman, and European is lost, and in like manner, the strict modes of Christianity as practised in Europe are lost also. This effect will extend itself still farther hereafter, and though this may appear to you as a strange idea, yet it is a very true one. I shall be able perhaps hereafter to explain myself better; in the meanwhile, let the following example serve as my first justification.

Let us suppose you and I to be travelling; we observe that in this house, to the right, lives a Catholic, who prays to God as he has been taught, and believes in transubstantiation; he works and raises wheat, he has a large family of children, all hale and robust; his belief, his prayers offend nobody. About one mile farther on the same road, his next neighbour may be a good honest plodding German Lutheran, who addresses himself to the same God, the God of all, agreeably to the modes he has been educated in, and believes in consubstantiation; by so doing he scandalises nobody; he also works in his fields, embellishes the earth, clears swamps, etc. What has the world to do with his Lutheran principles? He persecutes nobody, and nobody persecutes him, he visits his neighbours, and his neighbours visit him. Next to him lives a seceder, the most enthusiastic of all sectaries; his zeal is hot and fiery, but separated as he is from others of the same complexion, he has no congregation of his own to resort to, where he might cabal and mingle religious pride with worldly obstinacy. He likewise raises good crops, his house is handsomely painted, his orchard is one of the fairest in the neighbourhood. How does it concern the welfare of the country, or of the province at large, what this man's religious sentiments are, or really whether he has any at all? He is a good farmer, he is a sober, peaceable, good citizen: William Penn himself would not wish for more. This is the visible character, the invisible one is only guessed at, and is nobody's business. Next again lives a Low Dutchman, who implicitly believes the rules laid down by the synod of Dort. He conceives no other idea of a clergyman than that of a hired man; if he does his work well he will pay him the stipulated sum; if not he will dismiss him, and do without his sermons, and let his church be shut up for years. But notwithstanding this coarse idea, you will find his house and farm to be the neatest in all the country; and you will judge by his waggon and fat horses, that he thinks more of the affairs of this world than of those of the next. He is sober and laborious, therefore he is all he ought to be as to the affairs of this life; as for those of the next, he must trust to the great Creator. Each of these people instruct their children as well as they can, but these instructions are feeble compared to those which are given to the youth of the poorest class in Europe. Their children will therefore grow up less zealous and more indifferent in matters of religion than their parents. The foolish vanity, or rather the fury of making Proselytes, is unknown here; they have no time, the seasons call for all their attention, and thus in a few years, this mixed neighbourhood will exhibit a strange religious medley that will be neither pure Catholicism nor pure Calvinism. A very perceptible indifference even in the first generation, will become apparent; and it may happen that the daughter of the Catholic will marry the

son of the seceder, and settle by themselves at a distance from their parents. What religious education will they give their children? A very imperfect one. If there happens to be in the neighbourhood any place of worship, we will suppose a Quaker's meeting; rather than not show their fine clothes, they will go to it, and some of them may perhaps attach themselves to that society. Others will remain in a perfect state of indifference; the children of these zealous parents will not be able to tell what their religious principles are, and their grandchildren still less. The neighbourhood of a place of worship generally leads them to it, and the action of going thither, is the strongest evidence they can give of their attachment to any sect. The Quakers are the only people who retain a fondness for their own mode of worship; for be they ever so far separated from each other, they hold a sort of communion with the society, and seldom depart from its rules, at least in this country. Thus all sects are mixed as well as all nations; thus religious indifference is imperceptibly disseminated from one end of the continent to the other; which is at present one of the strongest characteristics of the Americans. Where this will reach no one can tell, perhaps it may leave a vacuum fit to receive other systems. Persecution, religious pride, the love of contradiction, are the food of what the world commonly calls religion. These motives have ceased here; zeal in Europe is confined; here it evaporates in the great distance it has to travel; there it is a grain of powder inclosed, here it burns away in the open air, and consumes without effect.

But to return to our back settlers. I must tell you, that there is something in the proximity of the woods, which is very singular. It is with men as it is with the plants and animals that grow and live in the forests; they are entirely different from those that live in the plains. I will candidly tell you all my thoughts but you are not to expect that I shall advance any reasons. By living in or near the woods, their actions are regulated by the wildness of the neighbourhood. The deer often come to eat their grain, the wolves to destroy their sheep, the bears to kill their hogs, the foxes to catch their poultry. This surrounding hostility immediately puts the gun into their hands; they watch these animals, they kill some; and thus by defending their property, they soon become professed hunters; this is the progress; once hunters, farewell to the plough. The chase renders them ferocious, gloomy, and unsociable; a hunter wants no neighbour, he rather hates them, because he dreads the competition. In a little time their success in the woods makes them neglect their tillage. They trust to the natural fecundity of the earth, and therefore do little; carelessness in fencing often exposes what little they sow to destruction; they are not at home to watch; in order therefore to make up the deficiency, they go often to the woods. That new mode of life brings along with it a new set of manners, which I cannot easily describe. These new manners being grafted on the old stock, produce a strange sort of lawless profligacy, the impressions of which are indeliblc. The manners of the Indian natives are respectable, compared with this European medley. Their wives and children live in sloth and inactivity; and having no proper pursuits, you may judge what education the latter receive. Their tender minds have nothing else to contemplate but the example of their parents; like them they grow up a mongrel breed, half civilised, half savage, except nature stamps on them some constitutional propensities. That rich, that voluptuous sentiment is gone that struck them so forcibly; the possession of their freeholds no longer conveys to their minds the same pleasure and pride. To all these reasons you must add, their lonely situation, and you cannot imagine what an effect on manners the great distances they live from each other has! Consider one of the last settlements in its first view: of what is it composed? Europeans who have not that sufficient share of knowledge they ought to have, in order to prosper; people who have suddenly passed from oppression, dread of government, and fear of laws, into the unlimited freedom of the woods. This sudden change must have a very great effect on most men, and on that class particularly. Eating of wild meat, whatever you may think, tends to alter their temper: though all the proof

I can adduce, is, that I have seen it: and having no place of worship to resort to, what little society this might afford is denied them. The Sunday meetings, exclusive of religious benefits, were the only social bonds that might have inspired them with some degree of emulation in neatness. Is it then surprising to see men thus situated, immersed in great and heavy labours, degenerate a little? It is rather a wonder the effect is not more diffusive. The Moravians and the Quakers are the only instances in exception to what I have advanced. The first never settle singly, it is a colony of the society which emigrates; they carry with them their forms, worship, rules, and decency: the others never begin so hard, they are always able to buy improvements, in which there is a great advantage, for by that time the country is recovered from its first barbarity. Thus our bad people are those who are half cultivators and half hunters; and the worst of them are those who have degenerated altogether into the hunting state. As old ploughmen and new men of the woods, as Europeans and new made Indians, they contract the vices of both; they adopt the moroseness and ferocity of a native, without his mildness, or even his industry at home. If manners are not refined, at least they are rendered simple and inoffensive by tilling the earth; all our wants are supplied by it, our time is divided between labour and rest, and leaves none for the commission of great misdeeds. As hunters it is divided between the toil of the chase, the idleness of repose, or the indulgence of inebriation. Hunting is but a licentious idle life, and if it does not always pervert good dispositions; yet, when it is united with bad luck, it leads to want: want stimulates that propensity to rapacity and injustice, too natural to needy men, which is the fatal gradation. After this explanation of the effects which follow by living in the woods, shall we yet vainly flatter ourselves with the hope of converting the Indians? We should rather begin with converting our back-settlers; and now if I dare mention the name of religion, its sweet accents would be lost in the immensity of these woods. Men thus placed are not fit either to receive or remember its mild instructions; they want temples and ministers, but as soon as men cease to remain at home, and begin to lead an erratic life, let them be either tawny or white, they cease to be its disciples.

Thus have I faintly and imperfectly endeavoured to trace our society from the sea to the woods! yet you must not imagine that every person who moves back, acts upon the same principles, or falls into the same degeneracy. Many families carry with them all their decency of conduct, purity of morals, and respect of religion; but these are scarce,

the power of example is sometimes irresistible. Even among these back-settlers, their depravity is greater or less, according to what nation or province they belong. Were I to adduce proofs of this, I might be accused of partiality. If there happens to be some rich intervals, some fertile bottoms, in those remote districts, the people will there prefer tilling the land to hunting, and will attach themselves to it; but even on these fertile spots you may plainly perceive the inhabitants to acquire a great degree of rusticity and selfishness. * * *

THOMAS PAINE (1737–1809)

Paine has been called "the epitome of a world in revolution." He came to America in 1774, bearing a somewhat spotted reputation and a guarded letter from Franklin. Born in England in 1737, he had worked for a time at his father's trade, corset making, had been twice appointed to and twice dismissed from the Excise, and had been sold out as a bankrupt. In Philadelphia he secured employment with the *Pennsylvania Gazette* and exhibited his real genius for journalism. Like a good reporter, he soon found the timely topic, made up his mind about it, and startled the more conservative colonists by coming out for independence.

He advanced his doctrine in an anonymous pamphlet entitled *Common Sense*, in January of 1776. The pamphlet was read in every corner of the new world and soon was reprinted in Europe. More than 100,000 copies were sold within three months. Those who were not in on the secret thought it was the work of Franklin or Adams. The pamphlet was effectively written and timely journalism. Paine perceived that the temper of the times had changed greatly in the eight years since Dickinson had written his calm letters, and he had seen at first hand conditions in England and America. So he went to the heart of the situation: the colonies were no longer British; to return to the fold would be less valuable than to strike for freedom; they had gone too far to turn back; they should follow the dictates of common sense.

Important as this was, Paine's greatest service to the cause of American independence came in December, 1776, amidst all the gloom caused by Washington's retreat across New Jersey. On December 18 Washington had written: "Between you and me, I think our affairs are in a very bad situation . . . if every nerve is not strained to the utmost to recruit the new army with all possible expedition, I think the game is pretty near up." Next day appeared the first issue of the *Crisis:* "These are the times that try men's souls." Washington had the pamphlet read to every regiment. From the end of 1776 until the end of 1783, thirteen regular issues of the *Crisis* and three additional publications in the series stirred America to fight for liberty.

When peace was made, Paine was a man without a revolution, and hurried to Europe to enter the political battle there raging. *The Rights of Man*, 1791, issued as a reply to Burke, won him a great reputation in Europe and indictment for treason

in England.   He escaped to France, where for a time he was in high favor with the
revolutionists.   When he remonstrated against violence to the king, he was sentenced
to death and saved from the guillotine only by intervention of the American consul.
While in Paris he wrote, primarily for the French people, *The Age of Reason*, a coarse
and slashing attack on traditional Christianity and an earnest statement of his own
deistical beliefs.   In 1802 he returned to America and in 1809 he died on his farm
in New York.

The most scholarly text is M. D. Conway's *The Writings of Thomas Paine*, 4 vols.,
1894–96.   The best short lives are by Leslie Stephen in *DNB* and by Crane Brinton
in *DAB*.   The best full-length biography is by M. D. Conway, 1892.   A convenient
volume of selections is *Thomas Paine* in the *AWS*, with an excellent introduction by
H. H. Clark, 1944.

From The Crisis
(December 19, 1776)

[*The Times That Try Men's Souls*]

These are the times that try men's souls.
The summer soldier and the sunshine patriot
will, in this crisis, shrink from the service of
their country; but he that stands it *now*, deserves the love and thanks of man and woman.
Tyranny, like hell, is not easily conquered;
yet we have this consolation with us, that the
harder the conflict, the more glorious the triumph.   What we obtain too cheap, we esteem
too lightly: it is dearness only that gives every
thing its value.   Heaven knows how to put a
proper price upon its goods, and it would be
strange indeed if so celestial an article as FREE-
DOM should not be highly rated.   Britain, with
an army to enforce her tyranny, has declared
that she has a right (*not only to* TAX) but "to
BIND *us in* ALL CASES WHATSOEVER," and if being
bound in that manner, is not slavery, then there
is not such a thing as slavery upon earth.
Even the expression is impious; for so unlimited a power can belong only to God.

Whether the independence of the continent
was declared too soon, or delayed too long,
I will not now enter into as an argument; my
own simple opinion is, that had it been eight
months earlier, it would have been much better.   We did not make a proper use of last
winter, neither could we, while we were in a
dependent state.   However, the fault, if it
were one, was all our own, we have none to
blame but ourselves.   But no great deal is lost
yet.   All that Howe has been doing for this
month past, is rather a ravage than a conquest, which the spirit of the Jerseys, a year
ago, would have quickly repulsed, and which
time and a little resolution will soon recover.

I have as little superstition in me as any
man living, but my secret opinion has ever
been, and still is, that God Almighty will not
give up a people to military destruction, or
leave them unsupportedly to perish, who have
so earnestly and so repeatedly sought to avoid
the calamities of war, by every decent method
which wisdom could invent.   Neither have I
so much of the infidel in me, as to suppose
that He has relinquished the government of
the world, and given us up to the care of
devils; and as I do not, I cannot see on what
grounds the king of Britain can look up to
heaven for help against us: a common murderer, a highwayman, or a housebreaker, has
as good a pretence as he.

'Tis surprising to see how rapidly a panic
will sometimes run through a country.   All
nations and ages have been subject to them:
Britain has trembled like an ague at the report
of a French fleet of flat bottomed boats; and
in the fourteenth century the whole English
army, after ravaging the kingdom of France,
was driven back like men petrified with fear;
and this brave exploit was performed by a
few broken forces collected and headed by a
woman, Joan of Arc.   Would that heaven
might inspire some Jersey maid to spirit up
her countrymen, and save her fair fellow suf-
ferers from ravage and ravishment!   Yet
panics, in some cases, have their uses; they
produce as much good as hurt.   Their duration is always short; the mind soon grows
through them, and acquires a firmer habit

than before. But their peculiar advantage is, that they are the touchstones of sincerity and hypocrisy, and bring things and men to light, which might otherwise have lain forever undiscovered. In fact, they have the same effect on secret traitors, which an imaginary apparition would have upon a private murderer. They sift out the hidden thoughts of man, and hold them up in public to the world. Many a disguised tory has lately shown his head, that shall penitentially solemnize with curses the day on which Howe arrived upon the Delaware.

As I was with the troops at Fort Lee, and marched with them to the edge of Pennsylvania, I am well acquainted with many circumstances, which those who live at a distance know but little or nothing of. Our situation there was exceedingly cramped, the place being a narrow neck of land between the North River and the Hackensack. Our force was inconsiderable, being not one fourth so great as Howe could bring against us. We had no army at hand to have relieved the garrison, had we shut ourselves up and stood on our defence. Our ammunition, light artillery, and the best part of our stores, had been removed, on the apprehension that Howe would endeavor to penetrate the Jerseys, in which case Fort Lee could be of no use to us; for it must occur to every thinking man, whether in the army or not, that these kind of field forts are only for temporary purposes, and last in use no longer than the enemy directs his force against the particular object, which such forts are raised to defend. Such was our situation and condition at Fort Lee on the morning of the 20th of November, when an officer arrived with information that the enemy with 200 boats had landed about seven miles above: Major General Green, who commanded the garrison, immediately ordered them under arms, and sent express to General Washington at the town of Hackensack, distant by the way of the ferry = six miles. Our first object was to secure the bridge over the Hackensack, which laid up the river between the enemy and us, about six miles from us, and three from them. General Washington arrived in about three quarters of an hour, and marched at the head of the troops towards the bridge, which place I

expected we should have a brush for; however, they did not choose to dispute it with us, and the greatest part of our troops went over the bridge, the rest over the ferry except some which passed at a mill on a small creek, between the bridge and the ferry, and made their way through some marshy grounds up to the town of Hackensack, and there passed the river. We brought off as much baggage as the wagons could contain, the rest was lost. The simple object was to bring off the garrison, and march them on till they could be strengthened by the Jersey or Pennsylvania militia, so as to be enabled to make a stand. We staid four days at Newark, collected our outposts with some of the Jersey militia, and marched out twice to meet the enemy, on being informed that they were advancing, though our numbers were greatly inferior to theirs. Howe, in my little opinion, committed a great error in generalship in not throwing a body of forces off from Staten Isand through Amboy, by which means he might have seized all our stores at Brunswick, and intercepted our march into Pennsylvania; but if we believe the power of hell to be limited, we must likewise believe that their agents are under some providential controul.

I shall not now attempt to give all the particulars of our retreat to the Delaware; suffice it for the present to say, that both officers and men, though greatly harassed and fatigued, frequently without rest, covering, or provision, the inevitable consequences of a long retreat, bore it with a manly and martial spirit. All their wishes centered in one, which was, that the country would turn out and help them to drive the enemy back. Voltaire has remarked that King William never appeared to full advantage but in difficulties and in action; the same remark may be made on General Washington, for the character fits him. There is a natural firmness in some minds which cannot be unlocked by trifles, but which, when unlocked, discovers a cabinet of fortitude; and I reckon it among those kind of public blessings, which we do not immediately see, that God hath blessed him with uninterrupted health, and given him a mind that can even flourish upon care.

I shall conclude this paper with some miscellaneous remarks on the state of our affairs;

and shall begin with asking the following question, Why is it that the enemy have left the New-England provinces, and made these middle ones the seat of war? The answer is easy: New-England is not infested with tories, and we are. I have been tender in raising the cry against these men, and used numberless arguments to show them their danger, but it will not do to sacrifice a world either to their folly or their baseness. The period is now arrived, in which either they or we must change our sentiments, or one or both must fall. And what is a tory? Good God! what is he? I should not be afraid to go with a hundred whigs against a thousand tories, were they to attempt to get into arms. Every tory is a coward; for servile, slavish, self-interested fear is the foundation of toryism; and a man under such influence, though he may be cruel, never can be brave.

But, before the line of irrecoverable separation be drawn between us, let us reason the matter together: Your conduct is an invitation to the enemy, yet not one in a thousand of you has heart enough to join him. Howe is as much deceived by you as the American cause is injured by you. He expects you will all take up arms, and flock to his standard, with muskets on your shoulders. Your opinions are of no use to him, unless you support him personally, for 'tis soldiers, and not tories, that he wants.

I once felt all that kind of anger, which a man ought to feel, against the mean principles that are held by the tories: a noted one who kept a tavern at Amboy, was standing at his door, with as pretty a child in his hand, about eight or nine years old, as ever I saw, and after speaking his mind as freely as he thought was prudent, finished with this unfatherly expression, "*Well! give me peace in my day.*" Not a man lives on the continent but fully believes that a separation must some time or other finally take place, and a generous parent should have said, "*If there must be trouble, let it be in my day, that my child may have peace;*" and this single reflection, well applied, is sufficient to awaken every man to duty. Not a place upon earth might be so happy as America. Her situation is remote from all the wrangling world, and she has nothing to do but to trade with them. A man can dis-

tinguish himself between temper and principle, and I am as confident, as I am that God governs the world, that America will never be happy till she gets clear of foreign dominion. Wars, without ceasing, will break out till that period arrives, and the continent must in the end be conqueror; for though the flame of liberty may sometimes cease to shine, the coal can never expire.

From The Age of Reason

(1794–96)

The Age of Reason, of which a part is reprinted below, is the most famous, or notorious, statement of late-eighteenth century deism. It "was scattered the length and breadth of the land. Newspapers advertised it, together with the counterblasts that conservatives wrote to overthrow it. Bishop Mead of Virginia found even Parson Weems selling the heretical tract at the tavern in Fairfax County Courthouse. The democratic clubs and the deistical societies used it as a textbook. College students swallowed it whole, to the great alarm of their preceptors; and humble men in villages from New Hampshire to Georgia and beyond the Alleghenies discussed it by tavern candlelight. The storm of criticism which the book brought forth for the time only seemed to feed the fire, nor did the epithets cast on Paine slow down the conflagration. He was abused as a filthy atheist, a dissolute drunkard, a malignant blasphemer, a superficial reasoner" (Curti, *The Growth of American Thought*, 159).

However one may today deplore the obvious defects of Paine's attack on Christianity, *The Age of Reason* is historically an important work, essential to an understanding of the time in which it was written. And as a work of literary art it shows, as Leslie Stephen said, "the power of wielding a fine vigorous English, a fit vehicle for fanatical passion."

[*A Deist's Belief*]

It has been my intention, for several years past, to publish my thoughts upon religion; I am well aware of the difficulties that attend the subject, and from that consideration, had reserved it to a more advanced period of life. I intended it to be the last offering I should make to my fellow-citizens of all nations, and that at a time when the purity of the motive that induced me to it, could not admit of a question, even by those who might disapprove the work.

The circumstance that has now taken place

in France of the total abolition of the whole national order of priesthood and of every thing appertaining to compulsive systems of religion, and compulsive articles of faith, has not only precipitated my intention, but rendered a work of this kind exceedingly necessary, lest, in the general wreck of superstition, of false systems of government, and false theology, we lose sight of morality, of humanity, and of the theology that is true.

As several of my colleagues, and others of my fellow-citizens of France, have given me the example of making their voluntary and individual profession of faith, I also will make mine; and I do this with all that sincerity and frankness with which the mind of man communicates with itself.

I believe in one God, and no more; and I hope for happiness beyond this life.

I believe in the equality of man; and I believe that religious duties consist in doing justice, loving mercy, and endeavoring to make our fellow creatures happy.

But, lest it should be supposed that I believe many other things in addition to these, I shall, in the progress of this work, declare the things I do not believe, and my reasons for not believing them.

I do not believe in the creed professed by the Jewish church, by the Roman church, by the Greek church, by the Turkish church, by the Protestant church, nor by any church that I know of. My own mind is my own church.

All national institutions of churches, whether Jewish, Christian, or Turkish, appear to me no other than human inventions, set up to terrify and enslave mankind, and monopolize power and profit.

I do not mean by this declaration to condemn those who believe otherwise; they have the same right to their belief as I have to mine. But it is necessary to the happiness of man, that he be mentally faithful to himself. Infidelity does not consist in believing, or in disbelieving; it consists in professing to believe what he does not believe.

It is impossible to calculate the moral mischief, if I may so express it, that mental lying has produced in society. When a man has so far corrupted and prostituted the chastity of his mind, as to subscribe his professional belief to things he does not believe, he has prepared himself for the commission of every other crime. He takes up the trade of a priest for the sake of gain, and, in order to qualify himself for that trade, he begins with a perjury. Can we conceive anything more destructive to morality than this?

Soon after I had published the pamphlet, "COMMON SENSE," in America, I saw the exceeding probability that a revolution in the system of government would be followed by a revolution in the system of religion. The adulterous connection of church and state, wherever it had taken place, whether Jewish, Christian, or Turkish, had so effectually prohibited, by pains and penalties, every discussion upon established creeds, and upon first principles of religion, that until the system of government should be changed, those subjects could not be brought fairly and openly before the world; but that whenever this should be done, a revolution in the system of religion would follow. Human inventions and priest-craft would be detected; and man would return to the pure, unmixed, and unadulterated belief of one God, and no more.

Every national church or religion has established itself by pretending some special mission from God, communicated to certain individuals. The Jews have their Moses; the Christians their Jesus Christ, their apostles and saints; and the Turks their Mahomet, as if the way to God was not open to every man alike.

Each of those churches show certain books, which they call *revelation*, or the word of God. The Jews say, that their word of God was given by God to Moses, face to face; the Christians say, that their word of God came by divine inspiration; and the Turks say, that their word of God (the Koran) was brought by an angel from Heaven. Each of those churches accuse the other of unbelief; and, for my own part, I disbelieve them all.

As it is necessary to affix right ideas to words, I will, before I proceed further into the subject, offer some other observations on the word *revelation*. Revelation when applied to religion, means something communicated *immediately* from God to man.

No one will deny or dispute the power of the Almighty to make such a communication, if he pleases. But admitting, for the sake of a case, that something has been revealed to a certain person, and not revealed to any other person, it is revelation to that person only. When he tells it to a second person, a second to a third, a third to a fourth, and so on, it ceases to be a revelation to all those persons. It is revelation to the first person only, and *hearsay* to every other, and, consequently, they are not obliged to believe it.

It is a contradiction in terms and ideas, to call anything a revelation that comes to us at second-hand, either verbally or in writing. Revelation is necessarily limited to the first communication — after this, it is only an account of something which that person says was a revelation made to him; and though he may find himself obliged to believe it, it cannot be incumbent on me to believe it in the same manner; for it was not a revelation made to *me*, and I have only his word for it that it was made to him.

When Moses told the children of Israel that he received the two tables of the commandments from the hands of God, they were not obliged to believe him, because they had no other authority for it than his telling them so; and I have no other authority for it than some historian telling me so. The commandments carry no internal evidence of divinity with them; they contain some good moral precepts such as any man qualified to be a lawgiver, or a legislator, could produce himself, without having recourse to supernatural intervention.

When I am told that the Koran was written in Heaven, and brought to Mahomet by an angel, the account comes too near the same kind of hearsay evidence and second-hand authority as the former. I did not see the angel myself, and, therefore, I have a right not to believe it.

When also I am told that a woman called the Virgin Mary, said, or gave out, that she was with child without any cohabitation with a man, and that her betrothed husband, Joseph, said that an angel told him so, I have a right to believe them or not; such a circumstance required a much stronger evidence than their bare word for it; but we have not even this — for neither Joseph nor Mary wrote any such matter themselves; it is only reported by others that *they said so* — it is

hearsay upon hearsay, and I do not choose to rest my belief upon such evidence.

It is, however, not difficult to account for the credit that was given to the story of Jesus Christ being the son of God. He was born when the heathen mythology had still some fashion and repute in the world, and that mythology had prepared the people for the belief of such a story. Almost all the extraordinary men that lived under the heathen mythology were reputed to be the sons of some of their gods. It was not a new thing, at that time, to believe a man to have been celestially begotten; the intercourse of gods with women was then a matter of familiar opinion. Their Jupiter, according to their accounts, had cohabited with hundreds; the story therefore had nothing in it either new, wonderful or obscene; it was conformable to the opinions that then prevailed among the people called Gentiles, or Mythologists, and it was those people only that believed it. The Jews, who had kept strictly to the belief of one God, and no more, and who had always rejected the heathen mythology, never credited the story.

It is curious to observe how the theory of what is called the Christian Church, sprung out of the tail of heathen mythology. A direct incorporation took place in the first instance, by making the reputed founder to be celestially begotten. The trinity of gods that then followed was no other than a reduction of the former plurality, which was about twenty or thirty thousand; the statue of Mary succeeded the statue of Diana of Ephesus; the deification of heroes change into the canonization of saints; the mythologists had gods for everything; the Christian Mythologists had saints for everything; the church became as crowded with the one, as the pantheon had been with the other; and Rome was the place of both. The Christian theory is little else than the idolatry of the ancient Mythologists, accommodated to the purposes of power and revenue; and it yet remains to reason and philosophy to abolish the amphibious fraud.

Nothing that is here said can apply even with the most distant disrespect, to the *real* character of Jesus Christ. He was a virtuous and an amiable man. The morality that he preached and practised was of the most benevolent kind; and though similar systems of morality had been preached by Confucius, and by some of the Greek philosophers, many years before; by the Quakers since; and by many good men in all ages, it has not been exceeded by any.

Jesus Christ wrote no account of himself, of his birth, parentage, or anything else; not a line of what is called the New Testament is of his own writing. The history of him is altogether the work of other people; and as to the account given of his resurrection and ascension, it was the necessary counterpart to the story of his birth. His historians, having brought him into the world in a supernatural manner, were obliged to take him out again in the same manner, or the first part of the story must have fallen to the ground.

The wretched contrivance with which this latter part is told, exceeds everything that went before it. The first part, that of the miraculous conception, was not a thing that admitted of publicity; and therefore the tellers of this part of the story had this advantage, that though they might not be credited, they could not be detected. They could not be expected to prove it, because it was not one of those things that admitted of proof, and it was impossible that the person to whom it was told could prove it himself.

But the resurrection of a dead person from the grave, and his ascension through the air, is a thing very different as to the evidence it admits of, to the invisible conception of a child in the womb. The resurrection and ascension, supposing them to have taken place, admitted of public and ocular demonstration, like that of the ascension of a balloon, or the sun at noon day, to all Jerusalem at least. A thing which everybody is required to believe, requires that the proof and evidence of it should be equal to all, and universal; and as the public visibility of this last related act, was the only evidence that could give sanction to the former part, the whole of it falls to the ground, because that evidence never was given. Instead of this, a small number of persons, not more than eight or nine, are introduced as proxies for the whole world, to say they saw it, and all the rest of the world are called upon to believe it. But it appears that Thomas did not believe the resur-

rection; and, as they say, would not believe without having ocular and manual demonstration himself. *So neither will I*, and the reason is equally as good for me, and for every other person, as for Thomas.

It is in vain to attempt to palliate or disguise this matter. The story, so far as relates to the supernatural part, has every mark of fraud and imposition stamped upon the face of it. Who were the authors of it is as impossible for us now to know, as it is for us to be assured, that the books in which the account is related, were written by the persons whose names they bear; the best surviving evidence we now have respecting this affair is the Jews. They are regularly descended from the people who lived in the time this resurrection and ascension is said to have happened, and they say, *it is not true*. It has long appeared to me a strange inconsistency to cite the Jews as a proof of the truth of the story. It is just the same as if a man were to say, I will prove the truth of what I have told you, by producing the people who say it is false.

That such a person as Jesus Christ existed, and that he was crucified, which was the mode of execution at that day, are historical relations strictly within the limits of probability. He preached most excellent morality, and the equality of man; but he preached also against the corruptions and avarice of the Jewish priests, and this brought upon him the hatred and vengeance of the whole order of priesthood. The accusation which those priests brought against him was that of sedition and conspiracy against the Roman government, to which the Jews were then subject and tributary; and it is not improbable that the Roman government might have some secret apprehensions of the effects of his doctrine as well as the Jewish priests; neither is it improbable that Jesus Christ had in contemplation the delivery of the Jewish nation from the bondage of the Romans. Between the two, however, this virtuous reformer and revolutionist lost his life. * * *

But some perhaps will say — Are we to have no word of God — no revelation? I answer, Yes: there is a word of God; there is a revelation.

THE WORD OF GOD IS THE CREATION WE BEHOLD: And it is in *this word*, which no human invention can counterfeit or alter, that God speaketh universally to man.

Human language is local and changeable, and is therefore incapable of being used as the means of unchangeable and universal information. The idea that God sent Jesus Christ to publish, as they say, the glad tidings to all nations, from one end of the earth to the other, is consistent only with the ignorance of those who knew nothing of the extent of the world, and who believed, as those world-saviours believed, and continued to believe, for several centuries, (and that in contradiction to the discoveries of philosophers and the experience of navigators,) that the earth was flat like a trencher; and that a man might walk to the end of it.

But how was Jesus Christ to make anything known to all nations? He could speak but one language, which was Hebrew; and there are in the world several hundred languages. Scarcely any two nations speak the same language, or understand each other; and as to translations, every man who knows anything of languages, knows that it was impossible to translate from one language to another, not only without losing a great part of the original, but frequently of mistaking the sense; and besides all this, the art of printing was wholly unknown at the time Christ lived.

It is always necessary that the means that are to accomplish any end, be equal to the accomplishment of that end, or the end cannot be accomplished. It is in this, that the difference between finite and infinite power and wisdom discovers itself. Man frequently fails in accomplishing his ends, from a natural inability of the power to the purpose; and frequently from the want of wisdom to apply power properly. But it is impossible for infinite power and wisdom to fail as man faileth. The means it useth are always equal to the end; but human language, more especially as there is not an universal language, is incapable of being used as an universal means of unchangeable and uniform information, and therefore it is not the means that God useth in manifesting himself universally to man.

It is only in the CREATION that all our ideas and conceptions of a *word of God* can unite. The Creation speaketh an universal language, independently of human speech or human language, multiplied and various as they be. It is an ever-existing original, which every man can read. It cannot be forged; it cannot be counterfeited; it cannot be lost; it cannot be altered; it cannot be suppressed. It does not depend upon the will of man whether it shall be published or not; it publishes itself from one end of the earth to the other. It preaches to all nations and to all worlds; and this *word of God* reveals to man all that is necessary for man to know of God.

Do we want to contemplate his power? We see it in the unchangeable order by which the incomprehensible whole is governed. Do we want to contemplate his munificence? We see it in the abundance with which he fills the earth. Do we want to contemplate his mercy? We see it in his not withholding that abundance even from the unthankful. In fine, do we want to know what God is? Search not the book called the Scripture, which any human hand might make, but the Scripture called the Creation.

The only idea man can affix to the name of God, is that of a *first cause*, the cause of all things. And, incomprehensible and difficult as it is for a man to conceive what a first cause is, he arrives at the belief of it, from the tenfold greater difficulty of disbelieving it. It is difficult beyond description to conceive that space can have no end; but it is more difficult to conceive an end. It is difficult beyond the power of man to conceive an eternal duration of what we call time; but it is more impossible to conceive a time when there shall be no time.

In like manner of reasoning, everything we behold carries in itself the internal evidence that it did not make itself. Every man is an evidence to himself, that he did not make himself; neither could his father make himself, nor his grandfather, nor any of his race; neither could any tree, plant, or animal make itself; and it is the conviction arising from this evidence, that carries us on, as it were, by necessity, to the belief of a first cause eternally existing, of a nature totally different to any material existence we know of, and by the power of which all things exist; and this first cause, man calls God.

It is only by the exercise of reason, that

man can discover God. Take away that reason, and he would be incapable of understanding any thing; and, in this case it would be just as consistent to read even the book called the Bible to a horse as to a man. How then is it that those people pretend to reject reason?

Almost the only parts in the book called the Bible, that convey to us any idea of God, are some chapters in Job, and the 19th Psalm; I recollect no other. Those parts are true *deistical* compositions; for they treat of the *Deity* through his works. They take the book of Creation as the word of God, they refer to no other book, and all the inferences they make are drawn from that volume.

I insert in this place the 19th Psalm, as paraphrased into English verse by Addison. I recollect not the prose, and where I write this I have not the opportunity of seeing it:

> The spacious firmament on high,
> With all the blue etherial sky,
> And spangled heavens, a shining frame,
> Their great original proclaim.
> The unwearied sun, from day to day,
> Does his Creator's power display,
> And publishes to every land,
> The work of an Almighty hand.
> Soon as the evening shades prevail,
> The moon takes up the wondrous tale,
> And nightly to the list'ning earth,
> Repeats the story of her birth;
> Whilst all the stars that round her burn,
> And all the planets, in their turn,
> Confirm the tidings as they roll,
> And spread the truth from pole to pole.
> What though in solemn silence all
> Move round this dark terrestrial ball;
> What though no real voice, nor sound,
> Amidst their radient orbs be found,
> In reason's ear they all rejoice,
> And utter forth a glorious voice,
> Forever singing as they shine,
> THE HAND THAT MADE US IS DIVINE.

What more does man want to know, than that the hand or power that made these things is Divine, is Omnipotent? Let him believe this with the force it is impossible to repel, if he permits his reason to act, and his rule of moral life will follow of course.

The allusions in Job have, all of them, the same tendency with this Psalm; that of deducing or proving a truth that would be otherwise unknown, from truths already known.

I recollect not enough of the passages in Job to insert them correctly: but there is one occurs to me that is applicable to the subject I am speaking upon. "Canst thou by searching find out God? Canst thou find out the Almighty to perfection?"

I know not how the printers have pointed this passage, for I keep no Bible; but it contains two distinct questions that admit of distinct answers.

First — Canst thou by searching find out God? Yes; because, in the first place, I know I did not make myself, and yet I have existence; and by *searching* into the nature of other things, I find that no other thing could make itself; and yet millions of other things exist; therefore it is, that I know, by positive conclusion resulting from this search, that there is a power superior to all those things, and that power is God.

Secondly — Canst thou find out the Almighty to *perfection?* No; not only because the power and wisdom He has manifested in the structure of the Creation that I behold is to me incomprehensible, but because even this manifestation, great as it is, is probably but a small display of that immensity of power and wisdom, by which millions of other worlds to me invisible by their distance, were created and continue to exist.

It is evident that both of these questions are put to the reason of the person to whom they are supposed to have been addressed; and it is only by admitting the first question to be answered affirmatively, that the second could follow. It would have been unnecessary, and even absurd, to have put a second question, more difficult than the first, if the first question had been answered negatively. The two questions have different objects; the first refers to the existence of God, the second to his attributes; reason can discover the one, but it falls infinitely short in discovering the whole of the other.

I recollect not a single passage in all the writings ascribed to the men called apostles, that convey any idea of what God is. Those writings are chiefly controversial; and the subject they dwell upon, that of a man dying in agony on a cross, is better suited to the gloomy genius of a monk in a cell, by whom it is not impossible they were written, than to any man breathing the open air of the Creation. The only passage that occurs to me, that has any reference to the works of God, by which only his power and wisdom can be known, is related to have been spoken by Jesus Christ, as a remedy against distrustful care. "Behold the lilies of the field, they toil not, neither do they spin." This, however, is far inferior to the allusions in Job and in the 19th Psalm; but it is similar in idea, and the modesty of the imagery is correspondent to the modesty of the man.

As to the Christian system of faith, it appears to me as a species of atheism — a sort of religious denial of God. It professes to believe in a man rather than in God. It is a compound made up chiefly of manism with but little deism, and is as near to atheism as twilight is to darkness. It introduces between man and his Maker an opaque body, which it calls a Redeemer, as the moon introduces her opaque self between the earth and the sun, and it produces by this means a religious or an irreligious eclipse of light. It has put the whole orbit of reason into shade.

The effect of this obscurity has been that of turning every thing upside down, and representing it in reverse; and among the revolutions it has thus magically produced, it has made a revolution in theology.

That which is now called natural philosophy, embracing the whole circle of science, of which astronomy occupies the chief place, is the study of the works of God, and of the power and wisdom of God in his works, and is the true theology.

As to the theology that is now studied in its place, it is the study of human opinions and of human fancies *concerning* God. It is not the study of God himself in the works that he has made, but in the works or writings that man has made; and it is not among the least of the mischiefs that the Christian system has done to the world, that it has abandoned the original and beautiful system of theology, like a beautiful innocent, to distress and reproach, to make room for the hag of superstition.

The Book of Job and the 19th Psalm, which even the Church admits to be more ancient than the chronological order in which they stand in the book called the Bible, are theological orations conformable to the original system of theology. The internal evidence of those orations proves to a demonstration that the study and contemplation of the works of creation, and of the power and wisdom of God, revealed and manifested in those works, made a great part of the religious devotion of the times in which they were written; and it was this devotional study and contemplation that led to the discovery of the principles upon which, what are now called sciences, are established; and it is to the discovery of these principles that almost all the arts that contribute to the convenience of human life, owe their existence. Every principal art has some science for its parent, though the person who mechanically performs the work does not always, and but very seldom, perceive the connection.

It is a fraud of the Christian system to call the sciences *human invention;* it is only the application of them that is human. Every science has for its basis a system of principles as fixed and unalterable as those by which the universe is regulated and governed. Man cannot make principles, he can only discover them.

For example — every person who looks at an almanac sees an account when an eclipse will take place, and he sees also that it never fails to take place according to the account there given. This shows that man is acquainted with the laws by which the heavenly bodies move. But it would be something worse than ignorance, were any Church on earth to say that those laws are a human invention. It would also be ignorance, or something worse, to say that the scientific principles, by the aid of which man is enabled to calculate and foreknow when an eclipse will take place, are a human invention. Man cannot invent a thing that is eternal and immutable; and the scientific principles he employs for this purpose must, and are, of necessity, as eternal and immutable as the laws by which the heavenly bodies move, or they could not be used as they are to ascertain the time when, and the manner how, an eclipse will take place.

The scientific principles that man employs to obtain the foreknowledge of an eclipse, or of any thing else, relating to the motion of the heavenly bodies, are contained chiefly in that part of science which is called trigonometry, or the properties of a triangle, which, when applied to the study of the heavenly bodies, is called astronomy; when applied to direct the course of a ship on the ocean, it is called navigation; when applied to the construction of figures drawn by rule and compass, it is called geometry; when applied to the construction of plans of edifices, it is called architecture; when applied to the measurement of any portion of the surface of the earth, it is called land-surveying. In fine, it is the soul of science; it is an eternal truth; it contains the *mathematical demonstration* of which man speaks, and the extent of its uses is unknown.

It may be said that man can make or draw a triangle, and therefore a triangle is an human invention.

But the triangle, when drawn, is no other than the image of the principle; it is a delineation to the eye, and from thence to the mind, of a principle that would otherwise be imperceptible. The triangle does not make the principle, any more than a candle taken into a room that was dark, makes the chairs and tables that before were invisible. All the properties of a triangle exist independently of the figure, and existed before any triangle was drawn or thought of by man. Man had no more to do in the formation of those properties or principles, than he had to do in making the laws by which the heavenly bodies move; and therefore the one must have the same Divine origin as the other.

In the same manner as, it may be said, that man can make a triangle, so also, may it be said, he can make the mechanical instrument called a lever; but the principle, by which the lever acts, is a thing distinct from the instrument, and would exist if the instrument did not; it attaches itself to the instrument after it is made; the instrument, therefore, can act no otherwise than it does act; neither can all the efforts of human invention make it act otherwise — that which, in all such cases, man calls the *effect*, is no other than the principle itself rendered perceptible to the senses.

Since, then, man cannot make principles, from whence did he gain a knowledge of them, so as to be able to apply them, not only to things on earth, but to ascertain the motion of bodies so immensely distant from him as all the heavenly bodies are? From whence, I ask, *could* he gain that knowledge, but from the study of the true theology?

It is the structure of the universe that has taught this knowledge to man. That structure is an ever-existing exhibition of every principle upon which every part of mathematical science is founded. The offspring of this science is mechanics; for mechanics is no other than the principles of science applied practically. The man who proportions the several parts of a mill, uses the same scientific principles, as if he had the power of constructing an universe; but as he cannot give to matter that invisible agency, by which all the component parts of the immense machine of the universe have influence upon each other, and act in motional unison together, without any apparent contract, and to which man has given the name of attraction, gravitation, and repulsion, he supplies the place of that agency by the humble imitation of teeth and cogs. All the parts of man's microcosm must visibly touch: but could he gain a knowledge of that agency, so as to be able to apply it in practice, we might then say that another *canonical book* of the Word of God had been discovered.

If man could alter the properties of the lever, so also could he alter the properties of the triangle; for a lever (taking that sort of lever which is called a steel-yard, for the sake of explanation) forms, when in motion, a triangle. The line it descends from, (one point of that line being in the fulcrum,) the line it descends to, and the cord of the arc, which the end of the lever describes in the air, are the three sides of a triangle. The other arm of the lever describes also a triangle; and the corresponding sides of those two triangles, calculated scientifically, or measured geometrically; and also the sines, tangents, and secants generated from the angles, and geometrically measured, have the same proportions to each other, as the different weights have that will balance each other on the lever, leaving the weight of the lever out of the case.

It may also be said, that man can make a wheel and axis; that he can put wheels of different magnitudes together, and produce a mill. Still the case comes back to the same point, which is, that he did not make the principle that gives the wheels those powers. That principle is as unalterable as in the former case, or rather it is the same principle under a different appearance to the eye.

The power that two wheels of different magnitudes have upon each other, is in the same proportion as if the semi-diameter of the two wheels were joined together and made into that kind of lever I have described, suspended at the part where the semi-diameters join; for the two wheels, scientifically considered, are no other than the two circles generated by the motion of the compound lever.

It is from the study of the true theology that all our knowledge of science is derived, and it is from that knowledge that all the arts have originated.

The Almighty Lecturer, by displaying the principles of science in the structure of the universe, has invited man to study and to imitation. It is as if He had said to the inhabitants of this globe, that we call ours, "I have made an earth for man to dwell upon, and I have rendered the starry heavens visible, to teach him science and the arts. He can now provide for his own comfort, AND LEARN FROM MY MUNIFICENCE TO ALL, TO BE KIND TO EACH OTHER."

Of what use is it, unless it be to teach man something that his eye is endowed with the power of beholding, to an incomprehensible distance, an immensity of worlds revolving in the ocean of space? Or of what use is it that this immensity of worlds is visible to man? What has man to do with the Pleiades, with Orion, with Sirius, with the star he calls the north star, with the moving orbs he has named Saturn, Jupiter, Mars, Venus, and Mercury, if no uses are to follow from their being visible? A less power of vision would have been sufficient for man, if the immensity he now possesses were given only to waste itself, as it were, on an immense desert of space glittering with shows.

It is only by contemplating what he calls the starry heavens, as the book and school of science, that he discovers any use in their being visible to him, or any advantage resulting from his immensity of vision. But when he contemplates the subject in this light, he sees an additional motive for saying, that *nothing was made in vain;* for in vain would be this power of vision if it taught man nothing.

As the Christian system of faith has made a revolution in theology, so also has it made a revolution in the state of learning. That which is now called learning, was not learning, originally. Learning does not consist, as the schools now make it consist, in the knowledge of languages, but in the knowledge of things to which language gives names.

The Greeks were a learned people, but learning with them did not consist in speaking Greek, any more than in a Roman's speaking Latin, or a Frenchman's speaking French, or an Englishman's speaking English. From what we know of the Greeks, it does not appear that they knew or studied any language but their own, and this was one cause of their becoming so learned; it afforded them more time to apply themselves to better studies. The schools of the Greeks were schools of science and philosophy, and not of languages; and it is in the knowledge of the things that science and philosophy teach, that learning consists.

Almost all the scientific learning that now exists, came to us from the Greeks, or the people who spoke the Greek language. It, therefore, became necessary for the people of other nations, who spoke a different language, that some among them should learn the Greek language, in order that the learning the Greeks had, might be made known in those nations, by translating the Greek books of science and philosophy into the mother tongue of each nation.

The study, therefore, of the Greek language (and in the same manner for the Latin) was no other than the drudgery business of a linguist; and the language thus obtained, was no other than the means, as it were, the tools, employed to obtain the learning the Greeks had. It made no part of the learning itself; and was so distinct from it, as to make it exceedingly probable that the persons who had studied Greek sufficiently to translate those works, such, for instance, as Euclid's Elements, did not understand any of the learning the works contained.

As there is now nothing new to be learned from the dead languages, all the useful books being already translated, the languages are become useless, and the time expended in teaching and learning them is wasted. So far as the study of languages may contribute to the progress and communication of knowledge (for it has nothing to do with the *creation* of knowledge,) it is only in the living languages that new knowledge is to be found; and certain it is, that, in general, a youth will learn more of a living language in one year, than of a dead language in seven; and it is but seldom that the teacher knows much of it himself. The difficulty of learning the dead languages does not arise from any superior abstruseness in the languages themselves but in their *being dead*, and the pronunciation entirely lost. It would be the same thing with any other language when it becomes dead. The best Greek linguist that now exists, does not understand Greek so well as a Grecian ploughman did, or a Grecian milkmaid: and the same for the Latin, compared with a ploughman or milkmaid of the Romans; it would therefore be advantageous to the state of learning to abolish the study of the dead languages, and to make learning consist, as it originally did, in scientific knowledge.

The apology that is sometimes made for continuing to teach the dead languages is, that they are taught at a time, when a child is not capable of exerting any other mental faculty than that of memory; but that is altogether erroneous. The human mind has a natural disposition to scientific knowledge, and to the things connected with it. The first and favorite amusement of a child, even before it begins to play, is that of imitating the works of man. It builds houses with cards or sticks; it navigates the little ocean of a bowl of water with a paper boat, or dams the stream of a gutter, and contrives something which it calls a mill; and it interests itself in the fate of its works with a care that resembles affection. It afterwards goes to school, where its genius is killed by the barren study of a dead language, and the philosopher is lost in the linguist.

But the apology that is now made for continuing to teach the dead languages, could not be the cause, at first, of cutting down learning to the narrow and humble sphere of linguistry; the cause, therefore, must be sought for elsewhere. In all researches of this kind, the best evidence that can be produced, is the internal evidence the thing carries with itself, and the evidence of circumstances that unites with it; both of which, in this case, are not difficult to be discovered.

Putting then aside, as a matter of distinct consideration, the outrage offered to the moral justice of God, by supposing him to make the innocent suffer for the guilty, and also the loose morality and low contrivance of supposing him to change himself into the shape of a man, in order to make an excuse to himself for not executing his supposed sentence upon Adam; putting, I say, those things aside as a matter of distinct consideration, it is certain that what is called the Christian system of faith, including in it the whimsical account of the creation — the strange story of Eve — the snake and the apple — the ambiguous idea of a man-god — the corporeal idea of the death of a god — the mythological idea of a family of gods, and the Christian system of arithmetic, that three are one, and one is three, are all irreconcilable not only to the divine gift of reason, that God hath given to man, but to the knowledge that man gains of the power and wisdom of God, by the aid of the sciences, and by studying the structure of the universe that God has made.

The setters-up, therefore, and the advocates of the Christian system of faith, could not but foresee that the continually progressive knowledge that man would gain, by the aid of science, of the power and wisdom of God, manifested in the structure of the universe, and in all the works of Creation, would militate against, and call into question, the truth of their system of faith; and therefore it became necessary to their purpose to cut learning down to a size less dangerous to their project, and this they effected by restricting the idea of learning to the dead study of dead languages.

They not only rejected the study of science out of the Christian schools, but they persecuted it; and it is only within about the last two centuries that the study has been revived. So late as 1610, Galileo, a Florentine, discovered and introduced the use of telescopes, and by applying them to observe the motions and appearance of the heavenly bodies, afforded additional means for ascertaining the true structure of the universe. Instead of being esteemed for those discoveries, he was sentenced to renounce them, or the opinions resulting from them, as a damnable heresy. And, prior to that time, Vigilius was condemned to be burned for asserting the antipodes, or in other words, that the earth was a globe, and habitable in every part where there was land; yet the truth of this is now too well known even to be told.

If the belief of errors not morally bad did no mischief, it would make no part of the moral duty of man to oppose and remove them. There was no moral ill in believing the earth was flat like a trencher, any more than there was moral virtue in believing that it was round like a globe; neither was there any moral ill in believing that the Creator made no other world than this, any more than there was moral virtue in believing that he made millions, and that the infinity of space is filled with worlds. But when a system of religion is made to grow out of a supposed system of creation that is not true, and to unite itself therewith in a manner almost inseparable therefrom, the case assumes an entirely different ground. It is then that errors, not morally bad, became fraught with the same mischiefs as if they were. It is then that the truth, though otherwise indifferent itself, becomes an essential, by becoming the criterion, that either confirms by corresponding evidence, or denies by contradictory evidence, the reality of the religion itself. In this view of the case, it is the moral duty of man to obtain every possible evidence that the structure of the heavens, or any other part of creation affords, with respect to systems of religion. But this, the supporters or partizans of the Christian system, as if dreading the result, incessantly opposed, and not only rejected the sciences, but persecuted the professors. Had Newton or Descartes lived three or four hundred years ago, and pursued their studies as they did, it is most probable they would not have lived to finish them; and had Franklin drawn lightning from the clouds at the same time, it would have been at the hazard of expiring for it in flames.

Later times have laid all the blame upon the Goths and Vandals; but, however unwilling the partizans of the Christian system may be to believe or to acknowledge it, it is nevertheless true, that the age of ignorance commenced with the Christian system. There was more knowledge in the world before that period, than for many centuries afterwards; and as to religious knowledge, the Christian system, as already said, was only another species of mythology; and the mythology to which it succeeded, was a corruption of an ancient system of theism.

It is owing to this long interregnum of science, *and to no other cause,* that we have now to look through a vast chasm of many hundred years to the respectable characters we call the ancients. Had the progression of knowledge gone on proportionably with the stock that before existed, that chasm would have been filled up with characters rising superior in knowledge to each other; and those ancients we now so much admire, would have appeared respectably in the background of the scene. But the Christian system laid all waste; and if we take our stand about the beginning of the sixteenth century, we look back through that long chasm, to the times of the ancients, as over a vast sandy desert, in which not a shrub appears to intercept the vision to the fertile hills beyond.

It is an inconsistency scarcely possible to be credited, that any thing should exist, under the name of a religion, that held it to be *irreligious* to study and contemplate the structure of the universe that God had made. But the fact is too well established to be denied. The event that served more than any other to break the first link in this long chain of despotic ignorance, is that known by the name of the Reformation by Luther. From that time, though it does not appear to have made any part of the intention of Luther, or of those who are called reformers, the sciences began to revive, and liberality, their natural associate, began to appear. * * *

THE FEDERALIST (1787-1788)

The greatest distinction of American letters during the Revolutionary period was not attained in fiction or in satiric or epic verse, but in political prose. State papers such as the Declaration of Independence and political essays such as *The Federalist* showed what America was capable of producing.

The eighty-five essays of *The Federalist* appeared in various New York newspapers during the years 1787 and 1788 over the signature "Publius." At that time ratification of the Constitution by New York state hung in the balance. In answer to essays by George Clinton and Robert Yates, *The Federalist* letters argued for ratification. They developed, as Parrington says, four main theses: "the necessity for taking effective action in view of the self-confessed failure of the Articles of Confederation; the urgent need of a sovereign, unitary state, to avoid the horrors which must follow from 'the political monster of an *imperium in imperio*'; the necessity of providing that justice shall prevail over the majority will; and the adaptability of the republican form to a great extent of territory and divergent interests." "*The Federalist* was at once adopted by its party as an unanswerable defense of the Constitution; and its fame has grown greater with the passing years. No other work on political theory in the American library has been rated so high, or been more frequently cited."

Alexander Hamilton (1757–1804) was the head architect of *The Federalist*. He had the aid of John Jay (1745–1829) and later James Madison (1751–1836). Of the eighty-five essays, it is known that Hamilton wrote fifty-one, Madison fourteen, and Jay five, while three were the joint work of Hamilton and Madison. The authorship of the remaining twelve is disputed by the friends of Hamilton and Madison, latest evidence favoring Madison.

The standard editions are those of H. C. Lodge, 1923, and P. L. Ford, 1898. A volume of *Selections from The Federalist* was edited by J. S. Bassett, 1921.

No. II. (John Jay)

[A Momentous Decision]

When the people of America reflect that they are now called upon to decide a question, which, in its consequences, must prove one of the most important that ever engaged their attention, the propriety of their taking a very comprehensive, as well as a very serious, view of it, will be evident.

Nothing is more certain than the indispensable necessity of government, and it is equally undeniable, that whenever and however it is instituted, the people must cede to it some of their natural rights, in order to vest it with requisite powers. It is well worthy of consideration, therefore, whether it would conduce more to the interest of the people of America that they should, to all general purposes, be one nation, under one federal government, or that they should divide themselves into separate confederacies, and give to the head of each the same kind of powers which they are advised to place in one national government.

It has until lately been a received and uncontradicted opinion, that the prosperity of the people of America depended on their continuing firmly united, and the wishes, prayers, and efforts of our best and wisest citizens have been constantly directed to that object. But politicians now appear, who insist that this opinion is erroneous, and that instead of looking for safety and happiness in union, we ought to seek it in a division of the States into distinct confederacies or sovereignties. However extraordinary this new doctrine may appear, it nevertheless has its advocates; and certain characters who were much opposed to it formerly, are at present of the number. Whatever may be the arguments or inducements which have wrought this change in the sentiments and declarations of these gentlemen, it certainly would not be wise in the people at large to adopt these new political tenets without being fully convinced that they are founded in truth and sound policy.

It has often given me pleasure to observe, that independent America was not composed of detached and distant territories, but that one connected, fertile, wide-spreading country was the portion of our western sons of liberty. Providence has in a particular manner blessed it with a variety of soils and productions, and watered it with innumerable streams, for the delight and accommodation of its inhabitants. A succession of navigable waters forms a kind of chain round its borders, as if to bind it together; while the most noble rivers in the world, running at convenient distances, present them with highways for the easy communication of friendly aids, and the mutual transportation and exchange of their various commodities.

With equal pleasure I have as often taken notice, that Providence has been pleased to give this one connected country to one united people — a people descended from the same ancestors, speaking the same language, professing the same religion, attached to the same principles of government, very similar in their manners and customs, and who, by their joint counsels, arms, and efforts, fighting side by side throughout a long and bloody war, have nobly established general liberty and independence.

This country and this people seem to have been made for each other, and it appears as if it was the design of Providence, that an inheritance so proper and convenient for a band of brethren, united to each other by the strongest ties, should never be split into a number of unsocial, jealous, and alien sovereignties.

Similar sentiments have hitherto prevailed among all orders and denominations of men among us. To all general purposes we have uniformly been one people; each individual citizen everywhere enjoying the same national rights, privileges, and protection. As a nation we have made peace and war; as a nation we have vanquished our common enemies; as a nation we have formed alliances, and made treaties, and entered into various compacts and conventions with foreign states.

A strong sense of the value and blessings of union induced the people, at a very early period, to institute a federal government to preserve and perpetuate it. They formed it almost as soon as they had a political existence; nay, at a time when their habitations were in flames, when many of their citizens were bleeding, and when the progress of hostility and desolation left little room for those calm and mature inquiries and reflections which must ever precede the formation of a wise and well-balanced government for a free people. It is not to be wondered at, that a government instituted in times so inauspicious, should on experiment be found greatly deficient and inadequate to the purpose it was intended to answer.

This intelligent people perceived and regretted these defects. Still continuing no less attached to union than enamoured of liberty, they observed the danger which immediately threatened the former and more remotely the latter; and being persuaded that ample security for both could only be found in a national government more wisely framed, they, as with one voice, convened the late convention at Philadelphia, to take that important subject under consideration.

This convention, composed of men who possessed the confidence of the people, and many of whom had become highly distinguished by their patriotism, virtue, and wisdom, in times which tried the minds and hearts of men, undertook the arduous task. In the mild season of peace, with minds unoccupied by other subjects, they passed many months in cool, uninterrupted, and daily consultation; and finally, without having been awed by power, or influenced by any passions except love for their country, they presented and recommended to the people the plan produced by their joint and very unanimous councils.

Admit, for so is the fact, that this plan is only *recommended*, not imposed, yet let it be remembered that it is neither recommended to *blind* approbation, nor to *blind* reprobation; but to that sedate and candid consideration which the magnitude and importance of the subject demand, and which it certainly ought to receive. But this (as was remarked in the foregoing number of this paper) is more to be wished than expected, that it may be so considered and examined. Experience on a former occasion teaches us not to be too sanguine in such hopes. It is not yet forgotten that well-grounded apprehensions of imminent danger induced the people of America to form the memorable Congress of 1774. That body recommended certain measures to their constituents, and the event proved their wisdom; yet it is fresh in our memories how soon the press began to teem with pamphlets and weekly papers against those very measures. Not only many of the officers of government, who obeyed the dictates of personal interest, but others, from a mistaken estimate of consequences, or the undue influence of former attachments, or whose ambition aimed at objects which did not correspond with the public good, were indefatigable in their efforts to persuade the people to reject the advice of that patriotic Congress. Many, indeed, were deceived and deluded, but the great majority of the people reasoned and decided judiciously; and happy they are in reflecting that they did so.

They considered that the Congress was composed of many wise and experienced men. That, being convened from different parts of the country, they brought with them and communicated to each other a variety of useful information. That, in the course of the time they passed together in inquiring into and discussing the true interests of their country, they must have acquired very accurate knowledge on that head. That they were individually interested in the public liberty and prosperity, and therefore that it was not less their inclination than their duty to recommend only such measures as, after the most mature deliberation, they really thought prudent and advisable.

These and similar considerations then induced the people to rely greatly on the judgment and integrity of the Congress; and they took their advice, notwithstanding the various arts and endeavours used to deter them from it. But if the people at large had reason to confide in the men of that Congress, few of whom had been fully tried or generally known, still greater reason have they now to respect the judgment and advice of the convention, for it is well known that some of the most distinguished members of that Congress, who have been since tried and justly approved for patriotism and abilities, and who have grown old in acquiring political information, were also members of this convention, and carried into it their accumulated knowledge and experience.

It is worthy of remark that not only the first, but every succeeding Congress, as well as the late convention, have invariably joined with the people in thinking that the prosperity of America depended on its Union. To preserve and perpetuate it was the great object of the people in forming that convention, and it is also the great object of the plan which the convention has advised them to adopt. With what propriety, therefore, or for what good purposes, are attempts at this particular period made by some men to depreciate the importance of the Union? Or why is it suggested that three or four confederacies would be better than one? I am persuaded in my own mind that the people have always thought right on this subject, and that their universal and uniform attachment to the cause of the Union rests on great and weighty reasons, which I shall endeavour to develop and explain in some ensuing papers. They who promote the idea of substituting a number of distinct confederacies in the room of the plan of the convention, seem clearly to foresee that the rejection of it would put the continuance of the Union in the utmost jeopardy. That certainly would be the case, and I sincerely wish that it may be as clearly foreseen by every good citizen, that whenever the dissolution of the Union arrives, America will have reason to exclaim in the words of the poet: "FAREWELL! A LONG FAREWELL TO ALL MY GREATNESS."   PUBLIUS.

No. X. (James Madison)
[Special Interests and the Union]

Among the numerous advantages promised by a well-constructed union, none deserves to be more accurately developed than its tendency to break and control the violence of faction. The friend of popular governments never finds himself so much alarmed for their character and fate as when he contemplates their propensity to this dangerous vice. He will not fail, therefore, to set a due value on any plan which, without violating the principles to which he is attached, provides a proper cure for it. The instability, injustice, and confusion introduced into the public councils have, in truth, been the mortal diseases under which popular governments have everywhere perished; as they continue to be the favorite and fruitful topics from which the adversaries to liberty derive their most specious declamations. The valuable improvements made by the American constitutions on the popular models, both ancient and modern, cannot certainly be too much admired; but it would be an unwarrantable partiality, to contend that they have as effectually obviated the danger on this side as was wished and expected. Complaints are everywhere heard from our most considerate and virtuous citizens, equally the friends of public and private faith and of public and personal liberty, that our governments are too unstable; that the public good is disregarded in the conflicts of rival parties; and that measures are too often decided, not according to the rules of justice, and the rights of the minor party, but by the superior force of an interested and overbearing majority. However anxiously we may wish that these complaints had no foundation, the evidence of known facts will not permit us to deny that they are in some degree true. It will be found, indeed, on a candid review of our situation, that some of the distresses under which we labor have been erroneously charged on the operation of our governments; but it will be found, at the same time, that other causes will not alone account for many of our heaviest misfortunes; and, particularly, for that prevailing and increasing distrust of public engagements, and alarm for private rights, which are echoed from one end of the continent to the other. These must be chiefly, if not wholly, effects of the unsteadiness and injustice with which a factious spirit has tainted our public administrations.

By a faction, I understand a number of citizens, whether amounting to a majority or minority of the whole, who are united and actuated by some common impulse of passion, or of interest, adverse to the rights of other citizens or to the permanent and aggregate interests of the community.

There are two methods of curing the mischiefs of faction: the one, by removing its causes; the other, by controlling its effects.

There are again two methods of removing the causes of faction: the one, by destroying the liberty which is essential to its existence; the other, by giving to every citizen the same opinions, the same passions, and the same interests.

It could never be more truly said than of the first remedy, that it was worse than the disease. Liberty is to faction what air is to fire, an ailment without which it instantly expires. But it could not be less folly to abolish liberty, which is essential to political life, because it nourishes faction, than it would be to wish the annihilation of air, which is essential to animal life, because it imparts to fire its destructive agency.

The second expedient is as impracticable as the first would be unwise. As long as the reason of man continues fallible, and he is at liberty to exercise it, different opinions will be formed. As long as the connection subsists between his reason and his self-love, his opinions and his passions will have a reciprocal influence on each other; and the former will be objects to which the latter will attach themselves. The diversity in the faculties of men, from which the rights of property originate, is not less an insuperable obstacle to a uniformity of interests. The protection of these faculties is the first object of government. From the protection of different and unequal faculties of acquiring property, the possession of different degrees and kinds of property immediately results; and from the influence of these on the sentiments and views of the respective proprietors ensues a division of the society into different interests and parties.

The latent causes of faction are thus sown in the nature of man; and we see them everywhere brought into different degrees of activity, according to the different circumstances of civil society. A zeal for different opinions concerning religion, concerning government and many other points, as well of speculation as of practice; an attachment to different leaders ambitiously contending for pre-eminence and power, or to persons of other descriptions whose fortunes have been interesting to the human passions, have, in turn, divided mankind into parties, inflamed them with mutual animosity, and rendered them much more disposed to vex and oppress each other, than to co-operate for their common good. So strong is this propensity of mankind to fall into mutual animosities, that where no substantial occasion presents itself, the most frivolous and fanciful distinctions have been sufficient to kindle their unfriendly passions and excite their most violent conflicts. But the most common and durable source of factions has been the various and unequal distribution of property. Those who hold and those who are without property have ever formed distinct interests in society. Those who are creditors and those who are debtors fall under a like discrimination. A landed interest, a manufacturing interest, a mercantile interest, a moneyed interest, with many lesser interests, grow up of necessity in civilized nations, and divide them into different classes, actuated by different sentiments and views. The regulation of these various and interfering interests forms the principal task of modern legislation, and involves the spirit of party and faction in the necessary and ordinary operations of the government.

No man is allowed to be a judge in his own cause; because his interest would certainly bias his judgment and, not improbably, corrupt his integrity. With equal, nay, with greater reason, a body of men are unfit to be both judges and parties at the same time; yet what are many of the most important acts of legislation, but so many judicial determinations, not indeed concerning the rights of single persons, but concerning the rights of large bodies of citizens? and what are the different classes of legislators, but advocates and parties to the causes which they determine? Is a law proposed concerning private debts? — it is a question to which the creditors are parties on one side, and the debtors on the other. Justice ought to hold the balance between them. Yet the parties are, and must be, themselves the judges; and the most numerous party, or,

in other words, the most powerful faction, must be expected to prevail. Shall domestic manufactures be encouraged, and in what degree by restrictions on foreign manufactures? are questions which would be differently decided by the landed and the manufacturing classes, and probably by neither with a sole regard to justice and the public good. The apportionment of taxes on the various descriptions of property is an act which seems to require the most exact impartiality; yet there is, perhaps, no legislative act in which greater opportunity and temptation are given to a predominant party, to trample on the rules of justice. Every shilling with which they overburden the inferior number is a shilling saved to their own pockets.

It is in vain to say that enlightened statesmen will be able to adjust these clashing interests and render them all subservient to the public good. Enlightened statesmen will not always be at the helm; nor, in many cases, can such an adjustment be made at all, without taking into view indirect and remote considerations, which will rarely prevail over the immediate interest which one party may find in disregarding the rights of another or the good of the whole.

The inference to which we are brought is that the causes of faction cannot be removed, and that relief is only to be sought in the means of controlling its effects.

If a faction consists of less than a majority, relief is supplied by the republican principle, which enables the majority to defeat its sinister views by regular vote. It may clog the administration, it may convulse the society; but it will be unable to execute and mask its violence under the forms of the Constitution. When a majority is included in a faction, the form of popular government, on the other hand, enables it to sacrifice to its ruling passion or interest both the public good and the rights of other citizens. To secure the public good, and private rights, against the danger of such a faction, and at the same time to preserve the spirit and the form of popular government, is then the great object to which our inquiries are directed. Let me add that it is the great *desideratum*, by which alone this form of government can be rescued from the opprobrium under which it has so long labored, and be recommended to the esteem and adoption of mankind.

By what means is this object attainable? Evidently by one of two only. Either the existence of the same passion or interest in a majority, at the same time, must be prevented; or the majority, having such coexistent passion or interest, must be rendered, by their number and local situation, unable to concert and carry into effect schemes of oppression. If the impulse and the opportunity be suffered to coincide, we well know that neither moral nor religious motives can be relied on as an adequate control. They are not found to be such on the injustice and violence of individuals, and lose their efficacy in proportion to the number combined together; that is, in proportion as their efficacy becomes needful.

From this view of the subject it may be concluded that a pure democracy, by which I mean a society consisting of a small number of citizens, who assemble and administer the government in person, can admit of no cure for the mischiefs of faction. A common passion or interest will, in almost every case, be felt by a majority of the whole; a communication and concert results from the form of government itself; and there is nothing to check the inducements to sacrifice the weaker party or an obnoxious individual. Hence it is that such democracies have ever been spectacles of turbulence and contention; have ever been found incompatible with personal security, or the rights of property, and have in general been as short in their lives as they have been violent in their deaths. Theoretic politicians, who have patronized this species of government, have erroneously supposed that by reducing mankind to a perfect equality in their political rights, they would at the same time be perfectly equalized and assimilated in their possessions, their opinions, and their passions.

A republic, by which I mean a government in which the scheme of representation takes place, opens a different prospect, and promises the cure for which we are seeking. Let us examine the points in which it varies from pure democracy, and we shall comprehend both the nature of the cure and the efficacy which it must derive from the union.

The two great points of difference between a democracy and a republic are: First, the delegation of the government, in the latter, to a small number of citizens elected by the rest; secondly, the greater number of citizens, and greater sphere of country, over which the latter may be extended.

The effect of the first difference is, on the one hand, to refine and enlarge the public views, by passing them through the medium of a chosen body of citizens, whose wisdom may best discern the true interest of their country, and whose patriotism and love of justice will be least likely to sacrifice it to temporary or partial considerations. Under such a regulation, it may well happen that the public voice, pronounced by the representatives of the people, will be more consonant to the public good than if pronounced by the people themselves, convened for the purpose. On the other hand, the effect may be inverted. Men of factious tempers, of local prejudices, or of sinister designs, may by intrigue, by corruption, or by other means, first obtain the suffrages, and then betray the interests of the people. The question resulting is, whether small or extensive republics are most favorable to the election of proper guardians of the public weal; and it is clearly decided in favor of the latter by two obvious considerations.

In the first place, it is to be remarked that, however small the republic may be, the representatives must be raised to a certain number, in order to guard against the cabals of a few; and that, however large it may be, they must be limited to a certain number, in order to guard against the confusion of a multitude. Hence, the number of representatives in the two cases not being in proportion to that of the constituents, and being proportionally greatest in the small republic, it follows that if the proportion of fit characters be not less in the large than in the small republic, the former will present a greater option, and consequently a greater probability of a fit choice.

In the next place, as each representative will be chosen by a greater number of citizens in the large than in the small republic, it will be more difficult for unworthy candidates to practise with success the vicious arts, by which elections are too often carried; and the suffrages of the people, being more free, will be more likely to centre in men who possess the most attractive merit and the most diffusive and established characters.

It must be confessed that in this as in most other cases, there is a mean, on both sides of which inconveniences will be found to lie. By enlarging too much the number of electors, you render the representative too little acquainted with all their local circumstances and lesser interests; as by reducing it too much, you render him unduly attached to these, and too little fit to comprehend and pursue great and national objects. The federal Constitution forms a happy combination in this respect; the great and aggregate interests being referred to the national, the local and particular to the State, legislatures.

The other point of difference is, the greater number of citizens and extent of territory which may be brought within the compass of republican than of democratic government; and it is this circumstance principally which renders factious combinations less to be dreaded in the former, than in the latter. The smaller the society, the fewer probably will be the distinct parties and interests composing it; the fewer the distinct parties and interests, the more frequently will a majority be found of the same party; and the smaller the number of individuals composing a majority, and the smaller the compass within which they are placed, the more easily will they concert and execute their plans of oppression. Extend the sphere, and you take in a greater variety of parties and interests; you make it less probable that a majority of the whole will have a common motive to invade the rights of other citizens; or if such a common motive exists, it will be more difficult for all who feel it to discover their own strength, and to act in unison with each other. Besides other impediments, it may be remarked that where there is a consciousness of unjust or dishonorable purposes, communication is always checked by distrust, in proportion to the number whose concurrence is necessary.

Hence it clearly appears that the same advantage which a republic has over a democracy, in controlling the effects of faction, is enjoyed by a large over a small republic — is enjoyed by the Union over the States composing it. Does the advantage consist in the substitution of representatives, whose enlightened views and virtuous sentiments render them superior to local prejudices, and to schemes of injustice? It will not be denied that the representation of the Union will be most likely to possess these requisite endowments. Does it consist in the greater security afforded by a greater variety of parties, against the event of any one party being able to outnumber and oppress the rest? In an equal degree does the increased variety of parties, comprised within the Union, increase this security. Does it, in fine, consist in the greater obstacles opposed to the concert and accomplishment of the secret wishes of an unjust and interested majority? Here, again, the extent of the Union gives it the most palpable advantage.

The influence of factious leaders may kindle a flame within their particular States, but will be unable to spread a general conflagration through the other States. A religious sect may degenerate into a political faction in a part of the confederacy; but the variety of sects dispersed over the entire face of it must secure the national councils against any danger from that source. A rage for paper money, for an abolition of debts, for an equal division of property, or for any other improper and wicked project will be less apt to pervade the whole body of the Union than a particular member of it; in the same proportion as such a malady is more likely to taint a particular county or district than an entire State.

In the extent and proper structure of the Union, therefore, we behold a republican remedy for the diseases most incident to republican government. And according to the degree of pleasure and pride we feel in being republicans, ought to be our zeal in cherishing the spirit and supporting the character of federalists.

THOMAS JEFFERSON (1743-1826)

Jefferson himself composed the epitaph which he wished: "Here was buried Thomas Jefferson, Author of the Declaration of Independence, the Statute of Virginia for Religious Freedom, and Father of the University of Virginia." Jefferson's choice of the three acts by which he wished to be remembered is significant. The three accomplishments represent movements toward liberty, — political, religious, and intellectual, — and they indicate how much Jefferson's career was a quest for liberty.

The outline of that career is too familiar to receive extended treatment here. Born in 1743 of a prominent Virginia family, educated at William and Mary College, law student and practising lawyer for a time, he was almost constantly in the political service of his state and nation from 1769, when he entered the Virginia House of Burgesses, until 1809, when he retired from the Presidency after declining a third term. He served with distinction as a member of the Continental Congress, as governor of Virginia (1779–81), as minister to France (1784–89), Secretary of State under Washington (1789–94), Vice-President (1797–1801), and President (1801–1809). In his later years he retired to his beautiful home, Monticello, and through a telescope watched the building of the University of Virginia. He died on July 4, 1826, the fiftieth anniversary of the adoption of his Declaration.

His works may be consulted in the 10-volume edition by P. L. Ford, 1892–99. Among the many biographies are those by A. J. Nock, 1926; G. Chinard (the best), 1929; J. T. Adams, 1936. C. Bowers has written on *The Young Jefferson*, 1945. On his thought see A. Koch, *The Philosophy of Thomas Jefferson*, 1943, and C. M. Wiltse, *The Jeffersonian Tradition in American Democracy*, 1935. C. Bowers's *Jefferson and Hamilton*, 1925, is biased in Jefferson's favor. There is a useful volume of selections from *Alexander Hamilton and Thomas Jefferson*, ed. by F. C. Prescott, in the *AWS*, 1934. *The Best Letters of Thomas Jefferson* were edited by J. G. de R. Hamilton, 1936.

From his Autobiography

(1821)

[*The Framing of the Declaration*]

It appearing in the course of these debates that the colonies of N. York, New Jersey, Pennsylvania, Delaware, Maryland, and South Carolina were not yet matured for falling from the parent stem, but that they were fast advancing to that state, it was thought most prudent to wait a while for them, and to postpone the final decision to July 1, but that this might occasion as little delay as possible a committee was appointed to prepare a declaration of independence. The commee were J. Adams, Dr. Franklin, Roger Sherman, Robert R. Livingston & myself. Committees were also appointed at the same time to prepare a plan of confederation for the colonies, and to state the terms proper to be proposed for foreign alliance. The committee for drawing the declaration of Independence desired me to do it. It was accordingly done, and being approved by them, I reported it to the house on Friday the 28th of June when it was read and ordered to lie on the table. On Monday, the 1st of July the house resolved itself into a commee of the whole & resumed the consideration of the original motion made by the delegates of Virginia, which being again debated through the day, was carried in the affirmative by the votes of N. Hampshire, Connecticut, Massachusetts, Rhode Island, N. Jersey, Maryland, Virginia, N. Carolina,

& Georgia. S. Carolina and Pennsylvania voted against it. Delaware having but two members present, they were divided. The delegates for New York declared they were for it themselves & were assured their constituents were for it, but that their instructions having been drawn near a twelvemonth before, when reconciliation was still the general object, they were enjoined by them to do nothing which should impede that object. They therefore thought themselves not justifiable in voting on either side, and asked leave to withdraw from the question, which was given them. The commee rose & reported their resolution to the house. Mr. Edward Rutledge of S. Carolina then requested the determination might be put off to the next day, as he believed his colleagues, tho' they disapproved of the resolution, would then join in it for the sake of unanimity. The ultimate question whether the house would agree to the resolution of the committee was accordingly postponed to the next day, when it was again moved and S. Carolina concurred in voting for it. In the meantime a third member had come post from the Delaware counties and turned the vote of that colony in favour of the resolution. Members of a different sentiment attending that morning from Pennsylvania also, their vote was changed, so that the whole 12 colonies who were authorized to vote at all, gave their voices for it; and within a few days, the convention of N. York approved of it and thus supplied the void occasioned by the withdrawing of her delegates from the vote.

Congress proceeded the same day to consider the declaration of Independence which had been reported & lain on the table the Friday preceding, and on Monday referred to a commee of the whole. The pusillanimous idea that we had friends in England worth keeping terms with, still haunted the minds of many. For this reason those passages which conveyed censures on the people of England were struck out, lest they should give them offence. The clause too, reprobating the enslaving the inhabitants of Africa, was struck out in complaisance to South Carolina and Georgia, who had never attempted to restrain the importation of slaves, and who on the contrary still wished to continue it. Our northern brethren also I believe felt a little tender under those censures; for tho' their people have very few slaves themselves yet they had been pretty considerable carriers of them to others. The debates having taken up the greater parts of the 2d 3d & 4th days of July were, in the evening of the last, closed, the declaration was reported by the commee, agreed to by the house and signed by every member present except Mr. Dickinson.

The Declaration of Independence
(1776)

When in the Course of human events, it becomes necessary for one people to dissolve the political bands which have connected them with another, and to assume among the powers of the earth, the separate and equal station to which the Laws of Nature and of Nature's God entitle them, a decent respect to the opinions of mankind requires that they should declare the causes which impel them to the separation.————We hold these truths to be self-evident, that all men are created equal, that they are endowed by their Creator with certain unalienable Rights, that among these are Life, Liberty and the pursuit of Happiness. — That to secure these rights, Governments are instituted among Men, deriving their just powers from the consent of the governed, — That whenever any Form of Government becomes destructive of these ends, it is the Right of the People to alter or to abolish it, and to institute new Government, laying its foundation on such principles and organizing its powers in such form, as to them shall seem most likely to effect their Safety and Happiness. Prudence, indeed, will dictate that Governments long established should not be changed for light and transient causes; and accordingly all experience hath shewn, that mankind are more disposed to suffer, while evils are sufferable, than to right themselves by abolishing the forms to which they are accustomed. But when a long train of abuses and usurpations, pursuing invariably the same Object evinces a design to reduce them under absolute Despotism, it is their right, it is their duty, to throw off such Government, and to provide new Guards for their future security. — Such has been the patient sufferance of these Colonies; and such is now the necessity which constrains them to alter their former Systems of Government. The history of the present King of Great Britain is a history of repeated injuries and usurpations, all having in direct object the establishment of an absolute Tyranny over these States. To prove this, let Facts be submitted to a candid world. —— He has refused his Assent to Laws, the most wholesome and necessary for the public good. —— He has forbidden his Governors to pass Laws of immediate and pressing importance, unless suspended in their operation till his Assent should be obtained; and when so suspended, he has utterly neglected to attend to them. —— He has refused to pass other Laws for the accommodation of large districts of people, unless those people would relinquish the right of Representation in the Legislature, a right inestimable to them and formidable to tyrants only. —— He has called together legislative bodies at places unusual, uncomfortable, and distant from the depository of their public Records, for the sole purpose of fatiguing them into compliance with his measures. —— He has dissolved Representative Houses repeatedly, for opposing with manly firmness his invasions on the rights of the people. —— He has refused for a long time, after such dissolutions, to cause others to be elected; whereby the Legislative powers, incapable of Annihilation, have returned to the People at large for their exercise; the State remaining in the mean time exposed to all the dangers of invasion from without, and convulsions within. —— He has endeavoured to prevent the population of these States; for that purpose obstructing the Laws for Naturalization of Foreigners; refusing to pass others to encourage their migrations hither, and raising the conditions of new Appropriations of Lands. —— He has obstructed the Administration of Justice, by refusing his Assent to Laws for establishing Judiciary powers. —— He has made Judges dependent on his Will alone, for the tenure of their offices, and the amount and payment of their salaries. —— He has erected a multitude of New Offices, and sent hither swarms of Officers to harass our people, and eat out their substance. —— He has kept among us, in times of peace, Standing Armies without the Consent of our legislatures. —— He has affected to render the Military independent of and superior to the Civil power. —— He has combined with others to subject us to a jurisdiction foreign to our constitution, and unacknowledged by our laws; giving his Assent to their Acts of pretended Legislation: — For Quartering large bodies of armed troops among us: — For protecting them, by a mock Trial, from punishment for any Murders which they should commit on the Inhabitants of these States: — For cutting off our Trade with all parts of the world: For imposing Taxes on us without our Consent: — For depriving us in many cases, of the benefits of Trial by Jury: — For transporting us beyond Seas to be tried for pretended offences: — For abolishing the free System of English Laws in a neighbouring Province, establishing therein an Arbitrary government, and enlarging its Boundaries so as to render it at once an example and fit instrument for introducing the same absolute rule into these Colonies: — For taking away our Charters, abolishing our most valuable Laws, and altering fundamentally the Forms of our Governments: — For suspending our own Legislatures, and declaring themselves invested with power to legislate for us in all cases whatsoever. — He has abdicated Government here, by declaring us out of his Protection and waging War against us: — He has plundered our seas, ravaged our Coasts, burnt our towns, and destroyed the lives of our people. — He is at this time transporting large Armies of foreign Mercenaries to compleat the works of death, desolation and tyranny, already begun with circumstances of Cruelty & perfidy scarcely paralleled in the most barbarous ages, and totally unworthy the Head of a civilized nation. — He has constrained our fellow Citizens taken Captive on the high Seas to bear Arms against their Country, to become the executioners of their friends and Brethren, or to fall themselves by their

Hands. — He has excited domestic insurrections amongst us, and has endeavoured to bring on the inhabitants of our frontiers, the merciless Indian Savages, whose known rule of warfare, is an undistinguished destruction of all ages, sexes and conditions. In every stage of these Oppressions We have Petitioned for Redress in the most humble terms: Our repeated Petitions have been answered only by repeated injury. A Prince, whose character is thus marked by every act which may define a Tyrant, is unfit to be the ruler of a free people. Nor have We been wanting in attentions to our British brethren. We have warned them from time to time of attempts by their legislature to extend an unwarrantable jurisdiction over us. We have reminded them of the circumstances of our emigration and settlement here. We have appealed to their native justice and magnanimity, and we have conjured them by the ties of our common kindred to disavow these usurpations, which, would inevitably interrupt our connections and correspondence. They too have been deaf to the voice of justice and of consanguinity. We must, therefore, acquiesce in the necessity, which denounces our Separation, and hold them, as we hold the rest of mankind, Enemies in War, in Peace Friends.

WE, THEREFORE, the Representatives of the UNITED STATES OF AMERICA, in General Congress Assembled, appealing to the Supreme Judge of the world for the rectitude of our intentions, do, in the Name and by Authority of the good People of these Colonies, solemnly publish and declare, That these United Colonies are, and of Right ought to be FREE AND INDEPENDENT STATES; that they are Absolved from all Allegiance to the British Crown, and that all political connection between them and the State of Great Britain, is and ought to be totally dissolved; and that as Free and Independent States, they have full Power to levy War, conclude Peace, contract Alliances, establish Commerce, and to do all other Acts and Things which Independent States may of right do. —— And for the support of this Declaration, with a firm reliance on the protection of divine Providence, we mutually pledge to each other our Lives, our Fortunes and our sacred Honour.

From Notes on Virginia
(1784)

According to G. B. Goode, Jefferson's *Notes on Virginia* was "the most important scientific work yet published in America," "the first comprehensive treatise upon the topography, natural history, and natural resources of one of the states." The student of American literature will however be more concerned with passages, like those below, on social and political matters.

[*No Dictators*]

In December 1776, our circumstances being much distressed, it was proposed in the house of delegates to create a *dictator*, invested with every power legislative, executive, and judiciary, civil and military, of life and of death, over our persons and over our properties; and in June 1781, again under calamity, the same proposition was repeated, and wanted a few votes only of being passed. One who entered into this contest from a pure love of liberty, and a sense of injured rights, who determined to make every sacrifice, and to meet every danger, for the reestablishment of those rights on a firm basis, who did not mean to expend his blood and substance for the wretched purpose of changing this matter for that, but to place the powers of governing him in a plurality of hands of his own choice, so that the corrupt will of no one man might in future oppress him, must stand confounded and dismayed when he is told, that a considerable portion of that plurality had meditated the surrender of them into a single hand, and, in lieu of a limited monarch, to deliver him over to a despotic one! How must he find his efforts and sacrifices abused and baffled, if he may still, by a single vote, be laid prostrate at the feet of one man!

In God's name, from whence have they derived this power? Is it from our ancient laws? None such can be produced. Is it from any principle in our new Constitution expressed or implied? Every lineament of that expressed or implied is in full opposition to it. Its fundamental principle is, that the State shall be governed as a commonwealth.

It provides a republican organization, proscribes under the name of *prerogative* the exercise of all powers undefined by the laws; places on this basis the whole system of our laws; and by consolidating them together, chooses that they shall be left to stand or fall together, never providing for any circumstances, nor admitting that such could arise, wherein either should be suspended; no, not for a moment. Our ancient laws expressly declare, that those who are but delegates themselves shall not delegate to others powers which require judgment and integrity in their exercise. Or was this proposition moved on a supposed right in the movers, of abandoning their posts in a moment of distress? The same laws forbid the abandonment of that post, even on ordinary occasions; and much more a transfer of their powers into other hands and other forms, without consulting the people. They never admit the idea that these, like sheep or cattle, may be given from hand to hand without an appeal to their own will. Was it from the necessity of the case? Necessities which dissolve a government do not convey its authority to an oligarchy or a monarchy. They throw back, into the hands of the people, the powers they had delegated, and leave them as individuals to shift for themselves. A leader may offer, but not impose himself, nor be imposed on them. Much less can their necks be submitted to his sword, their breath be held at his will or caprice. The necessity which should operate these tremendous effects should at least be palpable and irresistible. Yet in both instances, where it was feared, or pretended with us, it was belied by the event. It was belied, too, by the preceding experience of our sister States, several of whom had grappled through greater difficulties without abandoning their forms of government. When the proposition was first made, Massachusetts had found even the government of committees sufficient to carry them through an invasion. But we at the time of that proposition were under no invasion. When the second was made, there had been added to this example those of Rhode Island, New York, New Jersey, and Pennsylvania, in all of which the republican form had been found equal to the task of carrying them through

the severest trials. In this State alone did there exist so little virtue, that fear was to be fixed in the hearts of the people, and to become the motive of their exertions, and the principle of their government? The very thought alone was treason against the people; was treason against mankind in general; as riveting forever the chains which bow down their necks, by giving to their oppressors a proof, which they would have trumpeted through the universe of the imbecility of republican government, in times of pressing danger, to shield them from harm. Those who assume the right of giving away the reins of government in any case, must be sure that the herd, whom they hand on to the rods and hatchet of the dictator, will lay their necks on the block when he shall nod to them. But if our assemblies supposed such a resignation in the people, I hope they mistook their character. I am of opinion, that the government, instead of being braced and invigorated for greater exertions under their difficulties, would have been thrown back upon the bungling machinery of county committees for administration, till a convention could have been called, and its wheels again set into regular motion. What a cruel moment was this for creating such an embarrassment, for putting to the proof the attachment of our countrymen to republican government!

Those who meant well, of the advocates for this measure, (and most of them meant well, for I know them personally, had been their fellow-laborer in the common cause, and had often proved the purity of their principles), had been seduced in their judgment by the example of an ancient republic, whose constitution and circumstances were fundamentally different. They had sought this precedent in the history of Rome, where alone it was to be found, and where at length, too, it had proved fatal. They had taken it from a republic rent by the most bitter factions and tumults, where the government was of a heavy-handed unfeeling aristocracy, over a people ferocious, and rendered desperate by poverty and wretchedness; tumults which could not be allayed under the most trying circumstances, but by the omnipotent hand of a single despot. Their constitution, therefore, allowed a temporary tyrant to be erected, under the name of a dictator; and that temporary tyrant, after a few examples, became perpetual. They misapplied this precedent to a people mild in their dispositions, patient under their trial, united for the public liberty, and affectionate to their leaders. But if from the constitution of the Roman government there resulted to their senate a power of submitting all their rights to the will of one man, does it follow that the assembly of Virginia have the same authority? What clause in our constitution has substituted that of Rome, by way of residuary provision, for all cases not otherwise provided for? Or if they may step *ad libitum* into any other form of government for precedents to rule us by, for what oppression may not a precedent be found in this world of the *bellum omnium in omnia?* Searching for the foundations of this proposition, I can find none which may pretend a color of right or reason, but the defect before developed, that there being no barrier between the legislative, executive, and judiciary departments, the legislature may seize the whole; that having seized it, and possessing a right to fix their own quorum, they may reduce that quorum to one, whom they may call a chairman, speaker, dictator, or by any other name they please. Our situation is indeed perilous, and I hope my countrymen will be sensible of it, and will apply, at a proper season, the proper remedy; which is a convention to fix the constitution, to amend its defects, to bind up the several branches of government by certain laws, which, when they transgress, their acts shall become nullities; to render unnecessary an appeal to the people, or in other words a rebellion, on every infraction of their rights, on the peril that their acquiescence shall be construed into an intention to surrender those rights.

[*Education for Democracy*]

Another object of the revisal is to diffuse knowledge more generally through the mass of the people. This bill proposes to lay off every county into small districts of five or six miles square, called hundreds, and in each of them to establish a school for teaching reading, writing, and arithmetic. The tutor to be supported by the hundred, and every person in it entitled to send their children three years gratis, and as much longer as they please, paying for it. These schools to be under a visitor who is annually to choose the boy of best genius in the school, of those whose parents are too poor to give them further education, and to send him forward to one of the grammar schools, of which twenty are proposed to be erected in different parts of the country, for teaching Greek, Latin, geography, and the higher branches of numerical arithmetic. Of the boys thus sent in any one year, trial is to be made at the grammar schools one or two years, and the best genius of the whole selected, and continued six years, and the residue dismissed. By this means twenty of the best geniuses will be raked from the rubbish annually, and be instructed, at the public expense, so far as the grammar schools go. At the end of six years' instruction, one-half are to be discontinued (from among whom the grammar schools will probably be supplied with future masters); and the other half, who are to be chosen for the superiority of their parts and disposition, are to be sent and continued three years in the study of such sciences as they shall choose, at William and Mary College, the plan of which is proposed to be enlarged, as will be hereafter explained, and extended to all the useful sciences. The ultimate result of the whole scheme of education would be the teaching all the children of the State reading, writing, and common arithmetic; turning out ten annually, of superior genius, well taught in Greek, Latin, geography, and the higher branches of arithmetic; turning out ten others annually, of still superior parts, who, to those branches of learning, shall have added such of the sciences as their genius shall have led them to; the furnishing to the wealthier part of the people convenient schools at which their children may be educated at their own expense. The general objects of this law are to provide an education adapted to the years, to the capacity, and the condition of every one, and directed to their freedom and happiness.

Specific details were not proper for the

law. These must be the business of the visitors entrusted with its execution. The first stage of this education being the schools of the hundreds, wherein the great mass of the people will receive their instruction, the principal foundations of future order will be laid here. Instead, therefore, of putting the Bible and Testament into the hands of the children at an age when their judgments are not sufficiently matured for religious inquiries, their memories may here be stored with the most useful facts from Grecian, Roman, European and American history. The first elements of morality too may be instilled into their minds; such as, when further developed as their judgments advance in strength, may teach them how to work out their own greatest happiness, by showing them that it does not depend on the condition of life in which chance has placed them, but is always the result of a good conscience, good health, occupation, and freedom in all just pursuits. Those whom either the wealth of their parents or the adoption of the State shall destine to higher degrees of learning, will go on to the grammar schools, which constitute the next stage, there to be instructed in the languages. The learning Greek and Latin, I am told, is going into disuse in Europe. I know not what their manners and occupations may call for; but it would be very ill-judged in us to follow their example in this instance. There is a certain period of life, say from eight to fifteen or sixteen years of age, when the mind like the body is not yet firm enough for laborious and close operations. If applied to such, it falls an early victim to premature exertion; exhibiting, indeed, at first, in these young and tender subjects, the flattering appearance of their being men while they are yet children, but ending in reducing them to be children when they should be men. The memory is then most susceptible and tenacious of impressions; and the learning of languages being chiefly a work of memory, it seems precisely fitted to the powers of this period, which is long enough, too, for acquiring the most useful languages, ancient and modern. I do not pretend that language is science. It is only an instrument for the attainment of science. But that time is not lost which is employed in providing tools for future operation; more especially as in this case the books put into the hands of the youth for this purpose may be such as will at the same time impress their minds with useful facts and good principles. If this period be suffered to pass in idleness, the mind becomes lethargic and impotent, as would the body it inhabits if unexercised during the same time. The sympathy between body and mind during their rise, progress and decline, is too strict and obvious to endanger our being misled while we reason from the one to the other. As soon as they are of sufficient age, it is supposed they will be sent on from the grammar schools to the university, which constitutes our third and last stage, there to study those sciences which may be adapted to their views.

By that part of our plan which prescribes the selection of the youths of genius from among the classes of the poor, we hope to avail the State of those talents which nature has sown as liberally among the poor as the rich, but which perish without use, if not sought for and cultivated. But of all the views of this law none is more important, none more legitimate, than that of rendering the people the safe, as they are the ultimate, guardians of their own liberty. For this purpose the reading in the first stage, where *they* will receive their whole education, is proposed, as has been said, to be chiefly historical. History, by apprising them of the past, will enable them to judge of the future; it will avail them of the experience of other times and other nations; it will qualify them as judges of the actions and designs of men; it will enable them to know ambition under every disguise it may assume; and knowing it, to defeat its views. In every government on earth is some trace of human weakness, some germ of corruption and degeneracy, which cunning will discover, and wickedness insensibly open, cultivate, and improve. Every government degenerates when trusted to the rulers of the people alone. The people themselves, therefore, are its only safe depositories. And to render even them safe, their minds must be improved to a certain degree. This indeed is not all that is necessary, though it be essentially necessary. An amendment of our constitution must here come in aid of the public education. The influence over government must be shared among all the people. If every individual which composes their mass participates of the ultimate authority, the government will be safe; because the corrupting the whole mass will exceed any private resources of wealth; and public ones cannot be provided but by levies on the people. In this case every man would have to pay his own price. The government of Great Britain has been corrupted, because but one man in ten has a right to vote for members of parliament. The sellers of the government, therefore, get nine-tenths of their price clear. It has been thought that corruption is restrained by confining the right of suffrage to a few of the wealthier of the people; but it would be more effectually restrained by an extension of that right to such members as would bid defiance to the means of corruption.

Lastly, it is proposed, by a bill in this revisal, to begin a public library and gallery, by laying out a certain sum annually in books, paintings, and statues.

[Religious Freedom]

By our own act of assembly of 1705, c. 30, if a person brought up in the Christian religion denies the being of a God, or the Trinity, or asserts there are more gods than one, or denies the Christian religion to be true, or the scriptures to be of divine authority, he is punishable on the first offence by incapacity to hold any office or employment ecclesiastical, civil, or military; on the second by disability to sue, to take any gift or legacy, to be guardian, executor, or administrator, and by three years' imprisonment without bail. A father's right to the custody of his own children being founded in law on his right of guardianship, this being taken away, they may of course be severed from him, and put by the authority of a court into more orthodox hands. This is a summary view of that religious slavery under which a people have been willing to remain, who have lavished their lives and fortunes for the establishment of their civil freedom. The error seems not sufficiently

eradicated, that the operations of the mind, as well as the acts of the body, are subject to the coercion of the laws. But our rulers can have authority over such natural rights, only as we have submitted to them. The rights of conscience we never submitted, we could not submit. We are answerable for them to our God. The legitimate powers of government extend to such acts only as are injurious to others. But it does me no injury for my neighbor to say there are twenty gods, or no god. It neither picks my pocket nor breaks my leg. If it be said, his testimony in a court of justice cannot be relied on, reject it then, and be the stigma on him. Constraint may make him worse by making him a hypocrite, but it will never make him a truer man. It may fix him obstinately in his errors, but will not cure them. Reason and free inquiry are the only effectual agents against error. Give a loose to them, they will support the true religion by bringing every false one to their tribunal, to the test of their investigation. They are the natural enemies of error, and of error only. Had not the Roman government permitted free inquiry, Christianity could never have been introduced. Had not free inquiry been indulged, at the era of the Reformation, the corruptions of Christianity could not have been purged away. If it be restrained now, the present corruptions will be protected, and new ones encouraged. Was the government to prescribe to us our medicine and diet, our bodies would be in such keeping as our souls are now. Thus in France the emetic was once forbidden as a medicine, and the potato as an article of food. Government is just as infallible, too, when it fixes systems in physics. Galileo was sent to the Inquisition for affirming that the earth was a sphere; the government had declared it to be as flat as a trencher, and Galileo was obliged to adjure his error. This error, however, at length prevailed, the earth became a globe, and Descartes declared it was whirled round its axis by a vortex. The government in which he lived was wise enough to see that this was no question of civil jurisdiction, or we should all have been involved by authority in vortices. In fact, the vortices have been exploded, and the

Newtonian principle of gravitation is now more firmly established, on the basis of reason, than it would be were the government to step in, and to make it an article of necessary faith. Reason and experiment have been indulged, and error has fled before them.

It is error alone which needs the support of government. Truth can stand by itself. Subject opinion to coercion: whom will you make your inquisitors? Fallible men; men governed by bad passions, by private as well as public reasons. And why subject it to coercion? To produce uniformity. But is uniformity of opinion desirable? No more than of face and stature. Introduce the bed of Procrustes then, and as there is danger that the large men may beat the small, make us all of a size, by lopping the former and stretching the latter. Difference of opinion is advantageous in religion. The several sects perform the office of a *censor morum* over each other. Is uniformity attainable? Millions of innocent men, women, and children, since the introduction of Christianity, have been burnt, tortured, fined, imprisoned; yet we have not advanced one inch towards uniformity. What has been the effect of coercion? To make one-half the world fools, and the other half hypocrites. To support roguery and error all over the earth. Let us reflect that it is inhabited by a thousand millions of people. That these profess probably a thousand different systems of religion. That ours is but one of that thousand. That if there be but one right, and ours that one, we should wish to see the nine hundred and ninety-nine wandering sects gathered into the fold of truth. But against such a majority we cannot effect this by force. Reason and persuasion are the only practicable instruments. To make way for these, free inquiry must be indulged; and how can we wish others to indulge it while we refuse it ourselves.

But every state, says an inquisitor, has established some religion. No two, say I, have established the same. Is this a proof of the infallibility of establishments? Our sister States of Pennsylvania and New York, however, have long subsisted without any establishment at all. The experiment was new and doubtful when they made it. It has answered beyond conception. They flourish infinitely. Religion is well supported; of various kinds, indeed, but all good enough; all sufficient to preserve peace and order; or if a sect arises, whose tenets would subvert morals, good sense has fair play, and reasons and laughs it out of doors, without suffering the State to be troubled with it. They do not hang more malefactors than we do. They are not more disturbed with religious dissensions. On the contrary, their harmony is unparalleled, and can be ascribed to nothing but their unbounded tolerance, because there is no other circumstance in which they differ from every nation on earth. They have made the happy discovery, that the way to silence religious disputes, is to take no notice of them. Let us too give this experiment fair play, and get rid, while we may, of those tyrannical laws. It is true, we are as yet secured against them by the spirit of the times. I doubt whether the people of this country would suffer an execution for heresy, or a three years' imprisonment for not comprehending the mysteries of the Trinity. But is the spirit of the people an infallible, a permanent reliance? Is it government? Is this the kind of protection we receive in return for the rights we give up? Besides, the spirit of the times may alter, will alter. Our rulers will become corrupt, our people careless. A single zealot may commence persecutor, and better men be his victims. It can never be too often repeated, that the time for fixing every essential right on a legal basis is while our rulers are honest, and ourselves united. From the conclusion of this war we shall be going down hill. It will not then be necessary to resort every moment to the people for support. They will be forgotten, therefore, and their rights disregarded. They will forget themselves, but in the sole faculty of making money, and will never think of uniting to effect a due respect for their rights. The shackles, therefore, which shall not be knocked off at the conclusion of this war will remain on us long, will be made heavier and heavier, till our rights shall revive or expire in a convulsion.

[Negro Slavery]

There must doubtless be an unhappy influence on the manners of our people produced by the existence of slavery among us. The whole commerce between master and slave is a perpetual exercise of the most boisterous passions, the most unremitting despotism on the one part, and degrading submissions on the other. Our children see this, and learn to imitate it; for man is an imitative animal. This quality is the germ of all education in him. From his cradle to his grave he is learning to do what he sees others do. If a parent could find no motive either in his philanthropy or his self-love, for restraining the intemperance of passion towards his slave, it should always be a sufficient one that his child is present. But generally it is not sufficient. The parent storms, the child looks on, catches the lineaments of wrath, puts on the same airs in the circle of smaller slaves, gives a loose to the worst of passions, and thus nursed, educated, and daily exercised in tyranny, cannot but be stamped by it with odious peculiarities. The man must be a prodigy who can retain his manners and morals undepraved by such circumstances. And with what execration should the statesman be loaded, who, permitting one-half the citizens thus to trample on the rights of the other, transforms those into despots, and these into enemies, destroys the morals of the one part, and the *amor patriæ* of the other. For if a slave can have a country in this world, it must be any other in preference to that in which he is born to live and labor for another; in which he must lock up the faculties of his nature, contribute as far as depends on his individual endeavors to the evanishment of the human race, or entail his own miserable condition on the endless generations proceeding from him. With the morals of the people, their industry also is destroyed. For in a warm climate, no man will labor for himself who can make another labor for him. This is so true, that of the proprietors of slaves a very small proportion indeed are ever seen to labor. And can the liberties of a nation be thought secure when we have removed their only firm basis, a conviction in the minds of the people that

these liberties are of the gift of God? That they are not to be violated but with His wrath? Indeed I tremble for my country when I reflect that God is just; that his justice cannot sleep forever; that considering numbers, nature and natural means only, a revolution of the wheel of fortune, an exchange of situation is among possible events; that it may become probable by supernatural interference! The Almighty has no attribute which can take side with us in such a contest. But it is impossible to be temperate and to pursue this subject through the various considerations of policy, of morals, of history natural and civil. We must be contented to hope they will force their way into every one's mind. I think a change already perceptible, since the origin of the present revolution. The spirit of the master is abating, that of the slave rising from the dust, his condition mollifying, the way I hope preparing, under the auspices of heaven, for a total emancipation, and that this is disposed, in the order of events, to be with the consent of the masters, rather than by their extirpation.

First Inaugural Address

(1801)

Friends and Fellow-Citizens:

Called upon to undertake the duties of the first executive office of our country, I avail myself of the presence of that portion of my fellow-citizens which is here assembled, to express my grateful thanks for the favor with which they have been pleased to look towards me, to declare a sincere consciousness that the task is above my talents, and that I approach it with those anxious and awful presentiments which the greatness of the charge and the weakness of my powers so justly inspire. A rising nation spread over a wide and fruitful land, traversing all the seas with the rich productions of their industry, engaged in commerce with nations who feel power and forget right, advancing rapidly to destinies beyond the reach of mortal eye; when I contemplate these transcendent objects, and see the honor, the happiness, and the hopes of this beloved country committed to the issue and the auspices of this day, I shrink from the contemplation, and humble myself before the magnitude of the undertaking.

Utterly, indeed, should I despair, did not the presence of many whom I here see remind me that in the other high authorities provided by our constitution I shall find resources of wisdom, of virtue, and of zeal on which to rely under all difficulties. To you then, gentlemen, who are charged with the sovereign functions of legislation, and to those associated with you, I look with encouragement for that guidance and support which may enable us to steer with safety the vessel in which we are all embarked, amidst the conflicting elements of a troubled sea.

During the contest of opinion through which we have passed, the animation of discussions and of exertions has sometimes worn an aspect which might impose on strangers unused to think freely and to speak and to write what they think. But this being now decided by the voice of the nation, announced according to the rules of the Constitution, all will, of course, arrange themselves under the will of the law, and unite in common efforts for the common good. All too will bear in mind this sacred principle, that though the will of the majority is in all cases to prevail, that will, to be rightful, must be reasonable; that the minority possess their equal rights, which equal laws must protect, and to violate would be oppression. Let us then, fellow-citizens, unite with one heart and one mind; let us restore to social intercourse that harmony and affection without which liberty, and even life itself, are but dreary things. And let us reflect that having banished from our land that religious intolerance under which mankind so long bled and suffered, we have yet gained little if we countenance a political intolerance as despotic, as wicked, and capable of as bitter and bloody persecutions. During the throes and convulsions of the ancient world, during the agonizing spasms of infuriated man, seeking through blood and slaughter his long-lost liberty, it was not wonderful that the agitation of the billows should reach even this distant and peaceful

shore; that this should be more felt and feared by some and less by others; and should divide opinions as to measures of safety. But every difference of opinion is not a difference of principle. We have called by different names brethren of the same principle. We are all Republicans; we are all Federalists. If there be any among us who would wish to dissolve this Union, or to change its republican form, let them stand undisturbed as monuments of the safety with which error of opinion may be tolerated, where reason is left free to combat it. I know, indeed, that some honest men have feared that a republican government cannot be strong; that this Government is not strong enough. But would the honest patriot, in the full tide of successful experiment, abandon a government which has so far kept us free and firm, on the theoretic and visionary fear that this Government, the world's best hope, may by possibility want energy to preserve itself? I trust not. I believe this, on the contrary, the strongest government on earth. I believe it the only one where every man, at the call of the law would fly to the standard of the law; would meet invasions of the public order as his own personal concern. Sometimes it is said that man cannot be trusted with the government of himself. Can he then, be trusted with the government of others? Or have we found angels in the form of kings to govern him? Let history answer this question.

Let us then, pursue with courage and confidence our own federal and republican principles, our attachment to union and representative government. Kindly separated by nature and a wide ocean from the exterminating havoc of one quarter of the globe; too high-minded to endure the degradations of the others; possessing a chosen country, with room enough for our descendants to the hundredth and thousandth generation; entertaining a due sense of our equal right to the use of our own faculties, to the acquisitions of our own industry, to honor and confidence from our fellow-citizens, resulting not from birth, but from our actions and their sense of them; enlightened by a benign religion, professed indeed and practiced in various forms yet all of them inculcating honesty, truth, temperance, gratitude, and the love of man, acknowledging and adoring an overruling Providence, which by all its dispensations proves that it delights in the happiness of man here and his greater happiness hereafter: with all these blessings, what more is necessary to make us a happy and a prosperous people? Still one thing more, fellow-citizens — a wise and frugal government, which shall restrain men from injuring one another, shall leave them otherwise free to regulate their own pursuits of industry and improvement, and shall not take from the mouth of labor the bread it has earned. This is the sum of good government; and this is necessary to close the circle of our felicities.

About to enter, fellow-citizens, on the exercise of duties which comprehend everything dear and valuable to you, it is proper you should understand what I deem the essential principle of this government, and consequently those which ought to shape its administration. I will compress them in the narrowest compass they will bear, stating the general principle but not all its limitations. Equal and exact justice to all men of whatever state or persuasion, religious or political; peace, commerce and honest friendship with all nations, entangling alliances with none; the support of the state governments in all their rights, as the most competent administrations for our domestic concerns, and the surest bulwarks against anti-republican tendencies; the preservation of the general government in its whole constitutional vigor, as the sheet-anchor of our peace at home and safety abroad; a jealous care of the right of election by the people; a mild and safe corrective of abuses which are lopped by the sword of revolution, where peaceable remedies are unprovided; absolute acquiescence in the decisions of the majority, the vital principle of republics, from which is no appeal but to force, the vital principle and immediate parent of despotism; a well-disciplined militia, our best reliance in peace and for the first moments of war, till regulars may relieve them; the supremacy of the civil over the military authority — economy in the public expense, that labor may be lightly burdened; the honest payment of our debts, and sacred preservation of the public faith; encouragement of agriculture, and of commerce as its handmaid; the diffusion of information and arraignment of all abuses at the bar of the public reason; freedom of religion, freedom of the press, and freedom of person, under the protection of the habeas corpus; and trial by juries impartially selected. These principles form the bright constellation which has gone before us, and guided our steps through an age of revolution and reformation. The wisdom of our sages and blood of our heroes have been devoted to their attainment; they should be the creed of our political faith; the text of civic instruction; the touchstone by which to try the services of those we trust; and should we wander from them in moments of error or alarm, let us hasten to retrace our steps and to regain the road which alone leads to peace, liberty, and safety.

I repair then, fellow-citizens, to the post which you have assigned me. With experience enough in subordinate stations to know the difficulties of this, the greatest of all, I have learned to expect that it will rarely fall to the lot of imperfect man to retire from this station with the reputation and the favor which bring him into it. Without pretensions to that high confidence you reposed in our first and greatest revolutionary character, whose preëminent services had entitled him to the first place in his country's love, and had destined for him the fairest page in the volume of faithful history, I ask so much confidence only as may give firmness and effect to the legal administration of your affairs. I shall often go wrong through defect of judgment. When right, I shall often be thought wrong by those whose positions will not command a view of the whole ground. I ask your indulgence for my own errors, which will never be intentional; and your support against the errors of others who may condemn what they would not, if seen in all its parts. The approbation implied by your suffrage is a great consolation to me for the past; and my future solicitude will be to retain the good opinion of those who have bestowed it in advance, to conciliate that of others by doing them all the good in my power, and to be instrumental to the happiness and freedom of all.

Relying then on the patronage of your good-will, I advance with obedience to the work, ready to retire from it whenever you become sensible how much better choice it is in your power to make. And may that Infinite Power which rules the destinies of the universe lead our councils to what is best, and give them a favorable issue for your peace and prosperity.

Letters

[*Scientific Concerns*]

Paris, December 23, 1786.

Dear Sir, —

My last letter to you was dated August 14th. Yours of May 27th and June 28th were not then received, but have been since. I take the liberty of putting under your cover another letter to Mrs. Champis, as also an inquiry after a Dr. Griffiths. A letter to M. le Vieillard, from the person he had consulted about the essence L'Orient, will convey to you the result of my researches into that article. Your spring-block for assisting a vessel in sailing cannot be tried here, because the Seine, being not more than about forty toises wide, and running swiftly, there is no such thing on it as a vessel with sails. I thank you for the volume of the Philadelphia transactions, which came safely to hand, and is, in my opinion, a very valuable volume, and contains many precious papers. The paccan-nut is, as you conjecture, the Illinois nut. The former is the vulgar name south of the Potomac, as also with the Indians and Spaniards, and enters also into the botanical name which is Juglano Paccan. I have many volumes of the "Encyclopédie" for yourself and Dr. Franklin; but, as a winter passage is bad for books, and before the spring the packets will begin to sail from Havre to New York, I shall detain them till then. You must not presume too strongly that your comb-footed bird is known to M. de Buffon. He did not know our panther. I gave him the stripped skin of one I bought in Philadelphia, and it presents him a new species, which will appear in his next vol-

umes. I have convinced him that our deer is not a *chevreuil*, and would you believe that many letters to different acquaintances in Virginia, where this animal is so common, have never enabled me to present him with a large pair of their horns, a blue and red skin stuffed, to show him their colors, at different seasons. He has never seen the horns of what we call the elk. This would decide whether it be an elk or a deer. I am very much pleased with your project on the harmonica, and the prospect of your succeeding in the application of keys to it. It will be the greatest present which has been made to the musical world this century, not excepting the piano-forte. If its tone approaches that given by the finger as nearly only as the harpsichord does that of the harp, it will be very valuable. I have lately examined a foot-bass newly invented here, by the celebrated Krumfoltz. It is precisely a piano-forte, about ten feet long, eighteen inches broad, and nine inches deep. It is of one octave only, from fa to fa. The part where the keys are projects at the side in order to lengthen the levers of the keys. It is placed on the floor, and the harpsichord or other piano-forte is set over it, the foot acting in concert on that, while the fingers play on this. There are three unison chords to every note, of strong brass wire, and the lowest have wire wrapped on them as the lowest in the piano-forte. The chords give a fine, clear, deep tone, almost like the pipe of an organ. Have they connected you with our mint? My friend Monroe promised me he would take care for you in that, or perhaps the establishment of that at New York may have been incompatible with your residence in Philadelphia. A person here has invented a method of coining the French écu of six livres, so as to strike both faces and the edge at one stroke, and makes a coin as beautiful as a medal. No country has ever yet produced such a coin. They are made cheaper, too. As yet, he has only made a few to show the perfection of his manner. I am endeavoring to procure one to send to Congress as a model for their coinage. They will consider whether, on establishing a new mint, it will be worth while to buy his machines, if he will furnish them. A dislocation of my right wrist, which happened to me about a month after the date of my last letter to you, has disabled me from writing three months. I do it now in pain, and only in cases of necessity, or of strong inclination, having as yet no other use of my hand. I put under your cover a letter from my daughter to her friend. She joins me in respect to your good mother, to Mrs. Hopkinson and yourself, to whom I proffer assurances of the esteem with which I am, dear Sir, your sincere friend and servant.

[To Francis Hopkinson]

[Schools of Agriculture]

WASHINGTON, November 14, 1803

SIR:

The greatest evils of populous society have ever appeared to me to spring from the vicious distribution of its members among the occupations called for. I have no doubt that those nations are essentially right which leave this to individual choice, as a better guide to an advantageous distribution than any other which could be devised. But when, by a blind concourse, particular occupations are ruinously overcharged, and others left in want of hands, the national authorities can do much toward restoring the equilibrium. On the revival of letters, learning became the universal favorite. And with reason, because there was not enough of it existing to manage the affairs of a nation to the best advantage, nor to advance its individuals to the happiness of which they were susceptible, by improvements in their minds, their morals, their health, and in those conveniences which contribute to the comfort and embellishment of life. All the efforts of the society, therefore, were directed to the increase of learning, and the inducements of respect, ease, and profit were held up for its encouragement. Even the charities of the nation forgot that misery was their object, and spent themselves in founding schools to transfer to science the hardy sons of the plough. To these incitements were added the powerful fascinations of great cities. These circumstances have long since produced an overcharge in the class of competitors for learned occupation and great distress among the supernumerary candidates; and the more, as their habits of life have disqualified them for re-entering into the laborious class. The evil cannot be suddenly, nor perhaps ever, entirely cured; nor should I presume to say by what means it may be cured. Doubtless there are many engines which the nation might bring to bear on this object. Public opinion and public encouragement are among these. The class principally defective is that of agriculture. It is the first in utility, and ought to be the first in respect. The same artificial means which have been used to produce a competition in learning may be equally successful in restoring agriculture to its primary dignity in the eyes of men. It is a science of the very first order. It counts among its handmaids the most respectable sciences, such as Chemistry, Natural Philosophy, Mechanics, Mathematics generally, Natural History, Botany. In every college and university, a professorship of agriculture, and the class of its students, might be honored as the first. Young men closing their academical education with this, as the crown of all other sciences, fascinated with its solid charms, and at a time when they are to choose an occupation, instead of crowding the other classes, would return to the farms of their fathers, their own, or those of others, and replenish and invigorate a calling now languishing under contempt and oppression. The charitable schools, instead of storming their pupils with a lore which the present state of society does not call for, converted into schools of agriculture, might restore them to that branch qualified to enrich and honor themselves, and to increase the productions of the nation instead of consuming them. A gradual abolition of the useless offices so much accumulated in all governments might close this drain also from the labors of the field and lessen the burdens imposed on them. By these and the better means which will occur to others the surcharge of the learned might in time be drawn off to recruit the laboring class of citizens, the sum of industry be increased, and that of misery diminished.

Among the ancients, the redundance of population was sometimes checked by exposing infants. To the moderns, America has offered a more humane resource. Many who cannot find employment in Europe accordingly come here. Those who can labor do well, for the most part. Of the learned class of emigrants, a small portion find employments analogous to their talents. But many fail and return to complete their course of misery in the scenes where it began. Even here we find too strong a current from the country to the towns, and instances beginning to appear of that species of misery which you are so humanely endeavoring to relieve with you. Although we have in the old countries of Europe the lesson of their experience to warn us, yet I am not satisfied we shall have the firmness and wisdom to profit by it. The general desire of men to live by their heads rather than their hands, and the strong allurements of great cities to those who have any turn for dissipation, threaten to make them here, as in Europe, the sinks of voluntary misery. I perceive, however, that I have suffered my pen to run into a disquisition, when I had taken it up only to thank you for the volume you had been so kind as to send me, and to express my approbation of it. After apologizing, therefore, for having touched on a subject so much more familiar to you, and better understood, I beg leave to assure you of my high consideration and respect.

[To David Williams]

[Natural Aristocracy]

MONTICELLO, October 28, 1813.

***I agree with you that there is a natural aristocracy among men. The grounds of this are virtue and talents. Formerly, bodily powers gave place among the aristoi. But since the invention of gunpowder has armed the weak as well as the strong with missile death, bodily strength, like beauty, good humor, politeness and other accomplishments, has become but an auxiliary ground for distinction. There is also an artificial aristocracy, founded on wealth and birth, without either virtue or talents; for with these it would belong to the first class. The natural aristocracy I consider as the most precious gift of nature, for the instruction, the trusts, and government of society. And indeed, it would have been inconsistent in creation to have formed man for the social state, and not to have provided virtue and

wisdom enough to manage the concerns of the society. May we not even say, that that form of government is the best, which provides the most effectually for a pure selection of these natural aristoi into the offices of government? The artificial aristocracy is a mischievous ingredient in government, and provision should be made to prevent its ascendency. On the question, what is the best provision, you and I differ; but we differ as rational friends, using the free exercise of our own reason, and mutually indulging its errors. You think it best to put the pseudo-aristoi into a separate chamber of legislation, where they may be hindered from doing mischief by their co-ordinate branches, and where, also, they may be a protection to wealth against the Agrarian and plundering enterprises of the majority of the people. I think that to give them power in order to prevent them from doing mischief, is arming them for it, and increasing instead of remedying the evil. For if the co-ordinate branches can arrest their action, so may they that of the co-ordinates. Mischief may be done negatively as well as positively. Of this, a cabal in the Senate of the United States has furnished many proofs. Nor do I believe them necessary to protect the wealthy; because enough of these will find their way into every branch of the legislation, to protect themselves. From fifteen to twenty legislatures of our own, in action for thirty years past, have proved that no fears of an equalization of property are to be apprehended from them. I think the best remedy is exactly that provided by all our constitutions, to leave to the citizens the free election and separation of the aristoi from the pseudo-aristoi, of the wheat from the chaff. In general they will elect the really good and wise. In some instances, wealth may corrupt, and birth blind them; but not in sufficient degree to endanger the society.

It is probable that our difference of opinion may, in some measure, be produced by a difference of character in those among whom we live. From what I have seen of Massachusetts and Connecticut myself, and still more from what I have heard, and the character given of the former by yourself, who know them so much better, there seems to be in those two States a traditionary reverence for certain families, which has rendered the offices of the government nearly hereditary in those families. I presume that from an early period of your history, members of those families happening to possess virtue and talents, have honestly exercised them for the good of the people, and by their services have endeared their names to them. In coupling Connecticut with you, I mean it politically only, not morally. For having made the Bible the common law of their land, they seemed to have modeled their morality on the story of Jacob and Laban. But although this hereditary succession to office with you, may, in some degree, be founded in real family merit, yet in a much higher degree, it has proceeded from your strict alliance of Church and State. These families are canonised in the eyes of the people on common principles, "you tickle me, and I will tickle you." In Virginia we have nothing of this. Our clergy, before the revolution, having been secured against rivalship by fixed salaries, did not give themselves the trouble of acquiring influence over the people. Of wealth, there were great accumulations in particular families, handed down from generation to generation, under the English law of entails. But the only object of ambition for the wealthy was a seat in the King's Council. All their court then was paid to the crown and its creatures; and they Philipised in all collisions between the King and the people. Hence they were unpopular; and that unpopularity continues attached to their names. A Randolph, a Carter, or a Burwell must have great personal superiority over a common competitor to be elected by the people even at this day. At the first session of our legislature after the Declaration of Independence, we passed a law abolishing entails. And this was followed by one abolishing the privilege of primogeniture, and dividing the lands of intestates equally among all their children, or other representatives. These laws, drawn by myself, laid the ax to the foot of pseudo-aristocracy. And had another which I prepared been adopted by the legislature, our work would have been complete. It

was a bill for the more general diffusion of learning. This proposed to divide every county into wards of five or six miles square, like your townships; to establish in each ward a free school for reading, writing and common arithmetic; to provide for the annual selection of the best subjects from these schools, who might receive, at the public expense, a higher degree of education at a district school; and from these district schools to select a certain number of the most promising subjects, to be completed at an University, where all the useful sciences should be taught. Worth and genius would thus have been sought out from every condition of life, and completely prepared by education for defeating the competition of wealth and birth for public trusts. My proposition had, for a further object, to impart to these wards those portions of self-government for which they are best qualified, by confiding to them the care of their poor, their roads, police, elections, the nomination of jurors, administration of justice in small cases, elementary exercises of militia; in short, to have made them little republics, with a warden at the head of each, for all those concerns which, being under their eye, they would better manage than the larger republics of the county or State. A general call of ward meetings by their wardens on the same day through the State, would at any time produce the genuine sense of the people on any required point, and would enable the State to act in mass, as your people have so often done, and with so much effect by their town meetings. The law for religious freedom, which made a part of this system, having put down the aristocracy of the clergy, and restored to the citizen the freedom of the mind, and those of entails and descents nurturing an equality of condition among them, this on education would have raised the mass of the people to the high ground of moral respectability necessary to their own safety, and to orderly government; and would have completed the great object of qualifying them to select the veritable aristoi, for the trusts of government, to the exclusion of the pseudalists; and the same Theognis who has furnished the epigraphs of your two letters, assures us that

"Ουδεμιαν πω, Κυρν', αγαθοι πολιν ωλεσαν ανδρες." [Not any state, Curnus, have good men yet destroyed.]

Although this law has not yet been acted on but in a small and inefficient degree, it is still considered as before the legislature, with other bills of the revised code, not yet taken up, and I have great hope that some patriotic spirit will, at a favorable moment, call it up, and make it the key-stone of the arch of our government.

With respect to aristocracy, we should further consider, that before the establishment of the American States, nothing was known to history but the man of the old world, crowded within limits either small or overcharged, and steeped in the vices which that situation generates. A government adapted to such men would be one thing; but a very different one, that for the man of these States. Here every one may have land to labor for himself, if he chooses; or, preferring the exercise of any other industry, may exact for it such compensation as not only to afford a comfortable subsistence, but wherewith to provide for a cessation from labor in old age. Every one, by his property, or by his satisfactory situation, is interested in the support of law and order. And such men may safely and advantageously reserve to themselves a wholesome control over their public affairs, and a degree of freedom, which, in the hands of the *canaille* of the cities of Europe, would be instantly perverted to the demolition and destruction of everything public and private. The history of the last twenty-five years of France, and of the last forty years in America, nay of its last two hundred years, proves the truth of both parts of this observation.

But even in Europe a change has sensibly taken place in the mind of man. Science had liberated the ideas of those who read and reflect, and the American example had kindled feelings of right in the people. An insurrection has consequently begun, of science, talents, and courage, against rank and birth, which have fallen into contempt. It has failed in its first effort, because the mobs of the cities, the instrument used for its accomplishment, debased by ignorance, poverty and vice, could not be restrained to rational action. But the world will recover from the panic of this first catastrophe. Science is progressive and talents and enterprise on the alert. Resort may be had to the people of the country a more governable power from their principles and subordination; and rank and birth and tinsel-aristocracy will finally shrink into insignificance even there. This, however, we have no right to meddle with. It suffices for us, if the moral and physical condition of our own citizens qualifies them to select the able and good for the direction of their government, with a recurrence of elections at such short periods as will enable them to displace an unfaithful servant, before the mischief he meditates may be irremediable.

I have thus stated my opinion on a point on which we differ, not with a view to controversy, for we are both too old to change opinions which are the result of a long life of inquiry and reflection; but on the suggestions of a former letter of yours, that we ought not to die before we have explained ourselves to each other. We acted in perfect harmony, through a long and perilous contest for our liberty and independence. A constitution has been acquired, which, though neither of us thinks perfect, yet both consider as competent to render our fellow citizens the happiest and the securest on whom the sun has ever shone. If we do not think exactly alike as to its imperfections, it matters little to our country, which, after devoting to it long lives of disinterested labor, we have delivered over to our successors in life, who will be able to take care of it and of themselves.

Of the pamphlet on aristocracy which has been sent to you, or who may be its author, I have heard nothing but through your letter. If the person you suspect, it may be known from the quaint, mystical, and hyperbolical ideas, involved in affected, newfangled and pedantic terms which stamp his writings. Whatever it be, I hope your quiet is not to be affected at this day by the rudeness or intemperance of scribblers; but that you may continue in tranquillity to live and to rejoice in the prosperity of our country, until it shall be your own wish to take your seat among the aristoi who have gone before you. Ever and affectionately yours.

[To John Adams]

[*Portrait of Washington*]

MONTICELLO, January 2, 1814.

* * * I think I knew General Washington intimately and thoroughly; and were I called on to delineate his character, it should be in terms like these.

His mind was great and powerful, without being of the very first order; his penetration strong, though not so acute as that of a Newton, Bacon, or Locke; and as far as he saw, no judgment was ever sounder. It was slow in operation, being little aided by invention or imagination, but sure in conclusion. Hence the common remark of his officers, of the advantage he derived from councils of war, where hearing all suggestions, he selected whatever was best; and certainly no General ever planned his battles more judiciously. But if deranged during the course of the action, if any member of his plan was dislocated by sudden circumstances, he was slow in re-adjustment. The consequence was, that he often failed in the field, and rarely against an enemy in station, as at Boston and York. He was incapable of fear, meeting personal dangers with the calmest unconcern. Perhaps the strongest feature in his character was prudence, never acting until every circumstance, every consideration, was maturely weighed; refraining if he saw a doubt, but, when once decided, going through with his purpose, whatever obstacles opposed. His integrity was most pure, his justice the most inflexible I have ever known, no motives of interest or consanguinity, of friendship or hatred, being able to bias his decision. He was, indeed, in every sense of the words, a wise, a good, and a great man. His temper was naturally high toned; but reflection and resolution had obtained a firm and habitual ascendency over it. If ever, however, it broke its bonds, he was most tremendous in his wrath. In his expenses he was honorable, but exact; liberal in contributions to whatever promised utility; but frowning and unyielding on all visionary projects and all unworthy calls on his charity. His heart was not warm in its affections; but he exactly calculated every man's value, and gave him a solid esteem proportioned to it. His person, you know, was fine, his stature exactly what one would wish, his deportment easy, erect and noble; the best horseman of his age, and the most graceful figure that could be seen on horseback. Although in the circle of his friends, where he might be unreserved with safety, he took a free share in conversation, his colloquial talents were not above mediocrity, possessing neither copiousness of ideas, nor fluency of words. In public, when called on for a sudden opinion, he was unready, short and embarrassed. Yet he wrote readily, rather diffusely, in an easy and correct style. This he had acquired by conversation with the world, for his education was merely reading, writing, and common arithmetic, to which he added surveying at a later day. His time was employed in action chiefly, reading little, and that only in agriculture and English history. His correspondence became necessarily extensive, and, with journalizing his agricultural proceedings, occupied most of his leisure hours within doors. On the whole, his character was, in its mass, perfect, in nothing bad, in few points indifferent; and it may truly be said, that never did nature and fortune combine more perfectly to make a man great, and to place him in the same constellation with whatever worthies have merited from man an everlasting remembrance. For his was the singular destiny and merit, of leading the armies of his country successfully through an arduous war, for the establishment of its independence; of conducting its councils through the birth of a government, new in its forms and principles, until it had settled down into a quiet and orderly train; and of scrupulously obeying the laws through the whole of his career, civil and military, of which the history of the world furnishes no other example. * * *

[To Dr. Walter Jones]

[*The Sage of Monticello as Deist*]

The deism of Jefferson seems to have been largely inspired by Newtonian science. "Placed alongside Newton," he said, "every human character must appear diminutive." A moderate deist, especially in his later years, Jefferson was much concerned to "save" Christianity, that is, to rescue the simple gospel of Jesus, as he conceived, from "the religion of the priests," as the two following letters indicate.

MONTICELLO, June 25, 1819.

Your favor, Sir, of the 14th, has been duly received, and with it the book you were so kind as to forward to me. For this mark of attention, be pleased to accept my thanks. The science of the human mind is curious, but is one on which I have not indulged myself in much speculation. The times in which I have lived, and the scenes in which I have been engaged, have required me to keep the mind too much in action to have leisure to study minutely its laws of action. I am therefore little qualified to give an opinion on the comparative worth of books on that subject, and little disposed to do it on any book. Yours has brought the science within a small compass, and that is a merit of the first order; and especially with one to whom the drudgery of letter-writing often denies the leisure of reading a single page in a week. On looking over the summary of the contents of your book, it does not seem likely to bring into collision any of those sectarian differences which you suppose may exist between us. In that branch of religion which regards the moralities of life, and the duties of a social being, which teaches us to love our neighbors as ourselves, and to do good to all men, I am sure that you and I do not differ. We probably differ on the dogmas of theology, the foundation of all sectarianism, and on which no two sects dream alike; for if they did they would then be of the same. You say you are a Calvinist. I am not. I am of a sect by myself, as far as I know. I am not a Jew, and therefore do not adopt their theology, which supposes the God of infinite justice to punish the sins of the fathers upon their children, unto the third and fourth generation; and the benevolent and sublime Reformer of that religion has told us only that God is good and perfect, but has not defined Him. I am, therefore, of His theology, believing that we have neither words nor ideas adequate to that definition. And if we could all, after this example, leave the subject as undefinable, we should all be of one sect, doers of good, and eschewers of evil.

No doctrines of His lead to schism. It is the speculations of crazy theologists which have made a Babel of a religion the most moral and sublime ever preached to man, and calculated to heal, and not to create differences. These religious animosities I impute to those who call themselves His ministers, and who engraft their casuistries on the stock of His simple precepts. I am sometimes more angry with them than is authorized by the blessed charities which He preaches. To yourself I pray the acceptance of my great respect.

[To Ezra Stiles]

MONTICELLO, June 26, 1822.

DEAR SIR, —

I have received and read with thankfulness and pleasure your denunciation of the abuses of tobacco and wine. Yet, however sound in its principles, I expect it will be but a sermon to the wind. You will find it is as difficult to inculcate these sanative precepts on the sensualities of the present day, as to convince an Athanasian that there is but one God. I wish success to both attempts, and am happy to learn from you that the latter, at least, is making progress, and the more rapidly in proportion as our Platonizing Christians make more stir and noise about it. The doctrines of Jesus are simple, and tend all to the happiness of man.

1. That there is one only God, and He all perfect.

2. That there is a future state of rewards and punishments.

3. That to love God with all thy heart and thy neighbor as thyself is the sum of religion. These are the great points on which He endeavored to reform the religion of the Jews. But compare with these the demoralizing dogmas of Calvin.

1. That there are three Gods.

2. That good works, or the love of our neighbor, are nothing.

3. That faith is everything, and the more incomprehensible the proposition, the more merit in its faith.

4. That reason in religion is of unlawful use.

5. That God, from the beginning, elected certain individuals to be saved, and certain

others to be damned; and that no crimes of the former can damn them; no virtues of the latter save.

Now, which of these is the true and charitable Christian? He who believes and acts on the simple doctrines of Jesus? Or the impious dogmatists, as Athanasius and Calvin? Verily I say these are the false shepherds foretold as to enter not by the door into the sheepfold, but to climb up some other way. They are mere usurpers of the Christian name, teaching a counter-religion made up of the *deliria* of crazy imaginations, as foreign from Christianity as is that of Mahomet. Their blasphemies have driven thinking men into infidelity, who have too hastily rejected the supposed Author himself, with the horrors so falsely imputed to Him. Had the doctrines of Jesus been preached always as pure as they came from his lips, the whole civilized world would now have been Christian. I rejoice that in this blessed country of free inquiry and belief, which has surrendered its creed and conscience to neither kings nor priests, the genuine doctrine of one

only God is reviving, and I trust that there is not a *young man* now living in the United States who will not die an Unitarian.

But much I fear, that when this great truth shall be re-established, its votaries will fall into the fatal error of fabricating formulas of creed and confessions of faith, the engines which so soon destroyed the religion of Jesus, and made of Christendom a mere Aceldama; that they will give up morals for mysteries, and Jesus for Plato. How much wiser are the Quakers, who, agreeing in the fundamental doctrines of the gospel, schismatize about no mysteries, and, keeping within the pale of common sense, suffer no speculative differences of opinion, any more than of feature, to impair the love of their brethren. Be this the wisdom of Unitarians, this the holy mantle which shall cover within its charitable circumference all who believe in one God, and who love their neighbor! I conclude my sermon with sincere assurances of my friendly esteem and respect.

[To Benjamin Waterhouse]

PHILIP FRENEAU (1752–1832)

Freneau, says his latest editor, is "commonly recognised as our first important American poet — as the first man in America to love beauty for beauty's sake." Editor, sea-captain, farmer, school-teacher, Freneau devoted his life to the service of three things: poetry, liberty, and the sea.

Born of Huguenot stock in New York in 1752, he was well prepared for college by a tutor, graduated from the College of New Jersey (now Princeton) in 1771, and for a time decided to combine school teaching and writing. In 1775 he attained sudden fame as a political satirist. The next year he sailed for the West Indies to discover new poetical materials. During the voyage the mate died and Freneau took over the job. At once he discovered a great love for the sea. Most of his remaining years he divided between writing and roving. He was in the West Indies until 1778, and made a voyage to the Azores in 1779. Between 1781 and 1784 he was editor of *The Freeman's Journal;* for the next half-dozen years he was mainly on the sea in the Atlantic coast trade, and then for seven years more was active in journalism. He spent his later life, between long sea voyages, as a farmer in New Jersey. In 1832 he became lost in a blizzard and was frozen to death.

Born in the same year as Chatterton and dying in the same year with Walter Scott, Freneau not only lived through the American and French revolutions, but was coeval with the "Romantic Movement" in literature. In America he bridges the gap between the eighteenth-century writing of the colonial mind and that of the real romantic movement. He was famous in his own day for his satiric verse, evoked by political events of the time and written in Popean couplets. In many quarters he was infamous for the same verse: the barbs of his satire stung. His editorial career only got him the name "that rascal Freneau." Freneau was, as usual, at odds with his readers in that he deprecated his satirical verse; when he brought together his writings he subordinated the political verses. Today we are inclined to agree with Freneau. His best work belongs to the rising romantic movement; the great bulk of his satirical verse is slipshod and feeble beside such poems as "The Wild Honeysuckle" and "The Indian Burying Ground."

Freneau sometimes departed from conventionalized eighteenth-century diction, and illustrated for American poets the possibilities of nature and native subjects. "The Wild Honeysuckle" is the first memorable poem of nature in American literature.

The standard edition is *Poems of Philip Freneau*, edited by F. L. Pattee, 1902–07, in three volumes and including a biography. The most scholarly biography has been written by Lewis Leary, *That Rascal Freneau*, 1941. Indispensable for an understanding of Freneau's religious and philosophical speculations is N. F. Adkins' *Philip Freneau and the Cosmic Enigma*, 1949. See also the finely scholarly "Introduction" in *Poems of Freneau*, edited by H. H. Clark, 1929.

To the Memory of the Brave Americans

UNDER GENERAL GREENE, IN SOUTH CAROLINA, WHO FELL IN THE ACTION OF SEPTEMBER 8, 1781.

(1781)

At Eutaw Springs the valiant died;
  Their limbs with dust are covered o'er —
Weep on, ye springs, your tearful tide;
  How many heroes are no more!

If in this wreck of ruin, they   5
  Can yet be thought to claim a tear,
O smite your gentle breast, and say
  The friends of freedom slumber here!

Thou, who shalt trace this bloody plain,
  If goodness rules thy generous breast,   10
Sigh for the wasted rural reign;
  Sigh for the shepherds, sunk to rest!

Stranger, their humble graves adorn;
  You too may fall, and ask a tear;
'Tis not the beauty of the morn   15
  That proves the evening shall be clear. —

They saw their injured country's woe;
  The flaming town, the wasted field;
Then rushed to meet the insulting foe;
  They took the spear — but left the
    shield.   20

Led by thy conquering genius, Greene,
  The Britons they compelled to fly;
None distant viewed the fatal plain,
  None grieved, in such a cause to die —

But, like the Parthian, famed of old,   25
  Who, flying, still their arrows threw,
These routed Britons, full as bold,
  Retreated, and retreating slew.

Now rest in peace, our patriot band;
  Though far from nature's limits thrown, 30
We trust they find a happier land,
  A brighter sunshine of their own.

The Vanity of Existence

TO THYRSIS

(1781)

In youth, gay scenes attract our eyes,
  And not suspecting their decay
Life's flowery fields before us rise,
  Regardless of its winter day.

But vain pursuits, and joys as vain,   5
    Convince us life is but a dream.
Death is to wake, to rise again
    To that true life you best esteem.

So nightly on some shallow tide,
    Oft have I seen a splendid show;   10
Reflected stars on either side,
    And glittering moons were seen below.

But when the tide had ebbed away,
    The scene fantastic with it fled,
A bank of mud around me lay,   15
    And sea-weed on the river's bed.

On the Emigration to America

AND PEOPLING THE WESTERN COUNTRY

(1784)

To western woods, and lonely plains,
Palemon from the crowd departs,
Where Nature's wildest genius reigns,
To tame the soil, and plant the arts —
What wonders there shall freedom show,   5
What mighty STATES successive grow!

From Europe's proud, despotic shores
Hither the stranger takes his way,
And in our new found world explores
A happier soil, a milder sway,   10
Where no proud despot holds him down,
No slaves insult him with a crown.

What charming scenes attract the eye,
On wild Ohio's savage stream!
There Nature reigns, whose works outvie   15
The boldest pattern art can frame;
There ages past have rolled away,
And forests bloomed but to decay.

From these fair plains, these rural seats,
So long concealed, so lately known,   20
The unsocial Indian far retreats,
To make some other clime his own,
When other streams, less pleasing flow,
And darker forests round him grow.

Great Sire of floods! whose varied wave   25
Through climes and countries takes its way,
To whom creating Nature gave

Ten thousand streams to swell thy sway!
No longer shall *they* useless prove,
Nor idly through the forests rove;   30

Nor longer shall your princely flood
From distant lakes be swelled in vain,
Nor longer through a darksome wood
Advance, unnoticed, to the main,
Far other ends, the heavens decree —   35
And commerce plans new freights for thee.

While virtue warms the generous breast,
There heaven-born freedom shall reside,
Nor shall the voice of war molest,
Nor Europe's all-aspiring pride —   40
There Reason shall new laws devise,
And order from confusion rise.

Forsaking kings and regal state,
With all their pomp and fancied bliss,
The traveller owns, convinced though late,
No realm so free, so blest as this —   46
The east is half to slaves consigned,
Where kings and priests enchain the mind.

O come the time, and haste the day,
When man shall man no longer crush,   50
When Reason shall enforce her sway,
Nor these fair regions raise our blush,
Where still the *African* complains,
And mourns his yet unbroken chains.

Far brighter scenes a future age,   55
The muse predicts, these States will hail,
Whose genius may the world engage,
Whose deeds may over death prevail,
And happier systems bring to view,
Than all the eastern sages knew.   60

The Wild Honeysuckle

(1786)

Fair flower, that dost so comely grow,
Hid in this silent, dull retreat,
Untouched thy honied blossoms blow,
Unseen thy little branches greet;
    No roving foot shall crush thee here,   5
    No busy hand provoke a tear.

By Nature's self in white arrayed,
She bade thee shun the vulgar eye,
And planted here the guardian shade,

And sent soft waters murmuring by; 10
  Thus quietly thy summer goes,
  Thy days declining to repose.

Smit with those charms, that must decay,
I grieve to see your future doom;
They died — nor were those flowers more
    gay, 15
The flowers that did in Eden bloom:
  Unpitying frosts, and Autumn's power
  Shall leave no vestige of this flower.

From morning suns and evening dews
At first thy little being came: 20
If nothing once, you nothing lose,
For when you die you are the same;
  The space between, is but an hour,
  The frail duration of a flower.

Brevity of life

The Indian Burying Ground
(1788)

In spite of all the learned have said,
  I still my old opinion keep;
The posture, that we give the dead,
  Points out the soul's eternal sleep.

Not so the ancients of these lands — 5
  The Indian, when from life released,
Again is seated with his friends,
  And shares again the joyous feast.

His imaged birds, and painted bowl,
  And venison, for a journey dressed, 10
Bespeak the nature of the soul,
  Activity, that knows no rest.

His bow, for action ready bent,
  And arrows, with a head of stone,
Can only mean that life is spent, 15
  'And not the old ideas gone.

Thou, stranger, that shalt come this way,
  No fraud upon the dead commit —
Observe the swelling turf, and say
  They do not lie, but here they sit. 20

Here still a lofty rock remains,
  On which the curious eye may trace
(Now wasted, half, by wearing rains)
  The fancies of a ruder race.

Here still an aged elm aspires, 25
  Beneath whose far-projecting shade
(And which the shepherd still admires)
  The children of the forest played!

There oft a restless Indian queen
  (Pale Shebah, with her braided hair) 30
And many a barbarous form is seen
  To chide the man that lingers there.

By midnight moons, o'er moistening dews;
  In habit for the chase arrayed,
The hunter still the deer pursues, 35
  The hunter and the deer, a shade!

And long shall timorous fancy see
  The painted chief, and pointed spear,
And Reason's self shall bow the knee
  To shadows and delusions here. 40

To an Author
(1788)

Your leaves bound up compact and fair,
In neat array at length prepare,
To pass their hour on learning's stage,
To meet the surly critic's rage;
The statesman's slight, the smatterer's
    sneer — 5
Were these, indeed, your only fear,
You might be tranquil and resigned:
What most should touch your fluttering mind
Is that few critics will be found
To sift your works, and deal the wound. 10

Thus, when one fleeting year is past
On some bye-shelf your book is cast —
Another comes, with something new,
And drives you fairly out of view:

With some to praise, but more to blame, 15
The mind returns to — whence it came;
And some alive, who scarce could read
Will publish satires on the dead.

  Thrice happy Dryden, who could meet
Some rival bard in every street! 20
When all were bent on writing well
It was some credit to excel: —

Thrice happy Dryden, who could find
A Milbourne for his sport designed —
And Pope, who saw the harmless rage　25
Of Dennis bursting o'er his page
Might justly spurn the critic's aim,
Who only helped to swell his fame.

On these bleak climes by Fortune thrown,
Where rigid Reason reigns alone,　30
Where lovely Fancy has no sway,
Nor magic forms about us play —
Nor nature takes her summer hue
Tell me, what has the muse to do? —

An age employed in edging steel　35
Can no poetic raptures feel;
No solitude's attracting power,
No leisure of the noon day hour,
No shaded stream, no quiet grove
Can this fantastic century move,　40

The muse of love in no request —
Go — try your fortune with the rest,
One of the nine you should engage,
To meet the follies of the age: —

On one, we fear, your choice must fall —　45
The least engaging of them all —
Her visage stern — an angry style —
A clouded brow — malicious smile —
A mind on murdered victims placed —
She, only she, can please the taste!　50

Ode

(1791–1793)

This poem was sung at the "Civic Feast" in honor
of Citizen Genêt in Philadelphia, June 1, 1793.

God save the Rights of Man!
Give us a heart to scan
Blessings so dear;
Let them be spread around
Wherever man is found,　5
And with the welcome sound
Ravish his ear.

Let us with France agree,
And bid the world be free,
While tyrants fall!　10

Let the rude savage host
Of their vast numbers boast —
Freedom's almighty trust
Laughs at them all!

Though hosts of slaves conspire　15
To quench fair Gallia's fire,
Still shall they fail:
Though traitors round her rise,
Leagu'd with her enemies,
To war each patriot flies,　20
And will prevail.

No more is valour's flame
Devoted to a name,
Taught to adore —
Soldiers of Liberty　25
Disdain to bow the knee,
But teach Equality
To every shore.

The world at last will join
To aid thy grand design,　30
Dear Liberty!
To Russia's frozen lands
The generous flame expands:
On Afric's burning sands
Shall man be free!　35

In this our western world
Be Freedom's flag unfurl'd
Through all its shores!
May no destructive blast
Our heaven of joy o'ercast,　40
May Freedom's fabric last
While time endures.

If e'er her cause require!
Should tyrants e'er aspire
To aim their stroke,
May no proud despot daunt —　45
Should he his standard plant,
Freedom will never want
Her heart of oak!

On the Anniversary

OF THE STORMING OF THE BASTILLE
AT PARIS, JULY 14TH, 1789

(1793)

The chiefs that bow to Capet's reign,
In mourning, now, their weeds display;
But we, that scorn a monarch's chain,
Combine to celebrate the day
   To Freedom's birth that put the seal,   5
   And laid in dust the proud Bastille.

To Gallia's rich and splendid crown,
This mighty Day gave such a blow
As Time's recording hand shall own
No former age had power to do: 10
   No single gem some Brutus stole,
   But instant ruin seiz'd the whole.

Now Tyrant's rise, once more to bind
In royal chains a nation freed —
Vain hope! for they, to death consign'd,   15
Shall soon, like perjur'd Louis, bleed:
   O'er every king, o'er every queen
   Fate hangs the sword, and guillotine.

"Plung'd in a gulf of deep distress
France turns her back — (so traitors say)   20
Kings, priests, and nobles, round her press,
Resolv'd to seize their destin'd prey:
   Thus Europe swears (in arms combin'd)
   To Poland's doom is France consign'd."

Yet those, who now are thought so low   25
From conquests that were basely gain'd,
Shall rise tremendous from the blow
And free Two Worlds, that still are chain'd,
Restrict the Briton to his isle,
And Freedom plant in every soil.   30

Ye sons of this degenerate clime,
Haste, arm the barque, expand the sail;
Assist to speed that golden time
When Freedom rules, and monarchs fail;   34
   All left to France — new powers may join,
   And help to crush the cause divine.

Ah! while I write, dear France Allied,
My ardent wish I scarce restrain,
To throw these Sybil leaves aside,
And fly to join you on the main: 40
   Unfurl the topsail for the chace
   And help to crush the tyrant race!

The Republican Genius of Europe

(1795)

Emperors and kings! in vain you strive
   Your torments to conceal —
The age is come that shakes your thrones,
Tramples in dust despotic crowns,
   And bids the sceptre fail.   5

In western worlds the flame began:
   From thence to France it flew —
Through Europe, now, it takes its way,
Beams an insufferable day,
   And lays all tyrants low.   10

Genius of France! pursue the chace
   Till Reason's laws restore
Man to be Man, in every clime; —
That Being, active, great, sublime
   Debas'd in dust no more.   15

In dreadful pomp he takes his way
O'er ruin'd crowns, demolish'd thrones —
Pale tyrants shrink before his blaze —
Round him terrific lightnings play —
   With eyes of fire, he looks them through,   20
   Crushes the vile despotic crew,
   And Pride in ruin lays.

On a Honey Bee

DRINKING FROM A GLASS OF WINE
AND DROWNED THEREIN

(1809)

Thou, born to sip the lake or spring,
Or quaff the waters of the stream,
Why hither come on vagrant wing? —
Does Bacchus tempting seem —
Did he, for you, this glass prepare? —   5
Will I admit you to a share?

Did storms harass or foes perplex,
Did wasps or king-birds bring dismay —
Did wars distress, or labours vex,
Or did you miss your way? —   10
A better seat you could not take
Than on the margin of this lake.

Welcome! — I hail you to my glass:
All welcome, here, you find;

Here let the cloud of trouble pass,   15
Here, be all care resigned. —
This fluid never fails to please,
And drown the griefs of men or bees.

What forced you here, we cannot know;
And you will scarcely tell —   20
But cheery we would have you go
And bid a glad farewell:
On lighter wings we bid you fly,
Your dart will now all foes defy.

Yet take not, oh! too deep a drink,   25
And in this ocean die;
Here bigger bees than you might sink,
Even bees full six feet high.
Like Pharaoh, then, you would be said
To perish in a sea of red.   30

Do as you please, your will is mine;
Enjoy it without fear —
And your grave will be this glass of wine,
Your epitaph — a tear —
Go, take your seat in Charon's boat,   35
We'll tell the hive, you died afloat.

To a Caty-Did

(1815)

In a branch of willow hid
Sings the evening Caty-did:
From the lofty locust bough
Feeding on a drop of dew,
In her suit of green arrayed   5
Hear her singing in the shade
    Caty-did, Caty-did, Caty-did!

While upon a leaf you tread,
Or repose your little head,
On your sheet of shadows laid,   10
All the day you nothing said:
Half the night your cheery tongue
Reveled out its little song,
    Nothing else but Caty-did.

From your lodgings on the leaf   15
Did you utter joy or grief? —
Did you only mean to say,
I have had my summer's day,
And am passing, soon, away
To the grave of Caty-did: —   20
    Poor, unhappy Caty-did!

But you would have uttered more
Had you known of nature's power —
From the world when you retreat,
And a leaf's your winding sheet,   25
Long before your spirit fled,
Who can tell but nature said,
Live again, my Caty-did!
    Live and chatter, Caty-did.

Tell me, what did Caty do?   30
Did she mean to trouble you?
Why was Caty not forbid
To trouble little Caty-did?
Wrong indeed at you to fling,
Hurting no one while you sing   35
    Caty-did! Caty-did! Caty-did!

Why continue to complain?
Caty tells me, she again
Will not give you plague or pain: —
Caty says you may be hid   40
Caty will not go to bed
While you sing us Caty-did.
    Caty-did! Caty-did! Caty-did!

But while singing, you forgot
To tell us what did Caty not: 45
Caty did not think of cold,
Flocks retiring to the fold,
Winter, with his wrinkles old,
Winter, that yourself foretold
    When you gave us Caty-did.   50

Stay securely in your nest;
Caty now will do her best,
All she can to make you blest;
But, you want no human aid —
Nature, when she formed you, said,   55
"Independent you are made,
My dear little Caty-did:
Soon yourself must disappear
With the verdure of the year, —"
And to go, we know not where,   60
    With your song of Caty-did.

On the Uniformity and Perfection
of Nature

(1815)

This poem and the following are a direct expression of Freneau's deism.

On one fix'd point all nature moves,
Nor deviates from the track she loves;

Her system, drawn from reason's source,
She scorns to change her wonted course.

Could she descend from that great plan 5
To work unusual things for man,
To suit the insect of an hour —
This would betray a want of power,

Unsettled in its first design
And erring, when it did combine 10
The parts that form the vast machine,
The figures sketch'd on nature's scene.

Perfections of the great first cause
Submit to no contracted laws,
But all-sufficient, all-supreme, 15
Include no trivial views in them.

Who looks through nature with an eye
That would the scheme of heaven descry,
Observes her constant, still the same,
In all her laws, through all her frame. 20

No imperfection can be found
In all that is, above, around, —
All, nature made, in reason's sight
Is order all and all is right.

On the Religion of Nature
(1815)

The power that gives with liberal hand
  The blessings man enjoys, while here,
And scatters through a smiling land
  The abundant products of the year;
    That power of nature, ever bless'd, 5
    Bestow'd religion with the rest.

Born with ourselves, her early sway
  Inclines the tender mind to take
The path of right, fair virtue's way
  Its own felicity to make. 10
    This universally extends
    And leads to no mysterious ends.

Religion, such as nature taught,
  With all divine perfection suits;
Had all mankind this system sought 15
  Sophists would cease their vain disputes,
    And from this source would nations know
    All that can make their heaven below.

This deals not curses on mankind,
  Or dooms them to perpetual grief, 20
If from its aid no joys they find,
  It damns them not for unbelief;
    Upon a more exalted plan
    Creatress nature dealt with man —

Joy to the day, when all agree 25
  On such grand systems to proceed,
From fraud, design, and error free,
  And which to truth and goodness lead:
    Then persecution will retreat
    And man's religion be complete. 30

The Romantic Movement

"Incidents in Whale Fishing," after A. L. Garneray

The great task of the nineteenth-century American was to subdue nature in the interest of man. The American writer was equally absorbed in the significance of that task. Emerson and Whitman preached acceptance and imitation of nature, the good; Melville in *Moby Dick* made the whale the prototype of man's inscrutable and perhaps evil adversary in his struggle to understand and subdue the forces that opposed him.

Emerson welcomed "the movement which effected the elevation of . . . the lowest class in the state," even though he deplored the low growl of the political mob. After the election of Jackson, parties and politicians assiduously courted the common man.

"Stump Speaking," by George Caleb Bingham, 1854

Jefferson City, Missouri, about 1840

Along with canals and railroads, the steamboat and the growth of traffic on the
Mississippi and Missouri rivers gave impetus to the spread of culture in the new
West. Here is one of many similar state capitols, that in Jefferson City, Missouri,
as it looked about 1840.

By mid-century the impulse to push westward was balanced by an opposite tendency toward urbanism. In Whitman's poetry, both the crowded city and the epic
West found expression. This is the New York of Walt Whitman's day.

"Broadway in Winter," by H. Sebron, 1857

THE Romantic Movement

* *

WHAT WAS ROMANTICISM?

THE AGE OF ROMANTICISM arrived when the older generation, the rear guard of the retreating age of reason, was answered by the younger generation. Man, the younger generation affirmed, is something more than a thinking machine in a machine universe. He cannot be satisfied with ideas clear and consistent at the expense of truth; something is always left out. Reason, far from being completely trustworthy, may even lead us to conclusions that violate our sense of reality. Nor is common sense to be relied on for everything; it may be the way to wealth but it is not the way to the more abundant life. The world we live in is not a dead machine, but a living being. God is not outside the world, forgetting and forgotten, but in it and in us, an immanent presence. Man does not come into the world as a blank page, but trailing clouds of glory. A poet is not a deft tailor who dresses nature and human nature to advantage, but a man inspired with beauty or high truth, a prophet of the soul, a creative force; not a wit writing for town and court, but a man speaking to all men from the depth of his heart.

In this way did romanticism in Europe and later in America revolt against the complacency of the age of reason. The break was not, of course, complete. A new age, while throwing out what it does not like in the age before, keeps whatever it can use. So the romantic age took over and developed the deistic appreciation of the marvels of nature,

the idea of progress, the belief in democracy, sentimental sympathy based on the notion of man's natural goodness, the zeal for humanitarian reforms, the insistence upon freedom as opposed to authority of whatever sort.

To know what romanticism reacted against and what it retained from the eighteenth century is still not enough to define it. There have been many definitions, and they are all unsatisfactory.[1] Indeed it was in the very nature of the movement — an anti-intellectual movement — to elude close logical definition. This was true even of its thinkers, who were characteristically intangible, fluid in theory, untroubled by inconsistency (which Emerson called "the hobgoblin of little minds"). A later American philosopher, Josiah Royce, spoke of the German philosopher Schelling as "the prince of the romanticists" and described his attitude as follows:

His kaleidoscopic philosophy, which changed form with each new essay that he published, was like their whole scheme of life and of art. Trust your genius; follow your noble heart; change your doctrine whenever your heart changes, and change your heart often. Such is the practical creed of the romanticists. The world, you see, is after all the world of the inner life. . . . The world is essentially what men of genius make it. Let us be men of genius, and make what we choose.

It would be idle to look to Schelling or any other romantic theorist for an acceptable definition. But we are not entirely helpless.

[1] In a stimulating article, "Towards a Theory of Romanticism," *PMLA*, March, 1951, Morse Peckham reviews and reorganizes theories of the subject.

Even in the passage just quoted we can find a clue. The secret of life seems to lie not in the head but in the "heart." We are to seek reality not through conscious thought but through immediate unconscious perception. Somehow, the kingdom of God is within. Perhaps the true man is the will, his will as an ethical force presiding like a king over his appetites. But this is not the usual romantic view. The "heart" seems, rather, feeling, desire, aspiration, an expansive yearning for fulfillment, the Faustian spirit, the quest of the Blue Flower, and this, if one holds a different philosophy, may appear to be little more than castle-building, wishful thinking, escapism. But let us not hastily prejudge it. Man is complex, motives are mixed. However the romanticists may at times have deluded themselves, we shall not understand them till we have tried to grasp sympathetically what they conceived themselves to be. They conceived themselves to be emancipators of the human spirit, freeing it from the tyranny of everything exterior to itself, whether this was a Calvinistic dogma of depravity, or a cramping rationalism, or a common sense obsession with the pots and pans of practical life. Freed from these, the human spirit might regain the sense of wonder, the bloom of the world; might dwell upon the strange, the mysterious, the miraculous, might hope for a revelation here and now. Hence the romanticists thirsted for the freshness of inspiration, the directness of mysticism.

The inner life and its needs, they held, are not quite the same in all men. If men are born free and equal in worth as human beings, they are also born different, no two of them alike. Each should therefore be true to himself, express his very self, which is uniquely valuable. The romanticists accepted gladly the relativity of their subjectivism. It is perhaps not mere accident that the new words compounded with *self* in the nineteenth century were not often like the old *self-conceit*, *self-esteem*, *self-denial*, which now seemed unpleasant, but rather *self-expression*, *self-*

realization, *self-culture*, *self-help*, *self-reliance*, which seemed attractive.

ROMANTICISM IN THE UNITED STATES

America was ready to receive the new impulse from abroad. Two political revolutions — the American and the French — had occurred; an industrial revolution was on the way. The age of reason seemed to be fading into the dead past. A new nation looked to the future. "The older America of colonial days," as Parrington put it, "had been static, rationalistic, inclined to pessimism, fearful of innovation, tenacious of the customary. . . . The America that succeeded was a shifting, restless world, youthfully optimistic, eager to better itself, bent on finding easier roads to wealth than the plodding path of natural increase. It conceived of human nature as acquisitive, and accounting acquisitiveness a cardinal virtue, it set out to inquire what opportunities awaited it in the unexploited resources of the continent." A land of opportunity invited "economic romance," a romanticism of action. Indeed, Professor Turner's catalogue of frontier traits reads almost like a list of romantic traits: individualism, buoyancy, optimism, energy, etc. Men went to the West for adventure and material acquisition. They lived close to nature and were inclined to value the attributes of the natural man more highly than those of the civilized man.

One of the most pervasive romantic concepts of the mid-century was what has been called the "Myth of the Garden." The rich soil of the Middle West was the garden of the world to which the poor of all nations could come and live in happy, prosperous, democratic independence. The South resisted the myth — as it had to. According to Southern thinkers, the small farm which Horace Greeley wished to give every settler was not large enough to provide for the cultivated and refined maintenance of a family (as a plantation might), and labor in the fields was inimical to the individual's cultural and intellectual development. Hence, as one of them said, "None work in the fields who can help it. . . . [A] free society is in great measure dependent for its food and clothing on slave society." The Southerner, in other words, had a myth of his own — that of the possibility of a Greek democracy on American soil.[1]

The country as we know it today was beginning to take shape. By 1800 New York, not Philadelphia, was the largest town. By 1820 the United States contained about ten millions of people; by 1850, twenty-three millions. After 1845 immigration grew apace, especially from Germany and Ireland. From Virginia and the Carolinas pioneers moved into the valley of the Ohio and Mississippi; from New England, to the Middle West. Chicago, in 1833, had a population of only 350; by 1870 about 300,000. When California was annexed from Mexico in 1848, wide open spaces beckoned all the way to the Pacific, and with the purchase of Alaska in 1867 the domain of the United States became the fourth largest in the world. The Erie Canal linked East and Middle West, and then came the age of railroads, which, by 1860, had a mileage of 30,000. By 1860, also, the value of the country's manufactures equalled that of its agricultural production, even though the cotton crop in that year reached the enormous total of five million bales. Sectional differences were so great that, as one historian has said, the civilizations of North and South were as wide apart as those of Canada and Mexico today. It was the West — the land of the advancing frontier — that seemed the America of the future. As Emerson put it, "Europe stretches to the Alleghanies; America lies beyond."

If frontier optimism was favorable to romanticism, so was the sentiment of nationalism. The age of reason in Europe had been cosmopolitan. Under the leadership of France, European culture possessed a remarkable unity, with a common background in the ancient classics. In the nineteenth

[1] See H. N. Smith, *Virgin Land*, 1950, Book III: "The Garden of the World."

century the nations became aware of their diversity. Each sought to develop organically its own "genius," that which was native and therefore natural to it. A new, romantic dispensation made for both political and cultural patriotism. Now, for this aspect of romanticism America offered an obvious opportunity. We have already noted how the successful War of Independence roused a sentiment of nationalism that sought expression in literature. In the war of 1812 Andrew Jackson hurled a veteran British army back from the redoubts of New Orleans. By 1830 nationalism was militant, eager for a cultural outlet. One thing that America might celebrate was her physical self — her vast space, her scenery, her own birds and trees and flowers. In painting, the human portraiture of the age of reason was succeeded by the landscapes of the Hudson River School. Irving saw, if he did not fully use, the opportunity which America offered her writers:

Her mighty lakes, like oceans of liquid silver; her mountains, with their bright aerial tints; her valleys, teeming with wild fertility; her tremendous cataracts, thundering in their solitudes; her boundless plains, waving with spontaneous verdure; her broad deep rivers, rolling in solemn silence to the ocean; her trackless forests, where vegetation puts forth all its magnificence; her skies, kindling with the magic of summer clouds and glorious sunshine; — no, never need an American look beyond his own country for the sublime and beautiful of natural scenery.

America now had, also, a history of her own, accumulated through two hundred years: history, legend, tradition from the Puritan and Dutch colonial days, the struggles with the Indians, the contest with the French, the Revolution as a civil war and a war of freedom, the war with England in 1812, adventures in the forest and on the seas.

As a means to her own self-realization America also used the cultures of Europe. At this time the European countries, in response to the romantic impulse, were trying to be themselves, not by isolation but by turning to each other for fertilization. If the movement was scarcely cosmopolitan, it was at least international. While these countries looked to each other for usable ideas, examples, inspiration, the United States looked more or less to all of them. With its new national self-consciousness, it sought fructifying influences in contemporary foreign thought and literature, in Wordsworth, Coleridge, Carlyle, in Goethe, German romanticists, German philosophy. And its imagination was attracted by many past cultures whose very remoteness enhanced their romantic charm. England, "our old home," was explored; so were the old Germany and old Spain, the Middle Ages from northern Europe to Italy, ancient Greece seen with fresh eyes, and even the mystic Orient. Sensitive American minds turned wherever they could find the picturesque, the strange, the noble, wherever they could find sheer delight or suggestions for richer living. Not content with literary records and pictures, they went abroad to see with their own eyes or to study at the source. Ticknor, Everett, Bancroft, Motley, Hedge studied at German universities. Irving, Cooper, Emerson, Hawthorne, Longfellow, Lowell made long sojourns in various lands.

Another prominent feature of the American romantic movement was its humanitarianism. As a sentiment, a feeling of sympathy or essential identity with the common man, humanitarianism rose to an impressive climax in Walt Whitman. But characteristically it expressed itself in action, in support of practical reforms. Innumerable reforms were undertaken. In many states imprisonment for debt was abolished; in most states whipping was outlawed; there was better care for the insane; there was education for the blind; there was an energetic campaign for "temperance," for the rights of women, for world peace. But the energies of the humanitarian spirit went primarily into the abolition of Negro slavery. This reform, led by William Lloyd Garrison, whose first number of the *Liberator* appeared in 1831, became a burning issue that few writers could refuse to face. When the abolitionists had closed every

approach to emancipation except civil war, a political issue loomed even larger: the issue of union or disintegration. The desperate conflict of arms that preserved the union was also destined, as it turned out, to mark the end of the romantic movement.

One more feature of our romantic movement must be mentioned, one that sets it off from the European movement. On the Continent especially, romantic self-expression involved a great deal of loose living and a tendency to morbid and licentious literature. But not in America. When the romantic impulse reached our Puritan soil, "land of the pilgrims' pride," it was held in restraint by habits of living and thinking derived from a long discipline. Particularly in New England, where the movement centered, self-indulgence was alien to social traditions and personal values. Even Poe, whose life was irregular enough, managed to celebrate the beauty of woman as if he were sexless. But there is another explanation as well. As a new nation, a middle-class nation, the United States of this period was in its awkward age, self-conscious, sensitive to criticism, and its society was bent on demonstrating its elegance and refinement. Beginning with the sentimental novel of the age of reason, our society cherished an ideal of "female delicacy." According to E. Douglas Branch in *The Sentimental Years, 1836–1860*, we had in the period of romanticism "the most numerous reading public the world had yet known, the Sentimental generation in the United States." Women were a large part of this reading public, and their supposed delicacy of taste was sedulously respected by lesser and even by better authors. Thus Harriet Beecher Stowe, describing a slave trader, wrote: "His conversation was garnished at intervals with sundry profane expressions, which not even the desire to be graphic shall induce us to transcribe for our readers." From the point of view of many novelists today, she evidently missed her chance! Only Whitman, the last of our great romantics, made a complete break with what he called a "parlor and drawing-room literature for ladies" and introduced the frankness of realism. Of the movement as a whole it must be said that it produced perhaps the "cleanest" literature which the world has ever known. To what extent this is praise or dispraise the present reader will decide for himself.

HOW THE MOVEMENT DEVELOPED

The romantic spirit asserted itself first in England and Germany, where it flourished from the late eighteenth century till about 1830, then in France during the 1820's, and in Italy, and Spain, and Russia, coming to something like a close about 1850. In America this wave of idealism ("mania," William Dean Howells preferred to call it) arrived in strength in the 1820's and 30's.

Just at the time of a famous British jibe, Sydney Smith's question "Who reads an American book?" American literature was definitely launched by the publication of three significant works. They were *The Sketch Book*, 1819–20, by Washington Irving; *The Spy*, 1821, by James Fenimore Cooper; and the *Poems*, 1821, of William Cullen Bryant.

Irving, in his *Knickerbocker's History*, had previously romanticized old New York in a humorous way; now his imagination was charmed with England, not the England of the industrial revolution but that of a surviving older civilization and the memories associated with historic buildings and shrines. Later he gave his heart even more to the romantic past of Spain, and wrote romantic biographies of Columbus, Goldsmith, and Washington. Yet in his measured, urbane prose, reminiscent of the eighteenth century essayists, he still belonged to the age of neoclassicism. Cooper, in *The Spy*, wrote an historical novel of the American Revolution, and went on to build a series of novels, the Leatherstocking Tales, of the American forest, the noble savage, and an unforgettable frontiersman — novels fertile in invention, thrilling in action, poetic in their natural setting.

Bryant surpassed the English "graveyard school" in his first volume, and also showed his mastery of nature poetry in the Wordsworthian vein. Irving and Cooper lived in or near New York, and Bryant, though bred in western Massachusetts, resided in New York most of his life. Along with such minor authors as Drake, Halleck, and Willis, they came to be thought of as the "Knickerbocker" writers. Great newspapers were founded (Bryant edited the New York *Evening Post* for half a century), publishing houses were established, and New York was on the way to becoming the literary capital of the nation. From about 1825 to 1840, however, Philadelphia was the literary publishing center, and from 1850 to the end of the century New York had to share literary honors with Boston. The so-called New England Renaissance was a gradual growth between 1820 and 1850, but by the latter date most major American writers except Poe, Melville, and Whitman were credited to Massachusetts.

The most fruitful movement within American romanticism, a circle within a circle, was that known as Transcendentalism. It was perhaps poetic justice that Puritanism, superseded by deism, by Unitarianism, by a general drift to rationalism, should rise again with its old moral and spiritual ardor in the new outlook on life called transcendental. A group of fine minds, responsive to the romantic impulse from Europe, reacted against the climate of opinion left by the age of reason:

Unitarianism, [says Perry Miller] viewed in the larger perspective of modern intellectual history, was a form, the most institutionalized form, in which rationalism, "liberalism," and the cult of social conformity rather than of emotional intensity, were established in America. The protest of these few troubled spirits against what their society had confidently assumed was the crowning triumph of progress and enlightenment is therefore a portent for America, all the more because their protest was the result of no organized indoctrination, but was entirely spontaneous and instinctive. It was as native to the soil as the birch tree. It was an assertion that men in New England, and so in the New World, will refuse to live by sobriety and decorum alone, that there are requirements of the soul which demand satisfaction even though respectability must be defied and shocked. The Transcendentalists did not need to be unified upon any one creed or platform because they were already united in the community of the heart; they had all grown miserable and disgusted within what Emerson called the "corpse-cold Unitarianism of Brattle Street and Harvard College." This was the ethos of their youth; their ultimate condemnation of this ethos, after an agony of soul-searching and fumbling, is nothing less than the first of a succession of revolts by the youth of America against American Philistinism.[1]

A religious movement, Transcendentalism was also a philosophic movement, a social movement, a literary movement. Idealistic, mystical, individualistic, it was a general renovating force. It was "plain living and high thinking" rather than a systematic philosophy or creed. So far as it had a central belief, this belief was that there are "certain fundamental truths not derived from experience, not susceptible of proof, which transcend human life, and are perceived directly and intuitively by the human mind." What does this mean? In the pungent language of Emerson, it means: "God is, not was; He speaketh, not spake." It means: "Nothing can bring you peace but yourself. Nothing can bring you peace but the triumph of principles." It means: "Trust thyself: every heart vibrates to that iron string." It means: "If the single man plant himself indomitably on his instincts, and there abide, the huge world will come round to him." It means: "Give me health and a day, and I will make the pomp of emperors ridiculous."

A very small book published in September, 1836, proved to be the first important literary event of the new movement. It was called *Nature* and its author was later discovered to be Ralph Waldo Emerson. Emerson's place in Transcendentalism is rather hard to define. He was its Paul, but not its Peter; its spokesman and roving missionary yet never its militant captain. At times he seemed to be in the movement, but not of it.

[1] Reprinted by permission of the publishers from Perry Gilbert Eddy Miller, *The Transcendentalists: An Anthology.* Cambridge, Mass.: Harvard University Press, 1950.

He helped found the Transcendental Club, but was skeptical of the numerous schemes for reform, the ideal communities such as Brook Farm which were so popular among others of the group. "The sun and the evening sky do not look calmer than Alcott and his family at Fruitlands," he wrote in his journal. "I will not prejudge them successful. They look well in July. We will see them in December." Perhaps it was Emerson the Yankee whose good sense told him it might be better economics to live in Concord than on Brook Farm, while Emerson the poet sang with some abandon the doctrines of his time. This double aspect of Emerson's thought has long been recognized. His Yankee background included an impressive line of practical and sober New England ancestors. He drew his philosophy from

> "One in a Judean manger,
> And one by Avon's stream,
> One over against the mouths of Nile,
> And one in the Academe."

The four names represent four of the main sources of his thinking: Jesus, the Christian; Shakespeare, the Renaissance man; Plotinus, the Neo-Platonist and Oriental; and Plato himself, the Greek. He might also have mentioned the romantic thought of the times, mostly British, partly German, which came to him through Wordsworth, Coleridge, and Carlyle.

Close to Emerson was Henry Thoreau, "transcendental economist," who lived a year in his hut by Walden Pond at a cost of eight dollars; Bronson Alcott, who sought to learn the truths of life from the lips of children and himself talked endlessly and brilliantly; and Margaret Fuller, intellectual and passionate, who admired Goethe and claimed a fuller recognition for women. Others connected with the movement were Theodore Parker, a practical reformer, George Ripley, leader of the Brook Farm community, the poets Cranch and Very, and Orestes Brownson, who was successively a Unitarian, a Transcendentalist, and Roman Catholic.

Associated with the Transcendentalists at Brook Farm but in general aloof from the movement in its doctrinal aspects was Nathaniel Hawthorne. His solitary and brooding temperament made it hard for him to communicate even with such gifted neighbors as he had in Concord. He lived spiritually alone, whether in his birthplace — Salem of witchcraft memories — or in the Berkshire Hills, or in Liverpool or Concord.

Longfellow and Lowell lived in Cambridge. While the roots of the thought of transcendental Concord were deep in the idealism of the Greeks, the culture of literary Cambridge was grounded in medieval and modern Europe. The mood which often fitted Longfellow best was the *Sehnsucht* of the German poets, a romantic melancholy. Lowell, after a romantic start, became a sort of humanist of the New England Renaissance. Scholar, famous teacher of Dante at Harvard, poet, lecturer, essayist, he brought a wide and rich background to the task of criticism, was our best informed, and in many ways best, critic.

Holmes lived in Boston. His play of wit links him with the English and French eighteenth century, not with medieval Cambridge or transcendental Concord, though he too had his romantic side. There were also three historians of distinction: Motley who romanticized the Dutch, Prescott who romanticized the Spanish, and Parkman, ablest of the trio, who recorded memorably the struggle of France and England for America. Parkman combined the German scientific method with a literary approach that owed not a little to Scott and Byron. In Amesbury, not far from Boston, Whittier divided his time between poetry and the politics of humanitarianism. The novelist Melville, a New Englander on his father's side, wrote much of his masterpiece, *Moby-Dick*, on a farm in the Berkshires which was not far from the house to which his friend Hawthorne had moved after he finished *The Scarlet Letter*.

It was a man born in Boston (although his life was spent in the South and in Philadelphia and New York) who became the American Coleridge. Poe had Coleridge's interest in criticism and in the revival of wonder, but not his interest in Transcendental metaphysics. Poe had no like in America. Compare his "Eldorado" with Longfellow's "Excelsior." The poems have the same theme, but Poe's has an eery, exotic atmosphere which is not Concord, nor Cambridge, nor Salem, nor anything but Poe. This startling individuality produced striking verse, short stories written in a highly developed technique, and an important body of critical theory.

While New England was in the midst of its literary renaissance, the South passed from Jefferson's romantic theory of an agrarian democracy to the more curious dream of a "Greek democracy" (the phrase is Parrington's) in which there was to be a paternal rule of slaves. The literary center of the South was Charleston, South Carolina. It was natural that this city, whose cultural relations were less with the North than with England, should show in her literary production the distinguishing marks of the English romantic movement. Round William G. Simms gathered, in the years preceding the war, a coterie of writers whose romantic outlook on life and art was tempered with classical tastes and traditions. How far this romantic school might have gone — whether a writer of original power might have emerged from it — can never be known, for the clamor of war soon ended all hope of artistic achievement, and the prostration of the reconstruction age followed.

In 1855, nineteen years after the appearance of Emerson's *Nature*, Whitman published *Leaves of Grass* — 92 pages, twelve poems, and a sale probably not much in excess of twelve copies. Yet in literary history this little collection is comparable with the small volume published by Wordsworth and Coleridge in 1798. Each dates an epoch in national literary history; both have far-reaching international influences. Whitman's slight volume sums up American romanticism: it is the climax of the spirit which led men to attempt "the great American epic"; it is the summation of romantic natural goodness, the divinity of nature, individualism, freedom, humanitarianism. Whitman was the most expansive of democrats. No poet ever embraced the whole scheme of things with such enthusiasm. But while he sums up and transcends previous romanticism, he also marks the way for the age of realism that is to come. His free verse will reappear in a thousand poems written in revolt against the manner of romantic verse. His concern for common life will reappear in the revolt of the nineties and in the later regional novel and story. *Leaves of Grass* is a literary turning-point. The last great romanticist, Whitman looks backward to his teacher Emerson, and forward to his countless pupils in our own age.

Then came the war.

In 1861, says Lewis Mumford, "the Civil War cut a white gash through the history of the country. On one side lay the Golden Day, the period of an Elizabethan daring on the sea, of a well-balanced adjustment of farm and factory in the East, of a thriving regional culture operating through the lecture-lyceum and the provincial college. . . . When the curtain rose on this post-bellum scene, this old America was for all practical purposes demolished." The war crushed the South, dimmed the brightness of New England's renaissance, and pointed to the West as the land of material opportunity. Romanticism lived on stubbornly; it is not dead today. But the decade after Appomattox brought stirrings of change. By 1870 American thought had taken on a new temper. Out of the wreckage of the war, out of declining romantic faith and the bursting bubble of romantic economics, arose realism.

WASHINGTON IRVING (1783-1859)

America's first literary ambassador to Europe was born in New York City, on April 3, 1783, to a Scotch father and an English mother, and was named for the man who had just driven the British from the city. The boy was presented to General Washington (so the story goes), and Washington patted him on the head and told him to be a good boy. The advice was not too much heeded. He was a lively child. When he felt stuffy in the Presbyterian atmosphere of his home, he joined the Church of England. All his brothers were sent to Columbia College, but Washington was despaired of, and had no schooling after he was 16. He began to study law without much enthusiasm. In society he fared better. By 1804, when he attained his majority, he was a welcome guest in the best social circles, a mediocre law student, and something of a man about town.

In that year he went to Europe for his health, and traveled in France, Italy, and England. He returned to America in 1806, and, to the great surprise of everyone, was admitted to the New York bar. He practised little. During the next two years he and some friends wrote twenty humorous *Salmagundi* papers. Irving tried politics, lost interest quickly, then joined with his brother to write a parody of a pedantic guide-book to New York. Soon left to do the writing alone, Irving found his intention changing (see his own story below), and produced, instead of a parody, a humorous history. While at work on this, he suffered a tragedy in the death of his fiancée. He pulled himself together and finished the book, which was published in 1809 as *A History of New York, by Dietrich Knickerbocker*. Its success was enormous, but Irving was not yet ready to try literature as a profession. He joined his brothers' firm in 1810, and went abroad in 1815 to conduct the firm's business. He was to remain in Europe seventeen years.

The firm failed in 1818, and Irving found a literary career thrust upon him. The immediate result was the publication of *The Sketch Book* in 1819 and 1820. These stories and essays made him famous. He became a social lion in Britain as in New York, and was an intimate friend of Scott and other writers. *Bracebridge Hall* appeared in 1822 and *Tales of a Traveler* two years later. In 1826 he was in Spain as a member of the American Legation, and three years later established himself in a romantic home, the Alhambra, the subject of one of his most delightful books (1832). Other works growing out of his attachment to Spain were *The Life and Voyages of Columbus* and *The Conquest of Granada*. After spending the decade 1832–42 in America and publishing three works concerning the frontier, he was in Spain again for three years as American minister at the Court of Isabella II.

Irving's last works were biographical studies of Goldsmith, Mahomet, and Washington — the *Life of Washington* he considered his greatest book. For thirteen years he lived at Sunnyside, his home on the Hudson, and there he died.

The standard edition of his writings appeared in 21 vols. in 1860–61 (the same in 12 vols., 1881). The standard life is *Washington Irving*, 2 vols., by Stanley Williams, 1935. Stanley Williams also wrote the article in *DAB*. Van Wyck Brooks has described entertainingly the temper and attitudes of *The World of Washington Irving*, 1944. There is a useful volume of selections, *Washington Irving*, in the *AWS*, with an excellent introduction by H. A. Pochmann, 1934.

Rip Van Winkle

(The Sketch-Book, 1819–20)

"All of Irving's literary manipulation of his reading, his wandering life, and his melancholy were concentrated in a passion which made him compose the tale during a single night, pouring into it all he had ever felt concerning man's ceaseless enemy, 'time' . . ." (S. T. Williams, *LHUS*)

By Woden, God of Saxons,
From whenne comes Wensday, that is Wodensday.
Truth is a thing that ever I will keep
Unto thylke day in which I creep into
My sepulchre.   CARTWRIGHT.

Whoever has made a voyage up the Hudson must remember the Kaatskill Mountains. They are a dismembered branch of the great Appalachian family, and are seen away to the west of the river, swelling up to a noble height, and lording it over the surrounding country. Every change of season, every change of weather, indeed every hour of the day, produces some change in the magical hues and shapes of these mountains, and they are regarded by all the good wives, far and near, as perfect barometers. When the weather is fair and settled, they are clothed in blue and purple, and print their bold outlines on the clear evening sky; but sometimes when the rest of the landscape is cloudless they will gather a hood of gray vapors about their summits, which, in the last rays of the setting sun, will glow and light up like a crown of glory.

At the foot of these fairy mountains, the voyager may have described the light smoke curling up from a village, whose shingle-roofs gleam among the trees, just where the blue tints of the upland melt away into the fresh green of the nearer landscape. It is a little village of great antiquity, having been founded by some of the Dutch colonists in the early times of the province, just about the beginning of the government of the good Peter Stuyvesant, (may he rest in peace!) and there were some of the houses of the original settlers standing within a few years, built of small yellow bricks brought from Holland, having latticed windows and gable fronts, surmounted with weathercocks.

In the same village, and in one of these very houses (which, to tell the precise truth, was sadly time-worn and weather-beaten), there lived many years since, while the country was yet a province of Great Britain, a simple, good-natured fellow, of the name of Rip Van Winkle. He was a descendant of the Van Winkles who figured so gallantly in the chivalrous days of Peter Stuyvesant, and accompanied him to the siege of Fort Christina. He inherited, however, but little of the martial character of his ancestors. I have observed that he was a simple, good-natured man; he was, moreover, a kind neighbor, and an obedient henpecked husband. Indeed, to the latter circumstance might be owing that meekness of spirit which gained him such universal popularity; for those men are most apt to be obsequious and conciliating abroad, who are under the discipline of shrews at home. Their tempers, doubtless, are rendered pliant and malleable in the fiery furnace of domestic tribulation; and a curtain lecture is worth all the sermons in the world for teaching the virtues of patience and long-suffering. A termagant wife may, therefore, in some respects be considered a tolerable blessing, and if so, Rip Van Winkle was thrice blessed.

Certain it is, that he was a great favorite among all the good wives of the village, who, as usual with the amiable sex, took his part in all family squabbles; and never failed, whenever they talked those matters over in their evening gossipings, to lay all the blame on Dame Van Winkle. The children of the village, too, would shout with joy whenever he approached. He assisted at their sports, made their playthings, taught them to fly kites and shoot marbles, and told them long stories of ghosts, witches, and Indians. Whenever he went dodging about the village, he was surrounded by a troop of them, hanging on his skirts, clambering on his back, and playing a thousand tricks on him with impunity; and not a dog would bark at him throughout the neighborhood.

The great error in Rip's composition was an insuperable aversion to all kinds of profitable labor. It could not be from the want of assiduity or perseverance; for he would sit on a wet rock, with a rod as long and heavy as a Tartar's lance, and fish all day without a murmur, even though he should not be encouraged by a single nibble. He would carry a fowling-piece on his shoulder for hours together, trudging through woods and swamps, and up hill and down dale, to shoot a few squirrels or wild pigeons. He would never refuse to assist a neighbor, even in the roughest toil, and was a foremost man at all country frolics for husking Indian corn, or building stone-fences; the women of the village, too, used to employ him to run their errands, and to do such little odd jobs as their less obliging husbands would not do for them. In a word, Rip was ready to attend to anybody's business but his own; but as to doing family duty, and keeping his farm in order, he found it impossible.

In fact, he declared it was of no use to work on his farm; it was the most pestilent little piece of ground in the whole country; everything about it went wrong, and would go wrong, in spite of him. His fences were continually falling to pieces; his cow would either go astray or get among the cabbages; weeds were sure to grow quicker in his fields than anywhere else; the rain always made a point of setting in just as he had some outdoor work to do; so that though his patrimonial estate had dwindled away under his management, acre by acre, until there was little more left than a mere patch of Indian corn and potatoes, yet it was the worst-conditioned farm in the neighborhood.

His children, too, were as ragged and wild as if they belonged to nobody. His son Rip, an urchin begotten in his own likeness, promised to inherit the habits, with the old clothes of his father. He was generally seen trooping like a colt at his mother's heels, equipped in a pair of his father's cast-off galligaskins, which he had much ado to hold up with one hand, as a fine lady does her train in bad weather.

Rip Van Winkle, however, was one of those happy mortals, of foolish, well-oiled dispositions, who take the world easy, eat white bread or brown, whichever can be got with least thought or trouble, and would rather starve on a penny than work for a pound. If left to himself, he would have whistled life away in perfect contentment; but his wife kept continually dinning in his ears about his idleness, his carelessness, and the ruin he was bringing on his family. Morning, noon, and night her tongue was incessantly going, and everything he said or did was sure to produce a torrent of household eloquence. Rip had but one way of replying to all lectures of the kind, and that, by frequent use, had grown into a habit. He shrugged his shoulders, shook his head, cast up his eyes, but said nothing. This, however, always provoked a fresh volley from his wife; so that he was fain to draw off his forces, and take to the outside of the house — the only side which, in truth, belongs to a henpecked husband.

Rip's sole domestic adherent was his dog Wolf, who was as much henpecked as his master; for Dame Van Winkle regarded them as companions in idleness, and even looked upon Wolf with an evil eye, as the cause of his master's going so often astray. True it is, in all points of spirit befitting an honorable dog, he was as courageous an animal as ever scoured the woods — but what courage can withstand the ever-during and all-besetting terrors of a woman's tongue? The moment Wolf entered the house his crest fell, his tail drooped to the ground, or curled between his legs, he sneaked about with a gallows air, casting many a sidelong glance at Dame Van Winkle, and at the least flourish of a broomstick or ladle he would fly to the door with yelping precipitation.

Times grew worse and worse with Rip Van Winkle as years of matrimony rolled on; a tart temper never mellows with age, and a sharp tongue is the only edged tool that grows keener with constant use. For a long while he used to console himself, when driven from home, by frequenting a kind of perpetual club of the sages, philosophers, and other idle personages of the village; which held its sessions on a bench before a small inn, designated by a rubicund portrait of His Majesty George the Third. Here they used to sit in the shade through a long lazy summer's day, talking listlessly over village gossip, or telling endless sleepy stories about nothing. But it would have been worth any statesman's money to have heard the profound discussions that sometimes took place, when by chance an old newspaper fell into their hands, from some passing traveller.

How solemnly they would listen to the contents, as drawled out by Derrick Van Bummel, the school-master, a dapper learned little man, who was not to be daunted by the most gigantic word in the dictionary; and how sagely they would deliberate upon public events some months after they had taken place.

The opinions of this junto were completely controlled by Nicholas Vedder, a patriarch of the village, and landlord of the inn, at the door of which he took his seat from morning till night, just moving sufficiently to avoid the sun and keep in the shade of a large tree; so that the neighbors could tell the hour by his movements as accurately as by a sundial. It is true he was rarely heard to speak, but smoked his pipe incessantly. His adherents, however (for every great man has his adherents), perfectly understood him, and knew how to gather his opinions. When anything that was read or related displeased him, he was observed to smoke his pipe vehemently, and to send forth short, frequent and angry puffs; but when pleased, he would inhale the smoke slowly and tranquilly, and emit it in light and placid clouds; and sometimes, taking the pipe from his mouth, and letting the fragrant vapor curl about his nose, would gravely nod his head in token of perfect approbation.

From even this stronghold the unlucky Rip was at length routed by his termagant wife, who would suddenly break in upon the tranquillity of the assemblage and call the members all to naught; nor was that august personage, Nicholas Vedder himself, sacred from the daring tongue of this terrible virago, who charged him outright with encouraging her husband in habits of idleness.

Poor Rip was at last reduced almost to despair; and his only alternative, to escape from the labor of the farm and clamor of his wife, was to take gun in hand and stroll away into the woods. Here he would sometimes seat himself at the foot of a tree, and share the contents of his wallet with Wolf, with whom he sympathized as a fellow-sufferer in persecution. "Poor Wolf," he would say, "thy mistress leads thee a dog's life of it; but never mind, my lad, whilst I live thou shalt never want a friend to stand by thee!"

Wolf would wag his tail, look wistfully in his master's face, and if dogs can feel pity I verily believe he reciprocated the sentiment with all his heart.

In a long ramble of the kind on a fine autumnal day, Rip had unconsciously scrambled to one of the highest parts of the Kaatskill Mountains. He was after his favorite sport of squirrel shooting, and the still solitudes had echoed and reëchoed with the reports of his gun. Panting and fatigued, he threw himself, late in the afternoon, on a green knoll, covered with mountain herbage, that crowned the brow of a precipice. From an opening between the trees he could overlook all the lower country for many a mile of rich woodland. He saw at a distance the lordly Hudson, far, far below him, moving on its silent but majestic course, with the reflection of a purple cloud, or the sail of a lagging bark, here and there sleeping on its glassy bosom, and at last losing itself in the blue highlands.

On the other side he looked down into a deep mountain glen, wild, lonely, and shagged, the bottom filled with fragments from the impending cliffs, and scarcely lighted by the reflected rays of the setting sun. For some time Rip lay musing on this scene; evening was gradually advancing; the mountains began to throw their long blue shadows over the valleys; he saw that it would be dark long before he could reach the village, and he heaved a heavy sigh when he thought of encountering the terrors of Dame Van Winkle.

As he was about to descend, he heard a voice from a distance, hallooing, "Rip Van Winkle! Rip Van Winkle!" He looked round, but could see nothing but a crow winging its solitary flight across the mountain. He thought his fancy must have deceived him, and turned again to descend, when he heard the same cry ring through the still evening air: "Rip Van Winkle! Rip Van Winkle!" — at the same time; Wolf bristled up his back, and giving a low growl, skulked to his master's side, looking fearfully down into the glen. Rip now felt a vague apprehension stealing over him; he looked anxiously in the same direction, and perceived a strange figure slowly toiling up the rocks, and bending under the weight of something he carried on his back. He was surprised to see any human being in this lonely and unfrequented place; but supposing it to be some one of the neighborhood in need of his assistance, he hastened down to yield it.

On nearer approach he was still more surprised at the singularity of the stranger's appearance. He was a short, square-built old fellow, with thick bushy hair, and a grizzled beard. His dress was of the antique Dutch fashion: a cloth jerkin strapped round the waist, several pair of breeches, the outer one of ample volume, decorated with rows of buttons down the sides, and bunches at the knees. He bore on his shoulder a stout keg, that seemed full of liquor, and made signs for Rip to approach and assist him with the load. Though rather shy and distrustful of this new acquaintance, Rip complied with his usual alacrity; and mutually relieving one another, they clambered up a narrow gully, apparently the dry bed of a mountain torrent. As they ascended, Rip every now and then heard long rolling peals like distant thunder, that seemed to issue out of a deep ravine, or rather cleft, between lofty rocks, toward which their rugged path conducted. He paused for a moment, but supposing it to be the muttering of one of those transient thunder-showers which often take place in mountain heights, he proceeded. Passing through the ravine, they came to a hollow, like a small amphitheatre, surrounded by perpendicular precipices, over the brinks of which impending trees shot their branches, so that you only caught glimpses of the azure sky and the bright evening cloud. During the whole time Rip and his companion had labored on in silence; for though the former marvelled greatly what could be the object of carrying a keg of liquor up this wild mountain, yet there was something strange and incomprehensible about the unknown, that inspired awe and checked familiarity.

On entering the amphitheatre, new objects of wonder presented themselves. On a level spot in the centre was a company of odd-looking personages playing at ninepins. They were dressed in a quaint outlandish fashion; some wore short doublets, others jerkins, with long knives in their belts, and most of them had enormous breeches of similar style with that of the guide's. Their visages, too, were peculiar; one had a large beard, broad face, and small piggish eyes, the face of another seemed to consist entirely of nose, and was surmounted by a white sugar-loaf hat, set off with a little red cock's tail. They all had beards, of various shapes and colors. There was one who seemed to be the commander. He was a stout old gentleman, with a weather-beaten countenance; he wore a laced doublet, broad belt and hanger, high-crowned hat and feather, red stockings, and high-heeled shoes, with roses in them. The whole group reminded Rip of the figures in an old Flemish painting in the parlor of Dominie Van Shaick, the village parson, which had been brought over from Holland at the time of the settlement.

What seemed particularly odd to Rip was, that though these folks were evidently amusing themselves, yet they maintained the gravest faces, the most mysterious silence, and were, withal, the most melancholy party of pleasure he had ever witnessed. Nothing interrupted the stillness of the scene but the noise of the balls, which, whenever they were rolled, echoed along the mountains like rumbling peals of thunder.

As Rip and his companion approached them, they suddenly desisted from their play, and stared at him with such fixed, statue-like gaze, and such strange, uncouth, lack-lustre countenances, that his heart turned within him, and his knees smote together. His companion now emptied the contents of the keg into large flagons, and made signs to him to wait upon the company. He obeyed with fear and trembling; they quaffed the liquor in profound silence, and then returned to their game.

By degrees Rip's awe and apprehension subsided. He even ventured, when no eye was fixed upon him, to taste the beverage, which he found had much of the flavor of excellent Hollands. He was naturally a thirsty soul, and was soon tempted to repeat the draught. One taste provoked another; and he reiterated his visits to the flagon so often that at length his senses were overpowered, his eyes swam in his head, his head gradually declined, and he fell into a deep sleep.

On waking, he found himself on the green knoll whence he had first seen the old man of the glen. He rubbed his eyes — it was a bright, sunny morning. The birds were hopping and twittering among the bushes, and the eagle was wheeling aloft, and breasting the pure mountain breeze. "Surely," thought Rip, "I have not slept here all night." He recalled the occurrences before he fell asleep. The strange man with a keg of liquor — the mountain ravine — the wild retreat among the rocks — the woe-begone party at nine-pins — the flagon — "Oh! that flagon! that wicked flagon!" thought Rip — "what excuse shall I make to Dame Van Winkle?"

He looked round for his gun, but in place of the clean, well-oiled fowling-piece, he found an old firelock lying by him, the barrel incrusted with rust, the lock falling off, and the stock worm-eaten. He now suspected that the grave roisters of the mountain had put a trick upon him, and, having dosed him with liquor, had robbed him of his gun. Wolf, too, had disappeared, but he might have strayed away after a squirrel or partridge. He whistled after him, and shouted his name, but all in vain; the echoes repeated his whistle and shout, but no dog was to be seen.

He determined to revisit the scene of the last evening's gambol, and if he met with any of the party, to demand his dog and gun. As he rose to walk, he found himself stiff in the joints, and wanting in his usual activity. "These mountain beds do not agree with me," thought Rip, "and if this frolic should lay me up with a fit of the rheumatism, I shall have a blessed time with Dame Van Winkle." With some difficulty he got down into the glen: he found the gully up which he and his companion had ascended the preceding evening; but to his astonishment a mountain stream was now foaming down it, leaping from rock to rock, and filling the glen with babbling murmurs. He, however, made shift to scramble up its sides, working his toilsome way through thickets of birch, sassafras, and witch-hazel, and sometimes tripped up or entangled by the wild grape-

vines that twisted their coils or tendrils from tree to tree, and spread a kind of network in his path.

At length he reached to where the ravine had opened through the cliffs to the amphitheatre; but no traces of such opening remained. The rocks presented a high, impenetrable wall, over which the torrent came tumbling in a sheet of feathery foam, and fell into a broad, deep basin, black from the shadows of the surrounding forest. Here, then, poor Rip was brought to a stand. He again called and whistled after his dog; he was only answered by the cawing of a flock of idle crows, sporting high in air about a dry tree that overhung a sunny precipice; and who, secure in their elevation, seemed to look down and scoff at the poor man's perplexities. What was to be done? the morning was passing away, and Rip felt famished for want of his breakfast. He grieved to give up his dog and gun; he dreaded to meet his wife; but it would not do to starve among the mountains. He shook his head, shouldered the rusty firelock, and, with a heart full of trouble and anxiety, turned his steps homeward.

As he approached the village he met a number of people, but none whom he knew, which somewhat surprised him, for he had thought himself acquainted with every one in the country round. Their dress, too, was of a different fashion from that to which he was accustomed. They all stared at him with equal marks of surprise, and whenever they cast their eyes upon him, invariably stroked their chins. The constant recurrence of this gesture induced Rip, involuntarily, to do the same, when, to his astonishment, he found his beard had grown a foot long!

He had now entered the skirts of the village. A troop of strange children ran at his heels, hooting after him, and pointing at his gray beard. The dogs, too, not one of which he recognized for an old acquaintance, barked at him as he passed. The very village was altered; it was larger and more populous. There were rows of houses which he had never seen before, and those which had been his familiar haunts had disappeared. Strange names were over the doors — strange faces at the windows, — everything was strange. His mind now misgave him; he began to doubt whether both he and the world around him were not bewitched. Surely this was his native village, which he had left but the day before. There stood the Kaatskill Mountains — there ran the silver Hudson at a distance — there was every hill and dale precisely as it had always been — Rip was sorely perplexed — "That flagon last night," thought he, "has addled my poor head sadly!"

It was with some difficulty that he found the way to his own house, which he approached with silent awe, expecting every moment to hear the shrill voice of Dame Van Winkle. He found the house gone to decay — the roof fallen in, the windows shattered, and the doors off the hinges. A half-starved dog that looked like Wolf was skulking about it. Rip called him by name, but the cur snarled, showed his teeth, and passed on. This was an unkind cut indeed — "My very dog," sighed poor Rip, "has forgotten me!"

He entered the house, which, to tell the truth, Dame Van Winkle had always kept in neat order. It was empty, forlorn, and apparently abandoned. This desolateness overcame all his connubial fears — he called loudly for his wife and children — the lonely chambers rang for a moment with his voice, and then again all was silence.

He now hurried forth, and hastened to his old resort, the village inn — but it, too, was gone. A large, rickety wooden building stood in its place, with great gaping windows, some of them broken and mended with old hats and petticoats, and over the door was painted, "The Union Hotel, by Jonathan Doolittle." Instead of the great tree that used to shelter the quiet little Dutch inn of yore, there now was reared a tall naked pole, with something on the top that looked like a red night-cap, and from it was fluttering a flag, on which was a singular assemblage of stars and stripes — all this was strange and incomprehensible. He recognized on the sign, however, the ruby face of King George, under which he had smoked so many a peaceful pipe; but even this was singularly metamorphosed. The red coat was changed for one of blue and buff, a sword was held in the hand instead of a sceptre, the head was decorated with a cocked hat, and underneath was painted in large characters, GENERAL WASHINGTON.

There was, as usual, a crowd of folk about the door, but none that Rip recollected. The very character of the people seemed changed. There was a busy, bustling, disputatious tone about it, instead of the accustomed phlegm and drowsy tranquillity. He looked in vain for the sage Nicholas Vedder, with his broad face, double chin, and fair long pipe, uttering clouds of tobacco-smoke instead of idle speeches; or Van Bummel, the schoolmaster, doling forth the contents of an ancient newspaper. In place of these, a lean, bilious-looking fellow, with his pockets full of handbills, was haranguing vehemently about rights of citizens — elections — members of congress — liberty — Bunker's Hill — heroes of seventy-six — and other words, which were a perfect Babylonish jargon to the bewildered Van Winkle.

The appearance of Rip, with his long grizzled beard, his rusty fowling-piece, his uncouth dress, and an army of women and children at his heels, soon attracted the attention of the tavern-politicians. They crowded round him, eyeing him from head to foot with great curiosity. The orator bustled up to him, and, drawing him partly aside, inquired "on which side he voted?" Rip stared in vacant stupidity. Another short but busy little fellow pulled him by the arm, and, rising on tiptoe, inquired in his ear, "Whether he was Federal or Democrat?" Rip was equally at a loss to comprehend the question; when a knowing, self-important old gentleman, in a sharp cocked hat, made his way through the crowd, putting them to the right and left with his elbows as he passed, and planting himself before Van Winkle, with one arm akimbo, the other resting on his cane, his keen eyes and sharp hat penetrating, as it were, into his very soul, demanded in an austere tone, "what brought him to the election with a gun on his shoulder, and a mob at his heels, and whether he meant to breed a riot in the village?" — "Alas! gentlemen," cried Rip, somewhat dismayed, "I am a poor quiet man, a native of the place, and a loyal subject of the king, God bless him!"

Here a general shout burst from the by-standers — "A tory! a tory! a spy! a refugee! hustle him! away with him!" It was with great difficulty that the self-important man in the cocked hat restored order; and, having assumed a tenfold austerity of brow, demanded again of the unknown culprit what he came there for, and whom he was seeking? The poor man humbly assured him that he meant no harm, but merely came there in search of some of his neighbors, who used to keep about the tavern.

"Well — who are they? — name them."

Rip bethought himself a moment, and inquired, "Where's Nicholas Vedder?"

There was a silence for a little while, when an old man replied, in a thin, piping voice: "Nicholas Vedder! why, he is dead and gone these eighteen years! There was a wooden tombstone in the churchyard that used to tell all about him, but that is rotten and gone too."

"Where's Brom Dutcher?"

"Oh, he went off to the army in the beginning of the war; some say he was killed at the storming of Stony Point — others say he was drowned in a squall at the foot of Antony's Nose. I don't know — he never came back again."

"Where's Van Bummel, the school-master?"

"He went off to the wars too, was a great militia general, and is now in Congress."

Rip's heart died away at hearing of these sad changes in his home and friends, and finding himself thus alone in the world. Every answer puzzled him too, by treating of such enormous lapses of time, and of matters which he could not understand: war — Congress — Stony Point; he had no courage to ask after any more friends, but cried out in despair, "Does nobody here know Rip Van Winkle?"

"Oh, Rip Van Winkle!" exclaimed two or three, "Oh, to be sure! that's Rip Van Winkle yonder, leaning against the tree."

Rip looked, and beheld a precise counterpart of himself, as he went up the mountain: apparently as lazy, and certainly as ragged. The poor fellow was now completely confounded. He doubted his own identity, and whether he was himself or another man. In the midst of his bewilderment, the man in the cocked hat demanded who he was, and what was his name?

"God knows," exclaimed he, at his wit's end; "I'm not myself — I'm somebody else — that's me yonder — no — that's somebody else got into my shoes — I was myself, last night, but I fell asleep on the mountain and they've changed my gun, and everything's changed, and I'm changed, and I can't tell what's my name, or who I am!"

The bystanders began now to look at each other, nod, wink significantly, and tap their fingers against their foreheads. There was a whisper, also, about securing the gun, and keeping the old fellow from doing mischief, at the very suggestion of which the self-important man in the cocked hat retired with some precipitation. At this critical moment a fresh, comely woman pressed through the throng to get a peep at the gray-bearded man. She had a chubby child in her arms, which, frightened at his looks, began to cry. "Hush, Rip," cried she, "hush, you little fool; the old man won't hurt you." The name of the child, the air of the mother, the tone of her voice, all awakened a train of recollections in his mind. "What is your name, my good woman?" asked he.

"Judith Gardenier."

"And your father's name?"

"Ah, poor man, Rip Van Winkle was his name, but it's twenty years since he went away from home with his gun, and never has been heard of since, — his dog came home without him, but whether he shot himself, or was carried away by the Indians, nobody can tell. I was then but a little girl."

Rip had but one question more to ask; and he put it with a faltering voice:

"Where's your mother?"

"Oh, she too had died but a short time since; she broke a blood-vessel in a fit of passion at a New England peddler."

There was a drop of comfort, at least, in this intelligence. The honest man could contain himself no longer. He caught his daughter and her child in his arms. "I am your father!" cried he — "Young Rip Van Winkle once — old Rip Van Winkle now! Does nobody know poor Rip Van Winkle?"

All stood amazed, until an old woman,

tottering out from among the crowd, put her hand to her brow, and peering under it in his face for a moment, exclaimed, "Sure enough it is Rip Van Winkle — it is himself! Welcome home again, old neighbor — Why, where have you been these twenty long years?"

Rip's story was soon told, for the whole twenty years had been to him but as one night. The neighbors stared when they heard it; some were seen to wink at each other, and put their tongues in their cheeks; and the self-important man in the cocked hat, who, when the alarm was over, had returned to the field, screwed down the corners of his mouth, and shook his head — upon which there was a general shaking of the head throughout the assemblage.

It was determined, however, to take the opinion of old Peter Vanderdonk, who was seen slowly advancing up the road. He was a descendant of the historian of that name, who wrote one of the earliest accounts of the province. Peter was the most ancient inhabitant of the village, and well versed in all the wonderful events and traditions of the neighborhood. He recollected Rip at once and corroborated his story in the most satisfactory manner. He assured the company that it was a fact, handed down from his ancestor the historian, that the Kaatskill Mountains had always been haunted by strange beings. That it was affirmed that the great Hendrick Hudson, the first discoverer of the river and country, kept a kind of vigil there every twenty years, with his crew of the Half-moon; being permitted in this way to revisit the scenes of his enterprise, and keep a guardian eye upon the river and the great city called by his name. That his father had once seen them in their old Dutch dresses playing at ninepins in a hollow of the mountain; and that he himself had heard, one summer afternoon, the sound of their balls like distant peals of thunder.

To make a long story short, the company broke up, and returned to the more important concerns of the election. Rip's daughter took him home to live with her; she had a snug well-furnished house, and a stout cheery farmer for a husband, whom

Rip recollected for one of the urchins that used to climb upon his back. As to Rip's son and heir, who was the ditto of himself, seen leaning against the tree, he was employed to work on the farm, but evinced an hereditary disposition to attend to anything else but his business.

Rip now resumed his old walks and habits; he soon found many of his former cronies, though all rather the worse for the wear and tear of time, and preferred making friends among the rising generation, with whom he soon grew into great favor.

Having nothing to do at home, and being arrived at that happy age when a man can be idle with impunity, he took his place once more on the bench at the inn door, and was reverenced as one of the patriarchs of the village, and a chronicle of the old times "before the war." It was some time before he could get into the regular track of gossip, or could be made to comprehend the strange events that had taken place during his torpor. How that there had been a revolutionary war — that the country had thrown off the yoke of old England — and that, instead of being a subject of his Majesty George the Third, he was now a free citizen of the United States. Rip, in fact, was no politician; the changes of states and empires made but little impression on him; but there was one species of despotism under which he had long groaned, and that was — petticoat government. Happily that was at an end; he had got his neck out of the yoke of matrimony, and could go in and out whenever he pleased, without dreading the tyranny of Dame Van Winkle. Whenever her name was mentioned, however, he shook his head, shrugged his shoulders, and cast up his eyes, which might pass either for an expression of resignation to his fate, or joy at his deliverance.

He used to tell his story to every stranger that arrived at Mr. Doolittle's hotel. He was observed, at first, to vary on some points every time he told it, which was, doubtless, owing to his having so recently awaked. It at last settled down precisely to the tale I have related, and not a man, woman, or child in the neighborhood but knew it by heart. Some always pretended to doubt the reality of it, and insisted that Rip had been out of his head, and that this was one point on which he always remained flighty. The old Dutch inhabitants, however, almost universally gave it full credit. Even to this day they never hear a thunder-storm of a summer afternoon about the Kaatskill, but they say Hendrick Hudson and his crew are at their game of ninepins; and it is a common wish of all henpecked husbands in the neighborhood, when life hangs heavy on their hands, that they might have a quieting draught out of Rip Van Winkle's flagon.

The Legend of Sleepy Hollow

(*The Sketch-Book*, 1819–20)

A pleasing land of drowsy head it was,
Of dreams that wave before the half-shut eye;
And of gay castles in the clouds that pass,
For ever flushing round a summer sky.
CASTLE OF INDOLENCE.

In the bosom of one of those spacious coves which indent the eastern shore of the Hudson, at that broad expansion of the river denominated by the ancient Dutch navigators the Tappan Zee, and where they always prudently shortened sail, and implored the protection of St. Nicholas when they crossed, there lies a small market-town or rural port, which by some is called Greensburgh, but which is more generally and properly known by the name of Tarry Town. This name was given, we are told, in former days, by the good housewives of the adjacent country, from the inveterate propensity of their husbands to linger about the village tavern on market days. Be that as it may, I do not vouch for the fact, but merely advert to it, for the sake of being precise and authentic. Not far from this village, perhaps about two miles, there is a little valley, or rather lap of land, among high hills, which is one of the quietest places in the whole world. A small brook glides through it, with just murmur enough to lull one to repose; and the occasional whistle of a quail, or tapping of a woodpecker, is almost the only sound that ever breaks in upon the uniform tranquillity.

I recollect, that when a stripling, my first exploit in squirrel-shooting was in a grove of tall walnut-trees that shades one side of the valley. I had wandered into it at noon time, when all nature is peculiarly quiet, and was startled by the roar of my own gun, as it broke the Sabbath stillness around, and was prolonged and reverberated by the angry echoes. If ever I should wish for a retreat, whither I might steal from the world and its distractions, and dream quietly away the remnant of a troubled life, I know of none more promising than this little valley.

From the listless repose of the place, and the peculiar character of its inhabitants, who are descendants from the original Dutch settlers, this sequestered glen has long been known by the name of SLEEPY HOLLOW, and its rustic lads are called the Sleepy Hollow Boys throughout all the neighboring country. A drowsy, dreamy influence seems to hang over the land, and to pervade the very atmosphere. Some say that the place was bewitched by a high German doctor, during the early days of the settlement; others, that an old Indian chief, the prophet or wizard of his tribe, held his powwows there before the country was discovered by Master Hendrick Hudson. Certain it is, the place still continues under the sway of some witching power, that holds a spell over the minds of the good people, causing them to walk in a continual reverie. They are given to all kinds of marvellous beliefs; are subject to trances and visions; and frequently see strange sights, and hear music and voices in the air. The whole neighborhood abounds with local tales, haunted spots, and twilight superstitions; stars shoot and meteors glare oftener across the valley than in any other part of the country, and the nightmare, with her whole nine fold, seems to make it the favorite scene of her gambols.

The dominant spirit, however, that haunts this enchanted region, and seems to be commander-in-chief of all the powers of the air, is the apparition of a figure on horseback without a head. It is said by some to be the ghost of a Hessian trooper, whose head had been carried away by a cannon-ball, in some nameless battle during the revolutionary war; and who is ever and anon seen by the country folk, hurrying along in the gloom of night, as if on the wings of the wind. His haunts are not confined to the valley, but extend at times to the adjacent roads, and especially to the vicinity of a church at no great distance. Indeed, certain of the most authentic historians of those parts, who have been careful in collecting and collating the floating facts concerning this spectre, allege that the body of the trooper, having been buried in the church-yard, the ghost rides forth to the scene of battle in nightly quest of his head; and that the rushing speed with which he sometimes passes along the Hollow, like a midnight blast, is owing to his being belated, and in a hurry to get back to the church-yard before daybreak.

Such is the general purport of this legendary superstition, which has furnished materials for many a wild story in that region of shadows; and the spectre is known, at all the country firesides, by the name of the Headless Horseman of Sleepy Hollow.

It is remarkable that the visionary propensity I have mentioned is not confined to the native inhabitants of the valley, but is unconsciously imbibed by every one who resides there for a time. However wide awake they may have been before they entered that sleepy region, they are sure, in a little time, to inhale the witching influence of the air, and begin to grow imaginative — to dream dreams, and see apparitions.

I mention this peaceful spot with all possible laud; for it is in such little retired Dutch valleys, found here and there embosomed in the great State of New-York, that population, manners, and customs, remain fixed; while the great torrent of migration and improvement, which is making such incessant changes in other parts of this restless country, sweeps by them unobserved. They are like those little nooks of still water which border a rapid stream; where we may see the straw and bubble riding quietly at anchor, or slowly revolving in their mimic harbor, undisturbed by the rush of the passing current. Though many years have elapsed since I trod the drowsy shades of Sleepy Hollow, yet I question whether I should not still find the same trees and the same families vegetating in its sheltered bosom.

In this by-place of nature, there abode, in a remote period of American history, that is to say, some thirty years since, a worthy wight of the name of Ichabod Crane; who sojourned, or, as he expressed it, "tarried," in Sleepy Hollow, for the purpose of instructing the children of the vicinity. He was a native of Connecticut; a State which supplies the Union with pioneers for the mind as well as for the forest, and sends forth yearly its legions of frontier woodsmen and country school-masters. The cognomen of Crane was not inapplicable to his person. He was tall, but exceedingly lank, with narrow shoulders, long arms and legs, hands that dangled a mile out of his sleeves, feet that might have served for shovels, and his whole frame most loosely hung together. His head was small, and flat at top, with huge ears, large green glassy eyes, and a long snipe nose, so that it looked like a weather-cock, perched upon his spindle neck, to tell which way the wind blew. To see him striding along the profile of a hill on a windy day, with his clothes bagging and fluttering about him, one might have mistaken him for the genius of famine descending upon the earth, or some scarecrow eloped from a cornfield.

His school-house was a low building of one large room, rudely constructed of logs; the windows partly glazed, and partly patched with leaves of old copy-books. It was most ingeniously secured at vacant hours, by a withe twisted in the handle of the door, and stakes set against the window shutters; so that, though a thief might get in with perfect ease, he would find some embarrassment in getting out; an idea most probably borrowed by the architect, Yost Van Houten, from the mystery of an eel-pot. The school-house stood in a rather lonely but pleasant situation, just at the foot of a woody hill, with a brook running close by, and a formidable birch tree growing at one end of it. From hence the low murmur of his pupils' voices, conning over their lessons, might be heard in a drowsy summer's day, like the hum of a bee-hive; interrupted now and then by the authoritative voice of the master, in the tone of menace or command; or, peradventure, by the appalling sound of the birch, as he urged some tardy loiterer along the flowery path of knowledge. Truth to say, he was a conscientious man, and ever bore in mind the golden maxim, "Spare the rod and spoil the child." — Ichabod Crane's scholars certainly were not spoiled.

I would not have it imagined, however, that he was one of those cruel potentates of the school, who joy in the smart of their subjects; on the contrary, he administered justice with discrimination rather than severity; taking the burden off the backs of the weak, and laying it on those of the strong. Your mere puny stripling, that winced at the least flourish of the rod, was passed by with indulgence; but the claims of justice were satisfied by inflicting a double portion on some little, tough, wrong-headed, broad-skirted Dutch urchin, who sulked and swelled and grew dogged and sullen beneath the birch. All this he called "doing his duty by their parents;" and he never inflicted a chastisement without following it by the assurance, so consolatory to the smarting urchin, that "he would remember it, and thank him for it the longest day he had to live."

When school hours were over, he was even the companion and playmate of the larger boys; and on holiday afternoons would convoy some of the smaller ones home, who happened to have pretty sisters, or good housewives for mothers, noted for the comforts of the cupboard. Indeed it behooved him to keep on good terms with his pupils. The revenue arising from his school was small, and would have been scarcely sufficient to furnish him with daily bread, for he was a huge feeder, and though lank, had the dilating powers of an anaconda; but to help out his maintenance, he was, according to country custom in those parts, boarded and lodged at the houses of the farmers, whose children he instructed. With these he lived successively a week at a time; thus going the rounds of the neighborhood, with all his worldly effects tied up in a cotton handkerchief.

That all this might not be too onerous on the purses of his rustic patrons, who are apt to consider the costs of schooling a grievous burden, and schoolmasters as mere drones, he had various ways of rendering himself both useful and agreeable. He assisted the farmers occasionally in the lighter labors of their farms; helped to make hay; mended the fences; took the horses to water; drove the cows from pasture; and cut wood for the win-

ter fire. He laid aside, too, all the dominant dignity and absolute sway with which he lorded it in his little empire, the school, and became wonderfully gentle and ingratiating. He found favor in the eyes of the mothers, by petting the children, particularly the youngest; and like the lion bold, which whilom so magnanimously the lamb did hold, he would sit with a child on one knee, and rock a cradle with his foot for whole hours together.

In addition to his other vocations, he was the singing-master of the neighborhood, and picked up many bright shillings by instructing the young folks in psalmody. It was a matter of no little vanity to him, on Sundays, to take his station in front of the church gallery, with a band of chosen singers; where, in his own mind, he completely carried away the palm from the parson. Certain it is, his voice resounded far above all the rest of the congregation; and there are peculiar quavers still to be heard in that church, and which may even be heard half a mile off, quite to the opposite side of the mill-pond, on a still Sunday morning, which are said to be legitimately descended from the nose of Ichabod Crane. Thus, by divers little make-shifts in that ingenious way which is commonly denominated "by hook and by crook," the worthy pedagogue got on tolerably enough, and was thought, by all who understood nothing of the labor of headwork, to have a wonderfully easy life of it.

The schoolmaster is generally a man of some importance in the female circle of a rural neighborhood; being considered a kind of idle gentlemanlike personage, of vastly superior taste and accomplishments to the rough country swains, and, indeed, inferior in learning only to the parson. His appearance, therefore, is apt to occasion some little stir at the tea-table of a farmhouse, and the addition of a supernumerary dish of cakes or sweetmeats, or, peradventure, the parade of a silver tea-pot. Our man of letters, therefore, was peculiarly happy in the smiles of all the country damsels. How he would figure among them in the church-yard, between services on Sundays! gathering grapes for them from the wild vines that overrun the surrounding trees; reciting for their amusement all the epitaphs on the tombstones; or sauntering, with a whole bevy of them, along the banks of the adjacent mill-pond; while the more bashful country bumpkins hung sheepishly back, envying his superior elegance and address.

From his half itinerant life, also, he was a kind of travelling gazette, carrying the whole budget of local gossip from house to house; so that his appearance was always greeted with satisfaction. He was, moreover, esteemed by the women as a man of great erudition, for he had read several books quite through, and was a perfect master of Cotton Mather's history of New England witchcraft, in which, by the way, he most firmly and potently believed.

He was, in fact, an odd mixture of small shrewdness and simple credulity. His appetite for the marvellous, and his powers of digesting it, were equally extraordinary; and both had been increased by his residence in this spellbound region. No tale was too gross or monstrous for his capacious swallow. It was often his delight, after his school was dismissed in the afternoon, to stretch himself on the rich bed of clover, bordering the little brook that whimpered by his school-house, and there con over old Mather's direful tales, until the gathering dusk of the evening made the printed page a mere mist before his eyes. Then, as he wended his way, by swamp and stream and awful woodland, to the farmhouse where he happened to be quartered, every sound of nature, at that witching hour, fluttered his excited imagination; the moan of the whip-poor-will from the hill-side; the boding cry of the tree-toad, that harbinger of storm; the dreary hooting of the screech-owl, or the sudden rustling in the thicket of birds frightened from their roost. The fire-flies, too, which sparkled most vividly in the darkest places, now and then startled him, as one of uncommon brightness would stream across his path; and if, by chance, a huge blockhead of a beetle came winging his blundering flight against him, the poor varlet was ready to give up the ghost, with the idea that he was struck with a witch's token. His only resource on such occasions, either to drown thought, or drive away evil spirits, was to sing psalm tunes; — and the good people of Sleepy Hollow, as they sat by their doors of an evening, were often filled with awe, at hearing his nasal melody, "in linked sweetness long drawn out," floating from the distant hill, or along the dusky road.

Another of his sources of fearful pleasure was, to pass long winter evenings with the old Dutch wives, as they sat spinning by the fire, with a row of apples roasting and spluttering along the hearth, and listen to their marvellous tales of ghosts and goblins, and haunted fields, and haunted brooks, and haunted bridges, and haunted houses, and particularly of the headless horseman, or galloping Hessian of the Hollow, as they sometimes called him. He would delight them equally by his anecdotes of witchcraft, and of the direful omens and portentous sights and sounds in the air, which prevailed in the earlier times of Connecticut; and would frighten them wofully with speculations upon comets and shooting stars; and with the alarming fact that the world did absolutely turn round, and that they were half the time topsy-turvy!

But if there was a pleasure in all this, while snugly cuddling in the chimney corner of a chamber that was all of a ruddy glow from the crackling wood fire, and where, of course, no spectre dared to show his face, it was dearly purchased by the terrors of his subsequent walk homewards. What fearful shapes and shadows beset his path amidst the dim and ghastly glare of a snowy night! — With what wistful look did he eye every trembling ray of light streaming across the waste fields from some distant window! — How often was he appalled by some shrub covered with snow, which, like a sheeted spectre, beset his very path! — How often did he shrink with curdling awe at the sound of his own steps on the frosty crust beneath his feet; and dread to look over his shoulder, lest he should behold some uncouth being tramping close behind him! — and how often was he thrown into complete dismay by some rushing blast, howling among the trees, in the idea that it was the Galloping Hessian on one of his nightly scourings!

All these, however, were mere terrors of the night, phantoms of the mind that walk in darkness; and though he had seen many spectres in his time, and been more than once beset by Satan in divers shapes, in his lonely perambulations, yet daylight put an end to all these evils; and he would have passed a pleasant life of it, in despite of the devil and all his works, if his path had not been crossed by a being that causes more perplexity to mortal man than ghosts, goblins, and the whole race of witches put together, and that was — a woman.

Among the musical disciples who assembled, one evening in each week, to receive his instructions in psalmody, was Katrina Van Tassel, the daughter and only child of a substantial Dutch farmer. She was a blooming lass of fresh eighteen; plump as a partridge; ripe and melting and rosy cheeked as one of her father's peaches, and universally famed, not merely for her beauty, but her vast expectations. She was withal a little of a coquette, as might be perceived even in her dress, which was a mixture of ancient and modern fashions, as most suited to set off her charms. She wore the ornaments of pure yellow gold, which her great-great-grandmother had brought over from Saardam; the tempting stomacher of the olden time; and withal a provokingly short petticoat, to display the prettiest foot and ankle in the country round.

Ichabod Crane had a soft and foolish heart towards the sex; and it is not to be wondered at, that so tempting a morsel soon found favor in his eyes; more especially after he had visited her in her paternal mansion. Old Baltus Van Tassel was a perfect picture of a thriving, contented, liberal-hearted farmer. He seldom, it is true, sent either his eyes or his thoughts beyond the boundaries of his own farm; but within those every thing was snug, happy, and well-conditioned. He was satisfied with his wealth, but not proud of it; and piqued himself upon the hearty abundance, rather than the style in which he lived. His stronghold was situated on the banks of the Hudson, in one of those green, sheltered, fertile nooks, in which the Dutch farmers are so fond of nestling. A great elm-tree spread its broad branches over it; at the foot of which bubbled up a spring of the softest and sweetest water, in a little well, formed of a barrel; and then stole sparkling away through the grass, to a neighboring brook, that bubbled along among alders and dwarf willows. Hard by the farmhouse was a vast barn, that might have served for a church; every window and crevice of which seemed bursting forth with the treasures of the farm; the flail was busily resounding within it from morning to night; swallows and martins skimmed twittering about the eaves; and rows of pigeons, some with one eye turned up, as if watching the weather, some with their heads under their wings, or buried in their bosoms, and others swelling, and cooing, and bowing about their dames, were enjoying the sunshine on the roof. Sleek unwieldy porkers were grunting in the repose and abundance of their pens; whence sallied forth, now and then, troops of sucking pigs, as if to snuff the air. A stately squadron of snowy geese were riding in an adjoining pond, convoying whole fleets of ducks; regiments of turkeys were gobbling through the farmyard, and guinea fowls fretting about it, like ill-tempered housewives, with their peevish discontented cry. Before the barn door strutted the gallant cock, that pattern of a husband, a warrior, and a fine gentleman, clapping his burnished wings, and crowing in the pride and gladness of his heart — sometimes tearing up the earth with his feet, and then generously calling his ever-hungry family of wives and children to enjoy the rich morsel which he had discovered.

The pedagogue's mouth watered, as he looked upon this sumptuous promise of luxurious winter fare. In his devouring mind's eye, he pictured to himself every roasting-pig running about with a pudding in his belly, and an apple in his mouth; the pigeons were snugly put to bed in a comfortable pie, and tucked in with a coverlet of crust; the geese were swimming in their own gravy; and the ducks pairing cosily in dishes, like snug married couples, with a decent competency of onion sauce. In the porkers he saw carved out the future sleek side of bacon, and juicy relishing ham; not a turkey but he beheld daintily trussed up, with its gizzard under its wing, and, peradventure, a necklace of savory sausages; and even bright chanticleer himself lay sprawling on his back, in a side-dish, with uplifted claws, as if craving that quarter which his chivalrous spirit disdained to ask while living.

As the enraptured Ichabod fancied all this, and as he rolled his great green eyes over the fat meadow-lands, the rich fields of wheat, of rye, of buckwheat, and Indian corn, and the orchards burthened with ruddy fruit, which surrounded the warm tenement of Van Tassel, his heart yearned after the damsel who was to inherit these domains, and his imagination expanded with the idea, how they might be readily turned into cash, and the money invested in immense tracts of wild land, and shingle palaces in the wilderness. Nay, his busy fancy already realized his hopes, and presented to him the blooming Katrina, with a whole family of children, mounted on the top of a wagon loaded with household trumpery, with pots and kettles dangling beneath; and he beheld himself bestriding a pacing mare, with a colt at her heels, setting out for Kentucky, Tennessee, or the Lord knows where.

When he entered the house the conquest of his heart was complete. It was one of those spacious farmhouses, with highridged, but lowly-sloping roofs, built in the style handed down from the first Dutch settlers; the low projecting eaves forming a piazza along the front, capable of being closed up in bad weather. Under this were hung flails, harness, various utensils of husbandry, and nets for fishing in the neighboring river. Benches were built along the sides for summer use; and a great spinningwheel at one end, and a churn at the other, showed the various uses to which this important porch might be devoted. From this piazza the wondering Ichabod entered the hall, which formed the centre of the mansion and the place of usual residence. Here, rows of resplendent pewter, ranged on a long dresser, dazzled his eyes. In one corner stood a huge bag of wool ready to be spun; in another a quantity of linsey-woolsey just from the loom; ears of Indian corn, and strings of dried apples and peaches, hung in gay festoons along the walls, mingled with the gaud of red peppers; and a door left ajar gave him a peep into the best parlor, where the claw-footed chairs, and dark mahogany tables, shone like mirrors; andirons, with their accompanying shovel and tongs, glistened from their covert of asparagus tops; mock-oranges and conch-shells decorated the mantel-piece; strings of various colored birds' eggs were suspended above it: a great ostrich egg was hung from the centre of the room, and a corner cupboard, knowingly left open, displayed immense treasures of old silver and well-mended china.

From the moment Ichabod laid his eyes upon these regions of delight, the peace of his mind was at an end, and his only study was how to gain the affections of the peerless daughter of Van Tassel. In this enterprise, however, he had more real difficulties than generally fell to the lot of a knight-errant of yore, who seldom had any thing but giants, enchanters, fiery dragons, and such like easily-conquered adversaries, to contend with; and had to make his way merely through gates of iron and brass, and walls of adamant, to the castle keep, where the lady of his heart was confined; all which he achieved as easily as a man would carve his way to the centre of a Christmas pie; and then the lady gave him her hand as a matter of course. Ichabod, on the contrary, had to win his way to the heart of a country coquette, beset with a labyrinth of whims and caprices, which were for ever presenting new difficulties and impediments; and he had to encounter a host of fearful adversaries of real flesh and blood, the numerous rustic admirers, who beset every portal to her heart; keeping a watchful and angry eye upon each other, but ready to fly out in the common cause against any new competitor.

Among these the most formidable was a burly, roaring, roystering blade, of the name of Abraham, or, according to the Dutch abbreviation, Brom Van Brunt, the hero of the country round, which rang with his feats of strength and hardihood. He was broad-shouldered and double-jointed, with short curly black hair, and a bluff, but not unpleasant countenance, having a mingled air of fun and arrogance. From his Herculean frame and great powers of limb, he had received the nickname of BROM BONES, by which he was universally known. He was famed for great knowledge and skill in horsemanship, being as dexterous on horseback as a Tartar. He was foremost at all races and cock-fights; and, with the ascendency which bodily strength acquires in rustic life, was the umpire in all disputes, setting his hat on one side, and giving his decisions with an air and tone admitting of no gainsay or appeal. He was always ready for either a fight or a frolic; but had more mischief than ill-will in his composition; and, with all his overbearing roughness, there was a strong dash of waggish good humor at bottom. He had three or four boon companions, who regarded him as their model, and at the head of whom he scoured the country, attending every scene of feud or merriment for miles round. In cold weather he was distinguished by a fur cap, surmounted with a flaunting fox's tail; and when the folks at a country gathering descried this well-known crest at a distance, whisking about among a squad of hard riders, they always stood by for a squall. Sometimes his crew would be heard dashing along past the farm-houses at midnight, with whoop and halloo, like a troop of Don cossacks; and the old dames, startled out of their sleep, would listen for a moment till the hurry-scurry had clattered by, and then exclaim, "Ay, there goes Brom Bones and his gang!" The neighbors looked upon him with a mixture of awe, admiration, and good will; and when any madcap prank, or rustic brawl, occurred in the vicinity, always shook their heads, and warranted Brom Bones was at the bottom of it.

This rantipole hero had for some time singled out the blooming Katrina for the object of his uncouth gallantries, and though his amorous toyings were something like the gentle caresses and endearments of a bear, yet it was whispered that she did not altogether discourage his hopes. Certain it is, his advances were signals for rival candidates to retire, who felt no inclination to cross a lion in his amours; insomuch, that when his horse was seen tied to Van Tassel's paling, on a Sunday night, a sure sign that his master was courting, or, as it is termed, "sparking," within, all other suitors passed by in despair, and carried the war into other quarters.

Such was the formidable rival with whom Ichabod Crane had to contend, and, considering all things, a stouter man than he would have shrunk from competition, and a wiser man would have despaired. He had, however, a happy mixture of pliability and perseverance in his nature; he was in form and spirit like a supple-jack;—yielding, but tough; though he bent, he never broke;

and though he bowed beneath the slightest pressure, yet the moment it was away—jerk! he was as erect, and carried his head as high as ever.

To have taken the field openly against his rival would have been madness; for he was not a man to be thwarted in his amours, any more than that stormy lover, Achilles. Ichabod, therefore, made his advances in a quiet and gently insinuating manner. Under cover of his character of singing-master, he made frequent visits at the farmhouse; not that he had any thing to apprehend from the meddlesome interference of parents, which is so often a stumbling-block in the path of lovers. Balt Van Tassel was an easy indulgent soul; he loved his daughter better even than his pipe, and, like a reasonable man and an excellent father, let her have her way in every thing. His notable little wife, too, had enough to do to attend to her housekeeping and manage her poultry; for, as she sagely observed, ducks and geese are foolish things, and must be looked after, but girls can take care of themselves. Thus while the busy dame bustled about the house, or plied her spinning-wheel at one end of the piazza, honest Balt would sit smoking his evening pipe at the other, watching the achievements of a little wooden warrior, who, armed with a sword in each hand, was most valiantly fighting the wind on the pinnacle of the barn. In the mean time, Ichabod would carry on his suit with the daughter by the side of the spring under the great elm, or sauntering along in the twilight, that hour so favorable to the lover's eloquence.

I profess not to know how women's hearts are wooed and won. To me they have always been matters of riddle and admiration. Some seem to have but one vulnerable point, or door of access; while others have a thousand avenues, and may be captured in a thousand different ways. It is a great triumph of skill to gain the former, but a still greater proof of generalship to maintain possession of the latter, for the man must battle for his fortress at every door and window. He who wins a thousand common hearts is therefore entitled to some renown; but he who keeps undisputed sway over the heart of a coquette, is indeed a hero. Certain it is, this was not the case with the redoubtable Brom Bones; and from the moment Ichabod Crane made his advances, the interests of the former evidently declined; his horse was no longer seen tied at the palings on Sunday nights, and a deadly feud gradually arose between him and the preceptor of Sleepy Hollow.

Brom, who had a degree of rough chivalry in his nature, would fain have carried matters to open warfare, and have settled their pretensions to the lady, according to the mode of those most concise and simple reasoners, the knights-errant of yore — by single combat; but Ichabod was too conscious of the superior might of his adversary to enter the lists against him: he had overheard a boast of Bones, that he would "double the schoolmaster up, and lay him on a shelf of his own school-house;" and he was too wary to give him an opportunity. There was something extremely provoking in this obstinately pacific system; it left Brom no alternative but to draw upon the funds of rustic waggery in his disposition, and to play off boorish practical jokes upon his rival. Ichabod became the object of whimsical persecution to Bones, and his gang of rough riders. They harried his hitherto peaceful domains; smoked out his singing school, by stopping up the chimney; broke into the school-house at night, in spite of its formidable fastenings of withe and window stakes, and turned every thing topsy-turvy: so that the poor schoolmaster began to think all the witches in the country held their meetings there. But what was still more annoying, Brom took all opportunities of turning him into ridicule in presence of his mistress, and had a scoundrel dog whom he taught to whine in the most ludicrous manner, and introduced as a rival of Ichabod's to instruct her in psalmody.

In this way matters went on for some time, without producing any material effect on the relative situation of the contending powers. On a fine autumnal afternoon, Ichabod, in pensive mood, sat enthroned on the lofty stool whence he usually watched all the concerns of his little literary realm. In his hand he swayed a ferule, that sceptre of despotic power; the birch of justice reposed on three nails, behind the throne, a constant terror to evil doers; while on the desk before him might be seen sundry contraband articles and prohibited weapons, detected upon the persons of idle urchins; such as half-munched apples, popguns, whirligigs, fly-cages, and whole legions of rampant little paper game-cocks. Apparently there had been some appalling act of justice recently inflicted, for his scholars were all busily intent upon their books, or slyly whispering behind them with one eye kept upon the master; and a kind of buzzing stillness reigned throughout the school-room. It was suddenly interrupted by the appearance of a negro, in tow-cloth jacket and trowsers, a round-crowned fragment of a hat, like the cap of Mercury, and mounted on the back of a ragged, wild, half-broken colt, which he managed with a rope by way of halter. He came clattering up to the school door with an invitation to Ichabod to attend a merry-making or "quilting frolic," to be held that evening at Mynheer Van Tassel's; and having delivered his message with that air of importance, and effort at fine language, which a negro is apt to display on petty embassies of the kind, he dashed over the brook, and was seen scampering away up the hollow, full of the importance and hurry of his mission.

All was now bustle and hubbub in the late quiet schoolroom. The scholars were hurried through their lessons, without stopping at trifles; those who were nimble skipped over half with impunity, and those who were tardy, had a smart application now and then in the rear, to quicken their speed, or help them over a tall word. Books were flung aside without being put away on the shelves, inkstands were overturned, benches thrown down, and the whole school was turned loose an hour before the usual time, bursting forth like a legion of young imps, yelping and racketing about the green, in joy at their early emancipation.

The gallant Ichabod now spent at least an extra half hour at his toilet, brushing and furbishing up his best, and indeed only suit of rusty black, and arranging his looks by a bit of broken looking-glass, that hung up in the school-house. That he might make his appearance before his mistress in the true style of a cavalier, he borrowed a horse from the farmer with whom he was domiciliated, a choleric old Dutchman, of the name of Hans Van Ripper, and, thus gallantly mounted, issued forth, like a knight-errant in quest of adventures. But it is meet I should, in the true spirit of romantic story, give some account of the looks and equipments of my hero and his steed. The animal he bestrode was a brokendown plough-horse, that had outlived almost every thing but his viciousness. He was gaunt and shagged, with a ewe neck and a head like a hammer; his rusty mane and tail were tangled and knotted with burrs; one eye had lost its pupil, and was glaring and spectral; but the other had the gleam of a genuine devil in it. Still he must have had fire and mettle in his day, if we may judge from the name he bore of Gunpowder. He had, in fact, been a favorite steed of his master's, the choleric Van Ripper, who was a furious rider, and had infused, very probably, some of his own spirit into the animal; for, old and brokendown as he looked, there was more of the lurking devil in him than in any young filly in the country.

Ichabod was a suitable figure for such a steed. He rode with short stirrups, which brought his knees nearly up to the pommel of the saddle; his sharp elbows stuck out like grasshoppers'; he carried his whip perpendicularly in his hand, like a sceptre, and, as his horse jogged on, the motion of his arms was not unlike the flapping of a pair of wings. A small wool hat rested on the top of his nose, for so his scanty strip of forehead might be called; and the skirts of his black coat fluttered out almost to the horse's tail. Such was the appearance of Ichabod and his steed, as they shambled out of the gate of Hans Van Ripper, and it was altogether such an apparition as is seldom to be met with in broad daylight.

It was, as I have said, a fine autumnal day, the sky was clear and serene, and nature wore that rich and golden livery which we always associate with the idea of abundance. The forests had put on their sober brown and yellow, while some trees of the tenderer kind had been nipped by the frosts into brilliant dyes of orange, purple, and scarlet. Streaming files of wild ducks began to make their appearance high in the air; the bark of the squirrel might be heard from the groves of beech and hickory nuts, and tne pensive whistle of the quail at intervals from the neighboring stubble-field.

The small birds were taking their farewell banquets. In the fulness of their revelry, they fluttered, chirping and frolicking, from bush to bush, and tree to tree, capricious from the very profusion and variety around them. There was the honest cock-robin, the favorite game of stripling sportsmen, with its loud querulous note; and the twittering blackbirds flying in sable clouds; and the golden-winged woodpecker, with his crimson crest, his broad black gorget, and splendid plumage; and the cedar bird, with its red-tipt wings and yellow-tipt tail, and its little monteiro cap of feathers; and the blue jay, that noisy coxcomb in his gay light-blue coat and white under-clothes; screaming and chattering, nodding and bobbing and bowing, and pretnding to be on good terms with every songster of the grove.

As Ichabod jogged slowly on his way, his eye, ever open to every symptom of culinary abundance, ranged with delight over the treasures of jolly autumn. On all sides he beheld vast store of apples; some hanging in oppressive opulence on the trees; some gathered into baskets and barrels for the market; others heaped up in rich piles for the cider-press. Farther on he beheld great fields of Indian corn, with its golden ears peeping from their leafy coverts, and holding out the promise of cakes and hasty pudding; and the yellow pumpkins lying beneath them, turning up their fair round bellies to the sun, and giving ample prospects of the most luxurious of pies; and anon he passed the fragrant buckwheat fields, breathing the odor of the beehive, and as he beheld them, soft anticipations stole over his mind of dainty slapjacks, well buttered, and garnished with honey or treacle, by the delicate little dimpled hand of Katrina Van Tassel.

Thus feeding his mind with many sweet thoughts and "sugared suppositions," he journeyed along the sides of a range of hills which look out upon some of the goodliest scenes of the mighty Hudson. The sun gradually wheeled his broad disk down into the west. The wide bosom of the Tappan Zee lay motionless and glassy, excepting that here and there a gentle undulation waved and prolonged the blue shadow of the distant mountain. A few amber clouds floated in the sky, without a breath of air to move them. The horizon was of a fine golden tint, changing gradually into a pure apple green, and from that into the deep blue of the mid-heaven. A slanting ray lingered on the woody crests of the precipices that overhung some parts of the river, giving greater depth to the dark-gray and purple of their rocky sides. A sloop was loitering in the distance, dropping slowly down with the tide, her sail hanging uselessly against the mast; and as the reflection of the sky gleamed along the still water, it seemed as if the vessel was suspended in the air.

It was toward evening that Ichabod arrived at the castle of the Heer Van Tassel, which he found thronged with the pride and flower of the adjacent country. Old farmers, a spare leathern-faced race, in homespun coats and breeches, blue stockings, huge shoes, and magnificent pewter buckles. Their brisk withered little dames, in close crimped caps, long-waisted shortgowns, homespun petticoats, with scissors and pincushions, and gay calico pockets hanging on the outside. Buxom lasses, almost as antiquated as their mothers, excepting where a straw hat, a fine ribbon, or perhaps a white frock, gave symptoms of city innovation. The sons, in short squareskirted coats with rows of stupendous brass buttons, and their hair generally queued in the fashion of the times, especially if they could procure an eelskin for the purpose, it being esteemed, throughout the country, as a potent nourisher and strengthener of the hair.

Brom Bones, however, was the hero of the scene, having come to the gathering on his favorite steed Dare-devil, a creature, like himself, full of mettle and mischief, and which no one but himself could manage. He was, in fact, noted for preferring vicious animals, given to all kinds of tricks, which kept the rider in constant risk of his neck, for he held a tractable well-broken horse as unworthy of a lad of spirit.

Fain would I pause to dwell upon the world of charms that burst upon the enraptured gaze of my hero, as he entered the state parlor of Van Tassel's mansion. Not those of the bevy of buxom lasses, with their luxurious display of red and white; but the ample charms of a genuine Dutch country tea-table, in the sumptuous time of autumn. Such heaped-up platters of cakes of various and almost indescribable kinds, known only to experienced Dutch housewives! There was the doughty doughnut, the tenderer oly koek, and the crisp and crumbling cruller; sweet cakes and short cakes, ginger cakes and honey cakes, and the whole family of cakes. And then there were apple pies and peach pies and pumpkin pies; besides slices of ham and smoked beef; and moreover delectable dishes of preserved plums, and peaches, and pears, and quinces; not to mention broiled shad and roasted chickens; together with bowls of milk and cream, all mingled higgledy-piggledy, pretty much as I have enumerated them, with the motherly tea-pot sending up its clouds of vapor from the midst — Heaven bless the mark! I want breath and time to discuss this banquet as it deserves, and am too eager to get on with my story. Happily, Ichabod Crane was not in so great a hurry as his historian, but did ample justice to every dainty.

He was a kind and thankful creature, whose heart dilated in proportion as his skin was filled with good cheer; and whose spirits rose with eating as some men's do with drink. He could not help, too, rolling his large eyes round him as he ate and chuckling with the possibility that he might one day be lord of all this scene of almost unimaginable luxury and splendor. Then, he thought, how soon he'd turn his back upon the old schoolhouse; snap his fingers in the face of Hans Van Ripper, and every other niggardly patron, and kick any itinerant pedagogue out of doors that should dare to call him comrade!

Old Baltus Van Tassel moved about among his guests with a face dilated with content and good humor, round and jolly as the harvest moon. His hospitable attentions were brief, but expressive, being confined to a shake of the hand, a slap on the shoulder, a loud laugh, and a pressing invitation to "fall to, and help themselves."

And now the sound of the music from the common room, or hall, summoned to the dance. The musician was an old grayheaded negro, who had been the itinerant orchestra of the neighborhood for more than half a century. His instrument was as old and battered as himself. The greater part of the time he scraped on two or three strings, accompanying every movement of the bow with a motion of the head; bowing almost to the ground, and stamping with his foot whenever a fresh couple were to start.

Ichabod prided himself upon his dancing as much as upon his vocal powers. Not a limb, not a fibre about him was idle; and to have seen his loosely hung frame in full motion, and clattering about the room, you would have thought Saint Vitus himself, that blessed patron of the dance, was figuring before you in person. He was the admiration of all the negroes; who, having gathered, of all ages and sizes, from the farm and the neighborhood, stood forming a pyramid of shining black faces at every door and window, gazing with delight at the scene, rolling their white eye-balls, and showing grinning rows of ivory from ear to ear. How could the flogger of urchins be otherwise than animated and joyous? the lady of his heart was his partner in the dance, and smiling graciously in reply to all his amorous oglings; while Brom Bones, sorely smitten with love and jealousy, sat brooding by himself in one corner.

When the dance was at an end, Ichabod was attracted to a knot of the sager folks, who, with old Van Tassel, sat smoking at the end of the piazza, gossiping over former times, and drawing out long stories about the war.

This neighborhood, at the time of which I am speaking, was one of those highly-favored places which abound with chronicle and great men. The British and American line had run near it during the war; it had, therefore, been the scene of marauding, and infested with refugees, cow-boys, and all kinds of border chivalry. Just sufficient time had elapsed to enable each story-teller to dress up his tale with a little becoming fiction, and, in the indistinctness of his recollection, to make himself the hero of every exploit.

There was the story of Doffue Martling, a large bluebearded Dutchman, who had nearly taken a British frigate with an old iron nine-pounder from a mud breastwork, only that his gun burst at the sixth discharge. And there was an old gentleman who shall be nameless, being too rich a mynheer to be lightly mentioned, who, in the battle of Whiteplains, being an excellent master of defence, parried a musket ball with a small sword, insomuch that he absolutely felt it whiz round the blade, and glance off at the hilt: in proof of which, he was ready at any time to show the sword, with the hilt a little bent. There were several more that had been equally great in the field, not one of whom but was persuaded that he had a considerable hand in bringing the war to a happy termination.

But all these were nothing to the tales of ghosts and apparitions that succeeded. The neighborhood is rich in legendary treasures of the kind. Local tales and superstitions thrive best in these sheltered long-settled retreats; but are trampled under foot by the shifting throng that forms the population of most of our country places. Besides, there is no encouragement for ghosts in most of our villages, for they have scarcely had time to finish their first nap, and turn themselves in their graves, before their surviving friends have travelled away from the neighborhood; so that when they turn out at night to walk their rounds, they have no acquaintances left to call upon. This is perhaps the reason why we so seldom hear of ghosts except in our long-established Dutch communities.

The immediate cause, however, of the prevalence of supernatural stories in these parts, was doubtless owing to the vicinity of Sleepy Hollow. There was a contagion in the very air that blew from that haunted region; it breathed forth an atmosphere of dreams and fancies infecting all the land. Several of the Sleepy Hollow people were present at Van Tassel's, and, as usual, were doling out their wild and wonderful legends. Many dismal tales were told about funeral trains, and mourning cries and wailings heard and seen about the great tree where the unfortunate Major André was taken, and which stood in the neighborhood. Some mention was made also of the woman in white, that haunted the dark glen at Raven Rock, and was often heard to shriek on winter nights before a storm, having perished there in the snow. The chief part of the stories, however, turned upon the favorite spectre of Sleepy Hollow, the headless horseman, who had been heard several times of late, patrolling the country; and, it was said, tethered his horse nightly among the graves in the churchyard.

The sequestered situation of this church seems always to have made it a favorite haunt of troubled spirits. It stands on a knoll, surrounded by locust-trees and lofty elms, from among which its decent whitewashed walls shine modestly forth, like Christian purity beaming through the shades of retirement. A gentle slope descended from it to a silver sheet of water, bordered by high trees, between which peeps may be caught at the blue hills of the Hudson. To look upon its grass-grown yard, where the sunbeams seem to sleep so quietly, one would think that there at least the dead might rest in peace. On one side of the church extends a wide woody dell, along which raves a large brook among broken rocks and trunks of fallen trees. Over a deep black part of the stream, not far from the church, was formerly thrown a wooden bridge; the road that led to it, and the bridge itself, were thickly shaded by overhanging trees, which cast a gloom about it, even in the daytime; but occasioned a fearful darkness at night. This was one of the favorite haunts of the headless horseman; and the place where he was most frequently encountered. The tale was told of old Brouwer, a most heretical disbeliever in ghosts, how he met the horseman returning from his foray into Sleepy Hollow, and was obliged to get up behind him; how they galloped over bush and brake, over hill and swamp, until they reached the bridge; when the horseman suddenly turned into a skeleton, threw old Brouwer into the brook, and sprang away over the treetops with a clap of thunder.

This story was immediately matched by a thrice marvellous adventure of Brom Bones, who made light of the galloping Hessian as an arrant jockey. He affirmed that, on returning one night from the neighboring village of Sing Sing, he had been overtaken by this midnight trooper; that he had offered to race with him for a bowl of punch, and should have won it too, for Daredevil beat the goblin

horse all hollow, but, just as they came to the churchbridge, the Hessian bolted, and vanished in a flash of fire.

All these tales, told in that drowsy undertone with which men talk in the dark, the countenances of the listeners only now and then receiving a casual gleam from the glare of a pipe, sank deep in the mind of Ichabod. He repaid them in kind with large extracts from his invaluable author, Cotton Mather, and added many marvellous events that had taken place in his native State of Connecticut, and fearful sights which he had seen in his nightly walks about Sleepy Hollow.

The revel now gradually broke up. The old farmers gathered together their families in their wagons, and were heard for some time rattling along the hollow roads, and over the distant hills. Some of the damsels mounted on pillions behind their favorite swains, and their lighthearted laughter, mingling with the clatter of hoofs, echoed along the silent woodlands, sounding fainter and fainter until they gradually died away — and the late scene of noise and frolic was all silent and deserted. Ichabod only lingered behind, according to the custom of country lovers, to have a tête-à-tête with the heiress, fully convinced that he was now on the high road to success. What passed at this interview I will not pretend to say, for in fact I do not know. Something, however, I fear me, must have gone wrong, for he certainly sallied forth, after no very great interval, with an air quite desolate and chop-fallen. — Oh these women! these women! Could that girl have been playing off any of her coquettish tricks? — Was her encouragement of the poor pedagogue all a mere sham to secure her conquest of his rival? — Heaven only knows, not I! — Let it suffice to say, Ichabod stole forth with the air of one who had been sacking a hen-roost, rather than a fair lady's heart. Without looking to the right or left to notice the scene of rural wealth, on which he had so often gloated, he went straight to the stable, and with several hearty cuffs and kicks, roused his steed most uncourteously from the comfortable quarters in which he was soundly sleeping, dreaming of mountains of corn and oats, and whole valleys of timothy and clover.

It was the very witching time of night that

Ichabod, heavy-hearted and crest-fallen, pursued his travel homewards, along the sides of the lofty hills which rise above Tarry Town, and which he had traversed so cheerily in the afternoon. The hour was as dismal as himself. Far below him, the Tappan Zee spread its dusky and indistinct waste of waters, with here and there the tall mast of a sloop, riding quietly at anchor under the land. In the dead hush of midnight, he could even hear the barking of the watch dog from the opposite shore of the Hudson; but it was so vague and faint as only to give an idea of his distance from this faithful companion of man. Now and then, too, the long-drawn crowing of a cock, accidentally awakened, would sound far, far off, from some farm-house away among the hills — but it was like a dreaming sound in his ear. No signs of life occurred near him, but occasionally the melancholy chirp of a cricket, or perhaps the guttural twang of a bull-frog, from a neighboring marsh, as if sleeping uncomfortably, and turning suddenly in his bed.

All the stories of ghosts and goblins that he had heard in the afternoon, now came crowding upon his recollection. The night grew darker and darker; the stars seemed to sink deeper in the sky, and driving clouds occasionally hid them from his sight. He had never felt so lonely and dismal. He was, moreover, approaching the very place where many of the scenes of the ghost stories had been laid. In the centre of the road stood an enormous tulip-tree, which towered like a giant above all the other trees of the neighborhood, and formed a kind of landmark. Its limbs were gnarled, and fantastic, large enough to form trunks for ordinary trees, twisting down almost to the earth, and rising again into the air. It was connected with the tragical story of the unfortunate André, who had been taken prisoner hard by; and was universally known by the name of Major André's tree. The common people regarded it with a mixture of respect and superstition, partly out of sympathy for the fate of its ill-starred namesake, and partly from the tales of strange sights and doleful lamentations told concerning it.

As Ichabod approached this fearful tree, he began to whistle: he thought his whistle was answered — it was but a blast sweeping sharply through the dry branches. As he approached a little nearer, he thought he saw something white, hanging in the midst of the tree — he paused and ceased whistling; but on looking more narrowly, perceived that it was a place where the tree had been scathed by lightning, and the white wood laid bare. Suddenly he heard a groan — his teeth chattered and his knees smote against the saddle: it was but the rubbing of one huge bough upon another, as they were swayed about by the breeze. He passed the tree in safety, but new perils lay before him.

About two hundred yards from the tree a small brook crossed the road, and ran into a marshy and thickly-wooded glen, known by the name of Wiley's swamp. A few rough logs, laid side by side, served for a bridge over this stream. On that side of the road where the brook entered the wood, a group of oaks and chestnuts, matted thick with wild grape-vines, threw a cavernous gloom over it. To pass this bridge was the severest trial. It was at this identical spot that the unfortunate André was captured, and under the covert of those chestnuts and vines were the sturdy yeomen concealed who surprised him. This has ever since been considered a haunted stream, and fearful are the feelings of the schoolboy who has to pass it alone after dark.

As he approached the stream his heart began to thump; he summoned up, however, all his resolution, gave his horse half a score of kicks in the ribs, and attempted to dash briskly across the bridge; but instead of starting forward, the perverse old animal made a lateral movement, and ran broadside against the fence. Ichabod, whose fears increased with the delay, jerked the reins on the other side, and kicked lustily with the contrary foot: it was all in vain; his steed started, it is true, but it was only to plunge to the opposite side of the road into a thicket of brambles and alder bushes. The schoolmaster now bestowed both whip and heel upon the starveling ribs of old Gunpowder, who dashed forward, snuffling and snorting, but came to a stand just by the bridge, with a suddenness that had nearly sent his rider sprawling over his head. Just at this moment a plashy tramp by the side of the bridge caught the sensitive ear of Ichabod. In the dark shadow of the grove, on the margin of the brook, he beheld something huge, misshapen, black and towering. It stirred not, but seemed gathered up in the gloom, like some gigantic monster ready to spring upon the traveller.

The hair of the affrighted pedagogue rose upon his head with terror. What was to be done? To turn and fly was now too late; and besides, what chance was there of escaping ghost or goblin, if such it was, which could ride upon the wings of the wind? Summoning up, therefore, a show of courage, he demanded in stammering accents — "Who are you?" He received no reply. He repeated his demand in a still more agitated voice. Still there was no answer. Once more he cudgelled the sides of the inflexible Gunpowder, and, shutting his eyes, broke forth with involuntary fervor into a psalm tune. Just then the shadowy object of alarm put itself in motion, and, with a scramble and a bound, stood at once in the middle of the road. Though the night was dark and dismal, yet the form of the unknown might now in some degree be ascertained. He appeared to be a horseman of large dimensions, and mounted on a black horse of powerful frame. He made no offer of molestation or sociability, but kept aloof on one side of the road, jogging along on the blind side of old Gunpowder, who had now got over his fright and waywardness.

Ichabod, who had no relish for this strange midnight companion, and bethought himself of the adventure of Brom Bones with the Galloping Hessian, now quickened his steed, in hopes of leaving him behind. The stranger, however, quickened his horse to an equal pace. Ichabod pulled up, and fell into a walk, thinking to lag behind — the other did the same. His heart began to sink within him; he endeavored to resume his psalm tune, but his parched tongue clove to the roof of his mouth, and he could not utter a stave. There was something in the moody and dogged silence of this pertinacious companion, that was mysterious and appalling. It was soon fearfully accounted for. On mounting a rising ground, which brought the figure of his fellow-traveller in relief against the sky, gigantic in height, and muffled in a cloak,

Ichabod was horror-struck, on perceiving that he was headless! — but his horror was still more increased, on observing that the head, which should have rested on his shoulders, was carried before him on the pommel of the saddle: his terror rose to desperation; he rained a shower of kicks and blows upon Gunpowder, hoping, by a sudden movement, to give his companion the slip — but the spectre started full jump with him. Away then they dashed, through thick and thin; stones flying, and sparks flashing at every bound. Ichabod's flimsy garments fluttered in the air, as he stretched his long lank body away over his horse's head, in the eagerness of his flight.

They had now reached the road which turns off to Sleepy Hollow; but Gunpowder, who seemed possessed with a demon, instead of keeping up it, made an opposite turn, and plunged headlong down hill to the left. This road leads through a sandy hollow, shaded by trees for about a quarter of a mile, where it crosses the bridge famous in goblin story, and just beyond swells the green knoll on which stands the whitewashed church.

As yet the panic of the steed had given his unskilful rider an apparent advantage in the chase; but just as he had got half way through the hollow, the girths of the saddle gave way, and he felt it slipping from under him. He seized it by the pommel, and endeavored to hold it firm, but in vain; and had just time to save himself by clasping old Gunpowder round the neck, when the saddle fell to the earth, and he heard it trampled under foot by his pursuer. For a moment the terror of Hans Van Ripper's wrath passed across his mind — for it was his Sunday saddle; but this was no time for petty fears; the goblin was hard on his haunches; and (unskilful rider that he was!) he had much ado to maintain his seat; sometimes slipping on one side, sometimes on another, and sometimes jolted on the high ridge of his horse's backbone, with a violence that he verily feared would cleave him asunder.

An opening in the trees now cheered him with the hopes that the church bridge was at hand. The wavering reflection of a silver star in the bosom of the brook told him that he was not mistaken. He saw the walls of the church dimly glaring under the trees beyond. He recollected the place where Brom Bones's ghostly competitor had disappeared. "If I can but reach that bridge," thought Ichabod, "I am safe." Just then he heard the black steed panting and blowing close behind him; he even fancied that he felt his hot breath. Another convulsive kick in the ribs, and old Gunpowder sprang upon the bridge; he thundered over the resounding planks; he gained the opposite side; and now Ichabod cast a look behind to see if his pursuer should vanish, according to rule, in a flash of fire and brimstone. Just then he saw the goblin rising in his stirrups, and in the very act of hurling his head at him. Ichabod endeavored to dodge the horrible missile, but too late. It encountered his cranium with a tremendous crash — he was tumbled headlong into the dust, and Gunpowder, the black steed, and the goblin rider, passed by like a whirlwind.

The next morning the old horse was found without his saddle, and with the bridle under his feet, soberly cropping the grass at his master's gate. Ichabod did not make his appearance at breakfast — dinner-hour came, but no Ichabod. The boys assembled at the schoolhouse, and strolled idly about the banks of the brook; but no schoolmaster. Hans Van Ripper now began to feel some uneasiness about the fate of poor Ichabod, and his saddle. An inquiry was set on foot, and after diligent investigation they came upon his traces. In one part of the road leading to the church was found the saddle trampled in the dirt; the tracks of horses' hoofs deeply dented in the road, and evidently at furious speed, were traced to the bridge, beyond which, on the bank of a broad part of the brook, where the water ran deep and black, was found the hat of the unfortunate Ichabod, and close beside it a shattered pumpkin.

The brook was searched, but the body of the schoolmaster was not to be discovered. Hans Van Ripper, as executor of his estate, examined the bundle which contained all his worldly effects. They consisted of two shirts and a half; two stocks for the neck; a pair or two of worsted stockings; an old pair of corduroy smallclothes; a rusty razor; a book of psalm tunes, full of dogs' ears; and a broken pitchpipe. As to the books and furniture of the school-house, they belonged to the community, excepting Cotton Mather's "History of Witchcraft," a New England Almanac, and a book of dreams and fortune-telling; in which last was a sheet of foolscap much scribbled and blotted in several fruitless attempts to make a copy of verses in honor of the heiress of Van Tassel. These magic books and the poetic scrawl were forthwith consigned to the flames by Hans Van Ripper; who from that time forward determined to send his children no more to school; observing, that he never knew any good come of this same reading and writing. Whatever money the schoolmaster possessed, and he had received his quarter's pay but a day or two before, he must have had about his person at the time of his disappearance.

The mysterious event caused much speculation at the church on the following Sunday. Knots of gazers and gossips were collected in the church-yard, at the bridge, and at the spot where the hat and pumpkin had been found. The stories of Brouwer, of Bones, and a whole budget of others, were called to mind; and when they had diligently considered them all, and compared them with the symptoms of the present case, they shook their heads, and came to the conclusion that Ichabod had been carried off by the galloping Hessian. As he was a bachelor, and in nobody's debt, nobody troubled his head any more about him. The school was removed to a different quarter of the hollow, and another pedagogue reigned in his stead.

It is true, an old farmer, who had been down to New York on a visit several years after, and from whom this account of the ghostly adventure was received, brought home the intelligence that Ichabod Crane was still alive; that he had left the neighborhood, partly through fear of the goblin and Hans Van Ripper, and partly in mortification at having been suddenly dismissed by the heiress; that he had changed his quarters to a distant part of the country; had kept school and studied law at the same time, had been admitted to the bar, turned politician, electioneered, written for the newspapers, and finally had been made a justice of the Ten Pound Court. Brom Bones too, who shortly after his rival's disappearance conducted the blooming Katrina in triumph to the altar, was observed to look exceedingly knowing whenever the story of Ichabod was related, and always burst into a hearty laugh at the mention of the pumpkin; which led some to suspect that he knew more about the matter than he chose to tell.

The old country wives, however, who are the best judges of these matters, maintain to this day that Ichabod was spirited away by supernatural means; and it is a favorite story often told about the neighborhood round the winter evening fire. The bridge became more than ever an object of superstitious awe, and that may be the reason why the road has been altered of late years, so as to approach the church by the border of the mill-pond. ₅ The school-house being deserted, soon fell to decay, and was reported to be haunted by the ghost of the unfortunate pedagogue; and the ploughboy, loitering homeward of a still summer evening, has often fancied his voice at a distance, chanting a melancholy psalm tune among the tranquil solitudes of Sleepy Hollow.

JAMES FENIMORE COOPER (1789–1851)

Born at Burlington, New Jersey, in 1789, brought up in a pioneer settlement on Otsego Lake, New York, dismissed from Yale and sent to sea, Cooper wrote his first novel in 1820 to prove to his wife that he could produce a better book than the English work she was reading. He was dissatisfied with the effort. "Ashamed to have fallen into the track of imitation," he later explained, "I endeavoured to repay the wrong done to my own views, by producing a work that should be purely American, and of which love of country should be the theme." The first tangible expression of this purpose was *The Spy* (1821) with which, says Carl Van Doren, "American fiction may be said to have come of age."

The scene of this novel was Cooper's own New York, whose mountains, lakes, and wilderness trails he had well learned in his boyhood. Those boyhood experiences also furnished him the setting for his most famous series of novels, the Leather-Stocking tales: *The Pioneers* (1823), *The Last of the Mohicans* (1826), *The Prairie* (1827), *The Pathfinder* (1840), and *The Deerslayer* (1841). As the great character of *The Spy* was a patriotic peddler, unhandsome in outward appearance but heroic of soul, so the central character of the Leather-Stocking tales was one Natty Bumppo, a noble scout, who "stands as a protest, on behalf of simplicity and perfect freedom, against encroaching law and order." As civilization advances, Natty carries his virtues into the deeper forest, but at last is sought down and is compelled to yield the battle. New York, with its forest trails and wilderness legends, thus furnished Cooper with two great characters. His experiences before the mast furnished him with another, Long Tom Coffin. Long Tom is the chief character creation of *The Pilot* (1824), a story of the sea which has for its hero John Paul Jones.

In his later years Cooper wrote novels of social criticism, such as *Satanstoe* (1845), *The Chainbearer* (1846), and *The Redskins* (1846), fusing his fictional creation with an interest he had long had in social problems. This interest he had expressed repeatedly in such non-fictional publications as *Notions of the Americans* (1828), *A Letter to His Countrymen* (1834), *Gleanings in Europe* (1837, 1838), and *The American Democrat* (1838), from which selections are given in the text below to represent a side of Cooper not revealed in the Leather-Stocking Tales.

A good edition of *The Works of James Fenimore Cooper*, in 33 vols., was published in 1895–1900. R. E. Spiller ably edited a volume of selections in the *AWS*, 1936. The best biographies are by T. R. Lounsbury, 1883, H. W. Boynton, 1931, R. E. Spiller, 1931, and James Grossman, 1949.

Critical studies include Mark Twain's celebrated essay on "Fenimore Cooper's Literary Offences" in *How to Tell a Story, and Other Essays*, 1897, the essay on Cooper in W. C. Brownell's *American Prose Masters*, 1909, V. L. Parrington's *The Romantic Revolution in America*, pp. 222–237, and R. H. Pearce's "The Leatherstocking Tales Re-examined," *South Atlantic Quarterly*, October, 1947.

From Notions of the Americans [1]

(1828)

[*American Learning and Literature*]

The Americans have been placed, as respects moral and intellectual advancement, different from all other infant nations. They have never been without the wants of civilization, nor have they ever been entirely without the means of a supply. Thus pictures, and books, and statuary, and every thing else which appertains to elegant life, have always been known to them in an abundance, and of a quality exactly proportioned to their cost. Books, being the cheapest, and the nation having great leisure and prodigious zest for information, are not only the most common, as you will readily suppose, but they are probably more common than among any other people. I scarcely remember ever to have entered an American dwelling, however humble, without finding fewer or more books. As they form the most essential division of the subject, not only on account of their greater frequency, but on account of their far greater importance, I shall give them the first notice in this letter.

Unlike the progress of the two professions in the countries of our hemisphere, in America the printer came into existence before the author. Reprints of English works gave the first employment to the press. Then came almanacs, psalm-books, religious tracts, sermons, journals, political essays, and even rude attempts at poetry. All these preceded the revolution. The first journal was established in Boston at the commencement of the last century. There are several original polemical works of great originality and power that belong to the same period. I do not know that more learning and talents existed at that early day in the States of New-England than in Virginia, Maryland and the Carolinas, but there was certainly a stronger desire to exhibit them.* * *

Less attention is paid to classical learning here than in Europe; and, as the term of residence [in college] rarely exceeds four years, profound scholars are by no means common. This country possesses neither the population nor the endowments to maintain a large class of learned idlers, in order that one man in a hundred may contribute a mite to the growing stock of general knowledge. There is a luxury in this expenditure of animal force, to which the Americans have not yet attained. The good is far too problematical and remote, and the expense of man too certain, to be prematurely sought. I have heard, I will confess, an American legislator quote Horace and Cicero; but it is far from being the humour of the country. I thought the taste of the orator questionable. A learned quotation is rarely of any use in an argument, since few men are fools enough not to see that the application of any maxim to politics is liable to a thousand practical objections, and, nine times in ten, they are evidences of the want of a direct, natural, and vigorous train of thought. They are the affectations, but rarely the ebullitions of true talent. When a man feels strongly, or thinks strongly, or speaks strongly, he is just as apt to do it in his native tongue as he is to laugh when he is tickled, or to weep when in sorrow. The Americans are strong speakers and acute thinkers, but no great quoters of the morals and axioms of

[1] In this work, published anonymously, Cooper pretends to be an Englishman traveling in America.

a heathen age, because they happen to be recorded in Latin.

The higher branches of learning are certainly on the advance in this country. The gentlemen of the middle and southern States, before the revolution, were very generally educated in Europe, and they were consequently, in this particular, like our own people. Those who came into life during the struggle, and shortly after, fared worse. Even the next generation had little to boast of in the way of instruction. I find that boys entered the colleges so late as the commencement of the present century, who had read a part of the Greek Testament, and a few books of Cicero and Virgil, with perhaps a little of Horace. But great changes have been made, and are still making, in the degree of previous qualification. Still, it would be premature to say that there is any one of the American universities where classical knowledge, or even science, is profoundly attained, even at the present day. * * *

As respects authorship there is not much to be said. Compared to the books that are printed and read, those of native origin are few indeed. The principal reason of this poverty of original writers, is owing to the circumstance that men are not yet driven to their wits for bread. The United States are the first nation that possessed institutions, and, of course, distinctive opinions of its own, that was ever dependent on a foreign people for its literature. Speaking the same language as the English, and long in the habit of importing their books from the mother country, the revolution effected no immediate change in the nature of their studies, or mental amusements. The works were reprinted, it is true, for the purposes of economy, but they still continued English. Had the latter nation used this powerful engine with tolerable address, I think they would have secured such an ally in this country as would have rendered their own decline not only more secure, but as illustrious as had been their rise. There are many theories entertained as to the effect produced in this country by the falsehoods and jealous calumnies which have been undeniably uttered in the mother country, by means of the press, concerning her republican descendant. It is my own opinion that, like all

other ridiculous absurdities, they have defeated themselves, and that they are now more laughed at and derided, even here, than resented. By all that I can learn, twenty years ago, the Americans were, perhaps, far too much disposed to receive the opinions and to adopt the prejudices of their relatives; whereas, I think it is very apparent that they are now beginning to receive them with singular distrust. It is not worth our while to enter further into this subject, except as it has had, or is likely to have, an influence on the national literature.

It is quite obvious, that, so far as taste and forms alone are concerned, the literature of England and that of America must be fashioned after the same models. The authors, previously to the revolution, are common property, and it is quite idle to say that the American has not just as good a right to claim Milton, and Shakespeare, and all the old masters of the language, for his countrymen, as an Englishman. The Americans having continued to cultivate, and to cultivate extensively, an acquaintance with the writers of the mother country, since the separation, it is evident they must have kept pace with the trifling changes of the day. The only peculiarity that can, or ought to be expected in their literature, is that which is connected with the promulgation of their distinctive political opinions. They have not been remiss in this duty, as any one may see, who chooses to examine their books. * * *

The literature of the United States has, indeed, two powerful obstacles to conquer before (to use a mercantile expression) it can ever enter the markets of its own country on terms of perfect equality with that of England. Solitary and individual works of genius may, indeed, be occasionally brought to light, under the impulses of the high feeling which has conceived them; but, I fear, a good, wholesome, profitable and continued pecuniary support, is the applause that talent most craves. The fact, that an American publisher can get an English work without money, must for a few years longer, (unless legislative protection shall be extended to their own authors,) have a tendency to repress a national literature. No man will pay a writer for an epic, a tragedy, a sonnet, a history, or a romance, when he can get a work of equal merit for nothing. I have conversed with those who are conversant on the subject, and, I confess, I have been astonished at the information they imparted.

A capital American publisher has assured me that there are not a dozen writers in this country, whose works he should feel confidence in publishing at all, while he reprints hundreds of English books without the least hesitation. This preference is by no means so much owing to any difference in merit, as to the fact that, when the price of the original author is to be added to the uniform hazard which accompanies all literary speculations, the risk becomes too great. The general taste of the reading world in this country is better than that of England. The fact is both proved and explained by the circumstances that thousands of works that are printed and read in the mother country, are not printed and read here. The publisher on this side of the Atlantic has the advantage of seeing the reviews of every book he wishes to reprint, and, what is of far more importance, he knows, with the exception of books that he is sure of selling, by means of a name, the decision of the English critics before he makes his choice. Nine times in ten, popularity, which is all he looks for, is a sufficient test of general merit. Thus, while you find every English work of character, or notoriety, on the shelves of an American book-store, you may ask in vain for most of the trash that is so greedily devoured in the circulating libraries of the mother country, and which would be just as eagerly devoured here, had not a better taste been treated by a compelled abstinence. That taste must now be overcome before such works could be sold at all.

When I say that books are not rejected here, from any want of talent in the writers, perhaps I ought to explain. I wish to express something a little different. Talent is sure of too many avenues to wealth and honours, in America, to seek, unnecessarily, an unknown and hazardous path. It is better paid in the ordinary pursuits of life, than it would be likely to be paid by an adventure in which an extraordinary and skilful, because practised, foreign competition is certain. Perhaps high talent does not often make the trial with the American bookseller; but it is precisely for the reason I have named.

The second obstacle against which American literature has to contend, is in the poverty of materials. There is scarcely an ore which contributes to the wealth of the author, that is found, here, in veins as rich as in Europe. There are no annals for the historian; no follies (beyond the most vulgar and commonplace) for the satirist; no manners for the dramatist; no obscure fictions for the writer of romance; no gross and hardy offences against decorum for the moralist; nor any of the rich artificial auxiliaries of poetry. The weakest hand can extract a spark from the flint, but it would baffle the strength of a giant to attempt kindling a flame with a pudding-stone. I very well know there are theorists who assume that the society and institutions of this country are, or ought to be, particularly favourable to novelties and variety. But the experience of one month, in these States, is sufficient to show any observant man the falsity of their position. The effect of a promiscuous assemblage any where, is to create a standard of deportment; and great liberty permits every one to aim at its attainment. I have never seen a nation so much alike in my life, as the people of the United States, and what is more, they are not only like each other, but they are remarkably like that which common sense tells them they ought to resemble. No doubt, traits of character that are a little peculiar, without, however, being either very poetical, or very rich, are to be found in remote districts; but they are rare, and not always happy exceptions. In short, it is not possible to conceive a state of society in which more of the attributes of plain good sense, or fewer of the artificial absurdities of life, are to be found, than here. There is no costume for the peasant, (there is scarcely a peasant at all), no wig for the judge, no baton for the general, no diadem for the chief magistrate. The darkest ages of their history are illuminated by the light of truth; the utmost efforts of their chivalry are limited by the laws of God; and even the deeds of their sages and heroes are to be sung in a language that would differ but little from a version of the ten commandments. However useful and respectable all this may be in actual life, it indicates but one direction to the man of genius.

From England

(1837)

[*The Americans and the English*]

Beginning in 1826 Cooper was in Europe seven years, of which the chief literary product was six novels and a series of books on Switzerland, France, England, and Italy. *England* was probably written in 1828, but was not published till 1837, when it appeared in America, England, France, and Germany, the American edition bearing the title *Gleanings in Europe. England.* Cooper's comments, represented by the following selection, stirred up feeling against him both in England and in the United States.

He attacked Americans largely because of their slavish dependence on English opinion. In the same year in which Emerson pronounced his intellectual Declaration of Independence, Cooper called for a "mental emancipation" to tally the "declaration of political independence" (Preface to the first edition of *Gleanings in Europe. England*).

It would be an occupation of interest to note the changes, moral and physical, that time, climate, and different institutions have produced between the people of England, and those of America.

Physically, I do not think the change as great as is usually imagined. Dress makes a sensible difference in appearance, and I find that the Americans, who have been under the hands of the English tailors, are not easily distinguished from the English themselves. The principal points of distinction strike me to be these. We are taller, and less fleshy; more disposed to stoop; have more prominent features, and faces less full; are less ruddy, and more tanned; have much smaller hands and feet, anti-democratical as it may be; and are more slouching in gait. The exceptions, of course, are numerous; but I think these distinctions may be deemed national. The American, who has become Europeanized by dress, however, is so very different a looking animal from what he is at home, that too much stress is not to be laid on them. Then the great extent of the United States is creating certain physical differences in our own population, that render all such comparisons liable to many qualifications.

As to stature and physical force, I see no reason to think that the animal has deteriorated in America. As between England and the Old Atlantic states, the difference is not striking, after one allows for the disparity in numbers, and the density of the population here, the eye always seeking exceptions; but I incline to believe that the south-west will turn the scale to our side. I believe it to be a fact, that the aborigines of that portion of the Union were larger than those of our section of the country.

There are obvious physical differences among the English themselves. One county is said to have an undue proportion of red heads, another to have men taller than the common, this again men that are shorter, and all to show traces of their remote origins. It is probable that some of these peculiarities have descended to ourselves, though they have become blended by the unusual admixture of the population.

Morally, we live under the influence of systems so completely the converse of each other, that it is matter of surprise so many points of resemblance still remain. The immediate tendency of the English system is, to create an extreme deference in all the subordinate classes for their superiors; while that of the American is to run into the opposite feeling. The effects of both these tendencies are certainly observable; though relatively, that of our own much less, I think, than that of England. It gives good models a rather better chance here, than they have with us.

In England, the disaffected to the government are among precisely those who most sustain government in America; and the disaffected in America, (if so strong a word can properly be used, as applied to natives,) are of a class whose interests it is to sustain government in England. These facts give very different aspects to the general features of society. Walking in Regent-street lately, I witnessed an attempt of the police to compel some hackney coachmen to quit their boxes, and go with them before the magistrate. A crowd of a thousand people collected immediately, and its feeling was decidedly against the ministers of the law; so much so, indeed, as to render it doubtful whether the coachmen, whose conduct had been flagrantly criminal, would not be rescued. Now, in America, I think the feeling of such a crowd, would have been just the other way. It would have taken an interest in supporting the authorities of the country, instead of an interest in opposing them. This was not the case of a mob, you will remember, in which passion puts down reason; but an ordinary occurrence of the exercise of the power of the police. Instances of this nature might be multiplied, to show that the mass of the two people act under the influence of feelings diametrically opposed to each other.

On the other hand, Englishmen of the higher classes are, with very few exceptions, and these exceptions are usually instances of mere party opposition, attached to their system, sensitive of the subject of its merits or defects, and ever ready to defend it when assailed. The American of the same class is accustomed to sneer at democracy, to cavil at its fruits, and to colour and exaggerate its faults. Though this latter disposition may be, to a degree, accounted for by the facts, that all merit is comparative, and most of our people have not had the opportunities to compare; and that it is natural to resist most that which most annoys, although the substitution of any other for the actual system would produce even greater discontent; still, I think, the general tendency of aristocratical institutions on the one hand, and of democratical on the other, is to produce this broad difference in feeling, as between classes.

Both the Americans and the English are charged with being offensively boastful and arrogant as nations, and too much disposed to compare themselves advantageously with their neighbours. I have visited no country in which a similar disposition does not exist, and as communities are merely aggregations of men, I fancy that the disposition of a people to take this view of their own merits, is no more than carrying out the well known principle of individual vanity. The English and ourselves, however, well may, and probably do, differ from other nations in one circumstance connected with such a failing. The mass in both nations are better instructed, and are of more account than the mass in other countries, and their sentiments form more of a public opinion than else-

where. When the bulk of a people are in a condition to make themselves heard, one is not to expect much refinement or delicacy, in the sentiments they utter. The English do not strike me as being a vainer nation than the French, although, in the way of ordinary intercourse, I believe that both they and we are more boastful.

The English are to be particularly distinguished from the Americans in the circumstance of their being a proud people. This is a useful and even an ennobling quality, when it is sustained by facts, though apt to render a people both uncomfortable and unpleasant, when the glory on which they pique themselves is passed away. We are almost entirely wanting in national pride, though abundantly supplied with an irritable vanity that might rise to pride, had we greater confidence in our facts. Most intelligent Englishmen are ready enough to admit the obvious faults of their climate, and even of their social condition; but it is an uncommon American that will concede anything material on such points, unless it can be made to bear on democracy. We have the sensitiveness of provincials, increased by the consciousness of having our spurs to earn, on all matters of glory and renown, and our jealousy extends even to the reputations of the cats and dogs. It is but an indifferent compliment to human nature to add, that the man who will join complacently, and I may say ignorantly, in the abuse of foreigners against the institutions of the country, and even against its people, always reserving a saving clause in favour of his own particular class, will take fire if an innuendo is hazarded against its beef, or a suggestion made that the four thousand feet of the Round Peak are not equal to the thirteen thousand feet of the Jung Frau. The English are tolerably free from this weakness, and travelling is daily increasing this species of liberality, at least. I presume that the insular situation of England, and our own distance from Europe, are equally the causes of these traits; though there may be said to be a "property qualification" in the very nature of man, that disposes him to view his own things with complacency, and those of his neighbours with disgust. Bishop Heber, in one of his letters to Lord Grenville, in speaking of the highest peaks of the Himalayas, throws into a parenthesis, "which I feel some exultation in saying, is completely within the limits of the British empire;" a sort of sentiment, of which, I dare say, neither St. Chrysostom nor Polycarp was entirely free.

On the subject of sensibility to comments on their national habits and national characters, neither France nor England is by any means as philosophical or indifferent as one might suppose. As a rule, I believe all men are more easily enraged when their real faults are censured, than when their virtues are called in question; and if the defect happen to be unavoidable, or one for which they are not fairly responsible, the resentment is two-fold that which would attend a comment on a vice. The only difference I can discover between the English and ourselves in this particular, is easily to be traced to our greater provincialism, youth, and the consciousness that we are obliged to anticipate some of our renown. I should say that the English are *thin-skinned*, and the Americans *raw*. Both resent fair, frank, and manly comments with the same bad taste, resorting to calumny, blackguardism, and abuse, when wit and pleasantry would prove both more effective and wiser, and, perhaps, reformation wisest of all. I can only account for this peculiarity, by supposing that the institutions and political facts of the two countries have rendered vulgar-minded men of more account than is usually the case; and that their influence has created a species of public opinion which is less under the correction of taste, principles, and manners, than is the case in nations where the mass is more depressed. Of the fact itself, there can be no question.

In order to appreciate the effect of refinement on this nation, it will be necessary to recur to some of its statistical facts. England, including Wales, contains rather less than fifty-eight thousand square miles of territory; the state of New York, about forty-three thousand. On the former surface, there is a population of something like fifteen millions; on the latter, a population of less than two. One gives a proportion of about two hundred and sixty to the square mile,

and the other a proportion of less than fifty. These premises, alone would show us the immense advantage that any given portion of surface in England must possess over the same extent of surface in America, in all those arts and improvements that depend on physical force. If there were ten men of education, and refinement, and fortune, in a county of New York, of one thousand square miles in extent, there ought to be more than fifty men of the same character and means, in an English county of equal territory. This is supposing that the real premises offer nothing more against us than the disproportion between numbers and surface; whereas, in fact, time, wealth, and an older civilization more than quadruple the odds. Even these do not make up the sum of the adverse elements. Though England has but fifteen millions of souls, the empire she controls has nearly ten times that population, and a very undue proportion of the results of so great a physical force centre in this small spot.

The consideration of these truths suggest several useful heads of reflection. In the first place, they show us, if not the absolute impossibility, the great improbability, that the civilization, refinement, knowledge, wealth, and tastes of even the best portions of America can equal those of this country, and suggest the expediency of looking to other points for our sources of pride. I have said, that the two countries act under the influence of moral agencies that are almost the converse of each other. The condensation of improvement and cultivation is so great here, that even the base of society is affected by it, even to deportment; whereas, with us, these properties are so dispersed, as to render it difficult for those who are lucky enough to possess them, to keep what they have got, in face of the overshadowing influence of a lower school, instead of being able to impart them to society. Our standard, in nearly all things, as it is popular, is necessarily one of mediocrity; a highly respectable, and, circumstances considered, a singularly creditable one, but still a mediocrity; whereas, the condition of these people has enabled them to raise a standard which, however much it may be and is wanting in the better elements of a pure taste, has im-

mensely the advantage of our own in most of
the obvious blandishments of life. More than
half of the peculiarities of America — peculiarities for which it is usual to seek a cause
in the institutions, simply because they are
so peculiar themselves — are to be traced to
facts like these; or, in other words, to the disproportion between surface and numbers, the
want of any other commercial towns, and
our distance from the rest of the world.

Every condition of society has its own advantages, and its own disadvantages. To
claim perfection for any one in particular,
would be to deny the nature of man. Their
comparative merits are to be decided, only,
by the comparative gross results, and it is in
this sense, that I contend for the superiority
of our own. The utilitarian school, as it has
been popularly construed, is not to my taste,
either; for I believe there is great utility in
the grace and elegance of life, and no one
would feel more disposed to resist a system
in which these essential properties are pro-
scribed. That we are wanting in both, I am
ready to allow; but I think the reason is to
be found in facts entirely independent of the
institutions, and that the time will come when
the civilization of America will look down
that of any other section of the world, if the
country can pass that state of probation during which it is and will be exposed to the assaults of secret combinations to destroy it; and
during which, moreover, it is, in an especial
degree, liable to be affected by inherited
opinions, and opinions that have been obtained under a system that has so many of the
forms, while it has so few of the principles of
our own, as easily to be confounded with it,
by the ignorant and the unreflecting.

We over-estimate the effects of intelligence
as between ourselves and the English. The
mass of information, here, probably exceeds that of America, though it is less equally
distributed. In *general* knowledge of a practical nature, too, I think no people can compete with our own. But there is a species of
information, that is both useful and refining,
in which there are few European nations that
do not surpass us. I allude, in particular, to
most things that serve to embellish life. In
addition to this superiority, the Europeans of
the better classes very obviously possess over

us an important advantage, in their intimate
associations with each other, by which means
they insensibly imbibe a great deal of current knowledge, of which the similar classes in
America are nearly ignorant; or, which, if
known at all, is only known through the
medium of books. In the exhibition of this
knowledge, which embraces all that belongs
to what is commonly termed a knowledge
of the world, the difference between the
European and the American is the difference
that is seen between the man who has passed
all his days in good society, and the man who
has got his knowledge of it from novels and
plays.

In a correct estimate of their government,
and in an acquaintance with its general
action, the English are much our superiors,
though we know most of details. This arises
from the circumstances that the rights of an
Englishman are little more than franchises,
which require no very profound examination to be understood; while those of the
American depend on principles that demand study, and which are constantly exposed to the antagonist influence of opinions
that have been formed under another system.
It is true the English monarchy, as a monarchy and as it now exists, is a pure mystification; but the supremacy of parliament
being admitted, there can arise no great difficulty on the score of interpretation. The
American system, moreover, is complicated
and double, and the only true Whig and
Tory parties that can exist must have their
origin in the circumstance. To these reasons
may be added the general fact, that the
educated Englishman reasons on his institutions like an Englishman only; while his
American counterpart oftener reasons on
the institutions of the republic like an Englishman, too, than like an American. A
single fact will show you what I mean, although a hundred might be quoted. In
England the government is composed, in
theory, of three bases and one summit; in
America, it is composed of one base and three
summits. In one, there is supposed to be a
balance in the powers of the state; and, as
this is impossible in practice, it has resulted
in a consolidated authority in its action; in
the other, there is but one power, that of the

entire people, and the balance is in the action of their agents. A very little reflection will show that the maxims of two such systems ought to be as different as the systems themselves.

The English are to be distinguished from the Americans by greater independence of personal habits. Not only the institutions, but the physical condition of our own country has a tendency to reduce us all to the same level of usages. The steam-boats, the overgrown taverns, the speculative character of the enterprises, and the consequent disposition to do all things in common, aid the tendency of the system in bringing about such a result. In England a man dines by himself, in a room filled with other hermits; he eats at his leisure, drinks his wine in silence, reads the paper by the hour; and, in all things, encourages his individuality and insists on his particular humours. The American is compelled to submit to a common rule; he eats when others eat, sleeps when others sleep, and he is lucky, indeed, if he can read a paper in a tavern without having a stranger looking over each shoulder. The Englishman would stare at a proposal that should invade his habits under the pretence of a common wish, while the American would be very apt to yield tacitly, though this common wish should be no more than an impudent assertion of some one who had contrived to effect his own purposes, under the popular plea. The Englishman is so much attached to his independence that he instinctively resists every effort to invade it, and nothing would be more likely to arouse him than to say the mass thinks differently from himself; whereas the American ever seems ready to resign his own opinion to that which is made to seem to be the opinion of the public. I say *seems* to be, for so manifest is the power of public opinion, that one of the commonest expedients of all American managers, is to create an impression that the public thinks in a particular way, in order to bring the common mind in subjection. One often renders himself ridiculous by a foolish obstinacy, and the other is as often contemptible by a weak compliance. A portion of what may be called the *community* of character and habits in America is doubtless owing to

the rustic nature of its society, for one more easily maintains his independence in a capital than in a village, but I think the chief reasons are to be found in the practice of referring every thing to the common mind.

It is usual to ascribe the solitary and unsocial habits of English life to the natural dispositions of the people, but, I think, unjustly. The climate is made to bear the blame of no small portion of this peculiarity. Climate, probably, has an influence on us all, for we know that we are more elastic and more ready to be pleased in a clear bracing air, than in one that is close and *siroccoish*, but, on the whole I am led to think, the English owe their habits to their institutions, more than to any natural causes.

I know no subject, no feeling, nothing, on which an Englishman, as a rule, so completely loses sight of all the better points of his character, on which he is so uniformly bigoted and unjust, so ready to listen to misrepresentation and caricature, and so unwilling to receive truth — on which, in short, he is so little himself in general, as on those connected with America.

As the result of this hasty and imperfect comparison, I am led to believe, that a national character somewhere between the two, would be preferable to either, as it is actually found. This may be saying no more than that man does not exist in a condition of perfection; but were the inequalities named, pared off from both people, an ingenious critic might still find faults of sufficient magnitude to preserve the identity with the human race, and qualities of sufficient elevation, to entitle both to be considered among the greatest and best nations of modern, if not of any other, times.

In most things that pertain to taste, the English have greatly the advantage of us, though *taste* is certainly not the strong side of English character. On this point, alone, one might write a book, but a very few remarks must now satisfy you. In nothing, however, is this superiority more apparent, than in their simplicity, and, particularly, in their simplicity of language. They call a spade, a spade. I very well know, that neither men nor women, in America, who are properly educated, and who are accustomed to its really better tone, differ much, if any, from the English in this particular; but, in this case, as in most others, in which *national* peculiarities are sought, the better tone of America is over-shadowed by its mediocrity. Although I deem the government of this country the very quintessence of hocus pocus, having scarcely a single practice that does not violate its theory, I believe that there is more honesty of public sentiment in England, than in America. The defect at home, I ascribe, in common with the majority of our national failings, to the greater activity, and greater *unresisted* force of ignorance and cupidity, there, than here. High qualities are nowhere collected in a sufficient phalanx to present a front to the enemy, in America.

The besetting, the degrading vice of America, is the moral cowardice by which men are led to truckle to what is called public opinion; though this opinion is as inconstant as the winds — though, in all cases that enlist the feelings of factions, there are *two* and sometimes twenty, each differing from all the others, and though, nine times in ten, these opinions are mere engines set in motion by the most corrupt and the least respectable portion of the community, for unworthy purposes. The English are a more respectable and constant nation than the Americans, as relates to this peculiarity; probably, because the condensed masses of intelligence and character enable the superior portion of the community to produce a greater impression on the inferior, by their collective force. In standing prejudices, they strike me as being worse than ourselves; but in passing impressions, greatly our superiors.

For the last I have endeavoured to account, and I think the first may be ascribed to a system that is sustained by errors that it is not the interest of the more enlightened to remove, but which, instead of weakening in the ignorant, they rather encourage in themselves.

From The American Democrat

(1838)

[*An Aristocrat and a Democrat*]

With these opinions of Cooper's the reader may compare Thomas Jefferson's view that a "natural aristocracy" is a main feature of sound popular government (letter of Jefferson to John Adams, p. 101).

We live in an age when the words aristocrat and democrat are much used, without regard to the real significations. An aristocrat is one of a few who possess the political power of a country; a democrat, one of the many. The words are also properly applied to those who entertain notions favorable to aristocratical or democratical forms of government. Such persons are not necessarily either aristocrats or democrats in fact, but merely so in opinion. Thus a member of a democratical government may have an aristocratical bias, and vice versa.

To call a man who has the habits and opinions of a gentleman, an aristocrat from that fact alone, is an abuse of terms and betrays ignorance of the true principles of government, as well as of the world. It must be an equivocal freedom under which every one is not the master of his own innocent acts and associations; and he is a sneaking democrat indeed who will submit to be dictated to, in those habits over which neither law nor morality assumes a right of control.

Some men fancy that a democrat can only be one who seeks the level, social, mental and moral, of the majority, a rule that would at once exclude all men of refinement, education, and taste from the class. These persons are enemies of democracy, as they at once render it impracticable. They are usually great sticklers for their own associations and habits, too, though unable to comprehend any of a nature that are superior. They are, in truth, aristocrats in principle, though assuming a contrary pretension, the groundwork of all their feelings and arguments being self. Such is not the intention of liberty, whose aim is to leave every man to be the master of his own acts; denying hereditary honors, it is true, as unjust and unnecessary, but not denying the inevitable consequences of civilization.

The law of God is the only rule of conduct in this, as in other matters. Each man should do as he would be done by. Were the question put to the greatest advocate of indiscriminate association, whether he would submit to have his company and habits dictated to him, he would be one of the first to resist the tyranny; for they who are the most rigid in maintaining their own claims in such matters, are usually the loudest in decrying those whom they fancy to be better off than themselves. Indeed, it may be taken as a rule in social intercourse, that he who is the most apt to question the pretensions of others is the most conscious of the doubtful position he himself occupies; thus establishing the very claims he affects to deny, by letting his jealousy of it be seen. Manners, education, and refinement, are positive things, and they bring with them innocent tastes which are productive of high enjoyments; and it is as unjust to deny their possessors their indulgence as it would be to insist on the less fortunate's passing the time they would rather devote to athletic amusements, in listening to operas for which they have no relish, sung in a language they do not understand.

All that democracy means, is as equal a participation in rights as is practicable; and to pretend that social equality is a condition of popular institutions is to assume that the latter are destructive of civilization, for, as nothing is more self-evident than the impossibility of raising all men to the highest standard of tastes and refinement, the alternative would be to reduce the entire community to the lowest. The whole embarrassment on this point exists in the difficulty of making men comprehend qualities they do not themselves possess. We can all perceive the difference between ourselves and our inferiors, but when it comes to a question of the difference between us and our superiors, we fail to appreciate merits of which we have no proper conceptions. In face of this obvious difficulty, there is the safe and just governing rule, already mentioned, or that of permitting every one to be the undisturbed judge of his own habits and associations, so long as they are innocent and do not impair the rights of others to be equally judges for themselves. It follows, that social intercourse must regulate itself, independently of institutions, with the exception that the latter, while they withhold no natural, bestow no factitious advantages beyond those which are inseparable from the rights of property, and general civilization.

In a democracy, men are just as free to aim at the highest attainable places in society, as to attain the largest fortunes; and it would be clearly unworthy of all noble sentiment to say that the grovelling competition for money shall alone be free, while that which enlists all the liberal acquirements and elevated sentiments of the race, is denied the democrat. Such an avowal would be at once a declaration of the inferiority of the system, since nothing but ignorance and vulgarity could be its fruits.

The democratic gentleman must differ in many essential particulars from the aristocratical gentleman, though in their ordinary habits and tastes they are virtually identical. Their principles vary; and, to a slight degree, their deportment accordingly. The democrat, recognizing the right of all to participate in power, will be more liberal in his general sentiments, a quality of superiority in itself; but in conceding this much to his fellow man, he will proudly maintain his own independence of vulgar domination as indispensable to his personal habits. The same principles and manliness that would induce him to depose a royal despot would induce him to resist a vulgar tyrant.

There is no more capital, though more common error, than to suppose him an aristocrat who maintains his independence of habits; for democracy asserts the control of the majority, only in matters of law, and not in matters of custom. The very object of the institution is the utmost practicable personal liberty, and to affirm the contrary would be sacrificing the end to the means.

An aristocrat, therefore, is merely one who fortifies his exclusive privileges by positive institutions, and a democrat, one who is willing to admit of a free competition in all things. To say, however, that the last supposes this competition will lead to nothing is an assumption that means are employed without any reference to an end. He is the purest democrat who best maintains his rights, and no rights can be dearer to a man of cultivation than exemptions from unseasonable invasions on his time by the coarse minded and ignorant.

WILLIAM CULLEN BRYANT (1794-1878)

Eleven years younger than Irving, Bryant published his first important poem when Irving was speculating on the imminence of bankruptcy and the possibility of a literary career, and published his first important volume one year after Irving's *Sketch Book*. In the autobiographical account of his early years (which may be found in Godwin's *Life*, listed below) Bryant tells of his birth at Cummington, in the Berkshire Hills of Massachusetts, on November 3, 1794; of his father, a poetry-loving physician, his mother, descended from John and Priscilla Alden, and his maternal grandfather, a devout Calvinist in whose home he spent much of his childhood; of his experience in country activities — fishing, cornhusking, making maple syrup and cider; of his enthusiasm over Pope's translation of the *Iliad*, of his own first writing of verse, and his Popean political satire "The Embargo," published in 1808 and republished the next year; of his one year at Williams College, his law studies, and his admission to the bar; and of his reading just prior to the composition of "Thanatopsis."

The reception accorded "Thanatopsis," even in its early form (see note on poem), and the success of other early writings, lost Massachusetts a lawyer and gave America a man of letters. "Ah, Phillips, you have been imposed upon," said R. H. Dana to one of the editors of the *North American Review* who showed him the newly-submitted manuscript of "Thanatopsis." "No one on this side of the Atlantic is capable of writing such verses." In 1821 Bryant read the Phi Beta Kappa poem at Harvard and published his first important volume of verses. In 1825 he abandoned the practice of law and removed to New York to edit the *New York Review*. The following year he became assistant editor of the *New York Evening Post*, and three years later, in 1829, he became editor in chief and part owner.

Bryant's editorship of the *Evening Post* is a distinguished chapter in the history of American journalism. Says V. L. Parrington: "The journalist and critic who for fifty years sat in judgment on matters political and economic as well as cultural, who reflected in the *Evening Post* a refinement of taste and dignity of character before unequaled in American journalism, was of service to America quite apart from his contribution to our incipient poetry. He was the father of nineteenth-century American poetry. In the columns of the *Evening Post* the best liberalism of the times found a place, inspired and guided by Bryant's clear intelligence."

Bryant's poetical output was slight. He issued another volume in 1832, two years before his first visit to Europe, and in his later years found time to translate both the *Iliad* and *Odyssey* into English blank verse.

Parke Godwin's *A Biography of William Cullen Bryant*, 1883, is the standard life. Godwin's editions of Bryant's poems, 1883, and his prose works, 1889, are also standard. The Roslyn edition of the poems, 1903, is a good one-volume edition. For information on Bryant as journalist see *The Evening Post*, by Allan Nevins, 1922. There is a good volume of selections from Bryant, edited by T. McDowell, 1935, in the *AWS*. A critical revaluation by George Arms appears in the *University of Kansas City Review*, Spring, 1949.

Thanatopsis
(ca. 1811-21)

"My father brought home, I think from one of his visits to Boston, the *Remains of Henry Kirke White*, which had been republished in this country. I read the poems with great eagerness, and so often that I had committed several of them to memory, particularly the ode to the Rosemary. The melancholy tone which prevails in them deepened the interest with which I read them, for about that time I had, as young poets are apt to have, a liking for poetry of a querulous caste. I remember reading, at this time, that remarkable poem Blair's 'Grave,' and dwelling with great satisfaction upon its finer passages. I had the opportunity of comparing it with a poem on a kindred subject, also in blank verse, that of Bishop Porteus on 'Death,' and of observing how much the verse of the obscure Scottish minister excelled in originality of thought and vigor of expression that of the English prelate. In my father's library I found a small, thin volume of the miscellaneous poems of Southey, to which he had not called my attention, containing some of the finest of Southey's shorter poems. I read it greedily. Cowper's poems had been in my hands from an early age, and I now passed from his shorter poems, which are generally mere rhymed prose, to his 'Task,' the finer passages of which supplied a form of blank verse that captivated my admiration." The effect of this reading, and of Bryant's Calvinistic environment in the Berkshire forest, may be plainly seen in the poem that he now proceeded to write.

"Thanatopsis," or "view of death" (Greek θάνατος and ὄψις), was first published in the *North American Review*, September, 1817, in a shorter and inferior form beginning "Yet a few days" (line 18 of the present version) and ending "And make their bed with thee!" (line 66 of the present version). According to Bryant's own statement, it was written when he was but seventeen or eighteen years old, probably in his "solitary rambles in the woods." Though a sufficiently remarkable performance for a mere youth, it first became a masterpiece in the longer version published in 1821, when the poet was twenty-seven.

On the growth of the poem see "Thanatopsis, Old and New," by W. F. Johnson, *North American Review*, November, 1927, and "Bryant's Practice in Composition and Revision," by T. McDowell, *PMLA*, June, 1937.

To him who in the love of Nature holds
Communion with her visible forms, she speaks
A various language: for his gayer hours
She has a voice of gladness, and a smile
And eloquence of beauty; and she glides 5
Into his darker musings with a mild
And healing sympathy that steals away

Their sharpness ere he is aware. When thoughts
Of the last bitter hour come like a blight
Over thy spirit, and sad images 10
Of the stern agony and shroud and pall
And breathless darkness and the narrow house
Make thee to shudder and grow sick at heart,
Go forth under the open sky and list
To Nature's teachings, while from all around — 15
Earth and her waters and the depths of air —
Comes a still voice:

　　　　Yet a few days, and thee
The all-beholding sun shall see no more
In all his course; nor yet in the cold ground,
Where thy pale form was laid with many tears, 20
Nor in the embrace of ocean, shall exist
Thy image. Earth, that nourished thee shall claim
Thy growth, to be resolved to earth again
And, lost each human trace, surrendering up
Thine individual being, shalt thou go 25
To mix for ever with the elements,
To be a brother to the insensible rock
And to the sluggish clod, which the rude swain
Turns with his share and treads upon; the oak
Shall send his roots abroad and pierce thy mould. 30

Yet not to thine eternal resting-place
Shalt thou retire alone, nor couldst thou wish
Couch more magnificent. Thou shalt lie down
With patriarchs of the infant world, with kings,
The powerful of the earth, the wise, the good,
Fair forms, and hoary seers of ages past, 36
All in one mighty sepulchre. The hills
Rock-ribbed and ancient as the sun; the vales
Stretching in pensive quietness between;
The venerable woods, rivers that move 40
In majesty, and the complaining brooks
That make the meadows green; and, poured round all,
Old Ocean's gray and melancholy waste, —
Are but the solemn decorations all

Of the great tomb of man. The golden
       sun,   45
The planets, all the infinite host of heaven,
Are shining on the sad abodes of death,
Through the still lapse of ages. All that
       tread
The globe are but a handful to the tribes
That slumber in its bosom. Take the
       wings   50
Of morning, pierce the Barcan wilderness,
Or lose thyself in the continuous woods
Where rolls the Oregon, and hears no
       sound
Save his own dashings; yet the dead are
       there,
And millions in those solitudes, since first 55
The flight of years began, have laid them
       down
In their last sleep: the dead reign there
       alone.
So shalt thou rest; and what if thou with-
       draw
In silence from the living, and no friend
Take note of thy departure? All that
       breathe   60
Will share thy destiny. The gay will laugh
When thou art gone, the solemn brood of
       care
Plod on, and each one as before will chase
His favorite phantom; yet all these shall
       leave
Their mirth and their employments, and
       shall come   65
And make their bed with thee. As the long
       train
Of ages glide away, the sons of men —
The youth in life's green spring, and he who
       goes
In the full strength of years, matron and
       maid,
The speechless babe, and the gray-headed
       man —   70
Shall one by one be gathered to thy side
By those who in their turn shall follow them.

So live that when thy summons comes to
       join
The innumerable caravan which moves
To that mysterious realm where each shall
       take   75
His chamber in the silent halls of death,
Thou go not, like the quarry-slave at night,

Scourged to his dungeon, but, sustained and
       soothed
By an unfaltering trust, approach thy grave
Like one who wraps the drapery of his
       couch   80
About him and lies down to pleasant dreams.

The Yellow Violet
(1814)

While a law student at Bridgewater, Bryant became acquainted with the poems of Wordsworth
in *Lyrical Ballads.* "I shall never forget," Richard H. Dana wrote, "with what feeling my friend
Bryant, some years ago, described to me the effect
produced upon him by his meeting for the first
time with Wordsworth's ballads. He said that,
upon opening the book, a thousand springs seemed
to gush up at once in his heart, and the face of
Nature, of a sudden, to change into a strange freshness and life."
Compare this poem with Wordsworth's poems
on flowers, such as "To the Daisy" (beginning "In
youth from rock to rock I went").

When beechen buds begin to swell,
    And woods the bluebird's warble know,
The yellow violet's modest bell
    Peeps from the last year's leaves below.

Ere russet fields their green resume,   5
    Sweet flower, I love, in forest bare,
To meet thee, when thy faint perfume
    Alone is in the virgin air.

Of all her train, the hands of Spring
    First plant thee in the watery mould,   10
And I have seen thee blossoming
    Beside the snow-bank's edges cold.

Thy parent sun, who bade thee view
    Pale skies, and chilling moisture sip,
Has bathed thee in his own bright hue,   15
    And streaked with jet thy glowing lip.

Yet slight thy form, and low thy seat,
    And earthward bent thy gentle eye,
Unapt the passing view to meet,
    When loftier flowers are flaunting nigh. 20

Oft, in the sunless April day,
    Thy early smile has stayed my walk;
But midst the gorgeous blooms of May,
    I passed thee on thy humble stalk.

So they, who climb to wealth, forget   25
  The friends in darker fortunes tried.
I copied them — but I regret
  That I should ape the ways of pride.

And when again the genial hour
  Awakes the painted tribes of light,   30
I'll not o'erlook the modest flower
  That made the woods of April bright.

Inscription for the Entrance
to a Wood
(1815)

As first published in the *North American Review* in
1817, the poem ended at line 39. "The wood referred to was at Cummington, Mass., nearly in
front of the house now known as the Bryant Homestead" (P. Godwin).

Stranger, if thou hast learned a truth which
  needs
No school of long experience, that the world
Is full of guilt and misery, and hast seen
Enough of all its sorrows crimes and cares
To tire thee of it, enter this wild wood   5
And view the haunts of Nature. The calm
  shade
Shall bring a kindred calm; and the sweet
  breeze,
That makes the green leaves dance, shall
  waft a balm
To thy sick heart. Thou wilt find nothing
  here
Of all that pained thee in the haunts of
  men   10
And made thee loathe thy life. The primal
  curse
Fell, it is true, upon the unsinning earth,
But not in vengeance. God hath yoked to
  guilt
Her pale tormentor, misery. Hence these
  shades
Are still the abodes of gladness: the thick
  roof   15
Of green and stirring branches is alive
And musical with birds, that sing and sport
In wantonness of spirit; while, below,
The squirrel, with raised paws and form erect,
Chirps merrily. Throngs of insects in the
  shade   20
Try their thin wings and dance in the warm
  beam

That waked them into life. Even the green
  trees
Partake the deep contentment; as they bend
To the soft winds, the sun from the blue sky
Looks in and sheds a blessing on the scene.   25
Scarce less the cleft-born wild-flower seems
  to enjoy
Existence than the wingèd plunderer
That sucks its sweets. The mossy rocks
  themselves,
And the old and ponderous trunks of pros-
  trate trees
That lead from knoll to knoll a causey rude
Or bridge the sunken brook, and their dark
  roots,   31
With all their earth upon them, twisting high,
Breathe fixed tranquillity. The rivulet
Sends forth glad sounds, and, tripping o'er
  its bed
Of pebbly sands or leaping down the rocks,
Seems with continuous laughter to rejoice   36
In its own being. Softly tread the marge,
Lest from her midway perch thou scare the
  wren
That dips her bill in water. The cool wind,
That stirs the stream in play, shall come to
  thee,   40
Like one that loves thee nor will let thee pass
Ungreeted, and shall give its light embrace.

To a Waterfowl
(1815)

Written Dec. 15, 1815, in Plainfield, Mass.,
whither Bryant had walked to inquire into the opportunities offered there for beginning the practice
of law. Bryant "says in a letter that he felt, as he
walked up the hills, very forlorn and desolate indeed, not knowing what was to become of him in
the big world. . . . The sun had already set, leaving
behind it one of those brilliant seas of chrysolite and
opal which often flood the New England skies; and
while he was looking upon the rosy splendor with
rapt admiration, a solitary bird made wing along
the illuminated horizon. He watched the lone
wanderer until it was lost in the distance, asking
himself whither it had come and to what far home
it was flying. When he went to the house where
he was to stop for the night, his mind was still full
of what he had seen and felt, and he wrote those
lines, as imperishable as our language, 'The
Waterfowl' " (P. Godwin).

Whither, midst falling dew,
While glow the heavens with the last steps
  of day,

Far through their rosy depths dost thou
      pursue
      Thy solitary way?

Vainly the fowler's eye   5
Might mark thy distant flight to do thee
      wrong,
As, darkly seen against the crimson sky,
      Thy figure floats along.

Seek'st thou the plashy brink
Of weedy lake or marge of river wide,   10
Or where the rocking billows rise and sink
      On the chafed ocean-side?

There is a Power whose care
Teaches thy way along that pathless coast —
The desert and illimitable air, —   15
      Lone wandering, but not lost.

All day thy wings have fanned,
At that far height, the cold thin atmosphere,
Yet stoop not, weary, to the welcome land,
      Though the dark night is near.   20

And soon that toil shall end:
Soon shalt thou find a summer home, and
      rest,
And scream among thy fellows; reeds shall
      bend,
      Soon, o'er thy sheltered nest.

Thou'rt gone, the abyss of heaven   25
Hath swallowed up thy form; yet, on my
      heart
Deeply has sunk the lesson thou hast given,
      And shall not soon depart.

He who, from zone to zone,
Guides through the boundless sky thy certain
      flight,   30
In the long way, that I must tread alone,
      Will lead my steps aright.

I Cannot Forget with What Fervid Devotion

(1815–26)

"He became conscious of a certain change in
himself with respect to the external world such as is
often observed by subjective poets in their spiritual
experience as they pass from boyhood to manhood.
There was a feeling of having grown away from

something intimate and precious in his old joyless,
heedless association with nature. The scenes were
the same, but he had not the same power to identify himself with them as of old. Between him and
them was interposed a barrier of soilure and sophistication taken on through the worldly experience of life. Thought did not follow feeling with
the same exultant sense of inspiration as of old,
and the mood with which he viewed the objects
familiar to him since youth, was one of depression
and regretfulness. To these feelings, which have
received classical expression at the hands of Coleridge in the 'Lime-Tree Bower,' Bryant gives utterance a little rhetorically and awkwardly, but
not without a certain passionate sincerity, in the
poem entitled 'I Cannot Forget with What Fervid
Devotion' " (Bradley's Life).

I cannot forget with what fervid devotion
      I worshipped the visions of verse and of
      fame;
Each gaze at the glories of earth, sky, and
      ocean,
      To my kindled emotions, was wind over
      flame.

And deep were my musings in life's early
      blossom,   5
      Mid the twilight of mountain-groves wan-
      dering long;
How thrilled my young veins, and how
      throbbed my full bosom,
      When o'er me descended the spirit of song!

'Mong the deep-cloven fells that for ages had
      listened
      To the rush of the pebble-paved river
      between,   10
Where the kingfisher screamed and gray
      precipice glistened,
      All breathless with awe have I gazed on
      the scene;

Till I felt the dark power o'er my reveries
      stealing,
      From the gloom of the thicket that over
      me hung,
And the thoughts that awoke, in that rapture
      of feeling,   15
      Were formed into verse as they rose to my
      tongue.

Bright visions! I mixed with the world, and
      ye faded,
      No longer your pure rural worshipper now;

In the haunts your continual presence pervaded,
   Ye shrink from the signet of care on my
   brow.   20

In the old mossy groves on the breast of the
   mountain,
   In deep lonely glens where the waters complain,
By the shade of the rock, by the gush of the
   fountain,
   I seek your loved footsteps, but seek them
   in vain.

Oh, leave not forlorn and forever forsaken, 25
   Your pupil and victim to life and its tears!
But sometimes return, and in mercy awaken
   The glories ye showed to his earlier years.

O Fairest of the Rural Maids
(1820)

This poem Bryant addressed to his betrothed a
year before their marriage. It may be compared
with Wordsworth's "Three Years She Grew in Sun
and Shower."

O fairest of the rural maids!
Thy birth was in the forest shades;
Green boughs, and glimpses of the sky,
Were all that met thine infant eye.

Thy sports, thy wanderings, when a child, 5
Were ever in the sylvan wild;
And all the beauty of the place
Is in thy heart and on thy face.

The twilight of the trees and rocks
Is in the light shade of thy locks; 10
Thy step is as the wind, that weaves
Its playful way among the leaves.

Thine eyes are springs, in whose serene
And silent waters heaven is seen;
Their lashes are the herbs that look 15
On their young figures in the brook.

The forest depths, by foot unpressed,
Are not more sinless than thy breast;
The holy peace, that fills the air
Of those calm solitudes, is there. 20

I Broke the Spell that Held Me Long
(1824)

I broke the spell that held me long,
The dear, dear witchery of song.
I said, the poet's idle lore
Shall waste my prime of years no more,
For Poetry, though heavenly born, 5
Consorts with poverty and scorn.

I broke the spell — nor deemed its power
Could fetter me another hour.
Ah, thoughtless! how could I forget
Its causes were around me yet? 10
For wheresoe'er I looked, the while,
Was Nature's everlasting smile.

Still came and lingered on my sight
Of flowers and streams the bloom and light,
And glory of the stars and sun; — 15
And these and poetry are one.
They, ere the world had held me long,
Recalled me to the love of song.

Mutation
(1824)

They talk of short-lived pleasure — be it
   so —
   Pain dies as quickly: stern, hard-featured
   pain
Expires, and lets her weary prisoner go.
   The fiercest agonies have shortest reign;
   And after dreams of horror, comes again
The welcome morning with its rays of
   peace. 6
   Oblivion, softly wiping out the stain,
Makes the strong secret pangs of shame to
   cease:
Remorse is virtue's root; its fair increase
   Are fruits of innocence and blessedness: 10
Thus joy, o'erborne and bound, doth still
   release
   His young limbs from the chains that
   round him press.
Weep not that the world changes — did it
   keep
A stable, changeless state, 'twere cause indeed to weep.

A Forest Hymn

(1825)

The groves were God's first temples. Ere
    man learned
To hew the shaft, and lay the architrave,
And spread the roof above them — ere he
    framed
The lofty vault, to gather and roll back
The sound of anthems; in the darkling wood,
Amid the cool and silence, he knelt down, 6
And offered to the Mightiest solemn thanks
And supplication. For his simple heart
Might not resist the sacred influence
Which, from the stilly twilight of the place, 10
And from the gray old trunks that high in
    heaven
Mingled their mossy boughs, and from the
    sound
Of the invisible breath that swayed at once
All their green tops, stole over him, and
    bowed
His spirit with the thought of boundless
    power 15
And inaccessible majesty. Ah, why
Should we, in the world's riper years, neglect
God's ancient sanctuaries, and adore
Only among the crowd, and under roofs
That our frail hands have raised? Let me,
    at least, 20
Here, in the shadow of this aged wood,
Offer one hymn — thrice happy, if it find
Acceptance in His ear.
                Father, thy hand
Hath reared these venerable columns, thou
Didst weave this verdant roof. Thou didst
    look down 25
Upon the naked earth, and, forthwith, rose
All these fair ranks of trees. They, in thy
    sun,
Budded, and shook their green leaves in thy
    breeze,
And shot toward heaven. The century-
    living crow
Whose birth was in their tops, grew old and
    died 30
Among their branches, till at last they stood,
As now they stand, massy and tall and dark,
Fit shrine for humble worshipper to hold
Communion with his Maker. These dim
    vaults,

These winding isles, of human pomp or
    pride 35
Report not; no fantastic carvings show
The boast of our vain race to change the form
Of thy fair works. But thou art here — thou
    fill'st
The solitude. Thou art in the soft winds,
That run along the summit of these trees 40
In music; thou art in the cooler breath,
That from the inmost darkness of the place,
Comes, scarcely felt; the barky trunks, the
    ground,
The fresh moist ground, are all instinct with
    thee.
Here is continual worship: Nature, here, 45
In the tranquillity that thou dost love,
Enjoys thy presence. Noiselessly around,
From perch to perch, the solitary bird
Passes; and yon clear spring, that midst its
    herbs
Wells softly forth and, wandering, steeps the
    roots 50
Of half the mighty forest, tells no tale
Of all the good it does. Thou hast not left
Thyself without a witness, in these shades.
Of thy perfections: grandeur, strength, and
    grace
Are here to speak of thee. This mighty
    oak, 55
By whose immovable stem I stand and seem
Almost annihilated — not a prince,
In all that proud old world beyond the deep,
E'er wore his crown as loftily as he
Wears the green coronal of leaves with
    which 60
Thy hand has graced him. Nestled at his
    root
Is beauty such as blooms not in the glare
Of the broad sun: that delicate forest flower,
With scented breath and look so like a smile,
Seems, as it issues from the shapeless mould,
An emanation of the indwelling Life, 66
A visible token of the upholding Love,
That are the soul of this great universe.

My heart is awed within me when I think
Of the great miracle that still goes on, 70
In silence, round me — the perpetual work
Of thy creation, finished, yet renewed
Forever. Written on thy works I read
The lesson of thy own eternity:
Lo, all grow old and die; but see, again, 75

How on the faltering footsteps of decay
Youth presses, ever gay and beautiful youth
In all its beautiful forms. These lofty trees
Wave not less proudly that their ancestors
Moulder beneath them. Oh, there is not
    lost   80
One of earth's charms: upon her bosom yet,
After the flight of untold centuries,
The freshness of her far beginning lies
And yet shall lie. Life mocks the idle hate
Of his arch-enemy, Death; yea, seats him-
    self   85
Upon the tyrant's throne, the sepulchre,
And of the triumphs of his ghastly foe
Makes his own nourishment; for he came
    forth
From thine own bosom, and shall have no
    end.

    There have been holy men who hid them-
    selves   90
Deep in the woody wilderness, and gave
Their lives to thought and prayer, till they
    outlived
The generation born with them, nor seemed
Less aged than the hoary trees and rocks
Around them; and there have been holy
    men   95
Who deemed it were not well to pass life thus.
But let me often to these solitudes
Retire, and in thy presence reassure
My feeble virtue. Here its enemies,
The passions, at thy plainer footsteps
    shrink   100
And tremble and are still. O God! when
    thou
Dost scare the world with tempests, set on
    fire
The heavens with falling thunderbolts, or fill
With all the waters of the firmament
The swift dark whirlwind that uproots the
    woods   105
And drowns the villages; when, at thy call,
Uprises the great deep and throws himself
Upon the continent and overwhelms
Its cities; who forgets not, at the sight
Of these tremendous tokens of thy power, 110
His pride, and lays his strifes and follies by?
Oh, from these sterner aspects of thy face
Spare me and mine, nor let us need the wrath
Of the mad unchained elements to teach
Who rules them. Be it ours to meditate 115

In these calm shades thy milder majesty,
And to the beautiful order of thy works
Learn to conform the order of our lives.

To the Fringed Gentian
(1829)

Thou blossom bright with autumn dew,
And colored with the heaven's own blue,
That openest when the quiet light
Succeeds the keen and frosty night.

Thou comest not when violets lean   5
O'er wandering brooks and springs unseen,
Or columbines, in purple dressed,
Nod o'er the ground-bird's hidden nest.

Thou waitest late, and com'st alone,
When woods are bare and birds are flown, 10
And frosts and shortening days portend
The aged year is near his end.

Then doth thy sweet and quiet eye
Look through its fringes to the sky,
Blue — blue — as if that sky let fall   15
A flower from its cerulean wall.

I would that thus, when I shall see
The hour of death draw near to me,
Hope blossoming within my heart,
May look to heaven as I depart.   20

The Prairies
(1832)

    In 1832 Bryant crossed the Allegheny Moun-
tains by stage, went down the Ohio River by
steamboat, and traveled over Illinois by wagon
and on horseback.

These are the gardens of the Desert, these
The unshorn fields, boundless and beautiful,
For which the speech of England has no
    name —
The Prairies. I behold them for the first,
And my heart swells while the dilated sight 5
Takes in the encircling vastness. Lo, they
    stretch
In airy undulations, far away,
As if the Ocean, in his gentlest swell,
Stood still, with all his rounded billows fixed
And motionless forever. Motionless? 10

No, they are all unchained again: the clouds
Sweep over with their shadows, and, be-
    neath,
The surface rolls and fluctuates to the eye;
Dark hollows seem to glide along and chase
The sunny ridges. Breezes of the South, 15
Who toss the golden and the flame-like
    flowers,
And pass the prairie-hawk that, poised on
    high,
Flaps his broad wings, yet moves not, ye
    have played
Among the palms of Mexico and vines
Of Texas, and have crisped the limpid
    brooks 20
That from the fountains of Sonora glide
Into the calm Pacific: have ye fanned
A nobler or a lovelier scene than this?
Man hath no part in all this glorious work:
The hand that built the firmament hath
    heaved 25
And smoothed these verdant swells, and
    sown their slopes
With herbage, planted them with island
    groves,
And hedged them round with forests. Fit-
    ting floor
For this magnificent temple of the sky,
With flowers whose glory and whose multi-
    tude 30
Rival the constellations! The great heavens
Seem to stoop down upon the scene in love —
A nearer vault, and of a tenderer blue,
Than that which bends above our Eastern
    hills.

    As o'er the verdant waste I guide my steed,
Among the high rank grass that sweeps his
    sides, 36
The hollow beating of his footstep seems
A sacrilegious sound. I think of those
Upon whose rest he tramples: are they here,
The dead of other days? and did the dust 40
Of these fair solitudes once stir with life
And burn with passion? Let the mighty
    mounds
That overlook the rivers, or that rise
In the dim forest crowded with old oaks,
Answer. A race that long has passed away 45
Built them; a disciplined and populous race
Heaped, with long toil, the earth, while yet
    the Greek

Was hewing the Pentelicus to forms
Of symmetry, and rearing on its rock
The glittering Parthenon. These ample
    fields 50
Nourished their harvests; here their herds
    were fed,
When haply by their stalls the bison lowed,
And bowed his manèd shoulder to the yoke.
All day this desert murmured with their toils,
Till twilight blushed, and lovers walked, and
    wooed 55
In a forgotten language, and old tunes,
From instruments of unremembered form,
Gave the soft winds a voice. The red man
    came,
The roaming hunter tribes, warlike and fierce,
And the mound-builders vanished from the
    earth. 60
The solitude of centuries untold
Has settled where they dwelt. The prairie-
    wolf
Hunts in their meadows, and his fresh-dug
    den
Yawns by my path. The gopher mines the
    ground
Where stood their swarming cities. All is
    gone: 65
All save the piles of earth that hold their
    bones;
The platforms where they worshipped un-
    known gods;
The barriers which they builded from the
    soil
To keep the foe at bay, till o'er the walls
The wild beleaguerers broke, and, one by
    one, 70
The strongholds of the plain were forced and
    heaped
With corpses. The brown vultures of the
    wood
Flocked to those vast uncovered sepulchres,
And sat, unscared and silent, at their feast.
Haply some solitary fugitive, 75
Lurking in marsh and forest, till the sense
Of desolation and of fear became
Bitterer than death, yielded himself to die.
Man's better nature triumphed then: kind
    words
Welcomed and soothed him; the rude con-
    querors 80
Seated the captive with their chiefs; he chose
A bride among their maidens, and at length

Seemed to forget — yet ne'er forgot — the
    wife
Of his first love, and her sweet little ones
Butchered amid their shrieks, with all his
    race.   85

    Thus change the forms of being. Thus
      arise
Races of living things glorious in strength,
And perish, as the quickening breath of God
Fills them or is withdrawn. The red man,
    too,
Has left the blooming wilds he ranged so
    long,   90
And, nearer to the Rocky Mountains, sought
A wilder hunting-ground. The beaver builds
No longer by these streams, but far away,
On waters whose blue surface ne'er gave
    back
The white man's face, among Missouri's
    springs,   95
And pools whose issues swell the Oregon,
He rears his little Venice. In these plains
The bison feeds no more: twice twenty
    leagues
Beyond remotest smoke of hunter's camp,
Roams the majestic brute, in herds that
    shake   100
The earth with thundering steps — yet here
    I meet

His ancient footprints stamped beside the
    pool.

    Still this great solitude is quick with life.
Myriads of insects, gaudy as the flowers
They flutter over, gentle quadrupeds,   105
And birds that scarce have learned the fear
    of man,
Are here, and sliding reptiles of the ground,
Startlingly beautiful. The graceful deer
Bounds to the wood at my approach. The
    bee,
A more adventurous colonist than man,   110
With whom he came across the eastern deep,
Fills the savannas with his murmurings,
And hides his sweets, as in the golden age,
Within the hollow oak. I listen long
To his domestic hum, and think I hear   115
The sound of that advancing multitude
Which soon shall fill these deserts: from the
    ground
Comes up the laugh of children, the soft voice
Of maidens, and the sweet and solemn hymn
Of Sabbath worshippers; the low of herds   120
Blends with the rustling of the heavy grain
Over the dark-brown furrows. All at once
A fresher wind sweeps by and breaks my
    dream,
And I am in the wilderness alone.

EDGAR ALLAN POE (1809–1849)

Edgar Poe was born in Boston, January 19, 1809, to parents who were itinerant
actors. His parents died less than three years later, and he was taken into the Richmond home of Mr. and Mrs. John Allan, whose name he later adopted. Although
Poe's relation to them was never happy, they opened educational opportunities to the
orphan. From 1815 to 1820 he studied at schools in England and during the next
five years in Richmond. In February, 1826, he entered the University of Virginia,
soon acquired heavy gambling debts and a reputation as a hard drinker, and was
taken out of the University by Allan in December of the same year. Over the settlement of the debts they had the last and bitterest of many quarrels, and in 1827 Poe
enlisted, in Boston, in the United States battery of artillery. Another result of the
trip to Boston was *Tamerlane and Other Poems* "by a Bostonian," published 1827.

Within two years Poe had risen to the rank of sergeant-major, and had found time
to produce another volume of verse, *Al Aaraaf, Tamerlane, and Minor Poems* (1829).
Because of his honorable record in the battery he was recommended to a cadetship
at West Point, where he matriculated July 1, 1830. Less than eight months later he

secured his dismissal when he was disowned by his foster-father. From this time Poe was dependent on his pen for a livelihood.

A new volume of poems issued in 1831 showed a surer touch. The next four years he spent mostly in Baltimore, writing poems and stories. In 1833 the *Baltimore Saturday Visitor* awarded to him a prize of $100 for the best short story submitted to its contest. It was one of his few financial successes ("The Raven," in 1844, brought him much fame and ten dollars in cash). He was never free from want and poverty, and his personal habits were not conducive to conserving what he did make. In 1835 he removed to Richmond and became editor of the *Southern Literary Messenger*, for which publication his contributions won a great reputation. In 1836 he married his cousin, Virginia Clemm, a girl of thirteen. The next year he lost his position on the *Messenger*, because of frequent absence usually due to alcohol.

He spent a year in New York, then settled in Philadelphia, and became editor of *Graham's Magazine* (1841–42). His *Tales of the Grotesque and Arabesque* were published in 1840, and in 1843 "The Gold Bug" won him another $100 prize. His wife was an invalid and he was drinking more than ever when, soon after, he took his family to New York to seek new opportunities.

The Raven and Other Poems, 1845, made him famous, and in 1845 and 1846 (until the failure of the journal) he was editor of the *Broadway Journal*. In 1846 he contributed the "Literati" sections to *Godey's Lady's Book*. His wife died in 1847. The rest of his story is one of poverty, intoxication, mistaken love affairs, and, frequently, fine poems. In 1849 he visited Richmond for the last time, and became engaged to a sweetheart of his youth, then a wealthy widow. On his way south for the marriage, he celebrated the coming event with some acquaintances in Baltimore, was found unconscious on the street, and died four days later, October 7, 1849.

Much of Poe's writing is as sombre and tragic as his life. "The saddest and the strangest figure in American literary history," Campbell called him in *CHAL*. "Few writers have lived a life so full of struggle and disappointment, and none have lived and died more completely out of sympathy with their times . . . the widest differences of opinion have existed as to his place and his achievements. But there are few today who will not readily concede to him a place among the foremost writers of America, whether in prose or in verse, and there are not wanting those who account him one of the two or three writers of indisputable genius that America has produced."

The best collected edition of Poe is the Virginia edition, edited in 17 volumes by J. A. Harrison in 1902. The best edition of the poems alone is that by Killis Campbell, 1917. There is a good biography in the American Men of Letters series by George E. Woodberry, 1885, which was expanded into a 2-volume work, *The Life of Edgar Allan Poe*, 1909, admirably judicious and well written. A work of scholarship, thorough and cautious, is A. H. Quinn's *Edgar Allan Poe: A Critical Biography*, 1941. A number of Killis Campbell's learned articles were collected in *The Mind of Poe and Other Studies*, 1933. Poe's literary theory is the subject of the first chapter in N. Foerster's *American Criticism*, 1928. W. C. Brownell's study in *American Prose Masters*, 1909, is an acute criticism. Poe's letters have been collected by J. W. Ostrom, 1948.

Note. In addition to the following selected poems, see the poems that Poe included in his tales: "The Conqueror Worm," page 184, and "The Haunted Palace," pages 193–194.

Romance

(1829)

Romance, who loves to nod and sing,
With drowsy head and folded wing,
Among the green leaves as they shake
Far down within some shadowy lake,
To me a painted paroquet   5
Hath been — a most familiar bird —
Taught me my alphabet to say —
To lisp my very earliest words
While in the wild wood I did lie,
A child — with a most knowing eye.   10

Of late, eternal Condor years
So shake the very Heaven on high
With tumult as they thunder by,
I have no time for idle cares
Through gazing on the unquiet sky.   15
And when an hour with calmer wings
Its down upon my spirit flings —
That little time with lyre and rhyme
To while away — forbidden things!
My heart would feel to be a crime   20
Unless it trembled with the strings.

Sonnet — To Science

(1829)

Science! true daughter of Old Time thou art!
Who alterest all things with thy peering eyes.
Why preyest thou thus upon the poet's heart
Vulture, whose wings are dull realities?
How should he love thee? or how deem thee
     wise,   5
Who wouldst not leave him in his wandering
To seek for treasure in the jewelled skies,
Albeit he soared with an undaunted wing?
Hast thou not dragged Diana from her car?
And driven the Hamadryad from the wood   10
To seek a shelter in some happier star?
Hast thou not torn the Naiad from her flood,
The Elfin from the green grass, and from me
The summer dream beneath the tamarind
     tree?

A Dream Within a Dream

(1827, 1829, 1849)

Take this kiss upon the brow!
And, in parting from you now,
Thus much let me avow —

You are not wrong, who deem
That my days have been a dream;   5
Yet if hope has flown away
In a night, or in a day,
In a vision, or in none,
Is it therefore the less *gone?*
All that we see or seem   10
Is but a dream within a dream.

I stand amid the roar
Of a surf-tormented shore,
And I hold within my hand
Grains of the golden sand —   15
How few! yet how they creep
Through my fingers to the deep,
While I weep — while I weep!
O God! can I not grasp
Them with a tighter clasp?   20
O God! can I not save
One from the pitiless wave?
Is *all* that we see or seem
But a dream within a dream?

To Helen

(1831)

According to Poe's own statement, this poem was inspired by his love for Mrs. Jane Stith Stanard, of Richmond, whose home he had visited when a boy. "The truest, tenderest of this world's most womanly souls, and an angel to my forlorn and darkened nature," she became the object of "the first purely ideal love of my soul." After her death in 1824, the youth disconsolately cherished her memory.

Helen, thy beauty is to me
     Like those Nicéan barks of yore,
That gently, o'er a perfumed sea,
     The weary, way-worn wanderer bore
     To his own native shore.   5

On desperate seas long wont to roam,
     Thy hyacinth hair, thy classic face,
Thy Naiad airs have brought me home
     To the glory that was Greece,
     And the grandeur that was Rome.   10

Lo! in yon brilliant window-niche
     How statue-like I see thee stand,
The agate lamp within thy hand!
     Ah, Psyche, from the regions which
     Are Holy-Land!   15

Israfel
(1831)

"And the angel Israfel, whose heart-strings are a lute, and who has the sweetest voice of all God's creatures. — KORAN" (Poe's note, 1845). It may be noted that Poe is here quoting (and garbling), not the Koran itself, but Sale's *Preliminary Discourse* on the Koran, section IV: "the angel Israfil, who has the most melodious voice of all God's creatures." The interpolated phrase "whose heart-strings are a lute" Poe probably derived from Béranger's "Le Refus":
> "Son cœur est un luth suspendu;
>   Sitôt qu'on le touche, il résonne,"
— the same lines that he used for the motto of "The Fall of the House of Usher."

In Heaven a spirit doth dwell
    "Whose heart-strings are a lute;"
None sing so wildly well
As the angel Israfel,
And the giddy stars (so legends tell)   5
Ceasing their hymns, attend the spell
    Of his voice, all mute.

Tottering above
    In her highest noon,
    The enamoured moon   10
Blushes with love,
    While, to listen, the red levin
    (With the rapid Pleiads, even,
    Which were seven,)
    Pauses in Heaven.   15

And they say (the starry choir
    And the other listening things)
That Israfeli's fire
Is owing to that lyre
    By which he sits and sings —   20
The trembling living wire
Of those unusual strings.

But the skies that angel trod,
    Where deep thoughts are a duty —
Where Love's a grown-up God —   25
    Where the Houri glances are
Imbued with all the beauty
    Which we worship in a star.

Therefore, thou art not wrong,
    Israfeli, who despisest   30
An unimpassioned song;
To thee the laurels belong,

Best bard, because the wisest!
Merrily live, and long!

The ecstasies above   35
    With thy burning measures suit —
Thy grief, thy joy, thy hate, thy love,
    With the fervour of thy lute —
    Well may the stars be mute!

Yes, Heaven is thine; but this   40
    Is a world of sweets and sours;
    Our flowers are merely — flowers,
And the shadow of thy perfect bliss
    Is the sunshine of ours.

If I could dwell   45
Where Israfel
    Hath dwelt, and he where I,
He might not sing so wildly well
    A mortal melody,
While a bolder note than this might swell 50
    From my lyre within the sky.

The City in the Sea
(1831, 1845)

Lo! Death has reared himself a throne
In a strange city lying alone
Far down within the dim West,
Where the good and the bad and the worst
        and the best
Have gone to their eternal rest.   5
There shrines and palaces and towers
(Time-eaten towers that tremble not!)
Resemble nothing that is ours.
Around, by lifting winds forgot,
Resignedly beneath the sky   10
The melancholy waters lie.

No rays from the holy heaven come down
On the long night-time of that town;
But light from out the lurid sea
Streams up the turrets silently —   15
Gleams up the pinnacles far and free —
Up domes — up spires — up kingly halls —
Up fanes — up Babylon-like walls —
Up shadowy long-forgotten bowers
Of sculptured ivy and stone flowers —   20
Up many and many a marvellous shrine
Whose wreathèd friezes intertwine
The viol, the violet, and the vine.

Resignedly beneath the sky
The melancholy waters lie.   25
So blend the turrets and shadows there
That all seem pendulous in air,
While from a proud tower in the town
Death looks gigantically down.

There open fanes and gaping graves   30
Yawn level with the luminous waves;
But not the riches there that lie
In each idol's diamond eye —
Not the gayly-jewelled dead
Tempt the waters from their bed;   35
For no ripples curl, alas!
Along that wilderness of glass —
No swellings tell that winds may be
Upon some far-off happier sea —
No heavings hint that winds have been   40
On seas less hideously serene.

But lo, a stir is in the air!
The wave — there is a movement there!
As if the towers had thrust aside,
In slightly sinking, the dull tide —   45
As if their tops had feebly given
A void within the filmy Heaven.
The waves have now a redder glow —
The hours are breathing faint and low —
And when, amid no earthly moans,   50
Down, down that town shall settle hence,
Hell, rising from a thousand thrones,
Shall do it reverence.

The Sleeper

(1831)

At midnight, in the month of June,
I stand beneath the mystic moon.
An opiate vapor, dewy, dim,
Exhales from out her golden rim,
And, softly dripping, drop by drop,   5
Upon the quiet mountain top,
Steals drowsily and musically
Into the universal valley.
The rosemary nods upon the grave;
The lily lolls upon the wave;   10
Wrapping the fog about its breast,
The ruin moulders into rest;
Looking like Lethe, see! the lake
A conscious slumber seems to take,
And would not, for the world, awake.   15

All Beauty sleeps! — and lo! where lies
Irene, with her Destinies!

Oh, lady bright! can it be right —
This window open to the night?
The wanton airs, from the tree-top,   20
Laughingly through the lattice drop —
The bodiless airs, a wizard rout,
Flit through thy chamber in and out,
And wave the curtain canopy
So fitfully — so fearfully —   25
Above the closed and fringèd lid
'Neath which thy slumb'ring soul lies hid,
That, o'er the floor and down the wall,
Like ghosts the shadows rise and fall!
Oh, lady dear, has thou no fear?   30
Why and what art thou dreaming here?
Sure thou art come o'er far-off seas,
A wonder to these garden trees!
Strange is thy pallor! strange thy dress!
Strange, above all, thy length of tress,   35
And this all solemn silentness!

The lady sleeps! Oh, may her sleep,
Which is enduring, so be deep!
Heaven have her in its sacred keep!
This chamber changed for one more holy,   40
This bed for one more melancholy,
I pray to God that she may lie
Forever with unopened eye,
While the pale sheeted ghosts go by!
My love, she sleeps! Oh, may her sleep,   45
As it is lasting, so be deep!
Soft may the worms about her creep!
Far in the forest, dim and old,
For her may some tall vault unfold —
Some vault that oft hath flung its black   50
And wingèd panels fluttering back,
Triumphant, o'er the crested palls,
Of her grand family funerals —
Some sepulchre, remote, alone,
Against whose portal she hath thrown,   55
In childhood, many an idle stone —
Some tomb from out whose sounding door
She ne'er shall force an echo more,
Thrilling to think, poor child of sin!
It was the dead who groaned within.   60

Lenore

(1831, 1843, 1845)

To whom — if to any one — Poe refers, is not
known. The name Lenore, first used in the text of

1843, may have been derived from Bürger's famous romantic ballad "Lenore," which Scott and others had translated. The first and third stanzas are spoken by the relatives of the dead Lenore, the second and fourth by her lover, Guy De Vere.

Ah, broken is the golden bowl! the spirit
    flown forever!
Let the bell toll! — a saintly soul floats on the
    Stygian river;
And, Guy De Vere, hast *thou* no tear? —
    weep now or never more!
See! on yon drear and rigid bier low lies thy
    love, Lenore!
Come! let the burial rite be read — the fu-
    neral song be sung! —   5
An anthem for the queenliest dead that ever
    died so young —
A dirge for her the doubly dead in that she
    died so young.

"Wretches! ye loved her for her wealth and
    hated her for her pride,
"And when she fell in feeble health, ye
    blessed her — that she died!
"How *shall* the ritual, then, be read? — the
    requiem how be sung   10
"By you — by yours, the evil eye, — by
    yours, the slanderous tongue
"That did to death the innocence that died,
    and died so young?"

Peccavimus; but rave not thus! and let a Sab-
    bath song
Go up to God so solemnly the dead may feel
    no wrong!
The sweet Lenore hath "gone before," with
    Hope, that flew beside,   15
Leaving thee wild for the dear child that
    should have been thy bride —
For her, the fair and *debonair*, that now so
    lowly lies,
The life upon her yellow hair but not within
    her eyes —
The life still there, upon her hair — the death
    upon her eyes.

"Avaunt! to-night my heart is light. No
    dirge will I upraise.   20
"But waft the angel on her flight with a
    pæan of old days!
"Let *no* bell toll! — lest her sweet soul, amid
    its hallowed mirth,

"Should catch the note, as it doth float up
    from the damnèd Earth.
"To friends above, from fiends below, the
    indignant ghost is riven —
"From Hell unto a high estate far up within
    the Heaven —   25
"From grief and groan, to a golden throne,
    beside the King of Heaven."

The Valley of Unrest
(1831, 1845)

Once it smiled a silent dell
Where the people did not dwell;
They had gone unto the wars,
Trusting to the mild-eyed stars,
Nightly, from their azure towers,   5
To keep watch above the flowers,
In the midst of which all day
The red sun-light lazily lay.
Now each visiter shall confess
The sad valley's restlessness.   10
Nothing there is motionless —
Nothing save the airs that brood
Over the magic solitude.
Ah, by no wind are stirred those trees
That palpitate like the chill seas   15
Around the misty Hebrides!
Ah, by no wind those clouds are driven
That rustle through the unquiet Heaven
Uneasily, from morn till even,
Over the violets there that lie   20
In myriad types of the human eye —
Over the lilies there that wave
And weep above a nameless grave!
They wave: — from out their fragrant tops
Eternal dews come down in drops.   25
They weep: — from off their delicate stems
Perennial tears descend in gems.

The Coliseum
(1833)

Type of the antique Rome! Rich reliquary
Of lofty contemplation left to Time
By buried centuries of pomp and power!
At length — at length — after so many days
Of weary pilgrimage and burning thirst,   5
(Thirst for the springs of lore that in thee lie,)
I kneel, an altered and an humble man,
Amid thy shadows, and so drink within
My very soul thy grandeur, gloom, and glory!

Vastness! and Age! and Memories of Eld! 10
Silence! and Desolation! and dim Night!
I feel ye now — I feel ye in your strength —
O spells more sure than e'er Judæan king
Taught in the gardens of Gethsemane!
O charms more potent than the rapt Chaldee
Ever drew down from out the quiet stars! 16

Here, where a hero fell, a column falls!
Here, where the mimic eagle glared in gold,
A midnight vigil holds the swarthy bat!
Here, where the dames of Rome their gilded
    hair 20
Waved to the wind, now wave the reed and
    thistle!
Here, where on golden throne the monarch
    lolled,
Glides, spectre-like, unto his marble home,
Lit by the wan light of the hornèd moon,
The swift and silent lizard of the stones! 25

But stay! these walls — these ivy-clad ar-
    cades —
These mouldering plinths — these sad and
    blackened shafts —
These vague entablatures — this crumbling
    frieze —
These shattered cornices — this wreck — this
    ruin —
These stones — alas! these gray stones — are
    they all — 30
All of the famed and the colossal left
By the corrosive Hours to Fate and me?

"Not all" — the Echoes answer me — "not
    all!
Prophetic sounds and loud, arise forever
From us, and from all Ruin, unto the wise, 35
As melody from Memnon to the Sun.
We rule the hearts of mightiest men — we
    rule
With a despotic sway all giant minds.
We are not impotent — we pallid stones.
Not all our power is gone — not all our
    fame — 40
Not all the magic of our high renown —
Not all the wonder that encircles us —
Not all the mysteries that in us lie —
Not all the memories that hang upon
And cling around about us as a garment, 45
Clothing us in a robe of more than glory."

To One in Paradise
(ca. 1835)

Thou wast that all to me, love,
    For which my soul did pine —
A green isle in the sea, love,
    A fountain and a shrine,
All wreathed with fairy fruits and flowers, 5
    And all the flowers were mine.

Ah, dream too bright to last!
    Ah, starry Hope! that didst arise
But to be overcast!
    A voice from out the Future cries, 10
"On! on!" — but o'er the Past
    (Dim gulf!) my spirit hovering lies
Mute, motionless, aghast!

For, alas! alas! with me
    The light of Life is o'er! 15
No more — no more — no more —
    (Such language holds the solemn sea
To the sands upon the shore)
    Shall bloom the thunder-blasted tree,
Or the stricken eagle soar! 20

And all my days are trances,
    And all my nightly dreams
Are where thy grey eye glances,
    And where thy footstep gleams —
In what ethereal dances, 25
    By what eternal streams.

Dream-Land
(1844)

By a route obscure and lonely,
Haunted by ill angels only,
Where an Eidolon, named NIGHT,
On a black throne reigns upright,
I have reached these lands but newly 5
From an ultimate dim Thule —
From a wild weird clime that lieth, sublime,
    Out of SPACE — out of TIME.

Bottomless vales and boundless floods,
And chasms, and caves, and Titan woods,
With forms that no man can discover 11
For the tears that drip all over;
Mountains toppling evermore
Into seas without a shore;

Seas that restlessly aspire,   15
Surging, unto skies of fire;
Lakes that endlessly outspread
Their lone waters — lone and dead, —
Their still waters — still and chilly
With the snows of the lolling lily.   20

By the lakes that thus outspread
Their lone waters, lone and dead, —
Their sad waters, sad and chilly
With the snows of the lolling lily, —
By the mountains — near the river   25
Murmuring lowly, murmuring ever, —
By the grey woods, — by the swamp
Where the toad and the newt encamp, —
By the dismal tarns and pools
    Where dwell the Ghouls, —   30
By each spot the most unholy —
In each nook most melancholy, —
There the traveller meets, aghast,
Sheeted Memories of the Past —
Shrouded forms that start and sigh   35
As they pass the wanderer by —
White-robed forms of friends long given,
In agony, to the Earth — and Heaven.

For the heart whose woes are legion
'Tis a peaceful, soothing region —   40
For the spirit that walks in shadow
'Tis — oh 'tis an Eldorado!
But the traveller, travelling through it,
May not — dare not openly view it;
Never its mysteries are exposed   45
To the weak human eye unclosed;
So wills its King, who hath forbid
The uplifting of the fringèd lid;
And thus the sad Soul that here passes
Beholds it but through darkened glasses.   50

By a route obscure and lonely,
Haunted by ill angels only,
Where an Eidolon, named NIGHT,
On a black throne reigns upright,
I have wandered home but newly   55
From this ultimate dim Thule.

The Raven
(ca. 1842–44)

Poe's account of the composition of this poem
Is given in the prose essay "The Philosophy of

Composition" (see page 215). To what extent
this account is faithful to the facts is quite uncertain.

Once upon a midnight dreary, while I pondered, weak and weary,
Over many a quaint and curious volume of forgotten lore —
While I nodded, nearly napping, suddenly there came a tapping,
As of some one gently rapping, rapping at my chamber door.
"'Tis some visiter," I muttered, "tapping at my chamber door —
    Only this and nothing more."

Ah, distinctly I remember it was in the bleak December;
And each separate dying ember wrought its ghost upon the floor.
Eagerly I wished the morrow; — vainly I had sought to borrow
From my books surcease of sorrow — sorrow for the lost Lenore —   10
For the rare and radiant maiden whom the angels name Lenore —
    Nameless *here* for evermore.

And the silken, sad, uncertain rustling of each purple curtain
Thrilled me — filled me with fantastic terrors never felt before;
So that now, to still the beating of my heart, I stood repeating   15
"'Tis some visiter entreating entrance at my chamber door —
Some late visiter entreating entrance at my chamber door; —
    This it is and nothing more."

Presently my soul grew stronger; hesitating then no longer,
"Sir," said I, "or Madam, truly your forgiveness I implore;   20
But the fact is I was napping, and so gently you came rapping,
And so faintly you came tapping, tapping at my chamber door,
That I scarce was sure I heard you" — here I opened wide the door; —
    Darkness there and nothing more.

Deep into that darkness peering, long I stood there wondering, fearing,   25

Doubting, dreaming dreams no mortal ever
      dared to dream before;
But the silence was unbroken, and the still-
      ness gave no token,
And the only word there spoken was the
      whispered word, "Lenore!"
This I whispered, and an echo murmured
      back the word "Lenore!"
      Merely this and nothing more.   30

Back into the chamber turning, all my soul
      within me burning,
Soon again I heard a tapping somewhat
      louder than before.
"Surely," said I, "surely that is something at
      my window lattice;
Let me see, then, what thereat is, and this
      mystery explore —
Let my heart be still a moment and this mys-
      tery explore; —   35
      'Tis the wind and nothing more!"

Open here I flung the shutter, when, with
      many a flirt and flutter
In there stepped a stately Raven of the
      saintly days of yore.
Not the least obeisance made he; not a min-
      ute stopped or stayed he;
But, with mien of lord or lady, perched above
      my chamber door —   40
Perched upon a bust of Pallas just above my
      chamber door —
      Perched, and sat, and nothing more.

Then this ebony bird beguiling my sad fancy
      into smiling,
By the grave and stern decorum of the counte-
      nance it wore,
"Though thy crest be shorn and shaven,
      thou," I said, "art sure no craven,   45
Ghastly grim and ancient Raven wandering
      from the Nightly shore —
Tell me what thy lordly name is on the
      Night's Plutonian shore!"
      Quoth the Raven, "Nevermore."

Much I marvelled this ungainly fowl to hear
      discourse so plainly,
Though its answer little meaning — little
      relevancy bore;   50
For we cannot help agreeing that no living
      human being

Ever yet was blessed with seeing bird above
      his chamber door —
Bird or beast upon the sculptured bust above
      his chamber door,
      With such name as "Nevermore."

But the Raven, sitting lonely on the placid
      bust, spoke only   55
That one word, as if his soul in that one word
      he did outpour.
Nothing farther then he uttered — not a
      feather then he fluttered —
Till I scarcely more than muttered "Other
      friends have flown before —
On the morrow *he* will leave me, as my hopes
      have flown before."
      Then the bird said "Nevermore."   60

Startled at the stillness broken by reply so
      aptly spoken,
"Doubtless," said I, "what it utters is its only
      stock and store
Caught from some unhappy master whom
      unmerciful Disaster
Followed fast and followed faster till his songs
      one burden bore —
Till the dirges of his Hope that melancholy
      burden bore   65
      Of 'Never — nevermore.' "

But the Raven still beguiling all my fancy
      into smiling,
Straight I wheeled a cushioned seat in front
      of bird, and bust and door;
Then, upon the velvet sinking, I betook my-
      self to linking
Fancy unto fancy, thinking what this ominous
      bird of yore —   70
What this grim, ungainly, ghastly, gaunt, and
      ominous bird of yore
      Meant in croaking "Nevermore."

This I sat engaged in guessing, but no syllable
      expressing
To the fowl whose fiery eyes now burned into
      my bosom's core;
This and more I sat divining, with my head
      at ease reclining   75
On the cushion's velvet lining that the lamp-
      light gloated o'er,

But whose velvet violet lining with the lamp-
    light gloating o'er,
She shall press, ah, nevermore!

Then, methought, the air grew denser, per-
    fumed from an unseen censer
Swung by Seraphim whose foot-falls tinkled
    on the tufted floor.   80
"Wretch," I cried, "thy God hath lent thee
    — by these angels he hath sent thee
Respite — respite and nepenthe from thy
    memories of Lenore;
Quaff, oh quaff this kind nepenthe and forget
    this lost Lenore!"
    Quoth the Raven "Nevermore."

"Prophet!" said I, "thing of evil! prophet
    still, if bird or devil! —   85
Whether Tempter sent, or whether tempest
    tossed thee here ashore,
Desolate yet all undaunted, on this desert
    land enchanted —
On this home by Horror haunted — tell me
    truly, I implore —
Is there — *is* there balm in Gilead? — tell
    me — tell me, I implore!"
    Quoth the Raven "Nevermore."   90

"Prophet!" said I, "thing of evil! — prophet
    still, if bird or devil!
By that Heaven that bends above us — by
    that God we both adore —
Tell this soul with sorrow laden if, within the
    distant Aidenn,
It shall clasp a sainted maiden whom the
    angels name Lenore —
Clasp a rare and radiant maiden whom the
    angels name Lenore."   95
    Quoth the Raven "Nevermore."

"Be that word our sign of parting, bird or
    fiend!" I shrieked, upstarting —
"Get thee back into the tempest and the
    Night's Plutonian shore!
Leave no black plume as a token of that lie
    thy soul hath spoken!
Leave my loneliness unbroken! — quit the
    bust above my door!   100
Take thy beak from out my heart, and take
    thy form from off my door!"
    Quoth the Raven "Nevermore."

And the Raven, never flitting, still is sitting,
    still is sitting
On the pallid bust of Pallas just above my
    chamber door;
And his eyes have all the seeming of a demon's
    that is dreaming,   105
And the lamp-light o'er him streaming
    throws his shadow on the floor;
And my soul from out that shadow that lies
    floating on the floor
Shall be lifted — nevermore!

Ulalume
(1847)

On the meaning of this poem, consult the discussion in Campbell's edition of the poems, pages
269–71, beginning " 'Ulalume' has proved very
much of a riddle to the commentators."

The skies they were ashen and sober;
    The leaves they were crispèd and sere —
    The leaves they were withering and sere;
It was night in the lonesome October
    Of my most immemorial year;   5
It was hard by the dim lake of Auber,
    In the misty mid region of Weir —
It was down by the dank tarn of Auber,
    In the ghoul-haunted woodland of Weir.

Here once, through an alley Titanic,   10
    Of cypress, I roamed with my Soul —
    Of cypress, with Psyche, my Soul.
These were days when my heart was volcanic
    As the scoriac rivers that roll —
    As the lavas that restlessly roll   15
Their sulphurous currents down Yaanek
    In the ultimate climes of the pole —
That groan as they roll down Mount Yaanek
    In the realms of the boreal pole.

Our talk had been serious and sober,   20
    But our thoughts they were palsied and
    sere —
    Our memories were treacherous and
    sere —
For we knew not the month was October,
    And we marked not the night of the year —
    (Ah, night of all nights in the year!)   25
We noted not the dim lake of Auber —
    (Though once we have journeyed down
    here) —

Remembered not the dank tarn of Auber,
   Nor the ghoul-haunted woodland of Weir.

And now, as the night was senescent   30
   And star-dials pointed to morn —
   As the star-dials hinted of morn —
At the end of our path a liquescent
   And nebulous lustre was born,
Out of which a miraculous crescent   35
   Arose with a duplicate horn —
Astarte's bediamonded crescent
   Distinct with its duplicate horn.

And I said — "She is warmer than Dian:
   She rolls through an ether of sighs —   40
   She revels in a region of sighs:
She has seen that the tears are not dry on
   These cheeks, where the worm never dies
And has come past the stars of the Lion
   To point us the path to the skies —   45
   To the Lethean peace of the skies —
Come up, in despite of the Lion,
   To shine on us with her bright eyes —
Come up through the lair of the Lion,
   With love in her luminous eyes."   50

But Psyche, uplifting her finger,
   Said — "Sadly this star I mistrust —
   Her pallor I strangely mistrust:
Oh, hasten! — oh, let us not linger!
   Oh, fly! — let us fly! — for we must."   55
In terror she spoke, letting sink her
   Wings until they trailed in the dust —
In agony sobbed, letting sink her
   Plumes till they trailed in the dust —
   Till they sorrowfully trailed in the dust.   60

I replied — "This is nothing but dreaming:
   Let us on by this tremulous light!
   Let us bathe in this crystalline light!
Its Sibyllic splendor is beaming
   With Hope and in Beauty to-night: —   65
See! — it flickers up the sky through the
   night!
Ah, we safely may trust to its gleaming,
   And be sure it will lead us aright —
We safely may trust to a gleaming
   That cannot but guide us aright,   70
   Since it flickers up to Heaven through the
   night."

Thus I pacified Psyche and kissed her,
   And tempted her out of her gloom —
   And conquered her scruples and gloom;
And we passed to the end of the vista,   75
   But were stopped by the door of a tomb —
   By the door of a legended tomb;
And I said — "What is written, sweet sister,
   On the door of this legended tomb?"
She replied — "Ulalume — Ulalume —   80
   'Tis the vault of thy lost Ulalume!"

Then my heart it grew ashen and sober
   As the leaves that were crispèd and sere —
   As the leaves that were withering and sere,
And I cried — "It was surely October   85
   On this very night of last year
That I journeyed — I journeyed down
   here —
That I brought a dread burden down
   here —
   On this night of all nights in the year,
   Ah, what demon has tempted me here?   90
Well I know, now, this dim lake of Auber —
   This misty mid region of Weir —
Well I know, now, this dank tarn of Auber,
   This ghoul-haunted woodland of Weir."

The Bells

(1848–49)

I

Hear the sledges with the bells —
   Silver bells!
What a world of merriment their melody fore-
   tells!
   How they tinkle, tinkle, tinkle,
     In the icy air of night!   5
   While the stars that oversprinkle
   All the heavens, seem to twinkle
     With a crystalline delight;
     Keeping time, time, time,
     In a sort of Runic rhyme,   10
To the tintinnabulation that so musically
   wells
   From the bells, bells, bells, bells,
     Bells, bells, bells —
From the jingling and the tinkling of the bells.

II

Hear the mellow wedding bells —   15
   Golden bells!

What a world of happiness their harmony
    foretells!
Through the balmy air of night
How they ring out their delight! —
    From the molten-golden notes,   20
      And all in tune,
    What a liquid ditty floats
To the turtle-dove that listens, while she
    gloats
      On the moon!
Oh, from out the sounding cells,   25
What a gush of euphony voluminously wells!
      How it swells!
      How it dwells
    On the Future! — how it tells
    Of the rapture that impells   30
    To the swinging and the ringing
    Of the bells, bells, bells —
    Of the bells, bells, bells, bells,
      Bells, bells, bells —   34
To the rhyming and the chiming of the bells!

III

Hear the loud alarum bells —
    Brazen bells!
What a tale of terror, now their turbulency
    tells!
    In the startled ear of night
    How they scream out their affright!   40
      Too much horrified to speak,
      They can only shriek, shriek,
        Out of tune,
In a clamorous appealing to the mercy of the
    fire,
In a mad expostulation with the deaf and
    frantic fire,   45
      Leaping higher, higher, higher,
      With a desperate desire,
      And a resolute endeavor
    Now — now to sit, or never,
By the side of the pale-faced moon.   50
      Oh, the bells, bells, bells!
    What a tale their terror tells
      Of Despair!
How they clang, and clash, and roar!
What a horror they outpour   55
On the bosom of the palpitating air!
    Yet the ear, it fully knows,
      By the twanging,
      And the clanging,
    How the danger ebbs and flows;   60
    Yet the ear distinctly tells,

      In the jangling,
      And the wrangling,
    How the danger sinks and swells,
By the sinking or the swelling in the anger of
    the bells —   65
      Of the bells —
    Of the bells, bells, bells, bells,
      Bells, bells, bells —
In the clamor and the clanging of the bells!

IV

Hear the tolling of the bells —   70
    Iron bells!
What a world of solemn thought their mon-
    ody compels!
    In the silence of the night,
    How we shiver with affright
At the melancholy menace of their tone!
For every sound that floats   76
From the rust within their throats
      Is a groan.
And the people — ah, the people —
    They that dwell up in the steeple,   80
      All alone,
    And who, tolling, tolling, tolling,
      In that muffled monotone,
    Feel a glory in so rolling
      On the human heart a stone —   85
They are neither man nor woman —
They are neither brute nor human —
      They are Ghouls:
And their king it is who tolls —
And he rolls, rolls, rolls,   90
      Rolls
    A pæan from the bells!
And his merry bosom swells
    With the pæan of the bells!
And he dances, and he yells;   95
Keeping time, time, time,
In a sort of Runic rhyme,
    To the pæan of the bells: —
      Of the bells:
Keeping time, time, time,   100
In a sort of Runic rhyme,
    To the throbbing of the bells —
Of the bells, bells, bells —
    To the sobbing of the bells: —
Keeping time, time, time,   105
    As he knells, knells, knells,
In a happy Runic rhyme,
    To the rolling of the bells —
Of the bells, bells, bells: —

To the tolling of the bells —   110
Of the bells, bells, bells, bells,
    Bells, bells, bells —
To the moaning and the groaning of the bells.

For Annie

(1849)

For Mrs. Annie Richmond, of Lowell, Massachusetts, a friend of Poe's.

Thank Heaven! the crisis —
    The danger is past,
And the lingering illness
    Is over at last —
And the fever called "Living"   5
    Is conquered at last.

Sadly, I know
    I am shorn of my strength,
And no muscle I move
    As I lie at full length —   10
But no matter! — I feel
    I am better at length.

And I rest so composedly
    Now, in my bed,
That any beholder   15
    Might fancy me dead —
Might start at beholding me,
    Thinking me dead.

The moaning and groaning,
    The sighing and sobbing,   20
Are quieted now,
    With that horrible throbbing
At heart: — ah that horrible,
    Horrible throbbing!

The sickness — the nausea —   25
    The pitiless pain —
Have ceased with the fever
    That maddened my brain —
With the fever called "Living"
    That burned in my brain.   30

And oh! of all tortures
    That torture the worst
Has abated — the terrible
    Torture of thirst
For the napthaline river   35
    Of Passion accurst: —

I have drank of a water
    That quenches all thirst: —

Of a water that flows,
    With a lullaby sound,   40
From a spring but a very few
    Feet under ground —
From a cavern not very far
    Down under ground.

And ah! let it never   45
    Be foolishly said
That my room it is gloomy
    And narrow my bed;
For a man never slept
    In a different bed —   50
And, to sleep, you must slumber
    In just such a bed.

My tantalized spirit
    Here blandly reposes,
Forgetting, or never   55
    Regretting, its roses —
Its old agitations
    Of myrtles and roses:

For now, while so quietly
    Lying, it fancies   60
A holier odor
    About it, of pansies —
A rosemary odor,
    Commingled with pansies —
With rue and the beautiful   65
    Puritan pansies.

And so it lies happily,
    Bathing in many
A dream of the truth
    And the beauty of Annie —   70
Drowned in a bath
    Of the tresses of Annie.

She tenderly kissed me,
    She fondly caressed,
And then I fell gently   75
    To sleep on her breast —
Deeply to sleep
    From the heaven of her breast.

When the light was extinguished,
    She covered me warm,   80

And she prayed to the angels
　　To keep me from harm —
To the queen of the angels
　　To shield me from harm.

And I lie so composedly,　　　　　　85
　　Now, in my bed,
(Knowing her love)
　　That you fancy me dead —
And I rest so contentedly,
　　Now, in my bed,　　　　　　　90
(With her love at my breast)
　　That you fancy me dead —
That you shudder to look at me.
　　Thinking me dead: —

But my heart it is brighter　　　　95
　　Than all of the many
Stars of the sky,
　　For it sparkles with Annie —
It glows with the light
　　Of the love of my Annie —　　100
With the thought of the light
　　Of the eyes of my Annie.

Annabel Lee
(1849)

Generally held to have been written in memory
of Virginia Clemm, Poe's "child-wife."

It was many and many a year ago,
　　In a kingdom by the sea,
That a maiden there lived whom you may
　　know
By the name of ANNABEL LEE;
And this maiden she lived with no other
　　thought　　　　　　　　　　　　5
Than to love and be loved by me.

I was a child and *she* was a child,
　　In this kingdom by the sea,
But we loved with a love that was more than
　　love —
I and my ANNABEL LEE —　　　　10
With a love that the wingèd seraphs of heaven
　　Coveted her and me.

And this was the reason that, long ago,
　　In this kingdom by the sea,
A wind blew out of a cloud, chilling　　15
　　My beautiful ANNABEL LEE;

So that her high-born kinsmen came
　　And bore her away from me,
To shut her up in a sepulchre
　　In this kingdom by the sea.　　　　20

The angels, not half so happy in heaven,
　　Went envying her and me —
Yes! — that was the reason (as all men know,
　　In this kingdom by the sea)
That the wind came out of the cloud by
　　night,　　　　　　　　　　　　25
　　Chilling and killing my ANNABEL LEE.

But our love it was stronger by far than the
　　love
Of those who were older than we —
　　Of many far wiser than we —
And neither the angels in heaven above,　　30
　　Nor the demons down under the sea,
Can ever dissever my soul from the soul
　　Of the beautiful ANNABEL LEE:

For the moon never beams, without bringing
　　me dreams
Of the beautiful ANNABEL LEE;　　　35
And the stars never rise, but I feel the bright
　　eyes
Of the beautiful ANNABEL LEE:
And so, all the night-tide, I lie down by the
　　side
Of my darling — my darling — my life and
　　my bride,
In the sepulchre there by the sea —　　40
In her tomb by the sounding sea.

Eldorado
(1849)

Gaily bedight
　　A gallant knight,
In sunshine and in shadow,
　　Had journeyed long,
　　Singing a song,　　　　　　　5
In search of Eldorado.

But he grew old —
　　This knight so bold —
And o'er his heart a shadow
　　Fell as he found　　　　　　10
　　No spot of ground
That looked like Eldorado.

And, as his strength
Failed him at length,
He met a pilgrim shadow —   15
"Shadow," said he,
"Where can it be —
This land of Eldorado?"

"Over the Mountains
Of the Moon,   20
Down the Valley of the Shadow,
Ride, boldly ride,"
The shade replied, —
"If you seek for Eldorado."

Ligeia
(1838)

"In 'Ligeia,' which he regarded as his finest tale, he rewrote 'Morella,' but for much of its peculiar power he went back to the sources of his youngest inspiration. In 'Al Aaraaf' he had framed out of the breath of the night-wind and the idea of the harmony of universal nature a fairy creature, —
'Ligeia, Ligeia, my beautiful one!'
Now by a finer touch he incarnated the motions of the breeze and the musical voices of nature in the form of a woman: but the Lady Ligeia has still no human quality; her aspirations, her thoughts and capabilities, are those of a spirit; the very beam and glitter and silence of her ineffable eyes belong to the visionary world. She is, in fact, the maiden of Poe's dream, the Eidolon he served, the air-woven divinity in which he believed; for he had the true myth-making faculty, the power to make his senses aver what his imagination perceived. In revealing through 'Ligeia' the awful might of the soul in the victory of its will over death and in the eternity of its love, Poe worked in the very element of his reverie, in the liberty of a world as he would have it" (Woodberry, *Life*, I, 226–27).

And the will therein lieth, which dieth not. Who knoweth the mysteries of the will, with its vigor? For God is but a great will pervading all things by nature of its intentness. Man doth not yield himself to the angels, nor unto death utterly, save only through the weakness of his feeble will.
JOSEPH GLANVILL

I cannot, for my soul, remember how, when, or even precisely where, I first became acquainted with the lady Ligeia. Long years have since elapsed, and my memory is feeble through much suffering. Or, perhaps, I cannot *now* bring these points to mind, because, in truth, the character of my beloved, her rare learning, her singular yet placid cast of

beauty, and the thrilling and enthralling eloquence of her low musical language, made their way into my heart by paces so steadily and stealthily progressive that they have been unnoticed and unknown. Yet I believe that I met her first and most frequently in some large, old, decaying city near the Rhine. Of her family — I have surely heard her speak. That it is of a remotely ancient date cannot be doubted. Ligeia! Ligeia! Buried in studies of a nature more than all else adapted to deaden impressions of the outward world, it is by that sweet word alone — by Ligeia — that I bring before mine eyes in fancy the image of her who is no more. And now, while I write, a recollection flashes upon me that I have *never known* the paternal name of her who was my friend and my betrothed, and who became the partner of my studies, and finally the wife of my bosom. Was it a playful charge on the part of my Ligeia? or was it a test of my strength of affection, that I should institute no inquiries upon this point? or was it rather a caprice of my own — a wildly romantic offering on the shrine of the most passionate devotion? I but indistinctly recall the fact itself — what wonder that I have utterly forgotten the circumstances which originated or attended it? And, indeed, if ever that spirit which is entitled *Romance* — if ever she, the wan and the misty-winged Ashtophet of idolatrous Egypt, presided, as they tell, over marriages ill-omened, then most surely she presided over mine.

There is one dear topic, however, on which my memory fails me not. It is the *person* of Ligeia. In stature she was tall, somewhat slender, and, in her latter days, even emaciated. I would in vain attempt to portray the majesty, the quiet ease, of her demeanor, or the incomprehensible lightness and elasticity of her footfall. She came and departed as a shadow. I was never made aware of her entrance into my closed study, save by the dear music of her low sweet voice, as she placed her marble hand upon my shoulder. In beauty of face no maiden ever equalled her. It was the radiance of an opium-dream — an airy and spirit-lifting vision more wildly divine than the fantasies which hovered about the slumbering souls of the daughters of Delos. Yet her features were not of that regular mould which we have been falsely taught to worship in the classical labors of the heathen. "There is no exquisite beauty," says Bacon, Lord Verulam, speaking truly of all the forms and genera of beauty, "without some *strangeness* in the proportion." Yet, although I saw that the features of Ligeia were not of a classic regularity — although I perceived that her loveliness was indeed "exquisite," and felt that there was much of "strangeness" pervading it, yet I have tried in vain to detect the irregularity and to trace home my own perception of "the strange." I examined the contour of the lofty and pale forehead: it was faultless — how cold indeed that word when applied to a majesty so divine! — the skin rivalling the purest ivory, the commanding extent and repose, the gentle prominence of the regions above the temples; and then the raven-black, the glossy, the luxuriant, and naturally-curling tresses, setting forth the full force of the Homeric epithet, "hyacinthine!" I looked at the delicate outlines of the nose — and nowhere but in the graceful medallions of the Hebrews had I beheld a similar perfection. There were the same luxurious smoothness of surface, the same scarcely perceptible tendency to the aquiline, the same harmoniously curved nostrils speaking the free spirit. I regarded the sweet mouth. Here was indeed the triumph of all things heavenly — the magnificent turn of the short upper lip — the soft, voluptuous slumber of the under — the dimples which sported, and the color which spoke — the teeth glancing back, with a brilliancy almost startling, every ray of the holy light which fell upon them in her serene and placid, yet most exultingly radiant of all smiles. I scrutinized the formation of the chin: and here, too, I found the gentleness of breadth, the softness and the majesty, the fulness and the spirituality, of the Greek — the contour which the god Apollo revealed but in a dream to Cleomenes, the son of the Athenian. And then I peered into the large eyes of Ligeia.

For eyes we have no models in the remotely antique. It might have been, too, that in these eyes of my beloved lay the secret to which Lord Verulam alludes. They were, I must believe, far larger than the ordinary eyes of our own race. They were even fuller than the fullest of the gazelle eyes of the tribe of the valley of Nourjahad. Yet it was only at intervals — in moments of intense excitement — that this peculiarity became more than slightly noticeable in Ligeia. And at such moments was her beauty — in my heated fancy thus it appeared perhaps — the beauty of beings either above or apart from the earth, the beauty of the fabulous Houri of the Turk. The hue of the orbs was the most brilliant of black, and, far over them, hung jetty lashes of great length. The brows, slightly irregular in outline, had the same tint. The "strangeness," however, which I found in the eyes, was of a nature distinct from the formation, or the color, or the brilliancy of the features, and must, after all, be referred to the *expression*. Ah, word of no meaning! behind whose vast latitude of mere sound we intrench our ignorance of so much of the spiritual. The expression of the eyes of Ligeia! How for long hours have I pondered upon it! How have I, through the whole of a midsummer night, struggled to fathom it! What was it — that something more profound than the well of Democritus — which lay far within the pupils of my beloved? What *was* it? I was possessed with a passion to discover. Those eyes! those large, those shining, those divine orbs! they became to me twin stars of Leda, and I to them devoutest of astrologers.

There is no point, among the many incomprehensible anomalies of the science of mind, more thrillingly exciting than the fact — never, I believe, noticed in the schools — that in our endeavors to recall to memory something long forgotten, we often find ourselves *upon the very verge* of remembrance, without being able, in the end, to remember. And thus how frequently, in my intense scrutiny of Ligeia's eyes, have I felt approaching the full knowledge of their expression — felt it approaching, yet not quite be mine, and so at length entirely depart! And (strange, oh strangest mystery of all!) I found, in the commonest objects of the universe, a circle of analogies to that expression. I mean to say that, subsequently to the period when Ligeia's beauty passed into my spirit, there dwelling as in a shrine, I derived, from many existences in the material world, a sentiment such as I felt always aroused within me by her large and luminous orbs. Yet not the more could I define that sentiment, or analyze, or even steadily view it. I recognized it, let me repeat, sometimes in the survey of a rapidly growing vine — in the contemplation of a moth, a butterfly, a chrysalis, a stream of running water. I have felt it in the ocean; in the falling of a meteor. I have felt it in the glances of unusually aged people. And there are one or two stars in heaven, (one especially, a star of the sixth magnitude, double and changeable, to be found near the large star in Lyra,) in a telescopic scrutiny of which I have been made aware of the feeling. I have been filled with it by certain sounds from stringed instruments, and not unfrequently by passages from books. Among innumerable other instances, I well remember something in a volume of Joseph Glanvill, which (perhaps merely from its quaintness — who shall say?) never failed to inspire me with the sentiment: "And the will therein lieth, which dieth not. Who knoweth the mysteries of the will, with its vigor? For God is but a great will pervading all things by nature of its intentness. Man doth not yield him to the angels, nor unto death utterly, save only through the weakness of his feeble will."

Length of years and subsequent reflection have enabled me to trace, indeed, some remote connection between this passage in the English moralist and a portion of the character of Ligeia. An *intensity* in thought, action, or speech, was possibly, in her, a result, or at least an index, of that gigantic volition which, during our long intercourse, failed to give other and more immediate evidence of its existence. Of all the women whom I have ever known, she, the outwardly calm, the ever-placid Ligeia, was the most violently a prey to the tumultuous vultures of stern passion. And of such passion I could form no estimate, save by the miraculous expansion of those eyes which at once so delighted and appalled me — by the almost magical melody, modulation, distinctness, and placidity of her very low voice — and by the fierce energy (rendered doubly effective by contrast with her manner of utterance) of the wild words which she habitually uttered.

I have spoken of the learning of Ligeia: it was immense — such as I have never known in woman. In the classical tongues was she deeply proficient, and as far as my own acquaintance extended in regard to the modern dialects of Europe, I have never known her at fault. Indeed upon any theme of the most admired, because simply the most abstruse of the boasted erudition of the academy, have I *ever* found Ligeia at fault? How singularly, how thrillingly, this one point in the nature of my wife has forced itself, at this late period only, upon my attention! I said her knowledge was such as I have never known in woman — but where breathes the man who has traversed, and successfully, *all* the wide areas of moral, physical, and mathematical science? I saw not then what I now clearly perceive, that the acquisitions of Ligeia were gigantic, were astounding; yet I was sufficiently aware of her infinite supremacy to resign myself, with a child-like confidence, to her guidance through the chaotic world of metaphysical investigation at which I was most busily occupied during the earlier years of our marriage. With how vast a triumph, with how vivid a delight, with how much of all that is ethereal in hope, did I *feel*, as she bent over me in studies but little sought — but less known — that delicious vista by slow degrees expanding before me, down whose long, gorgeous, and all untrodden path, I might at length pass onward to the goal of a wisdom too divinely precious not to be forbidden!

How poignant, then, must have been the grief with which, after some years, I beheld my well-grounded expectations take wings to themselves and fly away! Without Ligeia I was but as a child groping benighted. Her presence, her readings alone, rendered vividly luminous the many mysteries of the transcendentalism in which we were immersed. Wanting the radiant lustre of her eyes, letters, lambent and golden, grew duller than Saturnian lead. And now those eyes shone less and less frequently upon the pages over which I pored. Ligeia grew ill. The wild eyes blazed with a too — too glorious effulgence; the pale fingers became of the transparent waxen hue of the grave; and the blue veins upon the lofty forehead swelled and sank impetuously with the tides of the most gentle emotion. I saw that she must die — and I struggled desperately in spirit with the grim Azrael. And the struggles of the passionate wife were, to my astonishment, even more energetic than my own. There had been much in her stern nature to impress me with the belief that, to her, death would have come without its terrors; but not so. Words are impotent to convey any just idea of the fierceness of resistance with which she wrestled with the Shadow. I groaned in anguish at the pitiable spectacle. I would have soothed — I would have reasoned; but, in the intensity of her wild desire for life — for life — *but* for life — solace and reason were alike the uttermost of folly. Yet not until the last instance, amid the most convulsive writhings of her fierce spirit, was shaken the external placidity of her demeanor. Her voice grew more gentle — grew more low — yet I would not wish to dwell upon the wild meaning of the quietly uttered words. My brain reeled as I hearkened, entranced, to a melody more than mortal — to assumptions and aspirations which mortality had never before known.

That she loved me I should not have doubted; and I might have been easily aware that, in a bosom such as hers, love would have reigned no ordinary passion. But in death only was I fully impressed with the strength of her affection. For long hours, detaining my hand, would she pour out before me the overflowing of a heart whose more than passionate devotion amounted to idolatry. How had I deserved to be so blessed by such confessions? How had I deserved to be so cursed with the removal of my beloved in the hour of her making them? But upon this subject I cannot bear to dilate. Let me say only, that in Ligeia's more than womanly abandonment to a love, alas! all unmerited, all unworthily bestowed, I at length recognized the principle of her longing, with so wildly earnest a desire, for the life which was now fleeing so rapidly away. It is this wild longing, it is this eager vehemence of desire for life — *but* for life, that I have no power to portray, no utterance capable of expressing.

At high noon of the night in which she departed, beckoning me peremptorily to her side; she bade me repeat certain verses composed by herself not many days before. I obeyed her. They were these:

Lo! 'tis a gala night
　Within the lonesome latter years!
An angel throng, bewinged, bedight
　In veils, and drowned in tears,
Sit in a theatre, to see
　A play of hopes and fears,
While the orchestra breathes fitfully
　The music of the spheres.

Mimes, in the form of God on high,
　Mutter and mumble low,
And hither and thither fly —
　Mere puppets they, who come and go
At bidding of vast formless things
　That shift the scenery to and fro,
Flapping from out their condor wings
　Invisible Woe!

That motley drama — oh, be sure
　It shall not be forgot!
With its Phantom chased for evermore,
　By a crowd that seize it not,
Through a circle that ever returneth in
　To the self-same spot,
And much of Madness, and more of Sin,
　And Horror the soul of the plot.

But see, amid the mimic rout
　A crawling shape intrude!
A blood-red thing that writhes from out
　The scenic solitude!
It writhes — it writhes! with mortal pangs
　The mimes become its food,
And seraphs sob at vermin fangs
　In human gore imbued.

Out — out are the lights — out all!
　And over each quivering form
The curtain, a funeral pall,
　Comes down with the rush of a storm,
While the angels, all pallid and wan,
　Uprising, unveiling, affirm
That the play is the tragedy, "Man,"
　And its hero, the Conqueror Worm.

"O God!" half shrieked Ligeia, leaping to her feet and extending her arms aloft with a spasmodic movement, as I made an end of these lines — "O God! O Divine Father! shall these things be undeviatingly so? shall this Conqueror be not once conquered? Are we not part and parcel in Thee? Who — who knoweth the mysteries of the will with its vigor? 'Man doth not yield him to the angels, *nor unto death utterly* save only through the weakness of his feeble will.'"

And now, as if exhausted with emotion, she suffered her white arms to fall, and returned solemnly to her bed of death. And as she breathed her last sighs, there came mingled with them a low murmur from her lips. I bent to them my ear, and distinguished, again, the concluding words of the passage in Glanvill: *"Man doth not yield him to the angels, nor unto death utterly, save only through the weakness of his feeble will."*

She died: and I, crushed into the very dust with sorrow, could no longer endure the lonely desolation of my dwelling in the dim and decaying city by the Rhine. I had no lack of what the world calls wealth. Ligeia had brought me far more, very far more, than ordinarily falls to the lot of mortals. After a few months, therefore, of weary and aimless wandering, I purchased, and put in some repair, an abbey, which I shall not name, in one of the wildest and least frequented portions of fair England. The gloomy and dreary grandeur of the building, the almost savage aspect of the domain, the many melancholy and time-honored memories connected with both, had much in unison with the feelings of utter abandonment which had driven me into that remote and unsocial region of the country. Yet although the external abbey, with its verdant decay hanging about it, suffered but little alteration, I gave way with a child-like perversity, and perchance with a faint hope of alleviating my sorrows, to a display of more than regal magnificence within. For such follies, even in childhood, I had imbibed a taste, and now they came back to me as if in the dotage of grief. Alas, I feel how much even of incipient madness might have been discovered in the gorgeous and fantastic draperies, in the solemn carvings of Egypt, in the wild cornices and furniture, in the Bedlam patterns of the carpets of tufted gold! I had become a bounden slave in the trammels of opium, and my labors and my orders had taken a coloring from my dreams. But these absurdities I must not pause to detail. Let me speak only of that one chamber, ever accursed, whither, in a moment of mental alienation, I led from the altar as my bride — as the successor of the unforgotten Ligeia — the fair-haired and blue-eyed Lady Rowena Trevanion, of Tremaine.

There is no individual portion of the architecture and decoration of that bridal chamber which is not now visibly before me. Where were the souls of the haughty family of the bride, when, through thirst of gold, they permitted to pass the threshold of an apartment so bedecked, a maiden and a daughter so beloved? I have said that I minutely remember the details of the chamber — yet I am sadly forgetful on topics of deep moment; and here there was no system, no keeping, in the fantastic display, to take hold upon the memory. The room lay in a high turret of the castellated abbey, was pentagonal in shape, and of capacious size. Occupying the whole southern face of the pentagon was the sole window — an immense sheet of unbroken glass from Venice — a single pane, and tinted of a leaden hue, so that the rays of either the sun or moon, passing through it, fell with a ghastly lustre on the objects within. Over the upper portion of this huge window extended the trellis-work of an aged vine, which clambered up the massy walls of the turret. The ceiling, of gloomy-looking oak, was excessively lofty, vaulted, and elaborately fretted with the wildest and most grotesque specimens of a semi-Gothic, semi-Druidical device. From out the most central recess of this melancholy vaulting depended, by a single chain of gold with long links, a huge censer of the same metal, Saracenic in pattern, and with many perforations so contrived that there writhed in and out of them, as if endued with a serpent vitality, a continual succession of parti-colored fires.

Some few ottomans and golden candelabra, of Eastern figure, were in various stations about; and there was the couch, too — the bridal couch — of an Indian model, and low, and sculptured of solid ebony, with a pall-like canopy above. In each of the angles of the chamber stood on end a gigantic sarcophagus of black granite, from the tombs of the kings over against Luxor, with their aged lids full of immemorial sculpture. But in the draping of the apartment lay, alas! the chief fantasy of all. The lofty walls, gigantic in height, even unproportionably so, were hung from summit to foot, in vast folds, with a heavy and massive-looking tapestry — tapestry of a material which was found alike as a carpet on the floor, as a covering for the ottomans and the ebony bed, as a canopy for the bed, and as the gorgeous volutes of the curtains which partially shaded the window.

The material was the richest cloth of gold. It was spotted all over, at irregular intervals, with arabesque figures, about a foot in diameter, and wrought upon the cloth in patterns of the most jetty black. But these figures partook of the true character of the arabesque only when regarded from a single point of view. By a contrivance now common, and indeed traceable to a very remote period of antiquity, they were made changeable in aspect. To one entering the room, they bore the appearance of simple monstrosities; but upon a farther advance, this appearance gradually departed; and, step by step, as the visitor moved his station in the chamber, he saw himself surrounded by an endless succession of the ghastly forms which belong to the superstition of the Norman, or arise in the guilty slumbers of the monk. The phantasmagoric effect was vastly heightened by the artificial introduction of a strong continual current of wind behind the draperies, giving a hideous and uneasy animation to the whole.

In halls such as these, in a bridal chamber such as this, I passed, with the Lady of Tremaine, the unhallowed hours of the first month of our marriage — passed them with but little disquietude. That my wife dreaded the fierce moodiness of my temper — that she shunned me, and loved me but little — I could not help perceiving; but it gave me rather pleasure than otherwise. I loathed her with a hatred belonging more to demon than to man. My memory flew back (oh, with what intensity of regret!) to Ligeia, the beloved, the august, the beautiful, the entombed. I revelled in recollections of her purity, of her wisdom, of her lofty, her ethereal nature, of her passionate, her idolatrous love. Now, then, did my spirit fully and freely burn with more than all the fires of her own. In the excitement of my opium dreams (for I was habitually fettered in the shackles of the drug), I would call aloud upon her name, during the silence of the night, or among the sheltered recesses of the glens by day, as if, through the wild eagerness, the solemn passion, the consuming ardor of my longing for the departed, I could restore her to the pathway she had abandoned — ah, *could* it be forever? — upon the earth.

About the commencement of the second month of the marriage, the Lady Rowena was attacked with sudden illness, from which her recovery was slow. The fever which consumed her, rendered her nights uneasy; and in her perturbed state of half-slumber, she spoke of sounds, and of motions, in and about the chamber of the turret, which I concluded had no origin save in the distemper of her fancy, or perhaps in the phantasmagoric influences of the chamber itself. She became at length convalescent — finally, well. Yet but a brief period elapsed, ere a second more violent disorder again threw her upon a bed of suffering; and from this attack her frame, at all times feeble, never altogether recovered. Her illnesses were, after this epoch, of alarming character, and of more alarming recurrence, defying alike the knowledge and the great exertions of her physicians. With the increase of the chronic disease, which had thus apparently taken too sure hold upon her constitution to be eradicated by human means, I could not fail to observe a similar increase in the nervous irritation of her temperament, and in her excitability by trivial causes of fear. She spoke again, and now more frequently and pertinaciously, of the sounds — of the slight sounds — and of the unusual motions among the tapestries, to which she had formerly alluded.

One night, near the closing in of September, she pressed this distressing subject with more than usual emphasis upon my attention. She had just awakened from an unquiet slumber, and I had been watching, with feelings half of anxiety, half of vague terror, the workings of her emaciated countenance. I sat by the side of her ebony bed, upon one of the ottomans of India. She partly arose, and spoke, in an earnest low whisper, of sounds which she *then* heard, but which I could not hear — of motions which she *then* saw, but which I could not perceive. The wind was rushing hurriedly behind the tapestries, and I wished to show her (what, let me confess it, I could not *all* believe) that those almost inarticulate breathings, and those very gentle variations of the figures upon the wall, were but the natural effects of that customary rushing of the wind. But a deadly pallor, overspreading her face, had proved to me that my exertions to reassure her would be fruitless.

She appeared to be fainting, and no attendants were within call. I remembered where was deposited a decanter of light wine which had been ordered by her physicians, and hastened across the chamber to procure it. But, as I stepped beneath the light of the censer, two circumstances of a startling nature attracted my attention. I had felt that some palpable although invisible object had passed lightly by my person; and I saw that there lay upon the golden carpet, in the very middle of the rich lustre thrown from the censer, a shadow — a faint, indefinite shadow of angelic aspect — such as might be fancied for the shadow of a shade. But I was wild with the excitement of an immoderate dose of opium, and heeded these things but little, nor spoke of them to Rowena. Having found the wine, I recrossed the chamber, and poured out a gobletful, which I held to the lips of the fainting lady. She had now partially recovered, however, and took the vessel herself, while I sank upon an ottoman near me, with my eyes fastened upon her person. It was then that I became distinctly aware of a gentle footfall upon the carpet, and near the couch; and in a second thereafter, as Rowena was in the act of raising the wine to her lips, I saw, or may have dreamed that I saw, fall within the goblet, as if from some invisible spring in the atmosphere of the room, three or four large drops of a brilliant and ruby-colored fluid. If this I saw — not so Rowena. She swallowed the wine unhesitatingly, and I forbore to speak to her of a circumstance which must after all, I considered, have been but the suggestion of a vivid imagination, rendered morbidly active by the terror of the lady, by the opium, and by the hour.

Yet I cannot conceal it from my own perception that, immediately subsequent to the fall of the ruby-drops, a rapid change for the worse took place in the disorder of my wife; so that, on the third subsequent night, the hands of her menials prepared her for the tomb, and on the fourth, I sat alone, with her shrouded body, in that fantastic chamber which had received her as my bride. Wild visions, opium-engendered, flitted shadow-like before me. I gazed with unquiet eye upon the sarcophagi in the angles of the room, upon the varying figures of the drapery, and upon the writhing of the particolored fires in the censer overhead. My eyes then fell, as I called to mind the circumstances of a former night, to the spot beneath the glare of the censer where I had seen the faint traces of the shadow. It was there, however, no longer; and breathing with greater freedom, I turned my glances to the pallid and rigid figure upon the bed. Then rushed upon me a thousand memories of Ligeia — and then came back upon my heart, with the turbulent violence of a flood, the whole of that unutterable woe with which I had regarded *her* thus enshrouded. The night waned; and still, with a bosom full of bitter thoughts of the one only and supremely beloved, I remained gazing upon the body of Rowena.

It might have been midnight, or perhaps earlier, or later, for I had taken no note of time, when a sob, low, gentle, but very distinct, startled me from my revery. I *felt* that it came from the bed of ebony — the bed of death. I listened in an agony of superstitious terror — but there was no repetition of the sound. I strained my vision to detect any motion in the corpse — but there was not the slightest perceptible. Yet I could not have been deceived. I *had* heard the noise, however faint, and my soul was awakened within me. I resolutely and perseveringly kept my attention riveted upon the body. Many minutes elapsed before any circumstance occurred tending to throw light upon the mystery. At length it became evident that a slight, a very feeble, and barely noticeable tinge of color had flushed up within the cheeks, and along the sunken small veins of the eyelids. Through a species of unutterable horror and awe, for which the language of mortality has no sufficiently energetic expression, I felt my heart cease to beat, my limbs grow rigid where I sat. Yet a sense of duty finally operated to restore my self-possession. I could no longer doubt that we had been precipitate in our preparations — that Rowena still lived. It was necessary that some immediate exertion be made; yet the turret was altogether apart from the portion of the abbey tenanted by the servants — there were none within call — I had no means of summoning them to my aid without leaving the room for many minutes — and this I could not venture to do. I therefore struggled alo.. > in my endeavors to call back the spirit still hovering. In a short period it was certain, however, that a relapse had taken place; the color disappeared from both eyelid and cheek, leaving a wanness even more than that of marble; the lips became doubly shrivelled and pinched up in the ghastly expression of death; a repulsive clamminess and coldness overspread rapidly the surface of the body; and all the usual rigorous stiffness immediately supervened. I fell back with a shudder upon the couch from which I had been so startlingly aroused, and again gave myself up to passionate waking visions of Ligeia.

An hour thus elapsed, when (could it be possible?) I was a second time aware of some vague sound issuing from the region of the bed. I listened — in extremity of horror. The sound came again — it was a sigh. Rushing to the corpse, I saw — distinctly saw — a tremor upon the lips. In a minute afterwards they relaxed, disclosing a bright line of the pearly teeth. Amazement now struggled in my bosom with the profound awe which had hitherto reigned there alone. I felt that my vision grew dim, that my reason wandered; and it was only by a violent effort that I at length succeeded in nerving myself to the task which duty thus once more had pointed out. There was now a partial glow upon the forehead and upon the cheek and throat; a perceptible warmth pervaded the whole frame; there was even a slight pulsation at the heart. The lady *lived;* and with redoubled ardor I betook myself to the task of restoration. I chafed and bathed the temples and the hands, and used every exertion which experience, and no little medical reading, could suggest. But in vain. Suddenly, the color fled, the pulsation ceased, the lips resumed the expression of the dead, and, in an instant afterward, the whole body took upon itself the icy chilliness, the livid hue, the intense rigidity, the sunken outline, and all the loathsome peculiarities of that which has been, for many days, a tenant of the tomb.

And again I sunk into visions of Ligeia — and again, (what marvel that I shudder while I write?) *again* there reached my ears a low sob from the region of the ebony bed. But why shall I minutely detail the unspeakable horrors of that night? Why shall I pause to relate how, time after time, until near the period of the gray dawn, this hideous drama of revivification was repeated; how each terrific relapse was only into a sterner and apparently more irredeemable death; how each agony wore the aspect of a struggle with some invisible foe; and how each struggle was succeeded by I know not what of wild change in the personal appearance of the corpse? Let me hurry to a conclusion.

The greater part of the fearful night had worn away, and she who had been dead, once again stirred — and now more vigorously than hitherto, although arousing from a dissolution more appalling in its utter helplessness than any. I had long ceased to struggle or to move, and remained sitting rigidly upon the ottoman, a helpless prey to a whirl of violent emotions, of which extreme awe was perhaps the least terrible, the least consuming. The corpse, I repeat, stirred, and now more vigorously than before. The hues of life flushed up with unwonted energy into the countenance — and limbs relaxed — and, save that the eyelids were yet pressed heavily together, and that the bandages and draperies of the grave still imparted their charnel character to the figure, I might have dreamed that Rowena had indeed shaken off, utterly, the fetters of Death. But if this idea was not, even then, altogether adopted, I could at least doubt no longer, when, arising from the bed, tottering, with feeble steps, with closed eyes, and with the manner of one bewildered in a dream, the thing that was enshrouded advanced bodily and palpably into the middle of the apartment.

I trembled not — I stirred not — for a crowd of unutterable fancies connected with the air, the stature, the demeanor of the figure, rushing hurriedly through my brain, had paralyzed — had chilled me into stone. I stirred not — but gazed upon the apparition. There was a mad disorder in my thoughts — a tumult unappeasable. Could it, indeed, be the *living* Rowena who confronted me? Could it indeed be Rowena *at all* — the fair-haired, the blue-eyed Lady Rowena Trevanion of Tremaine? Why, *why* should I doubt it? The bandage lay heavily about the mouth — but then might it not be the mouth of the breathing Lady of Tremaine? And the cheeks — there were the roses as in her noon of life — yes, these might indeed be the fair cheeks of the living Lady of Tremaine. And the chin, with its dimples, as in health, might it not be hers? but *had she then grown taller since her malady?* What inexpressible madness seized me with that thought? One bound, and I had reached her feet! Shrinking from my touch, she let fall from her head the ghastly cerements which had confined it, and there streamed forth, into the rushing atmosphere of the chamber, huge masses of long and dishevelled hair; *it was blacker than the raven wings of the midnight!* And now slowly opened *the eyes* of the figure which stood before me. "Here then, at least," I shrieked aloud, "can I never — can I never be mistaken — these are the full, and the black, and the wild eyes — of my lost love — of the lady — of the LADY LIGEIA."

The Fall of the House of Usher

(1839)

Son cœur est un luth suspendu;
Sitôt qu'on le touche il résonne.
                                   BÉRANGER.[1]

During the whole of a dull, dark, and soundless day in the autumn of the year, when the clouds hung oppressively low in the heavens, I had been passing alone, on horseback, through a singularly dreary tract of country; and at length found myself, as the shades of the evening drew on, within view of the melancholy House of Usher. I know not how it was — but, with the first glimpse of the building, a sense of insufferable gloom pervaded my spirit. I say insufferable; for the feeling was unrelieved by any of that half-pleasurable, because poetic, sentiment with which the mind usually receives even the sternest natural images of the desolate or terrible. I looked upon the scene before me — upon the mere house, and the simple landscape features of the domain, upon the bleak

[1] On the motto, see the note to "Israfel." For a general discussion of American "tales of terror" (Brockden Brown, Irving, Hawthorne, Poe) see E. Birkhead's study of *The Tale of Terror*, 1921, ch. XI.
   The motto may be translated: His heart is a lute suspended; whenever it is touched it sounds.

walls, upon the vacant eye-like windows, upon a few rank sedges, and upon a few white trunks of decayed trees — with an utter depression of soul which I can compare to no earthly sensation more properly than to the after-dream of the reveller upon opium; the bitter lapse into everyday life, the hideous dropping off of the veil. There was an iciness, a sinking, a sickening of the heart, an unredeemed dreariness of thought which no goading of the imagination could torture into aught of the sublime. What was it — I paused to think — what was it that so unnerved me in the contemplation of the House of Usher? It was a mystery all insoluble; nor could I grapple with the shadowy fancies that crowded upon me as I pondered. I was forced to fall back upon the unsatisfactory conclusion, that while, beyond doubt, there *are* combinations of very simple natural objects which have the power of thus affecting us, still the analysis of this power lies among considerations beyond our depth. It was possible, I reflected, that a mere different arrangement of the particulars of the scene, of the details of the picture, would be sufficient to modify, or perhaps to annihilate, its capacity for sorrowful impression; and acting upon this idea, I reined my horse to the precipitous brink of a black and lurid tarn that lay in unruffled lustre by the dwelling, and gazed down — but with a shudder even more thrilling than before — upon the remodelled and inverted images of the gray sedge, and the ghastly tree-stems, and the vacant and eye-like windows.

Nevertheless, in this mansion of gloom I now proposed to myself a sojourn of some weeks. Its proprietor, Roderick Usher, had been one of my boon companions in boyhood; but many years had elapsed since our last meeting. A letter, however, had lately reached me in a distant part of the country — a letter from him — which in its wildly importunate nature had admitted of no other than a personal reply. The MS. gave evidence of nervous agitation. The writer spoke of acute bodily illness, of a mental disorder which oppressed him, and of an earnest desire to see me, as his best and indeed his only personal friend, with a view of attempting, by the cheerfulness of my society, some alleviation of his malady. It was the manner in which all this, and much more, was said — it was the apparent *heart* that went with his request — which allowed me no room for hesitation; and I accordingly obeyed forthwith what I still considered a very singular summons.

Although as boys we had been even intimate associates, yet I really knew little of my friend. His reserve had been always excessive and habitual. I was aware, however, that his very ancient family had been noted, time out of mind, for a peculiar sensibility of temperament, displaying itself, through long ages, in many works of exalted art, and manifested of late in repeated deeds of munificent yet unobtrusive charity, as well as in a passionate devotion to the intricacies, perhaps even more than to the orthodox and easily recognizable beauties, of musical science. I had learned, too, the very remarkable fact that the stem of the Usher race, all time-honored as it was, had put forth at no period any enduring branch; in other words, that the entire family lay in the direct line of descent, and had always, with very trifling and very temporary variation, so lain. It was this deficiency, I considered, while running over in thought the perfect keeping of the character of the premises with the accredited character of the people, and while speculating upon the possible influence which the one, in the long lapse of centuries, might have exercised upon the other — it was this deficiency, perhaps of collateral issue, and the consequent undeviating transmission from sire to son of the patrimony with the name, which had, at length, so identified the two as to merge the original title of the estate in the quaint and equivocal appellation of the "House of Usher" — an appellation which seemed to include, in the minds of the peasantry who used it, both the family and the family mansion.

I have said that the sole effect of my somewhat childish experiment, that of looking down within the tarn, had been to deepen the first singular impression. There can be no doubt that the consciousness of the rapid increase of my superstition — for why should I not so term it? — served mainly to accelerate the increase itself. Such, I have long known,

is the paradoxical law of all sentiments having terror as a basis. And it might have been for this reason only, that, when I again uplifted my eyes to the house itself, from its image in the pool, there grew in my mind a strange fancy — a fancy so ridiculous, indeed, that I but mention it to show the vivid force of the sensations which oppressed me. I had so worked upon my imagination as really to believe that about the whole mansion and domain there hung an atmosphere peculiar to themselves and their immediate vicinity: an atmosphere which had no affinity with the air of heaven, but which had reeked up from the decayed trees, and the gray wall, and the silent tarn: a pestilent and mystic vapor, dull, sluggish, faintly discernible, and leaden-hued.

Shaking off from my spirit what *must* have been a dream, I scanned more narrowly the real aspect of the building. Its principal feature seemed to be that of an excessive antiquity. The discoloration of ages had been great. Minute fungi overspread the whole exterior, hanging in a fine tangled webwork from the eaves. Yet all this was apart from any extraordinary dilapidation. No portion of the masonry had fallen; and there appeared to be a wild inconsistency between its still perfect adaptation of parts and the crumbling condition of the individual stones. In this there was much that reminded me of the specious totality of old wood-work which has rotted for long years in some neglected vault, with no disturbance from the breath of the external air. Beyond this indication of extensive decay, however, the fabric gave little token of instability. Perhaps the eye of a scrutinizing observer might have discovered a barely perceptible fissure, which, extending from the roof of the building in front, made its way down the wall in a zigzag direction, until it became lost in the sullen waters of the tarn.

Noticing these things, I rode over a short causeway to the house. A servant in waiting took my horse, and I entered the Gothic archway of the hall. A valet, of stealthy step, thence conducted me, in silence, through many dark and intricate passages in my progress to the studio of his master. Much that I encountered on the way contributed, I know not how, to heighten the vague sentiments of which I have already spoken. While the objects around me — while the carvings of the ceilings, the sombre tapestries of the walls, the ebon blackness of the floors, and the phantasmagoric armorial trophies which rattled as I strode, were but matters to which, or to such as which, I had been accustomed from my infancy — while I hesitated not to acknowledge how familiar was all this — I still wondered to find how unfamiliar were the fancies which ordinary images were stirring up. On one of the staircases, I met the physician of the family. His countenance, I thought, wore a mingled expression of low cunning and perplexity. He accosted me with trepidation and passed on. The valet now threw open a door and ushered me into the presence of his master.

The room in which I found myself was very large and lofty. The windows were long, narrow, and pointed, and at so vast a distance from the black oaken floor as to be altogether inaccessible from within. Feeble gleams of encrimsoned light made their way through the trellised panes, and served to render sufficiently distinct the more prominent objects around; the eye, however, struggled in vain to reach the remoter angles of the chamber, or the recesses of the vaulted and fretted ceiling. Dark draperies hung upon the walls. The general furniture was profuse, comfortless, antique, and tattered. Many books and musical instruments lay scattered about, but failed to give any vitality to the scene. I felt that I breathed an atmosphere of sorrow. An air of stern, deep, and irredeemable gloom hung over and pervaded all.

Upon my entrance, Usher arose from a sofa on which he had been lying at full length, and greeted me with a vivacious warmth which had much in it, I at first thought, of an overdone cordiality — of the constrained effort of the *ennuyé* man of the world. A glance, however, at his countenance convinced me of his perfect sincerity. We sat down; and for some moments, while he spoke not, I gazed upon him with a feeling half of pity, half of awe. Surely man had never before so terribly altered, in so brief a period, as had Roderick Usher! It was with difficulty that I could bring myself to admit the identity of the wan being before me with the companion of my early boyhood. Yet the character of his face had been at all times remarkable. A cadaverousness of complexion; an eye large, liquid, and luminous beyond comparison; lips somewhat thin and very pallid, but of a surpassingly beautiful curve; a nose of a delicate Hebrew model, but with a breadth of nostril unusual in similar formations; a finely moulded chin, speaking, in its want of prominence, of a want of moral energy; hair of a more than web-like softness and tenuity; these features, with an inordinate expansion above the regions of the temple, made up altogether a countenance not easily to be forgotten. And now in the mere exaggeration of the prevailing character of these features, and of the expression they were wont to convey, lay so much of change that I doubted to whom I spoke. The now ghastly pallor of the skin, and the now miraculous lustre of the eye, above all things startled and even awed me. The silken hair, too, had been suffered to grow all unheeded, and as, in its wild gossamer texture, it floated rather than fell about the face, I could not, even with effort, connect its arabesque expression with any idea of simple humanity.

In the manner of my friend I was at once struck with an incoherence, an inconsistency; and I soon found this to arise from a series of feeble and futile struggles to overcome an habitual trepidancy, an excessive nervous agitation. For something of this nature I had indeed been prepared, no less by his letter than by reminiscences of certain boyish traits, and by conclusions deduced from his peculiar physical conformation and temperament. His action was alternately vivacious and sullen. His voice varied rapidly from a tremulous indecision (when the animal spirits seemed utterly in abeyance) to that species of energetic concision — that abrupt, weighty, unhurried, and hollow-sounding enunciation — that leaden, self-balanced and perfectly modulated guttural utterance — which may be observed in the lost drunkard, or the irreclaimable eater of opium, during the periods of his most intense excitement.

It was thus that he spoke of the object of my visit, of his earnest desire to see me, and of the solace he expected me to afford him. He entered, at some length, into what he conceived to be the nature of his malady. It was, he said, a constitutional and a family evil, and one for which he despaired to find a remedy — a mere nervous affection, he immediately added, which would undoubtedly soon pass off. It displayed itself in a host of unnatural sensations. Some of these, as he detailed them, interested and bewildered me; although, perhaps, the terms and the general manner of the narration had their weight. He suffered much from a morbid acuteness of the senses; the most insipid food was alone endurable; he could wear only garments of certain texture; the odors of all flowers were oppressive; his eyes were tortured by even a faint light; and there were but peculiar sounds, and these from stringed instruments, which did not inspire him with horror.

To an anomalous species of terror I found him a bounden slave. "I shall perish," said he, "I *must* perish in this deplorable folly. Thus, thus, and not otherwise, shall I be lost. I dread the events of the future, not in themselves, but in their results. I shudder at the thought of any, even the most trivial, incident, which may operate upon this intolerable agitation of soul. I have, indeed, no abhorrence of danger, except in its absolute effect — in terror. In this unnerved — in this pitiable condition, I feel that the period will sooner or later arrive when I must abandon life and reason together, in some struggle with the grim phantasm, FEAR."

I learned moreover at intervals, and through broken and equivocal hints, another singular feature of his mental condition. He was enchained by certain superstitious impressions in regard to the dwelling which he tenanted, and whence, for many years, he had never ventured forth — in regard to an influence whose supposititious force was conveyed in terms too shadowy here to be restated — an influence which some peculiarities in the mere form and substance of his family mansion, had, by dint of long sufferance, he said, obtained over his spirit — an effect which the physique of the gray walls and turrets, and of the dim tarn into which they all looked down, had, at length, brought about upon the morale of his existence.

He admitted, however, although with hesitation, that much of the peculiar gloom which thus afflicted him could be traced to a more natural and far more palpable origin — to the severe and long-continued illness, indeed to the evidently approaching dissolution, of a tenderly beloved sister — his sole companion for long years, his last and only relative on earth. "Her decease," he said, with a bitterness which I can never forget, "would leave him (him the hopeless and the frail) the last of the ancient race of the Ushers." While he spoke the lady Madeline (for so was she called) passed slowly through a remote portion of the apartment, and, without having noticed my presence, disappeared. I regarded her with an utter astonishment not unmingled with dread, and yet I found it impossible to account for such feelings. A sensation of stupor oppressed me, as my eyes followed her retreating steps. When a door, at length, closed upon her, my glance sought instinctively and eagerly the countenance of the brother; but he had buried his face in his hands, and I could only perceive that a far more than ordinary wanness had overspread the emaciated fingers through which trickled many passionate tears.

The disease of the lady Madeline had long baffled the skill of her physicians. A settled apathy, a gradual wasting away of the person, and frequent although transient affections of a partially cataleptical character, were the unusual diagnosis. Hitherto she had steadily borne up against the pressure of her malady, and had not betaken herself finally to bed; but, on the closing in of the evening of my arrival at the house, she succumbed (as her brother told me at night with inexpressible agitation) to the prostrating power of the destroyer; and I learned that the glimpse I had obtained of her person would thus probably be the last I should obtain — that the lady, at least while living, would be seen by me no more.

For several days ensuing, her name was unmentioned by either Usher or myself; and during this period I was busied in earnest endeavors to alleviate the melancholy of my friend. We painted and read together; or I listened, as if in a dream, to the wild improvisations of his speaking guitar. And thus, as a closer and still closer intimacy admitted me more unreservedly into the recesses of his spirit, the more bitterly did I perceive the futility of all attempt at cheering a mind from which darkness, as if an inherent positive quality, poured forth upon all objects of the moral and physical universe, in one unceasing radiation of gloom.

I shall ever bear about me a memory of the many solemn hours I thus spent alone with the master of the House of Usher. Yet I should fail in any attempt to convey an idea of the exact character of the studies, or of the occupations, in which he involved me, or led me the way. An excited and highly distempered ideality threw a sulphureous lustre over all. His long improvised dirges will ring forever in my ears. Among other things, I hold painfully in mind a certain singular perversion and amplification of the wild air of the last waltz of Von Weber. From the paintings over which his elaborate fancy brooded, and which grew, touch by touch, into vaguenesses at which I shuddered the more thrillingly because I shuddered knowing not why; — from these paintings (vivid as their images now are before me) I would in vain endeavor to educe more than a small portion which should lie within the compass of merely written words. By the utter simplicity, by the nakedness of his designs, he arrested and overawed attention. If ever mortal painted an idea, that mortal was Roderick Usher. For me at least, in the circumstances then surrounding me, there arose, out of the pure abstractions which the hypochondriac contrived to throw upon his canvas, an intensity of intolerable awe, no shadow of which felt I ever yet in the contemplation of the certainly glowing yet too concrete reveries of Fuseli.

One of the phantasmagoric conceptions of my friend, partaking not so rigidly of the spirit of abstraction, may be shadowed forth, although feebly, in words. A small picture presented the interior of an immensely long and rectangular vault or tunnel, with low walls, smooth, white, and without interruption or device. Certain accessory points of the design served well to convey the idea that this excavation lay at an exceeding depth below the surface of the earth. No outlet was observed in any portion of its vast extent, and no torch or other artificial source of light was discernible; yet a flood of intense rays rolled throughout, and bathed the whole in a ghastly and inappropriate splendor.

I have just spoken of that morbid condition of the auditory nerve which rendered all music intolerable to the sufferer, with the exception of certain effects of stringed instruments. It was, perhaps, the narrow limits to which he thus confined himself upon the guitar, which gave birth, in great measure, to the fantastic character of his performances. But the fervid *facility* of his impromptus could not be so accounted for. They must have been, and were, in the notes, as well as in the words of his wild fantasias (for he not unfrequently accompanied himself with rhymed verbal improvisations), the result of that intense mental collectedness and concentration to which I have previously alluded as observable only in particular moments of the highest artificial excitement. The words of one of these rhapsodies I have easily remembered. I was, perhaps, the more forcibly impressed with it, as he gave it, because, in the under or mystic current of its meaning, I fancied that I perceived, and for the first time, a full consciousness, on the part of Usher, of the tottering of his lofty reason upon her throne. The verses, which were entitled "The Haunted Palace," ran very nearly, if not accurately, thus:

I

In the greenest of our valleys
 By good angels tenanted,
Once a fair and stately palace —
 Radiant palace — reared its head.
In the monarch Thought's dominion,
 It stood there!
Never seraph spread a pinion
 Over fabric half so fair!

II

Banners yellow, glorious, golden,
 On its roof did float and flow,
(This — all this — was in the olden
 Time long ago)
And every gentle air that dallied,
 In that sweet day,
Along the ramparts plumed and pallid,
 A wingèd odor went away.

III

Wanderers in that happy valley,
 Through two luminous windows, saw
Spirits moving musically
 To a lute's well-tunèd law,

Round about a throne where, sitting,
  Porphyrogene!
In state his glory well befitting,
  The ruler of the realm was seen.

IV

And all with pearl and ruby glowing
  Was the fair palace door,
Through which came flowing, flowing, flowing
  And sparkling evermore,
A troop of Echoes, whose sweet duty
  Was but to sing,
In voices of surpassing beauty,
  The wit and wisdom of their king.

V

But evil things, in robes of sorrow,
  Assailed the monarch's high estate.
(Ah, let us mourn! — for never morrow
  Shall dawn upon him, desolate!)
And round about his home the glory
  That blushed and bloomed
Is but a dim-remembered story
  Of the old time entombed.

VI

And travellers, now, within that valley,
  Through the red-litten windows see
Vast forms that move fantastically
  To a discordant melody;
While, like a ghastly rapid river,
  Through the pale door
A hideous throng rush out forever,
  And laugh — but smile no more.

I well remember that suggestions arising
from this ballad led us into a train of thought,
wherein there became manifest an opinion of
Usher's which I mention not so much on
account of its novelty, (for other men [1] have
thought thus), as on account of the pertinacity with which he maintained it. This opinion, in its general form, was that of the sentience of all vegetable things. But in his disordered fancy the idea had assumed a more
daring character, and trespassed, under certain conditions, upon the kingdom of inorgan-
ization. I lack words to express the full extent, or the earnest *abandon* of his persuasion.
The belief, however, was connected (as I have
previously hinted) with the gray stones of the
home of his forefathers. The conditions of
the sentience had been here, he imagined, fulfilled in the method of collocation of these
stones — in the order of their arrangement,

as well as in that of the many fungi which
overspread them, and of the decayed trees
which stood around — above all, in the long
undisturbed endurance of this arrangement,
and in its reduplication in the still waters of
the tarn. Its evidence — the evidence of the
sentience — was to be seen, he said (and I
here started as he spoke), in the gradual yet
certain condensation of an atmosphere of
their own about the waters and the walls.
The result was discoverable, he added, in
that silent, yet importunate and terrible influence which for centuries had moulded the
destinies of his family, and which made *him*
what I now saw him — what he was. Such
opinions need no comment, and I will make
none.

Our books — the books which, for years,
had formed no small portion of the mental
existence of the invalid — were, as might be
supposed, in strict keeping with this character
of phantasm. We pored together over such
works as the *Ververt* and *Chartreuse* of Gresset;
the *Belphegor* of Machiavelli; the *Heaven and
Hell* of Swedenborg; the *Subterranean Voyage of
Nicholas Klimm* by Holberg; the *Chiromancy* of
Robert Flud, of Jean D'Indaginé, and of De
la Chambre; the *Journey into the Blue Distance*
of Tieck; and the *City of the Sun* of Campanella.
One favorite volume was a small octavo edition of the *Directorium Inquisitorum* by the
Dominican Eymeric de Gironne; and there
were passages in Pomponius Mela, about the
old African Satyrs and Ægipans, over which
Usher would sit dreaming for hours. His
chief delight, however, was found in the perusal of an exceedingly rare and curious book
in quarto Gothic — the manual of a forgotten
church — the *Vigiliæ Mortuorum Secundum
Chorum Ecclesiæ Maguntinæ.*[1]

I could not help thinking of the wild ritual
of this work, and of its probable influence
upon the hypochondriac, when one evening,
having informed me abruptly that the lady
Madeline was no more, he stated his intention of preserving her corpse for a fortnight,
(previously to its final interment,) in one of
the numerous vaults within the main walls of
the building. The worldly reason, however,
assigned for this singular proceeding, was one

---

[1] Watson, Dr. Percival, Spallanzani, and especially
the Bishop of Landaff. — See *Chemical Essays*, vol. v.
[Author's note.]

[1] Vigils for the dead according to the choir of the
church of Mayence.

which I did not feel at liberty to dispute. The brother had been led to his resolution (so he told me) by consideration of the unusual character of the malady of the deceased, of certain obtrusive and eager inquiries on the part of her medical men, and of the remote and exposed situation of the burial-ground of the family. I will not deny that when I called to mind the sinister countenance of the person whom I met upon the staircase, on the day of my arrival at the house, I had no desire to oppose what I regarded as at best but a harmless, and by no means an unnatural precaution.

At the request of Usher, I personally aided him in the arrangements for the temporary entombment. The body having been encoffined, we two alone bore it to its rest. The vault in which we placed it (and which had been so long unopened that our torches, half smothered in its oppressive atmosphere, gave us little opportunity for investigation) was small, damp, and entirely without means of admission for light; lying, at great depth, immediately beneath that portion of the building in which was my own sleeping apartment. It had been used, apparently, in remote feudal times, for the worst purposes of a donjon-keep, and in later days as a place of deposit for powder, or some other highly combustible substance, as a portion of its floor, and the whole interior of a long archway through which we reached it, were carefully sheathed with copper. The door, of massive iron, had been, also, similarly protected. Its immense weight caused an unusually sharp grating sound, as it moved upon its hinges.

Having deposited our mournful burden upon tressels within this region of horror, we partially turned aside the yet unscrewed lid of the coffin, and looked upon the face of the tenant. A striking similitude between the brother and sister now first arrested my attention; and Usher, divining, perhaps, my thoughts, murmured out some few words from which I learned that the deceased and himself had been twins, and that sympathies of a scarcely intelligible nature had always existed between them. Our glances, however, rested not long upon the dead — for we could not regard her unawed. The disease which had thus entombed the lady in the maturity of youth, had left, as usual in all maladies of a strictly cataleptical character, the mockery of a faint blush upon the bosom and the face, and that suspiciously lingering smile upon the lip which is so terrible in death. We replaced and screwed down the lid, and, having secured the door of iron, made our way, with toil, into the scarcely less gloomy apartments of the upper portion of the house.

And now, some days of bitter grief having elapsed, an observable change came over the features of the mental disorder of my friend. His ordinary manner had vanished. His ordinary occupations were neglected or forgotten. He roamed from chamber to chamber with hurried, unequal, and objectless step. The pallor of his countenance had assumed, if possible, a more ghastly hue — but the luminousness of his eye had utterly gone out. The once occasional huskiness of his tone was heard no more; and a tremulous quaver, as if of extreme terror, habitually characterized his utterance. There were times, indeed, when I thought his unceasingly agitated mind was laboring with some oppressive secret, to divulge which he struggled for the necessary courage. At times, again, I was obliged to resolve all into the mere inexplicable vagaries of madness, for I beheld him gazing upon vacancy for long hours, in an attitude of the profoundest attention, as if listening to some imaginary sound. It was no wonder that his condition terrified — that it infected me. I felt creeping upon me, by slow yet certain degrees, the wild influences of his own fantastic yet impressive superstitions.

It was, especially, upon retiring to bed late in the night of the seventh or eighth day after the placing of the lady Madeline within the donjon, that I experienced the full power of such feelings. Sleep came not near my couch, while the hours waned and waned away. I struggled to reason off the nervousness which had dominion over me. I endeavored to believe that much, if not all, of what I felt was due to the bewildering influence of the gloomy furniture of the room — of the dark and tattered draperies which, tortured into motion by the breath of a rising tempest, swayed fitfully to and fro upon the walls, and rustled uneasily about the decorations of the bed. But my efforts were fruitless. An irrepressible tremor gradually pervaded my frame; and at length there sat upon my very heart an incubus of utterly causeless alarm. Shaking this off with a gasp and a struggle, I uplifted myself upon the pillows, and, peering earnestly within the intense darkness of the chamber, hearkened — I know not why, except that an instinctive spirit prompted me — to certain low and indefinite sounds which came, through the pauses of the storm, at long intervals, I knew not whence. Overpowered by an intense sentiment of horror, unaccountable yet unendurable, I threw on my clothes with haste (for I felt that I should sleep no more during the night,) and endeavored to arouse myself from the pitiable condition into which I had fallen, by pacing rapidly to and fro through the apartment.

I had taken but few turns in this manner, when a light step on an adjoining staircase arrested my attention. I presently recognized it as that of Usher. In an instant afterward he rapped with a gentle touch at my door, and entered, bearing a lamp. His countenance was, as usual, cadaverously wan — but, moreover, there was a species of mad hilarity in his eyes — an evidently restrained hysteria in his whole demeanor. His air appalled me — but anything was preferable to the solitude which I had so long endured, and I even welcomed his presence as a relief.

"And you have not seen it?" he said abruptly, after having stared about him for some moments in silence — "you have not then seen it? — but, stay! you shall." Thus speaking, and having carefully shaded his lamp, he hurried to one of the casements, and threw it freely open to the storm.

The impetuous fury of the entering gust nearly lifted us from our feet. It was, indeed, a tempestuous yet sternly beautiful night, and one wildly singular in its terror and its beauty. A whirlwind had apparently collected its force in our vicinity; for there were frequent and violent alterations in the direction of the wind; and the exceeding density of the clouds (which hung so low as to press upon the turrets of the house) did not prevent our perceiving the life-like velocity with which they flew careering from all points against each other,

without passing away into the distance. I say that even their exceeding density did not prevent our perceiving this; yet we had no glimpse of the moon or stars, nor was there any flashing forth of the lightning. But the under surfaces of the huge masses of agitated vapor, as well as all terrestrial objects immediately around us, were glowing in the unnatural light of a faintly luminous and distinctly visible gaseous exhalation which hung about and enshrouded the mansion.

"You must not — you shall not behold this!" said I, shudderingly, to Usher, as I led him with a gentle violence from the window to a seat. "These appearances, which bewilder you, are merely electrical phenomena not uncommon — or it may be that they have their ghastly origin in the rank miasma of the tarn. Let us close this casement; the air is chilling and dangerous to your frame. Here is one of your favorite romances. I will read, and you shall listen; — and so we will pass away this terrible night together."

The antique volume which I had taken up was the *Mad Trist* of Sir Launcelot Canning; but I had called it a favorite of Usher's more in sad jest than in earnest; for, in truth, there is little in its uncouth and unimaginative prolixity which could have had interest for the lofty and spiritual ideality of my friend. It was, however, the only book immediately at hand; and I indulged a vague hope that the excitement which now agitated the hypochondriac might find relief (for the history of mental disorder is full of similar anomalies) even in the extremeness of the folly which I should read. Could I have judged, indeed, by the wild overstrained air of vivacity with which he hearkened, or apparently hearkened, to the words of the tale, I might well have congratulated myself upon the success of my design.

I had arrived at that well-known portion of the story where Ethelred, the hero of the *Trist*, having sought in vain for peaceable admission into the dwelling of the hermit, proceeds to make good an entrance by force. Here, it will be remembered, the words of the narrative run thus:

And Ethelred, who was by nature of a doughty heart, and who was now mighty withal, on account of the powerfulness of the wine which he had drunken, waited no longer to hold parley with the hermit, who, in sooth, was of an obstinate and maliceful turn, but, feeling the rain upon his shoulders, and fearing the rising of the tempest, uplifted his mace outright, and with blows made quickly room in the plankings of the door for his gauntleted hand; and now pulling therewith sturdily, he so cracked, and ripped, and tore all asunder, that the noise of the dry and hollow-sounding wood alarumed and reverberated throughout the forest.

At the termination of this sentence I started, and for a moment paused; for it appeared to me (although I at once concluded that my excited fancy had deceived me) — it appeared to me that from some very remote portion of the mansion there came, indistinctly, to my ears, what might have been, in its exact similarity of character, the echo (but a stifled and dull one certainly) of the very cracking and ripping sound which Sir Launcelot had so particularly described. It was, beyond doubt, the coincidence alone which had arrested my attention; for, amid the rattling of the sashes of the casements, and the ordinary commingled noises of the still increasing storm, the sound, in itself, had nothing, surely, which should have interested or disturbed me. I continued the story:

But the good champion Ethelred, now entering within the door, was sore enraged and amazed to perceive no signal of the maliceful hermit; but, in the stead thereof, a dragon of a scaly and prodigious demeanor, and of a fiery tongue, which sate in guard before a palace of gold, with a floor of silver; and upon the wall there hung a shield of shining brass with this legend enwritten —

Who entereth herein, a conqueror hath bin;
Who slayeth the dragon, the shield he shall win.

And Ethelred uplifted his mace, and struck upon the head of the dragon, which fell before him, and gave up his pesty breath, with a shriek so horrid and harsh, and withal so piercing, that Ethelred had fain to close his ears with his hands against the dreadful noise of it, the like whereof was never before heard.

Here again I paused abruptly, and now with a feeling of wild amazement; for there could be no doubt whatever that, in this instance, I did actually hear (although from what direction it proceeded I found it impossible to say) a low and apparently distant, but harsh, protracted, and most unusual screaming or grating sound — the exact counterpart of what my fancy had already conjured up for the dragon's unnatural shriek as described by the romancer.

Oppressed, as I certainly was, upon the occurrence of this second and most extraordinary coincidence, by a thousand conflicting sensations, in which wonder and extreme terror were predominant, I still retained sufficient presence of mind to avoid exciting, by any observation, the sensitive nervousness of my companion. I was by no means certain that he had noticed the sounds in question; although, assuredly, a strange alteration had during the last few minutes taken place in his demeanor. From a position fronting my own, he had gradually brought round his chair, so as to sit with his face to the door of the chamber; and thus I could but partially perceive his features, although I saw that his lips trembled as if he were murmuring inaudibly. His head had dropped upon his breast — yet I knew that he was not asleep, from the wide and rigid opening of the eye as I caught a glance of it in profile. The motion of his body, too, was at variance with this idea — for he rocked from side to side with a gentle yet constant and uniform sway. Having rapidly taken notice of all this, I resumed the narrative of Sir Launcelot, which thus proceeded:

And now, the champion, having escaped from the terrible fury of the dragon, bethinking himself of the brazen shield, and of the breaking up of the enchantment which was upon it, removed the carcass from out of the way before him, and approached valorously over the silver pavement of the castle to where the shield was upon the wall; which in sooth tarried not for his full coming, but fell down at his feet upon the silver floor, with a mighty great and terrible ringing sound.

No sooner had these syllables passed my lips, than — as if a shield of brass had indeed at the moment, fallen heavily upon a floor of silver — I became aware of a distinct, hollow, metallic and clangorous yet apparently muffled reverberation. Completely unnerved, I leaped to my feet; but the measured rocking movement of Usher was undisturbed. I rushed to the chair in which he sat. His eyes were bent fixedly before him, and throughout his whole countenance there reigned a stony rigidity. But as I placed my hand upon his shoulder, there came a strong shudder over his whole person; a sickly smile quivered about his lips; and I saw that he spoke in a low, hurried, and gibbering murmur, as if unconscious of my presence. Bending closely over him, I at length drank in the hideous import of his words.

"Not hear it? — yes, I hear it, and *have* heard it. Long — long — long — many minutes, many hours, many days, have I heard it — yet I dared not — oh, pity me, miserable wretch that I am! — I dared not — I *dared* not speak! *We have put her living in the tomb!* Said I not that my senses were acute? I *now* tell you that I heard her first feeble movements in the hollow coffin. I heard them — many, many days ago — yet I dared not — *I dared not speak!* And now — to-night — Ethelred — ha! ha! — the breaking of the hermit's door, and the death-cry of the dragon, and the clangor of the shield! — say, rather, the rending of her coffin, and the grating of the iron hinges of her prison, and her struggles within the coppered archway of the vault! Oh, whither shall I fly? Will she not be here anon? Is she not hurrying to upbraid me for my haste? Have I not heard her footstep on the stair? Do I not distinguish that heavy and horrible beating of her heart? Madman!" — here he sprang furiously to his feet, and shrieked out his syllables, as if in the effort he were giving up his soul — "*Madman! I tell you that she now stands without the door!*"

As if in the superhuman energy of his utterance there had been found the potency of a spell, the huge antique panels to which the speaker pointed threw slowly back, upon the instant, their ponderous and ebony jaws. It was the work of the rushing gust — but then without those doors there *did* stand the lofty and enshrouded figure of the lady Madeline of Usher. There was blood upon her white robes, and the evidence of some bitter struggle upon every portion of her emaciated frame. For a moment she remained trembling and reeling to and fro upon the threshold — then, with a low moaning cry, fell heavily inward upon the person of her brother, and, in her violent and now final death agonies, bore him to the floor a corpse, and a victim to the terrors he had anticipated.

From that chamber, and from that mansion, I fled aghast. The storm was still abroad in all its wrath as I found myself crossing the old causeway. Suddenly there shot along the path a wild light, and I turned to see whence a gleam so unusual could have issued; for the vast house and its shadows were alone behind me. The radiance was that of the full, setting, and blood-red moon, which now shone vividly through that once barely discernible fissure, of which I have before spoken as extending from the roof of the building, in a zigzag direction, to the base. While I gazed, this fissure rapidly widened — there came a fierce breath of the whirlwind — the entire orb of the satellite burst at once upon my sight — my brain reeled as I saw the mighty walls rushing asunder — there was a long tumultuous shouting sound like the voice of a thousand waters — and the deep and dank tarn at my feet closed sullenly and silently over the fragments of the "*House of Usher.*"

The Cask of Amontillado
(ca. 1846)

The thousand injuries of Fortunato I had borne as I best could, but when he ventured upon insult I vowed revenge. You, who so well know the nature of my soul, will not suppose, however, that I gave utterance to a threat. *At length* I would be avenged; this was a point definitely settled — but the very definitiveness with which it was resolved precluded the idea of risk. I must not only punish but punish with impunity. A wrong is unredressed when retribution overtakes its redresser. It is equally unredressed when the avenger fails to make himself felt as such to him who has done the wrong.

It must be understood that neither by word nor deed had I given Fortunato cause to doubt my good will. I continued, as was my wont, to smile in his face, and he did not perceive that my smile *now* was at the thought of his immolation.

He had a weak point — this Fortunato — although in other regards he was a man to be respected and even feared. He prided himself on his connoisseurship in wine.

Few Italians have the true virtuoso spirit. For the most part their enthusiasm is adopted to suit the time and opportunity, to practise imposture upon the British and Austrian *millionaires*. In painting and gemmary, Fortunato, like his countrymen, was a quack, but in the matter of old wines he was sincere. In this respect I did not differ from him materially; — I was skilful in the Italian vintages myself, and bought largely whenever I could.

It was about dusk, one evening during the supreme madness of the carnival season, that I encountered my friend. He accosted me with excessive warmth, for he had been drinking much. The man wore motley. He had on a tight-fitting parti-striped dress, and his head was surmounted by the conical cap and bells. I was so pleased to see him that I thought I should never have done wringing his hand.

I said to him — "My dear Fortunato, you are luckily met. How remarkably well you are looking today. But I have received a pipe of what passes for Amontillado, and I have my doubts."

"How?" said he. "Amontillado? A pipe? Impossible! And in the middle of the carnival!"

"I have my doubts," I replied; "and I was silly enough to pay the full Amontillado price without consulting you in the matter. You were not to be found, and I was fearful of losing a bargain."

"Amontillado!"

"I have my doubts."

"Amontillado!"

"And I must satisfy them."

"Amontillado!"

"As you are engaged, I am on my way to Luchresi. If any one has a critical turn it is he. He will tell me —"

"Luchresi cannot tell Amontillado from Sherry."

"And yet some fools will have it that his taste is a match for your own."

"Come, let us go."

"Whither?"

"To your vaults."

"My friend, no; I will not impose upon your good nature. I perceive you have an engagement. Luchresi —"

"I have no engagement; — come."

"My friend, no. It is not the engagement, but the severe cold with which I perceive you are afflicted. The vaults are insufferably damp. They are encrusted with nitre."

"Let us go, nevertheless. The cold is merely nothing. Amontillado! You have been imposed upon. And as for Luchresi, he cannot distinguish Sherry from Amontillado."

Thus speaking, Fortunato possessed himself of my arm; and putting on a mask of black silk and drawing a *roquelaire* closely about my person, I suffered him to hurry me to my palazzo.

There were no attendants at home; they had absconded to make merry in honor of the time. I had told them that I should not return until the morning, and had given them explicit orders not to stir from the house. These orders were sufficient, I well knew, to insure their immediate disappearance, one and all, as soon as my back was turned.

I took from their sconces two flambeaux, and giving one to Fortunato, bowed him through several suites of rooms to the archway that led into the vaults. I passed down a long and winding staircase, requesting him to be cautious as he followed. We came at length to the foot of the descent, and stood together upon the damp ground of the catacombs of the Montresors.

The gait of my friend was unsteady, and the bells upon his cap jingled as he strode.

"The pipe," he said.

"It is farther on," said I; "but observe the white web-work which gleams from these cavern walls."

He turned towards me, and looked into my eyes with two filmy orbs that distilled the rheum of intoxication.

"Nitre?" he asked, at length.

"Nitre," I replied. "How long have you had that cough?"

"Ugh! ugh! ugh! — ugh! ugh! ugh! — ugh! ugh! ugh! — ugh! ugh! ugh! — ugh! ugh!"

My poor friend found it impossible to reply for many minutes.

"It is nothing," he said, at last.

"Come," I said, with decision, "we will

go back; your health is precious. You are rich, respected, admired, beloved; you are happy, as once I was. You are a man to be missed. For me it is no matter. We will go back; you will be ill, and I cannot be responsible. Besides, there is Luchresi —"

"Enough," he said; "the cough is a mere nothing; it will not kill me. I shall not die of a cough."

"True — true," I replied; "and, indeed, I had no intention of alarming you unnecessarily — but you should use all proper caution. A draught of this Medoc will defend us from the damps."

Here I knocked off the neck of a bottle which I drew from a long row of its fellows that lay upon the mould.

"Drink," I said, presenting him the wine.

He raised it to his lips with a leer. He paused and nodded to me familiarly, while his bells jingled.

"I drink," he said, "to the buried that repose around us."

"And I to your long life."

He again took my arm, and we proceeded.

"These vaults," he said, "are extensive."

"The Montresors," I replied, "were a great and numerous family."

"I forget your arms."

"A huge human foot d'or, in a field azure; the foot crushes a serpent rampant whose fangs are imbedded in the heel."

"And the motto?"

"*Nemo me impune lacessit.*" [1]

"Good!" he said.

The wine sparkled in his eyes and the bells jingled. My own fancy grew warm with the Medoc. We had passed through long walls of piled skeletons, with casks and puncheons intermingling, into the inmost recesses of the catacombs. I paused again, and this time I made bold to seize Fortunato by an arm above the elbow.

"The nitre!" I said: "see, it increases. It hangs like moss upon the vaults. We are below the river's bed. The drops of moisture trickle among the bones. Come, we will go back ere it is too late. Your cough —"

"It is nothing," he said; "let us go on. But first, another draught of the Medoc."

[1] "No one can harm me with impunity."

I broke and reached him a flagon of De Grâve. He emptied it at a breath. His eyes flashed with a fierce light. He laughed and threw the bottle upwards with a gesticulation I did not understand.

I looked at him in surprise. He repeated the movement — a grotesque one.

"You do not comprehend?" he said.

"Not I," I replied.

"Then you are not of the brotherhood."

"How?"

"You are not of the masons."

"Yes, yes," I said; "yes, yes."

"You? Impossible! A mason?"

"A mason," I replied.

"A sign," he said, "a sign."

"It is this," I answered, producing from beneath the folds of my *roquelaire* a trowel.

"You jest," he exclaimed, recoiling a few paces. "But let us proceed to the Amontillado."

"Be it so," I said, replacing the tool beneath the cloak and again offering him my arm. He leaned upon it heavily. We continued our route in search of the Amontillado. We passed through a range of low arches, descended, passed on, and descending again, arrived at a deep crypt, in which the foulness of the air caused our flambeaux rather to glow than flame.

At the most remote end of the crypt there appeared another less spacious. Its walls had been lined with human remains, piled to the vault overhead, in the fashion of the great catacombs of Paris. Three sides of this interior crypt were still ornamented in this manner. From the fourth side the bones had been thrown down, and lay promiscuously upon the earth, forming at one point a mound of some size. Within the wall thus exposed by the displacing of the bones, we perceived a still interior crypt or recess, in depth about four feet, in width three, in height six or seven. It seemed to have been constructed for no especial use within itself, but formed merely the interval between two of the colossal supports of the roof of the catacombs, and was backed by one of their circumscribing walls of solid granite.

It was in vain that Fortunato, uplifting his dull torch, endeavored to pry into the depth of the recess. Its termination the feeble light did not enable us to see.

"Proceed," I said; "herein is the Amontillado. As for Luchresi —"

"He is an ignoramus," interrupted my friend, as he stepped unsteadily forward, while I followed immediately at his heels. In an instant he had reached the extremity of the niche, and finding his progress arrested by the rock, stood stupidly bewildered. A moment more and I had fettered him to the granite. In its surface were two iron staples, distant from each other about two feet, horizontally. From one of these depended a short chain, from the other a padlock. Throwing the links about his waist, it was but the work of a few seconds to secure it. He was too much astounded to resist. Withdrawing the key I stepped back from the recess.

"Pass your hand," I said, "over the wall; you cannot help feeling the nitre. Indeed, it is *very* damp. Once more let me *implore* you to return. No? Then I must positively leave you. But I must first render you all the little attentions in my power."

"The Amontillado!" ejaculated my friend, not yet recovered from his astonishment.

"True," I replied; "the Amontillado."

As I said these words I busied myself among the pile of bones of which I have before spoken. Throwing them aside, I soon uncovered a quantity of building stone and mortar. With these materials and with the aid of my trowel, I began vigorously to wall up the entrance of the niche.

I had scarcely laid the first tier of the masonry when I discovered that the intoxication of Fortunato had in a great measure worn off. The earliest indication I had of this was a low moaning cry from the depth of the recess. It was *not* the cry of a drunken man. There was then a long and obstinate silence. I laid the second tier, and the third, and the fourth; and then I heard the furious vibrations of the chain. The noise lasted for several minutes, during which, that I might hearken to it with the more satisfaction, I ceased my labors and sat down upon the bones. When at last the clanking subsided, I resumed the trowel, and finished without interruption the fifth, the sixth, and the seventh tier. The wall was now nearly upon a level with my breast. I again paused, and holding the flambeaux over the mason-work, threw a few feeble rays upon the figure within.

A succession of loud and shrill screams, bursting suddenly from the throat of the chained form, seemed to thrust me violently back. For a brief moment I hesitated, I trembled. Unsheathing my rapier, I began to grope with it about the recess; but the thought of an instant reassured me. I placed my hand upon the solid fabric of the catacombs, and felt satisfied. I reapproached the wall; I replied to the yells of him who clamored. I re-echoed, I aided, I surpassed them in volume and in strength. I did this, and the clamorer grew still.

It was now midnight, and my task was drawing to a close. I had completed the eighth, the ninth and the tenth tier. I had finished a portion of the last and the eleventh; there remained but a single stone to be fitted and plastered in. I struggled with its weight; I placed it partially in its destined position. But now there came from out the niche a low laugh that erected the hairs upon my head. It was succeeded by a sad voice, which I had difficulty in recognizing as that of the noble Fortunato. The voice said —

"Ha! ha! ha! — he! he! he! — a very good joke, indeed — an excellent jest. We will have many a rich laugh about it at the palazzo — he! he! he! — over our wine — he! he! he!"

"The Amontillado!" I said.

"He! he! he! — he! he! he! — yes, the Amontillado. But is it not getting late? Will not they be awaiting us at the palazzo, the Lady Fortunato and the rest? Let us be gone."

"Yes," I said, "let us be gone."

"For the love of God, Montresor!"

"Yes," I said, "for the love of God!"

But to these words I hearkened in vain for a reply. I grew impatient. I called aloud —

"Fortunato!"

No answer. I called again —

"Fortunato!"

No answer still. I thrust a torch through

the remaining aperture and let it fall within. There came forth in return only a jingling of the bells. My heart grew sick; it was the dampness of the catacombs that made it so. I hastened to make an end of my labor. I forced the last stone into its position; I plastered it up. Against the new masonry I re-erected the old rampart of bones. For the half of a century no mortal has disturbed them. *In pace requiescat!*

The Purloined Letter

(*ca.* 1845)

Nil sapientiae odiosius acumine nimio.[1]

SENECA.

At Paris, just after dark one gusty evening in the autumn of 18—, I was enjoying the twofold luxury of meditation and a meerschaum, in company with my friend C. Auguste Dupin, in his little back library, or book-closet, *au troisième, No. 33, Rue Dunôt, Faubourg St. Germain.* For one hour at least we had maintained a profound silence; while each, to any casual observer, might have seemed intently and exclusively occupied with the curling eddies of smoke that oppressed the atmosphere of the chamber. For myself, however, I was mentally discussing certain topics which had formed matter for conversation between us at an earlier period of the evening; I mean the affair of the Rue Morgue, and the mystery attending the murder of Marie Rogêt. I looked upon it, therefore, as something of a coincidence, when the door of our apartment was thrown open and admitted our old acquaintance, Monsieur G—, the Prefect of the Parisian police.

We gave him a hearty welcome; for there was nearly half as much of the entertaining as of the contemptible about the man, and we had not seen him for several years. We had been sitting in the dark, and Dupin now arose for the purpose of lighting a lamp, but sat down again, without doing so, upon G.'s saying that he had called to consult us, or rather to ask the opinion of my friend, about some official business which had occasioned a great deal of trouble.

"If it is any point requiring reflection," observed Dupin, as he forebore to enkindle the wick, "we shall examine it to better purpose in the dark."

"That is another of your odd notions," said the Prefect, who had a fashion of calling every thing "odd" that was beyond his comprehension, and thus lived amid an absolute legion of "oddities."

"Very true," said Dupin, as he supplied his visitor with a pipe, and rolled towards him a comfortable chair.

"And what is the difficulty now?" I asked. "Nothing more in the assassination way, I hope?"

"Oh no; nothing of that nature. The fact is, the business is *very* simple indeed, and I make no doubt that we can manage it sufficiently well ourselves; but then I thought Dupin would like to hear the details of it, because it is so excessively *odd.*"

"Simple and odd," said Dupin.

"Why, yes; and not exactly that, either. The fact is, we have all been a good deal puzzled because the affair *is* so simple, and yet baffles us altogether."

"Perhaps it is the very simplicity of the thing which puts you at fault," said my friend.

"What nonsense you *do* talk!" replied the Prefect, laughing heartily.

"Perhaps the mystery is a little *too* plain," said Dupin.

"Oh, good heavens! who ever heard of such an idea?"

"A little *too* self-evident."

"Ha! ha! ha! — ha! ha! ha! — ho! ho! ho!" — roared our visitor, profoundly amused, "oh, Dupin, you will be the death of me yet!"

"And what, after all, *is* the matter on hand?" I asked.

"Why, I will tell you," replied the Prefect, as he gave a long, steady, and contemplative puff, and settled himself in his chair. "I will tell you in a few words; but, before I begin, let me caution you that this is an affair demanding the greatest secrecy, and that I should most probably lose the position I now hold, were it known that I confided it to any one."

"Proceed," said I.

---

[1] "No part of wisdom is more odious than too great acumen."

"Or not," said Dupin.

"Well, then; I have received personal information, from a very high quarter, that a certain document of the last importance has been purloined from the royal apartments. The individual who purloined it is known; this beyond a doubt; he was seen to take it. It is known, also, that it still remains in his possession."

"How is this known?" asked Dupin.

"It is clearly inferred," replied the Prefect, "from the nature of the document, and from the non-appearance of certain results which would at once arise from its passing *out* of the robber's possession; — that is to say, from his employing it as he must design in the end to employ it."

"Be a little more explicit," I said.

"Well, I may venture so far as to say that the paper gives its holder a certain power in a certain quarter where such power is immensely valuable." The Prefect was fond of the cant of diplomacy.

"Still I do not quite understand," said Dupin.

"No? Well; the disclosure of the document to a third person who shall be nameless would bring in question the honor of a personage of most exalted station; and this fact gives the holder of the document an ascendancy over the illustrious personage whose honor and peace are so jeopardized."

"But this ascendancy," I interposed, "would depend upon the robber's knowledge of the loser's knowledge of the robber. Who would dare —"

"The thief," said G—, "is the Minister D—, who dares all things, those unbecoming as well as those becoming a man. The method of the theft was not less ingenious than bold. The document in question — a letter, to be frank — had been received by the personage robbed while alone in the royal *boudoir*. During its perusal she was suddenly interrupted by the entrance of the other exalted personage from whom especially it was her wish to conceal it. After a hurried and vain endeavor to thrust it in a drawer, she was forced to place it, open as it was, upon a table. The address, however, was uppermost, and, the contents thus unexposed, the letter escaped notice.

At this juncture enters the Minister D—. His lynx eye immediately perceives the paper, recognizes the handwriting of the address, observes the confusion of the personage addressed, and fathoms her secret. After some business transactions, hurried through in his ordinary manner, he produces a letter somewhat similar to the one in question, opens it, pretends to read it, and then places it in close juxtaposition to the other. Again he converses, for some fifteen minutes, upon the public affairs. At length, in taking leave, he takes also from the table the letter to which he had no claim. Its rightful owner saw, but, of course, dared not call attention to the act, in the presence of the third personage who stood at her elbow. The Minister decamped; leaving his own letter — one of no importance — upon the table."

"Here, then," said Dupin to me, "you have precisely what you demand to make the ascendancy complete — the robber's knowledge of the loser's knowledge of the robber."

"Yes," replied the Prefect; "and the power thus attained has, for some months past, been wielded, for political purposes, to a very dangerous extent. The personage robbed is more thoroughly convinced, every day, of the necessity of reclaiming her letter. But this, of course, cannot be done openly. In fine, driven to despair, she has committed the matter to me."

"Than whom," said Dupin, amid a perfect whirlwind of smoke, "no more sagacious agent could, I suppose, be desired, or even imagined."

"You flatter me," replied the Prefect; "but it is possible that some such opinion may have been entertained."

"It is clear," said I, "as you observe, that the letter is still in possession of the Minister; since it is this possession, and not any employment of the letter, which bestows the power. With the employment the power departs."

"True," said G—; "and upon this conviction I proceeded. My first care was to make thorough search of the Minister's hotel; and here my chief embarrassment lay in the necessity of searching without his knowledge. Beyond all things, I have been warned of the danger which would result from giving him reason to suspect our design."

"But," said I, "you are quite *au fait* in these investigations. The Parisian police have done this thing often before."

"Oh yes; and for this reason I did not despair. The habits of the Minister gave me, too, a great advantage. He is frequently absent from home all night. His servants are by no means numerous. They sleep at a distance from their master's apartment, and, being chiefly Neapolitans, are readily made drunk. I have keys, as you know, with which I can open any chamber or cabinet in Paris. For three months a night has not passed, during the greater part of which I have not been engaged, personally, in ransacking the D— Hôtel. My honor is interested, and, to mention a great secret, the reward is enormous. So I did not abandon the search until I had become fully satisfied that the thief is a more astute man than myself. I fancy that I have investigated every nook and corner of the premises in which it is possible that the paper can be concealed."

"But is it not possible," I suggested, "that although the letter may be in the possession of the Minister, as it unquestionably is, he may have concealed it elsewhere than upon his own premises?"

"This is barely possible," said Dupin. "The present peculiar condition of affairs at court, and especially of those intrigues in which D— is known to be involved, would render the instant availability of the document — its susceptibility of being produced at a moment's notice — a point of nearly equal importance with its possession."

"Its susceptibility of being produced?" said I.

"That is to say, of being *destroyed*," said Dupin.

"True," I observed; "the paper is clearly then upon the premises. As for its being upon the person of the Minister, we may consider that as out of the question."

"Entirely," said the Prefect. "He has been twice waylaid, as if by footpads, and his person rigorously searched under my own inspection."

"You might have spared yourself this trouble," said Dupin. "D—, I presume, is not altogether a fool, and, if not, must have anticipated these waylayings, as a matter of course."

"Not *altogether* a fool," said G—, "but then he's a poet, which I take to be only one remove from a fool."

"True," said Dupin, after a long and thoughtful whiff from his meerschaum, "although I have been guilty of certain doggerel myself."

"Suppose you detail," said I, "the particulars of your search."

"Why the fact is, we took our time, and we searched *every where*. I have had long experience in these affairs. I took the entire building, room by room; devoting the nights of a whole week to each. We examined, first, the furniture of each apartment. We opened every possible drawer; and I presume you know that, to a properly trained police agent, such a thing as a *secret* drawer is impossible. Any man is a dolt who permits a 'secret' drawer to escape him in a search of this kind. The thing is *so* plain. There is a certain amount of bulk — a space — to be accounted for in every cabinet. Then we have accurate rules. The fiftieth part of a line could not escape us. After the cabinets we took the chairs. The cushions we probed with the fine long needles you have seen me employ. From the tables we removed the tops."

"Why so?"

"Sometimes the top of a table, or other similarly arranged piece of furniture, is removed by the person wishing to conceal an article; then the leg is excavated, the article deposited within the cavity, and the top replaced. The bottoms and tops of bed-posts are employed in the same way."

"But could not the cavity be detected by sounding?" I asked.

"By no means, if, when the article is deposited, a sufficient wadding of cotton be placed around it. Besides, in our case, we were obliged to proceed without noise."

"But you could not have removed — you could not have taken to pieces *all* articles of furniture in which it would have been possible to make a deposit in the manner you mention. A letter may be compressed into a thin spiral roll, not differing much in shape or bulk from a large knitting-needle, and in this form it might be inserted into the rung of a chair, for example. You did not take to pieces all the chairs?"

"Certainly not; but we did better — we examined the rungs of every chair in the hotel, and, indeed, the jointings of every description of furniture, by the aid of a most powerful microscope. Had there been any traces of recent disturbance we should not have failed to detect it instantly. A single grain of gimlet-dust, for example, would have been as obvious as an apple. Any disorder in the glueing — any unusual gaping in the joints — would have sufficed to insure detection."

"I presume you looked to the mirrors, between the boards and the plates, and you probed the beds and the bed-clothes, as well as the curtains and carpets."

"That of course; and when we had absolutely completed every particle of the furniture in this way, then we examined the house itself. We divided its entire surface into compartments, which we numbered, so that none might be missed; then we scrutinized each individual square inch throughout the premises, including the two houses immediately adjoining, with the microscope, as before."

"The two houses adjoining!" I exclaimed; "you must have had a great deal of trouble."

"We had; but the reward offered is prodigious."

"You include the *grounds* about the houses?"

"All the grounds are paved with brick. They gave us comparatively little trouble. We examined the moss between the bricks, and found it undisturbed."

"You looked among D—'s papers, of course, and into the books of the library?"

"Certainly; we opened every package and parcel; we not only opened every book, but we turned over every leaf in each volume, not contenting ourselves with a mere shake, according to the fashion of some of our police officers. We also measured the thickness of every book-*cover*, with the most accurate admeasurement, and applied to each

the most jealous scrutiny of the microscope. Had any of the bindings been recently meddled with, it would have been utterly impossible that the fact should have escaped observation. Some five or six volumes, just from the hands of the binder, we carefully probed, longitudinally, with the needles."

"You explored the floors beneath the carpets?"

"Beyond doubt. We removed every carpet, and examined the boards with the microscope."

"And the paper on the walls?"

"Yes."

"You looked into the cellars?"

"We did."

"Then," I said, "you have been making a miscalculation, and the letter is *not* upon the premises, as you suppose."

"I fear you are right there," said the Prefect. "And now, Dupin, what would you advise me to do?"

"To make a thorough re-search of the premises."

"That is absolutely needless," replied G—. "I am not more sure that I breathe than I am that the letter is not at the Hôtel."

"I have no better advice to give you," said Dupin. "You have, of course, an accurate description of the letter?"

"Oh yes!" — And here the Prefect, producing a memorandum-book, proceeded to read aloud a minute account of the internal, and especially of the external appearance of the missing document. Soon after finishing the perusal of this description, he took his departure, more entirely depressed in spirits than I had ever known the good gentleman before.

In about a month afterwards he paid us another visit, and found us occupied very nearly as before. He took a pipe and a chair and entered into some ordinary conversation. At length I said, —

"Well, but G—, what of the purloined letter? I presume you have at last made up your mind that there is no such thing as overreaching the Minister?"

"Confound him, say I — yes; I made the re-examination, however, as Dupin suggested — but it was all labor lost, as I knew it would be."

"How much was the reward offered, did you say?" asked Dupin.

"Why, a very great deal — a *very* liberal reward — I don't like to say how much, precisely; but one thing I *will* say, that I wouldn't mind giving my individual cheque for fifty thousand francs to any one who could obtain me that letter. The fact is, it is becoming of more and more importance every day; and the reward has been lately doubled. If it were trebled, however, I could do no more than I have done."

"Why, yes," said Dupin, drawlingly, between the whiffs of his meerschaum, "I really — think, G—, you have not exerted yourself — to the utmost in this matter. You might — do a little more, I think, eh?"

"How? — in what way?"

"Why — puff, puff — you might — puff, puff — employ counsel in the matter, eh? — puff, puff, puff. Do you remember the story they tell of Abernethy?"

"No; hang Abernethy!"

"To be sure! hang him and welcome. But, once upon a time, a certain rich miser conceived the design of sponging upon this Abernethy for a medical opinion. Getting up, for this purpose, an ordinary conversation in a private company, he insinuated his case to his physician, as that of an imaginary individual.

"'We will suppose,' said the miser, 'that his symptoms are such and such; now, doctor, what would *you* have directed him to take?'"

"'Take!' said Abernethy, 'why, take *advice*, to be sure.'"

"But," said the Prefect, a little discomposed, "*I* am *perfectly* willing to take advice, and to pay for it. I would *really* give fifty thousand francs to any one who would aid me in the matter."

"In that case," replied Dupin, opening a drawer, and producing a cheque-book, "you may as well fill me up a cheque for the amount mentioned. When you have signed it, I will hand you the letter."

I was astounded. The Prefect appeared absolutely thunder-stricken. For some minutes he remained speechless and motionless, looking incredulously at my friend with open mouth, and eyes that seemed starting from their sockets; then, apparently recovering himself in some measure, he seized a pen, and after several pauses and vacant stares, finally filled up and signed a cheque for fifty thousand francs, and handed it across the table to Dupin. The latter examined it carefully and deposited it in his pocket-book; then, unlocking an *escritoire*, took thence a letter and gave it to the Prefect. This functionary grasped it in a perfect agony of joy, opened it with a trembling hand, cast a rapid glance at its contents, and then, scrambling and struggling to the door, rushed at length unceremoniously from the room and from the house, without having uttered a syllable since Dupin had requested him to fill up the cheque.

When he had gone, my friend entered into some explanations.

"The Parisian police," he said, "are exceedingly able in their way. They are persevering, ingenious, cunning, and thoroughly versed in the knowledge which their duties seem chiefly to demand. Thus, when G— detailed to us his mode of searching the premises at the Hôtel D—, I felt entire confidence in his having made a satisfactory investigation — so far as his labors extended."

"So far as his labors extended?" said I.

"Yes," said Dupin. "The measures adopted were not only the best of their kind, but carried out to absolute perfection. Had the letter been deposited within the range of their search, these fellows would, beyond a question, have found it."

I merely laughed — but he seemed quite serious in all that he said.

"The measures, then," he continued, "were good in their kind, and well executed; their defect lay in their being inapplicable to the case, and to the man. A certain set of highly ingenious resources are, with the Prefect, a sort of Procrustean bed, to which he forcibly adapts his designs. But he perpetually errs by being too deep or too shallow, for the matter in hand; and many a schoolboy is a better reasoner than he. I knew one about eight years of age, whose success at guessing in the game of 'even and odd' attracted universal admiration. This game is simple, and is played with marbles. One player holds in his hand a number of these toys, and demands of another whether that number is even or odd. If the guess is right, the guesser wins one; if wrong, he loses one. The boy to whom I allude won all the marbles of the school. Of course he had some principle of guessing; and this lay in mere observation and admeasurement of the astuteness of his opponents. For example, an arrant simpleton is his opponent, and, holding up his closed hand, asks, 'are they even or odd?' Our schoolboy replies, 'odd,' and loses; but upon the second trial he wins, for he then says to himself, 'the simpleton had them even upon the first trial, and his amount of cunning is just sufficient to make him have them odd upon the second; I will therefore guess odd'; — he guesses odd, and wins. Now, with a simpleton a degree above the first, he would have reasoned thus: 'This fellow finds that in the first instance I guessed odd, and, in the second, he will propose to himself upon the first impulse, a simple variation from even to odd, as did the first simpleton; but then a second thought will suggest that this is too simple a variation, and finally he will decide upon putting it even as before. I will therefore guess even'; — he guesses even, and wins. Now this mode of reasoning in the schoolboy, whom his fellows termed 'lucky,' — what, in its last analysis, is it?"

"It is merely," I said, "an identification of the reasoner's intellect with that of his opponent."

"It is," said Dupin; "and, upon inquiring of the boy by what means he effected the *thorough* identification in which his success consisted, I received answer as follows: 'When I wish to find out how wise, or how stupid, or how good, or how wicked is any one, or what are his thoughts at the moment, I fashion the expression of my face, as accurately as possible, in accordance with the expression of his, and then wait to see what thoughts or sentiments arise in my mind or heart, as if to match or correspond with the expression.' This response of the schoolboy lies at the bottom of all the spurious profundity which has been attributed to Rochefoucauld, to La Bougive, to Machiavelli, and to Campanella."

"And the identification," I said, "of the reasoner's intellect with that of his opponent, depends, if I understand you aright, upon the accuracy with which the opponent's intellect is admeasured."

"For its practical value it depends upon this," replied Dupin; "and the Prefect and his cohort fail so frequently, first, by default of this identification, and, secondly, by ill-admeasurement, or rather through non-admeasurement of the intellect with which they are engaged. They consider only their *own* ideas of ingenuity; and, in searching for anything hidden, advert only to the modes in which *they* would have hidden it. They are right in this much — that their own ingenuity is a faithful representative of that of *the mass*; but when the cunning of the individual felon is diverse in character from their own, the felon foils them, of course. This always happens when it is above their own, and very usually when it is below. They have no variation of principle in their investigations; at best, when urged by some unusual emergency — by some extraordinary reward — they extend or exaggerate their old modes of *practice*, without touching their principles. What, for example, in this case of D——, has been done to vary the principle of action? What is all this boring, and probing, and sounding, and scrutinizing with the microscope, and dividing the surface of the building into registered square inches — what is it all but an exaggeration *of the application* of the one principle or set of principles of search, which are based upon the one set of notions regarding human ingenuity, to which the Prefect, in the long routine of his duty, has been accustomed? Do you not see he has taken it for granted that *all* men proceed to conceal a letter — not exactly in a gimlet-hole bored in a chair-leg — but, at least, in *some* out-of-the-way hole or corner suggested by the same tenor of thought which would urge a man to secrete a letter in a gimlet-hole bored in a chair-leg? And do you not see also, that such *recherchés* nooks for concealment are adapted only for ordinary occasions, and would be adopted only by ordinary intellects; for, in all cases of concealment, a disposal of the article concealed — a disposal of it in this *recherché* manner — is, in the very first instance, presumable and presumed; and thus its discovery depends, not at all upon the acumen, but altogether upon the mere care, patience, and determination of the seekers; and where the case is of importance — or, what amounts to the same thing in the policial eyes, when the reward is of magnitude, — the qualities in question have *never* been known to fail? You will now understand what I meant in suggesting that, had the purloined letter been hidden any where within the limits of the Prefect's examination — in other words, had the principle of its concealment been comprehended within the principles of the Prefect — its discovery would have been a matter altogether beyond question. This functionary, however, has been thoroughly mystified; and the remote source of his defeat lies in the supposition that the Minister is a fool, because he has acquired renown as a poet. All fools are poets; this the Prefect *feels*; and he is merely guilty of a *non distributio medii*[1] in thence inferring that all poets are fools."

"But is this really the poet?" I asked. "There are two brothers, I know; and both have attained reputation in letters. The Minister I believe has written learnedly on the Differential Calculus. He is a mathematician, and no poet."

"You are mistaken; I know him well; he is both. As poet *and* mathematician, he would reason well; as mere mathematician, he could not have reasoned at all, and thus would have been at the mercy of the Prefect."

"You surprise me," I said, "by these opinions, which have been contradicted by the voice of the world. You do not mean to set at naught the well-digested idea of centuries. The mathematical reason has long been regarded as *the* reason *par excellence*."

" '*Il y a à parier*,' " replied Dupin, quoting from Chamfort, " '*que toute idée publique, toute convention reçue, est une sottise, car elle a convenu au plus grand nombre.*'[2] The mathe-

maticians, I grant you, have done their best to promulgate the popular error to which you allude, and which is none the less an error for its promulgation as truth. With an art worthy a better cause, for example, they have insinuated the term 'analysis' into application to algebra. The French are the originators of this particular deception; but if a term is of any importance — if words derive any value from applicability — then 'analysis' conveys 'algebra' about as much as, in Latin, '*ambitus*' implies 'ambition,' '*religio*' 'religion,' or '*homines honesti*' a set of *honorable* men."

"You have a quarrel on hand, I see," said I, "with some of the algebraists of Paris; but proceed."

"I dispute the availability, and thus the value, of that reason which is cultivated in any especial form other than the abstractly logical. I dispute, in particular, the reason educed by mathematical study. The mathematics are the science of form and quantity; mathematical reasoning is merely logic applied to observation upon form and quantity. The great error lies in supposing that even the truths of what is called *pure* algebra, are abstract or general truths. And this error is so egregious that I am confounded at the universality with which it has been received. Mathematical axioms are *not* axioms of general truth. What is true of *relation* — of form and quantity — is often grossly false in regard to morals, for example. In this latter science it is very usually *un*true that the aggregated parts are equal to the whole. In chemistry also the axiom fails. In the consideration of motive it fails; for two motives, each of a given value, have not, necessarily, a value when united, equal to the sum of their values apart. There are numerous other mathematical truths which are only truths within the limits of *relation*. But the mathematician argues, from his *finite truths*, through habit, as if they were of an absolutely general applicability — as the world indeed imagines them to be. Bryant, in his very learned 'Mythology,' mentions an analogous source of error, when he says that 'although the Pagan fables are not believed, yet we forget ourselves continually, and make inferences from them

---

[1] undistributed middle.
[2] "I'll wager, that every idea which is generally held, every set convention, is a stupidity; for it has suited the majority."

as existing realities.' With the algebraists, however, who are Pagans themselves, the 'Pagan fables' *are* believed, and the inferences are made, not so much through lapse of memory, as through an unaccountable addling of the brains. In short, I never yet encountered the mere mathematician who could be trusted out of equal roots, or one who did not clandestinely hold it as a point of his faith that $x^2 + px$ was absolutely and unconditionally equal to q. Say to one of these gentlemen, by way of experiment, if you please, that you believe occasions may occur where $x^2 + px$ is *not* altogether equal to q, and, having made him understand what you mean, get out of his reach as speedily as convenient, for, beyond doubt, he will endeavor to knock you down.

"I mean to say," continued Dupin, while I merely laughed at his last observations, "that if the Minister had been no more than a mathematician, the Prefect would have been under no necessity of giving me this check. I knew him, however, as both mathematician and poet, and my measures were adapted to his capacity, with reference to the circumstances by which he was surrounded. I knew him as a courtier, too, and as a bold *intriguant*. Such a man, I considered, could not fail to be aware of the ordinary policial modes of action. He could not have failed to anticipate — and events have proved that he did not fail to anticipate — the waylayings to which he was subjected. He must have foreseen, I reflected, the secret investigations of his premises. His frequent absences from home at night, which were hailed by the Prefect as certain aids to his success, I regarded only as *ruses*, to afford opportunity for thorough search to the police, and thus the sooner to impress them with the conviction to which G—, in fact, did finally arrive — the conviction that the letter was not upon the premises. I felt, also, that the whole train of thought, which I was at some pains in detailing to you just now, concerning the invariable principle of policial action in searches for articles concealed — I felt that this whole train of thought would necessarily pass through the mind of the Minister. It would imperatively lead him to despise all the ordinary *nooks* of concealment. *He* could not, I reflected, be so weak as not to see that the most intricate and remote recess of his hotel would be as open as his commonest closets to the eyes, to the probes, to the gimlets, and to the microscopes of the Prefect. I saw, in fine, that he would be driven, as a matter of course, to *simplicity*, if not deliberately induced to it as a matter of choice. You will remember, perhaps, how desperately the Prefect laughed when I suggested, upon our first interview, that it was just possible this mystery troubled him so much on account of its being so *very* self-evident."

"Yes," said I, "I remember his merriment well. I really thought he would have fallen into convulsions."

"The material world," continued Dupin, "abounds with the very strict analogies to the immaterial; and thus some color of truth has been given to the rhetorical dogma, that metaphor, or simile, may be made to strengthen an argument, as well as to embellish a description. The principle of the *vis inertiæ*, for example, seems to be identical in physics and metaphysics. It is not more true in the former, that a large body is with more difficulty set in motion than a smaller one, and that its subsequent *momentum* is commensurate with this difficulty, than it is, in the latter, that intellects of the vaster capacity, while more forcible, more constant, and more eventful in their movements than those of inferior grade, are yet the less readily moved, and more embarrassed and full of hesitation in the first few steps of their progress. Again: have you ever noticed which of the street signs, over the shop doors, are the most attractive of attention?"

"I have never given the matter a thought," I said.

"There is a game of puzzles," he resumed, "which is played upon a map. One party playing requires another to find a given word — the name of town, river, state or empire — any word, in short, upon the motley and perplexed surface of the chart. A novice in the game generally seeks to embarrass his opponents by giving them the most minutely lettered names; but the adept selects such words as stretch, in large characters, from one end of the chart to the other. These, like the over-largely lettered signs and placards of the street, escape observation by dint of being excessively obvious; and here the physical oversight is precisely analogous with the moral inapprehension by which the intellect suffers to pass unnoticed those considerations which are too obtrusively and too palpably self-evident. But this is a point, it appears, somewhat above or beneath the understanding of the Prefect. He never once thought it probable, or possible, that the Minister had deposited the letter immediately beneath the nose of the whole world, by way of best preventing any portion of that world from perceiving it.

"But the more I reflected upon the daring, dashing, and discriminating ingenuity of D—; upon the fact that the document must always have been *at hand*, if he intended to use it to good purpose; and upon the decisive evidence, obtained by the Prefect, that it was not hidden within the limits of that dignitary's ordinary search — the more satisfied I became that, to conceal this letter, the Minister had resorted to the comprehensive and sagacious expedient of not attempting to conceal it at all.

"Full of these ideas, I prepared myself with a pair of green spectacles, and called one fine morning, quite by accident, at the Ministerial hotel. I found D— at home, yawning, lounging, and dawdling, as usual, and pretending to be in the last extremity of *ennui*. He is, perhaps, the most really energetic human being now alive — but that is only when nobody sees him.

"To be even with him, I complained of my weak eyes, and lamented the necessity of the spectacles, under cover of which I cautiously and thoroughly surveyed the apartment, while seemingly intent only upon the conversation of my host.

"I paid especial attention to a large writing-table near which he sat, and upon which lay confusedly some miscellaneous letters and other papers, with one or two musical instruments and a few books. Here, however, after a long and very deliberate scrutiny, I saw nothing to excite particular suspicion.

"At length my eyes, in going the circuit of the room, fell upon a trumpery filigree card-rack of pasteboard, that hung dangling by a dirty blue ribbon, from a little brass knob just beneath the middle of the mantelpiece. In this rack, which had three or four compartments, were five or six visiting cards and a solitary letter. This last was much soiled and crumpled. It was torn nearly in two, across the middle — as if a design, in the first instance, to tear it entirely up as worthless, had been altered, or stayed, in the second. It had a large black seal, bearing the D— cipher *very* conspicuously, and was addressed, in a diminutive female hand, to D—, the Minister, himself. It was thrust carelessly, and even, as it seemed, contemptuously, into one of the upper divisions of the rack.

"No sooner had I glanced at this letter, than I concluded it to be that of which I was in search. To be sure, it was, to all appearance, radically different from the one of which the Prefect had read us so minute a description. Here the seal was large and black, with the D— cipher; there it was small and red, with the ducal arms of the S— family. Here, the address, to the Minister, was diminutive and feminine; there the superscription, to a certain royal personage, was markedly bold and decided; the size alone formed a point of correspondence. But, then, the *radicalness* of these differences, which was excessive; the dirt; the soiled and torn condition of the paper, so inconsistent with the *true* methodical habits of D—, and so suggestive of a design to delude the beholder into an idea of the worthlessness of the document; — these things, together with the hyperobtrusive situation of this document, full in the view of every visitor, and thus exactly in accordance with the conclusions to which I had previously arrived; these things, I say, were strongly corroborative of suspicion, in one who came with the intention to suspect.

"I protracted my visit as long as possible, and, while I maintained a most animated discussion with the Minister, on a topic which I knew well had never failed to interest and excite him, I kept my attention really riveted upon the letter. In this examination, I committed to memory its external appearance and arrangement in the rack; and also fell, at length, upon a discovery which set at rest whatever trivial doubt I might have entertained. In scrutinizing the edges of the paper, I observed them to be more *chafed* than seemed necessary. They presented the *broken* appearance which is manifested when a stiff paper, having been once folded and pressed with a folder, is refolded in a reversed direction, in the same creases or edges which had formed the original fold. This discovery was sufficient. It was clear to me that the letter had been turned, as a glove, inside out, re-directed, and re-sealed. I bade the Minister good morning, and took my departure at once, leaving a gold snuff-box upon the table.

"The next morning I called for the snuff-box, when we resumed, quite eagerly, the conversation of the preceding day. While thus engaged, however, a loud report, as if of a pistol, was heard immediately beneath the windows of the hotel, and was succeeded by a series of fearful screams, and the shoutings of a mob. D— rushed to a casement, threw it open, and looked out. In the meantime, I stepped to the card-rack, took the letter, put it in my pocket, and replaced it by a *fac-simile* (so far as regards externals), which I had carefully prepared at my lodgings; imitating the D— cipher, very readily, by means of a seal formed of bread.

"The disturbance in the street had been occasioned by the frantic behavior of a man with a musket. He had fired it among a crowd of women and children. It proved, however, to have been without ball, and the fellow was suffered to go his way as a lunatic or a drunkard. When he had gone, D— came from the window, whither I had followed him immediately upon securing the object in view. Soon afterwards I bade him farewell. The pretended lunatic was a man in my own pay."

"But what purpose had you," I asked, "in replacing the letter by a *fac-simile*? Would it not have been better, at the first visit, to have seized it openly, and departed?"

"D—," replied Dupin, "is a desperate man, and a man of nerve. His hotel, too, is not without attendants devoted to his interests. Had I made the wild attempt you suggest, I might never have left the Ministerial presence alive. The good people of Paris might have heard of me no more. But I had an object apart from these considerations. You know my political prepossessions. In this matter, I act as a partisan of the lady concerned. For eighteen months the Minister has had her in his power. She has now him in hers — since, being unaware that the letter is not in his possession, he will proceed with his exactions as if it was. Thus will he inevitably commit himself, at once, to his political destruction. His downfall, too, will not be more precipitate than awkward. It is all very well to talk about the *facilis descensus Averni*;[1] but in all kinds of climbing, as Catalani said of singing, it is far more easy to get up than to come down. In the present instance I have no sympathy — at least no pity — for him who descends. He is that *monstrum horrendum*,[2] an unprincipled man of genius. I confess, however, that I should like very well to know the precise character of his thoughts, when, being defied by her whom the Prefect terms 'a certain personage,' he is reduced to opening the letter which I left for him in the card-rack."

"How? did you put any thing particular in it?"

"Why — it did not seem altogether right to leave the interior blank — that would have been insulting. D—, at Vienna once, did me an evil turn, which I told him, quite good-humoredly, that I should remember. So, as I knew he would feel some curiosity in regard to the identity of the person who had outwitted him, I thought it a pity not to give him a clue. He is well acquainted with my MS., and I just copied into the middle of the blank sheet the words —

> "— *Un dessein si funeste,*
> *S'il n'est digne d'Atrée, est digne de*
> *Thyeste.*[3]

They are to be found in Crébillon's 'Atrée.'"

[1] "Easy descent to Hades."
[2] "Horrible monster."
[3] "So deadly a scheme, if it is not worthy of Atreus is at least worthy of Thyestes."

Hawthorne's Twice-Told Tales

(1842)

We said a few hurried words about Mr. Hawthorne in our last number, with the design of speaking more fully in the present. We are still, however, pressed for room, and must necessarily discuss his volumes more briefly and more at random than their high merits deserve.

The book professes to be a collection of *tales*, yet is, in two respects, misnamed. These pieces are now in their third republication, and, of course, are thrice-told. Moreover, they are by no means *all* tales, either in the ordinary or in the legitimate understanding of the term. Many of them are pure essays; for example, "Sights from a Steeple," "Sunday at Home," "Little Annie's Ramble," "A Rill from the Town Pump," "The Toll-Gatherer's Day," "The Haunted Mind," "The Sister Years," "Snow-Flakes," "Night Sketches," and "Foot-Prints on the Sea-Shore." We mention these matters chiefly on account of their discrepancy with that marked precision and finish by which the body of the work is distinguished.

Of the essays just named, we must be content to speak in brief. They are each and all beautiful, without being characterized by the polish and adaptation so visible in the tales proper. A painter would at once note their leading or predominant feature, and style it *repose*. There is no attempt at effect. All is quiet, thoughtful, subdued. Yet this repose may exist simultaneously with high originality of thought; and Mr. Hawthorne has demonstrated the fact. At every turn we meet with novel combinations; yet these combinations never surpass the limits of the quiet. We are soothed as we read; and withal is a calm astonishment that ideas so apparently obvious have never occurred or been presented to us before. Herein our author differs materially from Lamb or Hunt or Hazlitt — who, with vivid originality of manner and expression, have less of the true novelty of thought than is generally supposed, and whose originality, at best, has an uneasy and meretricious quaintness, replete with startling effects unfounded in nature, and inducing trains of reflection which lead to no satisfactory result. The Essays of Hawthorne have much of the character of Irving, with more of originality, and less of finish; while, compared with the Spectator, they have a vast superiority at all points. The Spectator, Mr. Irving, and Mr. Hawthorne have in common that tranquil and subdued manner which we have chosen to denominate *repose*; but, in the case of the two former, this repose is attained rather by the absence of novel combination, or of originality, than otherwise, and consists chiefly in the calm, quiet, unostentatious expression of commonplace thoughts, in an unambitious, unadulterated Saxon. In them, by strong effort, we are made to conceive the absence of all. In the essays before us the absence of effort is too obvious to be mistaken, and a strong undercurrent of *suggestion* runs continuously beneath the upper stream of the tranquil thesis. In short, these effusions of Mr. Hawthorne are the product of a truly imaginative intellect, restrained, and in some measure repressed, by fastidiousness of taste, by constitutional melancholy, and by indolence.

But it is of his tales that we desire principally to speak. The tale proper, in our opinion, affords unquestionably the fairest field for the exercise of the loftiest talent, which can be afforded by the wide domains of mere prose. Were we bidden to say how the highest genius could be most advantageously employed for the best display of its own powers, we should answer, without hesitation — in the composition of a rhymed poem, not to exceed in length what might be perused in an hour. Within this limit alone can the highest order of true poetry exist. We need only here say, upon this topic, that, in almost all classes of composition, the unity of effect or impression is a point of the greatest importance. It is clear, moreover, that this unity cannot be thoroughly preserved in productions whose perusal cannot be completed at one sitting. We may continue the reading of a prose composition, from the very nature of prose itself, much longer than we can persevere, to any good purpose, in the perusal of a poem. This latter, if truly fulfilling the demands of the poetic sentiment, induces an exaltation of the soul which cannot be long sustained. All high excitements are necessarily transient. Thus a long poem is a paradox. And, without unity of impression, the deepest effects cannot be brought about. Epics were the offspring of an imperfect sense of Art, and their reign is no more. A poem *too* brief may produce a vivid, but never an intense or enduring impression. Without a certain continuity of effort — without a certain duration or repetition of purpose — the soul is never deeply moved. There must be the dropping of the water upon the rock. De Béranger has wrought brilliant things — pungent and spirit-stirring — but, like all immassive bodies, they lack *momentum*, and thus fail to satisfy the Poetic Sentiment. They sparkle and excite, but, from want of continuity, fail deeply to impress. Extreme brevity will degenerate into epigrammatism; but the sin of extreme length is even more unpardonable. *In medio tutissimus ibis.* [You travel most safely the middle road.]

Were we called upon, however, to designate that class of composition which, next to such a poem as we have suggested, should best fulfil the demands of high genius — should offer it the most advantageous field of exertion — we should unhesitatingly speak of the prose tale, as Mr. Hawthorne has here exemplified it. We allude to the short prose narrative, requiring from a half-hour to one or two hours in its perusal. The ordinary novel is objectionable, from its length, for reasons already stated in substance. As it cannot be read at one sitting, it deprives itself, of course, of the immense force derivable from *totality*. Worldly interests intervening during the pauses of perusal, modify, annul, or counteract, in a greater or less degree, the impressions of the book. But simple cessation in reading would, of itself, be sufficient to destroy the true unity. In the brief tale, however, the author is enabled to carry out the fulness of his intention, be it what it may. During the hour of perusal the soul of the reader is at the writer's control. There are no external or extrinsic influences — resulting from weariness or interruption.

A skilful literary artist has constructed a tale. If wise, he has not fashioned his thoughts to accommodate his incidents; but having conceived, with deliberate care, a certain unique or single *effect* to be wrought out, he then invents such incidents — he then combines such events as may best aid him in establishing this preconceived effect. If his very initial sentence tend not to the outbringing of this effect, then he has failed in his first step. In the whole composition there should be no word written, of which the tendency, direct or indirect, is not to the one pre-established design. And by such means, with such care and skill, a picture is at length painted which leaves in the mind of him who contemplates it with a kindred art, a sense of the fullest satisfaction. The idea of the tale has been presented unblemished, because undisturbed; and this is an end unattainable by the novel. Undue brevity is just as exceptionable here as in the poem; but undue length is yet more to be avoided.

We have said that the tale has a point of superiority even over the poem. In fact, while the *rhythm* of this latter is an essential aid in the development of the poem's highest idea — the idea of the Beautiful — the artificialities of this rhythm are an inseparable bar to the development of all points of thought or expression which have their basis in *Truth*. But Truth is often, and in very great degree, the aim of the tale. Some of the finest tales are tales of ratiocination. Thus the field of this species of composition, if not in so elevated a region on the mountain of Mind, is a table-land of far vaster extent than the domain of the mere poem. Its products are never so rich, but infinitely more numerous, and more appreciable by the mass of mankind. The writer of the prose tale, in short, may bring to his theme a vast variety of modes or inflections of thought and expression — (the ratiocinative, for example, the sarcastic, or the humorous) which are not only antagonistical to the nature of the poem, but absolutely forbidden by one of its most peculiar and indispensable adjuncts; we allude, of course, to rhythm. It may be added here, *par parenthèse*, that the author who aims at the purely beautiful in a prose tale is laboring at a great disadvantage. For Beauty can be better treated in the poem. Not so with terror, or passion, or horror, or a multitude of such other points. And here it will be seen how full of prejudice are the usual animadversions against those *tales of effect*, many fine examples of which were found in the earlier numbers of *Blackwood*. The impressions produced were wrought in a legitimate sphere of action, and constituted a legitimate although sometimes an exaggerated interest. They were relished by every man of genius: although there were found many men of genius who condemned them without just ground. The true critic will but demand that the design intended be accomplished, to the fullest extent, by the means most advantageously applicable.

We have very few American tales of real merit — we may say, indeed, none, with the exception of *The Tales of a Traveller* of Washington Irving, and these *Twice-Told Tales* of Mr. Hawthorne. Some of the pieces of Mr. John Neal abound in vigor and originality; but, in general, his compositions of this class are excessively diffuse, extravagant, and indicative of an imperfect sentiment of Art. Articles at random are, now and then, met with in our periodicals which might be advantageously compared with the best effusions of the British Magazines; but, upon the whole, we are far behind our progenitors in this department of literature.

Of Mr. Hawthorne's tales we should say, emphatically, that they belong to the highest region of Art — an Art subservient to genius of a very lofty order. We had supposed, with good reason for so supposing, that he had been thrust into his present position by one of the impudent *cliques* which beset our literature, and whose pretensions it is our full purpose to expose at the earliest opportunity; but we have been most agreeably mistaken. We know of few compositions which the critic can more honestly commend than these *Twice-Told Tales*. As Americans, we feel proud of the book.

Mr. Hawthorne's distinctive trait is invention, creation, imagination, originality — a trait which, in the literature of fiction, is positively worth all the rest. But the nature of the originality, so far as regards its manifestation in letters, is but imperfectly understood. The inventive or original mind as frequently displays itself in novelty of *tone* as in novelty of matter. Mr. Hawthorne is original at *all* points.

It would be a matter of some difficulty to designate the best of these tales; we repeat that, without exception, they are beautiful. "Wakefield" is remarkable for the skill with which an old idea — a well-known incident — is worked up or discussed. A man of whims conceives the purpose of quitting his wife and residing *incognito*, for twenty years, in her immediate neighborhood. Something of this kind actually happened in London. The force of Mr. Hawthorne's tale lies in the analysis of the motives which must or might have impelled the husband to such folly, in the first instance, with the possible causes of his perseverance. Upon this thesis a sketch of singular power has been constructed.

"The Wedding Knell" is full of the boldest imagination — an imagination fully controlled by taste. The most captious critic could find no flaw in this production.

"The Minister's Black Veil" is a masterly composition, of which the sole defect is that to the rabble its exquisite skill will be *caviare*. The *obvious* meaning of this article will be found to smother its insinuated one. The *moral* put into the mouth of the dying minister will be supposed to convey the *true* import of the narrative; and that a crime of dark dye (having reference to the "young lady") has been committed, is a point which only minds congenial with that of the author will perceive.

"Mr. Higginbotham's Catastrophe" is vividly original, and managed most dexterously.

"Dr. Heidegger's Experiment" is exceedingly well imagined, and executed with surpassing ability. The artist breathes in every line of it.

"The White Old Maid" is objectionable even more than the "Minister's Black Veil," on the score of its mysticism. Even with the thoughtful and analytic, there will be much trouble in penetrating its entire import.

"The Hollow of the Three Hills" we would quote in full had we space; — not as evincing higher talent than any of the other pieces, but as affording an excellent example of the author's peculiar ability. The subject is commonplace. A witch subjects the Distant and the Past to the view of a mourner. It has been the fashion to describe, in such cases, a mirror in which the images of the absent appear; or a cloud of smoke is made to arise, and thence the figures are gradually unfolded. Mr. Hawthorne has wonderfully heightened his effect by making the ear, in place of the eye, the medium by which the fantasy is conveyed. The head of the mourner is enveloped in the cloak of the witch, and within its magic folds there arise sounds which have an all-sufficient intelligence. Throughout this article also, the artist is conspicuous — not more in positive than in negative merits. Not only is all done that should be done, but (what perhaps is an end with more difficulty attained) there is nothing done which should not be. Every word *tells*, and there is not a word which does *not* tell.

In "Howe's Masquerade" we observe something which resembles plagiarism — but which *may be* a very flattering coincidence of thought. We quote the passage in question.

[Quotation.] [1]

The idea here is, that the figure in the cloak is the phantom or reduplication of Sir William Howe; but in an article called "William Wilson," one of the *Tales of the Grotesque and Arabesque*, we have not only the same idea, but the same idea similarly presented in several respects. We quote two paragraphs, which our readers may compare with what has been already given. We have italicized, above, the immediate particulars of resemblance.

[Quotation.] [1]

Here it will be observed that, not only are the two general conceptions identical, but there are various *points* of similarity. In each case the figure seen is the wraith or duplication of the beholder. In each case the scene is a masquerade. In each case the figure is cloaked. In each, there is a quarrel — that is to say, angry words pass between the parties. In each the beholder is enraged. In each the cloak and sword fall upon the floor. The "villain, unmuffle yourself," of Mr. H. is precisely paralleled by a passage at page 56 of "William Wilson."

In the way of objection we have scarcely a word to say of these tales. There is, perhaps, a somewhat too general or prevalent *tone* — a tone of melancholy and mysticism. The subjects are insufficiently varied. There is not so much of *versatility* evinced as we might well be warranted in expecting from the high powers of Mr. Hawthorne. But beyond these trivial exceptions we have really none to make. The style is purity itself. Force abounds. High imagination gleams from every page. Mr. Hawthorne is a man of the truest genius. We only regret that the limits of our Magazine will not permit us to pay him that full tribute of commendation, which, under other circumstances, we should be so eager to pay.

The Philosophy of Composition
(1846)

Charles Dickens, in a note now lying before me, alluding to an examination I once made of the mechanism of *Barnaby Rudge*, says — "By the way, are you aware that Godwin wrote his *Caleb Williams* backwards? He first involved his hero in a web of difficulties, forming the second volume, and then, for the first, cast about him for some mode of accounting for what had been done."

I cannot think this the *precise* mode of procedure on the part of Godwin — and indeed what he himself acknowledges, is not altogether in accordance with Mr. Dickens' idea — but the author of *Caleb Williams* was too good an artist not to perceive the advantage derivable from at least a somewhat similar process. Nothing is more clear than that every plot, worth the name, must be elaborated to its *dénouement* before anything be attempted with the pen. It is only with the *dénouement* constantly in view that we can give a plot its indispensable air of consequence, or causation, by making the incidents, and especially the tone at all points, tend to the development of the intention.

There is a radical error, I think, in the usual mode of constructing a story. Either

[1] Omitted here, as in the text of the Virginia edition.

history affords a thesis — or one is suggested by an incident of the day — or, at best, the author sets himself to work in the combination of striking events to form merely the basis of his narrative — designing, generally, to fill in with description, dialogue, or autorial comment, whatever crevices of fact, or action, may, from page to page, render themselves apparent.

I prefer commencing with the consideration of an *effect*. Keeping originality *always* in view — for he is false to himself who ventures to dispense with so obvious and so easily attainable a source of interest — I say to myself, in the first place, "Of the innumerable effects, or impressions, of which the heart, the intellect, or (more generally) the soul is susceptible, what one shall I, on the present occasion, select!" Having chosen a novel, first, and secondly, a vivid effect, I consider whether it can be best wrought by incident or tone — whether by ordinary incidents and peculiar tone, or the converse, or by peculiarity both of incident and tone — afterward looking about me (or rather within) for such combinations of event, or tone, as shall best aid me in the construction of the effect.

I have often thought how interesting a magazine paper might be written by any author who would — that is to say who could — detail, step by step, the processes by which any one of his compositions attained its ultimate point of completion. Why such a paper has never been given to the world, I am much at a loss to say — but, perhaps, the autorial vanity has had more to do with the omission than any one other cause. Most writers — poets in especial — prefer having it understood that they compose by a species of fine frenzy — an ecstatic intuition — and would positively shudder at letting the public take a peep behind the scenes, at the elaborate and vacillating crudities of thought — at the true purposes seized only at the last moment — at the innumerable glimpses of idea that arrived not at the maturity of full view — at the fully matured fancies discarded in despair as unmanageable — at the cautious selections and rejections — at the painful erasures and interpolations — in a word, at the wheels and pinions — the

tackle for scene-shifting — the step-ladders and demon-traps — the cock's feathers, the red paint and the black patches, which, in ninety-nine cases out of the hundred, constitute the properties of the literary *histrio*.

I am aware, on the other hand, that the case is by no means common, in which an author is at all in condition to retrace the steps by which his conclusions have been attained. In general, suggestions, having arisen pell-mell, are pursued and forgotten in a similar manner.

For my own part, I have neither sympathy with the repugnance alluded to, nor, at any time the least difficulty in recalling to mind the progressive steps of any of my compositions; and, since the interest of an analysis, or reconstruction, such as I have considered a *desideratum*, is quite independent of any real or fancied interest in the thing analyzed, it will not be regarded as a breach of decorum on my part to show the *modus operandi* by which some one of my own works was put together. I select "The Raven," as most generally known. It is my design to render it manifest that no one point in its composition is referrible either to accident or intuition — that the work proceeded, step by step, to its completion with the precision and rigid consequence of a mathematical problem.

Let us dismiss, as irrelevant to the poem, *per se*, the circumstance — or say the necessity — which, in the first place, gave rise to the intention of composing *a* poem that should suit at once the popular and the critical taste.

We commence, then, with this intention.

The initial consideration was that of extent. If any literary work is too long to be read at one sitting, we must be content to dispense with the immensely important effect derivable from unity of impression — for, if two sittings be required, the affairs of the world interfere, and every thing like totality is at once destroyed. But since, *ceteris paribus*, no poet can afford to dispense with *any thing* that may advance his design, it but remains to be seen whether there is, in extent, any advantage to counterbalance the loss of unity which attends it. Here I say no, at once. What we term a long poem is, in fact, merely a succession of brief ones — that is to say, of brief poetical effects. It is needless to demonstrate that a poem is such, only inasmuch as it intensely excites, by elevating, the soul; and all intense excitements are, through a psychal necessity, brief. For this reason, at least one half of the *Paradise Lost* is essentially prose — a succession of poetical excitements interspersed, *inevitably*, with corresponding depressions — the whole being deprived, through the extremeness of its length, of the vastly important artistic element, totality, or unity, of effect.

It appears evident, then, that there is a distinct limit, as regards length, to all works of literary art — the limit of a single sitting — and that, although in certain classes of prose composition, such as *Robinson Crusoe* (demanding no unity), this limit may be advantageously overpassed, it can never properly be overpassed in a poem. Within this limit, the extent of a poem may be made to bear mathematical relation to its merit — in other words, to the excitement or elevation — again in other words, to the degree of the true poetical effect which it is capable of inducing; for it is clear that the brevity must be in direct ratio of the intensity of the intended effect: — this, with one proviso — that a certain degree of duration is absolutely requisite for the production of any effect at all.

Holding in view these considerations, as well as that degree of excitement which I deemed not above the popular, while not below the critical, taste, I reached at once what I conceived the proper *length* for my intended poem — a length of about one hundred lines. It is, in fact, a hundred and eight.

My next thought concerned the choice of an impression, or effect, to be conveyed: and here I may as well observe that, throughout the construction, I kept steadily in view the design of rendering the work *universally* appreciable. I should be carried too far out of my immediate topic were I to demonstrate a point upon which I have repeatedly insisted, and which, with the poetical, stands not in the slightest need of demonstration — the point, I mean, that Beauty is the sole legitimate province of the poem. A few words, however, in elucidation of my real meaning, which some of my friends have evinced a disposition to misrepresent. That pleasure which is at once the most intense, the most elevating, and the most pure, is I believe, found in the contemplation of the beautiful. When, indeed, men speak of Beauty, they mean, precisely, not a quality, as is supposed, but an effect — they refer, in short, just to that intense and pure elevation of *soul* — *not* of intellect, or of heart — upon which I have commented, and which is experienced in consequence of contemplating "the beautiful." Now I designate Beauty as the province of the poem, merely because it is an obvious rule of Art that effects should be made to spring from direct causes — that objects should be attained through means best adapted for their attainment — no one as yet having been weak enough to deny that the peculiar elevation alluded to is *most readily* attained in the poem. Now the object Truth, or the satisfaction of the intellect, and the object Passion, or the excitement of the heart, are, although attainable, to a certain extent, in poetry, far more readily attainable in prose. Truth, in fact, demands a precision, and Passion a *homeliness* (the truly passionate will comprehend me) which are absolutely antagonistic to that Beauty which, I maintain, is the excitement, or pleasurable elevation, of the soul. It by no means follows from any thing here said, that passion, or even truth, may not be introduced, and even profitably introduced, into a poem — for they may serve in elucidation, or aid the general effect, as do discords in music, by contrast — but the true artist will always contrive, first, to tone them into proper subservience to the predominant aim, and, secondly, to enveil them, as far as possible, in that Beauty which is the atmosphere and the essence of the poem.

Regarding, then, Beauty as my province, my next question referred to the *tone* of its highest manifestation — and all experience has shown that this tone is one of *sadness*. Beauty of whatever kind, in its supreme development, invariably excites the sensitive soul to tears. Melancholy is thus the most legitimate of all the poetical tones.

The length, the province, and the tone, being thus determined, I betook myself to ordinary induction, with the view of obtaining some artistic piquancy which might serve me as a key-note in the construction of the poem — some pivot upon which the whole structure might turn. In carefully thinking over all the usual artistic effects — or more properly *points*, in the theatrical sense — I did not fail to perceive immediately that no one had been so universally employed as that of the *refrain*. The universality of its employment sufficed to assure me of its intrinsic value, and spared me the necessity of submitting it to analysis. I considered it, however, with regard to its susceptibility of improvement, and soon saw it to be in a primitive condition. As commonly used, the *refrain*, or burden, not only is limited to lyric verse, but depends for its impression upon the force of monotone — both in sound and thought. The pleasure is deduced solely from the sense of identity — of repetition. I resolved to diversify, and so heighten, the effect, by adhering, in general, to the monotone of sound, while I continually varied that of thought: that is to say, I determined to produce continuously novel effects, by the variation *of the application* of the *refrain* — the *refrain* itself remaining, for the most part, unvaried.

These points being settled, I next bethought me of the *nature* of my *refrain*. Since its application was to be repeatedly varied, it was clear that the *refrain* itself must be brief, for there would have been an insurmountable difficulty in frequent variations of application in any sentence of length. In proportion to the brevity of the sentence, would, of course, be the facility of the variation. This led me at once to a single word as the best *refrain*.

The question now arose as to the *character* of the word. Having made up my mind to a *refrain*, the division of the poem into stanzas was, of course, a corollary: the *refrain* forming the close of each stanza. That such a close, to have force, must be sonorous and susceptible of protracted emphasis, admitted no doubt: and these considera-

tions inevitably led me to the long *o* as the most sonorous vowel, in connection with *r* as the most producible consonant.

The sound of the *refrain* being thus determined, it became necessary to select a word embodying this sound, and at the same time in the fullest possible keeping with that melancholy which I had predetermined as the tone of the poem. In such a search it would have been absolutely impossible to overlook the word "Nevermore." In fact, it was the very first which presented itself.

The next *desideratum* was a pretext for the continuous use of the one word "nevermore." In observing the difficulty which I at once found in inventing a sufficiently plausible reason for its continuous repetition, I did not fail to perceive that this difficulty arose solely from the pre-assumption that the word was to be so continuously or monotonously spoken by a *human* being — I did not fail to perceive, in short, that the difficulty lay in the reconciliation of this monotony with the exercise of reason on the part of the creature repeating the word. Here, then, immediately arose the idea of a *non*-reasoning creature capable of speech; and, very naturally, a parrot, in the first instance, suggested itself, but was superseded forthwith by a Raven, as equally capable of speech, and infinitely more in keeping with the intended *tone*.

I had now gone so far as the conception of a Raven — the bird of ill omen — monotonously repeating the one word, "Nevermore," at the conclusion of each stanza, in a poem of melancholy tone, and in length about one hundred lines. Now, never losing sight of the object *supremeness*, or perfection, at all points, I asked myself — "Of all melancholy topics, what, according to the *universal* understanding of mankind, is the *most* melancholy?" Death — was the obvious reply. "And when," I said, "is this most melancholy of topics most poetical?" From what I have already explained at some length, the answer, here also, is obvious — "When it most closely allies itself to *Beauty*: the death, then, of a beautiful woman is, unquestionably, the most poetical topic in the world — and equally is it beyond doubt that the lips best suited for such topic are those of a bereaved lover."

I had now to combine the two ideas, of a lover lamenting his deceased mistress and a Raven continuously repeating the word "Nevermore." — I had to combine these, bearing in mind my design of varying, at every turn, the *application* of the word repeated; but the only intelligible mode of such combination is that of imagining the Raven employing the word in answer to the queries of the lover. And here it was that I saw at once the opportunity afforded for the effect on which I had been depending — that is to say, the effect of the *variation of application.* I saw that I could make the first query propounded by the lover — the first query to which the Raven should reply "Nevermore" — that I could make this first query a commonplace one — the second less so — the third still less, and so on — until at length the lover, startled from his original *nonchalance* by the melancholy character of the word itself — by its frequent repetition — and by a consideration of the ominous reputation of the fowl that uttered it — is at length excited to superstition, and wildly propounds queries of a far different character — queries whose solution he has passionately at heart — propounds them half in superstition and half in that species of despair which delights in self-torture — propounds them not altogether because he believes in the prophetic or demoniac character of the bird (which, reason assures him, is merely repeating a lesson learned by rote) but because he experiences a frenzied pleasure in so modeling his questions as to receive from the *expected* "Nevermore" the most delicious because the most intolerable of sorrow. Perceiving the opportunity thus afforded me — or, more strictly, thus forced upon me in the progress of the construction — I first established in mind the climax, or concluding query — that query to which "Nevermore" should be in the last place an answer — that in reply to which this word "Nevermore" should involve the utmost conceivable amount of sorrow and despair.

Here then the poem may be said to have its beginning — at the end, where all works of art should begin — for it was here, at this point of my preconsiderations, that I first put pen to paper in the composition of the stanza:

"Prophet," said I, "thing of evil! prophet still if bird or devil!
By that heaven that bends above us — by that God we both adore,
Tell this soul with sorrow laden, if within the distant Aidenn,
It shall clasp a sainted maiden whom the angels name Lenore —
Clasp a rare and radiant maiden whom the angels name Lenore."
Quoth the raven "Nevermore."

I composed this stanza, at this point, first that, by establishing the climax, I might the better vary and graduate, as regards seriousness and importance, the preceding queries of the lover — and, secondly, that I might definitely settle the rhythm, the metre, and the length and general arrangement of the stanza — as well as graduate the stanzas which were to precede, so that none of them might surpass this in rhythmical effect. Had I been able, in the subsequent composition, to construct more vigorous stanzas, I should, without scruple, have purposely enfeebled them, so as not to interfere with the climacteric effect.

And here I may as well say a few words of the versification. My first object (as usual) was originality. The extent to which this has been neglected, in versification, is one of the most unaccountable things in the world. Admitting that there is little possibility of variety in mere *rhythm*, it is still clear that the possible varieties of metre and stanza are absolutely infinite — and yet, *for centuries, no man, in verse, has ever done, or ever seemed to think of doing, an original thing.* The fact is, that originality (unless in minds of very unusual force) is by no means a matter, as some suppose, of impulse or intuition. In general, to be found, it must be elaborately sought, and although a positive merit of the highest class, demands in its attainment less of invention than negation.

Of course, I pretend to no originality in either the rhythm or metre of the "Raven." The former is trochaic — the latter is octameter acatalectic, alternating with heptameter catalectic repeated in the *refrain* of the fifth verse, and terminating with tetrameter catalectic. Less pedantically — the feet employed throughout (trochees) consist of a long syllable followed by a short: the first line of the stanza consists of eight of these feet — the second of seven and a half (in effect two-thirds) — the third of eight — the fourth of seven and a half — the fifth the same — the sixth three and a half. Now, each of these lines, taken individually, has been employed before, and what originality the "Raven" has, is in their *combination into stanza*; nothing even remotely approaching this combination has ever been attempted. The effect of this originality of combination is aided by other unusual, and some altogether novel effects, arising from an extension of the application of the principles of rhyme and alliteration.

The next point to be considered was the mode of bringing together the lover and the Raven — and the first branch of this consideration was the *locale*. For this the most natural suggestion might seem to be a forest, or the fields — but it has always appeared to me that a close *circumscription of space* is absolutely necessary to the effect of insulated incident: — it has the force of a frame to a picture. It has an indisputable moral power in keeping concentrated the attention, and, of course, must not be confounded with mere unity of place.

I determined, then, to place the lover in his chamber — in a chamber rendered sacred to him by memories of her who had frequented it. The room is represented as richly furnished — this in mere pursuance of the ideas I have already explained on the subject of Beauty, as the sole true poetical thesis.

The *locale* being thus determined, I had now to introduce the bird — and the thought of introducing him through the window, was inevitable. The idea of making the lover suppose, in the first instance, that the flapping of the wings of the bird against the shutter, is a "tapping" at the door, originated in a wish to increase, by prolonging, the reader's curiosity, and in a desire to admit the incidental effect arising from the lover's throwing open the door, finding all dark, and thence adopting the half-fancy that it was the spirit of his mistress that knocked.

I made the night tempestuous, first, to account for the Raven's seeking admission, and secondly, for the effect of contrast with the (physical) serenity within the chamber.

I made the bird alight on the bust of Pallas, also for the effect of contrast between the marble and the plumage — it being understood that the bust was absolutely *suggested* by the bird — the bust of *Pallas* being chosen, first, as most in keeping with the scholarship of the lover, and, secondly, for the sonorousness of the word, Pallas, itself.

About the middle of the poem, also, I have availed myself of the force of contrast, with a view of deepening the ultimate impression. For example, an air of the fantastic — approaching as nearly to the ludicrous as was admissible — is given to the Raven's entrance. He comes in "with many a flirt and flutter."

Not the *least obeisance made he* — not a moment
   stopped or stayed he,
But with mien of lord or lady, perched above my
   chamber door.

In the two stanzas which follow, the design is more obviously carried out: —

Then this ebony bird beguiling my sad fancy into
   smiling
By the *grave and stern decorum of the countenance it wore*,
"Though thy *crest be shorn and shaven* thou," I said,
   "art sure no craven,
Ghastly grim and ancient Raven wandering from
   the nightly shore —
Tell me what thy lordly name is on the Night's
   Plutonian shore?"
   Quoth the Raven "Nevermore."

Much I marvelled *this ungainly fowl* to hear discourse so plainly
Though its answer little meaning — little relevancy
   bore;
For we cannot help agreeing that no living human
   being
*Ever yet was blessed with seeing bird above his chamber
   door* —
*Bird or beast upon the sculptured bust above his chamber
   door*,
   With such name as "Nevermore."

The effect of the *dénouement* being thus provided for, I immediately drop the fantastic for a tone of the most profound seriousness: — this tone commencing in the stanza directly following the one last quoted, with the line,

But the Raven, sitting lonely on that placid bust,
    spoke only, etc.

From this epoch the lover no longer jests — no longer sees any thing even of the fantastic in the Raven's demeanor. He speaks of him as a "grim, ungainly, ghastly, gaunt, and ominous bird of yore," and feels the "fiery eyes" burning into his "bosom's core." This revolution of thought, or fancy, on the lover's part, is intended to induce a similar one on the part of the reader — to bring the mind into a proper frame for the *dénouement* — which is now brought about as rapidly and as *directly* as possible.

With the *dénouement* proper — with the Raven's reply, "Nevermore," to the lover's final demand if he shall meet his mistress in another world — the poem, in its obvious phase, that of a simple narrative, may be said to have its completion. So far, every thing is within the limits of the accountable — of the real. A raven, having learned by rote the single word "Nevermore," and having escaped from the custody of its owner, is driven at midnight, through the violence of a storm, to seek admission at a window from which a light still gleams — the chamber-window of a student, occupied half in poring over a volume, half in dreaming of a beloved mistress deceased. The casement being thrown open at the fluttering of the bird's wings, the bird itself perches on the most convenient seat out of the immediate reach of the student, who, amused by the incident and the oddity of the visitor's demeanor, demands of it, in jest and without looking for a reply, its name. The raven addressed, answers with its customary word, "Nevermore" — a word which finds immediate echo in the melancholy heart of the student, who, giving utterance aloud to certain thoughts suggested by the occasion, is again startled by the fowl's repetition of "Nevermore." The student now guesses the state of the case, but is impelled, as I have before explained, by the human thirst for self-torture, and in part by superstition to propound such queries to the bird as will bring him, the lover, the most of the luxury of sorrow, through the anticipated answer "Nevermore." With the indulgence, to the extreme, of this self-torture, the narration,

in what I have termed its first or obvious phase, has a natural termination, and so far there has been no overstepping of the limits of the real.

But in subjects so handled, however skilfully, or with however vivid an array of incident, there is always a certain hardness or nakedness, which repels the artistical eye. Two things are invariably required — first, some amount of complexity, or more properly, adaptation; and, secondly, some amount of suggestiveness — some undercurrent, however indefinite, of meaning. It is this latter, in especial, which imparts to a work of art so much of that *richness* (to borrow from colloquy a forcible term) which we are too fond of confounding with *the ideal*. It is the *excess* of the suggested meaning — it is the rendering this the upper instead of the undercurrent of the theme — which turns into prose (and that of the very flattest kind) the so called poetry of the so called transcendentalists.

Holding these opinions, I added the two concluding stanzas of the poem — their suggestiveness being thus made to pervade all the narrative which has preceded them. The under-current of meaning is rendered first apparent in the lines —

"Take thy beak from out *my heart*, and take thy
    form from off my door!"
    Quoth the Raven "Nevermore!"

It will be observed the words, "from out my heart," involve the first metaphorical expression in the poem. They, with the answer, "Nevermore," dispose the mind to seek a moral in all that has been previously narrated. The reader begins now to regard the Raven as emblematical — but it is not until the very last line of the very last stanza, that the intention of making him emblematical of *Mournful and Never-ending Remembrance* is permitted distinctly to be seen:

And the Raven, never flitting, still is sitting, still is
    sitting,
On the pallid bust of Pallas, just above my cham-
    ber door;
And his eyes have all the seeming of a demon's that
    is dreaming,
And the lamplight o'er him streaming throws his
    shadow on the floor;
And my soul *from out that shadow* that lies floating
    on the floor
    Shall be lifted — nevermore.

RALPH WALDO EMERSON (1803-1882)

On May 25, 1803, Emerson was born in Boston. He numbered in his ancestry seven educated generations in America, and some of the staunchest families of New England, beginning with Peter Bulkeley, who founded Concord in 1636. His father, minister of the First (Unitarian) Church of Boston, died when Ralph Waldo was not quite eight years old, and the family was left in straitened circumstances. Nevertheless Mrs. Emerson managed the education of her children, and Ralph Waldo went to Harvard in 1817 and graduated in 1821 near the middle of his class. He wrote the class poem, but only after seven other seniors had declined. Three years of teaching school and he was back at Harvard Divinity School. In 1826 he was admitted to the ministry of the Unitarian Church — "If they had examined me," he said, "they never would have passed me" — and three years later he became pastor of the Second Church of Boston, the church of the Mathers. In 1829 he married Ellen Louisa Tucker, a beautiful girl. She died in 1831 and in this same year came the great turning point in his life: he resigned his pastorate because he could not conscientiously administer the Lord's Supper. Three months later he sailed for Europe.

There he established what was to be a lifelong friendship with Carlyle, met many important people and many important ideas, and returned in 1833, mended in spirit and health, to Concord. Here he lived quietly, except for brief intervals, the rest of his life. He began to lecture, married Lydia Jackson in 1835, and in 1836 published his first book, *Nature*. It had little sale, and few people found in it anything exciting. When he spoke some of the same doctrine the next year before the Phi Beta Kappa Society of Harvard College, the revolutionary nature of his thought was apparent. Oliver Wendell Holmes called the address "our intellectual Declaration of Independence"; others, "our Yankee version of a lecture by Abelard." Carlyle, with great admiration, said it was "a fearful work." His phrase proved pertinent: when Emerson applied the same thought to religion, before the graduating class of the Harvard Divinity School in 1838, the clergy was frightened. Emerson was called infidel and pagan. So it was throughout his life: the young men felt, as Holmes expressed it, "Thus saith the Lord"; the older men were not sure that it was not the devil speaking.

With the first volume of his collected essays in 1841, Emerson was fairly launched on his career. His main interest was in Concord, in quiet strolls by Walden Pond, conversations with Alcott, Thoreau, Margaret Fuller, and other kindred spirits, letters from Carlyle, and much writing. He helped found the Transcendentalist Club, edited the ill-fated *Dial* from 1842 until 1844, made many lecture tours that took him even west of the Mississippi, visited Europe several times, and published frequently. In 1844 appeared a second series of *Essays*, and in 1847 a first volume of *Poems*. *Representative Men* in 1850, *English Traits*, 1856, *The Conduct of Life*, 1860, *May Day and Other Poems*, 1867, and *Letters and Social Aims*, 1875, completed the list of his more important volumes. But J. Elliot Cabot had to be called in to order the muddle of manuscript for this last book, and Emerson failed steadily until his death, of pneumonia, on April 27, 1882.

Emerson was the heart of New England Transcendentalism, and still he was apart from much of it — the Brook Farm experiment, for instance. He raised no great philosophical system: "A foolish consistency is the hobgoblin of little minds," he said. He spoke as an oracle rather than as a schoolman. But from beginning to end he preached one doctrine — a higher individualism: "Trust thyself: every heart vibrates to that iron string." A great many avenues of the world's thought converged in him: Platonism and Neo-Platonism, Oriental wisdom, the Bible, Montaigne, Bacon, Shakespeare, Kant, Rousseau, Wordsworth and Coleridge, New England Puritan, New England Yankee. George E. Woodberry called him "the only great mind that America has produced in literature," and Matthew Arnold characterized him happily as "friend and aider of those who would live in the spirit."

The standard edition of Emerson is the Centenary, in 12 volumes, 1903. His *Journals* were published in 10 volumes, 1909–1914, a selection from which appears in Bliss Perry's *The Heart of Emerson's Journals*, 1926. The letters are in special collections and in a six-volume collection edited by R. L. Rusk, 1939. The standard biography is by R. L. Rusk, 1949. Norman Foerster has chapters on Emerson in *Nature in American Literature*, 1923, and in *American Criticism*, 1928. There are fresh and stimulating discussions in F. O. Matthiessen's *American Renaissance*, 1941. Indispensable for an understanding of the thought of Emerson's group is Perry Miller's *The Transcendentalists*, 1950, an anthology of their writings. Bliss Perry's *Emerson Today*, 1931, still serves as a good introduction, as does F. I. Carpenter's anthology in the American Writers Series, 1934. Useful for the study of Emerson's sources are J. S. Harrison, *The Teachers of Emerson*, 1910, and F. I. Carpenter, *Emerson and Asia*, 1930.

Thought

(1823)

I am not poor, but I am proud,
  Of one inalienable right,
Above the envy of the crowd, —
  Thought's holy light.

Better it is than gems or gold,   5
  And oh! it cannot die,
But thought will glow when the sun grows
    cold,
  And mix with Deity.

The Rhodora:

ON BEING ASKED, WHENCE IS THE FLOWER?

(1834)

In May, when sea-winds pierced our solitudes,
I found the fresh Rhodora in the woods,
Spreading its leafless blooms in a damp nook,

To please the desert and the sluggish brook.
The purple petals, fallen in the pool,   5
Made the black water with their beauty gay;
Here might the redbird come his plumes to
    cool,
And court the flower that cheapens his array.
Rhodora! if the sages ask thee why
This charm is wasted on the earth and sky, 10
Tell them, dear, that if eyes were made for
    seeing,
Then Beauty is its own excuse for being:
Why thou wert there, O rival of the rose!
I never thought to ask, I never knew:
But, in my simple ignorance, suppose 15
The self-same Power that brought me there
    brought you.

Each and All

(1834?)

"I remember when I was a boy going upon the beach and being charmed with the colors and forms of the shells. I picked up many and put them in my pocket. When I got home I could find nothing that I gathered — nothing but some dry,

ugly mussel and snail shells. Thence I learned
that Composition was more important than the
beauty of individual forms to Effect. On the
shore they lay wet and social, by the sea and under
the sky" (Journal, May 16, 1834).

Little thinks, in the field, yon red-cloaked
    clown
Of thee from the hill-top looking down;
The heifer that lows in the upland farm,
Far-heard, lows not thine ear to charm;
The sexton, tolling his bell at noon,   5
Deems not that great Napoleon
Stops his horse, and lists with delight,
Whilst his files sweep round yon Alpine
    height;
Nor knowest thou what argument
Thy life to thy neighbor's creed has lent.   10
All are needed by each one;
Nothing is fair or good alone.
I thought the sparrow's note from heaven,
Singing at dawn on the alder bough;
I brought him home, in his nest, at even;   15
He sings the song, but it cheers not now,
For I did not bring home the river and sky; —
He sang to my ear, — they sang to my eye.
The delicate shells lay on the shore;
The bubbles of the latest wave   20
Fresh pearls to their enamel gave,
And the bellowing of the savage sea
Greeted their safe escape to me.
I wiped away the weeds and foam,
I fetched my sea-born treasures home;   25
But the poor, unsightly, noisome things
Had left their beauty on the shore
With the sun and the sand and the wild
    uproar.
    The lover watched his graceful maid,
As 'mid the virgin train she strayed,   30
Nor knew her beauty's best attire
Was woven still by the snow-white choir.
At last she came to his hermitage,
Like the bird from the woodlands to the
    cage; —
The gay enchantment was undone,   35
A gentle wife, but fairy none.
Then I said, "I covet truth;
Beauty is unripe childhood's cheat;
I leave it behind with the games of youth:" —
As I spoke, beneath my feet   40
The ground-pine curled its pretty wreath,
Running over the club-moss burrs;
I inhaled the violet's breath;

Around me stood the oaks and firs;
Pine-cones and acorns lay on the ground;   45
Over me soared the eternal sky,
Full of light and of deity;
Again I saw, again I heard,
The rolling river, the morning bird; —
Beauty through my senses stole;   50
I yielded myself to the perfect whole.

The Apology
(1834?)

Think me not unkind and rude
    That I walk alone in grove and glen;
I go to the god of the wood
    To fetch his word to men.

Tax not my sloth that I   5
    Fold my arms beside the brook;
Each cloud that floated in the sky
    Writes a letter in my book.

Chide me not, laborious band,
    For the idle flowers I brought;   10
Every aster in my hand
    Goes home loaded with a thought.

There was never mystery
    But 'tis figured in the flowers;
Was never secret history   15
    But birds tell it in the bowers.

One harvest from thy field
    Homeward brought the oxen strong;
A second crop thine acres yield,
    Which I gather in a song.   20

Concord Hymn

SUNG AT THE COMPLETION OF THE BATTLE MONUMENT, JULY 4, 1837

(1837)

By the rude bridge that arched the flood,
    Their flag to April's breeze unfurled,
Here once the embattled farmers stood
    And fired the shot heard round the world.

The foe long since in silence slept;   5
    Alike the conqueror silent sleeps;
And Time the ruined bridge has swept
    Down the dark stream which seaward
    creeps.

On this green bank, by this soft stream,
  We set to-day a votive stone;   10
That memory may their deed redeem,
  When, like our sires, our sons are gone.

Spirit, that made those heroes dare
  To die, and leave their children free,
Bid Time and Nature gently spare   15
  The shaft we raise to them and thee.

The Humble-Bee

(1837?)

Burly, dozing humble-bee,
Where thou art is clime for me.
Let them sail for Porto Rique,
Far-off heats through seas to seek;
I will follow thee alone,   5
Thou animated torrid zone!
Zigzag steerer, desert cheerer,
Let me chase thy waving lines;
Keep me nearer, me thy hearer,
Singing over shrubs and vines.   10

Insect lover of the sun,
Joy of thy dominion!
Sailor of the atmosphere;
Swimmer through the waves of air;
Voyager of light and noon;   15
Epicurean of June;
Wait, I prithee, till I come
Within earshot of thy hum, —
All without is martyrdom.

When the south wind, in May days,   20
With a net of shining haze
Silvers the horizon wall,
And with softness touching all,
Tints the human countenance
With a color of romance,   25
And infusing subtle heats,
Turns the sod to violets,
Thou, in sunny solitudes,
Rover of the underwoods,
The green silence dost displace   30
With thy mellow, breezy bass.

Hot midsummer's petted crone,
Sweet to me thy drowsy tone
Tells of countless sunny hours,
Long days, and solid banks of flowers;   35

Of gulfs of sweetness without bound
In Indian wildernesses found;
Of Syrian peace, immortal leisure,
Firmest cheer, and bird-like pleasure.

Aught unsavory or unclean   40
Hath my insect never seen;
But violets and bilberrybells,
Maple-sap and daffodels,
Grass with green flag half-mast high,
Succory to match the sky,   45
Columbine with horn of honey,
Scented fern, and agrimony,
Clover, catchfly, adder's-tongue
And brier-roses, dwelt among;
All beside was unknown waste,   50
All was picture as he passed.

Wiser far than human seer,
Yellow-breeched philosopher!
Seeing only what is fair,
Sipping only what is sweet,   55
Thou dost mock at fate and care,
Leave the chaff, and take the wheat.
When the fierce northwestern blast
Cools sea and land so far and fast,
Thou already slumberest deep;   60
Woe and want thou canst outsleep;
Want and woe, which torture us,
Thy sleep makes ridiculous.

The Problem

(1839)

Cf. the Journal, August 28, 1838: "It is very
grateful to my feelings to go into a Roman Cathedral, yet I look as my countrymen do at the Roman
priesthood. It is very grateful to me to go into an
English Church and hear the liturgy read, yet
nothing would induce me to be the English priest.

"I find an unpleasant dilemma in this, nearer
home. I dislike to be a clergyman and refuse to be
one. Yet how rich a music would be to me a holy
clergyman in my town. It seems to me he cannot
be a man, quite and whole; yet how plain is the
need of one, and how high, yes, highest is the
function. Here is division of labor that I like not:
a man must sacrifice his manhood for the social
good. Something is wrong; I see not what."

I like a church; I like a cowl;
I love a prophet of the soul;
And on my heart monastic aisles
Fall like sweet strains, or pensive smiles;
Yet not for all his faith can see   5
Would I that cowlèd churchman be.

Why should the vest on him allure,
Which I could not on me endure?
Not from a vain or shallow thought
His awful Jove young Phidias brought;   10
Never from lips of cunning fell
The thrilling Delphic oracle;
Out from the heart of nature rolled
The burdens of the Bible old;
The litanies of nations came,   15
Like the volcano's tongue of flame,
Up from the burning core below, —
The canticles of love and woe:
The hand that rounded Peter's dome
And groined the aisles of Christian Rome   20
Wrought in a sad sincerity:
Himself from God he could not free;
He builded better than he knew; —
The conscious stone to beauty grew.

Know'st thou what wove yon woodbird's
      nest   25
Of leaves, and feathers from her breast?
Or how the fish outbuilt her shell,
Painting with morn her annual cell?
Or how the sacred pine-tree adds
To her old leaves new myriads?   30
Such and so grew these holy piles,
Whilst love and terror laid the tiles.
Earth proudly wears the Parthenon,
As the best gem upon her zone,
And Morning opes with haste her lids   35
To gaze upon the Pyramids;
O'er England's abbeys bends the sky,
As on its friends, with kindred eye;
For out of Thought's interior sphere
These wonders rose to upper air;   40
And Nature gladly gave them place,
Adopted them into her race,
And granted them an equal date
With Andes and with Ararat.

These temples grew as grows the grass;   45
Art might obey, but not surpass.
The passive Master lent his hand
To the vast soul that o'er him planned;
And the same power that reared the shrine
Bestrode the tribes that knelt within.   50
Ever the fiery Pentecost
Girds with one flame the countless host,
Trances the heart through chanting choirs,
And through the priest the mind inspires.
The word unto the prophet spoken   55

Was writ on tables yet unbroken;
The word by seers or sibyls told,
In groves of oak, or fanes of gold,
Still floats upon the morning wind,
Still whispers to the willing mind.   60
One accent of the Holy Ghost
The heedless world hath never lost.
I know what say the fathers wise, —
The Book itself before me lies,
Old *Chrysostom*, best Augustine,   65
And he who blent both in his line,
The younger *Golden Lips* or mines,
Taylor, the Shakespeare of divines.
His words are music in my ear,
I see his cowlèd portrait dear;   70
And yet, for all his faith could see,
I would not the good bishop be.

The Sphinx
(1841)

"Mr. Emerson wrote in his note-book in 1859:
'I have often been asked the meaning of the
"Sphinx." It is this: The perception of identity
unites all things and explains one by another, and
the most rare and strange is equally facile as the
most common. But if the mind live only in particulars, and see only differences (wanting the
power to see the whole — all in each), then the
world addresses to this mind a question it cannot
answer, and each new fact tears it in pieces and it
is vanquished by the distracting variety' " (E. W.
Emerson).

The Sphinx is drowsy,
    Her wings are furled:
Her ear is heavy,
    She broods on the world.
"Who'll tell me my secret,   5
    The ages have kept? —
I awaited the seer
    While they slumbered and slept: —

"The fate of the man-child,
    The meaning of man;   10
Known fruit of the unknown;
    Dædalian plan;
Out of sleeping a waking,
    Out of waking a sleep;
Life death overtaking;   15
    Deep underneath deep?

"Erect as a sunbeam,
    Upspringeth the palm;

The elephant browses,
  Undaunted and calm; 20
In beautiful motion
  The thrush plies his wings;
Kind leaves of his covert,
  Your silence he sings.

"The waves, unashamèd, 25
  In difference sweet,
Play glad with the breezes,
  Old playfellows meet;
The journeying atoms,
  Primordial wholes, 30
Firmly draw, firmly drive,
  By their animate poles.

"Sea, earth, air, sound, silence,
  Plant, quadruped, bird,
By one music enchanted, 35
  One deity stirred, —
Each the other adorning,
  Accompany still;
Night veileth the morning,
  The vapor the hill. 40

"The babe by its mother
  Lies bathèd in joy;
Glide its hours uncounted, —
  The sun is its toy;
Shines the peace of all being, 45
  Without cloud, in its eyes;
And the sum of the world
  In soft miniature lies.

"But man crouches and blushes,
  Absconds and conceals; 50
He creepeth and peepeth,
  He palters and steals;
Infirm, melancholy,
  Jealous glancing around,
An oaf, an accomplice, 55
  He poisons the ground.

"Out spoke the great mother,
  Beholding his fear; —
At the sound of her accents
  Cold shuddered the sphere: — 60
'Who has drugged my boy's cup?
  Who has mixed my boy's bread?
Who, with sadness and madness,
  Has turned my child's head?'"

I heard a poet answer 65
  Aloud and cheerfully,
"Say on, sweet Sphinx! thy dirges
  Are pleasant songs to me.
Deep love lieth under
  These pictures of time; 70
They fade in the light of
  Their meaning sublime.

"The fiend that man harries
  Is love of the Best;
Yawns the pit of the Dragon, 75
  Lit by rays from the Blest.
The Lethe of Nature
  Can't trance him again,
Whose soul sees the perfect,
  Which his eyes seek in vain. 80

"To vision profounder,
  Man's spirit must dive;
His aye-rolling orb
  At no goal will arrive;
The heavens that now draw him 85
  With sweetness untold,
Once found, — for new heavens
  He spurneth the old.

"Pride ruined the angels,
  Their shame them restores; 90
Lurks the joy that is sweetest
  In stings of remorse.
Have I a lover
  Who is noble and free? —
I would he were nobler 95
  Than to love me.

"Eterne alternation
  Now follows, now flies;
And under pain, pleasure, —
  Under pleasure, pain lies. 100
Love works at the centre,
  Heart-heaving alway;
Forth speed the strong pulses
  To the borders of day.

"Dull Sphinx, Jove keep thy five wits; 105
  Thy sight is growing blear;
Rue, myrrh, and cummin for the Sphinx,
  Her muddy eyes to clear!"
The old Sphinx bit her thick lip, —
  Said, "Who taught thee me to name? 110

I am thy spirit, yoke-fellow;
  Of thine eye I am eyebeam.

"Thou art the unanswered question;
  Couldst see thy proper eye,
Alway it asketh, asketh;   115
  And each answer is a lie.
So take thy quest through nature,
  It through thousand natures ply;
Ask on, thou clothed eternity;
  Time is the false reply."   120

Uprose the merry Sphinx,
  And crouched no more in stone;
She melted into purple cloud,
  She silvered in the moon;
She spired into a yellow flame;   125
  She flowered in blossoms red;
She flowed into a foaming wave:
  She stood Monadnoc's head.

Thorough a thousand voices
  Spoke the universal dame;   130
"Who telleth one of my meanings
  Is master of all I am."

The Snow-Storm

(1841)

Announced by all the trumpets of the sky,
Arrives the snow, and, driving o'er the fields,
Seems nowhere to alight: the whited air
Hides hills and woods, the river, and the
    heaven,
And veils the farm-house at the garden's
    end.   5
The sled and traveller stopped, the courier's
    feet
Delayed, all friends shut out, the housemates
    sit
Around the radiant fireplace, enclosed
In a tumultuous privacy of storm.

    Come see the north wind's masonry.   10
Out of an unseen quarry evermore
Furnished with tile, the fierce artificer
Curves his white bastions with projected
    roof
Round every windward stake, or tree, or door.
Speeding, the myriad-handed, his wild
    work   15

So fanciful, so savage, nought cares he
For number or proportion. Mockingly,
On coop or kennel he hangs Parian wreaths;
A swan-like form invests the hidden thorn;
Fills up the farmer's lane from wall to wall, 20
Maugre the farmer's sighs; and at the gate
A tapering turret overtops the work.
And when his hours are numbered, and the
    world
Is all his own, retiring, as he were not,
Leaves, when the sun appears, astonished
    Art   25
To mimic in slow structures, stone by stone,
Built in an age, the mad wind's night-work,
The frolic architecture of the snow.

Friendship

(1841)

A ruddy drop of manly blood
The surging sea outweighs,
The world uncertain comes and goes;
The lover rooted stays.
I fancied he was fled, —   5
And, after many a year,
Glowed unexhausted kindliness,
Like daily sunrise there.
My careful heart was free again,
O friend, my bosom said,   10
Through thee alone the sky is arched,
Through thee the rose is red;
All things through thee take nobler form,
And look beyond the earth,
The mill-round of our fate appears   15
A sun-path in thy worth.
Me too thy nobleness has taught
To master my despair;
The fountains of my hidden life
Are through thy friendship fair.   20

Forbearance

(1842)

Hast thou named all the birds without a
    gun?
Loved the wood-rose, and left it on its stalk?
At rich men's tables eaten bread and pulse?
Unarmed, faced danger with a heart of trust?
And loved so well a high behavior,   5
In man or maid, that thou from speech re-
    frained,

Nobility more nobly to repay?
O, be my friend, and teach me to be thine!

Grace

(1842)

How much, preventing God! how much I
 owe
To the defences thou hast round me set:
Example, custom, fear, occasion slow, —
These scornèd bondmen were my parapet.
I dare not peep over this parapet. 5
To gauge with glance the roaring gulf below,
The depths of sin to which I had descended,
Had not these me against myself defended.

Fable

(ca. 1845)

The mountain and the squirrel
Had a quarrel,
And the former called the latter "Little
 Prig";
Bun replied,
"You are doubtless very big; 5
But all sorts of things and weather
Must be taken in together,
To make up a year
And a sphere.
And I think it no disgrace 10
To occupy my place.
If I'm not so large as you,
You are not so small as I,
And not half so spry.
I'll not deny you make 15
A very pretty squirrel track;
Talents differ; all is well and wisely put;
If I cannot carry forests on my back,
Neither can you crack a nut."

Ode

INSCRIBED TO W. H. CHANNING

(1846)

"The circumstance which gave rise to this poem
though not known, can easily be inferred. Rev.
William Henry Channing, nephew of the great
Unitarian divine, a man most tender in his sympathies, with an apostle's zeal for right, had, no
doubt, been urging his friend to join the brave
band of men who were dedicating their lives to the
destruction of human slavery in the United States.
To these men Mr. Emerson gave honor and sympathy and active aid by word and presence on important occasions. He showed his colors from the
first, and spoke fearlessly on the subject in his lectures, but his method was the reverse of theirs,
affirmative not negative; he knew his office and
followed his genius. He said, 'I have quite other
slaves to free than those negroes, to wit, imprisoned
spirits, imprisoned thoughts'" (E. W. Emerson).

Though loath to grieve
The evil time's sole patriot,
I cannot leave
My honeyed thought
For the priest's cant, 5
Or statesman's rant.

If I refuse
My study for their politique,
Which at the best is trick,
The angry Muse 10
Puts confusion in my brain.

But who is he that prates
Of the culture of mankind,
Of better arts and life?
Go, blindworm, go, 15
Behold the famous States
Harrying Mexico
With rifle and with knife!

Or who, with accent bolder,
Dare praise the freedom-loving moun-
 taineer? 20
I found by thee, O rushing Contoocook!
And in thy valleys, Agiochook!
The jackals of the negro-holder.

The God who made New Hampshire
Taunted the lofty land 25
With little men: —
Small bat and wren
House in the oak: —

If earth-fire cleave
The upheaved land, and bury the folk, 30
The southern crocodile would grieve.
Virtue palters; Right is hence;
Freedom praised, but hid;
Funeral eloquence
Rattles the coffin-lid. 35

What boots thy zeal,
O glowing friend,
That would indignant rend
The northland from the south?
Wherefore? to what good end?   40
Boston Bay and Bunker Hill
Would serve things still; —
Things are of the snake.

The horseman serves the horse,
The neatherd serves the neat,   45
The merchant serves the purse,
The eater serves his meat;
'Tis the day of the chattel,
Web to weave, and corn to grind;
Things are in the saddle,   50
And ride mankind.

There are two laws discrete,
Not reconciled, —
Law for man, and law for thing;
The last builds town and fleet,   55
But it runs wild,
And doth the man unking.

'Tis fit the forest fall,
The steep be graded,
The mountain tunnelled,   60
The sand shaded,
The orchard planted,
The glebe tilled,
The prairie granted,
The steamer built.   65

Let man serve law for man;
Live for friendship, live for love,
For truth's and harmony's behoof;
The state may follow how it can,
As Olympus follows Jove.   70

    Yet do not I implore
The wrinkled shopman to my sounding
      woods,
Nor bid the unwilling senator
Ask votes of thrushes in the solitudes.
Every one to his chosen work; —   75
Foolish hands may mix and mar;
Wise and sure the issues are.
Round they roll till dark is light,
Sex to sex, and even to odd; —
The over-god   80
Who marries Right to Might,

Who peoples, unpeoples, —
He who exterminates
Races by stronger races,
Black by white faces, —   85
Knows to bring honey
Out of the lion;
Grafts gentlest scion
On pirate and Turk.
The Cossack eats Poland,   90
Like stolen fruit;
Her last noble is ruined,
Her last poet mute:
Straight, into double band
The victors divide;   95
Half for freedom strike and stand; —
The astonished Muse finds thousands at her
      side.

Bacchus

(1840)

Bring me wine, but wine which never grew
In the belly of the grape,
Or grew on vine whose tap-roots, reaching
      through
Under the Andes to the Cape,
Suffered no savour of the earth to scape.   5

Let its grapes the morn salute
From a nocturnal root,
Which feels the acrid juice
Of Styx and Erebus;
And turns the woe of Night,   10
By its own craft, to a more rich delight.

We buy ashes for bread;
We buy diluted wine;
Give me of the true, —
Whose ample leaves and tendrils curled   15
Among the silver hills of heaven,
Draw everlasting dew;
Wine of wine,
Blood of the world,
Form of forms, and mould of statures,   20
That I intoxicated,
And by the draught assimilated,
May float at pleasure through all natures;
The bird-language rightly spell,
And that which roses say so well.   25
Wine that is shed
Like the torrents of the sun
Up the horizon walls.

Or like the Atlantic streams, which run
When the South Sea calls. 30

Water and bread,
Food which needs no transmuting,
Rainbow-flowering, wisdom-fruiting
Wine which is already man,
Food which teach and reason can. 35

Wine which Music is, —
Music and wine are one, —
That I, drinking this,
Shall hear far Chaos talk with me;
Kings unborn shall walk with me; 40
And the poor grass shall plot and plan
What it will do when it is man.
Quickened so, will I unlock
Every crypt of every rock.

I thank the joyful juice 45
For all I know; —
Winds of remembering
Of the ancient being blow,
And seeming-solid walls of use
Open and flow. 50

Pour, Bacchus! the remembering wine;
Retrieve the loss of me and mine!
Vine for vine be antidote,
And the grape requite the lote!
Haste to cure the old despair, — 55
Reason in Nature's lotus drenched,
The memory of ages quenched;
Give them again to shine;
Let wine repair what this undid;

And where the infection slid, 60
A dazzling memory revive;
Refresh the faded tints,
Recut the aged prints,
And write my old adventures with the pen
Which on the first day drew, 65
Upon the tablets blue,
The dancing Pleiads and eternal men.

Hamatreya

(1847)

"The words 'I and mine' constitute ignorance.
"I have now given you a summary account of
the sovereigns of the earth. — These, and other
kings who with perishable frames have possessed
this ever-enduring world, and who, blinded with
deceptive notions of individual occupation, have
indulged the feeling that suggests 'This earth is
mine, — it is my son's, — it belongs to my dynasty,' — have all passed away. So, many who
reigned before them, many who succeeded them,
and many who are yet to come, have ceased or
will cease to be. Earth laughs, as if smiling, with
autumnal flowers to behold her kings unable to
effect the subjugation of themselves. I will repeat
to you, Maitreya, the stanzas that were chanted by
Earth, and which the Muni Asita communicated
to Janaka, whose banner was virtue. . . ." (*Journals*, 1845)

The poem was inspired by Emerson's reading in
the *Vishnu Purana* Book IV.

Bulkeley, Hunt, Willard, Hosmer, Meriam,
Flint,
Possessed the land which rendered to their
toil
Hay, corn, roots, hemp, flax, apples, wool
and wood.
Each of these landlords walked amidst his
farm,
Saying, "'Tis mine, my children's and my
name's. 5
How sweet the west wind sounds in my own
trees!
How graceful climb those shadows on my
hill!
I fancy these pure waters and the flags
Know me, as does my dog: we sympathize;
And, I affirm, my actions smack of the
soil."

Where are these men? Asleep beneath their
grounds:
And strangers, fond as they, their furrows
plough.
Earth laughs in flowers, to see her boastful
boys
Earth-proud, proud of the earth which is
not theirs;
Who steer the plough, but cannot steer their
feet 15
Clear of the grave.
They added ridge to valley, brook to pond,
And sighed for all that bounded their
domain;
"This suits me for a pasture; that's my park;
We must have clay, lime, gravel, granite-
ledge, 20
And misty lowland, where to go for peat.
The land is well, — lies fairly to the south.

'Tis good, when you have crossed the sea
  and back,
To find the sitfast acres where you left them."
Ah! the hot owner sees not Death, who
  adds   25
Him to his land, a lump of mould the more.
Hear what the Earth says:

EARTH-SONG

"Mine and yours;
Mine, not yours.
Earth endures;
Stars abide —
Shine down in the old sea;   5
Old are the shores;
But where are old men?
I who have seen much,
Such have I never seen.

"The lawyer's deed   10
Ran sure,
In tail,
To them, and to their heirs
Who shall succeed,
Without fail,   15
Forevermore.

"Here is the land,
Shaggy with wood,
With its old valley,
Mound and flood.   20
But the heritors? —
Fled like the flood's foam.
The lawyer, and the laws,
And the kingdom,
Clean swept herefrom.   25

"They called me theirs,
Who so controlled me;
Yet every one
Wished to stay, and is gone.
How am I theirs,   30
If they cannot hold me,
But I hold them?"

When I heard the Earth-song
I was no longer brave;
My avarice cooled   35
Like lust in the chill of the grave.

Days

(1851?)

Compare the following passage in the essay
"Works and Days": "The days are ever divine, as
to the first Aryans. They come and go like muffled and veiled figures, sent from a distant friendly
party; but they say nothing, and if we do not use
the gifts they bring, they carry them as silently
away."

Daughters of Time, the hypocritic Days,
Muffled and dumb like barefoot dervishes,
And marching single in an endless file,
Bring diadems and fagots in their hands.
To each they offer gifts after his will,   5
Bread, kingdoms, stars, and sky that holds
  them all.
I, in my pleachèd garden, watched the pomp,
Forgot my morning wishes, hastily
Took a few herbs and apples, and the Day
Turned and departed silent. I, too late,   10
Under her solemn fillet saw the scorn.

Two Rivers

(1856–57)

Thy summer voice, Musketaquit,
Repeats the music of the rain;
But sweeter rivers pulsing flit
Through thee, as thou through Concord
  Plain.

Thou in thy narrow banks are pent: 5
The stream I love unbounded goes
Through flood and sea and firmament;
Through light, through life, it forward flows.

I see the inundation sweet,
I hear the spending of the stream   10
Through years, through men, through Na-
  ture fleet,
Through love and thought, through power
  and dream.

Musketaquit, a goblin strong,
Of shard and flint makes jewels gay;
They lose their grief who hear his song,   15
And where he winds is the day of day.

So forth and brighter fares my stream, —
Who drink it shall not thirst again;
No darkness stains its equal gleam
And ages drop in it like rain.   20

Brahma

(1857)

This "Song of the Soul," as Emerson named the poem in his note-book, is both easier and harder than it is commonly regarded: easier because, as Emerson said of people who were puzzled, "If you tell them to say Jehovah instead of Brahma they will not feel any perplexity," and harder because it requires, for a full understanding, a richer religious and metaphysical background than most people possess. Useful suggestions may be found in the long note by E. W. Emerson in the Centenary edition of the *Poems*, 464–67.

If the red slayer think he slays,
 Or if the slain think he is slain,
They know not well the subtle ways
 I keep, and pass, and turn again.

Far or forgot to me is near;   5
 Shadow and sunlight are the same;
The vanished gods to me appear;
 And one to me are shame and fame.

They reckon ill who leave me out;
 When me they fly, I am the wings;   10
I am the doubter and the doubt,
 And I the hymn the Brahmin sings.

The strong gods pine for my abode,
 And pine in vain the sacred Seven;
But thou, meek lover of the good!   15
 Find me, and turn thy back on heaven.

Terminus

(*1860*)

It is time to be old,
To take in sail:
The god of bounds,
Who sets to seas a shore,
Came to me in his fatal rounds   5
And said: "No more!
No farther spread
Thy broad ambitious branches and thy root.
Fancy departs: no more invent;
Contract thy firmament   10
To compass of a tent.
There's not enough for this and that,
Make thy option which of two;
Economize the failing river,
Not the less revere the Giver;   15
Leave the many and hold the few.
Timely wise, accept the terms,

Soften the fall with wary foot;
A little while
Still plan and smile,
And, fault of novel germs,   20
Mature the unfallen fruit.
Curse, if thou wilt, thy sires,
Bad husbands of their fires,
Who, when they gave thee breath,   25
Failed to bequeath
The needful sinew stark as once,
The Baresark marrow to thy bones,
But left a legacy of ebbing veins,
Inconstant heat and nerveless reins;   30
Amid the Muses left thee deaf and dumb,
Amid the gladiators halt and numb."

As the bird trims her to the gale,
I trim myself to the storm of time;
I man the rudder, reef the sail,   35
Obey the voice at eve obeyed at prime:
"Lowly faithful, banish fear,
Right onward drive unharmed;
The port, well worth the cruise, is near,
And every wave is charmed."   40

Nature

(1836)

While on shipboard, returning from England in September, 1833, Emerson entered in his diary, "I like my book about Nature." The first part of the book, says Cabot in his *Memoir*, "appears to have been for some time in hand. This, I conjecture, may comprise the first five chapters. The seventh and eighth chapters (Spirit) seem to have been written after his removal to Concord; the sixth, Idealism, last of all, as the connection of the two."

As the book is a summary of Emerson's early inward life, so it is equally a foreshadowing of all his later work: "a Foundation and Ground-plan," as Carlyle said to him, "on which you may build whatsoever of great and true has been given you to build." Readers of Carlyle's *Sartor Resartus* (first published 1833–34) will find a comparison of that book and *Nature* enlightening. Students of philosophy will find a fascinating problem in conjecturing how far Emerson's thought is similar to that of the German Transcendental school and how far it is a continuation of Plato and the Neo-Platonists.

A subtle chain of countless rings
The next unto the farthest brings;
The eye reads omens where it goes,
And speaks all languages the rose;
And, striving to be man, the worm
Mounts through all the spires of form.
[Prefixed to the second edition, 1849.]

Introduction

Our age is retrospective. It builds the sepulchres of the fathers. It writes biographies, histories, and criticism. The foregoing generations beheld God and nature face to face; we, through their eyes. Why should not we also enjoy an original relation to the universe? Why should not we have a poetry and philosophy of insight and not a tradition, and a religion by revelation to us, and not the history of theirs? Embosomed for a season in nature, whose floods of life stream around and through us, and invite us, by the powers they supply, to action proportioned to nature, why should we grope among the dry bones of the past, or put the living generation into masquerade out of its faded wardrobe? The sun shines to-day also. There is more wool and flax in the fields. There are new lands, new men, new thoughts. Let us demand our own works and laws and worship.

Undoubtedly we have no questions to ask which are unanswerable. We must trust the perfection of the creation so far as to believe that whatever curiosity the order of things has awakened in our minds, the order of things can satisfy. Every man's condition is a solution in hieroglyphic to those inquiries he would put. He acts it as life, before he apprehends it as truth. In like manner, nature is already, in its forms and tendencies, describing its own design. Let us interrogate the great apparition that shines so peacefully around us. Let us inquire, to what end is nature?

All science has one aim, namely, to find a theory of nature. We have theories of races and of functions, but scarcely yet a remote approach to an idea of creation. We are now so far from the road to truth, that religious teachers dispute and hate each other, and speculative men are esteemed unsound and frivolous. But to a sound judgment, the most abstract truth is the most practical. Whenever a true theory appears, it will be its own evidence. Its test is, that it will explain all phenomena. Now many are thought not only unexplained but inexplicable; as language, sleep, madness, dreams, beasts, sex.

Philosophically considered, the universe is composed of Nature and the Soul. Strictly speaking, therefore, all that is separate from us, all which Philosophy distinguishes as the NOT ME, that is, both nature and art, all other men and my own body, must be ranked under this name, NATURE. In enumerating the values of nature and casting up their sum, I shall use the word in both senses; — in its common and in its philosophical import. In inquiries so general as our present one, the inaccuracy is not material; no confusion of thought will occur. *Nature*, in the common sense, refers to essences unchanged by man; space, the air, the river, the leaf. *Art* is applied to the mixture of his will with the same things, as in a house, a canal, a statue, a picture. But his operations taken together are so insignificant; a little chipping, baking, patching, and washing, that in an impression so grand as that of the world on the human mind, they do not vary the result.

I. Nature

To go into solitude, a man needs to retire as much from his chamber as from society. I am not solitary whilst I read and write, though nobody is with me. But if a man would be alone, let him look at the stars. The rays that come from those heavenly worlds will separate between him and what he touches. One might think the atmosphere was made transparent with this design, to give man, in the heavenly bodies, the perpetual presence of the sublime. Seen in the streets of cities, how great they are! If the stars should appear one night in a thousand years, how would men believe and adore; and preserve for many generations the remembrance of the city of God which had been shown! But every night come out these envoys of beauty, and light the universe with their admonishing smile.

The stars awaken a certain reverence, because though always present, they are inaccessible; but all natural objects make a kindred impression, when the mind is open to their influence. Nature never wears a mean appearance. Neither does the wisest man extort her secret, and lose his curiosity by finding out all her perfection. Nature never became a toy to a wise spirit. The flowers, the animals, the mountains, reflected the wisdom of his best hour, as much as they had delighted the simplicity of his childhood.

When we speak of nature in this manner, we have a distinct but most poetical sense in the mind. We mean the integrity of impression made by manifold natural objects. It is this which distinguishes the stick of timber of the wood-cutter, from the tree of the poet. The charming landscape which I saw this morning is indubitably made up of some twenty or thirty farms. Miller owns this field, Locke that, and Manning the woodland beyond. But none of them owns the landscape. There is a property in the horizon which no man has but he whose eye can integrate all the parts, that is, the poet. This is the best part of these men's farms, yet to this their warranty-deeds give no title.

To speak truly, few adult persons can see nature. Most persons do not see the sun. At least they have a very superficial seeing. The sun illuminates only the eye of the man, but shines into the eye and the heart of the child. The lover of nature is he whose inward and outward senses are still truly adjusted to each other; who has retained the spirit of infancy even into the era of manhood. His intercourse with heaven and earth becomes part of his daily food. In the presence of nature a wild delight runs through the man, in spite of real sorrows. Nature says, — he is my creature, and maugre all his impertinent griefs, he shall be glad with me. Not the sun or the summer alone, but every hour and season yields its tribute of delight; for every hour and change corresponds to and authorizes a different state of the mind, from breathless noon to grimmest midnight. Nature is a setting that fits equally well a comic or a mourning piece. In good health, the air is a cordial or incredible virtue. Crossing a bare common, in snow puddles, at twilight, under a clouded sky, without having in my thoughts any occurrence of special good fortune, I have enjoyed a perfect exhilaration. I am glad to the brink of fear. In the woods, too, a man casts off his years, as the snake his slough, and at what period soever of life, is always a child. In the woods is perpetual youth. Within these plantations of God, a decorum and sanctity reign, a perennial festival is dressed, and the guest sees not how he should tire of them in a thousand years. In the woods, we return to reason and faith. There I feel that nothing can befall me in life, — no disgrace, no calamity (leaving me my eyes), which nature cannot repair. Standing on the bare ground, — my head bathed by the blithe air, and uplifted into infinite space, — all mean egotism vanishes. I become a transparent eye-ball; I am nothing; I see all; the currents of the Universal Being circulate through me; I am part or parcel of God. The name of the nearest friend sounds then foreign and accidental: to be brothers, to be acquaintances, master or servant, is then a trifle and a disturbance. I am the lover of uncontained and immortal beauty. In the wilderness, I find something more dear and connate than in streets or villages. In the tranquil landscape, and especially in the distant line of the horizon, man beholds somewhat as beautiful as his own nature.

The greatest delight which the fields and woods minister is the suggestion of an occult relation between man and the vegetable. I am not alone and unacknowledged. They nod to me, and I to them. The waving of the boughs in the storm is new to me and old. It takes me by surprise, and yet is not unknown. Its effect is like that of a higher thought or a better emotion coming over me, when I deemed I was thinking justly or doing right.

Yet it is certain that the power to produce this delight does not reside in nature, but in man, or in a harmony of both. It is necessary to use these pleasures with great temperance. For nature is not always tricked in holiday attire, but the same scene which yesterday breathed perfume and glittered as for the frolic of the nymphs, is overspread with melancholy to-day. Nature always wears the colors of the spirit. To a man laboring under calamity, the heat of his own fire hath sadness in it. Then there is a kind of contempt of the landscape felt by him who has just lost by death a dear friend. The sky is less grand as it shuts down over less worth in the population.

II. *Commodity*

Whoever considers the final cause of the world will discern a multitude of uses that enter as parts into that result. They all admit of being thrown into one of the following classes: Commodity; Beauty; Language; and Discipline.

Under the general name of commodity, I rank all those advantages which our senses owe to nature. This, of course, is a benefit which is temporary and mediate, not ultimate, like its service to the soul. Yet although low, it is perfect in its kind, and is the only use of nature which all men apprehend. The misery of man appears like childish petulance, when we explore the steady and prodigal provision that has been made for his support and delight on this green ball which floats him through the heavens. What angels invented these splendid ornaments, these rich conveniences, this ocean of air above, this ocean of water beneath, this firmament of earth between? this zodiac of lights, this tent of dropping clouds, this striped coat of climates, this fourfold year? Beasts, fire, water, stones, and corn serve him. The field is at once his floor, his work-yard, his play-ground, his garden, and his bed.

> "More servants wait on man
> Than he'll take notice of."

Nature, in its ministry to man, is not only the material, but is also the process and the result. All the parts incessantly work into each other's hands for the profit of man. The wind sows the seed; the sun evaporates the sea; the wind blows the vapor to the field; the ice, on the other side of the planet, condenses rain on this; the rain feeds the plant; the plant feeds the animal; and thus the endless circulations of the divine charity nourish man.

The useful arts are reproductions or new combinations by the wit of man, of the same natural benefactors. He no longer waits for favoring gales, but by means of steam, he realizes the fable of Æolus's bag, and carries the two and thirty winds in the boiler of his boat. To diminish friction, he paves the road with iron bars, and, mounting a coach with a ship-load of men, animals, and mer-chandise behind him, he darts through the country, from town to town, like an eagle or a swallow through the air. By the aggregate of these aids, how is the face of the world changed, from the era of Noah to that of Napoleon! The private poor man hath cities, ships, canals, bridges, built for him. He goes to the post-office, and the human race run on his errands; to the book-shop, and the human race read and write of all that happens, for him; to the court-house, and nations repair his wrongs. He sets his house upon the road, and the human race go forth every morning, and shovel out the snow, and cut a path for him.

But there is no need of specifying particulars in this class of uses. The catalogue is endless, and the examples so obvious, that I shall leave them to the reader's reflection, with the general remark, that this mercenary benefit is one which has respect to a farther good. A man is fed, not that he may be fed, but that he may work.

III. *Beauty*

A nobler want of man is served by nature, namely, the love of Beauty.

The ancient Greeks called the world κόσμος, beauty. Such is the constitution of all things, or such the plastic power of the human eye, that the primary forms, as the sky, the mountain, the tree, the animal, give us a delight *in and for themselves;* a pleasure arising from outline, color, motion, and grouping. This seems partly owing to the eye itself. The eye is the best of artists. By the mutual action of its structure and of the laws of light, perspective is produced, which integrates every mass of objects, of what character soever, into a well colored and shaded globe, so that where the particular objects are mean and unaffecting, the landscape which they compose is round and symmetrical. And as the eye is the best composer, so light is the first of painters. There is no object so foul that intense light will not make beautiful. And the stimulus it affords to the sense, and a sort of infinitude which it hath, like space and time, make all matter gay. Even the corpse has its own beauty. But besides this general grace diffused over nature, almost all the individual forms are agreeable to the eye, as is proved by our endless imitations of some of them, as the acorn, the grape, the pine-cone, the wheat-ear, the egg, the wings and forms of most birds, the lion's claw, the serpent, the butterfly, seashells, flames, clouds, buds, leaves, and the forms of many trees, as the palm.

For better consideration, we may distribute the aspects of Beauty in a threefold manner.

1. First, the simple perception of natural forms is a delight. The influence of the forms and actions in nature is so needful to man, that, in its lowest functions, it seems to lie on the confines of commodity and beauty. To the body and mind which have been cramped by noxious work or company, nature is medicinal and restores their tone. The tradesman, the attorney comes out of the din and craft of the street and sees the sky and the woods, and is a man again. In their eternal calm, he finds himself. The health of the eye seems to demand a horizon. We are never tired, so long as we can see far enough.

But in other hours, Nature satisfies by its loveliness, and without any mixture of corporeal benefit. I see the spectacle of morning from the hill-top over against my house, from day-break to sun-rise, with emotions which an angel might share. The long slender bars of cloud float like fishes in the sea of crimson light. From the earth, as a shore, I look out into that silent sea. I seem to partake its rapid transformations; the active enchantment reaches my dust, and I dilate and conspire with the morning wind. How does Nature deify us with a few and cheap elements! Give me health and a day, and I will make the pomp of emperors ridiculous. The dawn is my Assyria; the sunset and moon-rise my Paphos, and unimaginable realms of faerie; broad noon shall be my England of the senses and the understanding; the night shall be my Germany of mystic philosophy and dreams.

Not less excellent, except for our less susceptibility in the afternoon, was the charm, last evening, of a January sunset. The western clouds divided and subdivided themselves into pink flakes modulated with tints of unspeakable softness, and the air had so much life and sweetness that it was a pain to come within doors. What was it that nature would say? Was there no meaning in the live repose of the valley behind the mill, and which Homer or Shakespeare could not reform for me in words? The leafless trees become spires of flame in the sunset, with the blue east for their background, and the stars of the dead calices of flowers, and every withered stem and stubble rimed with frost, contribute something to the mute music.

The inhabitants of cities suppose that the country landscape is pleasant only half the year. I please myself with the graces of the winter scenery, and believe that we are as much touched by it as by the genial influences of summer. To the attentive eye, each moment of the year has its own beauty, and in the same field, it beholds, every hour, a picture which was never seen before, and which shall never be seen again. The heavens change every moment, and reflect their glory or gloom on the plains beneath. The state of the crop in the surrounding farms alters the expression of the earth from week to week. The succession of native plants in the pastures and roadsides, which makes the silent clock by which time tells the summer hours, will make even the divisions of the day sensible to a keen observer. The tribes of birds and insects, like the plants punctual to their time, follow each other, and the year has room for all. By watercourses, the variety is greater. In July, the blue pontederia or pickerel-weed blooms in large beds in the shallow parts of our pleasant river, and swarms with yellow butterflies in continual motion. Art cannot rival this pomp of purple and gold. Indeed the river is a perpetual gala, and boasts each month a new ornament.

But this beauty of Nature which is seen and felt as beauty, is the least part. The shows of day, the dewy morning, the rainbow, mountains, orchards in blossom, stars, moonlight, shadows in still water, and the like, if too eagerly hunted, become shows merely, and mock us with their unreality. Go out of the house to see the moon, and 'tis mere tinsel; it will not please as when its light shines upon your necessary journey.

The beauty that shimmers in the yellow afternoons of October, who ever could clutch it? Go forth to find it, and it is gone; 'tis only a mirage as you look from the windows of diligence.

2. The presence of a higher, namely, of the spiritual element is essential to its perfection. The high and divine beauty which can be loved without effeminacy, is that which is found in combination with the human will. Beauty is the mark God sets upon virtue. Every natural action is graceful. Every heroic act is also decent, and causes the place and the bystanders to shine. We are taught by great actions that the universe is the property of every individual in it. Every rational creature has all nature for his dowry and estate. It is his, if he will. He may divest himself of it; he may creep into a corner, and abdicate his kingdom, as most men do, but he is entitled to the world by his constitution. In proportion to the energy of his thought and will, he takes up the world into himself. "All those things for which men plough, build, or sail, obey virtue;" said Sallust. "The winds and waves," said Gibbon, "are always on the side of the ablest navigators." So are the sun and moon and all the stars of heaven. When a noble act is done, — perchance in a scene of great natural beauty; when Leonidas and his three hundred martyrs consume one day in dying, and the sun and moon come each and look at them once in the steep defile of Thermopylæ; when Arnold Winkelried, in the high Alps, under the shadow of the avalanche, gathers in his side a sheaf of Austrian spears to break the line for his comrades; are not these heroes entitled to add the beauty of the scene to the beauty of the deed? When the bark of Columbus nears the shore of America; — before it, the beach lined with savages, fleeing out of all their huts of cane; the sea behind; and the purple mountains of the Indian Archipelago around, can we separate the man from the living picture? Does not the New World clothe his form with her palm-groves and savannahs as fit drapery? Ever does natural beauty steal in like air, and envelope great actions. When Sir Harry Vane was dragged up the Tower-hill, sitting on a sled, to suffer death as the champion of the English laws, one of the multitude cried out to him, "You never sate on so glorious a seat!" Charles II., to intimidate the citizens of London, caused the patriot Lord Russell to be drawn in an open coach through the principal streets of the city on his way to the scaffold. "But," his biographer says, "the multitude imagined they saw liberty and virtue sitting by his side." In private places, among sordid objects, an act of truth or heroism seems at once to draw to itself the sky as its temple, the sun as its candle. Nature stretches out her arms to embrace man, only let his thoughts be of equal greatness. Willingly does she follow his steps with the rose and the violet, and bend her lines of grandeur and grace to the decoration of her darling child. Only let his thoughts be of equal scope, and the frame will suit the picture. A virtuous man is in unison with her works, and makes the central figure of the visible sphere. Homer, Pindar, Socrates, Phocion, associate themselves fitly in our memory with the geography and climate of Greece. The visible heavens and earth sympathize with Jesus. And in common life whosoever has seen a person of powerful character and happy genius, will have remarked how easily he took all things along with him, — the persons, the opinions, and the day, and nature became ancillary to a man.

3. There is still another aspect under which the beauty of the world may be viewed, namely, as it becomes an object of the intellect. Beside the relation of things to virtue, they have a relation to thought. The intellect searches out the absolute order of things as they stand in the mind of God, and without the colors of affection. The intellectual and the active powers seem to succeed each other, and the exclusive activity of the one generates the exclusive activity of the other. There is something unfriendly in each to the other, but they are like the alternate periods of feeding and working in animals; each prepares and will be followed by the other. Therefore does beauty, which, in relation to actions, as we have seen, comes unsought, and comes because it is unsought, remain for the apprehension and pursuit of the intellect; and then again, in its turn, of

the active power. Nothing divine dies. All good is eternally reproductive. The beauty of nature re-forms itself in the mind, and not for barren contemplation, but for new creation.

All men are in some degree impressed by the face of the world; some men even to delight. This love of beauty is Taste. Others have the same love in such excess, that, not content with admiring, they seek to embody it in new forms. The creation of beauty is Art.

The production of a work of art throws a light upon the mystery of humanity. A work of art is an abstract or epitome of the world. It is the result or expression of nature, in miniature. For although the works of nature are innumerable and all different, the result or the expression of them all is similar and single. Nature is a sea of forms radically alike and even unique. A leaf, a sunbeam, a landscape, the ocean, make an analogous impression on the mind. What is common to them all, — that perfectness and harmony, is beauty. The standard of beauty is the entire circuit of natural forms, — the totality of nature; which the Italians expressed by defining beauty "il piu nell' uno." Nothing is quite beautiful alone; nothing but is beautiful in the whole. A single object is only so far beautiful as it suggests this universal grace. The poet, the painter, the sculptor, the musician, the architect, seek each to concentrate this radiance of the world on one point, and each in his several work to satisfy the love of beauty which stimulates him to produce. Thus is Art a nature passed through the alembic of man. Thus in art does Nature work through the will of a man filled with the beauty of her first works.

The world thus exists to the soul to satisfy the desire of beauty. This element I call an ultimate end. No reason can be asked or given why the soul seeks beauty. Beauty, in its largest and profoundest sense, is one expression for the universe. God is the all-fair. Truth, and goodness, and beauty, are but different faces of the same All. But beauty in nature is not ultimate. It is the herald of inward and eternal beauty, and is not alone a solid and satisfactory good. It must stand as a part, and not as yet the last or highest expression of the final cause of Nature.

IV. Language

Language is a third use which Nature subserves to man. Nature is the vehicle of thought, and in a simple, double, and threefold degree.

1. Words are signs of natural facts.
2. Particular natural facts are symbols of particular spiritual facts.
3. Nature is the symbol of spirit.

1. Words are signs of natural facts. The use of natural history is to give us aid in supernatural history; the use of the outer creation, to give us language for the beings and changes of the inward creation. Every word which is used to express a moral or intellectual fact, if traced to its root, is found to be borrowed from some material appearance. *Right* means *straight; wrong* means *twisted. Spirit* primarily means *wind; transgression,* the crossing of a *line; supercilious,* the *raising of the eyebrow.* We say the *heart* to express emotion, the *head* to denote thought; and *thought* and *emotion* are words borrowed from sensible things, and now appropriated to spiritual nature. Most of the process by which this transformation is made, is hidden from us in the remote time when language was framed; but the same tendency may be daily observed in children. Children and savages use only nouns or names of things, which they convert into verbs, and apply to analogous mental acts.

2. But this origin of all words that convey a spiritual import, — so conspicuous a fact in this history of language, — is our least debt to nature. It is not words only that are emblematic; it is things which are emblematic. Every natural fact is a symbol of some spiritual fact. Every appearance in nature corresponds to some state of the mind, and that state of the mind can only be described by presenting that natural appearance as its picture. An enraged man is a lion, a cunning man is a fox, a firm man is a rock, a learned man is a torch. A lamb is innocence; a snake is subtle spite; flowers express to us the delicate affections. Light

and darkness are our familiar expression for knowledge and ignorance; and heat for love. Visible distance behind and before us, is respectively our image of memory and hope. Who looks upon a river in a meditative hour and is not reminded of the flux of all things? Throw a stone into the stream, and the circles that propagate themselves are the beautiful type of all influence. Man is conscious of a universal soul within or behind his individual life, wherein, as in a firmament, the natures of Justice, Truth, Love, Freedom, arise and shine. The universal soul he calls Reason: it is not mine, or thine, or his, but we are its; we are its property and men. And the blue sky in which the private earth is buried, the sky with its eternal calm, and full of everlasting orbs, is the type of Reason. That which intellectually considered we call Reason, considered in relation to nature, we call Spirit. Spirit is the Creator. Spirit hath life in itself. And man in all ages and countries embodies it in his language as the FATHER.

It is easily seen that there is nothing lucky or capricious in these analogies, but that they are constant, and pervade nature. These are not the dreams of a few poets, here and there, but man is an analogist, and studies relations in all objects. He is placed in the centre of beings, and a ray of relation passes from every other being to him. And neither can man be understood without these objects, nor these objects without man. All the facts in natural history taken by themselves, have no value, but are barren, like a single sex. But marry it to human history, and it is full of life. While floras, all Linnæus' and Buffon's volumes, are dry catalogues of facts; but the most trivial of these facts, the habit of a plant, the organs, or work, or noise of an insect, applied to the illustration of a fact in intellectual philosophy, or in any way associated to human nature, affects us in the most lively and agreeable manner. The seed of a plant, — to what affecting analogies in the nature of man is that little fruit made use of, in all discourse, up to the voice of Paul, who calls the human corpse a seed, — "It is sown a natural body; it is raised a spiritual body." The motion of the earth round its axis and round the sun,

makes the day and the year. These are certain amounts of brute light and heat. But is there no intent of an analogy between man's life and the seasons? And do the seasons gain no grandeur or pathos from that analogy? The instincts of the ant are very unimportant considered as the ant's; but the moment a ray of relation is seen to extend from it to man, and the little drudge is seen to be a monitor, a little body with a mighty heart, then all its habits, even that said to be recently observed, that it never sleeps, become sublime.

Because of this radical correspondence between visible things and human thoughts, savages, who have only what is necessary, converse in figures. As we go back in history, language becomes more picturesque, until its infancy, when it is all poetry; or all spiritual facts are represented by natural symbols. The same symbols are found to make the original elements of all languages. It has moreover been observed, that the idioms of all languages approach each other in passages of the greatest eloquence and power. And as this is the first language, so is it the last. This immediate dependence of language upon nature, this conversion of an outward phenomenon into a type of somewhat in human life, never loses its power to affect us. It is this which gives that piquancy to the conversation of a strong-natured farmer or backwoodsman, which all men relish.

A man's power to connect his thought with its proper symbol, and so to utter it, depends on the simplicity of his character, that is, upon his love of truth and his desire to communicate it without loss. The corruption of man is followed by the corruption of language. When simplicity of character and the sovereignty of ideas is broken up by the prevalence of secondary desires, — the desire of riches, of pleasure, of power, and of praise, — and duplicity and falsehood take place of simplicity and truth, the power over nature as an interpreter of the will is in a degree lost; new imagery ceases to be created, and old words are perverted to stand for things which are not; a paper currency is employed, when there is no bullion in the vaults. In due time the fraud is manifest, and words lose all power to stimulate the understanding or the affections. Hundreds of writers may be found in every long-civilized nation who for a short time believe and made others believe that they see and utter truths, who do not of themselves clothe one thought in its natural garment, but who feed unconsciously on the language created by the primary writers of the country, those, namely, who hold primarily on nature.

But wise men pierce this rotten diction and fasten words again to visible things; so that picturesque language is at once a commanding certificate that he who employs it is a man in alliance with truth and God. The moment our discourse rises above the ground line of familiar facts and is inflamed with passion or exalted by thought, it clothes itself in images. A man conversing in earnest, if he watch his intellectual processes, will find that a material image more or less luminous arises in his mind, contemporaneous with every thought, which furnishes the vestment of the thought. Hence, good writing and brilliant discourse are perpetual allegories. This imagery is spontaneous. It is the blending of experience with the present action of the mind. It is proper creation. It is the working of the Original Cause through the instruments he has already made.

These facts may suggest the advantage which the country-life possesses, for a powerful mind, over the artificial and curtailed life of cities. We know more from nature than we can at will communicate. Its light flows into the mind evermore, and we forget its presence. The poet, the orator, bred in the woods, whose senses have been nourished by their fair and appeasing changes, year after year, without design and without heed, — shall not lose their lesson altogether, in the roar of cities or the broil of politics. Long hereafter, amidst agitation and terror in national council, — in the hour of revolution, — these solemn images shall reappear in their morning lustre, as fit symbols and words of the thoughts which the passing events shall awaken. At the call of a noble sentiment, again the woods wave, the pines murmur, the river rolls and shines, and the cattle low upon the mountains, as he saw and heard them in his infancy. And with these forms, the spells of persuasion, the keys of power are put into his hands.

3. We are thus assisted by natural objects in the expression of particular meanings. But how great a language to convey such pepper-corn informations! Did it need such noble races of creatures, this profusion of forms, this host of orbs in heaven, to furnish man with the dictionary and grammar of his municipal speech? Whilst we use this grand cipher to expedite the affairs of our pot and kettle, we feel that we have not yet put it to its use, neither are able. We are like travellers using the cinders of a volcano to roast their eggs. Whilst we see that it always stands ready to clothe what we would say, we cannot avoid the question whether the characters are not significant of themselves. Have mountains, and waves, and skies, no significance but what we consciously give them when we employ them as emblems of our thoughts? The world is emblematic. Parts of speech are metaphors, because the whole of nature is a metaphor of the human mind. The laws of moral nature answer to those of matter as face to face in a glass. "The visible world and the relation of its parts, is the dial plate of the invisible." The axioms of physics translate the laws of ethics. Thus, "the whole is greater than its part;" "reaction is equal to action;" "the smallest weight may be made to lift the greatest, the difference of weight being compensated by time;" and many the like propositions, which have an ethical as well as physical sense. These propositions have a much more extensive and universal sense when applied to human life, than when confined to technical use.

In like manner, the memorable words of history and the proverbs of nations consist usually of a natural fact, selected as a picture or parable of a moral truth. Thus: A rolling stone gathers no moss; A bird in the hand is worth two in the bush; A cripple in the right way will beat a racer in the wrong; Make hay while the sun shines: 'Tis hard to carry a full cup even; Vinegar is the son of wine; The last ounce broke the camel's back; Long-lived trees make roots first; — and the like. In their primary sense these are trivial facts, but we repeat them for the value of their analogical import. What is true of proverbs, is true of all fables, parables, and allegories.

This relation between the mind and matter is not fancied by some poet, but stands in the will of God, and so is free to be known by all men. It appears to men, or it does not appear. When in fortunate hours we ponder this miracle, the wise man doubts if at all other times he is not blind and deaf;

> "Can these things be,
> And overcome us like a summer's cloud,
> Without our special wonder?"

for the universe becomes transparent, and the light of higher laws than its own shines through it. It is the standing problem which has exercised the wonder and the study of every fine genius since the world began; from the era of the Egyptians and the Brahmins to that of Pythagoras, of Plato, of Bacon, of Leibnitz, of Swedenborg. There sits the Sphinx at the road-side, and from age to age, as each prophet comes by, he tries his fortune at reading her riddle. There seems to be a necessity in spirit to manifest itself in material forms; and day and night, river and storm, beast and bird, acid and alkali, pre-exist in necessary Ideas in the mind of God, and are what they are by virtue of preceding affections in the world of spirit. A fact is the end or last issue of spirit. The visible creation is the terminus or the circumference of the invisible world. "Material objects," said a French philosopher, "are necessarily kinds of *scoriæ* of the substantial thoughts of the Creator, which must always preserve an exact relation to their first origin; in other words, visible nature must have a spiritual and moral side."

This doctrine is abstruse, and though the images of "garment," "scoriæ," "mirror," etc., may stimulate the fancy, we must summon the aid of subtler and more vital expositors to make it plain. "Every scripture is to be interpreted by the same spirit which gave it forth," — is the fundamental law of criticism. A life in harmony with Nature, the love of truth and of virtue, will purge the eyes to understand her text. By degrees we may come to know the primitive sense of the permanent objects of nature, so that the world shall be to us an open book, and every form significant of its hidden life and final cause.

A new interest surprises us, whilst, under the view now suggested, we contemplate the fearful extent and multitude of objects; since "every object rightly seen, unlocks a new faculty of the soul." That which was unconscious truth, becomes, when interpreted and defined in an object, a part of the domain of knowledge, — a new weapon in the magazine of power.

V. *Discipline*

In view of the significance of nature, we arrive at once at a new fact, that nature is a discipline. This use of the world includes the preceding uses, as parts of itself.

Space, time, society, labor, climate, food, locomotion, the animals, the mechanical forces, give us sincerest lessons, day by day, whose meaning is unlimited. They educate both the Understanding and the Reason. Every property of matter is a school for the understanding, — its solidity or resistance, its inertia, its extension, its figure, its divisibility. The understanding adds, divides, combines, measures, and finds nutriment and room for its activity in this worthy scene. Meantime, Reason transfers all these lessons into its own world of thought, by perceiving the analogy that marries Matter and Mind.

1. Nature is a discipline of the understanding in intellectual truths. Our dealing with sensible objects is a constant exercise in the necessary lessons of difference, of likeness, of order, of being and seeming, of progressive arrangement; of ascent from particular to general; of combination to one end of manifold forces. Proportioned to the importance of the organ to be formed, is the extreme care with which its tuition is provided, — a care pretermitted in no single case. What tedious training, day after day, year after year, never ending, to form the common sense; what continual reproduction of annoyances, inconveniences, dilemmas; what rejoicing over us of little men; what disputing of prices, what reckonings of interest, — and all to form the Hand of the mind; — to instruct

us that "good thoughts are no better than good dreams, unless they be executed!"

The same good office is performed by Property and its filial systems of debt and credit. Debt, grinding debt, whose iron face the widow, the orphan, and the sons of genius fear and hate; — debt, which consumes so much time, which so cripples and disheartens a great spirit with cares that seem so base, is a preceptor whose lessons cannot be forgone, and is needed most by those who suffer from it most. Moreover, property, which has been well compared to snow, — "if it fall level today, it will be blown into drifts tomorrow," — is the surface action of internal machinery, like the index on the face of a clock. Whilst now it is the gymnastics of the understanding, it is hiving, in the foresight of the spirit, experience in profounder laws.

The whole character and fortune of the individual are affected by the least inequalities in the culture of the understanding; for example, in the perception of differences. Therefore is Space, and therefore Time, that man may know that things are not huddled and lumped, but sundered and individual. A bell and a plough have each their use, and neither can do the office of the other. Water is good to drink, coal to burn, wool to wear; but wool cannot be drunk, nor water spun, nor coal eaten. The wise man shows his wisdom in separation, in gradation, and his scale of creatures and of merits is as wide as nature. The foolish have no range in their scale, but suppose every man is as every other man. What is not good they call the worst, and what is not hateful, they call the best.

In like manner, what good heed Nature forms in us! She pardons no mistakes. Her yea is yea, and her nay, nay.

The first steps in Agriculture, Astronomy, Zoölogy (those first steps which the farmer, the hunter, and the sailor take), teach that Nature's dice are always loaded; that in her heaps and rubbish are concealed sure and useful results.

How calmly and genially the mind apprehends one after another the laws of physics! What noble emotions dilate the mortal as he enters into the councils of the creation, and feels by knowledge the privilege to BE! His insight refines him. The beauty of nature shines in his own breast. Man is greater that he can see this, and the universe less, because Time and Space relations vanish as laws are known.

Here again we are impressed and even daunted by the immense Universe to be explored. "What we know is a point to what we do not know." Open any recent journal of science, and weigh the problems suggested concerning Light, Heat, Electricity, Magnetism, Physiology, Geology, and judge whether the interest of natural science is likely to be soon exhausted.

Passing by many particulars of the discipline of nature, we must not omit to specify two.

The exercise of the Will, or the lesson of power, is taught in every event. From the child's successive possession of his several senses up to the hour when he saith, "Thy will be done!" he is learning the secret that he can reduce under his will, not only particular events but great classes, nay, the whole series of events, and so conform all facts to his character. Nature is thoroughly mediate. It is made to serve. It receives the dominion of man as meekly as the ass on which the Saviour rode. It offers all its kingdoms to man as the raw material which he may mould into what is useful. Man is never weary of working it up. He forges the subtile and delicate air into wise and melodious words, and gives them wing as angels of persuasion and command. One after another his victorious thought comes up with and reduces all things, until the world becomes at last only a realized will, — the double of the man.

2. Sensible objects conform to the premonitions of Reason and reflect the conscience. All things are moral; and in their boundless changes have an unceasing reference to spiritual nature. Therefore is nature glorious with form, color, and motion — that every globe in the remotest heaven, every chemical change from the rudest crystal up to the laws of life, every change of vegetation from the first principle of growth in the eye of a leaf, to the tropical forest and antediluvian coal-mine, every animal function from the sponge up to Hercules, shall hint or

thunder to man the laws of right and wrong, and echo the Ten Commandments. Therefore is Nature ever the ally of Religion — lends all her pomp and riches to the religious sentiment. Prophet and priest, David, Isaiah, Jesus, have drawn deeply from this source. This ethical character so penetrates the bone and marrow of nature, as to seem the end for which it was made. Whatever private purpose is answered by any member or part, this is its public and universal function, and is never omitted. Nothing in nature is exhausted in its first use. When a thing has served an end to the uttermost, it is wholly new for an ulterior service. In God, every end is converted into a new means. Thus the use of commodity, regarded by itself, is mean and squalid. But it is to the mind an education in the doctrine of Use, namely, that a thing is good only so far as it serves; that a conspiring of parts and efforts to the production of an end is essential to any being. The first and gross manifestations of this truth is our inevitable and hated training in values and wants, in corn and meat.

It has already been illustrated, that every natural process is a version of a moral sentence. The moral law lies at the centre of nature and radiates to the circumference. It is the pith and marrow of every substance, every relation, and every process. All things with which we deal, preach to us. What is a farm but a mute gospel? The chaff and the wheat, weeds and plants, blight, rain, insects, sun, — it is a sacred emblem from the first furrow of spring to the last stack which the snow of winter overtakes in the fields. But the sailor, the shepherd, the miner, the merchant, in their several resorts, have each an experience precisely parallel, and leading to the same conclusion: because all organizations are radically alike. Nor can it be doubted that this moral sentiment which thus scents the air, grows in the grain, and impregnates the waters of the world, is caught by man and sinks into his soul. The moral influence of nature upon every individual is that amount of truth which it illustrates to him. Who can estimate this? Who can guess how much firmness the sea-beaten rock has taught the fisherman? how much tranquillity has been reflected to man from the azure sky, over whose unspotted deeps the winds forevermore drive flocks of stormy clouds, and leave no wrinkle or stain? how much industry and providence and affection we have caught from the pantomime of brutes? What a searching preacher of self-command is the varying phenomenon of Health!

Herein is especially apprehended the unity of Nature, — the unity in variety, — which meets us everywhere. All the endless variety of things make an identical impression. Xenophanes complained in his old age that, look where he would, all things hastened back to Unity. He was weary of seeing the same entity in the tedious variety of forms. The fable of Proteus has a cordial truth. A leaf, a drop, a crystal, a moment of time, is related to the whole, and partakes of the perfection of the whole. Each particle is a microcosm, and faithfully renders the likeness of the world.

Not only resemblances exist in things whose analogy is obvious, as when we detect the type of the human hand in the flipper of the fossil saurus, but also in objects wherein there is great superficial unlikeness. Thus architecture is called "frozen music," by De Staël and Goethe. Vitruvius thought an architect should be a musician. "A Gothic church," said Coleridge, "is a petrified religion." Michael Angelo maintained that, to an architect, a knowledge of anatomy is essential. In Haydn's oratorios, the notes present to the imagination not only motions, as of the snake, the stag, and the elephant, but colors also; as the green grass. The law of harmonic sounds reappears in the harmonic colors. The granite is differenced in its laws only by the more or less of heat from the river that wears it away. The river, as it flows, resembles the air that flows over it; the air resembles the light which traverses it with more subtle currents; the light resembles the heat which rides with it through Space. Each creature is only a modification of the other; the likeness in them is more than the difference, and their radical law is one and the same. A rule of one art, or a law of one organization, holds true throughout nature. So intimate is this Unity, that, it is easily seen, it lies under the undermost garment of nature, and betrays its source in Universal Spirit. For it pervades Thought also. Every universal truth which we express in words, implies or supposes every other truth. *Omne verum vero consonat*. It is like a great circle on a sphere, comprising all possible circles; which, however, may be drawn and comprise it in like manner. Every such truth is the absolute Ens seen from one side. But it has innumerable sides.

The central Unity is still more conspicuous in actions. Words are finite organs of the infinite mind. They cannot cover the dimensions of what is in truth. They break, chop and impoverish it. An action is the perfection and publication of thought. A right action seems to fill the eye, and to be related to all nature. "The wise man, in doing one thing, does all; or, in the one thing he does rightly, he sees the likeness of all which is done rightly."

Words and actions are not the attributes of brute nature. They introduce us to the human form, of which all other organizations appear to be degradations. When this appears among so many that surround it, the spirit prefers it to all others. It says, "From such as this have I drawn joy and knowledge; in such as this have I found and beheld myself; I will speak to it; it can speak again; it can yield me thought already formed and alive." In fact, the eye, — the mind, — is always accompanied by these forms, male and female; and these are incomparably the richest informations of the power and order that lie at the heart of things. Unfortunately every one of them bears the marks as of some injury; is marred and superficially defective. Nevertheless, far different from the deaf and dumb nature around them, these all rest like fountain-pipes on the unfathomed sea of thought and virtue whereto they alone, of all organizations, are the entrances.

It were a pleasant inquiry to follow into detail their ministry to our education, but where would it stop? We are associated in adolescent and adult life with some friends, who, like skies and waters, are coextensive with our idea; who, answering each to a certain affection of the soul, satisfy our desire on that side; whom we lack power to put at such focal distance from us, that we can mend or even analyze them. We cannot choose but love them. When much intercourse with a friend has supplied us with a standard of excellence, and has increased our respect for the resources of God who thus sends a real person to outgo our ideal; when he has, moreover, become an object of thought, and, whilst his character retains all its unconscious effect, is converted in the mind into solid and sweet wisdom, — it is a sign to us that his office is closing, and he is commonly withdrawn from our sight in a short time.

VI. Idealism

Thus is the unspeakable but intelligible and practicable meaning of the world conveyed to man, the immortal pupil, in every object of sense. To this one end of Discipline; all parts of nature conspire.

A noble doubt perpetually suggests itself, — whether this end be not the Final Cause of the Universe; and whether nature outwardly exists. It is a sufficient account of that Appearance we call the World, that God will teach a human mind, and so makes it the receiver of a certain number of congruent sensations, which we call sun and moon, man and woman, house and trade. In my utter impotence to test the authenticity of the report of my senses, to know whether the impressions they make on me correspond with outlying objects, what difference does it make, whether Orion is up there in heaven, or some god paints the image in the firmament of the soul? The relations of parts and the end of the whole remaining the same, what is the difference, whether land and sea interact, and worlds revolve and intermingle without number or end, — deep yawning under deep, and galaxy balancing galaxy, throughout absolute space, — or whether, without relations of time and space, the same appearances are inscribed in the constant faith of man? Whether nature enjoy a substantial existence without, or is only in the apocalypse of the mind, it is alike useful and alike venerable to me. Be it what it may, it is ideal to me so long as I cannot try the accuracy of my senses.

The frivolous make themselves merry with the Ideal theory, as if its consequences were burlesque; as if it affected the stability of nature. It surely does not. God never jests with us, and will not compromise the end of nature by permitting any inconsequence in its procession. Any distrust of the permanence of laws would paralyze the faculties of man. Their permanence is sacredly respected, and his faith therein is perfect. The wheels and springs of man are all set to the hypothesis of the permanence of nature. We are not built like a ship to be tossed, but like a house to stand. It is a natural consequence of this structure, that so long as the active powers predominate over the reflective, we resist with indignation any hint that nature is more short-lived or mutable than spirit. The broker, the wheelwright, the carpenter, the tollman, are much displeased at the intimation.

But whilst we acquiesce entirely in the permanence of natural laws, the question of the absolute existence of nature still remains open. It is the uniform effect of culture on the human mind, not to shake our faith in the stability of particular phenomena, as of heat, water, azote; but to lead us to regard nature as phenomenon, not a substance; to attribute necessary existence to spirit; to esteem nature as an accident and an effect.

To the senses and the unrenewed understanding, belongs a sort of instinctive belief in the absolute existence of nature. In their view man and nature are indissolubly joined. Things are ultimates, and they never look beyond their sphere. The presence of Reason mars this faith. The first effort of thought tends to relax this despotism of the senses which binds us to nature as if we were a part of it, and shows us nature aloof, and, as it were, afloat. Until this higher agency intervened, the animal eye sees, with wonderful accuracy, sharp outlines and colored surfaces. When the eye of Reason opens, to outline and surface are at once added grace and expression. These proceed from imagination and affection, and abate somewhat of the angular distinctness of objects. If the Reason be stimulated to more earnest

vision, outlines and surfaces become transparent, and are no longer seen; causes and spirits are seen through them. The best moments of life are these delicious awakenings of the higher powers, and the reverential withdrawing of nature before its God.

Let us proceed to indicate the effects of culture.

1. Our first institution in the Ideal philosophy is a hint from Nature herself.

Nature is made to conspire with spirit to emancipate us. Certain mechanical changes, a small alteration in our local position, apprizes us of a dualism. We are strangely affected by seeing the shore from a moving ship, from a balloon, or through the tints of an unusual sky. The least change in our point of view gives the whole world a pictorial air. A man who seldom rides, needs only to get into a coach and traverse his own town, to turn the street into a puppet-show. The men, the women, — talking, running, bartering, fighting, — the earnest mechanic, the lounger, the beggar, the boys, the dogs, are unrealized at once, or, at least, wholly detached from all relation to the observer, and seen as apparent, not substantial beings. What new thoughts are suggested by seeing a face of country quite familiar, in the rapid movement of the railroad car! Nay, the most wonted objects, (make a very slight change in the point of vision,) please us most. In a camera obscura, the butcher's cart, and the figure of one of our own family amuse us. So a portrait of a well-known face gratifies us. Turn the eyes upside down, by looking at the landscape through your legs, and how agreeable is the picture, though you have seen it any time these twenty years!

In these cases, by mechanical means, is suggested the difference between the observer and the spectacle, — between man and nature. Hence arises a pleasure mixed with awe; I may say, a low degree of the sublime is felt, from the fact, probably, that man is hereby apprized that whilst the world is a spectacle, something in himself is stable.

2. In a higher manner the poet communicates the same pleasure. By a few strokes he delineates — as on air — the sun, the mountain, the camp, the city, the hero, the

maiden, not different from what we know them, but only lifted from the ground and afloat before the eye. He unfixes the land and the sea, makes them revolve around the axis of his primary thought, and disposes them anew. Possessed himself by a heroic passion, he uses matter as symbols of it. The sensual man conforms thoughts to things; the poet conforms things to his thoughts. The one esteems nature as rooted and fast; the other, as fluid, and impresses his being thereon. To him, the refractory world is ductile and flexible; he invests dust and stones with humanity, and makes them the words of the Reason. The Imagination may be defined to be the use which the Reason makes of the material world. Shakspeare possesses the power of subordinating nature for the purposes of expression, beyond all poets. His imperial muse tosses the creation like a bauble from hand to hand, and uses it to embody any caprice of thought that is uppermost in his mind. The remotest spaces of nature are visited, and the farthest sundered things are brought together, by a subtle spiritual connection. We are made aware that magnitude of material things is relative, and all objects shrink and expand to serve the passion of the poet. Thus in his sonnets, the lays of birds, the scents and dyes of flowers he finds to be the *shadow* of his beloved; time, which keeps her from him, is his *chest;* the suspicion she has awakened, is her *ornament:*

"The ornament of beauty is Suspect,
A crow which flies in heaven's sweetest air."

His passion is not the fruit of chance; it swells, as he speaks, to a city, or a state:

"No, it was builded far from accident;
It suffers not in smiling pomp, nor falls
Under the brow of thralling discontent;
It fears not policy, that heretic,
That works on leases of short numbered hours,
But all alone stands hugely politic."

In the strength of his constancy, the Pyramids seem to him recent and transitory. The freshness of youth and love dazzles him with its resemblance to morning:

"Take those lips away
Which so sweetly were forsworn;
And those eyes, — the break of day,
Lights that do mislead the morn."

The wild beauty of this hyperbole, I may say in passing, it would not be easy to match in literature.

This transfiguration which all material objects undergo through the passion of the poet, — this power which he exerts to dwarf the great, to magnify the small, — might be illustrated by a thousand examples from his plays. I have before me the Tempest, and will cite only these few lines:

"ARIEL. The strong based promontory
Have I made shake, and by the spurs plucked up
The pine and cedar."

Prospero calls for music to soothe the frantic Alonzo, and his companions:

"A solemn air, and the best comforter
To an unsettled fancy, cure thy brains
Now useless, boiled within thy skull."

Again:

"The charm dissolves apace,
And, as the morning steals upon the night,
Melting the darkness, so their rising senses
Begin to chase the ignorant fumes that mantle
Their clearer reason. Their understanding
Begins to swell: and the approaching tide
Will shortly fill the reasonable shores
That now lie foul and muddy."

The perception of real affinities between events (that is to say, of *ideal* affinities, for those only are real), enables the poet thus to make free with the most imposing forms and phenomena of the world, and to assert the predominance of the soul.

3. Whilst thus the poet animates nature with his own thoughts, he differs from the philosopher only herein, that the one proposes Beauty as his main end; the other Truth. But the philosopher, not less than the poet, postpones the apparent order and relations of things to the empire of thought. "The problem of philosophy," according to Plato, "is, for all that exists conditionally, to find a ground unconditioned and absolute." It proceeds on the faith that a law determines all phenomena, which being known, the phenomena can be predicted. That law, when in the mind, is an idea. Its beauty is infinite. The true philosopher and the true poet are one, and a beauty, which is truth, and a truth, which is beauty, is the aim of both. Is not the charm of one of Plato's or

Aristotle's definitions strictly like that of the Antigone of Sophocles? It is, in both cases, that a spiritual life has been imparted to nature; that the solid seeming block of matter has been pervaded and dissolved by a thought; that this feeble human being has penetrated the vast masses of nature with an informing soul, and recognized itself in their harmony, that is, seized their law. In physics, when this is attained, the memory disburthens itself of its cumbrous catalogues of particulars, and carries centuries of observation in a single formula.

Thus even in physics, the material is degraded before the spiritual. The astronomer, the geometer, rely on their irrefragable analysis, and disdain the results of observation. The sublime remark of Euler on his law of arches, "This will be found contrary to all experience, yet is true," had already transferred nature into the mind, and left matter like an outcast corpse.

4. Intellectual science has been observed to beget invariably a doubt of the existence of matter. Turgot said, "He that has never doubted the existence of matter, may be assured he has no aptitude for metaphysical inquiries." It fastens the attention upon immortal necessary uncreated natures, that is, upon Ideas; and in their presence we feel that the outward circumstance is a dream and a shade. Whilst we wait in this Olympus of gods, we think of nature as an appendix to the soul. We ascend into their region, and know that these are the thoughts of the Supreme Being. "These are they who were set up from everlasting, from the beginning, or ever the earth was. When he prepared the heavens, they were there; when he established the clouds above, when he strengthened the fountains of the deep. Then they were by him, as one brought up with him. Of them took he counsel."

Their influence is proportionate. As objects of science they are accessible to few men. Yet all men are capable of being raised by piety or by passion, into their region. And no man touches these divine natures, without becoming, in some degree, himself divine. Like a new soul, they renew the body. We become physically nimble and lightsome; we tread on air; life is no longer

irksome, and we think it will never be so. No man fears age or misfortune or death in their serene company, for he is transported out of the district of change. Whilst we behold unveiled the nature of Justice and Truth, we learn the difference between the absolute and the conditional or relative. We apprehend the absolute. As it were, for the first time, *we exist*. We become immortal, for we learn that time and space are relations of matter; that with a perception of truth or a virtuous will they have no affinity.

5. Finally, religion and ethics, which may be fitly called the practice of ideas, or the introduction of ideas into life, have an analogous effect with all lower culture, in degrading nature and suggesting its dependence on spirit. Ethics and religion differ herein; that the one is the system of human duties commencing from man; the other, from God. Religion includes the personality of God; Ethics does not. They are one to our present design. They both put nature under foot. The first and last lesson of religion is, "The things that are seen, are temporal; the things that are unseen, are eternal." It puts an affront upon nature. It does that for the unschooled, which philosophy does for Berkeley and Viasa. The uniform language that may be heard in the churches of the most ignorant sects is, — "Contemn the unsubstantial shows of the world; they are vanities, dreams, shadows, unrealities; seek the realities of religion." The devotee flouts nature. Some theosophists have arrived at a certain hostility and indignation towards matter, as the Manichean and Plotinus. They distrusted in themselves any looking back to these flesh-pots of Egypt. Plotinus was ashamed of his body. In short, they might all say of matter, what Michael Angelo said of external beauty, "It is the frail and weary weed, in which God dresses the soul which he has called into time."

It appears that motion, poetry, physical and intellectual science, and religion, all tend to affect our convictions of the reality of the external world. But I own there is something ungrateful in expanding too curiously the particulars of the general proposition, that all culture tends to imbue us with idealism. I have no hostility to nature, but a child's love to it. I expand and live in the warm day like corn and melons. Let us speak her fair. I do not wish to fling stones at my beautiful mother, nor soil my gentle nest. I only wish to indicate the true position of nature in regard to man, wherein to establish man all right education tends; as the ground which to attain is the object of human life, that is, of man's connection with nature. Culture inverts the vulgar views of nature, and brings the mind to call that apparent which it uses to call real, and that real which it uses to call visionary. Children, it is true, believe in the external world. The belief that it appears only, is an afterthought, but with culture this faith will as surely arise on the mind as did the first.

The advantage of the ideal theory over the popular faith is this, that it presents the world in precisely that view which is most desirable to the mind. It is, in fact, the view which Reason, both speculative and practical, that is, philosophy and virtue, take. For seen in the light of thought, the world always is phenomenal; and virtue subordinates it to the mind. Idealism sees the world in God. It beholds the whole circle of persons and things, of actions and events, of country and religion, not as painfully accumulated, atom after atom, act after act, in an aged creeping Past, but as one vast picture which God paints on the instant eternity for the contemplation of the soul. Therefore the soul holds itself off from a too trivial and microscopic study of the universal tablet. It respects the end too much to immerse itself in the means. It sees something more important in Christianity than the scandals of ecclesiastical history or the niceties of criticism; and, very incurious concerning persons or miracles, and not at all disturbed by chasms of historical evidence, it accepts from God the phenomenon, as it finds it, as the pure and awful form of religion in the world. It is not hot and passionate at the appearance of what it calls its own good or bad fortune, at the union or opposition of other persons. No man is its enemy. It accepts whatsoever befalls, as part of its lesson. It is a watcher more than a doer, and it is a doer, only that it may the better watch.

VII. Spirit

It is essential to a true theory of nature and of man, that it should contain somewhat progressive. Uses that are exhausted or that may be, and facts that end in the statement, cannot be all that is true of this brave lodging wherein man is harbored, and wherein all his faculties find appropriate and endless exercise. And all the uses of nature admit of being summed in one, which yields the activity of man an infinite scope. Through all its kingdoms, to the suburbs and outskirts of things, it is faithful to the cause whence it had its origin. It always speaks of Spirit. It suggests the absolute. It is a perpetual effect. It is a great shadow pointing always to the sun behind us.

The aspect of Nature is devout. Like the figure of Jesus, she stands with bended head, and hands folded upon the breast. The happiest man is he who learns from nature the lesson of worship.

Of that ineffable essence which we call Spirit, he that thinks most, will say least. We can foresee God in the coarse, and, as it were, distant phenomena of matter; but when we try to define and describe himself, both language and thought desert us, and we are as helpless as fools and savages. That essence refuses to be recorded in propositions, but when man has worshipped him intellectually, the noblest ministry of nature is to stand as the apparition of God. It is the organ through which the universal spirit speaks to the individual, and strives to lead back the individual to it.

When we consider Spirit, we see that the views already presented do not include the whole circumference of man. We must add some related thoughts.

Three problems are put by nature to the mind: What is matter? Whence is it? and Whereto? The first of these questions only, the ideal theory answers. Idealism saith: matter is a phenomenon, not a substance. Idealism acquaints us with the total disparity between the evidence of our own being and the evidence of the world's being. The one is perfect; the other, incapable of any assurance; the mind is a part of the nature of things; the world is a divine dream, from which we may presently awake to the glories and certainties of day. Idealism is a hypothesis to account for nature by other principles than those of carpentry and chemistry. Yet, if it only deny the existence of matter, it does not satisfy the demands of the spirit. It leaves God out of me. It leaves me in the splendid labyrinth of my perceptions, to wander without end. Then the heart resists it, because it balks the affections in denying substantive being to men and women. Nature is so pervaded with human life that there is something of humanity in all and in every particular. But this theory makes nature foreign to me, and does not account for that consanguinity which we acknowledge to it.

Let it stand then, in the present state of our knowledge, merely as a useful introductory hypothesis, serving to apprise us of the eternal distinction between the soul and the world.

But when, following the invisible steps of thought, we come to inquire, Whence is matter? and Whereto? many truths arise to us out of the recesses of consciousness. We learn that the highest is present to the soul of man; that the dread universal essence, which is not wisdom, or love, or beauty, or power, but all in one, and each entirely, is that for which all things exist, and that by which they are; that spirit creates; that behind nature, throughout nature, spirit is present; one and not compound it does not act upon us from without, that is, in space and time, but spiritually, or through ourselves: therefore, that spirit, that is, the Supreme Being, does not build up nature around us but puts it forth through us, as the life of the tree puts forth new branches and leaves through the pores of the old. As a plant upon the earth, so a man rests upon the bosom of God; he is nourished by unfailing fountains, and draws at his need inexhaustible power. Who can set bounds to the possibilities of man? Once inhale the upper air, being admitted to behold the absolute natures of justice and truth, and we learn that man has access to the entire mind of the Creator, is himself the creator in the finite. This view, which admonishes me where the sources of wisdom and power lie, and points to virtue as to

"The golden key
Which opes the palace of eternity,"

carries upon its face the highest certificate of truth, because it animates me to create my own world through the purification of my soul.

The world proceeds from the same spirit as the body of man. It is a remoter and inferior incarnation of God, a projection of God in the unconscious. But it differs from the body in one important respect. It is not, like that, now subjected to the human will. Its serene order is inviolable by us. It is, therefore, to us, the present expositor of the divine mind. It is a fixed point whereby we may measure our departure. As we degenerate, the contrast between us and our house is more evident. We are as much strangers in nature as we are aliens from God. We do not understand the notes of birds. The fox and the deer run away from us; the bear and tiger rend us. We do not know the uses of more than a few plants, as corn and the apple, the potato and the vine. Is not the landscape, every glimpse of which hath a grandeur, a face of him? Yet this may show us what discord is between man and nature, for you cannot freely admire a noble landscape if laborers are digging in the field hard by. The poet finds something ridiculous in his delight until he is out of the sight of men.

VIII. Prospects

In inquiries respecting the laws of the world and the frame of things, the highest reason is always the truest. That which seems faintly possible, it is so refined, is often faint and dim because it is deepest seated in the mind among the eternal verities. Empirical science is apt to cloud the sight, and by the very knowledge of functions and processes to bereave the student of the manly contemplation of the whole. The savant becomes unpoetic. But the best read naturalist who lends an entire and devout attention to truth, will see that there remains much to learn of his relation to the world, and that it is not to be learned by any addition or subtraction or other comparison of known quantities, but is arrived at by untaught sallies of the spirit, by a continual self-recovery, and by entire humility. He will perceive that there are far more excellent qualities in the student than preciseness and infallibility; that a guess is often more fruitful than an indisputable affirmation, and that a dream may let us deeper into the secret of nature than a hundred concerted experiments.

For the problems to be solved are precisely those which the physiologist and the naturalist omit to state. It is not so pertinent to man to know all the individuals of the animal kingdom, as it is to know whence and whereto is this tyrannizing unity in his constitution, which evermore separates and classifies things, endeavoring to reduce the most diverse to one form. When I behold a rich landscape, it is less to my purpose to recite correctly the order and superposition of the strata, than to know why all thought of multitude is lost in a tranquil sense of unity. I cannot greatly honor minuteness in details, so long as there is no hint to explain the relation between things and thoughts; no ray upon the *metaphysics* of conchology, of botany, of the arts, to show the relation of the forms of flowers, shells, animals, architecture, to the mind, and build science upon ideas. In a cabinet of natural history, we become sensible of a certain occult recognition and sympathy in regard to the most unwieldly and eccentric forms of beast, fish, and insect. The American who has been confined, in his own country, to the sight of buildings designed after foreign models, is surprised on entering York Minster or St. Peter's at Rome, by the feeling that these structures are imitations also, — faint copies of an invisible archetype. Nor has science sufficient humanity, so long as the naturalist overlooks that wonderful congruity which subsists between man and the world; of which he is lord, not because he is the most subtile inhabitant, but because he is its head and heart, and finds something of himself in every great and small thing, in every mountain stratum, in every new law of color, fact of astronomy, or atmospheric influence which observation or analysis lays open. A perception of this mystery inspires the muse of George Herbert, the beautiful psalmist of the seventeenth century. The following lines are part of his little poem on Man.

"Man is all symmetry,
Full of proportions, one limb to another,
    And to all the world besides.
    Each part may call the farthest, brother;
For head with foot hath private amity,
    And both with moons and tides.

"Nothing hath got so far
But man hath caught and kept it as his prey;
    His eyes dismount the highest star:
    He is in little all the sphere.
Herbs gladly cure our flesh, because that they
    Find their acquaintance there.

"For us, the winds do blow,
The earth doth rest, heaven move, and fountains
    flow.
    Nothing we see, but means our good,
    As our delight, or as our treasure;
The whole is either our cupboard of food,
    Or cabinet of pleasure.

"The stars have us to bed:
Night draws the curtain; which the sun withdraws,
    Music and light attend our head.
    All things unto our flesh are kind,
In their descent and being; to our mind,
    In their ascent and cause.

"More servants wait on man
Than he'll take notice of. In every path,
    He treads down that which doth befriend him
    When sickness makes him pale and wan.
Oh mighty love! Man is one world, and hath
    Another to attend him."

The perception of this class of truths makes the attraction which draws men to science, but the end is lost sight of in attention to the means. In view of this half-sight of science, we accept the sentence of Plato, that "poetry comes nearer to vital truth than history." Every surmise and vaticination of the mind is entitled to a certain respect, and we learn to prefer imperfect theories, and sentences which contain glimpses of truth, to digested systems which have no one valuable suggestion. A wise writer will feel that the ends of study and composition are best answered by announcing undiscovered regions of thought, and so communicating, through hope, new activity to the torpid spirit.

I shall therefore conclude this essay with some traditions of man and nature, which a certain poet sang to me; and which, as they have always been in the world, and perhaps reappear to every bard, may be both history and prophecy.

"The foundations of man are not in matter, but in spirit. But the element of spirit is eternity. To it, therefore, the longest series of events, the oldest chronologies are young and recent. In the cycle of the universal man, from whom the known individuals proceed, centuries are points, and all history is but the epoch of one degradation.

"We distrust and deny inwardly our sympathy with nature. We own and disown our relation to it, by turns. We are like Nebuchadnezzar, dethroned, bereft of reason, and eating grass like an ox. But who can set limits to the remedial force of spirit?

"A man is a god in ruins. When men are innocent, life shall be longer, and shall pass into the immortal as gently as we awake from dreams. Now, the world would be insane and rabid, if these disorganizations should last for hundreds of years. It is kept in check by death and infancy. Infancy is the perpetual Messiah, which comes into the arms of fallen men, and pleads with them to return to paradise.

"Man is the dwarf of himself. Once he was permeated and dissolved by spirit. He filled nature with his overflowing currents. Out from him sprang the sun and moon; from man the sun, from woman the moon. The laws of his mind, the periods of his actions externized themselves into day and night, into the year and the seasons. But, having made for himself this huge shell, his waters retired; he no longer fills the veins and veinlets; he is shrunk to a drop. He sees that the structure still fits him, but fits him colossally. Say, rather, once it fitted him, now it corresponds to him from far and on high. He adores timidly his own work. Now is man the follower of the sun, and woman the follower of the moon. Yet sometimes he starts in his slumber, and wonders at himself and his house, and muses strangely at the resemblance betwixt him and it. He perceives that if his law is still paramount, if still he have elemental power, if his word is sterling yet in nature, it is not conscious power, it is not inferior but superior to his will. It is instinct." Thus my Orphic poet sang.

At present, man applies to nature but half his force. He works on the world with his understanding alone. He lives in it and masters it by a penny-wisdom; and he that works most in it is but a half-man, and whilst his arms are strong and his digestion good, his mind is imbruted, and he is a selfish savage. His relation to nature, his power over it, is through the understanding, as by manure; the economic use of fire, wind, water, and the mariner's needle; steam, coal, chemical agriculture; the repairs of the human body by the dentist and the surgeon. This is such a resumption of power as if a banished king should buy his territories inch by inch, instead of vaulting at once into his throne. Meantime, in the thick darkness, there are not wanting gleams of a better light, — occasional examples of the action of man upon nature with his entire force, — with reason as well as understanding. Such examples are: the traditions of miracles in the earliest antiquity of all nations; the history of Jesus Christ; the achievements of a principle, as in religious and political revolutions, and in the abolition of the slave-trade; the miracles of enthusiasm, as those reported of Swedenborg, Hohenlohe, and the Shakers; many obscure and yet contested facts, now arranged under the name of Animal Magnetism; prayer; eloquence; self healing; and the wisdom of children. These are examples of Reason's momentary grasp of the sceptre; the exertions of a power which exists not in time or space, but an instantaneous instreaming causing power. The difference between the actual and the ideal force of man is happily figured by the schoolmen, in saying that the knowledge of man is an evening knowledge, *vespertina cognitio*, but that of God is a morning knowledge, *matutina cognitio*.

The problem of restoring to the world original and eternal beauty is solved by the redemption of the soul. The ruin or the blank that we see when we look at nature, is in our own eye. The axis of vision is not coincident with the axis of things, and so they appear not transparent but opaque. The reason why the world lacks unity, and lies broken and in heaps, is because man is disunited with himself. He cannot be a naturalist until he satisfies all the demands of the spirit. Love is as much its demand as perception. Indeed, neither can be perfect without the other. In the uttermost meaning of the words, thought is devout, and devotion is thought. Deep calls unto deep. But in actual life, the marriage is not celebrated. There are innocent men who worship God after the tradition of their fathers, but their sense of duty has not yet extended to the use of all their faculties. And there are patient naturalists, but they freeze their subject under the wintry light of the understanding. Is not prayer also a study of truth, — a sally of the soul into the unfound infinite? No man ever prayed heartily without learning something. But when a faithful thinker, resolute to detach every object from personal relations and see it in the light of thought, shall, at the same time, kindle science with the fire of the holiest affections, then will God go forth anew into the creation.

It will not need, when the mind is prepared for study, to search for objects. The invariable mark of wisdom is to see the miraculous in the common. What is a day? What is a year? What is summer? What is woman? What is a child? What is sleep? To our blindness, these things seem unaffecting. We make fables to hide the baldness of the fact and conform it, as we say, to the higher law of the mind. But when the fact is seen under the light of an idea, the gaudy fable fades and shrivels. We behold the real higher law. To the wise, therefore, a fact is true poetry, and the most beautiful of fables. These wonders are brought to our own door. You also are a man. Man and woman and their social life, poverty, labor, sleep, fear, fortune, are known to you. Learn that none of these things is superficial, but that each phenomenon has its roots in the faculties and affections of the mind. Whilst the abstract question occupies your intellect, nature brings it in the concrete to be solved by your hands. It were a wise inquiry for the closet, to compare, point by point, especially at remarkable crises in life, our daily history with the rise and progress of ideas in the mind.

So shall we come to look at the world with new eyes. It shall answer the endless inquiry of the intellect, — What is truth? and of the affections, — What is good? by yielding itself passive to the educated Will. Then shall come to pass what my poet said: "Nature is not fixed but fluid. Spirit alters, moulds, makes it. The immobility or bruteness of nature is the absence of spirit; to pure spirit it is fluid, it is volatile, it is obedient. Every spirit builds itself a house and beyond its house a world and beyond its world a heaven. Know then that the world exists for you. For you is the phenomenon perfect. What we are, that only can we see. All that Adam had, all that Cæsar could, you have and can do. Adam called his house, heaven and earth; Cæsar called his house, Rome; you perhaps call yours, a cobbler's trade; a hundred acres of ploughed land; or a scholar's garret. Yet line for line and point for point your dominion is as great as theirs, though without fine names. Build therefore your own world. As fast as you conform your life to the pure idea in your mind, that will unfold its great proportions. A correspondent revolution in things will attend the influx of the spirit. So fast will disagreeable appearances, swine, spiders, snakes, pests, mad-houses, prisons, enemies, vanish; they are temporary and shall be no more seen. The sordor and filths of nature, the sun shall dry up and the wind exhale. As when the summer comes from the south, the snow-banks melt and the face of the earth becomes green before it, so shall the advancing spirit create its ornaments along its path, and carry with it the beauty it visits and the song which enchants it; it shall draw beautiful faces, warm hearts, wise discourse, and heroic acts, around its way, until evil is no more seen. The kingdom of man over nature, which cometh not with observation, — a dominion such as now is beyond his dream of God, — he shall enter without more wonder than the blind man feels who is gradually restored to perfect sight."

The American Scholar
(1837)

An excellent opportunity to express his convictions came to Emerson in the invitation to deliver the Phi Beta Kappa oration in Cambridge on August 31, 1837, and well did he use it.

"This grand oration," wrote Oliver Wendell Holmes (*Ralph Waldo Emerson*, p. 88), "was our intellectual Declaration of Independence. Nothing like it had been heard in the halls of Harvard since Samuel Adams supported the affirmative of the question, 'Whether it be lawful to resist the chief magistrate, if the commonwealth cannot otherwise be preserved.' It was easy to find fault with an expression here and there. The dignity, not to say the formality, of an Academic assembly was startled by the realism that looked for the infinite in 'the meal in the firkin, the milk in the pan.' They could understand the deep thoughts suggested by 'the meanest flower that blows,' but these domestic illustrations had a kind of nursery homeliness about them which the grave professors and sedate clergymen were unused to expect on so stately an occasion. But the young men went out from it as if a prophet had been proclaiming to them 'Thus saith the Lord.' No listener ever forgot that address, and among all the notable utterances of the speaker it may be questioned if one ever contained more truth in language more like that of immediate inspiration."

MR. PRESIDENT AND GENTLEMEN, I greet you on the recommencement of our literary year. Our anniversary is one of hope, and, perhaps, not enough of labor. We do not meet for games of strength or skill, for the recitation of histories, tragedies, and odes, like the ancient Greeks; for parliaments of love and poesy, like the Troubadours; nor for the advancement of science, like our contemporaries in the British and European capitals. Thus far, our holiday has been simply a friendly sign of the survival of the love of letters amongst a people too busy to give to letters any more. As such it is precious as the sign of an indestructible instinct. Perhaps the time is already come when it ought to be, and will be, something else; when the sluggard intellect of this continent will look from under its iron lids and fill the postponed expectation of the world with something better than the exertions of mechanical skill. Our day of dependence, our long apprenticeship to the learning of other lands, draws to a close. The millions that around us are rushing into life, cannot always be fed on the sere remains of foreign harvests. Events, actions arise, that must be sung, that will sing themselves. Who can doubt that poetry will revive and lead in a new age, as the star in the constellation Harp, which now flames in our zenith, astronomers announce, shall one day be the pole-star for a thousand years?

In this hope I accept the topic which not only usage but the nature of our association seem to prescribe to this day, — the AMERICAN SCHOLAR. Year by year we come up hither to read one more chapter of his biography. Let us inquire what light new days and events have thrown on his character and his hopes.

It is one of those fables which out of an unknown antiquity convey an unlooked-for wisdom, that the gods, in the beginning, divided Man into men, that he might be more helpful to himself; just as the hand was divided into fingers, the better to answer its end.

The old fable covers a doctrine ever new and sublime; that there is One Man, — present to all particular men only partially, or through one faculty; and that you must take the whole society to find the whole man. Man is not a farmer, or a professor, or an engineer, but he is all. Man is priest, and scholar, and statesman, and producer, and soldier. In the *divided* or social state these functions are parcelled out to individuals, each of whom aims to do his stint of the joint work, whilst each other performs his. The fable implies that the individual, to possess himself, must sometimes return from his own labor to embrace all the other laborers. But, unfortunately, this original unit, this fountain of power, has been so distributed to multitudes, has been so minutely subdivided and peddled out, that it is spilled into drops, and cannot be gathered. The state of society is one in which the members have suffered amputation from the trunk, and strut about so many walking monsters, — a good finger, a neck, a stomach, an elbow, but never a man.

Man is thus metamorphosed into a thing, into many things. The planter, who is Man sent out into the field to gather food, is seldom cheered by any idea of the true dignity of his ministry. He sees his bushel and his cart, and nothing beyond, and sinks into the farmer, instead of Man on the farm. The tradesman scarcely ever gives an ideal worth to his work, but is ridden by the routine of his craft, and the soul is subject to dollars. The priest becomes a form; the attorney a statute-book; the mechanic a machine; the sailor a rope of the ship.

In this distribution of functions the scholar is the delegated intellect. In the right state he is *Man Thinking*. In the degenerate state, when the victim of society, he tends to become a mere thinker, or still worse, the parrot of other men's thinking.

In this view of him, as Man Thinking, the theory of his office is contained. Him Nature solicits with all her placid, all her monitory pictures; him the past instructs; him the future invites. Is not indeed every man a student, and do not all things exist for the student's behoof? And, finally, is not the true scholar the only true master? But the old oracle said, "All things have two handles: beware of the wrong one." In life, too often, the scholar errs with mankind and forfeits his privilege. Let us see him in his school, and consider him in reference to the main influences he receives.

I. The first in time and the first in importance of the influences upon the mind is that of nature. Every day, the sun; and, after the sunset, Night and her stars. Ever the winds blow; ever the grass grows. Every day, men and women, conversing, beholding and beholden. The scholar is he of all men whom this spectacle most engages. He must settle its value in his mind. What is nature to him? There is never a beginning, there is never an end, to the inexplicable continuity of this web of God, but always circular power returning into itself. Therein it resembles his own spirit, whose beginning, whose ending, he never can find, — so entire, so boundless. Far too as her splendors shine, system on system shooting like rays, upward, downward, without centre, without circumference, — in the mass and in the particle. Nature hastens to render account of herself to the mind. Classification begins. To the young mind every thing is individual, stands by itself. By and by, it finds how to join two things and see in them one nature; then three, then three thousand; and so, tyrannized over by its own unifying instinct, it goes on tying things together, diminishing

anomalies, discovering roots running under ground whereby contrary and remote things cohere and flower out from one stem. It presently learns that since the dawn of history there has been a constant accumulation and classifying of facts. But what is classification but the perceiving that these objects are not chaotic, and are not foreign, but have a law which is also a law of the human mind? The astronomer discovers that geometry, a pure abstraction of the human mind, is the measure of planetary motion. The chemist finds proportions and intelligible method throughout matter; and science is nothing but the finding of analogy, identity, in the most remote parts. The ambitious soul sits down before each refractory fact; one after another reduces all strange constitutions, all new powers, to their class and their law, and goes on forever to animate the last fibre of organization, the outskirts of nature, by insight.

Thus to him, to this school-boy under the bending dome of day, is suggested that he and it proceed from one root; one is leaf and one is flower; relation, sympathy, stirring in every vein. And what is that root? Is not that the soul of his soul? A thought too bold; a dream too wild. Yet when this spiritual light shall have revealed the law of more earthly natures, — when he has learned to worship the soul, and to see that the natural philosophy that now is, is only the first gropings of its gigantic hand, he shall look forward to an ever expanding knowledge as to a becoming creator. He shall see that nature is the opposite of the soul, answering to it part for part. One is seal and one is print. Its beauty is the beauty of his own mind. Its laws are the laws of his own mind. Nature then becomes to him the measure of his attainments. So much of nature as he is ignorant of, so much of his own mind does he not yet possess. And, in fine, the ancient precept, "Know thyself," and the modern precept, "Study nature," become at last one maxim.

II. The next great influence into the spirit of the scholar is the mind of the Past, — in whatever form, whether of literature, of art, of institutions, that mind is inscribed.

Books are the best type of the influence of the past, and perhaps we shall get at the truth, — learn the amount of this influence more conveniently, — by considering their value alone.

The theory of books is noble. The scholar of the first age received into him the world around; brooded thereon; gave it the new arrangement of his own mind, and uttered it again. It came into him life; it went out from him truth. It came to him short-lived actions; it went out from him immortal thoughts. It came to him business; it went from him poetry. It was dead fact; now, it is quick thought. It can stand, and it can go. It now endures, it now flies, it now inspires. Precisely in proportion to the depth of mind from which it issued, so high does it soar, so long does it sing.

Or, I might say, it depends on how far the process had gone, of transmuting life into truth. In proportion to the completeness of the distillation, so will the purity and imperishableness of the product be. But none is quite perfect. As no air-pump can by any means make a perfect vacuum, so neither can any artist entirely exclude the conventional, the local, the perishable from his book, or write a book of pure thought, that shall be as efficient, in all respects, to a remote posterity, as to contemporaries, or rather to the second age. Each age, it is found, must write its own books; or rather, each generation for the next succeeding. The books of an older period will not fit this.

Yet hence arises a grave mischief. The sacredness which attaches to the act of creation, the act of thought, is transferred to the record. The poet chanting was felt to be a divine man: henceforth the chant is divine also. The writer was a just and wise spirit: henceforward it is settled the book is perfect; as love of the hero corrupts into worship of his statue. Instantly the book becomes noxious: the guide is a tyrant. The sluggish and perverted mind of the multitude, slow to open to the incursions of Reason, having once so opened, having once received this book, stands upon it, and makes an outcry if it is disparaged. Colleges are built on it. Books are written on it by thinkers, not by Man Thinking; by men of talent, that is, who start wrong, who set out from accepted dogmas, not from their own sight of principles. Meek young men grow up in libraries, believing it their duty to accept the views which Cicero, which Locke, which Bacon, have given; forgetful that Cicero, Locke, and Bacon were only young men in libraries when they wrote these books.

Hence, instead of Man Thinking, we have the bookworm. Hence the book-learned class, who value books, as such; not as related to nature and the human constitution, but as making a sort of Third Estate with the world and the soul. Hence the restorers of readings, the emendators, the bibliomaniacs of all degrees.

Books are the best of things, well used; abused, among the worst. What is the right use? What is the one end which all means go to effect? They are for nothing but to inspire. I had better never see a book than to be warped by its attraction clean out of my own orbit, and made a satellite instead of a system. The one thing in the world, of value, is the active soul. This every man is entitled to; this every man contains within him, although in almost all men obstructed, and as yet unborn. The soul active sees absolute truth and utters truth, or creates. In this action it is genius; not the privilege of here and there a favorite, but the sound estate of every man. In its essence it is progressive. The book, the college, the school of art, the institution of any kind, stop with some past utterance of genius. This is good, say they, — let us hold by this. They pin me down. They look backward and not forward. But genius looks forward: the eyes of man are set in his forehead, not in his hindhead: man hopes: genius creates. Whatever talents may be, if the man create not, the pure efflux of the Deity is not his; — cinders and smoke there may be, but not yet flame. There are creative manners, there are creative actions, and creative words; manners, actions, words, that is, indicative of no custom or authority, but springing spontaneous from the mind's own sense of good and fair.

On the other part, instead of being its own seer, let it receive from another mind its truth, though it were in torrents of light, without periods of solitude, inquest, and self-recovery, and a fatal disservice is done. Genius is always sufficiently the enemy of genius by over-influence. The literature of every nation bears me witness. The English dramatic poets have Shakspearized now for two hundred years.

Undoubtedly there is a right way of reading, so it be sternly subordinated. Man Thinking must not be subdued by his instruments. Books are for the scholar's idle times. When he can read God directly, the hour is too precious to be wasted in other men's transcripts of their readings. But when the intervals of darkness come, as come they must, — when the sun is hid and the stars withdraw their shining, — we repair to the lamps which were kindled by their ray, to guide our steps to the East again, where the dawn is. We hear, that we may speak. The Arabian proverb says, "A fig tree, looking on a fig tree, becometh fruitful."

It is remarkable, the character of the pleasure we derive from the best books. They impress us with the conviction that one nature wrote and the same reads. We read the verses of one of the great English poets, of Chaucer, of Marvell, of Dryden, with the most modern joy, — with a pleasure, I mean, which is in great part caused by the abstraction of all *time* from their verses. There is some awe mixed with the joy of our surprise, when this poet, who lived in some past world, two or three hundred years ago, says that which lies close to my own soul, that which I also had well-nigh thought and said. But for the evidence thence afforded to the philosophical doctrine of the identity of all minds, we should suppose some preëstablished harmony, some foresight of souls that were to be, and some preparation of stores for their future wants, like the fact observed in insects, who lay up food before death for the young grub they shall never see.

I would not be hurried by any love of system, by any exaggeration of instincts, to underrate the Book. We all know, that as the human body can be nourished on any food, though it were boiled grass and the broth of shoes, so the human mind can be fed by any knowledge. And great and heroic men have existed who had almost no other

information than by the printed page. I only would say that it needs a strong head to bear that diet. One must be an inventor to read well. As the proverb says, "He that would bring home the wealth of the Indies, must carry out the wealth of the Indies." There is then creative reading as well as creative writing. When the mind is braced by labor and invention, the page of whatever book we read becomes luminous with manifold allusion. Every sentence is doubly significant, and the sense of our author is as broad as the world. We then see, what is always true, that as the seer's hour of vision is short and rare among heavy days and months, so is its record, perchance the least part of his volume. The discerning will read, in his Plato or Shakspeare, only that least part, — only the authentic utterances of the oracle; — all the rest he rejects, were it never so many times Plato's and Shakspeare's.

Of course there is a portion of reading quite indispensable to a wise man. History and exact science he must learn by laborious reading. Colleges, in like manner, have their indispensable office, — to teach elements. But they can only highly serve us when they aim not to drill, but to create; when they gather from far every ray of various genius to their hospitable halls, and by the concentrated fires, set the hearts of their youth on flame. Thought and knowledge are natures in which apparatus and pretension avail nothing. Gowns and pecuniary foundations, though of towns of gold, can never countervail the least sentence or syllable of wit. Forget this, and our American colleges will recede in their public importance, whilst they grow richer every year.

III. There goes in the world a notion that the scholar should be a recluse, a valetudinarian, — as unfit for any handiwork or public labor as a pen-knife for an axe. The so-called "practical men" sneer at speculative men, as if, because they speculate or *see*, they could do nothing. I have heard it said that the clergy, — who are always, more universally than any other class, the scholars of their day, — are addressed as women; that the rough, spontaneous conversation of men they do not hear, but only a mincing and diluted speech. They are often virtually disfranchised; and indeed there are advocates for their celibacy. As far as this is true of the studious classes, it is not just and wise. Action is with the scholar subordinate, but it is essential. Without it he is not yet man. Without it thought can never ripen into truth. Whilst the world hangs before the eye as a cloud of beauty, we cannot even see its beauty. Inaction is cowardice, but there can be no scholar without the heroic mind. The preamble of thought, the transition through which it passes from the unconscious to the conscious, is action. Only so much do I know, as I have lived. Instantly we know whose words are loaded with life, and whose not.

The world, — this shadow of the soul, or *other me*, — lies wide around. Its attractions are the keys which unlock my thoughts and make me acquainted with myself. I run eagerly into this resounding tumult. I grasp the hands of those next me, and take my place in the ring to suffer and to work, taught by an instinct that so shall the dumb abyss be vocal with speech. I pierce its order; I dissipate its fear; I dispose of it within the circuit of my expanding life. So much only of life as I know by experience, so much of the wilderness have I vanquished and planted, or so far have I extended my being, my dominion. I do not see how any man can afford, for the sake of his nerves and his nap, to spare any action in which he can partake. It is pearls and rubies to his discourse. Drudgery, calamity, exasperation, want, are instructors in eloquence and wisdom. The true scholar grudges every opportunity of action past by, as a loss of power. It is the raw material out of which the intellect moulds her splendid products. A strange process too, this by which experience is converted into thought, as a mulberry leaf is converted into satin. The manufacture goes forward at all hours.

The actions and events of our childhood and youth are now matters of calmest observation. They lie like fair pictures in the air. Not so with our recent actions, — with the business which we now have in hand. On this we are quite unable to speculate.

Our affections as yet circulate through it. We no more feel or know it than we feel the feet, or the hand, or the brain of our body. The new deed is yet a part of life, — remains for a time immersed in our unconscious life. In some contemplative hour it detaches itself from the life like a ripe fruit, to become a thought of the mind. Instantly it is raised, transfigured; the corruptible has put on incorruption. Henceforth it is an object of beauty, however base its origin and neighborhood. Observe too the impossibility of antedating this act. In its grub state, it cannot fly, it cannot shine, it is a dull grub. But suddenly, without observation, the selfsame thing unfurls beautiful wings, and is an angel of wisdom. So is there no fact, no event, in our private history, which shall not, sooner or later, lose its adhesive, inert form, and astonish us by soaring from our body into the empyrean. Cradle and infancy, school and playground, the fear of boys, and dogs, and ferules, the love of little maids and berries, and many another fact that once filled the whole sky, are gone already; friend and relative, profession and party, town and country, nation and world, must also soar and sing.

Of course, he who has put forth his total strength in fit actions has the richest return of wisdom. I will not shut myself out of this globe of action, and transplant an oak into a flower-pot, there to hunger and pine; nor trust the revenue of some single faculty, and exhaust one vein of thought, much like those Savoyards, who, getting their livelihood by carving shepherds, shepherdesses, and smoking Dutchmen, for all Europe, went out one day to the mountain to find stock, and discovered that they had whittled up the last of their pine-trees. Authors we have, in numbers, who have written out their vein, and who, moved by a commendable prudence, sail for Greece or Palestine, follow the trapper into the prairie, or ramble round Algiers, to replenish their merchantable stock.

If it were only for a vocabulary, the scholar would be covetous of action. Life is our dictionary. Years are well spent in country labors; in town; in the insight into trades and manufactures; in frank intercourse with many men and women; in science; in art;

to the one end of mastering in all their facts a language by which to illustrate and embody our perceptions. I learn immediately from any speaker how much he has already lived, through the poverty or the splendor of his speech. Life lies behind us as the quarry from whence we get tiles and copestones for the masonry of to-day. This is the way to learn grammar. Colleges and books only copy the language which the field and the work-yard made.

But the final value of action, like that of books, and better than books, is that it is a resource. That great principle of Undulation in nature, that shows itself in the inspiring and expiring of the breath; in desire and satiety; in the ebb and flow of the sea; in day and night; in heat and cold; and, as yet more deeply ingrained in every atom and every fluid, is known to us under the name of Polarity, — these "fits of easy transmission and reflection," as Newton called them, are the law of nature because they are the law of spirit.

The mind now thinks, now acts, and each fit reproduces the other. When the artist has exhausted his materials, when the fancy no longer paints, when thoughts are no longer apprehended and books are a weariness, — he has always the resource *to live*. Character is higher than intellect. Thinking is the function. Living is the functionary. The stream retreats to its source. A great soul will be strong to live, as well as strong to think. Does he lack organ or medium to impart his truth? He can still fall back on this elemental force of living them. This is a total act. Thinking is a partial act. Let the grandeur of justice shine in his affairs. Let the beauty of affection cheer his lowly roof. Those "far from fame," who dwell and act with him, will feel the force of his constitution in the doings and passages of the day better than it can be measured by any public and designed display. Time shall teach him that the scholar loses no hour which the man lives. Herein he unfolds the sacred germ of his instinct, screened from influence. What is lost in seemliness is gained in strength. Not out of those on whom systems of education have exhausted their culture, comes the helpful giant to destroy the old or to build

the new, but out of unhandselled savage nature; out of terrible Druids and Berserkers come at last Alfred and Shakspeare.

I hear therefore with joy whatever is beginning to be said of the dignity and necessity of labor to every citizen. There is virtue yet in the hoe and the spade, for learned as well as for unlearned hands. And labor is everywhere welcome; always we are invited to work; only be this limitation observed, that a man shall not for the sake of wider activity sacrifice any opinion to the popular judgments and modes of action.

I have now spoken of the education of the scholar by nature, by books, and by action. It remains to say somewhat of his duties.

They are such as become Man Thinking. They may all be comprised in self-trust. The office of the scholar is to cheer, to raise, and to guide men by showing them facts amidst appearances. He plies the slow, unhonored, and unpaid task of observation. Flamsteed and Herschel, in their glazed observatories, may catalogue the stars with the praise of all men, and the results being splendid and useful, honor is sure. But he, in his private observatory, cataloguing obscure and nebulous stars of the human mind, which as yet no man has thought of as such, — watching days and months sometimes for a few facts; correcting still his old records; — must relinquish display and immediate fame. In the long period of his preparation he must betray often an ignorance and shiftlessness in popular arts, incurring the disdain of the able who shoulder him aside. Long he must stammer in his speech; often forego the living for the dead. Worse yet, he must accept — how often! — poverty and solitude. For the ease and pleasure of treading the old road, accepting the fashions, the education, the religion of society, he takes the cross of making his own, and, of course, the self-accusation, the faint heart, the frequent uncertainty and loss of time, which are the nettles and tangling vines in the way of the self-relying and self-directed; and the state of virtual hostility in which he seems to stand to society, and especially to educated society. For all this loss and scorn, what offset? He is to find consolation in exercising the highest functions of human nature. He is one who raises himself from private considerations and breathes and lives on public and illustrious thoughts. He is the world's eye. He is the world's heart. He is to resist the vulgar prosperity that retrogrades ever to barbarism, by preserving and communicating heroic sentiments, noble biographies, melodious verse, and the conclusions of history. Whatsoever oracles the human heart, in all emergencies, in all solemn hours, has uttered as its commentary on the world of actions, — these he shall receive and impart. And whatsoever new verdict Reason from her inviolable seat pronounces on the passing men and events of today, — this he shall hear and promulgate.

These being his functions, it becomes him to feel all confidence in himself, and to defer never to the popular cry. He and he only knows the world. The world of any moment is the merest appearance. Some great decorum, some fetish of a government, some ephemeral trade, or war, or man, is cried up by half mankind and cried down by the other half, as if all depended on this particular up or down. The odds are that the whole question is not worth the poorest thought which the scholar has lost in listening to the controversy. Let him not quit his belief that a popgun is a popgun, though the ancient and honorable of the earth affirm it to be the crack of doom. In silence, in steadiness, in severe abstraction, let him hold by himself; add observation to observation, patient of neglect, patient of reproach, and bide his own time, — happy enough if he can satisfy himself alone that this day he has seen something truly. Success treads on every right step. For the instinct is sure, that prompts him to tell his brother what he thinks. He then learns that in going down into the secrets of his own mind he has descended into the secrets of all minds. He learns that he who has mastered any law in his private thoughts, is master to that extent of all men whose language he speaks, and of all into whose language his own can be translated. The poet, in utter solitude remembering his spontaneous thoughts and recording them, is found to have recorded that which men in crowded cities find true for them also. The

orator distrusts at first the fitness of his frank confessions, his want of knowledge of the persons he addresses, until he finds that he is the complement of his hearers; — that they drink his words because he fulfils for them their own nature; the deeper he dives into his privatest, secretest presentiment, to his wonder he finds this is the most acceptable, most public, and universally true. The people delight in it; the better part of every man feels, This is my music; this myself.

In self-trust all the virtues are comprehended. Free should the scholar be, — free and brave. Free even to the definition of freedom, "without any hindrance that does not arise out of his own constitution." Brave; for fear is a thing which a scholar by his very function puts behind him. Fear always springs from ignorance. It is a shame to him if his tranquillity, amid dangerous times, arise from the presumption that like children and women his is a protected class; or if he seek a temporary peace by the diversion of his thoughts from politics or vexed questions, hiding his head like an ostrich in the flowering bushes, peeping into microscopes, and turning rhymes, as a boy whistles to keep his courage up. So is the danger a danger still; so is the fear worse. Manlike let him turn and face it. Let him look into its eye and search its nature, inspect its origin, — see the whelping of this lion, — which lies no great way back; he will then find in himself a perfect comprehension of its nature and extent; he will have made his hands meet on the other side, and can henceforth defy it and pass on superior. The world is his who can see through its pretension. What deafness, what stone-blind custom, what overgrown error you behold is there only by sufferance, — by your sufferance. See it to be a lie, and you have already dealt it its mortal blow.

Yes, we are the cowed, — we the trustless. It is a mischievous notion that we are come late into nature; that the world was finished a long time ago. As the world was plastic and fluid in the hands of God, so it is ever to so much of his attributes as we bring to it. To ignorance and sin, it is flint. They adapt themselves to it as they may; but in proportion as a man has any thing in him divine, the firmament flows before him and takes his signet and form. Not he is great who can alter matter, but he who can alter my state of mind. They are the kings of the world who give the color of their present thought to all nature and all art, and persuade men by the cheerful serenity of their carrying the matter, that this thing which they do is the apple which the ages have desired to pluck, now at last ripe, and inviting nations to the harvest. The great man makes the great thing. Wherever Macdonald sits, there is the head of the table. Linnæus makes botany the most alluring of studies, and wins it from the farmer and the herb-woman; Davy, chemistry; and Cuvier, fossils. The day is always his who works in it with serenity and great aims. The unstable estimates of men crowd to him whose mind is filled with a truth, as the heaped waves of the Atlantic follow the moon.

For this self-trust, the reason is deeper than can be fathomed, — darker than can be enlightened. I might not carry with me the feeling of my audience in stating my own belief. But I have already shown the ground of my hope, in adverting to the doctrine that man is one. I believe man has been wronged; he has wronged himself. He has almost lost the light that can lead him back to his prerogatives. Men are become of no account. Men in history, men in the world of to-day, are bugs, are spawn, and are called "the mass" and "the herd." In a century, in a millennium, one or two men; that is to say, one or two approximations to the right state of every man. All the rest behold in the hero or the poet their own green and crude being, — ripened; yes, and are content to be less, so *that* may attain to its full stature. What a testimony, full of grandeur, full of pity, is borne to the demands of his own nature, by the poor clansman, the poor partisan, who rejoices in the glory of his chief. The poor and the low find some amends to their immense moral capacity, for their acquiescence in a political and social inferiority. They are content to be brushed like flies from the path of a great person, so that justice shall be done by him to that common nature which it is the dearest desire of all to see enlarged and glorified. They sun themselves in the great man's light, and feel it to be their own element. They cast the dignity of man from their downtrod selves upon the shoulders of a hero, and will perish to add one drop of blood to make that great heart beat, those giant sinews combat and conquer. He lives for us, and we live in him.

Men such as they are, very naturally seek money or power; and power because it is as good as money, — the "spoils," so called, "of office." And why not? for they aspire to the highest, and this, in their sleep-walking, they dream is highest. Wake them and they shall quit the false good and leap to the true, and leave governments to clerks and desks. This revolution is to be wrought by the gradual domestication of the idea of Culture. The main enterprise of the world for splendor, for extent, is the upbuilding of a man. Here are the materials strewn along the ground. The private life of one man shall be a more illustrious monarchy, more formidable to its enemy, more sweet and serene in its influence to its friend, than any kingdom in history. For a man, rightly viewed, comprehendeth the particular natures of all men. Each philosopher, each bard, each actor has only done for me, as by a delegate, what one day I can do for myself. The books which once we valued more than the apple of the eye, we have quite exhausted. What is that but saying that we have come up with the point of view which the universal mind took through the eyes of one scribe; we have been that man, and have passed on. First, one, then another, we drain all cisterns, and waxing greater by all these supplies, we crave a better and more abundant food. The man has never lived that can feed us ever. The human mind cannot be enshrined in a person who shall set a barrier on any one side to this unbounded, unboundable empire. It is one central fire, which, flaming now out of the lips of Etna, lightens the capes of Sicily, and now out of the throat of Vesuvius, illuminates the towers and vineyards of Naples. It is one light which beams out of a thousand stars. It is one soul which animates all men.

But I have dwelt perhaps tediously upon this abstraction of the Scholar. I ought not to delay longer to add what I have to say of nearer reference to the time and to this country.

Historically, there is thought to be a difference in the ideas which predominate over successive epochs, and there are data for marking the genius of the Classic, of the Romantic, and now of the Reflective or Philosophical age. With the views I have intimated of the oneness or the identity of the mind through all individuals, I do not much dwell on these differences. In fact, I believe each individual passes through all three. The boy is a Greek; the youth, romantic; the adult, reflective. I deny not, however, that a revolution in the leading idea may be distinctly enough traced.

Our age is bewailed as the age of Introversion. Must that needs be evil? We, it seems, are critical; we are embarrassed with second thoughts; we cannot enjoy any thing for hankering to know whereof the pleasure consists; we are lined with eyes; we see with our feet; the time is infected with Hamlet's unhappiness,

"Sicklied o'er with the pale cast of thought."

It is so bad then? Sight is the last thing to be pitied. Would we be blind? Do we fear lest we should outsee nature and God, and drink truth dry? I look upon the discontent of the literary class as a mere announcement of the fact that they find themselves not in the state of mind of their fathers, and regret the coming state as untried; as a boy dreads the water before he has learned that he can swim. If there is any period one would desire to be born in, is it not the age of Revolution; when the old and the new stand side by side and admit of being compared; when the energies of all men are searched by fear and by hope; when the historic glories of the old can be compensated by the rich possibilities of the new era? This time, like all times, is a very good one, if we but know what to do with it.

I read with some joy of the auspicious signs of the coming days, as they glimmer already through poetry and art, through philosophy and science, through church and state.

One of these signs is the fact that the same movement which effected the elevation of what was called the lowest class in the state, assumed in literature a very marked and as benign an aspect. Instead of the sublime and beautiful, the near, the low, the common, was explored and poetized. That which had been negligently trodden under foot by those who were harnessing and provisioning themselves for long journeys into far countries, is suddenly found to be richer than all foreign parts. The literature of the poor, the feelings of the child, the philosophy of the street, the meaning of household life, are the topics of the time. It is a great stride. It is a sign — is it not? — of new vigor when the extremities are made active, when currents of warm life run into the hands and the feet. I ask not for the great, the remote, the romantic; what is doing in Italy or Arabia; what is Greek art, or Provençal minstrelsy; I embrace the common, I explore and sit at the feet of the familiar, the low. Give me insight into to-day, and you may have the antique and future worlds. What would we really know the meaning of? The meal in the firkin; the milk in the pan; the ballad in the street; the news of the boat; the glance of the eye; the form and the gait of the body; — show me the ultimate reason of these matters; show me the sublime presence of the highest spiritual cause lurking, as always it does lurk, in these suburbs and extremities of nature; let me see every trifle bristling with the polarity that ranges it instantly on an eternal law; and the shop, the plough, and the ledger referred to the like cause by which light undulates and poets sing; — and the world lies no longer a dull miscellany and lumber-room, but has form and order; there is no trifle, there is no puzzle, but one design unites and animates the farthest pinnacle and the lowest trench.

This idea has inspired the genius of Goldsmith, Burns, Cowper, and, in a newer time, of Goethe, Wordsworth, and Carlyle. This idea they have differently followed and with various success. In contrast with their writing, the style of Pope, of Johnson, of Gibbon, looks cold and pedantic. This writing is blood-warm. Man is surprised to find that things near are not less beautiful and wondrous than things remote. The near explains the far. The drop is a small ocean. A man is related to all nature. This perception of the worth of the vulgar is fruitful in discoveries. Goethe, in this very thing the most modern of the moderns, has shown us as none ever did, the genius of the ancients.

There is one man of genius who has done much for this philosophy of life, whose literary value has never yet been rightly estimated; — I mean Emanuel Swedenborg. The most imaginative of men, yet writing with the precision of a mathematician, he endeavored to engraft a purely philosophical Ethics on the popular Christianity of his time. Such an attempt of course must have difficulty which no genius could surmount. But he saw and showed the connection between nature and the affections of the soul. He pierced the emblematic or spiritual character of the visible, audible, tangible world. Especially did his shade-loving muse hover over and interpret the lower parts of nature; he showed the mysterious bond that allies moral evil to the foul material forms, and has given in epical parables a theory of insanity, of beasts, of unclean and fearful things.

Another sign of our times, also marked by an analogous political movement, is the new importance given to the single person. Everything that tends to insulate the individual, — to surround him with barriers of natural respect, so that each man shall feel the world is his, and man shall treat with man as a sovereign state with a sovereign state, — tends to true union as well as greatness. "I learned," said the melancholy Pestalozzi, "that no man in God's wide earth is either willing or able to help any other man." Help must come from the bosom alone. The scholar is that man who must take up into himself all the ability of the time, all the contributions of the past, all the hopes of the future. He must be an university of knowledges. If there be one lesson more than another which should pierce his ear, it is, The world is nothing, the man is all; in yourself is the law of all nature, and you know not yet how a globule of sap ascends; in yourself slumbers the whole of Reason; it is for you to know all; it is for you to dare all. Mr. President and Gentlemen, this confidence in the unsearched might of man

belongs, by all motives, by all prophecy, by all preparation, to the American Scholar. We have listened too long to the courtly muses of Europe. The spirit of the American freeman is already suspected to be timid, imitative, tame. Public and private avarice make the air we breathe thick and fat. The scholar is decent, indolent, complaisant. See already the tragic consequence. The mind of this country, taught to aim at low objects, eats upon itself. There is no work for any but the decorous and the complaisant. Young men of the fairest promise, who begin life upon our shores, inflated by the mountain winds, shined upon by all the stars of God, find the earth below not in unison with these, but are hindered from action by the disgust which the principles on which business is managed inspire, and turn drudges, or die of disgust, some of them suicides. What is the remedy? They did not yet see, and thousands of young men as hopeful now crowding to the barriers for the career do not yet see, that if the single man plant himself indomitably on his instincts, and there abide, the huge world will come round to him. Patience, — patience; with the shades of all the good and great for company; and for solace the perspective of your own infinite life; and for work the study and the communication of principles, the making those instincts prevalent, the conversion of the world. Is it not the chief disgrace in the world, not to be an unit; — not to be reckoned one character; — not to yield that peculiar fruit which each man was created to bear, but to be reckoned in the gross, in the hundred, or the thousand, of the party, the section, to which we belong; and our opinion predicted geographically, as the north, or the south? Not so, brothers and friends, — please God, ours shall not be so. We will walk on our own feet; we will work with our own hands; we will speak our own minds. The study of letters shall be no longer a name for pity, for doubt, and for sensual indulgence. The dread of man and the love of man shall be a wall of defence and a wreath of joy around all. A nation of men will for the first time exist, because each believes himself inspired by the Divine Soul which also inspires all men.

Divinity School Address

(1838)

An address delivered before the Senior Class in Divinity College, Cambridge, Sunday evening, July 15, 1838. In his *Journal* Emerson had written on March 14: "I ought to sit and think, and then write a discourse to the American clergy, showing them the ugliness and unprofitableness of theology and churches at this day, and the glory and sweetness of the moral nature out of whose pale they are almost wholly shut." The Seniors in the Divinity School having invited him to make the Annual Address, Emerson spoke out, happy to have an opportunity to inspire these young men with "the glory and sweetness of the moral nature," and careless of the hostile reception he might expect at the hands of the clergy. The address did, indeed, cause "a profound sensation in religious circles, and led to a controversy," as Holmes says, "in which Emerson had little more than the part of Patroclus when the Greeks and Trojans fought over his body." The address, Holmes goes on to say, "is reverential, but it is also revolutionary. The file-leaders of Unitarianism drew back in dismay, and the ill names which had often been applied to them were now heard from their own lips as befitting this new heresy; if so mild a reproach as that of heresy belonged to this alarming manifesto." (*Ralph Waldo Emerson*, pp. 89–91.)

In this refulgent summer, it has been a luxury to draw the breath of life. The grass grows, the buds burst, the meadow is spotted with fire and gold in the tint of flowers. The air is full of birds, and sweet with the breath of the pine, the balm-of-Gilead, and the new hay. Night brings no gloom to the heart with its welcome shade. Through the transparent darkness the stars pour their almost spiritual rays. Man under them seems a young child, and his huge globe a toy. The cool night bathes the world as with a river, and prepares his eyes again for the crimson dawn. The mystery of nature was never displayed more happily. The corn and the wine have been freely dealt to all creatures, and the never-broken silence with which the old bounty goes forward has not yielded yet one word of explanation. One is constrained to respect the perfection of this world in which our senses converse. How wide; how rich; what invitation from every property it gives to every faculty of man! In its fruitful soils; in its navigable sea; in its mountains of metal and stone; in its forests of all woods; in its animals; in its chemical ingredients; in the

powers and path of light, heat, attraction and life, it is well worth the pith and heart of great men to subdue and enjoy it. The planters, the mechanics, the inventors, the astronomers, the builders of cities, and the captains, history delights to honor.

But when the mind opens and reveals the laws which traverse the universe and make things what they are, then shrinks the great world at once into a mere illustration and fable of this mind. What am I? and What is? asks the human spirit with a curiosity new-kindled, but never to be quenched. Behold these outrunning laws, which our imperfect apprehension can see tend this way and that, but not come full circle. Behold these infinite relations, so like, so unlike; many, yet one. I would study, I would know, I would admire forever. These works of thought have been the entertainments of the human spirit in all ages.

A more secret, sweet, and overpowering beauty appears to man when his heart and mind open to the sentiment of virtue. Then he is instructed in what is above him. He learns that his being is without bound; that to the good, to the perfect, he is born, low as he now lies in evil and weakness. That which he venerates is still his own, though he has not realized it yet. *He ought.* He knows the sense of that grand word, though his analysis fails to render account of it. When in innocency or when by intellectual perception he attains to say, — "I love the Right; Truth is beautiful within and without for evermore. Virtue, I am thine; save me; use me; thee will I serve, day and night, in great, in small, that I may be not virtuous, but virtue"; — then is the end of the creation answered, and God is well pleased.

The sentiment of virtue is a reverence and delight in the presence of certain divine laws. It perceives that this homely game of life we play, covers, under what seem foolish details, principles that astonish. The child amidst his baubles is learning the action of light, motion, gravity, muscular force; and in the game of human life, love, fear, justice, appetite, man, and God, interact. These laws refuse to be adequately stated. They will not be written out on paper, or spoken by the tongue. They elude our persevering thought;

yet we read them hourly in each other's faces, in each other's actions, in our own remorse. The moral traits which are all globed into every virtuous act and thought, — in speech we must sever, and describe or suggest by painful enumeration of many particulars. Yet, as this sentiment is the essence of all religion, let me guide your eye to the precise objects of the sentiment, by an enumeration of some of those classes of facts in which this element is conspicuous.

The intuition of the moral sentiment is an insight of the perfection of the laws of the soul. These laws execute themselves. They are out of time, out of space, and not subject to circumstance. Thus in the soul of man there is a justice whose retributions are instant and entire. He who does a noble deed is instantly ennobled. He who does a mean deed is by the action itself contracted. He who puts off impurity, thereby puts on purity. If a man is at heart just, then in so far is he God; the safety of God, the immortality of God, the majesty of God do enter into that man with justice. If a man dissemble, deceive, he deceives himself, and goes out of acquaintance with his own being. A man in the view of absolute goodness, adores, with total humility. Every step so downward, is a step upward. The man who renounces himself, comes to himself.

See how this rapid intrinsic energy worketh everywhere, righting wrongs, correcting appearances, and bringing up facts to a harmony with thoughts. Its operation in life, though slow to the senses, is at last as sure as in the soul. By it a man is made the Providence to himself, dispensing good to his goodness, and evil to his sin. Character is always known. Thefts never enrich; alms never impoverish; murder will speak out of stone walls. The least admixture of a lie, — for example, the taint of vanity, any attempt to make a good impression, a favorable appearance, — will instantly vitiate the effect. But speak the truth, and all nature and all spirits help you with unexpected furtherance. Speak the truth, and all things alive or brute are vouchers, and the very roots of the grass underground there do seem to stir and move to bear you witness. See again the perfection of the Law as it applies itself to the affections,

and becomes the law of society. As we are, so we associate. The good, by affinity, seek the good; the vile, by affinity, the vile. Thus of their own volition, souls proceed into heaven, into hell.

These facts have always suggested to man the sublime creed that the world is not the product of manifold power, but of one will, of one mind; and that one mind is everywhere active, in each ray of the star, in each wavelet of the pool; and whatever opposes that will is everywhere balked and baffled, because things are made so, and not otherwise. Good is positive. Evil is merely privative, not absolute: it is like cold, which is the privation of heat. All evil is so much death or nonentity. Benevolence is absolute and real. So much benevolence as a man hath, so much life hath he. For all things proceed out of this same spirit, which is differently named love, justice, temperance, in its different applications, just as the ocean receives different names on the several shores which it washes. All things proceed out of the same spirit, and all things conspire with it. Whilst a man seeks good ends, he is strong by the whole strength of nature. In so far as he roves from these ends, he bereaves himself of power, or auxiliaries; his being shrinks out of all remote channels, he becomes less and less, a mote, a point, until absolute badness is absolute death.

The perception of this law of laws awakens in the mind a sentiment which we call the religious sentiment, and which makes our highest happiness. Wonderful is its power to charm and to command. It is a mountain air. It is the embalmer of the world. It is myrrh and storax, and chlorine and rosemary. It makes the sky and the hills sublime, and the silent song of the stars is it. By it is the universe made safe and habitable, not by science or power. Thought may work cold and intransitive in things, and find no end or unity; but the dawn of the sentiment of virtue on the heart, gives and is the assurance that Law is sovereign over all natures; and the worlds, time, space, eternity, do seem to break out into joy.

This sentiment is divine and deifying. It is the beatitude of man. It makes him illimitable. Through it, the soul first knows itself.

It corrects the capital mistake of the infant man, who seeks to be great by following the great, and hopes to derive advantages *from another*, — by showing the fountain of all good to be in himself, and that he, equally with every man, is an inlet into the deeps of Reason. When he says, "I ought"; when love warms him; when he chooses, warned from on high, the good and great deed; then, deep melodies wander through his soul from Supreme Wisdom. — Then he can worship, and be enlarged by his worship; for he can never go behind this sentiment. In the sublimest flights of the soul, rectitude is never surmounted, love is never outgrown.

This sentiment lies at the foundation of society, and successively creates all forms of worship. The principle of veneration never dies out. Man fallen into superstition, into sensuality, is never quite without the visions of the moral sentiment. In like manner, all the expressions of this sentiment are sacred and permanent in proportion to their purity. The expressions of this sentiment affect us more than all other compositions. The sentences of the oldest time, which ejaculate this piety, are still fresh and fragrant. This thought dwelled always deepest in the minds of men in the devout and contemplative East; not alone in Palestine, where it reached its purest expression, but in Egypt, in Persia, in India, in China. Europe has always owed to oriental genius its divine impulses. What these holy bards said, all sane men found agreeable and true. And the unique impression of Jesus upon mankind, whose name is not so much written as ploughed into the history of this world, is proof of the subtle virtue of this infusion.

Meantime, whilst the doors of the temple stand open, day and night, before every man, and the oracles of this truth cease never, it is guarded by one stern condition; this, namely: it is an intuition. It cannot be received at second hand. Truly speaking, it is not instruction, but provocation, that I can receive from another soul. What he announces, I must find true in me, or reject; and on his word, or as his second, be he who he may, I can accept nothing. On the contrary, the absence of this primary faith is the presence of degradation. As is the flood, so is the ebb.

Let this faith depart, and the very words it spake and the things it made become false and hurtful. Then falls the church, the state, art, letters, life. The doctrine of the divine nature being forgotten, a sickness infects and dwarfs the constitution. Once man was all; now he is an appendage, a nuisance. And because the indwelling Supreme Spirit cannot wholly be got rid of, the doctrine of it suffers this perversion, that the divine nature is attributed to one or two persons, and denied to all the rest, and denied with fury. The doctrine of inspiration is lost; the base doctrine of the majority of voices usurps the place of the doctrine of the soul. Miracles, prophecy, poetry, the ideal life, the holy life, exist as ancient history merely; they are not in the belief, nor in the aspiration of society; but, when suggested, seem ridiculous. Life is comic or pitiful as soon as the high ends of being fade out of sight, and man becomes near-sighted, and can only attend to what addresses the senses.

These general views, which, whilst they are general, none will contest, find abundant illustration in the history of religion, and especially in the history of the Christian church. In that, all of us have had our birth and nurture. The truth contained in that, you, my young friends, are now setting forth to teach. As the Cultus, or established worship of the civilized world, it has great historical interest for us. Of its blessed words, which have been the consolation of humanity, you need not that I should speak. I shall endeavor to discharge my duty to you on this occasion, by pointing out two errors in its administration, which daily appear more gross from the point of view we have just now taken.

Jesus Christ belonged to the true race of prophets. He saw with open eye the mystery of the soul. Drawn by its severe harmony, ravished with its beauty, he lived in it, and had his being there. Alone in all history he estimated the greatness of man. One man was true to what is in you and me. He saw that God incarnates himself in man, and evermore goes forth anew to take possession of his World. He said, in this jubilee of sublime emotion, "I am divine. Through me, God acts; through me, speaks. Would you see

God, see me; or see thee, when thou also thinkest as I now think." But what a distortion did his doctrine and memory suffer in the same, in the next, and the following ages! There is no doctrine of the Reason which will bear to be taught by the Understanding. The understanding caught this high chant from the poet's lips, and said, in the next age, "This was Jehovah come down out of heaven. I will kill you, if you say he was a man." The idioms of his language and the figures of his rhetoric have usurped the place of his truth; and churches are not built on his principles, but on his tropes. Christianity became a Mythus, as the poetic teaching of Greece and of Egypt, before. He spoke of miracles; for he felt that man's life was a miracle, and all that man doth, and he knew that this daily miracle shines as the character ascends. But the word Miracle, as pronounced by Christian churches, gives a false impression; it is Monster. It is not one with the blowing clover and the falling rain.

He felt respect for Moses and the prophets, but no unfit tenderness at postponing their initial revelations to the hour and the man that now is; to the eternal revelation in the heart. Thus was he a true man. Having seen that the law in us is commanding, he would not suffer it to be commanded. Boldly, with hand, and heart, and life, he declared it was God. Thus is he, as I think, the only soul in history who has appreciated the worth of man.

1. In this point of view we become sensible of the first defect of historical Christianity. Historical Christianity has fallen into the error that corrupts all attempts to communicate religion. As it appears to us, and as it has appeared for ages, it is not the doctrine of the soul, but an exaggeration of the personal, the positive, the ritual. It has dwelt, it dwells, with noxious exaggeration about the *person* of Jesus. The soul knows no persons. It invites every man to expand to the full circle of the universe, and will have no preferences but those of spontaneous love. But by this eastern monarchy of a Christianity, which indolence and fear have built, the friend of man is made the injurer of man. The manner in which his name is surrounded with expressions which were once sallies of admiration and love, but are now petrified into official titles, kills all generous sympathy and liking. All who hear me, feel that the language that describes Christ to Europe and America is not the style of friendship and enthusiasm to a good and noble heart, but is appropriated and formal, — paints a demigod, as the Orientals or the Greeks would describe Osiris or Apollo. Accept the injurious impositions of our early catechetical instruction, and even honesty and self-denial were but splendid sins, if they did not wear the Christian name. One would rather be

"A pagan, suckled in a creed outworn,"

than to be defrauded of his manly right in coming into nature and finding not names and places, not land and professions, but even virtue and truth foreclosed and monopolized. You shall not be a man even. You shall not own the world; you shall not dare and live after the infinite Law that is in you, and in company with the infinite Beauty which heaven and earth reflect to you in all lovely forms; but you must subordinate your nature to Christ's nature; you must accept our interpretations, and take his portrait as the vulgar draw it.

That is always best which gives me to myself. The sublime is excited in me by the great stoical doctrine, Obey thyself. That which shows God in me, fortifies me. That which shows God out of me, makes me a wart and a wen. There is no longer a necessary reason for my being. Already the long shadows of untimely oblivion creep over me, and I shall decease forever.

The divine bards are the friends of my virtue, of my intellect, of my strength. They admonish me that the gleams which flash across my mind are not mine, but God's; that they had the like, and were not disobedient to the heavenly vision. So I love them. Noble provocations go out from them, inviting me to resist evil; to subdue the world; and to Be. And thus, by his holy thoughts, Jesus serves us, and thus only. To aim to convert a man by miracles is a profanation of the soul. A true conversion, a true Christ, is now, as always, to be made by the reception of beautiful sentiments. It is true that a great and rich soul, like his, falling among the simple, does so preponderate, that, as his did, it names the world. The world seems to exist for him, and they have not yet drunk so deeply of his sense as to see that only by coming again to themselves, or to God in themselves, can they grow forevermore. It is a low benefit to give me something; it is a high benefit to enable me to do somewhat of myself. The time is coming when all men will see that the gift of God to the soul is not a vaunting, overpowering, excluding sanctity, but a sweet, natural goodness, a goodness like thine and mine, and that so invites thine and mine to be and to grow.

The injustice of the vulgar tone of preaching is not less flagrant to Jesus than to the souls which it profanes. The preachers do not see that they make his gospel not glad, and shear him of the locks of beauty and the attributes of heaven. When I see a majestic Epaminondas, or Washington; when I see among my contemporaries a true orator, an upright judge, a dear friend; when I vibrate to the melody and fancy of a poem; I see beauty that is to be desired. And so lovely, and yet with more entire consent of my human being, sounds in my ear the severe music of the bards that have sung of the true God in all ages. Now do not degrade the life and dialogues of Christ out of the circle of this charm, by insulation and peculiarity. Let them lie as they befell, alive and warm, part of human life and of the landscape and of the cheerful day.

2. The second defect of the traditionary and limited way of using the mind of Christ is a consequence of the first; this namely: that the Moral Nature, that Law of laws whose revelations introduce greatness — yea, God himself — into the open soul, is not explored as the fountain of the established teaching in society. Men have come to speak of the revelation as somewhat long ago given and done, as if God were dead. The injury to faith throttles the preacher; and the goodliest of institutions becomes an uncertain and inarticulate voice.

It is very certain that it is the effect of conversation with the beauty of the soul, to beget a desire and need to impart to others the same knowledge and love. If utterance is denied, the thought lies like a burden on the man. Always the seer is a sayer. Somehow his dream is told; somehow he publishes it with solemn joy: sometimes with pencil on canvas; sometimes with chisel on stone; sometimes in towers and aisles of granite, his soul's worship is builded; sometimes in anthems of indefinite music; but clearest and most permanent, in words.

The man enamored of this excellency becomes its priest or poet. The office is coeval with the world. But observe the condition, the spiritual limitation of the office. The spirit only can teach. Not any profane man, not any sensual, not any liar, not any slave can teach, but only he can give, who has; he only can create, who is. The man on whom the soul descends, through whom the soul speaks, alone can teach. Courage, piety, love, wisdom, can teach; and every man can open his door to these angels, and they shall bring him the gift of tongues. But the man who aims to speak as books enable, as synods use, as the fashion guides, and as interest commands, babbles. Let him hush.

To this holy office you propose to devote yourselves. I wish you may feel your call in throbs of desire and hope. The office is the first in the world. It is of that reality that it cannot suffer the deduction of any falsehood. And it is my duty to say to you that the need was never greater of new revelation than now. From the views I have already expressed, you will infer the sad conviction, which I share, I believe, with numbers, of the universal decay and now almost death of faith in society. The soul is not preached. The Church seems to totter to its fall, almost all life extinct. On this occasion, any complaisance would be criminal which told you, whose hope and commission it is to preach the faith of Christ, that the faith of Christ is preached.

It is time that this ill-suppressed murmur of all thoughtful men against the famine of our churches; — this moaning of the heart because it is bereaved of the consolation, the hope, the grandeur that come alone out of the culture of the moral nature, — should be heard through the sleep of indolence, and over the din of routine. This great and perpetual office of the preacher is not discharged. Preaching is the expression of the moral sentiment in application to the duties of life. In how many churches, by how many prophets, tell me, is man made sensible that he is an infinite Soul; that the earth and heavens are passing into his mind; that he is drinking forever the soul of God? Where now sounds the persuasion, that by its very melody imparadises my heart, and so affirms its own origin in heaven? Where shall I hear words such as in elder ages drew men to leave all and follow, — father and mother, house and land, wife and child? Where shall I hear these august laws of moral being so pronounced as to fill my ear, and I feel ennobled by the offer of my uttermost action and passion? The test of the true faith, certainly, should be its power to charm and command the soul, as the laws of nature control the activity of the hands, — so commanding that we find pleasure and honor in obeying. The faith should blend with the light of rising and of setting suns, with the flying cloud, the singing bird, and the breath of flowers. But now the priest's Sabbath has lost the splendor of nature; it is unlovely; we are glad when it is done; we can make, we do make, even sitting in our pews, a far better, holier, sweeter, for ourselves.

Whenever the pulpit is usurped by a formalist, then is the worshipper defrauded and disconsolate. We shrink as soon as the prayers begin, which do not uplift, but smite and offend us. We are fain to wrap our cloaks about us, and secure, as best we can, a solitude that hears not. I once heard a preacher who sorely tempted me to say I would go to church no more. Men go, thought I, where they are wont to go, else had no soul entered the temple in the afternoon. A snow-storm was falling around us. The snow-storm was real, the preacher merely spectral, and the eye felt the sad contrast in looking at him, and then out of the window behind him into the beautiful meteor of the snow. He had lived in vain. He had no one word intimating that he had laughed or wept, was married or in love, had been commended, or cheated, or chagrined. If he had ever lived and acted, we were none the wiser for it. The capital secret of his profession, namely, to convert life into truth, he had not learned. Not one fact in all his experience had he yet imported into his doctrine. This man had ploughed and planted and talked and bought and sold; he had read books; he had eaten and drunken; his head aches, his heart throbs; he smiles and suffers; yet was there not a surmise, a hint, in all the discourse, that he had ever lived at all. Not a line did he draw out of real history. The true preacher can be known by this, that he deals out to his people his life, — life passed through the fire of thought. But of the bad preacher, it could not be told from his sermon what age of the world he fell in; whether he had a father or a child; whether he was a freeholder or a pauper; whether he was a citizen or a countryman; or any other fact of his biography. It seemed strange that the people should come to church. It seemed as if their houses were very unentertaining, that they should prefer this thoughtless clamor. It shows that there is a commanding attraction in the moral sentiment, that can lend a faint tint of light to dulness and ignorance coming in its name and place. The good hearer is sure he has been touched sometimes; is sure there is somewhat to be reached, and some word that can reach it. When he listens to these vain words, he comforts himself by their relation to his remembrance of better hours, and so they clatter and echo unchallenged.

I am not ignorant that when we preach unworthily, it is not always quite in vain. There is a good ear, in some men, that draws supplies to virtue out of very indifferent nutriment. There is poetic truth concealed in all the commonplaces of prayer and of sermons, and though foolishly spoken, they may be wisely heard; for each is some select expression that broke out in a moment of piety from some stricken or jubilant soul, and its excellency made it remembered. The prayers and even the dogmas of our church are like the zodiac of Denderah and the astronomical monuments of the Hindoos, wholly insulated from anything now extant in the life and business of the people. They mark the height to which the waters once rose. But this docility is a check upon the mischief from the good and devout. In a large portion of the community, the religious service gives rise to quite other thoughts and emotions. We need not chide the negligent servant. We are struck with pity, rather, at the swift retribution of his sloth. Alas for the unhappy man that is called to stand in the pulpit, and *not* give bread of life. Everything that befalls, accuses him. Would he ask contributions for the missions, foreign or domestic? Instantly his face is suffused with shame, to propose to his parish that they should send money a hundred or a thousand miles, to furnish such poor fare as they have at home and would do well to go the hundred or the thousand miles to escape. Would he urge people to a godly way of living; — and can he ask a fellow-creature to come to Sabbath meetings, when he and they all know what is the poor uttermost they can hope for therein? Will he invite them privately to the Lord's Supper? He dares not. If no heart warm this rite, the hollow, dry, creaking formality is too plain, than that he can face a man of wit and energy and put the invitation without terror. In the street, what has he to say to the bold village blasphemer? The village blasphemer sees fear in the face, form, and gait of the minister.

Let me not taint the sincerity of this plea by any oversight of the claims of good men. I know and honor the purity and strict conscience of numbers of the clergy. What life the public worship retains, it owes to the scattered company of pious men, who minister here and there in the churches, and who, sometimes accepting with too great tenderness the tenet of the elders, have not accepted from others, but from their own heart, the genuine impulses of virtue, and so still command our love and awe, to the sanctity of character. Moreover, the exceptions are not so much to be found in a few eminent preachers, as in the better hours, the truer inspirations of all, — nay, in the sincere moments of every man. But, with whatever exception, it is still true that tradition characterizes the preaching of this country; that it comes out of the memory, and not out of the soul; that it aims at what is usual, and not at what is necessary and eternal; that thus historical Christianity destroys the power of preaching, by withdrawing it from the exploration of the moral nature of man; where the sublime is, where are the resources of astonishment and power. What a cruel injustice it is to that Law, the joy of the whole earth, which alone can make the thought dear and rich; that Law whose fatal sureness the astronomical orbits poorly emulate; — that it is travestied and depreciated, that it is behooted and behowled, and not a trait, not a word of it articulated. The pulpit in losing sight of this Law, loses its reason, and gropes after it knows not what. And for want of this culture the soul of the community is sick and faithless. It wants nothing so much as a stern, high, stoical, Christian discipline, to make it know itself and the divinity that speaks through it. Now man is ashamed of himself; he skulks and sneaks through the world, to be tolerated, to be pitied, and scarcely in a thousand years does any man dare to be wise and good, and so draw after him the tears and blessings of his kind.

Certainly there have been periods when, from the inactivity of the intellect on certain truths, a greater faith was possible in names and persons. The Puritans in England and America found in the Christ of the Catholic Church and in the dogmas inherited from Rome, scope for their austere piety and their longings for civil freedom. But their creed is passing away, and none arises in its room. I think no man can go with his thoughts about him into one of our churches, without feeling that what hold the public worship had on men is gone, or going. It has lost its grasp on the affection of the good and the fear of the bad. In the country, neighborhoods, half parishes are *signing off*, to use the local term. It is already beginning to indicate character and religion to withdraw from the religious meetings. I have heard a devout person, who prized the Sabbath, say in bitterness of heart, "On Sundays, it seems wicked to go to church." And the motive that holds the best there is now only a hope and a waiting. What was once a mere circumstance, that the best and the worst men in the parish, the poor and the rich, the learned and the ignorant, young and old, should meet one day as fellows in one house, in sign of an equal right in the soul, has come to be a paramount motive for going thither.

My friends, in these two errors, I think, I find the causes of a decaying church and a wasting unbelief. And what greater calamity can fall upon a nation than the loss of worship? Then all things go to decay. Genius leaves the temple to haunt the senate or the market. Literature becomes frivolous. Science is cold. The eye of youth is not lighted by the hope of other worlds, and age is without honor. Society lives to trifles, and when men die we do not mention them.

And now, my brothers, you will ask, What in these desponding days can be done by us? The remedy is already declared in the ground of our complaint of the Church. We have contrasted the Church with the Soul. In the soul then let the redemption be sought. Wherever a man comes, there comes revolution. The old is for slaves. When a man comes, all books are legible, all things transparent, all religions are forms. He is religious. Man is the wonderworker. He is seen amid miracles. All men bless and curse. He saith yea and nay, only. The stationariness of religion; the assumption that the age of inspiration is past, that the Bible is closed; the fear of degrading the character of Jesus by representing him as a man; — indicate with sufficient clearness the falsehood of our theology. It is the office of a true teacher to show us that God is, not was; that He speaketh, not spake. The true Christianity, — a faith like Christ's in the infinitude of man, — is lost. None believeth in the soul of man, but only in some man or person old and departed. Ah me! no man goeth alone. All men go in flocks to this saint or that poet, avoiding the God who seeth in secret. They cannot see in secret; they love to be blind in public. They think society wiser than their soul, and know not that one soul, and their soul, is wiser than the whole world. See how nations and races flit by on the sea of time and leave no ripple to tell where they floated or sunk, and one good soul shall make the name of Moses, or of Zeno, or of Zoroaster, reverend forever. None assayeth the stern ambition to be the Self of the nation and of nature, but each would be an easy secondary to some Christian scheme, or sectarian connection, or some eminent man. Once leave your own knowledge of God, your own sentiment, and take secondary knowledge, as St. Paul's, or George Fox's, or Swedenborg's, and you get wide from God with every year this secondary form lasts, and if, as now, for centuries, — the chasm yawns to that breadth,

that men can scarcely be convinced there is in them anything divine.

Let me admonish you, first of all, to go alone; to refuse the good models, even those which are sacred to the imagination of men, and dare to love God without mediator or veil. Friends enough you shall find who will hold up to your emulation Wesleys and Oberlins, Saints and Prophets. Thank God for these good men, but say, "I also am a man." Imitation cannot go above its model. The imitator dooms himself to hopeless mediocrity. The inventor did it because it was natural to him, and so in him it has a charm. In the imitator something else is natural, and he bereaves himself of his own beauty, to come short of another man's.

Yourself a newborn bard of the Holy Ghost, cast behind you all conformity, and acquaint men at first hand with Deity. Look to it first and only, that fashion, custom, authority, pleasure, and money, are nothing to you, — are not bandages over your eyes, that you cannot see, — but live with the privilege of the immeasurable mind. Not too anxious to visit periodically all families and each family in your parish connection, — when you meet one of these men or women, be to them a divine man; be to them thought and virtue; let their timid aspirations find in you a friend; let their trampled instincts be genially tempted out in your atmosphere; let their doubts know that you have doubted, and their wonder feel that you have wondered. By trusting your own heart, you shall gain more confidence in other men. For all our penny-wisdom, for all our soul-destroying slavery to habit, it is not to be doubted that all men have sublime thoughts; that all men value the few real hours of life; they love to be heard; they love to be caught up into the vision of principles. We mark with light in the memory the few interviews we have had, in the dreary years of routine and of sin, with souls that made our souls wiser; that spoke what we thought; that told us what we knew; that gave us leave to be what we inly were. Discharge to men the priestly office, and, present or absent, you shall be followed with their love as by an angel.

And, to this end, let us not aim at common degrees of merit. Can we not leave, to such as love it, the virtue that glitters for the commendation of society, and ourselves pierce the deep solitudes of absolute ability and worth? We easily come up to the standard of goodness in society. Society's praise can be cheaply secured, and almost all men are content with those easy merits; but the instant effect of conversing with God will be to put them away. There are persons who are not actors, not speakers, but influences; persons too great for fame, for display; who disdain eloquence; to whom all we call art and artist, seems too nearly allied to show and by-ends, to the exaggeration of the finite and selfish, and loss of the universal. The orators, the poets, the commanders encroach on us only as fair women do, by our allowance and homage. Slight them by preoccupation of mind, slight them, as you can well afford to do, by high and universal aims, and they instantly feel that you have right, and that it is in lower places that they must shine. They also feel your right; for they with you are open to the influx of the all-knowing Spirit, which annihilates before its broad noon the little shades and gradations of intelligence in the compositions we call wiser and wisest.

In such high communion let us study the grand strokes of rectitude: a bold benevolence, an independence of friends, so that not the unjust wishes of those who love us shall impair our freedom, but we shall resist for truth's sake the freest flow of kindness, and appeal to sympathies far in advance; and — what is the highest form in which we know this beautiful element, — a certain solidity of merit, that has nothing to do with opinion, and which is so essentially and manifestly virtue, that it is taken for granted that the right, the brave, the generous step will be taken by it, and nobody thinks of commending it. You would compliment a coxcomb doing a good act, but you would not praise an angel. The silence that accepts merit as the most natural thing in the world, is the highest applause. Such souls, when they appear, are the Imperial Guard of Virtue, the perpetual reserve, the dictators of fortune. One needs not praise their courage, — they are the heart and soul of nature. O my friends, there are

resources in us on which we have not drawn. There are men who rise refreshed on hearing a threat; men to whom a crisis which intimidates and paralyzes the majority, — demanding not the faculties of prudence and thrift, but comprehension, immovableness, the readiness of sacrifice, — comes graceful and beloved as a bride. Napoleon said of Massena, that he was not himself until the battle began to go against him; then, when the dead began to fall in ranks around him, awoke his powers of combination, and he put on terror and victory as a robe. So it is in rugged crises, in unweariable endurance, and in aims which put sympathy out of the question, that the angel is shown. But these are heights that we can scarce remember and look up to without contrition and shame. Let us thank God that such things exist.

And now let us do what we can to rekindle the smouldering, nigh quenched fire on the altar. The evils of the church that now is are manifest. The question returns, What shall we do? I confess, all attempts to project and establish a Cultus with new rites and forms, seem to me vain. Faith makes us, and not we it, and faith makes its own forms. All attempts to contrive a system are as cold as the new worship introduced by the French to the goddess of Reason, — today, pasteboard and filigree, and ending tomorrow in madness and murder. Rather let the breath of new life be breathed by you through the forms already existing. For if once you are alive, you shall find they shall become plastic and new. The remedy to their deformity is first, soul, and second, soul, and evermore, soul. A whole popedom of forms one pulsation of virtue can uplift and vivify. Two inestimable advantages Christianity has given us; first the Sabbath, the jubilee of the whole world, whose light dawns welcome alike into the closet of the philosopher, into the garret of toil, and into prison-cells, and everywhere suggests, even to the vile, the dignity of spiritual being. Let it stand forevermore, a temple, which new love, new faith, new sight shall restore to more than its first splendor to mankind. And secondly, the institution of preaching, — the speech of man to men, — essentially the most flexible of all organs, of all forms. What hinders that now, everywhere, in pulpits, in lecture-rooms, in houses, in fields, wherever the invitation of men or your own occasions lead you, you speak the very truth, as your life and conscience teach it, and cheer the waiting, fainting hearts of men with new hope and new revelation?

I look for the hour when that supreme Beauty which ravished the souls of those Eastern men, and chiefly of those Hebrews, and through their lips spoke oracles to all time, shall speak in the West also. The Hebrew and Greek Scriptures contain immortal sentences, that have been bread of life to millions. But they have no epical integrity; are fragmentary; are not shown in their order to the intellect. I look for the new Teacher that shall follow so far those shining laws that he shall see them come full circle; shall see their rounding complete grace; shall see the world to be the mirror of the soul; shall see the identity of the law of gravitation with purity of heart; and shall show that the Ought, that Duty, is one thing with Science, with Beauty, and with Joy.

Self-Reliance
(1841)

This, perhaps the most famous of all Emerson's essays, is easily — and frequently — misunderstood. The reader must keep in mind Emerson's statement in an address of 1854: "self-reliance, the height and perfection of man, is reliance on God." For the "self" to be trusted is, according to Emerson, not the egoistic or "selfish" self, but the universal or divine self. "A curious example of the rudeness and inaccuracy of thought," he complains elsewhere, "is the inability to distinguish between the private and the universal consciousness. I never make that blunder when I write, but the critics who read impute their confusion to me." For further light on this distinction, see the discussion of subjectivism in Emerson's *Dial* paper entitled "Thoughts on Modern Literature" (in *Natural History of Intellect and Other Papers*).

I read the other day some verses written by an eminent painter which were original and not conventional. The soul always hears an admonition in such lines, let the subject be what it may. The sentiment they instil is of more value than any thought they may contain. To believe your own thought, to believe that what is true for you in your private heart is true for all men, — that is genius.

Speak your latent conviction, and it shall be the universal sense; for the inmost in due time becomes the outmost, and our first thought is rendered back to us by the trumpets of the Last Judgment. Familiar as the voice of the mind is to each, the highest merit we ascribe to Moses, Plato, and Milton is that they set at naught books and traditions, and spoke not what men, but what *they* thought. A man should learn to detect and watch that gleam of light which flashes across his mind from within, more than the lustre of the firmament of bards and sages. Yet he dismisses without notice his thought, because it is his. In every work of genius we recognize our own rejected thoughts; they come back to us with a certain alienated majesty. Great works of art have no more affecting lesson for us than this. They teach us to abide by our spontaneous impression with good-humored inflexibility then most when the whole cry of voices is on the other side. Else to-morrow a stranger will say with masterly good sense precisely what we have thought and felt all the time, and we shall be forced to take with shame our own opinion from another.

There is a time in every man's education when he arrives at the conviction that envy is ignorance; that imitation is suicide; that he must take himself for better for worse as his portion; that though the wide universe is full of good, no kernel of nourishing corn can come to him but through his toil bestowed on that plot of ground which is given to him to till. The power which resides in him is new in nature, and none but he knows what that is which he can do, nor does he know until he has tried. Not for nothing one face, one character, one fact, makes much impression on him and another none. This sculpture in the memory is not without preëstablished harmony. The eye was placed where one ray should fall, that it might testify of that particular ray. We but half express ourselves, and are ashamed of that divine idea which each of us represents. It may be safely trusted as proportionate and of good issues, so it be faithfully imparted, but God will not have his work made manifest by cowards. A man is relieved and gay when he has put his heart into his work and done his best; but what he has said or done otherwise shall give him no peace. It is a deliverance which does not deliver. In the attempt his genius deserts him; no muse befriends; no invention, no hope.

Trust thyself: every heart vibrates to that iron string. Accept the place the divine providence has found for you, the society of your contemporaries, the connection of events. Great men have always done so, and confided themselves childlike to the genius of their age, betraying their perception that the absolutely trustworthy was seated at their heart, working through their hands, predominating in all their being. And we are now men, and must accept in the highest mind the same transcendent destiny; and not minors and invalids in a protected corner, not cowards fleeing before a revolution, but guides, redeemers, and benefactors, obeying the Almighty effort and advancing on Chaos and the Dark.

What pretty oracles nature yields us on this text in the face and behavior of children, babes, and even brutes! That divided and rebel mind, that distrust of a sentiment because our arithmetic has computed the strength and means opposed to our purpose, these have not. Their mind being whole, their eye is as yet unconquered, and when we look in their faces we are disconcerted. Infancy conforms to nobody; all conform to it; so that one babe commonly makes four or five out of the adults who prattle and play to it. So God has armed youth and puberty and manhood no less with its own piquancy and charm, and made it enviable and gracious and its claims not to be put by, if it will stand by itself. Do not think the youth has no force, because he cannot speak to you and me. Hark! in the next room his voice is sufficiently clear and emphatic. It seems he knows how to speak to his contemporaries. Bashful or bold then, he will know how to make us seniors very unnecessary.

The nonchalance of boys who are sure of a dinner, and would disdain as much as a lord to do or say aught to conciliate one, is the healthy attitude of human nature. A boy is in the parlor what the pit is in the playhouse; independent, irresponsible, looking out from his corner on such people and facts as pass by, he tries and sentences them on their mer-

its, in the swift, summary ways of boys, as good, bad, interesting, silly, eloquent, troublesome. He cumbers himself never about consequences, about interests; he gives an independent, genuine verdict. You must court him; he does not court you. But the man is as it were clapped into jail by his consciousness. As soon as he has once acted or spoken with *éclat* he is a committed person, watched by the sympathy or the hatred of hundreds whose affections must now enter into his account. There is no Lethe for this. Ah, that he could pass again into his neutrality! Who can thus avoid all pledges and, having observed, observe again from the same unaffected, unbiased, unbribable, unaffrighted innocence, — must always be formidable. He would utter opinions on all passing affairs, which being seen to be not private but necessary, would sink like darts into the ear of men and put them in fear.

These are the voices which we hear in solitude, but they grow faint and inaudible as we enter into the world. Society everywhere is in conspiracy against the manhood of every one of its members. Society is a joint-stock company, in which the members agree, for the better securing of his bread to each shareholder, to surrender the liberty and culture of the eater. The virtue in most request is conformity. Self-reliance is its aversion. It loves not realities and creators, but names and customs.

Whoso would be a man, must be a nonconformist. He who would gather immortal palms must not be hindered by the name of goodness, but must explore if it be goodness. Nothing is at last sacred but the integrity of your own mind. Absolve you to yourself, and you shall have the suffrage of the world. I remember an answer which when quite young I was prompted to make to a valued adviser who was wont to importune me with the dear old doctrines of the church. On my saying, "What have I to do with the sacredness of traditions, if I live wholly from within?" my friend suggested, — "But these impulses may be from below, not from above." I replied, "They do not seem to me to be such; but if I am the Devil's child, I will live then from the Devil." No law can be sacred to me but that of my nature. Good and bad are but names very readily transferable to that or this; the only right is what is after my constitution; the only wrong what is against it. A man is to carry himself in the presence of all opposition as if everything were titular and ephemeral but he. I am ashamed to think how easily we capitulate to badges and names, to large societies and dead institutions. Every decent and well-spoken individual affects and sways me more than is right. I ought to go upright and vital, and speak the rude truth in all ways. If malice and vanity wear the coat of philanthropy, shall that pass? If an angry bigot assumes this bountiful cause of Abolition, and comes to me with his last news from Barbadoes, why should I not say to him, "Go love thy infant; love thy woodchopper; be good-natured and modest; have that grace; and never varnish your hard, uncharitable ambition with this incredible tenderness for black folk a thousand miles off. Thy love afar is spite at home." Rough and graceless would be such greeting, but truth is handsomer than the affectation of love. Your goodness must have some edge to it, — else it is none. The doctrine of hatred must be preached, as the counteraction of the doctrine of love, when that pules and whines. I shun father and mother and wife and brother when my genius calls me. I would write on the lintels of the doorpost, *Whim*. I hope it is somewhat better than whim at last, but we cannot spend the day in explanation. Expect me not to show cause why I seek or why I exclude company. Then again, do not tell me, as a good man did to-day, of my obligation to put all poor men in good situations. Are they *my* poor? I tell thee, thou foolish philanthropist, that I grudge the dollar, the dime, the cent I give to such men as do not belong to me and to whom I do not belong. There is a class of persons to whom by all spiritual affinity I am bought and sold; for them I will go to prison if need be; but your miscellaneous popular charities; the education at college of fools; the building of meeting-houses to the vain end to which many now stand; alms to sots, and the thousand-fold Relief Societies; — though I confess with shame I sometimes succumb and give the dollar, it is a wicked dollar, which by and by I shall have the manhood to withhold.

Virtues are, in the popular estimate, rather the exception than the rule. There is the man *and* his virtues. Men do what is called a good action, as some piece of courage or charity, much as they would pay a fine in expiation of daily non-appearance on parade. Their works are done as an apology or extenuation of their living in the world, — as invalids and the insane pay a high board. Their virtues are penances. I do not wish to expiate, but to live. My life is for itself and not for a spectacle. I much prefer that it should be of a lower strain, so it be genuine and equal, than that it should be glittering and unsteady. I wish it to be sound and sweet, and not to need diet and bleeding. I ask primary evidence that you are a man and refuse this appeal from the man to his actions. I know that for myself it makes no difference whether I do or forbear those actions which are reckoned excellent. I cannot consent to pay for a privilege where I have intrinsic right. Few and mean as my gifts may be, I actually am, and do not need for my own assurance or the assurance of my fellows any secondary testimony.

What I must do is all that concerns me, not what the people think. This rule, equally arduous in actual and in intellectual life, may serve for the whole distinction between greatness and meanness. It is the harder because you will always find those who think they know what is your duty better than you know it. It is easy in the world to live after the world's opinion; it is easy in solitude to live after our own; but the great man is he who in the midst of the crowd keeps with perfect sweetness the independence of solitude.

The objection to conforming to usages that have become dead to you is that it scatters your force. It loses your time and blurs the impression of your character. If you maintain a dead church, contribute to a dead Bible-society, vote with a great party either for the government or against it, spread your table like base housekeepers, — under all these screens I have difficulty to detect the precise man you are: and of course so much force is withdrawn from all your proper life. But do your work, and I shall know you. Do your work, and you shall reinforce yourself. A man must consider what a blind-man's-buff is this game of conformity. If I know your sect I anticipate your argument. I hear a preacher announce for his text and topic the expediency of one of the institutions of his church. Do I not know beforehand that not possibly can he say a new and spontaneous word? Do I not know that with all this ostentation of grounds of the institution he will do no such thing? Do I not know that he is pledged to himself not to look but at one side, the permitted side, not as a man, but as a parish minister? He is a retained attorney, and these airs of the bench are the emptiest affectation. Well, most men have bound their eyes with one or another handkerchief, and attached themselves to some one of these communities of opinion. This conformity makes them not false in a few particulars, authors of a few lies, but false in all particulars. Their every truth is not quite true. Their two is not the real two, their four not the real four; so that every word they say chagrins us and we know not where to begin to set them right. Meantime nature is not slow to equip us in the prison-uniform of the party to which we adhere. We come to wear one cut of face and figure, and acquire by degrees the gentlest asinine expression. There is a mortifying experience in particular, which does not fail to wreak itself also in the general history; I mean the "foolish face of praise," the forced smile which we put on in company where we do not feel at ease, in answer to conversation which does not interest us. The muscles, not spontaneously moved but moved by a low usurping wilfulness, grow tight about the outline of the face, with the most disagreeable sensation.

For nonconformity the world whips you with its displeasure. And therefore a man must know how to estimate a sour face. The by-standers look askance on him in the public street or in the friend's parlor. If this aversion had its origin in contempt and resistance like his own he might well go home with a sad countenance; but the sour faces of the multitude, like their sweet faces, have no deep cause, but are put on and off as the wind blows and a newspaper directs. Yet is the discontent of the multitude more formidable than that of the senate and the college. It is easy enough for a firm man who knows the

world to brook the rage of the cultivated classes. Their rage is decorous and prudent for they are timid, as being very vulnerable themselves. But when to their feminine rage the indignation of the people is added, when the ignorant and the poor are aroused, when the unintelligent brute force that lies at the bottom of society is made to growl and mow, it needs the habit of magnanimity and religion to treat it godlike as a trifle of no concernment.

The other terror that scares us from self-trust is our consistency; a reverence for our past act or word because the eyes of others have no other data for computing our orbit than our past acts, and we are loth to disappoint them.

But why should you keep your head over your shoulder? Why drag about this corpse of your memory, lest you contradict somewhat you have stated in this or that public place? Suppose you should contradict yourself; what then? It seems to be a rule of wisdom never to rely on your memory alone, scarcely even in acts of pure memory, but to bring the past for judgment into the thousand-eyed present, and live ever in a new day. In your metaphysics you have denied personality to the Deity, yet when the devout motions of the soul come, yield to them heart and life, though they should clothe God with shape and color. Leave your theory, as Joseph his coat in the hand of the harlot, and flee.

A foolish consistency is the hobgoblin of little minds, adored by little statesmen and philosophers and divines. With consistency a great soul has simply nothing to do. He may as well concern himself with his shadow on the wall. Speak what you think now in hard words and to-morrow speak what to-morrow thinks in hard words again, though it contradict everything you said to-day. — "Ah, so you shall be sure to be misunderstood." — Is it so bad then to be misunderstood? Pythagoras was misunderstood, and Socrates, and Jesus, and Luther, and Copernicus, and Galileo, and Newton, and every pure and wise spirit that ever took flesh. To be great is to be misunderstood.

I suppose no man can violate his nature. All the sallies of his will are rounded in by the law of his being, as the inequalities of Andes and Himmaleh are insignificant in the curve of the sphere. Nor does it matter how you gauge and try him. A character is like an acrostic or Alexandrian stanza; — read it forward, backward, or across, it still spells the same thing. In this pleasing contrite wood-life which God allows me, let me record day by day my honest thought without prospect or retrospect, and, I cannot doubt, it will be found symmetrical, though I mean it not and see it not. My book should smell of pines and resound with the hum of insects. The swallow over my window should interweave that thread or straw he carries in his bill into my web also. We pass for what we are. Character teaches above our wills. Men imagine that they communicate their virtue or vice only by overt actions, and do not see that virtue or vice emit a breath every moment.

There will be an agreement in whatever variety of actions, so they be each honest and natural in their hour. For of one will, the actions will be harmonious, however unlike they seem. These varieties are lost sight of at a little distance, at a little height of thought. One tendency unites them all. The voyage of the best ship is a zigzag line of a hundred tacks. See the line from a sufficient distance, and it straightens itself to the average tendency. Your genuine action will explain itself and will explain your other genuine actions. Your conformity explains nothing. Act singly, and what you have already done singly will justify you now. Greatness appeals to the future. If I can be firm enough to-day to do right and scorn eyes, I must have done so much right before as to defend me now. Be it how it will, do right now. Always scorn appearances and you always may. The force of character is cumulative. All the foregone days of virtue work their health into this. What makes the majesty of the heroes of the senate and the field, which so fills the imagination? The consciousness of a train of great days and victories behind. They shed a united light on the advancing actor. He is attended as by a visible escort of angels. That is it which throws thunder into Chatham's voice, and dignity into Washington's port, and America into Adams's eye. Honor is

venerable to us because it is no ephemera. It is always ancient virtue. We worship it to-day because it is not of to-day. We love it and pay it homage because it is not a trap for our love and homage, but is self-dependent, self-derived, and therefore of an old immaculate pedigree, even if shown in a young person.

I hope in these days we have heard the last of conformity and consistency. Let the words be gazetted and ridiculous henceforward. Instead of the gong for dinner, let us hear a whistle from the Spartan fife. Let us never bow and apologize more. A great man is coming to eat at my house. I do not wish to please him; I wish that he should wish to please me. I will stand here for humanity, and though I would make it kind, I would make it true. Let us affront and reprimand the smooth mediocrity and squalid contentment of the times, and hurl in the face of custom and trade and office, the fact which is the upshot of all history, that there is a great responsible Thinker and Actor working wherever a man works; that a true man belongs to no other time or place, but is the centre of things. Where he is there is nature. He measures you and all men and all events. Ordinarily, everybody in society reminds us of somewhat else, or of some other person. Character, reality, reminds you of nothing else; it takes place of the whole creation. The man must be so much that he must make all circumstances indifferent. Every true man is a cause, a country, and an age; requires infinite spaces and numbers and time fully to accomplish his design; — and posterity seem to follow his steps as a train of clients. A man Caesar is born, and for ages after we have a Roman Empire. Christ is born, and millions of minds so grow and cleave to his genius that he is confounded with virtue and the possible of man. An institution is the lengthened shadow of one man; as, Monachism, of the Hermit Antony; the Reformation, of Luther; Quakerism, of Fox; Methodism, of Wesley; Abolition, of Clarkson. Scipio, Milton called "the height of Rome"; and all history resolves itself very easily into the biography of a few stout and earnest persons.

Let a man then know his worth, and keep things under his feet. Let him not peep or steal, or skulk up and down with the air of a charity-boy, a bastard, or an interloper in the world which exists for him. But the man in the street, finding no worth in himself which corresponds to the force which built a tower or sculptured a marble god, feels poor when he looks on these. To him a palace, a statue, or a costly book have an alien and forbidding air, much like a gay equipage, and seem to say like that, "Who are you, Sir?" Yet they all are his, suitors for his notice, petitioners to his faculties that they will come out and take possession. The picture waits for my verdict; it is not to command me, but I am to settle its claims to praise. That popular fable of the sot who was picked up dead-drunk in the street, carried to the duke's house, washed and dressed and laid in the duke's bed, and, on his waking, treated with all obsequious ceremony like the duke, and assured that he had been insane, owes its popularity to the fact that it symbolizes so well the state of man, who is in the world a sort of sot, but now and then wakes up, exercises his reason and finds himself a true prince.

Our reading is mendicant and sycophantic. In history our imagination plays us false. Kingdom and lordship, power and estate, are a gaudier vocabulary than private John and Edward in a small house and common day's work; but the things of life are the same to both; the sum total of both is the same. Why all this deference to Alfred and Scanderbeg and Gustavus? Suppose they were virtuous; did they wear out virtue? As great a stake depends on your private act to-day as followed their public and renowned steps. When private men shall act with original views, the lustre will be transferred from the actions of kings to those of gentlemen.

The world has been instructed by its kings, who have so magnetized the eyes of nations. It has been taught by this colossal symbol the mutual reverence that is due from man to man. The joyful loyalty with which men have everywhere suffered the king, the noble, or the great proprietor to walk among them by a law of his own, make his own scale of men and things and reverse theirs, pay for benefits not with money but with honor, and represent the law in his person, was the hieroglyphic by which they obscurely signified

their consciousness of their own right and comeliness, the right of every man.

The magnetism which all original action exerts is explained when we inquire the reason of self-trust. Who is the Trustee? What is the aboriginal Self, on which a universal reliance may be grounded? What is the nature and power of that science-baffling star, without parallax, without calculable elements, which shoots a ray of beauty even into trivial and impure actions, if the least mark of independence appear? The inquiry leads us to that source, at once the essence of genius, of virtue, and of life, which we call Spontaneity or Instinct. We denote this primary wisdom as Intuition, whilst all later teachings are tuitions. In that deep force, the last fact behind which analysis cannot go, all things find their common origin. For the sense of being which in calm hours rises, we know not how, in the soul, is not diverse from things, from space, from light, from time, from man, but one with them and proceeds obviously from the same source whence their life and being also proceed. We first share the life by which things exist and afterwards see them as appearances in nature and forget that we have shared their cause. Here is the fountain of action and of thought. Here are the lungs of that inspiration which giveth man wisdom and which cannot be denied without impiety and atheism. We lie in the lap of immense intelligence, which makes us receivers of its truth and organs of its activity. When we discern justice, when we discern truth, we do nothing of ourselves, but allow a passage to its beams. If we ask whence this comes, if we seek to pry into the soul that causes, all philosophy is at fault. Its presence or its absence is all we can affirm. Every man discriminates between the voluntary acts of his mind and his involuntary perceptions, and knows that to his involuntary perceptions a perfect faith is due. He may err in the expression of them, but he knows that these things are so, like day and night, not to be disputed. My wilful actions and acquisitions are but roving; — the idlest reverie, the faintest native emotion, command my curiosity and respect. Thoughtless people contradict as readily the statement of perceptions as of opinions, or rather much more readily; for they do not distinguish between perception and notion. They fancy that I choose to see this or that thing. But perception is not whimsical, but fatal. If I see a trait, my children will see it after me, and in course of time all mankind, — although it may chance that no one has seen it before me. For my perception of it is as much a fact as the sun.

The relations of the soul to the divine spirit are so pure that it is profane to seek to interpose helps. It must be that when God speaketh he should communicate, not one thing, but all things; should fill the world with his voice; should scatter forth light, nature, time, souls, from the centre of the present thought; and new date and new create the whole. Whenever a mind is simple and receives a divine wisdom, old things pass away, — means, teachers, texts, temples fall; it lives now, and absorbs past and future into the present hour. All things are made sacred by relation to it, — one as much as another. All things are dissolved to their centre by their cause, and in the universal miracle petty and particular miracles disappear. If therefore a man claims to know and speak of God and carries you backward to the phraseology of some old mouldered nation in another country, in another world, believe him not. Is the acorn better than the oak which is its fulness and completion? Is the parent better than the child into whom he has cast his ripened being? Whence then this worship of the past? The centuries are conspirators against the sanity and authority of the soul. Time and space are but physiological colors which the eye makes, but the soul is light: where it is, is day; where it was, is night; and history is an impertinence and an injury if it be anything more than a cheerful apologue or parable of my being and becoming.

Man is timid and apologetic; he is no longer upright; he dares not say "I think," "I am," but quotes some saint or sage. He is ashamed before the blade of grass or the blowing rose. These roses under my window make no reference to former roses or to better ones; they are for what they are; they exist with God to-day. There is no time to them. There is simply the rose; it is perfect in every moment of its existence. Before a leaf-bud has burst, its whole life acts; in the full-blown flower there is no more; in the leafless root there is no less. Its nature is satisfied and it satisfies nature in all moments alike. But man postpones or remembers; he does not live in the present, but with reverted eye laments the past, or, heedless of the riches that surround him, stands on tiptoe to foresee the future. He cannot be happy and strong until he too lives with nature in the present, above time.

This should be plain enough. Yet see what strong intellects dare not yet hear God himself unless he speaks the phraseology of I know not what David, or Jeremiah, or Paul. We shall not always set so great a price on a few texts, on a few lives. We are like children who repeat by rote the sentences of grandames and tutors, and, as they grow older, of the men of talents and character they chance to see, — painfully recollecting the exact words they spoke; afterwards, when they come into the point of view which those had who uttered these sayings, they understand them and are willing to let the words go; for at any time they can use words as good when occasion comes. If we live truly, we shall see truly. It is as easy for the strong man to be strong, as it is for the weak to be weak. When we have new perception, we shall gladly disburden the memory of its hoarded treasures as old rubbish. When a man lives with God, his voice shall be as sweet as the murmur of the brook and the rustle of the corn.

And now at last the highest truth on this subject remains unsaid; probably cannot be said: for all that we say is the far-off remembering of the intuition. That thought by what I can now nearest approach to say it, is this. When good is near you, when you have life in yourself, it is not by any known or accustomed way; you shall not discern the footprints of any other; you shall not see face of man; you shall not hear any name; — the way, the thought, the good, shall be wholly strange and new. It shall exclude example and experience. You take the way from man, not to man. All persons that ever existed are its forgotten ministers. Fear and hope are alike beneath it. There is somewhat low even in hope. In the hour of vision there is nothing that can be called gratitude, nor properly joy. The soul raised over passion beholds identity and eternal causation, perceives the self-existence of Truth and Right, and calms itself with knowing that all things go well. Vast spaces of nature, the Atlantic Ocean, the South Sea; long intervals of time, years, centuries, are of no account. This which I think and feel underlay every former state of life and circumstances, as it does underlie my present, and what is called life and what is called death.

Life only avails, not the having lived. Power ceases in the instant of repose; it resides in the moment of transition from a past to a new state, in the shooting of the gulf, in the darting to an aim. This one fact the world hates; that the soul *becomes;* for that forever degrades the past, turns all riches to poverty, all reputation to a shame, confounds the saint with the rogue, shoves Jesus and Judas equally aside. Why then do we prate of self-reliance? Inasmuch as the soul is present there will be power not confident but agent. To talk of reliance is a poor external way of speaking. Speak rather of that which relies because it works and is. Who has more obedience than I masters me, though he should not raise his finger. Round him I must revolve by the gravitation of spirits. We fancy it rhetoric when we speak of eminent virtue. We do not yet see that virtue is Height, and that a man or a company of men, plastic and permeable to principles, by the law of nature must overpower and ride all cities, nations, kings, rich men, poets, who are not.

This is the ultimate fact which we so quickly reach on this, as on every topic, the resolution of all into the ever-blessed ONE. Self-existence is the attribute of the Supreme Cause, and it constitutes the measure of good by the degree in which it enters into all lower forms. All things real are so by so much virtue as they contain. Commerce, husbandry, hunting, whaling, war, eloquence, personal weight, are somewhat, and engage my respect as examples of its presence and impure action. I see the same law working in nature for conservation and growth. Power is, in nature, the essential measure of right. Nature suffers nothing to remain in her kingdoms which cannot help itself. The genesis and maturation of a planet, its poise and orbit, the bended tree recovering itself from the strong wind, the vital resources of every animal and vegetable, are demonstrations of the self-sufficing and therefore self-relying soul.

Thus all concentrates: let us not rove; let us sit at home with the cause. Let us stun and astonish the intruding rabble of men and books and institutions by a simple declaration of the divine fact. Bid the invaders take the shoes from off their feet, for God is here within. Let our simplicity judge them, and our docility to our own law demonstrate the poverty of nature and fortune beside our native riches.

But now we are a mob. Man does not stand in awe of man, nor is his genius admonished to stay at home, to put itself in communication with the internal ocean, but it goes abroad to beg a cup of water of the urns of other men. We must go alone. I like the silent church before the service begins, better than any preaching. How far off, how cool, how chaste the persons look, begirt each one with a precinct or sanctuary! So let us always sit. Why should we assume the faults of our friend, or wife, or father, or child, because they sit around our hearth, or are said to have the same blood? All men have my blood and I all men's. Not for that will I adopt their petulance or folly, even to the extent of being ashamed of it. But your isolation must not be mechanical, but spiritual, that is, must be elevation. At times the whole world seems to be in conspiracy to importune you with emphatic trifles. Friend, climate, child, sickness, fear, want, charity, all knock at once at thy closet door and say, — "Come out unto us." But keep thy state; come not into their confusion. The power men possess to annoy me I give them by a weak curiosity. No man can come near me but through my act. "What we love that we have, but by desire we bereave ourselves of the love."

If we cannot at once rise to the sanctities of obedience and faith, let us at least resist our temptations; let us enter into the state of war and wake Thor and Woden, courage and constancy, in our Saxon breasts. This is to be done in our smooth times by speaking the truth. Check this lying hospitality and lying affection. Live no longer to the expectation of these deceived and deceiving people with whom we converse. Say to them, "O father, O mother, O wife, O brother, O friend, I have lived with you after appearances hitherto. Henceforward I am the truth's. Be it known unto you that henceforward I obey no law less than the eternal law. I will have no covenants but proximities. I shall endeavor to nourish my parents, to support my family, to be the chaste husband of one wife, — but these relations I must fill after a new and unprecedented way. I appeal from your customs. I must be myself. I cannot break myself any longer for you, or you. If you can love me for what I am, we shall be the happier. If you cannot, I will still seek to deserve that you should. I will not hide my tastes or aversions. I will so trust that what is deep is holy, that I will do strongly before the sun and moon whatever inly rejoices me and the heart appoints. If you are noble, I will love you; if you are not, I will not hurt you and myself by hypocritical attentions. If you are true, but not in the same truth with me, cleave to your companions; I will seek my own. I do this not selfishly but humbly and truly. It is alike your interest, and mine, and all men's, however long we have dwelt in lies, to live in truth. Does this sound harsh to-day? You will soon love what is dictated by your nature as well as mine, and if we follow the truth it will bring us out safe at last." — But so may you give these friends pain. Yes, but I cannot sell my liberty and my power, to save their sensibility. Besides, all persons have their moments of reason, when they look out into the region of absolute truth; then will they justify me and do the same thing.

The populace think that your rejection of popular standards is a rejection of all standard, and mere antinomianism; and the bold sensualist will use the name of philosophy to gild his crimes. But the law of consciousness abides. There are two confessionals, in one or the other of which we must be shriven. You may fulfil your round of duties by clearing yourself in the *direct*, or in the *reflex* way. Consider whether you have satisfied your relations to father, mother, cousin, neighbor, town, cat and dog — whether any of these can upbraid you. But I may also neglect this reflex standard and absolve me to myself. I have my own stern claims and perfect circle. It denies the name of duty to many offices that are called duties. But if I can discharge its debts it enables me to dispense with the popular code. If any one imagines that this law is lax, let him keep its commandment one day.

And truly it demands something godlike in him who has cast off the common motives of humanity and has ventured to trust himself for a taskmaster. High be his heart, faithful his will, clear his sight, that he may in good earnest be doctrine, society, law, to himself, that a simple purpose may be to him as strong as iron necessity is to others!

If any man consider the present aspects of what is called by distinction *society*, he will see the need of these ethics. The sinew and heart of man seem to be drawn out, and we are become timorous, desponding whimperers. We are afraid of truth, afraid of fortune, afraid of death, and afraid of each other. Our age yields no great and perfect persons. We want men and women who shall renovate life and our social state, but we see that most natures are insolvent, cannot satisfy their own wants, have an ambition out of all proportion to their practical force and do lean and beg day and night continually. Our housekeeping is mendicant, our arts, our occupations, our marriages, our religion we have not chosen, but society has chosen for us. We are parlor soldiers. We shun the rugged battle of fate, where strength is born.

If our young men miscarry in their first enterprises they lose all heart. If the young merchant fails, men say he is *ruined*. If the finest genius studies at one of our colleges and is not installed in an office within one year afterwards in the cities or suburbs of Boston or New York, it seems to his friends and to himself that he is right in being disheartened and in complaining the rest of his life. A sturdy lad from New Hampshire or Vermont, who in turn tries all the professions, who *teams it, farms it, peddles*, keeps a school, preaches, edits a newspaper, goes to Congress, buys a township, and so forth, in successive years, and always like a cat falls on his feet, is worth a hundred of these city dolls.

He walks abreast with his days and feels no shame in not "studying a profession," for he does not postpone his life, but lives already. He has not one chance, but a hundred chances. Let a Stoic open the resources of man and tell men they are not leaning willows, but can and must detach themselves; that with the exercise of self-trust, new powers shall appear; that a man is the word made flesh, born to shed healing to the nations; that he should be ashamed of our compassion, and that the moment he acts from himself, tossing the laws, the books, idolatries and customs out of the window, we pity him no more but thank and revere him; — and that teacher shall restore the life of man to splendor and make his name dear to all history.

It is easy to see that a greater self-reliance must work a revolution in all the offices and relations of men; in their religion; in their education; in their pursuits; their modes of living; their association; in their property; in their speculative views.

1. In what prayers do men allow themselves! That which they call a holy office is not so much as brave and manly. Prayer looks abroad and asks for some foreign addition to come through some foreign virtue, and loses itself in endless mazes of natural and supernatural, and mediatorial and miraculous. Prayer that craves a particular commodity, anything less than all good, is vicious. Prayer is the contemplation of the facts of life from the highest point of view. It is the soliloquy of a beholding and jubilant soul. It is the spirit of God pronouncing his works good. But prayer as a means to effect a private end is meanness and theft. It supposes dualism and not unity in nature and consciousness. As soon as the man is at one with God, he will not beg. He will then see prayer in all action. The prayer of the farmer kneeling in his field to weed it, the prayer of the rower kneeling with the stroke of his oar, are true prayers heard throughout nature, though for cheap ends. Caratach, in Fletcher's *Bonduca*, when admonished to inquire the mind of the god Audate, replies, —

"His hidden meaning lies in our endeavors;
   Our valors are our best gods."

Another sort of false prayers are our regrets. Discontent is the want of self-reliance: it is infirmity of will. Regret calamities if you can thereby help the sufferer; if not attend your own work and already the evil begins to be repaired. Our sympathy is just as base. We come to them who weep foolishly and sit down and cry for company, instead of imparting to them truth and health in rough electric shocks, putting them once more in communication with their own reason. The secret of fortune is joy in our hands. Welcome evermore to gods and men is the self-helping man. For him all doors are flung wide; him all tongues greet, all honors crown, all eyes follow with desire. Our love goes out to him and embraces him because he did not need it. We solicitously and apologetically caress and celebrate him because he held on his way and scorned our disapprobation. The gods love him because men hated him. "To the persevering mortal," said Zoroaster, "the blessed Immortals are swift."

As men's prayers are a disease of the will, so are their creeds a disease of the intellect. They say with those foolish Israelites, "Let not God speak to us, lest we die. Speak thou, speak any man with us, and we will obey." Everywhere I am hindered of meeting God in my brother, because he has shut his own temple doors and recites fables merely of his brother's, or his brother's brother's God. Every new mind is a new classification. If it prove a mind of uncommon activity and power, a Locke, a Lavoisier, a Hutton, a Bentham, a Fourier, it imposes its classification on other men, and lo! a new system. In proportion to the depth of the thought, and so to the number of the objects it touches and brings within reach of the pupil, is his complacency. But chiefly is this apparent in creeds and churches, which are also classifications of some powerful mind acting on the elemental thought of duty and man's relation to the Highest. Such is Calvinism, Quakerism, Swedenborgism. The pupil takes the same delight in subordinating everything to the new terminology as a girl who has just learned botany in seeing a new earth and new seasons thereby. It will happen for a time that the pupil will find his intellectual power has grown by the study of his master's mind. But in all unbalanced minds the classification is idolized, passes for the end and not for a speedily exhaustible means, so that the walls of the system blend to their eye in the remote horizon with the walls of the universe; the luminaries of heaven seem to them hung on the arch their master built. They cannot imagine how you aliens have any right to see, — how you can see; "It must be somehow that you stole the light from us." They do not yet perceive that light, unsystematic, indomitable, will break into any cabin, even into theirs. Let them chirp awhile and call it their own. If they are honest and do well, presently their neat new pinfold will be too strait and low, will crack, will lean, will rot and vanish, and the immortal light, all young, and joyful, million-orbed, million-colored, will beam over the universe as on the first morning.

2. It is for want of self-culture that the superstition of Travelling, whose idols are Italy, England, Egypt, retains its fascination for all educated Americans. They who made England, Italy, or Greece venerable in the imagination, did so by sticking fast where they were, like an axis of the earth. In manly hours we feel that duty is our place. The soul is no traveller; the wise man stays at home, and when his necessities, his duties, on any occasion call him from his house, or into foreign lands, he is at home still and shall make men sensible by the expression of his countenance that he goes, the missionary of wisdom and virtue, and visits cities and men like a sovereign and not like an interloper or a valet.

I have no churlish objection to the circumnavigation of the globe for the purposes of art, of study, and benevolence, so that the man is first domesticated, or does not go abroad with the hope of finding somewhat greater than he knows. He who travels to be amused, or to get somewhat which he does not carry, travels away from himself, and grows old even in youth among old things. In Thebes, in Palmyra, his will and mind have become old and dilapidated as they. He carries ruins to ruins.

Travelling is a fool's paradise. Our first journeys discover to us the indifference of places. At home I dream that at Naples, at Rome, I can be intoxicated with beauty and lose my sadness. I pack my trunk, embrace my friends, embark on the sea and at last wake up in Naples, and there beside me is the stern fact, the sad self, unrelenting, identical, that I fled from. I seek the Vatican and the palaces. I affect to be intoxicated with sights and suggestions, but I am not intoxicated. My giant goes with me wherever I go.

3. But the rage of travelling is a symptom of a deeper unsoundness affecting the whole intellectual action. The intellect is vagabond, and our system of education fosters restlessness. Our minds travel when our bodies are forced to stay at home. We imitate; and what is imitation but the travelling of the mind? Our houses are built with foreign taste; our shelves are garnished with foreign ornaments; our opinions, our tastes, our faculties lean, and follow the Past and the Distant. The soul created the arts wherever they have flourished. It was in his own mind that the artist sought his model. It was an application of his own thought to the thing to be done and the conditions to be observed. And why need we copy the Doric or the Gothic model? Beauty, convenience, grandeur of thought and quaint expression are as near to us as to any, and if the American artist will study with hope and love the precise thing to be done by him, considering the climate, the soil, the length of the day, the wants of the people, the habit and form of the government, he will create a house in which all these will find themselves fitted, and taste and sentiment will be satisfied also.

Insist on yourself; never imitate. Your own gift you can present every moment with the cumulative force of a whole life's cultivation; but of the adopted talent of another you have only an extemporaneous half possession. That which each can do best, none but his Maker can teach him. No man yet knows what it is, nor can, till that person has exhibited it. Where is the master who could have taught Shakspeare? Where is the master who could have instructed Franklin, or Washington, or Bacon, or Newton? Every great man is a unique. The Scipionism of Scipio is precisely that part he could not borrow. Shakspeare will never be made by the study of Shakspeare. Do that which is assigned you, and you cannot hope too much or dare too much. There is at this moment for you an utterance brave and grand as that of the colossal chisel of Phidias, or trowel of the Egyptians, or the pen of Moses or Dante, but different from all these. Not possibly will the soul, all rich, all eloquent, with thousand-cloven tongue, deign to repeat itself; but if you can hear what these patriarchs say, surely you can reply to them in the same pitch of voice; for the ear and the tongue are two organs of one nature. Abide in the simple and noble regions of thy life, obey thy heart, and thou shall reproduce the Fore-world again.

4. As our Religion, our Education, our Art look abroad, so does our spirit of society. All men plume themselves on the improvement of society, and no man improves.

Society never advances. It recedes as fast on one side as it gains on the other. It undergoes continual changes; it is barbarous, it is civilized, it is christianized, it is rich, it is scientific; but this change is not amelioration. For everything that is given something is taken. Society acquires new arts and loses old instincts. What a contrast between the well-clad, reading, writing, thinking American, with a watch, a pencil, and a bill of exchange in his pocket, and the naked New Zealander, whose property is a club, a spear, a mat, and an undivided twentieth of a shed to sleep under! But compare the health of the two men and you shall see that the white man has lost his aboriginal strength. If the traveller tell us truly, strike the savage with a broad-axe and in a day or two the flesh shall unite and heal as if you struck the blow into soft pitch, and the same blow shall send the white to his grave.

The civilized man has built a coach, but has lost the use of his feet. He is supported on crutches, but lacks so much support of muscle. He has a fine Geneva watch, but he fails of the skill to tell the hour by the sun. A Greenwich nautical almanac he has, and so being sure of the information when he wants it, the man in the street does not know a star in the sky. The solstice he does not observe; the equinox he knows as little; and the whole bright calendar of the year is without a dial in his mind. His note-books impair his memory; his libraries overload his wit; the insurance-office increases the number of accidents; and it may be a question whether machinery does not encumber; whether we have not lost by refinement some energy, by a Christianity, entrenched in establishments and forms, some vigor of wild virtue. For every Stoic was a Stoic; but in Christendom where is the Christian?

There is no more deviation in the moral standard than in the standard of height or bulk. No greater men are now than ever were. A singular equality may be observed between the great men of the first and of the last ages; nor can all the science, art, religion, and philosophy of the nineteenth century avail to educate greater men than Plutarch's heroes, three or four and twenty centuries ago. Not in time is the race progressive. Phocion, Socrates, Anaxagoras, Diogenes, are great men, but they leave no class. He who is really of their class will not be called by their name, but will be his own man, and in his turn the founder of a sect. The arts and inventions of each period are only its costume and do not invigorate men. The harm of the improved machinery may compensate its good. Hudson and Behring accomplished so much in their fishing-boats as to astonish Parry and Franklin, whose equipment exhausted the resources of science and art. Galileo, with an opera-glass, discovered a more splendid series of celestial phenomena than any one since. Columbus found the New World in an undecked boat. It is curious to see the periodical disuse and perishing of means and machinery which were introduced with loud laudation a few years or centuries before. The great genius returns to essential man. We reckoned the improvements of the art of war among the triumphs of science, and yet Napoleon conquered Europe by the bivouac, which consisted of falling back on naked valor and disencumbering it of all aids. The Emperor held it impossible to make a perfect army, says Las Cases, "without abolishing our arms, magazines, commissaries, and carriages, until, in imitation of the Roman custom, the soldier should receive his supply of corn, grind it in his hand-mill and bake his bread himself."

Society is a wave. The wave moves onward, but the water of which it is composed does not. The same particle does not rise from the valley to the ridge. Its unity is only phenomenal. The persons who make up a nation to-day, next year die, and their experience dies with them.

And so the reliance on Property, including the reliance on governments which protect it, is the want of self-reliance. Men have looked away from themselves and at things so long that they have come to esteem the religious, learned, and civil institutions as guards of property, and they deprecate assaults on these, because they feel them to be assaults on property. They measure their esteem of each other by what each has, and not by what each is. But a cultivated man becomes ashamed of his property, out of new respect for his nature. Especially he hates what he has if he see that it is accidental, — came to him by inheritance, or gift, or crime; then he feels that it is not having; it does not belong to him, has no root in him and merely lies there because no revolution or no robber takes it away. But that which a man is, does always by necessity acquire; and what the man acquires, is living property, which does not wait the beck of rulers, or mobs, or revolutions, or fire, or storm, or bankruptcies, but perpetually renews itself wherever the man breathes. "Thy lot or portion of life," said the Caliph Ali, "is seeking after thee; therefore be at rest from seeking after it." Our dependence on these foreign goods leads us to our slavish respect for numbers. The political parties meet in numerous conventions; the greater the concourse and with each new uproar of announcement, The delegation from Essex! The Democrats from New Hampshire! The Whigs of Maine! the young patriot feels himself stronger than before by a new thousand of eyes and arms. In like manner the reformers summon conventions and vote and resolve in multitude. Not so, O friends! will the God deign to enter and inhabit you, but by a method precisely the reverse. It is only as a man puts off all foreign support and stands alone that I see him to be strong and to prevail. He is weaker by every recruit to his banner. Is not a man better than a town? Ask nothing of men, and, in the endless mutation, thou only firm column must presently appear the upholder of all that surrounds thee. He who knows that power is inborn, that he is weak because he has looked for good out of him and elsewhere, and, so perceiving, throws himself unhesitatingly on his thought, instantly rights himself, stands in the erect position, commands his limbs, works miracles; just as a man who stands on his feet is stronger than a man who stands on his head.

So use all that is called Fortune. Most men gamble with her, and gain all, and lose all, as her wheel rolls. But do thou leave as unlawful these winnings, and deal with Cause and Effect, the chancellors of God. In the Will work and acquire, and thou hast chained the wheel of Chance, and shall sit hereafter out of fear from her rotations. A political victory, a rise of rents, the recovery of your sick or the return of your absent friend, or some other favorable event raises your spirits, and you think good days are preparing for you. Do not believe it. Nothing can bring you peace but yourself. Nothing can bring you peace but the triumph of principles.

HENRY THOREAU (1817–1862)

The only native of Concord in the group that gathered there, Thoreau was born on July 12, 1817. He entered Harvard in 1833, and, when he graduated four years later, tried teaching school. "As I did not teach for the good of my fellow-men, but simply for a livelihood, this was a failure," he said. He began manufacturing pencils, but when he had made the best ones available in America and had no more worlds to conquer, he retired. Thereafter, except for a few brief trips, he lived close to nature in Concord. "I have traveled much in Concord," he said.

"I am a mystic, a Transcendentalist, and a natural philosopher." Individualism he carried to great lengths. He helped Emerson edit the *Dial*, surveyed occasionally, did odd jobs for his neighbors. He refused to pay his poll-tax on the ground that it was applied to the support of slavery, and he was imprisoned. Emerson (so the story goes) went to see him in prison, and asked, "Why are you in there, Henry?" "Why are you out there?" Thoreau answered reproachfully. He spoke for John Brown. He advocated civil disobedience. He built a hut by Walden Pond and lived there two years at an expense of eight dollars a year. He spent a number of years in Emerson's household. Then, by the irony of fate, this man who had always lived so familiarly with nature was stricken with tuberculosis, and died on May 6, 1862. Even on his deathbed he illustrated the Yankee practicality which was united in his personality with romantic individualism. He was asked if he could see anything of the land he was approaching. "One world at a time," answered Thoreau. "One world at a time."

In his lifetime Thoreau published only two books, *A Week on the Concord and Merrimac Rivers*, 1849, and *Walden: or Life in the Woods*, 1854. He also contributed to periodicals some poetry and a considerable amount of prose. In the years just following his death, essays and accounts of travel were published under the titles *Excursions*, *The Maine Woods*, and *Cape Cod;* also correspondence brought out by Emerson and later amplified as *Familiar Letters*. While the literary quality of all his writing is high, the reputation of Thoreau rests essentially on *Walden*.

In *Walden* Thoreau presented, in organic relation, a record of his two-year experiment (a sort of one-man Brook Farm), an individualist philosophy of life which has a perennial appeal, and a view of nature as a source of delight and spiritual discipline. To some readers, Thoreau at his best is equal or superior to Emerson. H. S. Canby (in *Classic Americans*, p. 218) has characterized him as "one of the masters of English prose, purer, stronger, racier, closer to a genuine life rhythm, than any one of his contemporaries, in England or America."

The best edition of Thoreau's works is the Walden, 1906, in 20 volumes, of which 14 are journals. *The Heart of Thoreau's Journals* was edited by Odell Shepard in 1927, *The Collected Poems of Henry Thoreau* by C. Bode, 1943. A pleasant little book by Emerson's son, E. W. Emerson, is *Henry Thoreau as Remembered by a Young Friend*, 1917. The best recent biographies are by H. S. Canby, 1939, and J. W. Krutch (American Men of Letters Series), 1950. Mark Van Doren has written *Henry David Thoreau, a Critical Study*, 1916, and N. Foerster's *Nature in American Literature*, 1923, contains a chapter on Thoreau's relation to nature. The centennial of Thoreau's experiment at Walden Pond brought forth an interpretive tribute by G. F. Whicher, *Walden Revisited*, 1945. B. V. Crawford's volume of selections in the *AWS*, 1934, is judiciously edited.

Smoke

(1843)

Light-winged smoke, Icarian bird,
Melting thy pinions in thy upward flight,
Lark without song, and messenger of
      dawn,

Circling above the hamlets as thy nest;
Or else, departing dream, and shadowy
      form   5
Of midnight vision, gathering up thy skirts;
By night star-veiling, and by day
Darkening the light and blotting out the
      sun;

Go thou my incense upward from this hearth,
And ask the Gods to pardon this clear
    flame.   10

Haze

(1843)

Woof of the sun, ethereal gauze,
Woven of Nature's richest stuffs,
Visible heat, air-water, and dry sea,
Last conquest of the eye;
Toil of the day displayed, sun-dust,   5
Aerial surf upon the shores of earth,
Ethereal estuary, frith of light,
Breakers of air, billows of heat,
Fine summer spray on inland seas;
Bird of the sun, transparent-winged,   10
Owlet of noon, soft-pinioned,
From heath or stubble rising without song, —
Establish thy serenity o'er the fields.

Inspiration

(1863)

If with light head erect I sing,
Though all the muses lend their force,
From my poor love of any thing,
The verse is weak and shallow as its source.

But if with bended neck I grope,   5
Listening behind me for my wit,
With faith superior to hope,
More anxious to keep back than forward it, —

Making my soul accomplice there
Unto the flame my heart hath lit, —   10
Then will the verse forever wear:
Time cannot bend the line which God hath
    writ.

I hearing get, who had but ears,
And sight, who had but eyes before;
I moments live, who lived but years,   15
And truth discern, who knew but learning's
    lore.

Now chiefly is my natal hour,
And only now my prime of life;
Of manhood's strength it is the flower,
'Tis peace's end and war's beginning strife. 20

It comes in summer's broadest noon,
By a gray wall, or some chance place,
Unseasoning time, insulting June,
And vexing day with its presuming face.

I will not doubt the love untold   25
Which not my worth nor want hath bought,
Which wooed me young, and wooes me old,
And to this evening hath me brought.

Civil Disobedience

(1849)

I heartily accept the motto, — "That government is best which governs least;" and I should like to see it acted up to more rapidly and systematically. Carried out, it finally amounts to this, which also I believe, — "That government is best which governs not at all;" and when men are prepared for it, that will be the kind of government which they will have. Government is at best but an expedient; but most governments are usually, and all governments are sometimes, inexpedient. The objections which have been brought against a standing army, and they are many and weighty, and deserve to prevail, may also at last be brought against a standing government. The standing army is only an arm of the standing government. The government itself, which is only the mode which the people have chosen to execute their will, is equally liable to be abused and perverted before the people can act through it. Witness the present Mexican war, the work of comparatively a few individuals using the standing government as their tool; for, in the outset, the people would not have consented to this measure.

This American government, — what is it but a tradition, though a recent one, endeavoring to transmit itself unimpaired to posterity, but each instant losing some of its integrity? It has not the vitality and force of a single living man; for a single man can bend it to his will. It is a sort of wooden gun to the people themselves. But it is not the less necessary for this; for the people must have some complicated machinery or other, and hear its din, to satisfy that idea of government which they have. Governments show thus how successfully men can be imposed on, even impose on themselves, for their own advantage. It is excellent, we must all allow. Yet this government never of itself furthered any enterprise, but by the alacrity with which it got out of its way. It does not keep the country free. It does not settle the West. It does not educate. The character inherent in the American people has done all that has been accomplished; and it would have done somewhat more, if the government had not sometimes got in its way. For government is an expedient by which men would fain succeed in letting one another alone; and, as has been said, when it is most expedient, the governed are most let alone by it. Trade and commerce, if they were not made of India-rubber, would never manage to bounce over the obstacles which legislators are continually putting in their way; and, if one were to judge these men wholly by the effects of their actions and not partly by their intentions, they would deserve to be classed and punished with those mischievous persons who put obstructions on the railroads.

But, to speak practically and as a citizen, unlike those who call themselves no-government men, I ask for, not at once no government, but *at once* a better government. Let every man make known what kind of government would command his respect, and that will be one step toward obtaining it.

After all, the practical reason why, when the power is once in the hands of the people, a majority are permitted, and for a long period continue, to rule is not because they are most likely to be in the right, nor because this seems fairest to the minority, but because they are physically the strongest. But a government in which the majority rule in all cases cannot be based on justice, even as far as men understand it. Can there not be a government in which majorities do not virtually decide right and wrong, but conscience? — in which majorities decide only those questions to which the rule of expediency is applicable? Must the citizen ever for a moment, or in the least degree, resign his conscience to the legislator? Why has every man a conscience, then? I think that we should be men first, and subjects afterward. It is not desirable to cultivate a respect for the law, so much as for the right. The only obligation which I have a right to assume is to do at any time what I think right. It is truly enough said, that a corporation has no conscience; but a corporation of conscientious men is a corporation *with* a conscience. Law never made men a whit more just; and, by means of their respect for it, even the well-disposed are daily made the agents of injustice. A common and natural result of an undue respect for law is, that you may see a file of soldiers, colonel, captain, corporal, privates, powder-monkeys, and all, marching in admirable order over hill and dale to the wars, against their wills, ay, against their common sense and consciences, which makes it very steep marching indeed, and produces a palpitation of the heart. They have no doubt that it is a damnable business in which they are concerned; they are all peaceably inclined. Now, what are they? Men at all? or small movable forts and magazines, at the service of some unscrupulous man in power? Visit the Navy-Yard, and behold a marine, such a man as an American government can make, or such as it can make a man with its black arts, — a mere shadow and reminiscence of humanity, a man laid out alive and standing, and already, as one may say, buried under arms with funeral accompaniments, though it may be,

"Not a drum was heard, not a funeral note,
   As his corse to the rampart we hurried;
Not a soldier discharged his farewell shot
   O'er the grave where our hero we buried."

The mass of men serve the state thus, not as men mainly, but as machines, with their bodies. They are the standing army, and the militia, jailers, constables, posse comitatus, etc. In most cases there is no free exercise whatever of the judgment or of the moral sense; but they put themselves on a level with wood and earth and stones; and wooden men can perhaps be manufactured that will serve the purpose as well. Such command no more respect than men of straw or a lump of dirt. They have the same sort of worth only as horses and dogs. Yet such as these even are commonly esteemed good citizens. Others — as most legislators, politicians, lawyers, ministers, and office-holders — serve the state chiefly with their heads; and, as they rarely make any moral distinctions, they are as likely to serve the Devil, without *intending* it, as God. A very few, as heroes, patriots, martyrs, reformers in the great sense, and *men*, serve the state with their consciences also, and so necessarily resist it for the most part; and they are commonly treated as enemies by it. A wise man will only be useful as a man, and will not submit to be "clay," and "stop a hole to keep the wind away," but leave that office to his dust at least:

"I am too high-born to be propertied,
   To be a secondary at control,
   Or useful serving-man and instrument
   To any sovereign state throughout the world."

He who gives himself entirely to his fellow-men appears to them useless and selfish; but he who gives himself partially to them is pronounced a benefactor and philanthropist.

How does it become a man to behave toward this American government today? I answer, that he cannot without disgrace be associated with it. I cannot for an instant recognize that political organization as *my* government which is the *slave's* government also.

All men recognize the right of revolution; that is, the right to refuse allegiance to, and to resist, the government, when its tyranny or its inefficiency are great and unendurable. But almost all say that such is not the case now. But such was the case, they think, in the Revolution of '75. If one were to tell me that this was a bad government because it taxed certain foreign commodities brought to its ports, it is most probable that I should not make an ado about it, for I can do without them. All machines have their friction; and possibly this does enough good to counterbalance the evil. At any rate, it is a great evil to make a stir about it. But when the friction comes to have its machine, and oppression and robbery are organized, I say, let us not have such a machine any longer. In other words, when a sixth of the population of a nation which has undertaken to be the refuge of liberty are slaves, and a whole

country is unjustly overrun and conquered by a foreign army, and subjected to military law, I think that it is not too soon for honest men to rebel and revolutionize. What makes this duty the more urgent is the fact that the country so overrun is not our own, but ours is the invading army.

Paley, a common authority with many on moral questions, in his chapter on the "Duty of Submission to Civil Government," resolves all civil obligation into expediency; and he proceeds to say, "that so long as the interest of the whole society requires it, that is, so long as the established government cannot be resisted or changed without public inconveniency, it is the will of God that the established government be obeyed, and no longer. . . . This principle being admitted, the justice of every particular case of resistance is reduced to a computation of the quantity of the danger and grievance on the one side, and of the probability and expense of redressing it on the other." Of this, he says, every man shall judge for himself. But Paley appears never to have contemplated those cases to which the rule of expediency does not apply, in which a people, as well as an individual, must do justice, cost what it may. If I have unjustly wrested a plank from a drowning man, I must restore it to him though I drown myself. This, according to Paley, would be inconvenient. But he that would save his life, in such a case, shall lose it. This people must cease to hold slaves, and to make war on Mexico, though it cost them their existence as a people.

In their practice, nations agree with Paley; but does any one think that Massachusetts does exactly what is right at the present crisis?

"A drab of state, a cloth-o'-silver slut,
To have her train borne up, and her soul trail in
   the dirt."

Practically speaking, the opponents to a reform in Massachusetts are not a hundred thousand politicians at the South, but a hundred thousand merchants and farmers here, who are more interested in commerce and agriculture than they are in humanity, and are not prepared to do justice to the slave and to Mexico, *cost what it may.* I quarrel not with far-off foes, but with those who, near at home, co-operate with, and do the bidding of, those far away, and without whom the latter would be harmless. We are accustomed to say, that the mass of men are unprepared; but improvement is slow, because the few are not materially wiser or better than the many. It is not so important that many should be as good as you, as that there be some absolute goodness somewhere; for that will leaven the whole lump. There are thousands who are *in opinion* opposed to slavery and to the war, who yet in effect do nothing to put an end to them; who, esteeming themselves children of Washington and Franklin, sit down with their hands in their pockets, and say that they know not what to do, and do nothing; who even postpone the question of freedom to the question of free-trade, and quietly read the prices-current along with the latest advices from Mexico, after dinner, and, it may be, fall asleep over them both. What is the price-current of an honest man and patriot to-day? They hesitate, and they regret, and sometimes they petition; but they do nothing in earnest and with effect. They will wait, well disposed, for others to remedy the evil, that they may no longer have it to regret. At most, they give only a cheap vote, and a feeble countenance and God-speed, to the right, as it goes by them. There are nine hundred and ninety-nine patrons of virtue to one virtuous man. But it is easier to deal with the real possessor of a thing than with the temporary guardian of it.

All voting is a sort of gaming, like checkers or backgammon, with a slight moral tinge to it, a playing with right and wrong, with moral questions; and betting naturally accompanies it. The character of the voters is not staked. I cast my vote, perchance, as I think right; but I am not vitally concerned that that right should prevail. I am willing to leave it to the majority. Its obligation, therefore, never exceeds that of expediency. Even voting *for the right* is *doing* nothing for it. It is only expressing to men feebly your desire that it should prevail. A wise man will not leave the right to the mercy of chance nor wish it to prevail through the power of the majority. There is but little virtue in

the action of masses of men. When the majority shall at length vote for the abolition of slavery, it will be because they are indifferent to slavery, or because there is but little slavery left to be abolished by their vote. *They* will then be the only slaves. Only *his* vote can hasten the abolition of slavery who asserts his own freedom by his vote.

I hear of a convention to be held at Baltimore, or elsewhere, for the selection of a candidate for the Presidency, made up chiefly of editors, and men who are politicians by profession; but I think, what is it to any independent, intelligent, and respectable man what decision they may come to? Shall we not have the advantage of his wisdom and honesty, nevertheless? Can we not count upon some independent votes? Are there not many individuals in the country who do not attend conventions? But no: I find that the respectable man, so called, has immediately drifted from his position, and despairs of his country, when his country has more reason to despair of him. He forthwith adopts one of the candidates thus selected as the only *available* one, thus proving that he is himself *available* for any purposes of the demagogue. His vote is of no more worth than that of any unprincipled foreigner or hireling native, who may have been bought. O for a man who is a *man*, and, as my neighbor says, has a bone in his back which you cannot pass your hand through! Our statistics are at fault: the population has been returned too large. How many *men* are there to a square thousand miles in this country? Hardly one. Does not America offer any inducement for men to settle here? The American has dwindled into an Odd Fellow, — one who may be known by the development of his organ of gregariousness, and a manifest lack of intellect and cheerful self-reliance; whose first and chief concern, on coming into the world, is to see that the Almshouses are in good repair; and, before yet he has lawfully donned the virile garb, to collect a fund for the support of the widows and orphans that may be; who, in short, ventures to live only by the aid of the Mutual Insurance company, which has promised to bury him decently.

It is not a man's duty, as a matter of course, to devote himself to the eradication of any, even the most enormous wrong; he may still properly have other concerns to engage him; but it is his duty, at least, to wash his hands of it, and, if he gives it no thought longer, not to give it practically his support. If I devote myself to other pursuits and contemplations, I must first see, at least, that I do not pursue them sitting upon another man's shoulders. I must get off him first, that he may pursue his contemplations too. See what gross inconsistency is tolerated. I have heard some of my townsmen say, "I should like to have them order me out to help put down an insurrection of the slaves, or to march to Mexico; — see if I would go;" and yet these very men have each, directly by their allegiance, and so indirectly, at least, by their money, furnished a substitute. The soldier is applauded who refuses to serve in an unjust war by those who do not refuse to sustain the unjust government which makes the war; is applauded by those whose own act and authority he disregards and sets at naught; as if the state were penitent to that degree that it hired one to scourge it while it sinned, but not to that degree that it left off sinning for a moment. Thus, under the name of Order and Civil Government, we are all made at last to pay homage to and support our own meanness. After the first blush of sin comes its indifference; and from immoral it becomes, as it were, unmoral, and not quite unnecessary to that life which we have made.

The broadest and most prevalent error requires the most disinterested virtue to sustain it. The slight reproach to which the virtue of patriotism is commonly liable, the noble are most likely to incur. Those who, while they disapprove of the character and measures of a government, yield to it their allegiance and support are undoubtedly its most conscientious supporters, and so frequently the most serious obstacles to reform. Some are petitioning the state to dissolve the Union, to disregard the requisitions of the President. Why do they not dissolve it themselves, — the union between themselves and the state, — and refuse to pay their quota into its treasury? Do not they stand in the same relation to the state that the state does to the Union? And have not the same reasons prevented the state from resisting the Union which have prevented them from resisting the state?

How can a man be satisfied to entertain an opinion merely, and enjoy *it*? Is there any enjoyment in it, if his opinion is that he is aggrieved? If you are cheated out of a single dollar by your neighbor, you do not rest satisfied with knowing that you are cheated, or with saying that you are cheated, or even with petitioning him to pay you your due; but you take effectual steps at once to obtain the full amount, and see that you are never cheated again. Action from principle, the perception and the performance of right, changes things and relations; it is essentially revolutionary, and does not consist wholly with anything which was. It not only divides states and churches, it divides families; ay, it divides the *individual*, separating the diabolical in him from the divine.

Unjust laws exist: shall we be content to obey them, or shall we endeavor to amend them, and obey them until we have succeeded, or shall we transgress them at once? Men generally, under such a government as this, think that they ought to wait until they have persuaded the majority to alter them. They think that, if they should resist, the remedy would be worse than the evil. But it is the fault of the government itself that the remedy *is* worse than the evil. *It* makes it worse. Why is it not more apt to anticipate and provide for reform? Why does it not cherish its wise minority? Why does it cry and resist before it is hurt? Why does it not encourage its citizens to be on the alert to point out its faults, and *do* better than it would have them? Why does it always crucify Christ, and excommunicate Copernicus and Luther, and pronounce Washington and Franklin rebels?

One would think, that a deliberate and practical denial of its authority was the only offense never contemplated by government; else, why has it not assigned its definite, its suitable and proportionate penalty? If a man who has no property refuses but once to earn nine shillings for the state, he is put in prison for a period unlimited by any law that

I know, and determined only by the discretion of those who placed him there; but if he should steal ninety times nine shillings from the state, he is soon permitted to go at large again.

If the injustice is part of the necessary friction of the machine of government, let it go, let it go: perchance it will wear smooth, — certainly the machine will wear out. If the injustice has a spring, or a pulley, or a rope, or a crank, exclusively for itself, then perhaps you may consider whether the remedy will not be worse than the evil; but if it is of such a nature that it requires you to be the agent of injustice to another, then, I say, break the law. Let your life be a counter friction to stop the machine. What I have to do is to see, at any rate, that I do not lend myself to the wrong which I condemn.

As for adopting the ways which the state has provided for remedying the evil, I know not of such ways. They take too much time, and a man's life will be gone. I have other affairs to attend to. I came into this world, not chiefly to make this a good place to live in, but to live in it, be it good or bad. A man has not everything to do, but something; and because he cannot do *everything*, it is not necessary that he should do *something* wrong. It is not my business to be petitioning the Governor or the Legislature any more than it is theirs to petition me; and if they should not hear my petition, what should I do then? But in this case the state has provided no way: its very Constitution is the evil. This may seem to be harsh and stubborn and unconciliatory; but it is to treat with the utmost kindness and consideration the only spirit that can appreciate or deserves it. So is all change for the better, like birth and death, which convulse the body.

I do not hesitate to say, that those who call themselves Abolitionists should at once effectually withdraw their support, both in person and property, from the government of Massachusetts, and not wait till they constitute a majority of one, before they suffer the right to prevail through them. I think that it is enough if they have God on their side, without waiting for that other one. Moreover, any man more right than his neighbors constitutes a majority of one already.

I meet this American government, or its representative, the state government, directly, and face to face, once a year — no more — in the person of its tax-gatherer; this is the only mode in which a man situated as I am necessarily meets it; and it then says distinctly, Recognize me; and the simplest, the most effectual, and, in the present posture of affairs, the indispensablest mode of treating with it on this head, of expressing your little satisfaction with and love for it is to deny it then. My civil neighbor, the tax-gatherer, is the very man I have to deal with, — for it is, after all, with men and not with parchment that I quarrel, — and he has voluntarily chosen to be an agent of the government. How shall he ever know well what he is and does as an officer of the government, or as a man, until he is obliged to consider whether he shall treat me, his neighbor, for whom he has respect, as a neighbor and well-disposed man, or as a maniac and disturber of the peace, and see if he can get over this obstruction to his neighborliness without a ruder and more impetuous thought or speech corresponding with his action. I know this well, that if one thousand, if one hundred, if ten men whom I could name, — if ten *honest* men only, — ay, if *one* HONEST man, in this State of Massachusetts, *ceasing to hold slaves*, were actually to withdraw from this copartnership, and be locked up in the county jail therefor, it would be the abolition of slavery in America. For it matters not how small the beginning may seem to be: what is once well done is done forever. But we love better to talk about it: that we say is our mission. Reform keeps many scores of newspapers in its service, but not one man. If my esteemed neighbor, the State's ambassador, who will devote his days to the settlement of the question of human rights in the Council Chamber, instead of being threatened with the prisons of Carolina, were to sit down the prisoner of Massachusetts, that State which is so anxious to foist the sin of slavery upon her sister, — though at present she can discover only an act of inhospitality to be the ground of a quarrel with her, — the Legislature would not wholly waive the subject the following winter.

Under a government which imprisons any

unjustly, the true place for a just man is also a prison. The proper place today, the only place which Massachusetts has provided for her freer and less desponding spirits, is in her prisons, to be put out and locked out of the State by her own act, as they have already put themselves out by their principles. It is there that the fugitive slave, and the Mexican prisoner on parole, and the Indian come to plead the wrongs of his race should find them; on that separate, but more free and honorable ground, where the State places those who are not *with* her, but *against* her, — the only house in a slave State in which a free man can abide with honor. If any think that their influence would be lost there, and their voices no longer afflict the ear of the State, that they would not be as an enemy within its walls, they do not know by how much truth is stronger than error, nor how much more eloquently and effectively he can combat injustice who has experienced a little in his own person. Cast your whole vote, not a strip of paper merely, but your whole influence. A minority is powerless while it conforms to the majority; it is not even a minority then; but it is irresistible when it clogs by its whole weight. If the alternative is to keep all just men in prison, or give up war and slavery, the State will not hesitate which to choose. If a thousand men were not to pay their tax-bills this year, that would not be a violent and bloody measure, as it would be to pay them, and enable the State to commit violence and shed innocent blood. This is, in fact, the definition of a peaceable revolution, if any such is possible. If the tax-gatherer, or any other public officer, asks me, as one has done, "But what shall I do?" my answer is, "If you really wish to do anything, resign your office." When the subject has refused allegiance, and the officer has resigned his office, then the revolution is accomplished. But even suppose blood should flow. Is there not a sort of blood shed when the conscience is wounded? Through this wound a man's real manhood and immortality flow out, and he bleeds to an everlasting death. I see this blood flowing now.

I have contemplated the imprisonment of the offender, rather than the seizure of his goods, — though both will serve the same purpose, — because they who assert the purest right, and consequently are most dangerous to a corrupt State, commonly have not spent much time in accumulating property. To such the State renders comparatively small service, and a slight tax is wont to appear exorbitant, particularly if they are obliged to earn it by special labor with their hands. If there were one who lived wholly without the use of money, the State itself would hesitate to demand it of him. But the rich man — not to make any invidious comparison — is always sold to the institution which makes him rich. Absolutely speaking, the more money, the less virtue; for money comes between a man and his objects, and obtains them for him; and it was certainly no great virtue to obtain it. It puts to rest many questions which he would otherwise be taxed to answer; while the only new question which it puts is the hard but superfluous one, how to spend it. Thus his moral ground is taken from under his feet. The opportunities of living are diminished in proportion as what are called the "means" are increased. The best thing a man can do for his culture when he is rich is to endeavor to carry out those schemes which he entertained when he was poor. Christ answered the Herodians according to their condition. "Show me the tribute-money," said he; — and one took a penny out of his pocket; — if you use money which has the image of Cæsar on it, and which he has made current and valuable, that is, *if you are men of the State*, and gladly enjoy the advantages of Cæsar's government, then pay him back some of his own when he demands it. "Render therefore to Cæsar that which is Cæsar's, and to God those things which are God's," — leaving them no wiser than before as to which was which; for they did not wish to know.

When I converse with the freest of my neighbors, I perceive that, whatever they may say about the magnitude and seriousness of the question, and their regard for the public tranquillity, the long and the short of the matter is, that they cannot spare the protection of the existing government, and they dread the consequences to their property and families of disobedience to it. For my own part, I should not like to think that I rely on the protection of the State. But, if I deny the authority of the State when it presents its tax-bill, it will soon take and waste all my property, and so harass me and my children without end. This is hard. This makes it impossible for a man to live honestly, and at the same time comfortably, in outward respects. It will not be worth the while to accumulate property; that would be sure to go again. You must hire or squat somewhere, and raise but a small crop, and eat that soon. You must live within yourself, and depend upon yourself always tucked up and ready for a start, and not have many affairs. A man may grow rich in Turkey even, if he will be in all respects a good subject of the Turkish government. Confucius said: "If a state is governed by the principles of reason, poverty and misery are subjects of shame; if a state is not governed by the principles of reason, riches and honors are the subjects of shame." No: until I want the protection of Massachusetts to be extended to me in some distant Southern port, where my liberty is endangered, or until I am bent solely on building up an estate at home by peaceful enterprise, I can afford to refuse allegiance to Massachusetts, and her right to my property and life. It costs me less in every sense to incur the penalty of disobedience to the State than it would to obey. I should feel as if I were worth less in that case.

Some years ago, the State met me in behalf of the Church, and commanded me to pay a certain sum toward the support of a clergyman whose preaching my father attended, but never I myself. "Pay," it said, "or be locked up in the jail." I declined to pay. But, unfortunately, another man saw fit to pay it. I did not see why the schoolmaster should be taxed to support the priest, and not the priest the schoolmaster; for I was not the State's schoolmaster, but I supported myself by voluntary subscription. I did not see why the lyceum should not present its tax-bill, and have the State to back its demand, as well as the Church. However, at the request of the selectmen, I condescended to make some such statement as this in writing:

—"Know all men by these presents, that I, Henry Thoreau, do not wish to be regarded as a member of any incorporated society which I have not joined." This I gave to the town clerk; and he has it. The State, having thus learned that I did not wish to be regarded as a member of that church, has never made a like demand on me since; though it said that it must adhere to its original presumption that time. If I had known how to name them, I should then have signed off in detail from all the societies which I never signed on to; but I did not know where to find a complete list.

I have paid no poll-tax for six years. I was put into a jail once on this account, for one night; and, as I stood considering the walls of solid stone, two or three feet thick, the door of wood and iron, a foot thick, and the iron grating which strained the light, I could not help being struck with the foolishness of that institution which treated me as if I were mere flesh and blood and bones, to be locked up. I wondered that it should have concluded at length that this was the best use it could put me to, and had never thought to avail itself of my services in some way. I saw that, if there was a wall of stone between me and my townsmen, there was a still more difficult one to climb or break through before they could get to be as free as I was. I did not for a moment feel confined, and the walls seemed a great waste of stone and mortar. I felt as if I alone of all my townsmen had paid my tax. They plainly did not know how to treat me, but behaved like persons who are underbred. In every threat and in every compliment there was a blunder; for they thought that my chief desire was to stand the other side of that stone wall. I could not but smile to see how industriously they locked the door on my meditations, which followed them out again without let or hindrance, and *they* were really all that was dangerous. As they could not reach me, they had resolved to punish my body; just as boys, if they cannot come at some person against whom they have a spite, will abuse his dog. I saw that the State was half-witted, that it was timid as a lone woman with her silver spoons, and that it did not know its friends from its foes, and I lost all my remaining respect for it, and pitied it.

Thus the State never intentionally confronts a man's sense, intellectual or moral, but only his body, his senses. It is not armed with superior wit or honesty, but with superior physical strength. I was not born to be forced. I will breathe after my own fashion. Let us see who is the strongest. What force has a multitude? They only can force me who obey a higher law than I. They force me to become like themselves. I do not hear of *men* being *forced* to live this way or that by masses of men. What sort of life were that to live? When I meet a government which says to me, "Your money or your life," why should I be in haste to give it my money? It may be in a great strait, and not know what to do: I cannot help that. It must help itself; do as I do. It is not worth the while to snivel about it. I am not responsible for the successful working of the machinery of society. I am not the son of the engineer. I perceive that, when an acorn and a chestnut fall side by side, the one does not remain inert to make way for the other, but both obey their own laws, and spring and grow and flourish as best they can, till one, perchance, overshadows and destroys the other. If a plant cannot live according to its nature, it dies; and so a man.

The night in prison was novel and interesting enough. The prisoners in their shirtsleeves were enjoying a chat and the evening air in the doorway, when I entered. But the jailer said, "Come, boys, it is time to lock up;" and so they dispersed, and I heard the sound of their steps returning into the hollow apartments. My room-mate was introduced to me by the jailer as "a first-rate fellow and a clever man." When the door was locked, he showed me where to hang my hat, and how he managed matters there. The rooms were whitewashed once a month; and this one, at least, was the whitest, most simply furnished, and probably the neatest apartment in the town. He naturally wanted to know where I came from, and what brought me there; and, when I had told him, I asked him in my turn how he came there, presuming him to be an honest man, of course; and, as the world goes, I believe he was. "Why," said he, "they accuse me of burning a barn; but I never did it." As near as I could discover, he had probably gone to bed in a barn when drunk, and smoked his pipe there; and so a barn was burnt. He had the reputation of being a clever man, had been there some three months waiting for his trial to come on, and would have to wait as much longer; but he was quite domesticated and contented, since he got his board for nothing, and thought that he was well treated.

He occupied one window, and I the other; and I saw that if one stayed there long, his principal business would be to look out the window. I had soon read all the tracts that were left there, and examined where former prisoners had broken out, and where a grate had been sawed off, and heard the history of the various occupants of that room; for I found that even here there was a history and a gossip which never circulated beyond the walls of the jail. Probably this is the only house in the town where verses are composed, which are afterward printed in a circular form, but not published. I was shown quite a long list of verses which were composed by some young men who had been detected in an attempt to escape, who avenged themselves by singing them.

I pumped my fellow-prisoner as dry as I could, for fear I should never see him again; but at length he showed me which was my bed, and left me to blow out the lamp.

It was like traveling into a far country, such as I had never expected to behold, to lie there for one night. It seemed to me that I never had heard the town-clock strike before, nor the evening sounds of the village; for we slept with the windows open, which were inside the grating. It was to see my native village in the light of the Middle Ages, and our Concord was turned into a Rhine stream, and visions of knights and castles passed before me. They were the voices of old burghers that I heard in the streets. I was an involuntary spectator and auditor of whatever was done and said in the kitchen of the adjacent village-inn, — a wholly new and rare experience to me. It was a closer view of my native town. I was fairly inside of it. I never had seen its institutions before. This is one of its peculiar institutions; for it is a shire town. I began to comprehend what its inhabitants were about.

In the morning, our breakfasts were put through the hole in the door, in small oblong-square tin pans, made to fit, and holding a pint of chocolate, with brown bread, and an iron spoon. When they called for the vessels again, I was green enough to return what bread I had left; but my comrade seized it, and said that I should lay that up for lunch or dinner. Soon after he was let out to work at haying in a neighboring field, whither he went every day, and would not be back till noon; so he bade me good-day, saying that he doubted if he should see me again.

When I came out of prison, — for some one interfered, and paid that tax, — I did not perceive that great changes had taken place on the common, such as he observed who went in a youth and emerged a tottering and gray-headed man; and yet a change had to my eyes come over the scene, — the town, and State, and country, — greater than any that mere time could effect. I saw yet more distinctly the State in which I lived. I saw to what extent the people among whom I lived could be trusted as good neighbors and friends; that their friendship was for summer weather only; that they did not greatly propose to do right; that they were a distinct race from me by their prejudices and super-stitions, as the Chinamen and Malays are; that in their sacrifices to humanity they ran no risks, not even to their property; that after all they were not so noble but they treated the thief as he had treated them, and hoped, by a certain outward observance and a few prayers, and by walking in a particular straight though useless path from time to time, to save their souls. This may be to judge my neighbors harshly; for I believe that many of them are not aware that they have such an institution as the jail in their village.

It was formerly the custom in our village, when a poor debtor came out of jail, for his acquaintances to salute him, looking through their fingers, which were crossed to represent the grating of a jail window, "How do ye do?" My neighbors did not thus salute me, but first looked at me, and then at one an-other, as if I had returned from a long journey. I was put into jail as I was going to the shoemaker's to get a shoe which was mended. When I was let out the next morn-ing, I proceeded to finish my errand, and, having put on my mended shoe, joined a huckleberry party, who were impatient to put themselves under my conduct; and in half an hour, — for the horse was soon tackled, — was in the midst of a huckleberry field, on one of our highest hills, two miles off, and then the State was nowhere to be seen.

This is the whole history of "My Prisons."

I have never declined paying the highway tax, because I am as desirous of being a good neighbor as I am of being a bad subject; and as for supporting schools, I am doing my part to educate my fellow-countrymen now. It is for no particular item in the tax-bill that I refuse to pay it. I simply wish to refuse allegiance to the State, to withdraw and stand aloof from it effectually. I do not care to trace the course of my dollar, if I could, till it buys a man or a musket to shoot one with, — the dollar is innocent, — but I am concerned to trace the effects of my alle-giance. In fact, I quietly declare war with the State, after my fashion, though I will still make what use and get what advantage of her I can, as is usual in such cases.

If others pay the tax which is demanded of me, from a sympathy with the State, they do but what they have already done in their own case, or rather they abet injustice to a greater extent than the State requires. If they pay the tax from a mistaken interest in the in-dividual taxed, to save his property, or prevent his going to jail, it is because they have not considered wisely how far they let their private feelings interfere with the public good.

This, then, is my position at present. But one cannot be too much on his guard in such a case, lest his action be biased by obstinacy or an undue regard for the opinions of men. Let him see that he does only what belongs to himself and to the hour.

I think sometimes, Why, this people mean well, they are only ignorant; they would do better if they knew how: why give your neighbors this pain to treat you as they are not inclined to? But I think again, This is no reason why I should do as they do, or permit others to suffer much greater pain of a different kind. Again, I sometimes say to myself, When many millions of men, without heat, without ill will, without personal feeling of any kind, demand of you a few shillings only, without the possibility, such is their constitution, of retracting or altering their present demand, and without the possibility, on your side, of appeal to any other millions, why expose yourself to this overwhelming brute force? You do not resist cold and hunger, the winds and the waves, thus obstinately; you quietly submit to a thousand similar necessities. You do not put your head into the fire. But just in proportion as I regard this as not wholly a brute force, but partly a human force, and consider that I have relations to those millions as to so many millions of men, and not of mere brute or inanimate things, I see that appeal is possible, first and instantaneously, from them to the Maker of them, and, secondly, from them to themselves. But if I put my head deliberately into the fire, there is no appeal to fire or to the Maker of fire, and I have only myself to blame. If I could convince myself that I have any right to be satisfied with men as they are, and to treat them accordingly, and not according, in some respects, to my requisitions and expectations of what they and I ought to be, then, like a good Mussulman and fatalist, I should endeavor to be satisfied with things as they are, and say it is the will of God. And, above all, there is this difference between resisting this and a purely brute or natural force, that I can resist this with some effect; but I cannot expect, like Orpheus, to change the nature of the rocks and trees and beasts.

I do not wish to quarrel with any man or nation. I do not wish to split hairs, to make fine distinctions, or set myself up as better than my neighbors. I seek rather, I may say, even an excuse for conforming to the laws of the land. I am but too ready to conform to them. Indeed, I have reason to suspect myself on this head; and each year, as the tax-gatherer comes round, I find myself disposed to review the acts and position of the general and State governments, and the spirit of the people, to discover a pretext for conformity.

> "We must affect our country as our parents,
> And if at any time we alienate
> Our love or industry from doing it honor,
> We must respect effects and teach the soul
> Matter of conscience and religion,
> And not desire of rule or benefit."

I believe that the State will soon be able to take all my work of this sort out of my hands, and then I shall be no better a patriot than my fellow-countrymen. Seen from a lower point of view, the Constitution, with all its faults, is very good; the law and the courts are very respectable; even this State and this American government are, in many respects, very admirable, and rare things, to be thankful for, such as a great many have described them; but seen from a point of view a little higher, they are what I have described them; seen from a higher still, and the highest, who shall say what they are, or that they are worth looking at or thinking of at all?

However, the government does not concern me much, and I shall bestow the fewest possible thoughts on it. It is not many moments that I live under a government, even in this world. If a man is thought-free, fancy-free, imagination-free, that which *is not* never for a long time appearing *to be* to him, unwise rulers or reformers cannot fatally interrupt him.

I know that most men think differently from myself; but those whose lives are by profession devoted to the study of these or kindred subjects content me as little as any. Statesmen and legislators, standing so completely within the institution, never distinctly and nakedly behold it. They speak of moving society, but have no resting-place without it. They may be men of a certain experience and discrimination, and have no doubt invented ingenious and even useful systems, for which we sincerely thank them; but all their wit and usefulness lie within certain not very wide limits. They are wont to forget that the world is not governed by policy and expediency. Webster never goes behind government, and so cannot speak with authority about it. His words are wisdom to those legislators who contemplate no essential reform in the existing government; but for thinkers, and those who legislate for all time, he never once glances at the subject. I know of those whose serene and wise speculations on this theme would soon reveal the limits of his mind's range and hospitality. Yet, compared with the cheap professions of most reformers, and the still cheaper wisdom and eloquence of politicians in general, his are almost the only sensible and valuable words, and we thank Heaven for him. Comparatively, he is always strong, original, and, above all, practical. Still, his quality is not wisdom, but prudence. The lawyer's truth is not Truth, but consistency or a consistent expediency. Truth is always in harmony with herself, and is not concerned chiefly to reveal the justice that may consist with wrong-doing. He well deserves to be called, as he has been called, the Defender of the Constitution. There are really no blows to be given by him but defensive ones. He is not a leader, but a follower. His leaders are the men of '87. "I have never made an effort," he says, "and never propose to make an effort; I have never countenanced an effort, and never mean to countenance an effort, to disturb the arrangement as originally made, by which the various States came into the Union." Still thinking of the sanction which the Constitution gives to slavery, he says, "Because it was a part of the original compact, — let it stand." Notwithstanding his special acuteness and ability, he is unable to take a fact out of its merely political relations, and behold it as it lies absolutely to be disposed of by the intellect, — what, for instance, it behooves a man to do here in America to-day with regard to slavery, — but ventures, or is driven, to make some such desperate answer as the following, while professing to speak absolutely, and as a private man, — from which what new and singular code of social duties might be inferred? "The manner," says he, "in which the governments of those States where slavery exists are to regulate it is for their own consideration, under their responsibility to their constituents, to the general laws of propriety, humanity, and justice, and to God. Associations formed elsewhere, springing from a feeling of human-ity, or any other cause, have nothing whatever to do with it. They have never received any encouragement from me, and they never will."

They who know of no purer sources of truth, who have traced up its stream no higher, stand, and wisely stand, by the Bible and the Constitution, and drink at it there with reverence and humility; but they who behold where it comes trickling into this lake or that pool, gird up their loins once more, and continue their pilgrimage toward its fountain-head.

No man with a genius for legislation has appeared in America. They are rare in the history of the world. There are orators, politicians, and eloquent men, by the thousand; but the speaker has not yet opened his mouth to speak who is capable of settling the much-vexed questions of the day. We love eloquence for its own sake, and not for any truth which it may utter, or any heroism it may inspire. Our legislators have not yet learned the comparative value of free-trade and of freedom, of union, and of rectitude, to a nation. They have no genius or talent for comparatively humble questions of taxation and finance, commerce and manufactures and agriculture. If we were left solely to the wordy wit of legislators in Congress for our guidance, uncorrected by the seasonable experience and the effectual complaints of the people, America would not long retain her rank among the nations. For eighteen hundred years, though perchance I have no right to say it, the New Testament has been written; yet where is the legislator who has wisdom and practical talent enough to avail himself of the light which it sheds on the science of legislation?

The authority of government, even such as I am willing to submit to, — for I will cheerfully obey those who know and can do better than I, and in many things even those who neither know nor can do so well, — is still an impure one: to be strictly just, it must have the sanction and consent of the governed. It can have no pure right over my person and property but what I concede to it. The progress from an absolute to a limited monarchy, from a limited monarchy to a democracy, is a progress toward a true respect for the individual. Even the Chinese philosopher was wise enough to regard the individual as the basis of the empire. Is a democracy, such as we know it, the last improvement possible in government? Is it not possible to take a step further towards recognizing and organizing the rights of man? There will never be a really free and enlightened State until the State comes to recognize the individual as a higher and independent power, from which all its own power and authority are derived, and treats him accordingly. I please myself with imagining a State at last which can afford to be just to all men, and to treat the individual with respect as a neighbor; which even would not think it inconsistent with its own repose if a few were to live aloof from it, not meddling with it, nor embraced by it, who fulfilled all the duties of neighbors and fellow-men. A State which bore this kind of fruit, and suffered it to drop off as fast as it ripened, would prepare the way for a still more perfect and glorious State, which also I have imagined, but not yet anywhere seen.

Economy

(*Walden*, 1854: ch. I)

"Thoreau lived in his Walden camp but two years, 1845–1847, and, as his narrative clearly shows, by no means exiled himself from home and companions. His hermitage was within easy walking distance of Concord; and, though his seclusion meant privacy at times, he was by no means debarred from society. The life in the woods was a characteristic expression of his stout independence of conditions, and served his purpose of living frugally and securing leisure for observation, reading, and writing." (Introductory note to *Walden* in the Walden edition of Thoreau's Writings.)

The long first chapter of *Walden*, entitled Economy, is represented below by salient passages. All of the other chapters printed here (Where I Lived, and What I Lived For; Sounds; and Conclusion) are complete.

When I wrote the following pages, or rather the bulk of them, I lived alone, in the woods, a mile from any neighbor, in a house which I had built myself, on the shore of Walden Pond, in Concord, Massachusetts, and earned my living by the labor of my hands only. I lived there two years and two

months. At present I am a sojourner in civilized life again.

I should not obtrude my affairs so much on the notice of my readers if very particular inquiries had not been made by my townsmen concerning my mode of life, which some would call impertinent, though they do not appear to me at all impertinent, but, considering the circumstances, very natural and pertinent. Some have asked what I got to eat; if I did not feel lonesome; if I was not afraid; and the like. Others have been curious to learn what portion of my income I devoted to charitable purposes; and some, who have large families, how many poor children I maintained. I will therefore ask those of my readers who feel no particular interest in me to pardon me if I undertake to answer some of these questions in this book. In most books, the *I*, or first person, is omitted; in this it will be retained; that, in respect to egotism, is the main difference. We commonly do not remember that it is, after all, always the first person that is speaking. I should not talk so much about myself if there were anybody else whom I knew as well. Unfortunately, I am confined to this theme by the narrowness of my experience. Moreover, I, on my side, require of every writer, first or last, a simple and sincere account of his own life, and not merely what he has heard of other men's lives; some such account as he would send to his kindred from a distant land; for if he has lived sincerely, it must have been in a distant land to me. Perhaps these pages are more particularly addressed to poor students. As for the rest of my readers, they will accept such portions as apply to them. I trust that none will stretch the seams in putting on the coat, for it may do good service to him whom it fits.

I would fain say something, not so much concerning the Chinese and Sandwich Islanders, as you who read these pages, who are said to live in New England; something about your condition, especially your outward condition or circumstances in this world, in this town, what it is, whether it is necessary that it be as bad as it is, whether it cannot be improved as well as not. I have traveled a good deal in Concord; and everywhere, in shops, and offices, and fields, the inhabitants have appeared to me to be doing penance in a thousand remarkable ways. What I have heard of Brahmins sitting exposed to four fires and looking in the face of the sun; or hanging suspended, with their heads downward, over flames; or looking at the heavens over their shoulders "until it becomes impossible for them to resume their natural position, while from the twist of the neck nothing but liquids can pass into the stomach"; or dwelling, chained for life, at the foot of a tree; or measuring with their bodies, like caterpillars, the breadth of vast empires; or standing on one leg on the tops of pillars, — even these forms of conscious penance are hardly more incredible and astonishing than the scenes which I daily witness. The twelve labors of Hercules were trifling in comparison with those which my neighbors have undertaken; for they were only twelve, and had an end; but I could never see that these men slew or captured any monster or finished any labor. They have no friend Iolas to burn with a hot iron the root of the hydra's head, but as soon as one head is crushed, two spring up.

I see young men, my townsmen, whose misfortune it is to have inherited farms, houses, barns, cattle, and farming tools; for these are more easily acquired than got rid of. Better if they had been born in the open pasture and suckled by a wolf, that they might have seen with clearer eyes what field they were called to labor in. Who made them serfs of the soil? Why should they eat their sixty acres, when man is condemned to eat only his peck of dirt? Why should they begin digging their graves as soon as they are born? They have got to live a man's life, pushing all these things before them, and get on as well as they can. How many a poor immortal soul have I met well nigh crushed and smothered under its load, creeping down the road of life, pushing before it a barn seventy-five feet by forty, its Augean stables never cleansed, and one hundred acres of land tillage, mowing, pasture, and wood-lot! The portionless, who struggle with no such unnecessary inherited encumbrances, find it labor enough to subdue and cultivate a few cubic feet of flesh. * * *

Near the end of March, 1845, I borrowed **an axe and went down to the woods by Wal-**den Pond, nearest to where I intended to build my house, and began to cut down some tall arrowy white pines, still in their youth, for timber. It is difficult to begin without borrowing, but perhaps it is the most generous course thus to permit your fellow-men to have an interest in your enterprise. The owner of the axe, as he released his hold on it, said that it was the apple of his eye; but I returned it sharper than I received it. It was a pleasant hillside where I worked, covered with pine woods, through which I looked out on the pond, and a small open field in the woods where pines and hickories were springing up. The ice in the pond was not yet dissolved, though there were some open spaces, and it was all dark colored and saturated with water. There were some slight flurries of snow during the days that I worked there; but for the most part when I came out on to the railroad, on my way home, its yellow sand heap stretched away gleaming in the hazy atmosphere, and the rails shone in the spring sun, and I heard the lark and pewee and other birds already come to commence another year with us. They were pleasant spring days, in which the winter of man's discontent was thawing as well as the earth, and the life that had lain torpid began to stretch itself. One day, when my axe had come off and I had cut a green hickory for a wedge, driving it with a stone, and had placed the whole to soak in a pond hole in order to swell the wood, I saw a striped snake run into the water, and he lay on the bottom, apparently without inconvenience, as long as I stayed there, or more than a quarter of an hour; perhaps because he had not yet fairly come out of the torpid state. It appeared to me that for a like reason men remain in their present low and primitive condition; but if they should feel the influence of the spring of springs arousing them, they would of necessity rise to a higher and more ethereal life. I had previously seen the snakes in frosty mornings in my path with portions of their bodies still numb and inflexible, waiting for the sun to thaw them. On the 1st of April it rained and melted the ice, and in the early part of the day, which was very foggy, I heard a stray goose groping about over the pond and cackling as if lost, or like the spirit of the fog.

So I went on for some days cutting and hewing timber, and also studs and rafters, all with my narrow axe, not having many communicable or scholar-like thoughts singing to myself, —

> Men say they know many things;
> But lo! they have taken wings, —
> The arts and sciences,
> And a thousand appliances;
> The wind that blows
> Is all that anybody knows.

I hewed the main timbers six inches square, most of the studs on two sides only, and the rafters and floor timbers on one side, leaving the rest of the bark on, so that they were just as straight and much stronger than sawed ones. Each stick was carefully mortised or tenoned by its stump, for I had borrowed other tools by this time. My days in the woods were not very long ones; yet I usually carried my dinner of bread and butter, and read the newspaper in which it was wrapped, at noon, sitting amid the green pine boughs which I had cut off, and to my bread was imparted some of their fragrance, for my hands were covered with a thick coat of pitch. Before I had done I was more the friend than the foe of the pine tree, though I had cut down some of them, having become better acquainted with it. Sometimes a rambler in the wood was attracted by the sound of my axe, and we chatted pleasantly over the chips which I had made.

By the middle of April, for I made no haste in my work, but rather made the most of it, my house was framed and ready for the raising. I had already bought the shanty of James Collins, an Irishman who worked on the Fitchburg Railroad, for boards. James Collins' shanty was considered an uncommonly fine one. When I called to see it he was not at home. I walked about the outside, at first unobserved from within, the window was so deep and high. It was of small dimensions, with a peaked cottage roof, and not much else to be seen, the dirt being raised five feet all around as if it were a compost heap. The roof was the soundest part, though a good deal warped and made brittle by the sun. Doorsill there was none, but a perennial passage for the hens under the door board. Mrs. C. came to the door and asked me to view it from the inside. The hens were driven in by my approach. It was dark, and had a dirt floor for the most part, dank, clammy, and aguish, only here a board and there a board which would not bear removal. She lighted a lamp to show me the inside of the roof and the walls, and also that the board floor extended under the bed, warning me not to step into the cellar, a sort of dust hole two feet deep. In her own words, they were "good boards overhead, good boards all around, and a good window," — of two whole squares originally, only the cat had passed out that way lately. There was a stove, a bed, and a place to sit, an infant in the house where it was born, a silk parasol, gilt-framed looking-glass, and a patent new coffeemill nailed to an oak sapling, all told. The bargain was soon concluded, for James had in the meanwhile returned. I to pay four dollars and twenty-five cents tonight, he to vacate at five tomorrow morning, selling to nobody else meanwhile: I to take possession at six. It were well, he said, to be there early, and anticipate certain indistinct but wholly unjust claims on the score of ground rent and fuel. This he assured me was the only encumbrance. At six I passed him and his family on the road. One large bundle held their all, — bed, coffeemill, looking-glass, hens, — all but the cat; she took to the woods and became a wild cat, and, as I learned afterward, trod in a trap set for woodchucks, and so became a dead cat at last.

I took down this dwelling the same morning, drawing the nails, and removed it to the pond side by small cartloads, spreading the boards on the grass there to bleach and warp back again in the sun. One early thrush gave me a note or two as I drove along the woodland path. I was informed treacherously by a young Patrick that neighbor Seeley, an Irishman, in the intervals of the carting, transferred the still tolerable straight, and drivable nails, staples, and spikes to his pocket, and then stood when I came back to pass the time of day, and look freshly up, unconcerned, with spring thoughts, at the devastation; there being a dearth of work, as he said. He was there to represent spectatordom, and help make this seemingly insignificant event one with the removal of the gods of Troy.

I dug my cellar in the side of a hill sloping

to the south, where a woodchuck had formerly dug his burrow, down through sumach and blackberry roots, and the lowest stain of vegetation, six feet square by seven deep, to a fine sand where potatoes would not freeze in any winter. The sides were left shelving, and not stoned; but the sun having never shone on them, the sand still keeps its place. It was but two hours' work. I took particular pleasure in this breaking of ground, for in almost all latitudes men dig into the earth for an equable temperature. Under the most splendid house in the city is still to be found the cellar where they store their roots as of old, and long after the superstructure has disappeared posterity remark its dent in the earth. The house is still but a sort of porch at the entrance of a burrow.

At length, in the beginning of May, with the help of some of my acquaintances, rather to improve so good an occasion for neighborliness than from any necessity, I set up the frame of my house. No man was ever more honored in the character of his raisers than I. They are destined, I trust, to assist at the raising of loftier structures one day. I began to occupy my house on the 4th of July, as soon as it was boarded and roofed, for the boards were carefully featheredged and lapped, so that it was perfectly impervious to rain; but before boarding I laid the foundation of a chimney at one end, bringing two cartloads of stones up the hill from the pond in my arms. I built the chimney after my hoeing in the fall, before a fire became necessary for warmth, doing my cooking in the meanwhile out of doors on the ground, early in the morning: which mode I still think is in some respects more convenient and agreeable than the usual one. When it stormed before my bread was baked, I fixed a few boards over the fire, and sat under them to watch my loaf, and passed some pleasant hours in that way. In those days, when my hands were much employed, I read but little, but the least scraps of paper which lay on the ground, my holder, or tablecloth, afforded me as much entertainment, in fact answered the same purpose as the Iliad. * * *

Before winter I built a chimney, and shingled the sides of my house, which were already impervious to rain, with imperfect and sappy shingles made of the first slice of the log, whose edges I was obliged to straighten with a plane.

I have thus a tight shingled and plastered house, ten feet wide by fifteen long, and eight-feet posts, with a garret and a closet, a large window on each side, two trap doors, one door at the end, and a brick fireplace opposite. The exact cost of my house, paying the usual price for such materials as I used, but not counting the work, all of which was done by myself, was as follows; and I give the details because very few are able to tell exactly what their houses cost, and fewer still, if any, the separate cost of the various materials which compose them: —

Boards............	$8.03½,	mostly shanty boards.
Refuse shingles for roof and sides....	4.00	
Laths.............	1.25	
Two secondhand windows with glass..........	2.43	
One thousand old brick...........	4.00	
Two casks of lime..	2.40	That was high.
Hair.............	.31	More than I needed.
Mantle-tree iron...	.15	
Nails.............	3.90	
Hinges and screws .	.14	
Latch.............	.10	
Chalk............	.01	
Transportation.....	1.40	I carried a good part on my back.
In all.........	$28.12½	

These are all the materials excepting the timber, stones, and sand, which I claimed by squatter's right. I have also a small woodshed adjoining, made chiefly of the stuff which was left after building the house.

I intend to build me a house which will surpass any on the main street in Concord in grandeur and luxury, as soon as it pleases me as much and will cost me no more than my present one.

I thus found that the student who wishes for a shelter can obtain one for a lifetime at an expense not greater than the rent which he now pays annually. If I seem to boast more than is becoming, my excuse is that I brag for humanity rather than for myself; and my shortcomings and inconsistencies do not affect the truth of my statement. Notwithstanding much cant and hypocrisy, — chaff which I find it difficult to separate from my wheat, but for which I am as sorry as any man, — I will breathe freely and stretch myself in this respect, it is such a relief to both the moral and physical system; and I am resolved that I will not through humility become the devil's attorney. I will endeavor to speak a good word for the truth. At Cambridge College the mere rent of a student's room, which is only a little larger than my own, is thirty dollars each year, though the corporation had the advantage of building thirty-two side by side and under one roof, and the occupant suffers the inconvenience of many and noisy neighbors, and perhaps a residence in the fourth story. I cannot but think that if we had more true wisdom in these respects, not only less education would be needed, because, forsooth, more would already have been acquired, but the pecuniary expense of getting an education would in a great measure vanish. Those conveniences which the student requires at Cambridge or elsewhere cost him or somebody else ten times as great a sacrifice of life as they would with proper management on both sides. Those things for which the most money is demanded are never the things which the student most wants. Tuition, for instance, is an important item in the term bill, while for the far more valuable education which he gets by associating with the most cultivated of his contemporaries no charge is made. The mode of founding a college is, commonly, to get up a subscription of dollars and cents, and then following blindly the principles of a division of labor to its extreme, a principle which should never be followed but with circumspection, — to call in a contractor who makes this a subject of speculation, and he employs Irishmen or other operatives actually to lay the foundations, while the students that are to be are said to be fitting themselves for it; and for these oversights successive generations have to pay. I think that it would be *better than this*, for the students, or those who desire to be benefited by it, even to lay the foundation themselves. The student who secures his coveted leisure and retirement by systematically shirking any labor necessary to man obtains but an ignoble and unprofitable leisure, defrauding himself of the experience which alone can make leisure fruitful. "But," says one, "you do not mean that the students should go to work with their hands instead of their heads?" I do not mean that exactly, but I mean something which he might think a good deal like that; I mean that they should not *play* life, or *study* it merely, while the community supports them at this expensive game, but earnestly *live* it from beginning to end. How could youths better learn to live than by at once trying the experiment of living? Methinks this would exercise their minds as much as mathematics. If I wished a boy to know something about the arts and sciences, for instance, I would not pursue the common course, which is merely to send him into the neighborhood of some professor, where anything is professed and practiced but the art of life; — to survey the world through a telescope or a microscope, and never with his natural eye; to study chemistry, and not learn how his bread is made, or mechanics, and not learn how it is earned; to discover new satellites to Neptune, and not detect the motes in his eyes, or to what vagabond he is a satellite himself; or to be devoured by the monsters that swarm all around him, while contemplating the monsters in a drop of vinegar. Which would have advanced the most at the end of a month, — the boy who had made his own jackknife from the ore which he had dug and smelted, reading as much as would be necessary for this, — or the boy who had attended the lectures on metallurgy at the Institute in the meanwhile, and had received a Rogers' penknife from his father? Which would be most likely to cut his fingers? . . . To my astonishment I was informed on leaving college that I had studied navigation! — why, if I had taken one turn down the harbor I should have known more about it. Even the *poor* student studies and is taught only *political* economy, while that economy of living which is synonymous with philosophy is not even sincerely professed in our colleges. The consequence is that while he is reading Adam Smith, Ricardo, and Say, he runs his father in debt irretrievably. * * *

Before I finished my house, wishing to earn ten or twelve dollars by some honest and agreeable method, in order to meet my unusual expenses, I planted about two acres and a half of light and sandy soil near it chiefly with beans, but also a small part with potatoes, corn, peas, and turnips. The whole lot contains eleven acres, mostly growing up to pines and hickories, and was sold the preceding season for eight dollars and eight cents an acre. One farmer said that it was "good for nothing but to raise cheeping squirrels on." I put no manure whatever on this land, not being the owner, but merely a squatter, and not expecting to cultivate so much again, and I did not quite hoe it all once. I got out several cords of stumps in plowing, which supplied me with fuel for a long time, and left small circles of virgin mold, easily distinguishable through the summer by the greater luxuriance of the beans there. The dead and for the most part unmerchantable wood behind my house, and the driftwood from the pond, have supplied the remainder of my fuel. I was obliged to hire a team and a man for the plowing, though I held the plow myself. My farm outgoes for the first season were, for implements, seed, work, etc., $14.72½. The seed corn was given me. This never costs anything to speak of, unless you plant more than enough. I got twelve bushels of beans, and eighteen bushels of potatoes, beside some peas and sweet corn. The yellow corn and turnips were too late to come to anything. My whole income from the farm was

	$23.44
Deducting the outgoes	14.72½
There are left..........................	$ 8.71½

besides produce consumed and on hand at the time this estimate was made of the value of $4.50, — the amount on hand much more than balancing a little grass which I did not raise. All things considered, that is, considering the importance of a man's soul and of today, notwithstanding the short time occupied by my experiment, nay, partly even because of its transient character, I believe that that was doing better than any farmer in Concord did that year.

The next year I did better still, for I spaded up all the land which I required, about a third of an acre, and I learned from the experience of both years, not being in the least awed by many celebrated works on husbandry, Arthur Young among the rest, that

if one would live simply and eat only the crop which he raised, and raise no more than he ate, and not exchange it for an insufficient quantity of more luxurious and expensive things, he would need to cultivate only a few rods of ground, and that it would be cheaper to spade up that than to use oxen to plow it, and to select a fresh spot from time to time than to manure the old, and he could do all his necessary farm work as it were with his left hand at odd hours in the summer; and thus he would not be tied to an ox, or horse, or cow, or pig, as at present. I desire to speak impartially on this point, and as one not interested in the success or failure of the present economical and social arrangements. I was more independent than any farmer in Concord, for I was not anchored to a house or farm, but could follow the bent of my genius, which is a very crooked one, every moment. Besides being better off than they already, if my house had been burned or my crops had failed, I should have been nearly as well off as before. * * *

By surveying, carpentry, and day-labor of various other kinds in the village in the meanwhile, for I have as many trades as fingers, I had earned $13.34. The expense of food for eight months, namely, from July 4th to March 1st, the time when these estimates were made, though I lived there more than two years, — not counting potatoes, a little green corn, and some peas, which I had raised, nor considering the value of what was on hand at the last date, was

Rice..............	$1.73½	
Molasses..........	1.73	Cheapest form of the saccharine.
Rye meal..........	1.04¾	
Indian meal.......	.99¾	Cheaper than rye.
Pork..............	.22	
Flour.............	.88	Costs more than Indian meal, both money and trouble.
Sugar.............	.80	All experiments which failed
Lard.............	.65	
Apples............	.25	
Dried apples.......	.22	
Sweet potatoes.....	.10	
One pumpkin......	.06	
One watermelon....	.02	
Salt..............	.03	

Yes, I did eat $8.74, all told; but I should not thus unblushingly publish my guilt, if I did not know that most of my readers were equally guilty with myself, and that their deeds would look no better in print. The next year I sometimes caught a mess of fish for my dinner, and once I went so far as to slaughter a woodchuck which ravaged my beanfield, — effect his transmigration, as a Tartar would say, — and devour him, partly for experiment's sake; but though it afforded me a momentary enjoyment, notwithstanding a musky flavor, I saw that the longest use would not make that a good practice, however it might seem to have your woodchucks ready dressed by the village butcher.

Clothing and some incidental expenses within the same dates, though little can be inferred from this item, amounted to . $8.40¾
Oil and some household utensils 2.00

So that all the pecuniary outgoes, excepting for washing and mending, which for the most part were done out of the house, and their bills have not yet been received, — and these are all and more than all the ways by which money necessarily goes out in this part of the world, — were

House $28.12½
Farm, one year 14.72½
Food eight months 8.74
Clothing, etc., eight months 8.40¾
Oil, etc., eight months 2.00
In all $61.99¾

I address myself now to those of my readers who have a living to get. And to meet this I have for farm produce sold

$23.44
Earned by day-labor 13.34
In all $36.78

which subtracted from the sum of the outgoes leaves a balance of $25.21¾ on the one side, — this being very nearly the means with which I started, and the measure of expenses to be incurred, — and on the other, besides the leisure and independence and health thus secured, a comfortable house for me as long as I choose to occupy it.

These statistics, however accidental and therefore uninstructive they may appear, as they have a certain completeness, have a certain value also. Nothing was given me of which I have not rendered some account. It appears from the above estimate, that my food alone cost me in money about twenty-seven cents a week. It was for nearly two years after this, rye and Indian meal, without yeast, potatoes, rice, a very little salt pork, molasses, and salt, and my drink, water. It was fit that I should live on rice, mainly, who loved so well the philosophy of India. To meet the objections of some inveterate cavilers, I may as well state that if I dined out occasionally, as I always had done, and I trust shall have opportunities to do again, it was frequently to the detriment of my domestic arrangements. But the dining out, being, as I have stated, a constant element, does not in the least affect a comparative statement like this.

I learned from my two years' experience that it would cost incredibly little trouble to obtain one's necessary food, even in this latitude; that a man may use as simple a diet as the animals, and yet retain health and strength. I have made a satisfactory dinner, satisfactory on several accounts, simply off a dish of purslane (*Portulaca oleracea*) which I gathered in my cornfield, boiled and salted. I give the Latin on account of the savoriness of the trivial name. And pray what more can a reasonable man desire, in peaceful times, in ordinary noons, than a sufficient number of ears of green sweet-corn boiled, with the addition of salt? Even the little variety that I used was a yielding to the demands of appetite, and not of health. Yet men have come to such a pass that they frequently starve, not for want of necessaries, but for want of luxuries; and I know a good woman who thinks that her son lost his life because he took to drinking water only. * * *

One young man of my acquaintance, who has inherited some acres, told me that he thought he should live as I did, *if he had the means.* I would not have any one adopt *my* mode of living on any account; for, besides that before he has fairly learned it I may have found out another for myself, I desire that there may be as many different persons in the world as possible; but I would have each one be very careful to find out and pursue *his own* way, and not his father's or his mother's or his neighbor's instead. The youth may build or plant or sail, only let him not be hindered from doing that which he tells me he would like to do. It is by a mathematical point only that we are wise, as the sailor or the fugitive slave keeps the polestar in his eye; but that is sufficient guidance for all our life. We may not arrive at our port within a calculable period, but we would preserve the true course.

Undoubtedly, in this case, what is true for one is truer still for a thousand, as a large house is not proportionally more expensive than a small one, since one roof may cover, one cellar underlie, and one wall separate several apartments. But for my part, I preferred the solitary dwelling. Moreover, it will commonly be cheaper to build the whole yourself than to convince another of the advantage of the common wall; and when you have done this, the common partition, to be much cheaper, must be a thin one, and that other may prove a bad neighbor, and also not keep his side in repair. The only coöperation which is commonly possible is exceedingly partial and superficial; and what little true coöperation there is, is as if it were not, being a harmony inaudible to men. If a man has faith he will coöperate with equal faith everywhere; if he has not faith, he will continue to live like the rest of the world, whatever company he is joined to. To coöperate, in the highest as well as the lowest sense, means *to get our living together*. I heard it proposed lately that two young men should travel together over the world, the one without money, earning his means as he went, before the mast and behind the plough, the other carrying a bill of exchange in his pocket. It was easy to see that they could not long be companions or coöperate, since one would not *operate* at all. They would part at the first interesting crisis in their adventures. Above all, as I have implied, the man who goes alone can start to-day; but he who travels with another must wait till that other is ready, and it may be a long time before they get off.

But all this is very selfish, I have heard some of my townsmen say. I confess that I have hitherto indulged very little in philanthropic enterprises. I have made some sacrifices to a sense of duty, and among others have sacrificed this pleasure also. There are those who have used all their arts to persuade me to undertake the support of some poor family in the town; and if I had nothing to do, — for the devil finds employment for the idle, — I might try my hand at some such pastime as that. However, when I have thought to indulge myself in this respect, and lay their Heaven under an obligation by maintaining certain poor persons in all respects as comfortably as I maintain myself, and have even ventured so far as to make them the offer, they have one and all unhesitatingly preferred to remain poor. While my townsmen and women are devoted in so many ways to the good of their fellows, I trust that one at least may be spared to other and less humane pursuits. You must have a genius for charity as well as for anything else. As for Doing-good, that is one of the professions which are full. Moreover, I have tried it fairly, and, strange as it may seem, am satisfied that it does not agree with my constitution. Probably I should not consciously and deliberately forsake my particular calling to do the good which society demands of me, to save the universe from annihilation; and I believe that a like but infinitely greater steadfastness elsewhere is all that now preserves it. But I would not stand between any man and his genius; and to him who does this work, which I decline, with his whole heart and soul and life, I would say, Persevere, even if the world call it doing evil, as it is most likely they will.

I am far from supposing that my case is a peculiar one; no doubt many of my readers would make a similar defence. At doing something, — I will not engage that my neighbors shall pronounce it good, — I do not hesitate to say that I should be a capital fellow to hire; but what that is, it is for my employer to find out. What *good* I do, in the common sense of that word, must be aside from my main path, and for the most part wholly unintended. Men say, practically, Begin where you are and such as you are, without aiming mainly to become of more worth, and with kindness aforethought go about doing good. If I were to preach at all in this strain, I should say rather, Set about being good. As if the sun should stop when he has kindled his fires up to the splendor of a moon or a star of the sixth magnitude, and go about like a Robin Goodfellow, peeping in at every cottage window, inspiring lunatics, and tainting meats, and making darkness visible, instead of steadily increasing his genial heat and beneficence till he is of such brightness that no mortal can look him in the face, and then, and in the meanwhile too, going about the world in his own orbit, doing it good, or rather, as a truer philosophy has discovered, the world going about him getting good. When Phaeton, wishing to prove his heavenly birth by his beneficence, had the sun's chariot but one day, and drove out of the beaten track, he burned several blocks of houses in the lower streets of heaven, and scorched the surface of the earth, and dried up every spring, and made the great desert of Sahara, till at length Jupiter hurled him headlong to the earth with a thunderbolt, and the sun, through grief at his death, did not shine for a year.

There is no odor so bad as that which arises from goodness tainted. It is human, it is divine, carrion. If I knew for a certainty that a man was coming to my house with the conscious design of doing me good, I should run for my life, as from that dry and parching wind of the African deserts called the simoom, which fills the mouth and nose and ears and eyes with dust till you are suffocated, for fear that I should get some of his good done to me, — some of its virus mingled with my blood. No, — in this case I would rather suffer evil the natural way. A man is not a good *man* to me because he will feed me if I should be starving, or warm me if I should be freezing, or pull me out of a ditch if I should ever fall into one. I can find you a Newfoundland dog that will do as much. Philanthropy is not love for one's fellow-man in the broadest sense. Howard was no doubt an exceedingly kind and worthy man in his way, and has his reward; but, comparatively speaking, what are a hundred Howards to *us*, if their philanthropy do not help *us* in our best estate, when we are most worthy to be helped? I never heard of a philanthropic meeting in which it was sincerely proposed to do any good to me, or the like of me.

The Jesuits were quite balked by those Indians who, being burned at the stake, suggested new modes of torture to their tormentors. Being superior to physical suffering, it sometimes chanced that they were superior to any consolation which the missionaries could offer; and the law to do as you would be done by fell with less persuasiveness on the ears of those who, for their part, did not care how they were done by, who loved their enemies after a new fashion, and came very near freely forgiving them all they did.

Be sure that you give the poor the aid they most need, though it be your example which leaves them far behind. If you give money, spend yourself with it, and do not merely abandon it to them. We make curious mistakes sometimes. Often the poor man is not so cold and hungry as he is dirty and ragged and gross. It is partly his taste, and not merely his misfortune. If you give him money, he will perhaps buy more rags with it. I was wont to pity the clumsy Irish laborers who cut ice on the pond, in such mean and ragged clothes, while I shivered in my more tidy and somewhat more fashionable garments, till, one bitter cold day, one who had slipped into the water came to my house to warm him, and I saw him strip off three pairs of pants and two pairs of stockings ere he got down to the skin, though they were dirty and ragged enough, it is true, and that he could afford to refuse the *extra* garments which I offered him, he had so many *intra* ones. This ducking was the very thing he needed. Then I began to pity myself, and I saw that it would be a greater charity to bestow on me a flannel shirt than a whole slop-shop on him. There are a thousand hacking at the branches of evil to one who is striking at the root, and it may be that he who bestows the largest amount of time and money on the needy is doing the most by his mode of life to produce that misery which he strives in vain to relieve. It is the pious slave-breeder devoting the proceeds of every tenth slave to buy a Sunday's liberty for the rest. Some show their kindness to the poor by employing them in their kitchens. Would they not be kinder if they employed themselves there? You boast of spending a tenth part of your income in charity; maybe you should spend the nine tenths so, and done with it. Society recovers only a tenth part of the property then. Is this owing to the generosity of him in whose possession it is found, or to the remissness of the officers of justice?

Philanthropy is almost the only virtue which is sufficiently appreciated by mankind. Nay, it is greatly overrated; and it is our selfishness which overrates it. A robust poor man, one sunny day here in Concord, praised a fellow-townsman to me, because, as he said, he was kind to the poor; meaning himself. The kind uncles and aunts of the race are more esteemed than its true spiritual fathers and mothers. I once heard a reverend lecturer on England, a man of learning and intelligence, after enumerating her scientific, literary, and political worthies, Shakspeare, Bacon, Cromwell, Milton, Newton, and others, speak next of her Christian heroes, whom, as if his profession required it of him, he elevated to a place far above all the rest, as the greatest of the great. They were Penn, Howard, and Mrs. Fry. Every one must feel the falsehood and cant of this. The last were not England's best men and women; only, perhaps, her best philanthropists.

I would not subtract anything from the praise that is due to philanthropy, but merely demand justice for all who by their lives and works are a blessing to mankind. I do not value chiefly a man's uprightness and benevolence, which are, as it were, his stem and leaves. Those plants of whose greenness withered we make herb tea for the sick, serve but a humble use, and are most employed by quacks. I want the flower and fruit of a man; that some fragrance be wafted over from him to me, and some ripeness flavor our intercourse. His goodness must not be a partial and transitory act, but a constant superfluity, which costs him nothing and of which he is unconscious. This is a charity which hides a multitude of sins. The philanthropist too often surrounds mankind with the remembrance of his own cast-off griefs as an atmosphere, and calls it sympathy. We should impart our courage, and not our despair, our health and ease, and not our

disease, and take care that this does not spread by contagion. From what southern plains comes up the voice of wailing? Under what latitudes reside the heathen to whom we send light? Who is that intemperate and brutal man whom we would redeem? If anything ail a man, so that he does not perform his functions, if he have a pain in his bowels even, — for that is the seat of sympathy, — he forthwith sets about reforming — the world. Being a microcosm himself, he discovers, and it is a true discovery, and he is the man to make it, — that the world has been eating green apples; to his eyes, in fact, the globe itself is a great green apple, which there is danger awful to think of that the children of men will nibble before it is ripe; and straightway his drastic philanthropy seeks out the Esquimau and the Patagonian, and embraces the populous Indian and Chinese villages; and thus, by a few years of philanthropic activity, the powers in the meanwhile using him for their own ends, no doubt, he cures himself of his dyspepsia, the globe acquires a faint blush on one or both of its cheeks, as if it were beginning to be ripe, and life loses its crudity and is once more sweet and wholesome to live. I never dreamed of any enormity greater than I have committed. I never knew, and never shall know, a worse man than myself.

I believe that what so saddens the reformer is not his sympathy with his fellows in distress, but, though he be the holiest son of God, is his private ail. Let this be righted, let the spring come to him, the morning rise over his couch, and he will forsake his generous companions without apology. My excuse for not lecturing against the use of tobacco is that I never chewed it; that is a penalty which reformed tobacco-chewers have to pay; though there are things enough I have chewed, which I could lecture against. If you should ever be betrayed into any of these philanthropies, do not let your left hand know what your right hand does, for it is not worth knowing. Rescue the drowning and tie your shoe-strings. Take your time, and set about some free labor.

Our manners have been corrupted by communication with the saints. Our hymn-books resound with a melodious cursing of

God and enduring him forever. One would say that even the prophets and redeemers had rather consoled the fears than confirmed the hopes of man. There is nowhere recorded a simple and irrepressible satisfaction with the gift of life, any memorable praise of God. All health and success does me good, however far off and withdrawn it may appear; all disease and failure helps to make me sad and does me evil, however much sympathy it may have with me or I with it. If, then, we would indeed restore mankind by truly Indian, botanic, magnetic, or natural means, let us first be as simple and well as Nature ourselves, dispel the clouds which hang over our own brows, and take up a little life into our pores. Do not stay to be an overseer of the poor, but endeavor to become one of the worthies of the world.

I read in the Gulistan, or Flower Garden, of Sheik Sadi of Shiraz, that "They asked a wise man, saying: Of the many celebrated trees which the Most High God has created lofty and umbrageous, they call none azad, or free, excepting the cypress, which bears no fruit; what mystery is there in this? He replied: Each has its appropriate produce, and appointed season, during the continuance of which it is fresh and blooming, and during their absence dry and withered; to neither of which states is the cypress exposed, being always flourishing; and of this nature are the azads, or religious independents. — Fix not thy heart on that which is transitory; for the Dijlah, or Tigris, will continue to flow through Bagdad after the race of caliphs is extinct: if thy hand has plenty, be liberal as the date tree; but if it affords nothing to give away, be an azad, or free man, like the cypress."

Where I Lived, and What I Lived For

(*Walden*, ch. II)

At a certain season of our life we are accustomed to consider every spot as the possible site of a house. I have thus surveyed the country on every side within a dozen miles of where I live. In imagination I have bought all the farms in succession, for all were to be bought, and I knew their price. I walked over each farmer's premises, tasted his wild apples, discoursed on husbandry with him, took his farm at his price, at any price, mortgaging it to him in my mind; even put a higher price on it, — took everything but a deed of it, — took his word for his deed, for I dearly love to talk, — cultivated it, and him too to some extent, I trust, and withdrew when I had enjoyed it long enough, leaving him to carry it on. This experience entitled me to be regarded as a sort of real-estate broker by my friends. Wherever I sat, there I might live, and the landscape radiated from me accordingly. What is a house but a *sedes*, a seat? — better if a country seat. I discovered many a site for a house not likely to be soon improved, which some might have thought too far from the village, but to my eyes the village was too far from it. Well, there I might live, I said; and there I did live, for an hour, a summer and a winter life; saw how I could let the years run off, buffet the winter through, and see the spring come in. The future inhabitants of this region, wherever they may place their houses, may be sure that they have been anticipated. An afternoon sufficed to lay out the land into orchard, wood-lot, and pasture, and to decide what fine oaks or pines should be left to stand before the door, and whence each blasted tree could be seen to the best advantage; and then I let it lie, fallow perchance, for a man is rich in proportion to the number of things which he can afford to let alone.

My imagination carried me so far that I even had the refusal of several farms, — the refusal was all I wanted, — but I never got my fingers burned by actual possession. The nearest that I came to actual possession was when I bought the Hollowell place, and had begun to sort my seeds, and collected materials with which to make a wheelbarrow to carry it on or off with; but before the owner gave me a deed of it, his wife — every man has such a wife — changed her mind and wished to keep it, and he offered me ten dollars to release him. Now, to speak the truth, I had but ten cents in the world, and it surpassed my arithmetic to tell, if I was that man who had ten cents, or who had a farm, or ten dollars, or all together. However, I let him keep the ten dollars and the farm too, for I had carried it far enough; or rather, to be generous, I sold him the farm for just what I gave for it, and, as he was not a rich man, made him a present of ten dollars, and still had my ten cents, and seeds, and materials for a wheelbarrow left. I found thus that I had been a rich man without any damage to my poverty. But I retained the landscape, and I have since annually carried off what it yielded without a wheelbarrow. With respect to landscapes, —

"I am monarch of all I *survey*,
My right there is none to dispute."

I have frequently seen a poet withdraw, having enjoyed the most valuable part of a farm, while the crusty farmer supposed that he had got a few wild apples only. Why, the owner does not know it for many years when a poet has put his farm in rhyme, the most admirable kind of invisible fence, has fairly impounded it, milked it, skimmed it, and got all the cream, and left the farmer only the skimmed milk.

The real attractions of the Hollowell farm, to me, were: its complete retirement, being about two miles from the village, half a mile from the nearest neighbor, and separated from the highway by a broad field; its bounding on the river, which the owner said protected it by its fogs from frosts in the spring, though that was nothing to me; the gray color and ruinous state of the house and barn, and the dilapidated fences, which put such an interval between me and the last occupant; the hollow and lichen-covered apple trees, gnawed by rabbits, showing what kind of neighbors I should have; but above all the recollection I had of it from my earliest voyages up the river, when the house was concealed behind a dense grove of red maples, through which I heard the house-dog bark. I was in haste to buy it, before the proprietor finished getting out some rocks, cutting down the hollow apple trees, and grubbing up some young birches which had sprung up in the pasture, or, in short, had made any more of his improvements. To enjoy these advantages I was ready to carry it on; like Atlas, to take the world on my shoulders, — I never heard what compensation he received for

that, — and do all those things which had no other motive or excuse but that I might pay for it and be unmolested in my possession of it; for I knew all the while that it would yield the most abundant crop of the kind I wanted, if I could only afford to let it alone. But it turned out as I have said.

All that I could say, then, with respect to farming on a large scale — I have always cultivated a garden — was, that I had had my seeds ready. Many think that seeds improve with age. I have no doubt that time discriminates between the good and the bad; and when at last I shall plant, I shall be less likely to be disappointed. But I would say to my fellows, once for all, As long as possible live free and uncommitted. It makes but little difference whether you are committed to a farm or the county jail.

Old Cato, whose *De Re Rusticâ* is my *Cultivator*, says, — and the only translation I have seen makes sheer nonsense of the passage, — "When you think of getting a farm turn it thus in your mind, not to buy greedily; nor spare your pains to look at it, and do not think it enough to go round it once. The oftener you go there the more it will please you, if it is good." I think I shall not buy greedily, but go round and round it as long as I live, and be buried in it first, that it may please me the more at last.

The present was my next experiment of this kind, which I purpose to describe more at length, for convenience putting the experience of two years into one. As I have said, I do not propose to write an ode to dejection, but to brag as lustily as chanticleer in the morning, standing on his roost, if only to wake my neighbors up.

When first I took up my abode in the woods, that is, began to spend my nights as well as days there, which, by accident, was on Independence Day, or the Fourth of July, 1845, my house was not finished for winter, but was merely a defence against the rain, without plastering or chimney, the walls being of rough, weather-stained boards, with wide chinks, which made it cool at night. The upright white hewn studs and freshly planed door and window casings gave it a clean and airy look, especially in the morning, when its timbers were saturated with dew, so that I fancied that by noon some sweet gum would exude from them. To my imagination it retained throughout the day more or less of this auroral character, reminding me of a certain house on a mountain which I had visited a year before. This was an airy and unplastered cabin, fit to entertain a travelling god, and where a goddess might trail her garments. The winds which passed over my dwelling were such as sweep over the ridges of mountains, bearing the broken strains, or celestial parts only, of terrestrial music. The morning wind forever blows, the poem of creation is uninterrupted: but few are the ears that hear it. Olympus is but the outside of the earth everywhere.

The only house I had been the owner of before, if I except a boat, was a tent, which I used occasionally when making excursions in the summer, and this is still rolled up in my garret; but the boat, after passing from hand to hand, has gone down the stream of time. With this more substantial shelter about me, I had made some progress toward settling in the world. This frame, so slightly clad, was a sort of crystallization around me, and reacted on the builder. It was suggestive somewhat as a picture in outlines. I did not need to go outdoors to take the air, for the atmosphere within had lost none of its freshness. It was not so much within-doors as behind a door where I sat, even in the rainiest weather. The Harivansa says, "An abode without birds is like a meat without seasoning." Such was not my abode, for I found myself suddenly neighbor to the birds; not by having imprisoned one, but having caged myself near them. I was not only nearer to some of those which commonly frequent the garden and the orchard, but to those wilder and more thrilling songsters of the forest which never, or rarely, serenade a villager, — the wood thrush, the veery, the scarlet tanager, the field sparrow, the whip-poor-will, and many others.

I was seated by the shore of a small pond, about a mile and a half south of the village of Concord and somewhat higher than it, in the midst of an extensive wood between that town and Lincoln, and about two miles south of that our only field known to fame, Concord

Battle Ground; but I was so low in the woods that the opposite shore, half a mile off, like the rest, covered with wood, was my most distant horizon. For the first week, whenever I looked out on the pond it impressed me like a tarn high up on the side of a mountain, its bottom far above the surface of other lakes, and, as the sun arose, I saw it throwing off its nightly clothing of mist, and here and there, by degrees, its soft ripples or its smooth reflecting surface was revealed, while the mists, like ghosts, were stealthily withdrawing in every direction into the woods, as at the breaking up of some nocturnal conventicle. The very dew seemed to hang upon the trees later into the day than usual, as on the sides of mountains.

This small lake was of most value as a neighbor in the intervals of a gentle rainstorm in August, when, both air and water being perfectly still, but the sky overcast, mid-afternoon had all the serenity of evening, and the wood thrush sang around, and was heard from shore to shore. A lake like this is never smoother than at such a time; and the clear portion of the air above it being shallow and darkened by clouds, the water, full of light and reflections, becomes a lower heaven itself so much the more important. From a hill-top near by, where the wood had been recently cut off, there was a pleasing vista southward across the pond, through a wide indentation in the hills which form the shore there, where their opposite sides sloping toward each other suggested a stream flowing out in that direction through a wooded valley, but stream there was none. That way I looked between and over the near green hills to some distant and higher ones in the horizon, tinged with blue. Indeed, by standing on tiptoe I could catch a glimpse of some of the peaks of the still bluer and more distant mountain ranges in the northwest, those true-blue coins from heaven's own mint, and also of some portion of the village. But in other directions, even from this point, I could not see over or beyond the woods which surrounded me. It is well to have some water in your neighborhood, to give buoyancy to and float the earth. One value even of the smallest well is, that when you look into it you see that earth is not continent but insular. This is as important as that it keeps butter cool. When I looked across the pond from this peak toward the Sudbury meadows, which in time of flood I distinguished elevated perhaps by a mirage in their seething valley, like a coin in a basin, all the earth beyond the pond appeared like a thin crust insulated and floated even by this small sheet of intervening water, and I was reminded that this on which I dwelt was but *dry land*.

Though the view from my door was still more contracted, I did not feel crowded or confined in the least. There was pasture enough for my imagination. The low shrub oak plateau to which the opposite shore arose stretched away toward the prairies of the West and the steppes of Tartary, affording ample room for all the roving families of men. "There are none happy in the world but beings who enjoy freely a vast horizon," — said Damodara,when his herds required new and larger pastures.

Both place and time were changed, and I dwelt nearer to those parts of the universe and to those eras in history which had most attracted me. Where I lived was as far off as many a region viewed nightly by astronomers. We are wont to imagine rare and delectable places in some remote and more celestial corner of the system, behind the constellation of Cassiopeia's Chair, far from noise and disturbance. I discovered that my house actually had its site in such a withdrawn, but forever new and unprofaned, part of the universe. If it were worth the while to settle in those parts near to the Pleiades or the Hyades, to Aldebaran or Altair, then I was really there, or at an equal remoteness from the life which I had left behind, dwindled and twinkling with as fine a ray to my nearest neighbor, and to be seen only in moonless nights by him. Such was that part of creation where I had squatted;

"There was a shepherd that did live,
    And held his thoughts as high
As where the mounts whereon his flocks
    Did hourly feed him by."

What should we think of the shepherd's life if his flocks always wandered to higher pastures than his thoughts?

Every morning was a cheerful invitation to make my life of equal simplicity, and I may say innocence, with Nature herself. I have been as sincere a worshipper of Aurora as the Greeks. I got up early and bathed in the pond; that was a religious exercise, and one of the best things which I did. They say that characters were engraven on the bathing tub of King Tching-thang to this effect: "Renew thyself completely each day; do it again, and again, and forever again." I can understand that. Morning brings back the heroic ages. I was as much affected by the faint hum of a mosquito making its invisible and unimaginable tour through my apartment at earliest dawn, when I was sitting with door and windows open, as I could be by any trumpet that ever sang of fame. It was Homer's requiem; itself an Iliad and Odyssey in the air, singing its own wrath and wanderings. There was something cosmical about it; a standing advertisement, till forbidden, of the everlasting vigor and fertility of the world. The morning, which is the most memorable season of the day, is the awakening hour. Then there is least somnolence in us; and for an hour, at least, some part of us awakes which slumbers all the rest of the day and night. Little is to be expected of that day, if it can be called a day, to which we are not awakened by our Genius, but by the mechanical nudgings of some servitor, are not awakened by our own newly acquired force and aspirations from within, accompanied by the undulations of celestial music, instead of factory bells, and a fragrance filling the air — to a higher life than we fell asleep from; and thus the darkness bear its fruit, and prove itself to be good, no less than the light. That man who does not believe that each day contains an earlier, more sacred, and auroral hour than he has yet profaned, has despaired of life, and is pursuing a descending and darkening way. After a partial cessation of his sensuous life, the soul of man, or its organs rather, are reinvigorated each day, and his Genius tries again what noble life it can make. All memorable events, I should say, transpire in morning time and in a morning atmosphere. The Vedas say, "All intelligences awake with the morning." Poetry and art, and the fairest and most memorable of the actions of men, date from such an hour. All poets and heroes, like Memnon, are the children of Aurora, and emit their music at sunrise. To him whose elastic and vigorous thought keeps pace with the sun, the day is a perpetual morning. It matters not what the clocks say or the attitudes and labors of men. Morning is when I am awake and there is a dawn in me. Moral reform is the effort to throw off sleep. Why is it that men give so poor an account of their day if they have not been slumbering? They are not such poor calculators. If they had not been overcome with drowsiness, they would have performed something. The millions are awake enough for physical labor; but only one in a million is awake enough for effective intellectual exertion, only one in a hundred millions to a poetic or divine life. To be awake is to be alive. I have never yet met a man who was quite awake. How could I have looked him in the face?

We must learn to reawaken and keep ourselves awake, not by mechanical aids, but by an infinite expectation of the dawn, which does not forsake us in our soundest sleep. I know of no more encouraging fact than the unquestionable ability of man to elevate his life by a conscious endeavor. It is something to be able to paint a particular picture, or to carve a statue, and so to make a few objects beautiful; but it is far more glorious to carve and paint the very atmosphere and medium through which we look, which morally we can do. To affect the quality of the day, that is the highest of arts. Every man is tasked to make his life, even in its details, worthy of the contemplation of his most elevated and critical hour. If we refused, or rather used up, such paltry information as we get, the oracles would distinctly inform us how this might be done.

I went to the woods because I wished to live deliberately, to front only the essential facts of life, and see if I could not learn what it had to teach, and not, when I came to die, discover that I had not lived. I did not wish to live what was not life, living is so dear; nor did I wish to practice resignation, unless it was quite necessary. I wanted to live deep and suck out all the marrow of life, to live so sturdily and Spartan-like as to put to rout all that was not life, to cut a broad swath and shave close, to drive life into a corner, and reduce it to its lowest terms, and, if it proved to be mean, why then to get the whole and genuine meanness of it, and publish its meanness to the world; or if it were sublime, to know it by experience, and be able to give a true account of it in my next excursion. For most men, it appears to me, are in a strange uncertainty about it, whether it is of the devil or of God, and have *somewhat hastily* concluded that it is the chief end of man here to "glorify God and enjoy him forever."

Still we live meanly, like ants; though the fable tells us that we were long ago changed into men; like pygmies we fight with cranes; it is error upon error, and clout upon clout, and our best virtue has for its occasion a superfluous and evitable wretchedness. Our life is frittered away by detail. An honest man has hardly need to count more than his ten fingers, or in extreme cases he may add his ten toes, and lump the rest. Simplicity, simplicity, simplicity! I say, let your affairs be as two or three, and not a hundred or a thousand; instead of a million count half a dozen, and keep your accounts on your thumb-nail. In the midst of this chopping sea of civilized life, such are the clouds and storms and quicksands and thousand-and-one items to be allowed for, that a man has to live, if he would not founder and go to the bottom and not make his port at all, by dead reckoning, and he must be a great calculator indeed who succeeds. Simplify, simplify. Instead of three meals a day, if it be necessary eat but one; instead of a hundred dishes, five; and reduce other things in proportion. Our life is like a German Confederacy, made up of petty states, with its boundary forever fluctuating, so that even a German cannot tell you how it is bounded at any moment. The nation itself, with all its so-called internal improvements, which, by the way are all external and superficial, is just such an unwieldy and overgrown establishment, cluttered with furniture and tripped up by its own traps, ruined by luxury and heedless expense, by want of calculation and a worthy aim, as the million households in the land; and the only cure for it, as for them, is in a rigid economy, a stern and more than Spartan simplicity of life and elevation of purpose. It lives too fast. Men think that it is essential that the *Nation* have commerce, and export ice, and talk through a telegraph, and ride thirty miles an hour, without a doubt, whether *they* do or not; but whether we should live like baboons or like men, is a little uncertain. If we do not get out sleepers, and forge rails, and devote days and nights to the work, but go to tinkering upon our *lives* to improve *them*, who will build railroads? And if railroads are not built, how shall we get to heaven in season? But if we stay at home and mind our business, who will want railroads? We do not ride on the railroad; it rides upon us. Did you ever think what those sleepers are that underlie the railroad? Each one is a man, an Irishman, or a Yankee man. The rails are laid on them, and they are covered with sand, and the cars run smoothly over them. They are sound sleepers, I assure you. And every few years a new lot is laid down and run over; so that, if some have the pleasure of riding on a rail, others have the misfortune to be ridden upon. And when they run over a man that is walking in his sleep, a supernumerary sleeper in the wrong position, and wake him up, they suddenly stop the cars, and make a hue and cry about it, as if this were an exception. I am glad to know that it takes a gang of men for every five miles to keep the sleepers down and level in their beds as it is, for this is a sign that they may sometime get up again.

Why should we live with such hurry and waste of life? We are determined to be starved before we are hungry. Men say that a stitch in time saves nine, and so they take a thousand stitches to-day to save nine to-morrow. As for *work*, we haven't any of any consequence. We have the Saint Vitus's dance, and cannot possibly keep our heads still. If I should only give a few pulls at the parish bell-rope, as for a fire, that is, without setting the bell, there is hardly a man on his farm in the outskirts of Concord, notwithstanding that press of engagements which was his excuse so many times this morning, nor a boy, nor a woman, I might almost say, but would forsake all and follow that sound, not mainly to save property from the flames,

but, if we will confess the truth, much more to see it burn, since burn it must, and we, be it known, did not set it on fire, — or to see it put out, and have a hand in it, if that is done as handsomely; yes, even if it were the parish church itself. Hardly a man takes a half-hour's nap after dinner, but when he wakes he holds up his head and asks, "What's the news?" as if the rest of mankind had stood his sentinels. Some give directions to be waked every half-hour, doubtless for no other purpose; and then, to pay for it, they tell what they have dreamed. After a night's sleep the news is as indispensable as the breakfast. "Pray tell me anything new that has happened to a man anywhere on this globe," — and he reads it over his coffee and rolls, that a man has had his eyes gouged out this morning on the Wachito River; never dreaming the while that he lives in the dark unfathomed mammoth cave of this world, and has but the rudiment of an eye himself.

For my part, I could easily do without the post-office. I think that there are very few important communications made through it. To speak critically, I never received more than one or two letters in my life — I wrote this some years ago — that were worth the postage. The penny-post is, commonly, an institution through which you seriously offer a man that penny for his thoughts which is so often safely offered in jest. And I am sure that I never read any memorable news in a newspaper. If we read of one man robbed, or murdered, or killed by accident, or one house burned, or one vessel wrecked, or one steamboat blown up, or one cow run over on the Western Railroad, or one mad dog killed, or one lot of grasshoppers in the winter, — we never need read of another. One is enough. If you are acquainted with the principle, what do you care for a myriad instances and applications? To a philosopher all *news*, as it is called, is gossip, and they who edit and read it are old women over their tea. Yet not a few are greedy after this gossip. There was such a rush, as I hear, the other day at one of the offices to learn the foreign news by the last arrival, that several large squares of plate glass belonging to the establishment were broken by the pressure, — news which I seriously think a ready wit might write a twelvemonth, or twelve years, beforehand with sufficient accuracy. As for Spain, for instance, if you know how to throw in Don Carlos and the Infanta, and Don Pedro and Seville and Granada, from time to time in the right proportions, — they may have changed the names a little since I saw the papers, — and serve up a bull-fight when other entertainments fail, it will be true to the letter, and give us as good an idea of the exact state or ruin of things in Spain as the most succinct and lucid reports under this head in the newspapers: and as for England, almost the last significant scrap of news from that quarter was the revolution of 1649; and if you have learned the history of her crops for an average year, you never need attend to that thing again, unless your speculations are of a merely pecuniary character. If one may judge who rarely looks into the newspapers, nothing new does ever happen in foreign parts, a French revolution not excepted.

What news! how much more important to know what that is which was never old! "Kieou-he-yu (great dignitary of the state of Wei) sent a man to Khoung-tseu to know his news. Khoung-tseu caused the messenger to be seated near him, and questioned him in these terms: What is your master doing? The messenger answered with respect: My master desires to diminish the number of his faults, but he cannot come to the end of them. The messenger being gone, the philosopher remarked: What a worthy messenger! What a worthy messenger!" The preacher, instead of vexing the ears of drowsy farmers on their day of rest at the end of the week, — for Sunday is the fit conclusion of an ill-spent week, and not the fresh and brave beginning of a new one, — with this one other draggle-tail of a sermon, should shout with thundering voice, "Pause! Avast! Why so seeming fast, but deadly slow?"

Shams and delusions are esteemed for soundest truths, while reality is fabulous. If men would steadily observe realities only, and not allow themselves to be deluded, life, to compare it with such things as we know, would be like a fairy tale and the Arabian Nights' Entertainments. If we respected only what is inevitable and has a right to be, music and poetry would resound along the streets. When we are unhurried and wise, we perceive that only great and worthy things have any permanent and absolute existence, that petty fears and petty pleasures are but the shadow of the reality. This is always exhilarating and sublime. By closing the eyes and slumbering, and consenting to be deceived by shows, men establish and confirm their daily life of routine and habit everywhere, which still is built on purely illusory foundations. Children, who play life, discern its true law and relations more clearly than men, who fail to live it worthily, but who think that they are wiser by experience, that is, by failure. I have read in a Hindoo book, that "there was a king's son, who, being expelled in infancy from his native city, was brought up by a forester, and, growing up to maturity in that state, imagined himself to belong to the barbarous race with which he lived. One of his father's ministers having discovered him, revealed to him what he was, and the misconception of his character was removed, and he knew himself to be a prince. So soul," continues the Hindoo philosopher, "from the circumstances in which it is placed, mistakes its own character, until the truth is revealed to it by some holy teacher, and then it knows itself to be *Brahme*." I perceive that we inhabitants of New England live this mean life that we do because our vision does not penetrate the surface of things. We think that that *is* which *appears* to be. If a man should walk through this town and see only the reality, where, think you, would the "Milldam" go to? If he should give us an account of the realities he beheld there, we should not recognize the place in his description. Look at a meeting-house, or a court-house, or a jail, or a shop, or a dwelling-house, and say what that thing really is before a true gaze, and they would all go to pieces in your account of them. Men esteem truth remote, in the outskirts of the system, behind the farthest star, before Adam and after the last man. In eternity there is indeed something true and sublime. But all these times and places and occasions are now and here. God himself culminates in the present moment, and will never be more divine in the lapse of all the ages. And we are enabled to apprehend at all what is sublime and noble only by the perpetual instilling and drenching of the reality that surrounds us. The universe constantly and obediently answers to our conceptions; whether we travel fast or slow, the track is laid for us. Let us spend our lives in conceiving then. The poet or the artist never yet had so fair and noble a design but some of his posterity at least could accomplish it.

Let us spend one day as deliberately as Nature, and not be thrown off the track by every nutshell and mosquito's wing that falls on the rails. Let us rise early and fast, or break fast, gently and without perturbation; let company come and let company go, let the bells ring and the children cry, — determined to make a day of it. Why should we knock under and go with the stream? Let us not be upset and overwhelmed in that terrible rapid and whirlpool called a dinner, situated in the meridian shallows. Weather this danger and you are safe, for the rest of the way is down hill. With unrelaxed nerves, with morning vigor, sail by it, looking another way, tied to the mast like Ulysses. If the engine whistles, let it whistle till it is hoarse for its pains. If the bell rings, why should we run? We will consider what kind of music they are like. Let us settle ourselves, and work and wedge our feet downward through the mud and slush of opinion, and prejudice, and tradition, and delusion, and appearance, that alluvion which covers the globe, through Paris and London, through New York and Boston and Concord, through Church and State, through poetry and philosophy and religion, till we come to a hard bottom and rocks in place, which we can call *reality*, and say, This is, and no mistake; and then begin, having a *point d'appui*, below freshet and frost and fire, a place where you might found a wall or a state, or set a lamp-post safely, or perhaps a gauge, not a Nilometer, but a Realometer, that future ages might know how deep a freshet of shams and appearances had gathered from time to time. If you stand right fronting and face to face to a fact, you will see the sun glimmer on both its surfaces, as if it were a cimeter, and feel

its sweet edge dividing you through the heart and marrow, and so you will happily conclude your mortal career. Be it life or death, we crave only reality. If we are really dying, let us hear the rattle in our throats and feel cold in the extremities; if we are alive, let us go about our business.

Time is but the stream I go a-fishing in. I drink at it; but while I drink I see the sandy bottom and detect how shallow it is. Its thin current slides away, but eternity remains. I would drink deeper; fish in the sky, whose bottom is pebbly with stars. I cannot count one. I know not the first letter of the alphabet. I have always been regretting that I was not as wise as the day I was born. The intellect is a cleaver; it discerns and rifts its way into the secret of things. I do not wish to be any more busy with my hands than is necessary. My head is hands and feet. I feel all my best faculties concentrated in it. My instinct tells me that my head is an organ for burrowing, as some creatures use their snout and fore paws, and with it I would mine and burrow my way through these hills. I think that the richest vein is somewhere hereabouts; so by the divining-rod and thin rising vapors I judge; and here I will begin to mine.

Sounds
(*Walden*, ch. IV)

But while we are confined to books, though the most select and classic, and read only particular written languages, which are themselves but dialects and provincial, we are in danger of forgetting the language which all things and events speak without metaphor, which alone is copious and standard. Much is published, but little printed. The rays which stream through the shutter will be no longer remembered when the shutter is wholly removed. No method nor discipline can supersede the necessity of being forever on the alert. What is a course of history, or philosophy, or poetry, no matter how well selected, or the best society, or the most admirable routine of life, compared with the discipline of looking always at what is to be seen? Will you be a reader, a student merely, or a seer? Read your fate, see what is before you, and walk on into futurity.

I did not read books the first summer; I hoed beans. Nay, I often did better than this. There were times when I could not afford to sacrifice the bloom of the present moment to any work, whether of the head or hands. I love a broad margin to my life. Sometimes, in a summer morning, having taken my accustomed bath, I sat in my sunny doorway from sunrise till noon, rapt in a revery, amidst the pines and hickories and sumachs, in undisturbed solitude and stillness, while the birds sang around or flitted noiseless through the house, until by the sun falling in at my west window, or the noise of some traveller's wagon on the distant highway, I was reminded of the lapse of time. I grew in those seasons like corn in the night, and they were far better than any work of the hands would have been. They were not time subtracted from my life, but so much over and above my usual allowance. I realized what the Orientals mean by contemplation and the forsaking of works. For the most part, I minded not how the hours went. The day advanced as if to light some work of mine; it was morning, and lo, now it is evening, and nothing memorable is accomplished. Instead of singing like the birds, I silently smiled at my incessant good fortune. As the sparrow had its trill, sitting on the hickory before my door, so had I my chuckle or suppressed warble which he might hear out of my nest. My days were not days of the week, bearing the stamp of any heathen deity, nor were they minced into hours and fretted by the ticking of a clock; for I lived like the Puri Indians, of whom it is said that "for yesterday, to-day, and to-morrow they have only one word, and they express the variety of meaning by pointing backward for yesterday, forward for to-morrow, and overhead for the passing day." This was sheer idleness to my fellow-townsmen, no doubt; but if the birds and flowers had tried me by their standard, I should not have been found wanting. A man must find his occasions in himself, it is true. The natural day is very calm, and will hardly reprove his indolence.

I had this advantage, at least, in my mode of life, over those who were obliged to look abroad for amusement, to society and the theatre, that my life itself was become my amusement and never ceased to be novel. It was a drama of many scenes and without an end. If we were always indeed getting our living, and regulating our lives according to the last and best mode we had learned, we should never be troubled with ennui. Follow your genius closely enough, and it will not fail to show you a fresh prospect every hour. Housework was a pleasant pastime. When my floor was dirty, I rose early, and, setting all my furniture out of doors on the grass, bed and bedstead making but one budget, dashed water on the floor, and sprinkled white sand from the pond on it, and then with a broom scrubbed it clean and white; and by the time the villagers had broken their fast the morning sun had dried my house sufficiently to allow me to move in again, and my meditations were almost uninterrupted. It was pleasant to see my whole household effects out on the grass, making a little pile like a gypsy's pack, and my three-legged table, from which I did not remove the books and pen and ink, standing amid the pines and hickories. They seemed glad to get out themselves, and as if unwilling to be brought in. I was sometimes tempted to stretch an awning over them and take my seat there. It was worth the while to see the sun shine on these things, and hear the free wind blow on them; so much more interesting most familiar objects look out doors than in the house. A bird sits on the next bough, life-everlasting grows under the table, and blackberry vines run round its legs; pine cones, chestnut burs, and strawberry leaves are strewn about. It looked as if this was the way these forms came to be transferred to our furniture, to tables, chairs and bedstead, — because they once stood in their midst.

My house was on the side of a hill, immediately on the edge of the larger wood, in the midst of a young forest of pitch pines and hickories, and half a dozen rods from the pond, to which a narrow footpath led down the hill. In my front yard grew the strawberry, blackberry, and life-everlasting, johns wort and goldenrod, shrub-oaks and sand-cherry, blueberry and ground-nut. Near the end of May, the sand-cherry (*cerasus pumila*) adorned the sides of the path with its delicate flowers arranged in umbels cylindrically about its short stems, which last, in the fall, weighed down with good-sized and handsome cherries, fell over in wreaths like rays on every side. I tasted them out of compliment to Nature, though they were scarcely palatable. The sumach (*rhus glabra*) grew luxuriantly about the house, pushing up through the embankment which I had made, and growing five or six feet the first season. Its broad pinnate tropical leaf was pleasant though strange to look on. The large buds, suddenly pushing out late in the spring from dry sticks which had seemed to be dead, developed themselves as by magic into graceful green and tender boughs, an inch in diameter; and sometimes, as I sat at my window, so heedlessly did they grow and tax their weak joints, I heard a fresh and tender bough suddenly fall like a fan to the ground, when there was not a breath of air stirring, broken off by its own weight. In August, the large masses of berries, which, when in flower, had attracted many wild bees, gradually assumed their bright velvety crimson hue, and by their weight again bent down and broke the tender limbs.

As I sit at my window this summer afternoon, hawks are circling about my clearing; the tantivy of wild pigeons, flying by twos and threes athwart my view, or perching restless on the white-pine boughs behind my house, gives a voice to the air; a fishhawk dimples the glassy surface of the pond and brings up a fish; a mink steals out of the marsh before my door and seizes a frog by the shore; the sedge is bending under the weight of the reed-birds flitting hither and thither; and for the last half hour I have heard the rattle of railroad cars, now dying away and then reviving like the beat of a partridge, conveying travellers from Boston to the country. For I did not live so out of the world as that boy who, as I hear, was put out to a farmer in the east part of the town, but erelong ran away and came home again, quite down at the heel and homesick. He had never seen such a dull and out-of-the-way place; the folks were all gone off; why,

you couldn't even hear the whistle! I doubt if there is such a place in Massachusetts now: —

"In truth, our village has become a butt
For one of those fleet railroad shafts, and o'er
Our peaceful plain its soothing sound is — Concord."

The Fitchburg Railroad touches the pond about a hundred rods south of where I dwell. I usually go to the village along its causeway, and am, as it were, related to society by this link. The men on the freight trains, who go over the whole length of the road, bow to me as to an old acquaintance, they pass me so often, and apparently they take me for an employee; and so I am. I too would fain be a track-repairer somewhere in the orbit of the earth.

The whistle of the locomotive penetrates my woods summer and winter, sounding like the scream of a hawk sailing over some farmer's yard, informing me that many restless city merchants are arriving within the circle of the town, or adventurous country traders from the other side. As they come under one horizon, they shout their warning to get off the track to the other, heard sometimes through the circles of two towns. Here come your groceries, country; your rations, countrymen! Nor is there any man so independent on his farm that he can say them nay. And here's your pay for them! screams the countryman's whistle; timber like long battering rams going twenty miles an hour against the city's walls, and chairs enough to seat all the weary and heavy laden that dwell within them. With such huge and lumbering civility the country hands a chair to the city. All the Indian huckleberry hills are stripped, all the cranberry meadows are raked into the city. Up comes the cotton, down goes the woven cloth; up comes the silk, down goes the woolen; up come the books, but down goes the wit that writes them.

When I meet the engine with its train of cars moving off with planetary motion,— or, rather, like a comet, for the beholder knows not if with that velocity and with that direction it will ever revisit this system, since its orbit does not look like a returning curve, — with its steam cloud like a banner streaming behind in golden and silver wreaths, like many a downy cloud which I have seen, high in the heavens, unfolding its masses to the light, — as if this travelling demigod, this cloud-compeller, would ere-long take the sunset sky for the livery of his train; when I hear the iron horse make the hills echo with his snort like thunder, shaking the earth with his feet, and breathing fire and smoke from his nostrils (what kind of winged horse or fiery dragon they will put into the new Mythology I don't know), it seems as if the earth had got a race now worthy to inhabit it. If all were as it seems, and men made the elements their servants for noble ends! If the cloud that hangs over the engine were the perspiration of heroic deeds, or as beneficent as that which floats over the farmer's fields, then the elements and Nature herself would cheerfully accompany men on their errands and be their escort.

I watch the passage of the morning cars with the same feeling that I do the rising of the sun, which is hardly more regular. Their train of clouds stretching far behind and rising higher and higher, going to heaven while the cars are going to Boston, conceals the sun for a minute and casts my distant field into the shade, a celestial train beside which the petty train of cars which hugs the earth is but the barb of the spear. The stabler of the iron horse was up early this winter morning by the light of the stars amid the mountains, to fodder and harness his steed. Fire, too, was awakened thus early to put the vital heat in him and get him off. If the enterprise were as innocent as it is early! If the snow lies deep, they strap on his snow-shoes, and with the giant plough plough a furrow from the mountains to the seaboard, in which the cars, like a following drill-barrow, sprinkle all the restless men and floating merchandise in the country for seed. All day the fire-steed flies over the country, stopping only that his master may rest, and I am awakened by his tramp and defiant snort at midnight, when in some remote glen in the woods he fronts the elements incased in ice and snow; and he will reach his stall only with the morning star, to start once more on his travels without rest or slumber. Or perchance, at evening, I hear him in his stable blowing off the superfluous energy of the day, that he may calm his nerves and cool his liver and brain for a few hours of iron slumber. If the enterprise were as heroic and commanding as it is protracted and unwearied!

Far through unfrequented woods on the confines of towns, where once only the hunter penetrated by day, in the darkest night dart these bright saloons without the knowledge of their inhabitants; this moment stopping at some brilliant station-house in town or city, where a social crowd is gathered, the next in the Dismal Swamp, scaring the owl and fox. The startings and arrivals of the cars are now the epochs in the village day. They go and come with such regularity and precision, and their whistle can be heard so far, that the farmers set their clocks by them, and thus one well-conducted institution regulates a whole country. Have not men improved somewhat in punctuality since the railroad was invented? Do they not talk and think faster in the depot than they did in the stage-office? There is something electrifying in the atmosphere of the former place. I have been astonished at the miracles it has wrought; that some of my neighbors, who, I should have prophesied, once for all, would never get to Boston by so prompt a conveyance, are on hand when the bell rings. To do things "railroad fashion" is now the by-word; and it is worth the while to be warned so often and so sincerely by any power to get off its track. There is no stopping to read the riot act, no firing over the heads of the mob, in this case. We have constructed a fate, an *Atropos*, that never turns aside. (Let that be the name of your engine.) Men are advertised that at a certain hour and minute these bolts will be shot toward particular points of the compass; yet it interferes with no man's business, and the children go to school on the other track. We live the steadier for it. We are all educated thus to be sons of Tell. The air is full of invisible bolts. Every path but your own is the path of fate. Keep on your own track, then.

What recommends commerce to me is its enterprise and bravery. It does not clasp its hands and pray to Jupiter. I see these men every day go about their business with more or less courage and content, doing more even than they suspect, and perchance better employed than they could have consciously devised. I am less affected by their heroism who stood up for half an hour in the front line at Buena Vista, than by the steady and cheerful valor of the men who inhabit the snow-plough for their winter quarters; who have not merely the three o'clock in the morning courage, which Bonaparte thought was the rarest, but whose courage does not go to rest so early, who go to sleep only when the storm sleeps or the sinews of their iron steed are frozen. On this morning of the Great Snow, perchance, which is still raging and chilling men's blood, I hear the muffled tone of their engine bell from out the fog bank of their chilled breath, which announces that the cars *are coming*, without long delay, notwithstanding the veto of a New England northeast snow storm, and I behold the ploughmen covered with snow and rime, their heads peering above the mouldboard which is turning down other than daisies and the nests of field-mice, like boulders of the Sierra Nevada, that occupy an outside place in the universe.

Commerce is unexpectedly confident and serene, alert, adventurous, and unwearied. It is very natural in its methods withal, far more so than many fantastic enterprises and sentimental experiments, and hence its singular success. I am refreshed and expanded when the freight train rattles past me, and I smell the stores which go dispensing their odors all the way from Long Wharf to Lake Champlain, reminding me of foreign parts, of coral reefs, and Indian oceans, and tropical climes, and the extent of the globe. I feel more like a citizen of the world at the sight of the palm-leaf which will cover so many flaxen New England heads the next summer, the Manilla hemp and cocoa-nut husks, the old junk, gunny bags, scrap iron, and rusty nails. This carload of torn sails is more legible and interesting now than if they should be wrought into paper and printed books. Who can write so graphically the history of the storms they have weathered as these rents have done? They are proof-sheets which need no correction. Here goes lumber from the Maine woods, which did not

go out to sea in the last freshet, risen four dollars on the thousand because of what did go out or was split up: pine, spruce, cedar, — first, second, third, and fourth qualities, so lately all of one quality, to wave over the bear, and moose, and caribou. Next rolls Thomaston lime, a prime lot, which will get far among the hills before it gets slacked. These rags in bales, of all hues and qualities, the lowest condition to which cotton and linen descend, the final result of dress, — of patterns which are now no longer cried up, unless it be in Milwaukee, as those splendid articles, English, French, or American prints, ginghams, muslins, &c., gathered from all quarters both of fashion and poverty, going to become paper of one color or a few shades only, on which forsooth will be written tales of real life, high and low, and founded on fact! This closed car smells of salt fish, the strong New England and commercial scent, reminding me of the Grand Banks and the fisheries. Who has not seen a salt fish, thoroughly cured for this world, so that nothing can spoil it, and putting the perseverance of the saints to the blush? with which you may sweep or pave the streets, and split your kindlings, and the teamster shelter himself and his lading against sun, wind, and rain behind it, — and the trader, as a Concord trader once did, hang it up by his door for a sign when he commences business, until at last his oldest customer cannot tell surely whether it be animal, vegetable, or mineral, and yet it shall be as pure as a snowflake, and if it be put into a pot and boiled, will come out an excellent dun fish for a Saturday's dinner. Next Spanish hides, with the tails still preserving their twist and the angle of elevation they had when the oxen that wore them were careering over the pampas of the Spanish main, — a type of all obstinacy, and evincing how almost hopeless and incurable are all constitutional vices. I confess that, practically speaking, when I have learned a man's real disposition, I have no hopes of changing it for the better or worse in this state of existence. As the Orientals say, "A cur's tail may be warmed, and pressed, and bound round with ligatures, and after a twelve years' labor bestowed upon it, still it will retain its natural form."

The only effectual cure for such inveteracies as these tails exhibit is to make glue of them, which I believe is what is usually done with them, and then they will stay put and stick. Here is a hogshead of molasses or of brandy directed to John Smith, Cuttingsville, Vermont, some trader among the Green Mountains, who imports for the farmers near his clearing, and now perchance stands over his bulk-head and thinks of the last arrivals on the coast, how they may affect the price for him, telling his customers this moment, as he has told them twenty times before this morning, that he expects some by the next train of prime quality. It is advertised in the Cuttingsville Times.

While these things go up other things come down. Warned by the whizzing sound, I look up from my book and see some tall pine, hewn on far northern hills, which has winged its way over the Green Mountains and the Connecticut, shot like an arrow through the township within ten minutes, and scarce another eye beholds it; going

> "to be the mast
> Of some great ammiral."

And hark! here comes the cattle-train bearing the cattle of a thousand hills, sheepcots, stables, and cow-yards in the air, drovers with their sticks, and shepherd boys in the midst of their flocks, all but the mountain pastures, whirled along like leaves blown from the mountains by the September gales. The air is filled with the bleating of calves and sheep, and the hustling of oxen, as if a pastoral valley were going by. When the old bell-wether at the head rattles his bell, the mountains do indeed skip like rams and the little hills like lambs. A car-load of drovers, too, in the midst, on a level with their droves now, their vocation gone, but still clinging to their useless sticks as their badge of office. But their dogs, where are they? It is a stampede to them; they are quite thrown out; they have lost the scent. Methinks I hear them barking behind the Peterboro' Hills, or panting up the western slope of the Green Mountains. They will not be in at the death. Their vocation, too, is gone. Their fidelity and sagacity are below par now. They will slink back to their kennels in disgrace, or

perchance run wild and strike a league with the wolf and the fox. So is your pastoral life whirled past and away. But the bell rings, and I must get off the track and let the cars go by:

> What's the railroad to me?
> I never go to see
> Where it ends.
> It fills a few hollows,
> And makes banks for the swallows,
> It sets the sand a-blowing,
> And the blackberries a-growing,

but I cross it like a cart-path in the woods. I will not have my eyes put out and my ears spoiled by its smoke and steam and hissing.

Now that the cars are gone by and all the restless world with them, and the fishes in the pond no longer feel their rumbling, I am more alone than ever. For the rest of the long afternoon, perhaps, my meditations are interrupted only by the faint rattle of a carriage or team along the distant highway.

Sometimes, on Sundays, I heard the bells, the Lincoln, Acton, Bedford, or Concord bell, when the wind was favorable, a faint, sweet, and, as it were, natural melody, worth importing into the wilderness. At a sufficient distance over the woods this sound acquires a certain vibratory hum, as if the pine needles in the horizon were the strings of a harp which it swept. All sound heard at the greatest possible distance produces one and the same effect, a vibration of the universal lyre, just as the intervening atmosphere makes a distant ridge of earth interesting to our eyes by the azure tint it imparts to it. There came to me in this case a melody which the air had strained, and which had conversed with every leaf and needle of the wood, that portion of the sound which the elements had taken up and modulated and echoed from vale to vale. The echo is, to some extent, an original sound, and therein is the magic and charm of it. It is not merely a repetition of what was worth repeating in the bell, but partly the voice of the wood; the same trivial words and notes sung by a wood-nymph.

At evening, the distant lowing of some cow in the horizon beyond the woods sounded sweet and melodious, and at first I would mistake it for the voices of certain minstrels by whom I was sometimes serenaded, who might be straying over hill and dale; but soon I was not unpleasantly disappointed when it was prolonged into the cheap and natural music of the cow. I do not mean to be satirical, but to express my appreciation of those youths' singing, when I state that I perceived clearly that it was akin to the music of the cow, and they were at length one articulation of Nature.

Regularly at half-past seven, in one part of the summer, after the evening train had gone by, the whippoorwills chanted their vespers for half an hour, sitting on a stump by my door, or upon the ridge pole of the house. They would begin to sing almost with as much precision as a clock, within five minutes of a particular time, referred to the setting of the sun, every evening. I had a rare opportunity to become acquainted with their habits. Sometimes I heard four or five at once in different parts of the wood, by accident one a bar behind another, and so near me that I distinguished not only the cluck after each note, but often that singular buzzing sound like a fly in a spider's web, only proportionally louder. Sometimes one would circle round and round me in the woods a few feet distant as if tethered by a string, when probably I was near its eggs. They sang at intervals throughout the night, and were again as musical as ever just before and about dawn.

When other birds are still the screech owls take up the strain, like mourning women their ancient u-lu-lu. Their dismal scream is truly Ben Jonsonian. Wise midnight hags! It is no honest and blunt tu-whit tu-who of the poets, but, without jesting, a most solemn grave-yard ditty, the mutual consolations of suicide lovers remembering the pangs and delights of supernal love in the infernal groves. Yet I love to hear their wailing, their doleful responses, trilled along the woodside; reminding me sometimes of music and singing birds; as if it were the dark and tearful side of music, the regrets and sighs that would fain be sung. They are the spirits, the low spirits and melancholy forebodings, of fallen souls that once in human shape night-walked the earth and did the deeds of darkness, now expiating their sins with their wailing hymns or threnodies in the scenery of their transgressions. They give me a new sense of the variety and capacity of that nature which is our common dwelling. *Oh-o-o-o-o that I never had been bor-r-r-rn!* sighs one on this side of the pond, and circles with the restlessness of despair to some new perch on the gray oaks. Then — *that I never had been bor-r-r-r-n!* echoes another on the farther side with tremulous sincerity, and — *bor-r-r-r-n!* comes faintly from far in the Lincoln woods.

I was also serenaded by a hooting owl. Near at hand you could fancy it the most melancholy sound in Nature, as if she meant by this to stereotype and make permanent in her choir the dying moans of a human being, — some poor weak relic of mortality who has left hope behind, and howls like an animal, yet with human sobs, on entering the dark valley, made more awful by a certain gurgling melodiousness, — I find myself beginning with the letters gl when I try to imitate it, — expressive of a mind which has reached the gelatinous mildewy stage in the mortification of all healthy and courageous thought. It reminded me of ghouls and idiots and insane howlings. But now one answers from far woods in a strain made really melodious by distance, — *Hoo hoo hoo hoorer hoo;* and indeed for the most part it suggested only pleasing associations, whether heard by day or night, summer or winter.

I rejoice that there are owls. Let them do the idiotic and maniacal hooting for men. It is a sound admirably suited to swamps and twilight woods which no day illustrates, suggesting a vast and undeveloped nature which men have not recognized. They represent the stark twilight and unsatisfied thoughts which all have. All day the sun has shone on the surface of some savage swamp, where the single spruce stands hung with usnea lichens, and small hawks circulate above, and the chickadee lisps amid the evergreens, and the partridge and rabbit skulk beneath; but now a more dismal and fitting day dawns, and a different race of creatures awakes to express the meaning of Nature there.

Late in the evening I heard the distant

rumbling of wagons over bridges, — a sound heard farther than almost any other at night, — the baying of dogs, and sometimes again the lowing of some disconsolate cow in a distant barn-yard. In the meanwhile all the shore rang with the trump of bullfrogs, the sturdy spirits of ancient wine-bibbers and wassailers, still unrepentant, trying to sing a catch in their Stygian lake, — if the Walden nymphs will pardon the comparison, for though there are almost no weeds, there are frogs there, — who would fain keep up the hilarious rules of their old festal tables, though their voices have waxed hoarse and solemnly grave, mocking at mirth, and the wine has lost its flavor, and become only liquor to distend their paunches, and sweet intoxication never comes to drown the memory of the past, but mere saturation and waterloggedness and distention. The most aldermanic, with his chin upon a heart-leaf, which serves for a napkin to his drooling chaps, under this northern shore quaffs a deep draught of the once scorned water, and passes round the cup with the ejaculation *tr-r-r-oonk,* *tr-r-r-oonk, tr-r-r-oonk!* and straightway comes over the water from some distant cove the same password repeated, where the next in seniority and girth has gulped down to his mark; and when this observance has made the circuit of the shores, then ejaculates the master of ceremonies, with satisfaction, *tr-r-r-oonk!* and each in his turn repeats the same down to the least distended, leakiest, and flabbiest-paunched, that there be no mistake; and then the bowl goes round again and again, until the sun disperses the morning mist, and only the patriarch is not under the pond, but vainly bellowing *troonk* from time to time, and pausing for a reply.

I am not sure that I ever heard the sound of cock-crowing from my clearing, and I thought that it might be worth the while to keep a cockerel for his music merely, as a singing bird. The note of this once wild Indian pheasant is certainly the most remarkable of any bird's, and if they could be naturalized without being domesticated, it would soon become the most famous sound in our woods, surpassing the clangor of the goose and the hooting of the owl; and then imagine the cackling of the hens to fill the pauses when their lords' clarions rested! No wonder that man added this bird to his tame stock, — to say nothing of the eggs and drumsticks. To walk in a winter morning in a wood where these birds abounded, their native woods, and hear the wild cockerels crow on the trees, clear and shrill for miles over the resounding earth, drowning the feebler notes of other birds, — think of it! It would put nations on the alert. Who would not be early to rise, and rise earlier and earlier every successive day of his life, till he became unspeakably healthy, wealthy, and wise? This foreign bird's note is celebrated by the poets of all countries along with the notes of their native songsters. All climates agree with brave Chanticleer. He is more indigenous even than the natives. His health is ever good, his lungs are sound, his spirits never flag. Even the sailor on the Atlantic and Pacific is awakened by his voice; but its shrill sound never roused me from my slumbers. I kept neither dog, cat, cow, pig, nor hens, so that you would have said there was a deficiency of domestic sound; neither the churn, nor the spinning-wheel, nor even the singing of the kettle, nor the hissing of the urn, nor children crying, to comfort one. An old-fashioned man would have lost his senses or died of ennui before this. Not even rats in the wall, for they were starved out, or rather were never baited in, — only squirrels on the roof and under the floor, a whippoorwill on the ridge pole, a blue-jay screaming beneath the window, a hare or woodchuck under the house, a screech-owl or a cat-owl behind it, a flock of wild geese or a laughing loon on the pond, and a fox to bark in the night. Not even a lark or an oriole, those mild plantation birds, ever visited my clearing. No cockerels to crow nor hens to cackle in the yard. No yard! but unfenced Nature reaching up to your very sills. A young forest growing up under your windows, and wild sumachs and blackberry vines breaking through into your cellar; sturdy pitch-pines rubbing and creaking against the shingles for want of room, their roots reaching quite under the house. Instead of a scuttle or a blind blown off in the gale, — a pine tree snapped off or torn up by the roots behind your house for fuel. Instead of no path to the front-yard gate in the Great Snow, — no gate — no frontyard, — and no path to the civilized world!

Conclusion
(*Walden*, Ch. XVIII)

To the sick the doctors wisely recommend a change of air and scenery. Thank Heaven, here is not all the world. The buckeye does not grow in New England, and the mocking-bird is rarely heard here. The wild goose is more of a cosmopolite than we; he breaks his fast in Canada, takes a luncheon in the Ohio, and plumes himself for the night in a southern bayou. Even the bison to some extent keeps pace with the seasons, cropping the pastures of the Colorado only till a greener and sweeter grass awaits him by the Yellowstone. Yet we think that if rail-fences are pulled down, and stone-walls piled up on our farms, bounds are henceforth set to our lives and our fates decided. If you are chosen town clerk, forsooth, you cannot go to Terra del Fuego this summer; but you may go to the land of infernal fire nevertheless. The universe is wider than our views of it.

Yet we should oftener look over the tafferel of our craft, like curious passengers, and not make the voyage like stupid sailors picking oakum. The other side of the globe is but the home of our correspondent. Our voyage is only great-circle sailing, and the doctors pre-scribe for diseases of the skin merely. One hastens to Southern Africa to chase the gi-raffe; but surely that is not the game he would be after. How long, pray, would a man hunt giraffes if he could? Snipes and woodcocks also may afford rare sport; but I trust it would be nobler game to shoot one's self. —

"Direct your eye right inward, and you'll find
   A thousand regions in your mind
   Yet undiscovered. Travel them, and be
   Expert in home-cosmography."

What does Africa, — what does the West stand for? Is not our own interior white on the chart? black though it may prove, like the coast, when discovered. Is it the source of the Nile, or the Niger, or the Mississippi, or a Northwest Passage around this continent that we would find? Are these the problems which most concern mankind? Is Franklin the only man who is lost, that his wife should be so earnest to find him? Does Mr. Grinnell know where he himself is? Be rather the Mungo Park, the Lewis and Clarke and Fro-bisher, of your own streams and oceans; ex-plore your own higher latitudes, — with ship-loads of preserved meats to support you, if they be necessary; and pile the empty cans sky-high for a sign. Were preserved meats invented to preserve meat merely? Nay, be a Columbus to whole new continents and worlds within you, opening new channels, not of trade, but of thought. Every man is the lord of a realm beside which the earthly empire of the Czar is but a petty state, a hum-mock left by the ice. Yet some can be pa-triotic who have no *self*-respect, and sacrifice the greater to the less. They love the soil which makes their graves, but have no sym-pathy with the spirit which may still animate their clay. Patriotism is a maggot in their heads. What was the meaning of that South Sea Exploring Expedition, with all its parade and expense, but an indirect recognition of the fact that there are continents and seas in the moral world, to which every man is an isthmus or an inlet, yet unexplored by him, but that it is easier to sail many thousand miles through cold and storm and cannibals, in a government ship, with five hundred men and boys to assist one, than it is to explore the private sea, the Atlantic and Pacific Ocean of one's being alone, —

"Erret, et extremos alter scrutetur Iberos.
   Plus habet hic vitæ, plus habet ille viæ."
"Let them wander and scrutinize the outlandish
      Australians.
I have more of God, they more of the road."

It is not worth the while to go round the world to count the cats in Zanzibar. Yet do this even till you can do better, and you may perhaps find some "Symmes' Hole" by which to get at the inside at last. England and France, Spain and Portugal, Gold Coast and Slave Coast, all front on this private sea; but no bark from them has ventured out sight of land, though it is without doubt the direct way to India. If you would learn to speak all tongues and conform to the customs of all na-tions, if you would travel farther than all travellers, be naturalized in all climes, and cause the Sphinx to dash her head against a stone, even obey the precept of the old philosopher, and Explore thyself. Herein are demanded the eye and the nerve. Only the defeated and deserters go to the wars, cowards that run away and enlist. Start now on that farthest western way, which does not pause at the Mississippi or the Pacific, nor conduct toward a wornout China or Japan, but leads on direct a tangent to this sphere, summer and winter, day and night, sun down, moon down, and at last earth down too.

It is said that Mirabeau took to highway robbery "to ascertain what degree of resolution was necessary in order to place one's self in formal opposition to the most sacred laws of society." He declared that "a soldier who fights in the ranks does not require half so much courage as a foot-pad," "that honor and religion have never stood in the way of a well-considered and a firm resolve." This was manly, as the world goes; and yet it was idle, if not desperate. A saner man would have found himself often enough "in formal opposition" to what are deemed "the most sacred laws of society," through obedience to yet more sacred laws, and so have tested his resolution without going out of his way. It is not for a man to put himself in such an attitude to society, but to maintain himself in whatever attitude he find himself through obedience to the laws of his being, which will never be one of opposition to a just government, if he should chance to meet with such.

I left the woods for as good a reason as I went there. Perhaps it seemed to me that I had several more lives to live, and could not spare any more time for that one. It is remarkable how easily and insensibly we fall into a particular route, and make a beaten track for ourselves. I had not lived there a week before my feet wore a path from my door to the pond-side; and though it is five or six years since I trod it, it is still quite distinct. It is true, I fear that others may have fallen into it, and so helped to keep it open. The surface of the earth is soft and impressible by the feet of men; and so with the paths which the mind travels. How worn and dusty, then, must be the highways of the world, how deep the ruts of tradition and conformity! I

did not wish to take a cabin passage, but rather to go before the mast and on the deck of the world, for there I could best see the moonlight amid the mountains. I do not wish to go below now.

I learned this, at least, by my experiment: that if one advances confidently in the direction of his dreams, and endeavors to live the life which he has imagined, he will meet with a success unexpected in common hours. He will put some things behind, will pass an invisible boundary; new, universal, and more liberal laws will begin to establish themselves around and within him; or the old laws be expanded, and interpreted in his favor in a more liberal sense, and he will live with the license of a higher order of beings. In proportion as he simplifies his life, the laws of the universe will appear less complex, and solitude will not be solitude, nor poverty poverty, nor weakness weakness. If you have built castles in the air, your work need not be lost; that is where they should be. Now put the foundations under them.

It is a ridiculous demand which England and America make, that you shall speak so that they can understand you. Neither men nor toadstools grow so. As if that were important, and there were not enough to understand you without them. As if Nature could support but one order of understandings, could not sustain birds as well as quadrupeds, flying as well as creeping things, and *hush* and *whoa*, which Bright can understand, were the best English. As if there were safety in stupidity alone. I fear chiefly lest my expression may not be *extra-vagant* enough, may not wander far enough beyond the narrow limits of my daily experience, so as to be adequate to the truth of which I have been convinced. *Extravagance!* it depends on how you are yarded. The migrating buffalo which seeks new pastures in another latitude, is not extravagant like the cow which kicks over the pail, leaps the cowyard fence, and runs after her calf, in milking-time. I desire to speak somewhere *without* bounds; like a man in a waking moment, to men in their waking moments; for I am convinced that I cannot exaggerate enough even to lay the foundation of a true expression. Who that has heard a strain of music feared then lest he should speak extravagantly any more forever? In view of the future of possible, we should live quite laxly and undefined in front, our outlines dim and misty on that side; as our shadows reveal an insensible perspiration toward the sun. The volatile truth of our words should continually betray the inadequacy of the residual statement. Their truth is instantly *translated;* its literal monument alone remains. The words which express our faith and piety are not definite; yet they are significant and fragrant like frankincense to superior natures.

Why level downward to our dullest perception always, and praise that as common sense? The commonest sense is the sense of men asleep, which they express by snoring. Sometimes we are inclined to class those who are once-and-a-half-witted with the half-witted, because we appreciate only a third part of their wit. Some would find fault with the morning-red, if they ever got up early enough. "They pretend," as I hear, "that the verses of Kabir have four different senses: illusion, spirit, intellect, and the exoteric doctrine of the Vedas;" but in this part of the world it is considered a ground for complaint if a man's writings admit of more than one interpretation. While England endeavors to cure the potato-rot, will not any endeavor to cure the brain-rot, which prevails so much more widely and fatally?

I do not suppose that I have attained to obscurity, but I should be proud if no more fatal fault were found with my pages on this score than was found with the Walden ice. Southern customers objected to its blue color, which is the evidence of its purity, as if it were muddy, and preferred the Cambridge ice, which is white, but tastes of weeds. The purity men love is like the mists which envelop the earth, and not like the azure ether beyond.

Some are dinning in our ears that we Americans, and moderns generally, are intellectual dwarfs compared with the ancients, or even the Elizabethan men. But what is that to the purpose? A living dog is better than a dead lion. Shall a man go and hang himself because he belongs to the race of pygmies, and not be the biggest pygmy that he can? Let every one mind his own business, and endeavor to be what he was made.

Why should we be in such desperate haste to succeed, and in such desperate enterprises? If a man does not keep pace with his companions, perhaps it is because he hears a different drummer. Let him step to the music which he hears, however measured or far away. It is not important that he should mature as soon as an apple tree or an oak. Shall he turn his spring into summer? If the condition of things which we were made for is not yet, what were any reality which we can substitute? We will not be shipwrecked on a vain reality. Shall we with pains erect a heaven of blue glass over ourselves, though when it is done we shall be sure to gaze still at the true ethereal heaven far above, as if the former were not?

There was an artist in the city of Kouroo who was disposed to strive after perfection. One day it came into his mind to make a staff. Having considered that in an imperfect work time is an ingredient, but into a perfect work time does not enter, he said to himself, It shall be perfect in all respects, though I should do nothing else in my life. He proceeded instantly to the forest for wood, being resolved that it should not be made of unsuitable material; and as he searched for and rejected stick after stick, his friends gradually deserted him, for they grew old in their works and died, but he grew not older by a moment. His singleness of purpose and resolution, and his elevated piety, endowed him, without his knowledge, with perennial youth. As he made no compromise with Time, Time kept out of his way, and only sighed at a distance because he could not overcome him. Before he had found a stock in all respects suitable the city of Kouroo was a hoary ruin, and he sat on one of its mounds to peel the stick. Before he had given it the proper shape the dynasty of the Candahars was at an end, and with the point of the stick he wrote the name of the last of that race in the sand, and then resumed his work. By the time he had smoothed and polished the staff Kalpa was no longer the pole-star; and ere he had put on the ferule and the head adorned with precious stones, Brahma had awoke and slumbered many times. But why do I stay to mention these things? When the finishing stroke was put to his work, it suddenly expanded before the eyes of the astonished artist into the fairest of all the creations of Brahma. He had made a new system in making a staff, a world with full and fair proportions; in which, though the old cities and dynasties had passed away, fairer and more glorious ones had taken their places. And now he saw by the heap of shavings still fresh at his feet, that, for him and his work, the former lapse of time had been an illusion, and that no more time had elapsed than is required for a single scintillation from the brain of Brahma to fall on and inflame the tinder of a mortal brain. The material was pure and his art was pure; how could the result be other than wonderful?

No face which we can give to a matter will stead us so well at last as the truth. This alone wears well. For the most part, we are not where we are, but in a false position. Through an infirmity of our natures, we suppose a case, and put ourselves into it, and hence are in two cases at the same time, and it is doubly difficult to get out. In sane moments we regard only the facts, the case that is. Say what you have to say, not what you ought. Any truth is better than make-believe. Tom Hyde, the tinker, standing on the gallows, was asked if he had anything to say. "Tell the tailors," said he, "to remember to make a knot in their thread before they take the first stitch." His companion's prayer is forgotten.

However mean your life is, meet it and live it; do not shun it and call it hard names. It is not so bad as you are. It looks poorest when you are richest. The fault-finder will find faults even in paradise. Love your life, poor as it is. You may perhaps have some pleasant, thrilling, glorious hours, even in a poorhouse. The setting sun is reflected from the windows of the almshouse as brightly as from the rich man's abode; the snow melts before its door as early in the spring. I do not see but a quiet mind may live as contentedly there, and have as cheering thoughts, as in a palace. The town's poor seem to me often to live the most independent lives of any. Maybe they are simply great enough to receive without misgiving. Most think that they are above being supported by the town; but it oftener happens that they are not above supporting themselves by dishonest means,

which should be more disreputable. Cultivate poverty like a garden herb, like sage. Do not trouble yourself much to get new things, whether clothes or friends. Turn the old; return to them. Things do not change; we change. Sell your clothes and keep your thoughts. God will see that you do not want society. If I were confined to a corner of a garret all my days, like a spider, the world would be just as large to me while I had my thoughts about me. The philosopher said: "From an army of three divisions one can take away its general, and put it in disorder; from the man the most abject and vulgar one cannot take away his thought." Do not seek so anxiously to be developed, to subject yourself to many influences to be played on; it is all dissipation. Humility like darkness reveals the heavenly lights. The shadows of poverty and meanness gather around us, "and lo! creation widens to our view." We are often reminded that if there were bestowed on us the wealth of Crœsus, our aims must still be the same, and our means essentially the same. Moreover, if you are restricted in your range by poverty, if you cannot buy books and newspapers, for instance, you are but confined to the most significant and vital experiences; you are compelled to deal with the material which yields the most sugar and the most starch. It is life near the bone where it is sweetest. You are defended from being a trifler. No man loses ever on a lower level by magnanimity on a higher. Superfluous wealth can buy superfluities only. Money is not required to buy one necessary of the soul.

I live in the angle of a leaden wall, into whose composition was poured a little alloy of bell metal. Often, in the repose of my midday, there reaches my ears a confused *tintinnabulum* from without. It is the noise of my contemporaries. My neighbors tell me of their adventures with famous gentlemen and ladies, what notabilities they met at the dinner-table; but I am no more interested in such things than in the contents of the *Daily Times*. The interest and the conversation are about costume and manners chiefly; but a goose is a goose still, dress it as you will. They tell me of California and Texas, of England and the Indies, of the Hon. Mr. —— of Georgia or of Massachusetts, all transient and fleeting phenomena, till I am ready to leap from their court-yard like the Mameluke bey. I delight to come to my bearings, — not walk in procession with pomp and parade, in a conspicuous place, but to walk even with the Builder of the universe, if I may, — not to live in this restless, nervous, bustling, trivial Nineteenth Century, but stand or sit thoughtfully while it goes by. What are men celebrating? They are all on a committee of arrangements, and hourly expect a speech from somebody. God is only the president of the day, and Webster is His orator. I love to weigh, to settle, to gravitate toward that which most strongly and rightfully attracts me; — not hang by the beam of the scale and try to weigh less, — not suppose a case, but take the case that is; to travel the only path I can, and that on which no power can resist me. It affords me no satisfaction to commence to spring an arch before I have got a solid foundation. Let us not play at kittly-benders. There is a solid bottom everywhere. We read that the traveller asked the boy if the swamp before him had a hard bottom. The boy replied that it had. But presently the traveller's horse sank in up to the girths, and he observed to the boy, "I thought you said that this bog had a hard bottom." "So it has," answered the latter, "but you have not got half way to it yet." So it is with the bogs and quicksands of society; but he is an old boy that knows it. Only what is thought, said, or done at a certain rare coincidence is good. I would not be one of those who will foolishly drive a nail into mere lath and plastering; such a deed would keep me awake nights. Give me a hammer, and let me feel for the furring. Do not depend on the putty. Drive a nail home and clinch it so faithfully that you can wake up in the night and think of your work with satisfaction, — a work at which you would not be ashamed to invoke the Muse. So will help you God, and so only. Every nail driven should be as another rivet in the machine of the universe, you carrying on the work.

Rather than love, than money, than fame, give me truth. I sat at a table where were rich food and wine in abundance, and obsequious attendance, but sincerity and truth were not; and I went away hungry from the inhospitable board. The hospitality was as cold as the ices. I thought that there was no need of ice to freeze them. They talked to me of the age of the wine and the fame of the vintage; but I thought of an older, a newer, and purer wine, of a more glorious vintage, which they had not got, and could not buy. The style, the house and grounds and "entertainment," pass for nothing with me. I called on the king, but he made me wait in his hall, and conducted like a man incapacitated for hospitality. There was a man in my neighborhood who lived in a hollow tree. His manners were truly regal. I should have done better had I called on him.

How long shall we sit in our porticos practising idle and musty virtues, which any work would make impertinent? As if one were to begin the day with long-suffering, and hire a man to hoe his potatoes; and in the afternoon go forth to practise Christian meekness and charity with goodness aforethought! Consider the China pride and stagnant self-complacency of mankind. This generation inclines a little to congratulate itself on being the last of an illustrious line; and in Boston and London and Paris and Rome, thinking of its long descent, it speaks of its progress in art and science and literature with satisfaction. There are the Records of the Philosophical Societies, and the public Eulogies of *Great Men!* It is the good Adam contemplating his own virtue. "Yes, we have done great deeds, and sung divine songs, which shall never die," — that is, as long as *we* can remember them. The learned societies and great men of Assyria, — where are they? What youthful philosophers and experimentalists we are! There is not one of my readers who has yet lived a whole human life. These may be but the spring months in the life of the race. If we have had the seven-years' itch, we have not seen the seventeen-year locust yet in Concord. We are acquainted with a mere pellicle of the globe on which we live. Most have not delved six feet beneath the surface, nor leaped as many above it. We know not where we are. Besides, we are sound asleep nearly half our time. Yet we esteem ourselves wise, and have an established order on the surface. Truly, we are deep thinkers, we are ambitious spirits! As I stand over the insect crawling amid the pine needles on the forest floor, and endeavoring to conceal itself from my sight, and ask myself why it will cherish those humble thoughts and hide its head from me who might, perhaps, be its benefactor and impart to its race some cheering information, I am reminded of the greater Benefactor and Intelligence that stands over me, the human insect.

There is an incessant influx of novelty into the world, and yet we tolerate incredible dulness. I need only suggest what kind of sermons are still listened to in the most enlightened countries. There are such words as joy and sorrow, but they are only the burden of a psalm, sung with a nasal twang, while we believe in the ordinary and mean. We think that we can change our clothes only. It is said that the British Empire is very large and respectable, and that the United States are a first-rate power. We do not believe that a tide rises and falls behind every man which can float the British Empire like a chip, if he should ever harbor it in his mind. Who knows what sort of seventeen-year locust will next come out of the ground? The government of the world I live in was not framed, like that of Britain, in after-dinner conversations over the wine.

The life in us is like the water in the river. It may rise this year higher than man has ever known it, and flood the parched uplands; even this may be the eventful year, which will drown out all our muskrats. It was not always dry land where we dwell. I see far inland the banks which the stream anciently washed, before science began to record its freshets. Every one has heard the story which has gone the rounds of New England, of a strong and beautiful bug which came out of the dry leaf of an old table of apple-tree wood, which had stood in a farmer's kitchen for sixty years, first in Connecticut, and afterward in Massachusetts, — from an egg deposited in the living tree many years earlier still, as appeared by counting the annual layers beyond it; which was heard gnawing out for several weeks, hatched perchance by the heat of an urn. Who does not feel his faith in a resurrection and immortality strengthened by hearing of this? Who knows what beautiful and winged life, whose egg has been buried for ages under many concentric layers of woodenness in the dead dry life of society, deposited at the first in the alburnum of the green and living tree, which has been gradually converted into the semblance of its well-seasoned tomb, — heard perchance gnawing out now for years by the astonished family of man, as they sat round the festive board, — may unexpectedly come forth from amidst society's most trivial and handselled furniture, to enjoy its perfect summer life at last!

I do not say that John or Jonathan will realize all this; but such is the character of that morrow which mere lapse of time can never make to dawn. The light which puts out our eyes is darkness to us. Only that day dawns to which we are awake. There is more day to dawn. The sun is but a morning star.

NATHANIEL HAWTHORNE (1804–1864)

Hawthorne came of an old Puritan family: his great-great-grandfather had been a judge in the witchcraft trials. Born in Salem on July 4, 1804, he lived there quietly — he said not twenty people in the town knew of his existence — until at the age of seventeen he entered Bowdoin College, where he found Longfellow and Franklin Pierce fellow students. Graduated in 1825, he returned to spend twelve more quiet years at home, seldom leaving his room except for a solitary walk, giving his days to reflection and reading and writing. Anonymously he published, in these years, a novel, *Fanshawe* (1828), in which the scene is laid at Bowdoin College in the eighteenth century, and, under various assumed names, sketches and tales which appeared in magazines and were partially collected, in 1837, in the first group of *Twice-Told Tales*.

Two years later he left Salem to take a post in the Boston Custom House secured for him by friends. When the administration changed, he lost his position and joined the community at Brook Farm. In 1842 he married, moved into the Old Manse in Concord, and published a second volume of *Twice-Told Tales*. He lived in the Manse till 1846, the year in which he published his *Mosses from an Old Manse*, and friends again came to his aid with a position as surveyor of the port of Salem. But another change of administration lost him this position in 1849, after which he lived successively in Lenox, West Newton, and Concord.

His great novel, *The Scarlet Letter*, appeared in 1850. When he followed it the next year with *The House of the Seven Gables*, his fame was secure. In another year he published *The Blithedale Romance*, and in 1853 Hawthorne was appointed consul to Liverpool by his college friend Franklin Pierce, who had just been elected to the Presidency. He served at Liverpool for four years, resigned in 1857, traveled in England and Italy until 1860 (when he published his last major work, *The Marble Faun*), and returned to America. He died at Plymouth, New Hampshire.

Hawthorne felt strongly the impulse of the romantic movement flourishing in his formative years, though he held aloof from Transcendental optimism. Still more deeply did he feel the meaning of his Puritan heritage, which lay for him not in its theology and ethical system (he reacted against these) but in the importance it gave to the moral life and especially to the problem of sin. The world of his fiction is therefore very different from Poe's. As Lewis E. Gates has said, "Ghastliness, mystery, horror, are never with Hawthorne ends in themselves. . . . His tone is always intensely human, never that of the cynical observer of men's foibles or of the dilettante elaborator of artistic effects. He loves life and believes in life; he believes in men and women; and his abounding tenderness and human sympathy are not really weakened or obscured by the aloofness he maintains in his art from the crude world of everyday experience."

The best of Hawthorne is in *The Scarlet Letter*, which every student of American letters should read thoughtfully. For an understanding of the range of his ideas and artistic methods a liberal selection of his sketches and tales is given below.

The standard edition of Hawthorne's works is the Riverside, in 12 volumes, 1883. *The American Notebooks* have been edited by Randall Stewart, 1932, *Short Stories of Hawthorne* by Newton Arvin, 1946. Good biographies are by G. E. Woodberry, 1902, and Randall Stewart, 1948. In addition to Poe's essay (see above, p. 212), some of the most penetrating criticism of Hawthorne as literary artist is W. C. Brownell's essay in *American Prose Masters*, 1909, and the treatment by F. O. Matthiessen in *American Renaissance*, 1941. Suggestive studies are *Hawthorne, the Artist*, by Leland Schubert, 1944, and *Hawthorne, Critic of Society*, by L. S. Hall, 1945. One of the best volumes in the *AWS* is that on Hawthorne by Austin Warren, 1934.

Young Goodman Brown

(1835)

On the materials for this tale, and on its significance, there is a judicious note by Austin Warren in his selections from Hawthorne in the *AWS*, pp. 361–62: "Hawthorne educes no positive counsel from this tale; he does not bid us put our trust in God instead of in men, or in virtue rather than the virtuous. He merely depicts a state of mind: a perilous sort of disillusionment. The historical setting adds color and eases the strain of the supernatural penumbra; but the tale is universal in its implications, and transcends its setting."

Young Goodman Brown came forth at sunset into the street at Salem village; but put his head back, after crossing the threshold, to exchange a parting kiss with his young wife. And Faith, as the wife was aptly named, thrust her own pretty head into the street, letting the wind play with the pink ribbons of her cap while she called to Goodman Brown.

"Dearest heart," whispered she, softly and rather sadly, when her lips were close to his ear, "prithee put off your journey until sunrise and sleep in your own bed to-night. A lone woman is troubled with such dreams and such thoughts that she's afeard of herself sometimes. Pray tarry with me this night, dear husband, of all nights in the year."

"My love and my Faith," replied young Goodman Brown, "of all nights in the year, this one night must I tarry away from thee. My journey, as thou callest it, forth and back again, must needs be done 'twixt now and sunrise. What, my sweet wife, dost thou doubt me already, and we but three months married?"

"Then God bless you!" said Faith, with the pink ribbons; "and may you find all well when you come back."

"Amen!" cried Goodman Brown. "Say thy prayers, dear Faith, and go to bed at dusk, and no harm will come to thee."

So they parted; and the young man pursued his way until, being about to turn the corner by the meeting-house, he looked back and saw the head of Faith still peeping after him with a melancholy air, in spite of her pink ribbons.

"Poor little Faith!" thought he, for his heart smote him, "What a wretch am I to leave her on such an errand! She talks of dreams, too. Methought as she spoke there was trouble in her face, as if a dream had warned her what work is to be done to-night. But no, no; 'twould kill her to think it. Well, she's a blessed angel on earth; and after this one night I'll cling to her skirts and follow her to heaven."

With this excellent resolve for the future, Goodman Brown felt himself justified in making more haste on his present evil purpose. He had taken a dreary road, darkened by all the gloomiest trees of the forest, which barely stood aside to let the narrow path creep through, and closed immediately behind. It was all as lonely as could be; and there is this peculiarity in such a solitude, that the traveller knows not who may be concealed by the innumerable trunks and the thick boughs overhead; so that with lonely footsteps he may yet be passing through an unseen multitude.

"There may be a devilish Indian behind every tree," said Goodman Brown to himself; and he glanced fearfully behind him as he added, "What if the devil himself should be at my very elbow!"

His head being turned back, he passed a crook of the road, and, looking forward again, beheld the figure of a man, in grave and decent attire, seated at the foot of an old tree. He arose at Goodman Brown's approach and walked onward side by side with him.

"You are late, Goodman Brown," said he. "The clock of the Old South was striking as I came through Boston, and that is full fifteen minutes agone."

"Faith kept me back a while," replied the young man, with a tremor in his voice, caused by the sudden appearance of his companion, though not wholly unexpected.

It was now deep dusk in the forest, and deepest in that part of it where these two were journeying. As nearly as could be discerned, the second traveller was about fifty years old, apparently in the same rank of life as Goodman Brown, and bearing a considerable resemblance to him, though perhaps more in expression than features. Still they might have been taken for father and son. And yet, though the elder person was as simply clad as the younger, and as simple in manner too, he had an indescribable air of one who knew the world, and who would not have felt abashed at the governor's dinner table or in King William's court, were it possible that his affairs should call him thither. But the only thing about him that could be fixed upon as remarkable was his staff, which bore the likeness of a great black snake, so curiously wrought that it might almost be seen to twist and wriggle itself like a living serpent. This, of course, must have been an ocular deception, assisted by the uncertain light.

"Come, Goodman Brown," cried his fellow-traveller, "this is a dull pace for the beginning of a journey. Take my staff, if you are so soon weary."

"Friend," said the other, exchanging his slow pace for a full stop, "having kept covenant by meeting thee here, it is my purpose now to return whence I came. I have scruples touching the matter thou wot'st of."

"Sayest thou so?" replied he of the serpent, smiling apart. "Let us walk on, nevertheless, reasoning as we go; and if I convince thee not thou shalt turn back. We are but a little way in the forest yet."

"Too far! too far!" exclaimed the goodman, unconsciously resuming his walk. "My father never went into the woods on such an errand, nor his father before him. We have been a race of honest men and good Christians since the days of the martyrs; and shall I be the first of the name of Brown that ever took this path and kept" —

"Such company, thou wouldst say," observed the elder person, interpreting his pause. "Well said, Goodman Brown! I have been as well acquainted with your family as with ever a one among the Puritans; and that's no trifle to say. I helped your grandfather, the constable, when he lashed the Quaker woman so smartly through the streets of Salem; and it was I that brought your father a pitch-pine knot, kindled at my own hearth, to set fire to an Indian village, in King Philip's war. They were my good friends, both; and many a pleasant walk have we had along this path, and returned merrily after midnight. I would fain be friends with you for their sake."

"If it be as thou sayest," replied Goodman Brown, "I marvel they never spoke of these matters; or, verily, I marvel not, seeing that the least rumor of the sort would have driven them from New England. We are a people of prayer, and good works to boot, and abide no such wickedness."

"Wickedness or not," said the traveller with the twisted staff, "I have a very general acquaintance here in New England. The deacons of many a church have drunk the communion wine with me; the selectmen of divers towns make me their chairman; and a majority of the Great and General Court are firm supporters of my interest. The governor and I, too — But these are state secrets."

"Can this be so?" cried Goodman Brown, with a stare of amazement at his undisturbed companion. "Howbeit, I have nothing to do with the governor and council; they have their own ways, and are no rule for a simple husbandman like me. But, were I to go on with thee, how should I meet the eye of that good old man, our minister, at Salem village? Oh, his voice would make me tremble both Sabbath day and lecture day."

Thus far the elder traveller had listened with due gravity; but now burst into a fit of irrepressible mirth, shaking himself so violently that his snake-like staff actually seemed to wriggle in sympathy.

"Ha! ha! ha!" shouted he again and again; then composing himself, "Well, go on, Goodman Brown, go on; but, prithee, don't kill me with laughing."

"Well, then, to end the matter at once," said Goodman Brown, considerably nettled, "there is my wife, Faith. It would break her dear little heart; and I'd rather break my own."

"Nay, if that be the case," answered the other, "e'en go thy ways, Goodman Brown. I would not for twenty old women like the one hobbling before us that Faith should come to any harm."

As he spoke he pointed his staff at a female figure on the path, in whom Goodman Brown recognized a very pious and exemplary dame, who had taught him his catechism in youth, and was still his moral and spiritual adviser, jointly with the minister and Deacon Gookin.

"A marvel, truly, that Goody Cloyse should be so far in the wilderness at nightfall," said he. "But with your leave, friend, I shall take a cut through the woods until we have left this Christian woman behind. Being a stranger to you, she might ask whom I was consorting with and whither I was going."

"Be it so," said his fellow-traveller. "Betake you to the woods, and let me keep the path."

Accordingly the young man turned aside, but took care to watch his companion, who advanced softly along the road until he had come within a staff's length of the old dame. She, meanwhile, was making the best of her way, with singular speed for so aged a woman, and mumbling some indistinct words — a prayer, doubtless — as she went. The traveller put forth his staff and touched her withered neck with what seemed the serpent's tail.

"The devil!" screamed the pious old lady.

"Then Goody Cloyse knows her old friend?" observed the traveller, confronting her and leaning on his writhing stick.

"Ah, forsooth, and is it your worship indeed?" cried the good dame. "Yea, truly is it, and in the very image of my old gossip, Goodman Brown, the grandfather of the silly fellow that now is. But — would your worship believe it? — my broomstick hath strangely disappeared, stolen, as I suspect, by that unhanged witch, Goody Cory, and that, too, when I was all anointed with the juice of smallage, and cinquefoil, and wolf's bane —"

"Mingled with fine wheat and the fat of a new-born babe," said the shape of old Goodman Brown.

"Ah, your worship knows the recipe," cried the old lady, cackling aloud. "So, as I was saying, being all ready for the meeting, and no horse to ride on, I made up my mind to foot it; for they tell me there is a nice young man to be taken into communion to-night. But now your good worship will lend me your arm, and we shall be there in a twinkling."

"That can hardly be," answered her friend. "I may not spare you my arm, Goody Cloyse; but here is my staff, if you will."

So saying, he threw it down at her feet, where, perhaps, it assumed life, being one of the rods which its owner had formerly lent to the Egyptian magi. Of this fact, however, Goodman Brown could not take cognizance. He had cast up his eyes in astonishment, and, looking down again, beheld neither Goody Cloyse nor the serpentine staff, but his fellow-traveller alone, who waited for him as calmly as if nothing had happened.

"That old woman taught me my catechism," said the young man; and there was a world of meaning in this simple comment.

They continued to walk onward, while the elder traveller exhorted his companion to make good speed and persevere in the path, discoursing so aptly that his arguments seemed rather to spring up in the bosom of his auditor than to be suggested by himself. As they went, he plucked a branch of maple to serve for a walking stick, and began to strip it of the twigs and little boughs, which were wet with evening dew. The moment his fingers touched them they became strangely withered and dried up as with a week's sunshine. Thus the pair proceeded, at a good free pace, until suddenly, in a gloomy hollow of the road, Goodman Brown sat himself down on the stump of a tree and refused to go any farther.

"Friend," said he, stubbornly, "my mind is made up. Not another step will I budge on this errand. What if a wretched old woman do choose to go to the devil when I thought she was going to heaven: is that any reason why I should quit my dear Faith and go after her?"

"You will think better of this by and by," said his acquaintance, composedly. "Sit here and rest yourself a while; and when you feel like moving again, there is my staff to help you along."

Without more words, he threw his companion the maple stick, and was as speedily out of sight as if he had vanished into the gloom. The young man sat a few moments by the roadside, applauding himself greatly, and thinking with how clear a conscience he should meet the minister in his morning walk, nor shrink from the eye of good old Deacon Gookin. And what calm sleep would be his that very night, which was to have been spent so wickedly, but so purely and sweetly now, in the arms of Faith! Amidst these pleasant and praiseworthy meditations, Goodman Brown heard the tramp of horses along the road, and deemed it advisable to conceal himself within the verge of the forest, conscious of the guilty purpose that had brought him thither, though now so happily turned from it.

On came the hoof tramps and the voices of the riders, two grave old voices, conversing soberly as they drew near. These mingled sounds appeared to pass along the road, within a few yards of the young man's hiding-place; but, owing doubtless to the depth of the gloom at that particular spot, neither the travellers nor their steeds were visible. Though their figures brushed the small boughs by the wayside, it could not be seen that they intercepted, even for a moment, the faint gleam from the strip of bright sky athwart which they must have passed. Goodman Brown alternately crouched and stood on tiptoe, pulling aside the branches and thrusting forth his head as far as he durst without discerning so much as a shadow. It vexed him the more, because he could have sworn, were such a thing possible, that he recognized the voices of the minister and Deacon Gookin, jogging along quietly, as they were wont to do, when bound to some ordination or ecclesiastical council. While yet within hearing, one of the riders stopped to pluck a switch.

"Of the two, reverend sir," said the voice like the deacon's, "I had rather miss an ordination dinner than to-night's meeting. They tell me that some of our community are to be here from Falmouth and beyond, and others from Connecticut and Rhode Island, besides several of the Indian powwows, who, after their fashion know almost as much deviltry as the best of us. Moreover, there is a goodly young woman to be taken into communion."

"Mighty well, Deacon Gookin!" replied the solemn old tones of the minister. "Spur up, or we shall be late. Nothing can be done, you know, until I get on the ground."

The hoofs clattered again; and the voices, talking so strangely in the empty air, passed on through the forest, where no church had ever been gathered or solitary Christian prayed. Whither, then, could these holy men be journeying so deep into the heathen wilderness? Young Goodman Brown caught hold of a tree for support, being ready to sink down on the ground, faint and overburdened with the heavy sickness of his heart. He looked up to the sky, doubting whether there really was a heaven above him. Yet there was the blue arch, and the stars brightening in it.

"With heaven above and Faith below, I will yet stand firm against the devil!" cried Goodman Brown.

While he still gazed upward into the deep arch of the firmament and had lifted his hands to pray, a cloud, though no wind was stirring, hurried across the zenith and hid the brightening stars. The blue sky was still visible, except directly overhead, where this black mass of cloud was sweeping swiftly northward. Aloft in the air, as if from the depths of the cloud, came a confused and doubtful sound of voices. Once the listener fancied that he could distinguish the accents of townspeople of his own, men and women, both pious and ungodly, many of whom he had met at the communion table, and had seen others rioting at the tavern. The next moment, so indistinct were the sounds, he doubted whether he had heard aught but the murmur of the old forest, whispering without a wind. Then came a stronger swell of those familiar tones, heard daily in the sunshine at Salem village, but never until now from a cloud of night. There was one voice, of a young woman, uttering lamentations, yet with an uncertain sorrow, and entreating for some favor, which, perhaps, it would grieve her to obtain; and all the unseen multitude, both saints and sinners, seemed to encourage her onward.

"Faith!" shouted Goodman Brown, in a voice of agony and desperation; and the echoes of the forest mocked him, crying, "Faith! Faith!" as if bewildered wretches were seeking her all through the wilderness.

The cry of grief, rage, and terror was yet piercing the night, when the unhappy husband held his breath for a response. There was a scream, drowned immediately in a louder murmur of voices, fading into far-off laughter, as the dark cloud swept away, leaving the clear and silent sky above Goodman Brown. But something fluttered lightly down through the air and caught on the branch of a tree. The young man seized it, and beheld a pink ribbon.

"My Faith is gone!" cried he, after one stupefied moment. "There is no good on earth; and sin is but a name. Come, devil; for to thee is this world given."

And, maddened with despair, so that he laughed loud and long, did Goodman Brown grasp his staff and set forth again, at such a rate that he seemed to fly along the forest path rather than to walk or run. The road grew wilder and drearier and more faintly traced, and vanished at length, leaving him in the heart of the dark wilderness, still rushing onward with the instinct that guides mortal man to evil. The whole forest was peopled with frightful sounds — the creaking of the trees, the howling of wild beasts, and the yell of Indians; while sometimes the wind tolled like a distant church bell, and sometimes gave a broad roar around the traveller, as if all Nature were laughing him to scorn. But he was himself the chief horror of the scene, and shrank not from its other horrors.

"Ha! ha! ha!" roared Goodman Brown when the wind laughed at him. "Let us hear which will laugh loudest. Think not to frighten me with your deviltry. Come witch, come wizard, come Indian powwow, come devil himself, and here comes Goodman Brown. You may as well fear him as he fear you."

In truth, all through the haunted forest there could be nothing more frightful than the figure of Goodman Brown. On he flew among the black pines, brandishing his staff with frenzied gestures, now giving vent to an inspiration of horrid blasphemy, and now shouting forth such laughter as set all the echoes of the forest laughing like demons around him. The fiend in his own shape is less hideous than when he rages in the breast of man. Thus sped the demoniac on his course, until, quivering among the trees, he saw a red light before him, as when the felled trunks and branches of a clearing have been set on fire, and throw up their lurid blaze against the sky, at the hour of midnight. He paused, in a lull of the tempest that had driven him onward, and heard the swell of what seemed a hymn, rolling solemnly from a distance with the weight of many voices. He knew the tune; it was a familiar one in the choir of the village meeting-house. The verse died heavily away, and was lengthened by a chorus, not of human voices, but of all the sounds of the benighted wilderness pealing in awful harmony together. Goodman Brown cried out, and his cry was lost to his own ear by its unison with the cry of the desert.

In the interval of silence he stole forward until the light glared full upon his eyes. At one extremity of an open space, hemmed in by the dark wall of the forest, arose a rock, bearing some rude, natural resemblance either to an altar or a pulpit, and surrounded by four blazing pines, their tops aflame, their stems untouched, like candles at an evening meeting. The mass of foliage that had overgrown the summit of the rock was all on fire, blazing high into the night and fitfully illuminating the whole field. Each pendent twig and leafy festoon was in a blaze. As the red light arose and fell, a numerous congregation alternately shone forth, then disappeared in shadow, and again grew, as it were, out of the darkness, peopling the heart of the solitary woods at once.

"A grave and dark-clad company," quoth Goodman Brown.

In truth they were such. Among them, quivering to and fro between gloom and splendor, appeared faces that would be seen next day at the council board of the province, and others which, Sabbath after Sabbath, looked devoutly heavenward, and benignantly over the crowded pews, from the holiest pulpits in the land. Some affirm that the lady of the governor was there. At least there were high dames well known to her, and wives of honored husbands, and widows, a great multitude, and ancient maidens, all of excellent repute, and fair young girls, who trembled lest their mothers should espy them. Either the sudden gleams of light flashing over the obscure field bedazzled Goodman Brown, or he recognized a score of the church members of Salem village famous for their especial sanctity. Good old Deacon Gookin had arrived, and waited at the skirts of that venerable saint, his revered pastor. But, irreverently consorting with these grave, reputable, and pious people, these elders of the church, these chaste dames and dewy virgins, there were men of dissolute lives and women of spotted fame, wretches given over to all mean and filthy vice, and suspected even of horrid crimes. It was strange to see that the good shrank not from the wicked, nor were the sinners abashed by the saints. Scattered also among their palefaced enemies were the Indian priests, or powwows, who had often scared their native forest with more hideous incantations than any known to English witchcraft.

"But where is Faith?" thought Goodman Brown; and, as hope came into his heart, he trembled.

Another verse of the hymn arose, a slow and mournful strain, such as the pious love, but joined to words which expressed all that our nature can conceive of sin, and darkly hinted at far more. Unfathomable to mere mortals is the lore of fiends. Verse after verse was sung; and still the chorus of the desert swelled between like the deepest tone of a mighty organ; and with the final peal of that dreadful anthem there came a sound, as if the roaring wind, the rushing streams, the howling beasts, and every other voice of the unconcerted wilderness were mingling and according with the voice of guilty man in homage to the prince of all. The four blazing pines threw up a loftier flame, and obscurely discovered shapes and visages of horror on the smoke wreaths above the impious assembly. At the same moment the fire on the rock shot redly forth and formed a glowing arch above its base, where now appeared a figure. With reverence be it spoken, the figure bore no slight similitude, both in garb and manner, to some grave divine of the New England churches.

"Bring forth the converts!" cried a voice that echoed through the field and rolled into the forest.

At the word, Goodman Brown stepped forth from the shadow of the trees and approached the congregation, with whom he felt a loathful brotherhood by the sympathy of all that was wicked in his heart. He could have well-nigh sworn that the shape of his own dead father beckoned him to advance, looking downward from a smoke wreath, while a woman, with dim features of despair, threw out her hand to warn him back. Was it his mother? But he had no power to retreat one step, nor to resist, even in thought, when the minister and good old Deacon Gookin seized his arms and led him to the blazing rock. Thither came also the slender form of a veiled female, led between Goody Cloyse, that pious teacher of the catechism, and Martha Carrier, who had received the devil's promise to be queen of hell. A rampant hag was she. And there stood the proselytes beneath the canopy of fire.

"Welcome, my children," said the dark figure, "to the communion of your race. Ye have found thus young your nature and your destiny. My children, look behind you!"

They turned; and flashing forth, as it were, in a sheet of flame, the fiend worshippers were seen; the smile of welcome gleamed darkly on every visage.

"There," resumed the sable form, "are all whom ye have reverenced from youth. Ye deemed them holier than yourselves, and shrank from your own sin, contrasting it with their lives of righteousness and prayerful aspirations heavenward. Yet here are they all in my worshipping assembly. This night it shall be granted you to know their secret deeds: how hoary-bearded elders of the church have whispered wanton words to the young maids of their households; how many a woman, eager for widows' weeds, has given her husband a drink at bedtime and let him sleep his last sleep in her bosom; how beardless youths have made haste to inherit their fathers' wealth: and how fair damsels — blush not, sweet ones — have dug little graves in the garden, and bidden me, the sole guest, to an infant's funeral. By the sympathy of your human hearts for sin ye shall scent out all the places — whether in church, bedchamber, street, field, or forest — where crime has been committed, and shall exult to behold the whole earth one stain of guilt, one mighty blood spot. Far more than this. It shall be yours to penetrate, in every bosom, the deep mystery of sin, the fountain of all wicked arts, and which inexhaustibly supplies more evil impulses than human power — than my power at its utmost — can make manifest in deeds. And now, my children, look upon each other."

They did so; and, by the blaze of the hell-kindled torches, the wretched man beheld his Faith, and the wife her husband, trembling before that unhallowed altar.

"Lo, there ye stand, my children," said the figure, in a deep and solemn tone, almost sad with its despairing awfulness, as if his once angelic nature could yet mourn for our miserable race. "Depending upon one another's hearts, ye had still hoped that virtue were not all a dream. Now are ye undeceived. Evil is the nature of mankind. Evil must be your only happiness. Welcome again, my children, to the communion of your race."

"Welcome," repeated the fiend worshippers, in one cry of despair and triumph.

And there they stood, the only pair, as it seemed, who were yet hesitating on the verge of wickedness in this dark world. A basin was hollowed, naturally, in the rock. Did it contain water, reddened by the lurid light? or was it blood? or, perchance, a liquid flame? Herein did the shape of evil dip his hand and prepare to lay the mark of baptism upon their foreheads, that they might be partakers of the mystery of sin, more conscious of the secret guilt of others, both in deed and thought, than they could now be of their own. The husband cast one look at his pale wife, and Faith at him. What polluted wretches would the next glance show them to each other, shuddering alike at what they disclosed and what they saw!

"Faith! Faith!" cried the husband, "look up to heaven, and resist the wicked one."

Whether Faith obeyed he knew not. Hardly had he spoken when he found himself amid calm night and solitude, listening to a roar of the wind which died heavily away through the forest. He staggered against the rock, and felt it chill and damp; while a hanging twig, that had been all on fire, besprinkled his cheek with the coldest dew.

The next morning young Goodman Brown came slowly into the street of Salem village, staring around him like a bewildered man. The good old minister was taking a walk along the graveyard to get an appetite for breakfast and meditate his sermon, and bestowed a blessing, as he passed, on Goodman Brown. He shrank from the venerable saint as if to avoid an anathema. Old Deacon Gookin was at domestic worship, and the holy words of his prayer were heard through the open window. "What God doth the wizard pray to?" quoth Goodman Brown. Goody Cloyse, that excellent old Christian, stood in the early sunshine at her own lattice, catechizing a little girl who had brought her a pint of morning's milk. Goodman Brown snatched away the child as from the grasp of the fiend himself. Turning the corner by the meeting-house, he spied the head of Faith, with the pink ribbons, gazing anxiously forth, and bursting into such joy at sight of him that she skipped along the street and almost kissed her husband before the whole village. But Goodman Brown looked sternly and sadly into her face, and passed on without a greeting.

Had Goodman Brown fallen asleep in the forest and only dreamed a wild dream of a witch-meeting?

Be it so if you will; but, alas! it was a dream of evil omen for young Goodman Brown. A stern, a sad, a darkly meditative, a distrustful, if not a desperate man did he become from the night of that fearful dream. On the Sabbath day, when the congregation were singing a holy psalm, he could not listen because an anthem of sin rushed loudly upon his ear and drowned all the blessed strain. When the minister spoke from the pulpit with power and fervid eloquence, and, with his hand on the open Bible, of the sacred truths of our religion, and of saint-like lives and triumphant deaths, and of future bliss or misery unutterable, then did Goodman Brown turn pale, dreading lest the roof should thunder down upon the gray blasphemer and his hearers. Often, awaking suddenly at midnight, he shrank from the bosom of Faith; and at morning or eventide, when the family knelt down at prayer, he scowled and muttered to himself, and gazed sternly at his wife, and turned away. And when he had lived long, and was borne to his grave a hoary corpse, followed by Faith, an aged woman, and children and grandchildren, a goodly procession, besides neighbors not a few, they carved no hopeful verse upon his tombstone, for his dying hour was gloom.

The Minister's Black Veil

A PARABLE [1]

(1836)

The sexton stood in the porch of Milford meeting-house, pulling busily at the bell-rope. The old people of the village came stooping

[1] Another clergyman in New England, Mr. Joseph Moody, of York, Maine, who died about eighty years since, made himself remarkable by the same eccentricity that is here related of the Reverend Mr. Hooper. In his case, however, the symbol had a different import. In early life he had accidentally killed a beloved friend; and from that day till the hour of his own death, he hid his face from men. [*Author's note.*]

along the street. Children, with bright faces, tripped merrily beside their parents, or mimicked a graver gait, in the conscious dignity of their Sunday clothes. Spruce bachelors looked sidelong at the pretty maidens, and fancied that the Sabbath sunshine made them prettier than on week days. When the throng had mostly streamed into the porch, the sexton began to toll the bell, keeping his eye on the Reverend Mr. Hooper's door. The first glimpse of the clergyman's figure was the signal for the bell to cease its summons.

"But what has good Parson Hooper got upon his face?" cried the sexton in astonishment.

All within hearing immediately turned about, and beheld the semblance of Mr. Hooper, pacing slowly his meditative way towards the meeting-house. With one accord they started, expressing more wonder than if some strange minister were coming to dust the cushions of Mr. Hooper's pulpit.

"Are you sure it is our parson?" inquired Goodman Gray of the sexton.

"Of a certainty it is good Mr. Hooper," replied the sexton. "He was to have exchanged pulpits with Parson Shute, of Westbury; but Parson Shute sent to excuse himself yesterday, being to preach a funeral sermon."

The cause of so much amazement may appear sufficiently slight. Mr. Hooper, a gentlemanly person, of about thirty, though still a bachelor, was dressed with due clerical neatness, as if a careful wife had starched his band, and brushed the weekly dust from his Sunday's garb. There was but one thing remarkable in his appearance. Swathed about his forehead, and hanging down over his face, so low as to be shaken by his breath, Mr. Hooper had on a black veil. On a nearer view it seemed to consist of two folds of crape, which entirely concealed his features, except the mouth and chin, but probably did not intercept his sight, further than to give a darkened aspect to all living and inanimate things. With this gloomy shade before him, good Mr. Hooper walked onward, at a slow and quiet pace, stooping somewhat, and looking on the ground, as is customary with abstracted men, yet nodding kindly to those of his parishioners who still waited on the meeting-house steps. But so wonder-struck were they that his greeting hardly met with a return.

"I can't really feel as if good Mr. Hooper's face was behind that piece of crape," said the sexton.

"I don't like it," muttered an old woman, as she hobbled into the meeting-house. "He has changed himself into something awful, only by hiding his face."

"Our parson has gone mad!" cried Goodman Gray, following him across the threshold.

A rumor of some unaccountable phenomenon had preceded Mr. Hooper into the meeting-house, and set all the congregation astir. Few could refrain from twisting their heads towards the door; many stood upright, and turned directly about; while several little boys clambered upon the seats, and came down again with a terrible racket. There was a general bustle, a rustling of the women's gowns and shuffling of the men's feet, greatly at variance with that hushed repose which should attend the entrance of the minister. But Mr. Hooper appeared not to notice the perturbation of his people. He entered with an almost noiseless step, bent his head mildly to the pews on each side, and bowed as he passed his oldest parishioner, a white-haired great-grandsire, who occupied an arm-chair in the centre of the aisle. It was strange to observe how slowly this venerable man became conscious of something singular in the appearance of his pastor. He seemed not fully to partake of the prevailing wonder, till Mr. Hooper had ascended the stairs, and showed himself in the pulpit, face to face with his congregation, except for the black veil. That mysterious emblem was never once withdrawn. It shook with his measured breath, as he gave out the psalm; it threw its obscurity between him and the holy page, as he read the Scriptures; and while he prayed, the veil lay heavily on his uplifted countenance. Did he seek to hide it from the dread Being whom he was addressing?

Such was the effect of this simple piece of crape, that more than one woman of delicate nerves was forced to leave the meeting-house. Yet perhaps the pale-faced congregation was almost as fearful a sight to the minister, as his black veil to them.

Mr. Hooper had the reputation of a good

preacher, but not an energetic one: he strove to win his people heavenward by mild, persuasive influences, rather than to drive them thither by the thunders of the Word. The sermon which he now delivered was marked by the same characteristics of style and manner as the general series of his pulpit oratory. But there was something, either in the sentiment of the discourse itself, or in the imagination of the auditors, which made it greatly the most powerful effort that they had ever heard from their pastor's lips. It was tinged, rather more darkly than usual, with the gentle gloom of Mr. Hooper's temperament. The subject had reference to secret sin, and those sad mysteries which we hide from our nearest and dearest, and would fain conceal from our own consciousness, even forgetting that the Omniscient can detect them. A subtle power was breathed into his words. Each member of the congregation, the most innocent girl, and the man of hardened breast, felt as if the preacher had crept upon them, behind his awful veil, and discovered their hoarded iniquity of deed or thought. Many spread their clasped hands on their bosoms. There was nothing terrible in what Mr. Hooper said, at least, no violence; and yet, with every tremor of his melancholy voice, the hearers quaked. An unsought pathos came hand in hand with awe. So sensible were the audience of some unwonted attribute in their minister, that they longed for a breath of wind to blow aside the veil, almost believing that a stranger's visage would be discovered, though the form, gesture, and voice were those of Mr. Hooper.

At the close of the services, the people hurried out with indecorous confusion, eager to communicate their pent-up amazement, and conscious of lighter spirits the moment they lost sight of the black veil. Some gathered in little circles, huddled closely together, with their mouths all whispering in the centre; some went homeward alone, wrapt in silent meditation; some talked loudly, and profaned the Sabbath day with ostentatious laughter. A few shook their sagacious heads, intimating that they could penetrate the mystery; while one or two affirmed that there was no mystery at all, but only that Mr. Hooper's eyes were so weakened by the midnight lamp, as to require a shade. After a brief interval, forth came good Mr. Hooper also, in the rear of his flock. Turning his veiled face from one group to another, he paid due reverence to the hoary heads, saluted the middle aged with kind dignity as their friend and spiritual guide, greeted the young with mingled authority and love, and laid his hands on the little children's heads to bless them. Such was always his custom on the Sabbath day. Strange and bewildered looks repaid him for his courtesy. None, as on former occasions, aspired to the honor of walking by their pastor's side. Old Squire Saunders, doubtless by an accidental lapse of memory, neglected to invite Mr. Hooper to his table, where the good clergyman had been wont to bless the food, almost every Sunday since his settlement. He returned, therefore, to the parsonage, and, at the moment of closing the door, was observed to look back upon the people, all of whom had their eyes fixed upon the minister. A sad smile gleamed faintly from beneath the black veil, and flickered about his mouth, glimmering as he disappeared.

"How strange," said a lady, "that a simple black veil, such as any woman might wear on her bonnet, should become such a terrible thing on Mr. Hooper's face!"

"Something must surely be amiss with Mr. Hooper's intellects," observed her husband, the physician of the village. "But the strangest part of the affair is the effect of this vagary, even on a sober-minded man like myself. The black veil, though it covers only our pastor's face, throws its influence over his whole person, and makes him ghostlike from head to foot. Do you not feel it so?"

"Truly do I," replied the lady; "and I would not be alone with him for the world. I wonder he is not afraid to be alone with himself!"

"Men sometimes are so," said her husband.

The afternoon service was attended with similar circumstances. At its conclusion, the bell tolled for the funeral of a young lady. The relatives and friends were assembled in the house, and the more distant acquaintances stood about the door, speaking of the good qualities of the deceased, when their talk was interrupted by the appearance of

Mr. Hooper, still covered with his black veil. It was now an appropriate emblem. The clergyman stepped into the room where the corpse was laid, and bent over the coffin, to take a last farewell of his deceased parishioner. As he stooped, the veil hung straight down from his forehead, so that, if her eyelids had not been closed forever, the dead maiden might have seen his face. Could Mr. Hooper be fearful of her glance, that he so hastily caught back the black veil? A person who watched the interview between the dead and living, scrupled not to affirm, that, at the instant when the clergyman's features were disclosed, the corpse had slightly shuddered, rustling the shroud and muslin cap, though the countenance retained the composure of death. A superstitious old woman was the only witness of this prodigy. From the coffin Mr. Hooper passed into the chamber of the mourners, and thence to the head of the staircase, to make the funeral prayer. It was a tender and heart-dissolving prayer, full of sorrow, yet so imbued with celestial hopes, that the music of a heavenly harp, swept by the fingers of the dead, seemed faintly to be heard among the saddest accents of the minister. The people trembled, though they but darkly understood him when he prayed that they, and himself, and all of mortal race, might be ready, as he trusted this young maiden had been, for the dreadful hour that should snatch the veil from their faces. The bearers went heavily forth, and the mourners followed, saddening all the street, with the dead before them, and Mr. Hooper in his black veil behind.

"Why do you look back?" said one in the procession to his partner.

"I had a fancy," replied she, "that the minister and the maiden's spirit were walking hand in hand."

"And so had I, at the same moment," said the other.

That night, the handsomest couple in Milford village were to be joined in wedlock. Though reckoned a melancholy man, Mr. Hooper had a placid cheerfulness for such occasions, which often excited a sympathetic smile where livelier merriment would have been thrown away. There was no quality of his disposition which made him more beloved than this. The company at the wedding awaited his arrival with impatience, trusting that the strange awe, which had gathered over him throughout the day, would now be dispelled. But such was not the result. When Mr. Hooper came, the first thing that their eyes rested on was the same horrible black veil, which had added deeper gloom to the funeral, and could portend nothing but evil to the wedding. Such was its immediate effect on the guests that a cloud seemed to have rolled duskily from beneath the black crape, and dimmed the light of the candles. The bridal pair stood up before the minister. But the bride's cold fingers quivered in the tremulous hand of the bridegroom, and her deathlike paleness caused a whisper that the maiden who had been buried a few hours before was come from her grave to be married. If ever another wedding were so dismal, it was that famous one where they tolled the wedding knell. After performing the ceremony, Mr. Hooper raised a glass of wine to his lips, wishing happiness to the new-married couple in a strain of mild pleasantry that ought to have brightened the features of the guests, like a cheerful gleam from the hearth. At that instant, catching a glimpse of his figure in the looking-glass, the black veil involved his own spirit in the horror with which it overwhelmed all others. His frame shuddered, his lips grew white, he spilt the untasted wine upon the carpet, and rushed forth into the darkness. For the Earth, too, had on her Black Veil.

The next day, the whole village of Milford talked of little else than Parson Hooper's black veil. That, and the mystery concealed behind it, supplied a topic for discussion between acquaintances meeting in the street, and good women gossiping at their open windows. It was the first item of news that the tavernkeeper told to his guests. The children babbled of it on their way to school. One imitative little imp covered his face with an old black handkerchief, thereby so affrighting his playmates that the panic seized himself, and he well-nigh lost his wits by his own waggery.

It was remarkable that of all the busybodies and impertinent people in the parish, not one ventured to put the plain question to

Mr. Hooper, wherefore he did this thing. Hitherto, whenever there appeared the slightest call for such interference, he had never lacked advisers, nor shown himself averse to be guided by their judgment. If he erred at all, it was by so painful a degree of self-distrust, that even the mildest censure would lead him to consider an indifferent action as a crime. Yet, though so well acquainted with this amiable weakness, no individual among his parishioners chose to make the black veil a subject of friendly remonstrance. There was a feeling of dread, neither plainly confessed nor carefully concealed, which caused each to shift the responsibility upon another, till at length it was found expedient to send a deputation of the church, in order to deal with Mr. Hooper about the mystery, before it should grow into a scandal. Never did an embassy so ill discharge its duties. The minister received them with friendly courtesy, but became silent, after they were seated, leaving to his visitors the whole burden of introducing their important business. The topic, it might be supposed, was obvious enough. There was the black veil swathed round Mr. Hooper's forehead, and concealing every feature above his placid mouth, on which, at times, they could perceive the glimmering of a melancholy smile. But that piece of crape, to their imagination, seemed to hang down before his heart, the symbol of a fearful secret between him and them. Were the veil but cast aside, they might speak freely of it, but not till then. Thus they sat a considerable time, speechless, confused, and shrinking uneasily from Mr. Hooper's eye, which they felt to be fixed upon them with an invisible glance. Finally, the deputies returned abashed to their constituents, pronouncing the matter too weighty to be handled, except by a council of the churches, if, indeed, it might not require a general synod.

But there was one person in the village unappalled by the awe with which the black veil had impressed all beside herself. When the deputies returned without an explanation, or even venturing to demand one, she, with the calm energy of her character, determined to chase away the strange cloud that appeared to be settling round Mr. Hooper, every moment more darkly than before. As his plighted wife, it should be her privilege to know what the black veil concealed. At the minister's first visit, therefore, she entered upon the subject with a direct simplicity, which made the task easier both for him and her. After he had seated himself, she fixed her eyes steadfastly upon the veil, but could discern nothing of the dreadful gloom that had so overawed the multitude: it was but a double fold of crape, hanging down from his forehead to his mouth, and slightly stirring with his breath.

"No," said she aloud, and smiling, "there is nothing terrible in this piece of crape, except that it hides a face which I am always glad to look upon. Come, good sir, let the sun shine from behind the cloud. First lay aside your black veil: then tell me why you put it on."

Mr. Hooper's smile glimmered faintly.

"There is an hour to come," said he, "when all of us shall cast aside our veils. Take it not amiss, beloved friend, if I wear this piece of crape till then."

"Your words are a mystery, too," returned the young lady. "Take away the veil from them, at least."

"Elizabeth, I will," said he, "so far as my vow may suffer me. Know, then, this veil is a type and a symbol, and I am bound to wear it ever, both in light and darkness, in solitude and before the gaze of multitudes, and as with strangers, so with my familiar friends. No mortal eye will see it withdrawn. This dismal shade must separate me from the world: even you, Elizabeth, can never come behind it!"

"What grievous affliction hath befallen you," she earnestly inquired, "that you should thus darken your eyes forever?"

"If it be a sign of mourning," replied Mr. Hooper, "I, perhaps, like most other mortals, have sorrows dark enough to be typified by a black veil."

"But what if the world will not believe that it is the type of an innocent sorrow?" urged Elizabeth. "Beloved and respected as you are, there may be whispers that you hide your face under the consciousness of secret sin. For the sake of your holy office, do away this scandal!"

The color rose into her cheeks as she intimated the nature of the rumors that were already abroad in the village. But Mr. Hooper's mildness did not forsake him. He even smiled again — that same sad smile, which always appeared like a faint glimmering of light, proceeding from the obscurity beneath the veil.

"If I hide my face for sorrow, there is cause enough," he merely replied; "and if I cover it for secret sin, what mortal might not do the same?"

And with this gentle, but unconquerable obstinacy did he resist all her entreaties. At length Elizabeth sat silent. For a few moments she appeared lost in thought, considering, probably, what new methods might be tried to withdraw her lover from so dark a fantasy, which, if it had no other meaning, was perhaps a symptom of mental disease. Though of a firmer character than his own, the tears rolled down her cheeks. But, in an instant, as it were, a new feeling took the place of sorrow: her eyes were fixed insensibly on the black veil, when, like a sudden twilight in the air, its terrors fell around her. She arose, and stood trembling before him.

"And do you feel it then, at last?" said he mournfully.

She made no reply, but covered her eyes with her hand, and turned to leave the room. He rushed forward and caught her arm.

"Have patience with me, Elizabeth!" cried he, passionately. "Do not desert me, though this veil must be between us here on earth. Be mine, and hereafter there shall be no veil over my face, no darkness between our souls! It is but a mortal veil — it is not for eternity! O! you know not how lonely I am, and how frightened, to be alone behind my black veil. Do not leave me in this miserable obscurity forever!"

"Lift the veil but once, and look me in the face," said she.

"Never! It cannot be!" replied Mr. Hooper.

"Then farewell!" said Elizabeth.

She withdrew her arm from his grasp, and slowly departed, pausing at the door, to give one long shuddering gaze, that seemed almost to penetrate the mystery of the black veil. But, even amid his grief, Mr. Hooper smiled to think that only a material emblem had separated him from happiness, though the horrors, which it shadowed forth, must be drawn darkly between the fondest of lovers.

From that time no attempts were made to remove Mr. Hooper's black veil, or, by a direct appeal, to discover the secret which it was supposed to hide. By persons who claimed a superiority to popular prejudice, it was reckoned merely an eccentric whim, such as often mingles with the sober actions of men otherwise rational, and tinges them all with its own semblance of insanity. But with the multitude, good Mr. Hooper was irreparably a bugbear. He could not walk the street with any peace of mind, so conscious was he that the gentle and timid would turn aside to avoid him, and that others would make it a point of hardihood to throw themselves in his way. The impertinence of the latter class compelled him to give up his customary walk at sunset to the burial ground; for when he leaned pensively over the gate, there would always be faces behind the gravestones, peeping at his black veil. A fable went the rounds that the stare of the dead people drove him thence. It grieved him, to the very depth of his kind heart, to observe how the children fled from his approach, breaking up their merriest sports, while his melancholy figure was yet afar off. Their instinctive dread caused him to feel more strongly than aught else, that a preternatural horror was interwoven with the threads of the black crape. In truth, his own antipathy to the veil was known to be so great, that he never willingly passed before a mirror, nor stooped to drink at a still fountain, lest, in its peaceful bosom, he should be affrighted by himself. This was what gave plausibility to the whispers, that Mr. Hooper's conscience tortured him for some great crime too horrible to be entirely concealed, or otherwise than so obscurely intimated. Thus, from beneath the black veil, there rolled a cloud into the sunshine, an ambiguity of sin or sorrow, which enveloped the poor minister, so that love or sympathy could never reach him. It was said that ghost and fiend consorted with him there. With self-shudderings and outward terrors, he walked continually in its shadow, groping darkly within his own soul, or gazing through a medium that saddened the whole world.

Even the lawless wind, it was believed, respected his dreadful secret, and never blew aside the veil. But still good Mr. Hooper sadly smiled at the pale visages of the worldly throng as he passed by.

Among all its bad influences, the black veil had the one desirable effect, of making its wearer a very efficient clergyman. By the aid of his mysterious emblem — for there was no other apparent cause — he became a man of awful power over souls that were in agony for sin. His converts always regarded him with a dread peculiar to themselves, affirming, though but figuratively, that, before he brought them to celestial light, they had been with him behind the black veil. Its gloom, indeed, enabled him to sympathize with all dark affections. Dying sinners cried aloud for Mr. Hooper, and would not yield their breath till he appeared; though ever, as he stooped to whisper consolation, they shuddered at the veiled face so near their own. Such were the terrors of the black veil, even when Death had bared his visage! Strangers came long distances to attend service at his church, with the mere idle purpose of gazing at his figure, because it was forbidden them to behold his face. But many were made to quake ere they departed! Once, during Governor Belcher's administration, Mr. Hooper was appointed to preach the election sermon. Covered with his black veil, he stood before the chief magistrate, the council, and the representatives, and wrought so deep an impression, that the legislative measures of that year were characterized by all the gloom and piety of our earliest ancestral sway.

In this manner Mr. Hooper spent a long life, irreproachable in outward act, yet shrouded in dismal suspicions; kind and loving, though unloved, and dimly feared; a man apart from men, shunned in their health and joy, but ever summoned to their aid in mortal anguish. As years wore on, shedding their snows above his sable veil, he acquired a name throughout the New England churches, and they called him Father Hooper. Nearly all his parishioners, who were of mature age when he was settled, had been borne away by many a funeral: he had one congregation in the church, and a more crowded one in the churchyard; and having wrought so late into the evening, and done his work so well, it was now good Father Hooper's turn to rest.

Several persons were visible by the shaded candle-light, in the death chamber of the old clergyman. Natural connections he had none. But there was the decorously grave, though unmoved physician, seeking only to mitigate the last pangs of the patient whom he could not save. There were the deacons, and other eminently pious members of his church. There, also, was the Reverend Mr. Clark, of Westbury, a young and zealous divine, who had ridden in haste to pray by the bedside of the expiring minister. There was the nurse, no hired handmaiden of death, but one whose calm affection had endured thus long in secrecy, in solitude, amid the chill of age, and would not perish, even at the dying hour. Who, but Elizabeth! And there lay the hoary head of good Father Hooper upon the death pillow, with the black veil still swathed about his brow, and reaching down over his face, so that each more difficult gasp of his faint breath caused it to stir. All through life that piece of crape had hung between him and the world: it had separated him from cheerful brotherhood and woman's love, and kept him in that saddest of all prisons, his own heart; and still it lay upon his face, as if to deepen the gloom of his darksome chamber, and shade him from the sunshine of eternity.

For some time previous, his mind had been confused, wavering doubtfully between the past and the present, and hovering forward, as it were, at intervals, into the indistinctness of the world to come. There had been feverish turns, which tossed him from side to side, and wore away what little strength he had. But in his most convulsive struggles, and in the wildest vagaries of his intellect, when no other thought retained its sober influence, he still showed an awful solicitude lest the black veil should slip aside. Even if his bewildered soul could have forgotten, there was a faithful woman at his pillow, who, with averted eyes, would have covered that aged face, which she had last beheld in the comeliness of manhood. At length the death-stricken old man lay quietly in the torpor of mental and bodily exhaustion, with an imperceptible pulse, and breath that grew fainter and fainter, except when a long, deep, and irregular inspiration seemed to prelude the flight of his spirit.

The minister of Westbury approached the bedside.

"Venerable Father Hooper," said he, "the moment of your release is at hand. Are you ready for the lifting of the veil that shuts in time from eternity?"

Father Hooper at first replied merely by a feeble motion of his head; then, apprehensive, perhaps, that his meaning might be doubtful, he exerted himself to speak.

"Yea," said he, in faint accents, "my soul hath a patient weariness until that veil be lifted."

"And is it fitting," resumed the Reverend Mr. Clark, "that a man so given to prayer, of such a blameless example, holy in deed and thought, so far as mortal judgment may pronounce; is it fitting that a father in the church should leave a shadow on his memory, that may seem to blacken a life so pure? I pray you, my venerable brother, let not this thing be! Suffer us to be gladdened by your triumphant aspect as you go to your reward. Before the veil of eternity be lifted, let me cast aside this black veil from your face!"

And thus speaking, the Reverend Mr. Clark bent forward to reveal the mystery of so many years. But, exerting a sudden energy, that made all the beholders stand aghast, Father Hooper snatched both his hands from beneath the bedclothes, and pressed them strongly on the black veil, resolute to struggle, if the minister of Westbury would contend with a dying man.

"Never!" cried the veiled clergyman. "On earth, never!"

"Dark old man!" exclaimed the affrighted minister, "with what horrible crime upon your soul are you now passing to the judgment?"

Father Hooper's breath heaved; it rattled in his throat; but, with a mighty effort, grasping forward with his hands, he caught hold of life, and held it back till he should speak. He even raised himself in bed; and there he sat, shivering with the arms of death around him, while the black veil hung down, awful, at that last moment, in the gathered terrors of a lifetime. And yet the faint, sad smile, so often there, now seemed to glimmer from its

obscurity, and linger on Father Hooper's lips.

"Why do you tremble at me alone?" cried he, turning his veiled face round the circle of pale spectators. "Tremble also at each other! Have men avoided me, and women shown no pity, and children screamed and fled, only for my black veil? What, but the mystery which it obscurely typifies, has made this piece of crape so awful? When the friend shows his inmost heart to his friend; the lover to his best beloved; when man does not vainly shrink from the eye of his Creator, loathsomely treasuring up the secret of his sin; then deem me a monster, for the symbol beneath which I have lived, and die! I look around me, and, lo! on every visage a Black Veil!"

While his auditors shrank from one another, in mutual affright, Father Hooper fell back upon his pillow, a veiled corpse, with a faint smile lingering on the lips. Still veiled, they laid him in his coffin, and a veiled corpse they bore him to the grave. The grass of many years has sprung up and withered on that grave, the burial stone is moss-grown, and good Mr. Hooper's face is dust; but awful is still the thought that it mouldered beneath the Black Veil!

The Maypole of Merry Mount[1]

(1835)

Bright were the days at Merry Mount, when the Maypole was the banner staff of that gay colony! They who reared it, should their banner be triumphant, were to pour sunshine over New England's rugged hills, and scatter flower seeds throughout the soil. Jollity and gloom were contending for an empire. Midsummer eve had come, bringing

[1] There is an admirable foundation for a philosophic romance in the curious history of the early settlement of Mount Wollaston, or Merry Mount. In the slight sketch here attempted, the facts, recorded on the grave pages of our New England annalists, have wrought themselves, almost spontaneously, into a sort of allegory. The masques, mummeries, and festive customs, described in the text, are in accordance with the manners of the age. Authority on these points may be found in Strutt's Book of English Sports and Pastimes. [*Author's note.*]

The "annalists" were Thomas Morton, *New English Canaan*, 1637, and William Bradford, *History of Plymouth Plantation*.

deep verdure to the forest, and roses in her lap, of a more vivid hue than the tender buds of Spring. But May, or her mirthful spirit, dwelt all the year round at Merry Mount, sporting with the Summer months, and revelling with Autumn, and basking in the glow of Winter's fireside. Through a world of toil and care she flitted with a dreamlike smile, and came hither to find a home among the lightsome hearts of Merry Mount.

Never had the Maypole been so gayly decked as at sunset on midsummer eve. This venerated emblem was a pine-tree, which had preserved the slender grace of youth, while it equalled the loftiest height of the old wood monarchs. From its top streamed a silken banner, colored like the rainbow. Down nearly to the ground the pole was dressed with birchen boughs, and others of the liveliest green, and some with silvery leaves, fastened by ribbons that fluttered in fantastic knots of twenty different colors, but no sad ones. Garden flowers, and blossoms of the wilderness, laughed gladly forth amid the verdure, so fresh and dewy that they must have grown by magic on that happy pine-tree. Where this green and flowery splendor terminated, the shaft of the Maypole was stained with the seven brilliant hues of the banner at its top. On the lowest green bough hung an abundant wreath of roses, some that had been gathered in the sunniest spots of the forest, and others, of still richer blush, which the colonists had reared from English seed. O, people of the Golden Age, the chief of your husbandry was to raise flowers!

But what was the wild throng that stood hand in hand about the Maypole? It could not be that the fauns and nymphs, when driven from their classic groves and homes of ancient fable, had sought refuge, as all the persecuted did, in the fresh woods of the West. These were Gothic monsters, though perhaps of Grecian ancestry. On the shoulders of a comely youth uprose the head and branching antlers of a stag; a second, human in all other points, had the grim visage of a wolf; a third, still with the trunk and limbs of a mortal man, showed the beard and horns of a venerable he-goat. There was the likeness of a bear erect, brute in all but his hind legs, which were adorned with pink silk stockings. And here again almost as wondrous, stood a real bear of the dark forest, lending each of his fore paws to the grasp of a human hand, and as ready for the dance as any in that circle. His inferior nature rose half way, to meet his companions as they stooped. Other faces wore the similitude of man or woman, but distorted or extravagant, with red noses pendulous before their mouths, which seemed of awful depth, and stretched from ear to ear in an eternal fit of laughter. Here might be seen the Salvage Man, well known in heraldry, hairy as a baboon, and girdled with green leaves. By his side, a noble figure, but still a counterfeit, appeared an Indian hunter, with feathery crest and wampum belt. Many of this strange company wore foolscaps, and had little bells appended to their garments, tinkling with a silvery sound, responsive to the inaudible music of their gleesome spirits. Some youths and maidens were of soberer garb, yet well maintained their places in the irregular throng by the expression of wild revelry upon their features. Such were the colonists of Merry Mount, as they stood in the broad smile of sunset round their venerated Maypole.

Had a wanderer, bewildered in the melancholy forest, heard their mirth, and stolen a half-affrighted glance, he might have fancied them the crew of Comus, some already transformed to brutes, some midway between man and beast, and the others rioting in the flow of tipsy jollity that foreran the change. But a band of Puritans, who watched the scene, invisible themselves, compared the masques to those devils and ruined souls with whom their superstition peopled the black wilderness.

Within the ring of monsters appeared the two airiest forms that had ever trodden on any more solid footing than a purple and golden cloud. One was a youth in glistening apparel, with a scarf of the rainbow pattern crosswise on his breast. His right hand held a gilded staff, the ensign of high dignity among the revellers, and his left grasped the slender fingers of a fair maiden, not less gayly decorated than himself. Bright roses glowed in contrast with the dark and glossy curls of each, and were scattered round their feet, or had sprung up spontaneously there. Behind this lightsome couple, so close to the Maypole that its boughs shaded his jovial face, stood the figure of an English priest, canonically dressed, yet decked with flowers, in heathen fashion, and wearing a chaplet of the native vine leaves. By the riot of his rolling eye, and the pagan decorations of his holy garb, he seemed the wildest monster there, and the very Comus of the crew.

"Votaries of the Maypole," cried the flower-decked priest, "merrily, all day long, have the woods echoed to your mirth. But be this your merriest hour, my hearts! Lo, here stand the Lord and Lady of the May, whom I, a clerk of Oxford, and high priest of Merry Mount, am presently to join in holy matrimony. Up with your nimble spirits, ye morris-dancers, green men, and glee maidens, bears and wolves, and horned gentlemen! Come; a chorus now, rich with the old mirth of Merry England, and the wilder glee of this fresh forest; and then a dance, to show the youthful pair what life is made of, and how airily they should go through it! All ye that love the Maypole, lend your voices to the nuptial song of the Lord and Lady of the May!"

This wedlock was more serious than most affairs of Merry Mount, where jest and delusion, trick and fantasy, kept up a continual carnival. The Lord and Lady of the May, though their titles must be laid down at sunset, were really and truly to be partners for the dance of life, beginning the measure that same bright eve. The wreath of roses, that hung from the lowest green bough of the Maypole, had been twined for them, and would be thrown over both their heads, in symbol of their flowery union. When the priest had spoken, therefore, a riotous uproar burst from the rout of monstrous figures.

"Begin you the stave, reverend Sir," cried they all; "and never did the woods ring to such a merry peal as we of the Maypole shall send up!"

Immediately a prelude of pipe, cithern, and viol, touched with practised minstrelsy, began to play from a neighboring thicket, in such a mirthful cadence that the boughs of the Maypole quivered to the sound. But the May Lord, he of the gilded staff, chancing to look into his Lady's eyes, was wonder struck at the almost pensive glance that met his own.

"Edith, sweet Lady of the May," whispered he reproachfully, "is yon wreath of roses a garland to hang above our graves, that you look so sad? O, Edith, this is our golden time! Tarnish it not by any pensive shadow of the mind; for it may be that nothing of futurity will be brighter than the mere remembrance of what is now passing."

"That was the very thought that saddened me! How came it in your mind too?" said Edith, in a still lower tone than he, for it was high treason to be sad at Merry Mount. "Therefore do I sigh amid this festive music. And besides, dear Edgar, I struggle as with a dream, and fancy that these shapes of our jovial friends are visionary, and their mirth unreal, and that we are no true Lord and Lady of the May. What is the mystery in my heart?"

Just then, as if a spell had loosened them down came a little shower of withering rose leaves from the Maypole. Alas, for the young lovers! No sooner had their hearts glowed with real passion than they were sensible of something vague and unsubstantial in their former pleasures, and felt a dreary presentiment of inevitable change. From the moment that they truly loved, they had subjected themselves to earth's doom of care and sorrow, and troubled joy, and had no more a home at Merry Mount. That was Edith's mystery. Now leave we the priest to marry them, and the masquers to sport round the Maypole, till the last sunbeam be withdrawn from its summit, and the shadows of the forest mingle gloomily in the dance. Meanwhile, we may discover who these gay people were.

Two hundred years ago, and more, the old world and its inhabitants became mutually weary of each other. Men voyaged by thousands to the West: some to barter glass beads, and such like jewels, for the furs of the Indian hunter; some to conquer virgin empires; and one stern band to pray. But none of these motives had much weight with the colonists of Merry Mount. Their leaders were men who had sported so long with life, that when Thought and Wisdom came, even these unwelcome guests were led astray by the crowd of vanities which they should have put to flight. Erring Thought and perverted Wisdom were made to put on masques, and play the fool. The men of whom we speak, after losing the heart's fresh gayety, imagined a wild philosophy of pleasure, and came hither to act out their latest day-dream. They gathered followers from all that giddy tribe whose whole life is like the festal days of soberer men. In their train were minstrels, not unknown in London streets: wandering players, whose theatres had been the halls of noblemen; mummers, rope-dancers, and mountebanks, who would long be missed at wakes, church ales, and fairs; in a word, mirth makers of every sort, such as abounded in that age, but now began to be discountenanced by the rapid growth of Puritanism. Light had their footsteps been on land, and as lightly they came across the sea. Many had been maddened by their previous troubles into a gay despair; others were as madly gay in the flush of youth, like the May Lord and his Lady; but whatever might be the quality of their mirth, old and young were gay at Merry Mount. The young deemed themselves happy. The elder spirits, if they knew that mirth was but the counterfeit of happiness, yet followed the false shadow wilfully, because at least her garments glittered brightest. Sworn triflers of a lifetime, they would not venture among the sober truths of life not even to be truly blest.

All the hereditary pastimes of Old England were transplanted hither. The King of Christmas was duly crowned, and the Lord of Misrule bore potent sway. On the Eve of St. John, they felled whole acres of the forest to make bonfires, and danced by the blaze all night, crowned with garlands, and throwing flowers into the flame. At harvest time, though their crop was of the smallest, they made an image with the sheaves of Indian corn, and wreathed it with autumnal garlands, and bore it home triumphantly. But what chiefly characterized the colonists of Merry Mount was their veneration for the Maypole. It has made their true history a poet's tale. Spring decked the hallowed emblem with young blossoms and fresh green boughs; Summer brought roses of the deepest blush, and the perfected foliage of the forest; Autumn enriched it with that red and yellow gorgeousness which converts each wildwood leaf into a painted flower; and Winter silvered it with sleet, and hung it round with icicles, till it flashed in the cold sunshine, itself a frozen sunbeam. Thus each alternate season did homage to the Maypole, and paid it a tribute of its own richest splendor. Its votaries danced round it, once, at least, in every month; sometimes they called it their religion, or their altar; but always, it was the banner staff of Merry Mount.

Unfortunately, there were men in the new world of a sterner faith than these Maypole worshippers. Not far from Merry Mount was a settlement of Puritans, most dismal wretches, who said their prayers before daylight, and then wrought in the forest or the cornfield till evening made it prayer time again. Their weapons were always at hand to shoot down the straggling savage. When they met in conclave, it was never to keep up the old English mirth, but to hear sermons three hours long, or to proclaim bounties on the heads of wolves and the scalps of Indians. Their festivals were fast days, and their chief pastime the singing of psalms. Woe to the youth or maiden who did but dream of a dance! The selectman nodded to the constable; and there sat the light-heeled reprobate in the stocks; or if he danced, it was round the whipping-post, which might be termed the Puritan Maypole.

A party of these grim Puritans, toiling through the difficult woods, each with a horseload of iron armor to burden his footsteps, would sometimes draw near the sunny precincts of Merry Mount. There were the silken colonists, sporting round their Maypole: perhaps teaching a bear to dance, or striving to communicate their mirth to the grave Indian; or masquerading in the skins of deer and wolves, which they had hunted for that especial purpose. Often, the whole colony were playing at blindman's buff, magistrates and all, with their eyes bandaged, except a single scapegoat, whom the blinded sinners pursued by the tinkling of the bells at his garments. Once, it is said, they were seen following a flower-decked corpse, with merriment and festive music, to his grave. But did the dead man laugh? In their quietest times, they sang ballads and told tales, for the edification of their pious visitors; or perplexed them with juggling tricks; or grinned at them through horse collars; and when sport itself grew wearisome, they made game of their own stupidity, and began a yawning match. At the very least of these enormities, the men of iron shook their heads and frowned so darkly that the revellers looked up, imagining that a momentary cloud had overcast the sunshine, which was to be perpetual there. On the other hand, the Puritans affirmed that, when a psalm was pealing from their place of worship, the echo which the forest sent them back seemed often like the chorus of a jolly catch, closing with a roar of laughter. Who but the fiend, and his bond slaves, the crew of Merry Mount, had thus disturbed them? In due time, a feud arose, stern and bitter on one side, and as serious on the other as anything could be among such light spirits as had sworn allegiance to the Maypole. The future complexion of New England was involved in this important quarrel. Should the grizzly saints establish their jurisdiction over the gay sinners, then would their spirits darken all the clime and make it a land of clouded visages, of hard toil, of sermon and psalm forever. But should the banner staff of Merry Mount be fortunate, sunshine would break upon the hills, and flowers would beautify the forest, and late posterity do homage to the Maypole.

After these authentic passages from history, we return to the nuptials of the Lord and Lady of the May. Alas! we have delayed too long, and must darken our tale too suddenly. As we glance again at the Maypole, a solitary sunbeam is fading from the summit, and leaves only a faint, golden tinge blended with the hues of the rainbow banner. Even that dim light is now withdrawn, relinquishing the whole domain of Merry Mount to the evening gloom, which has rushed so instantaneously from the black surrounding woods. But some of these black shadows have rushed forth in human shape.

Yes, with the setting sun, the last day of mirth had passed from Merry Mount. The ring of gay masquers was disordered and broken; the stag lowered his antlers in dismay; the wolf grew weaker than a lamb; the bells of the morris-dancers tinkled with tremulous affright. The Puritans had played a characteristic part in the Maypole mummer-

ies. Their darksome figures were intermixed with the wild shapes of their foes, and made the scene a picture of the moment, when waking thoughts start up amid the scattered fantasies of a dream. The leader of the hostile party stood in the centre of the circle, while the route of monsters cowered around him, like evil spirits in the presence of a dread magician. No fantastic foolery could look him in the face. So stern was the energy of his aspect, that the whole man, visage, frame and soul, seemed wrought of iron, gifted with life and thought, yet all of one substance with his headpiece and breastplate. It was the Puritan of Puritans; it was Endicott himself!

"Stand off, priest of Baal!" said he, with a grim frown, and laying no reverent hand upon the surplice. "I know thee, Blackstone![1] Thou art the man who couldst not abide the rule even of thine own corrupted church, and hast come hither to preach iniquity, and to give example of it in thy life. But now shall it be seen that the Lord hath sanctified this wilderness for his peculiar people. Woe unto them that would defile it! And first, for this flower-decked abomination, the altar of thy worship!"

And with his keen sword Endicott assaulted the hallowed Maypole. Nor long did it resist his arm. It groaned with a dismal sound; it showered leaves and rosebuds upon the remorseless enthusiast; and finally, with all its green boughs and ribbons and flowers, symbolic of departed pleasures, down fell the banner staff of Merry Mount. As it sank, tradition says, the evening sky grew darker, and the woods threw forth a more sombre shadow.

"There," cried Endicott, looking triumphantly on his work, "there lies the only Maypole in New England! The thought is strong within me that, by its fall, is shadowed forth the fate of light and idle mirth makers, amongst us and our posterity. Amen, saith John Endicott."

"Amen!" echoed his followers.

But the votaries of the Maypole gave one groan for their idol. At the sound, the Puri-

[1] Did Governor Endicott speak less positively, we should suspect a mistake here. The Rev. Mr. Blackstone, though an eccentric, is not known to have been an immoral man. We rather doubt his identity with the priest of Merry Mount. [*Author's note.*]

tan leader glanced at the crew of Comus, each a figure of broad mirth, yet, at this moment, strangely expressive of sorrow and dismay.

"Valiant captain," quoth Peter Palfrey, the Ancient of the band, "what order shall be taken with the prisoners?"

"I thought not to repent me of cutting down a Maypole," replied Endicott, "yet now I could find in my heart to plant it again, and give each of these bestial pagans one other dance round their idol. It would have served rarely for a whipping-post!"

"But there are pine-trees enow," suggested the lieutenant.

"True, good Ancient," said the leader. "Wherefore, bind the heathen crew, and bestow on them a small matter of stripes apiece, as earnest of our future justice. Set some of the rogues in the stocks to rest themselves, so soon as Providence shall bring us to one of our own well-ordered settlements, where such accommodations may be found. Further penalties, such as branding and cropping of ears, shall be thought of hereafter."

"How many stripes for the priest?" inquired Ancient Palfrey.

"None as yet," answered Endicott, bending his iron frown upon the culprit. "It must be for the Great and General Court to determine, whether stripes and long imprisonment, and other grievous penalty, may atone for his transgressions. Let him look to himself! For such as violate our civil order, it may be permitted us to show mercy. But woe to the wretch that troubleth our religion!"

"And this dancing bear," resumed the officer. "Must he share the stripes of his fellows?"

"Shoot him through the head!" said the energetic Puritan. "I suspect witchcraft in the beast."

"Here be a couple of shining ones," continued Peter Palfrey, pointing his weapon at the Lord and Lady of the May. "They seem to be of high station among these misdoers. Methinks their dignity will not be fitted with less than a double share of stripes."

Endicott rested on his sword, and closely surveyed the dress and aspect of the hapless pair. There they stood, pale, downcast, and apprehensive. Yet there was an air of mutual support, and of pure affection, seeking aid and giving it, that showed them to be man and wife, with the sanction of a priest upon their love. The youth, in the peril of the moment, had dropped his gilded staff, and thrown his arm about the Lady of the May, who leaned against his breast, too lightly to burden him, but with weight enough to express that their destinies were linked together, for good or evil. They looked first at each other, and then into the grim captain's face. There they stood, in the first hour of wedlock, while the idle pleasures, of which their companions were the emblems, had given place to the sternest cares of life, personified by the dark Puritans. But never had their youthful beauty seemed so pure and high as when its glow was chastened by adversity.

"Youth," said Endicott, "ye stand in an evil case, thou and thy maiden wife. Make ready presently, for I am minded that ye shall both have a token to remember your wedding day!"

"Stern man," cried the May Lord, "how can I move thee? Were the means at hand, I would resist to the death. Being powerless, I entreat! Do with me as thou wilt, but let Edith go untouched!"

"Not so," replied the immitigable zealot. "We are not wont to show an idle courtesy to that sex, which requireth the stricter discipline. What sayest thou, maid? Shall thy silken bridegroom suffer thy share of the penalty, besides his own?"

"Be it death," said Edith, "and lay it all on me!"

Truly, as Endicott had said, the poor lovers stood in a woful case. Their foes were triumphant, their friends captive and abased, their home desolate, the benighted wilderness around them, and a rigorous destiny, in the shape of the Puritan leader, their only guide. Yet the deepening twilight could not altogether conceal that the iron man was softened; he smiled at the fair spectacle of early love; he almost sighed for the inevitable blight of early hopes.

"The troubles of life have come hastily on this young couple," observed Endicott. "We will see how they comport themselves under their present trials ere we burden them with greater. If, among the spoil, there be any garments of a more decent fashion, let them be put upon this May Lord and his Lady, instead of their glistening vanities. Look to it, some of you."

"And shall not the youth's hair be cut?" asked Peter Palfrey, looking with abhorrence at the lovelock and long glossy curls of the young man.

"Crop it forthwith, and that in the true pumpkinshell fashion," answered the captain. "Then bring them along with us, but more gently than their fellows. There be qualities in the youth, which may make him valiant to fight, and sober to toil, and pious to pray; and in the maiden, that may fit her to become a mother in our Israel, bringing up babes in better nurture than her own hath been. Nor think ye, young ones, that they are the happiest, even in our lifetime of a moment, who misspend it in dancing round a Maypole!"

And Endicott, the severest Puritan of all who laid the rock foundation of New England, lifted the wreath of roses from the ruin of the Maypole, and threw it, with his own gauntleted hand, over the heads of the Lord and Lady of the May. It was a deed of prophecy. As the moral gloom of the world overpowers all systematic gayety, even so was their home of wild mirth made desolate amid the sad forest. They returned to it no more. But as their flowery garland was wreathed of the brightest roses that had grown there, so, in the tie that united them, were intertwined all the purest and best of their early joys. They went heavenward, supporting each other along the difficult path which it was their lot to tread, and never wasted one regretful thought on the vanities of Merry Mount.

Endicott and the Red Cross

(1837)

At noon of an autumnal day, more than two centuries ago, the English colors were displayed by the standard-bearer of the Salem trainband, which had mustered for martial exercise under the orders of John Endicott. It was a period when the religious exiles were accustomed often to buckle on their armor, and practise the handling of their weapons of war. Since the first settlement of New England, its prospects had never been so dismal. The dissensions between Charles the First and his subjects were then, and for several years afterwards, confined to the floor of Parliament. The measures of the King and ministry were rendered more tyrannically violent by an opposition, which had not yet acquired sufficient confidence in its own strength to resist royal injustice with the sword. The bigoted and haughty primate, Laud, Archbishop of Canterbury, controlled the religious affairs of the realm, and was consequently invested with powers which might have wrought the utter ruin of the two Puritan colonies, Plymouth and Massachusetts. There is evidence on record that our forefathers perceived their danger, but were resolved that their infant country should not fall without a struggle, even beneath the giant strength of the King's right arm.

Such was the aspect of the times when the folds of the English banner, with the Red Cross in its field, were flung out over a company of Puritans. Their leader, the famous Endicott, was a man of stern and resolute countenance, the effect of which was heightened by a grizzled beard that swept the upper portion of his breastplate. This piece of armor was so highly polished that the whole surrounding scene had its image in the glittering steel. The central object in the mirrored picture was an edifice of humble architecture with neither steeple nor bell to proclaim it — what nevertheless it was — the house of prayer. A token of the perils of the wilderness was seen in the grim head of a wolf, which had just been slain within the precincts of the town, and according to the regular mode of claiming the bounty, was nailed on the porch of the meeting-house. The blood was still plashing on the doorstep. There happened to be visible, at the same noontide hour, so many other characteristics of the times and manners of the Puritans, that we must endeavor to represent them in a sketch, though far less vividly than they were reflected in the polished breastplate of John Endicott.

In close vicinity to the sacred edifice appeared that important engine of Puritanic authority, the whipping-post — with the soil around it well trodden by the feet of evil doers, who had there been disciplined. At one corner of the meeting-house was the pillory, and at the other the stocks; and, by a singular good fortune for our sketch, the head of an Episcopalian and suspected Catholic was grotesquely incased in the former machine; while a fellow-criminal, who had boisterously quaffed a health to the king, was confined by the legs in the latter. Side by side, on the meeting-house steps, stood a male and a female figure. The man was a tall, lean, haggard personification of fanaticism, bearing on his breast this label, — A WANTON GOSPELLER, — which betokened that he had dared to give interpretations of Holy Writ unsanctioned by the infallible judgment of the civil and religious rulers. His aspect showed no lack of zeal to maintain his heterodoxies, even at the stake. The woman wore a cleft stick on her tongue, in appropriate retribution for having wagged that unruly member against the elders of the church; and her countenance and gestures gave much cause to apprehend that, the moment the stick should be removed, a repetition of the offence would demand new ingenuity in chastising it.

The above-mentioned individuals had been sentenced to undergo their various modes of ignominy, for the space of one hour at noonday. But among the crowd were several whose punishment would be life-long; some, whose ears had been cropped, like those of puppy dogs; others, whose cheeks had been branded with the initials of their misdemeanors; one, with his nostrils slit and seared; and another, with a halter about his neck, which he was forbidden ever to take off, or to conceal beneath his garments. Methinks he must have been grievously tempted to affix the other end of the rope to some convenient beam or bough. There was likewise a young woman, with no mean share of beauty, whose doom it was to wear the letter A on the breast of her gown, in the eyes of all the world and her own children. And even her own children knew what that initial signified. Sporting with her infamy, the lost and desperate creature had embroidered the fatal token in scarlet cloth, with gold thread and the nicest art of needlework; so that the capital A might

have been thought to mean Admirable, or anything rather than Adulteress.

Let not the reader argue, from any of these evidences of iniquity, that the times of the Puritans were more vicious than our own, when, as we pass along the very street of this sketch, we discern no badge of infamy on man or woman. It was the policy of our ancestors to search out even the most secret sins, and expose them to shame, without fear or favor, in the broadest light of the noonday sun. Were such the custom now, perchance we might find materials for a no less piquant sketch than the above.

Except the malefactors whom we have described, and the diseased or infirm persons, the whole male population of the town, between sixteen years and sixty, were seen in the ranks of the trainband. A few stately savages, in all the pomp and dignity of the primeval Indian, stood gazing at the spectacle. Their flint-headed arrows were but childish weapons compared with the matchlocks of the Puritans, and would have rattled harmlessly against the steel caps and hammered iron breastplates which inclosed each soldier in an individual fortress. The valiant John Endicott glanced with an eye of pride at his sturdy followers, and prepared to renew the martial toils of the day.

"Come, my stout hearts!" quoth he, drawing his sword. "Let us show these poor heathen that we can handle our weapons like men of might. Well for them, if they put us not to prove it in earnest!"

The iron-breasted company straightened their line, and each man drew the heavy butt of his matchlock close to his left foot, thus awaiting the orders of the captain. But, as Endicott glanced right and left along the front, he discovered a personage at some little distance with whom it behooved him to hold a parley. It was an elderly gentleman, wearing a black cloak and band, and a high-crowned hat, beneath which was a velvet skull-cap, the whole being the garb of a Puritan minister. This reverend person bore a staff which seemed to have been recently cut in the forest, and his shoes were bemired as if he had been travelling on foot through the swamps of the wilderness. His aspect was perfectly that of a pilgrim, heightened also by an apostolic dignity. Just as Endicott perceived him he laid aside his staff, and stooped to drink at a bubbling fountain which gushed into the sunshine about a score of yards from the corner of the meeting-house. But, ere the good man drank, he turned his face heavenward in thankfulness, and then, holding back his gray beard with one hand, he scooped up his simple draught in the hollow of the other.

"What, ho! good Mr. Williams," shouted Endicott. "You are welcome back again to our town of peace. How does our worthy Governor Winthrop? And what news from Boston?"

"The Governor hath his health, worshipful Sir," answered Roger Williams, now resuming his staff, and drawing near. "And for the news, here is a letter, which, knowing I was to travel hitherward to-day, his Excellency committed to my charge. Belike it contains tidings of much import; for a ship arrived yesterday from England."

Mr. Williams, the minister of Salem and of course known to all the spectators, had now reached the spot where Endicott was standing under the banner of his company, and put the Governor's epistle into his hand. The broad seal was impressed with Winthrop's coat of arms. Endicott hastily unclosed the letter and began to read, while, as his eye passed down the page, a wrathful change came over his manly countenance. The blood glowed through it, till it seemed to be kindling with an internal heat; nor was it unnatural to suppose that his breastplate would likewise become red-hot with the angry fire of the bosom which it covered. Arriving at the conclusion, he shook the letter fiercely in his hand, so that it rustled as loud as the flag above his head.

"Black tidings these, Mr. Williams," said he; "blacker never came to New England. Doubtless you know their purport?"

"Yea, truly," replied Roger Williams; "for the Governor consulted, respecting this matter, with my brethren in the ministry at Boston; and my opinion was likewise asked. And his Excellency entreats you by me, that the news be not suddenly noised abroad, lest the people be stirred up unto some outbreak, and thereby give the King and the Archbishop a handle against us."

"The Governor is a wise man — a wise man, and a meek and moderate," said Endicott, setting his teeth grimly. "Nevertheless, I must do according to my own best judgment. There is neither man, woman, nor child in New England, but has a concern as dear as life in these tidings; and if John Endicott's voice be loud enough, man, woman, and child shall hear them. Soldiers, wheel into a hollow square! Ho, good people! Here are news for one and all of you."

The soldiers closed in around their captain; and he and Roger Williams stood together under the banner of the Red Cross; while the women and the aged men pressed forward, and the mothers held up their children to look Endicott in the face. A few taps of the drum gave signal for silence and attention.

"Fellow-soldiers, — fellow-exiles," began Endicott, speaking under strong excitement, yet powerfully restraining it, "wherefore did ye leave your native country? Wherefore, I say, have we left the green and fertile fields, the cottages, or, perchance, the old gray halls, where we were born and bred, the churchyards where our forefathers lie buried? Wherefore have we come hither to set up our own tombstones in a wilderness? A howling wilderness it is! The wolf and the bear meet us within halloo of our dwellings. The savage lieth in wait for us in the dismal shadow of the woods. The stubborn roots of the trees break our ploughshares, when we would till the earth. Our children cry for bread, and we must dig in the sands of the sea-shore to satisfy them. Wherefore, I say again, have we sought this country of a rugged soil and wintry sky? Was it not for the enjoyment of our civil rights? Was it not for liberty to worship God according to our conscience?"

"Call you this liberty of conscience?" interrupted a voice on the steps of the meeting-house.

It was the Wanton Gospeller. A sad and quiet smile flitted across the mild visage of Roger Williams. But Endicott, in the excitement of the moment, shook his sword wrathfully at the culprit — an ominous gesture from a man like him.

"What hast thou to do with conscience, thou knave?" cried he. "I said liberty to worship God, not license to profane and ridicule him. Break not in upon my speech, or I will lay thee neck and heels till this time to-morrow! Hearken to me, friends, nor heed that accursed rhapsodist. As I was saying, we have sacrificed all things, and have come to a land whereof the old world hath scarcely heard, that we might make a new world unto ourselves, and painfully seek a path from hence to heaven. But what think ye now? This son of a Scotch tyrant — this grandson of a Papistical and adulterous Scotch woman, whose death proved that a golden crown doth not always save an anointed head from the block —"

"Nay, brother, nay," interposed Mr. Williams; "thy words are not meet for a secret chamber, far less for a public street."

"Hold thy peace, Roger Williams!" answered Endicott, imperiously. "My spirit is wiser than thine for the business now in hand. I tell ye, fellow-exiles, that Charles of England, and Laud, our bitterest persecutor, arch-priest of Canterbury, are resolute to pursue us even hither. They are taking counsel, saith this letter, to send over a governor-general, in whose breast shall be deposited all the law and equity of the land. They are minded, also, to establish the idolatrous forms of English Episcopacy; so that, when Laud shall kiss the Pope's toe, as cardinal of Rome, he may deliver New England, bound hand and foot, into the power of his master!"

A deep groan from the auditors, — a sound of wrath, as well as fear and sorrow, — responded to this intelligence.

"Look ye to it, brethren," resumed Endicott, with increasing energy. "If this king and this arch-prelate have their will, we shall briefly behold a cross on the spire of this tabernacle which we have builded, and a high altar within its walls, with wax tapers burning round it at noonday. We shall hear the sacring bell, and the voices of the Romish priests saying the mass. But think ye, Christian men, that these abominations may be suffered without a sword drawn? without a shot fired? without blood spilt, yea, on the very stairs of the pulpit? No, — be ye strong of hand and stout of heart! Here we stand on our own soil, which we have bought with our goods, which we have won with our swords, which we have cleared with our axes, which we have tilled with the sweat of our brows, which we have sanctified with our prayers to the God that brought us hither! Who shall enslave us here? What have we to do with this mitred prelate, — with this crowned king? What have we to do with England?"

Endicott gazed round at the excited countenances of the people, now full of his own spirit, and then turned suddenly to the standard-bearer, who stood close behind him.

"Officer, lower your banner!" said he.

The officer obeyed; and, brandishing his sword, Endicott thrust it through the cloth, and, with his left hand, rent the Red Cross completely out of the banner. He then waved the tattered ensign above his head.

"Sacrilegious wretch!" cried the high-churchman in the pillory, unable longer to restrain himself, "thou hast rejected the symbol of our holy religion!"

"Treason, treason!" roared the royalist in the stocks. "He hath defaced the King's banner!"

"Before God and man, I will avouch the deed," answered Endicott. "Beat a flourish, drummer! — shout, soldiers and people! — in honor of the ensign of New England. Neither Pope nor Tyrant hath part in it now!"

With a cry of triumph, the people gave their sanction to one of the boldest exploits which our history records. And forever honored be the name of Endicott! We look back through the mist of ages, and recognize in the rending of the Red Cross from New England's banner the first omen of that deliverance which our fathers consummated after the bones of the stern Puritan had lain more than a century in the dust.

David Swan

A FANTASY

(1837)

We can be but partially acquainted even with the events which actually influence our course through life, and our final destiny. There are innumerable other events — if such they may be called — which come close upon us, yet pass away without actual results, or even betraying their near approach, by the reflection of any light or shadow across our minds. Could we know all the vicissitudes of our fortunes, life would be too full of hope and fear, exultation or disappointment, to afford us a single hour of true serenity. This idea may be illustrated by a page from the secret history of David Swan.

We have nothing to do with David until we find him, at the age of twenty, on the high road from his native place to the city of Boston, where his uncle, a small dealer in the grocery line, was to take him behind the counter. Be it enough to say that he was a native of New Hampshire, born of respectable parents, and had received an ordinary school education, with a classic finish by a year at Gilmanton Academy. After journeying on foot from sunrise till nearly noon of a summer's day, his weariness and the increasing heat determined him to sit down in the first convenient shade, and await the coming up of the stagecoach. As if planted on purpose for him, there soon appeared a little tuft of maples, with a delightful recess in the midst, and such a fresh, bubbling spring that it seemed never to have sparkled for any wayfarer but David Swan. Virgin or not, he kissed it with his thirsty lips, and then flung himself along the brink, pillowing his head upon some shirts and a pair of pantaloons, tied up in a striped cotton handkerchief. The sunbeams could not reach him; the dust did not yet arise from the road after the heavy rain of yesterday; and his grassy lair suited the young man better than a bed of down. The spring murmured drowsily beside him; the branches waved dreamily across the blue sky overhead; and a deep sleep, perchance hiding dreams within its depths, fell upon David Swan. But we are to relate events which he did not dream of.

While he lay sound asleep in the shade, other people were wide awake, and passed to and fro, afoot, or horseback, and in all sorts of vehicles, along the sunny road by his bedchamber. Some looked neither to the right hand nor the left, and knew not that he was there; some merely glanced that way, without admitting the slumberer among their busy thoughts; some laughed to see how soundly he slept; and several, whose hearts were brimming full of scorn, ejected their venomous superfluity on David Swan. A middle-aged widow, when nobody else was near, thrust her head a little way into the recess, and vowed that the young fellow looked charming in his sleep. A temperance lecturer saw him, and wrought poor David into the texture of his evening's discourse, as an awful instance of dead drunkenness by the roadside. But censure, praise, merriment, scorn, and indifference were all one, or rather all nothing, to David Swan.

He had slept only a few moments when a brown carriage, drawn by a handsome pair of horses, bowled easily along, and was brought to a standstill nearly in front of David's resting place. A linchpin had fallen out, and permitted one of the wheels to slide off. The damage was slight, and occasioned merely a momentary alarm to an elderly merchant and his wife, who were returning to Boston in the carriage. While the coachman and a servant were replacing the wheel, the lady and gentleman sheltered themselves beneath the maple-trees, and there espied the bubbling fountain, and David Swan asleep beside it. Impressed with the awe which the humblest sleeper usually sheds around him, the merchant trod as lightly as the gout would allow; and his spouse took heed not to rustle her silk gown, lest David should start up all of a sudden.

"How soundly he sleeps!" whispered the old gentleman. "From what a depth he draws that easy breath! Such sleep as that, brought on without an opiate, would be worth more to me than half my income; for it would suppose health and an untroubled mind."

"And youth, besides," said the lady. "Healthy and quiet age does not sleep thus. Our slumber is no more like his than our wakefulness."

The longer they looked, the more did this elderly couple feel interested in the unknown youth, to whom the wayside and the maple shade were as a secret chamber, with the rich gloom of damask curtains brooding over him. Perceiving that a stray sunbeam glimmered down upon his face, the lady contrived to twist a branch aside, so as to intercept it. And having done this little act of kindness, she began to feel like a mother to him.

"Providence seems to have laid him here," whispered she to her husband, "and to have brought us hither to find him, after our disappointment in our cousin's son. Methinks I can see a likeness to our departed Henry. Shall we waken him?"

"To what purpose?" said the merchant, hesitating. "We know nothing of the youth's character."

"That open countenance!" replied his wife in the same hushed voice, yet earnestly. "This innocent sleep!"

While these whispers were passing, the sleeper's heart did not throb, nor his breath become agitated, nor his features betray the least token of interest. Yet Fortune was bending over him, just ready to let fall a burden of gold. The old merchant had lost his only son, and had no heir to his wealth except a distant relative, with whose conduct he was dissatisfied. In such cases people sometimes do stranger things than to act the magician, and awaken a young man to splendor who fell asleep in poverty.

"Shall we not waken him?" repeated the lady persuasively.

"The coach is ready, sir," said the servant, behind.

The old couple started, reddened, and hurried away, mutually wondering that they should ever have dreamed of doing anything so very ridiculous. The merchant threw himself back in the carriage, and occupied his mind with the plan of a magnificent asylum for unfortunate men of business. Meanwhile, David Swan enjoyed his nap.

The carriage could not have gone above a mile or two, when a pretty young girl came along with a tripping pace, which showed precisely how her little heart was dancing in her bosom. Perhaps it was this merry kind of motion that caused — is there any harm in saying it? — her garter to slip its knot. Conscious that the silken girth — if silk it were — was relaxing its hold, she turned aside into the shelter of the maple-trees, and there found a young man asleep by the spring! Blushing as red as any rose that she should have intruded into a gentleman's bedchamber, and for such a purpose, too, she was about to make her escape on tiptoe. But there was peril near the sleeper. A monster

of a bee had been wandering overhead — buzz, buzz, buzz — now among the leaves, now flashing through the strips of sunshine, and now lost in the dark shade, till finally he appeared to be settling on the eyelid of David Swan. The sting of a bee is sometimes deadly. As freehearted as she was innocent, the girl attacked the intruder with her handkerchief, brushed him soundly, and drove him from beneath the maple shade. How sweet a picture! This good deed accomplished, with quickened breath, and a deeper blush, she stole a glance at the youthful stranger for whom she had been battling with a dragon in the air.

"He is handsome!" thought she, and blushed redder yet.

How could it be that no dream of bliss grew so strong within him, that, shattered by its very strength, it should part asunder, and allow him to perceive the girl among its phantoms? Why, at least, did no smile of welcome brighten upon his face? She was come, the maid whose soul, according to the old and beautiful idea, had been severed from his own, and whom, in all his vague but passionate desires, he yearned to meet. Her, only, could he love with a perfect love; him, only, could she receive into the depths of her heart; and now her image was faintly blushing in the fountain by his side; should it pass away, its happy luster would never gleam upon his life again.

"How sound he sleeps!" murmured the girl.

She departed, but did not trip along the road so lightly as when she came.

Now, this girl's father was a thriving country merchant in the neighborhood, and happened, at that identical time, to be looking out for just such a young man as David Swan. Had David formed a wayside acquaintance with the daughter, he would have become the father's clerk, and all else in natural succession. So here, again, had good fortune — the best of fortunes — stolen so near that her garments brushed against him; and he knew nothing of the matter.

The girl was hardly out of sight when two men turned aside beneath the maple shade. Both had dark faces, set off by cloth caps, which were drawn down aslant over their brows. Their dresses were shabby, yet had a certain smartness. These were a couple of rascals who got their living by whatever the devil sent them, and now, in the interim of other business, had staked the joint profits of their next piece of villany on a game of cards, which was to have been decided here under the trees. But, finding David asleep by the spring, one of the rogues whispered to his fellow, —

"Hist! — Do you see that bundle under his head?"

The other villain nodded, winked, and leered.

"I'll bet you a horn of brandy," said the first, "that the chap has either a pocketbook, or a snug little hoard of small change, stowed away amongst his shirts. And if not there, we shall find it in his pantaloons pocket."

"But how if he wakes?" said the other.

His companion thrust aside his waistcoat, pointed to the handle of a dirk, and nodded.

"So be it!" muttered the second villain.

They approached the unconscious David, and, while one pointed the dagger towards his heart, the other began to search the bundle beneath his head. Their two faces, grim, wrinkled, and ghastly with guilt and fear, bent over their victim, looking horrible enough to be mistaken for fiends, should he suddenly awake. Nay, had the villains glanced aside into the spring, even they would hardly have known themselves as reflected there. But David Swan had never worn a more tranquil aspect, even when asleep on his mother's breast.

"I must take away the bundle," whispered one.

"If he stirs, I'll strike," muttered the other.

But, at this moment, a dog, scenting along the ground, came in beneath the maple-trees, and gazed alternately at each of these wicked men, then at the quiet sleeper. He then lapped out of the fountain.

"Pshaw!" said one villain. "We can do nothing now. The dog's master must be close behind."

"Let's take a drink and be off," said the other.

The man with the dagger thrust back the weapon into his bosom, and drew forth a pocket pistol, but not of that kind which kills by a single discharge. It was a flask of liquor, with a block-tin tumbler screwed upon the mouth. Each drank a comfortable dram, and left the spot, with so many jests, and such laughter at their unaccomplished wickedness, that they might be said to have gone on their way rejoicing. In a few hours they had forgotten the whole affair, nor once imagined that the recording angel had written down the crime of murder against their souls, in letters as durable as eternity. As for David Swan, he still slept quietly, neither conscious of the shadow of death when it hung over him, nor of the glow of renewed life when that shadow was withdrawn.

He slept, but no longer so quietly as at first. An hour's repose had snatched from his elastic frame the weariness with which many hours of toil had burdened it. Now, he stirred — now, moved his lips, without a sound — now, talked, in an inward tone, to the noon-day specters of his dream. But a noise of wheels came rattling louder and louder along the road, until it dashed through the dispersing mist of David's slumber — and there was the stagecoach. He started up with all his ideas about him.

"Halloo, driver! — take a passenger?" shouted he.

"Room on top!" answered the driver.

Up mounted David, and bowled away merrily towards Boston, without so much as a parting glance at that fountain of dreamlike vicissitude. He knew not that a phantom of Wealth had thrown a golden hue upon its waters — nor that one of Love had sighed softly to their murmur — nor that one of Death had threatened to crimson them with his blood — all, in the brief hour since he lay down to sleep. Sleeping or waking, we hear not the airy footsteps of the strange things that almost happen. Does it not argue a superintending Providence that, while viewless and unexpected events thrust themselves continually athwart our path, there should still be regularity enough in mortal life to render foresight even partially available?

Rappaccini's Daughter
(1844)

The theme of the story is the lust of knowledge, a source of evil which much occupied Hawthorne's mind. A main source of the story itself is suggested by his quotation, in his notebooks for 1839, from Sir Thomas Browne's *Vulgar Errors:* "A story there passeth of an Indian King that sent unto Alexander a fair woman, fed with aconite and other poisons, with this intent complexionally to destroy him!"

A young man, named Giovanni Guasconti, came, very long ago, from the more southern region of Italy, to pursue his studies at the University of Padua. Giovanni, who had but a scanty supply of gold ducats in his pocket, took lodgings in a high and gloomy chamber of an old edifice which looked not unworthy to have been the palace of a Paduan noble, and which, in fact, exhibited over its entrance the armorial bearings of a family long since extinct. The young stranger, who was not unstudied in the great poem of his country, recollected that one of the ancestors of this family, and perhaps an occupant of this very mansion, had been pictured by Dante as a partaker of the immortal agonies of his Inferno. These reminiscences and associations, together with the tendency to heartbreak natural to a young man for the first time out of his native sphere, caused Giovanni to sigh heavily as he looked around the desolate and ill-furnished apartment.

"Holy Virgin, signor!" cried old Dame Lisabetta, who, won by the youth's remarkable beauty of person, was kindly endeavoring to give the chamber a habitable air, "what a sigh was that to come out of a young man's heart! Do you find this old mansion gloomy? For the love of Heaven, then, put your head out of the window, and you will see as bright sunshine as you have left in Naples."

Guasconti mechanically did as the old woman advised, but could not quite agree with her that the Paduan sunshine was as cheerful as that of southern Italy. Such as it was, however, it fell upon a garden beneath the window and expended its fostering influences on a variety of plants, which seemed to have been cultivated with exceeding care.

"Does this garden belong to the house?" asked Giovanni.

"Heaven forbid, signor, unless it were fruitful of better pot herbs than any that grow there now," answered old Lisabetta. "No; that garden is cultivated by the own hands of Signor Giacomo Rappaccini, the famous doctor, who, I warrant him, has been heard of as far as Naples. It is said that he distils these plants into medicines that are as potent as a charm. Oftentimes you may see the signor doctor at work, and perchance the signora, his daughter, too, gathering the strange flowers that grow in the garden."

The old woman had now done what she could for the aspect of the chamber; and, commending the young man to the protection of the saints, took her departure.

Giovanni still found no better occupation than to look down into the garden beneath his window. From its appearance, he judged it to be one of those botanic gardens which were of earlier date in Padua than elsewhere in Italy or in the world. Or, not improbably, it might once have been the pleasure-place of an opulent family; for there was the ruin of a marble fountain in the centre sculptured with rare art, but so wofully shattered that it was impossible to trace the original design from the chaos of remaining fragments. The water, however, continued to gush and sparkle into the sunbeams as cheerfully as ever. A little gurgling sound ascended to the young man's window, and made him feel as if the fountain were an immortal spirit that sung its song unceasingly and without heeding the vicissitudes around it, while one century embodied it in marble and another scattered the perishable garniture on the soil. All about the pool into which the water subsided grew various plants, that seemed to require a plentiful supply of moisture for the nourishment of gigantic leaves, and, in some instances, flowers gorgeously magnificent. There was one shrub in particular, set in a marble vase in the midst of the pool, that bore a profusion of purple blossoms, each of which had the lustre and richness of a gem; and the whole together made a show so resplendent that it seemed enough to illuminate the garden, even had there been no sunshine. Every portion of the soil was peopled with plants and herbs, which, if less beautiful, still bore tokens of assiduous care, as if all had their individual virtues, known to the scientific mind that fostered them. Some were placed in urns, rich with old carving, and others in common garden pots; some crept serpent-like along the ground or climbed on high, using whatever means of ascent was offered them. One plant had wreathed itself round a statue of Vertumnus, which was thus quite veiled and shrouded in a drapery of hanging foliage, so happily arranged that it might have served a sculptor for a study.

While Giovanni stood at the window he heard a rustling behind a screen of leaves, and became aware that a person was at work in the garden. His figure soon emerged into view, and showed itself to be that of no common laborer, but a tall, emaciated, sallow, and sickly-looking man, dressed in a scholar's garb of black. He was beyond the middle term of life, with gray hair, a thin, gray beard, and a face singularly marked with intellect and cultivation, but which could never, even in his more youthful days, have expressed much warmth of heart.

Nothing could exceed the intentness with which this scientific gardener examined every shrub which grew in his path: it seemed as if he was looking into their inmost nature, making observations in regard to their creative essence, and discovering why one leaf grew in this shape and another in that, and wherefore such and such flowers differed among themselves in hue and perfume. Nevertheless, in spite of this deep intelligence on his part, there was no approach to intimacy between himself and these vegetable existences. On the contrary, he avoided their actual touch or the direct inhaling of their odors with a caution that impressed Giovanni most disagreeably; for the man's demeanor was that of one walking among malignant influences, such as savage beasts, or deadly snakes, or evil spirits, which, should he allow them one moment of license, would wreak upon him some terrible fatality. It was strangely frightful to the young man's imagination to see this air of insecurity in a person cultivating a garden, that most simple and innocent of human toils, and which had been alike the joy and labor of the unfallen parents of the race. Was this garden, then, the Eden of the present world? And this man, with such perception of harm in what his own hands caused to grow, — was he the Adam?

The distrustful gardener, while plucking away the dead leaves or pruning the too luxuriant growth of the shrubs, defended his hands with a pair of thick gloves. Nor were these his only armor. When, in his walk through the garden, he came to the magnificent plant that hung its purple gems beside the marble fountain, he placed a kind of mask over his mouth and nostrils, as if all this beauty did but conceal a deadlier malice; but, finding his task still too dangerous, he drew back, removed the mask, and called loudly, but in the infirm voice of a person affected with inward disease.

"Beatrice! Beatrice!"

"Here am I, my father. What would you?" cried a rich and youthful voice from the window of the opposite house — a voice as rich as a tropical sunset, and which made Giovanni, though he knew not why, think of deep hues of purple or crimson and of perfumes heavily delectable. "Are you in the garden?"

"Yes, Beatrice," answered the gardener, "and I need your help."

Soon there emerged from under a sculptured portal the figure of a young girl, arrayed with as much richness of taste as the most splendid of the flowers, beautiful as the day, and with a bloom so deep and vivid that one shade more would have been too much. She looked redundant with life, health, and energy; all of which attributes were bound down and compressed, as it were, and girdled tensely, in their luxuriance, by her virgin zone. Yet Giovanni's fancy must have grown morbid while he looked down into the garden; for the impression which the fair stranger made upon him was as if here were another flower, the human sister of those vegetable ones, as beautiful as they, more beautiful than the riches of them, but still to be touched only with a glove, nor to be approached without a mask. As Beatrice came down the garden path, it was observable that she handled and inhaled the odor of several of the plants which her father had most sedulously avoided.

"Here, Beatrice," said the latter, "see how many needful offices require to be done to our chief treasure. Yet, shattered as I am, my life might pay the penalty of approaching it so closely as circumstances demand. Henceforth, I fear, this plant must be consigned to your sole charge."

"And gladly will I undertake it," cried

again the rich tones of the young lady, as she bent towards the magnificent plant and opened her arms as if to embrace it. "Yes, my sister, my splendor, it shall be Beatrice's task to nurse and serve thee; and thou shalt reward her with thy kisses and perfumed breath, which to her is as the breath of life."

Then, with all the tenderness in her manner that was so strikingly expressed in her words, she busied herself with such attentions as the plant seemed to require; and Giovanni, at his lofty window, rubbed his eyes and almost doubted whether it were a girl tending her favorite flower, or one sister performing the duties of affection to another. The scene soon terminated. Whether Dr. Rappaccini had finished his labors in the garden, or that his watchful eye had caught the stranger's face, he now took his daughter's arm and retired. Night was already closing in; oppressive exhalations seemed to proceed from the plants and steal upward past the open window; and Giovanni, closing the lattice, went to his couch and dreamed of a rich flower and beautiful girl. Flower and maiden were different, and yet the same, and fraught with some strange peril in either shape.

But there is an influence in the light of morning that tends to rectify whatever errors of fancy, or even of judgment, we may have incurred during the sun's decline, or among the shadows of the night, or in the less wholesome glow of moonshine. Giovanni's first movement, on starting from sleep, was to throw open the window and gaze down into the garden which his dreams had made so fertile of mysteries. He was surprised and a little ashamed to find how real and matter-of-fact an affair it proved to be, in the first rays of the sun which gilded the dew-drops that hung upon leaf and blossom, and, while giving a brighter beauty to each rare flower, brought everything within the limits of ordinary experience. The young man rejoiced that, in the heart of the barren city, he had the privilege of overlooking this spot of lovely and luxuriant vegetation. It would serve, he said to himself, as a symbolic language to keep him in communion with Nature. Neither the sickly and thoughtworn Dr. Giacomo Rappaccini, it is true, nor his brilliant daughter, were now visible; so that Giovanni could

not determine how much of the singularity which he attributed to both was due to their own qualities and how much to his wonder-working fancy; but he was inclined to take a most rational view of the whole matter.

In the course of the day he paid his respects to Signor Pietro Baglioni, professor of medicine in the university, a physician of eminent repute, to whom Giovanni had brought a letter of introduction. The professor was an elderly personage, apparently of genial nature, and habits that might almost be called jovial. He kept the young man to dinner, and made himself very agreeable by the freedom and liveliness of his conversation, especially when warmed by a flask or two of Tuscan wine. Giovanni, conceiving that men of science, inhabitants of the same city, must needs be on familiar terms with one another, took an opportunity to mention the name of Dr. Rappaccini. But the professor did not respond with so much cordiality as he had anticipated.

"Ill would it become a teacher of the divine art of medicine," said Professor Pietro Baglioni, in answer to a question of Giovanni, "to withhold due and well-considered praise of a physician so eminently skilled as Rappaccini; but, on the other hand, I should answer it but scantily to my conscience were I to permit a worthy youth like yourself, Signor Giovanni, the son of an ancient friend, to imbibe erroneous ideas respecting a man who might hereafter chance to hold your life and death in his hands. The truth is, our worshipful Dr. Rappaccini has as much science as any member of the faculty — with perhaps one single exception — in Padua, or all Italy; but there are certain grave objections to his professional character."

"And what are they?" asked the young man.

"Has my friend Giovanni any disease of body or heart, that he is so inquisitive about physicians?" said the professor, with a smile. "But as for Rappaccini, it is said of him — and I, who know the man well, can answer for its truth — that he cares infinitely more for science than for mankind. His patients are interesting to him only as subjects for some new experiment. He would sacrifice human life, his own among the rest, or whatever else was dearest to him, for the sake of adding so much as a grain of mustard seed to the great heap of his accumulated knowledge."

"Methinks he is an awful man indeed," remarked Guasconti, mentally recalling the cold and purely intellectual aspect of Rappaccini. "And yet, worshipful professor, is it not a noble spirit? Are there many men capable of so spiritual a love of science?"

"God forbid," answered the professor, somewhat testily; "at least, unless they take sounder views of the healing art than those adopted by Rappaccini. It is his theory that all medicinal virtues are comprised within those substances which we term vegetable poisons. These he cultivates with his own hands, and is said even to have produced new varieties of poison, more horribly deleterious than Nature, without the assistance of this learned person, would ever have plagued the world withal. That the signor doctor does less mischief than might be expected with such dangerous substances is undeniable. Now and then, it must be owned, he has effected, or seemed to effect, a marvellous cure; but, to tell you my private mind, Signor Giovanni, he should receive little credit for such instances of success, — they being probably the work of chance, — but should be held strictly accountable for his failures, which may justly be considered his own work."

The youth might have taken Baglioni's opinions with many grains of allowance had he known that there was a professional warfare of long continuance between him and Dr. Rappaccini, in which the latter was generally thought to have gained the advantage. If the reader be inclined to judge for himself, we refer him to certain black-letter tracts on both sides, preserved in the medical department of the University of Padua.

"I know not, most learned professor," returned Giovanni, after musing on what had been said of Rappaccini's exclusive zeal for science, — "I know not how dearly this physician may love his art; but surely there is one object more dear to him. He has a daughter."

"Aha!" cried the professor, with a laugh. "So now our friend Giovanni's secret is out. You have heard of this daughter, whom all the young men in Padua are wild about, though not half a dozen have ever had the good hap to see her face. I know little of the Signora Beatrice save that Rappaccini is said to have instructed her deeply in his science, and that, young and beautiful as fame reports her, she is already qualified to fill a professor's chair. Perchance her father destines her for mine! Other absurd rumors there be, not worth talking about or listening to. So now, Signor Giovanni, drink off your glass of lachryma."

Guasconti returned to his lodgings somewhat heated with the wine he had quaffed, and which caused his brain to swim with strange fantasies in reference to Dr. Rappaccini and the beautiful Beatrice. On his way, happening to pass by a florist's he bought a fresh bouquet of flowers.

Ascending to his chamber, he seated himself near the window, but within the shadow thrown by the depth of the wall, so that he could look down into the garden with little risk of being discovered. All beneath his eye was a solitude. The strange plants were basking in the sunshine, and now and then nodding gently to one another, as if in acknowledgment of sympathy and kindred. In the midst, by the shattered fountain, grew the magnificent shrub, with its purple gems clustering all over it; they glowed in the air, and gleamed back again out of the depths of the pool, which thus seemed to overflow with colored radiance from the rich reflection that was steeped in it. At first, as we have said, the garden was a solitude. Soon, however, — as Giovanni had half hoped, half feared, would be the case, — a figure appeared beneath the antique sculptured portal, and came down between the rows of plants, inhaling their various perfumes as if she were one of those beings of old classic fable that lived upon sweet odors. On again beholding Beatrice, the young man was even startled to perceive how much her beauty exceeded his recollection of it; so brilliant, so vivid, was its character, that she glowed amid the sunlight, and, as Giovanni whispered to himself, positively illuminated the more shadowy intervals of the garden path. Her face being now more revealed than on the former occasion, he was struck by its expression of simplicity and sweetness, — qualities that had not entered into his idea of her character, and which made him ask anew what manner of mortal she might be. Nor did he fail again to observe, or imagine, an analogy between the beautiful girl and the gorgeous shrub that hung its gemlike flowers over the fountain, — a resemblance which Beatrice seemed to have indulged a fantastic humor in heightening, both by the arrangement of her dress and the selection of its hues.

Approaching the shrub, she threw open her arms, as with a passionate ardor, and drew its branches into an intimate embrace — so intimate that her features were hidden in its leafy bosom and her glistening ringlets all intermingled with the flowers.

"Give me thy breath, my sister," exclaimed Beatrice; "for I am faint with common air. And give me this flower of thine, which I separate with gentlest fingers from the stem and place it close beside my heart."

With these words the beautiful daughter of Rappaccini plucked one of the richest blossoms of the shrub, and was about to fasten it in her bosom. But now, unless Giovanni's draughts of wine had bewildered his senses, a singular incident occurred. A small orange-colored reptile, of the lizard or chameleon species, chanced to be creeping along the path, just at the feet of Beatrice. It appeared to Giovanni, — but, at the distance from which he gazed, he could scarcely have seen anything so minute, — it appeared to him, however, that a drop or two of moisture from the broken stem of the flower descended upon the lizard's head. For an instant the reptile contorted itself violently, and then lay motionless in the sunshine. Beatrice observed this remarkable phenomenon, and crossed herself, sadly, but without surprise; nor did she therefore hesitate to arrange the fatal flower in her bosom. There it blushed, and almost glimmered with the dazzling effect of a precious stone, adding to her dress and aspect the one appropriate charm which nothing else in the world could have supplied. But Giovanni, out of the shadow of his window, bent forward and shrank back, and murmured and trembled.

"Am I awake? Have I my senses?" said he to himself. "What is this being? Beautiful shall I call her, or inexpressibly terrible?"

Beatrice now strayed carelessly through the garden, approaching closer beneath Giovanni's window, so that he was compelled to thrust his head quite out of its concealment in order to gratify the intense and painful curiosity which she excited. At this moment there came a beautiful insect over the garden wall; it had, perhaps, wandered through the city, and found no flowers or verdure among those antique haunts of men until the heavy perfumes of Dr. Rappaccini's shrubs had lured it from afar. Without alighting on the flowers, this winged brightness seemed to be attracted by Beatrice, and lingered in the air and fluttered about her head. Now, here it could not be but that Giovanni Guasconti's eyes deceived him. Be that as it might, he fancied that, while Beatrice was gazing at the insect with childish delight, it grew faint and fell at her feet; its bright wings shivered; it was dead — from no cause that he could discern, unless it were the atmosphere of her breath. Again Beatrice crossed herself and sighed heavily as she bent over the dead insect.

An impulsive movement of Giovanni drew her eyes to the window. There she beheld the beautiful head of the young man — rather a Grecian than an Italian head, with fair, regular features, and a glistening of gold among his ringlets — gazing down upon her like a being that hovered in mid air. Scarcely knowing what he did, Giovanni threw down the bouquet which he had hitherto held in his hand.

"Signora," said he, "there are pure and healthful flowers. Wear them for the sake of Giovanni Guasconti."

"Thanks, signor," replied Beatrice, with her rich voice, that came forth as it were like a gush of music, and with a mirthful expression half childish and half woman-like. "I accept your gift, and would fain recompense it with this precious purple flower; but if I toss it into the air it will not reach you. So Signor Guasconti must even content himself with my thanks."

She lifted the bouquet from the ground, and then, as if inwardly ashamed at having stepped aside from her maidenly reserve to respond to a stranger's greeting, passed swiftly homeward through the garden. But few as the moments were, it seemed to Giovanni, when she was on the point of vanishing beneath the sculptured portal, that his beautiful bouquet was already beginning to wither in her grasp. It was an idle thought; there could be no possibility of distinguishing a faded flower from a fresh one at so great a distance.

For many days after this incident the young man avoided the window that looked into Dr. Rappaccini's garden, as if something ugly and monstrous would have blasted his eyesight had he been betrayed into a glance. He felt conscious of having put himself, to a certain extent, within the influence of an unintelligible power by the communication which he had opened with Beatrice. The wisest course would have been, if his heart were in any real danger, to quit his lodgings and Padua itself at once; the next wiser, to have accustomed himself, as far as possible, to the familiar and daylight view of Beatrice — thus bringing her rigidly and systematically within the limits of ordinary experience. Least of all, while avoiding her sight, ought Giovanni to have remained so near this extraordinary being that the proximity and possibility even of intercourse should give a kind of substance and reality to the wild vagaries which his imagination ran riot continually in producing. Guasconti had not a deep heart — or, at all events, its depths were not sounded now; but he had a quick fancy, and an ardent southern temperament, which rose every instant to a higher fever pitch. Whether or no Beatrice possessed those terrible attributes, that fatal breath, the affinity with those so beautiful and deadly flowers which were indicated by what Giovanni had witnessed, she had at least instilled a fierce and subtle poison into his system. It was not love, although her rich beauty was a madness to him; nor horror, even while he fancied her spirit to be imbued with the same baneful essence that seemed to pervade her physical frame; but a wild offspring of both love and horror that had each parent in it, and burned like one and shivered like the other. Giovanni knew not what to dread;

still less did he know what to hope; yet hope and dread kept a continual warfare in his breast, alternately vanquishing one another and starting up afresh to renew the contest. Blessed are all simple emotions, be they dark or bright! It is the lurid intermixture of the two that produces the illuminating blaze of the infernal regions.

Sometimes he endeavored to assuage the fever of his spirit by a rapid walk through the streets of Padua or beyond its gates: his footsteps kept time with the throbbings of his brain, so that the walk was apt to accelerate itself to a race. One day he found himself arrested; his arm was seized by a portly personage, who had turned back on recognizing the young man and expended much breath in overtaking him.

"Signor Giovanni! Stay, my young friend!" cried he. "Have you forgotten me? That might well be the case if I were as much altered as yourself."

It was Baglioni, whom Giovanni had avoided ever since their first meeting, from a doubt that the professor's sagacity would look too deeply into his secrets. Endeavoring to recover himself, he stared forth wildly from his inner world into the outer one and spoke like a man in a dream.

"Yes; I am Giovanni Guasconti. You are Professor Pietro Baglioni. Now let me pass!"

"Not yet, not yet, Signor Giovanni Guasconti," said the professor, smiling, but at the same time scrutinizing the youth with an earnest glance. "What! did I grow up side by side with your father? and shall his son pass me like a stranger in these old streets of Padua? Stand still, Signor Giovanni; for we must have a word or two before we part."

"Speedily, then, most worshipful professor, speedily," said Giovanni, with feverish impatience. "Does not your worship see that I am in haste?"

Now, while he was speaking there came a man in black along the street, stooping and moving feebly like a person in inferior health. His face was all overspread with a most sickly and sallow hue, but yet so pervaded with an expression of piercing and active intellect that an observer might easily have overlooked the merely physical attributes and have seen only this wonderful energy. As he passed, this person exchanged a cold and distant salutation with Baglioni, but fixed his eyes upon Giovanni with an intentness that seemed to bring out whatever was within him worthy of notice. Nevertheless, there was a peculiar quietness in the look, as if taking merely a speculative, not a human, interest in the young man.

"It is Dr. Rappaccini!" whispered the professor when the stranger had passed. "Has he ever seen your face before?"

"Not that I know," answered Giovanni, starting at the name.

"He *has* seen you! he must have seen you!" said Baglioni hastily. "For some purpose or other, this man of science is making a study of you. I know that look of his! It is the same that coldly illuminates his face as he bends over a bird, a mouse, or a butterfly, which, in pursuance of some experiment, he has killed by the perfume of a flower; a look as deep as Nature itself, but without Nature's warmth of love. Signor Giovanni, I will stake my life upon it, you are the subject of one of Rappaccini's experiments!"

"Will you make a fool of me?" cried Giovanni passionately. "*That*, signor professor, were an untoward experiment."

"Patience! patience!" replied the imperturbable professor. "I tell thee, my poor Giovanni, that Rappaccini has a scientific interest in thee. Thou hast fallen into fearful hands! And the Signora Beatrice, — what part does she act in this mystery?"

But Guasconti, finding Baglioni's pertinacity intolerable, here broke away, and was gone before the professor could again seize his arm. He looked after the young man intently and shook his head.

"This must not be," said Baglioni to himself. "The youth is the son of my old friend, and shall not come to any harm from which the arcana of medical science can preserve him. Besides, it is too insufferable an impertinence in Rappaccini, thus to snatch the lad out of my own hands, as I may say, and make use of him for his infernal experiments. This daughter of his! It shall be looked to. Perchance, most learned Rappaccini, I may foil you where you little dream of it!"

Meanwhile Giovanni had pursued a circuitous route, and at length found himself at the door of his lodgings. As he crossed the threshold he was met by old Lisabetta, who smirked and smiled, and was evidently desirous to attract his attention; vainly, however, as the ebullition of his feelings had momentarily subsided into a cold and dull vacuity. He turned his eyes full upon the withered face that was puckering itself into a smile, but seemed to behold it not. The old dame, therefore, laid her grasp upon his cloak.

"Signor! signor!" whispered she, still with a smile over the whole breadth of her visage, so that it looked not unlike a grotesque carving in wood, darkened by centuries. "Listen, signor! There is a private entrance into the garden!"

"What do you say?" exclaimed Giovanni, turning quickly about, as if an inanimate thing should start into feverish life. "A private entrance into Dr. Rappaccini's garden?"

"Hush! hush! not so loud!" whispered Lisabetta, putting her hand over his mouth. "Yes; into the worshipful doctor's garden, where you may see all his fine shrubbery. Many a young man in Padua would give gold to be admitted among those flowers."

Giovanni put a piece of gold into her hand.

"Show me the way," said he.

A surmise, probably excited by his conversation with Baglioni, crossed his mind, that this interposition of old Lisabetta might perchance be connected with the intrigue, whatever were its nature, in which the professor seemed to suppose that Dr. Rappaccini was involving him. But such a suspicion, though it disturbed Giovanni, was inadequate to restrain him. The instant that he was aware of the possibility of approaching Beatrice, it seemed an absolute necessity of his existence to do so. It mattered not whether she were angel or demon; he was irrevocably within her sphere, and must obey the law that whirled him onward, in ever-lessening circles, towards a result which he did not attempt to foreshadow; and yet, strange to say, there came across him a sudden doubt whether this intense interest on his part were not delusory; whether it were really of so deep and positive a nature as to justify him in now thrusting himself into an incalculable position; whether it were not merely the fantasy of a young man's brain, only slightly or not at all connected with his heart.

He paused, hesitated, turned half about, but again went on. His withered guide led him along several obscure passages, and finally undid a door, through which, as it was opened, there came the sight and sound of rustling leaves, with the broken sunshine slimmering among them. Giovanni stepped forth, and forcing himself through the entanglement of a shrub that wreathed its tendrils over the hidden entrance, stood beneath his own window in the open area of Dr. Rappaccini's garden.

How often is it the case that, when impossibilities have come to pass and dreams have condensed their misty substance into tangible realities, we find ourselves calm, and even coldly self-possessed, amid circumstances which it would have been a delirium of joy or agony to anticipate! Fate delights to thwart us thus. Passion will choose his own time to rush upon the scene, and lingers sluggishly behind when an appropriate adjustment of events would seem to summon his appearance. So was it now with Giovanni. Day after day his pulses had throbbed with feverish blood at the improbable idea of an interview with Beatrice, and of standing with her, face to face, in this very garden, basking in the Oriental sunshine of her beauty, and snatching from her full gaze the mystery which he deemed the riddle of his own existence. But now there was a singular and untimely equanimity within his breast. He threw a glance around the garden to discover if Beatrice or her father were present, and, perceiving that he was alone, began a critical observation of the plants.

The aspect of one and all of them dissatisfied him; their gorgeousness seemed fierce, passionate, and even unnatural. There was hardly an individual shrub which a wanderer, straying by himself through a forest, would not have been startled to find growing wild, as if an unearthly face had glared at him out of the thicket. Several also would have shocked a delicate instinct by an appearance of artificialness indicating that there had been such commixture, and, as it were, adultery, of various vegetable species, that the production was no longer of God's making, but the monstrous offspring of man's depraved fancy, glowing with only an evil mockery of beauty. They were probably the result of experiment, which in one or two cases had succeeded in mingling plants individually lovely into a compound possessing the questionable and ominous character that distinguished the whole growth of the garden. In fine, Giovanni recognized but two or three plants in the collection, and those of a kind that he well knew to be poisonous. While busy with these contemplations he heard the rustling of a silken garment, and, turning, beheld Beatrice emerging from beneath the sculptured portal.

Giovanni had not considered with himself what should be his deportment; whether he should apologize for his intrusion into the garden, or assume that he was there with the privity at least, if not by the desire, of Dr. Rappaccini or his daughter; but Beatrice's manner placed him at his ease, although leaving him still in doubt by what agency he had gained admittance. She came lightly along the path and met him near the broken fountain. There was surprise in her face, but brightened by a simple and kind expression of pleasure.

"You are a connoisseur in flowers, signor," said Beatrice, with a smile, alluding to the bouquet which he had flung her from the window. "It is no marvel, therefore, if the sight of my father's rare collection has tempted you to take a nearer view. If he were here, he could tell you many strange and interesting facts as to the nature and habits of these shrubs; for he has spent a lifetime in such studies, and this garden is his world."

"And yourself, lady," observed Giovanni, "if fame says true, — you likewise are deeply skilled in the virtues indicated by these rich blossoms and these spicy perfumes. Would you deign to be my instructress, I should prove an apter scholar than if taught by Signor Rappaccini himself."

"Are there such idle rumors?" asked Beatrice, with the music of a pleasant laugh.

"Do people say that I am skilled in my father's science of plants? What a jest is there! No; though I have grown up among these flowers, I know no more of them than their hues and perfume; and sometimes methinks I would fain rid myself of even that small knowledge. There are many flowers here, and those not the least brilliant, that shock and offend me when they meet my eye. But pray, signor, do not believe these stories about my science. Believe nothing of me save what you see with your own eyes."

"And must I believe all that I have seen with my own eyes?" asked Giovanni, pointedly, while the recollection of former scenes made him shrink. "No, signora; you demand too little of me. Bid me believe nothing save what comes from your own lips."

It would appear that Beatrice understood him. There came a deep flush to her cheek; but she looked full into Giovanni's eyes, and responded to his gaze of uneasy suspicion with a queenlike haughtiness.

"I do so bid you, signor," she replied. "Forget whatever you may have fancied in regard to me. If true to the outward senses, still it may be false in its essence; but the words of Beatrice Rappaccini's lips are true from the depths of the heart outward. Those you may believe."

A fervor glowed in her whole aspect and beamed upon Giovanni's consciousness like the light of truth itself; but while she spoke there was a fragrance in the atmosphere around her, rich and delightful, though evanescent, yet which the young man, from an indefinable reluctance, scarcely dared to draw into his lungs. It might be the odor of the flowers. Could it be Beatrice's breath which thus embalmed her words with a strange richness, as if by steeping them in her heart? A faintness passed like a shadow over Giovanni and flitted away; he seemed to gaze through the beautiful girl's eyes into her transparent soul, and felt no more doubt or fear.

The tinge of passion that had colored Beatrice's manner vanished; she became gay, and appeared to derive a pure delight from her communion with the youth not unlike what the maiden of a lonely island might have felt conversing with a voyager from the civilized world. Evidently her experience of life had been confined within the limits of that garden. She talked now about matters as simple as the daylight or summer clouds, and now asked questions in reference to the city, or Giovanni's distant home, his friends, his mother, and his sisters — questions indicating such seclusion, and such lack of familiarity with modes and forms, that Giovanni responded as if to an infant. Her spirit gushed out before him like a fresh rill that was just catching its first glimpse of the sunlight and wondering at the reflections of earth and sky which were flung into its bosom. There came thoughts, too, from a deep source, and fantasies of a gemlike brilliancy, as if diamonds and rubies sparkled upward among the bubbles of the fountain. Ever and anon there gleamed across the young man's mind a sense of wonder that he should be walking side by side with the being who had so wrought upon his imagination, whom he had idealized in such hues of terror, in whom he had positively witnessed such manifestations of dreadful attributes, — that he should be conversing with Beatrice like a brother, and should find her so human and so maidenlike. But such reflections were only momentary; the effect of her character was too real not to make itself familiar at once.

In this free intercourse they had strayed through the garden, and now, after many turns among its avenues, were come to the shattered fountain, beside which grew the magnificent shrub, with its treasury of glowing blossoms. A fragrance was diffused from it which Giovanni recognized as identical with that which he had attributed to Beatrice's breath, but incomparably more powerful. As her eyes fell upon it, Giovanni beheld her press her hand to her bosom as if her heart were throbbing suddenly and painfully.

"For the first time in my life," murmured she, addressing the shrub, "I had forgotten thee."

"I remember, signora," said Giovanni, "that you once promised to reward me with one of these living gems for the bouquet which I had the happy boldness to fling to your feet. Permit me now to pluck it as a memorial of this interview."

He made a step towards the shrub with extended hand; but Beatrice darted forward, uttering a shriek that went through his heart like a dagger. She caught his hand and drew it back with the whole force of her slender figure. Giovanni felt her touch thrilling through his fibres.

"Touch it not!" exclaimed she, in a voice of agony. "Not for thy life! It is fatal!"

Then, hiding her face, she fled from him and vanished beneath the sculptured portal. As Giovanni followed her with his eyes, he beheld the emaciated figure and pale intelligence of Dr. Rappaccini, who had been watching the scene, he knew not how long, within the shadow of the entrance.

No sooner was Guasconti alone in his chamber than the image of Beatrice came back to his passionate musings, invested with all the witchery that had been gathering around it ever since his first glimpse of her, and now likewise imbued with a tender warmth of girlish womanhood. She was human; her nature was endowed with all gentle and feminine qualities; she was worthiest to be worshipped; she was capable, surely, on her part, of the height and heroism of love. Those tokens which he had hitherto considered as proofs of a frightful peculiarity in her physical and moral system were now either forgotten, or, by the subtle sophistry of passion transmitted into a golden crown of enchantment, rendering Beatrice the more admirable by so much as she was the more unique. Whatever had looked ugly was now beautiful; or, if incapable of such a change, it stole away and hid itself among those shapeless half ideas which throng the dim region beyond the daylight of our perfect consciousness. Thus did he spend the night, nor fell asleep until the dawn had begun to awake the slumbering flowers in Dr. Rappaccini's garden, whither Giovanni's dreams doubtless led him. Up rose the sun in his due season, and, flinging his beams upon the young man's eyelids, awoke him to a sense of pain. When thoroughly aroused, he became sensible of a burning and tingling agony in his hand — in his right hand — the very hand which Beatrice had grasped in her own when he was on the point of plucking one of the gemlike flowers. On the back of that hand there was now a purple print like that of four small fingers, and the likeness of a slender thumb upon his wrist.

Oh, how stubbornly does love, — or even that cunning semblance of love which flourishes in the imagination, but strikes no depth of root into the heart, — how stubbornly does it hold its faith until the moment comes when it is doomed to vanish into thin mist! Giovanni wrapped a handkerchief about his hand and wondered what evil thing had stung him, and soon forgot his pain in a reverie of Beatrice.

After the first interview, a second was in the inevitable course of what we call fate. A third; a fourth; and a meeting with Beatrice in the garden was no longer an incident in Giovanni's daily life, but the whole space in which he might be said to live; for the anticipation and memory of that ecstatic hour made up the remainder. Nor was it otherwise with the daughter of Rappaccini. She watched for the youth's appearance, and flew to his side with confidence as unreserved as if they had been playmates from early infancy — as if they were such playmates still. If, by any unwonted chance, he failed to come at the appointed moment, she stood beneath the window and sent up the rich sweetness of her tones to float around him in his chamber and echo and reverberate throughout his heart: "Giovanni! Giovanni! Why tarriest thou? Come down!" And down he hastened into that Eden of poisonous flowers.

But, with all this intimate familiarity, there was still a reserve in Beatrice's demeanor, so rigidly and invariably sustained that the idea of infringing it scarcely occurred to his imagination. By all appreciable signs, they loved; they had looked love with eyes that conveyed the holy secret from the depths of one soul into the depths of the other, as if it were too sacred to be whispered by the way; they had even spoken love in those gushes of passion when their spirits darted forth in articulated breath like tongues of long-hidden flame; and yet there had been no seal of lips, no clasp of hands, nor any slightest caress such as love claims and hallows. He had never touched one of the gleaming ringlets of her hair; her garment — so marked was the physical barrier between them — had never been waved against him by a breeze. On the few occasions when Giovanni had seemed tempted to overstep the limit, Beatrice grew so sad, so stern, and withal wore such a look of desolate separation, shuddering at itself, that not a spoken word was requisite to repel him. At such times he was startled at the horrible suspicions that rose, monster-like, out of the caverns of his heart and stared him in the face; his love grew thin and faint as the morning mist; his doubts alone had substance. But, when Beatrice's face brightened again after the momentary shadow, she was transformed at once from the mysterious, questionable being whom he had watched with so much awe and horror; she was now the beautiful and unsophisticated girl whom he felt that his spirit knew with a certainty beyond all other knowledge.

A considerable time had now passed since Giovanni's last meeting with Baglioni. One morning, however, he was disagreeably surprised by a visit from the professor, whom he had scarcely thought of for whole weeks, and would willingly have forgotten still longer. Given up as he had long been to a pervading excitement, he could tolerate no companions except upon condition of their perfect sympathy with his present state of feeling. Such sympathy was not to be expected from Professor Baglioni.

The visitor chatted carelessly for a few moments about the gossip of the city and the university, and then took up another topic.

"I have been reading an old classic author lately," said he, "and met with a story that strangely interested me. Possibly you may remember it. It is of an Indian prince, who sent a beautiful woman as a present to Alexander the Great. She was as lovely as the dawn and gorgeous as the sunset; but what especially distinguished her was a certain rich perfume in her breath — richer than a garden of Persian roses. Alexander, as was natural to a youthful conqueror, fell in love at first sight with this magnificent stranger; but a certain sage physician, happening to be present, discovered a terrible secret in regard to her."

"And what was that?" asked Giovanni, turning his eyes downward to avoid those of the professor.

"That this lovely woman," continued Baglioni, with emphasis, "had been nourished with poisons from her birth upward, until her whole nature was so imbued with them that she herself had become the deadliest poison in existence. Poison was her element of life. With that rich perfume of her breath she blasted the very air. Her love would have been poison — her embrace death. Is not this a marvellous tale?"

"A childish fable," answered Giovanni, nervously starting from his chair. "I marvel how your worship finds time to read such nonsense among your graver studies."

"By the by," said the professor, looking uneasily about him, "what singular fragrance is this in your apartment? Is it the perfume of your gloves? It is faint, but delicious; and yet, after all, by no means agreeable. Were I to breathe it long, methinks it would make me ill. It is like the breath of a flower; but I see no flowers in the chamber."

"Nor are there any," replied Giovanni, who had turned pale as the professor spoke; "nor, I think, is there any fragrance except in your worship's imagination. Odors, being a sort of element combined of the sensual and the spiritual, are apt to deceive us in this manner. The recollection of a perfume, the bare idea of it, may easily be mistaken for a present reality."

"Ay; but my sober imagination does not often play such tricks," said Baglioni; "and, were I to fancy any kind of odor, it would be that of some vile apothecary drug, wherewith my fingers are likely enough to be imbued. Our worshipful friend Rappaccini, as I have heard, tinctures his medicaments with odors richer than those of Araby. Doubtless, likewise, the fair and learned Signora Beatrice would minister to her patients with draughts as sweet as a maiden's breath; but woe to him that sips them!"

Giovanni's face evinced many contending emotions. The tone in which the professor alluded to the pure and lovely daughter of Rappaccini was a torture to his soul; and yet the intimation of a view of her character, opposite to his own, gave instantaneous distinctness to a thousand dim suspicions, which now grinned at him like so many demons. But he strove hard to quell them and to respond to Baglioni with a true lover's perfect faith.

"Signor professor," said he, "you were my father's friend; perchance, too, it is your purpose to act a friendly part towards his son. I would fain feel nothing towards you save respect and deference; but I pray you to observe, signor, that there is one subject on which we must not speak. You know not the Signora Beatrice. You cannot, therefore, estimate the wrong — the blasphemy, I may even say — that is offered to her character by a light or injurious word."

"Giovanni! my poor Giovanni!" answered the professor, with a calm expression of pity, "I know this wretched girl far better than yourself. You shall hear the truth in respect to the poisoner Rappaccini and his poisonous daughter; yes, poisonous as she is beautiful. Listen; for, even should you do violence to my gray hairs, it shall not silence me. That old fable of the Indian woman has become a truth by the deep and deadly science of Rappaccini and in the person of the lovely Beatrice."

Giovanni groaned and hid his face.

"Her father," continued Baglioni, "was not restrained by natural affection from offering up his child in this horrible manner as the victim of his insane zeal for science; for, let us do him justice, he is as true a man of science as ever distilled his own heart in an alembic. What, then, will be your fate? Beyond a doubt you are selected as the material of some new experiment. Perhaps the result is to be death; perhaps a fate more awful still. Rappaccini, with what he calls the interest of science before his eyes, will hesitate at nothing."

"It is a dream," muttered Giovanni to himself; "surely it is a dream."

"But," resumed the professor, "be of good cheer, son of my friend. It is not yet too late for the rescue. Possibly we may even succeed in bringing back this miserable child within the limits of ordinary nature, from which her father's madness has estranged

her. Behold this little silver vase! It was wrought by the hands of the renowned Benvenuto Cellini, and is well worthy to be a love gift to the fairest dame in Italy. But its contents are invaluable. One little sip of this antidote would have rendered the most virulent poisons of the Borgias innocuous. Doubt not that it will be as efficacious against those of Rappaccini. Bestow the vase, and the precious liquid within it, on your Beatrice, and hopefully await the result."

Baglioni laid a small, exquisitely wrought silver vial on the table and withdrew, leaving what he had said to produce its effect upon the young man's mind.

"We will thwart Rappaccini yet," thought he, chuckling to himself, as he descended the stairs; "but, let us confess the truth of him, he is a wonderful man — a wonderful man indeed; a vile empiric, however, in his practice, and therefore not to be tolerated by those who respect the good old rules of the medical profession."

Throughout Giovanni's whole acquaintance with Beatrice, he had occasionally, as we have said, been haunted by dark surmises as to her character; yet so thoroughly had she made herself felt by him as a simple, natural, most affectionate, and guileless creature, that the image now held up by Professor Baglioni looked as strange and incredible as if it were not in accordance with his own original conception. True, there were ugly recollections connected with his first glimpses of the beautiful girl; he could not quite forget the bouquet that withered in her grasp, and the insect that perished amid the sunny air, by no ostensible agency save the fragrance of her breath. These incidents, however, dissolving in the pure light of her character, had no longer the efficacy of facts, but were acknowledged as mistaken fantasies, by whatever testimony of the senses they might appear to be substantiated. There is something truer and more real than what we can see with the eyes and touch with the finger. On such better evidence had Giovanni founded his confidence in Beatrice, though rather by the necessary force of her high attributes than by any deep and generous faith on his part. But now his spirit was incapable of sustaining

itself at the height to which the early enthusiasm of passion had exalted it; he fell
down, grovelling among earthly doubts, and
defiled therewith the pure whiteness of
Beatrice's image. Not that he gave her up; he
did but distrust. He resolved to institute
some decisive test that should satisfy him,
once for all, whether there were those dreadful peculiarities in her physical nature which
could not be supposed to exist without some
corresponding monstrosity of soul. His eyes,
gazing down afar, might have deceived him
as to the lizard, the insect, and the flowers;
but if he could witness, at the distance of a
few paces, the sudden blight of one fresh and
healthful flower in Beatrice's hand, there
would be room for no further question. With
this idea he hastened to the florist's and purchased a bouquet that was still gemmed
with the morning dew-drops.

It was now the customary hour of his daily
interview with Beatrice. Before descending
into the garden, Giovanni failed not to look
at his figure in the mirror, — a vanity to be
expected in a beautiful young man, yet, as
displaying itself at that troubled and feverish
moment, the token of a certain shallowness of
feeling and insincerity of character. He did
gaze, however, and said to himself that his
features had never before possessed so rich a
grace, nor his eyes such vivacity, nor his
cheeks so warm a hue of superabundant life.

"At least," thought he, "her poison has
not yet insinuated itself into my system. I
am no flower to perish in her grasp."

With that thought he turned his eyes on
the bouquet, which he had never once laid
aside from his hand. A thrill of indefinable
horror shot through his frame on perceiving
that those dewy flowers were already beginning to droop; they wore the aspect of things
that had been fresh and lovely yesterday.
Giovanni grew white as marble, and stood
motionless before the mirror, staring at his
own reflection there as at the likeness of
something frightful. He remembered Baglioni's remark about the fragrance that
seemed to pervade the chamber. It must
have been the poison in his breath! Then
he shuddered — shuddered at himself. Recovering from his stupor, he began to watch
with curious eye a spider that was busily at
work hanging its web from the antique
cornice of the apartment, crossing and re-
crossing the artful system of interwoven lines
— as vigorous and active a spider as ever
dangled from an old ceiling. Giovanni bent
towards the insect, and emitted a deep, long
breath. The spider suddenly ceased its toil;
the web vibrated with a tremor originating in
the body of the small artisan. Again Giovanni sent forth a breath, deeper, longer, and
imbued with a venomous feeling out of his
heart: he knew not whether he were wicked,
or only desperate. The spider made a convulsive gripe with his limbs and hung dead
across the window.

"Accursed! accursed!" muttered Giovanni,
addressing himself. "Hast thou grown so
poisonous that this deadly insect perishes by
thy breath?"

At that moment a rich, sweet voice came
floating up from the garden.

"Giovanni! Giovanni! It is past the
hour! Why tarriest thou? Come down!"

"Yes," muttered Giovanni again. "She
is the only being whom my breath may not
slay! Would that it might!"

He rushed down, and in an instant was
standing before the bright and loving eyes of
Beatrice. A moment ago his wrath and
despair had been so fierce that he could have
desired nothing so much as to wither her by a
glance; but with her actual presence there
came influences which had too real an existence to be at once shaken off: recollections of
the delicate and benign power of her feminine
nature, which had so often enveloped him in
a religious calm; recollections of many a holy
and passionate outgush of her heart, when
the pure fountain had been unsealed from its
depths and made visible in its transparency
to his mental eye; recollections which, had
Giovanni known how to estimate them,
would have assured him that all this ugly
mystery was but an earthly illusion, and that,
whatever mist of evil might seem to have
gathered over her, the real Beatrice was a
heavenly angel. Incapable as he was of such
high faith, still her presence had not utterly
lost its magic. Giovanni's rage was quelled
into an aspect of sullen insensibility. Beatrice, with a quick spiritual sense, immediately felt that there was a gulf of blackness

between them which neither he nor she could pass. They walked on together, sad and silent, and came thus to the marble fountain and to its pool of water on the ground, in the midst of which grew the shrub that bore gem-like blossoms. Giovanni was affrighted at the eager enjoyment — the appetite, as it were — with which he found himself inhaling the fragrance of the flowers.

"Beatrice," asked he, abruptly, "whence came this shrub?"

"My father created it," answered she, with simplicity.

"Created it! created it!" repeated Giovanni. "What mean you, Beatrice?"

"He is a man fearfully acquainted with the secrets of Nature," replied Beatrice; "and, at the hour when I first drew breath, this plant sprang from the soil, the offspring of his science, of his intellect, while I was but his earthly child. Approach it not!" continued she, observing with terror that Giovanni was drawing nearer to the shrub. "It has qualities that you little dream of. But I, dearest Giovanni, — I grew up and blossomed with the plant and was nourished with its breath. It was my sister, and I loved it with a human affection; for, alas! — hast thou not suspected it? — there was an awful doom."

Here Giovanni frowned so darkly upon her that Beatrice paused and trembled. But her faith in his tenderness reassured her, and made her blush that she had doubted for an instant.

"There was an awful doom," she continued, "the effect of my father's fatal love of science, which estranged me from all society of my kind. Until Heaven sent thee, dearest Giovanni, oh, how lonely was thy poor Beatrice!"

"Was it a hard doom?" asked Giovanni fixing his eyes upon her.

"Only of late have I known how hard it was," answered she, tenderly. "Oh, yes; but my heart was torpid, and therefore quiet."

Giovanni's rage broke forth from his sullen gloom like a lightning flash out of a dark cloud.

"Accursed one!" cried he, with venomous scorn and anger. "And, finding thy solitude wearisome, thou hast severed me likewise from all the warmth of life and enticed me into thy region of unspeakable horror!"

"Giovanni!" exclaimed Beatrice, turning her large bright eyes upon his face. The force of his words had not found its way into her mind; she was merely thunderstruck.

"Yes, poisonous thing!" repeated Giovanni, beside himself with passion. "Thou hast done it! Thou hast blasted me! Thou hast filled my veins with poison! Thou hast made me as hateful, as ugly, as loathsome and deadly a creature as thyself — a world's wonder of hideous monstrosity! Now, if our breath be happily as fatal to ourselves as to all others, let us join our lips in one kiss of unutterable hatred, and so die!"

"What has befallen me?" murmured Beatrice, with a low moan out of her heart. "Holy Virgin, pity me, a poor heartbroken child!"

"Thou, — dost thou pray?" cried Giovanni, still with the same fiendish scorn. "Thy very prayers, as they come from thy lips, taint the atmosphere with death. Yes, yes; let us pray! Let us to church and dip our fingers in the holy water at the portal! They that come after us will perish as by a pestilence! Let us sign crosses in the air! It will be scattering curses abroad in the likeness of holy symbols!"

"Giovanni," said Beatrice, calmly, for her grief was beyond passion, "why dost thou join thyself with me thus in those terrible words? I, it is true, am the horrible thing thou namest me. But thou, — what hast thou to do, save with one other shudder at my hideous misery to go forth out of the garden and mingle with thy race, and forget that there ever crawled on earth such a monster as poor Beatrice?"

"Dost thou pretend ignorance?" asked Giovanni, scowling upon her. "Behold! this power have I gained from the pure daughter of Rappaccini."

There was a swarm of summer insects flitting through the air in search of the food promised by the flower odors of the fatal garden. They circled round Giovanni's head, and were evidently attracted towards him by the same influence which had drawn them for an instant within the sphere of several of the shrubs. He sent forth a breath among them, and smiled bitterly at Beatrice as at least a score of the insects fell dead upon the ground.

"I see it! I see it!" shrieked Beatrice. "It is my father's fatal science! No, no, Giovanni; it was not I! Never! never! I dreamed only to love thee and be with thee a little time, and so to let thee pass away, leaving but thine image in mine heart; for, Giovanni, believe it, though my body be nourished with poison, my spirit is God's creature, and craves love as its daily food. But my father, — he has united us in this fearful sympathy. Yes; spurn me, tread upon me, kill me! Oh, what is death after such words as thine? But it was not I. Not for a world of bliss would I have done it."

Giovanni's passion had exhausted itself in its outburst from his lips. There now came across him a sense, mournful, and not without tenderness, of the intimate and peculiar relationship between Beatrice and himself. They stood, as it were, in an utter solitude, which would be made none the less solitary by the densest throng of human life. Ought not, then, the desert of humanity around them to press this insulated pair closer together? If they should be cruel to one another, who was there to be kind to them? Besides, thought Giovanni, might there not still be a hope of his returning within the limits of ordinary nature, and leading Beatrice, the redeemed Beatrice, by the hand? O, weak, and selfish, and unworthy spirit, that could dream of an earthly union and earthly happiness as possible, after such deep love had been so bitterly wronged as was Beatrice's love by Giovanni's blighting words! No, no; there could be no such hope. She must pass heavily, with that broken heart, across the borders of Time — she must bathe her hurts in some fount of paradise, and forget her grief in the light of immortality, and *there* be well.

But Giovanni did not know it.

"Dear Beatrice," said he, approaching her, while she shrank away as always at his approach, but now with a different impulse, "dearest Beatrice, our fate is not yet so desperate. Behold! there is a medicine, potent, as a wise physician has assured me, and almost divine in its efficacy. It is composed of ingredients the most opposite to those by which thy awful father has brought this calamity upon thee and me. It is distilled of blessed herbs. Shall we not quaff it together, and thus be purified from evil?"

"Give it me!" said Beatrice, extending her hand to receive the little silver vial which Giovanni took from his bosom. She added, with a peculiar emphasis, "I will drink; but do thou await the result."

She put Baglioni's antidote to her lips; and, at the same moment, the figure of Rappaccini emerged from the portal and came slowly towards the marble fountain. As he drew near, the pale man of science seemed to gaze with a triumphant expression at the beautiful youth and maiden, as might an artist who should spend his life in achieving a picture or a group of statuary and finally be satisfied with his success. He paused; his bent form grew erect with conscious power; he spread out his hands over them in the attitude of a father imploring a blessing upon his children; but those were the same hands that had thrown poison into the stream of their lives. Giovanni trembled. Beatrice shuddered nervously, and pressed her hand upon her heart.

"My daughter," said Rappaccini, "thou art no longer lonely in the world. Pluck one of those precious gems from thy sister shrub and bid thy bridegroom wear it in his bosom. It will not harm him now. My science and the sympathy between thee and him have so wrought within his system that he now stands apart from common men, as thou dost, daughter of my pride and triumph, from ordinary women. Pass on, then, through the world, most dear to one another and dreadful to all besides!"

"My father," said Beatrice, feebly, — and still as she spoke she kept her hand upon her heart, — "wherefore didst thou inflict this miserable doom upon thy child?"

"Miserable!" exclaimed Rappaccini. "What mean you, foolish girl? Dost thou deem it misery to be endowed with marvellous gifts against which no power nor strength could avail an enemy— misery, to be able to quell the mightiest with a breath —

misery, to be as terrible as thou art beautiful? Wouldst thou, then, have preferred the condition of a weak woman, exposed to all evil and capable of none?"

"I would fain have been loved, not feared," murmured Beatrice, sinking down upon the ground. "But now it matters not. I am going, father, where the evil which thou hast striven to mingle with my being will pass away like a dream — like the fragrance of these poisonous flowers, which will no longer taint my breath among the flowers of Eden. Farewell, Giovanni! Thy words of hatred are like lead within my heart; but they, too, will fall away as I ascend. Oh, was there not, from the first, more poison in thy nature than in mine?"

To Beatrice, — so radically had her earthly part been wrought upon by Rappaccini's skill, — as poison had been life, so the powerful antidote was death; and thus the poor victim of man's ingenuity and of thwarted nature, and of the fatality that attends all such efforts of perverted wisdom, perished there, at the feet of her father and Giovanni. Just at that moment Professor Pietro Baglioni looked forth from the window, and called loudly, in a tone of triumph mixed with horror, to the thunderstricken man of science.

"Rappaccini! Rappaccini! and is *this* the upshot of your experiment!"

Ethan Brand
(1851)

For sources, see a number of passages in the *American Notebooks*, July 29–September 9, 1838.

Bartram the lime-burner, a rough, heavy-looking man, begrimed with charcoal, sat watching his kiln, at nightfall, while his little son played at building houses with the scattered fragments of marble, when, on the hillside below them, they heard a roar of laughter, not mirthful, but slow, and even solemn, like a wind shaking the boughs of the forest.

"Father, what is that?" asked the little boy, leaving his play, and pressing betwixt his father's knees.

"Oh, some drunken man, I suppose," an-swered the lime-burner; "some merry fellow from the bar-room in the village, who dared not laugh loud enough within doors lest he should blow the roof of the house off. So here he is, shaking his jolly sides at the foot of Graylock."

"But, father," said the child, more sensitive than the obtuse, middle-aged clown, "he does not laugh like a man that is glad. So the noise frightens me!"

"Don't be a fool, child!" cried his father, gruffly. "You will never make a man, I do believe; there is too much of your mother in you. I have known the rustling of a leaf startle you. Hark! Here comes the merry fellow now. You shall see that there is no harm in him."

Bartram and his little son, while they were talking thus, sat watching the same lime-kiln that had been the scene of Ethan Brand's solitary and meditative life, before he began his search for the Unpardonable Sin. Many years, as we have seen, had now elapsed, since the portentous night when the IDEA was first developed. The kiln, however, on the mountain-side, stood unimpaired, and was in nothing changed since he had thrown his dark thoughts into the intense glow of its furnace, and melted them, as it were, into the one thought that took possession of his life. It was a rude, round, tower-like structure about twenty feet high, heavily built of rough stones, and with a hillock of earth heaped about the larger part of its circumference; so that the blocks and fragments of marble might be drawn by cart-loads, and thrown in at the top. There was an opening at the bottom of the tower, like an oven-mouth, but large enough to admit a man in a stooping posture, and provided with a massive iron door. With the smoke and jets of flame issuing from the chinks and crevices of this door, which seemed to give admittance into the hillside, it resembled nothing so much as the private entrance to the infernal regions, which the shepherds of the Delectable Mountains were accustomed to show to pilgrims.

There are many such lime-kilns in that tract of country, for the purpose of burning the white marble which composes a large part of the substance of the hills. Some of them, built years ago, and long deserted, with weeds growing in the vacant round of the interior, which is open to the sky, and grass and wild-flowers rooting themselves in the chinks of the stones, look already like relics of antiquity, and may yet be overspread with the lichens of centuries to come. Others, where the lime-burner still feeds his daily and night-long fire, afford points of interest to the wanderer among the hills, who seats himself on a log of wood or a fragment of marble, to hold a chat with the solitary man. It is a lonesome, and, when the character is inclined to thought, may be an intensely thoughtful occupation; as it proved in the case of Ethan Brand, who had mused to such strange purpose, in days gone by, while the fire in this very kiln was burning.

The man who now watched the fire was of a different order, and troubled himself with no thoughts save the very few that were requisite to his business. At frequent intervals, he flung back the clashing weight of the iron door, and, turning his face from the insufferable glare, thrust in huge logs of oak, or stirred the immense brands with a long pole. Within the furnace were seen the curling and riotous flames, and the burning marble, almost molten with the intensity of heat; while without, the reflection of the fire quivered on the dark intricacy of the surrounding forest, and showed in the foreground a bright and ruddy little picture of the hut, the spring beside its door, the athletic and coal-begrimed figure of the lime-burner, and the half-frightened child, shrinking into the protection of his father's shadow. And when again the iron door was closed, then reappeared the tender light of the half-full moon, which vainly strove to trace out the indistinct shapes of the neighboring mountains; and, in the upper sky, there was a flitting congregation of clouds, still faintly tinged with the rosy sunset, though thus far down into the valley the sunshine had vanished long and long ago.

The little boy now crept still closer to his father, as footsteps were heard ascending the hillside, and a human form thrust aside the bushes that clustered beneath the trees.

"Halloo! who is it?" cried the lime-burner, vexed at his son's timidity, yet half in-fected by it. "Come forward, and show yourself, like a man, or I'll fling this chunk of marble at your head!"

"You offer me a rough welcome," said a gloomy voice, as the unknown man drew nigh. "Yet I neither claim nor desire a kinder one, even at my own fireside."

To obtain a distincter view, Bartram threw open the iron door of the kiln, whence immediately issued a gush of fierce light, that smote full upon the stranger's face and figure. To a careless eye there appeared nothing very remarkable in his aspect, which was that of a man in a coarse, brown, country-made suit of clothes, tall and thin, with the staff and heavy shoes of a wayfarer. As he advanced, he fixed his eyes — which were very bright — intently upon the brightness of the furnace, as if he beheld, or expected to behold, some object worthy of note within it.

"Good evening, stranger," said the lime-burner; "whence come you, so late in the day?"

"I come from my search," answered the wayfarer; "for, at last, it is finished."

"Drunk! — or crazy!" muttered Bartram to himself. "I shall have trouble with the fellow. The sooner I drive him away, the better."

The little boy, all in a tremble, whispered to his father, and begged him to shut the door of the kiln, so that there might not be so much light; for that there was something in the man's face which he was afraid to look at, yet could not look away from. And, indeed, even the lime-burner's dull and torpid sense began to be impressed by an indescribable something in that thin, rugged, thoughtful visage, with the grizzled hair hanging wildly about it, and those deeply sunken eyes, which gleamed like fires within the entrance of a mysterious cavern. But, as he closed the door, the stranger turned towards him, and spoke in a quiet, familiar way, that made Bartram feel as if he were a sane and sensible man, after all.

"Your task draws to an end, I see," said he. "This marble has already been burning three days. A few hours more will convert the stone to lime."

"Why, who are you?" exclaimed the lime-burner. "You seem as well acquainted with my business as I am myself."

"And well I may be," said the stranger; "for I followed the same craft many a long year, and here, too, on this very spot. But you are a new-comer in these parts. Did you never hear of Ethan Brand?"

"The man that went in search of the Unpardonable Sin?" asked Bartram, with a laugh.

"The same," answered the stranger. "He has found what he sought, and therefore he comes back again."

"What! then you are Ethan Brand himself?" cried the lime-burner, in amazement. "I am a new-comer here, as you say, and they call it eighteen years since you left the foot of Graylock. But, I can tell you, the good folks still talk about Ethan Brand, in the village yonder, and what a strange errand took him away from his lime-kiln. Well, and so you have found the Unpardonable Sin?"

"Even so!" said the stranger, calmly.

"If the question is a fair one," proceeded Bartram, "where might it be?"

Ethan Brand laid his finger on his own heart.

"Here!" replied he.

And then, without mirth in his countenance, but as if moved by an involuntary recognition of the infinite absurdity of seeking throughout the world for what was the closest of all things to himself, and looking into every heart, save his own, for what was hidden in no other breast, he broke into a laugh of scorn. It was the same slow, heavy laugh, that had almost appalled the lime-burner when it heralded the wayfarer's approach.

The solitary mountain-side was made dismal by it. Laughter, when out of place, mistimed, or bursting forth from a disordered state of feeling, may be the most terrible modulation of the human voice. The laughter of one asleep, even if it be a little child, — the madman's laugh, — the wild, screaming laugh of a born idiot, — are sounds that we sometimes tremble to hear, and would always willingly forget. Poets have imagined no utterance of fiends or hobgoblins so fearfully appropriate as a laugh. And even the obtuse lime-burner felt his nerves shaken, as

this strange man looked inward at his own heart, and burst into laughter that rolled away into the night, and was indistinctly reverberated among the hills.

"Joe," said he to his little son, "scamper down to the tavern in the village, and tell the jolly fellows there that Ethan Brand has come back, and that he has found the Unpardonable Sin!"

The boy darted away on his errand, to which Ethan Brand made no objection, nor seemed hardly to notice it. He sat on a log of wood, looking steadfastly at the iron door of the kiln. When the child was out of sight, and his swift and light footsteps ceased to be heard treading first on the fallen leaves and then on the rocky mountain-path, the lime-burner began to regret his departure. He felt that the little fellow's presence had been a barrier between his guest and himself, and that he must now deal, heart to heart, with a man who, on his own confession, had committed the one only crime for which Heaven could afford no mercy. That crime, in its indistinct blackness, seemed to overshadow him. The lime-burner's own sins rose up within him, and made his memory riotous with a throng of evil shapes that asserted their kindred with the Master Sin, whatever it might be, which it was within the scope of man's corrupted nature to conceive and cherish. They were all of one family; they went to and fro between his breast and Ethan Brand's, and carried dark greetings from one to the other.

Then Bartram remembered the stories which had grown traditionary in reference to this strange man, who had come upon him like a shadow of the night, and was making himself at home in his old place, after so long absence that the dead people, dead and buried for years, would have had more right to be at home, in any familiar spot, than he. Ethan Brand, it was said, had conversed with Satan himself in the lurid blaze of this very kiln. The legend had been matter of mirth heretofore, but looked grisly now. According to this tale, before Ethan Brand departed on his search, he had been accustomed to evoke a fiend from the hot furnace of the lime-kiln, night after night, in order to confer with him about the Unpardonable

Sin; the man and the fiend each laboring to frame the image of some mode of guilt which could neither be atoned for nor forgiven. And, with the first gleam of light upon the mountain-top, the fiend crept in at the iron door, there to abide the intensest element of fire, until again summoned forth to share in the dreadful task of extending man's possible guilt beyond the scope of Heaven's else infinite mercy.

While the lime-burner was struggling with the horror of these thoughts, Ethan Brand rose from the log, and flung open the door of the kiln. The action was in such accordance with the idea in Bartram's mind, that he almost expected to see the Evil One issue forth, red-hot, from the raging furnace.

"Hold! hold!" cried he, with a tremulous attempt to laugh; for he was ashamed of his fears, although they overmastered him. "Don't, for mercy's sake, bring out your Devil now!"

"Man!" sternly replied Ethan Brand, "what need have I of the Devil? I have left him behind me, on my track. It is with such half-way sinners as you that he busies himself. Fear not, because I open the door. I do but act by old custom, and am going to trim your fire, like a lime-burner, as I was once."

He stirred the vast coals, thrust in more wood, and bent forward to gaze into the hollow prison-house of the fire, regardless of the fierce glow that reddened upon his face. The lime-burner sat watching him, and half suspected this strange guest of a purpose, if not to evoke a fiend, at least to plunge bodily into the flames, and thus vanish from the sight of man. Ethan Brand, however, drew quietly back, and closed the door of the kiln.

"I have looked," said he, "into many a human heart that was seven times hotter with sinful passions than yonder furnace is with fire. But I found not there what I sought. No, not the Unpardonable Sin!"

"What is the Unpardonable Sin?" asked the lime-burner; and then he shrank farther from his companion, trembling lest his question should be answered.

"It is a sin that grew within my own breast," replied Ethan Brand, standing erect, with a pride that distinguishes all enthusiasts of his stamp. "A sin that grew nowhere else! The sin of an intellect that triumphed over the sense of brotherhood with man and reverence for God, and sacrificed everything to its own mighty claims! The only sin that deserves a recompense of immortal agony! Freely, were it to do again, would I incur the guilt. Unshrinkingly I accept the retribution!"

"The man's head is turned," muttered the lime-burner to himself. "He may be a sinner like the rest of us, — nothing more likely, — but, I'll be sworn, he is a madman too."

Nevertheless, he felt uncomfortable at his situation, alone with Ethan Brand on the wild mountain-side, and was right glad to hear the rough murmur of tongues, and the footsteps of what seemed a pretty numerous party, stumbling over the stones and rustling through the underbrush. Soon appeared the whole lazy regiment that was wont to infest the village tavern, comprehending three or four individuals who had drunk flip beside the bar-room fire through all the winters, and smoked their pipes beneath the stoop through all the summers, since Ethan Brand's departure. Laughing boisterously, and mingling all their voices together in unceremonious talk, they now burst into the moonshine and narrow streaks of firelight that illuminated the open space before the lime-kiln. Bartram set the door ajar again, flooding the spot with light, that the whole company might get a fair view of Ethan Brand, and he of them.

There, among other old acquaintances, was a once ubiquitous man, now almost extinct, but whom we were formerly sure to encounter at the hotel of every thriving village throughout the country. It was the stage-agent. The present specimen of the genus was a wilted and smoke-dried man, wrinkled and red-nosed, in a smartly cut, brown, bobtailed coat, with brass buttons, who, for a length of time unknown, had kept his desk and corner in the bar-room, and was still puffing what seemed to be the same cigar that he had lighted twenty years before. He had great fame as a dry joker, though, perhaps, less on account of any intrinsic humor than from a certain flavor of brandy-toddy and tobacco-smoke, which impregnated all his ideas and expressions, as well as his person. Another well-remembered though strangely altered face was that of Lawyer Giles, as people still called him in courtesy; an elderly ragamuffin, in his soiled shirt-sleeves and tow-cloth trousers. This poor fellow had been an attorney, in what he called his better days, a sharp practitioner, and in great vogue among the village litigants; but flip, and sling, and toddy, and cocktails, imbibed at all hours, morning, noon, and night, had caused him to slide from intellectual to various kinds and degrees of bodily labor, till at last, to adopt his own phrase, he slid into a soap-vat. In other words, Giles was now a soap-boiler, in a small way. He had come to be but the fragment of a human being, a part of one foot having been chopped off by an axe, and an entire hand torn away by the devilish grip of a steam-engine. Yet, though the corporeal hand was gone, a spiritual member remained; for, stretching forth the stump, Giles steadfastly averred that he felt an invisible thumb and fingers with as vivid a sensation as before the real ones were amputated. A maimed and miserable wretch he was; but one, nevertheless, whom the world could not trample on, and had no right to scorn, either in this or any previous stage of his misfortunes, since he had still kept up the courage and spirit of a man, asked nothing in charity, and with his one hand — and that the left one — fought a stern battle against want and hostile circumstances.

Among the throng, too, came another personage, who, with certain points of similarity to Lawyer Giles, had many more of difference. It was the village doctor; a man of some fifty years, whom, at an earlier period of his life, we introduced as paying a professional visit to Ethan Brand during the latter's supposed insanity. He was now a purple-visaged, rude, and brutal, yet half-gentlemanly figure, with something wild, ruined, and desperate in his talk, and in all the details of his gesture and manners. Brandy possessed this man like an evil spirit, and made him as surly and savage as a wild beast, and as miserable as a lost soul; but

there was supposed to be in him such wonderful skill, such native gifts of healing, beyond any which medical science could impart, that society caught hold of him, and would not let him sink out of its reach. So, swaying to and fro upon his horse, and grumbling thick accents at the bedside, he visited all the sick-chambers for miles about among the mountain towns, and sometimes raised a dying man, as it were, by miracle, or quite as often, no doubt, sent his patient to a grave that was dug many a year too soon. The doctor had an everlasting pipe in his mouth, and, as somebody said, in allusion to his habit of swearing, it was always alight with hell-fire.

These three worthies pressed forward, and greeted Ethan Brand each after his own fashion, earnestly inviting him to partake of the contents of a certain black bottle, in which, as they averred, he would find something far better worth seeking for than the Unpardonable Sin. No mind, which has wrought itself by intense and solitary meditation into a high state of enthusiasm, can endure the kind of contact with low and vulgar modes of thought and feeling to which Ethan Brand was now subjected. It made him doubt — and, strange to say, it was a painful doubt — whether he had indeed found the Unpardonable Sin, and found it within himself. The whole question on which he had exhausted life, and more than life, looked like a delusion.

"Leave me," he said bitterly, "ye brute beasts, that have made yourselves so, shrivelling up your souls with fiery liquors! I have done with you. Years and years ago, I groped into your hearts, and found nothing there for my purpose. Get ye gone!"

"Why, you uncivil scoundrel," cried the fierce doctor, "is that the way you respond to the kindness of your best friends? Then let me tell you the truth. You have no more found the Unpardonable Sin than yonder boy Joe has. You are but a crazy fellow, — I told you so twenty years ago, — neither better nor worse than a crazy fellow, and the fit companion of old Humphrey, here!"

He pointed to an old man, shabbily dressed, with long white hair, thin visage, and unsteady eyes. For some years past this aged person had been wandering about among the hills, inquiring of all travelers whom he met for his daughter. The girl, it seemed, had gone off with a company of circus-performers; and occasionally tidings of her came to the village, and fine stories were told of her glittering appearance as she rode on horseback in the ring, or performed marvelous feats on the tight-rope.

The white-haired father now approached Ethan Brand, and gazed unsteadily into his face.

"They tell me you have been all over the earth," said he, wringing his hands with earnestness. "You must have seen my daughter, for she makes a grand figure in the world, and everybody goes to see her. Did she send any word to her old father, or say when she was coming back?"

Ethan Brand's eye quailed beneath the old man's. That daughter, from whom he so earnestly desired a word of greeting, was the Esther of our tale, the very girl whom, with such cold and remorseless purpose, Ethan Brand had made the subject of a psychological experiment, and wasted, absorbed, and perhaps annihilated her soul in the process.

"Yes," murmured he, turning away from the hoary wanderer; "it is no delusion. There is an Unpardonable Sin!"

While these things were passing, a merry scene was going forward in the area of cheerful light, beside the spring and before the door of the hut. A number of the youth of the village, young men and girls, had hurried up the hillside, impelled by curiosity to see Ethan Brand, the hero of so many a legend familiar to their childhood. Finding nothing, however, very remarkable in his aspect, — nothing but a sunburnt wayfarer, in plain garb and dusty shoes, who sat looking into the fire as if he fancied pictures among the coals, — these young people speedily grew tired of observing him. As it happened, there was other amusement at hand. An old German Jew, traveling with a diorama on his back, was passing down the mountain-road towards the village just as the party turned aside from it, and, in hopes of eking out the profits of the day, the showman had kept them company to the lime-kiln.

"Come, old Dutchman," cried one of the young men, "let us see your pictures, if you can swear they are worth looking at!"

"Oh, yes, Captain," answered the Jew, — whether as a matter of courtesy or craft, he styled everybody Captain, — "I shall show you, indeed, some very superb pictures!"

So, placing his box in a proper position, he invited the young men and girls to look through the glass orifices of the machine, and proceeded to exhibit a series of the most outrageous scratchings and daubings, as specimens of the fine arts, that ever an itinerant showman had the face to impose upon his circle of spectators. The pictures were worn out, moreover, tattered, full of cracks and wrinkles, dingy with tobacco-smoke, and otherwise in a most pitiable condition. Some purported to be cities, public edifices, and ruined castles in Europe; others represented Napoleon's battles and Nelson's sea-fights; and in the midst of these would be seen a gigantic, brown, hairy hand, — which might have been mistaken for the Hand of Destiny, though, in truth, it was only the showman's, — pointing its forefinger to various scenes of the conflict, while its owner gave historical illustrations. When, with much merriment at its abominable deficiency of merit, the exhibition was concluded, the German bade little Joe put his head into the box. Viewed through the magnifying-glasses, the boy's round, rosy visage assumed the strangest imaginable aspect of an immense Titanic child, the mouth grinning broadly, and the eyes and every other feature overflowing with fun at the joke. Suddenly, however, that merry face turned pale, and its expression changed to horror, for this easily impressed and excitable child had become sensible that the eye of Ethan Brand was fixed upon him through the glass.

"You make the little man to be afraid, Captain," said the German Jew, turning up the dark and strong outline of his visage, from his stooping posture. "But look again, and, by chance, I shall cause you to see somewhat that is very fine, upon my word!"

Ethan Brand gazed into the box for an instant, and then starting back, looked fixedly at the German. What had he seen? Nothing, apparently; for a curious youth, who had peeped in almost at the same moment, beheld only a vacant space of canvas.

"I remember you now," muttered Ethan Brand to the showman.

"Ah, Captain," whispered the Jew of Nuremberg, with a dark smile, "I find it to be a heavy matter in my show-box, — this Unpardonable Sin! By my faith, Captain, it has wearied my shoulders, this long day, to carry it over the mountain."

"Peace," answered Ethan Brand, sternly, "or get thee into the furnace yonder!"

The Jew's exhibition had scarcely concluded, when a great, elderly dog — who seemed to be his own master, as no person in the company laid claim to him — saw fit to render himself the object of public notice. Hitherto, he had shown himself a very quiet, well-disposed old dog, going round from one to another, and, by way of being sociable, offering his rough head to be patted by any kindly hand that would take so much trouble. But now, all of a sudden, this grave and venerable quadruped, of his own mere motion, and without the slightest suggestion from anybody else, began to run round after his tail, which, to heighten the absurdity of the proceeding, was a great deal shorter than it should have been. Never was seen such headlong eagerness in pursuit of an object that could not possibly be attained; never was heard such a tremendous outbreak of growling, snarling, barking, and snapping, — as if one end of the ridiculous brute's body were at deadly and most unforgivable enmity with the other. Faster and faster, round about went the cur; and faster and still faster fled the unapproachable brevity of his tail; and louder and fiercer grew his yells of rage and animosity; until, utterly exhausted, and as far from the goal as ever, the foolish old dog ceased his performance as suddenly as he had begun it. The next moment he was as mild, quiet, sensible, and respectable in his deportment, as when he first scraped acquaintance with the company.

As may be supposed, the exhibition was greeted with universal laughter, clapping of hands, and shouts of encore, to which the canine performer responded by wagging all that there was to wag of his tail, but appeared totally unable to repeat his very

successful effort to amuse the spectators.

Meanwhile, Ethan Brand had resumed his seat upon the log, and moved, it might be, by a perception of some remote analogy between his own case and that of this self-pursuing cur, he broke into the awful laugh, which, more than any other token, expressed the condition of his inward being. From that moment, the merriment of the party was at an end; they stood aghast, dreading lest the inauspicious sound should be reverberated around the horizon, and that mountain would thunder it to mountain, and so the horror be prolonged upon their ears. Then, whispering one to another that it was late, — that the moon was almost down, — that the August night was growing chill, — they hurried homewards, leaving the limeburner and little Joe to deal as they might with their unwelcome guest. Save for these three human beings, the open space on the hillside was a solitude, set in a vast gloom of forest. Beyond that darksome verge, the firelight glimmered on the stately trunks and almost black foliage of pines, intermixed with the lighter verdure of sapling oaks, maples, and poplars, while here and there lay the gigantic corpses of dead trees, decaying on the leaf-strewn soil. And it seemed to little Joe — a timorous and imaginative child — that the silent forest was holding its breath until some fearful thing should happen.

Ethan Brand thrust more wood into the fire, and closed the door of the kiln; then looking over his shoulder at the lime-burner and his son, he bade, rather than advised, them to retire to rest.

"For myself, I cannot sleep," said he. "I have matters that it concerns me to meditate upon. I will watch the fire, as I used to do in the old time."

"And call the Devil out of the furnace to keep you company, I suppose," muttered Bartram, who had been making intimate acquaintance with the black bottle above mentioned. "But watch, if you like, and call as many devils as you like! For my part, I shall be all the better for a snooze. Come, Joe!"

As the boy followed his father into the hut, he looked back at the wayfarer, and the tears came into his eyes, for his tender spirit had an intuition of the bleak and terrible loneliness in which this man had enveloped himself.

When they had gone, Ethan Brand sat listening to the crackling of the kindled wood, and looking at the little spirts of fire that issued through the chinks of the door. These trifles, however, once so familiar, had but the slightest hold of his attention, while deep within his mind he was reviewing the gradual but marvelous change that had been wrought upon him by the search to which he had devoted himself. He remembered how the night dew had fallen upon him, — how the dark forest had whispered to him, — how the stars had gleamed upon him, — a simple and loving man, watching his fire in the years gone by, and ever musing as it burned. He remembered with what tenderness, with what love and sympathy for mankind, and what pity for human guilt and woe, he had first begun to contemplate those ideas which afterwards became the inspiration of his life; with what reverence he had then looked into the heart of man, viewing it as a temple originally divine, and, however desecrated, still to be held sacred by a brother; with what awful fear he had deprecated the success of his pursuit, and prayed that the Unpardonable Sin might never be revealed to him. Then ensued that vast intellectual development, which, in its progress, disturbed the counterpoise between his mind and heart. The Idea that possessed his life had operated as a means of education; it had gone on cultivating his powers to the highest point of which they were susceptible; it had raised him from the level of an unlettered laborer to stand on a star-lit eminence, whither the philosophers of the earth, laden with the lore of universities, might vainly strive to clamber after him. So much for the intellect! But where was the heart? That, indeed, had withered, — had contracted, — had hardened, — had perished! It had ceased to partake of the universal throb. He had lost his hold of the magnetic chain of humanity. He was no longer a brother-man, opening the chambers or the dungeons of our common nature by the key of holy sympathy, which gave him a right to share in all its secrets; he was now a cold observer, looking on mankind as the subject of his experiment, and, at length, converting man and woman to be his puppets, and pulling the wires that moved them to such degrees of crime as were demanded for his study.

Thus Ethan Brand became a fiend. He began to be so from the moment that his moral nature had ceased to keep the pace of improvement with his intellect. And now, as his highest effort and inevitable development, — as the bright and gorgeous flower, and rich, delicious fruit of his life's labor, — he had produced the Unpardonable Sin!

"What more have I to seek? what more to achieve?" said Ethan Brand to himself. "My task is done, and well done!"

Starting from the log with a certain alacrity in his gait and ascending the hillock of earth that was raised against the stone circumference of the lime-kiln, he thus reached the top of the structure. It was a space of perhaps ten feet across, from edge to edge, presenting a view of the upper surface of the immense mass of broken marble with which the kiln was heaped. All these innumerable blocks and fragments of marble were red-hot and vividly on fire, sending up great spouts of blue flame, which quivered aloft and danced madly, as within a magic circle, and sank and rose again, with continual and multitudinous activity. As the lonely man bent forward over this terrible body of fire, the blasting heat smote up against his person with a breath that, it might be supposed, would have scorched and shrivelled him up in a moment.

Ethan Brand stood erect, and raised his arms on high. The blue flames played upon his face, and imparted the wild and ghastly light which alone could have suited its expression; it was that of a fiend on the verge of plunging into his gulf of intensest torment.

"O Mother Earth," cried he, "who art no more my Mother, and into whose bosom this frame shall never be resolved! O mankind, whose brotherhood I have cast off, and trampled thy great heart beneath my feet! O stars of heaven, that shone on me of old, as if to light me onward and upward! — farewell all, and forever. Come, deadly element of Fire, — henceforth my familiar frame! Embrace me, as I do thee!"

That night the sound of a fearful peal of laughter rolled heavily through the sleep of the lime-burner and his little son; dim shapes of horror and anguish haunted their dreams, and seemed still present in the rude hovel, when they opened their eyes to the daylight.

"Up, boy, up!" cried the lime-burner, staring about him. "Thank Heaven, the night is gone, at last; and rather than pass such another, I would watch my lime-kiln, wide awake, for a twelvemonth. This Ethan Brand, with his humbug of an Unpardonable Sin, has done me no such mighty favor, in taking my place!"

He issued from the hut, followed by little Joe, who kept fast hold of his father's hand. The early sunshine was already pouring its gold upon the mountain-tops, and though the valleys were still in shadow, they smiled cheerfully in the promise of the bright day that was hastening onward. The village, completely shut in by hills, which swelled away gently about it, looked as if it had rested peacefully in the hollow of the great hand of Providence. Every dwelling was distinctly visible; the little spires of the two churches pointed upwards, and caught a fore-glimmering of brightness from the sun-gilt skies upon their gilded weathercocks. The tavern was astir, and the figure of the old, smoke-dried stage-agent, cigar in mouth, was seen beneath the stoop. Old Graylock was glorified with a golden cloud upon his head. Scattered likewise over the breasts of the surrounding mountains, there were heaps of hoary mist, in fantastic shapes, some of them far down into the valley, others high up towards the summits, and still others, of the same family of mist or cloud, hovering in the gold radiance of the upper atmosphere. Stepping from one to another of the clouds that rested on the hills, and thence to the loftier brotherhood that sailed in air, it seemed almost as if a mortal man might thus ascend into the heavenly regions. Earth was so mingled with sky that it was a day-dream to look at it.

To supply that charm of the familiar and homely, which Nature so readily adopts into a scene like this, the stage coach was rattling down the mountain-road, and the driver sounded his horn, while Echo caught up the notes, and intertwined them into a rich and varied and elaborate harmony, of which the original performer could lay claim to little share. The great hills played a concert among themselves, each contributing a strain of airy sweetness.

Little Joe's face brightened at once.

"Dear father," cried he, skipping cheerily to and fro, "that strange man is gone, and the sky and the mountains all seem glad of it!"

"Yes," growled the lime-burner, with an oath, "but he has let the fire go down, and no thanks to him if five hundred bushels of lime are not spoiled. If I catch the fellow hereabouts again, I shall feel like tossing him into the furnace!"

With his long pole in his hand, he ascended to the top of the kiln. After a moment's pause, he called to his son.

"Come up here, Joe!" said he.

So little Joe ran up the hillock, and stood by his father's side. The marble was all burnt into perfect, snow-white lime. But on its surface, in the midst of the circle, — snow-white too, and thoroughly converted into lime — lay a human skeleton, in the attitude of a person who, after long toil, lies down to long repose. Within the ribs — strange to say — was the shape of a human heart.

"Was the fellow's heart made of marble?" cried Bartram, in some perplexity at this phenomenon. "At any rate, it is burnt into what looks like special good lime; and, taking all the bones together, my kiln is half a bushel the richer for him."

So saying, the rude lime-burner lifted his pole, and, letting it fall upon the skeleton, the relics of Ethan Brand were crumbled into fragments.

HERMAN MELVILLE (1819-1891)

Of New England ancestry, Melville was the son of a New York merchant who died early. He was educated at New York public schools and the Albany Academy, worked as a clerk and as a farm hand, and shipped before the mast, all before he was twenty. After a few years of teaching school, he signed on the whaler *Acushnet* for a voyage to the South Seas. Arriving at the Marquesas Islands in 1842, he deserted the ship, lived among the cannibal Typees, was picked up by an Australian whaler, participated in a mutiny, and was put ashore at Tahiti. Returning in the years 1843 and 1844 on an American ship bound around Cape Horn for Boston, he began to write autobiographic romances and romantic autobiographies, mixtures of his experiences and his imagination, fact and fiction: *Typee* (1846), *Omoo* (1847), *Redburn* (1849), *Mardi* (1849), *White-Jacket* (1850), and *Moby-Dick* (1851).

In the remarkable Melville revival that has come since the author's centenary, *Moby-Dick* has been acclaimed Melville's masterpiece and one of the greatest of American novels. "The time was propitious for such a book," says Carl Van Doren, *The American Novel*, 1921. "The golden age of the whalers was drawing to a close, though no decline had yet set in, and the native imagination had been stirred by tales of deeds done on remote oceans by the most heroic Yankees of the age in the arduous calling in which New England, and especially the hard little island of Nantucket, led and taught the world. A small literature of whaling had grown up, chiefly the records of actual voyages or novels like those of Cooper in which whaling was an incident of the nautical life. But the whalers still lacked any such romantic record as the frontier had. Melville brought to his task a sound knowledge of actual whaling, much curious learning in the literature of the subject, and, above all, an imagination which worked with great power upon the facts of his own experience."

The only way to secure a fair understanding of Melville's genius is to read the whole of *Moby-Dick*, now available in various editions. However, many aspects of his creative power may be seen in a story like *Benito Cereno*, given below. "*Benito Cereno* is a story of an adventure encountered by an American sea captain off the coast of South America. The framework of the narrative was taken almost verbatim from official records, but Melville touched the cold, lifeless facts of a captain's reports with the genius of a born story-teller, and the result is a perfect evocation of atmosphere. Over every word of the narrative hangs a nameless dread, a feeling of horror and disaster. The story creates a mood as well as does 'The Fall of the House of Usher,' but Poe could never get the reality into his lines that Melville achieved so deftly" (Blankenship, *American Literature*, 1931).

Melville's works were collected in the Standard Edition, 16 volumes, London, 1922–24. The first full-length life, R. M. Weaver's *Herman Melville, Mariner and Mystic*, did not appear till 1921. Then came John Freeman, *Herman Melville*, 1926, and Lewis Mumford, *Herman Melville*, 1929. Melville has been treated by F. O. Matthiessen in *American Renaissance*, 1941. On the development of his thought there is a critical study by William Ellery Sedgwick, *Herman Melville: The Tragedy of Mind*, 1944. A valuable volume of selections was edited by Willard Thorp for the *AWS*, 1938. Three volumes of a new and carefully edited "complete works" have appeared — *Poems*, 1947; *Piazza Tales*, 1948; *Pierre*, 1949. M. O. Percival's *A*

Reading of Moby-Dick, 1950, is rewarding. Richard Chase's *Herman Melville*, 1949, brings new critical methods to bear. Newton Arvin's *Herman Melville*, 1950, is the most distinguished and the best balanced critical study and biography to date.

Benito Cereno

(1855)

In this story Melville's art in the transformation of sailors' and travelers' tales into fiction reached a high point. "One of the most sensitively poised pieces of writing he had ever done," as F. O. Matthiessen calls it, the story followed its source closely and yet achieved a predetermined imaginative effect. It was based on chapter 18 of *A Narrative of Voyages and Travels*, 1817, by Amasa Delano; the chapter has been reprinted by H. C. Scudder in *PMLA*, June, 1928.

First published serially in *Putnam's Monthly Magazine*, the story was included in 1856 in the *Piazza Tales*.

In the year 1799, Captain Amasa Delano, of Duxbury, in Massachusetts, commanding a large sealer and general trader, lay at anchor with a valuable cargo, in the harbor of St. Maria — a small, desert, uninhabited island towards the southern extremity of the long coast of Chili. There he had touched for water.

On the second day, not long after dawn, while lying in his berth, his mate came below, informing him that a strange sail was coming into the bay. Ships were then not so plenty in those waters as now. He rose, dressed, and went on deck.

The morning was one peculiar to that coast. Everything was mute and calm; everything gray. The sea, though undulated into long roods of swells, seemed fixed, and was sleeked at the surface like waved lead that has cooled and set in the smelter's mould. The sky seemed a gray surtout. Flights of troubled gray fowl, kith and kin with flights of troubled gray vapors among which they were mixed, skimmed low and fitfully over the waters, as swallows over meadows before storms. Shadows present, foreshadowing deeper shadows to come.

To Captain Delano's surprise, the stranger, viewed through the glass, showed no colors; though to do so upon entering a haven, however unhabited in its shores, where but a single other ship might be lying, was the custom among peaceful seamen of all nations. Considering the lawlessness and loneliness of the spot, and the sort of stories, at that day, associated with those seas, Captain Delano's surprise might have deepened into some uneasiness had he not been a person of a singularly undistrustful good nature, not liable, except on extraordinary and repeated incentives, and hardly then, to indulge in personal alarms, any way involving the imputation of malign evil in man. Whether, in view of what humanity is capable, such a trait implies, along with a benevolent heart, more than ordinary quickness and accuracy of intellectual perception, may be left to the wise to determine.

But whatever misgivings might have obtruded on first seeing the stranger, would almost, in any seaman's mind, have been dissipated by observing that, the ship, in navigating into the harbor, was drawing too near the land; a sunken reef making out off her bow. This seemed to prove her a stranger, indeed, not only to the sealer, but the island; consequently, she could be no wonted freebooter on that ocean. With no small interest, Captain Delano continued to watch her — a proceeding not much facilitated by the vapors partly mantling the hull, through which the far matin light from her cabin streamed equivocally enough; much like the sun — by this time hemisphered on the rim of the horizon, and, apparently, in company with the strange ship, entering the harbor — which, wimpled by the same low, creeping clouds, showed not unlike a Lima intriguante's one sinister eye peering across the Plaza from the Indian loop-hole of her dusk *saya-y-manta*.

It might have been but a deception of the vapors, but, the longer the stranger was watched the more singular appeared her manoeuvres. Ere long it seemed hard to decide whether she meant to come in or no — what she wanted, or what she was about. The wind, which had breezed up a little during the night, was now extremely light and baffling, which the more increased the apparent uncertainty of her movements.

Surmising, at last, that it might be a ship in distress, Captain Delano ordered his whale-boat to be dropped, and, much to the wary opposition of his mate, prepared to board her, and, at the least, pilot her in. On the night previous, a fishing-party of the seamen had gone a long distance to some detached rocks out of sight from the sealer, and, an hour or two before daybreak, had returned, having met with no small success. Presuming that the stranger might have been long off soundings, the good captain put several baskets of the fish, for presents, into his boat, and so pulled away. From her continuing too near the sunken reef, deeming her in danger, calling to his men, he made all haste to apprise those on board of their situation. But, some time ere the boat came up, the wind, light though it was, having shifted, had headed the vessel off, as well as partly broken the vapors from about her.

Upon gaining a less remote view, the ship, when made signally visible on the verge of the leaden-hued swells, with the shreds of fog here and there raggedly furring her, appeared like a white-washed monastery after a thunderstorm, seen perched upon some dun cliff among the Pyrenees. But it was no purely fanciful resemblance which now, for a moment, almost led Captain Delano to think that nothing less than a ship-load of monks was before him. Peering over the bulwarks were what really seemed, in the hazy distance, throngs of dark cowls; while, fitfully revealed through the open port-holes, other dark moving figures were dimly descried, as of Black Friars pacing the cloisters.

Upon a still nigher approach, this appearance was modified, and the true character of the vessel was plain — a Spanish merchantman of the first class, carrying negro slaves, amongst other valuable freight, from one colonial port to another. A very large, and, in its time, a very fine vessel, such as in those days were at intervals encountered along that main; sometimes superseded Acapulco treasure-ships, or retired frigates of the Spanish king's navy, which, like superannuated Italian palaces, still, under a decline of masters, preserved signs of former state.

As the whale-boat drew more and more nigh, the cause of the peculiar pipe-clayed aspect of the stranger was seen in the slovenly neglect pervading her. The spars, ropes, and great part of the bulwarks, looked woolly, from long unacquaintance with the scraper, tar, and the brush. Her keel seemed laid, her ribs put together, and she launched, from Ezekiel's Valley of Dry Bones.

In the present business in which she was engaged, the ship's general model and rig appeared to have undergone no material change from their original warlike and Froissart pattern. However, no guns were seen.

The tops were large, and were railed about with what had once been octagonal network, all now in sad disrepair. These tops hung overhead like three ruinous aviaries, in one of which was seen perched on a ratlin, a white noddy, a strange fowl, so called from its lethargic somnambulistic character, being frequently caught by hand at sea. Battered and mouldy, the castellated forecastle seemed some ancient turret, long ago taken by assault, and then left to decay. Toward the stern, two high-raised quarter galleries — the balustrades here and there covered with dry, tindery sea-moss — opening out from the unoccupied state-cabin, whose dead-lights, for all the mild weather, were hermetically closed and calked — these tenantless balconies hung over the sea as if it were the grand Venetian canal. But the principal relic of faded grandeur was the ample oval of the shield-like stern-piece, intricately carved with the arms of Castile and Leon, medallioned about by groups of mythological or symbolical devices; uppermost and central of which was a dark satyr in a mask, holding his foot on the prostrate neck of a writhing figure, likewise masked.

Whether the ship had a figure-head, or only a plain beak, was not quite certain, owing to canvas wrapped about that part, either to protect it while undergoing a refurbishing, or else decently to hide its decay. Rudely painted or chalked, as in a sailor freak, along the forward side of a sort of pedestal below the canvas, was the sentence, *"Seguid vuestro jefe"* (follow your leader); while upon the tarnished head-boards, near by, appeared, in stately capitals, once gilt, the ship's name "SAN DOMINICK," each letter streakingly corroded with tricklings of copper-spike rust; while, like mourning weeds, dark festoons of sea-grass slimily swept to and fro over the name, with every hearse-like roll of the hull.

As, at last, the boat was hooked from the bow along toward the gangway amidship, its keel, while yet some inches separated from the hull, harshly grated as on a sunken coral reef. It proved a huge bunch of conglobated barnacles adhering below the water to the side like a wen — a token of baffling airs and long calms passed somewhere in those seas.

Climbing the side, the visitor was at once surrounded by a clamorous throng of whites and blacks, but the latter outnumbering the former more than could have been expected, negro transportation-ship as the stranger in port was. But, in one language, and as with one voice, all poured out a common tale of suffering; in which the negresses, of whom there were not a few, exceeded the others in their dolorous vehemence. The scurvy, together with a fever, had swept off a great part of their number, more especially the Spaniards. Off Cape Horn, they had narrowly escaped shipwreck; then, for days together, they had lain tranced without wind; their provisions were low; their water next to none; their lips that moment were baked.

While Captain Delano was thus made the mark of all eager tongues, his one eager glance took in all the faces, with every other object about him.

Always upon first boarding a large and populous ship at sea, especially a foreign one, with a nondescript crew such as Lascars or Manilla men, the impression varies in a peculiar way from that produced by first entering a strange house with strange inmates in a strange land. Both house and ship — the one by its walls and blinds, the other by its high bulwarks like ramparts — hoard from view their interiors till the last moment; but in the case of the ship there is this addition; that the living spectacle it contains, upon its sudden and complete disclosure, has, in contrast with the blank ocean which zones it, something of the effect of enchantment. The ship seems unreal; these strange costumes, gestures, and faces, but a shadowy tableau just emerged from the deep, which directly must receive back what it gave.

Perhaps it was some such influence, as above is attempted to be described, which, in Captain Delano's mind, heightened whatever, upon a staid scrutiny, might have seemed unusual; especially the conspicuous figures of four elderly grizzled negroes, their heads like black, doddered willow tops, who, in venerable contrast to the tumult below them, were couched sphynx-like, one on the starboard cat-head, another on the larboard, and the remaining pair face to face on the opposite bulwarks above the main-chains. They each had bits of unstranded old junk in their hands, and, with a sort of stoical self-content, were picking the junk into oakum, a small heap of which lay by their sides. They accompanied the task with a continuous, low, monotonous chant; droning and druling away like so many gray-headed bag-pipers playing a funeral march.

The quarter-deck rose into an ample elevated poop, upon the forward verge of which, lifted, like the oakum-pickers, some eight feet above the general throng, sat along in a row, separated by regular spaces, the cross-legged figures of six other blacks; each with a rusty hatchet in his hand, which, with a bit of brick and a rag, he was engaged like a scullion in scouring; while between each two was a small stack of hatchets, their rusted edges turned forward awaiting a like operation. Though occasionally the four oakum-pickers would briefly address some person or persons in the crowd below, yet the six hatchet-polishers neither spoke to others, nor breathed a whisper among themselves, but sat intent upon their task, except at intervals, when, with the peculiar love in negroes of uniting industry with pastime, two-and-two they sideways clashed their hatchets together, like cymbals, with a barbarous din. All six, unlike the generality, had the raw aspect of unsophisticated Africans.

But that first comprehensive glance which took in those ten figures, with scores less conspicuous, rested but an instant upon them, as, impatient of the hubbub of voices, the visitor turned in quest of whomsoever it might be that commanded the ship.

But as if not unwilling to let nature make known her own case among his suffering charge, or else in despair of restraining it for the time, the Spanish captain, a gentlemanly, reserved-looking, and rather young man to a stranger's eye, dressed with singular richness, but bearing plain traces of recent sleepless cares and disquietudes, stood passively by, leaning against the main-mast, at one moment casting a dreary, spiritless look upon his excited people, at the next an unhappy glance toward his visitor. By his side stood a black of small stature, in whose rude face, as occasionally, like a shepherd's dog, he mutely turned it up into the Spaniard's, sorrow and affection were equally blended.

Struggling through the throng, the American advanced to the Spaniard, assuring him of his sympathies, and offering to render whatever assistance might be in his power. To which the Spaniard returned, for the present but grave and ceremonious acknowledgments, his national formality dusked by the saturnine mood of ill-health.

But losing no time in mere compliments, Captain Delano, returning to the gangway, had his basket of fish brought up; and as the wind still continued light, so that some hours at least must elapse ere the ship could be brought to the anchorage, he bade his men return to the sealer, and fetch back as much water as the whale-boat could carry, with whatever soft bread the steward might have, all the remaining pumpkins on board, with a box of sugar, and a dozen of his private bottles of cider.

Not many minutes after the boat's pushing off, to the vexation of all, the wind entirely died away, and the tide turning, began drifting back the ship helplessly seaward. But trusting this would not long last, Captain Delano sought, with good hopes, to cheer up the strangers, feeling no small satisfaction that, with persons in their condition he could — thanks to his frequent voyages along the Spanish main — converse with some freedom in their native tongue.

While left alone with them, he was not long in observing some things tending to heighten his first impressions; but surprise was lost in pity, both for the Spaniards and blacks, alike evidently reduced from scarcity of water and provisions; while long-continued suffering seemed to have brought out the less good-natured qualities of the negroes, besides, at the same time, impairing the Spaniard's authority over them. But, under the circumstances, precisely this condition of things was to have been anticipated. In armies, navies, cities, or families, in nature herself, nothing more relaxes good order than misery. Still, Captain Delano was not without the idea, that had Benito Cereno been a man of greater energy, misrule would hardly have come to the present pass. But the debility, constitutional or induced by the hardships, bodily and mental, of the Spanish captain, was too obvious to be overlooked. A prey to settled dejection, as if long mocked with hope he would not now indulge it, even when it had ceased to be a mock, the prospect of that day or evening at furthest, lying at anchor, with plenty of water for his people, and a brother captain to counsel and befriend, seemed in no perceptible degree to encourage him. His mind appeared unstrung, if not still more seriously affected. Shut up in these oaken walls, chained to one dull round of command, whose unconditionality cloyed him, like some hypochondriac abbot he moved slowly about, at times suddenly pausing, starting, or staring, biting his lip, biting his finger-nail, flushing, paling, twitching his beard, with other symptoms of an absent or moody mind. This distempered spirit was lodged, as before hinted, in as distempered a frame. He was rather tall, but seemed never to have been robust, and now with nervous suffering was almost worn to a skeleton. A tendency to some pulmonary complaint appeared to have been lately confirmed. His voice was like that of one with lungs half gone — hoarsely suppressed, a husky whisper. No wonder that, as in this state he tottered about, his private servant apprehensively followed him. Sometimes the negro gave his master his arm, or took his handkerchief out of his pocket for him; performing these and similar offices with that affectionate zeal which transmutes into something filial or fraternal acts in themselves but menial; and which has gained for the negro the repute of making the most pleasing body-servant in the world; one, too, whom a master need be on no stiffly superior terms with, but may treat with familiar trust; less a servant than a devoted companion.

Marking the noisy indocility of the blacks in general, as well as what seemed the sullen inefficiency of the whites, it was not without humane satisfaction that Captain Delano witnessed the steady good conduct of Babo.

But the good conduct of Babo, hardly more than the ill-behavior of others, seemed to withdraw the half-lunatic Don Benito from his cloudy languor. Not that such precisely was the impression made by the Spaniard on the mind of his visitor. The Spaniard's individual unrest was, for the present, but noted as a conspicuous feature in the ship's general affliction. Still, Captain Delano was not a little concerned at what he could not help taking for the time to be Don Benito's unfriendly indifference toward himself. The Spaniard's manner, too, conveyed a sort of sour and gloomy disdain, which he seemed at no pains to disguise. But this the American in charity ascribed to the harassing effects of sickness, since, in former instances, he had noted that there are peculiar natures on whom prolonged physical suffering seems to cancel every social instinct of kindness; as if forced to black bread themselves, they deemed it but equity that each person coming nigh them should, indirectly, by some slight or affront, be made to partake of their fare.

But ere long Captain Delano bethought him that, indulgent as he was at the first, in judging the Spaniard, he might not, after all, have exercised charity enough. At bottom it was Don Benito's reserve which displeased him; but the same reserve was shown toward all but his personal attendant. Even the formal reports which, according to sea-usage, were at stated times made to him by some petty underling, either a white, mulatto or black, he hardly had patience enough to listen to, without betraying contemptuous aversion. His manner upon such occasions was, in its degree, not unlike that which might be supposed to have been his imperial countryman's, Charles V., just previous to the anchoritish retirement of that monarch from the throne.

This splenetic disrelish of his place was evinced in almost every function pertaining to it. Proud as he was moody, he condescended to no personal mandate. Whatever special orders were necessary, their delivery was delegated to his body-servant, who in turn transferred them to their ultimate destination, through runners, alert Spanish boys or slave boys, like pages or pilot-fish within easy call continually hovering round Don Benito. So that to have beheld this undemonstrative invalid gliding about, apathetic and mute, no landsman could have dreamed that in him was lodged a dictatorship beyond which, while at sea, there was no earthly appeal.

Thus, the Spaniard, regarded in his reserve, seemed as the involuntary victim of mental disorder. But, in fact, his reserve might, in some degree, have proceeded from design. If so, then here was evinced the unhealthy climax of that icy though conscientious policy, more or less adopted by all commanders of large ships, which, except in signal emergencies, obliterates alike the manifestation of sway with every trace of sociality; transforming the man into a block, or rather into a loaded cannon, which, until there is call for thunder, has nothing to say.

Viewing him in this light, it seemed but a natural token of the perverse habit induced by a long course of such hard self-restraint, that, notwithstanding the present condition of his ship, the Spaniard should still persist in a demeanor, which, however harmless, or it may be, appropriate, in a well-appointed vessel, such as the San Dominick might have been at the outset of the voyage, was anything but judicious now. But the Spaniard, perhaps, thought that it was with captains as with gods: reserve, under all events, must still be their cue. But probably this appearance of slumbering dominion might have been but an attempted disguise to conscious imbecility — not deep policy, but shallow device. But be all this as it might, whether Don Benito's manner was designed or not, the more Captain Delano noted its pervading reserve, the less he felt uneasiness at any particular manifestation of that reserve towards himself.

Neither were his thoughts taken up by the

captain alone. Wonted to the quiet order-liness of the sealer's comfortable family of a crew, the noisy confusion of the San Dominick's suffering host repeatedly challenged his eye. Some prominent breaches, not only of discipline but of decency, were observed. These Captain Delano could not but ascribe, in the main, to the absence of those subordinate deck-officers to whom, along with higher duties, is entrusted what may be styled the police department of a populous ship. True, the old oakum-pickers appeared at times to act the part of monitorial constables to their countrymen, the blacks; but though occasionally succeeding in allaying trifling outbreaks now and then between man and man, they could do little or nothing toward establishing general quiet. The San Dominick was in the condition of a transatlantic emigrant ship, among whose multitude of living freight are some individuals, doubtless, as little troublesome as crates and bales; but the friendly remonstrances of such with their ruder companions are of not so much avail as the unfriendly arm of the mate. What the San Dominick wanted was, what the emigrant ship has, stern superior officers. But on these decks not so much as a fourth-mate was to be seen.

The visitor's curiosity was roused to learn the particulars of those mishaps which had brought about such absenteeism, with its consequences; because, though deriving some inkling of the voyage from the wails which at the first moment had greeted him, yet of the details no clear understanding had been had. The best account would, doubtless, be given by the captain. Yet at first the visitor was loth to ask it, unwilling to provoke some distant rebuff. But plucking up courage, he at last accosted Don Benito, renewing the expression of his benevolent interest, adding, that did he (Captain Delano) but know the particulars of the ship's misfortunes, he would, perhaps, be better able in the end to relieve them. Would Don Benito favor him with the whole story.

Don Benito faltered; then, like some somnambulist suddenly interfered with, vacantly stared at his visitor, and ended by looking down on the deck. He maintained this posture so long, that Captain Delano, almost equally disconcerted, and involuntarily almost as rude, turned suddenly from him, walking forward to accost one of the Spanish seamen for the desired information. But he had hardly gone five paces when, with a sort of eagerness Don Benito invited him back, regretting his momentary absence of mind, and professing readiness to gratify him.

While most part of the story was being given, the two captains stood on the after part of the main-deck, a privileged spot, no one being near but the servant.

"It is now a hundred and ninety days," began the Spaniard, in his husky whisper, "that this ship, well officered and well manned, with several cabin passengers — some fifty Spaniards in all — sailed from Buenos Ayres bound to Lima, with a general cargo, Paraguay tea and the like — and," pointing forward, "that parcel of negroes, now not more than a hundred and fifty, as you see, but then numbering over three hundred souls. Off Cape Horn we had heavy gales. In one moment, by night, three of my best officers, with fifteen sailors, were lost, with the main-yard; the spar snapping under them in the slings, as they sought, with heavers, to beat down the icy sail. To lighten the hull, the heavier sacks of mata were thrown into the sea, with most of the water-pipes lashed on deck at the time. And this last necessity it was, combined with the prolonged detentions afterwards experienced, which eventually brought about our chief causes of suffering. When —"

Here there was a sudden fainting attack of his cough, brought on, no doubt, by his mental distress. His servant sustained him, and drawing a cordial from his pocket placed it to his lips. He a little revived. But unwilling to leave him unsupported while yet imperfectly restored, the black with one arm still encircled his master, at the same time keeping his eye fixed on his face, as if to watch for the first sign of complete restoration, or relapse, as the event might prove.

The Spaniard proceeded, but brokenly and obscurely, as one in a dream.

— "Oh, my God! rather than pass through what I have, with joy I would have hailed the most terrible gales; but —"

His cough returned and with increased violence; this subsiding, with reddened lips and closed eyes he fell heavily against his supporter.

"His mind wanders. He was thinking of the plague that followed the gales," plaintively sighed the servant; "my poor, poor master!" wringing one hand, and with the other wiping the mouth. "But be patient, Señor," again turning to Captain Delano, "these fits do not last long; master will soon be himself."

Don Benito reviving, went on; but as this portion of the story was very brokenly delivered, the substance only will here be set down.

It appeared that after the ship had been many days tossed in storms off the Cape, the scurvy broke out, carrying off numbers of the whites and blacks. When at last they had worked round into the Pacific, their spars and sails were so damaged, and so inadequately handled by the surviving mariners, most of whom were become invalids, that, unable to lay her northerly course by the wind, which was powerful, the unmanageable ship, for successive days and nights, was blown northwestward, where the breeze suddenly deserted her, in unknown waters, to sultry calms. The absence of the water-pipes now proved as fatal to life as before their presence had menaced it. Induced, or at least aggravated, by the more than scanty allowance of water, a malignant fever followed the scurvy; with the excessive heat of the lengthened calm, making such short work of it as to sweep away, as by billows, whole families of the Africans, and yet larger number, proportionably, of the Spaniards, including, by a luckless fatality, every remaining officer on board. Consequently, in the smart west winds eventually following the calm, the already rent sails, having to be simply dropped, not furled, at need, had been gradually reduced to the beggar's rags they were now. To procure substitutes for his lost sailors, as well as supplies of water and sails, the captain, at the earliest opportunity, had made for Baldivia, the southernmost civilized port of Chili and South America; but upon nearing the coast the thick weather had prevented him from so much as sighting that harbor. Since which period, almost without a crew, and almost without canvas and almost without water, and, at intervals, giving its added dead to the sea, the San Dominick had been battle-dored about by contrary winds, inveigled by currents, or grown weedy in calms. Like a man lost in woods, more than once she had doubled upon her own track.

"But throughout these calamities," huskily continued Don Benito, painfully turning in the half embrace of his servant, "I have to thank those negroes you see, who, though to your inexperienced eyes appearing unruly, have, indeed, conducted themselves with less of restlessness than even their owner could have thought possible under such circumstances."

Here he again fell faintly back. Again his mind wandered; but he rallied, and less obscurely proceeded.

"Yes, their owner was quite right in assuring me that no fetters would be needed with his blacks; so that while, as is wont in this transportation, those negroes have always remained upon deck — not thrust below, as in the Guinea-men — they have, also, from the beginning, been freely permitted to range within given bounds at their pleasure."

Once more the faintness returned — his mind roved — but, recovering, he resumed:

"But it is Babo here to whom, under God, I owe not only my own preservation, but likewise to him, chiefly, the merit is due, of pacifying his more ignorant brethren, when at intervals tempted to murmurings."

"Ah, master," sighed the black, bowing his face, "don't speak of me; Babo is nothing; what Babo has done was but duty."

"Faithful fellow!" cried Captain Delano. "Don Benito, I envy you such a friend; slave I cannot call him."

As master and man stood before him, the black upholding the white, Captain Delano could not but bethink him of the beauty of that relationship which could present such a spectacle of fidelity on the one hand and confidence on the other. The scene was heightened by the contrast in dress, denoting their relative positions. The Spaniard wore a loose Chili jacket of dark velvet; white small-clothes and stockings, with silver buckles at the knee and instep; a high-crowned sombrero, of fine grass; a slender sword, silver mounted, hung from a knot in his sash — the last being an almost invariable adjunct, more for utility than ornament, of a South American gentleman's dress to this hour. Excepting when his occasional nervous contortions brought about disarray, there was a certain precision in his attire, curiously at variance with the unsightly disorder around: especially in the belittered Ghetto, forward of the main-mast, wholly occupied by the blacks.

The servant wore nothing but wide trowsers, apparently, from their coarseness and patches, made out of some old topsail; they were clean, and confined at the waist by a bit of unstranded rope, which, with his composed, deprecatory air at times, made him look something like a begging friar of St. Francis.

However unsuitable for the time and place, at least in the blunt-thinking American's eyes, and however strangely surviving in the midst of all his afflictions, the toilette of Don Benito might not, in fashion at least, have gone beyond the style of the day among South Americans of his class. Though on the present voyage sailing from Buenos Ayres, he had avowed himself a native and resident of Chili, whose inhabitants had not so generally adopted the plain coat and once plebeian pantaloons; but, with a becoming modification, adhered to their provincial costume, picturesque as any in the world. Still, relatively to the pale history of the voyage, and his own pale face, there seemed something so incongruous in the Spaniard's apparel, as almost to suggest the image of an invalid courtier tottering about London streets in the time of the plague.

The portion of the narrative which, perhaps, most excited interest, as well as some surprise, considering the latitudes in question, was the long calms spoken of, and more particularly the ship's so long drifting about. Without communicating the opinion, of course, the American could not but impute at least part of the detentions both to clumsy seamanship and faulty navigation. Eyeing Don Benito's small, yellow hands, he easily inferred that the young captain had not got into command at the hawse-hole but the cabin-window; and if so, why wonder at incompetence, in youth, sickness, and gentility united?

But drowning criticism in compassion, after a fresh repetition of his sympathies, Captain Delano, having heard out his story, not only engaged, as in the first place, to see Don Benito and his people supplied in their immediate bodily needs, but, also, now further promised to assist him in procuring a large permanent supply of water, as well as some sails and rigging; and, though it would involve no small embarrassment to himself, yet he would spare three of his best seamen for temporary deck officers; so that without delay the ship might proceed to Conception, there fully to refit for Lima, her destined port.

Such generosity was not without its effect, even upon the invalid. His face lighted up; eager and hectic, he met the honest glance of his visitor. With gratitude he seemed overcome.

"This excitement is bad for master," whispered the servant, taking his arm, and with soothing words gently drawing him aside.

When Don Benito returned, the American was pained to observe that his hopefulness, like the sudden kindling in his cheek, was but febrile and transient.

Ere long, with a joyless mien, looking up towards the poop, the host invited his guest to accompany him there, for the benefit of what little breath of wind might be stirring.

As, during the telling of the story, Captain Delano had once or twice started at the occasional cymballing of the hatchet-polishers, wondering why such an interruption should be allowed, especially in that part of the ship, and in the ears of an invalid; and moreover, as the hatchets had anything but an attractive look, and the handlers of them still less so, it was, therefore, to tell the truth, not without some lurking reluctance, or even shrinking, it may be, that Captain Delano, with apparent complaisance, acquiesced in his host's invitation. The more so, since, with an untimely caprice of punctilio, rendered distressing by his cadaverous aspect, Don Benito, with Castilian bows, solemnly insisted upon his guest's preceding him up the ladder leading to the elevation; where, one on each side of the last step, sat for armorial supporters and sentries two of the ominous file. Gingerly enough stepped good Captain Delano between them, and in the instant of leaving them behind, like one running the gauntlet, he felt an apprehensive twitch in the calves of his legs.

But when, facing about, he saw the whole file, like so many organ-grinders, still stupidly intent on their work, unmindful of everything beside, he could not but smile at his late fidgety panic.

Presently, while standing with his host, looking forward upon the decks below, he was struck by one of those instances of insubordination previously alluded to. Three black boys, with two Spanish boys, were sitting together on the hatchets, scraping a rude wooden platter, in which some scanty mess had recently been cooked. Suddenly, one of the black boys, enraged at a word dropped by one of his white companions, seized a knife, and, though called to forbear by one of the oakum-pickers, struck the lad over the head, inflicting a gash from which blood flowed.

In amazement, Captain Delano inquired what this meant. To which the pale Don Benito dully muttered, that it was merely the sport of the lad.

"Pretty serious sport, truly," rejoined Captain Delano. "Had such a thing happened on board the Bachelor's Delight, instant punishment would have followed."

At these words the Spaniard turned upon the American one of his sudden, staring, half-lunatic looks; then, relapsing into his torpor, answered, "Doubtless, doubtless, Señor."

Is it, thought Captain Delano, that this helpless man is one of those paper captains I've known, who by policy wink at what by power they cannot put down? I know no sadder sight than a commander who has little of command but the name.

"I should think, Don Benito," he now said, glancing towards the oakum-picker who had sought to interfere with the boys, "that you would find it advantageous to keep all your blacks employed, especially the younger ones, no matter at what useless

task, and no matter what happens to the ship. Why, even with my little band, I find such a course indispensable. I once kept a crew on my quarter-deck thrumming mats for my cabin, when, for three days, I had given up my ship — mats, men, and all — for a speedy loss, owing to the violence of a gale, in which we could do nothing but helplessly drive before it."

"Doubtless, doubtless," muttered Don Benito.

"But," continued Captain Delano, again glancing upon the oakum-pickers and then at the hatchet-polishers, near by, "I see you keep some, at least, of your host employed."

"Yes," was again the vacant response.

"Those old men there, shaking their pows from their pulpits," continued Captain Delano, pointing to the oakum-pickers, "seem to act the part of old dominies to the rest, little heeded as their admonitions are at times. Is this voluntary on their part, Don Benito, or have you appointed them shepherds to your flock of black sheep?"

"What posts they fill, I appointed them," rejoined the Spaniard in an acrid tone, as if resenting some supposed satiric reflection.

"And these others, these Ashantee conjurors here," continued Captain Delano, rather uneasily eying the brandished steel of the hatchet-polishers, where, in spots, it had been brought to a shine, "this seems a curious business they are at, Don Benito?"

"In the gales we met," answered the Spaniard, "what of our general cargo was not thrown overboard was much damaged by the brine. Since coming into calm weather, I have had several cases of knives and hatchets daily brought up for overhauling and cleaning."

"A prudent idea, Don Benito. You are part owner of ship and cargo, I presume; but not of the slaves, perhaps?"

"I am owner of all you see," impatiently returned Don Benito, "except the main company of blacks, who belonged to my late friend Alexandro Aranda."

As he mentioned this name, his air was heart-broken; his knees shook; his servant supported him.

Thinking he divined the cause of such unusual emotion, to confirm his surmise,

Captain Delano, after a pause, said: "And may I ask, Don Benito, whether — since awhile ago you spoke of some cabin passengers — the friend, whose loss so afflicts you, at the outset of the voyage accompanied his blacks?"

"Yes."

"But died of the fever?"

"Died of the fever. — Oh, could I but —"

Again quivering, the Spaniard paused.

"Pardon me," said Captain Delano, lowly, "but I think that, by a sympathetic experience, I conjecture, Don Benito, what it is that gives the keener edge to your grief. It was once my hard fortune to lose at sea, a dear friend, my own brother, then supercargo. Assured of the welfare of his spirit, its departure I could have borne like a man; but that honest eye, that honest hand — both of which had so often met mine — and that warm heart; all, all — like scraps to the dogs — to throw all to the sharks! It was then I vowed never to have for fellow-voyager a man I loved, unless, unbeknown to him, I had provided every requisite, in case of a fatality, for embalming his mortal part for interment on shore. Were your friend's remains now on board this ship, Don Benito, not thus strangely would the mention of his name affect you."

"On board this ship?" echoed the Spaniard. Then, with horrified gestures, as directed against some spectre, he unconsciously fell into the ready arms of his attendant, who, with a silent appeal toward Captain Delano, seemed beseeching him not again to broach a theme so unspeakably distressing to his master.

This poor fellow now, thought the pained American, is the victim of that sad superstition which associates goblins with the deserted body of man, as ghosts with an abandoned house. How unlike are we made! What to me, in like case, would have been a solemn satisfaction, the bare suggestion, even, terrifies the Spaniard into this trance. Poor Alexandro Aranda! what would you say could you here see your friend — who, on former voyages, when you, for months, were left behind, has, I dare say, often longed, and longed, for one peep at you — now transported with terror at the least thought of having you anyway nigh him.

At this moment, with a dreary grave-yard toll, betokening a flaw, the ship's forecastle bell, smote by one of the grizzled oakum-pickers, proclaimed ten o'clock, through the leaden calm; when Captain Delano's attention was caught by the moving figure of a gigantic black, emerging from the general crowd below, and slowly advancing towards the elevated poop. An iron collar was about his neck, from which depended a chain, thrice wound round his body; the terminating links padlocked together at a broad band of iron, his girdle.

"How like a mute Atufal moves," murmured the servant.

The black mounted the steps of the poop, and, like a brave prisoner, brought up to receive sentence, stood in unquailing muteness before Don Benito, now recovered from his attack.

At the first glimpse of his approach, Don Benito had started, a resentful shadow swept over his face; and, as with the sudden memory of bootless rage, his white lips glued together.

This is some mulish mutineer, thought Captain Delano, surveying, not without a mixture of admiration, the colossal form of the negro.

"See, he waits your question, master," said the servant.

Thus reminded, Don Benito, nervously averting his glance, as if shunning, by anticipation, some rebellious response, in a disconcerted voice, thus spoke: —

"Atufal, will you ask my pardon now?"

The black was silent.

"Again, master," murmured the servant, with bitter upbraiding eyeing his countryman, "again, master; he will bend to master yet."

"Answer," said Don Benito, still averting his glance, "say but the one word, *pardon*, and your chains shall be off."

Upon this, the black, slowly raising both arms, let them lifelessly fall, his links clanking, his head bowed; as much as to say, "No, I am content."

"Go," said Don Benito, with inkept and unknown emotion.

Deliberately as he had come, the black obeyed.

"Excuse me, Don Benito," said Captain Delano, "but this scene surprises me; what means it, pray?"

"It means that that negro alone, of all the band, has given me peculiar cause of offence. I have put him in chains; I ——"

Here he paused; his hand to his head, as if there were a swimming there, or a sudden bewilderment of memory had come over him; but meeting his servant's kindly glance seemed reassured, and proceeded: —

"I could not scourge such a form. But I told him he must ask my pardon. As yet he has not. At my command, every two hours he stands before me."

"And how long has this been?"

"Some sixty days."

"And obedient in all else? And respectful?"

"Yes."

"Upon my conscience, then," exclaimed Captain Delano, impulsively, "he has a royal spirit in him, this fellow."

"He may have some right to it," bitterly returned Don Benito; "he says he was king in his own land."

"Yes," said the servant, entering a word, "those slits in Atufal's ears once held wedges of gold; but poor Babo here, in his own land, was only a poor slave; a black man's slave was Babo, who now is the white's."

Somewhat annoyed by these conversational familiarities, Captain Delano turned curiously upon the attendant, then glanced inquiringly at his master; but, as if long wonted to these little informalities, neither master nor man seemed to understand him.

"What, pray, was Atufal's offence, Don Benito?" asked Captain Delano; "if it was not something very serious, take a fool's advice, and, in view of his general docility, as well as in some natural respect for his spirit, remit his penalty."

"No, no, master never will do that," here murmured the servant to himself, "proud Atufal must first ask master's pardon. The slave there carries the padlock, but master here carries the key."

His attention thus directed, Captain Delano now noticed for the first time, that, suspended by a slender silken cord, from Don Benito's neck, hung a key. At once,

from the servant's muttered syllables, divining the key's purpose, he smiled and said: — "So, Don Benito — padlock and key — significant symbols, truly."

Biting his lip, Don Benito faltered.

Though the remark of Captain Delano, a man of such native simplicity as to be incapable of satire or irony, had been dropped in playful allusion to the Spaniard's singularly evidenced lordship over the black; yet the hypochondriac seemed in some way to have taken it as a malicious reflection upon his confessed inability thus far to break down, at least, on a verbal summons, the entrenched will of the slave. Deploring this supposed misconception, yet despairing of correcting it, Captain Delano shifted the subject; but finding his companion more than ever withdrawn, as if still slowly digesting the lees of the presumed affront above, mentioned, by-and-by Captain Delano likewise became less talkative, oppressed, against his own will, by what seemed the secret vindictiveness of the morbidly sensitive Spaniard. But the good sailor, himself of a quite contrary disposition, refrained, on his part, alike from the appearance as from the feeling of resentment, and if silent, was only so from contagion.

Presently the Spaniard, assisted by his servant somewhat discourteously crossed over from his guest; a procedure which, sensibly enough, might have been allowed to pass for idle caprice of ill-humor, had not master and man, lingering round the corner of the elevated skylight, began whispering together in low voices. This was unpleasing. And more: the moody air of the Spaniard, which at times had not been without a sort of valetudinarian stateliness, now seemed anything but dignified; while the menial familiarity of the servant lost its original charm of simple-hearted attachment.

In his embarrassment, the visitor turned his face to the other side of the ship. By so doing, his glance accidentally fell on a young Spanish sailor, a coil of rope in his hand, just stepped from the deck to the first round of the mizzen-rigging. Perhaps the man would not have been particularly noticed, were it not that, during his ascent to one of the yards, he, with a sort of covert intentness, kept his eye fixed on Captain Delano, from whom, presently, it passed, as if by a natural sequence, to the two whisperers.

His own attention thus redirected to that quarter, Captain Delano gave a slight start. From something in Don Benito's manner just then, it seemed as if the visitor had, at least partly, been the subject of the withdrawn consultation going on — a conjecture as little agreeable to the guest as it was little flattering to the host.

The singular alternations of courtesy and ill-breeding in the Spanish captain were unaccountable, except on one of two suppositions—innocent lunacy, or wicked imposture.

But the first idea, though it might naturally have occurred to an indifferent observer, and, in some respects, had not hitherto been wholly a stranger to Captain Delano's mind, yet, now that, in an incipient way, he began to regard the stranger's conduct something in the light of an intentional affront, of course the idea of lunacy was virtually vacated. But if not a lunatic, what then? Under the circumstances, would a gentleman, nay, any honest boor, act the part now acted by his host? The man was an impostor. Some low-born adventurer, masquerading as an oceanic grandee; yet so ignorant of the first requisites of mere gentlemanhood as to be betrayed into the present remarkable indecorum. That strange ceremoniousness, too, at other times evinced, seemed not uncharacteristic of one playing a part above his real level. Benito Cereno — Don Benito Cereno — a sounding name. One, too, at that period, not unknown, in the surname, to supercargoes and sea captains trading along the Spanish Main, as belonging to one of the most enterprising and extensive mercantile families in all those provinces; several members of it having titles; a sort of Castilian Rothschild, with a noble brother, or cousin, in every great trading town of South America. The alleged Don Benito was in early manhood, about twenty-nine or thirty. To assume a sort of roving cadetship in the maritime affairs of such a house, what more likely scheme for a young knave of talent and spirit? But the Spaniard was a pale invalid. Never mind. For even to the degree of simulating mortal disease, the craft

of some tricksters had been known to attain. To think that, under the aspect of infantile weakness, the most savage energies might be couched — those velvets of the Spaniard but the velvet paw to his fangs.

From no train of thought did these fancies come; not from within, but from without; suddenly, too, and in one throng, like hoar frost; yet as soon to vanish as the mild sun of Captain Delano's good-nature regained its meridian.

Glancing over once again towards his host — whose side-face, revealed above the skylight, was now turned toward him — he was struck by the profile, whose clearness of cut was refined by the thinness incident to ill-health, as well as ennobled about the chin by the beard. Away with suspicion. He was a true off-shoot of a true hidalgo Cereno.

Relieved by these and other better thoughts, the visitor, lightly humming a tune, now began indifferently pacing the poop, so as not to betray to Don Benito that he had at all mistrusted incivility, much less duplicity; for such mistrust would yet be proved illusory, and by the event; though, for the present, the circumstance which had provoked that distrust remained unexplained. But when that little mystery should have been cleared up, Captain Delano thought he might extremely regret it, did he allow Don Benito to become aware that he had indulged in ungenerous surmises. In short, to the Spaniard's black-letter text, it was best, for a while, to leave open margin.

Presently, his pale face twitching and overcast, the Spaniard, still supported by his attendant, moved over towards his guest, when, with even more than his usual embarrassment, and a strange sort of intriguing intonation in his husky whisper, the following conversation began: —

"Señor, may I ask how long you have lain at this isle?"

"Oh, but a day or two, Don Benito."

"And from what port are you last?"

"Canton."

"And there, Señor, you exchanged your seal-skins for teas and silks, I think you said?"

"Yes. Silks, mostly."

"And the balance you took in specie, perhaps?"

Captain Delano, fidgeting a little, answered —

"Yes; some silver; not a very great deal, though."

"Ah — well. May I ask how many men have you, Señor?"

Captain Delano slightly started, but answered —

"About five-and-twenty, all told."

"And at present, Señor, all on board, I suppose?"

"All on board, Don Benito," replied the Captain, now with satisfaction.

"And will be to-night, Señor?"

At this last question, following so many pertinacious ones, for the soul of him Captain Delano could not but look very earnestly at the questioner, who, instead of meeting the glance, with every token of craven discomposure dropped his eyes to the deck; presenting an unworthy contrast to his servant, who, just then, was kneeling at his feet, adjusting a loose shoe-buckle; his disengaged face meantime, with humble curiosity, turned openly up into his master's downcast one.

The Spaniard, still with a guilty shuffle, repeated his question:

"And — and will be to-night, Señor?"

"Yes, for aught I know," returned Captain Delano — "but nay," rallying himself into fearless truth, "some of them talked of going off on another fishing party about midnight."

"Your ships generally go — go more or less armed, I believe, Señor?"

"Oh, a six-pounder or two, in case of emergency," was the intrepidly indifferent reply, "with a small stock of muskets, sealing spears, and cutlasses, you know."

As he thus responded, Captain Delano again glanced at Don Benito, but the latter's eyes were averted; while abruptly and awkwardly shifting the subject, he made some peevish allusion to the calm, and then, without apology, once more, with his attendant, withdrew to the opposite bulwarks, where the whispering was resumed.

At this moment, and ere Captain Delano could cast a cool thought upon what had just passed, the young Spanish sailor, before mentioned, was seen descending from the rigging. In act of stooping over to spring inboard to the deck, his voluminous, unconfined frock, or shirt, of coarse woolen, much spotted with tar, opened out far down the chest, revealing a soiled under garment of what seemed the finest linen, edged, about the neck, with a narrow blue ribbon, sadly faded and worn. At this moment the young sailor's eye was again fixed on the whisperers, and Captain Delano thought he observed a lurking significance in it, as if silent signs, of some Freemason sort, had that instant been interchanged.

This once more impelled his own glance in the direction of Don Benito, and, as before, he could not but infer that himself formed the subject of the conference. He paused. The sound of the hatchet-polishing fell on his ears. He cast another swift side-look at the two. They had the air of conspirators. In connection with the late questionings, and the incident of the young sailor, these things now begat such return of involuntary suspicion, that the singular guilelessness of the American could not endure it. Plucking up a gay and humorous expression, he crossed over to the two rapidly, saying: — "Ha, Don Benito, your black here seems high in your trust; a sort of privy-counsellor, in fact."

Upon this, the servant looked up with a good-natured grin, but the master started as from a venomous bite. It was a moment or two before the Spaniard sufficiently recovered himself to reply; which he did, at last, with cold constraint: — "Yes, Señor, I have trust in Babo."

Here Babo, changing his previous grin of mere animal humor into an intelligent smile, not ungratefully eyed his master.

Finding that the Spaniard now stood silent and reserved, as if involuntarily, or purposely giving hint that his guest's proximity was inconvenient just then, Captain Delano, unwilling to appear uncivil even to incivility itself, made some trivial remark and moved off; again and again turning over in his mind the mysterious demeanor of Don Benito Cereno.

He had descended from the poop, and, wrapped in thought, was passing near a dark hatchway, leading down into the steerage, when, perceiving motion there, he looked to see what moved. The same instant there was a sparkle in the shadowy hatchway, and he saw one of the Spanish sailors, prowling there, hurriedly placing his hand in the bosom of his frock, as if hiding something. Before the man could have been certain who it was that was passing, he slunk below out of sight. But enough was seen of him to make it sure that he was the same young sailor before noticed in the rigging.

What was that which so sparkled? thought Captain Delano. It was no lamp — no match — no live coal. Could it have been a jewel? But how come sailors with jewels? — or with silk-trimmed under-shirts either? Has he been robbing the trunks of the dead cabin-passengers? But if so, he would hardly wear one of the stolen articles on board ship here. Ah, ah — if, now, that was, indeed, a secret sign I saw passing between this suspicious fellow and his captain while since; if I could only be certain that, in my uneasiness, my senses did not deceive me, then ——

Here, passing from one suspicious thing to another, his mind revolved the strange questions put to him concerning his ship.

By a curious coincidence, as each point was recalled, the black wizards of Ashantee would strike up with their hatchets, as in ominous comment on the white stranger's thoughts. Pressed by such enigmas and portents, it would have been almost against nature, had not, even into the least distrustful heart, some ugly misgivings obtruded.

Observing the ship now helplessly fallen into a current, with enchanted sails, drifting with increased rapidity seaward; and noting that, from a lately intercepted projection of the land, the sealer was hidden, the stout mariner began to quake at thoughts which he barely durst confess to himself. Above all, he began to feel a ghostly dread of Don Benito. And yet when he roused himself, dilated his chest, felt himself strong on his legs, and coolly considered it — what did all these phantoms amount to?

Had the Spaniard any sinister scheme, it must have reference not so much to him (Captain Delano) as to his ship (the Bachelor's Delight). Hence the present drifting away of the one ship from the other, instead of favoring any such possible scheme, was, for the time at least, opposed to it. Clearly any suspicion, combining such contradictions,

must need be delusive. Beside, was it not absurd to think of a vessel in distress — a vessel by sickness almost dismanned of her crew — a vessel whose inmates were parched for water — was it not a thousand times absurd that such a craft should, at present, be of a piratical character; or her commander, either for himself or those under him, cherish any desire but for speedy relief and refreshment? But then, might not general distress, and thirst in particular, be affected? And might not that same undiminished Spanish crew, alleged to have perished off to a remnant, be at that very moment lurking in the hold? On heart-broken pretence of entreating a cup of cold water, fiends in human form had got into lonely dwellings, nor retired until a dark deed had been done. And among the Malay pirates, it was no unusual thing to lure ships after them into their treacherous harbors, or entice boarders from a declared enemy at sea, by the spectacle of thinly manned or vacant decks, beneath which prowled a hundred spears with yellow arms ready to upthrust them through the mats. Not that Captain Delano had entirely credited such things. He had heard of them — and now, as stories, they recurred. The present destination of the ship was the anchorage. There she would be near his own vessel. Upon gaining that vicinity, might not the San Dominick, like a slumbering volcano, suddenly let loose energies now hid?

He recalled the Spaniard's manner while telling his story. There was a gloomy hesitancy and subterfuge about it. It was just the manner of one making up his tale for evil purposes, as he goes. But if that story was not true, what was the truth? That the ship had unlawfully come into the Spaniard's possession? But in many of its details, especially in reference to the more calamitous parts, such as the fatalities among the seamen, the consequent prolonged beating about, the past sufferings from obstinate calms, and still continued suffering from thirst; in all these points, as well as others, Don Benito's story had corroborated not only the wailing ejaculations of the indiscriminate multitude, white and black, but likewise — what seemed impossible to counterfeit — by the very expression and play of every human feature, which Captain Delano saw. If Don Benito's story was, throughout, an invention, then every soul on board, down to the youngest negress, was his carefully drilled recruit in the plot: an incredible inference. And yet, if there was ground for mistrusting his veracity, that inference was a legitimate one.

But those questions of the Spaniard. There, indeed, one might pause. Did they not seem put with much the same object with which the burglar or assassin, by daytime, reconnoitres the walls of a house? But, with ill purposes, to solicit such information openly of the chief person endangered, and so, in effect, setting him on his guard; how unlikely a procedure was that? Absurd, then, to suppose that those questions had been prompted by evil designs. Thus, the same conduct, which, in this instance, had raised the alarm, served to dispel it. In short, scarce any suspicion or uneasiness, however, apparently reasonable at the time, which was not now, with equal apparent reason, dismissed.

At last, he began to laugh at his former forebodings; and laugh at the strange ship for, in its aspect someway siding with them, as it were; and laugh, too, at the odd-looking blacks, particularly those old scissors-grinders, the Ashantees; and those bed-ridden old knitting women, the oakum-pickers; and almost at the dark Spaniard himself, the central hobgoblin of all.

For the rest, whatever in a serious way seemed enigmatical, was now good-naturedly explained away by the thought that, for the most part the poor invalid scarcely knew what he was about; either sulking in black vapors, or putting idle questions without sense or object. Evidently, for the present, the man was not fit to be intrusted with the ship. On some benevolent plea withdrawing the command from him, Captain Delano would yet have to send her to Conception in charge of his second mate, a worthy person and good navigator — a plan not more convenient for the San Dominick than for Don Benito; for, relieved from all anxiety, keeping wholly to his cabin, the sick man, under the good nursing of his servant, would probably, by the end of the passage, be in a measure restored to health, and with that he should also be restored to authority.

Such were the American's thoughts. They were tranquilizing. There was a difference between the idea of Don Benito's darkly pre-ordaining Captain Delano's fate, and Captain Delano's lightly arranging Don Benito's. Nevertheless, it was not without something of relief that the good seaman presently perceived his whale-boat in the distance. Its absence had been prolonged by unexpected detention at the sealer's side, as well as its returning trip lengthened by the continual recession of the goal.

The advancing speck was observed by the blacks. Their shouts attracted the attention of Don Benito, who, with a return of courtesy, approaching Captain Delano, expressed satisfaction at the coming of some supplies, slight and temporary as they must necessarily prove.

Captain Delano responded; but while doing so, his attention was drawn to something passing on the deck below: among the crowd climbing the landward bulwarks, anxiously watching the coming boat, two blacks, to all appearances accidentally incommoded by one of the sailors, violently pushed him aside, which the sailor someway resenting, they dashed him to the deck, despite the earnest cries of the oakum-pickers.

"Don Benito," said Captain Delano quickly, "do you see what is going on there? Look!"

But, seized by his cough, the Spaniard staggered, with both hands to his face, on the point of falling. Captain Delano would have supported him, but the servant was more alert, who, with one hand sustaining his master, with the other applied the cordial. Don Benito restored, the black withdrew his support, slipping aside a little, but dutifully remaining within call of a whisper. Such discretion was here evinced as quite wiped away, in the visitor's eyes, any blemish of impropriety which might have attached to the attendant, from the indecorous conferences before mentioned; showing, too, that if the servant were to blame, it might be more the master's fault than his own, since, when left to himself, he could conduct thus well.

His glance called away from the spectacle of disorder to the more pleasing one before him, Captain Delano could not avoid again congratulating his host upon possessing such a servant, who, though perhaps a little too forward now and then, must upon the whole be invaluable to one in the invalid's situation.

"Tell me, Don Benito," he added, with a smile — "I should like to have your man here, myself — what will you take for him? Would fifty doubloons be any object?"

"Master wouldn't part with Babo for a thousand doubloons," murmured the black, overhearing the offer, and taking it in earnest, and, with the strange vanity of a faithful slave, appreciated by his master, scorning to hear so paltry a valuation put upon him by a stranger. But Don Benito, apparently hardly yet completely restored, and again interrupted by his cough, made but some broken reply.

Soon his physical distress became so great, affecting his mind, too, apparently, that, as if to screen the sad spectacle, the servant gently conducted his master below.

Left to himself, the American, to while away the time till his boat should arrive, would have pleasantly accosted some one of the few Spanish seamen he saw; but recalling something that Don Benito had said touching their ill conduct, he refrained; as a shipmaster indisposed to countenance cowardice or unfaithfulness in seamen.

While, with these thoughts, standing with eye directed forward towards that handful of sailors, suddenly he thought that one or two of them returned the glance and with a sort of meaning. He rubbed his eyes, and looked again; but again seemed to see the same thing. Under a new form, but more obscure than any previous one, the old suspicions recurred, but, in the absence of Don Benito, with less of panic than before. Despite the bad account given of the sailors, Captain Delano resolved forthwith to accost one of them. Descending the poop, he made his way through the blacks, his movement drawing a queer cry from the oakum-pickers, prompted by whom, the negroes, twitching each other aside, divided before him; but, as if curious to see what was the object of this deliberate visit to their Ghetto, closing in

behind, in tolerable order, followed the white stranger up. His progress thus proclaimed as by mounted kings-at-arms, and escorted as by a Caffre guard of honor, Captain Delano, assuming a good-humored, offhand air, continued to advance; now and then saying a blithe word to the negroes, and his eye curiously surveying the white faces, here and there sparsely mixed in with the blacks, like stray white pawns venturously involved in the ranks of the chess-men opposed.

While thinking which of them to select for his purpose, he chanced to observe a sailor seated on the deck engaged in tarring the strap of a large block, a circle of blacks squatted round him inquisitively eyeing the process.

The mean employment of the man was in contrast with something superior in his figure. His hand, black with continually thrusting it into the tar-pot held for him by a negro, seemed not naturally allied to his face, a face which would have been a very fine one but for its haggardness. Whether this haggardness had aught to do with criminality, could not be determined; since, as intense heat and cold, though unlike, produce like sensations, so innocence and guilt, when, through casual association with mental pain, stamping any visible impress, use one seal — a hacked one.

Not again that this reflection occurred to Captain Delano at the time, charitable man as he was. Rather another idea. Because observing so singular a haggardness to be combined with a dark eye, averted as in trouble and shame, and then, again recalling Don Benito's confessed ill opinion of his crew, insensibly he was operated upon by certain general notions which, while disconnecting pain and abashment from virtue, as invariably link them with vice.

If, indeed, there be any wickedness on board this ship, thought Captain Delano, be sure that man there has fouled his hand in it, even as now he fouls it in the pitch. I don't like to accost him. I will speak to this other, this old Jack here on the windlass.

He advanced to an old Barcelona tar, in ragged red breeches and dirty nightcap, cheeks trenched and bronzed, whiskers dense as thorn hedges. Seated between two sleepy-looking Africans, this mariner, like his younger shipmate, was employed upon some rigging — splicing a cable — the sleepy-looking blacks performing the inferior function of holding the outer parts of the ropes for him.

Upon Captain Delano's approach, the man at once hung his head below its previous level; the one necessary for business. It appeared as if he desired to be thought absorbed, with more than common fidelity, in his task. Being addressed, he glanced up, but with what seemed a furtive, diffident air, which sat strangely enough on his weather-beaten visage, much as if a grizzly bear, instead of growling and biting, should simper and cast sheep's eyes. He was asked several questions concerning the voyage — questions purposely referring to several particulars in Don Benito's narrative, not previously corroborated by those impulsive cries greeting the visitor on first coming on board. The questions were briefly answered, confirming all that remained to be confirmed of the story. The negroes about the windlass joined in with the old sailor; but, as they became talkative, he by degrees became mute, and at length quite glum, seemed morosely unwilling to answer more questions, and yet, all the while, this ursine air was somehow mixed with his sheepish one.

Despairing of getting into unembarrassed talk with such a centaur, Captain Delano, after glancing round for more promising countenance, but seeing none, spoke pleasantly to the blacks to make way for him; and so, amid various grins and grimaces, returned to the poop, feeling a little strange at first, he could hardly tell why, but upon the whole with regained confidence in Benito Cereno.

How plainly, thought he, did that old whiskerando yonder betray a consciousness of ill desert. No doubt, when he saw me coming, he dreaded lest I, apprised by his Captain of the crew's general misbehavior, came with sharp words for him, and so down with his head. And yet — and yet, now that I think of it, that very old fellow, if I err not, was one of those who seemed so earnestly eying me here awhile since. Ah, these currents spin one's head round almost

as much as they do the ship. Ha, there now's a pleasant sort of sunny sight; quite sociable, too.

His attention had been drawn to a slumbering negress, partly disclosed through the lace-work of some rigging, lying, with youthful limbs carelessly disposed, under the lee of the bulwarks, like a doe in the shade of a woodland rock. Sprawling at her lapped breasts, was her wide-awake fawn, stark naked, its black little body half lifted from the deck, crosswise with its dam's; its hands, like two paws, clambering upon her; its mouth and nose ineffectually rooting to get at the mark; and meantime giving a vexatious half-grunt, blending with the composed snore of the negress.

The uncommon vigor of the child at length roused the mother. She started up, at a distance facing Captain Delano. But as if not at all concerned at the attitude in which she had been caught, delightedly she caught the child up, with maternal transports, covering it with kisses.

There's naked nature, now; pure tenderness and love, thought Captain Delano, well pleased.

This incident prompted him to remark the other negresses more particularly than before. He was gratified with their manners; like most uncivilized women, they seemed at once tender of heart and tough of constitution; equally ready to die for their infants or fight for them. Unsophisticated as leopardesses; loving as doves. Ah! thought Captain Delano, these, perhaps, are some of the very women whom Ledyard saw in Africa, and gave such a noble account of.

These natural sights somehow insensibly deepened his confidence and ease. At last he looked to see how his boat was getting on; but it was still pretty remote. He turned to see if Don Benito had returned; but he had not.

To change the scene, as well as to please himself with a leisurely observation of the coming boat, stepping over into the mizzen-chains, he clambered his way into the starboard quarter-gallery — one of those abandoned Venetian-looking water-balconies previously mentioned — retreats cut off from the deck. As his foot pressed the half-damp, half-dry sea-mosses matting the place, and a chance phantom cats-paw — an islet of breeze, unheralded, unfollowed — as this ghostly cats-paw came fanning his cheek; as his glance fell upon the row of small, round dead-lights — all closed like coppered eyes of the coffined — and the state-cabin door, once connecting with the gallery, even as the dead-lights had once looked out upon it, but now calked fast like a sarcophagus lid; and to a purple-black, tarred-over panel, threshold, and post; and he bethought him of the time, when that state-cabin and this state-balcony had heard the voices of the Spanish king's officers, and the forms of the Lima viceroy's daughters had perhaps leaned where he stood — as these and other images flitted through his mind, as the cats-paw through the calm, gradually he felt rising a dreamy inquietude, like that of one who alone on the prairie feels unrest from the repose of the noon.

He leaned against the carved balustrade, again looking off toward his boat; but found his eye falling upon the ribbon grass, trailing along the ship's waterline, straight as a border of green box; and parterres of seaweed, broad ovals and crescents, floating nigh and far, with what seemed long formal alleys between, crossing the terraces of swells, and sweeping round as if leading to the grottoes below. And overhanging all was the balustrade by his arm, which, partly stained with pitch and partly embossed with moss, seemed the charred ruin of some summerhouse in a grand garden long running to waste.

Trying to break one charm, he was but becharmed anew. Though upon the wide sea, he seemed in some far inland country; prisoner in some deserted château, left to stare at empty grounds, and peer out at vague roads, where never wagon or wayfarer passed.

But these enchantments were a little disenchanted as his eye fell on the corroded main-chains. Of an ancient style, massy and rusty in link, shackle and bolt, they seemed even more fit for the ship's present business than the one for which she had been built.

Presently he thought something moved nigh the chains. He rubbed his eyes, and looked hard. Groves of rigging were about the chains; and there, peering from behind a great stay, like an Indian from behind a hemlock, a Spanish sailor, a marlingspike in his hand, was seen, who made what seemed an imperfect gesture towards the balcony, but immediately, as if alarmed by some advancing step along the deck within, vanished into the recesses of the hempen forest, like a poacher.

What meant this? Something the man had sought to communicate, unbeknown to any one, even to his captain. Did the secret involve aught unfavourable to his captain? Were those previous misgivings of Captain Delano's about to be verified? Or, in his haunted mood at the moment, had some random, unintentional motion of the man, while busy with the stay, as if repairing it, been mistaken for a significant beckoning?

Not unbewildered, again he gazed off for his boat. But it was temporarily hidden by a rocky spur of the isle. As with some eagerness he bent forward, watching for the first shooting view of its beak, the balustrade gave way before him like charcoal. Had he not clutched an outreaching rope he would have fallen into the sea. The crash, though feeble, and the fall, though hollow, of the rotten fragments, must have been overheard. He glanced up. With sober curiosity peering down upon him was one of the old oakumpickers, slipped from his perch to an outside boom; while below the old negro, and, invisible to him, reconnoitering from a porthole like a fox from the mouth of its den, crouched the Spanish sailor again. From something suddenly suggested by the man's air, the mad idea now darted into Captain Delano's mind, that Don Benito's plea of indisposition, in withdrawing below, was but a pretense: that he was engaged there maturing some plot, of which the sailor, by some means gaining an inkling, had a mind to warn the stranger against; incited, it may be, by gratitude for a kind word on first boarding the ship. Was it from foreseeing some possible interference like this, that Don Benito had, beforehand, given such a bad character of his sailors, while praising the negroes; though, indeed, the former seemed as docile as the latter the contrary? The whites, too, by nature, were the shrewder race. A man with some evil design, would he not be likely to speak well of that stupidity which was blind to his depravity, and malign that intelligence from which it might not be hidden? Not unlikely, perhaps. But if the whites had dark secrets concerning Don Benito, could then Don Benito be any way in complicity with the blacks? But they were too stupid. Besides, who ever heard of a white so far a renegade as to apostatize from his very species almost, by leaguing in against it with negroes? These difficulties recalled former ones. Lost in their mazes, Captain Delano, who had now regained the deck, was uneasily advancing along it, when he observed a new face; an aged sailor seated cross-legged near the main hatchway. His skin was shrunk up with wrinkles like a pelican's empty pouch; his hair frosted; his countenance grave and composed. His hands were full of ropes, which he was working into a large knot. Some blacks were about him obligingly dipping the strands for him, here and there, as the exigencies of the operation demanded.

Captain Delano crossed over to him, and stood in silence surveying the knot; his mind, by a not uncongenial transition, passing from its own entanglements to those of the hemp. For intricacy such a knot he had never seen in an American ship, or indeed any other. The old man looked like an Egyptian priest, making Gordian knots for the temple of Ammon. The knot seemed a combination of double-bowline-knot, treble-crown-knot, back-handed-well-knot, knot-in-and-out-knot, and jamming-knot.

At last, puzzled to comprehend the meaning of such a knot, Captain Delano addressed the knotter:

"What are you knotting there, my man?"

"The knot," was the brief reply, without looking up.

"So it seems; but what is it for?"

"For some one else to undo," muttered back the old man, plying his fingers harder than ever, the knot being now nearly completed.

While Captain Delano stood watching him, suddenly the old man threw the knot towards him, saying in broken English, — the first heard in the ship, — something to this effect: "Undo it, cut it, quick." It was said lowly, but with such condensation of rapidity, that the long, slow words in Spanish, which had preceded and followed, almost operated as covers to the brief English between.

For a moment, knot in hand, and knot in head, Captain Delano stood mute; while, without further heeding him, the old man was now intent upon other ropes. Presently there was a slight stir behind Captain Delano. Turning, he saw the chained negro, Atufal, standing quietly there. The next moment the old sailor rose, muttering, and, followed by his subordinate negroes, removed to the forward part of the ship, where in the crowd he disappeared.

An elderly negro, in a clout like an infant's, and with a pepper and salt head, and a kind of attorney air, now approached Captain Delano. In tolerable Spanish, and with a good-natured, knowing wink, he informed him that the old knotter was simple-witted, but harmless; often playing his old tricks. The negro concluded by begging the knot, for of course the stranger would not care to be troubled with it. Unconsciously, it was handed to him. With a sort of congé, the negro received it, and, turning his back, ferreted into it like a detective custom-house officer after smuggled laces. Soon, with some African word, equivalent to pshaw, he tossed the knot overboard.

All this is very queer now, thought Captain Delano, with a qualmish sort of emotion; but, as one feeling incipient sea-sickness, he strove, by ignoring the symptoms, to get rid of the malady. Once more he looked off for his boat. To his delight, it was now again in view, leaving the rocky spur astern.

The sensation here experienced, after at first relieving his uneasiness, with unforeseen efficacy soon began to remove it. The less distant sight of that well-known boat — showing it, not as before, half blended with the haze, but with outline defined, so that its individuality, like a man's, was manifest; that boat, Rover by name, which, though now in strange seas, had often pressed the beach of Captain Delano's home, and, brought to its threshold for repairs, had familiarly lain there, as a Newfoundland dog; the sight of that household boat evoked a thousand trustful associations, which, contrasted with previous suspicions, filled him not only with lightsome confidence, but somehow with half humorous self-reproaches at his former lack of it.

"What, I, Amasa Delano — Jack of the Beach, as they called me when a lad — I, Amasa; the same that, duck-satchel in hand, used to paddle along the waterside to the school-house made from the old hulk — I, little Jack of the Beach, that used to go berrying with cousin Nat and the rest; I to be murdered here at the ends of the earth, on board a haunted pirate-ship by a horrible Spaniard? Too nonsensical to think of! Who would murder Amasa Delano? His conscience is clean. There is some one above. Fie, fie, Jack of the Beach! you are a child indeed; a child of the second childhood, old boy; you are beginning to dote and drule, I'm afraid."

Light of heart and foot, he stepped aft, and there was met by Don Benito's servant, who, with a pleasing expression, responsive to his own present feelings, informed him that his master had recovered from the effects of his coughing fit, and had just ordered him to go present his compliments to his good guest, Don Amasa, and say that he (Don Benito) would soon have the happiness to rejoin him.

There now, do you mark that? again thought Captain Delano, walking the poop. What a donkey I was. This kind gentleman who here sends me his kind compliments, he, but ten minutes ago, dark-lantern in hand, was dodging round some old grindstone in the hold, sharpening a hatchet for me, I thought. Well, well; these long calms have a morbid effect on the mind, I've often heard, though I never believed it before. Ha! glancing towards the boat; there's Rover; good dog; a white bone in her mouth. A pretty big bone though, seems to me. — What? Yes, she has fallen afoul of the bubbling tiderip there. It sets her the other way, too, for the time. Patience.

It was now about noon, though, from the grayness of everything, it seemed to be getting towards dusk.

The calm was confirmed. In the far distance, away from the influence of land, the leaden ocean seemed laid out and leaded up, its course finished, soul gone, defunct. But the current from landward, where the ship was, increased; silently sweeping her further and further towards the tranced waters beyond.

Still, from his knowledge of those latitudes, cherishing hopes of a breeze, and a fair and fresh one, at any moment, Captain Delano, despite present prospects, buoyantly counted upon bringing the San Dominick safely to anchor ere night. The distance swept over was nothing; since, with a good wind, ten minutes' sailing would retrace more than sixty minutes', drifting. Meantime, one moment turning to mark "Rover" fighting the tide-rip, and the next to see Don Benito approaching, he continued walking the poop.

Gradually he felt a vexation arising from the delay of his boat; this soon merged into uneasiness; and at last — his eye falling continually, as from a stage-box into the pit, upon the strange crowd before and below him, and, by-and-by, recognizing there the face — now composed to indifference — of the Spanish sailor who had seemed to beckon from the main-chains — something of his old trepidations returned.

Ah, thought he — gravely enough — this is like the ague: because it went off, it follows not that it won't come back.

Though ashamed of the relapse, he could not altogether subdue it; and so, exerting his good-nature to the utmost, insensibly he came to a compromise.

Yes, this is a strange craft; a strange history, too, and strange folks on board. But — nothing more.

By way of keeping his mind out of mischief till the boat should arrive, he tried to occupy it with turning over and over, in a purely speculative sort of way, some lesser peculiarities of the captain and crew. Among others, four curious points recurred:

First, the affair of the Spanish lad assailed with a knife by the slave boy; an act winked at by Don Benito. Second, the tyranny in Don Benito's treatment of Atufal, the black; as if a child should lead a bull of the Nile by the ring in his nose. Third, the trampling of the sailor by the two negroes; a piece of insolence passed over without so much as a reprimand. Fourth, the cringing submission to their master of all the ships' underlings, mostly blacks; as if by the least inadvertence they feared to draw down his despotic displeasure.

Coupling these points, they seemed somewhat contradictory. But what then, thought Captain Delano, glancing towards his now nearing boat — what then? Why, Don Benito is a very capricious commander. But he is not the first of the sort I have seen; though it's true he rather exceeds any other. But as a nation — continued he in his reveries — these Spaniards are all an odd set; the very word Spaniard has a curious, conspirator, Guy-Fawkish twang to it. And yet, I dare say, Spaniards in the main are as good folks as any in Duxbury, Massachusetts. Ah, good! At last "Rover" has come.

As, with its welcome freight, the boat touched the side, the oakum-pickers, with venerable gestures, sought to restrain the blacks, who, at the sight of three gurried water-casks in its bottom, and a pile of wilted pumpkins in its bow, hung over the bulwarks in disorderly raptures.

Don Benito, with his servant, now appeared; his coming, perhaps, hastened by hearing the noise. Of him Captain Delano sought permission to serve out the water, so that all might share alike, and none injure themselves by unfair excess. But sensible, and, on Don Benito's account, kind as this offer was, it was received with what seemed impatience; as if aware that he lacked energy as a commander, Don Benito, with the true jealousy of weakness, resented as an affront any interference. So, at least, Captain Delano inferred.

In another moment the casks were being hoisted in, when some of the eager negroes accidentally jostled Captain Delano, where he stood by the gangway; so that, unmindful of Don Benito, yielding to the impulse of the moment, with good-natured authority he bade the blacks stand back; to enforce his words making use of a half-mirthful, half-menacing gesture. Instantly the blacks paused, just where they were, each negro and negress suspended in his or her posture,

exactly as the word had found them — for a few seconds continuing so — while, as between the responsive posts of a telegraph, an unknown syllable ran from man to man among the perched oakum-pickers. While the visitor's attention was fixed by this scene, suddenly the hatchet-polishers half rose, and a rapid cry came from Don Benito.

Thinking that at the signal of the Spaniard he was about to be massacred, Captain Delano would have sprung for his boat, but paused, as the oakum-pickers, dropping down into the crowd with earnest exclamations, forced every white and every negro back, at the same moment, with gestures friendly and familiar, almost jocose, bidding him, in substance, not be a fool. Simultaneously the hatchet-polishers resumed their seats, quietly as so many tailors, and at once, as if nothing had happened, the work of hoisting in the casks was resumed, whites and blacks singing at the tackle.

Captain Delano glanced toward Don Benito. As he saw his meagre form in the act of recovering itself from reclining in the servant's arms, into which the agitated invalid had fallen, he could not but marvel at the panic by which himself had been surprised on the darting supposition that such a commander, who, upon a legitimate occasion, so trivial, too, as it now appeared, could lose all self-command, was, with energetic iniquity, going to bring about his murder.

The casks being on deck, Captain Delano was handed a number of jars and cups by one of the steward's aids, who, in the name of his captain, entreated him to do as he had proposed — dole out the water. He complied, with republican impartiality as to this republican element, which always seeks one level, serving the oldest white no better than the youngest black; excepting, indeed, poor Don Benito, whose condition, if not rank, demanded an extra allowance. To him, in the first place, Captain Delano presented a fair pitcher of the fluid; but, thirsting as he was for fresh water, the Spaniard quaffed not a drop until after several grave bows and salutes. A reciprocation of courtesies which the sight-loving Africans hailed with clapping of hands.

Two of the less wilted pumpkins being reserved for the cabin table, the residue were minced up on the spot for the general regalement. But the soft bread, sugar, and bottled cider, Captain Delano would have given the whites alone, and in chief Don Benito; but the latter objected; which disinterestedness not a little pleased the American; and so mouthfuls all around were given alike to whites and blacks; excepting one bottle of cider, which Babo insisted upon setting aside for his master.

Here it may be observed that as, on the first visit of the boat, the American had not permitted his men to board the ship, neither did he now; being unwilling to add to the confusion of the decks.

Not uninfluenced by the peculiar good-humor at present prevailing, and for the time oblivious of any but benevolent thoughts, Captain Delano, who, from recent indications, counted upon a breeze within an hour or two at furthest, dispatched the boat back to the sealer, with orders for all the hands that could be spared immediately to set about rafting casks to the watering-place and filling them. Likewise he bade word be carried to his chief officer, that if, against present expectation, the ship was not brought to anchor by sunset, he need be under no concern; for as there was to be a full moon that night, he (Captain Delano) would remain on board ready to play the pilot, come the wind soon or late.

As the two captains stood together, observing the departing boat — the servant, as it happened, having just spied a spot on his master's velvet sleeve, and silently engaged rubbing it out — the American expressed his regrets that the San Dominick had no boats; none, at least, but the unseaworthy old hulk of the long-boat, which, warped as a camel's skeleton in the desert, and almost as bleached, lay pot-wise inverted amidships, one side a little tipped, furnishing a subterraneous sort of den for family groups of the blacks, mostly women and small children; who, squatting on old mats below, or perched above in the dark dome, on the elevated seats, were descried, some distance within, like a social circle of bats, sheltering in some friendly cave; at in-

tervals, ebon flights of naked boys and girls, three or four years old, darting in and out of the den's mouth.

"Had you three or four boats now, Don Benito," said Captain Delano, "I think that, by tugging at the oars, your negroes here might help along matters some. Did you sail from port without boats, Don Benito?"

"They were stove in the gales, Señor."

"That was bad. Many men, too, you lost then. Boats and men. Those must have been hard gales, Don Benito."

"Past all speech," cringed the Spaniard.

"Tell me, Don Benito," continued his companion with increased interest, "tell me, were these gales immediately off the pitch of Cape Horn?"

"Cape Horn? — who spoke of Cape Horn?"

"Yourself did, when giving me an account of your voyage," answered Captain Delano, with almost equal astonishment at this eating of his own words, even as he ever seemed eating his own heart, on the part of the Spaniard. "You yourself, Don Benito, spoke of Cape Horn," he emphatically repeated.

The Spaniard turned, in a sort of stooping posture, pausing an instant, as one about to make a plunging exchange of elements, as from air to water.

At this moment a messenger-boy, a white, hurried by, in the regular performance of his function carrying the last expired half-hour forward to the forecastle, from the cabin time-piece, to have it struck at the ship's large bell.

"Master," said the servant, discontinuing his work on the coat sleeve, and addressing the rapt Spaniard with a sort of timid apprehensiveness, as one charged with a duty, the discharge of which, it was foreseen, would prove irksome to the very person who had imposed it, and for whose benefit it was intended, "master told me never mind where he was, or how engaged, always to remind him, to a minute, when shaving-time comes. Miguel has gone to strike the half-hour afternoon. It is *now*, master. Will master go into the cuddy?"

"Ah — yes," answered the Spaniard, starting, as from dreams into realities; then turning upon Captain Delano, he said that ere long he would resume the conversation.

"Then if master means to talk more to Don Amasa," said the servant, "why not let Don Amasa sit by master in the cuddy, and master can talk, and Don Amasa can listen, while Babo here lathers and strops."

"Yes," said Captain Delano, not unpleased with this sociable plan, "yes, Don Benito, unless you had rather not, I will go with you."

"Be it so, Señor."

As the three passed aft, the American could not but think it another strange instance of his host's capriciousness, this being shaved with such uncommon punctuality in the middle of the day. But he deemed it more than likely that the servant's anxious fidelity had something to do with the matter; inasmuch as the timely interruption served to rally his master from the mood which had evidently been coming upon him.

The place called the cuddy was a light deck-cabin formed by the poop, a sort of attic to the large cabin below. Part of it had formerly been the quarters of the officers; but since their death all the partitionings had been thrown down, and the whole interior converted into one spacious and airy marine hall; for absence of fine furniture and picturesque disarray of odd appurtenances, somewhat answering to the wide, cluttered hall of some eccentric bachelor-squire in the country, who hangs his shooting-jacket and tobacco-pouch on deer antlers, and keeps his fishing-rod, tongs, and walking-stick in the same corner.

The similitude was heightened, if not originally suggested, by glimpses of the surrounding sea; since, in one aspect, the country and the ocean seem cousins-german.

The floor of the cuddy was matted. Overhead, four or five old muskets were stuck into horizontal holes along the beams. On one side was a claw-footed old table lashed to the deck; a thumbed missal on it, and over it a small, meagre crucifix attached to the bulk-head. Under the table lay a dented cutlass or two, with a hacked harpoon, among some melancholy old rigging, like a heap of poor friars' girdles. There were also two long, sharp-ribbed settees of Malacca cane, black with age, and uncomfortable to look at as inquisitors' racks, with a large, misshapen arm-chair, which, furnished with a rude barber's crotch at the back, working with a screw, seemed some grotesque engine of torment. A flag locker was in one corner, exposing various colored bunting, some rolled up, others half unrolled, still others tumbled. Opposite was a cumbrous washstand, of black mahogany, all of one block, with a pedestal, like a font, and over it a railed shelf, containing combs, brushes, and other implements of the toilet. A torn hammock of stained grass swung near; the sheets tossed, and the pillow wrinkled up like a brow, as if whoever slept here slept but illy, with alternate visitations of sad thoughts and bad dreams.

The further extremity of the cuddy, overhanging the ship's stern, was pierced with three openings, windows or port-holes, according as men or cannon might peer, socially or unsocially, out of them. At present neither men nor cannon were seen, though huge ring-bolts and other rusty iron fixtures of the woodwork hinted of twenty-four-pounders.

Glancing towards the hammock as he entered, Captain Delano said, "You sleep here, Don Benito?"

"Yes, Señor, since we got into mild weather."

"This seems a sort of dormitory, sitting-room, sail-loft, chapel, armory, and private closet together, Don Benito," added Captain Delano, looking round.

"Yes, Señor; events have not been favorable to much order in my arrangements."

Here the servant, napkin on arm, made a motion as if waiting his master's good pleasure. Don Benito signified his readiness, when, seating him in the Malacca arm-chair, and for the guest's convenience drawing opposite one of the settees, the servant commenced operations by throwing back his master's collar and loosening his cravat.

There is something in the negro which, in a peculiar way, fits him for avocations about one's person. Most negroes are natural valets and hair-dressers; taking to the comb and brush congenially as to the castinets, and flourishing them apparently with almost equal satisfaction. There is, too, a smooth tact about them in this employment, with a marvelous, noiseless, gliding briskness, not ungraceful in its way, singularly pleasing to behold, and still more so to be the manipulated subject of. And above all is the great gift of good-humor. Not the mere grin or laugh is here meant. Those were unsuitable. But a certain easy cheerfulness, harmonious in every glance and gesture; as though God had set the whole negro to some pleasant tune.

When to all this is added the docility arising from the unaspiring contentment of a limited mind, and that susceptibility of blind attachment sometimes inhering in indisputable inferiors, one readily perceives why those hypochondriacs, Johnson and Byron — it may be something like the hypochondriac, Benito Cereno — took to their hearts, almost to the exclusion of the entire white race, their serving men, the negroes, Barber and Fletcher. But if there be that in the negro which exempts him from the inflicted sourness of the morbid or cynical mind, how, in his most prepossessing aspects, must he appear to a benevolent one? When at ease with respect to exterior things, Captain Delano's nature was not only benign, but familiarly and humorously so. At home, he had often taken rare satisfaction in sitting in his door, watching some free man of color at his work or play. If on a voyage he chanced to make a black sailor, invariably he was on chatty, and half-gamesome terms with him. In fact, like most men of a good, blithe heart, Captain Delano took to negroes, not philanthropically, but genially, just as other men to Newfoundland dogs.

Hitherto the circumstances in which he found the San Dominick had repressed the tendency. But in the cuddy, relieved from his former uneasiness, and, for various reasons, more sociably inclined than at any previous period of the day, and seeing the colored servant, napkin on arm, so debonair about his master, in a business so familiar as that of shaving, too, all his old weakness for negroes returned.

Among other things, he was amused with an odd instance of the African love of bright colors and fine shows, in the black's informally taking from the flag-locker a great piece of bunting of all hues, and lavishly tucking it under his master's chin for an apron.

The mode of shaving among the Spaniards is a little different from what it is with other nations. They have a basin, specially called a barber's basin, which on one side is scooped out, so as accurately to receive the chin, against which it is closely held in lathering; which is done, not with a brush, but with soap dipped in the water of the basin and rubbed on the face.

In the present instance salt-water was used for lack of better; and the parts lathered were only the upper lip, and low down under the throat, all the rest being cultivated beard.

These preliminaries being somewhat novel to Captain Delano he sat curiously eying them, so that no conversation took place, nor, for the present, did Don Benito appear disposed to renew any.

Setting down his basin, the negro searched among the razors, as for the sharpest, and having found it, gave it an additional edge by expertly stropping it on the firm, smooth, oily skin of his open palm; he then made a gesture as if to begin, but midway stood suspended for an instant, one hand elevating the razor, the other professionally dabbling among the bubbling suds on the Spaniard's lank neck. Not unaffected by the close sight of the gleaming steel, Don Benito nervously shuddered; his usual ghastliness was heightened by the lather, which lather, again, was intensified in its hue by the contrasting sootiness of the negro's body. Altogether the scene was somewhat peculiar, at least to Captain Delano, nor, as he saw the two thus postured, could he resist the vagary, that in the black he saw a headsman, and in the white a man at the block. But this was one of those antic conceits, appearing and vanishing in a breath, from which, perhaps, the best regulated mind is not free.

Meantime the agitation of the Spaniard had a little loosened the bunting from around him, so that one broad fold swept curtain-like over the chair-arm to the floor, revealing, amid a profusion of armorial bars and ground-colors — black, blue and yellow — a closed castle in a blood-red field diagonal with a lion rampant in a white.

"The castle and the lion," exclaimed Captain Delano — "why, Don Benito, this is the flag of Spain you use here. It's well it's only I, and not the King, that sees this," he added with a smile, "but" — turning towards the black, — "it's all one, I suppose, so the colors be gay;" which playful remark did not fail somewhat to tickle the negro.

"Now, master," he said, readjusting the flag, and pressing the head gently further back into the crotch of the chair; "now, master," and the steel glanced nigh the throat.

Again Don Benito faintly shuddered.

"You must not shake so, master. See, Don Amasa, master always shakes when I shave him. And yet master knows I never yet have drawn blood, though it's true, if master will shake so, I may some of these times. Now, master," he continued. "And now, Don Amasa, please go on with your talk about the gale, and all that; master can hear, and between times, master can answer."

"Ah yes, these gales," said Captain Delano; "but the more I think of your voyage, Don Benito, the more I wonder, not at the gales, terrible as they must have been, but at the disastrous interval following them. For here, by your account, have you been these two months and more getting from Cape Horn to St. Maria, a distance which I myself, with a good wind, have sailed in a few days. True, you had calms, and long ones, but to be becalmed for two months, that is, at least, unusual. Why, Don Benito, had almost any other gentleman told me such a story, I should have been half disposed to a little incredulity."

Here an involuntary expression came over the Spaniard, similar to that just before on the deck, and whether it was the start he gave, or a sudden gawky roll of the hull in the calm, or a momentary unsteadiness of the servant's hand, however, it was, just then the razor drew blood, spots of which stained the creamy lather under the throat; immediately the black barber drew back his steel, and remaining in his professional attitude, back to Captain Delano, and face to Don Benito, held up the trickling razor, saying, with a sort of half humorous sorrow, "See, master — you shook so — here's Babo's first blood."

No sword drawn before James the First of England, no assassination in that timid King's presence, could have produced a more terrified aspect than was now presented by Don Benito.

Poor fellow, thought Captain Delano, so nervous he can't even bear the sight of barber's blood; and this unstrung, sick man, is it credible that I should have imagined he meant to spill all my blood, who can't endure the sight of one little drop of his own? Surely, Amasa Delano, you have been beside yourself this day. Tell it not when you get home, sappy Amasa. Well, well, he looks like a murderer, doesn't he? More like as if himself were to be done for. Well, well, this day's experience shall be a good lesson.

Meantime, while these things were running through the honest seaman's mind, the servant had taken the napkin from his arm, and to Don Benito had said —"But answer Don Amasa, please, master, while I wipe this ugly stuff off the razor, and strop it again."

As he said the words, his face was turned half round, so as to be alike visible to the Spaniard and the American, and seemed, by its expression, to hint, that he was desirous, by getting his master to go on with the conversation, considerately to withdraw his attention from the recent annoying accident. As if glad to snatch the offered relief, Don Benito resumed, rehearsing to Captain Delano, that not only were the calms of unusual duration, but the ship had fallen in with obstinate currents; and other things he added, some of which were but repetitions of former statements, to explain how it came to pass that the passage from Cape Horn to St. Maria had been so exceedingly long; now and then mingling with his words, incidental praises, less qualified than before, to the blacks, for their general good conduct. These particulars were not given consecutively, the servant, at convenient times, using his razor, and so, between the intervals of shaving, the story and panegyric went on with more than usual huskiness.

To Captain Delano's imagination, now again not wholly at rest, there was something so hollow in the Spaniard's manner, with apparently some reciprocal hollowness in the servant's dusky comment of silence, that the idea flashed across him, that possibly master and man, for some unknown purpose, were acting out, both in word and deed, nay, to the very tremor of Don Benito's limbs, some juggling play before him. Neither did the suspicion of collusion lack apparent support, from the fact of those whispered conferences before mentioned. But then, what could be the object of enacting this play of the barber before him? At last, regarding the notion as a whimsy, insensibly suggested, perhaps, by the theatrical aspect of Don Benito in his harlequin ensign, Captain Delano speedily banished it.

The shaving over, the servant bestirred himself with a small bottle of scented waters, pouring a few drops on the head, and then diligently rubbing; the vehemence of the exercise causing the muscles of his face to twitch rather strangely.

His next operation was with comb, scissors and brush; going round and round, smoothing a curl here, clipping an unruly whisker-hair there, giving a graceful sweep to the temple-lock, with other impromptu touches evincing the hand of a master; while, like any resigned gentleman in barber's hands, Don Benito bore all, much less uneasily, at least, than he had done the razoring; indeed, he sat so pale and rigid now, that the negro seemed a Nubian sculptor finishing off a white statue-head.

All being over at last, the standard of Spain removed, tumbled up, and tossed back into the flag-locker, the negro's warm breath blowing away any stray hair which might have lodged down his master's neck; collar and cravat readjusted; a speck of lint whisked off the velvet lapel; all this being done; backing off a little space, and pausing with an expression of subdued self-complacency, the servant for a moment surveyed his master, as, in toilet at least, the creature of his own tasteful hands.

Captain Delano playfully complimented him upon his achievement; at the same time congratulating Don Benito.

But neither sweet waters, nor shampooing, nor fidelity, nor sociality, delighted the Spaniard. Seeing him relapsing into forbidding gloom, and still remaining seated, Captain Delano, thinking that his presence was undesired just then, withdrew, on pretense of seeing whether, as he had prophesied, any signs of a breeze were visible.

Walking forward to the mainmast, he stood awhile thinking over the scene, and not without some undefined misgivings, when he heard a noise near the cuddy, and turning, saw the negro, his hand to his cheek. Advancing, Captain Delano perceived that the cheek was bleeding. He was about to ask the cause, when the negro's wailing soliloquy enlightened him.

"Ah, when will master get better from his sickness; only the sour heart that sour sickness breeds made him serve Babo so; cutting Babo with the razor, because, only by accident, Babo had given master one little scratch; and for the first time in so many a day, too. Ah, ah, ah," holding his hand to his face.

Is it possible, thought Captain Delano; was it to wreak in private his Spanish spite against this poor friend of his, that Don Benito, by his sullen manner, impelled me to withdraw? Ah, this slavery breeds ugly passions in man. — Poor fellow!

He was about to speak in sympathy to the negro, but with a timid reluctance he now re-entered the cuddy.

Presently master and man came forth; Don Benito leaning on his servant as if nothing had happened.

But a sort of love-quarrel, after all, thought Captain Delano.

He accosted Don Benito, and they slowly walked together. They had gone but a few paces, when the steward — a tall, rajah-looking mulatto, orientally set off with a pagoda turban formed by three or four Madras handkerchiefs wound about his head, tier on tier — approaching with a salaam, announced lunch in the cabin.

On their way thither, the two captains were preceded by the mulatto, who, turning round as he advanced, with continual smiles and bows, ushered them in, a display of elegance which quite completed the insignificance of the small bare-headed Babo, who, as if not unconscious of inferiority, eyed askance the graceful steward. But in part, Captain Delano imputed his jealous watchfulness to that peculiar feeling which the full-blooded African entertains for the adulterated one. As for the steward, his manner, if not bespeaking much dignity of self-respect, yet evidenced his extreme desire to please; which is doubly meritorious, as at once Christian and Chesterfieldian.

Captain Delano observed with interest that while the complexion of the mulatto was hybrid, his physiognomy was European — classically so.

"Don Benito," whispered he, "I am glad to see this usher-of-the-golden-rod of yours; the sight refutes an ugly remark once made to me by a Barbados planter; that when a mulatto has a regular European face, look out for him; he is a devil. But see, your steward here has features more regular than King George's of England; and yet there he nods, and bows, and smiles; a king, indeed — the king of kind hearts and polite fellows. What a pleasant voice he has, too?"

"He has, Señor."

"But, tell me, has he not, so far as you have known him, always proved a good, worthy fellow?" said Captain Delano, pausing, while with a final genuflexion the steward disappeared into the cabin; "come, for the reason just mentioned, I am curious to know."

"Francesco is a good man," rather sluggishly responded Don Benito, like a phlegmatic appreciator, who would neither find fault nor flatter.

"Ah, I thought so. For it were strange, indeed, and not very creditable to us white-skins, if a little of our blood mixed with the African's, should, far from improving the latter's quality, have the sad effect of pouring vitriolic acid into black broth; improving the hue, perhaps, but not the wholesomeness."

"Doubtless, doubtless, Señor, but" — glancing at Babo — "not to speak of negroes, your planter's remark I have heard applied to the Spanish and Indian intermixtures in our provinces. But I know nothing about the matter," he listlessly added.

And here they entered the cabin.

The lunch was a frugal one. Some of Captain Delano's fresh fish and pumpkins, biscuit and salt beef, the reserved bottle of cider, and the San Dominick's last bottle of Canary.

As they entered, Francesco, with two or three colored aids, was hovering over the table giving the last adjustments. Upon perceiving their master they withdrew, Francesco making a smiling congé, and the Spaniard, without condescending to notice it, fastidiously remarking to his companion that he relished not superfluous attendance.

Without companions, host and guest sat down, like a childless married couple, at opposite ends of the table, Don Benito waving Captain Delano to his place, and, weak as he was, insisting upon that gentleman being seated before himself.

The negro placed a rug under Don Benito's feet, and a cushion behind his back, and then stood behind, not his master's chair, but Captain Delano's. At first, this a little surprised the latter. But it was soon evident that, in taking his position, the black was still true to his master; since by facing him he could the more readily anticipate his slightest want.

"This is an uncommonly intelligent fellow of yours, Don Benito," whispered Captain Delano across the table.

"You say true, Señor."

During the repast, the guest again reverted to parts of Don Benito's story, begging further particulars here and there. He inquired how it was that the scurvy and fever should have committed such wholesale havoc upon the whites, while destroying less than half of the blacks. As if this question reproduced the whole scene of plague before the Spaniard's eyes, miserably reminding him of his solitude in a cabin where before he had had so many friends and officers round him, his hand shook, his face became hueless, broken words escaped; but directly the sane memory of the past seemed replaced by insane terrors of the present. With starting eyes he stared before him at vacancy. For nothing was to be seen but the hand of his servant pushing the Canary over towards him. At length a few sips served partially to restore him. He made random reference to the different constitutions of races, enabling one to offer more resistance to certain maladies than another. The thought was new to his companion.

Presently Captain Delano, intending to say something to his host concerning the pecuniary part of the business he had under-taken for him, especially — since he was strictly accountable to his owners — with reference to the new suit of sails, and other things of that sort; and naturally preferring to conduct such affairs in private, was desirous that the servant should withdraw; imagining that Don Benito for a few minutes could dispense with his attendance. He, however, waited awhile; thinking that, as the conversation proceeded, Don Benito, without being prompted, would perceive the propriety of the step.

But it was otherwise. At last catching his host's eye, Captain Delano, with a slight, backward gesture of his thumb, whispered, "Don Benito, pardon me, but there is an interference with the full expression of what I have to say to you."

Upon this the Spaniard changed counte-nance; which was imputed to his resenting the hint, as in some way a reflection upon his servant. After a moment's pause, he assured his guest that the black's remaining with them could be of no disservice; because since losing his officers he had made Babo (whose original office, it now appeared, had been captain of the slaves) not only his constant attendant and companion, but in all things his confidant.

After this, nothing more could be said; though, indeed, Captain Delano could hardly avoid some little tinge of irritation upon being left ungratified in so inconsiderable a wish, by one, too, for whom he intended such solid services. But it is only his querulous-ness, thought he; and so filling his glass he proceeded to business.

The price of the sails and other matters was fixed upon. But while this was being done, the American observed that, though his original offer of assistance had been hailed with hectic animation, yet now when it was reduced to a business transaction, in-difference and apathy were betrayed. Don Benito, in fact, appeared to submit to hearing the details more out of regard to common propriety, than from any impression that weighty benefit to himself and his voyage was involved.

Soon, this manner became still more re-served. The effort was vain to seek to draw him into social talk. Gnawed by his splenetic mood, he sat twitching his beard, while to little purpose the hand of his servant, mute as that on the wall, slowly pushed over the Canary.

Lunch being over, they sat down on the cushioned transom; the servant placing a pillow behind his master. The long con-tinuance of the calm had now affected the atmosphere. Don Benito sighed heavily, as if for breath.

"Why not adjourn to the cuddy," said Captain Delano; "there is more air there." But the host sat silent and motionless.

Meantime his servant knelt before him with a large fan of feathers. And Francesco coming in on tiptoes, handed the negro a little cup of aromatic waters, with which at intervals he chafed his master's brow; smooth-ing the hair along the temples as a nurse does a child's. He spoke no word. He only rested his eye on his master's, as if, amid all Don Benito's distress, a little to refresh his spirit by the silent sight of fidelity.

Presently the ship's bell sounded two o'clock; and through the cabin-windows a slight rippling of the sea was discerned; and from the desired direction.

"There," exclaimed Captain Delano, "I told you so, Don Benito, look!"

He had risen to his feet, speaking in a very animated tone, with a view the more to rouse his companion. But though the crimson curtain of the stern-window near him that moment fluttered against his pale cheek, Don Benito seemed to have even less welcome for the breeze than the calm.

Poor fellow, thought Captain Delano, bitter experience has taught him that one ripple does not make a wind, any more than one swallow a summer. But he is mistaken for once. I will get his ship in for him, and prove it.

Briefly alluding to his weak condition, he urged his host to remain quietly where he was, since he (Captain Delano) would with pleasure take upon himself the responsibility of making the best use of the wind.

Upon gaining the deck, Captain Delano started at the unexpected figure of Atufal, monumentally fixed at the threshold, like one of those sculptured porters of black marble guarding the porches of Egyptian tombs. But this time the start was, perhaps, purely physical. Atufal's presence, singularly attesting docility even in sullenness, was contrasted with that of the hatchet-polishers, who in patience evinced their industry; while both spectacles showed, that lax as Don Benito's general authority might be, still, whenever he chose to exert it, no man so savage or colossal but must, more or less, bow.

Snatching a trumpet which hung from the bulwarks, with a free step Captain Delano advanced to the forward edge of the poop, issuing his orders in his best Spanish. The few sailors and many negroes, all equally pleased, obediently set about heading the ship toward the harbour.

While giving some directions about setting a lower stu'n'-sail, suddenly Captain Delano heard a voice faithfully repeating his orders. Turning, he saw Babo, now for the time acting, under the pilot, his original part of captain of the slaves. This assistance proved valuable. Tattered sails and warped yards were soon brought into some trim. And no brace or halyard was pulled but to the blithe songs of the inspirited negroes.

Good fellows, thought Captain Delano, a little training would make fine sailors of them. Why see, the very women pull and sing, too. These must be some of those Ashantee negresses that make such capital soldiers, I've heard. But who's at the helm? I must have a good hand there.

He went to see.

The San Dominick steered with a cumbrous tiller, with large horizontal pullies attached. At each pulley-end stood a subordinate black, and between them, at the tiller-head, the responsible post, a Spanish seaman, whose countenance evinced his due share in the general hopefulness and confidence at the coming of the breeze.

He proved the same man who had behaved with so shame-faced an air on the windlass. "Ah, — it is you, my man," exclaimed Captain Delano — "well, no more sheep's-eyes now; — look straight forward and keep the ship so. Good hand, I trust? And want to get into the harbor, don't you?"

The man assented with an inward chuckle, grasping the tiller-head firmly. Upon this,

unperceived by the American, the two blacks eyed the sailor intently.

Finding all right at the helm, the pilot went forward to the forecastle, to see how matters stood there.

The ship now had way enough to breast the current. With the approach of evening the breeze would be sure to freshen.

Having done all that was needed for the present, Captain Delano, giving his last orders to the sailors, turned aft to report affairs to Don Benito in the cabin; perhaps additionally incited to rejoin him by the hope of snatching a moment's private chat while his servant was engaged upon deck.

From opposite sides, there were, beneath the poop, two approaches to the cabin; one further forward than the other, and consequently communicating with a longer passage. Marking the servant still above, Captain Delano, taking the highest entrance — the one last named, and at whose porch Atufal still stood — hurried on his way, till, arrived at the cabin threshold, he paused an instant, a little to recover from his eagerness. Then, with the words of his intended business upon his lips, he entered. As he advanced toward the seated Spaniard, he heard another footstep, keeping time with his. From the opposite door, a salver in hand, the servant was likewise advancing.

"Confound the faithful fellow," thought Captain Delano; "what a vexatious coincidence."

Possibly, the vexation might have been something different, were it not for the brisk confidence inspired by the breeze. But even as it was, he felt a slight twinge, from a sudden indefinite association in his mind of Babo with Atufal.

"Don Benito," said he, "I give you joy; the breeze will hold, and will increase. By the way, your tall man and time-piece, Atufal, stands without. By your order, of course?"

Don Benito recoiled, as if at some bland satirical touch, delivered with such adroit garnish of apparent good breeding as to present no handle for retort.

He is like one flayed alive, thought Captain Delano; where may one touch him without causing a shrink?

The servant moved before his master, adjusting a cushion; recalled to civility, the Spaniard stiffly replied: "you are right. The slave appears where you saw him, according to my command; which is, that if at the given hour I am below, he must take his stand and abide my coming."

"Ah now, pardon me, but that is treating the poor fellow like an ex-king indeed. Ah, Don Benito," smiling, "for all the license you permit in some things, I fear lest, at bottom, you are a bitter hard master."

Again Don Benito shrank; and this time, as the good sailor thought, from a genuine twinge of his conscience.

Conversation now became constrained. In vain Captain Delano called attention to the now perceptible motion of the keel gently cleaving the sea; with lack-lustre eye, Don Benito returned words few and reserved.

By-and-by, the wind having steadily risen, and still blowing right into the harbor, bore the San Dominick swiftly on. Rounding a point of land, the sealer at distance came into open view.

Meantime Captain Delano had again repaired to the deck, remaining there some time. Having at last altered the ship's course, so as to give the reef a wide berth, he returned for a few moments below.

I will cheer up my poor friend, this time, thought he.

"Better and better, Don Benito,['] he cried as he blithely re-entered: "there will soon be an end to your cares, at least for awhile. For when, after a long, sad voyage, you know, the anchor drops into the haven, all its vast weight seems lifted from the captain's heart. We are getting on famously, Don Benito. My ship is in sight. Look through this side-light here; there she is; all a-taunt-o! The Bachelor's Delight, my good friend. Ah, how this wind braces one up. Come, you must take a cup of coffee with me this evening. My old steward will give you as fine a cup as ever any sultan tasted. What say you, Don Benito, will you?"

At first, the Spaniard glanced feverishly up, casting a longing look towards the sealer, while with mute concern his servant gazed into his face. Suddenly the old ague of coldness returned, and dropping back to his cushions he was silent.

"You do not answer. Come, all day you have been my host; would you have hospitality all on one side?"

"I cannot go," was the response.

"What? It will not fatigue you. The ships will lie together as near as they can, without swinging foul. It will be little more than stepping from deck to deck; which is but as from room to room. Come, come, you must not refuse me."

"I cannot go," decisively and repulsively repeated Don Benito.

Renouncing all but the last appearance of courtesy, with a sort of cadaverous sullenness, and biting his thin nails to the quick, he glanced, almost glared, at his guest, as if impatient that a stranger's presence should interfere with the full indulgence of his morbid hour. Meantime the sound of the parted waters came more and more gurglingly and merrily in at the windows; as reproaching him for his dark spleen; as telling him that, sulk as he might, and go mad with it, nature cared not a jot; since, whose fault was it, pray?

But the foul mood was now at its depth, as the fair wind at its height.

There was something in the man so far beyond any mere unsociality or sourness previously evinced, that even the forbearing good-nature of his guest could no longer endure it. Wholly at a loss to account for such demeanor, and deeming sickness with eccentricity, however extreme, no adequate excuse, well satisfied, too, that nothing in his own conduct could justify it, Captain Delano's pride began to be roused. Himself became reserved. But all seemed one to the Spaniard. Quitting him, therefore, Captain Delano once more went to the deck.

The ship was now within less than two miles of the sealer. The whaleboat was seen darting over the interval.

To be brief, the two vessels, thanks to the pilot's skill, ere long in neighborly style lay anchored together.

Before returning to his own vessel, Captain Delano had intended communicating to Don Benito the smaller details of the proposed services to be rendered. But, as it was, unwilling anew to subject himself to rebuffs, he resolved, now that he had seen the San Dominick safely moored, immediately to quit her, without further allusion to hospitality or business. Indefinitely postponing his ulterior plans, he would regulate his future actions according to future circumstances. His boat was ready to receive him; but his host still tarried below. Well, thought Captain Delano, if he has little breeding, the more need to show mine. He descended to the cabin to bid a ceremonious, and, it may be, tacitly rebukeful adieu. But to his great satisfaction, Don Benito, as if he began to feel the weight of that treatment with which his slighted guest had, not indecorously, retaliated upon him, now supported by his servant, rose to his feet, and grasping Captain Delano's hand, stood tremulous; too much agitated to speak. But the good augury hence drawn was suddenly dashed, by his resuming all his previous reserve, with augmented gloom, as, with half-averted eyes, he silently reseated himself on his cushions. With a corresponding return of his own chilled feelings, Captain Delano bowed and withdrew.

He was hardly midway in the narrow corridor, dim as a tunnel, leading from the cabin to the stairs, when a sound, as of the tolling for execution in some jail-yard, fell on his ears. It was the echo of the ship's flawed bell, striking the hour, drearily reverberated in this subterranean vault. Instantly, by a fatality not to be withstood, his mind, responsive to the portent, swarmed with superstitious suspicions. He paused. In images far swifter than these sentences, the minutest details of all his former distrusts swept through him.

Hitherto, credulous good-nature had been too ready to furnish excuses for reasonable fears. Why was the Spaniard, so superfluously punctilious at times, now heedless of common propriety in not accompanying to the side his departing guest? Did indisposition forbid? Indisposition had not forbidden more irksome exertion that day. His last equivocal demeanor recurred. He had risen to his feet, grasped his guest's hand, motioned toward his hat; then, in an instant, all was eclipsed in sinister muteness and gloom. Did this imply one brief, repentant relenting at the final moment, from some iniquitous plot, followed by remorseless re-

turn to it? His last glance seemed to express a calamitous, yet acquiescent farewell to Captain Delano forever. Why decline the invitation to visit the sealer that evening? Or was the Spaniard less hardened than the Jew, who refrained not from supping at the board of him whom the same night he meant to betray? What imported all those day-long enigmas and contradictions, except they were intended to mystify, preliminary to some stealthy blow? Atufal, the pretended rebel, but punctual shadow, that moment lurked by the threshold without. He seemed a sentry, and more. Who, by his own confession, had stationed him there? Was the negro now lying in wait?

The Spaniard behind — his creature before: to rush from darkness to light was the involuntary choice.

The next moment, with clenched jaw and hand, he passed Atufal, and stood unharmed in the light. As he saw his trim ship lying peacefully at her anchor, and almost within ordinary call; as he saw his household boat, with familiar faces in it, patiently rising and falling on the short waves by the San Dominick's side; and then, glancing about the decks where he stood, saw the oakum-pickers still gravely plying their fingers; and heard the low, buzzing whistle and industrious hum of the hatchet-polishers, still bestirring themselves over their endless occupation; and more than all, as he saw the benign aspect of nature, taking her innocent repose in the evening; the screened sun in the quiet camp of the west shining out like the mild light from Abraham's tent; as his charmed eye and ear took in all these, with the chained figure of the black, the clenched jaw and hand relaxed. Once again he smiled at the phantoms which had mocked him, and felt something like a tinge of remorse, that, by indulging them even for a moment, he should, by implication, have betrayed an almost atheist doubt of the ever-watchful Providence above.

There was a few minutes' delay, while, in obedience to his orders, the boat was being hooked along to the gangway. During this interval, a sort of saddened satisfaction stole over Captain Delano, at thinking of the kindly offices he had that day discharged for a stranger. Ah, thought he, after good actions one's conscience is never ungrateful, however much so the benefited party may be.

Presently, his foot, in the first act of descent into the boat, pressed the first round of the side-ladder, his face presented inward upon the deck. In the same moment, he heard his name courteously sounded; and, to his pleased surprise, saw Don Benito advancing — an unwonted energy in his air, as if, at the last moment, intent upon making amends for his recent discourtesy. With instinctive good feeling, Captain Delano, withdrawing his foot, turned and reciprocally advanced. As he did so, the Spaniard's nervous eagerness increased, but his vital energy failed; so that, the better to support him, the servant, placing his master's hand on his naked shoulder, and gently holding it there, formed himself into a sort of crutch.

When the two captains met, the Spaniard again fervently took the hand of the American, at the same time casting an earnest glance into his eyes, but, as before, too much overcome to speak.

I have done him wrong, self-reproachfully thought Captain Delano; his apparent coldness has deceived me; in no instance has he meant to offend.

Meantime, as if fearful that the continuance of the scene might too much unstring his master, the servant seemed anxious to terminate it. And so, still presenting himself as a crutch, and walking between the two captains, he advanced with them towards the gangway; while still, as if full of kindly contrition, Don Benito would not let go the hand of Captain Delano, but retained it in his, across the black's body.

Soon they were standing by the side, looking over into the boat, whose crew turned up their curious eyes. Waiting a moment for the Spaniard to relinquish his hold, the now embarrassed Captain Delano lifted his foot, to overstep the threshold of the open gangway; but still Don Benito would not let go his hand. And yet, with an agitated tone, he said, "I can go no further; here I must bid you adieu. Adieu, my dear, dear Don Amasa. Go — go!" suddenly tearing his hand loose, "go, and God guard you better than me, my best friend."

Not unaffected, Captain Delano would now have lingered; but catching the meekly admonitory eye of the servant, with a hasty farewell he descended into his boat, followed by the continual adieus of Don Benito, standing rooted in the gangway.

Seating himself in the stern, Captain Delano, making a last salute, ordered the boat shoved off. The crew had their oars on end. The bowsmen pushed the boat a sufficient distance for the oars to be lengthwise dropped. The instant that was done, Don Benito sprang over the bulwarks, falling at the feet of Captain Delano; at the same time, calling towards his ship, but in tones so frenzied, that none in the boat could understand him. But, as if not equally obtuse, three sailors, from three different and distant parts of the ship, splashed into the sea, swimming after their captain, as if intent upon his rescue.

The dismayed officer of the boat eagerly asked what this meant. To which, Captain Delano, turning a disdainful smile upon the unaccountable Spaniard, answered that, for his part, he neither knew nor cared; but it seemed as if Don Benito had taken it into his head to produce the impression among his people that the boat wanted to kidnap him. "Or else — give way for your lives," he wildly added, starting at a clattering hubhub in the ship, above which rang the tocsin of the hatchet-polishers; and seizing Don Benito by the throat he added, "this plotting pirate means murder!" Here, in apparent verification of the words, the servant, a dagger in his hand, was seen on the rail overhead, poised, in the act of leaping, as if with desperate fidelity to befriend his master to the last; while, seemingly to aid the black, the three Spanish sailors were trying to clamber into the hampered bow. Meantime, the whole host of negroes, as if inflamed at the sight of their jeopardized captain, impended in one sooty avalanche over the bulwarks.

All this, with what preceded, and what followed, occurred with such involutions of rapidity, that past, present, and future seemed one.

Seeing the negro coming, Captain Delano had flung the Spaniard aside, almost in the very act of clutching him and, by the unconscious recoil, shifting his place, with arms thrown up, so promptly grappled the servant in his descent, that with dagger presented at Captain Delano's heart, the black seemed of purpose to have leaped there as to his mark. But the weapon was wrenched away, and the assailant dashed down into the bottom of the boat, which now, with disentangled oars, began to speed through the sea.

At this juncture, the left hand of Captain Delano, on one side, again clutched the half-reclined Don Benito, heedless that he was in a speechless faint, while his right foot, on the other side, ground the prostrate negro; and his right arm pressed for added speed on the after oar, his eye bent forward, encouraging his men to their utmost.

But here, the officer of the boat, who had at last succeeded in beating off the towing sailors, and was now, with face turned aft, assisting the bowsman at his oar, suddenly called to Captain Delano, to see what the black was about; while a Portuguese oarsman shouted to him to give heed to what the Spaniard was saying.

Glancing down at his feet, Captain Delano saw the freed hand of the servant aiming with a second dagger — a small one, before concealed in his wool — with this he was snakishly writhing up from the boat's bottom, at the heart of his master, his countenance lividly vindictive, expressing the centred purpose of his soul; while the Spaniard, half-choked, was vainly shrinking away, with husky words, incoherent to all but the Portuguese.

That moment, across the long-benighted mind of Captain Delano, a flash of revelation swept, illuminating in unanticipated clearness his host's whole mysterious demeanor, with every enigmatic event of the day, as well as the entire past voyage of the San Dominick. He smote Babo's hand down, but his own heart smote him harder. With infinite pity he withdrew his hold from Don Benito. Not Captain Delano, but Don Benito, the black, in leaping into the boat, had intended to stab.

Both the black's hands were held, as, glancing up towards the San Dominick, Captain Delano, now with the scales dropped from his eyes, saw the negroes, not in misrule, not in tumult, not as if frantically concerned

for Don Benito, but with mask torn away, flourishing hatchets and knives, in ferocious piratical revolt. Like delirious black dervishes, the six Ashantees danced on the poop. Prevented by their foes from springing into the water, the Spanish boys were hurrying up to the topmost spars, while such of the few Spanish sailors, not already in the sea, less alert, were descried, helplessly mixed in, on deck, with the blacks.

Meantime Captain Delano hailed his own vessel, ordering the ports up, and the guns run out. But by this time the cable of the San Dominick had been cut; and the fag-end, in lashing out, whipped away the canvas shroud about the beak, suddenly revealing, as the bleached hull swung round towards the open ocean, death for the figurehead, in a human skeleton; chalky comment on the chalked words below, "*Follow your leader.*"

At the sight, Don Benito, covering his face, wailed out: "'Tis he, Aranda! my murdered, unburied friend!"

Upon reaching the sealer, calling for ropes, Captain Delano bound the negro, who made no resistance, and had him hoisted to the deck. He would then have assisted the now almost helpless Don Benito up the side; but Don Benito, wan as he was, refused to move, or be moved, until the negro should have been first put below out of view. When, presently assured that it was done, he no more shrank from the ascent.

The boat was immediately dispatched back to pick up the three swimming sailors. Meantime, the guns were in readiness, though, owing to the San Dominick having glided somewhat astern of the sealer, only the aftermost one could be brought to bear. With this, they fired six times; thinking to cripple the fugitive ship by bringing down her spars. But only a few inconsiderable ropes were shot away. Soon the ship was beyond the gun's range, steering broad out of the bay; the blacks thickly clustering round the bowsprit, one moment with taunting cries towards the whites, the next with upthrown gestures hailing the now dusky moors of ocean — cawing crows escaped from the hand of the fowler.

The first impulse was to slip the cables and give chase. But, upon second thoughts, to pursue with whale-boat and yawl seemed more promising.

Upon inquiring of Don Benito what fire-arms they had on board the San Dominick, Captain Delano was answered that they had none that could be used; because, in the earlier stages of the mutiny, a cabin-pas-senger, since dead, had secretly put out of order the locks of what few muskets there were. But with all his remaining strength, Don Benito entreated the American not to give chase, either with ship or boat; for the negroes had already proved themselves such desperadoes, that, in case of a present assault, nothing but a total massacre of the whites could be looked for. But, regarding this warning as coming from one whose spirit had been crushed by misery, the American did not give up his design.

The boats were got ready and armed. Captain Delano ordered twenty-five men into them. He was going himself when Don Benito grasped his arm.

"What! have you saved my life, Señor, and are you now going to throw away your own?"

The officers also, for reasons connected with their interests and those of the voyage, and a duty owing to the owners, strongly ob-jected against their commander's going. Weighing their remonstrances a moment, Captain Delano felt bound to remain; ap-pointing his chief mate — an athletic and resolute man, who had been a privateer's-man — to head the party. The more to encourage the sailors, they were told, that the Spanish captain considered his ship as good as lost; that she and her cargo, includ-ing some gold and silver, were worth more than a thousand doubloons. Take her, and no small part should be theirs. The sailors replied with a shout.

The fugitives had now almost gained an offing. It was nearly night; but the moon was rising. After hard, prolonged pulling, the boats came up on the ship's quarters, at a suitable distance laying upon their oars to discharge their muskets. Having no bullets to return, the negroes sent their yells. But, upon the second volley, Indian-like, they hurtled their hatchets. One took off a sailor's fingers. Another struck the whale-boat's bow, cutting off the rope there, and

remaining stuck in the gunwale like a wood-man's axe. Snatching it, quivering from its lodgment, the mate hurled it back. The returned gauntlet now stuck in the ship's broken quarter-gallery, and so re-mained.

The negroes giving too hot a reception, the whites kept a more respectful distance. Hovering now just out of reach of the hurtling hatchets, they, with a view to the close en-counter which must soon come, sought to decoy the blacks into entirely disarming themselves of their most murderous weapons in a hand-to-hand fight, by foolishly flinging them, as missiles, short of the mark, into the sea. But ere long, perceiving the stratagem, the negroes desisted, though not before many of them had to replace their lost hatchets with handspikes; an exchange which, as counted upon, proved, in the end, favorable to the assailants.

Meantime, with a strong wind, the ship still clove the water; the boats alternately falling behind, and pulling up, to discharge fresh volleys.

The fire was mostly directed towards the stern, since there, chiefly, the negroes, at present, were clustering. But to kill or maim the negroes was not the object. To take them, with the ship, was the object. To do it, the ship must be boarded; which could not be done by boats while she was sailing so fast.

A thought now struck the mate. Observ-ing the Spanish boys still aloft, high as they could get, he called to them to descend to the yards, and cut adrift the sails. It was done. About this time, owing to causes hereafter to be shown, two Spaniards, in the dress of sailors, and conspicuously showing themselves, were killed; not by volleys, but by deliberate marksman's shots; while, as it afterwards appeared, during one of the gen-eral discharges, Atufal, the black, and the Spaniard at the helm likewise were killed. What now, with the loss of the sails, and loss of leaders, the ship became unmanageable to the negroes.

With creaking masts, she came heavily round to the wind; the prow slowly swinging into view of the boats, its skeleton gleaming in the horizontal moonlight, and casting a gigantic ribbed shadow upon the water. One extended arm of the ghost seemed beckoning the whites to avenge it.

"Follow your leader!" cried the mate; and, one on each bow, the boats boarded. Sealing-spears and cutlasses crossed hatches and handspikes. Huddled upon the long-boat amidships, the negresses raised a wailing chant, whose chorus was the clash of the steel.

For a time the attack wavered; the negroes wedging themselves to beat it back; the half-repelled sailors, as yet unable to gain a footing, fighting as troopers in the saddle, one leg sideways flung over the bulwarks, and one without, plying their cutlasses like carters' whips. But in vain. They were almost overborne, when rallying themselves into a squad as one man, with a huzza, they sprang inboard, where, entangled, they involuntarily separated again. For a few breaths' space there was a vague, muffled, inner sound, as of submerged sword-fish rushing hither and thither through shoals of black-fish. Soon, in a reunited band, and joined by the Spanish seamen, the whites came to the surface, irresistibly driving the negroes toward the stern. But a barricade of casks and sacks, from side to side, had been thrown up by the mainmast. Here the negroes faced about, and though scorning peace or truce, yet fain would have had a respite. But, without pause, overleaping the barrier, the unflagging sailors again closed. Exhausted, the blacks now fought in despair. Their red tongues lolled, wolf-like, from their black mouths. But the pale sailors' teeth were set; not a word spoken; and, in five minutes more, the ship was won.

Nearly a score of the negroes were killed. Exclusive of those by the balls, many were mangled; their wounds — mostly inflicted by the long-edged sealing-spears — resembling those shaven ones of the English at Preston Pans, made by the poled scythes of the Highlanders. On the other side, none were killed, though several were wounded; some severely, including the mate. The surviving negroes were temporarily secured, and the ship, towed back into the harbor at midnight, once more lay anchored.

Omitting the incidents and arrangements ensuing, suffice it that, after two days spent in refitting, the two ships sailed in company for Conception in Chili, and thence for Lima in Peru; where, before the vice-regal courts, the whole affair, from the beginning, underwent investigation.

Though, midway on the passage, the ill-fated Spaniard, relaxed from constraint, showed some signs of regaining health with free-will; yet, agreeably to his own foreboding, shortly before arriving at Lima, he relapsed, finally becoming so reduced as to be carried ashore in arms. Hearing of his story and plight, one of the many religious institutions of the City of Kings opened an hospitable refuge to him, where both physician and priest were his nurses, and a member of the order volunteered to be his one special guardian and consoler, by night and by day.

The following extracts, translated from one of the official Spanish documents, will, it is hoped, shed light on the preceding narrative, as well as, in the first place, reveal the true port of departure and true history of the San Dominick's voyage, down to the time of her touching at the island of St. Maria.

But, ere the extracts come, it may be well to preface them with a remark.

The document selected, from among many others, for partial translation, contains the deposition of Benito Cereno; the first taken in the case. Some disclosures therein were, at the time, held dubious for both learned and natural reasons. The tribunal inclined to the opinion that the deponent, not undisturbed in his mind by recent events, raved of some things which could never have happened. But subsequent depositions of the surviving sailors, bearing out the revelations of their captain in several of the strangest particulars, gave credence to the rest. So that the tribunal, in its final decision, rested its capital sentences upon statements which, had they lacked confirmation, it would have deemed it but duty to reject.

I, DON JOSE DE ABOS AND PADILLA, His Majesty's Notary for the Royal Revenue, and Register of this Province, and Notary Public of the Holy Crusade of this Bishopric, etc.

Do certify and declare, as much as is requisite in law, that, in the criminal cause commenced the twenty-fourth of the month of September, in the year seventeen hundred and ninety-nine, against the Senegal negroes of the ship San Dominick, the following declaration before me was made:

Declaration of the first witness, DON BENITO CERENO.

The same day, and month, and year, His Honor, Doctor Juan Martinez de Rozas, Councilor of the Royal Audience of this Kingdom, and learned in the law of this Intendency, ordered the captain of the ship San Dominick, Don Benito Cereno, to appear; which he did in his litter, attended by the monk Infelez; of whom he received the oath, which he took by God, our Lord, and a sign of the Cross; under which he promised to tell the truth of whatever he should know and should be asked; — and being interrogated agreeably to the tenor of the act commencing the process, he said, that on the twentieth of May last, he set sail with his ship from the port of Valparaiso, bound to that of Callao; loaded with the produce of the country beside thirty cases of hardware and one hundred and sixty blacks, of both sexes, mostly belonging to Don Alexandro Aranda, gentleman, of the city of Mendoza; that the crew of the ship consisted of thirty-six men, beside the persons who went as passengers; that the negroes were in part as follows: . . .

[*Here, in the original, follows a list of some fifty names, descriptions, and ages, compiled from certain recovered documents of Aranda's, and also from recollections of the deponent, from which portions only are extracted.*]

— One, from about eighteen to nineteen years, named José, and this was the man that waited upon his master, Don Alexandro, and who speaks well the Spanish, having served him four or five years; . . . A mulatto, named Francesco, the cabin steward, of a good person and voice, having sung in the Valparaiso churches, native of the province of Buenos Ayres, aged about thirty-five years. A smart negro, named Dago, who had been for many years a grave-digger among the Spaniards, aged forty-six years. . . . Four old negroes, born in Africa, from sixty to seventy, but sound, caulkers by trade, whose names are as follows: — the first was named Muri, and he was killed (as was also his son named Diamelo); the second, Nacta; the third, Yola, likewise killed; the fourth, Ghofan; and six full-grown negroes, aged from thirty to forty-five, all raw, and born among the Ashantees — Matiluqui, Yan, Lecbe, Mapenda, Yambaio, Akim; four of whom were killed; . . . a powerful negro named Atufal, who being supposed to have been a chief in Africa, his owner set great store by him. . . . And a small negro of Senegal, but some years among the Spaniards, aged about thirty, which Negro's name was Babo; . . . that he does not remember the names of the others, but that still expecting the residue of Don Alexandro's papers will be found, will then take due account of them all, and remit to the court; . . . and thirty-nine women and children of all ages.

[*The catalogue over, the deposition goes on:*]

. . . That all the negroes slept upon deck, as is customary in this navigation, and none wore fetters, because the owner, his friend Aranda, told him that they were all tractable; . . . that on the seventh day after leaving port, at three o'clock in the morning, all the Spaniards being asleep except the two officers on the watch, who were the boatswain, Juan Robles, and the carpenter, Juan Bautista Gayete, and the helmsman and his boy, the negroes revolted suddenly, wounded dangerously the boatswain and the carpenter, and successively killed eighteen men of those who were sleeping upon deck, some with hand-spikes and hatchets, and others by throwing them alive overboard, after tying them; that of the Spaniards upon deck, they left about seven, as he thinks, alive and tied, to manoeuvre the ship, and three or four more who hid themselves, remained also alive. Although in the act of revolt the negroes made themselves masters of the hatchway, six or seven wounded went through it to the cockpit, without any hindrance on their part; that in the act of revolt, the mate and another person, whose name he does not recollect, attempted to come up through the hatchway, but being quickly wounded, were obliged to return to the cabin; that the deponent resolved at break of day to come up the companion-way, where the negro Babo was, being the ringleader, and Atufal, who assisted him, and having spoken to them, exhorted them to cease committing such atrocities, asking them, at the same time, what they wanted and intended to do, offering, himself, to obey their commands; that, notwithstanding this, they threw, in his presence, three men, alive and tied, overboard; that they told the deponent to come up, and that they would not kill him; which having done, the negro Babo asked him whether there were in those seas any negro countries where they might be carried, and he answered them, No; that the negro Babo afterwards told him to carry them to Senegal, or to the neighbouring islands of St. Nicholas; and he answered, that this was impossible, on account of the great distance, the necessity involved of rounding Cape Horn, the bad condition of the vessel, the want of provisions, sails, and water; but that the negro Babo replied to him he must carry them in any way; that they would do and conform themselves to everything the deponent should require as to eating and drinking; that after a long conference, being absolutely compelled to please them, for they threatened him to kill all the whites if they were not, at all events, carried to Senegal, he told them that what was most wanting for the voyage was water; that they would go near the coast to take it, and thence they would proceed on their course; that the negro Babo agreed to it; and the deponent steered towards the intermediate ports, hoping to meet some Spanish or foreign vessel that would save them; that within ten or eleven days they saw the land, and continued by it in the vicinity of Nasca; that the deponent observed that the negroes were not restless and mutinous, because he did not effect the taking in of water, the negro Babo having required, with threats, that it should be done, without fail, the following day; he told him he saw plainly that the coast was steep, and the rivers designated in the maps were not to be found, with other reasons suitable to the circumstances; that the best way would be to go to the island of Santa Maria, where they might water easily, it being a solitary island, as the foreigners did; that the deponent did not go to Pisco, that was near, nor make any other port of the coast, because the negro Babo had intimated to him several times, that he would kill all the whites the very moment he should perceive any city, town, or settlement of any kind on the shores to which they should be carried: that having determined to go to the island of Santa Maria, as the deponent had planned, for the purpose of trying whether, on the passage or near the island itself, they could find any vessel that should favor them, or whether he could escape from it in a boat to the neighbouring coast of Arruco, to adopt the necessary means he immediately changed his course, steering for the island; that the negroes Babo and Atufal held daily conferences, in which they discussed what was necessary for their design of returning to Senegal, whether they were to kill all the Spaniards, and particularly the deponent; that eight days after parting from the coast of Nasca, the deponent being on the watch a little after day-break, and soon after the negroes had their meeting, the negro Babo came to the place where the deponent was, and told him that he had determined to kill his master, Don Alexandro Aranda, both because he and his companions could not otherwise be sure of their liberty, and that to keep the seamen in subjection, he wanted to prepare a warning of what road they should be made to take did they or any of them oppose him; and that, by means of the death of Don Alexandro, that warning would best be given; but, that what this last meant, the deponent did not at the time comprehend, nor could not, further than that the death of Don Alexandro was intended; and moreover the negro Babo proposed to the deponent to call the mate Raneds, who was sleeping in the cabin, before the thing was done, for fear, as the deponent understood it, that the mate, who was a good navigator, should be killed with Don Alexandro and the rest; that the deponent, who was the friend, from youth of Don Alexandro, prayed and conjured, but all was useless; for the negro Babo answered him that the thing could not be prevented, and that all the Spaniards risked their death if they should attempt to frustrate his will in this matter, or any other; that, in this conflict, the deponent called the mate, Raneds, who was forced to go apart, and immediately the negro Babo commanded the Ashantee Martinqui and the Ashantee Lecbe to go and commit the murder; that those two went down with hatchets to the berth of Don Alexandro; that, yet half alive and mangled, they dragged him on deck; that they were going to throw him overboard in that state, but the negro Babo stopped them, bidding the murder be completed on the deck before him, which was done, when, by his orders, the body was carried below, forward; that nothing more was seen of it by the deponent for three days; . . . that Don Alonzo Sidonia, an old man, long resident at Valparaiso, and lately appointed to a civil office in Peru, whither he had taken passage, was at the time sleeping in the berth opposite Don Alexandro's; that awakening at his cries, surprised by them, and at the sight of the negroes with their bloody hatchets in their hands, he threw himself into the sea through a window which was near him and was drowned, without it being in the power of the deponent to assist or take him up; . . . that, a short time after killing Aranda, they brought upon deck his german-cousin, of middle-age, Don Francisco Masa, of Mendoza, and the young Don Joaquin, Marques de Aramboalaza, then lately from Spain, with his Spanish servant Ponce, and the three young clerks of Aranda, José Mozairi, Lorenzo Bargas, and Hermenegildo Gandix, all of Cadiz; that Don Joaquin and Hermenegildo Gandix, the negro Babo, for purposes hereafter to appear, preserved alive; but Don Francisco Masa, José Mozairi, and Lorenzo Bargas, with Ponce the servant, beside the boatswain, Juan Robles, the boatswain's mates, Manuel Viscaya and Roderigo Hurta, and four of the sailors, the negro Babo ordered to be thrown alive into the sea, although they made no resistance, nor begged for anything else but mercy; that the boatswain, Juan Robles, who knew how to swim, kept the longest above water, making acts of contrition, and, in the last words he uttered, charged this deponent to cause mass to be said for his soul to our Lady of Succor: . . . that, during the three days which followed, the deponent, uncertain what fate had befallen the remains of Don Alexandro, frequently asked the negro Babo where they were, and, if still on board, whether they were to be preserved for interment ashore, entreating him so to order it; that the negro Babo answered nothing till the fourth day, when at sunrise, the deponent coming on deck, the negro Babo showed him a skeleton, which had been substituted for the ship's proper figurehead — the image of Christopher Colon, the discoverer of the New World; that the negro Babo asked him whose skeleton that was, and whether, from its whiteness, he should not think it a white's; that, upon discovering his face, the negro Babo, coming close, said words to this effect: "Keep faith with the blacks from here to Senegal, or you shall in spirit, as now in body, follow your leader," pointing to the prow; . . . that the same morning the negro Babo took by succession each Spaniard forward, and asked him whose skeleton that was, and whether, from its whiteness, he should not think it a white's; that each Spaniard covered his face; that then to each the negro Babo repeated the words in the first place said to the deponent; . . . that they (the Spaniards), being then assembled aft, the negro Babo harangued them, saying that he had now done all; that the deponent (as navigator for the negroes) might pursue his course, warning him and all of them that they should, soul and body, go the way of Don Alexandro, if he saw them (the Spaniards) speak or plot anything against them (the negroes) — a threat which was repeated every day; that, before the events last mentioned, they had tied the cook to throw him overboard, for it is not known what thing they heard him speak, but finally the negro Babo spared his life, at the request of the deponent; that a few days after, the deponent, endeavoring not to omit any means to preserve the lives of the remaining whites, spoke to the negroes peace and tranquillity, and agreed to draw up a paper, signed by the deponent and the sailors who could write, as also by the negro Babo, for himself and all the blacks, in which the deponent obliged himself to carry them to Senegal, and they not to kill any more, and he formally to make over to them the ship, with the cargo, with which they were for that time satisfied and quieted. . . . But the next day, the more surely to guard against the sailors' escape, the negro Babo commanded all the boats to be destroyed but the long-boat, which was unseaworthy, and another, a cutter in good condition, which knowing it would yet be wanted for towing the water casks, he had it lowered down into the hold.

. . . .

[*Various particulars of the prolonged and perplexed navigation ensuing here follow, with incidents of a calamitous calm, from which portion one passage is extracted, to wit:*]

— That on the fifth day of the calm, all on board suffering much from the heat, and want of water, and five having died in fits, and mad, the negroes became irritable, and for a chance gesture, which they deemed suspicious — though it was harmless — made by the mate, Raneds, to the deponent in the act of handing a quadrant, they killed him; but that for this they were afterwards sorry, the mate being the only remaining navigator on board, except the deponent.

. . . .

— That omitting other events, which daily happened, and which can only serve uselessly to recall past misfortunes and conflicts, after seventy-three days' navigation, reckoned from the time they sailed from Nasca, during which they navigated under a scanty allowance of water, and were afflicted with the calms before mentioned, they at last arrived at the island of Santa Maria, on the seventeenth of the month of August, at about six o'clock in the afternoon, at which hour they cast anchor very near the American ship, Bachelor's Delight, which lay in the same bay, commanded by the generous Captain Amasa Delano; but at six o'clock in the morning, they had already descried the port, and the negroes became uneasy, as soon as at distance they saw the ship, not having expected to see one there; that the negro Babo pacified them, assuring them that no fear need be had; that straightway he ordered the figure on the

bow to be covered with canvas, as for repairs, and had the decks a little set in order; that for a time the negro Babo and the negro Atufal conferred; that the negro Atufal was for sailing away, but the negro Babo would not, and, by himself, cast about what to do; that at last he came to the deponent, proposing to him to say and do all that the deponent declares to have said and done to the American captain; . . . that the negro Babo warned him that if he varied in the least, or uttered any word, or gave any look that should give the least intimation of the past events or present state, he would instantly kill him, with all his companions, showing a dagger, which he carried hid, saying something which, as he understood it, meant that that dagger would be alert as his eye; that the negro Babo then announced the plan to all his companions, which pleased them; that he then, the better to disguise the truth, devised many expedients, in some of them uniting deceit and defense; that of this sort was the device of the six Ashantees before named, who were his bravoes; that them he stationed on the break of the poop, as if to clean certain hatchets (in cases, which were part of the cargo), but in reality to use them, and distribute them at need, and at a given word he told them; that, among other devices, was the device of presenting Atufal, his right hand man, as chained, though in a moment the chains could be dropped; that in every particular he informed the deponent what part he was expected to enact in every device, and what story he was to tell on every occasion, always threatening him with instant death if he varied in the least: that, conscious that many of the negroes would be turbulent, the negro Babo appointed the four aged negroes, who were calkers, to keep what domestic order they could on the decks; that again and again he harangued the Spaniards and his companions, informing them of his intent, and of his devices, and of the invented story that this deponent was to tell; charging them lest any of them varied from that story; that these arrangements were made and matured during the interval of two or three hours, between their first sighting the ship and the arrival on board of Captain Amasa Delano; that this happened at about half-past seven o'clock in the morning, Captain Amasa Delano coming in his boat, and all gladly receiving him; that the deponent, as well as he could force himself, acting then the part of principal owner, and a free captain of the ship, told Captain Amasa Delano, when called upon, that he came from Buenos Ayres, bound to Lima, with three hundred negroes; that off Cape Horn, and in a subsequent fever, many negroes had died; that also, by similar casualties, all the sea officers and the greatest part of the crew had died.

. . . .

[*And so the deposition goes on, circumstantially recounting the fictitious story dictated to the deponent by Babo, and through the deponent imposed*] *upon Captain Delano; and also recounting the friendly offers of Captain Delano, with other things, but all of which is here omitted. After the fictitious story, etc., the deposition proceeds:*]

— that the generous Captain Amasa Delano remained on board all the day, till he left the ship anchored at six o'clock in the evening, deponent speaking to him always of his pretended misfortunes, under the forementioned principles, without having had it in his power to tell a single word, or give him the least hint, that he might know the truth and state of things; because the negro Babo, performing the office of an officious servant with all the appearance of submission of the humble slave, did not leave the deponent one moment; that this was in order to observe the deponent's actions and words, for the negro Babo understands well the Spanish; and besides, there were thereabout some others who were constantly on the watch, and likewise understood the Spanish; ... that upon one occasion, while deponent was standing on the deck conversing with Amasa Delano, by a secret sign the negro Babo drew him (the deponent) aside, the act appearing as if originating with the deponent; that then, he being drawn aside, the negro Babo proposed to him to gain from Amasa Delano full particulars about his ship, and crew, and arms; that the deponent asked "For what?" that the negro Babo answered he might conceive; that, grieved at the prospect of what might overtake the generous Captain Amasa Delano, the deponent at first refused to ask the desired questions, and used every argument to induce the negro Babo to give up this new design; that the negro Babo showed the point of his dagger; that, after the information had been obtained the negro Babo again drew him aside, telling him that that very night he (the deponent) would be captain of two ships instead of one, for that, great part of the American's ship's crew being to be absent fishing, the six Ashantees, without any one else, would easily take it; that at this time he said other things to the same purpose; that no entreaties availed; that before Amasa Delano's coming on board, no hint had been given touching the capture of the American ship; that to prevent this project the deponent was powerless; ... — that in some things his memory is confused, he cannot distinctly recall every event; ... — that as soon as they had cast anchor at six of the clock in the evening, as has before been stated, the American Captain took leave, to return to his vessel; that upon a sudden impulse, which the deponent believes to have come from God and his angels, he, after the farewell had been said, followed the generous Captain Amasa Delano as far as the gunwale, where he stayed, under the pretense of taking leave, until Amasa Delano should have been seated in his boat; that on shoving off, the deponent sprang from the gunwale into the boat, and fell into it, he knows not how, God guarding him; that —

.   :   :   :   .   .   .   :   :

[*Here, in the original, follows the account of what further happened at the escape, and how the San Dominick was retaken, and of the passage to the coast; including in the recital many expressions of "eternal gratitude" to the "generous Captain Amasa Delano." The deposition then proceeds with recapitulatory remarks, and a partial renumeration of the negroes, making record of their individual part in the past events, with a view to furnishing, according to command of the court, the data whereon to found the criminal sentences to be pronounced. From this portion is the following:*]

— That he believes that all the negroes, though not in the first place knowing to the design of revolt, when it was accomplished, approved it. ... That the negro, José, eighteen years old, and in the personal service of Don Alexandro, was the one who communicated the information to the negro Babo, about the state of things in the cabin, before the revolt; that this is known, because, in the preceding midnight, he used to come from his berth, which was under his master's, in the cabin, to the deck where the ringleader and his associates were, and had secret conversations with the negro Babo, in which he was several times seen by the mate; that, one night, the mate drove him away twice; ... that this same negro José was the one who, without being commanded to do so by the negro Babo, as Lecbe and Martinqui were, stabbed his master, Don Alexandro, after he had been dragged half-lifeless to the deck; ... that the mulatto steward, Francesco, was of the first band of revolters, that he was, in all things, the creature and tool of the negro Babo; that, to make his court, he, just before a repast in the cabin, proposed, to the negro Babo, poisoning a dish for the generous Captain Amasa Delano; this is known and believed, because the negroes have said it; but that the negro Babo, having another design, forbade Francesco; ... that the Ashantee Lecbe was one of the worst of them; for that, on the day the ship was retaken, he assisted in the defense of her, with a hatchet in each hand, with one of which he wounded, in the breast, the chief mate of Amasa Delano, in the first act of boarding; this all knew; that, in sight of the deponent, Lecbe struck, with a hatchet, Don Francisco Masa when, by the negro Babo's orders, he was carrying him to throw him overboard, alive; beside participating in the murder, before mentioned, of Don Alexandro Aranda, and others of the cabin-passengers; that, owing to the fury with which the Ashantees fought in the engagement with the boats, but this Lecbe and Yan survived; that Yan was bad as Lecbe; that Yan was the man who, by Babo's command, willingly prepared the skeleton of Don Alexandro, in a way the negroes afterwards told the deponent, but which he, so long as reason is left him, can never divulge; that Yan and Lecbe were the two who, in a calm by night, riveted the skeleton to the bow; this also the negroes told him; that the negro Babo was he who traced the inscription below it; that the negro Babo was the plotter from first to last; he ordered every murder, and was the helm and keel of the revolt; that Atufal was his lieutenant in all; but Atufal, with his own hand, committed no murder; nor did the negro Babo; . . . that Atufal was shot, being killed in the fight with boats, ere boarding; . . . that the negresses, of age, were knowing to the revolt, and testified themselves satisfied at the death of their master, Don Alexandro; that, had the negroes not restrained them, they would have tortured to death, instead of simply killing, the Spaniards slain by command of the negro Babo; that the negresses used their utmost influence to have the deponent made away with; that, in the various acts of murder, they sang songs and danced — not gaily, but solemnly; and before the engagement with the boats, as well as during the action, they sang melancholy songs to the negroes, and that this melancholy tone was more inflaming than a different one would have been, and was so intended; that all this is believed because the negroes have said it.

— that of the thirty-six men of the crew, exclusive of the passengers (all of whom are now dead), which the deponent had knowledge of, six only remained alive, with four cabin-boys and ship-boys, not included with the crew; . . . — that the negroes broke an arm of one of the cabin-boys and gave him strokes with hatchets.

[*Then follow various random disclosures referring to various periods of time. The following are extracted:*]

— That during the presence of Captain Amasa Delano on board, some attempts were made by the sailors, and one by Hermenegildo Gandix, to convey hints to him of the true state of affairs; but that these attempts were ineffectual, owing to fear of incurring death, and, furthermore, owing to the devices which offered contradictions to the true state of affairs, as well as owing to the generosity and piety of Amasa Delano, incapable of sounding such wickedness; . . . that Luys Galgo, a sailor about sixty years of age, and formerly of the king's navy, was one of those who sought to convey tokens to Captain Amasa Delano; but his intent, though undiscovered, being suspected, he was, on a pretense, made to retire out of sight, and at last into the hold, and there was made away with. This the negroes have since said; . . . that one of the ship-boys feeling, from Captain Amasa Delano's presence, some hopes of release, and not having enough prudence, dropped some chance-word respecting his expectations, which being overheard and understood by a slave-boy with whom he was eating at the time, the latter struck him on the head with a knife, inflicting a bad wound, but of which the boy is now healing; that likewise, not long before the ship was brought to anchor, one of the seamen, steering at the time, endangered him-

self by letting the blacks remark some expression in his countenance, arising from some cause similar to the above; but this sailor, by his heedful after conduct, escaped; . . . that these statements are made to show the court that from the beginning to the end of the revolt, it was impossible for the deponent and his men to act otherwise than they did; . . . — that the third clerk, Hermenegildo Gandix, who before had been forced to live among the seamen, wearing a seaman's habit, and in all respects appearing to be one for the time; he, Gandix, was killed by a musket ball fired through mistake from the boats before boarding; having in his fright run up the mizzen-rigging, calling to the boats — "don't board," lest upon their boarding the negroes should kill him; that this inducing the Americans to believe he some way favored the cause of the negroes, they fired two balls at him, so that he fell wounded from the rigging, and was drowned in the sea; . . . — that the young Don Joaquin, Marques de Aramboalaza, like Hermenegildo Gandix, the third clerk, was degraded to the office and appearance of a common seaman; that upon one occasion, when Don Joaquin shrank, the negro Babo commanded the Ashantee Lecbe to take tar and heat it, and pour it upon Don Joaquin's hands; . . . — that Don Joaquin was killed owing to another mistake of the Americans, but one impossible to be avoided, as upon the approach of the boats, Don Joaquin, with a hatchet tied edge out and upright to his hand, was made by the negroes to appear on the bulwarks; whereupon, seen with arms in his hands and in a questionable attitude, he was shot for a renegade seaman; . . . — that on the person of Don Joaquin was found secreted a jewel, which, by papers that were discovered, proved to have been meant for the shrine of our Lady of Mercy in Lima; a votive offering, beforehand prepared and guarded, to attest his gratitude, when he should have landed in Peru, his last destination, for the safe conclusion of his entire voyage from Spain; . . . — that the jewel, with the other effects of the late Don Joaquin, is in the custody of the brethren of the Hospital de Sacerdotes, awaiting the disposition of the honorable court; . . . — that, owing to the condition of the deponent, as well as the haste in which the boats departed for the attack, the Americans were not forewarned that there were, among the apparent crew, a passenger and one of the clerks, disguised by the negro Babo; . . . — that, beside the negroes killed in the action, some were killed after the capture and reanchoring at night, when shackled to the ring-bolts on deck; that these deaths were committed by the sailors, ere they could be prevented. That so soon as informed of it, Captain Amasa Delano used all his authority, and, in particular with his own hand, struck down Martinez Gola, who, having found a razor in the pocket of an old jacket of his, which one of the shackled negroes had on, was aiming it at the negro's throat; that the noble Captain Amasa Delano also wrenched from the hand of Bartholomew Barlo, a dagger secreted at the time of the massacre of the whites, with which he was in the act of stabbing a shackled negro, who, the same day, with another negro, had thrown him down and jumped upon him; . . . — that, for all the events, befalling through so long a time, during which the ship was in the hands of the negro Babo, he cannot here give account; but that, what he has said is the most substantial of what occurs to him at present, and is the truth under the oath which he has taken; which declaration he affirmed and ratified, after hearing it read to him.

He said that he is twenty-nine years of age, and broken in body and mind; that when finally dismissed by the court, he shall not return home to Chili, but betake himself to the monastery on Mount Agonia without; and signed with his honor, and crossed himself, and, for the time, departed as he came, in his litter, with the monk Infelez, to the Hospital de Sacerdotes.

BENITO CERENO

DOCTOR ROZAS.

If the deposition have served as the key to fit into the lock of the complications which precede it, then, as a vault whose door has been flung back, the San Dominick's hull lies open to-day.

Hitherto the nature of this narrative, besides rendering the intricacies in the beginning unavoidable, has more or less required that many things, instead of being set down in the order of occurrence, should be retrospectively, or irregularly given; this last is the case with the following passages, which will conclude the account:

During the long, mild voyage to Lima, there was, as before hinted, a period during which the sufferer a little recovered his health, or, at least in some degree, his tranquillity. Ere the decided relapse which came, the two captains had many cordial conversations — their fraternal unreserve in singular contrast with former withdrawments.

Again and again, it was repeated, how hard it had been to enact the part forced on the Spaniard by Babo.

"Ah, my dear friend," Don Benito once said, "at those very times when you thought me so morose and ungrateful, nay when, as you now admit, you half thought me plotting your murder, at those very times my heart was frozen; I could not look at you, thinking of what, both on board this ship and your own, hung, from other hands, over my kind benefactor. And as God lives, Don Amasa, I know not whether desire for my own safety alone could have nerved me to that leap into your boat, had it not been for the thought that, did you, unenlightened, return to your ship, you, my best friend, with all who might be with you, stolen upon, that night, in your hammocks, would never in this world have wakened again. Do but think how you walked this deck, how you sat in this cabin, every inch of ground mined into honeycombs under you. Had I dropped the least hint, made the least advance towards an understanding between us, death, explosive death — yours as mine — would have ended the scene."

"True, true," cried Captain Delano, starting, "you saved my life, Don Benito, more than I yours; saved it, too, against my knowledge and will."

"Nay, my friend," rejoined the Spaniard, courteous even to the point of religion, "God charmed your life, but you saved mine. To think of some things you did — those smilings and chattings, rash pointings and gesturings. For less than these, they slew my mate, Raneds; but you had the Prince of Heaven's safe conduct through all ambuscades."

"Yes, all is owing to Providence, I know; but the temper of my mind that morning was more than commonly pleasant, while the sight of so much suffering, more apparent than real, added to my good-nature, compassion, and charity, happily interweaving the three. Had it been otherwise, doubtless, as you hint, some of my interferences might have ended unhappily enough. Besides, those feelings I spoke of enabled me to get the better of momentary distrust, at times when acuteness might have cost me my life, without saving another's. Only at the end did my suspicions get the better of me, and you know how wide of the mark they then proved."

"Wide indeed," said Don Benito, sadly; "you were with me all day; stood with me, sat with me, talked with me, looked at me, ate with me, drank with me; and yet, your last act was to clutch for a monster, not only an innocent man, but the most pitiable of all men. To such degree many malign machinations and deceptions impose. So far may even the best men err, in judging the conduct of one with the recesses of whose condition he is not acquainted. But you were forced to it; and you were in time undeceived. Would that, in both respects, it was so ever, and with all men."

"You generalize, Don Benito; and mournfully enough. But the past is passed; why moralize upon it? Forget it. See, yon bright sun has forgotten it all, and the blue sea, and the blue sky; these have turned over new leaves."

"Because they have no memory," he dejectedly replied; "because they are not human."

"But these mild trades that now fan your cheek, Don Benito, do they not come with a human-like healing to you? Warm friends, steadfast friends are the trades."

"With their steadfastness they but waft me to my tomb, Señor," was the foreboding response.

"You are saved," cried Captain Delano, more and more astonished and pained; "you are saved: what has cast such a shadow upon you?"

"The negro."

There was silence, while the moody man sat, slowly and unconciously gathering his mantle about him, as if it were a pall.

There was no more conversation that day.

But if the Spaniard's melancholy sometimes ended in muteness upon topics like the above, there were others upon which he never spoke at all; on which, indeed, all his old reserves were piled. Pass over the worst and, only to elucidate, let an item or two of these be cited. The dress so precise and costly, worn by him on the day whose events have been narrated, had not willingly been put on.

And that silver-mounted sword, apparent symbol of despotic command, was not, indeed, a sword, but the ghost of one. The scabbard, artificially stiffened, was empty.

As for the black — whose brain, not body, had schemed and led the revolt, with the plot — his slight frame, inadequate to that which it held, had at once yielded to the superior muscular strength of his captor, in the boat. Seeing all was over, he uttered no sound, and could not be forced to. His aspect seemed to say, since I cannot do deeds, I will not speak words. Put in irons in the hold, with the rest, he was carried to Lima. During the passage, Don Benito did not visit him. Nor then, nor at any time after, would he look at him. Before the tribunal he refused. When pressed by the judges he fainted. On the testimony of the sailors alone rested the legal identity of Babo.

Some months after, dragged to the gibbet at the tail of a mule, the black met his voiceless end. The body was burned to ashes; but for many days, the head, that hive of subtlety, fixed on a pole in the Plaza, met, unabashed, the gaze of the whites; and across the Plaza looked towards St. Bartholomew's church, in whose vaults slept then, as now, the recovered bones of Aranda: and across the Rimac bridge looked toward the monastery, on Mount Agonia without; where, three months after being dismissed by the court, Benito Cereno, borne on the bier, did, indeed, follow his leader.

JOHN GREENLEAF WHITTIER (1807–1892)

In the farmhouse at Haverhill, Mass., which he has romantically described in *Snow-Bound*, Whittier was born of Quaker parents whose ancestors had been in Massachusetts since 1638. Brought up in the busy life of a farm boy, Whittier at the age of fourteen read a volume of Burns and began to scribble verses. Some of these appeared in *The Free Press*, a weekly edited in Newburyport by William Lloyd Garrison. Garrison became interested in his young contributor and urged the boy's parents to supplement their son's scanty education by sending him to Haverhill Academy. Whittier studied at the academy during 1827 and 1828, and began his career as a cobbler, a teacher, and an editor of journals in Boston and Hartford.

In 1831 he published his first work, *Legends of New England in Prose and Verse*, and two years later entered the lists for abolition with a pamphlet entitled *Justice and Expediency*. That year, 1833, was a turning point in Whittier's career, just as 1832 had been a turning point in Emerson's. In *The Tent on the Beach* he described himself as

> a dreamer born,
> Who, with a mission to fulfill,
> Had left the Muses' haunts to turn
> The crank of an opinion mill.

The next three decades, the most vigorous years of his life, Whittier gave to his opinion mill. He was a delegate to the anti-slavery convention of 1833 in Philadelphia. He served in the Massachusetts legislature in 1835 and 1836. In this position, and publicly by prose, verse, and speech, he never ceased to argue against slavery. He risked his life before hostile mobs, he gave up his political career, and he spent strength and spirit on controversial publications that he might better have spent, many think, on other works. From 1838 until 1840 he edited *The Pennsylvania Freeman*. In 1843 he published *Lays of My Home*, and, in 1846, *Voices of Freedom*. A collected edition of his *Poems* appeared in 1848, and two years later *Songs of Labor*.

When the War of the Secession was at an end, Whittier settled down to the peaceful years he had earned. Almost three decades before this, he had established his home at Amesbury, and at this quiet spot he recalled his early years and wrote *Snow-Bound* in 1865. *The Tent on the Beach* was published in 1867 and *The Pennsylvania Pilgrim* in 1872. His seventieth and eightieth birthdays were celebrated by his readers throughout the country.

The standard edition is the Riverside, 7 volumes, 1888. H. E. Scudder edited the Cambridge edition of the poetical works, 1894. Standard early lives are by S. T. Pickard, 1894, and F. H. Underwood, 1884. These are superseded in some respects by Albert Mordell, 1941, and Whitman Bennett, 1941. Whittier's criticism has been collected by H. H. Clark and E. L. Cady, 1950. T. F. Currier's *Bibliography*, 1937, is an important reference work.

Forgiveness

(1846?)

My heart was heavy, for its trust had been
Abused, its kindness answered with foul
    wrong;
So, turning gloomily from my fellow-men,
One summer Sabbath day I strolled among
The green mounds of the village burial-
    place;   5
Where, pondering how all human love and
    hate
Find one sad level; and how, soon or late,
Wronged and wrongdoer, each with meek-
    ened face,
And cold hands folded over a still heart,

Pass the green threshold of our common
    grave,   10
Whither all footsteps tend, whence none
    depart,
Awed for myself, and pitying my race,
Our common sorrow, like a mighty wave,
Swept all my pride away, and trembling I
    forgave!

Ichabod

(1850)

"This poem," said Whittier, "was the outcome of the surprise and grief and forecast of evil consequences which I felt on reading the Seventh of March speech of Daniel Webster in support of the

'Compromise,' and the Fugitive Slave Law. No partisan or personal enmity dictated it. On the contrary my admiration of the splendid personality and intellectual power of the great senator was never stronger than when I laid down his speech, and, in one of the saddest moments of my life, penned my protest."

For the significance of the title, see 1 *Samuel*, IV, 19–22 ("And she named the child Ichabod, saying, The glory is departed from Israel").

So fallen! so lost! the light withdrawn
 Which once he wore!
The glory from his gray hairs gone
 Forevermore!

Revile him not, the Tempter hath 5
 A snare for all;
And pitying tears, not scorn and wrath,
 Befit his fall!

Oh, dumb be passion's stormy rage,
 When he who might   10
Have lighted up and led his age,
 Falls back in night.

Scorn! would the angels laugh, to mark
 A bright soul driven,
Fiend-goaded, down the endless dark, 15
 From hope and heaven!

Let not the land once proud of him
 Insult him now,
Nor brand with deeper shame his dim,
 Dishonored brow. 20

But let its humbled sons, instead,
 From sea to lake,
A long lament, as for the dead,
 In sadness make.

Of all we loved and honored, naught 25
 Save power remains;
A fallen angel's pride of thought,
 Still strong in chains.

All else is gone; from those great eyes
 The soul has fled: 30
When faith is lost, when honor dies,
 The man is dead!

Then pay the reverence of old days
 To his dead fame;
Walk backward, with averted gaze, 35
 And hide the shame!

First-Day Thoughts

(1852)

In calm and cool and silence, once again
 I find my old accustomed place among
 My brethren, where, perchance, no human tongue
 Shall utter words; where never hymn is sung,
 Nor deep-toned organ blown, nor censer swung, 5
Nor dim light falling through the pictured pane!
There, syllabled by silence, let me hear
The still small voice which reached the prophet's ear;
Read in my heart a still diviner law
Than Israel's leader on his tables saw! 10
There let me strive with each besetting sin
 Recall my wandering fancies, and restrain
 The sore disquiet of a restless brain;
 And, as the path of duty is made plain,
May grace be given that I may walk therein, 15
Not like the hireling, for his selfish gain,
With backward glances and reluctant tread,
Making a merit of his coward dread,
 But, cheerful, in the light around me thrown,
 Walking as one to pleasant service led; 20
 Doing God's will as if it were my own,
Yet trusting not in mine, but in his strength alone!

The Barefoot Boy

(1855)

Blessings on thee, little man,
Barefoot boy, with cheek of tan!
With thy turned-up pantaloons,
And thy merry whistled tunes;
With thy red lip, redder still 5
Kissed by strawberries on the hill;
With the sunshine on thy face,
Through thy torn brim's jaunty grace;
From my heart I give thee joy, —
I was once a barefoot boy! 10
Prince thou art, — the grown-up man
Only is republican.
Let the million-dollared ride!
Barefoot, trudging at his side,

Thou hast more than he can buy 15
In the reach of ear and eye, —
Outward sunshine, inward joy:
Blessings on thee, barefoot boy!

Oh for boyhood's painless play,
Sleep that wakes in laughing day, 20
Health that mocks the doctor's rules,
Knowledge never learned of schools,
Of the wild bee's morning chase,
Of the wild-flower's time and place,
Flight of fowl and habitude 25
Of the tenants of the wood;
How the tortoise bears his shell,
How the woodchuck digs his cell,
And the ground-mole sinks his well;
How the robin feeds her young, 30
How the oriole's nest is hung;
Where the whitest lilies blow,
Where the freshest berries grow,
Where the ground-nut trails its vine,
Where the wood-grape's clusters shine; 35
Of the black wasp's cunning way,
Mason of his walls of clay,
And the architectural plans
Of gray hornet artisans!
For, eschewing books and tasks, 40
Nature answers all he asks;
Hand in hand with her he walks,
Face to face with her he talks,
Part and parcel of her joy, —
Blessings on the barefoot boy! 45

Oh for boyhood's time of June,
Crowding years in one brief moon,
When all things I heard or saw,
Me, their master, waited for.
I was rich in flowers and trees, 50
Humming-birds and honey-bees;
For my sport the squirrel played,
Plied the snouted mole his spade;
For my taste the blackberry cone
Purpled over hedge and stone; 55
Laughed the brook for my delight
Through the day and through the night,
Whispering at the garden wall,
Talked with me from fall to fall;
Mine the sand-rimmed pickerel pond, 60
Mine the walnut slopes beyond,
Mine, on bending orchard trees,
Apples of Hesperides!
Still as my horizon grew,

Larger grew my riches too; 65
All the world I saw or knew
Seemed a complex Chinese toy,
Fashioned for a barefoot boy!

Oh, for festal dainties spread,
Like my bowl of milk and bread; 70
Pewter spoon and bowl of wood,
On the door-stone, gray and rude!
O'er me, like a regal tent,
Cloudy-ribbed, the sunset bent,
Purple-curtained, fringed with gold, 75
Looped in many a wind-swung fold;
While for music came the play
Of the pied frogs' orchestra;
And, to light the noisy choir,
Lit the fly his lamp of fire. 80
I was monarch: pomp and joy
Waited on the barefoot boy!

Cheerily, then, my little man,
Live and laugh, as boyhood can!
Though the flinty slopes be hard, 85
Stubble-speared the new-mown sward,
Every morn shall lead thee through
Fresh baptisms of the dew;
Every evening from thy feet
Shall the cool wind kiss the heat: 90
All too soon these feet must hide
In the prison cells of pride,
Lose the freedom of the sod,
Like a colt's for work be shod,
Made to tread the mills of toil, 95
Up and down in ceaseless moil:
Happy if their track be found
Never on forbidden ground;
Happy if they sink not in
Quick and treacherous sands of sin. 100
Ah! that thou couldst know thy joy,
Ere it passes, barefoot boy!

Skipper Ireson's Ride
(1828, 1857)

Of all the rides since the birth of time,
Told in story or sung in rhyme, —
On Apuleius's Golden Ass,
Or one-eyed Calender's horse of brass,
Witch astride of a human back, 5
Islam's prophet on Al-Borák, —
The strangest ride that ever was sped

Was Ireson's, out from Marblehead!
Old Floyd Ireson, for his hard heart,
　Tarred and feathered and carried in a cart
　　By the women of Marblehead!　　11

Body of turkey, head of owl,
Wings a-droop like a rained-on fowl,
Feathered and ruffled in every part,
Skipper Ireson stood in the cart.　　15
Scores of women, old and young,
Strong of muscle, and glib of tongue,
Pushed and pulled up the rocky lane,
Shouting and singing the shrill refrain:
　"Here's Flud Oirson, fur his horrd horrt,
　Torr'd an' futherr'd an' corr'd in a corrt　21
　　By the women o' Morble'ead!"

Wrinkled scolds with hands on hips,
Girls in bloom of cheek and lips,
Wild-eyed, free-limbed, such as chase　25
Bacchus round some antique vase,
Brief of skirt, with ankles bare,
Loose of kerchief and loose of hair,
With conch-shells blowing and fish-horns'
　　twang,
Over and over the Maenads sang:　　30
　"Here's Flud Oirson, fur his horrd horrt,
　Torr'd an' futherr'd an' corr'd in a corrt
　　By the women o' Morble'ead!"

Small pity for him! — He sailed away
From a leaking ship in Chaleur Bay, —　35
Sailed away from a sinking wreck,
With his own town's-people on her deck!
"Lay by! lay by!" they called to him.
Back he answered, "Sink or swim!
Brag of your catch of fish again!"　40
And off he sailed through the fog and rain!
Old Floyd Ireson, for his hard heart,
　Tarred and feathered and carried in a cart
　　By the women of Marblehead!

Fathoms deep in dark Chaleur　　45
That wreck shall lie forevermore.
Mother and sister, wife and maid,
Looked from the rocks of Marblehead
Over the moaning and rainy sea, —
Looked for the coming that might not be!　50
What did the winds and the sea-birds say
Of the cruel captain who sailed away —?
　Old Floyd Ireson, for his hard heart,

　Tarred and feathered and carried in a cart
　　By the women of Marblehead!　　55
Through the street, on either side,
Up flew windows, doors swung wide;
Sharp-tongued spinsters, old wives gray,
Treble lent the fish-horn's bray.
Sea-worn grandsires, cripple-bound,　50
Hulks of old sailors run aground,
Shock head, and fist, and hat, and cane,
And cracked with curses the hoarse refrain:
　"Here's Flud Oirson, fur his horrd horrt,
　Torr'd an' futherr'd an' corr'd in a corrt　65
　　By the women o' Morble'ead!"

Sweetly along the Salem road
Bloom of orchard and lilac showed.
Little the wicked skipper knew
Of the fields so green and the sky so blue.　70
Riding there in his sorry trim,
Like an Indian idol glum and grim,
Scarcely he seemed the sound to hear
Of voices shouting, far and near:
　"Here's Flud Oirson, fur his horrd horrt,　75
　Torr'd an' futherr'd an' corr'd in a corrt
　　By the women o' Morble'ead!"

"Hear me, neighbors!" at last he cried, —
"What to me is this noisy ride?
What is the shame that clothes the skin　80
To the nameless horror that lives within?
Waking or sleeping, I see a wreck,
And hear a cry from a reeling deck!
Hate me and curse me, — I only dread
The hand of God and the face of the dead!"
　Said old Floyd Ireson, for his hard heart,　86
　Tarred and feathered and carried in a cart
　　By the women of Marblehead!

Then the wife of the skipper lost at sea
Said, "God has touched him! why should
　　we!"　　90
Said an old wife mourning her only son,
"Cut the rogue's tether and let him run!"
So with soft relentings and rude excuse,
Half scorn, half pity, they cut him loose,
And gave him a cloak to hide him in,　95
And left him alone with his shame and sin.
　Poor Floyd Ireson, for his hard heart,
　Tarred and feathered and carried in a cart
　　By the women of Marblehead!

Telling the Bees

(1858)

"A remarkable custom, brought from the Old Country, formerly prevailed in the rural districts of New England. On the death of a member of the family, the bees were at once informed of the event, and their hives dressed in mourning. This ceremonial was supposed to be necessary to prevent the swarms from leaving their hives and seeking a new home" (Whittier). The place Whittier had in mind in writing this poem was his birthplace.

Here is the place; right over the hill
  Runs the path I took;
You can see the gap in the old wall still,
  And the stepping-stones in the shallow
    brook.

There is the house, with the gate red-barred,
  And the poplars tall;   6
And the barn's brown length, and the cattle-
    yard,
  And the white horns tossing above the wall.

There are the beehives ranged in the sun;
  And down by the brink   10
Of the brook are her poor flowers, weed-
    o'errun,
  Pansy and daffodil, rose and pink.

A year has gone, as the tortoise goes,
  Heavy and slow;
And the same rose blows, and the same sun
    glows,   15
  And the same brook sings of a year ago.

There's the same sweet clover-smell in the
    breeze;
  And the June sun warm
Tangles his wings of fire in the trees,
  Setting, as then, over Fernside farm.   20

I mind me how with a lover's care
  From my Sunday coat
I brushed off the burrs, and smoothed my
    hair,
  And cooled at the brookside my brow and
    throat.

Since we parted, a month had passed, —   25
  To love, a year;

Down through the beeches I looked at last
  On the little red gate and the well-sweep
    near.

I can see it all now, — the slantwise rain
  Of light through the leaves,   30
The sundown's blaze on her window-pane,
  The bloom of her roses under the eaves.

Just the same as a month before, —
  The house and the trees,
The barn's brown gable, the vine by the
    door, —   35
  Nothing changed but the hives of bees.

Before them, under the garden wall,
  Forward and back,
Went drearily singing the chore-girl small,
  Draping each hive with a shred of black.   40

Trembling, I listened: the summer sun
  Had the chill of snow;
For I knew she was telling the bees of one
  Gone on the journey we all must go!

Then I said to myself, "My Mary weeps   45
  For the dead to-day:
Haply her blind old grandsire sleeps
  The fret and the pain of his age away."

But her dog whined low; on the doorway sill,
  With his cane to his chin,   50
The old man sat; and the chore-girl still
  Sung to the bees stealing out and in.

And the song she was singing ever since
  In my ear sounds on: —
"Stay at home, pretty bees, fly not hence!   55
  Mistress Mary is dead and gone!"

Barbara Frietchie

(1863)

"The poem of 'Barbara Frietchie,'" Whittier said, "was written in good faith. The story was no invention of mine. It came to me from sources which I regarded as entirely reliable; it had been published in newspapers, and had gained public credence in Washington and Maryland before my poem was written. I had no reason to doubt its accuracy then, and I am still constrained to believe that it had foundation in fact." If the story did have "foundation in fact," it is probable that the fact was very freely elaborated in the version that Whittier followed.

Up from the meadows rich with corn,
Clear in the cool September morn,

The clustered spires of Frederick stand
Green-walled by the hills of Maryland.

Round about them orchards sweep, 5
Apple and peach tree fruited deep,

Fair as the garden of the Lord
To the eyes of the famished rebel horde,

On that pleasant morn of the early fall
When Lee marched over the mountain-
wall; 10

Over the mountains winding down,
Horse and foot, into Frederick town.

Forty flags with their silver stars,
Forty flags with their crimson bars,

Flapped in the morning wind: the sun 15
Of noon looked down, and saw not one.

Up rose old Barbara Frietchie then,
Bowed with her fourscore years and ten;

Bravest of all in Frederick town,
She took up the flag the men hauled down; 20

In her attic window the staff she set,
To show that one heart was loyal yet.

Up the street came the rebel tread,
Stonewall Jackson riding ahead.

Under his slouched hat left and right 25
He glanced; the old flag met his sight.

"Halt!" — the dust-brown ranks stood fast,
"Fire!" — out blazed the rifle-blast.

It shivered the window, pane and sash;
It rent the banner with seam and gash. 30

Quick, as it fell, from the broken staff
Dame Barbara snatched the silken scarf.

She leaned far out on the window-sill,
And shook it forth with a royal will.

"Shoot, if you must, this old gray head, 35
But spare your country's flag," she said.

A shade of sadness, a blush of shame,
Over the face of the leader came;

The nobler nature within him stirred
To life at that woman's deed and word; 40

"Who touches a hair on yon gray head
Dies like a dog! March on!" he said.

All day long through Frederick street
Sounded the tread of marching feet:

All day long that free flag tost 45
Over the heads of the rebel host.

Ever its torn folds rose and fell
On the loyal winds that loved it well;

And through the hill-gaps sunset light
Shone over it with a warm good-night. 50

Barbara Frietchie's work is o'er,
And the Rebel rides on his raids no more.

Honor to her! and let a tear
Fall, for her sake, on Stonewall's bier.

Over Barbara Frietchie's grave, 55
Flag of Freedom and Union, wave!

Peace and order and beauty draw
Round thy symbol of light and law;

And ever the stars above look down
On thy stars below in Frederick town! 60

Laus Deo!

(1865)

"The poem 'Laus Deo!' was suggested to Mr. Whittier as he sat in the Friends' meeting-house in Amesbury, and listened to the bells and the cannon which were proclaiming the passage of the constitutional amendment abolishing slavery, in 1865. It was the regular Fifth day meeting, and as the Friends sat in silence, their hearts responded to the joy that filled all the outside air" (Pickard, II, 488). "The poem," said Whittier, "wrote itself, or rather sang itself, while the bells rang."

It is done!
Clang of bell and roar of gun
Send the tidings up and down.
How the belfries rock and reel!
How the great guns, peal on peal,   5
Fling the joy from town to town!

Ring, O bells!
Every stroke exulting tells
Of the burial hour of crime.
Loud and long, that all may hear,   10
Ring for every listening ear
Of Eternity and Time!

Let us kneel:
God's own voice is in that peal,
And this spot is holy ground.   15
Lord, forgive us! What are we,
That our eyes this glory see,
That our ears have heard the sound!

For the Lord
On the whirlwind is abroad;   20
In the earthquake He has spoken:
He has smitten with this thunder
The iron walls asunder,
And the gates of brass are broken!

Loud and long   25
Lift the old exulting song;
Sing with Miriam by the sea,
He has cast the mighty down;
Horse and rider sink and drown;
"He hath triumphed gloriously!"   30

Did we dare,
In our agony of prayer,
Ask for more than He has done?
When was ever his right hand
Over any time or land   35
Stretched as now beneath the sun?

How they pale,
Ancient myth and song and tale,
In this wonder of our days,
When the cruel rod of war   40
Blossoms white with righteous law
And the wrath of man is praise!

Blotted out!
All within and all about
Shall a fresher life begin;   45

Freer breathe the universe
As it rolls its heavy curse
On the dead and buried sin!

It is done!
In the circuit of the sun   50
Shall the sound thereof go forth.
It shall bid the sad rejoice,
It shall give the dumb a voice,
It shall belt with joy the earth!

Ring and swing,   55
Bells of joy! On morning's wing
Send the song of praise abroad!
With a sound of broken chains
Tell the nations that He reigns,
Who alone is Lord and God!   60

The Eternal Goodness

(1865)

O Friends! with whom my feet have trod
The quiet aisles of prayer,
Glad witness to your zeal for God
And love of man I bear.

I trace your lines of argument;   5
Your logic linked and strong
I weigh as one who dreads dissent,
And fears a doubt as wrong.

But still my human hands are weak
To hold your iron creeds: 10
Against the words ye bid me speak
My heart within me pleads.

Who fathoms the Eternal Thought?
Who talks of scheme and plan?
The Lord is God! He needeth not   15
The poor device of man.

I walk with bare, hushed feet the ground
Ye tread with boldness shod;
I dare not fix with mete and bound
The love and power of God.   20

Ye praise his justice; even such
His pitying love I deem:
Ye seek a king; I fain would touch
The robe that hath no seam.

Ye see the curse which overbroods 25
   A world of pain and loss;
I hear our Lord's beatitudes
   And prayer upon the cross.

More than your schoolmen teach, within
   Myself, alas! I know: 30
Too dark ye cannot paint the sin,
   Too small the merit show.

I bow my forehead to the dust,
   I veil mine eyes for shame,
And urge, in trembling self-distrust, 35
   A prayer without a claim.

I see the wrong that round me lies,
   I feel the guilt within;
I hear, with groan and travail-cries,
   The world confess its sin. 40

Yet, in the maddening maze of things,
   And tossed by storm and flood,
To one fixed trust my spirit clings;
   I know that God is good!

Not mine to look where cherubim 45
   And seraphs may not see,
But nothing can be good in Him
   Which evil is in me.

The wrong that pains my soul below
   I dare not throne above, 50
I know not of his hate, — I know
   His goodness and his love.

I dimly guess from blessings known
   Of greater out of sight,
And, with the chastened Psalmist, own 55
   His judgments too are right.

I long for household voices gone,
   For vanished smiles I long,
But God hath led my dear ones on,
   And he can do no wrong. 60

I know not what the future hath
   Of marvel or surprise,
Assured alone that life and death
   His mercy underlies.

And if my heart and flesh are weak 65
   To bear an untried pain,

The bruisèd reed He will not break,
   But strengthen and sustain.

No offering of my own I have,
   Nor works my faith to prove; 70
I can but give the gifts He gave,
   And plead his love for love.

And so beside the Silent Sea
   I wait the muffled oar;
No harm from Him can come to me 75
   On ocean or on shore.

I know not where his islands lift
   Their fronded palms in air;
I only know I cannot drift
   Beyond his love and care. 80

O brothers! if my faith is vain,
   If hopes like these betray,
Pray for me that my feet may gain
   The sure and safer way.

And Thou, O Lord! by whom are seen 85
   Thy creatures as they be,
Forgive me if too close I lean
   My human heart on Thee!

Snow-Bound

A WINTER IDYL

(1865)

"The inmates of the family at the Whittier homestead who are referred to in the poem were my father, mother, my brother and two sisters, and my uncle and aunt, both unmarried. In addition, there was the district schoolmaster, who boarded with us. The 'not unfeared, half-welcome guest' was Harriet Livermore, daughter of Judge Livermore, of New Hampshire, a young woman of fine natural ability, enthusiastic, eccentric, with slight control over her violent temper, which sometimes made her religious profession doubtful. She was equally ready to exhort in school-house prayer-meetings and dance in a Washington ball-room, while her father was a member of Congress. She early embraced the doctrine of the Second Advent, and felt it her duty to proclaim the Lord's speedy coming. With this message she crossed the Atlantic and spent the greater part of a long life in travelling over Europe and Asia" (Whittier).

As the Spirits of Darkness be stronger in the dark, so Good Spirits, which be Angels of Light, are augmented not only by the Divine light of the

Sun, but also by our common VVood Fire: and as the Celestial Fire drives away dark spirits, so also this our Fire of VVood doth the same. — COR. AGRIPPA, *Occult Philosophy*, Book I. ch. v.

Announced by all the trumpets of the sky,
Arrives the snow, and, driving o'er the fields,
Seems nowhere to alight: the whited air
Hides hills and woods, the river and the heaven,
And veils the farm-house at the garden's end.
The sled and traveller stopped, the courier's feet
Delayed, all friends shut out, the housemates sit
Around the radiant fireplace, enclosed
In a tumultuous privacy of storm.
                    EMERSON. *The Snow Storm.*

The sun that brief December day
Rose cheerless over hills of gray,
And, darkly circled, gave at noon
A sadder light than waning moon.
Slow tracing down the thickening sky   5
Its mute and ominous prophecy,
A portent seeming less than threat,
It sank from sight before it set.
A chill no coat, however stout,
Of homespun stuff could quite shut out, · 10
A hard, dull bitterness of cold,
That checked, mid-vein, the circling race
Of life-blood in the sharpened face,
The coming of the snow-storm told.
The wind blew east; we heard the roar   15
Of Ocean on his wintry shore,
And felt the strong pulse throbbing there
Beat with low rhythm our inland air.

Meanwhile we did our nightly chores, —
Brought in the wood from out of doors,   20
Littered the stalls, and from the mows
Raked down the herd's-grass for the cows:
Heard the horse whinnying for his corn;
And, sharply clashing horn on horn,
Impatient down the stanchion rows   25
The cattle shake their walnut bows;
While, peering from his early perch
Upon the scaffold's pole of birch,
The cock his crested helmet bent
And down his querulous challenge sent.   30

Unwarmed by any sunset light
The gray day darkened into night,
A night made hoary with the swarm
And whirl-dance of the blinding storm,
As zigzag, wavering to and fro,   35
Crossed and recrossed the wingèd snow:
And ere the early bedtime came

The white drift piled the window-frame,
And through the glass the clothes-line posts
Looked in like tall and sheeted ghosts.   40

So all night long the storm roared on:
The morning broke without a sun;
In tiny spherule traced with lines
Of Nature's geometric signs,
In starry flake, and pellicle,   45
All day the hoary meteor fell;
And, when the second morning shone,
We looked upon a world unknown,
On nothing we could call our own.
Around the glistening wonder bent   50
The blue walls of the firmament,
No cloud above, no earth below, —
A universe of sky and snow!
The old familiar sights of ours
Took marvellous shapes; strange domes and
        towers   55
Rose up where sty or corn-crib stood,
Or garden-wall, or belt of wood;
A smooth white mound the brush-pile
        showed,
A fenceless drift what once was road;
The bridle-post an old man sat   60
With loose-flung coat and high cocked hat;
The well-curb had a Chinese roof;
And even the long sweep, high aloof,
In its slant splendor, seemed to tell
Of Pisa's leaning miracle.   65

A prompt, decisive man, no breath
Our father wasted: "Boys, a path!"
Well pleased (for when did farmer boy
Count such a summons less than joy?)
Our buskins on our feet we drew;   70
With mittened hands, and caps drawn low,
To guard our necks and ears from snow,
We cut the solid whiteness through.
And, where the drift was deepest, made
A tunnel walled and overlaid   75
With dazzling crystal: we had read
Of rare Aladdin's wondrous cave,
And to our own his name we gave,
With many a wish the luck were ours
To test his lamp's supernal powers.   80
We reached the barn with merry din,
And roused the prisoned brutes within.
The old horse thrust his long head out,
And grave with wonder gazed about;
The cock his lusty greeting said,   85

And forth his speckled harem led;
The oxen lashed their tails, and hooked,
And mild reproach of hunger looked;
The hornèd patriarch of the sheep,
Like Egypt's Amun roused from sleep,   90
Shook his sage head with gesture mute,
And emphasized with stamp of foot.

All day the gusty north-wind bore
The loosening drift its breath before;
Low circling round its southern zone,   95
The sun through dazzling snow-mist shone.
No church-bell lent its Christian tone
To the savage air, no social smoke
Curled over woods of snow-hung oak.
A solitude made more intense   100
By dreary-voicèd elements,
The shrieking of the mindless wind,
The moaning tree-boughs swaying blind,
And on the glass the unmeaning beat
Of ghostly finger-tips of sleet.   105
Beyond the circle of our hearth
No welcome sound of toil or mirth
Unbound the spell, and testified
Of human life and thought outside.
We minded that the sharpest ear   110
The buried brooklet could not hear.
The music of whose liquid lip
Had been to us companionship,
And, in our lonely life, had grown
To have an almost human tone.   115

As night drew on, and, from the crest
Of wooded knolls that ridged the west,
The sun, a snow-blown traveller, sank
From sight beneath the smothering bank,
We piled, with care, our nightly stack.   120
Of wood against the chimney-back, —
The oaken log, green, huge, and thick,
And on its top the stout back-stick;
The knotty forestick laid apart,
And filled between with curious art   125
The ragged brush; then, hovering near,
We watched the first red blaze appear,
Heard the sharp crackle, caught the gleam
On whitewashed wall and sagging beam,
Until the old, rude-furnished room   130
Burst, flower-like, into rosy bloom;
While radiant with a mimic flame
Outside the sparkling drift became,
And through the bare-boughed lilac-tree
Our own warm hearth seemed blazing free.

The crane and pendent trammels showed,   136
The Turks' heads on the andirons glowed:
While childish fancy, prompt to tell
The meaning of the miracle,
Whispered the old rhyme: "*Under the tree,*
When fire outdoors burns merrily,   141
There the witches are making tea."
The moon above the eastern wood
Shone at its full; the hill-range stood
Transfigured in the silver flood,   145
Its blown snows flashing cold and keen,
Dead white, save where some sharp ravine
Took shadow, or the sombre green
Of hemlocks turned to pitchy black
Against the whiteness at their back.   150
For such a world and such a night
Most fitting that unwarming light,
Which only seemed where'er it fell
To make the coldness visible.

Shut in from all the world without,   155
We sat the clean-winged hearth about,
Content to let the north-wind roar
In baffled rage at pane and door,
While the red logs before us beat
The frost-line back with tropic heat;   160
And ever, when a louder blast
Shook beam and rafter as it passed,
The merrier up its roaring draught
The great throat of the chimney laughed;
The house-dog on his paws outspread   165
Laid to the fire his drowsy head,
The cat's dark silhouette on the wall
A couchant tiger's seemed to fall;
And, for the winter fireside meet,
Between the andirons' straddling feet,   170
The mug of cider simmered slow,
The apples sputtered in a row,
And, close at hand, the basket stood
With nuts from brown October's wood.

What matter how the night behaved?   175
What matter how the north-wind raved?
Blow high, blow low, not all its snow
Could quench our hearth-fire's ruddy glow.
O Time and Change! — with hair as gray
As was my sire's that winter day,   180
How strange it seems, with so much gone
Of life and love, to still live on!
Ah, brother! only I and thou
Are left of all that circle now, —
The dear home faces whereupon   185

That fitful firelight paled and shone.
Henceforward, listen as we will,
The voices of that hearth are still;
Look where we may, the wide earth o'er
Those lighted faces smile no more.   190
We tread the paths their feet have worn,
    We sit beneath their orchard trees,
    We hear, like them, the hum of bees
And rustle of the bladed corn;
We turn the pages that they read,   195
    Their written words we linger o'er,
But in the sun they cast no shade,
No voice is heard, no sign is made,
    No step is on the conscious floor!
Yet Love will dream, and Faith will trust 200
(Since He who knows our need is just)
That somehow, somewhere, meet we must.
Alas for him who never sees
The stars shine through his cypress-trees!
Who, hopeless, lays his dead away,   205
Nor looks to see the breaking day
Across the mournful marbles play!
Who hath not learned, in hours of faith,
    The truth to flesh and sense unknown,
That Life is ever lord of Death,   210
    And Love can never lose its own!

We sped the time with stories old,
Wrought puzzles out, and riddles told,
Or stammered from our school-book lore
"The Chief of Gambia's golden shore."   215
How often since, when all the land
Was clay in Slavery's shaping hand,
As if a far-blown trumpet stirred
The languorous sin-sick air, I heard:
"*Does not the voice of reason cry,*   220
    Claim the first right which Nature gave,
From the red scourge of bondage fly,
    Nor deign to live a burdened slave!"
Our father rode again his ride
On Memphremagog's wooded side;   225
Sat down again to moose and samp
In trapper's hut and Indian camp;
Lived o'er the old idyllic ease
Beneath St. Francois' hemlock-trees;
Again for him the moonlight shone   230
On Norman cap and bodiced zone;
Again he heard the violin play
Which led the village dance away,
And mingled in its merry whirl
The grandam and the laughing girl.   235
Or, nearer home, our steps he led

Where Salisbury's level marshes spread
    Mile-wide as flies the laden bee;
Where merry mowers, hale and strong,
Swept, scythe on scythe, their swaths along
    The low green prairies of the sea.   241
We shared the fishing off Boar's Head,
    And round the rocky Isles of Shoals
    The hake-broil on the drift-wood coals;
The chowder on the sand-beach made,   245
Dipped by the hungry, steaming hot,
With spoons of clam-shell from the pot.
We heard the tales of witchcraft old,
And dream and sign and marvel told
To sleepy listeners as they lay   250
Stretched idly on the salted hay,
Adrift along the winding shores,
When favoring breezes deigned to blow
The square sail of the gundelow
And idle lay the useless oars.   255

Our mother, while she turned her wheel
Or run the new-knit stocking-heel,
Told how the Indian hordes came down
At midnight on Cocheco town,
And how her own great-uncle bore   260
His cruel scalp-mark to fourscore.
Recalling, in her fitting phrase,
    So rich and picturesque and free
    (The common unrhymed poetry
Of simple life and country ways),   265
The story of her early days, —
She made us welcome to her home;
Old hearths grew wide to give us room;
We stole with her a frightened look
At the gray wizard's conjuring-book,   270
The fame whereof went far and wide
Through all the simple country-side;
We heard the hawks at twilight play,
The boat-horn on Piscataqua,
The loon's weird laughter far away;   275
We fished her little trout-brook, knew
What flowers in wood and meadow grew,
What sunny hillsides autumn-brown
She climbed to shake the ripe nuts down,
Saw where in sheltered cove and bay   280
The ducks' black squadron anchored lay,
And heard the wild-geese calling loud
Beneath the gray November cloud.

Then, haply, with a look more grave,
And soberer tone, some tale she gave   285
From painful Sewel's ancient tome,

Beloved in every Quaker home,
Of faith fire-winged by martyrdom,
Or Chalkley's Journal, old and quaint, —
Gentlest of skippers, rare sea-saint! —   290
Who, when the dreary calms prevailed,
And water-butt and bread-cask failed,
And cruel, hungry eyes pursued
His portly presence mad for food,
With dark hints muttered under breath   295
Of casting lots for life or death,
Offered, if Heaven withheld supplies,
To be himself the sacrifice.
Then, suddenly, as if to save
The good man from his living grave,   300
A ripple on the water grew,
A school of porpoise flashed in view.
"Take, eat," he said, "and be content;
These fishes in my stead are sent
By Him who gave the tangled ram   305
To spare the child of Abraham."

Our uncle, innocent of books,
Was rich in lore of fields and brooks,
The ancient teachers never dumb
Of Nature's unhoused lyceum.   310
In moons and tides and weather wise,
He read the clouds as prophecies,
And foul or fair could well divine,
By many an occult hint and sign,
Holding the cunning-warded keys   315
To all the woodcraft mysteries;
Himself to Nature's heart so near
That all her voices in his ear
Of beast or bird had meanings clear,
Like Apollonius of old,   320
Who knew the tales the sparrows told,
Or Hermes, who interpreted
What the sage cranes of Nilus said;
A simple, guileless, childlike man,
Content to live where life began;   325
Strong only on his native grounds,
The little world of sights and sounds
Whose girdle was the parish bounds,
Whereof his fondly partial pride
The common features magnified,   330
As Surrey hills to mountains grew
In White of Selborne's loving view, —
He told how teal and loon he shot,
And how the eagle's eggs he got,
The feats on pond and river done,   335
The prodigies of rod and gun;
Till, warming with the tales he told,

Forgotten was the outside cold,
The bitter wind unheeded blew,
From ripening corn the pigeons flew,   340
The partridge drummed i' the wood, the mink
Went fishing down the river-brink;
In fields with bean or clover gay,
The woodchuck, like a hermit gray,
Peered from the doorway of his cell;   345
The muskrat plied the mason's trade,
And tier by tier his mud-walls laid;
And from the shagbark overhead
The grizzled squirrel dropped his shell.

Next, the dear aunt, whose smile of cheer   350
And voice in dreams I see and hear —
The sweetest woman ever Fate
Perverse denied a household mate,
Who, lonely, homeless, not the less
Found peace in love's unselfishness,   355
And welcome whereso'er she went,
A calm and gracious element,
Whose presence seemed the sweet income
And womanly atmosphere of home —
Called up her girlhood memories,   360
The huskings and the apple-bees,
The sleigh-rides and the summer sails,
Weaving through all the poor details
And homespun warp of circumstance
A golden woof-thread of romance.   365
For well she kept her genial mood
And simple faith of maidenhood;
Before her still a cloud-land lay,
The mirage loomed across her way;
The morning dew, that dries so soon   370
With others, glistened at her noon;
Through years of toil and soil and care,
From glossy tress to thin gray hair,
All unprofaned she held apart
The virgin fancies of the heart.   375
Be shame to him of woman born
Who hath for such but thought of scorn.

There, too, our elder sister plied
Her evening task the stand beside;
A full, rich nature, free to trust,   380
Truthful and almost sternly just,
Impulsive, earnest, prompt to act,
And make her generous thought a fact,
Keeping with many a light disguise
The secret of self-sacrifice.   385
O heart sore-tried! thou hast the best,
That Heaven itself could give thee, — rest,

Rest from all bitter thoughts and things!
　How many a poor one's blessing went
　With thee beneath the low green tent　390
Whose curtain never outward swings!

As one who held herself a part
Of all she saw, and let her heart
　Against the household bosom lean,
Upon the motley-braided mat　395
Our youngest and our dearest sat,
Lifting her large, sweet, asking eyes,
　Now bathed in the unfading green
And holy peace of Paradise.
Oh, looking from some heavenly hill,　400
　Or from the shade of saintly palms,
　Or silver reach of river calms,
Do those large eyes behold me still?
With me one little year ago: —
The chill weight of the winter snow　405
　For months upon her grave has lain;
And now, when summer south-winds blow
　And brier and harebell bloom again,
I tread the pleasant paths we trod,
I see the violet-sprinkled sod　410
Whereon she leaned, too frail and weak
The hillside flowers she loved to seek,
Yet following me where'er I went
With dark eyes full of love's content.
The birds are glad; the brier-rose fills　415
The air with sweetness; all the hills
Stretch green to June's unclouded sky,
But still I wait with ear and eye
For something gone which should be nigh,
A loss in all familiar things,　420
In flower that blooms, and bird that sings.
And yet, dear heart! remembering thee,
　Am I not richer than of old?
Safe in thy immortality,　424
　What change can reach the wealth I
　　hold?
What chance can mar the pearl and gold
Thy love hath left in trust with me?
And while in life's late afternoon,
　Where cool and long the shadows grow,
I walk to meet the night that soon　430
　Shall shape and shadow overflow,
I cannot feel that thou art far,
Since near at need the angels are;
And when the sunset gates unbar,
　Shall I not see thee waiting stand,　435
And, white against the evening star,
　The welcome of thy beckoning hand?

Brisk wielder of the birch and rule,
The master of the district school
Held at the fire his favored place,　440
Its warm glow lit a laughing face
Fresh-hued and fair, where scarce appeared
The uncertain prophecy of beard.
He teased the mitten-blinded cat,
Played cross-pins on my uncle's hat,　445
Sang songs, and told us what befalls
In classic Dartmouth's college halls.
Born the wild Northern hills among,
From whence his yeoman father wrung
By patient toil subsistence scant,　450
Not competence and yet not want,
He early gained the power to pay
His cheerful, self-reliant way;
Could doff at ease his scholar's gown
To peddle wares from town to town;　455
Or through the long vacation's reach
In lonely lowland districts teach,
Where all the droll experience found
At stranger hearths in boarding round,
The moonlit skater's keen delight,　460
The sleigh-drive through the frosty night,
The rustic-party, with its rough
Accompaniment of blind-man's-buff,
And whirling-plate, and forfeits paid,
His winter task a pastime made.　465
Happy the snow-locked homes wherein
He tuned his merry violin,
Or played the athlete in the barn,
Or held the good dame's winding-yarn,
Or mirth-provoking versions told　470
Of classic legends rare and old,
Wherein the scenes of Greece and Rome
Had all the commonplace of home,
And little seemed at best the odds
'Twixt Yankee pedlers and old gods;　475
Where Pindus-born Arachthus took
The guise of any grist-mill brook,
And dread Olympus at his will
Became a huckleberry hill.

A careless boy that night he seemed;　480
　But at his desk he had the look
And air of one who wisely schemed,
　And hostage from the future took
　In trainèd thought and lore of book.
Large-brained, clear-eyed, of such as he　485
Shall Freedom's young apostles be,
Who, following in War's bloody trail,
Shall every lingering wrong assail;

All chains from limb and spirit strike,
Uplift the black and white alike;   490
Scatter before their swift advance
The darkness and the ignorance,
The pride, the lust, the squalid sloth,
Which nurtured Treason's monstrous growth,
Made murder pastime, and the hell   495
Of prison-torture possible;
The cruel lie of caste refute,
Old forms remould, and substitute
For Slavery's lash the freeman's will,
For blind routine, wise-handed skill;   500
A school-house plant on every hill,
Stretching in radiate nerve-lines thence
The quick wires of intelligence;
Till North and South together brought
Shall own the same electric thought,   505
In peace a common flag salute,
And, side by side in labor's free
And unresentful rivalry,
Harvest the fields wherein they fought.

Another guest that winter night   510
Flashed back from lustrous eyes the light.
Unmarked by time, and yet not young,
The honeyed music of her tongue
And words of meekness scarcely told
A nature passionate and bold,   515
Strong, self-concentred, spurning guide,
Its milder features dwarfed beside
Her unbent will's majestic pride.
She sat among us, at the best,
A not unfeared, half-welcome guest,   520
Rebuking with her cultured phrase
Our homeliness of words and ways.
A certain pard-like, treacherous grace
Swayed the lithe limbs and dropped the lash,
Lent the white teeth their dazzling flash; 525
And under low brows, black with night,
Rayed out at times a dangerous light;
The sharp heat-lightnings of her face
Presaging ill to him whom Fate
Condemned to share her love or hate.   530
A woman tropical, intense
In thought and act, in soul and sense,
She blended in a like degree
The vixen and the devotee,
Revealing with each freak or feint   535
The temper of Petruchio's Kate,
The raptures of Siena's saint.
Her tapering hand and rounded wrist
Had facile power to form a fist;

The warm, dark languish of her eyes   540
Was never safe from wrath's surprise.
Brows saintly calm and lips devout
Knew every change of scowl and pout;
And the sweet voice had notes more high
And shrill for social battle-cry.   545

Since then what old cathedral town
Has missed her pilgrim staff and gown,
What convent-gate has held its lock
Against the challenge of her knock!
Through Smyrna's plague-hushed thorough-
        fares,   550
Up sea-set Malta's rocky stairs,
Gray olive slopes of hills that hem
    Thy tombs and shrines, Jerusalem,
Or startling on her desert throne
The crazy Queen of Lebanon   555
With claims fantastic as her own,
Her tireless feet have held their way;
And still, unrestful, bowed, and gray,
She watches under Eastern skies,
    With hope each day renewed and fresh,
    The Lord's quick coming in the flesh,   561
Whereof she dreams and prophesies!

Where'er her troubled path may be,
    The Lord's sweet pity with her go!
The outward wayward life we see,   565
    The hidden springs we may not know.
Nor is it given us to discern
    What threads the fatal sisters spun,
    Through what ancestral years has run
The sorrow with the woman born,   570
What forged her cruel chain of moods,
What set her feet in solitudes,
    And held the love within her mute,
What mingled madness in the blood,
    A life-long discord and annoy,   575
    Waters of tears with oil or joy,
And hid within the folded bud
    Perversities of flower and fruit.
It is not ours to separate
    The tangled skein of will and fate,   580
To show what metes and bounds should
        stand
Upon the soul's debatable land,
And between choice and Providence
Divide the circle of events;
But He who knows our frame is just,   585
Merciful and compassionate,
And full of sweet assurances

And hope for all the language is,
That He remembereth we are dust!

At last the great logs, crumbling low,   590
Sent out a dull and duller glow,
The bull's-eye watch that hung in view,
Ticking its weary circuit through,
Pointed with mutely warning sign
Its black hand to the hour of nine.   595
That sign the pleasant circle broke:
My uncle ceased his pipe to smoke,
Knocked from its bowl the refuse gray,
And laid it tenderly away;
Then roused himself to safely cover   600
The dull red brands with ashes over.
And while, with care, our mother laid
The work aside, her steps she stayed
One moment, seeking to express
Her grateful sense of happiness   605
For food and shelter, warmth and health,
And love's contentment more than wealth,
With simple wishes (not the weak,
Vain prayers which no fulfilment seek,
But such as warm the generous heart,   610
O'er-prompt to do with Heaven its part)
That none might lack, that bitter night,
For bread and clothing, warmth and light.

Within our beds awhile we heard
The wind that round the gables roared,   615
With now and then a ruder shock,
Which made our very bedsteads rock.
We heard the loosened clapboards tost,
The board-nails snapping in the frost;
And on us, through the unplastered wall,   620
Felt the light sifted snow-flakes fall.
But sleep stole on, as sleep will do
When hearts are light and life is new;
Faint and more faint the murmurs grew,
Till in the summer-land of dreams   625
They softened to the sound of streams,
Low stir of leaves, and dip of oars,
And lapsing waves on quiet shores.

Next morn we wakened with the shout
Of merry voices high and clear;   630
And saw the teamsters drawing near
To break the drifted highways out.
Down the long hillside treading slow
We saw the half-buried oxen go,
Shaking the snow from heads uptost,   635
Their straining nostrils white with frost.

Before our door the straggling train
Drew up, an added team to gain.
The elders threshed their hands a-cold,
Passed, with the cider-mug, their jokes   640
From lip to lip; the younger folks
Down the loose snow-banks, wrestling, rolled,
Then toiled again the cavalcade
O'er windy hill, through clogged ravine,
And woodland paths that wound be-
tween   645
Low drooping pine-boughs winter-weighed.
From every barn a team afoot,
At every house a new recruit,
Where, drawn by Nature's subtlest law,
Haply the watchful young men saw   650
Sweet doorway pictures of the curls
And curious eyes of merry girls,
Lifting their hands in mock defence
Against the snow-ball's compliments,
And reading in each missive tost   655
The charm with Eden never lost.

We heard once more the sleigh-bells' sound;
And, following where the teamsters led,
The wise old Doctor went his round,
Just pausing at our door to say,   660
In the brief autocratic way
Of one who, prompt at Duty's call,
Was free to urge her claim on all,
That some poor neighbor sick abed
At night our mother's aid would need.   665
For, one in generous thought and deed,
What mattered in the sufferer's sight
The Quaker matron's inward light,
The Doctor's mail of Calvin's creed?
All hearts confess the saints elect   670
Who, twain in faith, in love agree,
And melt not in an acid sect
The Christian pearl of charity!

So days went on: a week had passed
Since the great world was heard from
last.   675
The Almanac we studied o'er,
Read and reread our little store
Of books and pamphlets, scarce a score;
One harmless novel, mostly hid
From younger eyes, a book forbid,   680
And poetry (or good or bad,
A single book was all we had),
Where Ellwood's meek, drab-skirted Muse,
A stranger to the heathen Nine,

Sang, with a somewhat nasal whine, 685
The wars of David and the Jews.
At last the floundering carrier bore
The village paper to our door.
Lo! broadening outward as we read,
To warmer zones the horizon spread; 690
In panoramic length unrolled
We saw the marvels that it told.
Before us passed the painted Creeks,
And daft McGregor on his raids
  In Costa Rica's everglades. (695
And up Taygetos winding slow
Rode Ypsilanti's Mainote Greeks,
A Turk's head at each saddle-bow!
Welcome to us its week-old news,
Its corner for the rustic Muse, 700
  Its monthly gauge of snow and rain,
Its record, mingling in a breath
The wedding bell and dirge of death:
Jest, anecdote, and love-lorn tale,
The latest culprit sent to jail; 705
Its hue and cry of stolen and lost,
Its vendue sales and goods at cost,
  And traffic calling loud for gain.
We felt the stir of hall and street,
The pulse of life that round us beat; 710
The chill embargo of the snow
Was melted in the genial glow;
Wide swung again our ice-locked door,
And all the world was ours once more!

Clasp, Angel of the backward look 715
  And folded wings of ashen gray
  And voice of echoes far away,
The brazen covers of thy book;
The weird palimpsest old and vast,
Wherein thou hid'st the spectral past; 720
Where, closely mingling, pale and glow
The characters of joy and woe;
The monographs of outlived years,
Or smile-illumed or dim with tears,
  Green hills of life that slope to death, 725
And haunts of home, whose vistaed trees
Shade off to mournful cypresses
  With the white amaranths underneath.
Even while I look, I can but heed
  The restless sands' incessant fall, 730
Importunate hours that hours succeed,
Each clamorous with its own sharp need,
  And duty keeping pace with all.
Shut down and clasp the heavy lids;
I hear again the voice that bids 735

The dreamer leave his dream midway
For larger hopes and graver fears;
Life greatens in these later years,
The century's aloe flowers to-day!

Yet, haply, in some lull of life, 740
Some Truce of God which breaks its strife,
The worldling's eyes shall gather dew,
  Dreaming in throngful city ways
Of winter joys his boyhood knew;
And dear and early friends — the few 745
Who yet remain — shall pause to view
  These Flemish pictures of old days;
Sit with me by the homestead hearth,
And stretch the hands of memory forth
  To warm them at the wood-fire's blaze!
And thanks untraced to lips unknown 751
Shall greet me like the odors blown
From unseen meadows newly mown,
Or lilies floating in some pond,
Wood-fringed, the wayside gaze beyond; 755
The traveller owns the grateful sense
Of sweetness near, he knows not whence,
And, pausing, takes with forehead bare
The benediction of the air.

Abraham Davenport

(1866)

"The famous Dark Day of New England, May 19, 1780, was a physical puzzle for many years to our ancestors, but its occurrence brought something more than philosophical speculation into the minds of those who passed through it. The incident of Colonel Abraham Davenport's sturdy protest is a matter of history" (Whittier).

In the old days (a custom laid aside
With breeches and cocked hats) the people
    sent
Their wisest men to make the public laws.
And so, from a brown homestead, where the
    Sound
Drinks the small tribute of the Mianas, 5
Waved over by the woods of Rippowams,
And hallowed by pure lives and tranquil
    deaths,
Stamford sent up to the councils of the State
Wisdom and grace in Abraham Davenport.

'Twas on a May-day of the far old year 10
Seventeen hundred eighty, that there fell
Over the bloom and sweet life of the Spring,

Over the fresh earth and the heaven of noon,
A horror of great darkness, like the night
In day of which the Norland sagas tell, — 15
The Twilight of the Gods. The low-hung sky
Was black with ominous clouds, save where
    its rim
Was fringed with a dull glow, like that which
    climbs
The crater's sides from the red hell below.
Birds ceased to sing, and all the barn-yard
    fowls 20
Roosted; the cattle at the pasture bars
Lowed, and looked homeward; bats on
    leathern wings
Flitted abroad; the sounds of labor died;
Men prayed, and women wept; all ears grew
    sharp
To hear the doom-blast of the trumpet shat-
    ter 25
The black sky, that the dreadful face of
    Christ
Might look from the rent clouds, not as he
    looked
A loving guest at Bethany, but stern
As Justice and inexorable Law.

Meanwhile in the old State House, dim as
    ghosts 30
Sat the lawgivers of Connecticut,
Trembling beneath their legislative robes.
"It is the Lord's Great Day! Let us ad-
    journ,"
Some said; and then, as if with one accord,
All eyes were turned to Abraham Daven-
    port. 35
He rose, slow cleaving with his steady voice
The intolerable hush. "This well may be
The Day of Judgment which the world
    awaits;
But be it so or not, I only know
My present duty, and my Lord's command
To occupy till He come. So at the post 41
Where He hath set me in his providence,
I choose, for one, to meet Him face to face, —
No faithless servant frightened from my task,
But ready when the Lord of the harvest
    calls; 45
And therefore, with all reverence, I would
    say,
Let God do his work, we will see to ours.
Bring in the candles." And they brought
    them in.

Then by the flaring lights the Speaker read,
Albeit with husky voice and shaking hands,
An act to amend an act to regulate 51
The shad and alewive fisheries. Whereupon
Wisely and well spake Abraham Davenport,
Straight to the question, with no figures of
    speech
Save the ten Arab signs, yet not without 55
The shrewd dry humor natural to the man:
His awe-struck colleagues listening all the
    while,
Between the pauses of his argument,
To hear the thunder of the wrath of God
Break from the hollow trumpet of the
    cloud. 60

And there he stands in memory to this day,
Erect, self-poised, a rugged face, half seen
Against the background of unnatural dark,
A witness to the ages as they pass,
That simple duty hath no place for fear. 65

The Meeting

(1868)

This poem and "The Eternal Goodness" express
much of Whittier's spiritual experience. Compare
the following prose passages, given in Pickard's
Life, II, 262 fol.:
"We believe in the Scriptures, because they believe in us, because they repeat the warnings and
admonitions and promises of the indwelling Light
and Truth, because we find the law and prophets
in our souls. We agree with Luther, that 'the
Scriptures are not to be understood but by that
very spirit by which they were written,' and with
Calvin, that 'it is necessary that the same spirit
which spoke by the mouth of the prophets should
convince our hearts that they faithfully delivered
that which God committed to them.'
"My ground of hope for myself and for humanity is in that Divine fullness of love which was
manifested in the life, teachings, and self-sacrifice
of Christ. In the infinite mercy of God so revealed,
and not in any work or merit of our nature, I
humbly, yet very hopefully trust. I regard Christianity as a life, rather than a creed; and in judging
of my fellow-men I can use no other standard than
that which our Lord and Master has given us. 'By
their fruits ye shall know them.'"

The elder folks shook hands at last,
Down seat by seat the signal passed.
To simple ways like ours unused,
Half solemnized and half amused,

With long-drawn breath and shrug, my
    guest   5
His sense of glad relief expressed.
Outside, the hills lay warm in sun;
The cattle in the meadow-run
Stood half-leg deep; a single bird
The green repose above us stirred. 10
"What part or lot have you," he said,
"In these dull rites of drowsy-head?
Is silence worship? Seek it where
It soothes with dreams the summer air,
Not in this close and rude-benched hall, 15
But where soft lights and shadows fall,
And all the slow, sleep-walking hours
Glide soundless over grass and flowers!
From time and place and form apart,
Its holy ground the human heart, 20
Nor ritual-bound nor templeward
Walks the free spirit of the Lord!
Our common Master did not pen
His followers up from other men;
His service liberty indeed, 25
He built no church, He framed no creed;
But while the saintly Pharisee
Made broader his phylactery,
As from the synagogue was seen
The dusty-sandalled Nazarene 30
Through ripening cornfields lead the way
Upon the awful Sabbath day,
His sermons were the healthful talk
That shorter made the mountain-walk,
His wayside texts were flowers and birds, 35
Where mingled with his gracious words
The rustle of the tamarisk-tree
And ripple-wash of Galilee."

"Thy words are well, O friend," I said;
"Unmeasured and unlimited, 40
With noiseless slide of stone to stone,
The mystic Church of God has grown.
Invisible and silent stands
The temple never made with hands,
Unheard the voices still and small 45
Of its unseen confessional.
He needs no special place of prayer
Whose hearing ear is everywhere;
He brings not back the childish days
That ringed the earth with stones of praise, 50
Roofed Karnak's hall of gods, and laid
The plinths of Philae's colonnade.
Still less He owns the selfish good
And sickly growth of solitude, —

The worthless grace that, out of sight, 55
Flowers in the desert anchorite;
Dissevered from the suffering whole,
Love hath no power to save a soul.
Not out of Self, the origin
And native air and soil of sin, 60
The living waters spring and flow,
The trees with leaves of healing grow.

"Dream not, O friend, because I seek
This quiet shelter twice a week,
I better deem its pine-laid floor 65
Than breezy hill or sea-sung shore;
But nature is not solitude:
She crowds us with her thronging wood;
Her many hands reach out to us,
Her many tongues are garrulous; 70
Perpetual riddles of surprise
She offers to our ears and eyes;
She will not leave our senses still,
But drags them captive at her will:
And, making earth too great for heaven, 75
She hides the Giver in the given.

"And so I find it well to come
For deeper rest to this still room,
For here the habit of the soul
Feels less the outer world's control; 80
The strength of mutual purpose pleads
More earnestly our common needs;
And from the silence multiplied
By these still forms on either side,
The world that time and sense have known
Falls off and leaves us God alone. 86

"Yet rarely through the charmed repose
Unmixed the stream of motive flows,
A flavor of its many springs,
The tints of earth and sky it brings; 90
In the still waters needs must be
Some shade of human sympathy;
And here, in its accustomed place,
I look on memory's dearest face;
The blind by-sitter guesseth not 95
What shadow haunts that vacant spot;
No eyes save mine alone can see
The love wherewith it welcomes me!
And still, with those alone my kin,
In doubt and weakness, want and sin, 100
I bow my head, my heart I bare,
As when that face was living there,
And strive (too oft, alas! in vain)

The peace of simple trust to gain,
Fold fancy's restless wings, and lay   105
The idols of my heart away.

"Welcome the silence all unbroken,
Nor less the words of fitness spoken, —
Such golden words as hers for whom   109
Our autumn flowers have just made room;
Whose hopeful utterance through and
          through
The freshness of the morning blew;
Who loved not less the earth that light
Fell on it from the heavens in sight,   115
But saw in all fair forms more fair
The Eternal beauty mirrored there.
Whose eighty years but added grace
And saintlier meaning to her face, —
The look of one who bore away
Glad tidings from the hills of day,   120
While all our hearts went forth to meet
The coming of her beautiful feet!
Or haply hers, whose pilgrim tread
Is in the paths where Jesus led;
Who dreams her childhood's sabbath dream
By Jordan's willow-shaded stream,   126
And, of the hymns of hope and faith,
Sung by the monks of Nazareth,
Hears pious echoes, in the call
To prayer, from Moslem minarets fall,   130
Repeating where his works were wrought
The lesson that her Master taught,
Of whom an elder Sibyl gave,
The prophecies of Cumae's cave!

"I ask no organ's soulless breath   135
To drone the themes of life and death,
No altar candle-lit by day,
No ornate wordsman's rhetoric-play,
No cool philosophy to teach
Its bland audacities of speech   140
To double-tasked idolaters
Themselves their gods and worshippers,
No pulpit hammered by the fist
Of loud-asserting dogmatist,
Who borrows for the Hand of love   145
The smoking thunderbolts of Jove.
I know how well the fathers taught,
What work the later schoolmen wrought;
I reverence old-time faith and men,
But God is near us now as then;   150
His force of love is still unspent,
His hate of sin as imminent;

And still the measure of our needs
Outgrows the cramping bounds of creeds;
The manna gathered yesterday   155
Already savors of decay;
Doubts to the world's child-heart unknown
Question us now from star and stone;
Too little or too much we know,
And sight is swift and faith is slow;   160
The power is lost to self-deceive
With shallow forms of make-believe.
We walk at high noon, and the bells
Call to a thousand oracles,
But the sound deafens, and the light   165
Is stronger than our dazzled sight;
The letters of the sacred Book
Glimmer and swim beneath our look;
Still struggles in the Age's breast
With deepening agony of quest   170
The old entreaty: 'Art thou He,
Or look we for the Christ to be?'

"God should be most where man is least:
So, where is neither church nor priest,
And never rag of form or creed   175
To clothe the nakedness of need, —
Where farmer-folk in silence meet, —
I turn my bell-unsummoned feet;
I lay the critic's glass aside,
I tread upon my lettered pride,   180
And, lowest-seated, testify
To the oneness of humanity;
Confess the universal want,
And share whatever Heaven may grant.
He findeth not who seeks his own,   185
The soul is lost that's saved alone.
Not on one favored forehead fell
Of old the fire-tongued miracle,
But flamed o'er all the thronging host
The baptism of the Holy Ghost;   190
Heart answers heart: in one desire
The blending lines of prayer aspire;
'Where, in my name, meet two or three,'
Our Lord hath said, 'I there will be!'

"So sometimes comes to soul and sense   195
The feeling which is evidence
That very near about us lies
The realm of spiritual mysteries.
The sphere of the supernal powers
Impinges on this world of ours.   200
The low and dark horizon lifts,
To light the scenic terror shifts;

The breath of a diviner air
Blows down the answer of a prayer:
That all our sorrow, pain, and doubt   205
A great compassion clasps about,
And law and goodness, love and force,
Are wedded fast beyond divorce.
Then duty leaves to love its task,
The beggar Self forgets to ask;   210
With smile of trust and folded hands,
The passive soul in waiting stands
To feel, as flowers the sun and dew,
The One true Life its own renew.

"So to the calmly gathered thought   215
The innermost of truth is taught,
The mystery dimly understood,
That love of God is love of good,
And, chiefly, its divinest trace
In Him of Nazareth's holy face;   220
That to be saved is only this, —
Salvation from our selfishness,
From more than elemental fire,

The soul's unsanctified desire,
From sin itself, and not the pain   225
That warns us of its chafing chain;
That worship's deeper meaning lies
In mercy, and not sacrifice,
Not proud humilities of sense
And posturing of penitence,   230
But love's unforced obedience;
That Book and Church and Day are given
For man, not God, — for earth, not
      heaven, —
The blessed means to holiest ends,
Not masters, but benignant friends;   235
That the dear Christ dwells not afar,
The king of some remoter star,
Listening, at times, with flattered ear
To homage wrung from selfish fear,
But here, amidst the poor and blind,   240
The bound and suffering of our kind,
In works we do, in prayers we pray,
Life of our life, He lives to-day."

HENRY WADSWORTH LONGFELLOW (1807–1882)

Longfellow was born in Portland, Maine, February 27, 1807. His mother was a descendant of John Alden, his father a trustee of Bowdoin College, where Longfellow matriculated as a sophomore at the age of fifteen. One of his classmates was Nathaniel Hawthorne. When he graduated from Bowdoin in 1825, he had already shown enough ability at writing verse to make him desire a literary career. His father wished him to study law. Bowdoin settled the matter by offering him six hundred dollars a year for three years of European study to prepare him to teach modern languages. Longfellow went to Europe, returned with knowledge of German, French, Italian, and Spanish, and, late in 1829, joined the faculty of Bowdoin.

Six years later Harvard offered him the Smith professorship of modern languages, just vacated by Ticknor. He spent another year in Europe and began in 1836 his long residence in Cambridge. Installed in beautiful Craigie House, married again in 1843 (his first wife died in Europe), and happy amid congenial minds, the Smith Professor began to produce prose and verse rather than grammars and linguistic studies. *Outre Mer* appeared in 1835 and *Hyperion* and *Voices of the Night* in 1839. *Evangeline*, his most popular narrative, appeared in 1847, and *The Golden Legend* in 1851. In 1854 the poet had begun to chafe at the professor's duties, and he resigned his position after eighteen years of service during which he had introduced thousands of young men to the literatures of Europe. *The Song of Hiawatha* in 1855 at once caught the popular taste for Indian legend, and *The Courtship of Miles Standish*, three years later, sold ten thousand copies in London on the day of its appearance. Longfellow was famous throughout both Europe and America.

He suffered the great tragedy of his life in 1861, when his wife was burned to death. When he recovered from this, he put together a series of verse stories previously begun and somewhat in the nature of Chaucer's Canterbury Tales, *Tales of a Wayside Inn*, 1863. Later he buried himself in a translation of Dante's *Divina Commedia*, his version of which appeared in three volumes between 1867 and 1870. Another trip abroad brought him the highest academic honors of European universities. His last great work was *The Masque of Pandora, and Other Poems*, 1875.

Longfellow's verse, amazingly popular in his day, suffered from a severe reaction. Cooler judgment now sees the injustice of this reaction and places a surer value on his work. Beyond controversy this fact remains: no man of his day, possibly no man in America, did so much for the popularization of poetry. He was translated into nearly every European language, and in turn he translated from most European languages.

Longfellow's view of the right relation of American literature to foreign cultures was expressed in the novel *Kavanagh* (1849):

Nationality is a good thing to a certain extent, but universality is better. All that is best in the great poets of all countries is not what is national in them, but what is universal. Their roots are in their native soil; but their branches wave in the unpatriotic air that speaks the same language unto all men, and their leaves shine with the illimitable light that pervades all lands. Let us throw all the windows open; let us admit the light and air on all sides. As the blood of all nations is mingling with our own, so will their thoughts and feelings finally mingle in our literature. We shall draw from the Germans, tenderness; from the Spaniards, passion; from the French, vivacity, to mingle more and more with our English solid sense. And this will give us universality, so much to be desired.

The standard edition of Longfellow is the Riverside, 11 volumes, 1886. The standard biography is by Samuel Longfellow, *The Life of Henry Wadsworth Longfellow*, in 3 volumes, 1891. There is a short biography by T. W. Higginson, 1902. Aids to a critical reappraisal of Longfellow's poetry are the essay "Gentle Shades of Longfellow" in G. R. Elliott, *The Cycle of Modern Poetry*, 1929, and the Introduction to the volume of selections in the *AWS* by Odell Shepard, 1934.

Hymn to the Night

Ασπασίη, τρίλλιστος

(1839)

"Welcome, thrice prayed-for" (*Iliad*, VIII, 488) seemed the repose of the Night to Longfellow, "while sitting at my chamber window, on one of the balmiest nights of the year. I endeavored to reproduce the impression of the hour and scene."

I heard the trailing garments of the Night
Sweep through her marble halls!
I saw her sable skirts all fringed with light
From the celestial walls!

I felt her presence, by its spell of might,   5
Stoop o'er me from above;

The calm, majestic presence of the Night,
As of the one I love.

I heard the sounds of sorrow and delight,
The manifold, soft chimes,   10
That fill the haunted chambers of the Night,
Like some old poet's rhymes.

From the cool cisterns of the midnight air
My spirit drank repose;
The fountain of perpetual peace flows
there, —   15
From those deep cisterns flows.

O holy Night! from thee I learn to bear
What man has borne before!
Thou layest thy finger on the lips of Care,
And they complain no more.   20

Peace! Peace! Orestes-like I breathe this
    prayer!
Descend with broad-winged flight,
The welcome, the thrice-prayed for, the
    most fair,
    The best-beloved Night!

Serenade

(1840)

Stars of the summer night!
    Far in yon azure deeps,
Hide, hide your golden light!
    She sleeps!
My lady sleeps!
    Sleeps!   5

Moon of the summer night!
    Far down yon western steeps,
Sink, sink in silver light!
    She sleeps!
My lady sleeps!   10
    Sleeps!

Wind of the summer night!
    Where yonder woodbine creeps,
Fold, fold thy pinions light!
    She sleeps!   15
My lady sleeps!
    Sleeps!

Dreams of the summer night!
    Tell her, her lover keeps
Watch! while in slumbers light   20
    She sleeps!
My lady sleeps!
    Sleeps!

The Skeleton in Armor

(1840)

"A skeleton had been dug up at Fall River clad
in broken and corroded armor; and the idea occurred to me of connecting it with the Round
Tower at Newport." — Longfellow's note. This
tower was once thought to be of Norse origin.

    "Speak! speak! thou fearful guest!
Who, with thy hollow breast,
Still in rude armor drest,
    Comest to daunt me!
Wrapt not in Eastern balms,   5

But with thy fleshless palms
Stretched, as if asking alms,
    Why dost thou haunt me?"

Then from those cavernous eyes
Pale flashes seemed to rise,   10
As when the Northern skies
    Gleam in December;
And, like the water's flow
Under December's snow,
Came a dull voice of woe   15
    From the heart's chamber.

"I was a Viking old!
My deeds, though manifold,
No Skald in song has told,
    No Saga taught thee!   20
Take heed that in thy verse
Thou dost the tale rehearse,
Else dread a dead man's curse;
    For this I sought thee.

"Far in the Northern Land,   25
By the wild Baltic's strand,
I, with my childish hand,
    Tamed the gerfalcon;
And, with my skates fast-bound,
Skimmed the half-frozen Sound,   30
That the poor whimpering hound
    Trembled to walk on.

"Oft to his frozen lair
Tracked I the grisly bear,
While from my path the hare   35
    Fled like a shadow;
Oft through the forest dark
Followed the were-wolf's bark,
Until the soaring lark
    Sang from the meadow.   40

"But when I older grew,
Joining a corsair's crew,
O'er the dark sea I flew
    With the marauders.
Wild was the life we led;   45
Many the souls that sped,
Many the hearts that bled,
    By our stern orders.

"Many a wassail-bout
Wore the long winter out;   50

Often our midnight shout
　　Set the cocks crowing,
As we the Berserk's tale
Measured in cups of ale,
Draining the oaken pail　　　　　55
　　Filled to o'erflowing.

"Once as I told in glee
Tales of the stormy sea,
Soft eyes did gaze on me,
　　Burning yet tender;　　　　　60
And as the white stars shine
On the dark Norway pine,
On that dark heart of mine
　　Fell their soft splendor.

"I wooed the blue-eyed maid,　　65
Yielding, yet half afraid,
And in the forest's shade
　　Our vows were plighted.
Under its loosened vest
Fluttered her little breast,　　　70
Like birds within their nest
　　By the hawk frighted.

"Bright in her father's hall
Shields gleamed upon the wall,
Loud sang the minstrels all,　　75
　　Chanting his glory;
When of old Hildebrand
I asked his daughter's hand,
Mute did the minstrels stand
　　To hear my story.　　　　　80

"While the brown ale he quaffed,
Loud then the champion laughed,
And as the wind-gusts waft
　　The sea-foam brightly,
So the loud laugh of scorn　　85
Out of those lips unshorn,
From the deep drinking-horn
　　Blew the foam lightly.

"She was a Prince's child,
I but a Viking wild,　　　　　90
And though she blushed and smiled,
　　I was discarded!
Should not the dove so white
Follow the sea-mew's flight?
Why did they leave that night　　95
　　Her nest unguarded?

"Scarce had I put to sea,
Bearing the maid with me,
Fairest of all was she
　　Among the Norsemen!　　100
When on the white sea-strand,
Waving his armèd hand,
Saw we old Hildebrand,
　　With twenty horsemen.

"Then launched they to the blast,　105
Bent like a reed each mast,
Yet we were gaining fast,
　　When the wind failed us;
And with a sudden flaw
Came round the gusty Skaw,　　110
So that our foe we saw
　　Laugh as he hailed us.

"And as to catch the gale
Round veered the flapping sail,
'Death!' was the helmsman's hail,　115
　　'Death without quarter!'
Midships with iron keel
Struck we her ribs of steel;
Down her black hulk did reel
　　Through the black water!　　120

"As with his wings aslant,
Sails the fierce cormorant,
Seeking some rocky haunt,
　　With his prey laden, —
So toward the open main,　　　125
Beating to sea again,
Through the wild hurricane,
　　Bore I the maiden.

"Three weeks we westward bore,
And when the storm was o'er,　　130
Cloud-like we saw the shore
　　Stretching to leeward;
There for my lady's bower
Built I the lofty tower,
Which, to this very hour,　　　135
　　Stands looking seaward.

"There lived we many years;
Time dried the maiden's tears;
She had forgot her fears,
　　She was a mother;　　　　140
Death closed her mild blue eyes;
Under that tower she lies;
Ne'er shall the sun arise
　　On such another!

"Still grew my bosom then, 145
Still as a stagnant fen!
Hateful to me were men,
  The sunlight hateful!
In the vast forest here,
Clad in my warlike gear, 150
Fell I upon my spear,
  Oh, death was grateful!

"Thus, seamed with many scars,
Bursting these prison bars
Up to its native stars 155
  My soul ascended!
There from the flowing bowl
Deep drinks the warrior's soul,
Skoal! to the Northland! skoal!"
  Thus the tale ended. 160

Mezzo Cammin

(1842)

Half of my life is gone, and I have let
  The years slip from me and have not
    fulfilled
  The aspiration of my youth, to build
  Some tower of song with lofty parapet.
Not indolence, nor pleasure, nor the fret 5
  Of restless passions that would not be
    stilled,
  But sorrow, and a care that almost killed,
  Kept me from what I may accomplish yet;
Though, half-way up the hill, I see the Past
  Lying beneath me with its sounds and
    sights, — 10
  A city in the twilight dim and vast,
With smoking roofs, soft bells, and gleaming
    lights, —
  And hear above me on the autumnal blast
  The cataract of Death far thundering
    from the heights.

The Arsenal at Springfield

(1844)

On his wedding journey in the summer of 1843, Mr. Longfellow passed through Springfield, Massachusetts, and visited the United States arsenal there, in company with Mr. Charles Sumner. "While Mr. Sumner was endeavoring," says Mr. S. Longfellow, "to impress upon the attendant that the money expended upon these weapons of war would have been much better spent upon a great library, Mrs. Longfellow pleased her husband by remarking how like an organ looked the ranged and shining gun-barrels which covered the walls from floor to ceiling, and suggesting what mournful music Death would bring from them. 'We grew quite warlike against war,' she wrote, 'and I urged H. to write a peace poem.' " The poem was written some months later and published in Graham's Magazine, April, 1844 (Note in Riverside Edition).

This is the Arsenal. From floor to ceiling,
  Like a huge organ, rise the burnished arms;
But from their silent pipes no anthem pealing
  Startles the villages with strange alarms.

Ah! what a sound will rise, how wild and
    dreary, 5
  When the death-angel touches those swift
    keys!
What loud lament and dismal Miserere
  Will mingle with their awful symphonies!

I hear even now the infinite fierce chorus,
  The cries of agony, the endless groan, 10
Which, through the ages that have gone be-
    fore us,
  In long reverberations reach our own.

On helm and harness rings the Saxon ham-
    mer,
  Through Cimbric forest roars the Norse-
    man's song,
And loud, amid the universal clamor, 15
  O'er distant deserts sounds the Tartar
    gong.

I hear the Florentine, who from his palace
  Wheels out his battle-bell with dreadful
    din,
And Aztec priests upon their teocallis
  Beat the wild war-drum made of serpent's
    skin; 20

The tumult of each sacked and burning
    village:
  The shout that every prayer for mercy
    drowns;
The soldiers' revels in the midst of pillage;
  The wail of famine in beleaguered towns;

The bursting shell, the gateway wrenched
    asunder, 25
  The rattling musketry, the clashing blade;
And ever and anon, in tones of thunder,
  The diapason of the cannonade.

Is it, O man, with such discordant noises,
  With such accursed instruments as these,
Thou drownest Nature's sweet and kindly
      voices,   31
  And jarrest the celestial harmonies?

Were half the power, that fills the world
      with terror,
  Were half the wealth, bestowed on camps
      and courts,   34
Given to redeem the human mind from error,
  There were no need of arsenals nor forts:

The warrior's name would be a name ab-
      horrèd!
  And every nation, that should lift again
Its hand against a brother, on its forehead
  Would wear forevermore the curse of
      Cain!   40

Down the dark future, through long genera-
      tions,
  The echoing sounds grow fainter and then
      cease;
And like a bell, with solemn, sweet vibra-
      tions,
  I hear once more the voice of Christ say,
      "Peace!"

Peace! and no longer from its brazen por-
      tals   45
  The blast of War's great organ shakes the
      skies!
But beautiful as songs of the immortals,
  The holy melodies of love arise.

The Jewish Cemetery at Newport

(1852)

How strange it seems! These Hebrews in
      their graves,
  Close by the street of this fair seaport
      town,
Silent beside the never-silent waves,
  At rest in all this moving up and down!

The trees are white with dust, that o'er their
      sleep   5
  Wave their broad curtains in the south-
      wind's breath,

While underneath these leafy tents they keep
  The long, mysterious Exodus of Death.

And these sepulchral stones, so old and
      brown,
  That pave with level flags their burial-
      place,   10
Seem like the tablets of the Law, thrown
      down
  And broken by Moses at the mountain's
      base.

The very names recorded here are strange,
  Of foreign accent, and of different climes;
Alvares and Rivera interchange   15
  With Abraham and Jacob of old times.

"Blessed be God! for he created Death!"
  The mourners said, "and Death is rest and
      peace;"
Then added, in the certainty of faith,
  "And giveth Life that nevermore shall
      cease."   20

Closed are the portals of their Synagogue,
  No Psalms of David now the silence break,
No Rabbi reads the ancient Decalogue
  In the grand dialect the Prophets spake.

Gone are the living, but the dead remain, 25
  And not neglected; for a hand unseen,
Scattering its bounty, like a summer rain,
  Still keeps their graves and their remem-
      brance green.

How came they here? What burst of Chris-
      tian hate,
  What persecution, merciless and blind, 30
Drove o'er the sea — that desert desolate —
  These Ishmaels and Hagars of mankind?

They lived in narrow streets and lanes obscure,
  Ghetto and Judenstrass, in mirk and mire;
Taught in the school of patience to endure
  The life of anguish and the death of fire. 36

All their lives long, with the unleavened
      bread
  And bitter herbs of exile and its fears,
The wasting famine of the heart they fed,
  And slaked its thirst with marah of their
      tears.   40

Anathema maranatha! was the cry
  That rang from town to town, from street
    to street;
At every gate the accursed Mordecai
  Was mocked and jeered, and spurned by
    Christian feet.

Pride and humiliation hand in hand   45
  Walked with them through the world
    where'er they went;
Trampled and beaten were they as the sand,
  And yet unshaken as the continent.

For in the background figures vague and
    vast
  Of patriarchs and of prophets rose sub-
    lime,   50
And all the great traditions of the Past
  They saw reflected in the coming time.

And thus forever with reverted look
  The mystic volume of the world they read,
Spelling it backward, like a Hebrew book, 55
  Till life became a Legend of the Dead.

But ah! what once has been shall be no more!
  The groaning earth in travail and in pain
Brings forth its races, but does not restore,
  And the dead nations never rise again.   60

The Warden of the Cinque Ports

(1852)

The Warden was the Duke of Wellington, who
died September 13, 1852.

A mist was driving down the British Channel,
  The day was just begun,
And through the window-panes, on floor and
    panel,
  Streamed the red autumn sun.

It glanced on flowing flag and rippling
    pennon,   5
  And the white sails of ships;
And, from the frowning rampart, the black
    cannon
  Hailed it with feverish lips.

Sandwich and Romney, Hastings, Hithe,
    and Dover
  Were all alert that day,   10

To see the French war-steamers speeding
    over,
  When the fog cleared away.

Sullen and silent, and like couchant lions,
  Their cannon, through the night,
Holding their breath, had watched, in grim
    defiance,   15
  The sea-coast opposite.

And now they roared at drum-beat from
    their stations
  On every citadel;
Each answering each, with morning saluta-
    tions,
  That all was well.   20

And down the coast, all taking up the burden,
  Replied the distant forts,
As if to summon from his sleep the Warden
  And Lord of the Cinque Ports.

Him shall no sunshine from the fields of
    azure,   25
  No drum-beat from the wall,
No morning gun from the black fort's em-
    brasure,
  Awaken with its call!

No more, surveying with an eye impartial
  The long line of the coast,   30
Shall the gaunt figure of the old Field Marshal
  Be seen upon his post!

For in the night, unseen, a single warrior,
  In sombre harness mailed,
Dreaded of man, and surnamed the De-
    stroyer,   35
  The rampart wall had scaled.

He passed into the chamber of the sleeper,
  The dark and silent room,
And as he entered, darker grew, and deeper,
  The silence and the gloom.   40

He did not pause to parley or dissemble,
  But smote the Warden hoar;
Ah! what a blow! that made all England
    tremble
  And groan from shore to shore.

Meanwhile, without, the surly cannon
    waited,   45

The sun rose bright o'erhead;
Nothing in Nature's aspect intimated
That a great man was dead.

My Lost Youth
(1855)

Longfellow's *Journal:* "March 29, 1855 — At night as I lie in bed, a poem comes into my mind, — a memory of Portland, — my native town, the city by the sea.

    Siede la terra dove nato fui
    Sulla marina.

[The city where I was born sits by the side of the sea.]

"March 30 — Wrote the poem; and am rather pleased with it, and with the bringing in of the two lines of the old Lapland song.

    A boy's will is the wind's will,
  And the thoughts of youth are long, long thoughts."

The sea-fight referred to in the fifth stanza occurred in 1813: it "was the engagement," Longfellow said, "between the Enterprise and Boxer off the harbor of Portland, in which both captains were slain. They were buried side by side in the cemetery on Mountjoy."

Often I think of the beautiful town
  That is seated by the sea;
Often in thought go up and down
The pleasant streets of that dear old town,
  And my youth comes back to me.   5
    And a verse of a Lapland song
    Is haunting my memory still:
  "A boy's will is the wind's will,
And the thoughts of youth are long, long
    thoughts."

I can see the shadowy lines of its trees, 10
  And catch, in sudden gleams,
The sheen of the far-surrounding seas,
And islands that were the Hesperides
  Of all my boyish dreams.
    And the burden of that old song, 15
    It murmurs and whispers still:
  "A boy's will is the wind's will,
And the thoughts of youth are long, long
    thoughts."

I remember the black wharves and the slips,
  And the sea-tides tossing free; 20
And Spanish sailors with bearded lips,
And the beauty and mystery of the ships,
  And the magic of the sea.
    And the voice of that wayward song

Is singing and saying still: 25
  "A boy's will is the wind's will,
And the thoughts of youth are long, long
    thoughts."

I remember the bulwarks by the shore,
  And the fort upon the hill;
The sunrise gun, with its hollow roar, 30
The drum-beat repeated o'er and o'er,
  And the bugle wild and shrill.
    And the music of that old song
    Throbs in my memory still:
  "A boy's will is the wind's will, 35
And the thoughts of youth are long, long
    thoughts."

I remember the sea-fight far away,
  How it thundered o'er the tide!
And the dead captains, as they lay
In their graves, o'erlooking the tranquil
    bay 40
  Where they in battle died.
    And the sound of that mournful song
    Goes through me with a thrill:
  "A boy's will is the wind's will,
And the thoughts of youth are long, long
    thoughts." 45

I can see the breezy dome of groves,
  The shadows of Deering's Woods;
And the friendships old and the early loves
Come back with a Sabbath sound, as of doves
  In quiet neighborhoods. 50
    And the verse of that sweet old song,
    It flutters and murmurs still:
  "A boy's will is the wind's will,
And the thoughts of youth are long, long
    thoughts." 54

I remember the gleams and glooms that dart
  Across the school-boy's brain;
The song and the silence in the heart,
That in part are prophecies, and in part
  Are longings wild and vain.
    And the voice of that fitful song 60
    Sings on, and is never still:
  "A boy's will is the wind's will,
And the thoughts of youth are long, long
    thoughts."

There are things of which I may not speak;
  There are dreams that cannot die; 65

There are thoughts that make the strong
heart weak,
And bring a pallor into the cheek,
  And a mist before the eye.
    And the words of that fatal song
    Come over me like a chill: 70
"A boy's will is the wind's will,
And the thoughts of youth are long, long
thoughts."

Strange to me now are the forms I meet
  When I visit the dear old town;
But the native air is pure and sweet,   75
And the trees that o'ershadow each well-
known street,
  As they balance up and down,
    Are singing the beautiful song,
    Are sighing and whispering still:
      "A boy's will is the wind's will,   80
And the thoughts of youth are long, long
thoughts."

And Deering's Woods are fresh and fair,
  And with joy that is almost pain
My heart goes back to wander there,
And among the dreams of the days that were,
  I find my lost youth again.   86
    And the strange and beautiful song,
    The groves are repeating it still:
      "A boy's will is the wind's will,
And the thoughts of youth are long, long
thoughts."   90

Sandalphon
(1857)

Have you read in the Talmud of old,
In the Legends the Rabbins have told
  Of the limitless realms of the air,
Have you read it, — the marvellous story
Of Sandalphon, the Angel of Glory,   5
  Sandalphon, the Angel of Prayer?

How, erect, at the outermost gates
Of the City Celestial he waits,
  With his feet on the ladder of light,
That, crowded with angels unnumbered,   10
By Jacob was seen, as he slumbered
  Alone in the desert at night?

The Angels of Wind and of Fire
Chant only one hymn, and expire

With the song's irresistible stress;   15
Expire in their rapture and wonder,
As harp-strings are broken asunder
  By music they throb to express.

But serene in the rapturous throng,
Unmoved by the rush of the song,   20
  With eyes unimpassioned and slow,
Among the dead angels, the deathless
Sandalphon stands listening breathless
  To sounds that ascend from below; —

From the spirits on earth that adore,   25
From the souls that entreat and implore
  In the fervor and passion of prayer;
From the hearts that are broken with losses,
And weary with dragging the crosses
  Too heavy for mortals to bear.   30

And he gathers the prayers as he stands,
And they change into flowers in his hands,
  Into garlands of purple and red;
And beneath the great arch of the portal,
Through the streets of the City Immortal 35
  Is wafted the fragrance they shed.

It is but a legend, I know, —
A fable, a phantom, a show,
  Of the ancient Rabbinical lore;
Yet the old mediaeval tradition,   40
The beautiful, strange superstition,
  But haunts me and holds me the more.

When I look from my window at night,
And the welkin above is all white,
  All throbbing and panting with stars,   45
Among them majestic is standing
Sandalphon the angel, expanding
  His pinions in nebulous bars.

And the legend, I feel, is a part
Of the hunger and thirst of the heart,   50
  The frenzy and fire of the brain,
That grasps at the fruitage forbidden,
The golden pomegranates of Eden,
  To quiet its fever and pain.

Divina Commedia
(1864–67)

Although the popularity of Longfellow has
rested mainly on his long narrative poems and his
lyrics of sentiment or morals, latter-day critics have

perhaps oftenest singled out, as his finest achievement, the sonnets that he wrote from 1864 onward. Thus, P. E. More placed Longfellow "as a peer among the great sonnet writers of England" ("The Centenary of Longfellow," in *Shelburne Essays*, Fifth Series). In the centenary year, 1907, F. Greenslet edited a separate collection of *Longfellow's Sonnets*.

The series of sonnets headed "Divina Commedia" was written in connection with the long labor of translating Dante's great work — labor that constituted a refuge from the enduring sorrow that followed the death of his wife, by fire, in 1861. This sorrow finds restrained expression in the first sonnet, and again in "The Cross of Snow," page 454.

I

Oft have I seen at some cathedral door
A laborer, pausing in the dust and heat,
Lay down his burden, and with reverent feet
Enter, and cross himself, and on the floor
Kneel to repeat his paternoster o'er;   5
Far off the noises of the world retreat;
The loud vociferations of the street
Become an undistinguishable roar.
So, as I enter here from day to day,
And leave my burden at this minster gate,   10
Kneeling in prayer, and not ashamed to pray,
The tumult of the time disconsolate
To inarticulate murmurs dies away,
While the eternal ages watch and wait.

II

How strange the sculptures that adorn these
        towers!   15
This crowd of statues, in whose folded sleeves
Birds build their nests; while canopied with
        leaves
Parvis and portal bloom like trellised bowers,
And the vast minster seems a cross of flowers!
But fiends and dragons on the gargoyled
        eaves   20
Watch the dead Christ between the living
        thieves,
And, underneath, the traitor Judas lowers!
Ah! from what agonies of heart and brain,
What exultations trampling on despair,
What tenderness, what tears, what hate of
        wrong,   25
What passionate outcry of a soul in pain,
Uprose this poem of the earth and air,
This mediaeval miracle of song!

III

I enter, and I see thee in the gloom

Of the long aisles, O poet saturnine!   30
And strive to make my steps keep pace with
        thine.
The air is filled with some unknown perfume:
The congregation of the dead make room
For thee to pass; the votive tapers shine;
Like rooks that haunt Ravenna's groves of
        pine   35
The hovering echoes fly from tomb to tomb.
From the confessionals I hear arise
Rehearsals of forgotten tragedies,
And lamentations from the crypts below;
And then a voice celestial that begins   40
With the pathetic words, "Although your
        sins
As scarlet be," and ends with "as the snow."

IV

With snow-white veil and garments as of
        flame,
She stands before thee, who so long ago
Filled thy young heart with passion and the
        woe   45
From which thy song and all its splendors
        came;
And while with stern rebuke she speaks thy
        name,
The ice about thy heart melts as the snow
On mountain heights, and in swift overflow
Comes gushing from thy lips in sobs of
        shame.   50
Thou makest full confession; and a gleam,
As of the dawn on some dark forest cast,
Seems on thy lifted forehead to increase;
Lethe and Eunoë — the remembered dream
And the forgotten sorrow — bring at last   55
That perfect pardon which is perfect peace.

V

I lift mine eyes, and all the windows blaze
With forms of Saints and holy men who
        died,
Here martyred and hereafter glorified;
And the great Rose upon its leaves dis-
        plays   60
Christ's Triumph, and the angelic roundelays,
With splendor upon splendor multiplied;
And Beatrice again at Dante's side
No more rebukes, but smiles her words of
        praise.

And then the organ sounds, and unseen
    choirs   65
Sing the old Latin hymns of peace and love
And benedictions of the Holy Ghost;
And the melodious bells among the spires
O'er all the house-tops and through heaven
    above
Proclaim the elevation of the Host!   70

VI

O star of morning and of liberty!
O bringer of the light, whose splendor shines
Above the darkness of the Apennines,
Forerunner of the day that is to be!
The voices of the city and the sea,   75
The voices of the mountains and the pines,
Repeat thy song, till the familiar lines
Are footpaths for the thought of Italy!
Thy flame is blown abroad from all the
    heights,
Through all the nations, and a sound is
    heard,   80
As of a mighty wind, and men devout,
Strangers of Rome, and the new proselytes,
In their own language hear the wondrous
    word,
And many are amazed and many doubt.

Chaucer
(1873)

An old man in a lodge within a park;
The chamber walls depicted all around
With portraitures of huntsman, hawk, and
    hound,
And the hurt deer. He listeneth to the lark,
Whose song comes with the sunshine through
    the dark   5
Of painted glass in leaden lattice bound;
He listeneth and he laugheth at the sound,
Then writeth in a book like any clerk.
He is the poet of the dawn, who wrote
The Canterbury Tales, and his old age   10
Made beautiful with song; and as I read
I hear the crowing cock, I hear the note
Of lark and linnet, and from every page
Rise odors of ploughed field or flowery mead.

Milton
(1873)

I pace the sounding sea-beach and behold
    How the voluminous billows roll and run,

Upheaving and subsiding, while the sun
    Shines through their sheeted emerald far
        unrolled,
And the ninth wave, slow gathering fold by
        fold   5
    All its loose-flowing garments into one,
    Plunges upon the shore, and floods the
        dun
    Pale reach of sands, and changes them to
        gold.
So in majestic cadence rise and fall
    The mighty undulations of thy song,   10
    O sightless bard, England's Maeonides!
And ever and anon, high over all
    Uplifted, a ninth wave superb and strong,
    Floods all the soul with its melodious seas.

Venice
(1875)

White swan of cities, slumbering in thy nest
    So wonderfully built among the reeds
    Of the lagoon, that fences thee and feeds,
    As sayeth thy old historian and thy guest!
White water-lily, cradled and caressed   5
    By ocean streams, and from the silt and
        weeds
    Lifting thy golden filaments and seeds,
    Thy sun-illumined spires, thy crown and
        crest!
White phantom city, whose untrodden
    streets
    Are rivers, and whose pavements are the
        shifting   10
    Shadows of palaces and strips of sky;
I wait to see thee vanish like the fleets
    Seen in mirage, or towers of cloud up-
        lifting
    In air their unsubstantial masonry.

Nature
(1876)

As a fond mother, when the day is o'er,
Leads by the hand her little child to bed,
Half willing, half reluctant to be led,
And leave his broken playthings on the floor,
Still gazing at them through the open door,   5
Nor wholly reassured and comforted
By promises of others in their stead,

Which, though more splendid, may not
    please him more;
So Nature deals with us, and takes away
Our playthings one by one, and by the
    hand   10
Leads us to rest so gently, that we go
Scarce knowing if we wish to go or stay,
Being too full of sleep to understand
How far the unknown transcends the what
    we know.

The Three Silences of Molinos

TO JOHN GREENLEAF WHITTIER

(1877)

Three Silences there are: the first of speech,
The second of desire, the third of thought;
This is the lore a Spanish monk, distraught
With dreams and visions, was the first to
    teach.   4
These Silences, commingling each with each,
Made up the perfect Silence that he sought
And prayed for, and wherein at times he
    caught
Mysterious sounds from realms beyond our
    reach.
O thou, whose daily life anticipates
The life to come, and in whose thought and
    word   10
The spiritual world preponderates,
Hermit of Amesbury! thou too hast heard
Voices and melodies from beyond the gates,
And speakest only when thy soul is stirred!

The Cross of Snow

(1879)

In the long, sleepless watches of the night,
A gentle face — the face of one long dead —
Looks at me from the wall, where round its
    head
The night-lamp casts a halo of pale light.
Here in this room she died; and soul more
    white   5
Never through martyrdom of fire was led
To its repose; nor can in books be read
The legend of a life more benedight.
There is a mountain in the distant West,
That, sun-defying, in its deep ravines   10
Displays a cross of snow upon its side.
Such is the cross I wear upon my breast

These eighteen years, through all the chang-
    ing scenes   65
And seasons, changeless since the day she
    died.

The Bells of San Blas

(1882)

Suggested by an article on Mexico in the March,
1882, issue of *Harper's Magazine*. This is Longfellow's last poem. The concluding stanza was written nine days before his death.

What say the Bells of San Blas
To the ships that southward pass
    From the harbor of Mazatlan?
To them it is nothing more
Than the sound of surf on the shore, —   5
    Nothing more to master or man.

But to me, a dreamer of dreams,
To whom what is and what seems
    Are often one and the same, —
The Bells of San Blas to me   10
Have a strange, wild melody,
    And are something more than a name.

For bells are the voice of the church;
They have tones that touch and search
    The hearts of young and old;   15
One sound to all, yet each
Lends a meaning to their speech,
    And the meaning is manifold.

They are a voice of the Past
Of an age that is fading fast,   20
    Of a power austere and grand;
When the flag of Spain unfurled
Its folds o'er this western world,
    And the Priest was lord of the land.

The chapel that once looked down   25
On the little seaport town
    Has crumbled into the dust;
And on oaken beams below
The bells swing to and fro,
    And are green with mould and rust.   30

"Is, then, the old faith dead,"
They say, "and in its stead
    Is some new faith proclaimed,
That we are forced to remain
Naked to sun and rain,   35
    Unsheltered and ashamed?

"Once in our tower aloof
We rang over wall and roof
   Our warnings and our complaints;
And round about us there   40
The white doves filled the air,
   Like the white souls of the saints.

"The saints! Ah, have they grown
Forgetful of their own?
   Are they asleep, or dead,   45
That open to the sky
Their ruined Missions lie,
   No longer tenanted?

"Oh, bring us back once more
The vanished days of yore,   50
   When the world with faith was filled;

Bring back the fervid zeal,
The hearts of fire and steel,
   The hands that believe and build.

"Then from our tower again   55
We will send over land and main
   Our voices of command,
Like exiled kings who return
To their thrones, and the people learn
   That the Priest is lord of the land!"   60

O Bells of San Blas, in vain
Ye call back the Past again!
   The Past is deaf to your prayer;
Out of the shadows of night
The world rolls into light;
   It is daybreak everywhere.   65

JAMES RUSSELL LOWELL (1819-1891)

Few American university chairs can boast a succession of more distinguished occupants than the Smith professorship at Harvard. George Ticknor, the historian of Spanish literature, was succeeded by Longfellow, and Longfellow by James Russell Lowell. Lowell was thirty-seven when he began to teach at Harvard. He was born and bred in Cambridge, — born February 22, 1819, in Elmwood, the colonial house where he spent most of his life. His ancestors had long been in Massachusetts, and his home was rich in books. He entered Harvard in 1834 and graduated in 1838. He studied law, received an LL.B. from Harvard in 1840, but found letters more to his taste, and law less, as time passed.

His decision to follow a literary career was furthered in 1840 by his engagement to Maria White, who was to become his wife four years later. Miss White read contemporary poetry, wrote verse, sympathised with the abolitionists, and inclined to mysticism. " 'They say,' " Lowell reported, "that she is 'transcendental.' " Her influence and that of her romantic associates is visible in two volumes of poems which Lowell published during this period. He contributed to periodicals, edited an unsuccessful one, The Pioneer, for a short time, and made important literary acquaintances.

A second series of Poems in 1847 was followed by Biglow Papers, first series, A Fable for Critics, and The Vision of Sir Launfal, all in 1848. He first visited Europe in 1851 and 1852. The following year his wife died. A course of lectures delivered in Boston in 1854 and 1855 led to his appointment as Smith professor of Modern Languages at his alma mater, and from this time Lowell turned more and more toward the production of critical prose. In 1857 he married again, and the same year became editor of the Atlantic Monthly. Two years later he left this journal to join Charles Eliot Norton on the North American Review, of which publication he became editor in 1863, and continued in the position for ten years. In 1864, three months after peace was declared, he wrote his Commemoration Ode. In 1867 he brought out a second series of

Biglow Papers, and then began his long series of critical essays with *Among My Books*, first series, in 1870, and *My Study Windows*, the following year.

In 1877 he was appointed Minister to Spain, as Irving had been thirty-five years before. After three years in Madrid he was made Minister to England, where he served with distinction until 1885. "During my reign no ambassador or minister has created so much interest or won so much regard," said Queen Victoria. After 1885 Lowell traveled extensively, returned to Elmwood, and died there.

The best edition of Lowell is the Elmwood, 16 volumes, 1904. The standard biography is by H. E. Scudder, 2 volumes, 1901. F. Greenslet's *James Russell Lowell*, 1905, is both delightful and scholarly. A valuable article entitled "Lowell — Humanitarian, Nationalist, or Humanist?" by H. H. Clark, appeared in the journal *Studies in Philology* in 1930. For studies of Lowell as critic, see W. C. Brownell's *American Prose Masters*, 1909, 299–316, and N. Foerster's *American Criticism*, 1928, ch. 3. H. H. Clark and N. Foerster edited Lowell in the *AWS*, 1947.

From The Biglow Papers

In these poems, as the casual reader may perceive, Lowell broke away from foreign models. It is worth remarking, however, on the other hand, that he used the old verse forms, pointed out the English origin of the Yankee dialect, and insisted upon the English basis of the New England character. Furthermore, the romantic elements — largely European in origin — of his apprenticeship years reappear in these poems — the passion for freedom, for brotherhood, for peace, the emphasis on feeling and imagination, the love of nature — and are expressed so memorably that the two series of *The Biglow Papers* may be viewed, in one way, as the culmination of Lowell's early poetry.

Although the actual authorship of the Papers was no secret, they appeared ostensibly as contributions by a Yankee youth named Hosea Biglow, supported by a Parson Wilbur, erudite minister of the town of Jaalam.

A Letter from Mr. Ezekiel Biglow of Jaalam to the Hon. Joseph T. Buckingham, Editor of the Boston Courier, Inclosing a Poem of His Son, Mr. Hosea Biglow

(1846)

"The act of May 13, 1846, authorized President Polk to employ the militia, and call out 50,000 volunteers, if necessary. He immediately called for the full number of volunteers, asking Massachusetts for 777 men. On May 26 Governor Briggs issued a proclamation for the enrolment of the regiment. As the President's call was merely a request and not an order, many Whigs and the Abolitonists were for refusing it. *The Liberator* for June 5 severely censured the governor for complying, and accused him of not carrying out the resolutions of the last Whig Convention, which had pledged the party 'to present as firm a front of opposition to the institution as was consistent with

their allegiance to the Constitution.'" (Note in the Riverside and Cambridge editions.)

JAYLEM, june 1846.

MISTER EDDYTER, — Our Hosea wuz down to Boston last week, and he see a cruetin Sarjunt a struttin round as popler as a hen with 1 chicking, with 2 fellers a drummin and fifin arter him like all nater. the sarjunt he thout Hosea hedn't gut his teeth cut cos he looked a kindo's though he'd jest com down, so he cal'lated to hook him in, but Hosy woodn't take none o' his sarse for all he hed much as 20 Rooster's tales stuck onto his hat and eenamost enuf brass a bobbin up and down on his shoulders and figureed onto his coat and trousis, let alone wut nater hed sot in his featers, to make a 6 pounder out on.

wal, Hosea he com home considerabal riled, and arter I'd gone to bed I heern Him a thrashin round like a short-tailed Bull in flitime. The old Woman ses she to me ses she, Zekle, ses she, our Hosee's gut the chollery or suthin anuther ses she, don't you Bee skeered, ses I, he's oney amakin pottery ses i, he's ollers on hand at that ere busynes like Da & martin, and shure enuf, cum mornin, Hosy he cum down stares full chizzle, hare on eend and cote tales flyin, and sot rite of to go reed his varses to Parson Wilbur bein he haint aney grate shows o' book larnin himself, bimeby he cum back and sed the parson wuz dreffle tickled with 'em as i hoop you will Be, and said they wuz True grit.

Hosea ses taint hardly fair to call' em hisn now, cos the parson kind o' slicked off sum

o' the last varses, but he told Hosee he didn't
want to put his ore in to tetch to the Rest on
'en, bein they wuz verry well As thay wuz,
and then Hosy ses he sed suthin a nuther
about Simplex Mundishes or sum sech feller,
but I guess Hosea kind o' didn't hear him, for
I never hearn o' nobody o' that name in this
villadge, and I've lived here man and boy
76 year cum next tater diggin, and thair
aint no wheres a kitting spryer'n I be.

If you print 'em I wish you'd jest let folks
know who hosy's father is, cos my ant Keziah
used to say it's nater to be curus ses she, she
aint livin though and he's a likely kind o'
lad.

EZEKIEL BIGLOW

Thrash away, you'll *hev* to rattle
   On them kittle-drums o' yourn, —
'Taint a knowin' kind o' cattle
   Thet is ketched with mouldy corn;
Put in stiff, you fifer feller, 5
   Let folks see how spry you be, —
Guess you'll toot till you are yeller
   'Fore you git ahold o' me!

Thet air flag's a leetle rotten,
   Hope it aint your Sunday's best; — 10
Fact! it takes a sight o' cotton
   To stuff out a soger's chest:
Sence we farmers hev to pay fer't,
   Ef you must wear humps like these,
S'posin' you should try salt hay fer't, 15
   It would du ez slick ez grease.

'Twouldn't suit them Suthun fellers,
   They're a dreffle graspin' set,
We must ollers blow the bellers
   Wen they want their irons het; 20
May be it's all right ez preachin',
   But *my* narves it kind o' grates,
Wen I see the overreachin'
   O' them nigger-drivin' States.

Them thet rule us, them slave-traders, 25
   Haint they cut a thunderin' swarth
(Helped by Yankee renegaders),
   Thru the vartu o' the North!
We begin to think it's nater
   To take sarse an' not be riled; — 30
Who'd expect to see a tater
   All on eend at bein' biled?

Ez fer war, I call it murder, —
   There you hev it plain an' flat;
I don't want to go no furder 35
   Than my Testyment fer that;
God hez sed so plump an' fairly,
   It's ez long ez it is broad,
An' you've gut to git up airly
   Ef you want to take in God. 40

'Taint your eppyletts an' feathers
   Make the thing a grain more right;
'Taint afollerin' your bell-wethers
   Will excuse ye in His sight;
Ef you take a sword an' dror it, 45
   An' go stick a feller thru,
Guv'ment aint to answer for it,
   God'll send the bill to you.

Wut's the use o' meetin'-goin'
   Every Sabbath, wet or dry, 50
Ef it's right to go amowin'
   Feller-men like oats an' rye?
I dunno but wut it's pooty
   Trainin' round in bobtail coats, —
But it's curus Christian dooty 55
   This 'ere cuttin' folks's throats.

They may talk o' Freedom's airy
   Tell they're pupple in the face, —
It's a grand gret cemetary
   Fer the barthrights of our race; 60
They jest want this Californy
   So's to lug new slave-States in
To abuse ye, an' to scorn ye,
   An' to plunder ye like sin.

Aint it cute to see a Yankee 65
   Take sech everlastin' pains,
All to get the Devil's thankee
   Helpin' on 'em weld their chains?
Wy, it's jest ez clear ez figgers,
   Clear ez one an' one make two, 70
Chaps thet make black slaves o' niggers
   Want to make wite slaves o' you.

Tell ye jest the eend I've come to
   Arter cipherin' plaguy smart,
An' it makes a handy sum, tu, 75
   Any gump could larn by heart;
Laborin' man an' laborin' woman
   Hev one glory an' one shame.
Ev'y thin' thet's done inhuman
   Injers all on 'em the same. 80

'Taint by turnin' out to hack folks
  You're agoin' to git your right,
Nor by lookin' down on black folks
  Coz you're put upon by wite;
Slavery aint o' nary color,   85
  'Taint the hide thet makes it wus,
All it keers fer in a feller
  'S jest to make him fill its pus.

Want to tackle me in, du ye?
  I expect you'll hev to wait;   90
Wen cold lead puts daylight thru ye
  You'll begin to kal'late;
S'pose the crows wun't fall to pickin'
  All the carkiss from your bones,
Coz you helped to give a lickin'   95
  To them poor half-Spanish drones?

Jest go home an' ask our Nancy
  Wether I'd be sech a goose
Ez to jine ye, — guess you'd fancy
  The etarnal bung wuz loose!   100
She wants me fer home consumption,
  Let alone the hay's to mow, —
Ef you're arter folks o' gumption,
  You've a darned long row to hoe.

Take them editors that's crowin'   105
  Like a cockerel three months old, —
Don't ketch any on 'em goin',
  Though they be so blasted bold;
Aint they a prime lot o' fellers?
  'Fore they think on't guess they'll sprout
(Like a peach thet's got the yellers),   111
  With the meanness bustin' out.

Wall, go 'long to help 'em stealin',
  Bigger pens to cram with slaves,
Help the men thet's ollers dealin'   115
  Insults on your fathers' graves;
Help the strong to grind the feeble,
  Help the many agin the few,
Help the men thet call your people
  Witewashed slaves an' peddlin' crew!   120

Massachusetts, God forgive her,
  She's akneelin' with the rest,
She, thet ough' to ha' clung ferever
  In her grand old eagle-nest;
She thet ough' to stand so fearless   125
  W'ile the wracks are round her hurled,
Holdin' up a beacon peerless
  To the oppressed of all the world!

Ha'n't they sold your colored seamen?
  Ha'n't they made your env'ys w'iz?   130
Wut'll make ye act like freemen?
  Wut'll git your dander riz?
Come, I'll tell ye wut I'm thinkin'
  Is our dooty in this fix,
They'd ha' done't ez quick ez winkin'   135
  In the days o' seventy-six.

Clang the bells in every steeple,
  Call all true men to disown
The tradoocers of our people,
  The enslavers o' their own;   140
Let our dear old Bay State proudly
  Put the trumpet to her mouth,
Let her ring this messidge loudly
  In the ears of all the South: —

"I'll return ye good fer evil   145
  Much ez we frail mortils can,
But I wun't go help the Devil
  Makin' man the cus o' man;
Call me coward, call me traiter,
  Jest ez suits your mean idees, —   150
Here I stand a tyrant-hater,
  An' the friend o' God an' Peace!"

Ef I'd my way I hed ruther
  We should go to work an' part,
They take one way, we take t'other,   155
  Guess it wouldn't break my heart;
Man hed ough' to put asunder
  Them thet God has noways jined;
An' I shouldn't gretly wonder
  Ef there's thousands o' my mind.   160

[The first recruiting sergeant on record I
conceive to have been that individual who is
mentioned in the Book of Job as *going to and
fro in the earth, and walking up and down in it.*
Bishop Latimer will have him to have been a
bishop, but to me that other calling would
appear more congenial. The sect of Cainites
is not yet extinct, who esteemed the first-born
of Adam to be the most worthy, not only
because of that privilege of primogeniture,
but inasmuch as he was able to overcome and
slay his younger brother. That was a wise
saying of the famous Marquis Pescara to the
Papal Legate, that *it was impossible for men
to serve Mars and Christ at the same time.* Yet
in time past the profession of arms was

judged to be κατ᾽ ἐξοχήν that of a gentleman, nor does this opinion want for strenuous upholders even in our day. Must we suppose, then, that the profession of Christianity was only intended for losels, or, at best, to afford an opening for plebeian ambition? Or shall we hold with that nicely metaphysical Pomeranian, Captain Vratz, who was Count Königsmark's chief instrument in the murder of Mr. Thynne, that the Scheme of Salvation has been arranged with an especial eye to the necessities of the upper classes, and that "God would consider *a gentleman* and deal with him suitably to the condition and profession he had placed him in"? It may be said of us all, *Exemplo plus quam ratione vivimus.* — H. W.]

What Mr. Robinson Thinks

(1847)

"George Nixon Briggs was the Whig governor of Massachusetts from 1844 to 1851. The campaign referred to here is that of 1847. Governor Briggs was renominated by acclamation and supported by his party with great enthusiasm. His opponent was Caleb Cushing, then in Mexico, and raised by President Polk to the rank of Brigadier-General. Cushing was defeated by a majority of 14,060" (note in the Riverside and Cambridge editions).

"John Paul Robinson (1799–1864) was a resident of Lowell, a lawyer of considerable ability, and a thorough classical scholar. He represented Lowell in the State Legislature in 1829, 1830, 1831, 1833, and 1842, and was Senator from Middlesex in 1836. Late in the gubernatorial contest of 1847 it was rumored that Robinson, heretofore a zealous Whig, and a delegate to the recent Springfield Convention, had gone over to the Democratic or, as it was then styled, the 'Loco' camp. The editor of the *Boston Palladium* wrote to him to learn the truth, and Robinson replied in an open letter avowing his intention to vote for Cushing" (*Ibid.*).

Guvener B. is a sensible man;
 He stays to his home an' looks arter his
  folks;
He draws his furrer ez straight ez he can,
An' into nobody's tater-patch pokes;
   But John P.   5
   Robinson he
 Sez he wunt vote fer Guvener B.

My! aint it terrible? Wut shall we du?

We can't never choose him o' course, —
  thet's flat;
Guess we shall hev to come round (don't
  you?)   10
An' go in fer thunder an' guns, an' all that;
   Fer John P.
   Robinson he
 Sez he wunt vote fer Guvener B.

Ginral C. is a dreffle smart man: 15
 He's ben on all sides thet give places or
  pelf;
But consistency still wuz a part of his plan, —
 He's ben true to *one* party, — an' thet is
  himself; —
   So John P.
   Robinson he   20
 Sez he shall vote fer Ginral C.

Ginral C. he goes in fer the war;
 He don't vally princerple more'n an old
  cud;
Wut did God make us raytional creeturs fer,
 But glory an' gunpowder, plunder an'
  blood?   25
   So John P.
   Robinson he
 Sez he shall vote fer Ginral C.

We were gittin' on nicely up here to our
  village,
 With good old idees o' wut's right an' wut
  aint,
We kind o' thought Christ went agin war   30
  an' pillage,
 An' thet eppyletts worn't the best mark of
  a saint;
   But John P.
   Robinson he
 Sez this kind o' thing's an exploded idee. 35

The side of our country must ollers be took,
 An' President Polk, you know, *he* is our
  country.
An' the angel thet writes all our sins in a
  book
 Puts the *debit* to him, an' to us the *per
  contry*
   An' John P.   40
   Robinson he
 Sez this is his view o' the thing to a T.

Parson Wilbur he calls all these argimunts
  lies;
  Sez they're nothin' on airth but jest *fee,
    faw, fum*
An' thet all this big talk of our destinies   45
  Is half on it ign'ance, an' t'other half rum;
        But John P.
       Robinson he
  Sez it ain't no sech thing; an' of course, so
    must we.

Parson Wilbur sez *he* never heerd in his
  life   50
Thet th' Apostles rigged out in their swaller-
  tail coats,
An' marched round in front of a drum an' a
  fife,
  To git some on 'em office, an' some on 'em
    votes;
        But John P.
       Robinson he   55
  Sez they didn't know everythin' down
    in Judee.

Wal, it's a marcy we've gut folks to tell us
  The rights an' the wrongs o' these matters,
    I vow, —
God sends country lawyers, an' other wise
  fellers,
  To start the world's team wen it gits in a
    slough;   60
        Fer John P
       Robinson he
  Sez the world'll go right, ef he hollers
    out Gee!

[The attentive reader will doubtless have
perceived in the foregoing poem an allusion
to that pernicious sentiment, "Our country,
right or wrong." It is an abuse of language
to call a certain portion of land, much more,
certain personages, elevated for the time being
to high station, our country. I would not
sever nor loosen a single one of those ties by
which we are united to the spot of our birth,
nor minish by a tittle the respect due to the
Magistrate. I love our own Bay State too
well to do the one, and as for the other, I
have myself for nigh forty years exercised,
however unworthily, the function of Justice
of the Peace, having been called thereto by
the unsolicited kindness of that most excellent man and upright patriot, Caleb Strong.
Patriæ fumus igne alieno luculentior is best
qualified with this, — *Ubi libertas, ibi patria.*
We are inhabitants of two worlds, and owe a
double, not a divided, allegiance. In virtue
of our clay, this little ball of earth exacts a
certain loyalty of us, while, in our capacity as
spirits, we are admitted citizens of an invisible and holier fatherland. There is a patriotism of the soul whose claim absolves us
from our other and terrene fealty. Our true
country is that ideal realm which we represent to ourselves under the names of
religion, duty, and the like. Our terrestrial
organizations are but far-off approaches to so
fair a model, and all they are verily traitors
who resist not any attempt to divert them
from this their original intendment. When,
therefore, one would have us to fling up our
caps and shout with the multitude, "*Our
country, however bounded!*" he demands of us
that we sacrifice the larger to the less, the
higher to the lower, and that we yield to the
imaginary claims of a few acres of soil our
duty and privilege as liegemen of Truth.
Our true country is bounded on the north
and the south, on the east and the west, by
Justice, and when she oversteps that invisible boundary-line by so much as a hair's-
breadth, she ceases to be our mother, and
chooses rather to be looked upon *quasi
noverca.* That is a hard choice when our
earthly love of country calls upon us to tread
one path and our duty points us to another.
We must make as noble and becoming an
election as did Penelope between Icarius and
Ulysses. Veiling our faces, we must take
silently the hand of Duty to follow her. * * *
                      H. W.]

The Courtin'
(1848–66)

God makes sech nights, all white an' still
  Fur'z you can look or listen,
Moonshine an' snow on field an' hill,
  All silence an' all glisten.

Zekle crep' up quite unbeknown   5
  An' peeked in thru' the winder,
An' there sot Huldy all alone,
  'ith no one nigh to hender.

A fireplace filled the room's one side
  With half a cord o' wood in —   10
There warn't no stoves (tell comfort died)
  To bake ye to a puddin'.

The wa'nut logs shot sparkles out
  Towards the pootiest, bless her,
An' leetle flames danced all about   15
  The chiny on the dresser.

Agin the chimbley crook-necks hung,
  An' in amongst 'em rusted
The ole queen's-arm thet gran'ther Young
  Fetched back f'om Concord busted.   20

The very room, coz she was in,
  Seemed warm f'om floor to ceilin',
An' she looked full ez rosy agin
  Ez the apples she was peelin'.

'Twas kin' o' kingdom-come to look   25
  On sech a blessed cretur,
A dogrose blushin' to a brook
  Ain't modester nor sweeter.

He was six foot o' man, A 1,
  Clear grit an' human natur',   30
None couldn't quicker pitch a ton
  Nor dror a furrer straighter.

He'd sparked it with full twenty gals,
  Hed squired 'em, danced 'em, druv 'em,
Fust this one, an' then thet, by spells —   35
  All is, he couldn't love 'em.

But long o' her his veins 'ould run
  All crinkly like curled maple,
The side she breshed felt full o' sun
  Ez a south slope in Ap'il.   40

She thought no v'ice hed sech a swing
  Ez hisn in the choir;
My! when he made Ole Hunderd ring,
  She *knowed* the Lord was nigher.

An' she'd blush scarlit, right in prayer,   45
  When her new meetin'-bunnet
Felt somehow thru' its crown a pair
  O' blue eyes sot upun it.

Thet night, I tell ye, she looked *some!*
  She seemed to 've gut a new soul,   50

For she felt sartin-sure he'd come,
  Down to her very shoe-sole.

She heered a foot, an' knowed it tu,
  A-raspin' on the scraper, —
All ways to once her feelin's flew   55
  Like sparks in burnt-up paper.

He kin' o' l'itered on the mat,
  Some doubtfle o' the sekle,
His heart kep' goin' pity-pat,
  But hern went pity Zekle.   60

An' yit she gin her cheer a jerk
  Ez though she wished him furder,
An' on her apples kep' to work,
  Parin' away like murder.

"You want to see my Pa, I s'pose?"   65
  "Wal . . . no . . . I come dasignin' " —
"To see my Ma? She's sprinklin' clo'es
  Agin to-morrer's i'nin'."

To say why gals acts so or so,
  Or don't, 'ould be persumin';   70
Mebby to mean *yes* an' say *no*
  Comes nateral to women.

He stood a spell on one foot fust,
  Then stood a spell on t'other,
An' on which one he felt the wust   75
  He couldn't ha' told ye nuther.

Says he, "I'd better call agin!"
  Says she, "Think likely, Mister":
Thet last word pricked him like a pin,
  An' . . . Wal, he up an' kist her.   80

When Ma bimeby upon 'em slips,
  Huldy sot pale ez ashes,
All kin' o' smily roun' the lips
  An' teary roun' the lashes.

For she was jes' the quiet kind   85
  Whose naturs never vary,
Like streams that keep a summer mind
  Snowhid in Jenooary.

The blood clost roun' her heart felt glued
  Too tight for all expressin',   90
Tell mother see how metters stood,
  An' gin 'em both her blessin'.

Then her red come back like the tide
  Down to the Bay o' Fundy,
An' all I know is they was cried   95
  In meetin' come nex' Sunday.

Sunthin' in the Pastoral Line

(1862)

Once git a smell o' musk into a draw,
An' it clings hold like precedents in law:
Your gra'ma'am put it there, — when, good-
    ness knows, —
To jes' this-worldify her Sunday-clo'es;
But the old chist wun't sarve her gran'son's
    wife   5
(For, 'thout new funnitoor, wut good in
    life?),
An' so ole clawfoot, from the precinks dread
O' the spare chamber, slinks into the shed,
Where, dim with dust, it fust or last subsides
To holdin' seeds an' fifty things besides; 10
But better days stick fast in heart an' husk,
An' all you keep in't gits a scent o' musk.

Jes' so with poets: wut thy've airly read
Gits kind o' worked into their heart an' head,
So's 't they can't seem to write but jest on
    sheers   15
With furrin countries or played-out ideers
Nor hev a feelin', ef it doosn't smack
O' wut some critter chose to feel 'way back:
This makes 'em talk o' daisies, larks, an'
    things,
Ez though we'd nothin' here that blows an'
    sings   20
(Why, I'd give more for one live bobolink
Than a square mile o' larks in printer's
    ink), —
This makes 'em think our fust o' May is May,
Which 'tain't, for all the almanicks can say.

O little city-gals, don't never go it   25
Blind on the word o' noospaper or poet!
They're apt to puff, an' May-day seldom
    looks
Up in the country ez 't doos in books;
They're no more like than hornets'-nests an'
    hives,
Or printed sarmons be to holy lives.   30
I, with my trouses perched on cowhide boots,
Tuggin' my foundered feet out by the roots,
Hev seen ye come to fling on April's hearse

Your muslin nosegays from the milliner's,
Puzzlin' to find dry ground your queen to
    choose,   35
An' dance your throats sore in morocker
    shoes:
I've seen ye an' felt proud, thet, come wut
    would,
Our Pilgrim stock wuz pethed with hardi-
    hood.
Pleasure doos make us Yankees kind o'
    winch,
Ez though 'twuz sunthin' paid for by the
    inch;   40
But yit we du contrive to worry thru,
Ef Dooty tells us thet the thing's to du,
An' kerry a hollerday, ef we set out,
Ez stiddily ez though 'twuz a redoubt.   44

I, country-born an' bred, know where to find
Some blooms thet make the season suit the
    mind,
An' seem to metch the doubtin' bluebird's
    notes, —
Half-vent'rin' liverworts in furry coats,
Bloodroots, whose rolled-up leaves ef you
    oncurl,
Each on 'em's cradle to a baby-pearl, —   50
But these are jes' Spring's pickets; sure ez
    sin,
The rebble frosts'll try to drive 'em in;
For half our May's so awfully like Mayn't,
'twould rile a Shaker or an evrige saint;
Though I own up I like our back'ard springs
Thet kind o' haggle with their greens an'
    things,   56
An' when you 'most give up, 'uthout more
    words
Toss the fields full o' blossoms, leaves, an
    birds;
Thet's Northun natur', slow an' apt to doubt,
But when it *doos* git stirred, ther' 's no gin-
    out!   60

Fust come the blackbirds clatt'rin' in tall
    trees,
An' settlin' things in windy Congresses, —
Queer politicians, though, for I'll be skinned
Ef all on 'em don't head aginst the wind.
'fore long the trees begin to show belief, — 65
The maple crimsons to a coral-reef,
Then saffern swarms swing off from all the
    willers

So plump they look like yaller caterpillars,
Then gray hossches'nuts lettle hands unfold
Softer'n a baby's be at three days old: 70
Thet's robin-redbreast's almanick; he knows
Thet arter this ther' 's only blossom-snows;
So, choosin' out a handy crotch an' spouse,
He goes to plast'rin' his adobë house.

Then seems to come a hitch, — things lag
     behind,   75
Till some fine mornin' Spring makes up her
     mind,
An' ez, when snow-swelled rivers cresh their
     dams
Heaped-up with ice thet dovetails in an'
     jams
A leak comes spirtin' thru some pin-hole cleft,
Grows stronger, fercer, tears out right an'
     left,   80
Then all the waters bow themselves an' come,
Suddin, in one gret slope o' shedderin' foam,
Jes' so our Spring gits everythin' in tune
An' gives one leap from Aperl into June:
Then all comes crowdin' in; afore you
     think   85
Young oak-leaves mist the side-hill woods
     with pink;
The catbird in the laylock-bush is loud;
The orchards turn to heaps o' rosy cloud;
Red-cedars blossom tu, though few folks know
     it,
An' look all dipt in sunshine like a poet;   90
The lime-trees pile their solid stacks o' shade
An' drows'ly simmer with the bees' sweet
     trade;
In ellum-shrouds the flashin' hangbird clings
An' for the summer vy'ge his hammock
     slings;
All down the loose-walled lanes in archin'
     bowers   95
The barb'ry droops its strings o' golden
     flowers,
Whose shrinkin' hearts the school-gals love
     to try
With pins, — they'll worry yourn so, boys,
     bimeby!
But I don't love your cat'logue style, — do
     you? —
Ez ef to sell off Natur' by vendoo;   100
One word with blood in't 's twice ez good ez
     two:
'nuff sed, June's bridesman, poet o' the year,

Gladness on wings, the bobolink, is here;
Half-hid in tip-top apple-blooms he swings,
Or climbs aginst the breeze with quiverin'
     wings,   105
Or, givin' way to 't in a mock despair,
Runs down, a brook o' laughter, thru the air.
I ollus feel the sap start in my veins
In Spring, with curus heats an' prickly pains,
Thet drive me, when I git a chance, to
     walk   110
Off by myself to hev a privit talk
With a queer critter thet can't seem to 'gree
Along o' me like most folks, — Mister Me.
Ther' 's times when I'm unsoshle ez a stone,
An' sort o' suffercate to be alone, —   115
I'm crowded jes' to think thet folks are nigh,
An' can't bear nothin' closer than the sky;
Now the wind's full ez shifty in the mind
Ez wut it is ou'-doors, ef I ain't blind,
An' sometimes, in the fairest sou'west
     weather,   120
My innard vane points east for weeks to-
     gether,
My natur' gits all goose-flesh, an' my sins
Come drizzlin' on my conscience sharp ez
     pins:
Wal, et sech times I jes' slip out o' sight
An' take it out in a fair stan'-up fight   125
With the one cuss I can't lay on the shelf,
The crook'dest stick in all the heap, — My-
     self.

'Twuz so las' Sabbath arter meetin'-time:
Findin' my feelin's wouldn't noways rhyme
With nobody's, but off the hendle flew   130
An' took things from an east-wind pint o'
     view,
I started off to lose me in the hills
Where the pines be, up back o' 'Siah's Mills:
Pines, ef you're blue, are the best friends I
     know,
They mope an' sigh an' sheer your feelin's
     so, —   135
They hesh the ground beneath so, tu, I swan,
You half-forgit you've gut a body on.
Ther' 's a small school'us' there where four
     roads meet,
The door-steps hollered out by little feet,
An' side-posts carved with names whose
     owners grew   140
To gret men, some on 'em, an' deacons, tu;
'taint used no longer, coz the town hez gut

A high-school, where they teach the Lord
    knows wut:
Three-story larnin' 's pop'lar now; I guess
We thriv' ez wal on jes' two stories less,   145
For it strikes me ther' 's sech a thing ez
    sinnin'
By overloadin' children's underpinnin':
Wal, here it wuz I larned my A B C,
An' it's a kind o' favorite spot with me.

We're curus critters: Now ain't jes' the
    minute   150
Thet ever fits us easy while we're in it;
Long ez 'twuz futur', 'twould be perfect
    bliss, —
Soon ez it's past, *thet* time's wuth ten o' this;
An' yet there ain't a man thet need be told
Thet Now's the only bird lays eggs o' gold.
A knee-high lad, I used to plot an' plan   156
An' think 'twuz life's cap-sheaf to be a man;
Now, gittin' gray, there's nothin' I enjoy
Like dreamin' back along into a boy:
So the ole school'us' is a place I choose   160
Afore all others, ef I want to muse;
I set down where I used to set, an' git
My boyhood back, an' better things with
    it, —
Faith, Hope, an' sunthin', ef it isn't Cher-
    rity,
It's want o' guile, an' thet's ez gret a rerrity,
While Fancy's cushin', free to Prince and
    Clown,   166
Makes the hard bench ez soft ez milk-weed-
    down.

Now, 'fore I knowed, thet Sabbath arternoon
When I sot out to tramp myself in tune,
I found me in the school'us' on my seat,   170
Drummin' the march to No-wheres with my
    feet.
Thinkin' o' nothin', I've heerd ole folks say
Is a hard kind o' dooty in its way:
It's thinkin' everythin' you ever knew,
Or ever hearn, to make your feelin's blue.
I sot there tryin' thet on for a spell: 176
I thought o' the Rebellion, then o' Hell,
Which some folks tell ye now is jest a metter-
    for
(A the'ry, p'raps, it wun't *feel* none the bet-
    ter for);
I thought o' Reconstruction, wut we'd
    win   180

Patchin' our patent self-blow-up agin:
I thought ef this 'ere milkin' o' the wits,
So much a month, warn't givin' Natur'
    fits, —
Ef folks warn't druv, findin' their own milk
    fail,
To work the cow thet hez an iron tail,   185
An' ef idees 'thout ripenin' in the pan
Would send up cream to humor ary man:
From this to thet I let my worryin' creep,
Till finally I must ha' fell asleep.

Our lives in sleep are some like streams thet
    glide   190
'twixt flesh an' sperrit boundin' on each side,
Where both shores' shadders kind o' mix an'
    mingle
In sunthin' thet ain't jes' like either single;
An' when you cast off moorin's from To-day,
An' down towards To-morrer drift away,   195
The imiges thet tengle on the stream
Make a new upside-down'ard world o'
    dream:
Sometimes they seem like sunrise-streaks an'
    warnin's
O' wut'll be in Heaven on Sabbath-mornin's,
An', mixed right in ez ef jest out o' spite,
Sunthin' thet says your supper ain't gone
    right.   201
I'm gret on dreams, an' often when I wake,
I've lived so much it makes my mem'ry ache,
An' can't skurce take a cat-nap in my cheer
'thout hevin' 'em, some good, some bad, all
    queer.   205

Now I wuz settin' where I'd ben, it seemed,
An' ain't sure yit whether I r'ally dreamed,
Nor, ef I did, how long I might ha' slep',
When I hearn some un stompin' up the step,
An' lookin' round, ef two an' two make
    four,   210
I see a Pilgrim Father in the door.
He wore a steeple-hat, tall boots, an' spurs
With rowels to 'em big ez ches'nut-burrs,
An' his gret sword behind him sloped away
Long'z a man's speech thet dunno wut to
    say. —   215
"Ef your name's Biglow, an' your given-
    name
Hosee," sez he, "it's arter you I came;
I'm your gret-gran'ther multiplied by
    three." —

"My *wut?*" sez I. — "Your gret-gret-gret,"
        sez he:
"You wouldn't ha' never ben here but for
        me.   220
Two hundred an' three year ago this May
The ship I come in sailed up Boston Bay;
I'd been a cunnle in our Civil War, —
But wut on airth hev *you* gut up one for?
Coz we du things in England, 'tain't for you
To git a notion you can du 'em tu;   226
I'm told you write in public prints: ef true,
It's nateral you should know a thing or
        two." —
"Thet air's an argymunt I can't endorse, —
'twould prove, coz you wear spurs, you kep'
        a horse: 230
For brains," sez I, "wutever you may think,
Ain't boun' to cash the drafs o' pen-an'-ink, —
Though mos' folks write ez ef they hoped jes'
        quickenin'
The churn would argoo skim-milk into
        thickenin';
But skim-milk ain't a thing to change its
        view   235
O' wut it's meant for more'n a smoky flue.
But du pray tell me, 'fore we furder go,
How in all Natur' did you come to know
'bout our affairs," sez I, "in Kingdom-
        Come?" —
"Wal, I worked round at sperrit-rappin'
        some,   240
An' danced the tables till their legs wuz gone,
In hopes o' larnin' wut wuz goin' on,"
Sez he, "but mejums lie so like all-split
Thet I concluded it wuz best to quit.
But, come now, ef you wun't confess to
        knowin',   245
You've some conjectures how the thing's
        a-goin'." —
"Gran'ther," sez I, "a vane warn't never
        known
Nor asked to hev a jedgment of its own;
An' yit, ef 'tain't gut rusty in the jints,
It's safe to trust its say on certin pints: 250
It knows the wind's opinions to a T,
An' the wind settles wut the weather'll be."
"I never thought a scion of our stock
Could grow the wood to make a weathercock;
When I wuz younger'n you, skurce more'n a
        shaver,   255
No airthly wind," sez he, "could make me
        waver!"

(Ez he said this, he clinched his jaw an' fore-
        head,
Hitchin' his belt to bring his sword-hilt for-
        rard.) —
"Jes so it wuz with me," sez I, "I swow,
When *I* wuz younger'n wut you see me
        now, —   260
Nothin' from Adam's fall to Huldy's bonnet
Thet I warn't full-cocked with my jedgment
        on it;
But now I'm gettin' on in life, I find
It's a sight harder to make up my mind, —
Nor I don't often try tu, when events   265
Will du it for me free of all expense.
The moral question's ollus plain enough, —
It's jes' the human-natur' side thet's tough;
Wut's best to think mayn't puzzle me nor
        you, —
The pinch comes in decidin' wut to *du*;   270
Ef you *read* History, all runs smooth ez
        grease,
Coz there the men ain't nothin' more'n
        idees, —
But come to *make* it, ez we must to-day,
Th' idees hev arms an' legs an' stop the way:
It's easy fixin' things in facts an' figgers, —
They can't resist, nor warn't brought up
        with niggers;   276
But come to try your the'ry on, — why, then
Your facts an' figgers change to ign'ant men
Actin' ez ugly —" — "Smite 'em hip an'
        thigh!"
Sez gran'ther, "and let every man-child
        die!   280
Oh for three weeks o' Crommle an' the Lord!
Up, Isr'el, to your tents an' grind the
        sword!" —
"Thet kind o' thing worked wal in ole Judee,
But you forgit how long it's ben A.D.;
You think thet's ellerkence, — I call it
        shoddy,   285
A thing," sez I, "wun't cover soul nor body;
I like the plain all-wool o' common-sense,
Thet warms ye now, an' will a twelvemonth
        hence.
You took to follerin' where the Prophets
        beckoned,
An', fust you knowed on, back come Charles
        the Second;   290
Now wut I want's to hev all *we* gain stick,
An' not to start Millennium too quick;
We hain't to punish only, but to keep,

An' the cure's gut to go a cent'ry deep."
"Wall, milk-an'-water ain't the best o'
  glue,"   295
Sez he, "an' so you'll find afore you're thru;
Ef reshness venters sunthin', shilly-shally
Loses ez often wut's ten times the vally.
Thet exe of ourn, when Charles's neck gut
  split,
Opened a gap thet ain't bridged over yit: 300
Slav'ry's your Charles, the Lord hez gin the
  exe" —
"Our Charles," sez I, "hez gut eight million
  necks.
The hardest question ain't the black man's
  right,
The trouble is to 'mancipate the white;
One's chained in body an' can be sot free, 305
But t'other's chained in soul to an idee:
It's a long job, but we shall worry thru it;
Ef bagnets fail, the spellin'-book must du it."
"Hosee," sez he, "I think you're goin' to
  fail:

The rettlesnake ain't dangerous in the tail; 310
This 'ere rebellion's nothing but the rettle, —
You'll stomp on thet an' think you've won
  the bettle;
It's Slavery thet's the fangs an' thinkin' head,
An' ef you want selvation, cresh it dead, —
An' cresh it suddin, or you'll larn by waitin'
Thet Chance wun't stop to listen to de-
  batin'!"   316
"God's truth!" sez I, — "an' ef I held the
  club,
An' knowed jes' where to strike, — but
  there's the rub!" —
"Strike soon," sez he, "or you'll be deadly
  ailin', —
Folks thet's afeared to fail are sure o' failin';
God hates your sneakin' creturs thet be-
  lieve   321
He'll settle things they run away an' leave!"
He brought his foot down fercely, ez he
  spoke,
An' give me sech a startle thet I woke.

OLIVER WENDELL HOLMES (1809–1894)

Holmes's quality is expertly summed up by Odell Shepard: "Holmes contained in himself the man of wit, the man of imagination, and the man of science, and all three of them were continually diving into what he calls 'the infinite ocean of simili-tudes and analogies that rolls through the universe.' No doubt it was this triple equipment that enabled him to make his unerring gannetlike plunges out of the skies of abstract thought upon the one minute and distant object that could best illustrate and drive home his meaning. For he was quite wrong, of course, in implying that everyone can do this sort of thing. He came near the truth when he said, 'Just according to the intensity and extension of our mental being we shall see the many in the one and the one in the many.' " (*LHUS*, Vol. I, p. 600)

Holmes was born in Cambridge. He was born into the so-called Brahmin caste of New England, and, during his long life in Boston, became one of the pillars of that society, one of its favorite physicians, and its chief wit. He attended Phillips Academy at Andover, entered Harvard in 1825, and graduated in due course of four years. A year in the law school followed, in which he did not let his law studies interfere too much with his verse writing. While still a law student, in 1830, he wrote a fiery lyric that made his name known throughout the country, "Old Ironsides." The same year he found a new interest that would compete more successfully with his writing than would the law, and he spent four years in hard study of medicine in Boston and Paris, later in other Continental cities.

Returning to America in 1835, he began to practice medicine in Boston (he took as his motto "the smallest fevers thankfully received"), and wrote and lectured on the side. His first volume of poems had been issued in 1833, and he continued to produce occasional verses, essays, and medicinal dissertations. In 1838 he began a short period as professor of anatomy at Dartmouth College, and in 1847 entered upon thirty-five years of successful teaching as professor of anatomy and physiology in the Harvard Medical School.

When Lowell became editor of the *Atlantic Monthly* in 1857 he accepted the position on the condition that Holmes should contribute constantly. To the early numbers of this new magazine, Holmes sent *The Autocrat of the Breakfast Table*, published in 1858. *The Professor at the Breakfast Table* followed a year later, *Elsie Venner*, a novel, in 1861, and *The Poet at the Breakfast Table* in 1872. He wrote more essays, more "medicated novels," and some excellent familiar verse. When he visited Europe in 1886, at the age of 77, he captivated London just as he had won Boston. Oxford gave him a D.C.L., Cambridge and Edinburgh, LL.D. Holmes died in Boston, the last survivor of the great New England group.

The standard edition is the Riverside, in 13 volumes, 1891. The standard biography is *Life and Letters of Oliver Wendell Holmes*, by J. T. Morse, 2 volumes, 1896. There are good essays on Holmes by Leslie Stephen, *Studies of a Biographer*, 1907, vol. II, and by H. H. Clark, "Dr. Holmes: Re-interpretation," *New England Quarterly*, 1939. S. I. Hayakawa and H. M. Jones edited the selections in the *AWS*, 1939.

The Ballad of the Oysterman

(1830)

It was a tall young oysterman lived by the
    river-side,
His shop was just upon the bank, his boat was
    on the tide;
The daughter of a fisherman, that was so
    straight and slim,
Lived over on the other bank, right opposite
    to him.

It was the pensive oysterman that saw a
    lovely maid,   5
Upon a moonlight evening, a-sitting in the
    shade:
He saw her wave her handkerchief, as much
    as if to say,
"I'm wide awake, young oysterman, and all
    the folks away."

Then up arose the oysterman, and to himself
    said he,
"I guess I'll leave the skiff at home, for fear
    that folks should see;   10
I read it in the story-book, that, for to kiss his
    dear,
Leander swam the Hellespont, — and I will
    swim this here."

And he has leaped into the waves, and crossed
    the shining stream,
And he has clambered up the bank, all in the
    moonlight gleam;
Oh there were kisses sweet as dew, and words
    as soft as rain, —   15
But they have heard her father's step, and in
    he leaps again!

Out spoke the ancient fisherman, — "Oh,
    what was that, my daughter?"
"'Twas nothing but a pebble, sir, I threw
    into the water."
"And what is that, pray tell me, love, that
    paddles off so fast?"
"It's nothing but a porpoise, sir, that's been
    a-swimming past."   20

Out spoke the ancient fisherman, — "Now
    bring me my harpoon!
I'll get into my fishing-boat, and fix the fel-
    low soon."
Down fell that pretty innocent, as falls a
    snow-white lamb,
Her hair drooped round her pallid cheeks,
    like seaweed on a clam.

Alas for those two loving ones! she waked not
    from her swound,   25
And he was taken with the cramp, and in the
    waves was drowned;

But Fate has metamorphosed them, in pity of
their woe,
And now they keep an oyster-shop for mermaids down below.

Old Ironsides

(1830)

"The frigate Constitution, historic indeed, but
old and unseaworthy, then lying in the navy
yard at Charlestown, was condemned by the
Navy Department to be destroyed. Holmes read
this in a newspaper paragraph, and it stirred
him. On a scrap of paper, with a lead pencil, he
rapidly shaped the impetuous stanzas of 'Old
Ironsides,' and sent them to the *Daily Advertiser*, of
Boston. Fast and far they travelled through the
newspaper press of the country; they were even
printed in hand-bills and circulated about the
streets of Washington. An occurrence, which
otherwise would probably have passed unnoticed,
now stirred a national indignation. The astonished Secretary made haste to retrace a step which
he had taken quite innocently in the way of business. The Constitution's tattered ensign was *not*
torn down. The ringing, spirited verses gave the
gallant ship a reprieve, which satisfied sentimen-
tality, and a large part of the people of the United
States had heard of O. W. Holmes, law student at
Cambridge, who had only come of age a month
ago" (Morse's *Life*, I, 79–80).

Ay, tear her tattered ensign down!
  Long has it waved on high,
And many an eye has danced to see
  That banner in the sky;
Beneath it rung the battle shout,   5
  And burst the cannon's roar; —
The meteor of the ocean air
  Shall sweep the clouds no more.

Her deck, once red with heroes' blood,
  Where knelt the vanquished foe,   10
When winds were hurrying o'er the flood,
  And waves were white below,
No more shall feel the victor's tread,
  Or know the conquered knee; —
The harpies of the shore shall pluck   15
  The eagle of the sea!

Oh, better that her shattered hulk
  Should sink beneath the wave;
Her thunders shook the mighty deep,
  And there should be her grave;   20

Nail to the mast her holy flag,
  Set every threadbare sail,
And give her to the god of storms,
  The lightning and the gale!

My Aunt

(1831)

My aunt! my dear unmarried aunt!
  Long years have o'er her flown;
Yet still she strains the aching clasp
  That binds her virgin zone;
I know it hurts her, — though she looks   5
  As cheerful as she can;
Her waist is ampler than her life,
  For life is but a span.

My aunt! my poor deluded aunt!
  Her hair is almost gray;   10
Why will she train that winter curl
  In such a spring-like way?
How can she lay her glasses down,
  And say she reads as well,
When through a double convex lens   15
  She just makes out to spell?

Her father — grandpapa! forgive
  This erring lip its smiles —
Vowed she should make the finest girl
  Within a hundred miles;   20
He sent her to a stylish school;
  'Twas in her thirteenth June;
And with her, as the rules required,
  "Two towels and a spoon."

They braced my aunt against a board,   25
  To make her straight and tall;
They laced her up, they starved her down,
  To make her light and small;
They pinched her feet, they singed her hair,
  They screwed it up with pins; —   30
Oh, never mortal suffered more
  In penance for her sins.

So, when my precious aunt was done,
  My grandsire brought her back
(By daylight, lest some rabid youth   35
  Might follow on the track);
"Ah!" said my grandsire, as he shook
  Some powder in his pan,
"What could this lovely creature do
  Against a desperate man!"   40

Alas! nor chariot, nor barouche,
  Nor bandit cavalcade,
Tore from the trembling father's arms
  His all-accomplished maid.
For her how happy had it been!   45
  And Heaven had spared to me
To see one sad, ungathered rose
  On my ancestral tree.

The Last Leaf

(1831 or 1832)

"The poem was suggested by the sight of a figure
well known to Bostonians [in 1831 or 1832], that
of Major Thomas Melville, 'the last of the cocked
hats,' as he was sometimes called. The Major had
been a personable young man, very evidently, and
retained evidence of it in
      The monumental pomp of age —
which had something imposing and something odd
about it for youthful eyes like mine. He was often
pointed at as one of the 'Indians' of the famous
'Boston Tea-Party' of 1774. His aspect among the
crowds of a later generation reminded me of a
withered leaf which has held to its stem through
the storms of autumn and winter, and finds itself
still clinging to its bough while the new growths of
spring are bursting their buds and spreading their
foliage all around it. I make this explanation for
the benefit of those who have been puzzled by the
lines,
      The last leaf upon the tree
        In the spring."

I saw him once before,
As he passed by the door,
  And again
The pavement stones resound,
As he totters o'er the ground   5
  With his cane.

They say that in his prime,
Ere the pruning-knife of Time
  Cut him down,
Not a better man was found   10
By the Crier on his round
  Through the town.

But now he walks the streets,
And he looks at all he meets
  Sad and wan,   15
And he shakes his feeble head,
That it seems as if he said,
  "They are gone."

The mossy marbles rest
On the lips that he has prest   20
  In their bloom,
And the names he loved to hear
Have been carved for many a year
  On the tomb.

My grandmamma has said ·   25
  Poor old lady, she is dead
  Long ago —
That he had a Roman nose,
And his cheek was like a rose
  In the snow;   30

But now his nose is thin,
And it rests upon his chin
  Like a staff,
And a crook is in his back,
And a melancholy crack   35
  In his laugh.

I know it is a sin
For me to sit and grin
  At him here;
But the old three-cornered hat,   40
And the breeches, and all that,
  Are so queer!

And if I should live to be
The last leaf upon the tree
  In the spring,   45
Let them smile, as I do now,
At the old forsaken bough
  Where I cling.

The Chambered Nautilus

(1858)

Embedded in *The Autocrat of the Breakfast-Table*
are a number of Holmes's poems of 1857–58, including "The Chambered Nautilus," "The Living
Temple," and "The Deacon's Masterpiece, or,
The Wonderful 'One-Hoss Shay.'" These three
are reprinted in the present volume, the first two
among Holmes's poems, and the "One-Hoss-
Shay" in its original setting among the selections
from *The Autocrat* (see pp. 489–90).
  "The Chambered Nautilus" is introduced by
the Autocrat as follows: "— Did I not say to you a
little while ago that the universe swam in an ocean
of similitudes and analogies? I will not quote
Cowley, or Burns, or Wordsworth, just now, to
show you what thoughts were suggested to them
by the simplest natural objects, such as a flower or

a leaf; but I will read you a few lines, if you do not object, suggested by looking at a section of one of those chambered shells to which is given the name of Pearly Nautilus. . . . If you will look into Roget's Bridgewater Treatise, you will find a figure of one of these shells and a section of it. The last will show you the series of enlarging compartments successively dwelt in by the animal that inhabits the shell, which is built in a widening spiral. Can you find no lesson in this?"

This is the ship of pearl, which, poets feign,
    Sails the unshadowed main, —
    The venturous bark that flings
On the sweet summer wind its purpled wings
    In gulfs enchanted, where the Siren sings. 5
    And coral reefs lie bare,
Where the cold sea-maids rise to sun their
    streaming hair.

Its webs of living gauze no more unfurl;
    Wrecked is the ship of pearl!
    And every chambered cell,   10
Where its dim dreaming life was wont to
    dwell,
As the frail tenant shaped his growing shell,
    Before thee lies revealed, —
Its irised ceiling rent, its sunless crypt un-
    sealed!

Year after year beheld the silent toil 15
    That spread his lustrous coil;
    Still, as the spiral grew,
He left the past year's dwelling for the new,
Stole with soft step its shining archway
    through,
    Built up its idle door,   20
Stretched in his last-found home, and knew
    the old no more.

Thanks for the heavenly message brought by
    thee,
    Child of the wandering sea,
    Cast from her lap, forlorn!
From thy dead lips a clearer note is born 25
Than ever Triton blew from wreathèd horn!
    While on mine ear it rings,
Through the deep caves of thought I hear a
    voice that sings: —

Build thee more stately mansions, O my soul,
    As the swift seasons roll! 30
    Leave thy low-vaulted past!

Let each new temple, nobler than the last,
Shut thee from heaven with a dome more
    vast,
    Till thou at length art free,
Leaving thine outgrown shell by life's unrest-
    ing sea!

The Living Temple

(1858)

"Having read our company so much of the Professor's talk about age and other subjects connected with physical life, I took the next Sunday morning to repeat to them the following poem of his, which I have had by me for some time. He calls it — I suppose for his professional friends — 'The Anatomist's Hymn,' but I shall name it 'The Living Temple' " (*The Autocrat*).

Not in the world of light alone,
Where God has built his blazing throne,
Nor yet alone in earth below,
With belted seas that come and go,
And endless isles of sunlit green, 5
Is all thy Maker's glory seen:
Look in upon thy wondrous frame, —
Eternal wisdom still the same!

The smooth, soft air with pulse-like waves
Flows murmuring through its hidden caves,
Whose streams of brightening purple rush, 11
Fired with a new and livelier blush,
While all their burden of decay
The ebbing current steals away,
And red with Nature's flame they start 15
From the warm fountains of the heart.

No rest that throbbing slave may ask,
Forever quivering o'er his task,
While far and wide a crimson jet
Leaps forth to fill the woven net 20
Which in unnumbered crossing tides
The flood of burning life divides,
Then, kindling each decaying part,
Creeps back to find the throbbing heart.

But warmed with that unchanging flame 25
Behold the outward moving frame,
Its living marbles jointed strong
With glistening band and silvery thong,
And linked to reason's guiding reins
By myriad rings in trembling chains, 30
Each graven with the threaded zone
Which claims it as the master's own.

See how yon beam of seeming white
Is braided out of seven-hued light,
Yet in those lucid globes no ray   35
By any chance shall break astray.
Hark how the rolling surge of sound,
Arches and spirals circling round,
Wakes the hushed spirit through thine ear
With music it is heaven to hear.   40

Then mark the cloven sphere that holds
All thought in its mysterious folds;
That feels sensation's faintest thrill,
And flashes forth the sovereign will;
Think on the stormy world that dwells   45
Locked in its dim and clustering cells!
The lightning gleams of power it sheds
Along its hollow glassy threads!

O Father! grant thy love divine
To make these mystic temples thine!   50
When wasting age and wearying strife
Have sapped the leaning walls of life,
When darkness gathers over all,
And the last tottering pillars fall,
Take the poor dust thy mercy warms,   55
And mould it into heavenly forms!

To My Readers

(1862)

Prologue to the collected edition of Holmes's
poems, 1862.

Nay, blame me not; I might have spared
  Your patience many a trivial verse,
Yet these my earlier welcome shared,
  So, let the better shield the worse.

And some might say, "Those ruder songs   5
  Had freshness which the new have lost;
To spring the opening leaf belongs,
  The chestnut-burs await the frost."

When those I wrote, my locks were brown,
  When these I write — ah, well-a-day!   10
The autumn thistle's silvery down
  Is not the purple bloom of May!

Go, little book, whose pages hold
  Those garnered years in loving trust;
How long before your blue and gold   15
  Shall fade and whiten in the dust?

O sexton of the alcoved tomb,
  Where souls in leathern cerements lie,
Tell me each living poet's doom!
  How long before his book shall die?   20

It matters little, soon or late,
  A day, a month, a year, an age, —
I read oblivion in its date,
  And Finis on its title-page.

Before we sighed, our griefs were told;   25
  Before we smiled, our joys were sung;
And all our passions shaped of old
  In accents lost to mortal tongue.

In vain a fresher mould we seek, —
  Can all the varied phrases tell   30
That Babel's wandering children speak
  How thrushes sing or lilacs smell?

Caged in the poet's lonely heart,
  Love wastes unheard its tenderest tone;
The soul that sings must dwell apart,   35
  Its inward melodies unknown.

Deal gently with us, ye who read!
  Our largest hope is unfulfilled, —
The promise still outruns the deed, —
  The tower, but not the spire, we build. 40

Our whitest pearl we never find;
  Our ripest fruit we never reach;
The flowering moments of the mind
  Drop half their petals in our speech.

These are my blossoms; if they wear   45
  One streak of morn or evening's glow,
Accept them; but to me more fair
  The buds of song that never blow.

Dorothy Q.

A FAMILY PORTRAIT

(1871)

Grandmother's mother: her age, I guess,
Thirteen summers, or something less;
Girlish bust, but womanly air;
Smooth, square forehead with uprolled hair;
Lips that lover has never kissed;   5
Taper fingers and slender wrist;

Hanging sleeves of stiff brocade;
So they painted the little maid.

On her hand a parrot green
Sits unmoving and broods serene.   10
Hold up the canvas full in view, —
Look! there's a rent the light shines through,
Dark with a century's fringe of dust, —
That was a Red-Coat's rapier-thrust!
Such is the tale the lady old,   15
Dorothy's daughter's daughter, told.

Who the painter was none may tell, —
One whose best was not over well;
Hard and dry, it must be confessed,
Flat as a rose that has long been pressed;   20
Yet in her cheek the hues are bright,
Dainty colors of red and white,
And in her slender shape are seen
Hint and promise of stately mien.

Look not on her with eyes of scorn, —   25
Dorothy Q. was a lady born!
Ay! since the galloping Normans came,
England's annals have known her name;
And still to the three-hilled rebel town
Dear is that ancient name's renown,   30
For many a civic wreath they won,
The youthful sire and the gray-haired son.

O Damsel Dorothy! Dorothy Q.!
Strange is the gift that I owe to you;
Such a gift as never a king   35
Save to daughter or son might bring, —
All my tenure of heart and hand,
All my title to house and land;
Mother and sister and child and wife
And joy and sorrow and death and life!   40

What if a hundred years ago
Those close-shut lips had answered No,
When forth the tremulous question came
That cost the maiden her Norman name.
And under the folds that look so still   45
The bodice swelled with the bosom's thrill?
Should I be I, or would it be
One tenth another, to nine tenths me?

Soft is the breath of a maiden's YES:
Not the light gossamer stirs with less;   50
But never a cable that holds so fast
Through all the battles of wave and blast,

And never an echo of speech or song
That lives in the babbling air so long!
There were tones in the voice that whispered
    then   55
You may hear to-day in a hundred men.

O lady and lover, how faint and far
Your images hover, — and here we are,
Solid and stirring in flesh and bone, —
Edward's and Dorothy's — all their own, —
A goodly record for Time to show   61
Of a syllable spoken so long ago! —
Shall I bless you, Dorothy, or forgive
For the tender whisper that bade me live?

It shall be a blessing, my little maid!   65
I will heal the stab of the Red-Coat's blade,
And freshen the gold of the tarnished frame,
And gild with a rhyme your household name;
So you shall smile on us brave and bright
As first you greeted the morning's light,   70
And live untroubled by woes and fears
Through a second youth of a hundred years.

At the Saturday Club
(1884)

"Nothing could be further from the ordinary
idea of the romantic 'man of genius,' " Mrs. James
T. Fields said of Holmes, "than was his well-
trimmed little figure, and nothing more surprising
and delightful than the way in which his childish-
ness of nature would break out and assert itself.
. . . Given a dinner-table, with light and color and
somebody occasionally to throw the ball, his spirits would rise and coruscate astonishingly. He
was not unaware if men whom he considered his
superiors were present; he was sure to make them
understand that he meant to sit at their feet and
listen to them, even if his own excitement ran
away with him."

Among the best of Holmes's opportunities to
"coruscate astonishingly" were the meetings of the
famous Saturday Club. "It was natural enough,"
said Holmes himself, "that such men as Emerson,
Longfellow, Agassiz, Peirce, with Hawthorne,
Motley, Sumner, when within reach, and others
who would be good company for them, should
meet and dine together once in a while, as they
did, in point of fact, every month, and as some who
are still living, with other and newer members,
still meet and dine."

In 1883 Holmes wrote to Lowell: "I go to the
Saturday Club quite regularly, but the company
is more of ghosts than of flesh and blood for me.
I carry a stranger there now and then, introduce
him to the members who happen to be there, and
then say: There at that end used to sit Agassiz;

here at this end Longfellow; Emerson used to be
there, and Lowell often next him; on such an
occasion Hawthorne was with us, at another time
Motley, and Sumner, and smaller constellations, —
nebulæ if you will, but luminous more or less in
the provincial firmament."

This is our place of meeting; opposite
That towered and pillared building: look at
    it;
King's Chapel in the Second George's day,
Rebellion stole its regal name away, —
Stone Chapel sounded better; but at last   5
The poisoned name of our provincial past
Had lost its ancient venom; then once more
Stone Chapel was King's Chapel as before.
(So let rechristened North Street, when it
    can,
Bring back the days of Marlborough and
    Queen Anne!)   10
  Next the old church your wandering eye
    will meet —
A granite pile that stares upon the street —
Our civic temple; slanderous tongues have
    said
Its shape was modelled from St. Botolph's
    head
Lofty, but narrow; jealous passers-by   15
Say Boston always held her head too high.
  Turn half-way round, and let your look
    survey
The white façade that gleams across the
    way, —
The many-windowed building, tall and wide,
The palace-inn that shows its northern side   20
In grateful shadow when the sunbeams beat
The granite wall in summer's scorching heat.
This is the place; whether its name you spell
Tavern, or caravansera, or hotel.
Would I could steal its echoes! you should
    find   25
Such store of vanished pleasures brought to
    mind:
Such feasts! the laughs of many a jocund hour
That shook the mortar from King George's
    tower;
Such guests! What famous names its record
    boasts,   29
Whose owners wander in the mob of ghosts!
Such stories! Every beam and plank is filled
With juicy wit the joyous talkers spilled,
Ready to ooze, as once the mountain pine
The floors are laid with oozed its turpentine!

A month had flitted since The Club had
    met;   35
The day came round; I found the table set,
The waiters lounging round the marble stairs,
Empty as yet the double row of chairs.
I was a full half hour before the rest,
Alone, the banquet-chamber's single guest.
So from the table's side a chair I took,   41
And having neither company nor book
To keep me waking, by degrees there crept
A torpor over me, — in short, I slept.

Loosed from its chain, along the wreck-
    strown track   45
Of the dead years my soul goes travelling
    back;
My ghosts take on their robes of flesh; it
    seems
Dreaming is life; nay, life less life than
    dreams,
So real are the shapes that meet my eyes.
They bring no sense of wonder, no surprise,   50
No hint of other than an earth-born source;
All seems plain daylight, everything of course.
  How dim the colors are, how poor and faint
This palette of weak words with which I
    paint!
Here sit my friends; if I could fix them so   55
As to my eyes they seem, my page would glow
Like a queen's missal, warm as if the brush
Of Titian or Velasquez brought the flush
Of life into their features. *Ay de mi!*
If syllables were pigments, you should see   60
Such breathing portraitures as never man
Found in the Pitti or the Vatican.

  Here sits our POET, Laureate, if you will.
Long has he worn the wreath, and wears it
    still.
Dead? Nay, not so; and yet they say his
    bust   65
Looks down on marbles covering royal dust,
Kings by the Grace of God, or Nature's grace;
Dead! No! Alive! I see him in his place,
Full-featured, with the bloom that heaven
    denies
Her children, pinched by cold New England
    skies,   70
Too often, while the nursery's happier few
Win from a summer cloud its roseate hue.
Kind, soft-voiced, gentle, in his eye there
    shines

The ray serene that filled Evangeline's.
Modest he seems, not shy; content to wait
Amid the noisy clamor of debate   76
The looked-for moment when a peaceful
        word
Smooths the rough ripples louder tongues
        have stirred.
In every tone I mark his tender grace
And all his poems hinted in his face;   80
What tranquil joy his friendly presence gives!
How could I think him dead? He lives! He
        lives!

There, at the table's further end I see
In his old place our Poet's *vis-à-vis*,
The great PROFESSOR, strong, broad-shoul-
        dered, square,   85
In life's rich noontide, joyous, debonair.
His social hour no leaden care alloys,
His laugh rings loud and mirthful as a
        boy's, —
That lusty laugh the Puritan forgot, —
What ear has heard it and remembers not? 90
How often, halting at some wide crevasse
Amid the windings of his Alpine pass,
High up the cliffs, the climbing mountaineer,
Listening the far-off avalanche to hear,
Silent, and leaning on his steel-shod staff, 95
Has heard that cheery voice, that ringing
        laugh,
From the rude cabin whose nomadic walls
Creep with the moving glacier as it crawls!
How does vast Nature lead her living train
In ordered sequence through that spacious
        brain,   100
As in the primal hour when Adam named
The new-born tribes that young creation
        claimed! —
How will her realm be darkened, losing thee,
Her darling, whom we call *our* AGASSIZ!

But who is he whose massive frame belies
The maiden shyness of his downcast eyes? 106
Who broods in silence till, by questions
        pressed,
Some answer struggles from his laboring
        breast?
An artist Nature meant to dwell apart,
Locked in his studio with a human heart, 110
Tracking its caverned passions to their lair,
And all its throbbing mysteries laying bare.
Count it no marvel that he broods alone

Over the heart he studies, — 'tis his own;
So in his page, whatever shape it wear, 115
The Essex wizard's shadowed self is there, —
The great ROMANCER, hid beneath his veil
Like the stern preacher of his sombre tale;
Virile in strength, yet bashful as a girl,
Prouder than Hester, sensitive as Pearl. 120

From his mild throng of worshippers re-
        leased,
Our Concord Delphi sends its chosen priest,
Prophet or poet, mystic, sage, or seer,
By every title always welcome here.
Why that ethereal spirit's frame describe? 125
You know the race-marks of the Brahmin
        tribe, —
The spare, slight form, the sloping shoulder's
        droop,
The calm, scholastic mien, the clerkly stoop,
The lines of thought the sharpened features
        wear,
Carved by the edge of keen New England
        air.   130
        List! for he speaks! As when a king would
        choose
The jewels for his bride, he might refuse
This diamond for its flaw, — find that less
        bright
Than those, its fellows, and a pearl less white
Than fits her snowy neck, and yet at last, 135
The fairest gems are chosen, and made fast
In golden fetters; so, with light delays
He seeks the fittest word to fill his phrase;
Nor vain nor idle his fastidious quest,
His chosen word is sure to prove the best. 140
        Where in the realm of thought, whose air
        is song,
Does he, the Buddha of the West, belong?
He seems a wingèd Franklin, sweetly wise,
Born to unlock the secrets of the skies;
And which the nobler calling, — if 'tis fair
Terrestrial with celestial to compare, — 146
To guide the storm-cloud's elemental flame,
Or walk the chambers whence the lightning
        came,
Amidst the sources of its subtile fire,
And steal their effluence for his lips and
        lyre?   150
        If lost at times in vague aerial flights,
None treads with firmer footstep when he
        lights;
A soaring nature, ballasted with sense,

Wisdom without her wrinkles or pretence,
In every Bible he has faith to read,   155
And every altar helps to shape his creed.
Ask you what name this prisoned spirit
    bears
While with ourselves this fleeting breath it
    shares?
Till angels greet him with a sweeter one
In heaven, on earth we call him EMERSON. 160

I start; I wake; the vision is withdrawn;
Its figures fading like the stars at dawn;
Crossed from the roll of life their cherished
    names,
And memory's pictures fading in their
    frames;   164
Yet life is lovelier for these transient gleams
Of buried friendships; blest is he who dreams!

From The Autocrat of the
Breakfast-Table

(1857–58)

When, with the first issue of the *Atlantic Monthly*,
the *Autocrat* instalments began to appear, it was
evident that a new prose writer of high distinction
and wide appeal had been discovered. Holmes
was then already forty-eight years old. A quarter
of a century earlier, he had published, soon after
his graduation from college, two papers under the
title of "The Autocrat of the Breakfast-Table" in
the *New England Magazine*. To these early papers
Holmes wittily refers when he begins his *Atlantic*
series with the words, "I was just going to say,
when I was interrupted...." With these words
he embarks upon his rambling monologues before
a group of boarders, whose portraits are gradually
painted as the talk proceeds. But the center of
interest is the Autocrat's (Holmes's) mind, with
its apparently inexhaustible flow of Gallic wit,
worldly wisdom, penetrating logic, and poetic
feeling.

* * * Who was that boarder that just whispered something about the Macaulay-flowers
of literature? — There was a dead silence. —
I said calmly, I shall henceforth consider any
interruption by a pun as a hint to change my
boarding-house. Do not plead my example.
If *I* have used any such, it has been only as
a Spartan father would show up a drunken
helot. We have done with them.   50
    — If a logical mind ever found out any-
thing with its logic? — I should say that its

most frequent work was to build a *pons
asinorum* over chasms which shrewd people
can bestride without such a structure. You
can hire logic, in the shape of a lawyer, to
prove anything that you want to prove. You   5
can buy treatises to show that Napoleon
never lived, and that no battle of Bunker-hill
was ever fought. The great minds are those
with a wide span,[1] which couple truths related to, but far removed from, each other.   10
Logicians carry the surveyor's chain over the
track of which these are the true explorers.
I value a man mainly for his primary relations with truth, as I understand truth, — not
for any secondary artifice in handling his   15
ideas. Some of the sharpest men in argument
are notoriously unsound in judgment. I
should not trust the counsel of a clever de-
bater, any more than that of a good chess-
player. Either may of course advise wisely,   20
but not necessarily because he wrangles or
plays well.

The old gentleman who sits opposite got
his hand up, as a pointer lifts his forefoot, at
the expression, "his relations with truth, as I 25
understand truth," and when I had done,
sniffed audibly, and said I talked like a transcendentalist. For his part, common sense
was good enough for him.
    Precisely so, my dear sir, I replied; common 30
sense, *as you understand it*. We all have to
assume a standard of judgment in our own
minds, either of things or persons. A man
who is willing to take another's opinion has
to exercise his judgment in the choice of   35
whom to follow, which is often as nice a matter as to judge of things for one's self. On the
whole, I had rather judge men's minds by
comparing their thoughts with my own, than
judge of thoughts by knowing who utter   40
them. I must do one or the other. It does
not follow, of course, that I may not recognize another man's thoughts as broader and
deeper than my own; but that does not necessarily change my opinion, otherwise this   45
would be at the mercy of every superior mind
that held a different one. How many of our
most cherished beliefs are like those drinking-
glasses of the ancient pattern, that serve us

[1] There is something like this in J. H. Newman's
Grammar of Assent. See *Characteristics*, arranged by
W. S. Lilly, p. 81. [*Author's note.*]

well so long as we keep them in our hand, but spill all if we attempt to set them down! I have sometimes compared conversation to the Italian game of *mora*, in which one player lifts his hand with so many fingers extended, and the other gives the number if he can. I show my thought, another his; if they agree, well; if they differ, we find the largest common factor, if we can, but at any rate avoid disputing about remainders and fractions, which is to real talk what tuning an instrument is to playing on it.

— What if, instead of talking this morning, I should read you a copy of verses, with critical remarks by the author? Any of the company can retire that like.

ALBUM VERSES

When Eve had led her lord away,
   And Cain had killed his brother,
The stars and flowers, the poets say,
   Agreed with one another

To cheat the cunning tempter's art,
   And teach the race its duty,
By keeping on its wicked heart
   Their eyes of light and beauty.

A million sleepless lids, they say,
   Will be at least a warning;
And so the flowers would watch by day,
   The stars from eve to morning.

On hill and prairie, field and lawn,
   Their dewy eyes upturning,
The flowers still watch from reddening dawn
   Till western skies are burning.

Alas! each hour of daylight tells
   A tale of shame so crushing,
That some turn white as sea-bleached shells,
   And some are always blushing.

But when the patient stars look down
   On all their light discovers,
The traitor's smile, the murderer's frown,
   The lips of lying lovers,

They try to shut their saddening eyes,
   And in the vain endeavor
We see them twinkling in the skies,
   And so they wink forever.

What do *you* think of these verses, my friends? — Is that piece an impromptu? said my landlady's daughter. (Aet. 19+. Ten-

der-eyed blonde. Long ringlets. Cameo pin. Gold pencil-case on a chain. Locket. Bracelet. Album. Autograph book. Accordeon. Reads Byron, Tupper, and Sylvanus Cobb, Junior, while her mother makes the puddings. Says "Yes?" when you tell her anything.) — *Oui et non, ma petite,* — Yes and no, my child. Five of the seven verses were written off-hand; the other two took a week, — that is, were hanging round the desk in a ragged, forlorn, unrhymed condition as long as that. All poets will tell you just such stories. *C'est le* DERNIER *pas qui coûte.* Don't you know how hard it is for some people to get out of a room after their visit is really over? They want to be off, and you want to have them off, but they don't know how to manage it. One would think they had been built in your parlor or study, and were waiting to be launched. I have contrived a sort of ceremonial inclined plane for such visitors, which being lubricated with certain smooth phrases, I back them down, metaphorically speaking, stern-foremost, into their "native element," the great ocean of out-doors. Well, now, there are poems as hard to get rid of as these rural visitors. They come in glibly, use up all the serviceable rhymes, *day, ray, beauty, duty, skies, eyes, other, brother, mountain, fountain,* and the like; and so they go on until you think it is time for the wind-up, and the wind-up won't come on any terms. So they lie about until you get sick of the sight of them, and end by thrusting some cold scrap of a final couplet upon them, and turning them out of doors. I suspect a good many "impromptus" could tell just such a story as the above. — Here turning to our landlady, I used an illustration which pleased the company much at the time, and has since been highly commended. "Madam," I said, "you can pour three gills and three quarters of honey from that pint jug, if it is full, in less than one minute; but, Madam, you could not empty that last quarter of a gill though you were turned into a marble Hebe, and held the vessel upside down for a thousand years."

One gets tired to death of the old, old rhymes, such as you see in that copy of verses — which I don't mean to abuse, or to praise either. I always feel as if I were a cobbler, putting new top-leathers to an old pair of

boot-soles and bodies, when I am fitting sentiments to these venerable jingles.

.   .   .   .   youth
.   .   .   .   morning
.   .   .   .   truth
.   .   .   .   warning.

Nine tenths of the "Juvenile Poems" written spring out of the above musical and suggestive coincidences.

"Yes?" said our landlady's daughter.

I did not address the following remark to
her, and I trust, from her limited range of
reading, she will never see it; I said it softly
to my next neighbor.

When a young female wears a flat circular
side-curl, gummed on each temple, — when
she walks with a male, not arm in arm, but
his arm against the back of hers, — and when
she says "Yes?" with the note of interroga-
tion, you are generally safe in asking her
what wages she gets, and who the "feller"
was you saw her with.

"What were you whispering?" said the
daughter of the house, moistening her lips, as
she spoke, in a very engaging manner.

"I was only laying down a principle of
social diagnosis."

"Yes?"

* * * I really believe some people save
their bright thoughts as being too precious
for conversation. What do you think an admiring friend said the other day to one that
was talking good things, — good enough to
print? "Why," said he, "you are wasting
merchantable literature, a cash article, at the
rate, as nearly as I can tell, of fifty dollars an
hour." The talker took him to the window
and asked him to look out and tell what he
saw.

"Nothing but a very dusty street," he said,
"and a man driving a sprinkling-machine
through it."

"Why don't you tell the man he is wasting
that water? What would be the state of the
highways of life, if we did not drive our
thought-sprinklers through them with the
valves open, sometimes?

"Besides, there is another thing about this
talking, which you forget. It shapes our
thoughts for us; — the waves of conversation
roll them as the surf rolls the pebbles on the
shore. Let me modify the image a little. I
rough out my thoughts in talk as an artist
models in clay. Spoken language is so plastic, — you can pat and coax, and spread and
shave, and rub out, and fill up, and stick on
so easily, when you work that soft material,
that there is nothing like it for modelling.
Out of it come the shapes which you turn into
marble or bronze in your immortal books, if
you happen to write such. Or, to use another illustration, writing or printing is like
shooting with a rifle; you may hit your reader's mind, or miss it; — but talking is like
playing at a mark with the pipe of an engine;
if it is within reach, and you have time
enough, you can't help hitting it."

The company agreed that this last illustration was of superior excellence, or, in the
phrase used by them, "Fust-rate." I acknowledged the compliment, but gently re-
buked the expression. "Fust-rate," "prime,"
"a prime article," "a superior piece of goods,"
"a handsome garment," "a gent in a flowered
vest," — all such expressions are final. They
blast the lineage of him or her who utters
them, for generations up and down. * * *

The whole force of conversation depends
on how much you can take for granted. Vulgar chess-players have to play their game out;
nothing short of the brutality of an actual
checkmate satisfies their dull apprehensions.
But look at two masters of that noble game!
White stands well enough, so far as you can
see; but Red says, Mate in six moves; —
White looks, — nods; — the game is over.
Just so in talking with first-rate men; especially when they are good-natured and expansive, as they are apt to be at table. That
blessed clairvoyance which sees into things
without opening them, — that glorious license, which, having shut the door and driven
the reporter from its keyhole, calls upon
Truth, majestic virgin! to get down from her
pedestal and drop her academic poses, and
take a festive garland and the vacant place on
the medius lectus, — that carnival-shower of
questions and replies and comments, large
axioms bowled over the mahogany like
bomb-shells from professional mortars, and
explosive wit dropping its trains of many-
colored fire, and the mischief-making rain of
bon-bons pelting everybody that shows himself, — the picture of a truly intellectual ban-

quet is one which the old Divinities might well have attempted to reproduce in their —

— "Oh, oh, oh!" cried the young fellow whom they call John, — "that is from one of your lectures!"

I know it, I replied, — I concede it, I confess it, proclaim it. * * *

— Do not think, because I talk to you of many subjects briefly, that I should not find it much lazier work to take each one of them and dilute it down to an essay. Borrow some of my old college themes and water my remarks to suit yourselves, as the Homeric heroes did with their *melas oinos,* — that black, sweet, syrupy wine which they used to alloy with three parts or more of the flowing stream. [Could it have been *melasses,* as Webster and his provincials spell it, — or *Molossa's,* as dear old smattering, chattering, would-be-College-President, Cotton Mather, has it in the "Magnalia"? Ponder thereon, ye small antiquaries who make barn-door-fowl flights of learning in "Notes and Queries!" — ye Historical Societies, in one of whose venerable triremes I, too, ascend the stream of time, while other hands tug at the oars! — ye Amines of parasitical literature, who pick up your grains of native-grown food with a bodkin, having gorged upon less honest fare, until, like the great minds Goethe speaks of, you have "made a Golgotha" of your pages! — ponder thereon!] * * *

Just as we find a mathematical rule at the bottom of many of the bodily movements, just so thought may be supposed to have its regular cycles. Such or such a thought comes round periodically, in its turn. Accidental suggestions, however, so far interfere with the regular cycles, that we may find them practically beyond our power of recognition. Take all this for what it is worth, but at any rate you will agree that there are certain particular thoughts which do not come up once a day, nor once a week, but that a year would hardly go round without your having them pass through your mind. Here is one which comes up at intervals in this way. Some one speaks of it, and there is an instant and eager smile of assent in the listener or listeners. Yes, indeed; they have often been struck by it:

All at once a conviction flashes through us that

we have been in the same precise circumstances as at the present instant, once or many times before.

O, dear, yes! — said one of the company, — everybody has had that feeling.

The landlady didn't know anything about such notions; it was an idee in folks' heads, she expected.

The schoolmistress said, in a hesitating sort of way, that she knew the feeling well, and didn't like to experience it; it made her think she was a ghost, sometimes.

The young fellow whom they call John said he knew all about it; he had just lighted a cheroot the other day, when a tremendous conviction all at once came over him that he had done just the same thing ever so many times before. I looked severely at him, and his countenance immediately fell — *on the side toward me;* I cannot answer for the other, for he can wink and laugh with either half of his face without the other half's knowing it.

— I have noticed — I went on to say — the following circumstances connected with these sudden impressions. First, that the condition which seems to be the duplicate of a former one is often very trivial, — one that might have presented itself a hundred times. Secondly, that the impression is very evanescent, and that it is rarely, if ever, recalled by any voluntary effort, at least after any time has elapsed. Thirdly, that there is a disinclination to record the circumstances, and a sense of incapacity to reproduce the state of mind in words. Fourthly, I have often felt that the duplicate condition had not only occurred once before, but that it was familiar and, as it seemed, habitual. Lastly, I have had the same convictions in my dreams.

How do I account for it? — Why, there are several ways that I can mention, and you may take your choice. The first is that which the young lady hinted at; — that these flashes are sudden recollections of a previous existence. I don't believe that; for I remember a poor student I used to know told me he had such a conviction one day when he was blacking his boots, and I can't think he had ever lived in another world where they use Day and Martin.

Some think that Dr. Wigan's doctrine of the brain's being a double organ, its hemispheres working together like the two eyes, accounts for it. One of the hemispheres hangs fire, they suppose, and the small interval between the perceptions of the nimble and the sluggish half seems an indefinitely long period and therefore the second perception appears to be the copy of another, ever so old. But even allowing the centre of perception to be double, I can see no good reason for supposing this indefinite lengthening of the time, nor any analogy that bears it out. It seems to me most likely that the coincidence of circumstances is very partial, but that we take this partial resemblance for identity, as we occasionally do resemblances of persons. A momentary posture of circumstances is so far like some preceding one that we accept it as exactly the same, just as we accost a stranger occasionally, mistaking him for a friend. The apparent similarity may be owing perhaps, quite as much to the mental state at the time, as to the outward circumstances. * * *

— There is a natural tendency in many persons to run their adjectives together in *triads*, as I have heard them called, — thus He was honorable, courteous, and brave; she was graceful, pleasing, and virtuous. Dr. Johnson is famous for this; I think it was Bulwer who said you could separate a paper in the "Rambler" into three distinct essays. Many of our writers show the same tendency, — my friend, the Professor, especially. Some think it is in humble imitation of Johnson, — some that it is for the sake of the stately sound only. I don't think they get to the bottom of it. It is, I suspect, an instinctive and involuntary effort of the mind to present a thought or image with the *three dimensions* which belong to every solid, — an unconscious handling of an idea as if it had length, breadth, and thickness. It is a great deal easier to say this than to prove it, and a great deal easier to dispute it than to disprove it. But mind this: the more we observe and study, the wider we find the range of the automatic and instinctive principles in body, mind, and morals, and the narrower the limits of the self-determining conscious movement.

— I have often seen piano-forte players and singers make such strange motions over their instruments or song-books that I wanted to laugh at them. "Where did our friends pick up all these fine ecstatic airs?" I would say to myself. Then I would remember My Lady in "Marriage à la Mode," and amuse myself with thinking how affectation was the same thing in Hogarth's time and in our own. But one day I bought me a Canary-bird and hung him up in a cage at my window. By-and-by he found himself at home, and began to pipe his little tunes; and there he was, sure enough, swimming and waving about, with all the droopings and liftings and languishing side-turnings of the head that I had laughed at. And now I should like to ask, WHO taught him all this? — and me, through him, that the foolish head was not the one swinging itself from side to side and bowing and nodding over the music, but that other which was passing its shallow and self-satisfied judgment on a creature made of finer clay than the frame which carried that same head upon its shoulders?

— Do you want an image of the human will or the self-determining principle, as compared with its pre-arranged and impassable restrictions? A drop of water, imprisoned in a crystal; you may see such alone in any mineralogical collection. One little fluid particle in the crystalline prism of the solid universe!

— Weaken moral obligations? — No, not weaken but define them. When I preach that sermon I spoke of the other day, I shall have to lay down some principles not fully recognized in some of your textbooks.

I should have to begin with one most formidable preliminary. You saw an article the other day in one of the journals, perhaps, in which some old Doctor or other said quietly that patients were very apt to be fools and cowards. But a great many of the clergyman's patients are not only fools and cowards, but also liars.

[Immense sensation at the table. — Sudden retirement of the angular female in oxydated bombazine. Movement of adhesion — as they say in the Chamber of Deputies — on the part of the young fellow they call John. Falling of the old-gentleman-opposite's lower jaw — (gravitation is beginning to get the better of him.) Our landlady to Benjamin Franklin, briskly, — Go to school right off, there's a good boy! Schoolmistress curious. — takes a quick glance at divinity-student, Divinity-student slightly flushed; draws his shoulders back a little, as if a big falsehood, — or truth, — had hit him in the forehead. Myself calm.]

— I should not make such a speech as that, you know, without having pretty substantial indorsers to fall back upon, in case my credit should be disputed. Will you run upstairs, Benjamin Franklin (for B. F. had *not* gone right off, of course), and bring down a small volume from the left upper corner of the right-hand shelves?

[Look at the precious little black, ribbed backed, clean-typed, vellum-papered 32mo. "DESIDERII ERASMI COLLOQUIA. Amstelodami. Typis Ludovici Elzevirii. 1650." Various names written on title-page. Most conspicuous this: Gul. Cookeson, E. Coll. Omn. Anim. 1725. Oxon.

— O William Cookeson, of All-Souls College, Oxford, — then writing as I now write, — now in the dust, where I shall lie, — is this line all that remains to thee of earthly remembrance? Thy name is at least once more spoken by living men; — is it a pleasure to thee? Thou shalt share with me my little draught of immortality, — its week, its month, its year, — whatever it may be, — and then we will go together into the solemn archives of Oblivion's Uncatalogued Library!]

— If you think I have used rather strong language, I shall have to read something to you out of the book of this keen and witty scholar, — the great Erasmus, — who "laid the egg of the Reformation which Luther hatched." Oh, you never read his *Naufragium*, or "Shipwreck," did you? Of course not; for, if you had, I don't think you would have given me credit, — or discredit, — for entire originality in that speech of mine. That men are cowards in the contemplation of futurity he illustrates by the extraordinary antics of many on board the sinking vessel; that they are fools, by their praying to the sea, and making promises to bits of wood from the true cross, and all manner of similar nonsense; that they are fools, cowards, and liars all at once, by this story: I will put it into rough English for you. — "I couldn't help laughing to hear one fellow bawling out, so that he might be sure to be heard, a promise to Saint Christopher of Paris — the monstrous statue in the great church there, — that he would give him a wax taper as big as himself. 'Mind what you promise!' said an acquaintance who stood near him, poking him with his elbow; 'you couldn't pay for it, if you sold all your things at auction.' 'Hold your tongue, you donkey!' said the fellow, — but softly, so that Saint Christopher should not hear him, — 'do you think I'm in earnest? If I once get my foot on dry ground, catch me giving him so much as a tallow candle!' "

Now, therefore, remembering that those who have been loudest in their talk about the great subject of which we were speaking have not necessarily been wise, brave, and true men, but, on the contrary, have very often been wanting in one or two or all of the qualities these words imply, I should expect to find a good many doctrines current in the schools which I should be obliged to call foolish, cowardly, and false.

— So you would abuse other people's beliefs, Sir, and yet not tell us your own creed! — said the divinity-student, coloring up with a spirit for which I liked him all the better.

— I have a creed, — I replied; — none better, and none shorter. It is told in two words, — the two first of the Paternoster. And when I say these words I mean them. And when I compared the human will to a drop in a crystal, and said I meant to *define* moral obligations, and not weaken them, this was what I intended to express: that the fluent, self-determining power of human beings is a very strictly limited agency in the universe. The chief planes of its enclosing solid are, of course, organization, education, condition. Organization may reduce the power of the will to nothing, as in some idiots; and from this zero the scale mounts upwards by slight gradations. Education is only second to nature. Imagine all the infants born this year in Boston and Timbuctoo to change places! Condition does less, but "Give me neither poverty nor riches" was the prayer of Agur, and with good reason. If there is any improvement in modern theology, it is in getting out of the region of pure abstractions and taking these every-day working forces into account. The great theological question now heaving and throbbing in the minds of Christian men is this: —

No, I won't talk about these things now. My remarks might be repeated, and it would give my friends pain to see with what personal incivilities I should be visited. Besides, what business has a mere boarder to be talking about such things at a breakfast-table? Let him make puns. To be sure, he was brought up among the Christian fathers, and learned his alphabet out of a quarto "Concilium Tridentinum." He has also heard many thousand theological lectures by men of various denominations; and it is not at all to the credit of these teachers, if he is not fit by this time to express an opinion on theological matters.

I know well enough that there are some of you who had a great deal rather see me stand on my head than use it for any purpose of thought. Does not my friend, the Professor, receive at least two letters a week, requesting him to ...., — on the strength of some youthful antic of his, which, no doubt, authorizes the intelligent constituency of autograph-hunters to address him as a harlequin?

— Well, I can't be savage with you for wanting to laugh, and I like to make you laugh well enough, when I can. But then observe this: if the sense of the ridiculous is one side of an impressible nature, it is very well; but if that is all there is in a man, he had better have been an ape at once, and so have stood at the head of his profession. Laughter and tears are meant to turn the wheels of the same machinery of sensibility; one is wind-power, and the other water-power; that is all. I have often heard the Professor talk about hysterics as being Nature's cleverest illustration of the reciprocal convertibility of the two states of which these acts are the manifestations. But you may see it every day in children; and if you want to choke with stifled tears at the sight of the transition, as it shows itself in older years, go and see Mr. Blake play *Jesse Rural*.

It is a very dangerous thing for a literary man to indulge his love for the ridiculous. People laugh *with* him just so long as he amuses them; but if he attempts to be serious, they must still have their laugh, and so they laugh *at* him. There is in addition, however, a deeper reason for this than would at first appear. Do you know that you feel a little superior to every man who makes you laugh, whether by making faces or verses? Are you aware that you have a pleasant sense of patronizing him, when you condescend so far as to let him turn somersets, literal or literary, for your royal delight? Now if a man can only be allowed to stand on a daïs, or raised platform, and look down on his neighbor who is exerting his talent for him, oh, it is all right! — first-rate performance! — and all the rest of the fine phrases. But if all at once the performer asks the gentleman to come upon the floor, and, stepping upon the platform, begins to talk down at him, — ah, that wasn't in the programme!

I have never forgotten what happened when Sydney Smith — who, as everybody knows, was an exceedingly sensible man, and a gentleman, every inch of him — ventured to preach a sermon on the Duties of Royalty. The "Quarterly," "so savage and tartarly," came down upon him in the most contemptuous style, as "a joker of jokes," a "diner-out of the first water," in one of his own phrases; sneering at him, insulting him, as nothing but a toady of a court, sneaking behind the anonymous, would ever have been mean enough to do a man of his position and genius, or to any decent person even. — If I were giving advice to a young fellow of talent, with two or three facets to his mind, I would tell him by all means to keep his wit in the background until after he had made a reputation by his more solid qualities. And so to an actor: *Hamlet* first, and *Bob Logic* afterwards, if you like; but don't think, as they say poor Liston used to, that people will be ready to allow that you can do anything great with *Macbeth's* dagger after flourishing about with *Paul Pry's* umbrella. Do you know, too, that the majority of men look upon all who challenge their attention, — for a while, at least, — as beggars, and nuisances? They always try to get off as cheaply as they can; and the cheapest of all things they can give a literary man — pardon the forlorn pleasantry! — is the *funny*-bone. That is all very well so far as it goes, but satisfies no man, and makes a good many angry, as I told you on a former occasion.

— Oh, indeed, no! — I am not ashamed to make you laugh, occasionally. I think I could read you something I have in my desk which would probably make you smile. Perhaps I will read it one of these days, if you are patient with me when I am sentimental and reflective; not just now. The ludicrous has its place in the universe; it is not a human invention, but one of the Divine ideas, illustrated in the practical jokes of kittens and monkeys long before Aristophanes or Shakspeare. How curious it is that we always consider solemnity and the absence of all gay surprises and encounter of wits as essential to the idea of the future life of those whom we thus deprive of half their faculties and then call *blessed!* There are not a few who, even in this life, seem to be preparing themselves for that smileless eternity to which they look forward, by banishing all gayety from their hearts and all joyousness from their countenances. I meet one such in the street not unfrequently, a person of intelligence and education, but who gives me (and all that he passes) such a rayless and chilling look of recognition, — something as if he were one of Heaven's assessors, come down to "doom" every acquaintance he met, — that I have sometimes begun to sneeze on the spot, and gone home with a violent cold, dating from that instant. I don't doubt he would cut his kitten's tail off, if he caught her playing with it. Please tell me, who taught her to play with it?

No, no! — give me a chance to talk to you, my fellow-boarders, and you need not be afraid that I shall have any scruples about entertaining you, if I can do it, as well as giving you some of my serious thoughts, and perhaps my sadder fancies. I know nothing in English or any other literature more admirable than that sentiment of Sir Thomas Browne, "EVERY MAN TRULY LIVES, SO LONG AS HE ACTS HIS NATURE, OR SOME WAY MAKES GOOD THE FACULTIES OF HIMSELF." * * *

Now I tell you a poem must be kept *and used*, like a meerschaum, or a violin. A poem is just as porous as the meerschaum; — the more porous it is, the better. I mean to say that a genuine poem is capable of absorbing an indefinite amount of the essence of our own humanity, — its tenderness, its heroism, its regrets, its aspirations, so as to be gradu-

ally stained through with a divine secondary color derived from ourselves. So you see it must take time to bring the sentiment of a poem into harmony with our nature, by staining ourselves through every thought and image our being can penetrate.

Then again as to the mere music of a new poem, why, who can expect anything more from that than from the music of a violin fresh from the maker's hands? Now you know very well that there are no less than fifty-eight different pieces in a violin. These pieces are strangers to each other, and it takes a century, more or less, to make them thoroughly acquainted. At last they learn to vibrate in harmony and the instrument becomes an organic whole, as if it were a great seed-capsule which had grown from a garden-bed in Cremona, or elsewhere. Besides, the wood is juicy and full of sap for fifty years or so, but at the end of fifty or a hundred more gets tolerably dry and comparatively resonant.

Don't you see that all this is just as true of a poem? Counting each word as a piece, there are more pieces in an average copy of verses than in a violin. The poet has forced all these words together, and fastened them, and they don't understand it at first. But let the poem be repeated aloud and murmured over in the mind's muffled whisper often enough, and at length the parts become knit together in such absolute solidarity that you could not change a syllable without the whole world's crying out against you for meddling with the harmonious fabric. * * *

Did you never, in walking in the fields, come across a large flat stone, which had lain, nobody knows how long, just where you found it, with the grass forming a little hedge, as it were, all round it, close to its edges, — and have you not, in obedience to a kind of feeling that told you it had been lying there long enough, insinuated your stick or your foot or your fingers under its edge and turned it over as a housewife turns a cake, when she says to herself, "It's done brown enough by this time"? What an odd revelation, and what an unforeseen and unpleasant surprise to a small community, the very existence of which you had not suspected, until the sudden dismay and scattering among its members produced by your turning the old stone over! Blades of grass flattened down, colorless, matted together, as if they had been bleached and ironed; hideous crawling creatures, some of them coleopterous or horny-shelled, — turtle-bugs one wants to call them; some of them softer, but cunningly spread out and compressed like Lepine watches; (Nature never loses a crack or a crevice, mind you, or a joint in a tavern bedstead, but she always has one of her flat-pattern live timekeepers to slide into it;) black, glossy crickets, with their long filaments sticking out like the whips of four-horse stage-coaches; motionless, slug-like creatures, young larvæ, perhaps more horrible in their pulpy stillness than even in the infernal wriggle of maturity! But no sooner is the stone turned and the wholesome light of day let upon this compressed and blinded community of creeping things, than all of them which enjoy the luxury of legs — and some of them have a good many — rush round wildly, butting each other and everything in their way, and end in a general stampede for underground retreats from the region poisoned by sunshine. *Next year* you will find the grass growing tall and green where the stone lay; the ground-bird builds her nest where the beetle had his hole; the dandelion and the buttercup are growing there, and the broad fans of insect-angels open and shut their golden disks, as the rhythmic waves of blissful consciousness pulsate through their glorified being.

— The young fellow whom they call John saw fit to say, in his very familiar way, — at which I do not choose to take offence, but which I sometimes think it necessary to repress, that I was coming it rather strong on the butterflies.

No, I replied; there is meaning in each of those images, — the butterfly as well as the others. The stone is ancient error. The grass is human nature borne down and bleached of all its color by it. The shapes which are found beneath are the crafty beings that thrive in darkness, and the weaker organisms kept helpless by it. He who turns the stone over is whosoever puts the staff of truth to the old lying incubus, no matter whether he do it with a serious face or a laughing one. The next year stands for the coming time.

Then shall the nature which had lain blanched and broken rise in its full stature and native hues in the sunshine. Then shall God's minstrels build their nests in the hearts of a newborn humanity. Then shall beauty — Divinity taking outlines and color — light upon the souls of men as the butterfly, image of the beautified spirit rising from the dust, soars from the shell that held a poor grub, which would never have found wings had not the stone been lifted.

You never need think you can turn over any old falsehood without a terrible squirming and scattering of the horrid little population that dwells under it. * * *

Sin has many tools, but a lie is the handle which fits them all.

— I think, Sir, — said the divinity-student, — you must intend that for one of the sayings of the Seven Wise Men of Boston you were speaking of the other day.

I thank you, my young friend, — was my reply, — but I must say something better than that, before I could pretend to fill out the number.

— The schoolmistress wanted to know how many of these sayings there were on record, and what, and by whom said.

— Why, let us see, — there is that one of Benjamin Franklin, "the great Bostonian," after whom this lad was named. To be sure, he said a great many wise things, — and I don't feel sure he didn't borrow this, — he speaks as if it were old. But then he applied it so neatly! —

"He that has once done you a kindness will be more ready to do you another than he whom you yourself have obliged."

Then there is that glorious Epicurean paradox, uttered by my friend, the Historian, in one of his flashing moments: —

"Give us the luxuries of life, and we will dispense with its necessaries."

To these must certainly be added that other saying of one of the wittiest of men: —

"Good Americans, when they die, go to Paris."

— The divinity-student looked grave at this, but said nothing.

The schoolmistress spoke out, and said she didn't think the wit meant any irreverence.

It was only another way of saying, Paris is a heavenly place after New York or Boston.

A jaunty-looking person, who had come in with the young fellow they call John, — evidently a stranger, — said there was one more wise man's saying that he had heard; it was about our place, but he didn't know who said it. — A civil curiosity was manifested by the company to hear the fourth wise saying. I heard him distinctly whispering to the young fellow who brought him to dinner, *Shall I tell it?* To which the answer was, *Go ahead!* — Well, — he said, — this was what I heard: —

"Boston State-House is the hub of the solar system. You couldn't pry that out of a Boston man if you had the tire of all creation straightened out for a crowbar."

Sir, — said I, — I am gratified with your remark. It expresses with pleasing vivacity that which I have sometimes heard uttered with malignant dulness. The satire of the remark is essentially true of Boston, — and of all other considerable, — and inconsiderable, — places with which I have had the privilege of being acquainted. Cockneys think London is the only place in the world. Frenchmen — you remember the line about Paris, the Court, the World, etc. — I recollect well, by the way, a sign in that city which ran thus: "Hotel de l'Univers et des États Unis"; and as Paris *is* the universe to a Frenchman, of course the United States are outside of it. — "See Naples and then die." It is quite as bad with smaller places. I have been about, lecturing, you know, and have found the following propositions to hold true of all of them.

1. The axis of the earth sticks out visibly through the centre of each and every town or city.

2. If more than fifty years have passed since its foundation, it is affectionately styled by the inhabitants the "*good old* town of" — (whatever its name may happen to be).

3. Every collection of its inhabitants that comes together to listen to a stranger is invariably declared to be a "remarkably intelligent audience."

4. The climate of the place is particularly favorable to longevity.

5. It contains several persons of vast talent little known to the world. (One or two of them, you may perhaps chance to remember, sent short pieces to the "Pactolian" some time since, which were "respectfully declined.")

Boston is just like other places of its size; — only, perhaps, considering its excellent fish-market, paid fire-department, superior monthly publications, and correct habit of spelling the English language, it has some right to look down on the mob of cities. I'll tell you, though, if you want to know it, what is the real offence of Boston. It drains a large water-shed of its intellect, and will not itself be drained. If it would only send away its first-rate men, instead of its second-rate ones (no offence to the well-known exceptions, of which we are always proud), we should be spared such epigrammatic remarks as that which the gentleman has quoted. There can never be a real metropolis in this country, until the biggest centre can drain the lesser ones of their talent and wealth. — I have observed, by the way, that the people who really live in two great cities are by no means so jealous of each other as are those of smaller cities situated within the intellectual basin, or *suction-range,* of one large one, of the pretensions of any other. Don't you see why? Because their promising young author and rising lawyer and large capitalist have been drained off to the neighboring big city, their prettiest girl has been exported to the same market; all their ambition points there, and all their thin gilding of glory comes from there. I hate little toad-eating cities.

— Would I be so good as to specify any particular example? — Oh, — an example? Did you ever see a bear-trap? Never? Well, shouldn't you like to see me put my foot into one? With sentiments of the highest consideration I must beg leave to be excused.

Besides, some of the smaller cities are charming. If they have an old church or two, a few stately mansions of former grandees, here and there an old dwelling with the second story projecting (for the convenience of shooting the Indians knocking at the front-door with their tomahawks), — if they have, scattered about, those mighty square houses built something more than half a century ago, and standing like architectural boulders dropped by the former diluvium of wealth, whose refluent wave has left them as its monument, — if they have gardens with elbowed apple-trees that push their branches over the high board-fence and drop their fruit on the side-walk, — if they have a little grass in the side-streets, enough to betoken quiet without proclaiming decay, — I think I could go to pieces, after my life's work were done, in one of those tranquil places, as sweetly as in any cradle that an old man may be rocked to sleep in. I visit such spots always with infinite delight. My friend, the Poet, says, that rapidly growing towns are most unfavorable to the imaginative and reflective faculties. Let a man live in one of these old quiet places, he says, and the wine of his soul which is kept thick and turbid by the rattle of busy streets, settles, and, as you hold it up, you may see the sun through it by day and the stars by night.

— Do I think that the little villages have the conceit of the great towns? — I don't believe there is much difference. You know how they read Pope's line in the smallest town in our State of Massachusetts? — Well, they read it

"All are but parts of one stupendous HULL!"

* * * Men who exercise chiefly those faculties of the mind which work independently of the will, — poets and artists, for instance, who follow their imagination in their creative moments, instead of keeping it in hand as your logicians and practical men do with their reasoning faculty, — such men are too apt to call in the mechanical appliances to help them govern their intellects.

— He means they get drunk, — said the young fellow already alluded to by name.

Do you think men of true genius are apt to indulge in the use of inebriating fluids? — said the divinity-student.

If you think you are strong enough to bear what I am going to say, — I replied, — I will talk to you about this. But mind, now, these are the things that some foolish people call *dangerous* subjects, — as if these vices which burrow into people's souls, as the Guinea-worm burrows into the naked feet of West-Indian slaves, would be more mischievous when seen than out of sight. Now the true way to deal with those obstinate animals, which are a dozen feet long, some of them, and no bigger than a horse hair, is to get a piece of silk round their *heads*, and pull them out very cautiously. If you only break them off, they grow worse than ever, and sometimes kill the person who has the misfortune to harbor one of them. Whence it is plain that the first thing to do is to find out where the head lies.

Just so of all the vices, and particularly of this vice of intemperance. What is the head of it, and where does it lie? For you may depend upon it, there is not one of these vices that has not a head of its own, — an intelligence, — a meaning, — a certain virtue, I was going to say, — but that might, perhaps, sound paradoxical. I have heard an immense number of moral physicians lay down the treatment of moral Guinea-worms, and the vast majority of them would always insist that the creature had no head at all, but was all body and tail. So I have found a very common result of their method to be that the string slipped, or that a piece only of the creature was broken off, and the worm soon grew again, as bad as ever. The truth is, if the Devil could only appear in church by attorney, and make the best statement that the facts would bear him out in doing on behalf of his special virtues (what we commonly call vices), the influence of good teachers would be much greater than it is. For the arguments by which the Devil prevails are precisely the ones that the Devil-queller most rarely answers. The way to argue down a vice is not to tell lies about it, — to say that it has no attractions, when everybody knows that it has, — but rather to let it make out its case just as it certainly will in the moment of temptation, and then meet it with the weapons furnished by the Divine armory. Ithuriel did not spit the toad on his spear, you remember, but touched him with it, and the blasted angel took the sad glories of his true shape. If he had shown fight then, the fair spirits would have known how to deal with him.

That all spasmodic cerebral action is an evil is not perfectly clear. Men get fairly intoxicated with music, with poetry, with religious excitement, — oftenest with love. Ninon de l'Enclos said she was so easily excited that her soup intoxicated her, and convalescents have been made tipsy by a beefsteak.

There are forms and stages of alcoholic exaltation which, in themselves, and without regard to their consequences, might be considered as positive improvements of the persons affected. When the sluggish intellect is roused, the slow speech quickened, the cold nature warmed, the latent sympathy developed, the flagging spirit kindled, — before the trains of thought become confused, or the will perverted, or the muscles relaxed, — just at the moment when the whole human zoöphyte flowers out like a full-blown rose, and is ripe for the subscription-paper or the contribution box, — it would be hard to say that a man was, at that very time, worse, or less to be loved, than when driving a hard bargain with all his meaner wits about him. The difficulty is, that the alcoholic virtues don't wash; but until the water takes their colors out, the tints are very much like those of the true celestial stuff.

[Here I was interrupted by a question which I am very willing to report, but have confidence enough in those friends who examine these records to commit to their candor.

A person at table asked me whether I "went in for rum as a steady drink?" — His manner made the question highly offensive, but I restrained myself, and answered thus:]

Rum I take to be the name which unwashed moralists apply alike to the product distilled from molasses and the noblest juices of the vineyard. Burgundy "in all its sunset glow" is rum. Champagne, soul of "the foaming grape of Eastern France," is rum. Hock, which our friend, the Poet, speaks of as

"The Rhine's breastmilk, gushing cold and bright,
  Pale as the moon, and maddening as her light,"

is rum. Sir, I repudiate the loathsome vulgarism as an insult to the first miracle wrought by the Founder of our religion! I address myself to the company. — I believe in temperance, nay, almost in abstinence, as a rule for healthy people. I trust that I practice both. But let me tell you, there are companies of men of genius into which I sometimes go, where the atmosphere of intellect and sentiment is so much more stimulating than alcohol, that, if I thought fit to take wine, it would be to keep me sober.

Among the gentlemen that I have known, few, if any, were ruined by drinking. My few drunken acquaintances were generally ruined before they became drunkards. The habit of drinking is often a vice, no doubt, — sometimes a misfortune, — as when an almost irresistible hereditary propensity exists to indulge in it, — but oftenest of all a *punishment*.

Empty heads, — heads without ideas in wholesome variety and sufficient number to furnish food for the mental clockwork, — ill-regulated heads, where the faculties are not under the control of the will, — these are the ones that hold the brains which their owners are so apt to tamper with, by introducing the appliances we have been talking about. Now, when a gentleman's brain is empty or ill-regulated, it is, to a great extent, his own fault; and so it is simple retribution, that, while he lies slothfully sleeping or aimlessly dreaming, the fatal habit settles on him like a vampire, and sucks his blood, fanning him all the while with its hot wings into deeper slumber or idler dreams! I am not such a hard-souled being as to apply this to the neglected poor, who have had no chance to fill their heads with wholesome ideas, and to be taught the lesson of self-government. I trust the tariff of Heaven has an *ad valorem* scale for them, — and all of us.

But to come back to poets and artists; — if they really are more prone to the abuse of stimulants, — and I fear that this is true, — the reason of it is only too clear. A man abandons himself to a fine frenzy, and the power which flows through him, as I once explained to you, makes him the medium of a great poem or a great picture. The creative action is not voluntary at all, but automatic; we can only put the mind into the proper attitude, and wait for the wind, that blows where it listeth, to breathe over it. Thus the true state of creative genius is allied to *reverie*, or dreaming. If mind and body were both healthy and had food enough and fair play, I doubt whether any men would be more temperate than the imaginative classes. But body and mind often flag, —

perhaps they are ill-made to begin with, underfed with bread or ideas, overworked, or abused in some way. The automatic action, by which genius wrought its wonders, fails. There is only one thing which can rouse the machine: not will, — that cannot reach it, nothing but a ruinous agent, which hurries the wheels a while and soon eats out the heart of the mechanism. The dreaming faculties are always the dangerous ones, because their mode of action can be imitated by artificial excitement; the reasoning ones are safe, because they imply continued voluntary effort.

I think you will find it true, that, before any vice can fasten on a man, body, mind, or moral nature must be debilitated. The mosses and fungi gather on sickly trees, not thriving ones; and the odious parasites which fasten on the human frame choose that which is already enfeebled. Mr. Walker, the hygeian humorist, declared that he had such a healthy skin it was impossible for any impurity to stick to it, and maintained that it was an absurdity to wash a face which was of necessity always clean. I don't know how much fancy there was in this; but there is no fancy in saying that the lassitude of tired-out operatives, and the languor of imaginative natures in their periods of collapse, and the vacuity of minds untrained to labor and discipline, fit the soul and body for the germination of the seeds of intemperance.

Whenever the wandering demon of Drunkenness finds a ship adrift, — no steady wind in its sails, no thoughtful pilot directing its course, — he steps on board, takes the helm, and steers straight for the maelstrom. * * *

And since I am talking of early recollections, I don't know why I shouldn't mention some others that still cling to me, — not that you will attach any very particular meaning to these same images so full of significance to me, but that you will find something parallel to them in your own memory. You remember, perhaps, what I said one day about smells. There were certain *sounds* also which had a mysterious suggestiveness to me, — not so intense, perhaps, as that connected with the other sense, but yet peculiar, and never to be forgotten.

The first was the creaking of the woodsled, bringing their loads of oak and walnut from the country, as the slow-swinging oxen trailed them along over the complaining snow, in the cold, brown light of early morning. Lying in bed and listening to their dreary music had a pleasure in it akin to the Lucretian luxury, or that which Byron speaks of as to be enjoyed in looking on at a battle by one "who hath no friend, no brother there."

There was another sound, in itself so sweet, and so connected with one of those simple and curious superstitions of childhood of which I have spoken, that I can never cease to cherish a sad sort of love for it. — Let me tell the superstitious fancy first. The Puritan "Sabbath," as everybody knows, began at "sundown" on Saturday evening. To such observance of it I was born and bred. As the large, round disk of day declined, a stillness, a solemnity, a somewhat melancholy hush came over us all. It was time for work to cease, and for playthings to be put away. The world of active life passed into the shadow of an eclipse, not to emerge until the sun should sink again beneath the horizon.

It was in this stillness of the world without and of the soul within that the pulsating lullaby of the evening crickets used to make itself most distinctly heard — so that I well remember I used to think that the purring of these little creatures, which mingled with the batrachian hymns from the neighboring swamp, *was peculiar to Saturday evenings.* I don't know that anything could give a clearer idea of the quieting and subduing effect of the old habit of observance of what was considered holy time, than this strange, childish fancy.

Yes, and there was still another sound which mingled its solemn cadences with the waking and sleeping dreams of my boyhood. It was heard only at times, — a deep, muffled roar, which rose and fell, not loud, but vast, — a whistling boy would have drowned it for his next neighbor, but it must have been heard over the space of a hundred square miles. I used to wonder what this might be. Could it be the roar of the thousand wheels and the ten thousand footsteps jarring and trampling along the stones of the neighboring city? That would be continuous; but this, as I have said, rose and fell in regular rhythm. I remember being told, and I suppose this to have been the true solution, that it was the sound of the waves, after a high wind, breaking on the long beaches many miles distant. I should really like to know whether any observing people living ten miles, more or less, inland from long beaches, — in such a town, for instance, as Cantabridge, in the eastern part of the Territory of the Massachusetts, — have ever observed any such sound, and whether it was rightly accounted for as above. * * *

Sir, — said I, — all men love all women. That is the *primâ-facie* aspect of the case. The Court of Nature assumes the law to be, that all men do so; and the individual man is bound to show cause why he does not love any particular woman. A man, says one of my old black-letter law-books, may show divers good reasons, as thus: He hath not seen the person named in the indictment; she is of tender age, or the reverse of that; she hath certain personal disqualifications, — as, for instance, she is a blackamoor, or hath an ill-favored countenance; or, his capacity of loving being limited, his affections are engrossed by a previous comer; and so of other conditions. Not the less is it true that he is bound by duty and inclined by nature to love each and every woman. Therefore it is that each woman virtually summons every man to show cause why he doth not love her. This is not by written document, or direct speech, for the most part, but by certain signs of silk, gold, and other materials, which say to all men, — Look on me and love, as in duty bound. Then the man pleadeth this special incapacity, whatsoever that may be, — as, for instance, impecuniosity, or that he hath one or many wives in his household, or that he is of mean figure, or small capacity; of which reasons it may be noted, that the first is, according to late decisions, of chiefest authority. — So far the old law-book. But there is a note from an older authority, saying that every woman doth also love each and every man, except there be some good reason to the contrary; and a very observing friend of mine, a young unmarried clergyman, tells me, that, so far as his experience goes, he has reason to think the ancient author had fact to justify his statement. * * *

[The company looked a little flustered one morning when I came in, — so much so, that I inquired of my neighbor, the divinity-student, what had been going on. It appears that the young fellow whom they call John had taken advantage of my being a little late (I having been rather longer than usual dressing that morning) to circulate several questions involving a quibble or play upon words, — in short, containing that indignity to the human understanding, condemned in the passages from the distinguished moralist of the last century and the illustrious historian of the present, which I cited on a former occasion, and known as a *pun*. After breakfast, one of the boarders handed me a small roll of paper containing some of the questions and their answers. I subjoin two or three of them, to show what a tendency there is to frivolity and meaningless talk in young persons of a certain sort, when not restrained by the presence of more reflective natures. — It was asked, "Why tertian and quartan fevers were like certain short-lived insects." Some interesting physiological relation would be naturally suggested. The inquirer blushes to find that the answer is in the paltry equivocation, that they *skip* a day or two. — "Why an Englishman must go to the Continent to weaken his grog or punch." The answer proves to have no relation whatever to the temperance-movement, as no better reason is given than that island- (or, as it is absurdly written, *ile and*) water won't mix. — But when I came to the next question and its answer, I felt that patience ceased to be a virtue. "Why an onion is like a piano" is a query that a person of sensibility would be slow to propose; but that in an educated community an individual could be found to answer it in these words, — "Because it smell odious," *quasi*, it's melodi-ous, — is not credible, but too true. I can show you the paper.

Dear reader, I beg your pardon for repeating such things. I know most conversations reported in books are altogether above such trivial details, but folly will come up at every table as surely as purslain and chickweed and sorrel will come up in gardens. This young fellow ought to have talked philosophy, I know perfectly well; but he didn't, — he made jokes.]

I am willing, — I said, — to exercise your

ingenuity in a rational and contemplative manner. — No, I do not proscribe certain forms of philosophical speculation which involve an approach to the absurd or the ludicrous, such as you may find, for example, in 5 the folio of the Reverend Father Thomas Sanchez, in his famous Disputations, "De Sancto Matrimonio." I will therefore turn this levity of yours to profit by reading you a rhymed problem, wrought out by my friend 10 the Professor:

THE DEACON'S MASTERPIECE:
OR THE WONDERFUL "ONE-HOSS-SHAY"
A LOGICAL STORY

Have you heard of the wonderful one-hoss-shay,
That was built in such a logical way
It ran a hundred years to a day,
And then, of a sudden, it — ah, but stay,
I'll tell you what happened without delay,
Scaring the parson into fits,
Frightening people out of their wits, —

Have you ever heard of that, I say?
Seventeen hundred and fifty-five,
Georgius Secundus was then alive, —
Snuffy old drone from the German hive;
That was the year when Lisbon-town
Saw the earth open and gulp her down,
And Braddock's army was done so brown,
Left without a scalp to its crown.
It was on the terrible earthquake-day
That the Deacon finished the one-hoss-shay.

Now in building of chaises, I tell you what,
There is always *somewhere* a weakest spot, —
In hub, tire, felloe, in spring or thill,
In panel, or crossbar, or floor, or sill,
In screw, bolt, thoroughbracc, — lurking still,
Find it somewhere you must and will, —
Above or below, or within or without, —
And that's the reason, beyond a doubt,
A chaise *breaks down*, but doesn't *wear out*.

But the Deacon swore (as Deacons do,
With an "I dew vum," or an "I tell *yeou*,")
He would build one shay to beat the taown
'n' the keounty 'n' all the kentry raoun';
It should be so built that it *couldn'* break daown,
— "Fur," said the Deacon, "'t's mighty plain
Thut the weakes' place mus' stan' the strain;
'n' the way t' fix it, uz I maintain,
        Is only jest
T' make that place uz strong uz the rest."

So the Deacon inquired of the village folk
Where he could find the strongest oak,
That couldn't be split nor bent nor broke, —
That was for spokes and floor and sills;

He sent for lancewood to make the thills;
The crossbars were ash, from the straightest trees,
The panels of white-wood, that cuts like cheese,
But lasts like iron for things like these;
The hubs of logs from the "Settler's ellum," —
Last of its timber, — they couldn't sell 'em,
Never an axe had seen their chips,
And the wedges flew from between their lips,
Their blunt ends frizzled like celery-tips;
Step and prop-iron, bolt and screw,
Spring, tire, axle, and linchpin too,
Steel of the finest, bright and blue;
Thoroughbrace bison-skin, thick and wide;
Boot, top, dasher, from tough old hide
Found in the pit when the tanner died.
That was the way he "put her through." —
15 "There!" said the Deacon, "naow she'll dew."

Do! I tell you, I rather guess
She was a wonder, and nothing less!
Colts grew horses, beards turned gray,
Deacon and deaconess dropped away,
Children and grand-children — where were they?
But there stood the stout old one-hoss-shay
As fresh as on Lisbon-earthquake-day!

EIGHTEEN HUNDRED; — it came and found
25 The Deacon's Masterpiece strong and sound.
Eighteen hundred increased by ten; —
"Hahnsum kerridge" they called it then.
Eighteen hundred and twenty came; —
Running as usual; much the same.
30 Thirty and forty at last arrive,
And then come fifty, and FIFTY-FIVE.

Little of all we value here
Wakes on the morn of its hundredth year
Without both feeling and looking queer.
35 In fact, there's nothing that keeps its youth,
So far as I know, but a tree and truth.
(This is a moral that runs at large;
Take it. — You're welcome. — No extra charge.)
40 FIRST OF NOVEMBER, — the Earthquake-day. —
There are traces of age in the one-hoss-shay.

A general flavor of mild decay,
But nothing local, as one may say.
45 There couldn't be, — for the Deacon's art
Had made it so like in every part
That there wasn't a chance for one to start.
For the wheels were just as strong as the thills,
And the floor was just as strong as the sills,
50 And the panels just as strong as the floor,
And the whippletree neither less nor more,
And the back-crossbar as strong as the fore,
And spring and axle and hub *encore*.
And yet, *as a whole*, it is past a doubt
55 In another hour it will be *worn out*!

First of November, 'Fifty-five!
This morning the parson takes a drive.
Now, small boys, get out of the way!
60 Here comes the wonderful one-hoss-shay,
Drawn by a rat-tailed, ewe-necked bay.
"Huddup!" said the parson. — Off went they.

The parson was working his Sunday's text, —
Had got to *fifthly*, and stopped perplexed
At what the — Moses — was coming next.
All at once the horse stood still,
Close by the meet'n'-house on the hill.
— First a shiver, and then a thrill,
Then something decidedly like a spill, —
And the parson was sitting upon a rock,
At half-past nine by the meet'n'-house clock, —
Just the hour of the Earthquake shock!
— What do you think the parson found,

When he got up and stared around?
The poor old chaise in a heap or mound,
As if it had been to the mill and ground.
You see, of course, if you're not a dunce,
How it went to pieces all at once, —
All at once, and nothing first, —
Just as bubbles do when they burst.

End of the wonderful one-hoss-shay.
Logic is logic. That's all I say.

ABRAHAM LINCOLN (1809–1865)

To Lincoln's brief autobiography printed below only a few facts need here be added. As he says, "What I have done since that is pretty well known." There was the senatorial campaign of 1858, and the great debates with Douglas. Lincoln lost the election, but when the Republican national convention met in Chicago two years later he was nominated for the Presidency on the third ballot. With 180 electoral votes to his opponents' 123, he was elected to the office and began four stormy years in the White House.

Lincoln's part in the war need not be discussed here. When the result of the conflict was still in doubt, he was reëlected to the Presidency by an overwhelming majority in the electoral college. Inaugurated March 4, 1865, he had served little more than a month of his second term when an assassin's bullet ended his life.

Lincoln has won a place in American letters by salient ideas expressed in a flexible style, clear yet rich, and vivid with the imagery of the frontier of which he was a product.

The standard edition of Lincoln is *The Complete Works of Abraham Lincoln*, edited, 1894, by J. G. Nicolay and John Hay. For studies of Lincoln as literary artist, see R. P. Basler, ed., *Abraham Lincoln: His Speeches and Writings*, 1946, and *Abraham Lincoln, Master of Words*, by D. K. Dodge. The standard biography is the ten-volume *Abraham Lincoln, A History*, 1890, by his official editors. There is a one-volume abridgment by Nicolay, 1904. Among others: Brand Whitlock's *Abraham Lincoln*, 1909, revised 1916; Lord Charnwood's *Abraham Lincoln*, which gives an English point of view; *Abraham Lincoln, the Prairie Years*, by Carl Sandburg, 2 volumes, 1926, and *Abraham Lincoln, the War Years*, 2 volumes, 1939.

Autobiography

(*1859*)

Lincoln sent this short sketch of his life to J. W. Fell on December 20, 1859, in order that it might be used for campaign purposes.

I was born February 12, 1809, in Hardin County, Kentucky. My parents were both born in Virginia, of undistinguished families — second families, perhaps I should say. My mother, who died in my tenth year, was of a family of the name of Hanks, some of whom now reside in Adams, and others in Macon County, Illinois. My paternal grandfather, Abraham Lincoln, emigrated from Rockingham County, Virginia, to Kentucky about 1781 or 1782, where a year or two later he was killed by the Indians, not in battle, but by stealth, when he was laboring to open a farm in the forest. His ancestors, who were Quakers, went to Virginia from Berks County, Pennsylvania. An effort to identify them with the New England family of the same name ended in nothing more definite than a similarity of Christian names in both families, such as Enoch, Levi, Mordecai, Solomon, Abraham, and the like.

My father, at the death of his father, was but six years of age, and he grew up literally without education. He removed from Kentucky to what is now Spencer County, Indiana, in my eighth year. We reached our new home about the time the state came into the Union. It was a wild region, with many bears and other wild animals still in the woods. There I grew up. There were some schools, so called, but no qualification was ever required of a teacher beyond "readin', writin', and cipherin'," to the rule of three. If a straggler supposed to understand Latin happened to sojourn in the neighborhood, he was looked upon as a wizard. There was absolutely nothing to excite ambition for education. Of course, when I came of age I did not know much. Still, somehow, I could read, write, and cipher to the rule of three, but that was all. I have not been to school since. The little advance I now have upon this store of education, I have picked up from time to time under the pressure of necessity.

I was raised to farm work, which I continued till I was twenty-two. At twenty-one I came to Illinois, Macon County. Then I got to New Salem, at that time in Sangamon, now in Menard County, where I remained a year as a sort of clerk in a store. Then came the Black Hawk War; and I was elected a captain of volunteers, a success which gave me more pleasure than any I have had since. I went the campaign, was elated, ran for the legislature the same year (1832), and was beaten — the only time I ever have been beaten by the people. The next and three succeeding biennial elections I was elected to the legislature. I was not a candidate afterward. During this legislative period I had studied law, and removed to Springfield to practice it. In 1846 I was once elected to the lower House of Congress. Was not a candidate for reëlection. From 1849 to 1854, both inclusive, practiced law more assiduously than ever before. Always a Whig in politics; and generally on the Whig electoral tickets, making active canvasses. I was losing interest in politics when the repeal of the Missouri Compromise aroused me again. What I have done since that is pretty well known.

If any personal description of me is thought desirable, it may be said I am, in height, six feet four inches, nearly; lean in flesh, weighing on an average one hundred and eighty pounds; dark complexion, with coarse black hair and gray eyes. No other marks or brands recollected.

Farewell Speech to His Friends in Springfield
(1861)

My Friends: No one, not in my situation, can appreciate my feeling of sadness at this parting. To this place, and the kindness of these people, I owe everything. Here I have lived a quarter of a century, and have passed from a young to an old man. Here my children have been born, and one is buried. I now leave, not knowing when or whether ever I may return, with a task before me greater than that which rested upon Washington. Without the assistance of that Divine Being who ever attended him, I cannot succeed. With that assistance, I cannot fail. Trusting in Him who can go with me, and remain with you, and be everywhere for good, let us confidently hope that all will yet be well. To His care commending you, as I hope in your prayers you will commend me, I bid you an affectionate farewell.

Letter to Horace Greeley

EXECUTIVE MANSION, WASHINGTON,
August 22, 1862

HON. HORACE GREELEY.

Dear Sir: I have just read yours of the 19th, addressed to myself through the New York *Tribune.* If there be in it any statements or assumptions of fact which I may know to be erroneous, I do not, now and here, controvert them. If there be in it any inferences which I may believe to be falsely drawn, I do not, now and here, argue against them. If there be perceptible in it an impatient and dictatorial tone, I waive it in deference to an old friend whose heart I have always supposed to be right.

As to the policy I "seem to be pursuing," as you say, I have not meant to leave any one in doubt.

I would save the Union. I would save it the shortest way under the Constitution. The sooner the national authority can be restored, the nearer the Union will be "the Union as it was." If there be those who would not save the Union unless they could at the same time save slavery, I do not agree with them. If there be those who would not save the Union unless they could at the same time destroy slavery, I do not agree with them. My paramount object in this struggle is to save the Union, and is not either to save or to destroy slavery. If I could save the Union without freeing any slave, I would do it; and if I could save it by freeing all the slaves, I would do it; and if I could save it by freeing some and leaving others alone, I would also do that. What I do about slavery and the coloured race, I do because I believe it helps to save the Union; and what I forbear, I forbear because I do not believe it would help to save the Union. I shall do less whenever I shall believe what I am doing hurts the cause, and I shall do more whenever I shall believe doing more will help the cause. I shall try to correct errors when shown to be errors, and I shall adopt new views so fast as they shall appear to be true views.

I have here stated my purpose according to my view of official duty; and I intend no modification of my oft-expressed personal wish that all men everywhere could be free.

Yours,
A. LINCOLN

The Gettysburg Address

(1863)

Fourscore and seven years ago our fathers brought forth on this continent a new nation, conceived in liberty, and dedicated to the proposition that all men are created equal.

Now we are engaged in a great civil war, testing whether that nation, or any nation so conceived and so dedicated, can long endure. We are met on a great battlefield of that war. We have come to dedicate a portion of that field as a final resting place for those who here gave their lives that that nation might live. It is altogether fitting and proper that we should do this.

But, in a larger sense, we cannot dedicate — we cannot consecrate — we cannot hallow — this ground. The brave men, living and dead, who struggled here, have consecrated it far above our poor power to add or detract. The world will little note nor long remember what we say here, but it can never forget what they did here. It is for us, the living, rather, to be dedicated here to the unfinished work which they who fought here have thus far so nobly advanced. It is rather for us to be here dedicated to the great task remaining before us — that from these honored dead we take increased devotion to that cause for which they gave the last full measure of devotion; that we here highly resolve that these dead shall not have died in vain; that this nation, under God, shall have a new birth of freedom; and that government of the people, by the people, for the people, shall not perish from the earth.

Letter to Mrs. Bixby

"Among the letters, perhaps the most impressive is that written to Mrs. Bixby, the mother of five sons who had died fighting for the Union in the armies of the North. It is short, and it deals with a theme on which hundreds of letters are written daily. But I do not know where the nobility of self-sacrifice for a great cause, and of the consolation which the thought of a sacrifice so made should bring, is set forth with such simple and pathetic beauty. Deep must be the fountains from which there issues so pure a stream" (James Bryce).

EXECUTIVE MANSION, WASHINGTON
November 21, 1864

MRS. BIXBY, Boston, Massachusetts.

DEAR MADAM: I have been shown in the files of the War Department a statement of the Adjutant-General of Massachusetts that you are the mother of five sons who have died gloriously on the field of battle. I feel how weak and fruitless must be any words of mine which should attempt to beguile you from the grief of a loss so overwhelming. But I cannot refrain from tendering to you the consolation that may be found in the thanks of the Republic they died to save. I pray that our heavenly Father may assuage the anguish of your bereavement, and leave you only the cherished memory of the loved and lost, and the solemn pride that must be yours to have laid so costly a sacrifice upon the altar of freedom.

Yours very sincerely and respectfully,
ABRAHAM LINCOLN

Second Inaugural Address

(1865)

FELLOW-COUNTRYMEN: At this second appearing to take the oath of the presidential office, there is less occasion for an extended address than there was at the first. Then a statement, somewhat in detail, of a course to be pursued, seemed fitting and proper. Now, at the expiration of four years, during which public declarations have been constantly called forth on every point and phase of the great contest which still absorbs the attention and engrosses the energies of the nation, little that is new could be presented. The progress of our arms, upon which all else chiefly depends, is as well known to the public as to myself; and it is, I trust, reasonably satisfactory and encouraging to all. With high hope for the future, no prediction in regard to it is ventured.

On the occasion corresponding to this four years ago, all thoughts were anxiously directed to an impending civil war. All dreaded it — all sought to avert it. While the inaugural address was being delivered from this place, devoted altogether to saving the Union without war, insurgent agents were in the city seeking to destroy it without war — seeking to dissolve the Union, and divide effects, by negotiation. Both parties deprecated war; but one of them would make war rather than let the nation survive; and the other would accept war rather than let it perish. And the war came.

One-eighth of the whole population were colored slaves, not distributed generally over the Union, but localized in the Southern part of it. These slaves constituted a peculiar and powerful interest. All knew that this interest was, somehow, the cause of the war. To strengthen, perpetuate, and extend this interest was the object for which the insurgents would rend the Union even by war; while the government claimed no right to do more than to restrict the territorial enlargement of it.

Neither party expected for the war the magnitude or the duration which it has already attained. Neither anticipated that the cause of the conflict might cease with, or even before, the conflict itself should cease. Each looked for an easier triumph, and a result less fundamental and astounding. Both read the same Bible, and pray to the same God; and each invokes his aid against the other. It may seem strange that any men should dare to ask a just God's assistance in wringing their bread from the sweat of other men's faces; but let us judge not, that we be not judged. The prayers of both could not be answered — that of neither has been answered fully.

The Almighty has his own purposes. "Woe unto the world because of offences! for it must needs be that offences come; but woe to that man by whom the offence cometh." If we shall suppose that American slavery is one of those offences which, in the providence of God, must needs come, but which, having continued through his appointed time, he now wills to remove, and that he gives to both North and South this terrible war, as the woe due to those by whom the offence came, shall we discern therein any departure from those divine attributes which the believers in a living God always ascribe to him? Fondly do we hope — fervently do we pray — that this mighty scourge of war may speedily pass away. Yet, if God wills that it continue until all the wealth piled by the bondmen's two hundred and fifty years of unrequited toil shall be sunk, and until every drop of blood drawn with the lash shall be paid by another drawn with the sword, as was said three thousand years ago, so still it must be said, "The judgments of the Lord are true and righteous altogether."

With malice toward none; with charity for all; with firmness in the right, as God gives us to see the right, let us strive on to finish the work we are in; to bind up the nation's wounds; to care for him who shall have borne the battle, and for his widow, and his orphan — to do all which may achieve and cherish a just and lasting peace among ourselves, and with all nations.

WALT WHITMAN (1819-1892)

Walter Whitman was born at West Hills, Long Island. His ancestors were English and Dutch, some of them Quakers. The Whitmans moved to Brooklyn when Walt was small, and he felt the dual influence of a large city and a pleasant countryside near enough to be always available. He left school at the age of eleven. Office-boy, type-setter, occasional author, he became an itinerant country school teacher in 1836 and continued in this position until 1841 except for one brief flier in newspaper editing. In his spare time he learned the printing business, and in 1841 he definitely cast his lot with journalism in New York.

In five years he rose to be editor of the *Daily Brooklyn Eagle*, but lost his position in 1848 and was glad to accept another on a paper just starting in New Orleans. Three months in the South and he resigned his position and returned, by way of Chicago, to Brooklyn. Here he made his headquarters until 1862, as journalist, proprietor of a book store, builder, and poet. In 1855 he collected the verse he had recently been writing and published it in a thin volume.

Whitman himself seems to have expected *Leaves of Grass* to be a bombshell. The book, however, was scarcely noticed. It received one important comment: Emerson wrote, "I greet you at the beginning of a great career." Whitman used this sentence, without permission, to advertise the second edition published the next year. This edition contained thirty-two poems, twenty more than the first edition. All his life Whitman continued to supplement, rewrite, and revise *Leaves of Grass*. It was his "letter to the world."

Late in 1862 he went down to Fredericksburg to care for a younger brother who had been slightly wounded. The next three years he gave freely of his health and heart as a nurse among the wounded in hospitals in and near Washington. He still found time to write vivid accounts of what he saw, and occasional poems such as "O Captain! My Captain!" He gathered the poems in *Drum Taps* in 1865. The same year he was forced out of a governmental clerkship because a superior thought his poems indecent. His friends came to his aid — one of them with a pamphlet entitled *The Good Gray Poet*, a name which stuck to Whitman thereafter, — and he was established as a clerk in another department. Whitman never married; toward men he apparently had an abnormal attraction.

In 1873, two years after he had issued *Democratic Vistas*, he was stricken with paralysis and settled in Camden, New Jersey, where he lived until his death on March 26, 1892. He revised his work, sent out a few articles, received many letters from friends in Europe and America, and made occasional journeys. In 1891 and 1892 he issued the ninth edition of *Leaves of Grass*, containing all the poems as we have them.

Both the poetic technique and the poetic ideas of Whitman have been a center of ever-renewed controversy. His ideas and attitudes, historically speaking, were chiefly those of the Romantic Movement. In his response to nature, his subjective individualism, his compassionate feeling for all men, he was akin to such predecessors as Rousseau, Wordsworth, Shelley, and Emerson. His acceptance of modern science, and of the idea of progress which in his day seemed to be supported by the theory of evolution, was fitted into an essentially romantic ideology. On the other hand his technique appears to have pointed rather to the future. It can be seen now that he was preparing the way for the "free verse" of the early twentieth century. Upon later poets who shared his outlook and spirit and upon later poets who did not, his technical experiments exerted a considerable influence. On the whole, his place is that of a transitional figure between the romantic and the realistic dispensations. And it was a figure of such size that he is among the greatest writers in American letters.

The Complete Writings of Walt Whitman was issued in 10 volumes, 1902. E. Holloway's *Leaves of Grass, Inclusive Edition*, is the best edition of that book. Good biographical and critical studies are by Bliss Perry, 1906, Newton Arvin, 1938, H. S. Canby, 1943, and Frederik Schyberg (translated from the Danish), 1951. Among other interpretations may be mentioned the laudatory view of his friend and disciple, John Burroughs, *Whitman*, 1895; the hostile view of G. Santayana in the chapter "The Poetry of Barbarism" in *Interpretations of Poetry and Religion*, 1900; S. P. Sherman's essay on Whitman in *Americans*, 1922; N. Foerster's study of his literary theory in *American Criticism*, 1928; Malcolm Cowley's articles in the *New Republic*, March 18 and April 8, 1946. Floyd Stovall edited Whitman for the *AWS*, 1934. G. W. Allen is the author of a *Walt Whitman Handbook*, 1946.

FROM Song of Myself
(1855, 1881)

Leaves of Grass, 1855 (in which volume this poem is the first and longest), came rather late in Whitman's career, and upon it many influences converged: his ancestral heritage, his scant schooling, his contact with nature and with the human life of cities, his reading in literature ancient and modern, his responsiveness to the time-spirit (the humanitarian impulse, the romantic and Transcendental mood of revolt and emphasis on the self, etc.).

The first edition of Whitman's book, published in July, 1855, amounted to fewer than 900 copies, most of which he gave to critics and friends. It contained a preface of 10 pages and 95 pages of poems printed without titles. The Preface (now in *Prose Works*) is vague and incoherent in expression; a better, far more lucid statement of Whitman's purpose may be found in *Democratic Vistas*, written many years later, after Whitman had come to see his total drift more clearly. (Selections from it are given on pp. 532–34 of the present volume.) The 1855 Preface has been summarized by B. Perry: "The book is scarcely to be understood without it, and in the long list of dissertations by poets upon the nature of poetry, it would be difficult to point to one more vigorous and impassioned, although much of it is as inconsecutive as the essays of Emerson which helped to inspire it. Its general theme is the inspiration which the United States offers to the great poet. America does not repel the past, he declares, although the life has gone out of the past. Here, in this teeming nation of nations, is the fullest poetical nature known to history. The genius of the United States

is best shown in the common people, and the American poet must express their life. He must love the earth and sun and the animals, despise riches, give alms to every one that asks, stand up for the stupid and crazy. He must reëxamine all that he has been told at school or church or in any book, and dismiss whatever insults his own soul. Thus his very flesh becomes a great poem. He is at one with the universe, and feels the harmony of things with man. He brings all things to bear upon the individual character. The 'art of art' is simplicity; it is to speak in literature with the perfect rectitude of animals and trees. Thus the great poet is marked by unconstraint and defiance of precedent. He sees that the soul is as great as anything outside of it; that there is no antagonism between poetry and science, or between the natural and the supernatural, — everything being miraculous and divine. General laws rule, and these make for happiness. The poet, furthermore, must be a champion of political liberty. He must recognize that the actual facts of the American republic are superior to fiction and romance. . . . The work of the priests is done. Every man shall henceforth be his own priest, finding his inspiration in the real objects of today, in America. The English language — 'the speech of the proud and melancholy races and of all who aspire' — is to be the chosen tongue. The poems distilled from other poems will probably pass away, but the soul of the nations will advance half way to meet the soul of its true poets."

After this Preface come the twelve poems of the

---

[1] Throughout the poems by Whitman here given, the first date is "that of the earliest known publication of the poem in whole or in part," and the last date is "that of its first appearance in final form and with final title" (E. Holloway, Inclusive Edition of *Leaves of Grass*, 1924).

1855 edition, without heading, but later entitled: "Song of Myself," "A Song for Occupations," "To Think of Time," "The Sleepers," "I Sing the Body Electric," "Faces," "Song of the Answerer," "Europe," "A Boston Ballad," "There Was a Child Went Forth," "Who Learns My Lesson Complete," and "Great Are the Myths." The poems given in our text indicate the contents and spirit of the 1855 edition. Note, however, that our version is the final, not the original; although the differences are, generally, insignificant.

1

I celebrate myself, and sing myself,
And what I assume you shall assume,
For every atom belonging to me as good belongs to you.

I loafe and invite my soul,
I lean and loafe at my ease observing a spear of summer grass.   5

My tongue, every atom of my blood, form'd from this soil, this air,
Born here of parents born here from parents the same, and their parents the same,
I, now thirty-seven years old in perfect health begin,
Hoping to cease not till death.

Creeds and schools in abeyance,   10
Retiring back a while sufficed at what they are, but never forgotten,
I harbor for good or bad, I permit to speak at every hazard,
Nature without check with original energy.

2

Houses and rooms are full of perfumes, the shelves are crowded with perfumes,
I breathe the fragrance myself and know it and like it,   15
The distillation would intoxicate me also, but I shall not let it.

The atmosphere is not a perfume, it has no taste of the distillation, it is odorless,
It is for my mouth forever, I am in love with it,
I will go to the bank by the wood and become undisguised and naked,
I am mad for it to be in contact with me.   20

The smoke of my own breath,
Echoes, ripples, buzz'd whispers, love-root, silk-thread, crotch and vine,
My respiration and inspiration, the beating of my heart, the passing of blood and air
         through my lungs,
The sniff of green leaves and dry leaves, and of the shore and dark-color'd sea-rocks,
         and of hay in the barn,
The sound of the belch'd words of my voice loos'd to the eddies of the wind,   25
A few light kisses, a few embraces, a reaching around of arms,
The play of shine and shade on the trees as the supple boughs wag,
The delight alone or in the rush of the streets, or along the fields and hill-sides,
The feeling of health, the full-noon trill, the song of me rising from bed and meeting
         the sun.

Have you reckon'd a thousand acres much? have you reckon'd the earth much?   30
Have you practis'd so long to learn to read?
Have you felt so proud to get at the meaning of poems?

Stop this day and night with me and you shall possess the origin of all poems,
You shall possess the good of the earth and sun, (there are millions of suns left,)
You shall no longer take things at second or third hand, nor look through the eyes of
    the dead, nor feed on the spectres in books,   35
You shall not look through my eyes either, nor take things from me,
You shall listen to all sides and filter them from your self.

3

I have heard what the talkers were talking, the talk of the beginning and the end,
But I do not talk of the beginning or the end.

There was never any more inception than there is now,   40
Nor any more youth or age than there is now,
And will never be any more perfection than there is now,
Nor any more heaven or hell than there is now.

Urge and urge and urge,
Always the procreant urge of the world.   45
Out of the dimness opposite equals advance, always substance and increase, always
    sex,
Always a knit of identity, always distinction, always a breed of life.

To elaborate is no avail, learn'd and unlearn'd feel that it is so.

Sure as the most certain sure, plumb in the uprights, well entretied, braced in
    the beams,
Stout as a horse, affectionate, haughty, electrical,   50
I and this mystery here we stand.

Clear and sweet is my soul, and clear and sweet is all that is not my soul.

Lack one lacks both, and the unseen is proved by the seen,
Till that becomes unseen and receives proof in its turn.

Showing the best and dividing it from the worst age vexes age,   55
Knowing the perfect fitness and equanimity of things, while they discuss I am silent,
    and go bathe and admire myself.

Welcome is every organ and attribute of me, and of any man hearty and clean,
Not an inch nor a particle of an inch is vile, and none shall be less familiar than
    the rest.

I am satisfied — I see, dance, laugh, sing;
As the hugging and loving bed-fellow sleeps at my side through the night, and
    withdraws at the peep of the day with stealthy tread,   60
Leaving the baskets cover'd with white towels swelling the house with their plenty,
Shall I postpone my acceptation and realization and scream at my eyes,
That they turn from gazing after and down the road,
And forthwith cipher and show me to a cent,
Exactly the value of one and exactly the value of two, and which is ahead?   65

4

Trippers and askers surround me,
People I meet, the effect upon me of my early life or the ward and city I live in, or
    the nation,
The latest dates, discoveries, inventions, societies, authors old and new,
My dinner, dress, associates, looks, compliments, dues,
The real or fancied indifference of some man or woman I love,   70
The sickness of one of my folks or of myself, or ill-doing or loss or lack of money, or
    depressions or exaltations,
Battles, the horrors of fratricidal war, the fever of doubtful news, the fitful events;
These come to me days and nights and go from me again,
But they are not the Me myself.

Apart from the pulling and hauling stands what I am,   75
Stands amused, complacent, compassionating, idle, unitary,
Looks down, is erect, or bends an arm on an impalpable certain rest,
Looking with side-curved head curious what will come next,
Both in and out of the game and watching and wondering at it.

Backward I see in my own days where I sweated through fog with linguists and
    contenders,   80
I have no mockings or arguments, I witness and wait.

5

I believe in you my soul, the other I am must not abase itself to you,
And you must not be abased to the other.

Loafe with me on the grass, loose the stop from your throat,
Not words, not music or rhyme I want, not custom or lecture, not even the best,   85
Only the lull I like, the hum of your valvèd voice.

I mind how once we lay such a transparent summer morning,
How you settled your head athwart my hips and gently turn'd over upon me,
And parted the shirt from my bosom-bone, and plunged your tongue to my bare-
    stript heart,
And reach'd till you felt my beard, and reach'd till you held my feet.   90

Swiftly arose and spread around me the peace and knowledge that pass all the
    argument of the earth,
And I know that the hand of God is the promise of my own,
And I know that the spirit of God is the brother of my own,
And that all the men ever born are also my brothers, and the women my sisters and
    lovers,
And that a kelson of the creation is love,   95
And limitless are leaves stiff or drooping in the fields,
And brown ants in the little wells beneath them,
And mossy scabs of the worm fence, heap'd stones, elder, mullein and poke-weed.

6

A child said *What is the grass?* fetching it to me with full hands,
How could I answer the child?   I do not know what it is any more than he.   100

I guess it must be the flag of my disposition, out of hopeful green stuff woven.
Or I guess it is the handkerchief of the Lord,
A scented gift and remembrancer designedly dropt,
Bearing the owner's name someway in the corners, that we may see and remark,
    and say *Whose?*

Or I guess the grass is itself a child, the produced babe of the vegetation.   105

Or I guess it is a uniform hieroglyphic,
And it means, Sprouting alike in broad zones and narrow zones,
Growing among black folks as among white,
Kanuck, Tuckahoe, Congressman, Cuff, I give them the same, I receive them the
    same.

And now it seems to me the beautiful uncut hair of graves.   110

Tenderly will I use you curling grass,
It may be you transpire from the breasts of young men,
It may be if I had known them I would have loved them,
It may be you are from old people, or from offspring taken soon out of their mothers'
    laps,
And here you are the mothers' laps.   115

This grass is very dark to be from the white heads of old mothers,
Darker than the colorless beards of old men,
Dark to come from under the faint red roofs of mouths.

O I perceive after all so many uttering tongues,
And I perceive they do not come from the roofs of mouths for nothing.   120

I wish I could translate the hints about the dead young men and women,
And the hints about old men and mothers, and the offspring taken soon out of their
    laps.

What do you think has become of the young and old men?
And what do you think has become of the women and children?

They are alive and well somewhere,   125
The smallest sprout shows there is really no death,
And if ever there was it led forward life, and does not wait at the end to arrest it,
And ceas'd the moment life appear'd.

All goes onward and outward, nothing collapses,
And to die is different from what any one supposed, and luckier.   130

7

Has any one supposed it lucky to be born?
I hasten to inform him or her it is just as lucky to die, and I know it.

I pass death with the dying and birth with the new-wash'd babe, and am not con-
    tain'd between my hat and boots,

And peruse manifold objects, no two alike and every one good,
The earth good and the stars good, and their adjuncts all good.   135

I am not an earth nor an adjunct of an earth,
I am the mate and companion of people, all just as immortal and fathomless as
    myself,
(They do not know how immortal, but I know.)

Every kind for itself and its own, for me mine male and female,
For me those that have been boys and that love women,   140
For me the sweet-heart and the old maid, for me mothers and the mothers of
    mothers,
For me lips that have smiled, eyes that have shed tears,
For me children and the begetters of children.

Undrape! you are not guilty to me, nor stale nor discarded,   145
I see through the broadcloth and gingham whether or no,
And am around, tenacious, acquisitive, tireless, and cannot be shaken away.

8

The little one sleeps in its cradle,
I lift the gauze and look a long time, and silently brush away flies with my hand.

The youngster and the red-faced girl turn aside up the bushy hill,   150
I peeringly view them from the top.

The suicide sprawls on the bloody floor of the bedroom,
I witness the corpse with its dabbled hair, I note where the pistol has fallen.

The blab of the pave, tires of carts, sluff of boot-soles, talk of the promenaders,
The heaving omnibus, the driver with his interrogating thumb, the clank of the shod
    horses on the granite floor,   155
The snow-sleighs, clinking, shouted jokes, pelts of snow-balls,
The hurrahs for popular favorites, the fury of rous'd mobs,
The flap of the curtain'd litter, a sick man inside borne to the hospital,
The meeting of enemies, the sudden oath, the blows and fall,
The excited crowd, the policeman with his star quickly working his passage to the
    centre of the crowd,   160
The impassive stones that receive and return so many echoes,
What groans of over-fed or half-starv'd who fall sunstruck or in fits,
What exclamations of women taken suddenly who hurry home and give birth to
    babes,
What living and buried speech is always vibrating here, what howls restrain'd by
    decorum,
Arrests of criminals, slights, adulterous offers made, acceptances, rejections with
    convex lips,   165
I mind them or the show or resonance of them — I come and I depart.

20

Who goes there? hankering, gross, mystical, nude;
How is it I extract strength from the beef I eat?   390
What is a man anyhow? what am I? what are you?

All I mark as my own you shall offset it with your own,
Else it were time lost listening to me.

I do not snivel that snivel the world over,
That months are vacuums and the ground but wallow and filth.   395

Whimpering and truckling fold with powders for invalids, conformity goes to the
     fourth remov'd,
I wear my hat as I please indoors or out.
Why should I pray? why should I venerate and be ceremonious?

Having pried through the strata, analyzed to a hair, counsel'd with doctors and cal-
     culated close,
I find no sweeter fat than sticks to my own bones.   400

In all people I see myself, none more and not one a barley-corn less,
And the good or bad I say of myself I say of them.

I know I am solid and sound,
To me the converging objects of the universe perpetually flow,
All are written to me, and I must get what the writing means.   405

I know I am deathless,
I know this orbit of mine cannot be swept by a carpenter's compass,
I know I shall not pass like a child's carlacue cut with a burnt stick at night.

I know I am august,
I do not trouble my spirit to vindicate itself or be understood,   410
I see that the elementary laws never apologize,
(I reckon I behave no prouder than the level I plant my house by, after all.)

I exist as I am, that is enough,
If no other in the world be aware I sit content,
And if each and all be aware I sit content.   415

One world is aware and by the far largest to me, and that is myself,
And whether I come to my own to-day or in ten thousand or ten million years,
I can cheerfully take it now, or with equal cheerfulness I can wait.

My foothold is tenon'd and mortis'd in granite,
I laugh at what you call dissolution,   420
And I know the amplitude of time.

21

I am the poet of the Body and I am the poet of the Soul,
The pleasures of heaven are with me and the pains of hell are with me,
The first I graft and increase upon myself, the latter I translate into a new tongue.

I am the poet of the woman the same as the man,   425
And I say it is as great to be a woman as to be a man,
And I say there is nothing greater than the mother of men.

I chant the chant of dilation or pride,
We have had ducking and deprecating about enough,
I show that size is only development.   430

Have you outstript the rest? are you the President?
It is a trifle, they will more than arrive there every one, and still pass on.

I am he that walks with the tender and growing night,
I call to the earth and sea half-held by the night.

Press close bare-bosom'd night — press close magnetic nourishing night!   435
Night of south winds — night of the large few stars!
Still nodding night — mad naked summer night.

Smile O voluptuous cool-breath'd earth!
Earth of the slumbering and liquid trees!
Earth of departed sunset — earth of the mountains misty-topt!   440
Earth of the vitreous pour of the full moon just tinged with blue!
Earth of shine and dark mottling the tide of the river!
Earth of the limpid gray of clouds brighter and clearer for my sake!
Far-swooping elbow'd earth — rich apple-blossom'd earth!
Smile, for your lover comes.   445

Prodigal, you have given me love — therefore I to you give love!
O unspeakable passionate love.

22

You sea! I resign myself to you also — I guess what you mean,
I behold from the beach your crooked inviting fingers,
I believe you refuse to go back without feeling of me,   450
We must have a turn together, I undress, hurry me out of sight of the land,
Cushion me soft, rock me in billowy drowse,
Dash me with amorous wet, I can repay you.

Sea of stretch'd ground-swells,
Sea breathing broad and convulsive breaths,   455
Sea of the brine of life and of unshovell'd yet always-ready graves,
Howler and scooper of storms, capricious and dainty sea,
I am integral with you, I too am of one phase and of all phases.

Partaker of influx and efflux, I, extoller of hate and conciliation,
Extoller of amies and those that sleep in each others' arms.   460

I am he attesting sympathy,
(Shall I make my list of things in the house and skip the house that supports them?)

I am not the poet of goodness only, I do not decline to be the poet of wickedness also.

What blurt is this about virtue and about vice?
Evil propels me and reform of evil propels me, I stand indifferent,   465
My gait is no fault-finder's or rejecter's gait,
I moisten the roots of all that has grown.

Did you fear some scrofula out of the unflagging pregnancy?
Did you guess the celestial laws are yet to be work'd over and rectified?

I find one side a balance and the antipodal side a balance,   470
Soft doctrine as steady help as stable doctrine,
Thoughts and deeds of the present our rouse and early start.

This minute that comes to me over the past decillions,
There is no better than it and now.

What behaved well in the past or behaves well to-day is not such a wonder,   475
The wonder is always and always how there can be a mean man or an infidel.

23

Endless unfolding of words of ages!
And mine a word of the modern, the word En-Masse.

A word of the faith that never balks,
Here or henceforward it is all the same to me, I accept Time absolutely.   480
It alone is without flaw, it alone rounds and completes all,
That mystic baffling wonder alone completes all.

I accept Reality and dare not question it,
Materialism first and last imbuing.

Hurrah for positive science! long live exact demonstration!   485
Fetch stonecrop mixt with cedar and branches of lilac,
This is the lexicographer, this the chemist, this made a grammar of the old car-
    touches,
These mariners put the ship through dangerous unknown seas,
This is the geologist, this works with the scalpel, and this is a mathematician.

Gentlemen, to you the first honors always!   490
Your facts are useful, and yet they are not my dwelling,
I but enter by them to an area of my dwelling.

Less the reminders of properties told my words,
And more the reminders they of life untold, and of freedom and extrication,
And make short account of neuters and geldings, and favor men and women fully
    equipt,   495
And beat the gong of revolt. and stop with fugitives and them that plot and conspire.

24

Walt Whitman, a kosmos, of Manhattan the son,
Turbulent, fleshy, sensual, eating, drinking and breeding,
No sentimentalist, no stander above men and women or apart from them,
No more modest than immodest.   500

Unscrew the locks from the doors!
Unscrew the doors themselves from their jambs!

Whoever degrades another degrades me,
And whatever is done or said returns at last to me.

Through me the afflatus surging and surging, through me the current and index. 505

I speak the pass-word primeval, I give the sign of democracy,
By God! I will accept nothing which all cannot have their counterpart of on the
        same terms.

Through me many long dumb voices,
Voices of the interminable generations of prisoners and slaves,
Voices of the diseas'd and despairing and of thieves and dwarfs,   510
Voices of cycles of preparation and accretion,
And of the threads that connect the stars, and of wombs and of the father-stuff,
And of the rights of them the others are down upon,
Of the deform'd, trivial, flat, foolish, despised,
Fog in the air, beetles rolling balls of dung.   515

Through me forbidden voices,
Voices of sexes and lusts, voices veil'd and I remove the veil,
Voices indecent by me clarified and transfigur'd.

I do not press my fingers across my mouth,
I keep as delicate around the bowels as around the head and heart,   520
Copulation is no more rank to me than death is.

I believe in the flesh and the appetites,
Seeing, hearing, feeling, are miracles, and each part and tag of me is a miracle.
Divine am I inside and out, and I make holy whatever I touch or am touch'd from,
The scent of these arm-pits aroma finer than prayer,   525
This head more than churches, bibles, and all the creeds.

If I worship one thing more than another it shall be the spread of my own body, or
        any part of it,
Translucent mould of me it shall be you!
Shaded ledges and rests it shall be you!
Firm masculine colter it shall be you!   530
Whatever goes to the tilth of me it shall be you!
You my rich blood! your milky stream pale strippings of my life!
Breast that presses against other breasts it shall be you!
My brain it shall be your occult convolutions!
Root of wash'd sweet-flag! timorous pond-snipe! nest of guarded duplicate eggs!
        it shall be you!   535

Mix'd tussled hay of head, beard, brawn, it shall be you!
Trickling sap of maple, fibre of manly wheat, it shall be you!
Sun so generous it shall be you!
Vapors lighting and shading my face it shall be you!
You sweaty brooks and dews it shall be you!   540
Winds whose soft-tickling genitals rub against me it shall be you!
Broad muscular fields, branches of live oak, loving lounger in my winding paths,
        it shall be you!
Hands I have taken, face I have kiss'd, mortal I have ever touch'd, it shall be you.

I dote on myself, there is that lot of me and all so luscious,
Each moment and whatever happens thrills me with joy,   545
I cannot tell how my ankles bend, nor whence the cause of my faintest wish,
Nor the cause of the friendship I emit, nor the cause of the friendship I take again.

That I walk up my stoop, I pause to consider if it really be,
A morning-glory at my window satisfies me more than the metaphysics of books.

To behold the day-break!   550
The little light fades the immense and diaphanous shadows,
The air tastes good to my palate.

Hefts of the moving world at innocent gambols silently rising, freshly exuding,
Scooting obliquely high and low.

Something I cannot see puts upward libidinous prongs,   555
Seas of bright juice suffuse heaven.

The earth by the sky staid with, the daily close of their junction,
The heav'd challenge from the east that moment over my head,
The mocking taunt, See then whether you shall be master!

25

Dazzling and tremendous how quick the sun-rise would kill me,   560
If I could not now and always send sun-rise out of me.

We also ascend dazzling and tremendous as the sun,
We found our own O my soul in the calm and cool of the daybreak.

My voice goes after what my eyes cannot reach,
With the twirl of my tongue I encompass worlds and volumes of worlds.   565
Speech is the twin of my vision, it is unequal to measure itself,
It provokes me forever, it says sarcastically,
Walt you contain enough, why don't you let it out then?

Come now I will not be tantalized, you conceive too much of articulation,
Do you not know O speech how the buds beneath you are folded?   570
Waiting in gloom, protected by frost,
The dirt receding before my prophetical screams,
I underlying causes to balance them at last,
My knowledge my live parts, it keeping tally with the meaning of all things,
Happiness, (which whoever hears me let him or her set out in search of this day.)   575

My final merit I refuse you, I refuse putting from me what I really **am,**
Encompass worlds, but never try to encompass me,
I crowd your sleekest and best by simply looking toward you.

Writing and talk do not prove me,
I carry the plenum of proof and every thing else in my face,   580
With the hush of my lips I wholly confound the skeptic.

26

Now I will do nothing but listen,
To accrue what I hear into this song, to let sounds contribute toward it.

I hear bravuras of birds, bustle of growing wheat, gossip of flames, clack of sticks
    cooking my meals,
I hear the sound I love, the sound of the human voice,   585
I hear all sounds running together, combined, fused or following,
Sounds of the city and sounds out of the city, sounds of the day and night,
Talkative young ones to those that like them, the loud laugh of work-people at
    their meals,
The angry base of disjointed friendship, the faint tones of the sick,
The judge with hands tight to the desk, his pallid lips pronouncing a death-
    sentence,   590
The heave'e'yo of stevedores unlading ships by the wharves, the refrain of the anchor-
    lifters,
The ring of alarm-bells, the cry of fire, the whirr of swift-streaking engines and hose-
    carts with premonitory tinkles and color'd lights,
The steam-whistle, the solid roll of the train of approaching cars,
The slow march play'd at the head of the association marching two and two,
(They go to guard some corpse, the flag-tops are draped with black muslin.)   595

I hear the violoncello, ('tis the young man's heart's complaint,)
I hear the key'd cornet, it glides quickly in through my ears,
It shakes mad-sweet pangs through my belly and breast.
I hear the chorus, it is a grand opera,
Ah this indeed is music — this suits me.   600

A tenor large and fresh as the creation fills me,
The orbic flex of his mouth is pouring and filling me full.

I hear the train'd soprano (what work with hers is this?)
The orchestra whirls me wider than Uranus flies,
It wrenches such ardors from me I did not know I possess'd them,   605
It sails me, I dab with bare feet, they are lick'd by the indolent waves,
I am cut by bitter and angry hail, I lose my breath,
Steep'd amid honey'd morphine, my windpipe throttled in fakes of death,
At length let up again to feel the puzzle of puzzles,
And that we call Being.   610

27

To be in any form, what is that?
(Round and round we go, all of us, and ever come back thither,)
If nothing lay more develop'd the quahaug in its callous shell were enough.

Mine is no callous shell,
I have instant conductors all over me whether I pass or stop, 615
They seize every object and lead it harmlessly through me.

I merely stir, press, feel with my fingers, and am happy,
To touch my person to some one else's is about as much as I can stand.

28

Is this then a touch? quivering me to a new identity,
Flames and ether making a rush for my veins, 620
Treacherous tip of me reaching and crowding to help them,
My flesh and blood playing out lightning to strike what is hardly different from
    myself,
On all sides prurient provokers stiffening my limbs,
Straining the udder of my heart for its withheld drip,
Behaving licentious toward me, taking no denial, 625
Depriving me of my best as for a purpose,
Unbuttoning my clothes, holding me by the bare waist,
Deluding my confusion with the calm of the sunlight and pasture-fields,
Immodestly sliding the fellow-senses away,
They bribed to swap off with touch and go and graze at the edges of me, 630
No consideration, no regard for my draining strength or my anger,
Fetching the rest of the herd around to enjoy them a while,
Then all uniting to stand on a headland and worry me.

The sentries desert every other part of me,
They have left me helpless to a red marauder, 635
They all come to the headland to witness and assist against me.

I am given up by traitors,
I talk wildly, I have lost my wits, I and nobody else am the greatest traitor,
I went myself first to the headland, my own hands carried me there.

You villain touch! what are you doing? my breath is tight in its throat, 640
Unclench your floodgates, you are too much for me.

29

Blind loving wrestling touch, sheath'd hooded sharp-tooth'd touch!
Did it make you ache so, leaving me?

Parting track'd by arriving, perpetual payment of perpetual loan,
Rich showering rain, and recompense richer afterward. 645
Sprouts take and accumulate, stand by the curb prolific and vital,
Landscapes projected masculine, full-sized and golden.

30

All truths wait in all things,
They neither hasten their own delivery nor resist it,
They do not need the obstetric forceps of the surgeon, 650
The insignificant is as big to me as any,
(What is less or more than a touch?)

Logic and sermons never convince,
The damp of the night drives deeper into my soul.

(Only what proves itself to every man and woman is so,   655
Only what nobody denies is so.)

A minute and a drop of me settle my brain,
I believe the soggy clods shall become lovers and lamps,
And a compend of compends is the meat of a man or woman,
And a summit and flower there is the feeling they have for each other,   660
And they are to branch boundlessly out of that lesson until it becomes omnific,
And until one and all shall delight us, and we them.

31

I believe a leaf of grass is no less than the journey-work of the stars,
And the pismire is equally perfect, and a grain of sand, and the egg of the wren,
And the tree-toad is a chef-d'œuvre for the highest,   665
And the running blackberry would adorn the parlors of heaven,
And the narrowest hinge in my hand puts to scorn all machinery,
And the cow crunching with depress'd head surpasses any statue,
And a mouse is miracle enough to stagger sextillions of infidels.   669

I find I incorporate gneiss, coal, long-threaded moss, fruits, grains, esculent roots,
And am stucco'd with quadrupeds and birds all over,
And have distanced what is behind me for good reasons,
But call any thing back again when I desire it.

In vain the speeding or shyness,
In vain the plutonic rocks send their old heat against my approach,   675
In vain the mastodon retreats beneath its own powder'd bones,
In vain objects stand leagues off and assume manifold shapes,
In vain the ocean settling in hollows and the great monsters lying low,
In vain the buzzard houses herself with the sky,
In vain the snake slides through the creepers and logs,   680
In vain the elk takes to the inner passes of the woods,
In vain the razor-bill'd auk sails far north to Labrador,
I follow quickly, I ascend to the nest in the fissure of the cliff.

32

I think I could turn and live with animals, they're so placid and self-contain'd,
I stand and look at them long and long.   685

They do not sweat and whine about their condition,
They do not lie awake in the dark and weep for their sins,
They do not make me sick discussing their duty to God,
Not one is dissatisfied, not one is demented with the mania of owning things,
Not one kneels to another, nor to his kind that lived thousands of years ago,   690
Not one is respectable or unhappy over the whole earth.

So they show their relations to me and I accept them,
They bring me tokens of myself, they evince them plainly in their possession.

I wonder where they get those tokens,
Did I pass that way huge times ago and negligently drop them?   695

Myself moving forward then and now and forever,
Gathering and showing more always and with velocity,
Infinite and omnigenous, and the like of these among them,
Not too exclusive toward the reachers of my remembrancers,
Picking out here one that I love, and now go with him on brotherly terms.   700

A gigantic beauty of a stallion, fresh and responsive to my caresses,
Head high in the forehead, wide between the ears,
Limbs glossy and supple, tail dusting the ground,
Eyes full of sparkling wickedness, ears finely cut, flexibly moving.

His nostrils dilate as my heels embrace him,   705
His well-built limbs tremble with pleasure as we race around and return.
I but use you a minute, then I resign you, stallion,
Why do I need your paces when I myself out-gallop them?
Even as I stand or sit passing faster than you.

39

The friendly and flowing savage, who is he?
Is he waiting for civilization, or past it and mastering it?

Is he some Southwesterner rais'd out-doors? is he Kanadian?
Is he from the Mississippi country? Iowa, Oregon, California?
The mountains? prairie-life? bush-life? or sailor from the sea?   980

Wherever he goes men and women accept and desire him,
They desire he should like them, touch them, speak to them, stay with them.

Behavior lawless as snow-flakes, words simple as grass, uncomb'd head, laughter, and
    naïveté,
Slow-stepping feet, common features, common modes and emanations,
They descend in new forms from the tips of his fingers,   985
They are wafted with the odor of his body or breath, they fly out of the glance of his
    eyes.

43

I do not despise you priests, all time, the world over,
My faith is the greatest of faiths and the least of faiths,
Enclosing worship ancient and modern and all between ancient and modern,
Believing I shall come again upon the earth after five thousand years,
Waiting responses from oracles, honoring the gods, saluting the sun,   1100
Making a fetich of the first rock or stump, powowing with sticks in the circle of
    obis,
Helping the llama or brahmin as he trims the lamps of the idols,
Dancing yet through the streets in a phallic procession, rapt and austere in the woods
    a gymnosophist,
Drinking mead from the skull-cup, to Shastas and Vedas admirant, minding the
    Koran,

Walking the teokallis, spotted with gore from the stone and knife, beating the
　　　serpent-skin drum,　　　　　　　　　　　　　　　　　　　　　　　1105
Accepting the Gospels, accepting him that was crucified, knowing assuredly that
　　　he is divine,
To the mass kneeling or the puritan's prayer rising, or sitting patiently in a pew,
Ranting and frothing in my insane crisis, or waving dead-like till my spirit arouses
　　　me,
Looking forth on pavement and land, or outside of pavement and land,
Belonging to the winders of the circuit of circuits.　　　　　　　　　　　1110

One of that centripetal and centrifugal gang I turn and talk like a man leaving
　　　charges before a journey.

Down-hearted doubters dull and excluded,
Frivolous, sullen, moping, angry, affected, dishearten'd, atheistical,
I know every one of you, I know the sea of torment, doubt, despair and unbelief.

How the flukes splash!　　　　　　　　　　　　　　　　　　　　　　　1115
How they contort rapid as lightning, with spasms and spouts of blood!
Be at peace bloody flukes of doubters and sullen mopers,

I take my place among you as much as among any,
The past is the push of you, me, all, precisely the same,
And what is yet untried and afterward is for you, me, all, precisely the same.　1120

I do not know what is untried and afterward,
But I know it will in its turn prove sufficient, and cannot fail.

Each who passes is consider'd, each who stops is consider'd, not a single one can
　　　it fail.

It cannot fail the young man who died and was buried,
Nor the young woman who died and was put by his side,　　　　　　　　1125
Nor the little child that peep'd in at the door, and then drew back and was never
　　　seen again,
Nor the old man who has lived without purpose, and feels it with bitterness worse
　　　than gall,
Nor him in the poor house tubercled by rum and the bad disorder,
Nor the numberless slaughter'd and wreck'd, nor the brutish koboo call'd the
　　　ordure of humanity,
Nor the sacs merely floating with open mouths for food to slip in,　　　　1130
Nor any thing in the earth, or down in the oldest graves of the earth,
Nor any thing in the myriads of spheres, nor the myriads of myriads that inhabit
　　　them,
Nor the present, nor the least wisp that is known.

44

It is time to explain myself — let us stand up.

What is known I strip away.　　　　　　　　　　　　　　　　　　　　1135
I launch all men and women forward with me into the Unknown.

The clock indicates the moment — but what does eternity indicate?

We have thus far exhausted trillions of winters and summers,
There are trillions ahead, and trillions ahead of them.

Births have brought us richness and variety,   1140
And other births will bring us richness and variety.

I do not call one greater and one smaller,
That which fills its period and place is equal to any.

Were mankind murderous or jealous upon you, my brother, my sister?
I am sorry for you, they are not murderous or jealous upon me,   1145
All has been gentle with me, I keep no account with lamentation,
(What have I to do with lamentation?)

I am an acme of things accomplish'd, and I an encloser of things to be.

My feet strike an apex of the apices of the stairs,
On every step bunches of ages, and larger bunches between the steps, 1150
All below duly travel'd, and still I mount and mount.

Rise after rise bow the phantoms behind me,
Afar down I see the huge first Nothing, I know I was even there,
I waited unseen and always, and slept through the lethargic mist,
And took my time, and took no hurt from the fetid carbon.   1155

Long I was hugg'd close — long and long.

Immense have been the preparations for me,
Faithful and friendly the arms that have help'd me.

Cycles ferried my cradle, rowing and rowing like cheerful boatmen,
For room to me stars kept aside in their own rings,   1160
They sent influences to look after what was to hold me.

Before I was born out of my mother generations guided me,
My embryo has never been torpid, nothing could overlay it.

For it the nebula cohered to an orb,
The long slow strata piled to rest it on,   1165
Vast vegetables gave it sustenance,
Monstrous sauroids transported it in their mouths and deposited it with care.

All forces have been steadily employ'd to complete and delight me,
Now on this spot I stand with my robust soul.

48

I have said that the soul is not more than the body,
And I have said that the body is not more than the soul,   1270
And nothing, not God, is greater to one than one's self is,

And whoever walks a furlong without sympathy walks to his own funeral drest in
    his shroud,
And I or you pocketless of a dime may purchase the pick of the earth,
And to glance with an eye or show a bean in its pod confounds the learning of all
    times,
And there is no trade or employment but the young man following it may become
    a hero,   1275
And there is no object so soft but it makes a hub for the wheel'd universe,
And I say to any man or woman, Let your soul stand cool and composed before a
    million universes.

And I say to mankind, Be not curious about God,
For I who am curious about each am not curious about God,   1279
(No array of terms can say how much I am at peace about God and about death.)

I hear and behold God in every object, yet understand God not in the least,
Nor do I understand who there can be more wonderful than myself.

Why should I wish to see God better than this day?
I see something of God each hour of the twenty-four, and each moment then,
In the faces of men and women I see God, and in my own face in the glass,   1285
I find letters from God dropt in the street, and every one is sign'd by God's name,
And I leave them where they are, for I know that wheresoe'er I go,
Others will punctually come for ever and ever.

49

And as to you Death, and you bitter hug of mortality, it is idle to try to alarm
    me.

To his work without flinching the accoucheur comes,   1290
I see the elder-hand pressing receiving supporting,
I recline by the sills of the exquisite flexible doors,
And mark the outlet, and mark the relief and escape.

And as to you Corpse I think you are good manure, but that does not offend me,
I smell the white roses sweet-scented and growing,   1295
I reach to the leafy lips, I reach to the polish'd breasts of melons.

And as to you Life I reckon you are the leavings of many deaths,
(No doubt I have died myself ten thousand times before.)

I hear you whispering there O stars of heaven,
O suns — O grass of graves — O perpetual transfers and promotions,   1300
If you do not say any thing how can I say any thing?

Of the turbid pool that lies in the autumn forest,
Of the moon that descends the steeps of the soughing twilight,
Toss, sparkles of day and dusk — toss on the black stems that decay in the muck,
Toss to the moaning gibberish of the dry limbs.   1305

I ascend from the moon, I ascend from the night,
I perceive that the ghastly glimmer is noonday sunbeams reflected,
And debouch to the steady and central from the offspring great or small.

50

There is that in me — I do not know what it is — but I know it is in me.

Wrench'd and sweaty — calm and cool then my body becomes, 1310
I sleep — I sleep long.

I do not know it — it is without name — it is a word unsaid,
It is not in any dictionary, utterance, symbol.

Something it swings on more than the earth I swing on,
To it the creation is the friend whose embracing awakes me. 1315

Perhaps I might tell more. Outlines! I plead for my brothers and sisters.

Do you see O my brothers and sisters?
It is not chaos or death — it is form, union, plan — it is eternal life — it is Happiness.

51

The past and present wilt — I have fill'd them, emptied them,
And proceed to fill my next fold of the future. 1320

Listener up there! what have you to confide to me?
Look in my face while I snuff the sidle of evening,
(Talk honestly, no one else hears you, and I stay only a minute longer.)

Do I contradict myself?
Very well then I contradict myself, 1325
(I am large, I contain multitudes.)

I concentrate toward them that are nigh, I wait on the door-slab.

Who has done his day's work? who will soonest be through with his supper?
Who wishes to walk with me?

Will you speak before I am gone? will you prove already too late? 1330

52

The spotted hawk swoops by and accuses me, he complains of my gab and my
loitering.

I too am not a bit tamed, I too am untranslatable,
I sound my barbaric yawp over the roofs of the world.

The last scud of day holds back for me,
It flings my likeness after the rest and true as any on the shadow'd wilds, 1335
It coaxes me to the vapor and the dusk.

I depart as air, I shake my white locks at the runaway sun,
I effuse my flesh in eddies, and drift it in lacy jags.

I bequeath myself to the dirt to grow from the grass I love,
If you want me again look for me under your boot-soles. 1340

You will hardly know who I am or what I mean,
But I shall be good health to you nevertheless,
And filter and fibre your blood.

Failing to fetch me at first keep encouraged,
Missing me one place search another,   1345
I stop somewhere waiting for you.

There Was a Child Went Forth

(1855, 1871)

Among the *Leaves* of 1855 is this autobiographical summary of Whitman's early experience — his parents, the men and women in the streets, the wonderful life of nature inland and by the sea — the shaping influences on the child that went forth into the world.

There was a child went forth every day,
And the first object he look'd upon, that object he became,
And that object became part of him for the day or a certain part of the day,
Or for many years or stretching cycles of years.

The early lilacs became part of this child,   5
And grass and white and red morning-glories, and white and red clover, and the
    song of the phœbe-bird,
And the Third-month lambs and the sow's pink-faint litter, and the mare's foal
    and the cow's calf,
And the noisy brood of the barnyard or by the mire of the pond-side,
And the fish suspending themselves so curiously below there, and the beautiful
    curious liquid,
And the water-plants with their graceful flat heads, all became part of him.   10

The field-sprouts of Fourth-month and Fifth-month became part of him,
Winter-grain sprouts and those of the light-yellow corn, and the esculent roots
    of the garden,
And the apple-trees cover'd with blossoms and the fruit afterward, and wood-berries,
    and the commonest weeds by the road,
And the old drunkard staggering home from the outhouse of the tavern whence he
    had lately risen,
And the schoolmistress that pass'd on her way to the school,   15
And the friendly boys that pass'd, and the quarrelsome boys,
And the tidy and fresh-cheek'd girls, and the barefoot Negro boy and girl,
And all the changes of city and country wherever he went.
His own parents, he that had father'd him and she that had conceiv'd him in her
    womb and birth'd him,
They gave this child more of themselves than that,   20
They gave him afterward every day, they became part of him.

The mother at home quietly placing the dishes on the supper-table,
The mother with mild words, clean her cap and gown, a wholesome odor falling
    off her person and clothes as she walks by,
The father, strong, self-sufficient, manly, mean, anger'd, unjust,
The blow, the quick loud word, the tight bargain, the crafty lure, 25
The family usages, the language, the company, the furniture, the yearning and
    swelling heart,

Affection that will not be gainsay'd, the sense of what is real, the thought if after all
      it should prove unreal,
The doubts of day-time and the doubts of night-time, the curious whether and
      how,
Whether that which appears so is so, or is it all flashes and specks?
Men and women crowding fast in the streets, if they are not flashes and specks what
      are they?   30
The streets themselves and the façades of houses, and goods in the windows,
Vehicles, teams, the heavy-plank'd wharves, the huge crossing at the ferries,
The village on the highland seen from afar at sunset, the river between,
Shadows, aureola and mist, the light falling on roofs and gables of white or brown
      two miles off,
The schooner near by sleepily dropping down the tide, the little boat slack-tow'd
      astern,   35
The hurrying tumbling waves, quick-broken crests, slapping,
The strata of color'd clouds, the long bar of maroon-tint away solitary by itself, the
      spread of purity it lies motionless in,
The horizon's edge, the flying sea-crow, the fragrance of salt marsh and shore mud,
These became part of that child who went forth every day, and who now goes, and
      will always go forth every day.

Who Learns My Lesson Complete?

(1855, 1867)

In *Leaves*, 1855. Watts-Dunton's well-known description of the romantic movement as "the Renascence of Wonder" may be considered in connection with this poem and many passages in other poems of Whitman. "The phrase, the Renascence of Wonder," said Watts-Dunton, "merely indicates that there are two great impulses governing man,

and probably not man only, but the entire world of conscious life; the impulse of acceptance — the impulse to take unchallenged and for granted all the phenomena of the outer world as they are — and the impulse to confront these phenomena with eyes of inquiry and wonder" (*Poetry and the Renascence of Wonder*, pp. 237–38).

Who learns my lesson complete?
Boss, journeyman, apprentice, churchman and atheist,
The stupid and the wise thinker, parents and offspring, merchant, clerk, porter
      and customer,
Editor, author, artist, and schoolboy — draw nigh and commence;
It is no lesson — it lets down the bars to a good lesson,   5
And that to another, and every one to another still.

The great laws take and effuse without argument,
I am of the same style, for I am their friend,
I love them quits and quits, I do not halt and make salaams.

I lie abstracted and hear beautiful tales of things and the reasons of things,   10
They are so beautiful I nudge myself to listen.

I cannot say to any person what I hear — I cannot say it to myself — it is very
      wonderful.
It is no small matter, this round and delicious globe moving so exactly in its orbit for
      ever and ever, without one jolt or the untruth of a single second,
I do not think it was made in six days, nor in ten thousand years, nor ten billions of
      years,

Nor plann'd and built one thing after another as an architect plans and builds a
house.   15

I do not think seventy years is the time of a man or woman,
Nor that seventy millions of years is the time of a man or woman,
Nor that years will ever stop the existence of me, or any one else.

Is it wonderful that I should be immortal? as every one is immortal;
I know it is wonderful, but my eyesight is equally wonderful, and how I was conceived in my mother's womb is equally wonderful,   20
And pass'd from a babe in the creeping trance of a couple of summers and winters to
articulate and walk — all this is equally wonderful.

And that my soul embraces you this hour, and we affect each other without ever
seeing each other, and never perhaps to see each other, is every bit as wonderful.

And that I can think such thoughts as these is just as wonderful,
And that I can remind you, and you think them and know them to be true, is just
as wonderful.

And that the moon spins round the earth and on with the earth, is equally wonderful,   25
And that they balance themselves with the sun and stars is equally wonderful.

Out of the Cradle Endlessly Rocking

(1859, 1860, 1881)

As first printed, in the New York *Saturday Press*, Dec. 24, 1859, this poem bore the title "A Child's Reminiscence." It is, says Binns (*Life*, 12), "a memory of the May days when the boy discovered a mocking-bird's nest containing four pale green eggs, among the briers by the beach, and watched over them there from day to day till presently the mother-bird disappeared; and then of those September nights when, escaping from his bed, he ran barefoot down on to the shore through the windy moonlight, flung himself upon the sand, and listened to the desolate singing of the widowed he-bird close beside the surf. There, in the night, with the sea and the wind, he lay utterly absorbed in the sweet, sad singing of that passion, some

mystic response awakening in his soul; till in an ecstasy of tears which flooded his young cheeks, he felt, rather than understood, the world-meaning hidden in the thought of death."

Gay Allen (*Walt Whitman Handbook*, p. 143), quoting the Danish critic, Frederik Schyberg, contrasts the "word unsaid" in line 1312 of "Song of Myself" with the "word final" in line 161 of "Out of the Cradle Endlessly Rocking," and suggests that in the four years between the publication of the two poems Whitman's ultimate reality ceased to be "form, union, plan . . . eternal life . . . happiness," and became "chaos and death — but primarily death."

Out of the cradle endlessly rocking,
Out of the mocking-bird's throat, the musical shuttle,
Out of the Ninth-month midnight,
Over the sterile sands and the fields beyond, where the child leaving his bed wan-
der'd alone, bareheaded, barefoot,
Down from the shower'd halo,   5
Up from the mystic play of shadows twining and twisting as if they were alive,
Out from the patches of briers and blackberries,
From the memories of the bird that chanted to me,
From your memories sad brother, from the fitful risings and fallings I heard,
From under that yellow half-moon late-risen and swollen as if with tears,   10

From those beginning notes of yearning and love there in the mist,
From the thousand responses of my heart never to cease,
From the myriad thence-arous'd words,
From the word stronger and more delicious than any,
From such as now they start the scene revisiting,   15
As a flock, twittering, rising, or overhead passing,
Borne hither, ere all eludes me, hurriedly,
A man, yet by these tears a little boy again,
Throwing myself on the sand, confronting the waves,
I, chanter of pains and joys, uniter of here and hereafter,   20
Taking all hints to use them, but swiftly leaping beyond them,
A reminiscence sing.

Once Paumanok,
When the lilac-scent was in the air and Fifth-month grass was growing,
Up this seashore in some briers,   25
Two feather'd guests from Alabama, two together,
And their nest, and four light-green eggs spotted with brown,
And everyday the he-bird to and fro near at hand,
And every day the she-bird crouch'd on her nest, silent, with bright eyes,
And every day I, a curious boy, never too close, never disturbing them,   30
Cautiously peering, absorbing, translating.

Shine! shine! shine!
Pour down your warmth, great sun!
While we bask, we two together,

Two together!   35
Winds blow south, or winds blow north,
Day come white, or night come black,
Home, or rivers and mountains from home,
Singing all time, minding no time,
While we two keep together.   40

Till of a sudden,
May-be kill'd, unknown to her mate,
One forenoon that she-bird crouch'd not on the nest,
Nor return'd that afternoon, nor the next,
Nor ever appear'd again.   45

And thenceforward all summer in the sound of the sea,
And at night under the full of the moon in calmer weather,
Over the hoarse surging of the sea,
Or flitting from brier to brier by day,
I saw, I heard at intervals the remaining one, the he-bird,   50
The solitary guest from Alabama.

Blow! blow! blow!
Blow up sea-winds along Paumanok's shore;
I wait and I wait till you blow my mate to me.

Yes, when the stars glisten'd, **55**
All night long on the prong of a moss-scallop'd stake,
Down almost amid the slapping waves,
Sat the lone singer wonderful causing tears.

He call'd on his mate,
He pour'd forth the meanings which I of all men know. **60**

Yes my brother I know,
The rest might not, but I have treasur'd every note,
For more than once dimly down to the beach gliding,
Silent, avoiding the moonbeams, blending myself with the shadows,
Recalling now the obscure shapes, the echoes, the sounds and sights after their
　　sorts, **65**
The white arms out in the breakers tirelessly tossing,
I, with bare feet, a child, the wind wafting my hair,
Listen'd long and long.

Listen'd to keep, to sing, now translating the notes,
Following you my brother. **70**

Soothe! soothe! soothe!
Close on its wave soothes the wave behind,
And again another behind embracing and lapping, every one close,
But my love soothes not me, not me.

Low hangs the moon, it rose late, **75**
It is lagging — O I think it is heavy with love, with love.

O madly the sea pushes upon the land,
With love, with love.

O night! do I not see my love fluttering out among the breakers?
What is that little black thing I see there in the white? **80**

Loud! loud! loud!
Loud I call to you, my love!
High and clear I shoot my voice over the waves,
Surely you must know who is here, is here,
You must know who I am, my love. **85**

Low-hanging moon!
What is that dusky spot in your brown yellow?

O it is the shape, the shape of my mate!
O moon do not keep her from me any longer.

Land! land! O land! **90**
Whichever way I turn, O I think you could give me my mate back again if you only would,
For I am almost sure I see her dimly whichever way I look.

O rising stars!
Perhaps the one I want so much will rise, will rise with one of you.

O throat! O trembling throat!   95
Sound clearer through the atmosphere!
Pierce the woods, the earth,
Somewhere listening to catch you must be the one I want.

Shake out carols!
Solitary here, the night's carols!   100
Carols of lonesome love! death's carols!
Carols under that lagging, yellow, waning moon!
O under that moon where she droops almost down into the sea!
O reckless despairing carols.

But soft! sink low!   105
Soft! let me just murmur,
And do you wait a moment you husky-nois'd sea,
For somewhere I believe I heard my mate responding to me,
So faint, I must be still, be still to listen,
But not altogether still, for then she might not come immediately to me.   110

Hither my love!
Here I am! here!
With this just-sustain'd note I announce myself to you,
This gentle call is for you my love, for you.

Do not be decoy'd elsewhere,   115
That is the whistle of the wind, it is not my voice,
That is the fluttering, the fluttering of the spray,
Those are the shadows of leaves.

O darkness! O in vain!
O I am very sick and sorrowful.   120

O brown halo in the sky near the moon, drooping upon the sea!
O troubled reflection in the sea!
O throat! O throbbing heart!
And I singing uselessly, uselessly all the night.

O past! O happy life! O songs of joy!   125
In the air, in the woods, over fields,
Loved! loved! loved! loved! loved!
But my mate no more, no more with me!
We two together no more.

The aria sinking,   130
All else continuing, the stars shining,
The winds blowing, the notes of the bird continuous echoing,
With angry moans the fierce old mother incessantly moaning,
On the sands of Paumanok's shore gray and rustling,

The yellow half-moon enlarged, sagging down, drooping, the face of the sea almost
    touching,   135
The boy ecstatic, with his bare feet the waves, with his hair the atmosphere dallying,
The love in the heart long pent, now loose, now at last tumultuously bursting,
The aria's meaning, the ears, the soul, swiftly depositing,
The strange tears down the cheeks coursing,
The colloquy there, the trio, each uttering,   140
The undertone, the savage old mother incessantly crying,
To the boy's soul's questions sullenly timing, some drown'd secret hissing,
To the outsetting bard.

Demon or bird! (said the boy's soul,)
Is it indeed toward your mate you sing? or is it really to me?   145
For I, that was a child, my tongue's use sleeping, now I have heard you,
Now in a moment I know what I am for, I awake,
And already a thousand singers, a thousand songs, clearer, louder and more sorrow-
    ful than yours,
A thousand warbling echoes have started to life within me, never to die.

O you singer solitary, singing by yourself, projecting me,   150
O solitary me listening, never more shall I cease perpetuating you,
Never more shall I escape, never more the reverberations,
Never more the cries of unsatisfied love be absent from me,
Never again leave me to be the peaceful child I was before what there in the night,
By the sea under the yellow and sagging moon,   155
The messenger there arous'd, the fire, the sweet hell within,
The unknown want, the destiny of me.

O give me the clew! (it lurks in the night here somewhere,)
O if I am to have so much, let me have more!

A word then, (for I will conquer it,)   160
The word final, superior to all,
Subtle, sent up — what is it? — I listen;
Are you whispering it, and have been all the time, you sea-waves?
Is that it from your liquid rims and wet sands?

Whereto answering, the sea,   165
Delaying not, hurrying not,
Whisper'd me through the night, and very plainly before daybreak,
Lisp'd to me the low and delicious word death,
And again death, death, death, death,
Hissing melodious, neither like the bird nor like my arous'd child's heart,   170
But edging near as privately for me rustling at my feet,
Creeping thence steadily up to my ears and laving me softly all over,
Death, death, death, death, death.

Which I do not forget,
But fuse the song of my dusky demon and brother,   175
That he sang to me in the moonlight on Paumanok's gray beach,
With the thousand responsive songs at random,
My own songs awaked from that hour,

And with them the key, the word up from the waves,
The word of the sweetest song and all songs,   180
That strong and delicious word which, creeping to my feet,
(Or like some old crone rocking the cradle, swathed in sweet garments, bending
     aside,)
The sea whisper'd me.

A Noiseless Patient Spider

(1862–63, 1881)

A noiseless patient spider,
I mark'd where on a little promontory it stood isolated,
Mark'd how to explore the vacant vast surrounding,
It launch'd forth filament, filament, filament, out of itself,
Ever unreeling them, ever tirelessly speeding them.   5

And you O my soul where you stand,
Surrounded, detached, in measureless oceans of space,
Ceaselessly musing, venturing, throwing, seeking the spheres to connect them,
Till the bridge you will need be form'd, till the ductile anchor hold,
Till the gossamer thread you fling catch somewhere, O my soul.   10

When I Heard the Learn'd Astronomer

(1865, 1867)

When I heard the learn'd astronomer;
When the proofs, the figures, were ranged in columns before me;
When I was shown the charts and the diagrams, to add, divide, and measure them.
When I, sitting, heard the astronomer, where he lectured with much applause in the
     lecture-room,
How soon, unaccountable, I became tired and sick,   5
Till rising and gliding out, I wander'd off by myself,
In the mystical moist night-air, and from time to time,
Look'd up in perfect silence at the stars.

Come Up from the Fields Father

(1865, 1867)

This, like the ensuing poems evoked by the war, was published in *Drum-Taps*, 1865.

Come up from the fields father, here's a letter from our Pete,
And come to the front door mother, here's a letter from thy dear son.

Lo, 'tis autumn,
Lo, where the trees, deeper green, yellower and redder,
Cool and sweeten Ohio's villages with leaves fluttering in the moderate wind,   5
Where apples ripe in the orchards hang and grapes on the trellis'd vines,
(Smell you the smell of the grapes on the vines?
Smell you the buckwheat where the bees were lately buzzing?)

Above all, lo, the sky so calm, so transparent after the rain, and with wondrous
      clouds,
Below too, all calm, all vital and beautiful, and the farm prospers well.   10

Down in the fields all prospers well,
But now from the fields come father, come at the daughter's call,
And come to the entry mother, to the front door come right away.
Fast as she can she hurries, something ominous, her steps trembling,
She does not tarry to smooth her hair nor adjust her cap.   15

Open the envelope quickly,
O this is not our son's writing, yet his name is sign'd,
O a strange hand writes for our dear son, O stricken mother's soul!
All swims before her eyes, flashes with black, she catches the main words only,

Sentences broken, *gunshot wound in the breast, cavalry skirmish, taken to hospital,*   20
At present low, but will soon be better.

Ah now the single figure to me,
Amid all teeming and wealthy Ohio with all its cities and farms,
Sickly white in the face and dull in the head, very faint,
By the jamb of a door leans.   25

Grieve not so, dear mother, (the just-grown daughter speaks through her sobs,
The little sisters huddle around speechless and dismay'd,)
See, dearest mother, the letter says Pete will soon be better.

Alas poor boy, he will never be better, (nor may-be needs to be better, that brave
      and simple soul,)
While they stand at home at the door he is dead already,   30
The only son is dead.

But the mother needs to be better,
She with thin form presently drest in black,
By day her meals untouch'd, then at night fitfully sleeping, often waking,
In the midnight waking, weeping, longing with one deep longing,   35
O that she might withdraw unnoticed, silent from life escape and withdraw,
To follow, to seek, to be with her dear dead son.

As Toilsome I Wander'd Virginia's Woods

(1865, 1867)

As toilsome I wander'd Virginia's woods,
To the music of rustling leaves kick'd by my feet, (for 'twas autumn,)
I mark'd at the foot of a tree the grave of a soldier;
Mortally wounded he and buried on the retreat, (easily all could I understand.)
The halt of a mid-day hour, when up! no time to lose — yet this sign left,   5
On a tablet scrawl'd and nail'd on the tree by the grave,
Bold, cautious, true, and my loving comrade.

When Lilacs Last in the Dooryard Bloom'd
(1865–66, 1881)

Whitman often brooded on death and the grave. From boyhood on, he was fond of musing in cemeteries. He was always devoted to Bryant, "one of the best poets in the world," whose indebtedness to the eighteenth-century English "graveyard school" of writers has been noted. See his review of Bryant, nine years before *Leaves of Grass*, in *Uncollected Poetry and Prose*, I, 128–29, and his earliest

extant poems, *ibid.*, 1–31, (especially the first poem of all, "Our Future Lot," published in a newspaper in 1838, when Whitman was nineteen.)

It was lilac time in Brooklyn when Lincoln died, April 15, 1865, in Washington; he was laid to rest in his home town, Springfield, Illinois, on the 4th of May.

1

When lilacs last in the dooryard bloom'd,
And the great star early droop'd in the western sky in the night,
I mourn'd, and yet shall mourn with ever-returning spring.

Ever-returning spring, trinity sure to me you bring,
Lilac blooming perennial and drooping star in the west,   5
And thought of him I love.

2

O powerful western fallen star!
O shades of night — O moody, tearful night!
O great star disappear'd — O the black murk that hides the star!
O cruel hands that hold me powerless — O helpless soul of me!   10
O harsh surrounding cloud that will not free my soul.

3

In the dooryard fronting an old farm-house near the white-wash'd palings,
Stands the lilac-bush tall-growing with heart-shaped leaves of rich green,
With many a pointed blossom rising delicate, with the perfume strong I love,
With every leaf a miracle — and from this bush in the dooryard,   15
With delicate-color'd blossoms and heart-shaped leaves of rich green,
A sprig with its flower I break.

4

In the swamp in secluded recesses,
A shy and hidden bird is warbling a song.

Solitary the thrush,   20
The hermit withdrawn to himself, avoiding the settlements
Sings by himself a song.

Song of the bleeding throat,
Death's outlet song of life, (for well dear brother I know,
If thou wast not granted to sing thou would'st surely die.)   25

5

Over the breast of the spring, the land, amid cities,
Amid lanes and through old woods, where lately the violets peep'd from the ground
      spotting the gray debris,
Amid the grass in the fields each side of the lanes, passing the endless grass,

Passing the yellow-spear'd wheat, every grain from its shroud in the dark-brown
    fields uprisen,
Passing the apple-tree blows of white and pink in the orchards,   30
Carrying a corpse to where it shall rest in the grave,
Night and day journeys a coffin.

6

Coffin that passes through lanes and streets,
Through day and night with the great cloud darkening the land,
With the pomp of the inloop'd flags with the cities draped in black,   35
With the show of the states themselves as of crape-veil'd women standing,
With processions long and winding and the flambeaus of the night,
With the countless torches lit, with the silent sea of faces and the unbared heads,
With the waiting depot, the arriving coffin, and the sombre faces,
With dirges through the night, with the thousand voices rising strong and solemn,
With all the mournful voices of the dirges pour'd around the coffin,   41
The dim-lit churches and the shuddering organs — where amid these you journey,
With the tolling tolling bells' perpetual clang,
Here, coffin that slowly passes,
I give you my sprig of lilac.   45

7

(Nor for you, for one alone,
Blossoms and branches green to coffins all I bring,
For fresh as the morning, thus would I chant a song for you O sane and sacred death.

All over bouquets of roses,
O death, I cover you over with roses and early lilies,   50
But mostly and now the lilac that blooms the first,
Copious I break, I break the sprigs from the bushes,
With loaded arms I come, pouring for you,
For you and the coffins all of you O death.)

8

O western orb sailing the heaven,   55
Now I know what you must have meant as a month since I walk'd,
As I walk'd in silence the transparent shadowy night,
As I saw you had something to tell as you bent to me night after night,
As you droop'd from the sky low down as if to my side, (while the other stars all
    look'd on,)
As we wander'd together the solemn night, (for something I know not what kept me
    from sleep,)   60
As the night advanced, and I saw on the rim of the west how full you were of woe,
As I stood on the rising ground in the breeze in the cool transparent night,
As I watch'd where you pass'd and was lost in the netherward black of the night,
As my soul in its trouble dissatisfied sank, as where you sad orb,
Concluded, dropt in the night, and was gone.   65

9

Sing on there in the swamp,
O singer bashful and tender, I hear your notes, I hear your call,
I hear, I come presently, I understand you,

But a moment I linger, for the lustrous star has detain'd me,
The star my departing comrade holds and detains me.   **70**

10

O how shall I warble myself for the dead one there I loved?
And how shall I deck my song for the large sweet soul that has gone?
And what shall my perfume be for the grave of him I love?

Sea-winds blown from east and west,
Blown from the Eastern sea and blown from the Western sea, till there on the prairies meeting,   **75**
These and with these and the breath of my chant,
I'll perfume the grave of him I love.

11

O what shall I hang on the chamber walls?
And what shall the pictures be that I hang on the walls,
To adorn the burial-house of him I love?   **80**

Pictures of growing spring and farms and homes,
With the Fourth-month eve at sundown, and the gray smoke lucid and bright,
With floods of the yellow gold of the gorgeous, indolent, sinking sun, burning, expanding the air,
With the fresh sweet herbage under foot, and the pale green leaves of the trees prolific,
In the distance the flowing glaze, the breast of the river, with a wind-dapple here and there,   **85**
With ranging hills on the banks, with many a line against the sky, and shadows,
And the city at hand with dwellings so dense, and stacks of chimneys,
And all the scenes of life and the workshops, and the workmen homeward returning.

12

Lo, body and soul — this land,
My own Manhattan with spires, and the sparkling and hurrying tides, and the ships,   **90**
The varied and ample land, the South and the North in the light, Ohio's shores and flashing Missouri,
And ever the far-spreading prairies cover'd with grass and corn.

Lo, the most excellent sun so calm and haughty,
The violet and purple morn with just-felt breezes,
The gentle soft-born measureless light,   **95**
The miracle spreading bathing all, the fulfill'd noon,
The coming eve delicious, the welcome night and the stars,
Over my cities shining all, enveloping man and land.

13

Sing on, sing on you gray-brown bird,
Sing from the swamps, the recesses, pour your chant from the bushes,   **100**
Limitless out of the dusk, out of the cedars and pines.

Sing on dearest brother, warble your reedy song,
Loud human song, with voice of uttermost woe.

O liquid and free and tender!
O wild and loose to my soul — O wondrous singer!   105
You only I hear — yet the star holds me, (but will soon depart,)
Yet the lilac with mastering odor holds me.

14

Now while I sat in the day and look'd forth,
In the close of the day with its light and the fields of spring, and the farmers prepar-
        ing their crops,
In the large unconscious scenery of my land with its lakes and forests,   110
In the heavenly aerial beauty, (after the perturb'd winds and the storms,)
Under the arching heavens of the afternoon swift passing, and the voices of children
        and women,
The many-moving sea-tides, and I saw the ships how they sail'd,
And the summer approaching with richness, and the fields all busy with labor,
And the infinite separate houses, how they all went on, each with its meals and mi-
        nutia of daily usages,   115
And the streets how their throbbings throbb'd, and the cities pent — lo, then and
        there,
Falling upon them all and among them all, enveloping me with the rest,
Appear'd the cloud, appear'd the long black trail,
And I knew death, its thought, and the sacred knowledge of death.

Then with the knowledge of death as walking one side of me,   120
And the thought of death close-walking the other side of me,
And I in the middle as with companions, and as holding the hands of companions,
I fled forth to the hiding receiving night that talks not,
Down to the shores of the water, the path by the swamp in the dimness,
To the solemn shadowy cedars and ghostly pines so still.   125

And the singer so shy to the rest receiv'd me,
The gray-brown bird I know receiv'd us comrades three,
And he sang the carol of death, and a verse for him I love.

From deep secluded recesses,
From the fragrant cedars and the ghostly pines so still,   130
Came the carol of the bird.

And the charm of the carol rapt me,
As I held as if by their hands my comrades in the night,
And the voice of my spirit tallied the song of the bird.

Come lovely and soothing death,   135
Undulate round the world, serenely arriving, arriving,
In the day, in the night, to all, to each,
Sooner or later delicate death.

Prais'd be the fathomless universe,
For life and joy, and for objects and knowledge curious,   140
And for love, sweet love — but praise! praise! praise!
For the sure-enwinding arms of cool-enfolding death.

Dark mother always gliding near with soft feet,
Have none chanted for thee a chant of fullest welcome?
Then I chant it for thee, I glorify thee above all,   145
I bring thee a song that when thou must indeed come, come unfalteringly.

Approach strong deliveress,
When it is so, when thou hast taken them, I joyously sing the dead,
Lost in the loving floating ocean of thee,
Laved in the flood of thy bliss O death.   150

From me to thee glad serenades,
Dances for thee I propose saluting thee, adornments and feastings for thee,
And the sights of the open landscape and the high-spread sky are fitting,
And life and the fields, and the huge and thoughtful night.

The night in silence under many a star,   155
The ocean shore and the husky whispering wave whose voice I know,
And the soul turning to thee O vast and well-veil'd death,
And the body gratefully nestling close to thee.

Over the tree-tops I float thee a song,
Over the rising and sinking waves, over the myriad fields and the prairies wide,   160
Over the dense-pack'd cities all and the teeming wharves and ways,
I float this carol with joy, with joy to thee O death.

15

To the tally of my soul,
Loud and strong kept up the gray-brown bird,
With pure deliberate notes spreading filling the night.   165
Loud in the pines and cedars dim,
Clear in the freshness moist and swamp-perfume,
And I with my comrades there in the night.

While my sight that was bound in my eyes unclosed,
As to long panoramas of visions.   170

And I saw askant the armies,
I saw as in noiseless dreams hundreds of battle-flags,
Borne through the smoke of the battles and pierc'd with missiles I saw them,
And carried hither and yon through the smoke, and torn and bloody,
And at last but a few shreds left on the staffs, (and all in silence,)   175
And the staffs all splinter'd and broken.

I saw battle-corpses, myriads of them,
And the white skeletons of young men, I saw them,
I saw the debris and debris of all the slain soldiers of the war,
But I saw they were not as was thought,   180
They themselves were fully at rest, they suffer'd not,
The living remain'd and suffer'd, the mother suffer'd,
And the wife and the child and the musing comrade suffer'd,
And the armies that remain'd suffer'd.

16

Passing the visions, passing the night,   185
Passing, unloosing the hold of my comrades' hands,
Passing the song of the hermit bird and the tallying song of my soul,
Victorious song, death's outlet song, yet varying ever-altering song,
As low and wailing, yet clear the notes, rising and falling, flooding the night,
Sadly sinking and fainting, as warning and warning, and yet again bursting with
     joy,   190
Covering the earth and filling the spread of the heaven,
As that powerful psalm in the night I heard from recesses,
Passing, I leave thee lilac with heart-shaped leaves,
I leave thee there in the door-yard, blooming, returning with spring.

I cease from my song for thee,   195
From my gaze on thee in the west, fronting the west, communing with thee,
O comrade lustrous with silver face in the night.
Yet each to keep and all, retrievements out of the night,
The song, the wondrous chant of the gray-brown bird,
And the tallying chant, the echo arous'd in my soul,   200
With the lustrous and drooping star with the countenance full of woe,
With the holders holding my hand hearing the call of the bird,
Comrades mine and I in the midst, and their memory ever to keep, for the dead I
     loved so well,
For the sweetest, wisest soul of all my days and lands — and this for his dear sake,
Lilac and star and bird twined with the chant of my soul,   205
There in the fragrant pines and the cedars dusk and dim.

Years of the Modern

(1865, 1881)

Years of the modern! years of the unperform'd!
Your horizon rises, I see it parting away for more august dramas,
I see not America only, not only Liberty's nation but other nations preparing,
I see tremendous entrances and exits, new combinations, the solidarity of races,
I see that force advancing with irresistible power on the world's stage,   5
(Have the old forces, the old wars, played their parts? are the acts suitable to them
    closed?)
I see Freedom, completely arm'd and victorious and very haughty, with Law on one
    side and Peace on the other,
A stupendous trio all issuing forth against the idea of caste;
What historic denouements are these we so rapidly approach?
I see men marching and countermarching by swift millions,   10
I see the frontiers and boundaries of the old aristocracies broken,
I see the landmarks of European kings removed,
I see this day the People beginning their landmarks, (all others give way;)
Never were such sharp questions ask'd as this day,
Never was average man, his soul, more energetic, more like a God,   15
Lo, how he urges and urges, leaving the masses no rest!
His daring foot is on land and sea everywhere, he colonizes the Pacific, the archi-
    pelagoes,
With the steamship, the electric telegraph, the newspaper, the wholesale engines of
    war,

With these and the world-spreading factories he interlinks all geography, all lands;
What whispers are these O lands, running ahead of you, passing under the seas?   20
Are all nations communing? is there going to be but one heart to the globe?
Is humanity forming en-masse? for lo, tyrants tremble, crowns grow dim,
The earth, restive, confronts a new era, perhaps a general divine war,
No one knows what will happen next, such portents fill the days and nights;
Years prophetical! the space ahead as I walk, as I vainly try to pierce it, is full of
    phantoms,   25
Unborn deeds, things soon to be, project their shapes around me,
This incredible rush and heat, this strange ecstatic fever of dreams O years!
Your dreams O years, how they penetrate through me! (I know not whether I sleep
    or wake;)
The perform'd America and Europe grow dim, retiring in shadow behind me,
The unperform'd, more gigantic than ever, advance, advance upon me.   30

To a Locomotive in Winter

(1876, 1881)

Thee for my recitative,
Thee in the driving storm even as now, the snow, the winter-day declining,
Thee in thy panoply, thy measur'd dual throbbing and thy beat convulsive,
Thy black cylindric body, golden brass and silvery steel,
Thy ponderous side-bars, parallel and connecting rods, gyrating, shuttling at thy
    sides,   5
Thy metrical, now swelling pant and roar, now tapering in the distance,
Thy great protruding head-light fix'd in front,
Thy long, pale, floating vapor-pennants, tinged with delicate purple,
The dense and murky clouds out-belching from thy smoke-stack,
Thy knitted frame, thy springs and valves, the tremulous twinkle of thy wheels,   10
Thy train of cars behind, obedient, merrily following,
Through gale or calm, now swift, now slack, yet steadily careering;
Type of the modern — emblem of motion and power — pulse of the continent,
For once come serve the Muse and merge in verse, even as here I see thee,
With storm and buffeting gusts of wind and falling snow,   15
By day thy warning ringing bell to sound its notes,
By night thy silent signal lamps to swing.

Fierce-throated beauty!
Roll through my chant with all thy lawless music, thy swinging lamps at night,
Thy madly-whistled laughter, echoing, rumbling like an earthquake, rousing all,   20
Law of thyself complete, thine own track firmly holding,
(No sweetness debonair of tearful harp or glib piano thine,)
Thy trills of shrieks by rocks and hills return'd,
Launch'd o'er the prairies wide, across the lakes,
To the free skies unpent and glad and strong.   25

To Foreign Lands

(1860, 1871)

I heard that you ask'd for something to prove this puzzle the New World,
And to define America, her athletic Democracy,
Therefore I send you my poems that you behold in them what you wanted.

From Democratic Vistas

(1871)

[American Democracy, Actual and Ideal]

For my part, I would alarm and caution even the political and business reader, and to the utmost extent, against the prevailing delusion that the establishment of free political institutions, and plentiful intellectual smartness, with general good order, physical plenty, industry, etc., (desirable and precious advantages as they all are,) do, of themselves, determine and yield to our experiment of democracy the fruitage of success. With such advantages at present fully, or almost fully, possess'd — the Union just issued, victorious, from the struggle with the only foes it need ever fear, (namely, those within itself, the interior ones,) and with unprecedented materialistic advancement — society, in these States, is canker'd, crude, superstitious, and rotten. Political, or law-made society is, and private, or voluntary society, is also. In any vigor, the element of the moral conscience, the most important, the verteber to State or man, seems to me either entirely lacking, or seriously enfeebled or ungrown.

I say we had best look our times and lands searchingly in the face, like a physician diagnosing some deep disease. Never was there, perhaps, more hollowness at heart than at present, and here in the United States. Genuine belief seems to have left us. The underlying principles of the States are not honestly believ'd in, (for all this hectic glow, and these melo-dramatic screamings,) nor is humanity itself believ'd in. What penetrating eye does not everywhere see through the mask? The spectacle is appalling. We live in an atmosphere of hypocrisy throughout. The men believe not in the women, nor the women in the men. A scornful superciliousness rules in literature. The aim of all the *littérateurs* is to find something to make fun of. A lot of churches, sects, etc., the most dismal phantasms I know, usurp the name of religion. Conversation is a mass of badinage. From deceit in the spirit, the mother of all false deeds, the offspring is already incalculable. An acute and candid person, in the revenue department in Washington, who is led by the course of his employment to regularly visit the cities, north, south and west, to investigate frauds, has talk'd much with me about his discoveries. The depravity of the business classes of our country is not less than has been supposed, but infinitely greater. The official services of America, national, state, and municipal, in all their branches and departments, except the judiciary, are saturated in corruption, bribery, falsehood, mal-administration; and the judiciary is tainted. The great cities reek with respectable as much as non-respectable robbery and scoundrelism. In fashionable life, flippancy, tepid amours, weak infidelism, small aims, or no aims at all, only to kill time. In business, (this all-devouring modern word, business,) the one sole object is, by any means, pecuniary gain. The magician's serpent in the fable ate up all the other serpents; and money-making is our magician's serpent, remaining to-day sole master of the field. The best class we show, is but a mob of fashionably dress'd speculators and vulgarians. True, indeed, behind this fantastic farce, enacted on the visible stage of society, solid things and stupendous labors are to be discover'd, existing crudely and going on in the background, to advance and tell themselves in time. Yet the truths are none the less terrible. I say that our New World democracy, however great a success in uplifting the masses out of their sloughs, in materialistic development, products, and in a certain highly-deceptive superficial popular intellectuality, is, so far, an almost complete failure in its social aspects, and in really grand religious, moral, literary, and esthetic results. In vain do we march with unprecedented strides to empire so colossal, outvying the antique, beyond Alexander's, beyond the proudest sway of Rome. In vain have we annex'd Texas, California, Alaska, and reach north for Canada and south for Cuba. It is as if we were somehow being endow'd with a vast and more and more thoroughly-appointed body, and then left with little or no soul.

Let me illustrate further, as I write, with current observations, localities, etc. The subject is important, and will bear repetition. After an absence, I am now again (September, 1870) in New York city and Brooklyn, on a few weeks' vacation. The splendor, picturesqueness, and oceanic amplitude and rush of these great cities, the unsurpass'd situation, rivers and bay, sparkling sea-tides, costly and lofty new buildings, façades of marble and iron, of original grandeur and elegance of design, with the masses of gay color, the preponderance of white and blue, the flags flying, the endless ships, the tumultuous streets, Broadway, the heavy, low, musical roar, hardly ever intermitted, even at night; the jobbers' houses, the rich shops, the wharves, the great Central Park, and the Brooklyn Park of hills, (as I wander among them this beautiful fall weather, musing, watching, absorbing) — the assemblages of the citizens in their groups, conversations, trades, evening amusements, or along the by-quarters — these, I say, and the like of these, completely satisfy my senses of power, fulness, motion, etc., and give me, through such senses and appetites, and through my esthetic conscience, a continued exaltation and absolute fulfilment. Always and more and more, as I cross the East and North rivers, the ferries, or with the pilots in their pilot-houses, or pass an hour in Wall street, or the gold exchange, I realize, (if we must admit such partialisms,) that not Nature alone is great in her fields of freedom and the open air, in her storms, the shows of night and day, the mountains, forests, seas — but in the artificial, the work of man too is equally great — in this profusion of teeming humanity — in these ingenuities, streets, goods, houses, ships — these hurrying, feverish, electric crowds of men, their complicated business genius, (not least among the geniuses,) and all this mighty, many-threaded wealth and industry concentrated here.

But sternly discarding, shutting our eyes to the glow and grandeur of the general superficial effect, coming down to what is of the only real importance, Personalities, and examining minutely, we question, we ask, Are there, indeed, *men* here worthy the name? Are there athletes? Are there perfect women, to match the generous material luxuriance? Is there a pervading atmosphere of beautiful manners? Are there crops of fine youths, and majestic old persons? Are there arts worthy

freedom and a rich people? Is there a great moral and religious civilization — the only justification of a great material one? Confess that to severe eyes, using the moral microscope upon humanity, a sort of dry and flat Sahara appears, these cities, crowded with petty grotesques, malformations, phantoms, playing meaningless antics. Confess that everywhere, in shop, street, church, theatre, bar-room, official chair, are pervading flippancy and vulgarity, low cunning, infidelity — everywhere the youth puny, impudent, foppish, prematurely ripe — everywhere an abnormal libidinousness, unhealthy forms, male, female, painted, padded, dyed, chignon'd, muddy complexions, bad blood, the capacity for good motherhood deceasing or deceas'd, shallow notions of beauty, with a range of manners, or rather lack of manners, (considering the advantages enjoy'd,) probably the meanest to be seen in the world.[1]

Of all this, and these lamentable conditions, to breathe into them the breath recuperative of sane and heroic life, I say a new founded literature, not merely to copy and reflect existing surfaces, or pander to what is called taste — not only to amuse, pass away time, celebrate the beautiful, the refined, the past, or exhibit technical, rhythmic, or grammatical dexterity — but a literature underlying life, religious, consistent with science, handling the elements and forces with competent power, teaching and training men — and, as perhaps the most precious of its results, achieving the entire redemption of woman out of these incredible holds and webs of silliness, millinery, and every kind of dys-

[1] Of these rapidly sketch'd hiatuses, the two which seem to me most serious are, for one, the condition, absence, or perhaps the singular abeyance, of moral conscientious fibre all through American society; and, for another, the appalling depletion of women in their powers of sane athletic maternity, their crowning attribute, and ever making the woman, in loftiest spheres, superior to the man.

I have sometimes thought, indeed, that the sole avenue and means of a reconstructed sociology depended, primarily, on a new birth, elevation, expansion, invigoration of woman, affording, for races to come, (as the conditions that antedate birth are indispensable,) a perfect motherhood. Great, great, indeed, far greater than they know, is the sphere of women. But doubtless the question of such new sociology all goes together, includes many varied and complex influences and premises, and the man as well as the woman, and the woman as well as the man. [*Author's note.*]

peptic depletion — and thus insuring to the States a strong and sweet Female Race, a race of perfect Mothers — is what is needed.

And now, in the full conception of these facts and points, and all that they infer, pro and con — with yet unshaken faith in the elements of the American masses, the composites, of both sexes, and even consider'd as individuals — and ever recognizing in them the broadest bases of the best literary and esthetic appreciation — I proceed with my speculations, Vistas.

First, let us see what we can make out of a brief, general, sentimental consideration of political democracy, and whence it has arisen, with regard to some of its current features, as an aggregate, and as the basic structure of our future literature and authorship. We shall, it is true, quickly and continually find the origin-idea of the singleness of man, individualism, asserting itself, and cropping forth, even from the opposite ideas. But the mass, or lump character, for imperative reasons, is to be ever carefully weigh'd, borne in mind, and provided for. Only from it, and from its proper regulation and potency, comes the other, comes the chance of individualism. The two are contradictory, but our task is to reconcile them.[1]

The political history of the past may be summ'd up as having grown out of what underlies the words, order, safety, caste, and especially out of the need of some prompt deciding authority, and of cohesion at all cost. Leaping time, we come to the period within the memory of people now living, when, as from some lair where they had slumber'd long, accumulating wrath, sprang

up and are yet active, (1790, and on even to the present, 1870,) those noisy eructations, destructive iconoclasms, a fierce sense of wrongs, amid which moves the form, well known in modern history, in the old world, stain'd with much blood, and mark'd by savage reactionary clamors and demands. These bear, mostly, as on one inclosing point of need.

For after the rest is said — after the many time-honor'd and really true things for subordination, experience, rights of property, etc., have been listen'd to and acquiesced in — after the valuable and well-settled statement of our duties and relations in society is thoroughly conn'd over and exhausted — it remains to bring forward and modify everything else with the idea of that Something a man is, (last precious consolation of the drudging poor,) standing apart from all else, divine in his own right, and a woman in hers, sole and untouchable by any canons of authority, or any rule derived from precedent, state-safety, the acts of legislatures, or even from what is called religion, modesty, or art. The radiation of this truth is the key of the most significant doings of our immediately preceding three centuries, and has been the political genesis and life of America. Advancing visibly, it still more advances invisibly. Underneath the fluctuations of the expressions of society, as well as the movements of the politics of the leading nations of the world, we see steadily pressing ahead and strengthening itself, even in the midst of immense tendencies toward aggregation, this image of completeness in separatism, of individual personal dignity, of a single person, either male or female, characterized in the main, not from extrinsic acquirements or position, but in the pride of himself or herself alone; and, as an eventual conclusion and summing up, (or else the entire scheme of things is aimless, a cheat, a crash,) the simple idea that the last, best dependence is to be upon humanity itself, and its own inherent, normal, full-grown qualities, without any superstitious support whatever. * * *

[1] The question hinted here is one which time only can answer. Must not the virtue of modern Individualism, continually enlarging, usurping all, seriously affect, perhaps keep down entirely, in America, the like of the ancient virtue of Patriotism, the fervid and absorbing love of general country? I have no doubt myself that the two will merge, and will mutually profit and brace each other, and that from them a greater product, a third, will arise. But I feel that at present they and their oppositions form a serious problem and paradox in the United States. [*Author's note.*]

Realism and Naturalism

"Held Up by Buffalo," by Newbold Trotter

Not buffalo nor Indians nor mountain ranges could stay the tide of settlement or the march of technology.

Vanderbilt Mansion

Back East, the profits of settlement and technology were taking the shape of mansions like that of Cornelius Vanderbilt in New York; and in Edith Wharton's social world the new plutocracy was to break through the insularity of the old "family" aristocracy.

"*Family Group,*" *by Eastman Johnson, 1871*

It has been said that although the family is "at the center of the essential mythology of our social and economic life," Howells was the only nineteenth-century writer of large reputation who dealt with it directly and immediately. Johnson's painting dates from a time when family life was more than a myth.

"*The Wyndham Sisters,*" *by J. S. Sargent*

John Singer Sargent's portraits of "society" people are as far from the spirit of Howells as they are close to that of Henry James, an admirer of Sargent. Both James and Sargent were preoccupied with subtlety, refinement, and the graces of character and civilization.

Realism and Naturalism

★★★

REALISM AND SCIENCE

"Every ship is romantic except that we are sailing in," said Emerson. For a number of decades the more sensitive minds of Europe and America had imagined how strange or beautiful other ships might be, or how full of high meaning their own ship might be when viewed in "the light that never was, on sea or land."

A new period was at hand when men turned from the ideal ship to the actual ship, from the land of heart's desire to the not so rosy facts of life. They now proposed to give up dreams and face the truth, to avoid warm enthusiasm and begin cool observation, to abandon wishful thinking and adopt the integrity of science — to be disinterested, objective, exact, to see things as they really are. In harmony with the scientific-industrial civilization of the modern world, they would produce an impersonal literature, subordinating or suppressing personal preferences, confidences, and confessions, all the illusions of the inner life, and endeavor in complete honesty to picture with truth the world outside the individual consciousness, the world we actually live in.

Authority for the new outlook and the new literature they found in the concepts of the "real" and "natural," generally ignoring the fact that previous movements had appealed to the same concepts. The Puritans of the Christian tradition were overwhelmed with the reality of a personal God and Satan; the rationalists of the eighteenth century, developing the classical faith in reason, were equally convinced of the reality of their intellectual abstractions; the romanticists were no less convinced of the realities suggested by their feelings and intuitions. It remained for the realists to assume or declare that the true reality is to be found in the concrete and tangible world which is the subject of science.

As the romantic movement had done, the realistic movement spread over Europe. While it reshaped all literary forms, it developed most typically in the novel. In England it had previously appeared, without the intentness of the scientific spirit, in Fielding and Smollett and Jane Austen, who were followed during the Victorian era by Dickens, Thackeray, George Eliot, Trollope, and others. In Russia the realistic novel was created by Gogol, Turgenev, Dostoevski, Tolstoy, and it appeared in Germany, the Scandinavian countries, indeed everywhere. But it was in logical France that its possibilities were explored most clearly. In France a new period opened about 1830 with Stendhal, who was soon succeeded by Balzac and Flaubert. Balzac was generally regarded as the chief founder of the realistic novel in Europe. He enunciated the central principles of realistic fiction in the preface to his great series, the *Comédie humaine*, summarized as follows by R. D. Jameson. (1) "The function of the novelist is to describe social animals in the same way that the scientist describes other animals. Man lives in society, and the variations in human character are due to the variations in human environment." (2) "The novelist becomes the historian of contemporary society. Not only must he record the manners of the people of his time, but he must record their culture, he must describe their clothes, their houses, their business — all, in fact, that will serve to help future generations towards an understanding." (3) "The social historian who writes novels must not content himself merely with a description of society; he must show the relations between causes and events. He is above all a scientist, and it is his task to separate the various causes which lead to a given result."

The relation of realism and science was suggested by an American novelist, William Dean Howells, in a little book on *Criticism and Fiction*. The final criterion of art he conceives to be "the scientific spirit," the "natural" and "honest." It is the business of the critic "to classify and analyze the fruits of the human mind very much as the naturalist classifies the objects of his study, rather than to praise or blame them." Similarly, the novelist, in his view of human life, is not to "declare this thing or that thing unworthy of notice, any more than the scientist can declare a fact of the material world beneath the dignity of his inquiry." Fidelity is the prime virtue of the novelist, "the historian of feeling and character." Like the historian, like the scientist, the novelist must choose a portion of human experience to write about. He must be a specialist. "Formerly, all science could be grasped by a single mind; but now the man who hopes to become great or useful in science must devote himself to a single department. It is so in everything — all arts, all trades; and the novelist is not superior to the universal rule against universality." Howells finds American fiction writers, quite properly, striving to record "each part of the country and each phase of our civilization."

With science, with realism in the arts, came a new sense of fact. While science of course uses reason in its operations, its funda-mental interest is in fact — in what is, what has been. As Carl Becker has remarked, "The essential quality of modern opinion is factual rather than rational. . . . The trend of modern thought is away from an overdone rationalism of the facts to a more careful and disinterested examination of the facts themselves." At last, it seemed, science was unfolding the true facts about man and the universe. The results came, in the nineteenth century, largely in geology and biology. The notion of a static world-machine was destroyed when Lyell, before the middle of the century, demonstrated the gradual evolution of the earth itself. Then Darwin, in 1859, seemed to make it quite clear that the idea of a special creation of man in the image of God must be abandoned in favor of the concept of gradual evolution by natural selection.

But scientific and philosophic doctrines are never as important as what people do with them and how they interpret them for their own needs and wishes. The idea of evolution was interpreted both optimistically and pessimistically, both positively and negatively. To some writers (like Whitman) the belief that man had evolved from something lower was a sign that he would evolve to something higher. To others, the idea that man's conduct is conditioned by his heredity and environment was justification for believing that moral free will was mostly illusory and that man is caught in a deterministic trap. Some thinkers quickly and painlessly adjusted their religious beliefs to the new thought, or simply declared that Darwinism was irrelevant in the religious domain. Others saw in Darwinism the doom of Christian tradition and supernaturalism. Some economists and sociologists found in evolutionism the groundwork for theories which would lead to the infinite improvement of human society through control of social forces. Others thought that evolutionism proved the futility of trying to tamper with the free action of social energy, and implied that society would advance more rapidly if those unable to compete were allowed to die. The only common denominators for all thinkers in the new scientific age seemed to be a universal respect for observed fact, and a belief in the capacity of man increasingly to master his environment and control it for his comfort and profit. But comfort and profit seemed, to a few, to be assuming the mastery of man.

SOCIETY AND LITERATURE

An orgy of materialism followed the Civil War. The prostrate South lay helpless under Northern misgovernment. New England, transformed by emigration to the West and immigration from Europe, as well as by the development of industry, saw the Golden Day of her culture fade into mellow twilight. Destiny pointed to the West, to the valley of the Mississippi, the great plains beyond, the Rockies and the Pacific Coast. There lay unimaginable acres, virgin resources, waiting for use wise or reckless. The American people preferred to be reckless. In their vast vitality, their exuberant energy, they proceeded to ravage a continent and each other. Railroads were thrown across all barriers, cattle replaced the buffalos, settlers rushed to the new lands, the earth gave up its coal, iron, and precious metals, great forests were leveled, agricultural lands were depleted, factories and inventions multiplied, fortunes were carved, irresponsibility reigned in business, finance, and politics. Rugged individualism, plutocracy, jungle ethics gave capitalism a mad revel.

After 1865 the frontier rushed swiftly to the Pacific, rebounded, and went back eastward to capture the land it had overleaped. Over the Rockies toiled, in turn, the same procession that had long before scaled the Alleghanies: the buffalo, the Indian, the scout, trader, trapper, cattle-raiser, farmer. The progress of the frontier was lighted by red-fire; it echoed log chopping and gun-fire. Hard on the heels of the settler followed the speculator and the exploiter. In this mad age, says Lewis Mumford, "the old America was for all practical purposes demolished; industrialism had entered overnight, had transformed the

practices of agriculture, had encouraged a mad exploitation of mineral oil, natural gas, and coal, and had made the unscrupulous master of finances, fat with war-profits, the central figure of the situation." Of course, the scramble for new land had to stop some time. The report of the superintendent of the census of 1890 contained this paragraph:

Up to and including 1880 the country had a frontier of settlement, but at present the unsettled area has been so broken into by isolated bodies of settlement that there can hardly be said to be a frontier line. In the discussion of its extent, its westward movement, etc., it can not, therefore, any longer have a place in the census reports.

For three centuries Americans had always been able to look westward at virgin land. The frontier had taught them much; it had contributed to the national temper much more than the "preëmption, exploitation, progress" which was Parrington's summary. Of course the frontier spirit was not at an end with the passing of the frontier: America is still largely a nation of pioneers. But the passing of the free land and the cessation of a vague and romantic idea of "opportunity in the West" helped to rear a realistic civilization on the ashes of a romantic one.

The Civil War crushed the last powerful aristocracy that remained in the country. The middle class became suddenly the ruling class, and the new kings had machines for armor and banks for castles. A few decades after the war, machines sang a raucous song of triumph from the factories of a thousand cities.

The growth of cities was an inevitable result of the creation of a more nearly static society and of the rise of industrialism. People moved to the cities because there industry could be most efficiently conducted. New York had only a few more than 200,000 people in 1840. In 1870 it had nearly 1,500,000; by 1890, it had about 2,500,000. Pittsburgh, Cleveland, Cincinnati, St. Louis, Chicago, even cities on the plains and on the coast — Minneapolis, Kansas City, Omaha, Denver, Salt Lake City, San Francisco, Los Angeles —

began to erect a prosperous urban civilization. As urban concentration helped science to function more efficiently, so did science in turn make life easier for city dwellers. Inventors produced a bewildering array of mechanisms — machines for light, food, transportation, communication, entertainment, even culture. Waited on by machines, waiting on machines, increasingly told by his scientists, philosophers, and psychologists how much he resembled a machine — this is the American who at length succeeded the Western pioneer and the Concord philosopher.

Cities and machines had a devastating effect on the agrarian dream Americans had persisted in since the time of Jefferson. The old ideal conceived of the independent yeoman living happily on a subsistence farm small enough to be managed by the family. But in an acquisitive America in which wealth and high living were becoming conspicuous, fewer and fewer people were satsified with mere subsistence. The rich lands of the Midwest produced more than farmers could use, especially with the development of farm machinery. Staple farming promised cash returns, but distant markets could be reached only with the help of steamboat and railroad. Larger investments in farms required banking facilities. Banks, steamboats, railroads, and machinery hastened the growth of cities, and, economically, cities dominated farming districts. Thus the "yeoman" in "the garden" was caught in the complex net of capitalism, industrialism, and urbanism. Hence the irony that the Homestead Act of 1862 helped to destroy the type of homestead (described in Whittier's *Snow-Bound*) which it was intended to foster.

Rich, progressive post-war America did not produce writers of the stature of the great romantics, some of whom lived on into the eighties and nineties and exerted, to the end of the century, far greater influence on the imaginations of the people than the new realists. Romantic poetry lapsed into convention. In proportion as the inner impulse flagged,

the reliance on models became more conspicuous. The younger generation of poets were usually content to imitate the masters whose shadows had fallen across their reading — the earlier English and American romantics and a few of their Victorian successors, notably Tennyson. The most prominent "school" of this post-bellum poetry was a group of accomplished versemen who gathered in New York: Taylor, Aldrich, Stoddard, Stedman, Gilder, and others. These men wrote beautifully after the fashion of their romantic models, and receded farther and farther from the vital images and rhythms of American life. Lanier was often closer than they to the realities, and was at the same time a more genuine romantic spirit, while Emily Dickinson, heir to transcendental subjectivism and ancestor of the poetic modes of the next century, was capable of a startling, stabbing reality and utter directness of speech. But, on the whole, the vital literary activity of the decades following the war tended rather to express itself in realistic prose.

In prose a significant movement was taking place, a movement that might be called the literary discovery and settlement of America. Hitherto, American literature had developed along the Atlantic seaboard, North and South. Though Whitman had sounded a new note, his influence on poets was not important until the nineties. The younger poets, by gathering in New York, elected to continue the Atlantic tradition. Then, almost suddenly, the literary frontier was extended all the way to the Pacific. Writers of novels and short stories found available a plenty of "real" material. Realism appeared first in American literature as an attempt to make a realistic transcript or inventory of a new-found country and its folk.

It may be significant that the first great American novelist who considered that his business should be realistic transcription came from the land west of the Alleghanies. William Dean Howells was born and educated in Ohio, and came East to write in New York and later to edit in Boston the

Atlantic Monthly — a circumstance itself symbolic of the change in the literary temper of the country. In a long series of books he faithfully set down American life as he saw it. Henry James, another seeker after realism, was born in New York, was educated in Europe, and stayed there to write and to become the greatest of American expatriate artists. While both men were devoted to the cause of truthful transcription, their subjects were different. James, with remarkable subtlety, wrote the record of the European American; Howells, with grace and calmness, recorded the "realism of the commonplace" in the America about him.

Other writers were discovering America. Mark Twain found that the people of the Mississippi valley made excellent literary subjects, and that dialect might be extremely effective in print. Bret Harte found a literary gold mine in the Far West where so many other prospectors had failed. John Hay wrote *Jim Bludso* in the dialect of Pike County, and started a deluge of ballads and ballad collections — Pike County ballads, cowboy ballads, railroad ballads, mountain ballads. And then, in the late seventies and the eighties, came that astonishing flood of local color literature that put dialect and humble life and regionalism on the pages of the best writers in the land.

These writers found that America was made up of many different kinds of people, and that each kind had special oddities, idiosyncrasies, and attractions — racial, individual, or environmental. Furthermore, these "quaint" people were fast disappearing. Southern local colorists — George W. Cable of Louisiana, Joel Chandler Harris of Georgia, Mary Murfree of Tennessee — strove to preserve the Southern past by writing of pre-war days or of those regions of the South which had been least affected by modern progress. Sarah Orne Jewett and Mary Wilkins Freeman found their materials in those parts of New England which had been by-passed by urbanism and industrialism. It is a fact worth pondering that much of the best writing of the period, including that of Mark Twain, was retrospective, and found its values in the old America rather than in the new.

THE EIGHTEEN-NINETIES

"The more smiling aspects of life," which William Dean Howells found to be typically American, had begun to look rather dubious by the beginning of the last decade of the century. This was true even in the Middle West, where frontier soddies, log-cabins, clearings, and razor-back hogs had been replaced by comfortable frame houses, huge barns, neat fields, and fat cattle, as well as towns with banks, libraries, high schools, often colleges, and here and there great cities humming with machinery and enterprise. In 1890 came the Populist revolt, which, in the fall elections, captured four seats in the Senate and over fifty in the House, and prepared the way for the revival of the Democratic party under Bryan. In 1890 there were more strikes than in any other year of the century, and in the next years came the great Homestead steel strike and the Pullman strike. At the Middle Border a land boom ended in deflation, in foreclosures by the thousands in Kansas alone, where farmers turned eastward again with wagons bearing the scrawl *In God we trusted, in Kansas we busted.* In 1893 the stock market collapsed, and the next year was the darkest Americans had known since the Civil War. The dismal fall of wages and prices, the abortive strikes of half a million workers, the sinister fires lighting up hobo camps, the march of "Coxey's Army" of 20,000 unemployed from the Middle West to Washington, the portent of Bellamy Clubs inspired by the Utopian novel *Looking Backward* — such signs seemed convincing evidence that government of the people, by the people, and for the people, so solemnly reaffirmed in the war, had failed.

At the end of the decade a few American idealists were perceiving another kind of failure — a failure of national morality. The economy was feeling a need for new world markets. As the naval theorist, Captain Mahan, put it, "Whether they will or no, Americans must now begin to look outward." Hitherto only languidly interested in foreign affairs, they looked outward upon a world of rival imperialisms, of international struggles for markets and sources of supply. As the nineteenth century drew toward a close, Great Britain, France, and Germany engaged in colonial expansion with a zest similar to that of America in her westward movement. The United States joined the procession. It accepted the Manifest Destiny thrust upon it. As the Washington *Post* expressed the new outlook:

> Ambition, interest, land hunger, pride, the mere joy of fighting, whatever it may be, we are animated by a new sensation. We are face to face with a strange destiny. The taste of Empire is in the mouth of the people even as the taste of blood in the jungle. It means an Imperial policy, the Republic, renascent, taking her place with the armed nations.

In 1893 the stars and stripes were unfurled at Honolulu. In 1898 we fought what John Hay called "a splendid little war" with Spain. The next year we began a less splendid war against the Filipinos which roused Mark Twain's sardonic suggestion that Old Glory should have "the white stripes painted black and the stars replaced by the skull and cross bones." After an imperialist spree lasting a decade, grown-up America owned Hawaii, Midway, Wake, Guam, Tutuila, the Philippine Islands, and Puerto Rico, held protectorates over Cuba, Panama, and Nicaragua, and asserted a stake in the Far East. The old thirteen colonies on the Atlantic seaboard had developed into a world power.

It was a world which seemed to be dominated and motivated by force rather than by principle. Men of principle, like William Vaughn Moody and Henry Adams, understood and protested, but writers of fiction, who were equally concerned with principle, needed a philosophy and a method by which they could realistically reveal the operation of force in the physical and moral world. That philosophy and method had been developing

in France since the eighteen-sixties, and its name was "naturalism." Used here as a literary and historical term, it may be defined as one kind of realism.

"What we call nature," said Taine, "is this brood of secret impulses, often maleficent, generally vulgar, always blind, which trouble and fret within us, ill-covered by the cloak of decency and reason under which we try to disguise them; we think we lead them and they lead us; we think our actions our own, they are theirs." During the American Civil War, Taine published a history of English literature in which he used a deterministic formula of race, place, and time. As a literary school, however, naturalism begins with Emile Zola in 1871, a fact suggested by the definition of literary naturalism in *Webster's Dictionary* as the theory that "literature should conform to nature; ... specifically, the principles and characteristics of certain nineteenth-century realistic writers, notably Zola and Maupassant." To form an adequate view of Zola's naturalism, with its admixture of romanticism, one should know one or two of his novels, such as *Nana*. But Zola also set forth his views in a book on *The Experimental Novel*, from which a few quotations are worth noting:

> Naturalism does not belong to me, it belongs to the century. It acts in society, in the sciences, in letters and in art, and in politics.

> Science enters into the domain of us novelists, who are today the analyzers of man, in his individual and social relations. We are continuing, by our observations and experiments, the work of the physiologist, who has continued that of the physicist and the chemist. We are making use, in a certain way, of scientific psychology to complete scientific physiology; and to finish the series we have only to bring into our studies of nature and man the decisive tool of the experimental method. In one word, we should operate on the characters, the passions, on the human and social data, in the same way that the chemist and the physicist operate on inanimate beings, and as the physiologist operates on living beings. Determinism dominates everything.

> To give your reader a scrap of human life, that is the whole purpose of the naturalistic novel.

> It is impersonal; I mean to say by that that the novelist is but a recorder who is forbidden to judge and to conclude.

We tell everything, we do not make a choice, neither do we idealize; and this is why they accuse us of taking pleasure in obscenity.

Such was the theory, as conceived by Zola and, with variations, by subsequent naturalists in America. The practice did not always tally with the theory. "We do not make a choice," said Zola. Yet he himself made a most momentous choice when he tried to impose upon life the naturalistic philosophy. And he made other choices when he poured a romantic enthusiasm and unreality into his novels, and when he espoused the sentiment and reformatory spirit of humanitarianism. According to Howells, many naturalists, while professing to find the ugly as well as the beautiful worthy of celebration, "seem to regard it as rather more worthy." And many American naturalists, while forbidden by their theory to judge and to conclude, nevertheless have written with a passionate humanitarian concern for the victims of the struggle for existence. Our naturalists, that is to say our radical realists, have commonly been radical as well in their economic and social outlook.

Some of the early work of Hamlin Garland has a resemblance to naturalism. His *Main-Travelled Roads*, a collection of short stories published in 1891, is local color with a difference, not picturesquely romantic but unflinchingly "real." Here is a realism quite other than Howells' genial celebration of the commonplace. The commonplace, according to Garland, was a distressing sight to behold; on the main-traveled road of life "the poor and the weary predominate." As westering trailmakers the Garland family had sung:

> We'll reign like kings in fairy land,
> Lords of the soil.

The disillusioned next generation sang instead:

> There's a dear old homestead on Nebraska's fertile
>   plain,
>   There I toiled my manhood's strength away:
> All that labor now is lost to me, but it is Shylock's
>   gain,
>   For that dear old home he claims today.

Brooding over his experience in the light of his reading of Taine, Spencer, Henry George, Whitman, and others, Garland wrote an acrid protest.

In the same decade the naturalism of Zola arrived,—a name associated, in genteel circles, with all that was bestial, obscene, and decadent. When Stephen Crane in 1892 offered his novel *Maggie: A Girl of the Streets*, no publisher would touch it; he printed it privately, and published it only in 1896. Crane's best book is *The Red Badge of Courage*, in which he strips war of all romance. Another novelist, Frank Norris, devoted to Zola (at one period, according to his brother, he was never without a novel of Zola in his hand), published *McTeague*, a novel of lower and middle class life in San Francisco, *The Octopus*, on the struggle of California ranchers against the railroads, and *The Pit*, on speculators in the Chicago wheat exchange. A third naturalist, Jack London, tutored by a rough life and by Darwin, Spencer, Nietzsche, and Marx, wrote short stories of the primitive Far North, but was at his best in his novels, particularly *The Call of the Wild*, 1903, which has as its "hero" a dog, and glorifies brute strength and cunning. In other works he wrote of the ruthless captain of a sealing ship, of a prizefighter, of prehistoric savages, and other subjects involving primitive and individualistic qualities, while at the same time he was engaged in collectivistic propaganda.

Consciously or unconsciously, every major author who was writing in the nineties recognized that the end of an age was at hand; that established Victorian values were being discarded or ignored; and that a new age was beginning whose values could not be predicted. The "gay nineties" were indeed superficially gay, but under the surface they were deeply troubled. The year 1900 cannot be considered a fixed dividing line between the old and the new, but between 1890 and 1914 the nineteenth century died and our own culture was born.

WILLIAM DEAN HOWELLS (1837–1920)

Two recent anthologies of Howells' work (by C. and R. Kirk, and H. S. Commager, both 1950) are a sign of renewed interest in the first great realistic American novelist, "in himself almost an entire literary movement, almost an academy." He was born in ante-bellum Ohio and lived there, as printer, newspaper correspondent, and editor, until after he had reached manhood. His early life and the environment that partly shaped him are the subjects of two charming and revealing books, *A Boy's Town*, 1890, and *Years of My Youth*, 1916. He virtually educated himself, by a long course of devoted reading described in *My Literary Passions*, 1895. In 1860, Howells had become well enough known as a journalist in Ohio to be asked to write a campaign biography of Lincoln. The following year he was appointed consul to Venice, and during the Civil War years went on reading, especially in Dante, Goldoni, and other Italians. He returned to America in 1865, served for a short time on the staff of the *Nation*, and then went to Boston to serve on the staff of the *Atlantic*. In 1872, at the age of thirty-five, he was made editor.

The young editor soon proved to be a leader, in criticism and fiction alike, away from romance and toward realism. In 1871 he had published *Suburban Sketches*, which mingled essay and story in a gracious delineation of New England life. Later in the 70's came several New England novels. After he had resigned from the *Atlantic* in 1881, he produced his finest creations: *A Modern Instance*, 1882, and *The Rise of Silas Lapham*, 1885, both of them gently accurate pictures of New England life and character which illustrate plainly his conception of the art of fiction. That conception was similar to Jane Austen's, his "divine Jane," rather than to that of Tolstoy, whom he later extolled in the highest terms but never really emulated.

Howells settled in New York in 1885, when it had become apparent that Boston was no longer the literary capital of the country. He served on the staff of *Harper's* and wrote a long series of novels, without excelling the two named above. He tried his hand at the short story and the drama, doing acceptable but not distinguished work. He was made president of the American Academy, received the gold medal of the National Institute, and lived to see realism at its height in America.

As a novelist and as a force for realism Howells will probably be best remembered. He "produced in his fourscore books," says Carl Van Doren, "the most considerable transcript of American life yet made by one man." As a realistic critic of literature he wrote urbanely, as in the little book *Criticism and Fiction*, which shows a mind sensitive to both American democracy and modern science. He came to be known as the "dean of American letters," and he was useful in sponsoring the work of such young realists as Frank Norris, Stephen Crane, and Hamlin Garland.

There is no complete collected edition of his works. *Life in Letters*, 2 volumes, 1928, was edited by his daughter Mildred Howells. Critical studies have been done by D. G. Cooke, 1922, and O. W. Firkins, 1924. Firkins also wrote the article in *DAB*. Chapters on Howells may be found in Carl Van Doren, *The American Novel*, 1921, and W. F. Taylor, *The Economic Novel in America*, 1942.

From Criticism and Fiction

(1892)

[Criticism and Realism]

. . . I do not pin my faith to the saying of one whom I heard denying, the other day, that a thing of beauty was a joy forever. He contended that Keats's line should have read, "Some things of beauty are sometimes joys forever," and that any assertion beyond this was too hazardous.

I should, indeed, prefer another line of Keats's, if I were to profess any formulated creed, and should feel much safer with his "Beauty is Truth, Truth Beauty," than even with my friend's reformation of the more quoted verse. It brings us back to the solid ground taken by Mr. Symonds, which is not essentially different from that taken in the great Mr. Burke's Essay on the Sublime and the Beautiful. . . .

"As for those called critics," the author [Burke] says, "they have generally sought the rule of the arts in the wrong place; they have sought among poems, pictures, engravings, statues, and buildings; but art can never give the rules that make an art. This is, I believe, the reason why artists in general, and poets principally, have been confined in so narrow a circle; they have been rather imitators of one another than of nature. Critics follow them, and therefore can do little as guides. I can judge but poorly of anything while I measure it by no other standard than itself. The true standard of the arts is in every man's power; and an easy observation of the most common, sometimes of the meanest things, in nature will give the truest lights, where the greatest sagacity and industry that slights such observation must leave us in the dark, or, what is worse, amuse and mislead us by false lights."

If this should happen to be true — and it certainly commends itself to acceptance — it might portend an immediate danger to the vested interests of criticism, only that it was written a hundred years ago; and we shall probably have the "sagacity and industry that slights the observation" of nature long enough yet to allow most critics the time to learn some more useful trade than criticism as they pursue it. Nevertheless, I am in hopes that the communistic era in taste foreshadowed by Burke is approaching, and that it will occur within the lives of men now overawed by the foolish old superstition that literature and art are anything but the expression of life, and are to be judged by any other test than that of their fidelity to it. The time is coming, I hope, when each new author, each new artist, will be considered, not in his proportion to any other author or artist, but in his relation to the human nature, known to us all, which it is his privilege, his high duty, to interpret. "The true standard of the artist is in every man's power" already, as Burke says; Michelangelo's "light of the piazza," the glance of the common eye, is and always was the best light on a statue; Goethe's "boys and blackbirds" have in all ages been the real connoisseurs of berries; but hitherto the mass of common men have been afraid to apply their own simplicity, naturalness, and honesty to the appreciation of the beautiful. They have always cast about for the instruction of some one who professed to know better, and who browbeat wholesome common-sense into the self-distrust that ends in sophistication. They have fallen generally to the worst of this bad species, and have been "amused and misled" (how pretty that quaint old use of amuse is!) "by the false lights" of critical vanity and self-righteousness. They have been taught to compare what they see and what they read, not with the things that they have observed and known, but with the things that some other artist or writer has done. Especially if they have themselves the artistic impulse in any direction they are taught to form themselves, not upon life, but upon the masters who became masters only by forming themselves upon life. The seeds of death are planted in them, and they can produce only the still-born, the academic. They are not told to take their work into the public square and see if it seems true to the chance passer, but to test it by the work of the very men who refused and decried any other test of their own work. The young writer who attempts to report the phrase and carriage of every-day life, who tries to tell just how he has heard men talk and seen them look, is made to feel guilty of something low and unworthy by the stupid people who would like to have him show how Shakespeare's men talked and looked, or Scott's, or Thackeray's, or Balzac's, or Hawthorne's, or Dickens's; he is instructed to idealize his personages, that is, to take the life-likeness out of them, and put the book-likeness into them. He is approached in the spirit of the wretched pedantry into which learning, much or little, always decays when it withdraws itself and stands apart from experience in an attitude of imagined superiority, and which would say with the same confidence to the scientist: "I see that you are looking at a grasshopper there which you have found in the grass, and I suppose you intend to describe it. Now don't waste your time and sin against culture in that way. I've got a grasshopper here, which has been evolved at considerable pains and expense out of the grasshopper in general; in fact, it's a type. It's made up of wire and card-board, very prettily painted in a conventional tint, and it's perfectly indestructible. It isn't very much like a real grasshopper, but it's a great deal nicer, and it's served to represent the notion of a grasshopper ever since man emerged from barbarism. You may say that it's artificial. Well, it is artificial; but then it's ideal too; and what you want to do is to cultivate the ideal. You'll find the books full of my kind of grasshopper, and scarcely a trace of yours in any of them. The thing that you are proposing to do is commonplace; but if you say that it isn't commonplace, for the very reason that it hasn't been done before, you'll have to admit that it's photographic."

As I said, I hope the time is coming when not only the artist, but the common, average man, who always "has the standard of the arts in his power," will have also the courage to apply it, and will reject the ideal grasshopper wherever he finds it, in science, in literature, in art, because it is not "simple, natural, and honest," because it is not like a real grasshopper. But I will own that I think the time is yet far off, and that the people who have been brought up on the ideal grasshopper, the heroic grasshopper, the impassioned grasshopper, the self-devoted, adventureful, good old romantic card-board grasshopper, must die out before the simple, honest, and natural grasshopper can have a fair field. I am in no haste to compass the end of these good people, whom I find in the mean time very amusing. It is delightful to meet one of them, either in print or out of it — some sweet elderly lady or excellent gentleman whose youth was pastured on the literature of thirty or forty years ago — and to witness the confidence with which they preach their favorite authors as all the law and the prophets. They have commonly read little or nothing since, or, if they have, they have judged it by a standard taken from these authors, and never dreamed of judging it by nature; they are destitute of the documents in the case of the later writers; they suppose that Balzac was the beginning of realism, and that Zola is its wicked end; they are quite ignorant, but they are ready to talk you down, if you differ from them, with an assumption of knowledge sufficient for any occasion. The horror, the resentment, with which they receive any question of their literary saints is genuine; you descend at once very far in the moral and social scale, and anything short of offensive personality is too good for you; it is expressed to you that you are one to be avoided, and put down even a little lower than you have naturally fallen.

These worthy persons are not to blame; it is part of their intellectual mission to represent the petrifaction of taste, and to preserve an image of a smaller and cruder and emptier world than we now live in, a world which was feeling its way towards the simple, the natural, the honest, but was a good deal "amused and misled" by lights now no longer mistakable for heavenly luminaries. They belong to a time, just passing away, when certain authors were considered authorities in certain kinds, when they must be accepted entire and not questioned in any particular. Now we are beginning to see and to say that no author is an authority except in those moments when he held his ear close to Nature's lips and caught her very accent. These moments are not continuous with any authors in the past, and they are rare with all. Therefore I am not afraid to say now that the greatest classics are sometimes not at all great, and that we can profit by them only when we hold them, like our meanest contemporaries, to a strict accounting, and verify their work by the standard of the arts which we all have in our power, the simple, the natural, and the honest.

Those good people, these curious and interesting if somewhat musty back-numbers, must always have a hero, an idol of some sort, and it is droll to find Balzac, who suffered from their sort such bitter scorn and hate for his realism while he was alive, now become a fetich in his turn, to be shaken in the faces of those who will not blindly worship him. But it is no new thing in the history of literature: whatever is established is sacred with those who do not think. At the beginning of the century, when romance was making the same fight against effete classicism which realism is making to-day against effete romanticism, the Italian poet Monti declared that "the romantic was the cold grave of the Beautiful," just as the realistic is now supposed to be. The romantic of that day and the real of this are in certain degree the same. Romanticism then sought, as realism seeks now, to widen the bounds of sympathy, to level every barrier against æsthetic freedom, to escape from the paralysis of tradition. It exhausted itself in this impulse; and it remained for realism to assert that fidelity to experience and probability of motive are essential conditions of a great imaginative literature. It is not a new theory, but it has never before universally characterized literary endeavor. When realism becomes false to itself, when it heaps up facts merely, and maps life instead of picturing it, realism will perish too. Every true realist instinctively knows this, and it is perhaps the reason why he is careful of every fact, and feels himself bound to express or to indicate its meaning at the risk of over-moralizing. In life he finds nothing insignificant; all tells for destiny and character; nothing that God has made is contemptible. He cannot look upon human life and declare this thing or that thing unworthy of notice, any more than the scientist can declare a fact of the material world beneath the dignity of his inquiry. He feels in every nerve the equality of things and the unity of men; his soul is exalted, not by vain shows and shadows and ideals, but by realities, in which alone the truth lives. In

criticism it is his business to break the images of false gods and misshapen heroes, to take away the poor silly toys that many grown people would still like to play with. He cannot keep terms with Jack the Giant-killer or Puss in Boots, under any name or in any place, even when they reappear as the convict Vautrec, or the Marquis de Montrivaut, or the Sworn Thirteen Noblemen. He must say to himself that Balzac, when he imagined these monsters, was not Balzac, he was Dumas; he was not realistic, he was romantic. * * *

[The English Novel since Jane Austen]

Which brings us again, after this long way about, to the divine Jane and her novels, and that troublesome question about them. She was great and they were beautiful, because she and they were honest, and dealt with nature nearly a hundred years ago as realism deals with it to-day. Realism is nothing more and nothing less than the truthful treatment of material, and Jane Austen was the first and the last of the English novelists to treat material with entire truthfulness. Because she did this, she remains the most artistic of the English novelists, and alone worthy to be matched with the great Scandinavian and Slavic and Latin artists. It is not a question of intellect, or not wholly that. The English have mind enough; but they have not taste enough; or, rather, their taste has been perverted by their false criticism, which is based upon personal preference, and not upon principle; which instructs a man to think that what he likes is good, instead of teaching him first to distinguish what is good before he likes it. The art of fiction, as Jane Austen knew it, declined from her through Scott, and Bulwer, and Dickens, and Charlotte Brontë, and Thackeray, and even George Eliot, because the mania of romanticism had seized upon all Europe, and these great writers could not escape the taint of their time; but it has shown few signs of recovery in England, because English criticism, in the presence of the Continental masterpieces, has continued provincial and special and personal, and has expressed a love and a hate which had to do with the quality of the artist rather than the character of his work. It was inevitable that in their time the English romanticists should treat, as Señor Valdés says, "the barbarous customs of the Middle Ages, softening and disfiguring them, as Walter Scott and his kind did"; that they should "devote themselves to falsifying nature, refining and subtilizing sentiment, and modifying psychology after their own fancy," like Bulwer and Dickens, as well as like Rousseau and Madame de Staël, not to mention Balzac, the worst of all that sort at his worst. This was the natural course of the disease; but it really seems as if it were their criticism that was to blame for the rest: not, indeed, for the performance of this writer or that, for criticism can never affect the actual doing of a thing; but for the esteem in which this writer or that is held through the perpetuation of false ideals. The only observer of English middle-class life since Jane Austen worthy to be named with her was not George Eliot, who was first ethical and then artistic, who transcended her in everything but the form and method most essential to art, and there fell hopelessly below her. It was Anthony Trollope who was most like her in simple honesty and instinctive truth, as unphilosophized as the light of common day; but he was so warped from a wholesome ideal as to wish at times to be like the caricaturist Thackeray, and to stand about in his scene, talking it over with his hands in his pockets, interrupting the action, and spoiling the illusion in which alone the truth of art resides. Mainly, his instinct was too much for his ideal, and with a low view of life in its civic relations and a thoroughly bourgeois soul, he yet produced works whose beauty is surpassed only by the effect of a more poetic writer in the novels of Thomas Hardy. Yet if a vote of English criticism even at this late day, when all continental Europe has the light of æsthetic truth, could be taken, the majority against these artists would be overwhelmingly in favor of a writer who had so little artistic sensibility, that he never hesitated on any occasion, great or small, to make a foray among his characters, and catch them up to show them to the reader and tell him how beautiful or ugly they were; and cry out over their amazing properties.

Doubtless the ideal of those poor islanders

will be finally changed. If the truth could become a fad it would be accepted by all their "smart people," but truth is something rather too large for that; and we must await the gradual advance of civilization among them. Then they will see that their criticism has misled them; and that it is to this false guide they owe, not precisely the decline of fiction among them, but its continued debasement as an art. * * *

[Democracy and the American Novel]

I would have our American novelists be as American as they unconsciously can. Matthew Arnold complained that he found no "distinction" in our life, and I would gladly persuade all artists intending greatness in any kind among us that the recognition of the fact pointed out by Mr. Arnold ought to be a source of inspiration to them, and not discouragement. We have been now some hundred years building up a state on the affirmation of the essential equality of men in their rights and duties, and whether we have been right or been wrong the gods have taken us at our word, and have responded to us with a civilization in which there is no "distinction" perceptible to the eye that loves and values it. Such beauty and such grandeur as we have is common beauty, common grandeur, or the beauty and grandeur in which the quality of solidarity so prevails that neither distinguishes itself to the disadvantage of anything else. It seems to me that these conditions invite the artist to the study and the appreciation of the common, and to the portrayal in every art of those finer and higher aspects which unite rather than sever humanity, if he would thrive in our new order of things. The talent that is robust enough to front the every-day world and catch the charm of its work-worn, care-worn, brave, kindly face, need not fear the encounter, though it seems terrible to the sort nurtured in the superstition of the romantic, the bizarre, the heroic, the distinguished, as the things alone worthy of painting or carving or writing. The arts must become democratic, and then we shall have the expression of America in art; and the reproach which Mr. Arnold was half right in making us shall have no justice in it any longer; we shall be "distinguished." * * *

[Decency and the American Novel]

One of the great newspapers the other day invited the prominent American authors to speak their minds upon a point in the theory and practice of fiction which had already vexed some of them. It was the question of how much or how little the American novel ought to deal with certain facts of life which are not usually talked of before young people, and especially young ladies. Of course the question was not decided, and I forget just how far the balance inclined in favor of a larger freedom in the matter. But it certainly inclined that way; one or two writers of the sex which is somehow supposed to have purity in its keeping (as if purity were a thing that did not practically concern the other sex, preoccupied with serious affairs) gave it a rather vigorous tilt to that side. In view of this fact it would not be the part of prudence to make an effort to dress the balance; and indeed I do not know that I was going to make any such effort. But there are some things to say, around and about the subject, which I should like to have some one else say, and which I may myself possibly be safe in suggesting.

One of the first of these is the fact, generally lost sight of by those who censure the Anglo-Saxon novel for its prudishness, that it is really not such a prude after all; and that if it is sometimes apparently anxious to avoid those experiences of life not spoken of before young people, this may be an appearance only. Sometimes a novel which has this shuffling air, this effect of truckling to propriety, might defend itself, if it could speak for itself, by saying that such experiences happened not to come within its scheme, and that, so far from maiming or mutilating itself in ignoring them, it was all the more faithfully representative of the tone of modern life in dealing with love that was chaste, and with passion so honest that it could be openly spoken of before the tenderest society bud at dinner. It might say that the guilty intrigue, the betrayal, the extreme flirtation even, was the exceptional thing in life, and unless the scheme of the story necessarily involved it, that it would be bad art to lug it in, and as bad taste as to introduce such topics in a mixed company. It could say very justly that the novel in our civilization now always addresses a mixed company, and that the vast majority of the company are ladies, and that very many, if not most, of these ladies are young girls. If the novel were written for men and for married women alone, as in continental Europe, it might be altogether different. But the simple fact is that it is not written for them alone among us, and it is a question of writing, under cover of our universal acceptance, things for young girls to read which you would be put out-of-doors for saying to them, or frankly giving notice of your intention, and so cutting yourself off from the pleasure — and it is a very high and sweet one — of appealing to these vivid, responsive intelligences, which are none the less brilliant and admirable because they are innocent.

One day a novelist who liked, after the manner of other men, to repine at his hard fate, complained to his friend, a critic, that he was tired of the restriction he had put upon himself in this regard; for it is a mistake, as can be readily shown, to suppose that others impose it. "See how free those French fellows are!" he rebelled. "Shall we always be shut up to our tradition of decency?"

"Do you think it's much worse than being shut up to their tradition of indecency?" said his friend.

Then that novelist began to reflect, and he remembered how sick the invariable motive of the French novel made him. He perceived finally that, convention for convention, ours was not only more tolerable, but on the whole was truer to life, not only to its complexion, but also to its texture. No one will pretend that there is not vicious love beneath the surface of our society; if he did, the fetid explosions of the divorce trials would refute him; but if he pretended that it was in any just sense characteristic of our society, he could be still more easily refuted. Yet it exists, and it is unquestionably the material of tragedy, the stuff from which intense effects are wrought. The question, after owning this fact, is whether these intense effects are not rather cheap effects. I incline to think they are, and I will try to say why I think so, if I may do so without offence. The material itself, the mere mention of it, has an instant fascination; it arrests, it detains, till the last word is said, and while there is anything to be hinted. This is what makes a love intrigue of some sort all but essential to the popularity of any fiction. Without such an intrigue the intellectual equipment of the author must be of the highest, and then he will succeed only with the highest class of readers. But any author who will deal with a guilty love intrigue holds all readers in his hand, the highest with the lowest, as long as he hints the slightest hope of the smallest potential naughtiness. He need not at all be a great author; he may be a very shabby wretch, if he has but the courage or the trick of that sort of thing. The critics will call him "virile" and "passionate"; decent people will be ashamed to have been limed by him; but the low average will only ask another chance of flocking into his net. If he happens to be an able writer, his really fine and costly work will be unheeded, and the lure to the appetite will be chiefly remembered. There may be other qualities which make reputations for other men, but in his case they will count for nothing. He pays this penalty for his success in that kind; and every one pays some such penalty who deals with some such material. It attaches in like manner to the triumphs of the writers who now almost form a school among us, and who may be said to have established themselves in an easy popularity simply by the study of erotic shivers and fervors. They may find their account in the popularity, or they may not; there is no question of the popularity.

But I do not mean to imply that their case covers the whole ground. So far as it goes, though, it ought to stop the mouths of those who complain that fiction is enslaved to propriety among us. It appears that of a certain kind of impropriety it is free to give us all it will, and more. But this is not what serious men and women writing fiction mean when they rebel against the limitations of their art in our civilization. They have no desire to deal with nakedness, as painters and sculptors freely do in the worship of beauty; or with certain facts of life, as the stage does, in the service of sensation. But they ask why, when the conventions of the plastic and histrionic arts liberate their followers to the portrayal of almost any phase of the physical or of the emotional nature, an American novelist may not write a story on the lines of Anna Karenina or Madame Bovary. Sappho they put aside, and from Zola's work they avert their eyes. They do not condemn him or Daudet, necessarily, or accuse their motives; they leave them out of the question: they do not want to do that kind of thing. But they do sometimes wish to do another kind, to touch one of the most serious and sorrowful problems of life in the spirit of Tolstoi and Flaubert, and they ask why they may not. At one time, they remind us, the Anglo-Saxon novelist did deal with such problems — De Foe in his spirit, Richardson in his, Goldsmith in his. At what moment did our fiction lose this privilege? In what fatal hour did the Young Girl arise and seal the lips of Fiction, with a touch of her finger, to some of the most vital interests of life?

Whether I wished to oppose them in their aspiration for greater freedom, or whether I wished to encourage them, I should begin to answer them by saying that the Young Girl had never done anything of the kind. The manners of the novel have been improving with those of its readers; that is all. Gentlemen no longer swear or fall drunk under the table, or abduct young ladies and shut them up in lonely country-houses, or so habitually set about the ruin of their neighbors' wives, as they once did. Generally, people now call a spade an agricultural implement; they have not grown decent without having also grown a little squeamish, but they have grown comparatively decent; there is no doubt about that. They require of a novelist whom they respect unquestionable proof of his seriousness, if he proposes to deal with certain phases of life; they require a sort of scientific decorum. He can no longer expect to be received on the ground of entertainment only; he assumes a higher function, something like that of a physician or a priest, and they expect him to be bound by laws as sacred as those of such professions; they hold him solemnly pledged not to betray them or abuse their confidence. If he will accept the conditions, they give him their confidence, and he may then treat to his greater honor, and not at all to his disadvantage, of such experiences, such relations of men and women as George Eliot treats in Adam Bede, in Daniel Deronda, in Romola, in almost all her books; such as Hawthorne treats in the Scarlet Letter; such as Dickens treats in David Copperfield; such as Thackeray treats in Pendennis, and glances at in every one of his fictions; such as most of the masters of English fiction have at some time treated more or less openly. It is quite false or quite mistaken to suppose that our novels have left untouched these most important realities of life. They have only not made them their stock in trade; they have kept a true perspective in regard to them; they have relegated them in their pictures of life to the space and place they occupy in life itself, as we know it in England and America. They have kept a correct proportion, knowing perfectly well that unless the novel is to be a map, with everything scrupulously laid down in it, a faithful record of life in far the greater extent could be made to the exclusion of guilty love and all its circumstances and consequences.

I justify them in this view not only because I hate what is cheap and meretricious, and hold in peculiar loathing the cant of the critics who require "passion" as something in itself admirable and desirable in a novel, but because I prize fidelity in the historian of feeling and character. Most of these critics who demand "passion" would seem to have no conception of any passion but one. Yet there are several other passions; the passion of grief, the passion of avarice, the passion of pity, the passion of ambition, the passion of hate, the passion of envy, the passion of devotion, the passion of friendship; and all these have a greater part in the drama of life than the passion of love, and infinitely greater than the passion of guilty love. Wittingly or unwittingly, English fiction and American fiction have recognized this truth, not fully, not in the measure it merits, but in greater degree than most other fiction.

MARK TWAIN (1835–1910)

Howells had come out of the West to absorb New England traditions, and had been adopted by New England. On Samuel Langhorne Clemens the hand of the West lay more heavily. He went to school to the flying frontier, to the prairies and the Mississippi, long before he was taken under the literary wing of Howells, and he won literary success in the mining camps of California long before New England learned to read him. He was probably the most important single contribution of the frontier to American literature. "Here at last," says Parrington, "was an authentic American — a native writer thinking his own thoughts, using his own eyes, speaking his own dialect — everything European fallen away, the last shred of feudal culture gone, local and western yet continental."

Clemens was born November 30, 1835, in Florida, Missouri, of a family which had followed the lure of the West. Four years after his birth, the family settled in the sleepy little slave-holding town of Hannibal, and there, among the hills and beside the great river, a few miles above Pike County and a hundred miles from St. Louis, the boy lived the adventurous life described in Tom Sawyer and Huckleberry Finn. His first venture was journalism. Upon the death of his father, the boy of twelve was apprenticed to the printer of his brother's paper in Hannibal. In 1853 he set out to see the world, and worked as a printer in St. Louis, Chicago, Philadelphia, Keokuk, and Cincinnati. In the spring of 1857 he took passage for New Orleans, apparently with the intention of proceeding to South America, where he had an idea for making cocoa at the headwaters of the Amazon. On this trip he met the pilot, Horace Bixby, and with characteristic impulsiveness, engaged himself as apprentice. He "learned the river," and acquired "his richest store of literary material."

In 1861, we find him in Nevada, prospector, journalist, unsuccessful speculator. In San Francisco Bret Harte encouraged him and taught him to tell a story. In 1865 he made his first success with the story of *Jim Smiley and His Jumping Frog*. In 1866 he lectured on the Sandwich Islands to a convulsed audience in San Francisco. After that, there was no stopping his career. *The Innocents Abroad* (1869) was the result of traveling in Europe and the Holy Land. He moved to Hartford, Connecticut, in 1871, and wrote the story of his western experiences, *Roughing It*. In the next decade he produced three of his greatest books: *Tom Sawyer* (1876), *Life on the Mississippi* (1883), and *Huckleberry Finn* (1884). *A Connecticut Yankee in King Arthur's Court* followed in 1889, *Pudd'nhead Wilson* in 1894, and his own favorite among his books, *Joan of Arc*, two years later.

Royalties and lectures made him a fortune, but he lost it in bad investments, and in 1895, when he was sixty years old, found himself bankrupt. A triumphal lecturing tour of the world and new books restored his financial status, and with a new fortune he built himself a mansion at Redding, Connecticut, where he died on April 21, 1910. After his death came his pessimistic novel *The Mysterious Stranger*, 1916, his *Letters*, 1917, and his *Autobiography*, 1924.

The best edition of Mark Twain is the Definitive, in 35 volumes, 1922. The official biography is by A. B. Paine, 3 volumes, 1912. *My Mark Twain*, by William Dean Howells, 1912, is a vivid personal impression. More recent biographical and critical studies are Bernard De Voto's *Mark Twain's America*, 1932, and *Mark Twain at Work*, 1942; G. C. Bellamy's *Mark Twain as a Literary Artist*, 1950; K. R. Andrews' *Nook Farm: Mark Twain's Hartford Circle*, 1950; and lives by Edward Wagenknecht, 1935, and J. De L. Ferguson, 1943.

The Celebrated Jumping Frog of Calaveras County

(1865)

In compliance with the request of a friend of mine, who wrote me from the East, I called on good-natured, garrulous old Simon Wheeler, and inquired after my friend's friend, *Leonidas W.* Smiley, as requested to do, and I hereunto append the result. I have a lurking suspicion that *Leonidas W.* Smiley is a myth; that my friend never knew such a personage; and that he only conjectured that, if I asked old Wheeler about him, it would remind him of his infamous *Jim* Smiley, and he would go to work and bore me nearly to death with some infernal reminiscence of him as long and tedious as it should be useless to me. If that was the design, it certainly succeeded.

I found Simon Wheeler dozing comfortably by the bar-room stove of the old, dilapidated tavern in the ancient mining camp of Angel's, and I noticed that he was fat and bald-headed, and had an expression of winning gentleness and simplicity upon his tranquil countenance. He roused up and gave me good-day. I told him a friend of mine had commissioned me to make some inquiries about a cherished companion of his boyhood named *Leonidas W.* Smiley — *Rev. Leonidas W.* Smiley — a young minister of the Gospel, who he had heard was at one time a resident of Angel's Camp. I added that, if Mr. Wheeler could tell me anything about this Rev. Leonidas W. Smiley, I would feel under many obligations to him.

Simon Wheeler backed me into a corner and blockaded me there with his chair, and then sat me down and reeled off the monotonous narrative which follows this paragraph.

He never smiled, he never frowned, he never changed his voice from the gentle-flowing key to which he tuned the initial sentence, he never betrayed the slightest suspicion of enthusiasm; but all through the interminable narrative there ran a vein of impressive earnestness and sincerity, which showed me plainly that, so far from his imagining that there was anything ridiculous or funny about his story, he regarded it as a really important matter, and admired its two heroes as men of transcendent genius in *finesse*. To me, the spectacle of a man drifting serenely along through such a queer yarn without ever smiling, was exquisitely absurd. As I said before, I asked him to tell me what he knew of Rev. Leonidas W. Smiley, and he replied as follows. I let him go on in his own way, and never interrupted him once:

There was a feller here once by the name of *Jim* Smiley, in the winter of '49 — or may be it was the spring of '50 — I don't recollect exactly, somehow, though what makes me think it was one or the other is because I remember the big flume wasn't finished when he first came to the camp; but any way, he was the curiosest man about always betting on any thing that turned up you ever see, if he could get any body to bet on the other side; and if he couldn't, he'd change sides. Any way that suited the other men would suit him — any way just so's he got a bet, *he* was satisfied. But still he was lucky, uncommon lucky; he most always come out winner. He was always ready and laying for a chance; there couldn't be no solitary thing mentioned but that feller'd offer to bet on it, and take any side you please, as I was just telling you. If there was a horse-race, you'd find him flush, or you'd find him busted at the end of it; if there was a dog-fight, he'd bet on it; if there was a cat-fight, he'd bet on it; if there was a chicken-fight, he'd bet on it; why, if there was two birds setting on a fence, he would bet you which one would fly first; or if there was a camp-meeting, he would be there reg'lar, to bet on Parson Walker, which he judged to be the best exhorter about there, and so he was, too, and a good man. If he even seen a straddle-bug start to go anywheres, he would bet you

how long it would take him to get wherever he was going to, and if you took him up, he would follow that straddle-bug to Mexico but what he would find out where he was bound for and how long he was on the road. Lots of the boys here has seen that Smiley, and can tell you about him. Why, it never made no difference to *him* — he would bet on *any* thing — the dangdest feller. Parson Walker's wife laid very sick once, for a good while, and it seemed as if they warn't going to save her; but one morning he come in, and Smiley asked how she was, and he said she was considerable better — thank the Lord for his inf'nit mercy — and coming on so smart that, with the blessing of Prov'dence she'd get well yet; and Smiley, before he thought, says, "Well, I'll risk two-and-a-half that she won't, any way."

Thish-yer Smiley had a mare — the boys called her the fifteen-minute nag, but that was only in fun, you know, because, of course, she was faster than that — and he used to win money on that horse, for all she was so slow and always had the asthma, or the distemper, or the consumption, or something of that kind. They used to give her two or three hundred yards start, and then pass her under way; but always at the fag-end of the race she'd get excited and desperate-like, and come cavorting and straddling up, and scattering her legs around limber, sometimes in the air, and sometimes out to one side amongst the fences, and kicking up m-o-r-e dust, and raising m-o-r-e racket with her coughing and sneezing and blowing her nose — and always fetch up at the stand just about a neck ahead, as near as you could cypher it down.

And he had a little small bull pup, that to look at him you'd think he wa'n't worth a cent, but to set around and look ornery, and lay for a chance to steal something. But as soon as money was up on him, he was a different dog; his under-jaw'd begin to stick out like the fo'castle of a steamboat, and his teeth would uncover, and shine savage like the furnaces. And a dog might tackle him, and bully-rag him, and bite him, and throw him over his shoulder two or three times, and Andrew Jackson — which was the name of the pup — Andrew Jackson would never let on but what *he* was satisfied, and hadn't expected nothing else — and the bets being doubled and doubled on the other side all the time, till the money was all up; and then all of a sudden he would grab that other dog jest by the j'int of his hind leg and freeze to it — not chaw, you understand, but only jest grip and hang on till they throwed up the sponge, if it was a year. Smiley always come out winner on that pup, till he harnessed a dog once that didn't have no hind legs, because they'd been sawed off by a circular saw, and when the thing had gone along far enough, and the money was all up, and he come to make a snatch for his pet holt, he saw in a minute how he'd been imposed on, and how the other dog had him in the door, so to speak, and he 'peared surprised, and then he looked sorter discouraged-like, and didn't try no more to win the fight, and so he got shucked out bad. He give Smiley a look, as much as to say his heart was broke, and it was *his* fault, for putting up a dog that hadn't no hind legs for him to take holt of, which was his main dependence in a fight, and then he limped off a piece and laid down and died. It was a good pup, was that Andrew Jackson, and would have made a name for hisself if he'd lived, for the stuff was in him, and he had genius — I know it, because he hadn't had no opportunity to speak of, and it don't stand to reason that a dog could make such a fight as he could under them circumstances, if he hadn't no talent. It always makes me feel sorry when I think of that last fight of his'n, and the way it turned out.

Well, thish-yer Smiley had rat-tarriers, and chicken cocks, and tom-cats, and all them kind of things, till you couldn't rest, and you couldn't fetch nothing for him to bet on but he'd match you. He ketched a frog one day, and took him home, and said he cal'klated to edercate him; and so he never done nothing for three months but set in his back yard and learn that frog to jump. And you bet he *did* learn him, too. He'd give him a little punch behind, and the next minute you'd see that frog whirling in the air like a doughnut — see him turn one summerset, or may be a couple, if he got a good start, and come down flat-footed and all right, like a cat. He got him up so in the matter of catching flies, and kept him in practice so constant, that he'd nail a fly every time as far as he could see him. Smiley said all a frog wanted was education, and he could do most anything — and I believe him. Why, I've seen him set Dan'l Webster down here on this floor — Dan'l Webster was the name of the frog — and sing out, "Flies, Dan'l, flies!" and quicker'n you could wink, he'd spring straight up, and snake a fly off'n the counter there, and flop down on the floor again as solid as a gob of mud, and fall to scratching the side of his head with his hind foot as indifferent as if he hadn't no idea he'd been doin' any more'n any frog might do. You never see a frog so modest and straightfor'ard as he was, for all he was so gifted. And when it come to fair and square jumping on a dead level, he could get over more ground at one straddle than any animal of his breed you ever see. Jumping on a dead level was his strong suit, you understand; and when it come to that, Smiley would ante up money on him as long as he had a red. Smiley was monstrous proud of his frog, and well he might be, for fellers that had traveled and been everywheres, all said he laid over any frog that ever *they* see.

Well Smiley kept the beast in a little lattice box, and he used to fetch him down town sometimes and lay for a bet. One day a feller — a stranger in the camp, he was — come across him with his box, and says:

"What might it be that you've got in the box?"

And Smiley says, sorter indifferent like, "It might be a parrot, or it might be a canary, may be, but it ain't — it's only just a frog."

And the feller took it, and looked at it careful, and turned it round this way and that, and says, "H'm — so 'tis. Well, what's *he* good for?"

"Well," Smiley says, easy and careless, "he's good enough for *one* thing, I should judge — he can outjump ary frog in Calaveras county."

The feller took the box again, and took another long, particular look, and give it back to Smiley, and says, very deliberate, "Well, I don't see no p'ints about that frog that's any better'n any other frog."

"May be you don't," Smiley says. "May be you understand frogs, and may be you don't understand 'em; may be you've had experience, and may be you an't only a amature, as it were. Anyways, I've got *my* opinion, and I'll risk forty dollars he can out-jump any frog in Calaveras county."

And the feller studied a minute, and then says, kinder sad like, "Well, I'm only a stranger here, and I ain't got no frog, but if I had a frog, I'd bet you."

And then Smiley says, "That's all right — that's all right — if you'll hold my box a minute, I'll go and get you a frog." And so the feller took the box, and put up his forty dollars along with Smiley's, and set down to wait.

So he set there a good while thinking and thinking to hisself, and then he got the frog out and prized his mouth open and took a teaspoon and filled him full of quail shot — filled him pretty near up to his chin — and set him on the floor. Smiley he went to the swamp and slopped around in the mud for a long time, and finally he ketched a frog, and fetched him in, and give him to this feller, and says:

"Now, if you're ready, set him alongside of Dan'l, with his fore-paws just even with Dan'l, and I'll give the word." Then he says, "one — two — three — jump!" and him and the feller touched up the frogs from behind, and the new frog hopped off, but Dan'l give a heave, and hysted up his shoulders — so — like a Frenchman, but it want no use — couldn't budge; he was planted as solid as an anvil, and he couldn't no more stir than if he was anchored out. Smiley was a good deal surprised, and he was disgusted too, but he didn't have no idea what the matter was, of course.

The feller took the money and started away; and when he was going out of the door, he sorter jerked his thumb over his shoulders — this way — at Dan'l, and says again, very deliberate, "Well, *I* don' see no p'ints about that frog that's any better'n any other frog."

Smiley he stood scratching his head and looking down at Dan'l a long time, and at last he says, "I do wonder what in the nation that frog throw'd off for — I wonder if there ain't something the matter with him — he 'pears to look mighty baggy, somehow." And he ketched Dan'l by the nap of the neck, and lifted him up and says, "Why, blame my cats, if he don't weigh five pound!" and

turned him upside down, and he belched out a double handful of shot. And then he see how it was, and he was the maddest man — he set the frog down and took out after that feller, but he never ketched him. And —

[Here Simon Wheeler heard his name called from the front yard, and got up to see what was wanted.] And turning to me as he moved away, he said: "Just set where you are, stranger, and rest easy — I an't going to be gone a second."

But, by your leave, I did not think that a continuation of the history of the enterprising vagabond *Jim* Smiley would be likely to afford me much information concerning the Rev. *Leonidas W.* Smiley, and so I started away.

At the door I met the sociable Wheeler returning, and he buttonholed me and recommenced:

"Well, thish-yer Smiley had a yaller one-eyed cow that didn't have no tail, only jest a short stump like a bannanner, and —"

"Oh! hang Smiley and his afflicted cow!" I muttered, good-naturedly, and bidding the old gentleman good-day, I departed.

From Roughing It

(1872)

[*Buck Fanshaw's Funeral*]

Somebody has said that in order to know a community, one must observe the style of its funerals and know what manner of men they bury with most ceremony. I cannot say which class we buried with most éclat in our "flush times," the distinguished public benefactor or the distinguished rough — possibly the two chief grades or grand divisions of society honored their illustrious dead about equally; and hence, no doubt, the philosopher I have quoted from would have needed to see two representative funerals in Virginia before forming his estimate of the people.

There was a grand time over Buck Fanshaw when he died. He was a representative citizen. He had "killed his man" — not in his own quarrel, it is true, but in defence of a stranger unfairly beset by numbers. He had kept a sumptuous saloon. He had been the proprietor of a dashing help-meet whom he could have discarded without the formality of a divorce. He held a high position in the fire department and had been a very Warwick in politics. When he died there was a great lamentation throughout the town, but especially in the vast bottom-stratum of society.

On the inquest it was shown that Buck Fanshaw, in the delirium of a wasting typhoid fever, had taken arsenic, shot himself through the body, cut his throat, and jumped out of a four-storey window and broken his neck — and after due deliberation, the jury, sad and tearful, but with intelligence unblinded by its sorrow, brought a verdict of death "by the visitation of God." What could the world do without juries?

Prodigious preparations were made for the funeral. All the vehicles in town were hired, all the saloons put in mourning, all the municipal and fire-company flags hung at half-mast, and all the firemen ordered to muster in uniform and bring their machines duly draped in black. Now — let us remark in parenthesis — as all the peoples of the earth had representative adventurers in Silverland, and as each adventurer had brought the slang of his nation or his locality with him, the combination made the slang of Nevada the richest and the most infinitely varied and copious that had ever existed anywhere in the world, perhaps, except in the mines of California in the "early days." Slang was the language of Nevada. It was hard to preach a sermon without it, and to be understood. Such phrases as "You bet!" "Oh, no, I reckon not!" "No Irish need apply," and a hundred others, became so common as to fall from the lips of a speaker unconsciously — and very often when they did not touch the subject under discussion and consequently failed to mean anything.

After Buck Fanshaw's inquest, a meeting of the short-haired brotherhood was held, for nothing can be done on the Pacific coast without a public meeting and an expression of sentiment. Regretful resolutions were passed and various committees appointed; among others, a committee of one was deputed to call on the minister, a fragile, gentle, spirituel new fledgling from an Eastern theological seminary, and as yet unacquainted with the ways of the mines. The committeeman, "Scotty" Briggs, made his visit; and in after days it was worth some-

thing to hear the minister tell about it. Scotty was a stalwart rough, whose customary suit, when on weighty official business, like committee work, was a fire helmet, flaming red flannel shirt, patent leather belt with spanner and revolver attached, coat hung over his arm, and pants stuffed into boot tops. He formed something of a contrast to the pale theological student. It is fair to say of Scotty, however, in passing, that he had a warm heart, and a strong love for his friends, and never entered into a quarrel when he could reasonably keep out of it. Indeed, it was commonly said that whenever one of Scotty's fights were investigated, it always turned out that it had originally been no affair of his, but that out of native goodheartedness he had dropped in of his own accord to help the man who was getting the worst of it. He and Buck Fanshaw were bosom friends, for years, and had often taken adventurous "potluck" together. On one occasion, they had thrown off their coats and taken the weaker side in a fight among strangers, and after gaining a hard-earned victory, turned and found that the men they were helping had deserted early, and not only that, but had stolen their coats and made off with them! But to return to Scotty's visit to the minister. He was on a sorrowful mission, now, and his face was the picture of woe. Being admitted to the presence he sat down before the clergyman, placed his fire-hat on an unfinished manuscript sermon under the minister's nose, took from it a red silk handkerchief, wiped his brow and heaved a sigh of dismal impressiveness, explanatory of his business. He choked, and even shed tears; but with an effort he mastered his voice and said in lugubrious tones:

"Are you the duck that runs the gospelmill next door?"

"Am I the — pardon me, I believe I do not understand?"

With another sigh, and half-sob, Scotty rejoined:

"Why you see we are in a bit of trouble, and the boys thought maybe you would give us a lift, if we'd tackle you — that is, if I've got the rights of it and you are the head clerk of the doxology-works next door."

"I am the shepherd in charge of the flock whose fold is next door."

" The which?"

"The spiritual adviser of the little company of believers whose sanctuary adjoins these premises."

Scotty scratched his head, reflected a moment, and then said:

"You ruther hold over me, pard. I reckon I can't call that hand. Ante and pass the buck."

"How? I beg pardon. What did I understand you to say?"

"Well, you've ruther got the bulge on me. Or maybe we've both got the bulge somehow. You bulge somehow. You don't smoke me and I don't smoke you. You see one of the boys has passed in his checks and we want to give him a good send-off, and so the thing I'm on now is to roust out somebody to jerk a little chin-music for us and waltz him through handsome."

"My friend, I seem to grow more and more bewildered. Your observations are wholly incomprehensible to me. Cannot you simplify them in some way? At first I thought perhaps I understood you, but I grope now. Would it not expedite matters if you restricted yourself to categorical statements of fact unencumbered with obstructing accumulations of metaphor and allegory?"

Another pause, and more reflection. Then, said Scotty:

"I'll have to pass, I judge."

"How?"

"You've raised me out, pard."

"I still fail to catch your meaning."

"Why, that last lead of yourn is too many for me — that's the idea. I can't neither trump nor follow suit."

The clergyman sank back in his chair perplexed. Scotty leaned his head on his hand and gave himself up to thought. Presently his face came up, sorrowful but confident.

"I've got it now, so's you can savvy," he said. "What we want is a gospel-sharp. See?"

"A what?"

"Gospel-sharp. Parson."

"Oh! Why did you not say so before? I am a clergyman — a parson."

"Now you talk! You see my blind and straddle it like a man. Put it there!" — extending a brawny paw, which closed over the minister's small hand and gave it a shake indicative of fraternal sympathy and fervent gratification.

"Now we're all right, pard. Let's start fresh. Don't you mind my snuffling a little — becuz we're in a power of trouble. You see one of the boys has gone up the flume —"

"Gone where?"

"Up the flume — throwed up the sponge, you understand."

"Thrown up the sponge?"

"Yes — kicked the bucket —"

"Ah — has departed to that mysterious country from whose bourne no traveler returns."

"Return! I reckon not. Why pard, he's *dead!*"

"Yes, I understand."

"Oh, you do? Well I thought maybe you might be getting tangled some more. Yes, you see he's dead again —"

"*Again?* Why, has he ever been dead before?"

"Dead before? No! Do you reckon a man has got as many lives as a cat? But you bet you he's awful dead now, poor old boy, and I wish I'd never seen this day. I don't want no better friend than Buck Fanshaw. I knowed him by the back; and when I know a man and like him, I freeze to him — you hear *me*. Take him all round, pard, there never was a bullier man in the mines. No man ever knowed Buck Fanshaw to go back on a friend. But it's all up, you know, it's all up. It ain't no use. They've scooped him."

"Scooped him?"

"Yes — death has. Well, well, well, we've got to give him up. Yes indeed. It's a kind of a hard world, after all, *ain't* it? But pard, he was a rustler! You ought to see him get started once. He was a bully boy with a glass eye! Just spit in his face and give him room according to his strength, and it was just beautiful to see him peel and go in. He was the worst son of a thief that ever drawed breath. Pard, he was *on* it! He was on it bigger than an Injun!"

"On it? On what?"

"On the shoot. On the shoulder. On the fight, you understand. *He* didn't give a continental for *any*body. *Beg* your pardon, friend, for coming so near saying a cuss-word — but you see I'm on an awful strain, in this palaver, on account of having to camp down and draw everything so mild. But we've got to give him up. There ain't any getting around that, I don't reckon. Now if we can get you to help plant him —"

"Preach the funeral discourse? Assist at the obsequies?"

"Obs'quies is good. Yes. That's it — that's our little game. We are going to get the thing up regardless, you know. He was always nifty himself, and so you bet you his funeral ain't going to be no slouch — solid silver door-plate on his coffin, six plumes on the hearse, and a nigger on the box in a biled shirt and a plug hat — how's that for high? And we'll take care of *you*, pard. We'll fix you all right. There'll be a kerridge for you; and whatever you want, you just 'scape out and we'll tend to it. We've got a shebang fixed up for you to stand behind, in No. 1's house, and don't you be afraid. Just go in and toot your horn, if you don't sell a clam. Put Buck through as bully as you can, pard, for anybody that knowed him will tell you that he was one of the whitest men that was ever in the mines. You can't draw it too strong. He never could stand it to see things going wrong. He's done more to make this town quiet and peaceable than any man in it. I've seen him lick four Greasers in eleven minutes, myself. If a thing wanted regulating, *he* warn't a man to go browsing around after somebody to do it, but he would prance in and regulate it himself. He warn't a Catholic. Scasely. He was down on 'em. His word was, 'No Irish need apply!' But it didn't make no difference about that when it came down to what a man's rights was — and so, when some roughs jumped the Catholic bone-yard and started in to stake out town-lots in it he *went* for 'em! And he *cleaned* 'em, too! I was there, pard, and I seen it myself."

"That was very well indeed — at least the impulse was — whether the act was strictly defensible or not. Had deceased any religious convictions? That is to say, did he feel a dependance upon, or acknowledge allegiance to a higher power?"

More reflection.

"I reckon you've stumped me again, pard. Could you say it over once more, and say it slow?"

"Well, to simplify it somewhat, was he, or rather had he ever been connected with any organization sequestered from secular concerns and devoted to self-sacrifice in the interests of morality?"

"All down but nine — set 'em up on the other alley, pard."

"What did I understand you to say?"

"Why, you're most too many for me, you know. When you get in with your left I hunt grass every time. Every time you draw, you fill; but I don't seem to have any luck. Let's have a new deal."

"How? Begin again?"

"That's it."

"Very well. Was he a good man, and —"

"There — I see that; don't put up another chip till I look at my hand. A good man, says you? Pard, it ain't no name for it. He was the best man that ever — pard, you would have doted on that man. He could lam any galoot of his inches in America. It was him that put down the riot last election before it got a start; and everybody said he was the only man that could have done it. He waltzed in with a spanner in one hand and a trumpet in the other, and sent fourteen men home on a shutter in less than three minutes. He had that riot all broke up and prevented nice before anybody ever got a chance to strike a blow. He was always for peace, and he would *have* peace — he could not stand disturbances. Pard, he was a great loss to this town. It would please the boys if you could chip in something like that and do him justice. Here once when the Micks got to throwing stones through the Methodis' Sunday-school windows, Buck Fanshaw, all of his own notion, shut up his saloon and took a couple of six-shooters and mounted guard over the Sunday school. Says he, 'No Irish need apply!' And they didn't. He was the bulliest man in the mountains, pard! He could run faster, jump higher, hit harder, and hold more tangle-foot whisky without spilling it than any man in seventeen counties. Put that in, pard — it'll please the boys more than anything you could say. And you can say, pard, that he never shook his mother."

"Never shook his mother?"

"That's it — any of the boys will tell you so."

"Well, but why *should* he shake her?"

"That's what *I* say — but some people does."

"Not people of any repute?"

"Well, some that averages pretty so-so."

"In my opinion the man that would offer personal violence to his own mother, ought to —"

"Cheese it, pard; you've banked your ball clean outside the string. What I was drivin' at, was, that he never *throwed off* on his mother — don't you see? No indeedy. He gave her a house to live in, and town lots, and plenty of money; and he looked after her and took care of her all the time; and when she was down with the small-pox I'm d—d if he didn't set up nights and nuss her himself! *Beg* your pardon for saying it, but it hopped out too quick for yours truly. You've treated me like a gentleman, pard, and I ain't the man to hurt your feelings intentional. I think you're white. I think you're a square man, pard. I like you, and I'll lick any man that don't. I'll lick him till he can't tell himself from a last year's corpse! Put it *there!*" [Another fraternal hand-shake — and exit.]

The obsequies were all that "the boys" could desire. Such a marvel of funeral pomp had never been seen in Virginia. The plumed hearse, the dirge-breathing brass bands, the closed marts of business, the flags drooping at half-mast, the long, plodding procession of uniformed secret societies, military battalions and fire companies, draped engines, carriages of officials; and citizens in vehicles and on foot, attracted multitudes of spectators to the sidewalks, roofs and windows; and for years afterward, the degree of grandeur attained by any civic display in Virginia was determined by comparison with Buck Fanshaw's funeral.

Scotty Briggs, as a pall-bearer and a mourner, occupied a prominent place at the funeral, and when the sermon was finished and the last sentence of the prayer for the dead man's soul ascended, he responded, in a low voice, but with feeling:

"AMEN. No Irish need apply."

As the bulk of the response was without apparent relevancy, it was probably nothing more than a humble tribute to the memory of the friend that was gone; for, as Scotty had once said, it was "his word."

Scotty Briggs, in after days, achieved the distinction of becoming the only convert to religion that was ever gathered from the Virginia roughs; and it transpired that the man who had it in him to espouse the quarrel of the weak out of inborn nobility of spirit was no mean timber whereof to construct a Christian. The making him one did not warp his generosity or diminish his courage; on the contrary it gave intelligent direction to the one and a broader field to the other. If his Sunday-school class progressed faster than the other classes, was it matter for wonder? I think not. He talked to his pioneer small-fry in a language they understood! It was my large privilege, a month before he died, to hear him tell the beautiful story of Joseph and his brethren to his class "without looking at the book." I leave it to the reader to fancy what it was like, as it fell, riddled with slang, from the lips of that grave, earnest teacher, and was listened to by his little learners with a consuming interest that showed that they were as unconscious as he was that any violence was being done to the sacred proprieties!

[Mark Twain Tries a Lecture]

After half a year's luxurious vagrancy in the Islands, I took shipping in a sailing vessel, and regretfully returned to San Francisco — a voyage in every way delightful, but without an incident; unless lying two long weeks in a dead calm, eighteen hundred miles from the nearest land, may rank as an incident. Schools of whales grew so tame that day after day they played about the ship among the porpoises and the sharks without the least apparent fear of us, and we pelted them with empty bottles for lack of better sport. Twenty-four hours afterward these bottles would be still lying on the glassy water under our noses, showing that the ship had not moved out of her place in all that time. The calm was absolutely breathless, and the surface of the sea absolutely without a wrinkle. For a whole day and part of a night we lay so close to another ship that had drifted to our vicinity, that we carried on conversations with her passengers, introduced each other by name, and became pretty intimately acquainted with people we had never heard of before, and have never heard of since. This was the only vessel we saw during the whole lonely voyage. We had fifteen passengers, and to show how hard pressed they were at last for occupation and amusement, I will mention that the gentlemen gave a good part of their time every day, during the calm, to trying to sit on an empty champagne bottle (lying on its side) and thread a needle without touching their heels to the deck, or falling over; and the ladies sat in the shade of the mainsail, and watched the enterprise with absorbing interest. We were at sea five Sundays; and yet, but for the almanac, we never would have known but that all the other days were Sundays too.

I was home again, in San Francisco, without means and without employment. I tortured my brain for a saving scheme of some kind, and at last a public lecture occurred to me! I sat down and wrote one, in a fever of hopeful anticipation. I showed it to several friends, but they all shook their heads. They said nobody would come to hear me, and I would make a humiliating failure of it. They said that as I had never spoken in public, I would break down in the delivery, anyhow. I was disconsolate now. But at last an editor slapped me on the back and told me to "go ahead." He said, "Take the largest house in town, and charge a dollar a ticket." The audacity of the proposition was charming; it seemed fraught with practical worldly wisdom, however. The proprietor of the several theaters endorsed the advice, and said I might have his handsome new opera house at half price — fifty dollars. In sheer desperation I took it — on credit, for sufficient reasons. In three days I did a hundred and fifty dollars' worth of printing and advertising, and was the most distressed and frightened creature on the Pacific coast.

I could not sleep — who could, under such circumstances? For other people there was facetiousness in the last line of my posters, but to me it was plaintive with a pang when I wrote it:

"Doors open at 7½. The trouble will begin at 8."

That line has done good service since. Showmen have borrowed it frequently. I have even seen it appended to a newspaper advertisement reminding school pupils in vacation what time next term would begin. As those three days of suspense dragged by, I grew more and more unhappy. I had sold two hundred tickets among my personal friends, but I feared they might not come. My lecture, which had seemed "humorous" to me, at first, grew steadily more and more dreary, till not a vestige of fun seemed left, and I grieved that I could not bring a coffin on the stage and turn the thing into a funeral. I was so panic-stricken, at last, that I went to three old friends, giants in stature, cordial by nature, and stormy-voiced, and said:

"This thing is going to be a failure; the jokes in it are so dim that nobody will ever see them; I would like to have you sit in the parquette, and help me through."

They said they would. Then I went to the wife of a popular citizen, and said that if she was willing to do me a very great kindness, I would be glad if she and her husband would sit prominently in the left-hand stage-box, where the whole house could see them. I explained that I should need help, and would turn toward her and smile, as a signal, when I had been delivered of an obscure joke — "and then," I added, "don't wait to investigate, but *respond!*"

She promised. Down the street I met a man I never had seen before. He had been drinking, and was beaming with smiles and good nature. He said:

"My name's Sawyer. You don't know me, but that don't matter. I haven't got a cent, but if you knew how bad I wanted to laugh, you'd give me a ticket. Come, now, what do you say?"

"Is your laugh hung on a hair-trigger? —

that is, is it critical, or can you get it off *easy?*"

My drawling infirmity of speech so affected him that he laughed a specimen or two that struck me as being about the article I wanted, and I gave him a ticket, and appointed him to sit in the second circle, in the center, and be responsible for that division of the house. I gave him minute instructions about how to detect indistinct jokes, and then went away, and left him chuckling placidly over the novelty of the idea.

I ate nothing on the last of the three eventful days — I only suffered. I had advertised that on this third day the box-office would be opened for the sale of reserved seats. I crept down to the theater at four in the afternoon to see if any sales had been made. The ticket-seller was gone, the box-office was locked up. I had to swallow suddenly, or my heart would have got out. "No sales," I said to myself; "I might have known it." I thought of suicide, pretended illness, flight. I thought of these things in earnest, for I was very miserable and scared. But of course I had to drive them away, and prepare to meet my fate. I could not wait for half-past seven — I wanted to face the horror, and end it — the feeling of many a man doomed to hang, no doubt. I went down back streets at six o'clock, and entered the theater by the back door. I stumbled my way in the dark among the ranks of canvas scenery, and stood on the stage. The house was gloomy and silent, and its emptiness depressing. I went into the dark among the scenes again, and for an hour and a half gave myself up to the horrors, wholly unconscious of everything else. Then I heard a murmur; it rose higher and higher, and ended in a crash, mingled with cheers. It made my hair raise, it was so close to me, and so loud. There was a pause, and then another; presently came a third, and before I well knew what I was about, I was in the middle of the stage, staring at a sea of faces, bewildered by the fierce glare of the lights, and quaking in every limb with a terror that seemed like to take my life away. The house was full, aisles and all!

The tumult in my heart and brain and legs continued a full minute before I could gain any command over myself. Then I recognized the charity and the friendliness in the faces before me, and little by little my fright melted away, and I began to talk. Within three or four minutes I was comfortable, and even content. My three chief allies, with three auxiliaries, were on hand, in the parquette, all sitting together, all armed with bludgeons, and all ready to make an onslaught upon the feeblest joke that might show its head. And whenever a joke did fall, their bludgeons came down and their faces seemed to split from ear to ear; Sawyer, whose hearty countenance was seen looming redly in the center of the second circle, took it up, and the house was carried handsomely. Inferior jokes never fared so royally before. Presently, I delivered a bit of serious matter with impressive unction (it was my pet), and the audience listened with an absorbed hush that gratified me more than any applause; and as I dropped the last word of the clause, I happened to turn and catch Mrs. ——'s intent and waiting eye; my conversation with her flashed upon me and in spite of all I could do I smiled. She took it for the signal, and promptly delivered a mellow laugh that touched off the whole audience; and the explosion that followed was the triumph of the evening. I thought that that honest man Sawyer would choke himself; and as for the bludgeons, they performed like pile-drivers. But my poor little morsel of pathos was ruined. It was taken in good faith as an intentional joke, and the prize one of the entertainment, and I wisely let it go at that.

All the papers were kind in the morning; my appetite returned; I had abundance of money. All's well that ends well.

From Life on the Mississippi
(1875, 1883)

The Boys' Ambition

When I was a boy, there was but one permanent ambition among my comrades in our village [1] on the west bank of the Mississippi River. That was, to be a steamboatman. We had transient ambitions of other sorts, but they were only transient. When a

[1] Hannibal, Missouri. [*Author's note.*]

circus came and went, it left us all burning to become clowns; the first negro minstrel show that ever came to our section left us all suffering to try that kind of life; now and then we had a hope that, if we lived and were good, God would permit us to be pirates. These ambitions faded out, each in its turn; but the ambition to be a steamboatman always remained.

Once a day a cheap, gaudy packet arrived upward from St. Louis, and another downward from Keokuk. Before these events, the day was glorious with expectancy; after them, the day was a dead and empty thing. Not only the boys, but the whole village, felt this. After all these years I can picture that old time to myself now, just as it was then: the white town drowsing in the sunshine of a summer's morning; the streets empty, or pretty nearly so; one or two clerks sitting in front of the Water Street stores, with their splint-bottomed chairs tilted back against the walls, chins on breasts, hats slouched over their faces, asleep — with shingle-shavings enough around to show what broke them down; a sow and a litter of pigs loafing along the sidewalk, doing a good business in watermelon rinds and seeds; two or three lonely little freight piles scattered about the "levee"; a pile of "skids" on the slope of the stone-paved wharf, and the fragrant town drunkard asleep in the shadow of them; two or three wood flats at the head of the wharf, but nobody to listen to the peaceful lapping of the wavelets against them; the great Mississippi, the majestic, the magnificent Mississippi, rolling its mile-wide tide along, shining in the sun; the dense forest away on the other side; the "point" above the town, and the "point" below, bounding the river-glimpse and turning it into a sort of sea, and withal a very still and brilliant and lonely one. Presently a film of dark smoke appears above one of those remote "points"; instantly a negro drayman, famous for his quick eye and prodigious voice, lifts up the cry, "S-t-e-a-m-boat a-comin'!" and the scene changes! The town drunkard stirs, the clerks wake up, a furious clatter of drays follows, every house and store pours out a human contribution, and all in a twinkling the dead town is alive and moving. Drays, carts, men, boys, all go hurrying from many quarters to a common center, the wharf. Assembled there, the people fasten their eyes upon the coming boat as upon a wonder they are seeing for the first time. And the boat *is* rather a handsome sight, too. She is long and sharp and trim and pretty; she has two tall, fancy-topped chimneys, with a gilded device of some kind swung between them; a fanciful pilot-house, all glass and "gingerbread," perched on top of the "texas" deck behind them; the paddle-boxes are gorgeous with a picture or with gilded rays above the boat's name; the boiler-deck, the hurricane-deck, and the texas deck are fenced and ornamented with clean while railings; there is a flag gallantly flying from the jack-staff; the furnace doors are open and the fires glaring bravely; the upper decks are black with passengers; the captain stands by the big bell, calm, imposing, the envy of all; great volumes of the blackest smoke are rolling and tumbling out of the chimneys — a husbanded grandeur created with a bit of pitch-pine just before arriving at a town; the crew are grouped on the forecastle; the broad stage is run far out over the port bow, and an envied deck-hand stands picturesquely on the end of it with a coil of rope in his hand; the pent steam is screaming through the gauge-cocks; the captain lifts his hand, a bell rings, the wheels stop; then they turn back, churning the water to foam, and the steamer is at rest. Then such a scramble as there is to get aboard, and to get ashore, and to take in freight and to discharge freight, all at one and the same time; and such a yelling and cursing as the mates facilitate it all with! Ten minutes later the steamer is under way again, with no flag on the jack-staff and no black smoke issuing from the chimneys. After ten more minutes the town is dead again, and the town drunkard asleep by the skids once more.

My father was a justice of the peace, and I supposed he possessed the power of life and death over all men, and could hang anybody that offended him. This was distinction enough for me as a general thing; but the desire to be a steamboatman kept intruding, nevertheless. I first wanted to be a cabin-boy, so that I could come out with a white apron on and shake a table-cloth over the side, where all my old comrades could see me; later I thought I would rather be the deck-hand who stood on the end of the stage-plank with the coil of rope in his hand, because he was particularly conspicuous. But these were only day-dreams — they were too heavenly to be contemplated as real possibilities. By and by one of our boys went away. He was not heard of for a long time. At last he turned up as apprentice engineer or "striker" on a steamboat. This thing shook the bottom out of all my Sunday-school teachings. That boy had been notoriously worldly, and I just the reverse; yet he was exalted to this eminence, and I left in obscurity and misery. There was nothing generous about this fellow in his greatness. He would always manage to have a rusty bolt to scrub while his boat tarried at our town, and he would sit on the inside guard and scrub it, where we all could see him and envy him and loathe him. And whenever his boat was laid up he would come home and swell around the town in his blackest and greasiest clothes, so that nobody could help remembering that he was a steamboatman; and he used all sorts of steamboat technicalities in his talk, as if he were so used to them that he forgot common people could not understand them. He would speak of the "labboard" side of a horse in an easy, natural way that would make one wish he was dead. And he was always talking about "St. Looy" like an old citizen; he would refer casually to occasions when he was "coming down Fourth Street," or when he was "passing by the Planter's House," or when there was a fire and he took a turn on the brakes of "the old Big Missouri"; and then he would go on and lie about how many towns the size of ours were burned down there that day. Two or three of the boys had long been persons of consideration among us because they had been to St. Louis once and had a vague general knowledge of its wonders, but the day of their glory was over now. They lapsed into a humble silence, and learned to disappear when the ruthless "cub"-engineer approached. This fellow had money, too, and hair-oil. Also an ignorant silver watch and a showy brass watch-chain. He wore a leather belt and used no suspenders. If ever a youth was cordially admired and hated by his comrades, this one was. No girl could withstand his charms. He "cut out" every boy in the village. When his boat blew up at last, it diffused a tranquil contentment among us such as we had not known for months. But when he came home the next week, alive, renowned, and appeared in church all battered up and bandaged, a shining hero, stared at and wondered over by everybody, it seemed to us that the partiality of Providence for an undeserving reptile had reached a point where it was open to criticism.

This creature's career could produce but one result, and it speedily followed. Boy after boy managed to get on the river. The minister's son became an engineer. The doctor's and the postmaster's sons became "mud clerks"; the wholesale liquor dealer's son became a barkeeper on a boat; four sons of the chief merchant, and two sons of the county judge, became pilots. Pilot was the grandest position of all. The pilot, even in those days of trivial wages, had a princely salary — from a hundred and fifty to two hundred and fifty dollars a month, and no board to pay. Two months of his wages would pay a preacher's salary for a year. Now some of us were left disconsolate. We could not get on the river — at least our parents would not let us.

So, by and by, I ran away. I said I would never come home again till I was a pilot and could come in glory. But somehow I could not manage it. I went meekly aboard a few of the boats that lay packed together like sardines at the long St. Louis wharf, and humbly inquired for the pilots, but got only a cold shoulder and short words from mates and clerks. I had to make the best of this sort of treatment for the time being, but I had comforting day-dreams of a future when I should be a great and honored pilot, with plenty of money, and could kill some of these mates and clerks and pay for them.

I Want to be a Cub-Pilot

Months afterward the hope within me struggled to a reluctant death, and I found myself without an ambition. But I was ashamed to go home. I was in Cincinnati, and I set to work to map out a new career. I had been reading about the recent exploration of the river Amazon by an expedition sent out by our government. It was said that the expedition, owing to difficulties, had not thoroughly explored a part of the country lying about the headwaters, some four thousand miles from the mouth of the river. It was only about fifteen hundred miles from Cincinnati to New Orleans, where I could doubtless get a ship. I had thirty dollars left; I would go and complete the exploration of the Amazon. This was all the thought I gave to the subject. I never was great in matters of detail. I packed my valise, and took passage on an ancient tub called the *Paul Jones*, for New Orleans. For the sum of sixteen dollars I had the scarred and tarnished splendors of "her" main saloon principally to myself, for she was not a creature to attract the eye of wiser travelers.

When we presently got under way and went poking down the broad Ohio, I became a new being, and the subject of my own admiration. I was a traveler! A word never had tasted so good in my mouth before. I had an exultant sense of being bound for mysterious lands and distant climes which I never have felt in so uplifting a degree since. I was in such a glorified condition that all ignoble feelings departed out of me, and I was able to look down and pity the untraveled with a compassion that had hardly a trace of contempt in it. Still, when we stopped at villages and wood-yards, I could not help lolling carelessly upon the railings of the boiler-deck to enjoy the envy of the country boys on the bank. If they did not seem to discover me, I presently sneezed to attract their attention, or moved to a position where they could not help seeing me. And as soon as I knew they saw me I gaped and stretched, and gave other signs of being mightily bored with traveling.

I kept my hat off all the time, and stayed where the wind and the sun could strike me, because I wanted to get the bronzed and weather-beaten look of an old traveler. Before the second day was half gone I experienced a joy which filled me with the purest gratitude; for I saw that the skin had begun to blister and peel off my face and neck. I wished that the boys and girls at home could see me now.

We reached Louisville in time — at least the neighborhood of it. We stuck hard and fast on the rocks in the middle of the river, and lay there four days. I was now beginning to feel a strong sense of being a part of the boat's family, a sort of infant son to the captain and younger brother to the officers. There is no estimating the pride I took in this grandeur, or the affection that began to swell and grow in me for those people. I could not know how the lordly steamboatman scorns that sort of presumption in a mere landsman. I particularly longed to acquire the least trifle of notice from the big stormy mate, and I was on the alert for an opportunity to do him a service to that end. It came at last. The riotous pow-wow of setting a spar was going on down on the forecastle, and I went down there and stood around in the way — or mostly skipping out of it — till the mate suddenly roared a general order for somebody to bring him a capstan bar. I sprang to his side and said: "Tell me where it is — I'll fetch it!"

If a rag-picker had offered to do a diplomatic service for the Emperor of Russia, the monarch could not have been more astounded than the mate was. He even stopped swearing. He stood and stared down at me. It took him ten seconds to scrape his disjointed remains together again. Then he said impressively: "Well, if this don't beat h——l!" and turned to his work with the air of a man who had been confronted with a problem too abstruse for solution.

I crept away, and courted solitude for the rest of the day. I did not go to dinner; I stayed away from supper until everybody else had finished. I did not feel so much like a member of the boat's family now as before. However, my spirits returned, in instalments, as we pursued our way down the river. I was sorry I hated the mate so, because it was not in (young) human nature not to admire him. He was huge and muscular, his face was bearded and whiskered all over; he had a red woman and a blue woman tattooed on his right arm — one on each side of a blue anchor with a red rope to it; and in the matter of profanity he was sublime. When he was getting out cargo at a landing, I was always where I could see and hear. He felt all the majesty of his great position, and made the world feel it, too. When he gave even the simplest order, he discharged it like a blast of lightning, and sent a long, reverberating peal of profanity thundering after it. I could not help contrasting the way in which the average landsman would give an order with the mate's way of doing it. If the landsman should wish the gangplank moved a foot farther forward, he would probably say: "James, or William, one of you push that plank forward, please"; but put the mate in his place, and he would roar out: "Here, now, start that gang-plank for'ard! Lively, now! *What*'re you about? Snatch it! *snatch* it! There! there! Aft again! aft again! Don't you hear me? Dash it to dash! are you going to *sleep* over it! '*Vast* heaving. 'Vast heaving, I tell you! Going to heave it clear astern? WHERE're you going with that barrel! *for'ard* with it 'fore I make you swallow it, you dash-dash-dash-*dashed* split between a tired mud-turtle and a crippled hearse-horse!"

I wished I could talk like that.

When the soreness of my adventure with the mate had somewhat worn off, I began timidly to make up to the humblest official connected with the boat — the night watchman. He snubbed my advances at first, but I presently ventured to offer him a new chalk pipe, and that softened him. So he allowed me to sit with him by the big bell on the hurricane-deck, and in time he melted into conversation. He could not well have helped it, I hung with such homage on his words and so plainly showed that I felt honored by his notice. He told me the names of dim capes and shadowy islands as we glided by them in the solemnity of the night, under the winking stars, and by and by got to talking about himself. He seemed over-sentimental for a man whose salary was six dollars a week — or rather he might have seemed so to an older person than I. But I drank in his words hungrily, and with a faith that might have moved mountains if it had been applied judiciously. What was it to me that he was soiled and seedy and fragrant with gin? What was it to me that his grammar was bad, his construction worse, and his profanity so void of art that it was an element of weakness rather than strength in his conversation? He was a wronged man, a man who had seen trouble, and that was enough for me. As he mellowed into his plaintive history his tears dripped upon the lantern in his lap, and I cried, too, from sympathy. He said he was the son of an English nobleman — either an earl or an alderman, he could not remember which, but believed was both; his father, the nobleman, loved him, but his mother hated him from the cradle; and so while he was still a little boy he was sent to "one of them old, ancient colleges" — he couldn't remember which; and by and by his father died and his mother seized the property and "shook" him, as he phrased it. After his mother shook him, members of the nobility with whom he was acquainted used their influence to get him the position of "loblolly-boy in a ship"; and from that point my watchman threw off all trammels of date and locality and branched out into a narrative that bristled all along with incredible adventures; a narrative that was so reeking with bloodshed, and so crammed with hair-breadth escapes and the most engaging and unconscious personal villainies, that I sat speechless, enjoying, shuddering, wondering, worshiping.

It was a sore blight to find out afterward that he was a low, vulgar, ignorant, sentimental, half-witted humbug, an untraveled native of the wilds of Illinois, who had absorbed wildcat literature and appropriated its marvels, until in time he had woven odds and ends of the mess into this yarn, and then gone on telling it to fledglings like me, until he had come to believe it himself.

A Cub-Pilot's Experience

What with lying on the rocks four days at Louisville, and some other delays, the poor old *Paul Jones* fooled away about two weeks in making the voyage from Cincinnati to New Orleans. This gave me a chance to get acquainted with one of the pilots, and he taught me how to steer the boat, and thus made the fascination of river life more potent than ever for me.

It also gave me a chance to get acquainted with a youth who had taken deck passage — more's the pity; for he easily borrowed six dollars of me on a promise to return to the boat and pay it back to me the day after we should arrive. But he probably died or forgot, for he never came. It was doubtless the former, since he had said his parents were wealthy, and he only traveled deck passage because it was cooler.[1]

I soon discovered two things. One was that a vessel would not be likely to sail for the mouth of the Amazon under ten or twelve years; and the other was that the nine or ten dollars still left in my pocket would not suffice for so impossible an exploration as I had planned, even if I could afford to wait for a ship. Therefore it followed that I must contrive a new career. The *Paul Jones* was now bound for St. Louis. I planned a siege against my pilot, and at the end of three hard days he surrendered. He agreed to teach me the Mississippi River from New Orleans to St. Louis for five hundred dollars, payable out of the first wages I should receive after graduating. I entered upon the small enterprise of "learning" twelve or thirteen hundred miles of the great Mississippi River with the easy confidence of my time of life. If I had really known what I was about to require of my faculties, I should not have had the courage to begin. I supposed that all a pilot had to do was to keep his boat in the river, and I did not consider that that could be much of a trick, since it was so wide.

The boat backed out from New Orleans at four in the afternoon, and it was "our watch" until eight. Mr. Bixby, my chief, "straightened her up," plowed her along past the sterns of the other boats that lay at the Levee, and then said, "Here, take her; shave those steamships as close as you'd peel an apple." I took the wheel, and my heartbeat fluttered up into the hundreds; for it seemed to me that we were about to scrape the side off every ship in the line, we were so close. I held my breath and began to claw the boat away from the danger; and I had my own opinion of the pilot who had known no better than to get us into such peril, but I was too wise to express it. In half a minute I had a wide margin of safety intervening between the *Paul Jones* and the ships; and within ten seconds more I was set aside in disgrace, and Mr. Bixby was going into danger again and flaying me alive with abuse of my cowardice. I was stung, but I was obliged to admire the easy confidence with which my chief loafed from side to side of his wheel, and trimmed the ships so closely that disaster seemed ceaselessly imminent. When he had cooled a little he told me that the easy water was close ashore and the current outside, and therefore we must hug the bank, up-stream, to get the benefit of the former, and stay well out, down-stream, to take advantage of the latter. In my own mind I resolved to be a downstream pilot and leave the up-streaming to people dead to prudence.

Now and then Mr. Bixby called my attention to certain things. Said he, "This is Six-Mile Point." I assented. It was pleasant enough information, but I could not see the bearing of it. I was not conscious that it was a matter of any interest to me. Another time he said, "This is Nine-Mile Point." Later he said, "This is Twelve-Mile Point." They were all about level with the water's edge; they all looked about alike to me; they were monotonously unpicturesque. I hoped Mr. Bixby would change the subject. But no; he would crowd up around a point, hugging the shore with affection, and then say: "The slack water ends here, abreast this bunch of China trees; now we cross over." So he crossed over. He gave me the wheel once or twice, but I had no luck. I either came near chipping off the edge of a sugar-plantation, or I yawed too far from shore, and so dropped back into disgrace again and got abused.

The watch was ended at last, and we took supper and went to bed. At midnight the glare of a lantern shone in my eyes, and the night watchman said:

"Come, turn out!"

And then he left. I could not understand this extraordinary procedure; so I presently gave up trying to, and dozed off to sleep. Pretty soon the watchman was back again,

[1] "Deck" passage — *i.e.*, steerage passage. [*Author's note.*]

and this time he was gruff. I was annoyed. I said:

"What do you want to come bothering around here in the middle of the night for? Now, as like as not, I'll not get to sleep again to-night."

The watchman said:

"Well, if this ain't good, I'm blessed."

The "off-watch" was just turning in, and I heard some brutal laughter from them, and such remarks as "Hello, watchman! ain't the new cub turned out yet? He's delicate, likely. Give him some sugar in a rag, and send for the chambermaid to sing 'Rock-a-by Baby,' to him."

About this time Mr. Bixby appeared on the scene. Something like a minute later I was climbing the pilot-house steps with some of my clothes on and the rest in my arms. Mr. Bixby was close behind, commenting. Here was something fresh — this thing of getting up in the middle of the night to go to work. It was a detail in piloting that had never occurred to me at all. I knew that boats ran all night, but somehow I had never happened to reflect that somebody had to get up out of a warm bed to run them. I began to fear that piloting was not quite so romantic as I had imagined it was; there was something very real and worklike about this new phase of it.

It was a rather dingy night, although a fair number of stars were out. The big mate was at the wheel, and he had the old tub pointed at a star and was holding her straight up the middle of the river. The shores on either hand were not much more than half a mile apart, but they seemed wonderfully far away and ever so vague and indistinct. The mate said:

"We've got to land at Jones's plantation, sir."

The vengeful spirit in me exulted. I said to myself, "I wish you joy of your job, Mr. Bixby; you'll have a good time finding Mr. Jones's plantation such a night as this; and I hope you never *will* find it as long as you live."

Mr. Bixby said to the mate:

"Upper end of the plantation, or the lower?"

"Upper."

"I can't do it. The stumps there are out of water at this stage. It's no great distance to the lower, and you'll have to get along with that."

"All right, sir. If Jones don't like it, he'll have to lump it, I reckon."

And then the mate left. My exultation began to cool and my wonder to come up. Here was a man who not only proposed to find this plantation on such a night, but to find either end of it you preferred. I dreadfully wanted to ask a question, but I was carrying about as many short answers as my cargo-room would admit of, so I held my peace. All I desired to ask Mr. Bixby was the simple question whether he was ass enough to really imagine he was going to find that plantation on a night when all plantations were exactly alike and all of the same color. But I held in. I used to have fine inspirations of prudence in those days.

Mr. Bixby made for the shore and soon was scraping it, just the same as if it had been daylight. And not only that, but singing:

"Father in heaven, the day is declining," etc.

It seemed to me that I had put my life in the keeping of a peculiarly reckless outcast. Presently he turned on me and said:

"What's the name of the first point above New Orleans?"

I was gratified to be able to answer promptly, and I did. I said I didn't know.

"Don't *know?*"

This manner jolted me. I was down at the foot again, in a moment. But I had to say just what I had said before.

"Well, you're a smart one!" said Mr. Bixby. "What's the name of the *next* point?"

Once more I didn't know.

"Well, this beats anything. Tell me the name of *any* point or place I told you."

I studied awhile and decided that I couldn't.

"Look here! What do you start out from, above Twelve-Mile Point, to cross over?"

"I — I — don't know."

"You — you — don't know?" mimicking my drawling manner of speech. "What *do* you know?"

"I — I — nothing, for certain."

"By the great Cæsar's ghost, I believe you! You're the stupidest dunderhead I ever saw or ever heard of, so help me Moses! The idea of *you* being a pilot — *you!* Why, you don't know enough to pilot a cow down a lane."

Oh, but his wrath was up! He was a nervous man, and he shuffled from one side of his wheel to the other as if the floor was hot. He would boil awhile to himself, and then overflow and scald me again.

"Look here! What do you suppose I told you the names of those points for?"

I tremblingly considered a moment, and then the devil of temptation provoked me to say:

"Well — to — to — be entertaining, I thought."

This was a red rag to the bull. He raged and stormed so (he was crossing the river at the time) that I judged it made him blind, because he ran over the steering-oar of a trading-scow. Of course the traders sent up a volley of red-hot profanity. Never was a man so grateful as Mr. Bixby was; because he was brimful, and here were subjects who could *talk back*. He threw open a window, thrust his head out, and such an irruption followed as I never had heard before. The fainter and farther away the scowmen's curses drifted, the higher Mr. Bixby lifted his voice and the weightier his adjectives grew. When he closed the window he was empty. You could have drawn a seine through his system and not caught curses enough to disturb your mother with. Presently he said to me in the gentlest way:

"My boy, you must get a little memorandum-book; and every time I tell you a thing, put it down right away. There's only one way to be a pilot, and that is to get this entire river by heart. You have to know it just like A B C."

That was a dismal revelation to me; for my memory was never loaded with anything but blank cartridges. However, I did not feel discouraged long. I judged that it was best to make some allowance, for doubtless Mr. Bixby was "stretching." Presently he pulled a rope and struck a few strokes on the big bell. The stars were all gone now, and the night was as black as ink. I could hear the wheels churn along the bank, but I was not entirely certain that I could see the shore. The voice of the invisible watchman called up from the hurricane-deck:

"What's this, sir?"

"Jones's plantation."

I said to myself, "I wish I might venture to offer a small bet that it isn't." But I did not chirp. I only waited to see. Mr. Bixby handled the engine-bells, and in due time the boat's nose came to the land, a torch glowed from the forecastle, a man skipped ashore, a darkey's voice on the bank said: "Gimme de k'yarpet-bag, Mass' Jones," and the next moment we were standing up the river again, all serene. I reflected deeply awhile, and then said — but not aloud — "Well, the finding of that plantation was the luckiest accident that ever happened; but it couldn't happen again in a hundred years." And I fully believed it *was* an accident, too.

By the time we had gone seven or eight hundred miles up the river, I had learned to be a tolerably plucky up-stream steersman, in daylight; and before we reached St. Louis I had made a trifle of progress in night work, but only a trifle. I had a note-book that fairly bristled with the names of towns, "points," bars, islands, bends, reaches, etc.; but the information was to be found only in the note-book — none of it was in my head. It made my heart ache to think I had only got half of the river set down; for as our watch was four hours off and four hours on, day and night, there was a long four-hour gap in my book for every time I had slept since the voyage began.

My chief was presently hired to go on a big New Orleans boat, and I packed my satchel and went with him. She was a grand affair. When I stood in her pilot-house I was so far above the water that I seemed perched on a mountain; and her decks stretched so far away, fore and aft, below me, that I wondered how I could ever have considered the little *Paul Jones* a large craft. There were other differences, too. The *Paul Jones's* pilot-house was a cheap, dingy, battered rattle trap, cramped for room; but here was a sumptuous glass temple; room enough to have a dance in; showy red and gold window-curtains; an imposing sofa; leather cushions and a back to the high bench where visiting pilots sit, to spin yarns and "look at the river"; bright, fanciful "cuspidores," instead of a broad wooden box filled with sawdust; nice new oilcloth on the floor; a hospitable big stove for winter; a wheel as high as my head, costly with inlaid work; a wire tiller-rope; bright brass knobs for the bells; and a tidy, white-aproned, black "texas-tender," to bring up tarts and ices and coffee during mid-watch, day and night. Now this was "something like"; and so I began to take heart once more to believe that piloting was a romantic sort of occupation after all. The moment we were under way I began to prowl about the great steamer and fill myself with joy. She was as clean and as dainty as a drawing-room; when I looked down her long, gilded saloon, it was like gazing through a splendid tunnel; she had an oil-picture, by some gifted sign-painter, on every state-room door; she glittered with no end of prism-fringed chandeliers; the clerk's office was elegant, the bar was marvelous, and the bar-keeper had been barbered and uphol-stered at incredible cost. The boiler-deck (*i.e.*, the second story of the boat, so to speak) was as spacious as a church, it seemed to me; so with the forecastle; and there was no piti-ful handful of deck-hands, firemen, and roustabouts down there, but a whole battalion of men. The fires were fiercely glaring from a long row of furnaces, and over them were eight huge boilers! This was unutterable pomp. The mighty engines — but enough of this. I had never felt so fine before. And when I found that the regiment of natty servants respectfully "sir'd" me, my satis-faction was complete.

A Daring Deed

When I returned to the pilot-house St. Louis was gone, and I was lost. Here was a piece of river which was all down in my book, but I could make neither head nor tail of it: you understand, it was turned around. I had seen it when coming up-stream, but I had never faced about to see how it looked when it was behind me. My heart broke again, for it was plain that I had got to learn this troublesome river *both ways*.

The pilot-house was full of pilots, going down to "look at the river." What is called the "upper river" (the two hundred miles between St. Louis and Cairo, where the Ohio comes in) was low; and the Mississippi changes its channel so constantly that the pilots used to always find it necessary to run down to Cairo to take a fresh look, when their boats were to lie in port a week; that is, when the water was at a low stage. A deal of this "looking at the river" was done by poor fellows who seldom had a berth, and whose only hope of getting one lay in their being always freshly posted and therefore ready to drop into the shoes of some reputa-ble pilot, for a single trip, on account of such pilot's sudden illness, or some other necessity. And a good many of them constantly ran up and down inspecting the river, not because they ever really hoped to get a berth, but because (they being guests of the boat) it was cheaper to "look at the river" than stay ashore and pay board. In time these fellows grew dainty in their tastes, and only infested boats that had an established reputation for setting good tables. All visiting pilots were useful, for they were always ready and willing, winter or summer, night or day, to go out in the yawl and help buoy the channel or assist the boat's pilots in any way they could. They were likewise welcomed because all pilots are tireless talkers, when gathered to-gether, and as they talk only about the river they are always understood and are always interesting. Your true pilot cares nothing about anything on earth but the river, and his pride in his occupation surpasses the pride of kings.

We had a fine company of these river in-spectors along this trip. There were eight or ten, and there was abundance of room for them in our great pilot-house. Two or three of them wore polished silk hats, elaborate shirt-fronts, diamond breastpins, kid gloves, and patent-leather boots. They were choice in their English, and bore themselves with a dignity proper to men of solid means and prodigious reputation as pilots. The others were more or less loosely clad, and wore upon their heads tall felt cones that were sug-gestive of the days of the commonwealth. I was a cipher in this august company, and felt subdued, not to say torpid. I was not even of sufficient consequence to assist at the wheel when it was necessary to put the tiller hard down in a hurry; the guest that stood nearest did that when occasion required — and this was pretty much all the time, because of the crookedness of the channel and the scant water. I stood in a corner; and the talk I listened to took the hope all out of me. One visitor said to another:

"Jim, how did you run Plum Point, coming up?"

"It was in the night, there, and I ran it the way one of the boys on the *Diana* told me; started out about fifty yards above the wood-pile on the false point, and held on the cabin under Plum Point till I raised the reef — quarter less twain — then straightened up for the middle bar till I got well abreast the old one-limbed cottonwood in the bend, then got my stern on the cottonwood, and head on the low place above the point, and came through a-booming — nine and a half."

"Pretty square crossing, an't it?"

"Yes, but the upper bar's working down fast."

Another pilot spoke up and said:

"I had better water than that, and ran it lower down; started out from the false point — marked twain — raised the second reef abreast the big snag in the bend, and had quarter less twain."

One of the gorgeous ones remarked:

"I don't want to find fault with your leadsmen, but that's a good deal of water for Plum Point, it seems to me."

There was an approving nod all around as this quiet snub dropped on the boaster and "settled" him. And so they went on talk-talk-talking. Meantime, the thing that was running in my mind was, "Now, if my ears hear aright, I have not only to get the names of all the towns and islands and bends, and so on, by heart, but I must even get up a warm personal acquaintanceship with every old snag and one-limbed cottonwood and obscure wood-pile that ornaments the banks of this river for twelve hundred miles; and more than that, I must actually know where these things are in the dark, unless these guests are gifted with eyes that can pierce through two miles of solid blackness. I wish

the piloting business was in Jericho and I had never thought of it."

At dusk Mr. Bixby tapped the big bell three times (the signal to land), and the captain emerged from his drawing-room in the forward end of the "texas," and looked up inquiringly. Mr. Bixby said:

"We will lay up here all night, captain."

"Very well, sir."

That was all. The boat came to shore and was tied up for the night. It seemed to me a fine thing that the pilot could do as he pleased, without asking so grand a captain's permission. I took my supper and went immediately to bed, discouraged by my day's observations and experiences. My late voyage's note-booking was but a confusion of meaningless names. It had tangled me all up in a knot every time I had looked at it in the daytime. I now hoped for respite in sleep; but no, it reveled all through my head till sunrise again, a frantic and tireless nightmare.

Next morning I felt pretty rusty and low-spirited. We went booming along, taking a good many chances, for we were anxious to "get out of the river" (as getting out to Cairo was called) before night should overtake us. But Mr. Bixby's partner, the other pilot, presently grounded the boat, and we lost so much time getting her off that it was plain the darkness would overtake us a good long way above the mouth. This was a great misfortune, especially to certain of our visiting pilots, whose boats would have to wait for their return, no matter how long that might be. It sobered the pilot-house talk a good deal. Coming up-stream, pilots did not mind low water or any kind of darkness; nothing stopped them but fog. But downstream work was different; a boat was too nearly helpless, with a stiff current pushing behind her; so it was not customary to run down-stream at night in low water.

There seemed to be one small hope, however: if we could get through the intricate and dangerous Hat Island crossing before night, we could venture the rest, for we would have plainer sailing and better water. But it would be insanity to attempt Hat Island at night. So there was a deal of looking at watches all the rest of the day, and a constant ciphering upon the speed we were making; Hat Island was the eternal subject; sometimes hope was high and sometimes we were delayed in a bad crossing, and down it went again. For hours all hands lay under the burden of this suppressed excitement; it was even communicated to me, and I got to feeling so solicitous about Hat Island, and under such an awful pressure of responsibility, that I wished I might have five minutes on shore to draw a good, full, relieving breath, and start over again. We were standing no regular watches. Each of our pilots ran such portions of the river as he had run when coming up-stream, because of his greater familiarity with it; but both remained in the pilot-house constantly.

An hour before sunset Mr. Bixby took the wheel, and Mr. W. stepped aside. For the next thirty minutes every man held his watch in his hand and was restless, silent, and uneasy. At last somebody said, with a doomful sigh:

"Well, yonder's Hat Island — and we can't make it."

All the watches closed with a snap, everybody sighed and muttered something about its being "too bad, too bad — ah, if we could *only* have got here half an hour sooner!" and the place was thick with the atmosphere of disappointment. Some started to go out, but loitered, hearing no bell-tap to land. The sun dipped behind the horizon, the boat went on. Inquiring looks passed from one guest to another; and one who had his hand on the door-knob and had turned it, waited, then presently took away his hand and let the knob turn back again. We bore steadily down the bend. More looks were exchanged and nods of surprised admiration — but no words. Insensibly the men drew together behind Mr. Bixby, as the sky darkened and one or two dim stars came out. The dead silence and sense of waiting became oppressive. Mr. Bixby pulled the cord, and two deep, mellow notes from the big bell floated off on the night. Then a pause, and one more note was struck. The watchman's voice followed, from the hurricane-deck:

"Labboard lead, there! Stabbord lead!"

The cries of the leadsmen began to rise out of the distance, and were gruffly repeated by the word-passers on the hurricane-deck.

"M-a-r-k three! M-a-r-k three! Quarter-less-three! Half twain! Quartertwain! M-a-r-k twain! Quarter-less ——"

Mr. Bixby pulled two bell-ropes, and was answered by faint jinglings far below in the engine-room, and our speed slackened. The steam began to whistle through the gauge-cocks. The cries of the leadsmen went on — and it is a weird sound, always, in the night. Every pilot in the lot was watching now, with fixed eye, and talking under his breath. Nobody was calm and easy but Mr. Bixby. He would put his wheel down and stand on a spoke, and as the steamer swung into her (to me) utterly invisible marks — for we seemed to be in the midst of a wide and gloomy sea — he would meet and fasten her there. Out of the murmur of half-audible talk, one caught a coherent sentence now and then — such as:

"There; she's over the first reef all right!"

After a pause, another subdued voice:

"Her stern's coming down just *exactly* right, by *George!*"

"Now she's in the marks; over she goes!"

Somebody else muttered:

"Oh, it was done beautiful — *beautiful!*"

Now the engines were stopped altogether, and we drifted with the current. Not that I could see the boat drift, for I could not, the stars being all gone by this time. This drifting was the dismalest work; it held one's heart still. Presently I discovered a blacker gloom than that which surrounded us. It was the head of the island. We were closing right down upon it. We entered its deeper shadow, and so imminent seemed the peril that I was likely to suffocate; and I had the strongest impulse to do *something*, anything, to save the vessel. But still Mr. Bixby stood by his wheel, silent, intent as a cat, and all the pilots stood shoulder to shoulder at his back.

"She'll not make it!" somebody whispered.

The water grew shoaler and shoaler, by the leadsman's cries, till it was down to:

"Eight-and-a-half! E-i-g-h-t feet! E-i-g-h-t feet! Seven-and ——"

Mr. Bixby said warningly through his speaking-tube to the engineer:

"Stand by, now!"

"Ay, ay, sir!"

"Seven-and-a-half! Seven feet! *Six-and*——"

We touched bottom! Instantly Mr. Bixby set a lot of bells ringing, shouted through the tube, "*Now*, let her have it — every ounce you've got!" then to his partner, "Put her hard down! snatch her! snatch her!" The boat rasped and ground her way through the sand, hung upon the apex of disaster a single tremendous instant, and then over she went! And such a shout as went up at Mr. Bixby's back never loosened the roof of a pilot-house before!

There was no more trouble after that. Mr. Bixby was a hero that night; and it was some little time, too, before his exploit ceased to be talked about by river-men.

Fully to realize the marvelous precision required in laying the great steamer in her marks in that murky waste water, one should know that not only must she pick her intricate way through snags and blind reefs, and then shave the head of the island so closely as to brush the overhanging foliage with her stern, but at one place she must pass almost within arm's reach of a sunken and invisible wreck that would snatch the hull timbers from under her if she should strike it, and destroy a quarter of a million dollars' worth of steamboat and cargo in five minutes, and maybe a hundred and fifty human lives into the bargain.

The last remark I heard that night was a compliment to Mr. Bixby, uttered in soliloquy and with unction by one of our guests. He said:

"By the Shadow of Death, but he's a lightning pilot!"

The Man That Corrupted Hadleyburg

(1899)

This short story was first published in *Harper's Magazine* for December, 1899, and the next year was placed in the volume *The Man that Corrupted Hadleyburg and Other Stories and Essays*. Written about the same time as *What is Man?* and *The Mysterious Stranger*, it represents the pessimistic attitude of Mark Twain in his late years.

1

It was many years ago. Hadleyburg was the most honest and upright town in all the region round about. It had kept that reputation unsmirched during three generations, and was prouder of it than of any other of its possessions. It was so proud of it, and so anxious to insure its perpetuation, that it began to teach the principles of honest dealing to its babies in the cradle, and made the like teachings the staple of their culture thenceforward through all the years devoted to their education. Also, throughout the formative years temptations were kept out of the way of the young people, so that their honesty could have every chance to harden and solidify, and become a part of their very bone. The neighboring towns were jealous of this honorable supremacy, and affected to sneer at Hadleyburg's pride in it and call it vanity; but all the same they were obliged to acknowledge that Hadleyburg was in reality an incorruptible town; and if pressed they would also acknowledge that the mere fact that a young man hailed from Hadleyburg was all the recommendation he needed when he went forth from his natal town to seek for responsible employment.

But at last, in the drift of time, Hadleyburg had the ill luck to offend a passing stranger — possibly without knowing it, certainly without caring, for Hadleyburg was sufficient unto itself, and cared not a rap for strangers or their opinions. Still, it would have been well to make an exception in this one's case, for he was a bitter man and revengeful. All through his wanderings during a whole year he kept his injury in mind, and gave all his leisure moments to trying to invent a compensating satisfaction for it. He contrived many plans, and all of them were good, but none of them was quite sweeping enough; the poorest of them would hurt a great many individuals, but what he wanted was a plan which would comprehend the entire town, and not let so much as one person escape unhurt. At last he had a fortunate idea, and when it fell into his brain it lit up his whole head with an evil joy. He began to form a plan at once, saying to himself, "That is the thing to do — I will corrupt the town."

5

Six months later he went to Hadleyburg, and arrived in a buggy at the house of the old cashier of the bank about ten at night. He got a sack out of the buggy, shouldered it, and staggered with it through the cottage yard, and knocked at the door. A woman's voice said "Come in," and he entered, and set his sack behind the stove in the parlor, saying politely to the old lady who sat reading the *Missionary Herald* by the lamp:

"Pray keep your seat, madam, I will not disturb you. There — now it is pretty well concealed; one would hardly know it was there. Can I see your husband a moment, madam?"

No, he was gone to Brixton, and might not return before morning.

"Very well, madam, it is no matter. I merely wanted to leave that sack in his care, to be delivered to the rightful owner when he shall be found. I am a stranger; he does not know me; I am merely passing through the town tonight to discharge a matter which has been long in my mind. My errand is now completed, and I go pleased and a little proud, and you will never see me again. There is a paper attached to the sack which will explain everything. Good-night, madam."

The old lady was afraid of the mysterious big stranger, and was glad to see him go. But her curiosity was roused, and she went straight to the sack and brought away the paper. It began as follows:

"TO BE PUBLISHED; or, *the right man sought out by private inquiry — either will answer. This sack contains gold coin weighing a hundred and sixty pounds four ounces —*"

"Mercy on us, and the door not locked!" Mrs. Richards flew to it all in a tremble and locked it, then pulled down the window-shades and stood frightened, worried, and wondering if there was anything else she could do toward making herself and the money more safe. She listened awhile for burglars, then surrendered to curiosity and went back to the lamp and finished reading the paper:

"*I am a foreigner, and am presently going back to my own country, to remain there permanently. I am grateful to America for what I have received at her hands during my stay under her flag; and to one of her citizens — a citizen of Hadleyburg — I am especially grateful for a great kindness done me a year or two ago. Two great kindnesses; in fact. I will explain. I was a gambler. I say I WAS. I was a ruined gambler. I arrived in this village at night, hungry and without a penny. I asked for help — in the dark; I was ashamed to beg in the light. I begged of the right man. He gave me twenty dollars — that is to say, he gave me life, as I considered it. He also gave me fortune; for out of that money I have made myself rich at the gaming-table. And finally, a remark which he made to me has remained with me to this day, and has at last conquered me; and in conquering has saved the remnant of my morals; I shall gamble no more. Now I have no idea who that man was, but I want him found, and I want him to have this money, to give away, throw away, or keep, as he pleases. It is merely my way of testifying my gratitude to him. If I could stay, I would find him myself; but no matter, he will be found. This is an honest town, an incorruptible town, and I know I can trust it without fear. This man can be identified by the remark which he made to me; I feel persuaded that he will remember it.*

"*And now my plan is this: If you prefer to conduct the inquiry privately, do so. Tell the contents of this present writing to any one who is likely to be the right man. If he shall answer, 'I am the man; the remark I made was so-and-so,' apply the test — to wit: open the sack, and in it you will find a sealed envelope containing that remark. If the remark mentioned by the candidate tallies with it, give him the money, and ask no further questions, for he is certainly the right man.*

"*But if you shall prefer a public inquiry, then publish this present writing in the local paper — with these instructions added, to wit: Thirty days from now, let the candidate appear at the town-hall at eight in the evening (Friday), and hand his remark, in a sealed envelope, to the Rev. Mr. Burgess (if he will be kind enough to act); and let Mr. Burgess there and then destroy the seals on the sack, open it, and see if the remark is correct; if correct, let the money be delivered, with my sincere gratitude, to my benefactor thus identified.*"

Mrs. Richards sat down, gently quivering with excitement, and was soon lost in thinking — after this pattern: "What a strange thing it is! . . . And what a fortune for that kind man who set his bread afloat upon the waters! . . . If it had only been my husband that did it! — for we are so poor, so old and poor! . . ." Then, with a sigh — "But it was not my Edward; no, it was not he that gave a stranger twenty dollars. It is a pity too; I see it now. . . ." Then, with a shudder — "But it is *gambler's* money! the wages of sin; we couldn't take it; we couldn't touch it. I don't like to be near it; it seems a defilement." She moved to a farther chair. . . . "I wish Edward would come, and take it to the bank; a burglar might come at any moment; it is dreadful to be here all alone with it."

At eleven Mr. Richards arrived, and while his wife was saying, "I am *so* glad you've come!" he was saying, "I'm so tired — tired clear out; it is dreadful to be poor, and have to make these dismal journeys at my time of life. Always at the grind, grind, grind, on a salary — another man's slave, and he sitting at home in his slippers, rich and comfortable."

"I am so sorry for you, Edward, you know that; but be comforted; we have our livelihood; we have our good name ——"

"Yes, Mary, and that is everything. Don't mind my talk — it's just a moment's irritation and doesn't mean anything. Kiss me — there, it's all gone now, and I am not complaining any more. What have you been getting? What's in the sack?"

Then his wife told him the great secret. It dazed him for a moment; then he said:

"It weighs a hundred and sixty pounds? Why, Mary, it's for-ty thou-sand dollars — think of it — a whole fortune! Not ten men in this village are worth that much. Give me the paper."

He skimmed through it and said:

"Isn't it an adventure! Why, it's a romance; it's like the impossible things one reads about in books, and never sees in life." He was well stirred up now; cheerful, even gleeful. He tapped his old wife on the cheek, and said, humorously, "Why, we're rich, Mary, rich; all we've got to do is to bury the money and burn the papers. If the gambler ever comes to inquire, we'll merely look coldly upon him and say: 'What is this nonsense you are talking? We have never heard of you and your sack of gold before;' and then he would look foolish, and ——"

"And in the mean time, while you are running on with your jokes, the money is still here, and it is fast getting along toward burglar-time."

"True. Very well, what shall we do — make the inquiry private? No, not that; it would spoil the romance. The public method is better. Think what a noise it will make! And it will make all the other towns jealous; for no stranger would trust such a thing to any town but Hadleyburg, and they know it.

It's a great card for us. I must get to the printing-office now, or I shall be too late."

"But stop — stop — don't leave me here alone with it, Edward!"

But he was gone. For only a little while, however. Not far from his own house he met the editor-proprietor of the paper, and gave him the document, and said, "Here is a good thing for you, Cox — put it in."

"It may be too late, Mr. Richards, but I'll see."

At home again he and his wife sat down to talk the charming mystery over; they were in no condition for sleep. The first question was, Who could the citizen have been who gave the stranger the twenty dollars? It seemed a simple one; both answered it in the same breath —

"Barclay Goodson."

"Yes," said Richards, "he could have done it, and it would have been like him, but there's not another in the town."

"Everybody will grant that, Edward — grant it privately, anyway. For six months, now, the village has been its own proper self once more — honest, narrow, self-righteous, and stingy."

"It is what he always called it, to the day of his death — said it right out publicly, too."

"Yes, and he was hated for it."

"Oh, of course; but he didn't care. I reckon he was the best-hated man among us, except the Reverend Burgess."

"Well, Burgess deserves it — he will never get another congregation here. Mean as the town is, it knows how to estimate *him*. Edward, doesn't it seem odd that the stranger should appoint Burgess to deliver the money?"

"Well, yes — it does. That is — that is ——"

"Why so much that-*is*-ing? Would *you* select him?"

"Mary, maybe the stranger knows him better than this village does."

"Much *that* would help Burgess!"

The husband seemed perplexed for an answer; the wife kept a steady eye upon him, and waited. Finally Richards said, with the hesitancy of one who is making a statement which is likely to encounter doubt,

"Mary, Burgess is not a bad man."

His wife was certainly surprised.

"Nonsense!" she exclaimed.

"He is not a bad man. I know. The whole of his unpopularity had its foundation in that one thing — the thing that made so much noise."

"That 'one thing,' indeed! As if that 'one thing' wasn't enough, all by itself."

"Plenty. Plenty. Only he wasn't guilty of it."

"How you talk! Not guilty of it! Everybody knows he *was* guilty."

"Mary, I give you my word — he was innocent."

"I can't believe it, and I don't. How do you know?"

"It is a confession. I am ashamed, but I will make it. I was the only man who knew he was innocent. I could have saved him, and — and — well, you know how the town was wrought up — I hadn't the pluck to do it. It would have turned everybody against me. I felt mean, ever so mean; but I didn't dare; I hadn't the manliness to face that."

Mary looked troubled, and for a while was silent. Then she said, stammeringly:

"I — I don't think it would have done for you to — to — One mustn't — er — public opinion — one has to be so careful — so —" It was a difficult road, and she got mired; but after a little she got started again. "It was a great pity, but — Why, we couldn't afford it, Edward — we couldn't indeed. Oh, I wouldn't have had you do it for anything!"

"It would have lost us the good-will of so many people, Mary; and then — and then —"

"What troubles me now is, what *he* thinks of us, Edward."

"He? *He* doesn't suspect that I could have saved him."

"Oh," exclaimed the wife, in a tone of relief, "I am glad of that. As long as he doesn't know that you could have saved him, he — he — well, that makes it a great deal better. Why, I might have known he didn't know, because he is always trying to be friendly with us, as little encouragement as we give him. More than once people have twitted me with it. There's the Wilsons, and the Wilcoxes, and the Harknesses, they take a mean pleasure in saying,

'*Your friend* Burgess,' because they know it pesters me. I wish he wouldn't persist in liking us so; I can't think why he keeps it up."

"I can explain it. It's another confession. When the thing was new and hot, and the town made a plan to ride him on a rail, my conscience hurt me so that I couldn't stand it, and I went privately and gave him notice, and he got out of the town and staid out till it was safe to come back."

"Edward! If the town had found it out —"

"*Don't!* It scares me yet, to think of it. I repented of it the minute it was done; and I was even afraid to tell you, lest your face might betray it to somebody. I didn't sleep any that night, for worrying. But after a few days I saw that no one was going to suspect me, and after that I got to feeling glad I did it. And I feel glad yet, Mary — glad through and through."

"So do I, now, for it would have been a dreadful way to treat him. Yes, I'm glad; for really you did owe him that, you know. But, Edward, suppose it should come out yet, some day!"

"It won't."

"Why!"

"Because everybody thinks it was Goodson."

"Of course they would!"

"Certainly. And of course *he* didn't care. They persuaded poor old Sawlsberry to go and charge it on him, and he went blustering over there and did it. Goodson looked him over, like as if he was hunting for a place on him that he could despise the most, then he says, 'So you are the Committee of Inquiry, are you?' Sawlsberry said that was about what he was. 'Hm. Do they require particulars, or do you reckon a kind of a *general* answer will do?' 'If they require particulars, I will come back, Mr. Goodson; I will take the general answer first.' 'Very well, then, tell them to go to hell — I reckon that's general enough. And I'll give you some advice, Sawlsberry; when you come back for the particulars, fetch a basket to carry the relics of yourself home in.'"

"Just like Goodson; it's got all the marks. He had only vanity; he thought he could give advice better than any other person."

"It settled the business, and saved us, Mary. The subject was dropped."

"Bless you, I'm not doubting *that*."

Then they took up the gold-sack mystery again, with strong interest. Soon the conversation began to suffer breaks — interruptions caused by absorbed thinkings. The breaks grew more and more frequent. At last Richards lost himself wholly in thought. He sat long, gazing vacantly at the floor, and by-and-by he began to punctuate his thoughts with little nervous movements of his hands that seemed to indicate vexation. Meantime his wife too had relapsed into a thoughtful silence, and her movements were beginning to show a troubled discomfort. Finally Richards got up and strode aimlessly about the room, ploughing his hands through his hair, much as a somnambulist might do who was having a bad dream. Then he seemed to arrive at a definite purpose; and without a word he put on his hat and passed quickly out of the house. His wife sat brooding, with a drawn face, and did not seem to be aware that she was alone. Now and then she murmured, "Lead us not into t . . . but — but — we are so poor, so poor! . . . Lead us not into . . . Ah, who would be hurt by it? — and no one would ever know. . . . Lead us . . ." The voice died out in mumblings. After a little she glanced up and muttered in a half-frightened, half-glad way —

"He is gone! But, oh dear, he may be too late — too late. . . . Maybe not — maybe there is still time." She rose and stood thinking, nervously clasping and unclasping her hands. A slight shudder shook her frame, and she said, out of a dry throat, "God forgive me — it's awful to think such things — but . . . Lord, how we are made — how strangely we are made!"

She turned the light low, and slipped stealthily over and kneeled down by the sack and felt of its ridgy sides with her hands, and fondled them lovingly; and there was a gloating light in her poor old eyes. She fell into fits of absence; and came half out of them at times to mutter, "If we had only waited! — oh, if we had only waited a little, and not been in such a hurry!"

Meantime Cox had gone home from his office and told his wife all about the strange thing that had happened, and they had talked it over eagerly, and guessed that the late Goodson was the only man in the town who could have helped a suffering stranger with so noble a sum as twenty dollars. Then there was a pause, and the two became thoughtful and silent. And by-and-by nervous and fidgety. At last the wife said, as if to herself,

"Nobody knows this secret but the Richardses . . . and us . . . nobody."

The husband came out of his thinkings with a slight start, and gazed wistfully at his wife, whose face was become very pale; then he hesitatingly rose, and glanced furtively at his hat, then at his wife — a sort of mute inquiry. Mrs. Cox swallowed once or twice, with her hand at her throat, then in place of speech she nodded her head. In a moment she was alone, and mumbling to herself.

And now Richards and Cox were hurrying through the deserted streets, from opposite directions. They met, panting, at the foot of the printing-office stairs; by the night-light there they read each other's face. Cox whispered,

"Nobody knows about this but us?"

The whispered answer was,

"Not a soul — on honor, not a soul!"

"If it isn't too late to —"

The men were starting up-stairs; at this moment they were overtaken by a boy, and Cox asked,

"Is that you, Johnny?"

"Yes, sir."

"You needn't ship the early mail — nor *any* mail; wait till I tell you."

"It's already gone, sir."

"*Gone?*" It had the sound of an unspeakable disappointment in it.

"Yes, sir. Time-table for Brixton and all the towns beyond changed to-day, sir — had to get the papers in twenty minutes earlier than common. I had to rush; if I had been two minutes later —"

The men turned and walked slowly away, not waiting to hear the rest. Neither of them spoke during ten minutes; then Cox said, in a vexed tone,

"What possessed you to be in such a hurry, *I* can't make out."

The answer was humble enough:

"I see it now, but somehow I never thought, you know, until it was too late. But the next time —"

"Next time be hanged! It won't come in a thousand years."

Then the friends separated without a good-night, and dragged themselves home with the gait of mortally stricken men. At their homes their wives sprang up with an eager "Well?" — then saw the answer with their eyes and sank down sorrowing, without waiting for it to come in words. In both houses a discussion followed of a heated sort — a new thing; there had been discussions before, but not heated ones, not ungentle ones. The discussions to-night were a sort of seeming plagiarisms of each other. Mrs. Richards said,

"If you had only waited, Edward — if you had only stopped to think; but no, you must run straight to the printing-office and spread it all over the world."

"It *said* publish it."

"That is nothing; it also said do it privately, if you liked. There, now — is that true, or not?"

"Why, yes — yes, it is true; but when I thought what a stir it would make, and what a compliment it was to Hadleyburg that a stranger should trust it so —"

"Oh, certainly, I know all that; but if you had only stopped to think, you would have seen that you *couldn't* find the right man, because he is in his grave, and hasn't left chick nor child nor relation behind him; and as long as the money went to somebody that awfully needed it, and nobody would be hurt by it, and — and —"

She broke down, crying. Her husband tried to think of some comforting thing to say, and presently came out with this:

"But after all, Mary, it must be for the best — it *must* be; we know that. And we must remember that it was so ordered —"

"Ordered! Oh, everything's *ordered*, when a person has to find some way out when he has been stupid. Just the same, it was *ordered* that the money should come to us in this special way, and it was you that must take it on yourself to go meddling with the designs of Providence — and who gave you the right? It was wicked, that is what it was — just blasphemous presumption, and no more becoming to a meek and humble professor of —"

"But, Mary, you know how we have been trained all our lives long, like the whole village, till it is absolutely second nature to us to stop not a single moment to think when there's an honest thing to be done —"

"Oh, I know it, I know it — it's been one everlasting training and training and training in honesty — honesty shielded, from the very cradle, against every possible temptation, and so it's *artificial* honesty, and weak as water when temptation comes, as we have seen this night. God knows I never had shade nor shadow of a doubt of my petrified and indestructible honesty until now — and now, under the very first big and real temptation, I — Edward, it is my belief that this town's honesty is as rotten as mine is; as rotten as yours is. It is a mean town, a hard, stingy town, and hasn't a virtue in the world but this honesty it is so celebrated for and so conceited about; and so help me, I do believe that if ever the day comes that its honesty falls under great temptation, its grand reputation will go to ruin like a house of cards. There, now, I've made confession, and I feel better; I am a humbug, and I've been one all my life, without knowing it. Let no man call me honest again — I will not have it."

"I — Well, Mary, I feel a good deal as you do; I certainly do. It seems strange, too, so strange. I never could have believed it — never."

A long silence followed; both were sunk in thought. At last the wife looked up and said,

"I know what you are thinking, Edward."

Richards had the embarrassed look of a person who is caught.

"I am ashamed to confess it, Mary, but —"

"It's no matter, Edward, I was thinking the same question myself."

"I hope so. State it."

"You were thinking, if a body could only guess out *what the remark was* that Goodson made to the stranger."

"It's perfectly true. I feel guilty and ashamed. And you?"

"I'm past it. Let us make a pallet here; we've got to stand watch till the bank vault opens in the morning and admits the sack. ... Oh, dear, oh, dear — if we hadn't made the mistake!"

The pallet was made, and Mary said:

"The open sesame — what could it have been? I do wonder what that remark could have been? But come; we will get to bed now."

"And sleep?"

"No; think."

"Yes, think."

By this time the Coxes too had completed their spat and their reconciliation, and were turning in — to think, to think, and toss, and fret, and worry over what the remark could possibly have been which Goodson made to the stranded derelict: that golden remark; that remark worth forty thousand dollars, cash.

The reason that the village telegraph-office was open later than usual that night was this: The foreman of Cox's paper was the local representative of the Associated Press. One might say its honorary representative, for it wasn't four times a year that he could furnish thirty words that would be accepted. But this time it was different. His despatch stating what he had caught got an instant answer:

"*Send the whole thing — all the details — twelve hundred words.*"

A colossal order! The foreman filled the bill; and he was the proudest man in the State. By breakfast-time the next morning the name of Hadleyburg the Incorruptible was on every lip in America, from Montreal to the Gulf, from the glaciers of Alaska to the orange-groves of Florida; and millions and millions of people were discussing the stranger and his money-sack, and wondering if the right man would be found, and hoping some more news about the matter would come soon — right away.

2

Hadleyburg village woke up world-celebrated — astonished — happy — vain. Vain beyond imagination. Its nineteen principal citizens and their wives went about shaking hands with each other, and beaming, and smiling, and congratulating, and saying *this* thing adds a new word to the dictionary — *Hadleyburg*, synonym for *incorruptible* — destined to live in dictionaries forever! And the minor and unimportant citizens and their wives went around acting in much the same way. Everybody ran to the bank to see the gold-sack; and before noon grieved and envious crowds began to flock in from Brixton and all neighboring towns; and that afternoon and next day reporters began to arrive from everywhere to verify the sack and its history and write the whole thing up anew, and make dashing free-hand pictures of the sack and of Richards's house, and the bank, and the Presbyterian church, and the Baptist church, and the public square, and the town-hall where the test would be applied and the money delivered; and damnable portraits of the Richardses, and Pinkerton the banker, and Cox, and the foreman, and Reverend Burgess, and the postmaster — and even of Jack Halliday, who was the loafing, good-natured, no-account, irreverent fisherman, hunter, boys' friend, stray-dogs' friend, typical "Sam Lawson" of the town. The little mean, smirking, oily Pinkerton showed the sack to all comers, and rubbed his sleek palms together pleasantly, and enlarged upon the town's fine old reputation for honesty and upon this wonderful endorsement of it, and hoped and believed that the example would now spread far and wide over the American world, and be epoch-making in the matter of moral regeneration. And so on, and so on.

By the end of a week things had quieted down again; the wild intoxication of pride and joy had sobered to a soft, sweet, silent delight — a sort of deep, nameless, unutterable content. All faces bore a look of peaceful, holy happiness.

Then a change came. It was a gradual change: so gradual that its beginnings were hardly noticed; maybe were not noticed at all, except by Jack Halliday, who always noticed everything; and always made fun of it, too, no matter what it was. He began to throw out chaffing remarks about people not looking quite so happy as they did a day or two ago; and next he claimed that the new aspect was deepening to positive sadness; next, that it was taking on a sick look; and finally he said that everybody was become so moody, thoughtful, and absent-minded that he could rob the meanest man in town of a cent out of the bottom of his breeches pocket and not disturb his revery.

At this stage — or at about this stage — a saying like this was dropped at bedtime — with a sigh, usually — by the head of each of the nineteen principal households:

"Ah, what *could* have been the remark that Goodson made!"

And straightway — with a shudder — came this, from the man's wife:

"Oh, *don't!* What horrible thing are you mulling in your mind? Put it away from you, for God's sake!"

But that question was wrung from those men again the next night — and got the same retort. But weaker.

And the third night the men uttered the question yet again — with anguish, and absently. This time — and the following night — the wives fidgeted feebly, and tried to say something. But didn't.

And the night after that they found their tongues and responded — longingly,

"Oh, if we *could* only guess!"

Halliday's comments grew daily more and more sparklingly disagreeable and disparaging. He went diligently about, laughing at the town, individually and in mass. But his laugh was the only one left in the village: it fell upon a hollow and mournful vacancy and emptiness. Not even a smile was findable anywhere. Halliday carried a cigar-box around on a tripod, playing that it was a camera, and halted all passers and aimed the thing and said, "Ready! — now look pleasant, please," but not even this capital joke could surprise the dreary faces into any softening.

So three weeks passed — one week was left. It was Saturday evening — after supper. Instead of the aforetime Saturday-evening flutter and bustle and shopping and larking, the streets were empty and desolate. Richards and his old wife sat apart in their little parlor — miserable and thinking. This was become their evening habit now: the life-long habit which had preceded it, of reading, knitting, and contented chat, or receiving or paying neighborly calls, was dead and gone and forgotten, ages ago — two or three weeks ago; nobody talked now, nobody read, nobody visited — the whole village sat at home, sighing, worrying, silent. Trying to guess out that remark.

The postman left a letter. Richards glanced listlessly at the superscription and the post-mark — unfamiliar, both — and tossed the letter on the table and resumed his might-have-beens and his hopeless dull miseries where he had left them off. Two or three hours later his wife got wearily up and was going away to bed without a good-night — custom now — but she stopped near the letter and eyed it awhile with a dead interest, then broke it open, and began to skim it over. Richards, sitting there with his chair tilted back against the wall and his chin between his knees, heard something fall. It was his wife. He sprang to her side, but she cried out:

"Leave me alone, I am too happy. Read the letter — read it!"

He did. He devoured it, his brain reeling. The letter was from a distant State, and it said:

"I am a stranger to you, but no matter: I have something to tell. I have just arrived home from Mexico, and learned about that episode. Of course you do not know who made that remark, but I know, and I am the only person living who does know. It was GOODSON. *I knew him well, many years ago. I passed through your village that very night, and was his guest till the midnight train came along. I overheard him make that remark to the stranger in the dark — it was in Hale Alley. He and I talked of it the rest of the way home, and while smoking in his house. He mentioned many of your villagers in the course of his talk — most of them in a very uncomplimentary way, but two or three favorably: among these latter yourself. I say 'favorably' — nothing stronger. I remember his saying he did not actually* LIKE *any person in the town — not one; but that you —* I THINK *he said you — am almost sure — had done him a very great service once, possibly without knowing the full value of it, and he wished he had a fortune, he would leave it to you when he died, and a curse apiece for the rest of the citizens. Now, then, if it was you that did him that service, you are his legitimate heir, and entitled to the sack of gold. I know that I can trust to your honor and honesty, for in a citizen of Hadleyburg these virtues are an unfailing inheritance, and so I am going to reveal to you the remark, well satisfied that if you are not the right man you will seek and find the right one and see that poor Goodson's debt of gratitude for the service referred to is paid. This is the remark:* 'YOU ARE FAR FROM BEING A BAD MAN: GO, AND REFORM.'* "HOWARD L. STEPHENSON."*

"Oh, Edward, the money is ours, and I am so grateful, *oh*, so grateful — kiss me, dear, it's forever since we kissed — and we needed it so — the money — and now you are free of Pinkerton and his bank, and nobody's slave any more; it seems to me I could fly for joy."

It was a happy half-hour that the couple spent there on the settee caressing each other; it was the old days come again — days that had begun with their courtship and lasted without a break till the stranger brought the deadly money. By-and-by the wife said:

"Oh, Edward, how lucky it was you did him that grand service, poor Goodson! I never liked him, but I love him now. And it was fine and beautiful of you never to mention it or brag about it." Then, with a touch of reproach, "But you ought to have told *me*, Edward, you ought to have told your wife, you know."

"Well, I — er — well, Mary, you see ——"

"Now stop hemming and hawing, and tell me about it, Edward. I always loved you, and now I'm proud of you. Everybody believes there was only one good generous soul in this village, and now it turns out that you — Edward, why don't you tell me?"

"Well — er — er — Why, Mary, I can't!"

"You *can't*? *Why* can't you?"

"You see, he — well, he — he made me promise I wouldn't."

The wife looked him over, and said, very slowly,

"Made — you — promise? Edward, what do you tell me that for?"

"Mary, do you think I would lie?"

She was troubled and silent for a moment, then she laid her hand within his and said:

"No . . . no. We have wandered far enough from our bearings — God spare us that! In all your life you have never uttered a lie. But now — now that the foundations of things seem to be crumbling from under us, we — we —" She lost her voice for a moment, then said, brokenly, "Lead us not into temptation. . . . I think you made the promise, Edward. Let it rest so. Let us keep away from that ground. Now — that is all gone by; let us be happy again; it is no time for clouds."

Edward found it something of an effort to comply, for his mind kept wandering — trying to remember what the service was that he had done Goodson.

The couple lay awake the most of the night, Mary happy and busy, Edward busy, but not so happy. Mary was planning what she would do with the money. Edward was trying to recall that service. At first his conscience was sore on account of the lie he had told Mary — if it was a lie. After much reflection — suppose it *was* a lie? What then? Was it such a great matter? Aren't we always *acting* lies? Then why not *tell* them? Look at Mary — look what she had done. While he was hurrying off on his honest errand, what was she doing? Lamenting because the papers hadn't been destroyed and the money kept! Is theft better than lying?

That point lost its sting — the lie dropped into the background and left comfort behind it. The next point came to the front: *had* he rendered that service? Well, here was Goodson's own evidence as reported in Stephenson's letter; there could be no better evidence than that — it was even *proof* that he had rendered it. Of course. So that point was settled. . . . No, not quite. He recalled with a wince that this unknown Mr. Stephenson was just a trifle unsure as to whether the performer of it was Richards or some other — and, oh dear, he had put Richards on his honor! He must himself decide whither that money must go — and Mr. Stephenson was not doubting that if he was the wrong man he would go honorably and find the right one. Oh, it was odious to put a man in such a situation — ah, why couldn't Stephenson have left out that doubt! What did he want to intrude that for?

Further reflection. How did it happen that *Richards's* name remained in Stephenson's mind as indicating the right man, and not some other man's name? That looked good. Yes, that looked very good. In fact, it went on looking better and better, straight along — until by-and-by it grew into positive *proof*. And then Richards put the matter at once out of his mind, for he had a private instinct that a proof once established is better left so.

He was feeling reasonably comfortable

now, but there was still one other detail that kept pushing itself on his notice: of course he had done that service — that was settled; but what *was* that service? He must recall it — he would not go to sleep till he had recalled it; it would make his peace of mind perfect. And so he thought and thought. He thought of a dozen things — possible services, even probable services — but none of them seemed adequate, none of them seemed large enough, none of them seemed worth the money — worth the fortune Goodson had wished he could leave in his will. And besides, he couldn't remember having done them, anyway. Now, then — now, then — what *kind* of a service would it be that would make a man so inordinately grateful? Ah — the saving of his soul! That must be it. Yes, he could remember, now, how he once set himself the task of converting Goodson, and labored at it as much as — he was going to say three months; but upon closer examination it shrunk to a month, then to a week, then to a day, then to nothing. Yes, he remembered now, and with unwelcome vividness, that Goodson had told him to go to thunder and mind his own business — *he* wasn't hankering to follow Hadleyburg to heaven!

So that solution was a failure — he hadn't saved Goodson's soul. Richards was discouraged. Then after a little came another idea: had he saved Goodson's property? No, that wouldn't do — he hadn't any. His life? That is it! Of course. Why, he might have thought of it before. This time he was on the right track, sure. His imagination-mill was hard at work in a minute, now.

Thereafter during a stretch of two exhausting hours he was busy saving Goodson's life. He saved it in all kinds of difficult and perilous ways. In every case he got it saved satisfactorily up to a certain point; then, just as he was beginning to get well persuaded that it had really happened, a troublesome detail would turn up which made the whole thing impossible. As in the matter of drowning, for instance. In that case he had swum out and tugged Goodson ashore in an unconscious state with a great crowd looking on and applauding, but when he had got it all thought out and was just beginning to remember all about it a whole swarm of disqualifying details arrived on the ground: the town would have known of it, it would glare like a limelight in his own memory instead of being an inconspicuous service which he had possibly rendered "without knowing its full value." And at this point he remembered that he couldn't swim, anyway.

Ah — *there* was a point which he had been overlooking from the start: it had to be a service which he had rendered "possibly without knowing the full value of it." Why, really, that ought to be an easy hunt — much easier than those others. And sure enough, by-and-by he found it. Goodson, years and years ago, came near marrying a very sweet and pretty girl, named Nancy Hewitt, but in some way or other the match had been broken off; the girl died, Goodson remained a bachelor, and by-and-by became a soured one and a frank despiser of the human species. Soon after the girl's death the village found out, or thought it had found out, that she carried a spoonful of negro blood in her veins. Richards worked at these details a good while, and in the end he thought he remembered things concerning them which must have gotten mislaid in his memory through long neglect. He seemed to dimly remember that it was *he* that found out about the negro blood; that it was he that told the village; that the village told Goodson where they got it; that he thus saved Goodson from marrying the tainted girl; that he had done him this great service "without knowing the full value of it," in fact without knowing that he *was* doing it; but that Goodson knew the value of it, and what a narrow escape he had had, and so went to his grave grateful to his benefactor and wishing he had a fortune to leave him. It was all clear and simple now, and the more he went over it the more luminous and certain it grew; and at last, when he nestled to sleep satisfied and happy, he remembered the whole thing just as if it had been yesterday. In fact, he dimly remembered Goodson's *telling* him his gratitude once. Meantime Mary had spent six thousand dollars on a new house for herself and a pair of slippers for her pastor, and then had fallen peacefully to rest.

That same Saturday evening the postman had delivered a letter to each of the other principal citizens — nineteen letters in all. No two of the envelopes were alike, and no two of the superscriptions were in the same hand, but the letters inside were just like each other in every detail but one. They were exact copies of the letter received by Richards — handwriting and all — and were all signed by Stephenson, but in place of Richards's name each receiver's own name appeared.

All night long eighteen principal citizens did what their caste-brother Richards was doing at the same time — they put in their energies trying to remember what notable service it was that they had unconsciously done Barclay Goodson. In no case was it a holiday job; still they succeeded.

And while they were at this work, which was difficult, their wives put in the night spending the money, which was easy. During that one night the nineteen wives spent an average of seven thousand dollars each out of the forty thousand in the sack — a hundred and thirty-three thousand altogether.

Next day there was a surprise for Jack Halliday. He noticed that the faces of the nineteen chief citizens and their wives bore that expression of peaceful and holy happiness again. He could not understand it, neither was he able to invent any remarks about it that could damage it or disturb it. And so it was his turn to be dissatisfied with life. His private guesses at the reasons for the happiness failed in all instances, upon examination. When he met Mrs. Wilcox and noticed the placid ecstasy in her face, he said to himself, "Her cat has had kittens" — and went and asked the cook; it was not so; the cook had detected the happiness, but did not know the cause. When Halliday found the duplicate ecstasy in the face of "Shadbelly" Billson (village nickname), he was sure some neighbor of Billson's had broken his leg, but inquiry showed that this had not happened. The subdued ecstasy in Gregory Yates's face could mean but one thing — he was a mother-in-law short; it was another mistake. "And Pinkerton — Pinkerton — he has collected ten cents that he

thought he was going to lose." And so on, and so on. In some cases the guesses had to remain in doubt, in the others they proved distinct errors. In the end Halliday said to himself, "Anyway, it foots up that there's nineteen Hadleyburg families temporarily in heaven: I don't know how it happened; I only know Providence is off duty to-day."

An architect and builder from the next State had lately ventured to set up a small business in this unpromising village, and his sign had now been hanging out a week. Not a customer yet; he was a discouraged man, and sorry he had come. But his weather changed suddenly now. First one and then another chief citizen's wife said to him privately:

"Come to my house Monday week — but say nothing about it for the present. We think of building."

He got eleven invitations that day. That night he wrote his daughter and broke off her match with her student. He said she could marry a mile higher than that.

Pinkerton the banker and two or three other well-to-do men planned country-seats — but waited. That kind don't count their chickens until they are hatched.

The Wilsons devised a grand new thing — a fancy-dress ball. They made no actual promises, but told all their acquaintanceship in confidence that they were thinking the matter over and thought they should give it — "and if we do, you will be invited, of course." People were surprised, and said, one to another, "Why, they are crazy, those poor Wilsons, they can't afford it." Several among the nineteen said privately to their husbands, "It is a good idea, we will keep still till their cheap thing is over, then *we* will give one that will make it sick."

The days drifted along, and the bill of future squanderings rose higher and higher, wilder and wilder, more and more foolish and reckless. It began to look as if every member of the nineteen would not only spend his whole forty thousand dollars before receiving-day, but be actually in debt by the time he got the money. In some cases light-headed people did not stop with planning to spend, they really spent — on credit. They bought land, mortgages, farms, speculative stocks, fine clothes, horses, and various other things, paid down the bonus, and made themselves liable for the rest — at ten days. Presently the sober second thought came, and Halliday noticed that a ghastly anxiety was beginning to show up in a good many faces. Again he was puzzled, and didn't know what to make of it. "The Wilcox kittens aren't dead, for they weren't born; nobody's broken a leg; there's no shrinkage in mother-in-laws; *nothing* has happened — it is an insolvable mystery."

There was another puzzled man, too — the Rev. Mr. Burgess. For days, wherever he went, people seemed to follow him or to be watching out for him; and if he ever found himself in a retired spot, a member of the nineteen would be sure to appear, thrust an envelope privately into his hand, whisper "To be opened at the town hall Friday evening," then vanish away like a guilty thing. He was expecting that there might be one claimant for the sack — doubtful, however, Goodson being dead — but it never occurred to him that all this crowd might be claimants. When the great Friday came at last, he found that he had nineteen envelopes.

3

The town-hall had never looked finer. The platform at the end of it was backed by a showy draping of flags; at intervals along the walls were festoons of flags; the gallery fronts were clothed in flags; the supporting columns were swathed in flags; all this was to impress the stranger, for he would be there in considerable force, and in a large degree he would be connected with the press. The house was full. The 412 fixed seats were occupied; also the 68 extra chairs which had been packed into the aisles; the steps of the platform were occupied; some distinguished strangers were given seats on the platform; at the horseshoe of tables which fenced the front and sides of the platform sat a strong force of special correspondents who had come from everywhere. It was the best-dressed house the town had ever produced. There were some tolerably expensive toilets there, and in several cases the ladies who wore them had the look of being unfamiliar

with that kind of clothes. At least the town thought they had that look, but the notion could have arisen from the town's knowledge of the fact that these ladies had never inhabited such clothes before.

The gold-sack stood on a little table at the front of the platform where all the house could see it. The bulk of the house gazed at it with a burning interest, a mouth-watering interest, a wistful and pathetic interest; a minority of nineteen couples gazed at it tenderly, lovingly, proprietarily, and the male half of this minority kept saying over to themselves the moving little impromptu speeches of thankfulness for the audience's applause and congratulations which they were presently going to get up and deliver. Every now and then one of these got a piece of paper out of his vest pocket and privately glanced at it to refresh his memory.

Of course there was a buzz of conversation going on — there always is; but at last when the Rev. Mr. Burgess rose and laid his hand on the sack he could hear his microbes gnaw, the place was so still. He related the curious history of the sack, then went on to speak in warm terms of Hadleyburg's old and well-earned reputation for spotless honesty, and of the town's just pride in this reputation. He said that this reputation was a treasure of priceless value; that under Providence its value had now become inestimably enhanced, for the recent episode had spread this fame far and wide, and thus had focussed the eyes of the American world upon this village, and made its name for all time, as he hoped and believed, a synonym for commercial incorruptibility. [*Applause.*] "And who is to be the guardian of this noble treasure — the community as a whole? No! The responsibility is individual, not communal. From this day forth each and every one of you is in his own person its special guardian, and individually responsible that no harm shall come to it. Do you — does each of you — accept this great trust? [*Tumultuous assent.*] Then all is well. Transmit it to your children and to your children's children. To-day your purity is beyond reproach — see to it that it shall remain so. To-day there is not a person in your community who could be beguiled to touch a penny not his own —

see to it that you abide in this grace. [*"We will! we will!"*] This is not the place to make comparisons between ourselves and other communities — some of them ungracious toward us; they have their ways, we have ours; let us be content. [*Applause.*] I am done. Under my hand, my friends, rests a stranger's eloquent recognition of what we are: through him the world will always henceforth know what we are. We do not know who he is, but in your name I utter your gratitude, and ask you to raise your voices in endorsement."

The house rose in a body and made the walls quake with the thunders of its thankfulness for the space of a long minute. Then it sat down, and Mr. Burgess took an envelope out of his pocket. The house held its breath while he slit the envelope open and took from it a slip of paper. He read its contents — slowly and impressively — the audience listening with tranced attention to this magic document, each of whose words stood for an ingot of gold:

" '*The remark which I made to the distressed stranger was this: "You are very far from being a bad man; go, and reform."* ' " Then he continued: "We shall know in a moment now whether the remark here quoted corresponds with the one concealed in the sack; and if that shall prove to be so — and it undoubtedly will — this sack of gold belongs to a fellow-citizen who will henceforth stand before the nation as the symbol of the special virtue which has made our town famous throughout the land — Mr. Billson!"

The house had gotten itself all ready to burst into a proper tornado of applause; but instead of doing it, it seemed stricken with a paralysis; there was a deep hush for a moment or two, then a wave of whispered murmurs swept the place — of about this tenor: "*Billson!* oh, come, this is *too* thin! Twenty dollars to a stranger — or *anybody* — *Billson!* Tell it to the marines!" And now at this point the house caught its breath all of a sudden in a new access of astonishment, for it discovered that whereas in one part of the hall Deacon Billson was standing up with his head meekly bowed, in another part of it Lawyer Wilson was doing the same. There was a wondering silence now for a while.

Everybody was puzzled, and nineteen couples were surprised and indignant.

Billson and Wilson turned and stared at each other. Billson asked, bitingly,

"Why do *you* rise, Mr. Wilson?"

"Because I have a right to. Perhaps you will be good enough to explain to the house why *you* rise?"

"With great pleasure. Because I wrote that paper."

"It is an impudent falsity! I wrote it myself."

It was Burgess's turn to be paralyzed. He stood looking vacantly at first one of the men and then the other, and did not seem to know what to do. The house was stupefied. Lawyer Wilson spoke up, now, and said,

"I ask the Chair to read the name signed to that paper."

That brought the Chair to itself, and it read out the name,

" 'John Wharton *Billson*.' "

"There!" shouted Billson, "what have you got to say for yourself, now? And what kind of apology are you going to make to me and to this insulted house for the imposture which you have attempted to play here?"

"No apologies are due, sir; and as for the rest of it, I publicly charge you with pilfering my note from Mr. Burgess and substituting a copy of it signed with your own name. There is no other way by which you could have gotten hold of the test-remark; I alone, of living men, possessed the secret of its wording."

There was likely to be a scandalous state of things if this went on; everybody noticed with distress that the short-hand scribes were scribbling like mad; many people were crying "Chair, Chair! Order! order!" Burgess rapped with his gavel, and said:

"Let us not forget the proprieties due. There has evidently been a mistake somewhere, but surely that is all. If Mr. Wilson gave me an envelope — and I remember now that he did — I still have it."

He took one out of his pocket, opened it, glanced at it, looked surprised and worried, and stood silent a few moments. Then he waved his hand in a wandering and mechanical way, and made an effort or two to say something, then gave it up, despondently. Several voices cried out:

"Read it! read it! What is it?"

So he began in a dazed and sleep-walker fashion:

" ' *The remark which I made to the unhappy stranger was this:* "*You are far from being a bad man.* [The house gazed at him, marvelling.] *Go, and reform.*" ' [*Murmurs:* "Amazing! what can this mean?"] This one," said the Chair, "is signed Thurlow G. Wilson."

"There!" cried Wilson, "I reckon that settles it! I knew perfectly well my note was purloined."

"Purloined!" retorted Billson. "I'll let you know that neither you nor any man of your kidney must venture to —"

The Chair. "Order, gentlemen, order! Take your seats, both of you, please."

They obeyed, shaking their heads and grumbling angrily. The house was profoundly puzzled; it did not know what to do with this curious emergency. Presently Thompson got up. Thompson was the hatter. He would have liked to be a Nineteener; but such was not for him; his stock of hats was not considerable enough for the position. He said:

"Mr. Chairman, if I may be permitted to make a suggestion, can both of these gentlemen be right? I put it to you, sir, can both have happened to say the very same words to the stranger? It seems to me —"

The tanner got up and interrupted him. The tanner was a disgruntled man; he believed himself entitled to be a Nineteener, but he couldn't get recognition. It made him a little unpleasant in his ways and speech. Said he:

"Sho, *that's* not the point! *That* could happen — twice in a hundred years — but not the other thing. *Neither* of them gave the twenty dollars!" [*A ripple of applause.*]

Billson. "I did!"

Wilson. "I did!"

Then each accused the other of pilfering.

The Chair. "Order! Sit down, if you please — both of you. Neither of the notes has been out of my possession at any moment."

A Voice. "Good — that settles *that!*"

The Tanner. "Mr. Chairman, one thing is now plain: one of these men has been eavesdropping under the other one's bed, and filching family secrets. If it is not unparlia-

mentary to suggest it, I will remark that both are equal to it. [*The Chair.* "Order! order!"] I withdraw the remark, sir, and will confine myself to suggesting that *if* one of them has overheard the other reveal the test-remark to his wife, we shall catch him now."

A Voice. "How?"

The Tanner. "Easily. The two have not quoted the remark in exactly the same words. You would have noticed that, if there hadn't been a considerable stretch of time and an exciting quarrel inserted between the two readings."

A Voice. "Name the difference."

The Tanner. "The word *very* is in Billson's note, and not in the other."

Many Voices. "That's so — he's right."

The Tanner. "And so, if the Chair will examine the test-remark in the sack, we shall know which of these two frauds — [*The Chair.* "Order!"] — which of these two adventurers — [*The Chair.* "Order! order!"] — which of these two gentlemen — [*laughter and applause*] — is entitled to wear the belt as being the first dishonest blatherskite ever bred in this town — which he has dishonored, and which will be a sultry place for him from now out!" [*Vigorous applause.*]

Many Voices. "Open it! — open the sack!"

Mr. Burgess made a slit in the sack, slid his hand in and brought out an envelope. In it were a couple of folded notes. He said:

"One of these is marked, 'Not to be examined until all written communications which have been addressed to the Chair — if any — shall have been read.' The other is marked '*The Test.*' Allow me. It is worded — to wit:

" 'I do not require that the first half of the remark which was made to me by my benefactor shall be quoted with exactness, for it was not striking, and could be forgotten; but its closing fifteen words are quite striking, and I think easily rememberable; unless *these* shall be accurately reproduced, let the applicant be regarded as an impostor. My benefactor began by saying he seldom gave advice to any one, but that it always bore the hall-mark of high value when he did give it. Then he said this — and it has never faded from my memory: *You are far from being a bad man —*' ' "

Fifty Voices. "That settles it — the money's

Wilson's! Wilson! Wilson! Speech! Speech!"

People jumped up and crowded around Wilson, wringing his hand and congratulating fervently — meantime the Chair was hammering with the gavel and shouting:

"Order, gentlemen! Order! Order! Let me finish reading, please." When quiet was restored, the reading was resumed — as follows:

" ' "*Go, and reform — or, mark my words — some day, for your sins, you will die and go to hell or Hadleyburg* — TRY AND MAKE IT THE FORMER.*" ' "

A ghastly silence followed. First an angry cloud began to settle darkly upon the faces of the citizenship; after a pause the cloud began to rise, and a tickled expression tried to take its place; tried so hard that it was only kept under with great and painful difficulty; the reporters, the Brixtonites, and other strangers bent their heads down and shielded their faces with their hands, and managed to hold in by main strength and heroic courtesy. At this most inopportune time burst upon the stillness the roar of a solitary voice — Jack Halliday's:

"*That's* got the hall-mark on it!"

Then the house let go, strangers and all. Even Mr. Burgess's gravity broke down presently, then the audience considered itself officially absolved from all restraint, and it made the most of its privilege. It was a good long laugh, and a tempestuously wholehearted one, but it ceased at last — long enough for Mr. Burgess to try to resume, and for the people to get their eyes partially wiped; then it broke out again; and afterward yet again; then at last Burgess was able to get out these serious words:

"It is useless to try to disguise the fact — we find ourselves in the presence of a matter of grave import. It involves the honor of your town, it strikes at the town's good name. The difference of a single word between the test-remarks offered by Mr. Wilson and Mr. Billson was itself a serious thing, since it indicated that one or the other of these gentlemen had committed a theft —"

The two men were sitting limp, nerveless, crushed; but at these words both were electrified into movement, and started to get up —

"Sit down!" said the Chair, sharply, and

they obeyed. "That, as I have said, was a serious thing. And it was — but for only one of them. But the matter has become graver; for the honor of *both* is now in formidable peril. Shall I go even further, and say in inextricable peril? *Both* left out the crucial fifteen words." He paused. During several moments he allowed the pervading stillness to gather and deepen its impressive effects, then added: "There would seem to be but one way whereby this could happen. I ask these gentlemen — Was there *collusion?* — agreement?"

A low murmur sifted through the house; its import was, "He's got them both."

Billson was not used to emergencies; he sat in a helpless collapse. But Wilson was a lawyer. He struggled to his feet, pale and worried, and said:

"I ask the indulgence of the house while I explain this most painful matter. I am sorry to say what I am about to say, since it must inflict irreparable injury upon Mr. Billson, whom I have always esteemed and respected until now, and in whose invulnerability to temptation I entirely believed — as did you all. But for the preservation of my own honor I must speak — and with frankness. I confess with shame — and I now beseech your pardon for it — that I said to the ruined stranger all of the words contained in the test-remark, including the disparaging fifteen. [*Sensation.*] When the late publication was made I recalled them, and I resolved to claim the sack of coin, for by every right I was entitled to it. Now I will ask you to consider this point, and weigh it well: that stranger's gratitude to me that night knew no bounds; he said himself that he could find no words for it that were adequate, and that if he should ever be able he would repay me a thousandfold. Now, then, I ask you this: could I expect — could I believe — could I even remotely imagine — that, feeling as he did, he would do so ungrateful a thing as to add those quite unnecessary fifteen words to his test? — set a trap for me? — expose me as a slanderer of my own town before my own people assembled in a public hall? It was preposterous; it was impossible. His test would contain only the kindly opening clause of my remark. Of that I had no shadow of doubt. You would have thought as I did.

You would not have expected a base betrayal from one whom you had befriended and against whom you had committed no offence. And so, with perfect confidence, perfect trust, I wrote on a piece of paper the opening words — ending with 'Go, and reform,' — and signed it. When I was about to put it in an envelope I was called into my back office, and without thinking I left the paper lying open on my desk." He stopped, turned his head slowly toward Billson, waited a moment, then added: "I ask you to note this: when I returned, a little later, Mr. Billson was retiring by my street door." (*Sensation.*)

In a moment Billson was on his feet and shouting:

"It's a lie! It's an infamous lie!"

The Chair. "Be seated, sir! Mr. Wilson has the floor."

Billson's friends pulled him into his seat and quieted him, and Wilson went on:

"Those are the simple facts. My note was now lying in a different place on the table from where I had left it. I noticed that, but attached no importance to it, thinking a draught had blown it there. That Mr. Billson would read a private paper was a thing which could not occur to me; he was an honorable man, and he would be above that. If you will allow me to say it, I think his extra word '*very*' stands explained; it is attributable to a defect of memory. I was the only man in the world who could furnish here any detail of the test-mark — by *honorable* means. I have finished."

There is nothing in the world like a persuasive speech to fuddle the mental apparatus and upset the convictions and debauch the emotions of an audience not practised in the tricks and delusions of oratory. Wilson sat down victorious. The house submerged him in tides of approving applause; friends swarmed to him and shook him by the hand and congratulated him, and Billson was shouted down and not allowed to say a word. The Chair hammered and hammered with its gavel, and kept shouting,

"But let us proceed, gentlemen, let us proceed!"

At last there was a measurable degree of quiet, and the hatter said,

"But what is there to proceed with, sir, but to deliver the money?"

Voices. "That's it! That's it! Come forward, Wilson!"

The Hatter. "I move three cheers for Mr. Wilson, Symbol of the special virtue which —"

The cheers burst forth before he could finish; and in the midst of them — and in the midst of the clamor of the gavel also — some enthusiasts mounted Wilson on a big friend's shoulder and were going to fetch him in triumph to the platform. The Chair's voice now rose above the noise —

"Order! To your places! You forget that there is still a document to be read." When quiet had been restored he took up the document, and was going to read it, but laid it down again, saying, "I forgot; this is not to be read until all written communications received by me have first been read." He took an envelope out of his pocket, removed its enclosure, glanced at it — seemed astonished — held it out and gazed at it — stared at it.

Twenty or thirty voices cried out:

"What is it? Read it! read it!"

And he did — slowly, and wondering:

" 'The remark which I made to the stranger — [*Voices.* "Hello! how's this?"] — was this: "You are far from being a bad man. [*Voices.* "Great Scott!"] Go, and reform." ' [*Voice.* "Oh, saw my leg off!"] Signed by Mr. Pinkerton the banker."

The pandemonium of delight which turned itself loose now was of a sort to make the judicious weep. Those whose withers were unwrung laughed till the tears ran down; the reporters, in throes of laughter, set down disordered pothooks which would never in the world be decipherable; and a sleeping dog jumped up, scared out of its wits, and barked itself crazy at the turmoil. All manner of cries were scattered through the din: "We're getting rich — *two* Symbols of Incorruptibility! — without counting Billson!" "*Three!* — count Shadbelly in — we can't have too many!" "All right — Billson's elected!" "Alas, poor Wilson — victim of *two* thieves!"

A Powerful Voice. "Silence! The Chair's fished up something more out of its pocket."

Voices. "Hurrah! Is it something fresh? Read it! read! read!"

The Chair [*reading*]. " 'The remark which I

made,' etc. 'You are far from being a bad man. Go,' etc. Signed, 'Gregory Yates.' "

Tornado of Voices. "Four Symbols!" " 'Rah for Yates!" "Fish again!"

The house was in a roaring humor now, and ready to get all the fun out of the occasion that might be in it. Several Nineteeners, looking pale and distressed, got up and began to work their way toward the aisles, but a score of shouts went up:

"The doors, the doors — close the doors; no Incorruptible shall leave this place! Sit down, everybody!"

The mandate was obeyed.

"Fish again! Read! read!"

The Chair fished again, and once more the familiar words began to fall from its lips —

" 'You are far from being a bad man —' "

"Name! name! What's his name?"

" 'L. Ingoldsby Sargent.' "

"Five elected! Pile up the Symbols! Go on, go on!"

" 'You are far from being a bad —' "

"Name! name!"

" 'Nicholas Whitworth.' "

"Hooray! hooray! it's a symbolical day!"

Somebody wailed in, and began to sing this rhyme (leaving out "it's") to the lovely "Mikado" tune of "When a man's afraid of a beautiful maid"; the audience joined in, with joy; then, just in time, somebody contributed another line —

"And don't you this forget ——"

The house roared it out. A third line was at once furnished —

"Corruptibles far from Hadleyburg are ——"

The house roared that one too. As the last note died, Jack Halliday's voice rose high and clear, freighted with a final line —

"But the Symbols are here, you bet!"

That was sung, with booming enthusiasm. Then the happy house started in at the beginning and sang the four lines through twice, with immense swing and dash, and finished up with a crashing three-times-three and a tiger for "Hadleyburg the Incorruptible and all Symbols of it which we shall find worthy to receive the hall-mark to-night."

Then the shoutings at the Chair began again, all over the place:

"Go on! go on! Read! read some more! Read all you've got!"

"That's it — go on! We are winning eternal celebrity!"

A dozen men got up now and began to protest. They said that this farce was the work of some abandoned joker, and was an insult to the whole community. Without a doubt these signatures were all forgeries —

"Sit down! sit down! Shut up! You are confessing. We'll find *your* names in the lot."

"Mr. Chairman, how many of those envelopes have you got?"

The Chair counted.

"Together with those that have been already examined, there are nineteen."

A storm of derisive applause broke out.

"Perhaps they all contain the secret. I move that you open them all and read every signature that is attached to a note of that sort — and read also the first eight words of the note."

"Second the motion!"

It was put and carried — uproariously. Then poor old Richards got up, and his wife rose and stood at his side. Her head was bent down, so that none might see that she was crying. Her husband gave her his arm, and so supporting her, he began to speak in a quavering voice:

"My friends, you have known us two — Mary and me — all our lives, and I think you have liked us and respected us —"

The Chair interrupted him:

"Allow me. It is quite true — that which you are saying, Mr. Richards; this town *does* know you two; it *does* like you; it *does* respect you; more — it honors you and *loves* you —"

Halliday's voice rang out:

"That's the hall-marked truth, too! If the Chair is right, let the house speak up and say it. Rise! Now, then — hip! hip! hip! — all together!"

The house rose in mass, faced toward the old couple eagerly, filled the air with a snowstorm of waving handkerchiefs, and delivered the cheers with all its affectionate heart.

The Chair then continued:

"What I was going to say is this: We know your good heart, Mr. Richards, but this is not a time for the exercise of charity toward offenders. [Shouts of "Right! right!"] I see your generous purpose in your face, but I cannot allow you to plead for these men —"

"But I was going to —"

"Please take your seat, Mr. Richards. We must examine the rest of these notes — simple fairness to the men who have already been exposed requires this. As soon as that has been done — I give you my word for this — you shall be heard."

Many Voices. "Right! — the Chair is right — no interruption can be permitted at this stage! Go on! — the names! the names! — according to the terms of the motion!"

The old couple sat reluctantly down, and the husband whispered to the wife, "It is pitifully hard to have to wait; the shame will be greater than ever when they find we were only going to plead for *ourselves.*"

Straightway the jollity broke loose again with the reading of the names.

" 'You are far from being a bad man —' Signature, 'Robert J. Titmarsh.'

" 'You are far from being a bad man —' Signature, 'Eliphalet Weeks.'

" 'You are far from being a bad man —' Signature, 'Oscar B. Wilder.' "

At this point the house lit upon the idea of taking the eight words out of the Chairman's hands. He was not unthankful for that. Thenceforward he held up each note in its turn, and waited. The house droned out the eight words in a massed and measured and musical deep volume of sound (with a daringly close resemblance to a well-known church chant) — " 'You are f-a-r from being a b-a-a-a-d man.' " Then the Chair said, "Signature, 'Archibald Wilcox.' " And so on, and so on, name after name, and everybody had an increasingly and gloriously good time except the wretched Nineteen. Now and then, when a particularly shining name was called, the house made the Chair wait while it chanted the whole of the test-remark from the beginning to the closing words, "And go to hell or Hadleyburg — try and make it the for-or-m-e-r!" and in these special cases they added a grand and agonized and imposing "A-a-a-a-*men!*"

The list dwindled, dwindled, dwindled, poor old Richards keeping tally of the count, wincing when a name resembling his own was pronounced, and waiting in miserable suspense for the time to come when it would be his humiliating privilege to rise with Mary and finish his plea, which he was intending to word thus: ". . . for until now we have never done any wrong thing, but have gone our humble way unreproached. We are very poor, we are old, and have no chick nor child to help us; we were sorely tempted, and we fell. It was my purpose when I got up before to make confession and beg that my name might not be read out in this public place, for it seemed to us that we could not bear it; but I was prevented. It was just; it was our place to suffer with the rest. It has been hard for us. It is the first time we have ever heard our name fall from any one's lips — sullied. Be merciful — for the sake of the better days; make our shame as light to bear as in your charity you can." At this point in his revery Mary nudged him, perceiving that his mind was absent. The house was chanting, "You are f-a-r," etc.

"Be ready," Mary whispered. "Your name comes now; he has read eighteen."

The chant ended.

"Next! next! next!" came volleying from all over the house.

Burgess put his hand into his pocket. The old couple, trembling, began to rise, Burgess fumbled a moment, then said,

"I find I have read them all."

Faint with joy and surprise, the couple sank into their seats, and Mary whispered,

"Oh, bless God, we are saved! — he has lost ours — I wouldn't give this for a hundred of those sacks!"

The house burst out with its "Mikado" travesty, and sang it three times with ever-increasing enthusiasm, rising to its feet when it reached for the third time the closing line —

"But the Symbols are here, you bet!"

and finishing up with cheers and a tiger for "Hadleyburg purity and our eighteen immortal representatives of it."

Then Wingate, the saddler, got up and proposed cheers "for the cleanest man in town, the one solitary important citizen in it who didn't try to steal that money — Edward Richards."

They were given with great and moving heartiness; then somebody proposed that

Richards be elected sole Guardian and Symbol of the now Sacred Hadleyburg Tradition, with power and right to stand up and look the whole sarcastic world in the face.

Passed, by acclamation; then they sang the "Mikado" again, and ended it with,

"And there's *one* Symbol left, you bet!"

There was a pause; then —

A Voice. "Now, then, who's to get the sack?"

The Tanner (with bitter sarcasm). "That's easy. The money has to be divided among the eighteen Incorruptibles. They gave the suffering stranger twenty dollars apiece — and that remark — each in his turn — it took twenty-two minutes for the procession to move past. Staked the stranger — total contribution, $360. All they want is just the loan back — and interest — forty thousand dollars altogether."

Many Voices [derisively]. "That's it! Divvy! divvy! Be kind to the poor — don't keep them waiting!"

The Chair. "Order! I now offer the stranger's remaining document. It says: 'If no claimant shall appear [*grand chorus of groans*], I desire that you open the sack and count out the money to the principal citizens of your town, they to take it in trust [*Cries of "Oh! Oh! Oh!"*], and use it in such ways as to them shall seem best for the propagation and preservation of your community's noble reputation for incorruptible honesty [*more cries*] — a reputation to which their names and their efforts will add a new and far-reaching lustre.' [*Enthusiastic outburst of sarcastic applause.*] That seems to be all. No — here is a postscript:

" 'P. S. — CITIZENS OF HADLEYBURG: There is no test-remark — nobody made one. [*Great sensation.*] There wasn't any pauper stranger, nor any twenty-dollar contribution, nor any accompanying benediction and compliment — these are all inventions. [*General buzz and hum of astonishment and delight.*] Allow me to tell my story — it will take but a word or two. I passed through your town at a certain time, and received a deep offense which I had not earned. Any other man would have been content to kill one or two of you and call it square, but to me that would have been a triv-

ial revenge, and inadequate; for the dead do not *suffer*. Besides, I could not kill you all — and, anyway, made as I am, even that would not have satisfied me. I wanted to damage every man in the place, and every woman — and not in their bodies or in their estate, but in their vanity — the place where feeble and foolish people are most vulnerable. So I disguised myself and came back and studied you. You were easy game. You had an old and lofty reputation for honesty, and naturally you were proud of it — it was your treasure of treasures, the very apple of your eye. As soon as I found out that you carefully and vigilantly kept yourselves and your children *out of temptation*, I knew how to proceed. Why, you simple creatures, the weakest of all weak things is a virtue which has not been tested in the fire. I laid a plan, and gathered a list of names. My project was to corrupt Hadleyburg the Incorruptible. My idea was to make liars and thieves of nearly half a hundred smirchless men and women who had never in their lives uttered a lie or stolen a penny. I was afraid of Goodson. He was neither born nor reared in Hadleyburg. I was afraid that if I started to operate my scheme by getting my letter laid before you, you would say to yourselves, "Goodson is the only man among us who would give away twenty dollars to a poor devil" — and then you might not bite at my bait. But Heaven took Goodson; then I knew I was safe, and I set my trap and baited it. It may be that I shall not catch all the men to whom I mailed the pretended test secret, but I shall catch the most of them, if I know Hadleyburg nature. [*Voices.* "Right — he got every last one of them."] I believe they will even steal ostensible *gamble*-money, rather than miss, poor, tempted, and mistrained fellows. I am hoping to eternally and everlastingly squelch your vanity and give Hadleyburg a new renown — one that will *stick* — and spread far. If I have succeeded, open the sack and summon the Committee on Propagation and Preservation of the Hadleyburg Reputation.' "

A Cyclone of Voices. "Open it! Open it! The Eighteen to the front! Committee on Propagation of the Tradition! Forward — the Incorruptibles!"

The Chair ripped the sack wide, and gathered up a handful of bright, broad, yellow coins, shook them together, then examined them —

"Friends, they are only gilded disks of lead!"

There was a crashing outbreak of delight over this news, and when the noise had subsided, the tanner called out:

"By right of apparent seniority in this business, Mr. Wilson is Chairman of the Committee on Propagation of the Tradition. I suggest that he step forward on behalf of his pals, and receive in trust the money."

A Hundred Voices. "Wilson! Wilson! Wilson! Speech! Speech!"

Wilson [in a voice trembling with anger]. "You will allow me to say, and without apologies for my language, *damn* the money!"

A Voice. "Oh, and him a Baptist!"

A Voice. "Seventeen Symbols left! Step up, gentlemen, and assume your trust!"

There was a pause — no response.

The Saddler. "Mr. Chairman, we've got *one* clean man left, anyway, out of the late aristocracy; and he needs money, and deserves it. I move that you appoint Jack Halliday to get up there and auction off that sack of gilt twenty-dollar pieces, and give the result to the right man — the man whom Hadleyburg delights to honor — Edward Richards."

This was received with great enthusiasm, the dog taking a hand again; the saddler started the bids at a dollar, the Brixton folk and Barnum's representative fought hard for it, the people cheered every jump that the bids made, the excitement climbed moment by moment higher and higher, the bidders got on their mettle and grew steadily more and more daring, more and more determined, the jumps went from a dollar up to five, then to ten, then to twenty, then fifty, then to a hundred, then —

At the beginning of the auction Richards whispered in distress to his wife: "Oh, Mary, can we allow it? It — it — you see, it is an honor-reward, a testimonial to purity of character, and — and — can we allow it? Hadn't I better get up and — Oh, Mary, what ought we to do? — what do you think we —" [*Halliday's voice.* "Fifteen I'm bid! — fifteen for the sack! — twenty! — ah, thanks! — thirty — thanks again! Thirty, thirty, thirty! — do I hear forty? — forty it is! Keep the ball rolling, gentlemen, keep it rolling! — fifty! — thanks, noble Roman! — going at fifty, fifty, fifty! — seventy! — ninety! — splendid! — a hundred! — pile it up, pile it up! — hundred and twenty — forty! — just in time! — hundred and fifty! — TWO hundred! — superb! Do I hear two h— thanks! — two hundred and fifty! —"*]

"It is another temptation, Edward — I'm all in a tremble — but, oh, we've escaped *one* temptation, and that ought to warn us, to — [*"Six did I hear? — thanks! — six fifty, six f— SEVEN hundred!"*] And yet, Edward, when you think — nobody susp — [*"Eight hundred dollars! — hurrah! — make it nine! — Mr. Parsons, did I hear you say — thanks! — nine! — this noble sack of virgin lead going at only nine hundred dollars, gilding and all — come! do I hear — a thousand! — gratefully yours! — did some one say eleven? — a sack which is going to be the most celebrated in the whole Uni——"*] Oh, Edward" (*beginning to sob*), "we are *so* poor! — but — but — do as you think best — do as you think best."

Edward fell — that is, he sat still; sat with a conscience which was not satisfied, but which was overpowered by circumstances.

Meantime a stranger, who looked like an amateur detective gotten up as an impossible English earl, had been watching the evening's proceedings with manifest interest, and with a contented expression in his face; and he had been privately commenting to himself. He was now soliloquizing somewhat like this: "None of the Eighteen are bidding; that is not satisfactory; I must change that — the dramatic unities require it; they must buy the sack they tried to steal; they must pay a heavy price, too — some of them are rich. And another thing, when I make a mistake in Hadleyburg nature the man that puts that error upon me is entitled to a high honorarium, and some one must pay it. This poor old Richards has brought my judgment to shame; he is an honest man; — I don't understand it, but I acknowledge it. Yes, he saw my deuces — *and* with a straight flush, and by rights the pot is his. And it shall be a jackpot, too, if I can manage it. He disappointed me, but let that pass."

He was watching the bidding. At a thousand, the market broke; the prices tumbled swiftly. He waited — and still watched. One competitor dropped out; then another, and another. He put in a bid or two, now. When the bids had sunk to ten dollars, he added a five; some one raised him a three; he waited a moment, then flung in a fifty-dollar jump, and the sack was his — at $1282. The house broke out in cheers — then stopped; for he was on his feet, and had lifted his hand. He began to speak.

"I desire to say a word, and ask a favor. I am a speculator in rarities, and I have dealings with persons interested in numismatics all over the world. I can make a profit on this purchase, just as it stands; but there is a way, if I can get your approval, whereby I can make every one of these leaden twenty-dollar pieces worth its face in gold, and perhaps more. Grant me that approval, and I will give part of my gains to your Mr. Richards, whose invulnerable probity you have so justly and so cordially recognized to-night; his share shall be ten thousand dollars, and I will hand him the money to-morrow. [*Great applause from the house.* But the "invulnerable probity" made the Richardses blush prettily; however, it went for modesty, and did no harm.] If you will pass my proposition by a good majority — I would like a two-thirds vote — I will regard that as the town's consent, and that is all I ask. Rarities are always helped by any device which will rouse curiosity and compel remark. Now if I may have your permission to stamp upon the faces of each of these ostensible coins the names of the eighteen gentlemen who —"

Nine-tenths of the audience were on their feet in a moment — dog and all — and the proposition was carried with a whirlwind of approving applause and laughter.

They sat down, and all the Symbols except "Dr." Clay Harkness got up, violently protesting against the proposed outrage, and threatening to —

"I beg you not to threaten me," said the stranger, calmly. "I know my legal rights, and am not accustomed to being frightened at bluster." [*Applause.*] He sat down. "Dr." Harkness saw an opportunity here. He was one of the two very rich men of the place, and Pinkerton was the other. Harkness was pro-

prietor of a mint; that is to say, a popular patent medicine. He was running for the Legislature on one ticket, and Pinkerton on the other. It was a close race and a hot one, and getting hotter every day. Both had strong appetites for money; each had bought a great tract of land, with a purpose; there was going to be a new railway, and each wanted to be in the Legislature and help locate the route to his own advantage; a single vote might make the decision, and with it two or three fortunes. The stake was large, and Harkness was a daring speculator. He was sitting close to the stranger. He leaned over while one or another of the other Symbols was entertaining the house with protests and appeals, and asked, in a whisper,

"What is your price for the sack?"

"Forty thousand dollars."

"I'll give you twenty."

"No."

"Twenty-five."

"No."

"Say thirty."

"The price is forty thousand dollars; not a penny less."

"All right, I'll give it. I will come to the hotel at ten in the morning. I don't want it known; will see you privately."

"Very good." Then the stranger got up and said to the house:

"I find it late. The speeches of these gentlemen are not without merit, not without interest, not without grace; yet if I may be excused I will take my leave. I thank you for the great favor which you have shown me in granting my petition. I ask the Chair to keep the sack for me until to-morrow, and to hand these three five-hundred-dollar notes to Mr. Richards." They were passed up to the Chair. "At nine I will call for the sack, and at eleven will deliver the rest of the ten thousand to Mr. Richards in person, at his home. Good-night."

Then he slipped out, and left the audience making a vast noise, which was composed of a mixture of cheers, the "Mikado" song, dog-disapproval, and the chant, "You are f-a-r from being a b-a-a-d man — a-a-a-a-men!"

At home the Richardses had to endure congratulations and compliments until midnight. Then they were left to themselves.

They looked a little sad, and they sat silent and thinking. Finally Mary sighed and said,

"Do you think we are to blame, Edward — *much* to blame?" and her eyes wandered to the accusing triplet of big bank-notes lying on the table, where the congratulators had been gloating over them and reverently fingering them. Edward did not answer at once; then he brought out a sigh and said, hesitatingly:

"We — we couldn't help it, Mary. It — well, it was ordered. *All* things are."

Mary glanced up and looked at him steadily, but he didn't return the look. Presently she said:

"I thought congratulations and praises always tasted good. But — it seems to me, now — Edward?"

"Well?"

"Are you going to stay in the bank?"

"N-no."

"Resign?"

"In the morning — by note."

"It does seem best."

Richards bowed his head in his hands and muttered:

"Before, I was not afraid to let oceans of people's money pour through my hands, but — Mary, I am so tired, so tired —"

"We will go to bed."

At nine in the morning the stranger called for the sack and took it to the hotel in a cab. At ten Harkness had a talk with him privately. The stranger asked for and got five checks on a metropolitan bank — drawn to "Bearer," — four for $1500 each, and one for $34,000. He put one of the former in his pocket-book, and the remainder, representing $38,500, he put in an envelope, and with these he added a note, which he wrote after Harkness was gone. At eleven he called at the Richards house and knocked. Mrs. Richards peeped through the shutters, then went and received the envelope, and the stranger disappeared without a word. She came back flushed and a little unsteady on her legs, and gasped out:

"I am sure I recognized him! Last night it seemed to me that maybe I had seen him somewhere before."

"He is the man that brought the sack here?"

"I am almost sure of it."

"Then he is the ostensible Stephenson too, and sold every important citizen in this town with his bogus secret. Now if he has sent checks instead of money, we are sold too, after we thought we had escaped. I was beginning to feel fairly comfortable once more, after my night's rest, but the look of that envelope makes me sick. It isn't fat enough; $8500 in even the largest bank-notes makes more bulk than that."

"Edward, why do you object to checks?"

"Checks signed by Stephenson! I am resigned to take the $8500 if it could come in bank-notes — for it does seem that it was so ordered, Mary — but I have never had much courage, and I have not the pluck to try to market a check signed with that disastrous name. It would be a trap. That man tried to catch me; we escaped somehow or other; and now he is trying a new way. If it is checks ——"

"Oh, Edward, it is *too* bad!" and she held up the checks and began to cry.

"Put them in the fire! quick! we mustn't be tempted. It is a trick to make the world laugh at *us*, along with the rest, and — Give them to *me*, since you can't do it!" He snatched them and tried to hold his grip till he could get to the stove; but he was human, he was a cashier, and he stopped a moment to make sure of the signature. Then he came near to fainting.

"Fan me, Mary, fan me! They are the same as gold!"

"Oh, how lovely, Edward! Why?"

"Signed by Harkness. What can the mystery of that be, Mary?"

"Edward, do you think ——"

"Look here — look at this! Fifteen — fifteen — fifteen — thirty-four. Thirty-eight thousand five hundred! Mary, the sack isn't worth twelve dollars, and Harkness — apparently — has paid about par for it."

"And does it all come to us, do you think — instead of the ten thousand?"

"Why, it looks like it. And the checks are made to 'Bearer,' too."

"Is that good, Edward? What is it for?"

"A hint to collect them at some distant bank, I reckon. Perhaps Harkness doesn't want the matter known. What is that — a note?"

"Yes. It was with the checks."

It was in the "Stephenson" handwriting, but there was no signature. It said:

"I am a disappointed man. Your honesty is beyond the reach of temptation. I had a different idea about it, but I wronged you in that, and I beg pardon, and do it sincerely. I honor you — and that is sincere, too. This town is not worthy to kiss the hem of your garment. Dear sir, I made a square bet with myself that there were nineteen debauchable men in your self-righteous community. I have lost. Take the whole pot, you are entitled to it."

Richards drew a deep sigh, and said:

"It seems written with fire — it burns so. Mary — I am miserable again."

"I, too. Ah, dear, I wish ——"

"To think, Mary — he *believes* in me."

"Oh, don't, Edward — I can't bear it."

"If those beautiful words were deserved, Mary — and God knows I believed I deserved them once — I think I could give the forty thousand dollars for them. And I would put that paper away, as representing more than gold and jewels, and keep it always. But now — We could not live in the shadow of its accusing presence, Mary."

He put it in the fire.

A messenger arrived and delivered an envelope. Richards took from it a note and read it; it was from Burgess.

"You saved me, in a difficult time. I saved you last night. It was at cost of a lie, but I made the sacrifice freely, and out of a grateful heart. None in this village knows so well as I know how brave and good and noble you are. At bottom you cannot respect me, knowing as you do of that matter of which I am accused, and by the general voice condemned; but I beg that you will at least believe that I am a grateful man; it will help me to bear my burden.

[*Signed*] "BURGESS."

"Saved, once more. And on such terms!" He put the note in the fire. "I — I wish I were dead, Mary, I wish I were out of it all."

"Oh, these are bitter, bitter days, Edward. The stabs, through their very generosity, are so deep — and they come so fast!"

Three days before the election each of two thousand voters suddenly found himself in possession of a prized memento — one of the renowned bogus double-eagles. Around one of its faces was stamped these words: "THE REMARK I MADE TO THE POOR STRANGER WAS —" Around the other face was stamped these: "GO, AND REFORM. [SIGNED] PINKER-TON." Thus the entire remaining refuse of the renowned joke was emptied upon a single head, and with calamitous effect. It revived the recent vast laugh and concentrated it upon Pinkerton; and Harkness's election was a walk-over.

Within twenty-four hours after the Richardses had received their checks their consciences were quieting down, discouraged; the old couple were learning to reconcile themselves to the sin which they had committed. But they were to learn, now, that a sin takes on new and real terrors when there seems a chance that it is going to be found out. This gives it a fresh and most substantial and important aspect. At church the morning sermon was of the usual pattern; it was the same old things said in the same old way; they had heard them a thousand times and found them innocuous, next to meaningless, and easy to sleep under; but now it was different: the sermon seemed to bristle with accusations; it seemed aimed straight and specially at people who were concealing deadly sins. After church they got away from the mob of congratulators as soon as they could, and hurried homeward, chilled to the bone at they did not know what — vague, shadowy, indefinite fears. And by chance they caught a glimpse of Mr. Burgess as he turned a corner. He paid no attention to their nod of recognition! He hadn't seen it; but they did not know that. What could his conduct mean? It might mean — it might mean — oh, a dozen dreadful things. Was it possible that he knew that Richards could have cleared him of guilt in that bygone time, and had been silently waiting for a chance to even up accounts? At home, in their distress they got to imagining that their servant might have been in the next room listening when Richards revealed the secret to his wife that he knew of Burgess's innocence; next, Richards began to imagine that he had heard the swish of a gown in there at that time; next, he was sure he *had* heard it. They would call Sarah in, on a pretext, and watch her face: if she had been betraying them to Mr. Burgess, it would show in her manner. They asked her some questions — questions which were so random and incoherent and seemingly purposeless that the girl felt sure that the old people's minds had been affected by their sudden good fortune; the sharp and watchful gaze which they bent upon her frightened her, and that completed the business. She blushed, she became nervous and confused, and to the old people these were plain signs of guilt — guilt of some fearful sort or other — without doubt she was a spy and a traitor. When they were alone again they began to piece many unrelated things together and get horrible results out of the combination. When things had got about to the worst, Richards was delivered of a sudden gasp, and his wife asked,

"Oh, what is it? — what is it?"

"The note — Burgess's note! Its language was sarcastic, I see it now." He quoted: "'At bottom you cannot respect me, *knowing*, as you do, of *that matter* of which I am accused' — oh, it is perfectly plain, now, God help me! He knows that I know! You see the ingenuity of the phrasing. It was a trap — and like a fool, I walked into it. And Mary —?"

"Oh, it is dreadful — I know what you are going to say — he didn't return your transcript of the pretended test-remark."

"No — kept it to destroy us with. Mary, he has exposed us to some already. I know it I know it well. I saw it in a dozen faces after church. Ah, he wouldn't answer our nod of recognition — *he* knew what he had been doing!"

In the night the doctor was called. The news went around in the morning that the old couple were rather seriously ill — prostrated by the exhausting excitement growing out of their great windfall, the congratulations, and the late hours, the doctor said. The town was sincerely distressed; for these old people were about all it had left to be proud of, now.

Two days later the news was worse. The old couple were delirious, and were doing strange things. By witness of the nurses, Richards had exhibited checks — for $8500? No — for an amazing sum — $38,500! What could be the explanation of this gigantic piece of luck?

The following day the nurses had more news — and wonderful. They had concluded to hide the checks, lest harm come to them; but when they searched they were gone from under the patient's pillow — vanished away. The patient said:

"Let the pillow alone; what do you want?"

"We thought it best that the checks ——"

"You will never see them again — they are destroyed. They came from Satan. I saw the hell-brand on them, and I knew they were sent to betray me to sin." Then he fell to gabbling strange and dreadful things which were not clearly understandable, and which the doctor admonished them to keep to themselves.

Richards was right; the checks were never seen again.

A nurse must have talked in her sleep, for within two days the forbidden gabblings were the property of the town; and they were of a surprising sort. They seemed to indicate that Richards had been a claimant for the sack himself, and that Burgess had concealed that fact and then maliciously betrayed it.

Burgess was taxed with this and stoutly denied it. And he said it was not fair to attach weight to the chatter of a sick old man who was out of his mind. Still, suspicion was in the air, and there was much talk.

After a day or two it was reported that Mrs. Richards's delirious deliveries were getting to be duplicates of her husband's. Suspicion flamed up into conviction, now, and the town's pride in the purity of its one undiscredited important citizen began to dim down and flicker toward extinction.

Six days passed, then came more news. The old couple were dying. Richards's mind cleared in his latest hour, and he sent for Burgess. Burgess said:

"Let the room be cleared. I think he wishes to say something in privacy."

"No!" said Richards; "I want witnesses. I want you all to hear my confession, so that I may die a man, and not a dog. I was clean — artificially — like the rest; and like the rest I fell when temptation came. I signed a lie, and claimed the miserable sack. Mr. Burgess remembered that I had done him a service, and in gratitude (and ignorance) he suppressed my claim and saved me. You know the thing that was charged against Burgess years ago. My testimony, and mine alone, could have cleared him, and I was a coward, and left him to suffer disgrace —"

"No — no — Mr. Richards, you ——"

"My servant betrayed my secret to him —"

"No one has betrayed anything to me ——"

— "and then he did a natural and justifiable thing, he repented of the saving kindness 5 which he had done me, and he *exposed* me — as I deserved —"

"Never! — I make oath ——"

"Out of my heart I forgive him."

Burgess's impassioned protestations fell 10 upon deaf ears; the dying man passed away without knowing that once more he had done poor Burgess a wrong. The old wife died that night.

The last of the sacred Nineteen had fallen a prey to the fiendish sack; the town was stripped of the last rag of its ancient glory. Its mourning was not showy, but it was deep.

By act of the Legislature — upon prayer and petition — Hadleyburg was allowed to change its name to (never mind what — I will not give it away), and leave one word out of the motto that for many generations had graced the town's official seal.

It is an honest town once more, and the man will have to rise early that catches it napping again.

BRET HARTE (1836-1902)

The Far West, more than any other region, made "local color" prevail in American literature during the period of rising realism. This was largely the achievement of Bret Harte and Joaquin Miller. Ever since their time, the West has been a favorite theme of American writers and readers.

Harte was, to be sure, something of a stranger in the West. Born in Albany, New York, he was nineteen before he went with his mother to California. Here from 1856 to 1871 he led a varied life, in city and country, and acquired a fund of knowledge for his writing. In 1857 he was employed by the San Francisco *Golden Era*, in the columns of which appeared his earliest extant writings. In 1864 he was made secretary of the California Mint. He helped Mark Twain establish *The Californian* and became editor of the *Overland Monthly* when that publication was founded in 1868. In this journal he published the writings that suddenly extended his reputation from California to the Atlantic seaboard and England: "The Luck of Roaring Camp" (1868), "The Outcasts of Poker Flat" (1869), and "Plain Language from Truthful James," or "The Heathen Chinee" (1870).

No sooner had Harte thus given the Far West and the gold rush a place in American literature than he abandoned the land of his literary apprenticeship and made a triumphal return to the East. The *Atlantic Monthly* paid him ten thousand dollars for one year's writing. For seven years he wrote in New York. Two more he spent as consul in Crefeld, Germany, and the next five as consul at Glasgow. Thereafter he lived in England, continuing to write of California. He died in London.

Harte's works were collected in 20 volumes, 1896-1914. Short biographies are by G. R. Stewart, Jr. in *DAB* and John Erskine in *Leading American Novelists*, 1910; longer ones, by H. W. Boynton, 1903, H. C. Merwin, 1911, G. R. Stewart, Jr., 1931. *The Letters of Bret Harte* were edited by his son, G. B. Harte, 1926. On his place in American letters see F. L. Pattee, *American Literature Since 1870*, ch. 4, and *Development of the American Short Story*, ch. 10; also W. Blair, *Native American Humor*, 1937. Bret Harte is the subject of a well-informed book by J. B. Harrison in the *AWS*, 1941.

The Outcasts of Poker Flat

(1869)

As Mr. John Oakhurst, gambler, stepped into the main street of Poker Flat on the morning of the 23d of November, 1850, he was conscious of a change in its moral atmosphere since the preceding night. Two or three men, conversing earnestly together, ceased as he approached, and exchanged significant glances. There was a Sabbath lull in the air, which, in a settlement unused to Sabbath influences, looked ominous.

Mr. Oakhurst's calm, handsome face betrayed small concern in these indications. Whether he was conscious of any predisposing cause was another question. "I reckon they're after somebody," he reflected; "likely it's me." He returned to his pocket the handkerchief with which he had been whipping away the red dust of Poker Flat from his neat boots, and quietly discharged his mind of any further conjecture.

In point of fact, Poker Flat was "after somebody." It had lately suffered the loss of several thousand dollars, two valuable horses, and a prominent citizen. It was experiencing a spasm of virtuous reaction, quite as lawless and ungovernable as any of the acts that had provoked it. A secret committee had determined to rid the town of all improper persons. This was done permanently in regard of two men who were then hanging from the boughs of a sycamore in the gulch, and temporarily in the banishment of certain other objectionable characters. I regret to say that some of these were ladies. It is but due to the sex, however, to state that their impropriety was professional, and it was only in such easily established standards of evil that Poker Flat ventured to sit in judgment.

Mr. Oakhurst was right in supposing that he was included in this category. A few of the committee had urged hanging him as a possible example and a sure method of reimbursing themselves from his pockets of the sums he had won from them. "It's agin justice," said Jim Wheeler, "to let this yer young man from Roaring Camp — an entire stranger — carry away our money." But a crude sentiment of equity residing in the breasts of those who had been fortunate enough to win from Mr. Oakhurst overruled this narrower local prejudice.

Mr. Oakhurst received his sentence with philosophic calmness, none the less coolly that he was aware of the hesitation of his judges. He was too much of a gambler not to accept fate. With him life was at best an uncertain game, and he recognized the usual percentage in favor of the dealer.

A body of armed men accompanied the deported wickedness of Poker Flat to the outskirts of the settlement. Besides Mr. Oakhurst, who was known to be a coolly desperate man, and for whose intimidation the armed escort was intended, the expatriated party consisted of a young woman familiarly known as "The Duchess"; another who had won the title of "Mother Shipton"; and "Uncle Billy," a suspected sluice-robber and confirmed drunkard. The cavalcade provoked no comments from the spectators, nor was any word uttered by the escort. Only when the gulch which marked the uttermost limit of Poker Flat was reached, the leader spoke briefly and to the point. The exiles were forbidden to return at the peril of their lives.

As the escort disappeared, their pent-up feelings found vent in a few hysterical tears from the Duchess, some bad language from Mother Shipton, and a Parthian volley of expletives from Uncle Billy. The philosophic Oakhurst alone remained silent. He listened calmly to Mother Shipton's desire to cut somebody's heart out, to the repeated statements of the Duchess that she would die in the road, and to the alarming oaths that seemed to be bumped out of Uncle Billy as he rode forward. With the easy good humor characteristic of his class, he insisted upon exchanging his own riding-horse, "Five-Spot," for the sorry mule which the Duchess rode. But even this act did not draw the party into any closer sympathy. The young woman readjusted her somewhat draggled plumes with a feeble, faded coquetry: Mother Shipton eyed the possessor of "Five-Spot" with malevolence, and Uncle Billy included the whole party in one sweeping anathema.

The road to Sandy Bar — a camp that, not having as yet experienced the regenerating influences of Poker Flat, consequently seemed to offer some invitation to the emigrants — lay over a steep mountain range. It was distant a day's severe travel. In that advanced season the party soon passed out of the moist, temperate regions of the foothills into the dry, cold, bracing air of the Sierras. The trail was narrow and difficult. At noon the Duchess, rolling out of her saddle upon the ground, declared her intention of going no farther, and the party halted.

The spot was singularly wild and impressive. A wooded amphitheatre, surrounded on three sides by precipitous cliffs of naked granite, sloped gently toward the crest of another precipice that overlooked the valley. It was, undoubtedly, the most suitable spot for a camp, had camping been advisable. But Mr. Oakhurst knew that scarcely half the journey to Sandy Bar was accomplished, and the party were not equipped or provisioned for delay. This fact he pointed out to his companions curtly, with a philosophic commentary on the folly of "throwing up their hand before the game was played out." But they were furnished with liquor, which in this emergency stood them in place of food, fuel, rest, and prescience. In spite of his remonstrances, it was not long before they were more or less under its influence. Uncle Billy passed rapidly from a bellicose state into one of stupor, the Duchess became maudlin, and Mother Shipton snored. Mr. Oakhurst alone remained erect leaning against a rock calmly surveying them.

Mr. Oakhurst did not drink. It interfered with a profession which required coolness, impassiveness, and presence of mind, and, in his own language, he "couldn't afford it." As he gazed at his recumbent fellow exiles, the loneliness begotten of his pariah trade, his habits of life, his very vices, for the first time seriously oppressed him. He bestirred himself in dusting his black clothes, washing his hands and face, and other acts characteristic of his studiously neat habits and for a moment forgot his annoyance. The thought of deserting his weaker and more pitiable companions never perhaps occurred to him. Yet he could not help feeling the want of that excitement which, singularly enough, was most conducive to that calm equanimity for which he was notorious. He looked at the

gloomy walls that rose a thousand feet sheer above the circling pines around him, at the sky ominously clouded, at the valley below, already deepening into shadow; and, doing so, suddenly he heard his own name called.

A horseman slowly ascended the trail. In the fresh, open face of the newcomer Mr. Oakhurst recognized Tom Simson, otherwise known as "The Innocent," of Sandy Bar. He had met him some months before over a "little game," and had, with perfect equanimity, won the entire fortune — amounting to some forty dollars — of that guileless youth. After the game was finished, Mr. Oakhurst drew the youthful speculator behind the door and thus addressed him: "Tommy, you're a good little man, but you can't gamble worth a cent. Don't try it over again." He then handed him his money back, pushed him gently from the room, and so made a devoted slave of Tom Simson.

There was a remembrance of this in his boyish and enthusiastic greeting of Mr. Oakhurst. He had started, he said, to go to Poker Flat to seek his fortune. "Alone?" No, not exactly alone; in fact (a giggle), he had run away with Piney Woods. Didn't Mr. Oakhurst remember Piney? She that used to wait on the table at the Temperance House? They had been engaged a long time, but old Jake Woods had objected, and so they had run away, and were going to Poker Flat to be married, and here they were. And they were tired out, and how lucky it was they had found a place to camp, and company. All this the Innocent delivered rapidly, while Piney, a stout, comely damsel of fifteen emerged from behind the pine-tree, where she had been blushing unseen, and rode to the side of her lover.

Mr. Oakhurst seldom troubled himself with sentiment, still less with propriety; but he had a vague idea that the situation was not fortunate. He retained, however, his presence of mind sufficiently to kick Uncle Billy, who was about to say something, and Uncle Billy was sober enough to recognize in Mr. Oakhurst's kick a superior power that would not bear trifling. He then endeavored to dissuade Tom Simson from delaying further, but in vain. He even pointed out the fact that there was no provision nor means of making a camp. But, unluckily, the Innocent met this objection by assuring the party that he was provided with an extra mule loaded with provisions, and by the discovery of a rude attempt at a log house near the trail. "Piney can stay with Mrs. Oakhurst," said the Innocent, pointing to the Duchess, "and I can shift for myself."

Nothing but Mr. Oakhurst's admonishing foot saved Uncle Billy from bursting into a roar of laughter. As it was, he felt compelled to retire up the cañon until he could recover his gravity. There he confided the joke to the tall pine-trees, with many slaps of his leg, contortions of his face, and the usual profanity. But when he returned to the party, he found them seated by a fire — for the air had grown strangely chill and the sky overcast — in apparently amicable conversation. Piney was actually talking in an impulsive girlish fashion to the Duchess, who was listening with an interest and animation she had not shown for many days. The Innocent was holding forth, apparently with equal effect, to Mr. Oakhurst and Mother Shipton, who was actually relaxing into amiability. "Is this yer a d—d picnic?" said Uncle Billy, with inward scorn, as he surveyed the sylvan group, the glancing firelight, and the tethered animals in the foreground. Suddenly an idea mingled with the alcoholic fumes that disturbed his brain. It was apparently of a jocular nature, for he felt impelled to slap his leg again and cram his fist into his mouth.

As the shadows crept slowly up the mountain, a slight breeze rocked the tops of the pine-trees and moaned through their long and gloomy aisles. The ruined cabin, patched and covered with pine boughs, was set apart for the ladies. As the lovers parted, they unaffectedly exchanged a kiss, so honest and sincere that it might have been heard above the swaying pines. The frail Duchess and the malevolent Mother Shipton were probably too stunned to remark upon this last evidence of simplicity, and so turned without a word to the hut. The fire was replenished, the men lay down before the door, and in a few minutes were asleep.

Mr. Oakhurst was a light sleeper. Toward morning he awoke benumbed and cold. As he stirred the dying fire, the wind, which was now blowing strongly, brought to his cheek that which caused the blood to leave it, — snow!

He started to his feet with the intention of awakening the sleepers, for there was no time to lose. But turning to where Uncle Billy had been lying, he found him gone. A suspicion leaped to his brain, and a curse to his lips. He ran to the spot where the mules had been tethered — they were no longer there. The tracks were already rapidly disappearing in the snow.

The momentary excitement brought Mr. Oakhurst back to the fire with his usual calm. He did not waken the sleepers. The Innocent slumbered peacefully, with a smile on his good-humored, freckled face; the virgin Piney slept beside her frailer sisters as sweetly as though attended by celestial guardians; and Mr. Oakhurst, drawing his blanket over his shoulders, stroked his mustaches and waited for the dawn. It came slowly in a whirling mist of snowflakes that dazzled and confused the eye. What could be seen of the landscape appeared magically changed. He looked over the valley, and summed up the present and future in two words, "Snowed in!"

A careful inventory of the provisions, which fortunately for the party, had been stored within the hut, and so escaped the felonious fingers of Uncle Billy, disclosed the fact that with care and prudence they might last ten days longer. "That is," said Mr. Oakhurst *sotto voce* to the Innocent, "if you're willing to board us. If you ain't — and perhaps you'd better not — you can wait till Uncle Billy gets back with provisions." For some occult reason, Mr. Oakhurst could not bring himself to disclose Uncle Billy's rascality, and so offered the hypothesis that he had wandered from the camp and had accidentally stampeded the animals. He dropped a warning to the Duchess and Mother Shipton, who of course knew the facts of their associate's defection. "They'll find out the truth about us *all* when they find out anything," he added significantly, "and there's no good frightening them now."

Tom Simson not only put all his worldly store at the disposal of Mr. Oakhurst, but seemed to enjoy the prospect of their enforced seclusion. "We'll have a good camp for a week, and then the snow'll melt, and we'll all go back together." The cheerful gayety of the young man and Mr. Oakhurst's calm infected the others. The Innocent with the aid of pine boughs, extemporized a thatch for the roofless cabin, and the Duchess directed Piney in the rearrangement of the interior with a taste and tact that opened the blue eyes of that provincial maiden to their fullest extent. "I reckon now you're used to fine things at Poker Flat," said Piney. The Duchess turned away sharply to conceal something that reddened her cheeks through their professional tint, and Mother Shipton requested Piney not to "chatter." But when Mr. Oakhurst returned from a weary search for the trail, he heard the sound of happy laughter echoed from the rocks. He stopped in some alarm, and his thoughts first naturally reverted to the whiskey, which he had prudently cachéd. "And yet it don't somehow sound like whiskey," said the gambler. It was not until he caught sight of the blazing fire through the still blinding storm, and the group around it, that he settled to the conviction that it was "square fun."

Whether Mr. Oakhurst had cachéd his cards with the whiskey as something debarred the free access of the community, I cannot say. It was certain that, in Mother Shipton's words, he "didn't say 'cards' once" during that evening. Haply the time was beguiled by an accordion, produced somewhat ostentatiously by Tom Simson from his pack. Notwithstanding some difficulties attending the manipulation of this instrument, Piney Woods managed to pluck several reluctant melodies from its keys, to an accompaniment by the Innocent on a pair of bone castanets. But the crowning festivity of the evening was reached in a rude camp-meeting hymn, which the lovers, joining hands, sang with great earnestness and vociferation. I fear that a certain defiant tone and Covenanter's swing to its chorus, rather than any devotional quality, caused it speedily to infect the others, who at last joined in the refrain:

"I'm proud to live in the service of the Lord,
    And I'm bound to die in His army."

The pines rocked, the storm eddied and whirled above the miserable group, and the flames of their altar leaped heavenward, as if in token of the vow.

At midnight the storm abated, the rolling clouds parted, and the stars glittered keenly above the sleeping camp. Mr. Oakhurst, whose professional habits had enabled him to live on the smallest possible amount of sleep, in dividing the watch with Tom Simson, somehow managed to take upon himself the greater part of that duty. He excused himself to the Innocent by saying that he had "often been a week without sleep." "Doing what?" asked Tom. "Poker!" replied Oakhurst sententiously. "When a man gets a streak of luck — nigger-luck — he don't get tired. The luck gives in first. Luck," continued the gambler reflectively, "is a mighty queer thing. All you know about it for certain is that it's bound to change. And it's finding out when it's going to change that makes you. We've had a streak of bad luck since we left Poker Flat — you come along, and slap you get into it, too. If you can hold your cards right along you're all right. For," added the gambler, with cheerful irrelevance —

" 'I'm proud to live in the service of the Lord,
        And I'm bound to die in His army.' "

The third day came, and the sun, looking through the white-curtained valley, saw the outcasts divide their slowly decreasing store of provisions for the morning meal. It was one of the peculiarities of that mountain climate that its rays diffused a kindly warmth over the wintry landscape, as if in regretful commiseration of the past. But it revealed drift on drift of snow piled high around the hut — a hopeless, uncharted, trackless sea of white lying below the rocky shores to which the castaways still clung. Through the marvelously clear air the smoke of the pastoral village of Poker Flat rose miles away. Mother Shipton saw it, and from a remote pinnacle of her rocky fastness hurled in that direction a final malediction. It was her last vituperative attempt, and perhaps for that reason was invested with a certain degree of sublimity. It did her good, she privately informed the Duchess. "Just you go out there and cuss, and see." She then set herself to the task of amusing "the child," as she and the Duchess were pleased to call Piney. Piney was no chicken, but it was a soothing and original theory of the pair thus to account for the fact that she didn't swear and wasn't improper.

When night crept up again through the gorges, the reedy notes of the accordion rose and fell in fitful spasms and long-drawn gasps by the flickering campfire. But music failed to fill entirely the aching void left by insufficient food, and a new diversion was proposed by Piney — story-telling. Neither Mr. Oakhurst nor his female companions caring to relate their personal experiences, this plan would have failed too, but for the Innocent. Some months before he had chanced upon a stray copy of Mr. Pope's ingenious translation of the Iliad. He now proposed to narrate the principal incidents of that poem — having thoroughly mastered the argument and fairly forgotten the words — in the current vernacular of Sandy Bar. And so for the rest of that night the Homeric demigods again walked the earth. Trojan bully and wily Greek wrestled in the winds, and the great pines in the cañon seemed to bow to the wrath of the son of Peleus. Mr. Oakhurst listened with quiet satisfaction. Most especially was he interested in the fate of "Ash-heels," as the Innocent persisted in denominating the "swift-footed Achilles."

So, with small food and much of Homer and the accordion, a week passed over the heads of the outcasts. The sun again forsook them, and again from leaden skies the snowflakes were sifted over the land. Day by day closer around them drew the snowy circle, until at last they looked from their prison over drifted walls of dazzling white, that towered twenty feet above their heads. It became more and more difficult to replenish their fires, even from the fallen trees beside them, now half hidden in the drifts. And yet no one complained. The lovers turned from the dreary prospect and looked into each other's eyes, and were happy. Mr. Oakhurst settled himself coolly to the losing game before him. The Duchess, more cheerful than she had been, assumed the care of Piney. Only Mother Shipton — once the strongest of the party — seemed to sicken

and fade. At midnight on the tenth day she called Oakhurst to her side. "I'm going," she said, in a voice of querulous weakness, "but don't say anything about it. Don't waken the kids. Take the bundle from under my head, and open it." Mr. Oakhurst did so. It contained Mother Shipton's rations for the last week, untouched. "Give 'em to the child," she said, pointing to the sleeping Piney. "You've starved yourself," said the gambler. "That's what they call it," said the woman querulously, as she lay down again, and, turning her face to the wall, passed quietly away.

The accordion and the bones were put aside that day, and Homer was forgotten. When the body of Mother Shipton had been committed to the snow, Mr. Oakhurst took the Innocent aside, and showed him a pair of snow shoes, which he had fashioned from the old pack-saddle. "There's one chance in a hundred to save her yet," he said, pointing to Piney; "but it's there," he added, pointing toward Poker Flat. "If you can reach there in two days she's safe." "And you?" asked Tom Simson. "I'll stay here," was the curt reply.

The lovers parted with a long embrace. "You are not going, too?" said the Duchess, as she saw Mr. Oakhurst apparently waiting to accompany him. "As far as the cañon," he replied. He turned suddenly and kissed the Duchess, leaving her pallid face aflame, and her trembling limbs rigid with amazement.

Night came, but not Mr. Oakhurst. It brought the storm again and the whirling snow. Then the Duchess, feeding the fire, found that some one had quietly piled beside the hut enough fuel to last a few days longer. The tears rose to her eyes, but she hid them from Piney.

The women slept but little. In the morning, looking into each other's faces, they read their fate. Neither spoke, but Piney, accepting the position of the stronger, drew near and placed her arm around the Duchess's waist. They kept this attitude for the rest of the day. That night the storm reached its greatest fury, and rending asunder the protecting vines, invaded the very hut.

Toward morning they found themselves

unable to feed the fire, which gradually died away. As the embers slowly blackened, the Duchess crept closer to Piney, and broke the silence of many hours: "Piney, can you pray?" "No, dear," said Piney simply. The Duchess, without knowing exactly why, felt relieved, and, putting her head upon Piney's shoulder, spoke no more. And so reclining, the younger and purer pillowing the head of her soiled sister upon her virgin breast, they fell asleep.

The wind lulled as if it feared to waken them. Feathery drifts of snow, shaken from the long pine boughs, flew like white winged birds, and settled about them as they slept. The moon through the rifted clouds looked down upon what had been the camp. But all human stain, all trace of earthly travail, was hidden beneath the spotless mantle mercifully flung from above.

They slept all that day and the next, nor did they waken when voices and footsteps broke the silence of the camp. And when pitying fingers brushed the snow from their wan faces, you could scarcely have told from the equal peace that dwelt upon them which was she that had sinned. Even the law of Poker Flat recognized this, and turned away, leaving them still locked in each other's arms.

But at the head of the gulch, on one of the largest pine-trees, they found the deuce of clubs pinned to the bark with a bowie-knife. It bore the following, written in pencil in a firm hand:

†

BENEATH THIS TREE
LIES THE BODY
OF
JOHN OAKHURST,
WHO STRUCK A STREAK OF BAD LUCK
ON THE 23D OF NOVEMBER 1850,
AND
HANDED IN HIS CHECKS
ON THE 7TH DECEMBER, 1850.

⸸

And pulseless and cold, with a Derringer by his side and a bullet in his heart, though still calm as in life, beneath the snow lay he who at once was the strongest and yet the weakest of the outcasts of Poker Flat.

SIDNEY LANIER (1842–1881)

Lanier's was the first poetic work of high promise to emerge from the desolate South of the Reconstruction days. Of his more distinguished Southern contemporaries, Henry Timrod of Charleston had died in 1867, having published but one small volume of poems; and Paul Hamilton Hayne, who later collected Timrod's verse, produced little during the post-war period. All three were Confederate veterans whose careers and fortunes were wrecked by the War, and who endured, as Timrod put it, "beggary, starvation, . . . bitter grief, utter want of hope." From them to the Southern Agrarians and William Faulkner there is a demonstrable continuity of thought and feeling on the subject of Southern land, life, and ideals.

Born in Macon, Georgia, graduated from Oglethorpe College, Georgia, in 1860, Lanier had served four years in the Confederate army, had been captured running a blockade, and emerged from a Federal prison at the end of the war with tuberculosis. He tried school teaching, he tried the law, he wrote a novel (*Tiger Lilies*, 1867), he wrote and printed poems. An excellent musician, he was appointed first flutist of the Peabody Symphony Orchestra of Baltimore in 1873, and two years later he drew considerable attention to his writing with the poem "Corn," which he published in *Lippincott's Magazine*.

The promise of this and other work gained him the friendship of Bayard Taylor, through whom he was selected to write the cantata for the Centennial Exposition in

Philadelphia. He published a volume of *Poems* in 1877, and was made lecturer on English literature in Johns Hopkins University in 1879. The next year appeared *The Science of English Verse*. But tuberculosis was upon him. He fled to the Carolina mountains, and died there at the age of thirty-nine.

Like Poe and Whitman and many other moderns, Lanier held music to be the supreme art. His flute-playing vied with his writing as a medium of expression; the relation of music to verse was the theme of *The Science of English Verse;* and his own achievement in the writing of musical poetry is noteworthy.

The Centennial edition of Lanier was published in 10 volumes in 1946. There are lives by Edwin Mims, 1905, and A. H. Starke, 1932. Selected poems and a critical estimate are included in the useful collection of *Southern Poets* edited for the *AWS* by E. W. Parks, 1936.

The Symphony

(1875)

"O Trade!   O Trade! would thou wert
    dead!
The Time needs heart — 'tis tired of head:
We're all for love," the violins said.
"Of what avail the rigorous tale
Of bill for coin and box for bale?   5
Grant thee, O Trade! thine uttermost hope:
Level red gold with blue sky-slope,
And base it deep as devils grope:
When all's done, what hast thou won
Of the only sweet that's under the sun?   10
Ay, canst thou buy a single sigh
Of true love's least, least ecstasy?"
Then, with a bridegroom's heart-beats trem-
    bling,
All the mightier strings assembling
Ranged them on the violins' side   15
As when the bridegroom leads the bride,
And, heart in voice, together cried:
"Yea, what avail the endless tale
Of gain by cunning and plus by sale?
Look up the land, look down the land,   20
The poor, the poor, the poor, they stand
Wedged by the pressing of Trade's hand
Against an inward-opening door
That pressure tightens evermore:
They sigh a monstrous foul-air sigh   25
For the outside leagues of liberty,
Where Art, sweet lark, translates the sky
Into a heavenly melody.
'Each day, all day' (these poor folks say),
'In the same old year-long, drear-long way,
We weave in the mills and heave in the
    kilns,   31
We sieve mine-meshes under the hills.

And thieve much gold from the Devil's bank
    tills,
To relieve, O God, what manner of ills? —
The beasts, they hunger, and eat, and die;   35
And so do we, and the world's a sty;
Hush, fellow-swine: why nuzzle and cry?
Swinehood hath no remedy
Say many men, and hasten by,
Clamping the nose and blinking the eye.   40
But who said once, in the lordly tone,
Man shall not live by bread alone
But all that cometh from the Throne?
      Hath God said so?
      But Trade saith *No:*   45
And the kilns and the curt-tongued mills say
      Go!
There's plenty that can, if you can't: we know.
Move out, if you think you're underpaid.
The poor are prolific; we're not afraid;
Trade is trade.' "   50
Thereat this passionate protesting
Meekly changed, and softened till
It sank to sad requesting
And suggesting sadder still:
"And oh, if men might sometime see   55
How piteous-false the poor decree
That trade no more than trade must be!
Does business mean. *Die, you — live, I?*
Then 'Trade is trade' but sings a lie:
'Tis only war grown miserly.   60
If business is battle, name it so:
War-crimes less will shame it so,
And widows less will blame it so.
Alas, for the poor to have some part
In yon sweet living lands of Art,   65
Makes problem not for head, but heart.
Vainly might Plato's brain revolve it:
Plainly the heart of a child could solve it."

And then, as when from words that seem but
　　rude
We pass to silent pain that sits abrood　　70
Back in our heart's great dark and solitude,
So sank the strings to gentle throbbing
Of long chords change-marked with sob-
　　bing —
Motherly sobbing, not distinctlier heard
Than half wing-openings of the sleeping
　　bird
Some dream of danger to her young hath
　　stirred.　　76
Then stirring and demurring ceased, and lo!
Every least ripple of the strings' song-flow
Died to a level with each level bow
And made a great chord tranquil-surfaced
　　so,　　80
As a brook beneath his curving bank doth go
To linger in the sacred dark and green
Where many boughs the still pool overlean
And many leaves make shadow with their
　　sheen.
　　　　But presently　　85
A velvet flute-note fell down pleasantly
Upon the bosom of that harmony,
And sailed and sailed incessantly,
As if a petal from a wild-rose blown
Had fluttered down upon that pool of tone
And boatwise dropped o' the convex side　　91
And floated down the glassy tide
And clarified and glorified
The solemn spaces where the shadows bide.
From the warm concave of that fluted note
Somewhat, half song, half odor, forth did
　　float,　　96
As if a rose might somehow be a throat:
"When Nature from her far-off glen
Flutes her soft messages to men,
　　The flute can say them o'er again;　　100
　　Yea, Nature, singing sweet and lone,
Breathes through life's strident polyphone
The flute-voice in the world of tone.
　　　Sweet friends,
　　Man's love ascends　　105
To finer and diviner ends
Than man's mere thought e'er comprehends:
For I, e'en I,
As here I lie,
A petal on a harmony,　　110
Demand of Science whence and why
Man's tender pain, man's inward cry,
When he doth gaze on earth and sky?

I am not overbold:
　　I hold　　115
Full powers from Nature manifold.
I speak for each no-tonguèd tree
That, spring by spring, doth nobler be,
And dumbly and most wistfully
His mighty prayerful arms outspreads　　120
Above men's oft-unheeding heads,
And his big blessing downward sheds.
I speak for all-shaped blooms and leaves,
Lichens on stones and moss on eaves,
Grasses and grains in ranks and sheaves;　　125
Broad-fronded ferns and keen-leaved canes,
And briery mazes bounding lanes,
And marsh-plants, thirsty-cupped for rains,
And milky stems and sugary veins;
For every long-armed woman-vine　　130
That round a piteous tree doth twine;
For passionate odors, and divine
Pistils, and petals crystalline;
All purities of shady springs,
All shynesses of film-winged things　　135
That fly from tree-trunks and bark-rings;
All modesties of mountain-fawns
That leap to covert from wild lawns,
And tremble if the day but dawns;
All sparklings of small beady eyes　　140
Of birds, and sidelong glances wise
Wherewith the jay hints tragedies;
All piquancies of prickly burs,
And smoothnesses of downs and furs,
Of eiders and of minevers;　　145
All limpid honeys that do lie
At stamen-bases, nor deny
The humming-birds' fine roguery,
Bee-thighs, nor any butterfly;
All gracious curves of slender wings,　　150
Bark-mottlings, fibre-spiralings,
Fern-wavings and leaf-flickerings;
Each dial-marked leaf and flower-bell
Wherewith in every lonesome dell
Time to himself his hours doth tell;　　155
All tree-sounds, rustlings of pine-cones,
Wind-sighings, doves' melodious moans,
And night's unearthly under-tones;
All placid lakes and waveless deeps,
All cool reposing mountain-steeps,　　160
Vale-calms and tranquil lotos-sleeps; —
Yea, all fair forms, and sounds, and lights,
And warmths, and mysteries, and nights,
Of Nature's utmost depths and heights.
— These doth my timid tongue present,　　165

Their mouthpiece and leal instrument
And servant, all love-eloquent.
I heard, when '*All for love*' the violins cried:
So, Nature calls through all her system
    wide,
Give me thy love, O man, so long denied. 170
Much time is run, and man hath changed
    his ways,
Since Nature, in the antique fable-days,
Was hid from man's true love by proxy fays,
False fauns and rascal gods that stole her
    praise.
The nymphs, cold creatures of man's colder
    brain, 175
Chilled Nature's streams till man's warm
    heart was fain
Never to lave its love in them again.
Later, a sweet Voice *Love thy neighbor* said,
Then first the bounds of neighborhood out-
    spread
Beyond all confines of old ethnic dread. 180
Vainly the Jew might wag his covenant head:
'*All men are neighbors,*' so the sweet Voice said.
So, when man's arms had circled all man's
    race,
The liberal compass of his warm embrace
Stretched bigger yet in the dark bounds of
    space; 185
With hands a-grope he felt smooth Nature's
    grace,
Drew her to breast and kissed her sweet-heart
    face:
Yea, man found neighbors in great hills and
    trees
And streams and clouds and suns and birds
    and bees,
And throbbed with neighbor-loves in loving
    these. 190
But oh, the poor! the poor! the poor!
That stand by the inward-opening door
Trade's hand doth tighten ever more,
And sigh their monstrous foul-air sigh
For the outside hills of liberty, 195
Where Nature spreads her wild blue sky
For Art to make into melody!
Thou Trade! thou king of the modern days!
    Change thy ways,
    Change thy ways; 200
Let the sweaty laborers file
    A little while,
    A little while,
Where Art and Nature sing and smile.

Trade! is thy heart all dead, all dead? 205
And hast thou nothing but a head?
I'm all for heart," the flute-voice said.
And into sudden silence fled,
Like as a blush that while 'tis red
Dies to a still, still white instead. 210
    Thereto a thrilling calm succeeds,
Till presently the silence breeds
A little breeze among the reeds
That seems to blow by sea-marsh weeds:
Then from the gentle stir and fret 215
Sings out the melting clarionet,
Like as a lady sings while yet
Her eyes with salty tears are wet.
"O Trade! O Trade!" the Lady said,
"I too will wish thee utterly dead 220
If all thy heart is in thy head.
For O my God! and O my God!
What shameful ways have women trod
At beckoning of Trade's golden rod!
Alas when sighs are traders' lies, 225
And heart's-ease eyes and violet eyes
    Are merchandise!
O purchased lips that kiss with pain!
O cheeks coin-spotted with smirch and stain!
O trafficked hearts that break in twain! 230
— And yet what wonder at my sisters'
    crime?
So hath Trade withered up Love's sinewy
    prime,
Men love not women as in olden time.
Ah, not in these cold merchantable days
Deem men their life an opal gray, where
    plays 235
The one red Sweet of gracious ladies'-praise.
Now, comes a suitor with sharp prying eye —
Says, *Here, you Lady, if you'll sell, I'll buy:*
Come, heart for heart — a trade? What! weep-
    ing? why?
Shame on such wooers' dapper mercery! 240
I would my lover kneeling at my feet
In humble manliness should cry, O sweet!
I know not if thy heart my heart will greet:
I ask not if thy love my love can meet:
Whate'er thy worshipful soft tongue shall say, 245
I'll kiss thine answer, be it yea or nay:
I do but know I love thee, and I pray
To be thy knight until my dying day.
Woe him that cunning trades in hearts con-
    trives!
Base love good women to base loving
    drives. 250

If men loved larger, larger were our lives;
And wooed they nobler, won they nobler
    wives.''

There thrust the bold straightforward horn
To battle for that lady lorn,
With heartsome voice of mellow scorn,   255
Like any knight in knighthood's morn.
    "Now comfort thee," said he,
        "Fair Lady.
For God shall right thy grievous wrong,
And man shall sing thee a true-love song,   260
Voiced in act his whole life long,
    Yea, all thy sweet life long,
        Fair Lady.
Where's he that craftily hath said,
The day of chivalry is dead?   265
I'll prove that lie upon his head,
    Or I will die instead,
        Fair Lady.
Is Honor gone into his grave?
Hath Faith become a caitiff knave,   270
And Selfhood turned into a slave
    To work in Mammon's cave,
        Fair Lady?
Will Truth's long blade ne'er gleam again?
Hath Giant Trade in dungeons slain   275
All great contempts of mean-got gain
    And hates of inward stain,
        Fair Lady?
For aye shall name and fame be sold,
And place be hugged for the sake of gold,
And smirch-robed Justice feebly scold   281
    At Crime all money-bold,
        Fair Lady?
Shall self-wrapt husbands aye forget
Kiss-pardons for the daily fret   285
Wherewith sweet wifely eyes are wet —
    Blind to lips kiss-wise set —
        Fair Lady?
Shall lovers higgle, heart for heart,
Till wooing grows a trading mart   290
Where much for little, and all for part,
    Make love a cheapening art,
        Fair Lady?
Shall woman scorch for a single sin
That her betrayer may revel in,   295
And she be burnt, and he but grin
    When that the flames begin,
        Fair Lady?
Shall ne'er prevail the woman's plea,
We maids would far, far whiter be   300

If that our eyes might sometimes see
    Men maids in purity,
        Fair Lady?
Shall Trade aye salve his conscience-aches
With jibes at Chivalry's old mistakes —   305
The wars that o'erhot knighthood makes
    For Christ's and ladies' sakes,
        Fair Lady?
Now by each knight that e'er hath prayed
To fight like a man and love like a maid,   310
Since Pembroke's life, as Pembroke's blade,
    I' the scabbard, death, was laid,
        Fair Lady,
I dare avouch my faith is bright
That God doth right and God hath might.
Nor time hath changed His hair to white,   316
    Nor His dear love to spite,
        Fair Lady.
I doubt no doubts: I strive, and shrive my
        clay,
And fight my fight in the patient modern
        way   320
For true love and for thee — ah me! and pray
    To be thy knight until my dying day,
        Fair Lady.''
Made end that knightly horn, and spurred
        away
Into the thick of the melodious fray.   325
And then the hautboy played and smiled,
And sang like any large-eyed child,
Cool-hearted and all undefiled.
    "Huge Trade!" he said,
"Would thou wouldst lift me on thy head
And run where'er my finger led!   331
Once said a Man — and wise was He —
Never shalt thou the heavens see,
Save as a little child thou be.''
Then o'er sea-lashings of commingling tunes
The ancient wise bassoons,   336
        Like weird,
        Gray-beard
Old harpers sitting on the high sea-dunes,
        Chanted runes: 340
"Bright-waved gain, gray-waved loss,
The sea of all doth lash and toss,
One wave forward and one across:
But now 'twas trough, now 'tis crest,
And worst doth foam and flash to best,   345
    And curst to blest.

"Life! Life! thou sea-fugue, writ from east
    to west,

Love, Love alone can pore
On thy dissolving score
Of harsh half-phrasings,   350
   Blotted ere writ,
And double erasings
   Of chords most fit.
Yea, Love, sole music-master blest,
May read thy weltering palimpsest.   355
To follow Time's dying melodies through,
And never to lose the old in the new,
And ever to solve the discords true —
   Love alone can do.
And ever Love hears the poor-folks' cry-
   ing,   360
And ever Love hears the women's sighing,
And ever sweet knighthood's death-defying,
And ever wise childhood's deep implying,
But never a trader's glozing and lying.
"And yet shall Love himself be heard,   365
Though long deferred, though long deferred:
O'er the modern waste a dove hath whirred:
Music is Love in search of a word."

The Mocking Bird

(1877)

Superb and sole, upon a plumèd spray
That o'er the general leafage boldly grew,
He summ'd the woods in song; or typic drew
The watch of hungry hawks, the lone dismay
Of languid doves when long their lovers
   stray,   5
And all birds' passion-plays that sprinkle
   dew
At morn in brake or bosky avenue.
Whate'er birds did or dreamed, this bird
   could say.
Then down he shot, bounced airily along
The sward, twitched in a grasshopper, made
   song   10
Midflight, perched, prinked, and to his art
   again.
Sweet Science, this large riddle read me plain:
How may the death of that dull insect be
The life of yon trim Shakspere on the tree?

EMILY DICKINSON (1830-1886)

An Indian-summer flower of romanticism on the Puritan ground of New England, Emily Dickinson was also a precursor of the poets of the early twentieth century. Born in Amherst, Massachusetts, she numbered among her ancestors a founder of the town. Her father, lawyer, treasurer of Amherst College, a pillar of the First Church, is described as haughty and austere, shy and gentle, laconic and strict. Her mother was "an exquisite little lady of the old school." In 1847 Emily entered Mount Holyoke Female Seminary, a school where Christmas was celebrated by meditation and fasting, and where young ladies were trained to become "mates" (not wives) of missionaries. After her return from Mount Holyoke she lived quietly in her father's home in Amherst. During her twenties she was in the life of the village if not exactly of it, but by 1870 she had become a recluse: "I do not cross my father's ground to any house or town."

Among the few friends who counted heavily in her life was Ben Newton, a young law student who recognized and encouraged her gift of poetry, and gave her books including the *Poems* of Emerson (not yet — in 1850 — regarded as an accepted sage but rather as what we would call a "radical"). In the opinion of Professor Whicher, "There is nothing to show that Emily Dickinson, though she loved Newton as an elder brother, ever considered him as a possible husband." In 1853 he died. "Much as she mourned for Newton, . . . the man who of all others became her support and comforter while he lived, and when he died her 'Heavenly Father,' was the Reverend Charles Wadsworth. . . . At the time of their first meeting, in May, 1854, he was just forty years old, at the height of his great powers, happily married, and immersed in

the multifarious concerns of his pastorate.   She was twenty-three, and not yet inured
to loneliness" (Whicher).   After his death on April 1, 1882, she wrote: "All other
surprise is at last monotonous, but the Death of the Loved is all Moments — *now*.
Love has but one Date — 'The first of April.' "   Such expressions indicate the depth
of her feeling for Charles Wadsworth, but do not require us to assume that he was
attached to her in the same manner.   Much of Emily Dickinson's poetry bears upon
her experience of love for a man she could not marry.

Doubtless her one passionate experience sharpened her already keen sensibilities
and intelligence.   As her poetry shows, she found strange beauty and startling suggestion in the simplest things — a bee's hum, a stone in the road, the glance of a
friend, a sentence in a book.   As an English critic has said in our own century, "It is
almost terrible to reflect that, in the heyday of our confident Victorianism, a solitary
woman should have plumbed these depths, should not only have discarded the serene
assurance of the time but should have pierced through to the lower layer, the reserves of the army of its consolations, so that her verse expresses, with achieved in-
transigence, many a thought with which the rebellious spirits of today are but beginning to grapple."

This is why her poetry became so popular in the questioning 1920's.   Upon her
own time it had no effect whatever, for the simple reason that (with the exception of
three poems) all of it was first published after her death in 1886.   Four years later it
began to appear in small books.   Collected editions appeared in 1924, 1930, and
1937.   A volume of new poems, *Bolts of Melody*, followed in 1945.   Lives are by
Martha Dickinson Bianchi, 1924; Genevieve Taggard, 1930; and G. F. Whicher,
1938 — the last and best of these bears the title *This Was a Poet*.

The Thought Beneath

The thought beneath so slight a film
  Is more distinctly seen, —
As laces just reveal the surge,
  Or mists the Apennine.

How Happy Is the Little Stone

How happy is the little stone
That rambles in the road alone,
And doesn't care about careers,
And exigencies never fears;
Whose coat of elemental brown   5
A passing universe put on;
And independent as the sun,
Associates or glows alone,
Fulfilling absolute decree
In casual simplicity.   10

A Route of Evanescence

A route of evanescence
With a revolving wheel;
A resonance of emerald,

A rush of cochineal;
And every blossom on the bush   5
Adjusts its tumbled head, —
The mail from Tunis, probably,
An easy morning's ride.

Where Ships of Purple

Where ships of purple gently toss
On seas of daffodil,
Fantastic sailors mingle,
And then — the wharf is still.

The Sky Is Low

The sky is low, the clouds are mean,
A travelling flake of snow
Across a barn or through a rut
Debates if it will go.

A narrow wind complains all day   5
How some one treated him;
Nature, like us, is sometimes caught
Without her diadem.

The Day Came Slow

The day came slow, till five o'clock,
Then sprang before the hills
Like hindered rubies, or the light
A sudden musket spills.

The purple could not keep the east,   5
The sunrise shook from fold,
Like breadths of topaz, packed a night,
The lady just unrolled.

The happy winds their timbrels took;
The birds, in docile rows,   10
Arranged themselves around their prince
(The wind is prince of those).

The orchard sparkled like a Jew, —
How mighty 'twas, to stay
A guest in this stupendous place,   15
The parlor of the day!

To Hear an Oriole

To hear an oriole sing
May be a common thing,
Or only a divine.

It is not of the bird
Who sings the same, unheard,   5
As unto crowd.

The fashion of the ear
Attireth that it hear
In dun or fair.

So whether it be rune,   10
Or whether it be none,
Is of within;

The "tune is in the tree,"
The sceptic showeth me;
"No, sir! In thee!"   15

There's a Certain Slant of Light

There's a certain slant of light,
On winter afternoons,
That oppresses, like the weight
Of cathedral tunes.

Heavenly hurt it gives us;   5
We can find no scar,

But internal difference
Where the meanings are.

None may teach it anything
'Tis the seal, despair, —   10
An imperial affliction
Sent us of the air.

When it comes, the landscape listens,
Shadows hold their breath;
When it goes, 'tis like the distance   15
On the look of death.

Apparently with No Surprise

Apparently with no surprise
To any happy flower,
The frost beheads it at its play
In accidental power.
The blond assassin passes on,   5
The sun proceeds unmoved
To measure off another day
For an approving God.

The Last Night

The last night that she lived,
It was a common night,
Except the dying; this to us
Made nature different.

We noticed smallest things, —   5
Things overlooked before,
By this great light upon our minds
Italicized, as 'twere.

That others could exist
While she must finish quite,   10
A jealousy for her arose
So nearly infinite.

We waited while she passed;
It was a narrow time,
Too jostled were our souls to speak,   15
At length the notice came.

She mentioned, and forgot;
Then lightly as a reed
Bent to the water, shivered scarce,
Consented, and was dead.   20

And we, we placed the hair,
And drew the head erect;
And then an awful leisure was,
Our faith to regulate.

The Bustle in a House

The bustle in a house
The morning after death
Is solemnest of industries
Enacted upon earth, —

The sweeping up the heart,   5
And putting love away
We shall not want to use again
Until eternity.

That Such Have Died

That such have died enables us
   The tranquiller to die;
That such have lived, certificate
   For immortality.

A Death-Blow Is a Life-Blow

A death-blow is a life-blow to some
Who, till they died, did not alive become;
Who, had they lived, had died, but when
They died, vitality begun.

He Preached upon "Breadth"

He preached upon "breadth" till it argued
      him narrow, —
The broad are too broad to define;
And of "truth" until it proclaimed him a
      liar, —
The truth never flaunted a sign.

Simplicity fled from his counterfeit presence
As gold the pyrites would shun.   6
What confusion would cover the innocent
      Jesus
To meet so enabled a man!

Exultation

Exultation is the going
Of an inland soul to sea, —
Past the houses, past the headlands,
Into deep eternity!

Bred as we, among the mountains,   5
Can the sailor understand
The divine intoxication
Of the first league out from land?

I Many Times Thought Peace

I many times thought peace had come,
When peace was far away;
As wrecked men deem they sight the land
At centre of the sea,

And struggle slacker, but to prove,   5
As hopelessly as I,
How many the fictitious shores
Before the harbor lie.

I Know That He Exists

I know that he exists
Somewhere, in silence.
He has hid his rare life
From our gross eyes.

'Tis an instant's play,   5
'Tis a fond ambush,
Just to make bliss
Earn her own surprise!

But should the play
Prove piercing earnest,   10
Should the glee glaze
In death's stiff stare,

Would not the fun
Look too expensive?
Would not the jest   15
Have crawled too far?

I Never Saw a Moor

I never saw a moor,
I never saw the sea;
Yet know I how the heather looks,
And what a wave must be.

I never spoke with God,   5
Nor visited in heaven;
Yet certain am I of the spot
As if the chart were given.

We Never Know How High

We never know how high we are
   Till we are called to rise;
And then, if we are true to plan,
   Our statures touch the skies.

The heroism we recite   5
   Would be a daily thing,
Did not ourselves the cubits warp
   For fear to be a king.

It Dropped so Low in My Regard

It dropped so low in my regard
   I heard it hit the ground,
And go to pieces on the stones
   At bottom of my mind;

Yet blamed the fate that fractured, less   5
   Than I reviled myself
For entertaining plated wares
   Upon my silver shelf.

Much Madness Is Divinest Sense

Much madness is divinest sense
To a discerning eye;
Much sense the starkest madness.
'Tis the majority
In this, as all, prevails.   5
Assent, and you are sane;
Demur, — you're straightway dangerous,
And handled with a chain.

To Fight Aloud

To fight aloud is very brave,
   But gallanter, I know,
Who charge within the bosom,
   The cavalry of woe.

Who win, and nations do not see,   5
   Who fall, and none observe,
Whose dying eyes no country
   Regards with patriot love.

We trust, in plumed procession,
   For such the angels go,   10
Rank after rank, with even feet
   And uniforms of snow.

The Soul Selects

The soul selects her own society,
   Then shuts the door;
On her divine majority
   Obtrude no more.

Unmoved, she notes the chariot's pausing   5
   At her low gate;
Unmoved, an emperor is kneeling
   Upon her mat.

I've known her from an ample nation
   Choose one;   10
Then close the valves of her attention
   Like stone.

He Ate and Drank the Precious Words

He ate and drank the precious words,
   His spirit grew robust;
He knew no more that he was poor,
   Nor that his frame was dust.

He danced along the dingy days,   5
   And this bequest of wings
Was but a book. What liberty
   A loosened spirit brings!

'Tis Little I Could Care for Pearls

'Tis little I could care for pearls
   Who own the ample sea;
Or brooches, when the Emperor
   With rubies pelteth me;

Or gold, who am the Prince of Mines;   5
   Or diamonds, when I see
A diadem to fit a dome
   Continual crowning me.

It's Such a Little Thing to Weep

It's such a little thing to weep,
   So short a thing to sigh;
And yet by trades the size of these
   We men and women die!

Presentiment

Presentiment is that long shadow on the lawn
Indicative that suns go down;

The notice to the startled grass
That darkness is about to pass.

A Thought Went up My Mind

A thought went up my mind to-day
That I have had before,
But did not finish, — some way back,
I could not fix the year,

Nor where it went, nor why it came   5
The second time to me,
Nor definitely what it was,
Have I the art to say.

But somewhere in my soul, I know
I've met the thing before;   10
It just reminded me — 'twas all —
And came my way no more.

I Like to See It Lap the Miles

I like to see it lap the miles,
And lick the valleys up,
And stop to feed itself at tanks;
And then, prodigious, step

Around a pile of mountains,   5
And, supercilious, peer
In shanties by the sides of roads;
And then a quarry pare

To fit its sides, and crawl between,
Complaining all the while   10
In horrid, hooting stanza;
Then chase itself down hill

And neigh like Boanerges;
Then, punctual as a star,
Stop — docile and omnipotent —   15
At its own stable door.

A Narrow Fellow in the Grass

A narrow fellow in the grass
Occasionally rides;
You may have met him, — did you not?
His notice sudden is.

The grass divides as with a comb,   5
A spotted shaft is seen;
And then it closes at your feet
And opens further on.

He likes a boggy acre,
A floor too cool for corn.   10
Yet when a child, and barefoot,
I more than once, at morn,

Have passed, I thought, a whiplash
Unbraiding in the sun, —
When, stooping to secure it,   15
It wrinkled, and was gone.

Several of nature's people
I know, and they know me;
I feel for them a transport
Of cordiality;   20

But never met this fellow,
Attended or alone,
Without a tighter breathing,
And zero at the bone.

Because I Could Not Stop

Because I could not stop for Death,
He kindly stopped for me;
The carriage held but just ourselves
And Immortality.

We slowly drove, he knew no haste,   5
And I had put away
My labor and my leisure too,
For his civility.

We passed the school where children played
At wrestling in a ring;   10
We passed the fields of gazing grain,
We passed the setting sun.

We paused before a house that seemed
A swelling of the ground;
The roof was scarcely visible,   15
The cornice but a mound.

Since then 't is centuries; but each
Feels shorter than the day
I first surmised the horses' heads
Were toward eternity.   20

HENRY JAMES (1843–1916)

Son of Henry James, Senior, friend of Emerson, brother of William James, the philosopher and psychologist of pragmatism, Henry James was born in 1843 in New York. Because his father thought the best education was obtainable abroad, he was taken to Europe in infancy and was educated under tutors in several countries and in German universities. The greater part of his life he spent abroad, especially in England, and in 1915, the year before he died, he became a British subject, as a protest against the neutrality of his native country.

He was a "Passionate Pilgrim" to Europe himself, and first effectively expressed himself in a long short story of that title, published in 1871. The first important ones among his many novels were *Roderick Hudson* (1875) and — one of his best — *The American* (1876–77), both of which appeared as serials in the *Atlantic Monthly*. When *The European* appeared in 1878, James stood forth as a master of the international novel. Well acquainted with Americans and Europeans, he contrasted the culture of America with that of Europe. He approached his subject as a writer seeking the "air of reality" through psychological analysis conducted in the spirit of the scientist and through observation conducted in the spirit of the painter. Though early under the spell of Hawthorne, he soon drew closer to the nineteenth century European realists — George Eliot, Turgenev, Balzac, Flaubert, Maupassant, etc. "It was his tendency always to subordinate incident to character, to subordinate character as such to situation — or the relations among the characters; and in situation or character, to prefer something rather out of the ordinary, some aspect or type not too obviously interesting but calling for insight and subtlety in their interpretation. . . . Each tale of James is thus an 'initiation' into some social or artistic or spiritual value not obvious to the vulgar. And each tale is a quiet picture, a social study. . . ." (J. W. Beach).

Although primarily a novelist and writer of short and long tales, James is also a leading American literary critic. Reflecting with penetration on the work of contemporary authors, he wrote *French Poets and Novelists* (1878), *Hawthorne* (1879), *Partial Portraits* (1888), *Essays in London and Elsewhere* (1893), *Notes on Novelists* (1914), and *Notes and Reviews* (1921). Reflecting in much the same manner on his own work, James wrote the remarkable prefaces for the New York Edition of his prose fiction (1907–1917) conveniently gathered by R. P. Blackmur under the title *The Art of the Novel*, 1934.

The Novels and Stories of Henry James were published in a complete edition in 1921–1923. *The Notebooks of Henry James* were edited by F. O. Matthiessen and K. B. Murdock, 1947. *The Letters of Henry James* were edited in 2 volumes by Percy Lubbock, 1920. Pelham Edgar, *Henry James: Man and Author*, 1927, is descriptive and critical; Van Wyck Brooks, *The Pilgrimage of Henry James*, 1925, is interpretive in psychological terms. James's fictional technique has been studied by J. W. Beach in *The Method of Henry James*, 1918, and by F. O. Matthiessen in *Henry James: The Major Phase*, 1944, and his critical writing by Morris Roberts in *Henry James's Criticism*, 1929. Twenty-six estimates of James's achievement were gathered in *The Question of Henry James*, edited by F. W. Dupee, 1945. The volume in the *AWS* is the work of L. N. Richardson, 1941.

The Real Thing

(1893)

I

When the porter's wife (she used to answer the house-bell), announced "A gentleman — with a lady, sir," I had, as I often had in those days, for the wish was father to the thought, an immediate vision of sitters. Sitters my visitors in this case proved to be; but not in the sense I should have preferred. However, there was nothing at first to indicate that they might have come for a portrait. The gentleman, a man of fifty, very high and very straight, with a moustache slightly grizzled and a dark grey walking-coat admirably fitted, both of which I noted professionally — I don't mean as a barber or yet as a tailor — would have struck me as a celebrity if celebrities often were striking. It was a truth of which I had for some time been conscious that a figure with a good deal of frontage was, as one might say, almost never a public institution. A glance at the lady helped to remind me of this paradoxical law: she also looked too distinguished to be a "personality." Moreover one would scarcely come across two variations together.

Neither of the pair spoke immediately — they only prolonged the preliminary gaze which suggested that each wished to give the other a chance. They were visibly shy; they stood there letting me take them in — which, as I afterwards perceived, was the most practical thing they could have done. In this way their embarrassment served their cause. I had seen people painfully reluctant to mention that they desired anything so gross as to be represented on canvas; but the scruples of my new friends appeared almost insurmountable. Yet the gentleman might have said "I should like a portrait of my wife," and the lady might have said "I should like a portrait of my husband." Perhaps they were not husband and wife — this naturally would make the matter more delicate. Perhaps they wished to be done together — in which case they ought to have brought a third person to break the news.

"We come from Mr. Rivet," the lady said at last, with a dim smile which had the effect of a moist sponge passed over a "sunk" piece of painting, as well as of a vague allusion to vanished beauty. She was as tall and straight, in her degree, as her companion, and with ten years less to carry. She looked as sad as a woman could look whose face was not charged with expression; that is, her tinted oval mask showed friction as an exposed surface shows it. The hand of time had played over her freely, but only to simplify. She was slim and stiff, and so well-dressed, in dark blue cloth, with lappets and pockets and buttons, that it was clear she employed the same tailor as her husband. The couple had an indefinable air of prosperous thrift — they evidently got a good deal of luxury for their money. If I was to be one of their luxuries it would behoove me to consider my terms.

"Ah, Claude Rivet recommended me?" I inquired; and I added that it was very kind of him, though I could reflect that, as he only painted landscape, this was not a sacrifice.

The lady looked very hard at the gentleman, and the gentleman looked round the room. Then staring at the floor a moment and stroking his moustache, he rested his pleasant eyes on me with the remark: "He said you were the right one."

"I try to be, when people want to sit."

"Yes, we should like to," said the lady anxiously.

"Do you mean together?"

My visitors exchanged a glance. "If you could do anything with *me*, I suppose it would be double," the gentleman stammered.

"Oh yes, there's naturally a higher charge for two figures than for one."

"We should like to make it pay," the husband confessed.

"That's very good of you," I returned, appreciating so unwonted a sympathy — for I supposed he meant pay the artist.

A sense of strangeness seemed to dawn on the lady. "We mean for the illustrations — Mr. Rivet said you might put one in."

"Put one in — an illustration?" I was equally confused.

"Sketch her off, you know," said the gentleman, colouring.

It was only then that I understood the service Claude Rivet had rendered me; he had told them that I worked in black and white, for magazines, for story-books, for sketches of contemporary life, and consequently had frequent employment for models. These things were true, but it was not less true (I may confess it now — whether because the aspiration was to lead to everything or to nothing I leave the reader to guess), that I couldn't get the honours, to say nothing of the emoluments, of a great painter of portraits out of my head. My "illustrations" were my pot-boilers; I looked to a different branch of art (far and away the most interesting it had always seemed to me), to perpetuate my fame. There was no shame in looking to it also to make my fortune; but that fortune was by so much further from being made from the moment my visitors wished to be "done" for nothing. I was disappointed; for in the pictorial sense I had immediately *seen* them. I had seized their type — I had already settled what I would do with it. Something that wouldn't absolutely have pleased them, I afterwards reflected.

"Ah, you're — you're — a — ?" I began, as soon as I had mastered my surprise. I couldn't bring out the dingy word "models"; it seemed to fit the case so little.

"We haven't had much practice," said the lady.

"We've got to *do* something, and we've thought that an artist in your line might perhaps make something of us," her husband threw off. He further mentioned that they didn't know many artists and that they had gone first, on the off-chance (he painted views of course, but sometimes put in figures — perhaps I remembered), to Mr. Rivet, whom they had met a few years before at a place in Norfolk where he was sketching.

"We used to sketch a little ourselves," the lady hinted.

"It's very awkward, but we absolutely *must* do something," her husband went on.

"Of course, we're not so *very* young," she admitted, with a wan smile.

With the remark that I might as well know something more about them, the husband had handed me a card extracted from a neat new pocket-book (their appurtenances were all of the freshest) and inscribed with the words "Major Monarch." Impressive as these words were they didn't carry my knowledge much further; but my visitor presently added: "I've left the army, and we've had the misfortune to lose our money. In fact our means are dreadfully small."

"It's an awful bore," said Mrs. Monarch.

They evidently wished to be discreet — to take care not to swagger because they were gentlefolks. I perceived they would have been willing to recognise this as something of a drawback, at the same time that I guessed at an underlying sense — their consolation in adversity — that they *had* their points. They certainly had; but these advantages struck me as preponderantly social; such for instance as would help to make a drawing-room look well. However, a drawing-room was always, or ought to be, a picture.

In consequence of his wife's allusion to their age Major Monarch observed: "Naturally, it's more for the figure that we thought of going in. We can still hold ourselves up." On the instant I saw that the figure was indeed their strong point. His "naturally" didn't sound vain, but it lighted up the question. "*She* has got the best," he continued, nodding at his wife, with a pleasant after-dinner absence of circumlocution. I could only reply, as if we were in fact sitting over our wine, that this didn't prevent his own from being very good; which led him in turn to rejoin: "We thought that if you ever have to do people like us, we might be something like it. *She*, particularly — for a lady in a book, you know."

I was so amused by them that, to get more of it, I did my best to take their point of view; and though it was an embarrassment to find myself appraising physically, as if they were animals on hire or useful blacks, a pair whom I should have expected to meet only in one of the relations in which criticism is tacit, I looked at Mrs. Monarch judicially enough to be able to exclaim, after a moment, with conviction: "Oh yes, a lady in a book!" She was singularly like a bad illustration.

"We'll stand up, if you like," said the Major; and he raised himself before me with a really grand air.

I could take his measure at a glance — he

was six feet two and a perfect gentleman. It would have paid any club in process of formation and in want of a stamp to engage him at a salary to stand in the principal window. What struck me immediately was that in coming to me they had rather missed their vocation; they could surely have been turned to better account for advertising purposes. I couldn't of course see the thing in detail, but I could see them make someone's fortune — I don't mean their own. There was something in them for a waistcoat maker, an hotel-keeper or a soap-vendor. I could imagine "We always use it" pinned on their bosoms with the greatest effect; I had a vision of the promptitude with which they would launch a table d'hôte.

Mrs. Monarch sat still, not from pride but from shyness, and presently her husband said to her: "Get up my dear and show how smart you are." She obeyed, but she had no need to get up to show it. She walked to the end of the studio, and then she came back blushing, with her fluttered eyes on her husband. I was reminded of an incident I had accidentally had a glimpse of in Paris — being with a friend there, a dramatist about to produce a play — when an actress came to him to ask to be intrusted with a part. She went through her paces before him, walked up and down as Mrs. Monarch was doing. Mrs. Monarch did it quite as well, but I abstained from applauding. It was very odd to see such people apply for such poor pay. She looked as if she had ten thousand a year. Her husband had used the word that described her: she was, in the London current jargon, essentially and typically "smart." Her figure was, in the same order of ideas, conspicuously and irreproachably "good." For a woman of her age her waist was surprisingly small; her elbow moreover had the orthodox crook. She held her head at the conventional angle; but why did she come to *me!* She ought to have tried on jackets at a big shop. I feared my visitors were not only destitute, but "artistic" — which would be a great complication. When she sat down again I thanked her, observing that what a draughtsman most valued in his model was the faculty of keeping quiet.

"Oh, *she* can keep quiet," said Major Monarch. Then he added, jocosely: "I've always kept her quiet."

"I'm not a nasty fidget, am I?" Mrs. Monarch appealed to her husband.

He addressed his answers to me. "Perhaps it isn't out of place to mention — because we ought to be quite business-like, oughtn't we? — that when I married her she was known as the Beautiful Statue."

"Oh dear!" said Mrs. Monarch, ruefully.

"Of course I should want a certain amount of expression," I rejoined.

"Of *course!*" they both exclaimed.

"And then I suppose you know that you'll get awfully tired."

"Oh, we *never* get tired!" they eagerly cried.

"Have you had any kind of practice?"

They hesitated — they looked at each other. "We've been photographed, *immensely*," said Mrs. Monarch.

"She means the fellows have asked us," added the Major.

"I see — because you're so good-looking."

"I don't know what they thought, but they were always after us."

"We always got our photographs for nothing," smiled Mrs. Monarch.

"We might have brought some, my dear," her husband remarked.

"I'm not sure we have any left. We've given quantities away," she explained to me.

"With our autographs and that sort of thing," said the Major.

"Are they to be got in the shops?" I inquired, as a harmless pleasantry.

"Oh, yes; *hers* — they used to be."

"Not now," said Mrs. Monarch, with her eyes on the floor.

II

I could fancy the "sort of thing" they put on the presentation-copies of their photographs, and I was sure they wrote a beautiful hand. It was odd how quickly I was sure of everything that concerned them. If they were now so poor as to have to earn shillings and pence, they never had had much of a margin. Their good looks had been their capital, and they had good-humouredly made the most of the career that this resource marked out for them. It was in their faces, the blankness, the deep intellectual repose of the twenty years of country-house visiting which had given them pleasant intonations. I could see the sunny drawing-rooms, sprinkled with periodicals she didn't read, in which Mrs. Monarch had continuously sat; I could see the wet shrubberies in which she had walked, equipped to admiration for either exercise. I could see the rich covers the Major had helped to shoot and the wonderful garments in which, late at night, he repaired to the smoking-room to talk about them. I could imagine their leggings and waterproofs, their knowing tweeds and rugs, their rolls of sticks and cases of tackle and neat umbrellas; and I could evoke the exact appearance of their servants and the compact variety of their luggage on the platforms of country stations.

They gave small tips, but they were liked; they didn't do anything themselves, but they were welcome. They looked so well everywhere; they gratified the general relish for stature, complexion and "form." They knew it without fatuity or vulgarity, and they respected themselves in consequence. They were not superficial; they were thorough and kept themselves up — it had been their line. People with such a taste for activity had to have some line. I could feel how, even in a dull house, they could have been counted upon for cheerfulness. At present something had happened — it didn't matter what, their little income had grown less, it had grown least — and they had to do something for pocket-money. Their friends liked them, but didn't like to support them. There was something about them that represented credit — their clothes, their manners, their type; but if credit is a large empty pocket in which an occasional chink reverberates, the chink at least must be audible. What they wanted of me was to help to make it so. Fortunately they had no children — I soon divined that. They would also perhaps wish our relations to be kept secret: this was why it was "for the figure" — the reproduction of the face would betray them.

I liked them — they were so simple; and I had no objection to them if they would suit. But, somehow, with all their perfections I didn't easily believe in them. After all they were amateurs, and the ruling passion of my life was the detestation of the amateur. Combined with this was another perversity — an innate preference for the represented subject over the real one: the defect of the real one was so apt to be a lack of representation. I liked things that appeared; then one was sure. Whether they *were* or not was a subordinate and almost always a profitless question. There were other considerations, the first of which was that I already had two or three people in use, notably a young person with big feet, in alpaca, from Kilburn, who for a couple of years had come to me regularly for my illustrations and with whom I was still — perhaps ignobly — satisfied. I frankly explained to my visitors how the case stood; but they had taken more precautions than I supposed. They had reasoned out their opportunity, for Claude Rivet had told them of the projected *édition de luxe* of one of the writers of our day — the rarest of the novelists — who, long neglected by the multitudinous vulgar and dearly prized by the attentive (need I mention Philip Vincent?) had had the happy fortune of seeing, late in life, the dawn and then the full light of a higher criticism — an estimate in which, on the part of the public, there was something really of expiation. The edition in question, planned by a publisher of taste, was practically an act of high reparation; the woodcuts with which it was to be enriched were the homage of English art to one of the most independent representatives of English letters. Major and Mrs. Monarch confessed to me that they had hoped I might be able to work *them* into my share of the enterprise. They knew I was to do the first of the books, "Rutland Ramsay," but I had to make clear to them that my participation in the rest of the affair — this first book was to be a test — was to depend on the satisfaction I should give. If this should be limited my employers would drop me without a scruple. It was therefore a crisis for me, and naturally I was making special preparations, looking about for new people, if they should be necessary, and securing the best types. I admitted however that I should like to settle down to two or three good models who would do for everything.

"Should we have often to — a — put on

special clothes?" Mrs. Monarch timidly demanded.

"Dear, yes — that's half the business."

"And should we be expected to supply our own costumes?"

"Oh, no; I've got a lot of things. A painter's models put on — or put off — anything he likes."

"And do you mean — a — the same?"

"The same?"

Mrs. Monarch looked at her husband again.

"Oh, she was just wondering," he explained, "if the costumes are in *general* use." I had to confess that they were, and I mentioned further that some of them (I had a lot of genuine, greasy last-century things), had served their time, a hundred years ago, on living, world-stained men and women. "We'll put on anything that *fits*," said the Major.

"Oh, I arrange that — they fit in the pictures."

"I'm afraid I should do better for the modern books. I would come as you like," said Mrs. Monarch.

"She has got a lot of clothes at home: they might do for contemporary life," her husband continued.

"Oh, I can fancy scenes in which you'd be quite natural." And indeed I could see the slipshod rearrangements of stale properties — the stories I tried to produce pictures for without the exasperation of reading them — whose sandy tracts the good lady might help to people. But I had to return to the fact that for this sort of work — the daily mechanical grind — I was already equipped; the people I was working with were fully adequate.

"We only thought we might be more like *some* characters," said Mrs. Monarch mildly, getting up.

Her husband also rose; he stood looking at me with a dim wistfulness that was touching in so fine a man. "Wouldn't it be rather a pull sometimes to have — a — to have?" He hung fire; he wanted me to help him by phrasing what he meant. But I couldn't — I didn't know. So he brought it out, awkwardly: "The *real* thing; a gentleman, you know, or a lady." I was quite ready to give a general assent — I admitted that there was a great deal in that. This encouraged Major Monarch to say, following up his appeal with an unacted gulp: "It's awfully hard — we've tried everything." The gulp was communicative; it proved too much for his wife. Before I knew it Mrs. Monarch had dropped again upon a divan and burst into tears. Her husband sat down beside her, holding one of her hands; whereupon she quickly dried her eyes with the other, while I felt embarrassed as she looked up at me. "There isn't a confounded job I haven't applied for — waited for — prayed for. You can fancy we'd be pretty bad first. Secretaryships and that sort of thing? You might as well ask for a peerage. I'd be *anything* — I'm strong; a messenger or a coalheaver. I'd put on a gold-laced cap and open carriage-doors in front of the haberdasher's; I'd hang about a station, to carry portmanteaus; I'd be a postman. But they won't *look* at you; there are thousands, as good as yourself, already on the ground. *Gentlemen*, poor beggars, who have drunk their wine, who have kept their hunters!"

I was as reassuring as I knew how to be, and my visitors were presently on their feet again while, for the experiment, we agreed on an hour. We were discussing it when the door opened and Miss Churm came in with a wet umbrella. Miss Churm had to take the omnibus to Maida Vale and then walk half-a-mile. She looked a trifle blowsy and slightly splashed. I scarcely ever saw her come in without thinking afresh how odd it was that, being so little in herself, she should yet be so much in others. She was a meagre little Miss Churm, but she was an ample heroine of romance. She was only a freckled cockney, but she could represent everything, from a fine lady to a shepherdess; she had the faculty, as she might have had a fine voice or long hair. She couldn't spell, and she loved beer, but she had two or three "points," and practice, and a knack, and mother-wit, and a kind of whimsical sensibility, and a love of the theatre, and seven sisters, and not an ounce of respect, especially for the *h*. The first thing my visitors saw was that her umbrella was wet, and in their spotless perfection they visibly winced at it. The rain had come on since their arrival.

"I'm all in a soak; there *was* a mess of

people in the 'bus. I wish you lived near a stytion," said Miss Churm. I requested her to get ready as quickly as possible, and she passed into the room in which she always changed her dress. But before going out she asked me what she was to get into this time.

"It's the Russian princess, don't you know?" I answered; "the one with the 'golden eyes,' in black velvet, for the long thing in the *Cheapside*."

"Golden eyes? I *say!*" cried Miss Churm, while my companions watched her with intensity as she withdrew. She always arranged herself, when she was late, before I could turn round; and I kept my visitors a little, on purpose, so that they might get an idea, from seeing her, what would be expected of themselves. I mentioned that she was quite my notion of an excellent model — she was really very clever.

"Do you think she looks like a Russian princess?" Major Monarch asked, with lurking alarm.

"When I make her, yes."

"Oh, if you have to *make* her —!" he reasoned, acutely.

"That's the most you can ask. There are so many that are not makeable."

"Well now, *here's* a lady" — and with a persuasive smile he passed his arm into his wife's — "who's already made!"

"Oh, I'm not a Russian princess," Mrs. Monarch protested, a little coldly. I could see that she had known some and didn't like them. There, immediately, was a complication of a kind that I never had to fear with Miss Churm.

This young lady came back in black velvet — the gown was rather rusty and very low on her lean shoulders — and with a Japanese fan in her red hands. I reminded her that in the scene I was doing she had to look over someone's head. "I forget whose it is; but it doesn't matter. Just look over a head."

"I'd rather look over a stove," said Miss Churm; and she took her station near the fire. She fell into position, settled herself into a tall attitude, gave a certain backward inclination to her head and a certain forward droop to her fan, and looked, at least to my prejudiced sense, distinguished and charming, foreign and dangerous. We left her

looking so, while I went down-stairs with Major and Mrs. Monarch.

"I think I could come about as near it as that," said Mrs. Monarch.

"Oh, you think she's shabby, but you must allow for the alchemy of art."

However, they went off with an evident increase of comfort, founded on their demonstrable advantage in being the real thing. I could fancy them shuddering over Miss Churm. She was very droll about them when I went back, for I told her what they wanted.

"Well, if *she* can sit I'll tyke to bookkeeping," said my model.

"She's very lady-like," I replied, as an innocent form of aggravation.

"So much the worse for *you*. That means she can't turn round."

"She'll do for the fashionable novels."

"Oh yes, she'll *do* for them!" my model humorously declared. "Ain't they bad enough without her?" I had often sociably denounced them to Miss Churm.

III

It was for the elucidation of a mystery in one of these works that I first tried Mrs. Monarch. Her husband came with her, to be useful if necessary — it was sufficiently clear that as a general thing he would prefer to come with her. At first I wondered if this were for "propriety's" sake — if he were going to be jealous and meddling. The idea was too tiresome, and if it had been confirmed it would speedily have brought our acquaintance to a close. But I soon saw there was nothing in it and that if he accompanied Mrs. Monarch it was (in addition to the chance of being wanted), simply because he had nothing else to do. When she was away from him his occupation was gone — she never *had* been away from him. I judged, rightly, that in their awkward situation their close union was their main comfort and that this union had no weak spot. It was a real marriage, an encouragement to the hesitating, a nut for pessimists to crack. Their address was humble (I remember afterwards thinking it had been the only thing about them that was really professional), and I could fancy the lamentable lodgings in which the Major would have been left alone. He could bear them with his wife — he couldn't bear them without her.

He had too much tact to try and make himself agreeable when he couldn't be useful; so he simply sat and waited, when I was too absorbed in my work to talk. But I liked to make him talk — it made my work, when it didn't interrupt it, less sordid, less special. To listen to him was to combine the excitement of going out with the economy of staying at home. There was only one hindrance: that I seemed not to know any of the people he and his wife had known. I think he wondered extremely, during the term of our intercourse, whom the deuce I *did* know. He hadn't a stray sixpence of an idea to fumble for; so we didn't spin it very fine — we confined ourselves to questions of leather and even of liquor (saddlers and breeches-makers and how to get good claret cheap), and matters like "good trains" and the habits of small game. His lore on these last subjects was astonishing, he managed to interweave the station-master with the ornithologist. When he couldn't talk about greater things he could talk cheerfully about smaller, and since I couldn't accompany him into reminiscences of the fashionable world he could lower the conversation without a visible effort to my level.

So earnest a desire to please was touching in a man who could so easily have knocked one down. He looked after the fire and had an opinion on the draught of the stove, without my asking him, and I could see that he thought many of my arrangements not half clever enough. I remember telling him that if I were only rich I would offer him a salary to come and teach me how to live. Sometimes he gave a random sigh, of which the essence was: "Give me even such a bare old barrack as *this*, and I'd do something with it!" When I wanted to use him he came alone; which was an illustration of the superior courage of women. His wife could bear her solitary second floor, and she was in general more discreet; showing by various small reserves that she was alive to the propriety of keeping our relations markedly professional — not letting them slide into sociability. She wished it to remain clear that she and the

Major were employed, not cultivated, and if she approved of me as a superior, who could be kept in his place, she never thought me quite good enough for an equal.

She sat with great intensity, giving the whole of her mind to it, and was capable of remaining for an hour almost as motionless as if she were before a photographer's lens. I could see she had been photographed often, but somehow the very habit that made her good for that purpose unfitted her for mine. At first I was extremely pleased with her lady-like air, and it was a satisfaction, on coming to follow her lines, to see how good they were and how far they could lead the pencil. But after a few times I began to find her too insurmountably stiff; do what I would with it my drawing looked like a photograph or a copy of a photograph. Her figure had no variety of expression — she herself had no sense of variety. You may say that this was my business, was only a question of placing her. I placed her in every conceivable position, but she managed to obliterate their differences. She was always a lady certainly, and into the bargain was always the same lady. She was the real thing, but always the same thing. There were moments when I was oppressed by the serenity of her confidence that she *was* the real thing. All her dealings with me and all her husband's were an implication that this was lucky for *me*. Meanwhile I found myself trying to invent types that approached her own, instead of making her own transform itself — in the clever way that was not impossible, for instance, to poor Miss Churm. Arrange as I would and take the precautions I would, she always, in my pictures, came out too tall — landing me in the dilemma of having represented a fascinating woman as seven feet high, which, out of respect perhaps to my own very much scantier inches, was far from my idea of such a personage.

The case was worse with the Major — nothing I could do would keep *him* down, so that he became useful only for the representation of brawny giants. I adored variety and range, I cherished human accidents, the illustrative note; I wanted to characterise closely, and the thing in the world I most hated was the danger of being ridden by a type. I had quarrelled with some of my friends about it — I had parted company with them for maintaining that one *had* to be, and that if the type was beautiful (witness Raphael and Leonardo), the servitude was only a gain. I was neither Leonardo nor Raphael; I might only be a presumptuous young modern searcher, but I held that everything was to be sacrificed sooner than character. When they averred that the haunting type in question could easily *be* character, I retorted, perhaps superficially: "Whose?" It couldn't be everybody's — it might end in being nobody's.

After I had drawn Mrs. Monarch a dozen times I perceived more clearly than before that the value of such a model as Miss Churm resided precisely in the fact that she had no positive stamp, combined of course with the other fact that what she did have was a curious and inexplicable talent for imitation. Her usual appearance was like a curtain which she could draw up at request for a capital performance. This performance was simply suggestive; but it was a word to the wise — it was vivid and pretty. Sometimes, even, I thought it, though she was plain herself, too insipidly pretty; I made it a reproach to her that the figures drawn from her were monotonously (*bêtement*, as we used to say) graceful. Nothing made her more angry: it was so much her pride to feel that she could sit for characters that had nothing in common with each other. She would accuse me at such moments of taking away her "reputytion."

It suffered a certain shrinkage, this queer quantity, from the repeated visits of my new friends. Miss Churm was greatly in demand, never in want of employment, so I had no scruple in putting her off occasionally, to try them more at my ease. It was certainly amusing at first to do the real thing — it was amusing to do Major Monarch's trousers. They *were* the real thing, even if he did come out colossal. It was amusing to do his wife's back hair (it was so mathematically neat,) and the particular "smart" tension of her tight stays. She lent herself especially to positions in which the face was somewhat averted or blurred; she abounded in ladylike back views and *profils perdus*. When she stood

erect she took naturally one of the attitudes in which court-painters represent queens and princesses; so that I found myself wondering whether, to draw out this accomplishment, I couldn't get the editor of the *Cheapside* to publish a really royal romance, "A Tale of Buckingham Palace." Sometimes, however, the real thing and the make-believe came into contact; by which I mean that Miss Churm, keeping an appointment or coming to make one on days when I had much work in hand, encountered her invidious rivals. The encounter was not on their part, for they noticed her no more than if she had been the housemaid; not from intentional loftiness, but simply because, as yet, professionally, they didn't know how to fraternise, as I could guess that they would have liked — or at least that the Major would. They couldn't talk about the omnibus — they always walked; and they didn't know what else to try — she wasn't interested in good trains or cheap claret. Besides, they must have felt — in the air — that she was amused at them, secretly derisive of their ever knowing how. She was not a person to conceal her scepticism if she had had a chance to show it. On the other hand Mrs. Monarch didn't think her tidy; for why else did she take pains to say to me (it was going out of the way, for Mrs. Monarch), that she didn't like dirty women?

One day when my young lady happened to be present with my other sitters (she even dropped in, when it was convenient, for a chat), I asked her to be so good as to lend a hand in getting tea — a service with which she was familiar and which was one of a class that, living as I did in a small way, with slender domestic resources, I often appealed to my models to render. They liked to lay hands on my property, to break the sitting, and sometimes the china — I made them feel Bohemian. The next time I saw Miss Churm after this incident she surprised me greatly by making a scene about it — she accused me of having wished to humiliate her. She had not resented the outrage at the time, but had seemed obliging and amused, enjoying the comedy of asking Mrs. Monarch, who sat vague and silent, whether she would have cream and sugar, and putting an exaggerated simper into the question. She had tried intonations — as if she too wished to pass for the real thing; till I was afraid my other visitors would take offence.

Oh, *they* were determined not to do this; and their touching patience was the measure of their great need. They would sit by the hour, uncomplaining, till I was ready to use them; they would come back on the chance of being wanted and would walk away cheerfully if they were not. I used to go to the door with them to see in what magnificent order they retreated. I tried to find other employment for them — I introduced them to several artists. But they didn't "take," for reasons I could appreciate, and I became conscious, rather anxiously, that after such disappointments they fell back upon me with a heavier weight. They did me the honour to think that it was I who was most *their* form. They were not picturesque enough for the painters, and in those days there were not so many serious workers in black and white. Besides, they had an eye to the great job I had mentioned to them — they had secretly set their hearts on supplying the right essence for my pictorial vindication of our fine novelist. They knew that for this undertaking I should want no costume-effects, none of the frippery of past ages — that it was a case in which everything would be contemporary and satirical and, presumably, genteel. If I could work them into it their future would be assured, for the labour would of course be long and the occupation steady.

One day Mrs. Monarch came without her husband — she explained his absence by his having had to go to the City. While she sat there in her usual anxious stiffness there came, at the door, a knock which I immediately recognised as the subdued appeal of a model out of work. It was followed by the entrance of a young man whom I easily perceived to be a foreigner and who proved in fact an Italian acquainted with no English word but my name, which he uttered in a way that made it seem to include all others. I had not then visited his country, nor was I proficient in his tongue; but as he was not so meanly constituted — what Italian is? — as to depend only on that member for expression he conveyed to me, in familiar but graceful mimicry, that he was in search of exactly the employment in which the lady before me was engaged. I was not struck with him at first, and while I continued to draw I emitted rough sounds of discouragement and dismissal. He stood his ground, however, not importunately, but with a dumb, dog-like fidelity in his eyes which amounted to innocent impudence — the manner of a devoted servant (he might have been in the house for years), unjustly suspected. Suddenly I saw that this very attitude and expression made a picture, whereupon I told him to sit down and wait till I should be free. There was another picture in the way he obeyed me, and I observed as I worked that there were others still in the way he looked wonderingly, with his head thrown back, about the high studio. He might have been crossing himself in St. Peter's. Before I finished I said to myself: "The fellow's a bankrupt orange-monger, but he's a treasure."

When Mrs. Monarch withdrew he passed across the room like a flash to open the door for her, standing there with the rapt, pure gaze of the young Dante spellbound by the young Beatrice. As I never insisted, in such situations, on the blankness of the British domestic, I reflected that he had the making of a servant (and I needed one, but couldn't pay him to be only that), as well as of a model; in short I made up my mind to adopt my bright adventurer if he would agree to officiate in the double capacity. He jumped at my offer, and in the event my rashness (for I had known nothing about him) was not brought home to me. He proved a sympathetic though a desultory ministrant, and had in a wonderful degree the *sentiment de la pose*. It was uncultivated, instinctive; a part of the happy instinct which had guided him to my door and helped him to spell out my name on the card nailed to it. He had had no other introduction to me than a guess, from the shape of my high north window, seen outside, that my place was a studio and that as a studio it would contain an artist. He had wandered to England in search of fortune, like other itinerants, and had embarked, with a partner and a small green handcart, on the sale of penny ices. The ices had melted away and the partner had dissolved in their train. My young man wore tight yellow trousers with reddish stripes and his name was Oronte. He was sallow but fair, and when I put him into some old clothes of my own he looked like an Englishman. He was as good as Miss Churm, who could look, when required, like an Italian.

IV

I thought Mrs. Monarch's face slightly convulsed when, on her coming back with her husband, she found Oronte installed. It was strange to have to recognise in a scrap of a lazzarone a competitor to her magnificent Major. It was she who scented danger first, for the Major was anecdotically unconscious. But Oronte gave us tea, with a hundred eager confusions (he had never seen such a queer process), and I think she thought better of me for having at last an "establishment." They saw a couple of drawings that I had made of the establishment, and Mrs. Monarch hinted that it never would have struck her that he had sat for them. "Now the drawings you make from *us*, they look exactly like us," she reminded me, smiling in triumph; and I recognised that this was indeed just their defect. When I drew the Monarchs I couldn't, somehow, get away from them — get into the character I wanted to represent; and I had not the least desire my model should be discoverable in my picture. Miss Churm never was, and Mrs. Monarch thought I hid her, very properly, because she was vulgar; whereas if she was lost it was only as the dead who go to heaven are lost — in the gain of an angel the more.

By this time I had got a certain start with "Rutland Ramsay," the first novel in the great projected series; that is, I had produced a dozen drawings, several with the help of the Major and his wife, and I had sent them in for approval. My understanding with the publishers, as I have already hinted, had been that I was to be left to do my work, in this particular case, as I liked, with the whole book committed to me; but my connection with the rest of the series was only contingent. There were moments when, frankly, it *was* a comfort to have the real thing under one's hand; for there were characters in "Rutland Ramsay" that were very much like it. There were people presumably as straight as the Major and women of as good a fashion as Mrs. Monarch. There was a great deal of country-house life — treated, it is true, in a fine, fanciful, ironical, generalised way — and there was a considerable implication of knickerbockers and kilts. There were certain things I had to settle at the outset; such things for instance as the exact appearance of the hero, the particular bloom of the heroine. The author of course gave me a lead, but there was a margin for interpretation. I took the Monarchs into my confidence, I told them frankly what I was about, I mentioned my embarrassments and alternatives. "Oh, take *him!*" Mrs. Monarch murmured sweetly, looking at her husband; and "What could you want better than my wife?" the Major inquired, with the comfortable candour that now prevailed between us.

I was not obliged to answer these remarks — I was only obliged to place my sitters. I was not easy in mind, and I postponed, a little timidly perhaps, the solution of the question. The book was a large canvas, the other figures were numerous, and I worked off at first some of the episodes in which the hero and the heroine were not concerned. When once I had set *them* up I should have to stick to them — I couldn't make my young man seven feet high in one place and five feet nine in another. I inclined on the whole to the latter measurement, though the Major more than once reminded me that *he* looked about as young as anyone. It was indeed quite possible to arrange him, for the figure, so that it would have been difficult to detect his age. After the spontaneous Oronte had been with me a month, and after I had given him to understand several different times that his native exuberance would presently constitute an insurmountable barrier to our further intercourse, I waked to a sense of his heroic capacity. He was only five feet seven, but the remaining inches were latent. I tried him almost secretly at first, for I was really rather afraid of the judgment my other models would pass on such a choice. If they regarded Miss Churm as little better than a snare, what would they think of the representation by a person so little the real thing as an Italian street-vendor of a protagonist formed by a public school?

If I went a little in fear of them it was not because they bullied me, because they had got an oppressive foothold, but because in their really pathetic decorum and mysteriously permanent newness they counted on me so intensely. I was therefore very glad when Jack Hawley came home: he was always of such good counsel. He painted badly himself, but there was no one like him for putting his finger on the place. He had been absent from England for a year; he had been somewhere — I don't remember where — to get a fresh eye. I was in a good deal of dread of any such organ, but we were old friends; he had been away for months and a sense of emptiness was creeping into my life. I hadn't dodged a missile for a year.

He came back with a fresh eye, but with the same old black velvet blouse, and the first evening he spent in my studio we smoked cigarettes till the small hours. He had done no work himself, he had only got the eye; so the field was clear for the production of my little things. He wanted to see what I had done for the *Cheapside*, but he was disappointed in the exhibition. That at least seemed the meaning of two or three comprehensive groans which, as he lounged on my big divan, on a folded leg, looking at my latest drawings, issued from his lips with the smoke of the cigarette.

"What's the matter with you?" I asked.

"What's the matter with *you!*"

"Nothing save that I'm mystified."

"You are indeed. You're quite off the hinge. What's the meaning of this new fad?" And he tossed me, with visible irreverence, a drawing in which I happened to have depicted both my majestic models. I asked if he didn't think it good, and he replied that it struck him as execrable, given the sort of thing I had always represented myself to him as wishing to arrive at; but I let that pass, I was so anxious to see exactly what he meant. The two figures in the picture looked colossal, but I supposed this was *not* what he meant, inasmuch as, for aught he knew to the contrary, I might have been trying for that. I maintained that I was working exactly in the same way as when he last had done me the honour to commend me. "Well, there's a big hole somewhere," he

answered; "wait a bit and I'll discover it." I depended upon him to do so: where else was the fresh eye? But he produced at last nothing more luminous than "I don't know — I don't like your types." This was lame, for a critic who had never consented to discuss with me anything but the question of execution, the direction of strokes and the mystery of values.

"In the drawings you've been looking at I think my types are very handsome."

"Oh, they won't do!"

"I've had a couple of new models."

"I see you have. *They* won't do."

"Are you very sure of that?"

"Absolutely — they're stupid."

"You mean *I* am — for I ought to get round that."

"You *can't* — with such people. Who are they?"

I told him, as far as was necessary, and he declared, heartlessly: *"Ce sont des gens qu'il faut mettre à la porte."*

"You've never seen them; they're awfully good," I compassionately objected.

"Not seen them? Why, all this recent work of yours drops to pieces with them. It's all I want to see of them."

"No one else has said anything against it — the *Cheapside* people are pleased."

"Everyone else is an ass, and the *Cheapside* people the biggest asses of all. Come, don't pretend, at this time of day, to have pretty illusions about the public, especially about publishers and editors. It's not for *such* animals you work — it's for those who know, *coloro che sanno;* so keep straight for *me* if you can't keep straight for yourself. There's a certain sort of thing you tried for from the first — and a very good thing it is. But this twaddle isn't *in* it." When I talked with Hawley later about "Rutland Ramsay" and its possible successors he declared that I must get back into my boat again or I would go to the bottom. His voice in short was the voice of warning.

I noted the warning, but I didn't turn my friends out of doors. They bored me a good deal; but the very fact that they bored me admonished me not to sacrifice them — if there was anything to be done with them — simply to irritation. As I look back at this phase they seem to me to have pervaded my life not a little. I have a vision of them as most of the time in my studio, seated, against the wall, on an old velvet bench to be out of the way, and looking like a pair of patient courtiers in a royal ante-chamber. I am convinced that during the coldest weeks of the winter they held their ground because it saved them fire. Their newness was losing its gloss, and it was impossible not to feel that they were objects of charity. Whenever Miss Churm arrived they went away, and after I was fairly launched in "Rutland Ramsay" Miss Churm arrived pretty often. They managed to express to me tacitly that they supposed I wanted her for the low life of the book, and I let them suppose it, since they had attempted to study the work — it was lying about the studio — without discovering that it dealt only with the highest circles. They had dipped into the most brilliant of our novelists without deciphering many passages. I still took an hour from them, now and again, in spite of Jack Hawley's warning: it would be time enough to dismiss them, if dismissal should be necessary, when the rigour of the season was over. Hawley had made their acquaintance — he had met them at my fireside — and thought them a ridiculous pair. Learning that he was a painter they tried to approach him, to show him too that they were the real thing; but he looked at them, across the big room, as if they were miles away: they were a compendium of everything that he most objected to in the social system of his country. Such people as that, all convention and patent-leather, with ejaculations that stopped conversation, had no business in a studio. A studio was a place to learn to see, and how could you see through a pair of feather beds?

The main inconvenience I suffered at their hands was that, at first, I was shy of letting them discover how my artful little servant had begun to sit to me for "Rutland Ramsay." They knew that I had been odd enough (they were prepared by this time to allow oddity to artists,) to pick a foreign vagabond out of the streets, when I might have had a person with whiskers and credentials; but it was some time before they learned how high I rated his accomplish-

ments. They found him in an attitude more than once, but they never doubted I was doing him as an organ-grinder. There were several things they never guessed, and one of them was that for a striking scene in the novel, in which a footman briefly figured, it occurred to me to make use of Major Monarch as the menial. I kept putting this off, I didn't like to ask him to don the livery — besides the difficulty of finding a livery to fit him. At last, one day late in the winter, when I was at work on the despised Oronte (he caught one's idea in an instant), and was in the glow of feeling that I was going very straight, they came in, the Major and his wife, with their society laugh about nothing (there was less and less to laugh at), like country-callers — they always reminded me of that — who have walked across the park after church and are presently persuaded to stay to luncheon. Luncheon was over, but they could stay to tea — I knew they wanted it. The fit was on me, however, and I couldn't let my ardour cool and my work wait, with the fading daylight, while my model prepared it. So I asked Mrs. Monarch if she would mind laying it out — a request which, for an instant, brought all the blood to her face. Her eyes were on her husband's for a second, and some mute telegraphy passed between them. Their folly was over the next instant; his cheerful shrewdness put an end to it. So far from pitying their wounded pride, I must add, I was moved to give it as complete a lesson as I could. They bustled about together and got out the cups and saucers and made the kettle boil. I know they felt as if they were waiting on my servant, and when the tea was prepared I said: "He'll have a cup, please — he's tired." Mrs. Monarch brought him one where he stood, and he took it from her as if he had been a gentleman at a party, squeezing a crush-hat with an elbow.

Then it came over me that she had made a great effort for me — made it with a kind of nobleness — and that I owed her a compensation. Each time I saw her after this I wondered what the compensation could be. I couldn't go on doing the wrong thing to oblige them. Oh, it *was* the wrong thing, the stamp of the work for which they sat —

Hawley was not the only person to say it now. I sent in a large number of the drawings I had made for "Rutland Ramsay," and I received a warning that was more to the point than Hawley's. The artistic adviser of the house for which I was working was of opinion that many of my illustrations were not what had been looked for. Most of these illustrations were the subjects in which the Monarchs had figured. Without going into the question of what *had* been looked for, I saw at this rate I shouldn't get the other books to do. I hurled myself in despair upon Miss Churm, I put her through all her paces. I not only adopted Oronte publicly as my hero, but one morning when the Major looked in to see if I didn't require him to finish a figure for the *Cheapside*, for which he had begun to sit the week before, I told him that I had changed my mind — I would do the drawing from my man. At this my visitor turned pale and stood looking at me. "Is *he* your idea of an English gentleman?" he asked.

I was disappointed, I was nervous, I wanted to get on with my work; so I replied with irritation: "Oh, my dear Major — I can't be ruined for *you!*"

He stood another moment; then, without a word, he quitted the studio. I drew a long breath when he was gone, for I said to myself that I shouldn't see him again. I had not told him definitely that I was in danger of having my work rejected, but I was vexed at his not having felt the catastrophe in the air, read with me the moral of our fruitless collaboration, the lesson that, in the deceptive atmosphere of art, even the highest respectability may fail of being plastic.

I didn't owe my friends money, but I did see them again. They re-appeared together, three days later, and under the circumstances there was something tragic in the fact. It was a proof to me that they could find nothing else in life to do. They had threshed the matter out in a dismal conference — they had digested the bad news that they were not in for the series. If they were not useful to me even for the *Cheapside* their function seemed difficult to determine, and I could only judge at first that they had come, forgivingly, decorously, to take a last leave.

This made me rejoice in secret that I had little leisure for a scene; for I had placed both my other models in position together and I was pegging away at a drawing from which I hoped to derive glory. It had been suggested by the passage in which Rutland Ramsay, drawing up a chair to Artemisia's piano-stool, says extraordinary things to her while she ostensibly fingers out a difficult piece of music. I had done Miss Churm at the piano before — it was an attitude in which she knew how to take on an absolutely poetic grace. I wished the two figures to "compose" together, intensely, and my little Italian had entered perfectly into my conception. The pair were vividly before me, the piano had been pulled out; it was a charming picture of blended youth and murmured love, which I had only to catch and keep. My visitors stood and looked at it, and I was friendly to them over my shoulder.

They made no response, but I was used to silent company and went on with my work, only a little disconcerted (even though exhilarated by the sense that *this* was at least the ideal thing), at not having got rid of them after all. Presently I heard Mrs. Monarch's sweet voice beside, or rather above me: "I wish her hair was a little better done." I looked up and she was staring with a strange fixedness at Miss Churm whose back was turned to her. "Do you mind my just touching it?" she went on — a question which made me spring up for an instant, as with the instinctive fear that she might do the young lady a harm. But she quieted me with a glance I shall never forget — I confess I should like to have been able to paint *that* — and went for a moment to my model. She spoke to her softly, laying a hand upon her shoulder and bending over her; and as the girl, understandingly, gratefully assented, she disposed her rough curls, with a few quick passes, in such a way as to make Miss Churm's head twice as charming. It was one of the most heroic personal services I have ever seen rendered. Then Mrs. Monarch turned away with a low sigh and, looking about her as if for something to do, stooped to the floor with a noble humility and picked up a dirty rag that had dropped out of my paint-box.

The Major meanwhile had also been looking for something to do and, wandering to the other end of the studio, saw before him my breakfast things, neglected, unremoved. "I say, can't I be useful *here?*" he called out to me with an irrepressible quaver. I assented with a laugh that I fear was awkward and for the next ten minutes, while I worked, I heard the light clatter of china and the tinkle of spoons and glass. Mrs. Monarch assisted her husband — they washed up my crockery, they put it away. They wandered off into my little scullery, and I afterwards found that they had cleaned my knives and that my slender stock of plate had an unprecedented surface. When it came over me, the latent eloquence of what they were doing, I confess that my drawing was blurred for a moment — the picture swam. They had accepted their failure, but they couldn't accept their fate. They had bowed their heads in bewilderment to the perverse and cruel law in virtue of which the real thing could be so much less precious than the unreal; but they didn't want to starve. If my servants were my models, my models might be my servants. They would reverse the parts — the others would sit for the ladies and gentlemen, and *they* would do the work. They would still be in the studio — it was an intense dumb appeal to me not to turn them out. "Take us on," they wanted to say — "we'll do *anything*."

When all this hung before me the *afflatus* vanished — my pencil dropped from my hand. My sitting was spoiled and I got rid of my sitters, who were also evidently rather mystified and awestruck. Then, alone with the Major and his wife, I had a most uncomfortable moment. He put their prayer into a single sentence: "I say, you know — just let *us* do for you, can't you?" I couldn't — it was dreadful to see them emptying my slops; but I pretended I could, to oblige them, for about a week. Then I gave them a sum of money to go away; and I never saw them again. I obtained the remaining books, but my friend Hawley repeats that Major and Mrs. Monarch did me a permanent harm, got me into a second-rate trick. If it be true I am content to have paid the price — for the memory.

The Death of the Lion

(1894, 1895, 1909)

I

I had simply, I suppose, a change of heart, and it must have begun when I received my manuscript back from Mr. Pinhorn. Mr. Pinhorn was my "chief," as he was called in the office: he had accepted the high mission of bringing the paper up. This was a weekly periodical, which had been supposed to be almost past redemption when he took hold of it. It was Mr. Deedy who had let the thing down so dreadfully: he was never mentioned in the office now save in connexion with that misdemeanour. Young as I was I had been in a manner taken over from Mr. Deedy, who had been owner as well as editor; forming part of a promiscuous lot, mainly plant and office-furniture, which poor Mrs. Deedy, in her bereavement and depression, parted with at a rough valuation. I could account for my continuity but on the supposition that I had been cheap. I rather resented the practice of fathering all flatness on my late protector, who was in his unhonoured grave; but as I had my way to make I found matter enough for complacency in being on a "staff." At the same time I was aware of my exposure to suspicion as a product of the old lowering system. This made me feel I was doubly bound to have ideas, and had doubtless been at the bottom of my proposing to Mr. Pinhorn that I should lay my lean hands on Neil Paraday. I remember how he looked at me — quite, to begin with, as if he had never heard of this celebrity, who indeed at that moment was by no means in the centre of the heavens; and even when I had knowingly explained he expressed but little confidence in the demand for any such stuff. When I had reminded him that the great principle on which we were supposed to work was just to create the demand we required, he considered a moment and then returned: "I see — you want to write him up."

"Call it that if you like."

"And what's your inducement?"

"Bless my soul — my admiration!"

Mr. Pinhorn pursed his mouth. "Is there much to be done with him?"

"Whatever there is we should have it all to ourselves, for he hasn't been touched."

This argument was effective and Mr. Pinhorn responded. "Very well, touch him." Then he added: "But where can you do it?"

"Under the fifth rib!"

Mr. Pinhorn stared. "Where's that?"

"You want me to go down and see him?" I asked when I had enjoyed his visible search for the obscure suburb I seemed to have named.

"I don't 'want' anything — the proposal's your own. But you must remember that that's the way we do things *now*," said Mr. Pinhorn with another dig at Mr. Deedy.

Unregenerate as I was I could read the queer implications of this speech. The present owner's superior virtue as well as his deeper craft spoke in his reference to the late editor as one of that baser sort who deal in false representations. Mr. Deedy would as soon have sent me to call on Neil Paraday as he would have published a "holiday-number"; but such scruples presented themselves as mere ignoble thrift to his successor, whose own sincerity took the form of ringing door-bells and whose definition of genius was the art of finding people at home. It was as if Mr. Deedy had published reports without his young men's having, as Mr. Pinhorn would have said, really been there. I was unregenerate, as I have hinted, and couldn't be concerned to straighten out the journalistic morals of my chief, feeling them indeed to be an abyss over the edge of which it was better not to peer. Really to be there this time moreover was a vision that made the idea of writing something subtle about Neil Paraday only the more inspiring. I would be as considerate as even Mr. Deedy could have wished, and yet I should be as present as only Mr. Pinhorn could conceive. My allusion to the sequestered manner in which Mr. Paraday lived — it had formed part of my explanation, though I knew of it only by hearsay — was, I could divine, very much what had made Mr. Pinhorn nibble. It truck him as inconsistent with the success

of his paper that any one should be so sequestered as that. And then wasn't an immediate exposure of everything just what the public wanted? Mr. Pinhorn effectually called me to order by reminding me of the promptness with which I had met Miss Braby at Liverpool on her return from her fiasco in the States. Hadn't we published, while its freshness and flavour were unimpaired, Miss Braby's own version of that great international episode? I felt somewhat uneasy at this lumping of the actress and the author, and I confess that after having enlisted Mr. Pinhorn's sympathies I procrastinated a little. I had succeeded better than I wished, and I had, as it happened, work nearer at hand. A few days later I called on Lord Crouchley and carried off in triumph the most unintelligible statement that had yet appeared of his lordship's reasons for his change of front. I thus set in motion in the daily papers columns of virtuous verbiage. The following week I ran down to Brighton for a chat, as Mr. Pinhorn called it, with Mrs. Bounder, who gave me, on the subject of her divorce, many curious particulars that had not been articulated in court. If ever an article flowed from the primal fount it was that article on Mrs. Bounder. By this time, however, I became aware that Neil Paraday's new book was on the point of appearing and that its approach had been the ground of my original appeal to Mr. Pinhorn, who was now annoyed with me for having lost so many days. He bundled me off — we would at least not lose another. I've always thought his sudden alertness a remarkable example of the journalistic instinct. Nothing had occurred, since I first spoke to him, to create a visible urgency, and no enlightenment could possibly have reached him. It was a pure case of professional *flair* — he had smelt the coming glory as an animal smells its distant prey.

II

I may as well say at once that this little record pretends in no degree to be a picture either of my introduction to Mr. Paraday or of certain proximate steps and stages. The scheme of my narrative allows no space for these things, and in any case a prohibitory sentiment would hang about my recollection of so rare an hour. These meagre notes are essentially private, so that if they see the light the insidious forces that, as my story itself shows, make at present for publicity will simply have overmastered my precautions. The curtain fell lately enough on the lamentable drama. My memory of the day I alighted at Mr. Paraday's door is a fresh memory of kindness, hospitality, compassion, and of the wonderful illuminating talk in which the welcome was conveyed. Some voice of the air had taught me the right moment, the moment of his life at which an act of unexpected young allegiance might most come home to him. He had recently recovered from a long, grave illness. I had gone to the neighbouring inn for the night, but I spent the evening in his company, and he insisted the next day on my sleeping under his roof. I hadn't an indefinite leave: Mr. Pinhorn supposed us to put our victims through on the gallop. It was later, in the office, that the rude motions of the jig were set to music. I fortified myself, however, as my training had taught me to do, by the conviction that nothing could be more advantageous for my article than to be written in the very atmosphere. I said nothing to Mr. Paraday about it, but in the morning, after my removal from the inn, while he was occupied in his study, as he had notified me he should need to be, I committed to paper the main heads of my impression. Then thinking to commend myself to Mr. Pinhorn by my celerity, I walked out and posted my little packet before luncheon. Once my paper was written I was free to stay on, and if it was calculated to divert attention from my levity in so doing I could reflect with satisfaction that I had never been so clever. I don't mean to deny of course that I was aware it was much too good for Mr. Pinhorn; but I was equally conscious that Mr. Pinhorn had the supreme shrewdness of recognising from time to time the cases in which an article was not too bad only because it was too good. There was nothing he loved so much as to print on the right occasion a thing he hated. I had begun my visit to the great

man on a Monday, and on the Wednesday his book came out. A copy of it arrived by the first post, and he let me go out into the garden with it immediately after breakfast. I read it from beginning to end that day, and in the evening he asked me to remain with him the rest of the week and over the Sunday.

That night my manuscript came back from Mr. Pinhorn, accompanied with a letter the gist of which was the desire to know what I meant by trying to fob off on him such stuff. That was the meaning of the question, if not exactly its form, and it made my mistake immense to me. Such as this mistake was I could not only look it in the face and accept it. I knew where I had failed, but it was exactly where I couldn't have succeeded. I had been sent down to be personal and then in point of fact hadn't been personal at all: what I had dispatched to London was just a little finicking feverish study of my author's talent. Anything less relevant to Mr. Pinhorn's purpose couldn't well be imagined, and he was visibly angry at my having (at his expense, with a second-class ticket), approached the subject of our enterprise only to stand off so helplessly. For myself, I knew but too well what had happened, and how a miracle — as pretty as some old miracle of legend — had been wrought on the spot to save me. There had been a big brush of wings, the flash of an opaline robe, and then, with a great cool stir of the air, the sense of an angel's having swooped down and caught me to his bosom. He held me only till the danger was over, and it all took place in a minute. With my manuscript back on my hands I understood the phenomenon better, and the reflexions I made on it are what I meant, at the beginning of this anecdote, by my change of heart. Mr. Pinhorn's note was not only a rebuke decidedly stern, but an invitation immediately to send him — it was the case to say so — the genuine article, the revealing and reverberating sketch to the promise of which, and of which alone, I owed my squandered privilege. A week or two later I recast my peccant paper and, giving it a particular application to Mr. Paraday's new book, obtained for it the hospitality of another journal, where, I must admit, Mr. Pinhorn was so far vindicated as that it attracted not the least attention.

III

I was frankly, at the end of three days, a very prejudiced critic, so that one morning when, in the garden, my great man had offered to read me something I quite held my breath as I listened. It was the written scheme of another book — something put aside long ago, before his illness, but that he had lately taken out again to reconsider. He had been turning it round when I came down on him, and it had grown magnificently under this second hand. Loose liberal confident, it might have passed for a great gossiping eloquent letter — the overflow into talk of an artist's amorous plan. The theme I thought singularly rich, quite the strongest he had yet treated; and this familiar statement of it, full too of fine maturities, was really, in summarised splendour, a mine of gold, a precious independent work. I remember rather profanely wondering whether the ultimate production could possibly keep at the pitch. His reading of the fond epistle, at any rate, made me feel as if I were, for the advantage of posterity, in close correspondence with him — were the distinguished person to whom it had been affectionately addressed. It was a high distinction simply to be told such things. The idea he now communicated had all the freshness, the flushed fairness, of the conception untouched and untried: it was Venus rising from the sea and before the airs had blown upon her. I had never been so throbbingly present at such an unveiling. But when he had tossed the last bright word after the others, as I had seen cashiers in banks, weighing mounds of coin, drop a final sovereign into the tray, I knew a sudden prudent alarm.

"My dear master, how, after all, are you going to do it? It's infinitely noble, but what time it will take, what patience and independence, what assured, what perfect conditions! Oh for a lone isle in a tepid sea!"

"Isn't this practically a lone isle, and aren't you, as an encircling medium, tepid enough?" he asked, alluding with a laugh to the wonder of my young admiration and the narrow limits of his little provincial home. "Time isn't what I've lacked hitherto: the question hasn't been to find it, but to use it. Of course my illness made, while it lasted, a great hole — but I dare say there would have been a great hole at any rate. The earth we tread has more pockets than a billiard-table. The great thing is now to keep on my feet."

"That's exactly what I mean."

Neil Paraday looked at me with eyes — such pleasant eyes as he had — in which, as I now recall their expression, I seem to have seen a dim imagination of his fate. He was fifty years old, and his illness had been cruel, his convalescence slow. "It isn't as if I weren't all right."

"Oh if you weren't all right I wouldn't look at you!" I tenderly said.

We had both got up, quickened as by this clearer air, and he had lighted a cigarette. I had taken a fresh one, which with an intenser smile, by way of answer to my exclamation, he applied to the flame of his match. "If I weren't better I shouldn't have thought of *that!*" He flourished his script in his hand.

"I don't want to be discouraging, but that's not true," I returned. "I'm sure that during the months you lay here in pain you had visitations sublime. You thought of a thousand things. You think of more and more all the while. That's what makes you, if you'll pardon my familiarity, so respectable. At a time when so many people are spent you come into your second wind. But, thank God, all the same, you're better! Thank God too you're not, as you were telling me yesterday, 'successful.' If *you* weren't a failure what would be the use of trying? That's my one reserve on the subject of your recovery — that it makes you 'score,' as the newspapers say. It looks well in the newspapers, and almost anything that does that's horrible. 'We are happy to announce that Mr. Paraday, the celebrated author, is again in the enjoyment of excellent health.' Somehow I shouldn't like to see it."

"You won't see it; I'm not in the least celebrated — my obscurity protects me. But couldn't you bear even to see I was dying or dead?" my host enquired.

"Dead — *passe encore*;[1] there's nothing so safe. One never knows what a living artist may do — one has mourned so many. However, one must make the worst of it. You must be as dead as you can."

"Don't I meet that condition in having just published a book?"

"Adequately, let us hope; for the book's verily a masterpiece."

At this moment the parlour-maid appeared in the door that opened from the garden: Paraday lived at no great cost, and the frisk of petticoats, with a timorous "Sherry, sir?" was about his modest mahogany. He allowed half his income to his wife, from whom he had succeeded in separating without redundancy of legend. I had a general faith in his having behaved well, and I had once, in London, taken Mrs. Paraday down to dinner. He now turned to speak to the maid, who offered him, on a tray, some card or note, while, agitated, excited, I wandered to the end of the precinct. The idea of his security became supremely dear to me, and I asked myself if I were the same young man who had come down a few days before to scatter him to the four winds. When I retraced my steps he had gone into the house, and the woman — the second London post had come in — had placed my letters and a newspaper on a bench. I sat down there to the letters, which were a brief business, and then, without heeding the address, took the paper from its envelope. It was the journal of highest renown, *The Empire* of that morning. It regularly came to Paraday, but I remembered that neither of us had yet looked at the copy already delivered. This one had a great mark on the "editorial" page, and, uncrumpling the wrapper, I saw it to be directed to my host and stamped with the name of his publishers. I instantly divined that *The Empire* had spoken of him, and I've not forgotten the odd little shock of the circumstance. It checked all eagerness and made me drop the paper a moment. As I sat there conscious of a palpitation I think I had a vision of what was to be. I had also

[1] Admitted, granted.

a vision of the letter I would presently address to Mr. Pinhorn, breaking, as it were, with Mr. Pinhorn. Of course, however, the next minute the voice of *The Empire* was in my ears.

The article wasn't, I thanked heaven, a review; it was a "leader," the last of three, presenting Neil Paraday to the human race. His new book, the fifth from his hand, had been but a day or two out, and *The Empire*, already aware of it, fired, as if on the birth of a prince, a salute of a whole column. The guns had been booming these three hours in the house without our suspecting them. The big blundering newspaper had discovered him, and now he was proclaimed and anointed and crowned. His place was assigned him as publicly as if a fat usher with a wand had pointed to the topmost chair; he was to pass up and still up, higher and higher, between the watching faces and the envious sounds — away up to the dais and the throne. The article was "epoch-making," a landmark in his life; he had taken rank at a bound, waked up a national glory. A national glory was needed, and it was an immense convenience he was there. What all this meant rolled over me, and I fear I grew a little faint — it meant so much more than I could say "yea" to on the spot. In a flash, somehow, all was different; the tremendous wave I speak of had swept something away. It had knocked down, I suppose, my little customary altar, my twinkling tapers and my flowers, and had reared itself into the likeness of a temple vast and bare. When Neil Paraday should come out of the house he would come out a contemporary. That was what had happened: the poor man was to be squeezed into his horrible age. I felt as if he had been overtaken on the crest of the hill and brought back to the city. A little more and he would have dipped down the short cut to posterity and escaped.

IV

When he came out it was exactly as if he had been in custody, for beside him walked a stout man with a big black beard, who, save that he wore spectacles, might have been a policeman, and in whom at a second glance I recognised the highest contemporary enterprise.

"This is Mr. Morrow," said Paraday, looking, I thought, rather white: "he wants to publish heaven knows what about me."

I winced as I remembered that this was exactly what I myself had wanted. "Already?" I cried with a sort of sense that my friend had fled to me for protection.

Mr. Morrow glared, agreeably, through his glasses: they suggested the electric headlights of some monstrous modern ship, and I felt as if Paraday and I were tossing terrified under his bows. I saw his momentum was irresistible. "I was confident that I should be the first in the field. A great interest is naturally felt in Mr. Paraday's surroundings," he heavily observed.

"I hadn't the least idea of it," said Paraday, as if he had been told he had been snoring.

"I find he hasn't read the article in *The Empire*," Mr. Morrow remarked to me. "That's so very interesting — it's something to start with," he smiled. He had begun to pull off his gloves, which were violently new, and to look encouragingly round the little garden. As a "surrounding" I felt how I myself had already been taken in; I was a little fish in the stomach of a bigger one. "I represent," our visitor continued, "a syndicate of influential journals, no less than thirty-seven, whose public — whose publics, I may say — are in peculiar sympathy with Mr. Paraday's line of thought. They would greatly appreciate any expression of his views on the subject of the art he so nobly exemplifies. In addition to my connexion with the syndicate just mentioned I hold a particular commission from *The Tatler*, whose most prominent department, 'Smatter and Chatter' — I dare say you've often enjoyed it — attracts such attention. I was honoured only last week, as a representative of *The Tatler*, with the confidence of Guy Walsingham, the brilliant author of 'Obsessions.' She pronounced herself thoroughly pleased with my sketch of her method; she went so far as to say that I had made her genius more comprehensible even to herself."

Neil Paraday had dropped on the garden-bench and sat there at once detached and confounded; he looked hard at a bare spot in the lawn, as if with an anxiety that had suddenly made him grave. His movement had been interpreted by his visitor as an invitation to sink sympathetically into a wicker chair that stood hard by, and while Mr. Morrow so settled himself I felt he had taken official possession and that there was no undoing it. One had heard of unfortunate people's having "a man in the house," and this was just what *we* had. There was a silence of a moment, during which we seemed to acknowledge in the only way that was possible the presence of universal fate; the sunny stillness took no pity, and my thought, as I was sure Paraday's was doing, performed within the minute a great distant revolution. I saw just how emphatic I should make my rejoinder to Mr. Pinhorn, and that having come, like Mr. Morrow, to betray, I must remain as long as possible to save. Not because I had brought my mind back, but because our visitor's last words were in my ear, I presently enquired with gloomy irrelevance if Guy Walsingham were a woman.

"Oh yes, a mere pseudonym — rather pretty, isn't it? — and convenient, you know, for a lady who goes in for the larger latitude. 'Obsessions, by Miss So-and-so,' would look a little odd, but men are more naturally indelicate. Have you peeped into 'Obsessions'?" Mr. Morrow continued sociably to our companion.

Paraday, still absent, remote, made no answer, as if he hadn't heard the question; a form of intercourse that appeared to suit the cheerful Mr. Morrow as well as any other. Imperturbably bland, he was a man of resources — he only needed to be on the spot. He had pocketed the whole poor place while Paraday and I were wool-gathering, and I could imagine that he had already got his "heads." His system, at any rate, was justified by the inevitability with which I replied, to save my friend the trouble: "Dear no — he hasn't read it. He doesn't read such things!" I unwarily added.

"Things that are *too* far over the fence, eh?" I was indeed a godsend to Mr. Morrow. It was the psychological moment; it determined the appearance of his note-book, which, however, he at first kept slightly behind him, even as the dentist approaching his victim keeps the horrible forceps. "Mr. Paraday holds with the good old proprieties — I see!" And thinking of the thirty-seven influential journals, I found myself, as I found poor Paraday, helplessly assisting at the promulgation of this ineptitude. "There's no point on which distinguished views are so acceptable as on this question — raised perhaps more strikingly than ever by Guy Walsingham — of the permissibility of the larger latitude. I've an appointment, precisely in connexion with it, next week, with Dora Forbes, author of 'The Other Way Round,' which everybody's talking about. Has Mr. Paraday glanced at 'The Other Way Round'?" Mr. Morrow now frankly appealed to me. I took on myself to repudiate the supposition, while our companion, still silent, got up nervously and walked away. His visitor paid no heed to his withdrawal, but opened out the notebook with a more fatherly pat. "Dora Forbes, I gather, takes the ground, the same as Guy Walsingham's, that the larger latitude has simply got to come. He holds that it has got to be squarely faced. Of course his sex makes him a less prejudiced witness. But an authoritative word from Mr. Paraday — from the point of view of *his* sex, you know — would go right round the globe. He takes the line that we *haven't* got to face it?"

I was bewildered: it sounded somehow as if there were three sexes. My interlocutor's pencil was poised, my private responsibility great. I simply sat staring, none the less, and only found presence of mind to say: "Is this Miss Forbes a gentleman?"

Mr. Morrow had a subtle smile. "It wouldn't be 'Miss' — there's a wife!"

"I mean is she a man?"

"The wife?" — Mr. Morrow was for a moment as confused as myself. But when I explained that I alluded to Dora Forbes in person he informed me, with visible amusement at my being so out of it, that this was the "pen-name" of an indubitable male — he had a big red moustache. "He goes in for the slight mystification because the ladies are such popular favourites. A great deal of interest is felt in his acting on that idea

— which *is* clever, isn't it? — and there's every prospect of its being widely imitated." Our host at this moment joined us again, and Mr. Morrow remarked invitingly that he should be happy to make a note of any observation the movement in question, the bid for success under a lady's name, might suggest to Mr. Paraday. But the poor man, without catching the allusion, excused himself, pleading that, though greatly honoured by his visitor's interest, he suddenly felt unwell and should have to take leave of him — have to go and lie down and keep quiet. His young friend might be trusted to answer for him, but he hoped Mr. Morrow didn't expect great things even of his young friend. His young friend, at this moment, looked at Neil Paraday with an anxious eye, greatly wondering if he were doomed to be ill again; but Paraday's own kind face met his question reassuringly, seemed to say in a glance intelligible enough: "Oh I'm not ill, but I'm scared; get him out of the house as quietly as possible." Getting newspapermen out of the house was odd business for an emissary of Mr. Pinhorn, and I was so exhilarated by the idea of it that I called after him as he left us: "Read the article in *The Empire* and you'll soon be all right!"

V

"Delicious my having come down to tell him of it!" Mr. Morrow ejaculated. "My cab was at the door twenty minutes after *The Empire* had been laid on my breakfast-table. Now what have you got for me?" he continued, dropping again into his chair, from which, however, he the next moment eagerly rose. "I was shown into the drawing-room, but there must be more to see — his study, his literary sanctum, the little things he has about, or other domestic objects and features. He wouldn't be lying down on his study-table? There's a great interest always felt in the scene of an author's labours. Sometimes we're favoured with very delightful peeps. Dora Forbes showed me all his table-drawers, and almost jammed my hand into one into which I made a dash! I don't ask that of you, but if we could talk things over right there where he sits I feel as if I should get the keynote."

I had no wish whatever to be rude to Mr. Morrow, I was too much initiated not to tend to more diplomacy; but I had a quick inspiration, and I entertained an insurmountable, an almost superstitious objection to his crossing the threshold of my friend's little lonely shabby consecrated workshop. "No, no — we shan't get at his life that way," I said. "The way to get at his life is to — But wait a moment!" I broke off and went quickly into the house, whence I in three minutes reappeared before Mr. Morrow with the two volumes of Paraday's new book. "His life's here," I went on, "and I'm so full of this admirable thing that I can't talk of anything else. The artist's life's his work, and this is the place to observe him. What he has to tell us he tells us with *this* perfection. My dear sir, the best interviewer's the best reader."

Mr. Morrow good-humouredly protested. "Do you mean to say that no other source of information should be open to us?"

"None other till this particular one — by far the most copious — has been quite exhausted. Have you exhausted it, my dear sir? Had you exhausted it when you came down here? It seems to me in our time almost wholly neglected, and something should surely be done to restore its ruined credit. It's the course to which the artist himself at every step, and with such pathetic confidence, refers us. This last book of Mr. Paraday's is full of revelations."

"Revelations?" panted Mr. Morrow, whom I had forced again into his chair.

"The only kind that count. It tells you with a perfection that seems to me quite final all the author thinks, for instance, about the advent of the 'larger latitude.' "

"Where does it do that?" asked Mr. Morrow, who had picked up the second volume and was insincerely thumbing it.

"Everywhere — in the whole treatment of his case. Extract the opinion, disengage the answer — those are the real acts of homage."

Mr. Morrow, after a minute, tossed the book away. "Ah but you mustn't take me for a reviewer."

"Heaven forbid I should take you for anything so dreadful! You came down to perform a little act of sympathy, and so, I may confide to you, did I. Let us perform our little act together. These pages overflow with the testimony we want: let us read them and taste them and interpret them. You'll of course have perceived for yourself that one scarcely does read Neil Paraday till one reads him aloud; he gives out to the ear an extraordinary full tone, and it's only when you expose it confidently to that test that you really get near his style. Take up your book again and let me listen, while you pay it out, to that wonderful fifteenth chapter. If you feel you can't do it justice, compose yourself to attention while I produce for you — I think I can! — this scarcely less admirable ninth."

Mr. Morrow gave me a straight look which was as hard as a blow between the eyes; he had turned rather red, and a question had formed itself in his mind which reached my sense as distinctly as if he had uttered it: "What sort of damned fool are *you?*" Then he got up, gathering together his hat and gloves, buttoning his coat, projecting hungrily all over the place the big transparency of his mask. It seemed to flare over Fleet Street and somehow made the actual spot distressingly humble: there was so little for it to feed on unless he counted the blisters of our stucco or saw his way to do something with the roses. Even the poor roses were common kinds. Presently his eyes fell on the manuscript from which Paraday had been reading to me and which still lay on the bench. As my own followed them I saw it looked promising, looked pregnant, as if it gently throbbed with the life the reader had given it. Mr. Morrow indulged in a nod at it and a vague thrust of his umbrella. "What's that?"

"Oh, it's a plan — a secret."

"A secret!" There was an instant's silence, and then Mr. Morrow made another movement. I may have been mistaken, but it affected me as the translated impulse of the desire to lay hands on the manuscript, and this led me to indulge in a quick anticipatory grab which may very well have seemed ungraceful, or even impertinent, and which at any rate left Mr. Paraday's two admirers very erect, glaring at each other while one of them held a bundle of papers well behind him. An instant later Mr. Morrow quitted me abruptly, as if he had really carried something off with him. To reassure myself, watching his broad back recede, I only grasped my manuscript the tighter. He went to the back door of the house, the one he had come out from, but on trying the handle he appeared to find it fastened. So he passed round into the front garden, and by listening intently enough I could presently hear the outer gate close behind him with a bang. I thought again of the thirty-seven influential journals and wondered what would be his revenge. I hasten to add that he was magnanimous: which was just the most dreadful thing he could have been. *The Tatler* published a charming chatty familiar account of Mr. Paraday's "Home-life," and on the wings of the thirty-seven influential journals it went, to use Mr. Morrow's own expression, right round the globe.

VI

A week later, early in May, my glorified friend came up to town, where, it may be veraciously recorded, he was the king of the beasts of the year. No advancement was ever more rapid, no exaltation more complete, no bewilderment more teachable. His book sold but moderately, though the article in *The Empire* had done unwonted wonders for it; but he circulated in person to a measure that the libraries might well have envied. His formula had been found — he was a "revelation." His momentary terror had been real, just as mine had been — the overclouding of his passionate desire to be left to finish his work. He was far from unsociable, but he had the finest conception of being let alone that I've ever met. For the time, none the less, he took his profit where it seemed most to crowd on him, having in his pocket the portable sophistries about the nature of the artist's task. Observation too was a kind of work and experience a kind of success; London dinners were all material and London ladies were fruitful soil. "No one has the faintest conception of what I'm trying for," he said to me, "and not many have read three pages that I've written; but I must dine with them first —

they'll find out why when they've time." It was rather rude justice perhaps; but the fatigue had the merit of being a new sort, while the phantasmagoric town was probably after all less of a battlefield than the haunted study. He once told me that he had had no personal life to speak of since his fortieth year, but had had more than was good for him before. London closed the parenthesis and exhibited him in relations; one of the most inevitable of these being that in which he found himself to Mrs. Weeks Wimbush, wife of the boundless brewer and proprietress of the universal menagerie. In this establishment, as everybody knows, on occasions when the crush is great, the animals rub shoulders freely with the spectators and the lions sit down for whole evenings with the lambs.

It had been ominously clear to me from the first that in Neil Paraday this lady, who, as all the world agreed, was tremendous fun, considered that she had secured a prime attraction, a creature of almost heraldic oddity. Nothing could exceed her enthusiasm over her capture, and nothing could exceed the confused apprehensions it excited in me. I had an instinctive fear of her which I tried without effect to conceal from her victim, but which I let her notice with perfect impunity. Paraday heeded it, but she never did, for her conscience was that of a romping child. She was a blind violent force to which I could attach no more idea of responsibility than to the creaking of a sign in the wind. It was difficult to say what she conduced to but circulation. She was constructed of steel and leather, and all I asked of her for our tractable friend was not to do him to death. He had consented for a time to be of india-rubber, but my thoughts were fixed on the day he should resume his shape or at least get back into his box. It was evidently all right, but I should be glad when it was well over. I had a special fear — the impression was ineffaceable of the hour when, after Mr. Morrow's departure, I had found him on the sofa in his study. That pretext of indisposition had not in the least been meant as a snub to the envoy of *The Tatler* — he had gone to lie down in very truth. He had felt a pang of his old pain, the result of the agitation wrought in him by this forcing open of a new period. His old programme, his old ideal even had to be changed. Say what one would, success was a complication and recognition had to be reciprocal. The monastic life, the pious illumination of the missal in the convent-cell were things of the gathered past. It didn't engender despair, but at least it required adjustment. Before I left him on that occasion we had passed a bargain, my part of which was that I should make it my business to take care of him. Let whoever would represent the interest in his presence (I must have had a mystical prevision of Mrs. Weeks Wimbush) I should represent the interest in his work — or otherwise expressed in his absence. These two interests were in their essence opposed; and I doubt, as youth is fleeting, if I shall ever again know the intensity of joy with which I felt that in so good a cause I was willing to make myself odious.

One day in Sloane Street I found myself questioning Paraday's landlord, who had come to the door in answer to my knock. Two vehicles, a barouche and a smart hansom, were drawn up before the house.

"In the drawing-room, sir? Mrs. Weeks Wimbush."

"And in the dining-room?"

"A young lady, sir — waiting: I think a foreigner."

It was three o'clock, and on days when Paraday didn't lunch out he attached a value to these appropriated hours. On which days, however, didn't the dear man lunch out? Mrs. Wimbush, at such a crisis, would have rushed round immediately after her own repast. I went into the dining-room first, postponing the pleasure of seeing how, upstairs, the lady of the barouche would, on my arrival, point the moral of my sweet solicitude. No one took such an interest as herself in his doing only what was good for him, and she was always on the spot to see that he did it. She made appointments with him to discuss the best means of economising his time and protecting his privacy. She further made his health her special business, and had so much sympathy with my own zeal for it that she was the author of pleasing fictions on the subject of what my devotion had led me to give up. I gave up nothing (I don't count Mr. Pinhorn) because I had nothing, and all I had as yet achieved was to find myself also in the menagerie. I had dashed in to save my friend, but I had only got domesticated and wedged; so that I could do little more for him than exchange with him over people's heads looks of intense but futile intelligence.

VII

The young lady in the dining-room had a brave face, black hair, blue eyes, and in her lap a big volume. "I've come for his autograph," she said when I had explained to her that I was under bonds to see people for him when he was occupied. "I've been waiting half an hour, but I'm prepared to wait all day." I don't know whether it was this that told me she was American, for the propensity to wait all day is not in general characteristic of her race. I was enlightened probably not so much by the spirit of the utterance as by some quality of its sound. At any rate I saw she had an individual patience and a lovely frock, together with an expression that played among her pretty features like a breeze among flowers. Putting her book on the table she showed me a massive album, showily bound and full of autographs of price. The collection of faded notes, of still more faded "thoughts," of quotations, platitudes, signatures, represented a formidable purpose.

I could only disclose my dread of it. "Most people apply to Mr. Paraday by letter, you know."

"Yes, but he doesn't answer. I've written three times."

"Very true," I reflected; "the sort of letter you mean goes straight into the fire."

"How do you know the sort I mean?" My interlocutress had blushed and smiled, and in a moment she added: "I don't believe he gets many like them!"

"I'm sure they're beautiful, but he burns without reading." I didn't add that I had convinced him he ought to.

"Isn't he then in danger of burning things of importance?"

"He would perhaps be so if distinguished men hadn't an infallible nose for nonsense."

She looked at me a moment — her face was sweet and gay. "Do *you* burn without reading too?" — in answer to which I assured her that if she'd trust me with her repository I'd see that Mr. Paraday should write his name in it.

She considered a little. "That's very well, but it wouldn't make me see him."

"Do you want very much to see him?" It seemed ungracious to catechise so charming a creature, but somehow I had never yet taken my duty to the great author so seriously.

"Enough to have come from America for the purpose."

I stared. "All alone?"

"I don't see that that's exactly your business, but if it will make me more seductive I'll confess that I'm quite by myself. I had to come alone or not come at all."

She was interesting; I could imagine she had lost parents, natural protectors — could conceive even she had inherited money. I was at a pass of my own fortunes when keeping hansoms at doors seemed to me pure swagger. As a trick of this bold and sensitive girl, however, it became romantic — a part of the general romance of her freedom, her errand, her innocence. The confidence of young Americans was notorious, and I speedily arrived at a conviction that no impulse could have been more generous than the impulse that had operated here. I foresaw at the moment that it would make her my peculiar charge, just as circumstances had made Neil Paraday. She would be another person to look after, so that one's honour would be concerned in guiding her straight. These things became clearer to me later on; at the instant I had scepticism enough to observe to her, as I turned the pages of her volume, that her net had all the same caught many a big fish. She appeared to have had fruitful access to the great ones of the earth; there were people moreover whose signatures she had presumably secured without a personal interview. She couldn't have worried George Washington and Friedrich Schiller and Hannah More. She met this argument, to

my surprise, by throwing up the album without a pang. It wasn't even her own; she was responsible for none of its treasures. It belonged to a girl-friend in America, a young lady in a western city. This young lady had insisted on her bringing it, to pick up more autographs: she thought they might like to see, in Europe, in what company they would be. The "girl-friend," the western city, the immortal names, the curious errand, the idyllic faith, all made a story as strange to me, and as beguiling, as some tale in the Arabian Nights. Thus it was that my informant had encumbered herself with the ponderous tome; but she hastened to assure me that this was the first time she had brought it out. For her visit to Mr. Paraday it had simply been a pretext. She didn't really care a straw that he should write his name; what she did want was to look straight into his face.

I demurred a little. "And why do you require to do that?"

"Because I just love him!" Before I could recover from the agitating effect of this crystal ring my companion had continued: "Hasn't there ever been any face that *you've* wanted to look into?"

How could I tell her so soon how much I appreciated the opportunity of looking into hers? I could only assent in general to the proposition that there were certainly for every one such yearnings, and even such faces; and I felt the crisis demanded all my lucidity, all my wisdom. "Oh yes, I'm a student of physiognomy. Do you mean," I pursued, "that you've a passion for Mr. Paraday's books?"

"They've been everything to me and a little more beside — I know them by heart. They've completely taken hold of me. There's no author about whom I'm in such a state as I'm in about Neil Paraday."

"Permit me to remark then," I presently returned, "that you're one of the right sort."

"One of the enthusiasts? Of course I am!"

"Oh there are enthusiasts who are quite of the wrong. I mean you're one of those to whom an appeal can be made."

"An appeal?" Her face lighted as with the chance of some great sacrifice.

If she was ready for one it was only waiting for her, and in a moment I mentioned it. "Give up this crude purpose of seeing him. Go away without it. That will be far better."

She looked mystified, then turned visibly pale. "Why, hasn't he any personal charm?" The girl was terrible and laughable in her bright directness.

"Ah that dreadful word 'personal'!" I wailed; "we're dying of it, for you women bring it out with murderous effect. When you meet with a genius as fine as this idol of ours let him off the dreary duty of being a personality as well. Know him only by what's best in him and spare him for the same sweet sake."

My young lady continued to look at me in confusion and mistrust, and the result of her reflexion on what I had just said was to make her suddenly break out: "Look here, sir — what's the matter with him?"

"The matter with him is that if he doesn't look out people will eat a great hole in his life."

She turned it over. "He hasn't any disfigurement?"

"Nothing to speak of!"

"Do you mean that social engagements interfere with his occupations?"

"That but feebly expresses it."

"So that he can't give himself up to his beautiful imagination?"

"He's beset, badgered, bothered — he's pulled to pieces on the pretext of being applauded. People expect him to give them his time, his golden time, who wouldn't themselves give five shillings for one of his books."

"Five? I'd give five thousand!"

"Give your sympathy — give your forbearance. Two thirds of those who approach him only do it to advertise themselves."

"Why it's too bad!" the girl exclaimed with the face of an angel. "It's the first time I was ever called crude!" she laughed.

I followed up my advantage. "There's a lady with him now who's a terrible complication, and who yet hasn't read, I'm sure, ten pages he ever wrote."

My visitor's wide eyes grew tenderer. "Then how does she talk ——"

"Without ceasing. I only mention her as a single case. Do you want to know how to show a superlative consideration? Simply avoid him."

"Avoid him?" she despairingly breathed.

"Don't force him to have to take account of you; admire him in silence, cultivate him at a distance and secretly appropriate his message. Do you want to know," I continued, warming to my idea, "how to perform an act of homage really sublime?" Then as she hung on my words: "Succeed in never seeing him at all!"

"Never at all?" — she suppressed a shriek for it.

"The more you get into his writings the less you'll want to, and you'll be immensely sustained by the thought of the good you're doing him."

She looked at me without resentment or spite, and at the truth I had put before her with candour, credulity, pity. I was afterwards happy to remember that she must have gathered from my face the liveliness of my interest in herself. "I think I see what you mean."

"Oh I express it badly, but I should be delighted if you'd let me come to see you — to explain it better."

She made no response to this, and her thoughtful eyes fell on the big album, on which she presently laid her hands as if to take it away. "I did use to say out West that they might write a little less for autographs — to all the great poets, you know — and study the thoughts and style a little more."

"What do they care for the thoughts and style? They didn't even understand you. I'm not sure," I added, "that I do myself, and I dare say that you by no means make me out."

She had got up to go, and though I wanted her to succeed in not seeing Neil Paraday I wanted her also, inconsequently, to remain in the house. I was at any rate far from desiring to hustle her off. As Mrs. Weeks Wimbush, upstairs, was still saving our friend in her own way, I asked my young lady to let me briefly relate, in illustration of my point, the little incident of my having gone down into the country for a profane purpose and been converted on the spot to holiness. Sinking again into her chair to listen she showed a deep interest in the anecdote. Then thinking it over gravely she returned with her odd intonation: "Yes, but you do see him!" I had to admit that this was the case; and I wasn't so prepared with an effective attenuation as I could have wished. She eased the situation off, however, by the charming quaintness with which she finally said: "Well, I wouldn't want him to be lonely!" This time she rose in earnest, but I persuaded her to let me keep the album to show Mr. Paraday. I assured her I'd bring it back to her myself. "Well, you'll find my address somewhere in it on a paper!" she sighed all resignedly at the door.

VIII

I blush to confess it, but I invited Mr. Paraday that very day to transcribe into the album one of his most characteristic passages. I told him how I had got rid of the strange girl who had brought it — her ominous name was Miss Hunter and she lived at an hotel; quite agreeing with him moreover as to the wisdom of getting rid with equal promptitude of the book itself. This was why I carried it to Albemarle Street no later than on the morrow. I failed to find her at home, but she wrote to me and I went again: she wanted so much to hear more about Neil Paraday. I returned repeatedly, I may briefly declare, to supply her with this information. She had been immensely taken, the more she thought of it, with that idea of mine about the act of homage: it had ended by filling her with a rapturous rapture. She positively desired to do something sublime for him, though indeed I could see that, as this particular flight was difficult, she appreciated the fact that my visits kept her up. I had it on my conscience to keep her up; I neglected nothing that would contribute to it, and her conception of our cherished author's independence became at last as fine as his very own. "Read him, read him — *that* will be an education in decency," I constantly repeated; while, seeking him in his works even as God in nature, she represented herself as convinced that, according to my as-

surance, this was the system that had, as she expressed it, weaned her. We read him together when I could find time, and the generous creature's sacrifice was fed by our communion. There were twenty selfish women about whom I told her and who stirred her to a beautiful rage. Immediately after my first visit her sister, Mrs. Milsom, came over from Paris, and the two ladies began to present, as they called it, their letters. I thanked our stars that none had been presented to Mr. Paraday. They received invitations and dined out, and some of these occasions enabled Fanny Hunter to perform, for consistency's sake, touching feats of submission. Nothing indeed would now have induced her even to look at the object of her admiration. Once, hearing his name announced at a party, she instantly left the room by another door and then straightway quitted the house. At another time when I was at the opera with them — Mrs. Milsom had invited me to their box — I attempted to point Mr. Paraday out to her in the stalls. On this she asked her sister to change places with her and, while that lady devoured the great man through a powerful glass, presented, all the rest of the evening, her inspired back to the house. To torment her tenderly I pressed the glass upon her, telling her how wonderfully near it brought our friend's handsome head. By way of answer she simply looked at me in charged silence, letting me see that tears had gathered in her eyes. These tears, I may remark, produced an effect on me of which the end is not yet. There was a moment when I felt it my duty to mention them to Neil Paraday, but I was deterred by the reflexion that there were questions more relevant to his happiness.

These questions indeed, by the end of the season, were reduced to a single one — the question of reconstituting so far as might be possible the conditions under which he had produced his best work. Such conditions could never all come back, for there was a new one that took up too much place; but some perhaps were not beyond recall. I wanted above all things to see him sit down to the subject he had, on my making his acquaintance, read me that admirable sketch of. Something told me there was no security but in his doing so before the new factor, as we used to say at Mr. Pinhorn's, should render the problem incalculable. It only half-reassured me that the sketch itself was so copious and so eloquent that even at the worst there would be the making of a small but complete book, a tiny volume which, for the faithful, might well become an object of adoration. There would even not be wanting critics to declare, I foresaw, that the plan was a thing to be more thankful for than the structure to have been reared on it. My impatience for the structure, none the less, grew and grew with the interruptions. He had on coming up to town begun to sit for his portrait to a young painter, Mr. Rumble, whose little game, as we also used to say at Mr. Pinhorn's, was to be the first to perch on the shoulders of renown. Mr. Rumble's studio was a circus in which the man of the hour, and still more the woman, leaped through the hoops of his showy frames almost as electrically as they burst into telegrams and "specials." He pranced into the exhibitions on their back; he was the reporter on canvas, the Vandyke up to date, and there was one roaring year in which Mrs. Bounder and Miss Braby, Guy Walsingham and Dora Forbes proclaimed in chorus from the same pictured walls that no one had yet got ahead of him.

Paraday had been promptly caught and saddled, accepting with characteristic good humour his confidential hint that to figure in his show was not so much a consequence as a cause of immortality. From Mrs. Wimbush to the last "representative" who called to ascertain his twelve favourite dishes, it was the same ingenuous assumption that he would rejoice in the repercussion. There were moments when I fancied I might have had more patience with them if they hadn't been so fatally benevolent. I hated at all events Mr. Rumble's picture, and had my bottled resentment ready when, later on, I found my distracted friend had been stuffed by Mrs. Wimbush into the mouth of another cannon. A young artist in whom she was intensely interested, and who had no connexion with Mr. Rumble, was to show how far *he* could make him go. Poor Paraday, in return, was naturally to write something somewhere about the young artist. She played her victims against each other with admirable ingenuity, and hei establishment was a huge machine in which the tiniest and the biggest wheels went round to the same treadle. I had a scene with her in which I tried to express that the function of such a man was to exercise his genius — not to serve as a hoarding for pictorial posters. The people I was perhaps angriest with were the editors of magazines who had introduced what they called new features, so aware were they that the newest feature of all would be to make him grind their axes by contributing his views on vital topics and taking part in the periodical prattle about the future of fiction. I made sure that before I should have done with him there would scarcely be a current form of words left me to be sick of; but meanwhile I could make surer still of my animosity to bustling ladies for whom he drew the water that irrigated their social flower-beds.

I had a battle with Mrs. Wimbush over the artist she protected, and another over the question of a certain week, at the end of July, that Mr. Paraday appeared to have contracted to spend with her in the country. I protested against this visit; I intimated that he was too unwell for hospitality without a *nuance*, for caresses without imagination; I begged he might rather take the time in some restorative way. A sultry air of promises, of ponderous parties, hung over his August, and he would greatly profit by the interval of rest. He hadn't told me he was ill again — that he had had a warning; but I hadn't needed this, for I found his reticence his worst symptom. The only thing he said to me was that he believed a comfortable attack of something or other would set him up: it would put out of the question everything but the exemptions he prized. I'm afraid I shall have presented him as a martyr in a very small cause if I fail to explain that he surrendered himself much more liberally than I surrendered him. He filled his lungs, for the most part, with the comedy of his queer fate: the tragedy was in the spectacles through which I chose to look. He was conscious of inconvenience, and above all of a great renouncement; but how could he have heard a mere dirge in the bells of his accession? The sagacity and the jealousy were mine, and his the impressions and the harvest. Of course, as regards Mrs. Wimbush, I was worsted in my encounters, for wasn't the state of his health the very reason for his coming to her at Prestidge? Wasn't it precisely at Prestidge that he was to be coddled, and wasn't the dear Princess coming to help her coddle him? The dear Princess, now on a visit to England, was of a famous foreign house, and, in her gilded cage, with her retinue of keepers and feeders, was the most expensive specimen in the good lady's collection. I don't think her august presence had had to do with Paraday's consenting to go, but it's not impossible he had operated as a bait to the illustrious stranger. The party had been made up for him, Mrs. Wimbush averred, and every one was counting on it, the dear Princess most of all. If he was well enough he was to read them something absolutely fresh, and it was on that particular prospect the Princess had set her heart. She was so fond of genius in *any* walk of life, and was so used to it and understood it so well: she was the greatest of Mr. Paraday's admirers, she devoured everything he wrote. And then he read like an angel. Mrs. Wimbush reminded me that he had again and again given her, Mrs. Wimbush, the privilege of listening to him.

I looked at her a moment. "What has he read to you?" I crudely enquired.

For a moment too she met my eyes, and for the fraction of a moment she hesitated and coloured. "Oh all sorts of things!"

I wondered if this were an imperfect recollection or only a perfect fib, and she quite understood my unuttered comment on her measure of such things. But if she could forget Neil Paraday's beauties she could of course forget my rudeness, and three days later she invited me, by telegraph, to join the party at Prestidge. This time she might indeed have had a story about what I had given up to be near the master. I addressed from that fine residence several communications to a young lady in London, a young lady whom, I confess, I quitted with

reluctance and whom the reminder of what she herself could give up was required to make me quit at all. It adds to the gratitude I owe her on other grounds that she kindly allows me to transcribe from my letters a few of the passages in which that hateful sojourn is candidly commemorated.

IX

"I suppose I ought to enjoy the joke of what's going on here," I wrote, "but somehow it doesn't amuse me. Pessimism on the contrary possesses me and cynicism deeply engages. I positively feel my own flesh sore from the brass nails in Neil Paraday's social harness. The house is full of people who like him, as they mention, awfully, and with whom his talent for talking nonsense has prodigious success. I delight in his nonsense myself; why is it therefore that I grudge these happy folk their artless satisfaction? Mystery of the human heart — abyss of the critical spirit! Mrs. Wimbush thinks she can answer that question, and as my want of gaiety has at last worn out her patience she has given me a glimpse of her shrewd guess. I'm made restless by the selfishness of the insincere friend — I want to monopolise Paraday in order that he may push me on. To be intimate with him's a feather in my cap; it gives me an importance that I couldn't naturally pretend to, and I seek to deprive him of social refreshment because I fear that meeting more disinterested people may enlighten him as to my real motive. All the disinterested people here are his particular admirers and have been carefully selected as such. There's supposed to be a copy of his last book in the house, and in the hall I come upon ladies, in attitudes, bending gracefully over the first volume. I discreetly avert my eyes, and when I next look round the precarious joy has been superseded by the book of life. There's a sociable circle or a confidential couple, and the relinquished volume lies open on its face and as dropped under extreme coercion. Somebody else presently finds it and transfers it, with its air of momentary desolation, to another piece of furniture. Every one's asking every one about it all day, and every one's telling every one where they put it last. I'm sure it's rather smudgy about the twentieth page. I've a strong impression too that the second volume is lost — has been packed in the bag of some departing guest; and yet everybody has the impression that somebody else has read to the end. You see therefore that the beautiful book plays a great part in our existence. Why should I take the occasion of such distinguished honours to say that I begin to see deeper into Gustave Flaubert's doleful refrain about the hatred of literature? I refer you again to the perverse constitution of man.

"The Princess is a massive lady with the organisation of an athlete and the confusion of tongues of a *valet de place*. She contrives to commit herself extraordinarily little in a great many languages, and is entertained and conversed with in detachments and relays, like an institution which goes on from generation to generation or a big building contracted for under a forfeit. She can't have a personal taste any more than, when her husband succeeds, she can have a personal crown, and her opinion in any matter is rusty and heavy and plain — made, in the night of ages, to last and be transmitted. I feel as if I ought to 'tip' some *custode* for my glimpse of it. She has been told everything in the world and has never perceived anything, and the echoes of her education respond awfully to the rash footfall — I mean the casual remark — in the cold Valhalla of her memory. Mrs. Wimbush delights in her wit and says there's nothing so charming as to hear Mr. Paraday draw it out. He's perpetually detailed for this job, and he tells me it has a peculiarly exhausting effect. Every one's beginning — at the end of two days — to sidle obsequiously away from her, and Mrs. Wimbush pushes him again and again into the breach. None of the uses I have yet seen him put to infuriate me quite so much. He looks very fagged and has at last confessed to me that his condition makes him uneasy — has even promised me he'll go straight home instead of returning to his final engagements in town. Last night I had some talk with him about going to-day, cutting his visit short; so sure am I that he'll be better as soon as he's shut up in his lighthouse. He told me that this is what he would like to do; reminding me, however, that the first lesson of his greatness has been precisely that he can't do what he likes. Mrs. Wimbush would never forgive him if he should leave her before the Princess has received the last hand. When I hint that a violent rupture with our hostess would be the best thing in the world for him he gives me to understand that if his reason assents to the proposition his courage hangs woefully back. He makes no secret of being mortally afraid of her, and when I ask what harm she can do him that she hasn't already done he simply repeats: 'I'm afraid, I'm afraid! Don't enquire too closely,' he said last night; 'only believe that I feel a sort of terror. It's strange, when she's so kind! At any rate, I'd as soon overturn that piece of priceless Sèvres as tell her I must go before my date.' It sounds dreadfully weak, but he has some reason, and he pays for his imagination, which puts him (I should hate it) in the place of others and makes him feel, even against himself, their feelings, their appetites, their motives. It's indeed inveterately against himself that he makes his imagination act. What a pity he has such a lot of it! He's too beastly intelligent. Besides, the famous reading's still to come off, and it has been postponed a day to allow Guy Walsingham to arrive. It appears this eminent lady's staying at a house a few miles off, which means of course that Mrs. Wimbush has forcibly annexed her. She's to come over in a day or two — Mrs. Wimbush wants her to hear Mr. Paraday.

"To-day's wet and cold, and several of the company, at the invitation of the Duke, have driven over to luncheon at Bigwood. I saw poor Paraday wedge himself, by command, into the little supplementary seat of a brougham in which the Princess and our hostess were already ensconced. If the front glass isn't open on his dear old back perhaps he'll survive. Bigwood, I believe, is very grand and frigid, all marble and precedence, and I wish him well out of the adventure. I can't tell you how much more and more *your* attitude to him, in the midst of all this, shines out by contrast. I never willingly talk to these people about him, but see what a comfort I find it to scribble to you! I appreciate it — it keeps me warm; there are no fires in the house. Mrs. Wimbush goes by the calendar, the temperature goes by the weather, the weather goes by God knows what, and the Princess is easily heated. I've nothing but my acrimony to restore my circulation. Coming in an hour ago I found Lady Augusta Minch rummaging about the hall. When I asked her what she was looking for she said she had mislaid something that Mr. Paraday had lent her. I ascertained in a moment that the article in question is a manuscript, and I've a foreboding that it's the noble morsel he read me six weeks ago. When I expressed my surprise that he should have bandied about anything so precious (I happen to know it's his only copy — in the most beautiful hand in all the world) Lady Augusta confessed to me that she hadn't had it from himself, but from Mrs. Wimbush, who had wished to give her a glimpse of it as a salve for her not being able to stay and hear it read.

"'Is that the piece he's to read,' I asked, 'when Guy Walsingham arrives?'

"'It's not for Guy Walsingham they're waiting now, it's Dora Forbes,' Lady Augusta said. 'She's coming, I believe, early to-morrow. Meanwhile Mrs. Wimbush has found out about *him*, and is actively wiring to him. She says he also must hear him.'

"'You bewilder me a little,' I replied; 'in the age we live in one gets lost among the genders and the pronouns. The clear thing is that Mrs. Wimbush doesn't guard such a treasure so jealously as she might.'

"'Poor dear, she has the Princess to guard! Mr. Paraday lent her the manuscript to look over.'

"'She spoke, you mean, as if it were the morning paper?'

"Lady Augusta stared — my irony was lost on her. 'She didn't have time, so she gave me a chance first; because unfortunately I go to-morrow to Bigwood.'

"'And your chance has only proved a chance to lose it?'

"'I haven't lost it. I remember now — it was very stupid of me to have forgotten. I told my maid to give it to Lord Dorimont — or at least to his man.'

"'And Lord Dorimont went away directly after luncheon.'

"'Of course he gave it back to my maid — or else his man did,' said Lady Augusta. 'I dare say it's all right.'

"The conscience of these people is like a summer sea. They haven't time to look over a priceless composition; they've only time to kick it about the house. I suggested that the 'man,' fired with a noble emulation, has perhaps kept the work for his own perusal; and her ladyship wanted to know whether, if the thing shouldn't reappear for the grand occasion appointed by our hostess, the author wouldn't have something else to read that would do just as well. Their questions are too delightful! I declared to Lady Augusta briefly that nothing in the world can ever do so well as the thing that does best; and at this she looked a little disconcerted. But I added that if the manuscript had gone astray our little circle would have the less of an effort of attention to make. The piece in question was very long — it would keep them three hours.

"'Three hours! Oh the Princess will get up!' said Lady Augusta.

"'I thought she was Mr. Paraday's greatest admirer.'

"'I dare say she is — she's so awfully clever. But what's the use of being a Princess ——'

"'If you can't dissemble your love?' I asked as Lady Augusta was vague. She said at any rate that she'd question her maid; and I'm hoping that when I go down to dinner I shall find the manuscript has been recovered."

X

"It has *not* been recovered," I wrote early the next day, "and I'm moreover much troubled about our friend. He came back from Bigwood with a chill and, being allowed to have a fire in his room, lay down a while before dinner. I tried to send him to bed and indeed thought I had put him in the way of it; but after I had gone to dress Mrs. Wimbush came up to see him, with the inevitable result that when I returned I found him under arms and flushed and feverish, though decorated with the rare flower she had brought him for his button-hole. He came down to dinner, but Lady Augusta Minch was very shy of him. To-day he's in great pain, and the advent of *ces dames* — I mean of Guy Walsingham and Dora Forbes — doesn't at all console me. It does Mrs. Wimbush, however, for she has consented to his remaining in bed so that he may be all right to-morrow for the listening circle. Guy Walsingham's already on the scene, and the doctor for Paraday also arrived early. I haven't yet seen the author of 'Obsessions,' but of course I've had a moment by myself with the Doctor. I tried to get him to say that our invalid must go straight home — I mean to-morrow or next day; but he quite refuses to talk about the future. Absolute quiet and warmth and the regular administration of an important remedy are the points he mainly insists on. He returns this afternoon, and I'm to go back to see the patient at one o'clock, when he next takes his medicine. It consoles me a little that he certainly won't be able to read — an exertion he was already more than unfit for. Lady Augusta went off after breakfast, assuring me her first care would be to follow up the lost manuscript. I can see she thinks me a shocking busybody and doesn't understand my alarm, but she'll do what she can, for she's a good-natured woman. 'So are they all honourable men.' That was precisely what made her give the thing to Lord Dorimont and made Lord Dorimont bag it. What use *he* has for it God only knows. I've the worst forebodings, but somehow I'm strangely without passion — desperately calm. As I consider the unconscious, the well-meaning ravages of our appreciative circle I bow my head in submission to some great natural, some universal accident; I'm rendered almost indifferent, in fact quite gay (ha-ha!) by the sense of immitigable fate. Lady Augusta promises me to trace the precious object and let me have it through the post by the time Paraday's well enough to play his part with it. The last evidence is that her maid did give it to his lordship's valet. One would suppose it some thrilling number of *The Family Budget.* Mrs. Wimbush, who's aware of the accident, is much less agitated by it than she would doubtless be were she not for the hour inevitably engrossed with Guy Walsingham."

Later in the day I informed my correspondent, for whom indeed I kept a loose diary of the situation, that I had made the acquaintance of this celebrity and that she was a pretty little girl who wore her hair in what used to be called a crop. She looked so juvenile and so innocent that if, as Mr. Morrow had announced, she was resigned to the larger latitude, her superiority to prejudice must have come to her early. I spent most of the day hovering about Neil Paraday's room, but it was communicated to me from below that Guy Walsingham, at Prestidge, was a success. Toward evening I became conscious somehow that her superiority was contagious, and by the time the company had separated for the night I was sure the larger latitude had been generally accepted. I thought of Dora Forbes and felt that he had no time to lose. Before dinner I received a telegram from Lady Augusta Minch. "Lord Dorimont thinks he must have left bundle in train — enquire." How could I enquire — if I was to take the word as a command? I was too worried and now too alarmed about Neil Paraday. The Doctor came back, and it was an immense satisfaction to me to be sure he was wise and interested. He was proud of being called to so distinguished a patient, but he admitted to me that night that my friend was gravely ill. It was really a relapse, a recrudescence of his old malady. There could be no question of moving him: we must at any rate see first, on the spot, what turn his condition would take. Meanwhile, on the morrow, he was to have a nurse. On the morrow the dear man was easier, and my spirits rose to such cheerfulness that I could almost laugh over Lady Augusta's second telegram: "Lord Dorimont's servant been to station — nothing found. Push enquiries." I did laugh, I'm sure, as I remembered this to be the mystic scroll I had scarcely allowed poor Mr. Morrow to point his umbrella at. Fool that I had been: the thirty-seven influential journals wouldn't have destroyed it, they'd only have printed it. Of course I said nothing to Paraday.

When the nurse arrived she turned me out of the room, on which I went down-stairs. I should premise that at breakfast the news that our brilliant friend was doing well excited universal complacency, and the Princess graciously remarked that he was only to be commiserated for missing the society of Miss Collop. Mrs. Wimbush, whose social gift never shone brighter than in the dry decorum with which she accepted this fizzle in her fireworks, mentioned to me that Guy Walsingham had made a very favourable impression on her Imperial High-ness. Indeed I think every one did so, and that, like the money-market or the national honour, her Imperial Highness was consti-tutionally sensitive. There was a certain gladness, a perceptible bustle in the air, however, which I thought slightly anomalous in a house where a great author lay critically ill. "Le roy est mort — vive le roy": I was reminded that another great author had already stepped into his shoes. When I came down again after the nurse had taken pos-session I found a strange gentleman hanging about the hall and pacing to and fro by the closed door of the drawing-room. This per-sonage was florid and bald; he had a big red moustache and wore showy knicker-bockers — characteristics all that fitted to my conception of the identity of Dora Forbes. In a moment I saw what had happened: the author of "The Other Way Round" had just alighted at the portals of Prestidge, but had suffered a scruple to restrain him from penetrating further. I recognised his scruple when, pausing to listen at his gesture of caution, I heard a shrill voice lifted in a sort of rhythmic uncanny chant. The famous reading had begun, only it was the author of "Obsessions" who now furnished the sac-rifice. The new visitor whispered to me that he judged something was going on he oughtn't to interrupt.

"Miss Collop arrived last night," I smiled, "and the Princess has a thirst for the *inédit*." [1]

Dora Forbes raised his bushy brows. "Miss Collop?"

"Guy Walsingham, your distinguished confrère — or shall I say your formidable rival?"

[1] Unpublished.

"Oh!" growled Dora Forbes. Then he added: "Shall I spoil it if I go in?"

"I should think nothing could spoil it!" I ambiguously laughed.

Dora Forbes evidently felt the dilemma; he gave an irritated crook to his moustache. "*Shall* I go in?" he presently asked.

We looked at each other hard a moment; then I expressed something bitter that was in me, expressed it in an infernal "Do!" After this I got out into the air, but not so fast as not to hear, when the door of the drawing-room opened, the disconcerted drop of Miss Collop's public manner: she must have been in the midst of the larger latitude. Producing with extreme rapidity, Guy Wal-singham has just published a work in which amiable people who are not initiated have been pained to see the genius of a sister-novelist held up to unmistakeable ridicule; so fresh an exhibition does it seem to them of the dreadful way men have always treated women. Dora Forbes, it's true, at the present hour, is immensely pushed by Mrs. Wimbush and has sat for his portrait to the young artists she protects, sat for it not only in oils but in monumental alabaster.

What happened at Prestidge later in the day is of course contemporary history. If the interruption I had whimsically sanc-tioned was almost a scandal, what is to be said of that general scatter of the company which, under the Doctor's rule, began to take place in the evening? His rule was soothing to behold, small comfort as I was to have at the end. He decreed in the inter-est of his patient an absolutely soundless house and a consequent break-up of the party. Little country practitioner as he was, he literally packed off the Princess. She de-parted as promptly as if a revolution had broken out, and Guy Walsingham emigrated with her. I was kindly permitted to re-main, and this was not denied even to Mrs. Wimbush. The privilege was withheld in-deed from Dora Forbes; so Mrs. Wimbush kept her latest capture temporarily con-cealed. This was so little, however, her usual way of dealing with her eminent friends that a couple of days of it exhausted her patience and she went up to town with him in great publicity. The sudden turn for the worse her afflicted guest had, after a brief improvement, taken on the third night, raised an obstacle to her seeing him before her retreat; a fortunate circumstance doubtless, for she was fundamentally disappointed in him. This was not the kind of performance for which she had invited him to Prestidge, let alone invited the Princess. I must add that none of the generous acts marking her patronage of intellectual and other merit have done so much for her reputation as her lending Neil Paraday the most beautiful of her numerous homes to die in. He took advantage to the utmost of the singular favour. Day by day I saw him sink, and I roamed alone about the empty terraces and gardens. His wife never came near him, but I scarcely noticed it: as I paced there with rage in my heart I was too full of another wrong. In the event of his death it would fall to me perhaps to bring out in some charming form, with notes, with the tenderest editorial care, that precious heritage of his written project. But where *was* that precious heritage, and were both the author and the book to have been snatched from us? Lady Augusta wrote me she had done all she could and that poor Lord Dorimont, who had really been worried to death, was extremely sorry. I couldn't have the matter out with Mrs. Wimbush, for I didn't want to be taunted by her with desiring to aggrandise myself by a public connexion with Mr. Paraday's sweepings. She had signified her willingness to meet the expense of all advertising, as indeed she was always ready to do. The last night of the horrible series, the night before he died, I put my ear closer to his pillow.

"That thing I read you that morning, you know."

"In your garden that dreadful day? Yes?"

"Won't it do as it is?"

"It would have been a glorious book."

"It *is* a glorious book," Neil Paraday murmured. "Print it as it stands — beautifully."

"Beautifully!" I passionately promised.

It may be imagined whether, now that he's gone, the promise seems to me less sacred. I'm convinced that if such pages had appeared in his lifetime the Abbey would hold

him to-day. I've kept the advertising in my own hands, but the manuscript has not been recovered. It's impossible, and at any rate intolerable, to suppose it can have been wantonly destroyed. Perhaps some hazard of a blind hand, some brutal fatal ignorance has lighted kitchen-fires with it. Every stupid and hideous accident haunts my meditations. My undiscourageable search for the lost treasure would make a long chapter. Fortunately I've a devoted associate in the person of a young lady who has every day a fresh indignation and a fresh idea, and who maintains with intensity that the prize will still turn up. Sometimes I believe her, but I've quite ceased to believe it myself. The only thing for us at all events is to go on seeking and hoping together, and we should be closely united by this firm tie even were we not at present by another.

The Art of Fiction

(1884)

I should not have affixed so comprehensive a title to these few remarks, necessarily wanting in any completeness upon a subject the full consideration of which would carry us far, did I not seem to discover a pretext for my temerity in the interesting pamphlet lately published under this name by Mr. Walter Besant. Mr. Besant's lecture at the Royal Institution — the original form of his pamphlet — appears to indicate that many persons are interested in the art of fiction, and are not indifferent to such remarks, as those who practise it may attempt to make about it. I am therefore anxious not to lose the benefit of this favourable association, and to edge in a few words under cover of the attention which Mr. Besant is sure to have excited. There is something very encouraging in his having put into form certain of his ideas on the mystery of story-telling.

It is a proof of life and curiosity — curiosity on the part of the brotherhood of novelists as well as on the part of their readers. Only a short time ago it might have been supposed that the English novel was not what the French call *discutable*. It had no air of having a theory, a conviction, a consciousness of itself behind it — of being the expression of an artistic faith, the result of choice and comparison. I do not say it was necessarily the worse for that: it would take much more courage than I possess to intimate that the form of the novel as Dickens and Thackeray (for instance) saw it had any taint of incompleteness. It was, however, *naïf* (if I may help myself out with another French word); and evidently if it be destined to suffer in any way for having lost its *naïveté* it has now an idea of making sure of the corresponding advantages. During the period I have alluded to there was a comfortable, good-humoured feeling abroad that a novel is a novel, as a pudding is a pudding, and that our only business with it could be to swallow it. But within a year or two, for some reason or other, there have been signs of returning animation — the era of discussion would appear to have been to a certain extent opened. Art lives upon discussion, upon experiment, upon curiosity, upon variety of attempt, upon the exchange of views and the comparison of standpoints; and there is a presumption that those times when no one has anything particular to say about it, and has no reason to give for practice or preference, though they may be times of honour, are not times of development — are times, possibly even, a little of dulness. The successful application of any art is a delightful spectacle, but the theory too is interesting; and though there is a great deal of the latter without the former I suspect there has never been a genuine success that has not had a latent core of conviction. Discussion, suggestion, formulation, these things are fertilising when they are frank and sincere. Mr. Besant has set an excellent example in saying what he thinks, for his part, about the way in which fiction should be written, as well as about the way in which it should be published; for his view of the "art," carried on into an appendix, covers that too. Other labourers in the same field will doubtless take up the argument, they will give it the light of their experience, and the effect will surely be to make our interest in the novel a little more what it had for some time threatened to fail to be — a serious, active, inquiring interest, under protection of which this delightful study may, in moments of confidence, venture to say a little more what it thinks of itself.

It must take itself seriously for the public to take it so. The old superstition about fiction being "wicked" has doubtless died out in England; but the spirit of it lingers in a certain oblique regard directed toward any story which does not more or less admit that it is only a joke. Even the most jocular novel feels in some degree the weight of the proscription that was formerly directed against literary levity: the jocularity does not always succeed in passing for orthodoxy. It is still expected, though perhaps people are ashamed to say it, that a production which is after all only a "make-believe" (for what else is a "story"?) shall be in some degree apologetic — shall renounce the pretension of attempting really to represent life. This, of course, any sensible, wide-awake story declines to do, for it quickly perceives that the tolerance granted to it on such a condition is only an attempt to stifle it disguised in the form of generosity. The old evangelical hostility to the novel, which was as explicit as it was narrow, and which regarded it as little less favourable to our immortal part than a stage-play, was in reality far less insulting. The only reason for the existence of a novel is that it does attempt to represent life. When it relinquishes this attempt, the same attempt that we see on the canvas of the painter, it will have arrived at a very strange pass. It is not expected of the picture that it will make itself humble in order to be forgiven; and the analogy between the art of the painter and the art of the novelist is, so far as I am able to see, complete. Their inspiration is the same, their process (allowing for the different quality of the vehicle) is the same, their success is the same. They may learn from each other, they may explain and sustain each other. Their cause is the same, and the honour of one is the honour of another. The Mahometans think a picture an unholy thing, but it is a long time since any Christian did, and it is therefore the more odd that in the Christian mind the traces (dissimulated though they may be) of a suspicion of the sister art should linger to this day. The only effectual way to lay it to rest is to emphasise the analogy to which I just alluded — to insist on the fact that as the picture is reality, so the novel is history. That is the only general description (which does it justice) that we may give of the novel. But history also is allowed to represent life; it is not, any more than painting, expected to apologise. The subject-matter of fiction is stored up likewise in documents and records, and if it will not give itself away, as they say in California, it must speak with assurance, with the tone of the historian. Certain accomplished novelists have a habit of giving themselves away which must often bring tears to the eyes of people who take their fiction seriously. I was lately struck, in reading over many pages of Anthony Trollope, with his want of discretion in this particular. In a digression, a parenthesis or an aside, he concedes to the reader that he and this trusting friend are only "making believe." He admits that the events he narrates have not really happened, and that he can give his narrative any turn the reader may like best. Such a betrayal of a sacred office seems to me, I confess, a terrible crime; it is what I mean by the attitude of apology, and it shocks me every whit as much in Trollope as it would have shocked me in Gibbon or Macaulay. It implies that the novelist is less occupied in looking for the truth (the truth, of course I mean, that he assumes, the premises that we must grant him, whatever they may be), than the historian, and in doing so it deprives him at a stroke of all his standing-room. To represent and illustrate the past, the actions of men, is the task of either writer, and the only difference that I can see is, in proportion as he succeeds, to the honour of the novelist, consisting as it does in his having more difficulty in collecting his evidence, which is so far from being purely literary. It seems to me to give him a great character, the fact that he has at once so much in common with the philosopher and the painter; this double analogy is a magnificent heritage.

It is of all this evidently that Mr. Besant is full when he insists upon the fact that fiction is one of the *fine* arts, deserving in its turn of all the honours and emoluments that have hitherto been reserved for the successful profession of music, poetry, painting, architecture. It is impossible to insist too much on so important a truth, and the place that Mr. Besant demands for the work of the novelist may be represented, a trifle less abstractly, by saying that he demands not only that it shall be reputed artistic, but that it shall be reputed very artistic indeed. It is excellent that he should have struck this note, for his doing so indicates that there was need of it, that his proposition may be to many people a novelty. One rubs one's eyes at the thought; but the rest of Mr. Besant's essay confirms the revelation. I suspect in truth that it would be possible to confirm it still further, and that one would not be far wrong in saying that in addition to the people to whom it has never occurred that a novel ought to be artistic, there are a great many others who, if this principle were urged upon them, would be filled with an indefinable mistrust. They would find it difficult to explain their repugnance, but it would operate strongly to put them on their guard. "Art," in our Protestant communities, where so many things have got so strangely twisted about, is supposed in certain circles to have some vaguely injurious effect upon those who make it an important consideration, who let it weigh in the balance. It is assumed to be opposed in some mysterious manner to morality, to amusement, to instruction. When it is embodied in the work of the painter (the sculptor is another affair!) you know what it is: it stands there before you, in the honesty of pink and green and a gilt frame; you can see the worst of it at a glance, and you can be on your guard. But when it is introduced into literature it becomes more insidious — there is danger of its hurting you before you know it. Literature should be either instructive or amusing, and there is in many minds an impression that these artistic preoccupations, the search for form, contribute to neither end, interfere indeed with both. They are too frivolous to be edifying, and too serious to be diverting; and they are moreover priggish and paradoxical and superfluous. That, I think, represents the manner in which the latent thought of many people who read novels as an exercise in skipping would explain itself if it were to become articulate. They would argue, of course, that a novel ought to be "good," but they would interpret this term in a fashion of their own, which indeed would vary considerably from one critic to another. One would say that being good means representing virtuous and aspiring characters, placed in prominent positions; another would say that it depends on a "happy ending," on a distribution at the last of prizes, pensions, husbands, wives, babies, millions, appended paragraphs, and cheerful remarks. Another still would say that it means being full of incident and movement, so that we shall wish to jump ahead, to see who was the mysterious stranger, and if the stolen will was ever found, and shall not be distracted from this pleasure by any tiresome analysis or "description." But they would all agree that the "artistic" idea would spoil some of their fun. One would hold it accountable for all the description, another would see it revealed in the absence of sympathy. Its hostility to a happy ending would be evident, and it might even in some cases render any ending at all impossible. The "ending" of a novel is, for many persons, like that of a good dinner, a course of dessert and ices, and the artist in fiction is regarded as a sort of meddlesome doctor who forbids agreeable aftertastes. It is therefore true that this conception of Mr. Besant's of the novel as a superior form encounters not only a negative but a positive indifference. It matters little that as a work of art it should really be as little or as much of its essence to supply happy endings, sympathetic characters, and an objective tone, as if it were a work of mechanics: the association of ideas, however incongruous, might easily be too much for it if an eloquent voice were not sometimes raised to call attention to the fact that it is at once as free and as serious a branch of literature as any other.

Certainly this might sometimes be doubted in presence of the enormous number of works of fiction that appeal to the credulity of our generation, for it might easily seem that there could be no great character in a commodity so quickly and easily produced. It must be admitted that good novels are much compromised by bad ones, and that the field at large suffers discredit from overcrowding. I think, however, that this injury is only superficial, and that the superabundance of written fiction proves nothing against the principle itself. It has been vulgarised, like all other kinds of literature, like everything else to-day, and it has proved more than some kinds accessible to vulgarisation. But there is as much difference as there ever was between a good novel and a bad one: the bad is swept with all the daubed canvases and spoiled marble into some unvisited limbo, or infinite rubbish-yard beneath the back-windows of the world, and the good subsists and emits its light and stimulates our desire for perfection. As I shall take the liberty of making but a single criticism of Mr. Besant, whose tone is so full of the love of his art, I may as well have done with it at once. He seems to me to mistake in attempting to say so definitely beforehand what sort of an affair the good novel will be. To indicate the danger of such an error as that has been the purpose of these few pages; to suggest that certain traditions on the subject, applied *a priori*, have already had much to answer for, and that the good health of an art which undertakes so immediately to reproduce life must demand that it be perfectly free. It lives upon exercise, and the very meaning of exercise is freedom. The only obligation to which in advance we may hold a novel, without incurring the accusation of being arbitrary, is that it be interesting. That general responsibility rests upon it, but it is the only one I can think of. The ways in which it is at liberty to accomplish this result (of interesting us) strike me as innumerable, and such as can only suffer from being marked out or fenced in by prescription. They are as various as the temperament of man, and they are successful in proportion as they reveal a particular mind, different from others. A novel is in its broadest definition a personal, a direct impression of life: that, to begin with, constitutes its value, which is greater or less according to the intensity of the impression. But there will be no intensity at all, and therefore no value, unless there is freedom to feel and say. The tracing of a line to be followed, of a tone to be taken, of a form to be filled out, is a limita- tion of that freedom and a suppression of the very thing that we are most curious about. The form, it seems to me, is to be appreciated after the fact; then the author's choice has been made, his standard has been indicated; then we can follow lines and directions and compare tones and resemblances. Then in a word we can enjoy one of the most charm- ing of pleasures, we can estimate quality, we can apply the test of execution. The execution belongs to the author alone; it is what is most personal to him, and we meas- ure him by that. The advantage, the luxury, as well as the torment and responsibility of the novelist, is that there is no limit to what he may attempt as an executant — no limit to his possible experiments, efforts, dis- coveries, successes. Here it is especially that he works, step by step, like his brother of the brush, of whom we may always say that he has painted his picture in a manner best known to himself. His manner is his secret, not necessarily a jealous one. He cannot dis- close it as a general thing if he would; he would be at a loss to teach it to others. I say this with a due recollection of having in- sisted on the community of method of the artist who paints a picture and the artist who writes a novel. The painter *is* able to teach the rudiments of his practice, and it is possi- ble, from the study of good work (granted the aptitude), both to learn how to paint and to learn how to write. Yet it remains true, without injury to the *rapprochement*, that the literary artist would be obliged to say to his pupil much more than the other, "Ah, well, you must do it as you can!" It is a question of degree, a matter of delicacy. If there are exact sciences, there are also exact arts, and the grammar of painting is so much more definite that it makes the difference.

I ought to add, however, that if Mr. Besant says at the beginning of his essay that the "laws of fiction may be laid down and taught with as much precision and exactness as the laws of harmony, perspective, and proportion," he mitigates what might appear to be an extravagance by applying his re- mark to "general" laws, and by expressing most of these rules in a manner with which it would certainly be unaccommodating to

disagree. That the novelist must write from his experience, that his "characters must be real and such as might be met with in actual life;" that "a young lady brought up in a quiet country village should avoid descrip- tions of garrison life," and "a writer whose friends and personal experiences belong to the lower middle-class should carefully avoid introducing his characters into society"; that one should enter one's notes in a com- mon-place book; that one's figures should be clear in outline; that making them clear by some trick of speech or of carriage is a bad method, and "describing them at length" is a worse one; that English Fiction should have a "conscious moral purpose"; that "it is almost impossible to estimate too highly the value of careful workmanship — that is, of style"; that "the most important point of all is the story," that "the story is everything": these are principles with most of which it is surely impossible not to sympathise. That remark about the lower middle-class writer and his knowing his place is perhaps rather chilling; but for the rest I should find it diffi- cult to dissent from any one of these recom- mendations. At the same time, I should find it difficult positively to assent to them, with the exception, perhaps, of the injunction as to entering one's notes in a common-place book. They scarcely seem to me to have the quality that Mr. Besant attributes to the rules of the novelist — the "precision and exactness" of "the laws of harmony, per- spective, and proportion." They are sugges- tive, they are even inspiring, but they are not exact, though they are doubtless as much so as the case admits of: which is a proof of that liberty of interpretation for which I just contended. For the value of these different injunctions — so beautiful and so vague — is wholly in the meaning one attaches to them. The characters, the situation, which strike one as real will be those that touch and inter- est one most, but the measure of reality is very difficult to fix. The reality of Don Quixote or of Mr. Micawber is a very deli- cate shade; it is a reality so coloured by the author's vision that, vivid as it may be, one would hesitate to propose it as a model: one would expose one's self to some very embar- rassing questions on the part of a pupil. It goes without saying that you will not write a good novel unless you possess the sense of reality; but it will be difficult to give you a recipe for calling that sense into being. Humanity is immense, and reality has a myriad forms; the most one can affirm is that some of the flowers of fiction have the odour of it, and others have not; as for telling you in advance how your nosegay should be composed, that is another affair. It is equally excellent and inconclusive to say that one must write from experience; to our supposititious aspirant such a declaration might savour of mockery. What kind of experience is intended, and where does it begin and end? Experience is never limited, and it is never complete; it is an immense sensibility, a kind of huge spiderweb of the finest silken threads suspended in the chamber of consciousness, and catching every air-borne particle in its tissue. It is the very atmosphere of the mind; and when the mind is imaginative — much more when it happens to be that of a man of genius — it takes to itself the faintest hints of life, it converts the very pulses of the air into revelations. The young lady living in a village has only to be a damsel upon whom nothing is lost to make it quite unfair (as it seems to me) to declare to her that she shall have nothing to say about the military. Greater miracles have been seen than that, imagination assisting, she should speak the truth about some of these gentlemen. I remember an English novelist, a woman of genius, telling me that she was much commended for the impression she had managed to give in one of her tales of the nature and way of life of the French Protestant youth. She had been asked where she learned so much about this recondite being, she had been congratulated on her peculiar opportunities. These opportunities consisted in her having once, in Paris, as she ascended a staircase, passed an open door where, in the household of a *pasteur*, some of the young Protestants were seated at table round a finished meal. The glimpse made a picture; it lasted only a moment, but that moment was experience. She had got her direct personal impression, and she turned out her type. She knew what youth was, and what Protestantism; she also had the advantage of having seen what it was to be French, so that she converted these ideas into a concrete image and produced a reality. Above all, however, she was blessed with the faculty which when you give it an inch takes an ell, and which for the artist is a much greater source of strength than any accident of residence or of place in the social scale. The power to guess the unseen from the seen, to trace the implication of things, to judge the whole piece by the pattern, the condition of feeling life in general so completely that you are well on your way to knowing any particular corner of it — this cluster of gifts may almost be said to constitute experience, and they occur in country and in town, and in the most differing stages of education. If experience consists of impressions, it may be said that impressions *are* experience, just as (have we not seen it?) they are the very air we breathe. Therefore, if I should certainly say to a novice, "Write from experience and experience only," I should feel that this was rather a tantalising monition if I were not careful immediately to add, "Try to be one of the people on whom nothing is lost!"

I am far from intending by this to minimise the importance of exactness — of truth of detail. One can speak best from one's own taste, and I may therefore venture to say that the air of reality (solidity of specification) seems to me to be the supreme virtue of a novel — the merit on which all its other merits (including that conscious moral purpose of which Mr. Besant speaks) helplessly and submissively depend. If it be not there they are all as nothing, and if these be there, they owe their effect to the success with which the author has produced the illusion of life. The cultivation of this success, the study of this exquisite process, form, to my taste, the beginning and the end of the art of the novelist. They are his inspiration, his despair, his reward, his torment, his delight. It is here in very truth that he competes with life; it is here that he competes with his brother the painter in *his* attempt to render the look of things, the look that conveys their meaning, to catch the colour, the relief, the expression, the surface, the substance of the human spectacle. It is in regard to this that Mr. Besant is well inspired when he bids him take notes. He cannot possibly take too many, he cannot possibly take enough. All life solicits him, and to "render" the simplest surface, to produce the most momentary illusion, is a very complicated business. His case would be easier, and the rule would be more exact, if Mr. Besant had been able to tell him what notes to take. But this, I fear, he can never learn in any manual; it is the business of his life. He has to take a great many in order to select a few, he has to work them up as he can, and even the guides and philosophers who might have most to say to him must leave him alone when it comes to the application of precepts, as we leave the painter in communion with his palette. That his characters "must be clear in outline," as Mr. Besant says — he feels that down to his boots; but how he shall make them so is a secret between his good angel and himself. It would be absurdly simple if he could be taught that a great deal of "description" would make them so, or that on the contrary the absence of description and the cultivation of dialogue, or the absence of dialogue and the multiplication of "incident," would rescue him from his difficulties. Nothing, for instance, is more possible than that he be of a turn of mind for which this odd, literal opposition of description and dialogue, incident and description, has little meaning and light. People often talk of these things as if they had a kind of internecine distinctness, instead of melting into each other at every breath, and being intimately associated parts of one general effort of expression. I cannot imagine composition existing in a series of blocks, nor conceive, in any novel worth discussing at all, of a passage of description that is not in its intention narrative, a passage of dialogue that is not in its intention descriptive, a touch of truth of any sort that does not partake of the nature of incident, or an incident that derives its interest from any other source than the general and only source of the success of a work of art — that of being illustrative. A novel is a living thing, all one and continuous, like any other organism, and in proportion as it lives will it be found, I think, that in each of the parts there is something of each of the other parts.

The critic who over the close texture of a finished work shall pretend to trace a geography of items will mark some frontiers as artificial, I fear, as any that have been known to history. There is an old-fashioned distinction between the novel of character and the novel of incident which must have cost many a smile to the intending fabulist who was keen about his work. It appears to me as little to the point as the equally celebrated distinction between the novel and the romance — to answer as little to any reality. There are bad novels and good novels, as there are bad pictures and good pictures; but that is the only distinction in which I see any meaning, and I can as little imagine speaking of a novel of character as I can imagine speaking of a picture of character. When one says picture one says of character, when one says novel one says of incident, and the terms may be transposed at will. What is character but the determination of incident? What is incident but the illustration of character? What is either a picture or a novel that is *not* of character? What else do we seek in it and find in it? It is an incident for a woman to stand up with her hand resting on a table and look out at you in a certain way; or if it be not an incident I think it will be hard to say what it is. At the same time it is an expression of character. If you say you don't see it (character in *that — allons donc!*), this is exactly what the artist who has reasons of his own for thinking he *does* see it undertakes to show you. When a young man makes up his mind that he has not faith enough after all to enter the church as he intended, that is an incident, though you may not hurry to the end of the chapter to see whether perhaps he doesn't change once more. I do not say that these are extraordinary or startling incidents. I do not pretend to estimate the degree of interest proceeding from them, for this will depend upon the skill of the painter. It sounds almost puerile to say that some incidents are intrinsically much more important than others, and I need not take this precaution after having professed my sympathy for the major ones in remarking that the only classification of the novel that I can understand is into that which has life and that which has it not.

The novel and the romance, the novel of incident and that of character — these clumsy separations appear to me to have been made by critics and readers for their own convenience, and to help them out of some of their occasional queer predicaments, but to have little reality or interest for the producer, from whose point of view it is of course that we are attempting to consider the art of fiction. The case is the same with another shadowy category which Mr. Besant apparently is disposed to set up — that of the "modern English novel"; unless indeed it be that in this matter he has fallen into an accidental confusion of standpoints. It is not quite clear whether he intends the remarks in which he alludes to it to be didactic or historical. It is as difficult to suppose a person intending to write a modern English as to suppose him writing an ancient English novel: that is a label which begs the question. One writes the novel, one paints the picture, of one's language and of one's time, and calling it modern English will not, alas! make the difficult task any easier. No more, unfortunately, will calling this or that work of one's fellow-artist a romance — unless it be, of course, simply for the pleasantness of the thing, as for instance when Hawthorne gave this heading to his story of *Blithedale*. The French, who have brought the theory of fiction to remarkable completeness, have but one name for the novel, and have not attempted smaller things in it, that I can see, for that. I can think of no obligation to which the "romancer" would not be held equally with the novelist; the standard of execution is equally high for each. Of course it is of execution that we are talking — that being the only point of a novel that is open to contention. This is perhaps too often lost sight of, only to produce interminable confusions and cross-purposes. We must grant the artist his subject, his idea, his *donnée*: our criticism is applied only to what he makes of it. Naturally I do not mean that we are bound to like it or find it interesting: in case we do not our course is perfectly simple — to let it alone. We may believe that of a certain idea even the most sincere novelist can make nothing at all, and the event may perfectly justify our belief; but the failure will have been a failure to execute, and it **is** in the execution that the fatal weakness is recorded. If we pretend to respect the artist at all, we must allow him his freedom of choice, in the face, in particular cases, of innumerable presumptions that the choice will not fructify. Art derives a considerable part of its beneficial exercise from flying in the face of presumptions, and some of the most interesting experiments of which it is capable are hidden in the bosom of common things. Gustave Flaubert has written a story about the devotion of a servant-girl to a parrot, and the production, highly finished as it is, cannot on the whole be called a success. We are perfectly free to find it flat, but I think it might have been interesting; and I, for my part, am extremely glad he should have written it; it is a contribution to our knowledge of what can be done — or what cannot. Ivan Turgénieff has written a tale about a deaf and dumb serf and a lap-dog, and the thing is touching, loving, a little masterpiece. He struck the note of life where Gustave Flaubert missed it — he flew in the face of a presumption and achieved a victory.

Nothing, of course, will ever take the place of the good old fashion of "liking" a work of art or not liking it: the most improved criticism will not abolish that primitive, that ultimate test. I mention this to guard myself from the accusation of intimating that the idea, the subject, of a novel or a picture, does not matter. It matters, to my sense, in the highest degree, and if I might put up a prayer it would be that artists should select none but the richest. Some, as I have already hastened to admit, are much more remunerative than others, and it would be a world happily arranged in which persons intending to treat them should be exempt from confusions and mistakes. This fortunate condition will arrive only, I fear, on the same day that critics become purged from error. Meanwhile, I repeat, we do not judge the artist with fairness unless we say to him, "Oh, I grant you your starting-point, because if I did not I should seem to prescribe to you, and heaven forbid I should take that responsibility. If I pretend to tell you what you must not take, you will call upon me to tell you then what you must take; in which case I shall be prettily caught. Moreover, it isn't till I have accepted your data that I can begin to measure you. I have the standard, the pitch; I have no right to tamper with your flute and then criticise your music. Of course I may not care for your idea at all; I may think it silly, or stale, or unclean; in which case I wash my hands of you altogether. I may content myself with believing that you will not have succeeded in being interesting, but I shall, of course, not attempt to demonstrate it, and you will be as indifferent to me as I am to you. I needn't remind you that there are all sorts of tastes: who can know it better? Some people, for excellent reasons, don't like to read about carpenters; others, for reasons even better, don't like to read about courtesans. Many object to Americans. Others (I believe they are mainly editors and publishers) won't look at Italians. Some readers don't like quiet subjects; others don't like bustling ones. Some enjoy a complete illusion, others the consciousness of large concessions. They choose their novels accordingly, and if they don't care about your idea they won't, *a fortiori*, care about your treatment."

So that it comes back very quickly, as I have said, to the liking: in spite of M. Zola, who reasons less powerfully than he represents, and who will not reconcile himself to this absoluteness of taste, thinking that there are certain things that people ought to like, and that they can be made to like. I am quite at a loss to imagine anything (at any rate in this matter of fiction) that people *ought* to like or to dislike. Selection will be sure to take care of itself, for it has a constant motive behind it. That motive is simply experience. As people feel life, so they will feel the art that is most closely related to it. This closeness of relation is what we should never forget in talking of the effort of the novel. Many people speak of it as a factitious, artificial form, a product of ingenuity, the business of which is to alter and arrange the things that surround us, to translate them into conventional, traditional moulds. This, however, is a view of the matter which carries us but a very short way, condemns the art to an eternal repetition of a few familiar *clichés*, cuts short its development, and leads us straight up to a dead wall. Catching the very note and trick, the strange irregular rhythm of life, that is the attempt whose strenuous force keeps Fiction upon her feet. In proportion as in what she offers us we see life *without* rearrangement do we feel that we are touching the truth; in proportion as we see it *with* rearrangement do we feel that we are being put off with a substitute, a compromise and convention. It is not uncommon to hear an extraordinary assurance of remark in regard to this matter of rearranging, which is often spoken of as if it were the last word of art. Mr. Besant seems to me in danger of falling into the great error with his rather unguarded talk about "selection." Art is essentially selection, but it is a selection whose main care is to be typical, to be inclusive. For many people art means rose-coloured windowpanes, and selection means picking a bouquet for Mrs. Grundy. They will tell you glibly that artistic considerations have nothing to do with the disagreeable, with the ugly; they will rattle off shallow commonplaces about the province of art and the limits of art till you are moved to some wonder in return as to the province and the limits of ignorance. It appears to me that no one can ever have made a seriously artistic attempt without becoming conscious of an immense increase — a kind of revelation — of freedom. One perceives in that case — by the light of a heavenly ray — that the province of art is all life, all feeling, all observation, all vision. As Mr. Besant so justly intimates, it is all experience. That is a sufficient answer to those who maintain that it must not touch the sad things of life, who stick into its divine unconscious bosom little prohibitory inscriptions on the end of sticks, such as we see in public gardens — "It is forbidden to walk on the grass; it is forbidden to touch the flowers; it is not allowed to introduce dogs or to remain after dark; it is requested to keep to the right." The young aspirant in the line of fiction whom we continue to imagine will do nothing without taste, for in that case his freedom would be of little use to him; but the first advantage of his taste will be to reveal to him the absurdity of the little sticks and tickets. If he have taste, I must add, of course he will have ingenuity, and my disrespectful reference to that quality just now was not meant to imply that it is useless in fiction. But it is only a secondary aid; the first is a capacity for receiving straight impressions.

Mr. Besant has some remarks on the question of "the story" which I shall not attempt to criticise, though they seem to me to contain a singular ambiguity, because I do not think I understand them. I cannot see what is meant by talking as if there were a part of a novel which is the story and part of it which for mystical reasons is not — unless indeed the distinction be made in a sense in which it is difficult to suppose that any one should attempt to convey anything. "The story," if it represents anything, represents the subject, the idea, the *donnée* of the novel; and there is surely no "school" — Mr. Besant speaks of a school — which urges that a novel should be all treatment and no subject. There must assuredly be something to treat; every school is intimately conscious of that. This sense of the story being the idea, the starting-point, of the novel, is the only one that I see in which it can be spoken of as something different from its organic whole; and since in proportion as the work is successful the idea permeates and penetrates it, informs and animates it, so that every word and every punctuation-point contribute directly to the expression, in that proportion do we lose our sense of the story being a blade which may be drawn more or less out of its sheath. The story and the novel, the idea and the form, are the needle and thread, and I never heard of a guild of tailors who recommended the use of the thread without the needle, or the needle without the thread. Mr. Besant is not the only critic who may be observed to have spoken as if there were certain things in life which constitute stories, and certain others which do not. I find the same odd implication in an entertaining article in the *Pall Mall Gazette*, devoted, as it happens, to Mr. Besant's lecture. "The story is the thing!" says this graceful writer, as if with a tone of opposition to some other idea. I should think it was, as every painter who, as the time for "sending in" his picture

looms in the distance, finds himself still in quest of a subject — as every belated artist not fixed about his theme will heartily agree. There are some subjects which speak to us and others which do not, but he would be a clever man who should undertake to give a rule — an index expurgatorius — by which the story and the no story should be known apart. It is impossible (to me at least) to imagine any such rule which shall not be altogether arbitrary. The writer in the *Pall Mall* opposes the delightful (as I suppose) novel of *Margot la Balafrée* to certain tales in which "Bostonian nymphs" appear to have "rejected English dukes for psychological reasons." I am not acquainted with the romance just designated, and can scarcely forgive the *Pall Mall* critic for not mentioning the name of the author, but the title appears to refer to a lady who may have received a scar in some heroic adventure. I am inconsolable at not being acquainted with this episode, but am utterly at a loss to see why it is a story when the rejection (or acceptance) of a duke is not, and why a reason, psychological or other, is not a subject when a cicatrix is. They are all particles of the multitudinous life with which the novel deals, and surely no dogma which pretends to make it lawful to touch the one and unlawful to touch the other will stand for a moment on its feet. It is the special picture that must stand or fall, according as it seem to possess truth or to lack it. Mr. Besant does not, to my sense, light up the subject by intimating that a story must, under penalty of not being a story, consist of "adventures." Why of adventures more than of green spectacles? He mentions a category of impossible things, and among them he places "fiction without adventure." Why without adventure, more than without matrimony, or celibacy, or parturition, or cholera, or hydropathy, or Jansenism? This seems to me to bring the novel back to the hapless little *rôle* of being an artificial, ingenious thing — bring it down from its large, free character of an immense and exquisite correspondence with life. And what *is* adventure, when it comes to that, and by what sign is the listening pupil to recognise it? It is an adventure — an immense one

— for me to write this little article; and for a Bostonian nymph to reject an English duke is an adventure only less stirring, I should say, than for an English duke to be rejected by a Bostonian nymph. I see dramas within dramas in that, and innumerable points of view. A psychological reason is, to my imagination, an object adorably pictorial; to catch the tint of its complexion — I feel as if that idea might inspire one to Titianesque efforts. There are few things more exciting to me, in short, than a psychological reason, and yet, I protest, the novel seems to me the most magnificent form of art. I have just been reading, at the same time, the delightful story of *Treasure Island*, by Mr. Robert Louis Stevenson and, in a manner less consecutive, the last tale from M. Edmond de Goncourt, which is entitled *Chérie*. One of these works treats of murders, mysteries, islands of dreadful renown, hairbreadth escapes, miraculous coincidences and buried doubloons. The other treats of a little French girl who lived in a fine house in Paris, and died of wounded sensibility because no one would marry her. I call *Treasure Island* delightful, because it appears to me to have succeeded wonderfully in what it attempts; and I venture to bestow no epithet upon *Chérie*, which strikes me as having failed deplorably in what it attempts — that is in tracing the development of the moral consciousness of a child. But one of these productions strikes me as exactly as much of a novel as the other, and as having a "story" quite as much. The moral consciousness of a child is as much a part of life as the islands of the Spanish Main, and the one sort of geography seems to me to have those "surprises" of which Mr. Besant speaks quite as much as the other. For myself (since it comes back in the last resort, as I say, to the preference of the individual), the picture of the child's experience has the advantage that I can at successive steps (an immense luxury, near to the "sensual pleasure" of which Mr. Besant's critic in the *Pall Mall* speaks) say Yes or No, as it may be, to what the artist puts before me. I have been a child in fact, but I have been on a quest for a buried treasure only in supposition, and it is a simple accident that with

M. de Goncourt I should have for the most part to say No. With George Eliot, when she painted that country with a far other intelligence, I always said Yes.

The most interesting part of Mr. Besant's lecture is unfortunately the briefest passage — his very cursory allusion to the "conscious moral purpose" of the novel. Here again it is not very clear whether he be recording a fact or laying down a principle; it is a great pity that in the latter case he should not have developed his idea. This branch of the subject is of immense importance, and Mr. Besant's few words point to considerations of the widest reach, not to be lightly disposed of. He will have treated the art of fiction but superficially who is not prepared to go every inch of the way that these considerations will carry him. It is for this reason that at the beginning of these remarks I was careful to notify the reader that my reflections on so large a theme have no pretension to be exhaustive. Like Mr. Besant, I have left the question of the morality of the novel till the last, and at the last I find I have used up my space. It is a question surrounded with difficulties, as witness the very first that meets us, in the form of a definite question, on the threshold. Vagueness, in such a discussion, is fatal, and what is the meaning of your morality and your conscious moral purpose? Will you not define your terms and explain how (a novel being a picture) a picture can be either moral or immoral? You wish to paint a moral picture or carve a moral statue: will you not tell us how you would set about it? We are discussing the Art of Fiction; questions of art are questions (in the widest sense) of execution; questions of morality are quite another affair, and will you not let us see how it is that you find it so easy to mix them up? These things are so clear to Mr. Besant that he has deduced from them a law which he sees embodied in English Fiction, and which is "a truly admirable thing and a great cause for congratulation." It is a great cause for congratulation indeed when such thorny problems become as smooth as silk. I may add that in so far as Mr. Besant perceives that in point of fact English Fiction has addressed itself preponderantly to these delicate questions he will appear to many people to have made a vain discovery. They will have been positively struck, on the contrary, with the moral timidity of the usual English novelist; with his (or with her) aversion to face the difficulties with which on every side the treatment of reality bristles. He is apt to be extremely shy (whereas the picture that Mr. Besant draws is a picture of boldness), and the sign of his work, for the most part, is a cautious silence on certain subjects. In the English novel (by which of course I mean the American as well), more than in any other, there is a traditional difference between that which people know and that which they agree to admit that they know, that which they see and that which they speak of, that which they feel to be a part of life and that which they allow to enter into literature. There is the great difference, in short, between what they talk of in conversation and what they talk of in print. The essence of moral energy is to survey the whole field, and I should directly reverse Mr. Besant's remark and say not that the English novel has a purpose, but that it has a diffidence. To what degree a purpose in a work of art is a source of corruption I shall not attempt to inquire; the one that seems to me least dangerous is the purpose of making a perfect work. As for our novel, I may say lastly on this score that as we find it in England to-day it strikes me as addressed in a large degree to "young people," and that this in itself constitutes a presumption that it will be rather shy. There are certain things which it is generally agreed not to discuss, not even to mention, before young people. That is very well, but the absence of discussion is not a symptom of the moral passion. The purpose of the English novel — "a truly admirable thing, and a great cause for congratulation" — strikes me therefore as rather negative.

There is one point at which the moral sense and the artistic sense lie very near together; that is in the light of the very obvious truth that the deepest quality of a work of art will always be the quality of the mind of the producer. In proportion as that intelligence is fine will the novel, the picture, the statue partake of the substance of beauty and truth. To be constituted of such elements is, to my vision, to have purpose enough. No good novel will ever proceed from a superficial mind; that seems to me an axiom which, for the artist in fiction, will cover all needful moral ground: if the youthful aspirant take it to heart it will illuminate for him many of the mysteries of "purpose." There are many other useful things that might be said to him, but I have come to the end of my article, and can only touch them as I pass. The critic in the *Pall Mall Gazette*, whom I have already quoted, draws attention to the danger, in speaking of the art of fiction, of generalising. The danger that he has in mind is rather, I imagine, that of particularising, for there are some comprehensive remarks which, in addition to those embodied in Mr. Besant's suggestive lecture, might without fear of misleading him be addressed to the ingenuous student. I should remind him first of the magnificence of the form that is open to him, which offers to sight so few restrictions and such innumerable opportunities. The other arts, in comparison, appear confined and hampered; the various conditions under which they are exercised are so rigid and definite. But the only condition that I can think of attaching to the composition of the novel is, as I have already said, that it be sincere. This freedom is a splendid privilege, and the first lesson of the young novelist is to learn to be worthy of it. "Enjoy it as it deserves," I should say to him; "take possession of it, explore it to its utmost extent, publish it, rejoice in it. All life belongs to you, and do not listen either to those who would shut you up into corners of it and tell you that it is only here and there that art inhabits, or to those who would persuade you that this heavenly messenger wings her way outside of life altogether, breathing a superfine air, and turning away her head from the truth of things. There is no impression of life, no manner of seeing it and feeling it, to which the plan of the novelist may not offer a place; you have only to remember talents so dissimilar as those of Alexandre Dumas and Jane Austen, Charles Dickens and Gustave Flaubert have worked in this field with equal glory. Do not think too much about optimism and pessimism; try and catch the colour of life itself. In France to-day we see a prodigious effort (that of Emile Zola, to whose solid and serious work no explorer of the capacity of the novel can allude without respect), we see an extraordinary effort, vitiated by a spirit of pessimism on a narrow basis. M. Zola is magnificent, but he strikes an English reader as ignorant; he has an air of working in the dark; if he had as much light as energy, his results would be of the highest value. As for the aberrations of a shallow optimism, the ground (of English fiction especially) is strewn with their brittle particles as with broken glass. If you must indulge in conclusions, let them have the taste of a wide knowledge. Remember that your first duty is to be as complete as possible — to make as perfect a work. Be generous and delicate and pursue the prize."

HAMLIN GARLAND (1860–1940)

Hamlin Garland was "a son of the Middle Border." Born on a farm in Wisconsin, he spent much of his youth in Iowa, graduated from Cedar Valley Seminary at Osage, Iowa, taught and tramped through the country for two years, and finally in 1884 sold a claim in Dakota for enough money to take him to Boston. He attended the Boston School of Oratory, then taught there. In 1887 he revisited the Middle Border country of his youth. "This was an epoch-making experience for me," he said, "for my three years in Boston had given me perspective on the life of the prairie farmer. I perceived with new vision the loneliness and drudgery of the farmers' wives. All across northwestern Iowa and up through central Dakota I brooded darkly over the problem presented, and this bitter mood was deepened by the condition in which I found my mother on a treeless farm just above Ordway. It was in this mood of resentment that I began to write (immediately after returning to Boston) the stories which later made up the first volume of *Main-Travelled Roads*."

Between 1887 and 1889 Garland wrote, according to his own statement, all the stories that appeared in *Main-Travelled Roads* (1891) and in *Other Main-Travelled Roads* (1910). These stories established his reputation. Of his later writings, none equals them in rugged strength save *A Son of the Middle Border* (1917), his autobiographical account of pioneer life in the upper Middle West. *In Crumbling Idols* (1894) he expressed in a series of essays his revolt from conventionalism in art, holding that "to spread the reign of justice should everywhere be the design and intent of the artist." But after 1895 his realistic vein thinned out, and by 1900 he was writing romantic stories of the Far West which attracted large audiences and offended nobody but his former admirers. Only his return to pioneer life in the reminiscent Middle Border series, beginning in 1917, restored his critical reputation. He was awarded the Pulitzer Prize in 1921.

Critical interpretations may be found in V. L. Parrington, *The Beginnings of Critical Realism in America*, 1930; F. L. Pattee, *The Development of the American Short Story*, ch. on "The Revolt of the 'Nineties"; C. Van Doren, *The American Novel*, 1940, ch. on "Emergence of Naturalism"; W. F. Taylor, *The Economic Novel in America*, 1942, ch. IV.

Under the Lion's Paw

(1889)

It was the last of autumn and first day of winter coming together. All day long the plowmen on their prairie farms had moved to and fro in their wide level fields through the falling snow, which melted as it fell, wetting them to the skin — all day, notwithstanding the frequent squalls of snow, the dripping, desolate clouds, and the muck of the furrows, black and tenacious as tar.

Under their dripping harness the horses swung to and fro silently, with that marvelous uncomplaining patience which marks the horse. All day the wild geese, honking wildly, as they sprawled sidewise down the wind, seemed to be fleeing from an enemy behind, and with neck outthrust and wings extended, sailed down the wind, soon lost to sight.

Yet the plowman behind his plow, though the snow lay on his ragged great-coat, and the cold clinging mud rose on his heavy boots, fettering him like gyves, whistled in the very beard of the gale. As day passed, the snow, ceasing to melt, lay along the plowed land, and lodged in the depth of the stubble, till on each slow round the last furrow stood out black and shining as jet between the plowed land and the gray stubble.

When night began to fall, and the geese, flying low, began to alight invisibly in the near corn-field, Stephen Council was still at work "finishing a land." He rode on his sulky plow when going with the wind, but walked when facing it. Sitting bent and cold but cheery under his slouch hat, he talked encouragingly to his four-in-hand.

"Come round there, boys! — Round agin! We got t' finish this land. Come in there, Dan! *Stiddy*, Kate, — stiddy! None o' y'r tantrums, Kittie. It's purty tuff, but got a be did. *Tchk! tchk!* Step along, Pete! Don't let Kate git y'r single-tree on the wheel. *Once* more!"

They seemed to know what he meant, and that this was the last round, for they worked with greater vigor than before.

"Once more, boys, an' then, sez I, oats an' a nice warm stall, an' sleep f'r all."

By the time the last furrow was turned on the land it was too dark to see the house, and the snow was changing to rain again. The tired and hungry man could see the light from the kitchen shining through the leafless hedge, and he lifted a great shout, "Supper f'r a half a dozen!"

It was nearly eight o'clock by the time he had finished his chores and started for supper. He was picking his way carefully through the mud, when the tall form of a man loomed up before him with a premonitory cough.

"Waddy ye want?" was the rather startled question of the farmer.

"Well, ye see," began the stranger, in a deprecating tone, "we'd like t' git in f'r the night. We've tried every house f'r the last two miles, but they hadn't any room f'r us. My wife's jest about sick, 'n' the children are cold and hungry ——"

"Oh, y' want 'o stay all night, eh?"

"Yes, sir; it 'ud be a great accom ——"

"Wall, I don't make it a practice t' turn anybuddy way hungry, not on sech nights as this. Drive right in. We ain't got much, but sech as it is ——"

But the stranger had disappeared. And soon his steaming, weary team, with drooping heads and swinging single-trees, moved past the well to the block beside the path. Council stood at the side of the "schooner" and helped the children out — two little half-sleeping children — and then a small woman with a babe in her arms.

"There ye go!" he shouted jovially, to the children. "*Now* we're all right! Run right along to the house there, an' tell Mam' Council you wants sumpthin' t' eat. Right this way, Mis' — keep right off t' the right there. I'll go an' git a lantern. Come," he said to the dazed and silent group at his side.

"Mother," he shouted, as he neared the fragrant and warmly lighted kitchen, "here are some wayfarers an' folks who need sumpthin' t' eat an' a place t' snooze." He ended by pushing them all in.

Mrs. Council, a large, jolly, rather coarse-looking woman, took the children in her arms. "Come right in, you little rabbits. 'Most asleep, hey? Now here's a drink o' milk f'r each o' ye. I'll have s'm tea in a minute. Take off y'r things and set up t' the fire."

While she set the children to drinking milk,

Council got out his lantern and went out to the barn to help the stranger about his team, where his loud, hearty voice could be heard as it came and went between the haymow and the stalls.

The woman came to light as a small, timid, and discouraged-looking woman, but still pretty, in a thin and sorrowful way.

"Land sakes! An' you've traveled all the way from Clear Lake t'-day in this mud! Waal! waal! No wonder you're all tired out. Don't wait f'r the men, Mis'——" She hesitated, waiting for the name.

"Haskins."

"Mis' Haskins, set right up to the table an' take a good swig o' tea whilst I make y' s'm toast. It's green tea, an' it's good. I tell Council as I git older I don't seem to enjoy Young Hyson n'r Gunpowder. I want the reel green tea, jest as it comes off'n the vines. Seems t'have more heart in it, some way. Don't s'pose it has. Council says it's all in m' eye." Going on in this easy way, she soon had the children filled with bread and milk and the woman thoroughly at home, eating some toast and sweet-melon pickles, and sipping the tea.

"See the little rats!" she laughed at the children. "They're full as they can stick now, and they want to go to bed. Now, don't git up, Mis' Haskins; set right where you are an' let me look after 'em. I know all about young ones, though I'm all alone now. Jane went an' married last fall. But, as I tell Council, it's lucky we keep our health. Set right there, Mis' Haskins; I won't have you stir a finger."

It was an unmeasured pleasure to sit there in the warm, homely kitchen, the jovial chatter of the housewife driving out and holding at bay the growl of the impotent, cheated wind.

The little woman's eyes filled with tears which fell down upon the sleeping baby in her arms. The world was not so desolate and cold and hopeless, after all.

"Now I hope Council won't stop out there and talk politics all night. He's the greatest man to talk politics an' read the *Tribune* — How old is it?"

She broke off and peered down at the face of the babe.

"Two months 'n' five days," said the mother, with a mother's exactness.

"Ye don't say! I want 'o know! The dear little pudzy-wudzy!" she went on, stirring it up in the neighborhood of the ribs with her fat forefinger. "Pooty tough on 'oo to go galivant'n' 'cross lots this way——"

"Yes, that's so; a man can't lift a mountain," said Council, entering the door. "Mother, this is Mr. Haskins, from Kansas. He's been eat up 'n' drove out by grasshoppers."

"Glad t' see yeh! — Pa, empty that washbasin 'n' give him a chance t' wash."

Haskins was a tall man, with a thin, gloomy face. His hair was a reddish brown, like his coat, and seemed equally faded by the wind and sun, and his sallow face, though hard and set, was pathetic somehow. You would have felt that he had suffered much by the line of his mouth showing under his thin, yellow mustache.

"Hain't Ike got home yet, Sairy?"

"Hain't seen 'im."

"W-a-a-l, set right up, Mr. Haskins; wade right into what we've got; 'tain't much, but we manage to live on it — she gits fat on it," laughed Council, pointing his thumb at his wife.

After supper, while the women put the children to bed, Haskins and Council talked on, seated near the huge cooking-stove, the steam rising from their wet clothing. In the Western fashion Council told as much of his own life as he drew from his guest. He asked but few questions, but by and by the story of Haskins' struggles and defeat came out. The story was a terrible one, but he told it quietly, seated with his elbows on his knees, gazing most of the time at the hearth.

"I didn't like the looks of the country, anyhow," Haskins said, partly rising and glancing at his wife. "I was ust t' northern Ingyannie, where we have lots o' timber 'n' lots o' rain, 'n' I didn't like the looks o' that dry prairie. What galled me the worst was goin' s' far away acrosst so much fine land layin' all through here vacant."

"And the 'hoppers eat ye four years, hand runnin', did they?"

"Eat! They wiped us out. They chawed everything that was green. They jest set around waitin' f'r us to die t' eat us, too. My God! I ust t' dream of 'em sittin' 'round on the bedpost, six feet long, workin' their jaws. They eet the fork-handles. They got worse 'n' worse till they jest rolled on one another, piled up like snow in winter. Well, it ain't no use. If I was t' talk all winter I couldn't tell nawthin'. But all the while I couldn't help thinkin' of all that land back here that nobuddy was usin' that I ought 'o had 'stead o' bein' out there in that cussed country."

"Waal, why didn't ye stop an' settle here?" asked Ike, who had come in and was eating his supper.

"Fer the simple reason that you fellers wantid ten 'r fifteen dollars an acre fer the bare land, and I hadn't no money fer that kind o' thing."

"Yes, I do my own work," Mrs. Council was heard to say in the pause which followed. "I'm a-gettin' purty heavy t' be on m' laigs all day, but we can't afford t' hire, so I keep rackin' around somehow, like a foundered horse. S' lame — I tell Council he can't tell how lame I am, f'r I'm jest as lame in one laig as t' other." And the good soul laughed at the joke on herself as she took a handful of flour and dusted the biscuit-board to keep the dough from sticking.

"Well, I hain't *never* been very strong," said Mrs. Haskins. "Our folks was Canadians an' small-boned, and then since my last child I hain't got up again fairly. I don't like t' complain. Tim has about all he can bear now — but they was days this week when I jes wanted to lay right down an' die."

"Waal, now, I'll tell ye," said Council, from his side of the stove, silencing everybody with his good-natured roar, "I'd go down and *see* Butler, *anyway,* if I was you. I guess he'd let you have his place purty cheap; the farm's all run down. He's ben anxious t' let t' somebuddy next year. It 'ud be a good chance fer you. Anyhow, you go to bed and sleep like a babe. I've got some plowin' t' do, anyhow, an' we'll see if somethin' can't be done about your case. Ike, you go out an' see if the horses is all right, an' I'll show the folks t' bed."

When the tired husband and wife were ly-ing under the generous quilts of the spare bed, Haskins listened a moment to the wind in the eaves, and then said, with a slow and solemn tone, "There are people in this world who are good enough t' be angels, an' only haff t' die to *be* angels."

II

Jim Butler was one of those men called in the West "land poor." Early in the history of Rock River he had come into the town and started in the grocery business in a small way, occupying a small building in a mean part of the town. At this period of his life he earned all he got, and was up early and late sorting beans, working over butter, and carting his goods to and from the station. But a change came over him at the end of the second year, when he sold a lot of land for four times what he paid for it. From that time forward he believed in land speculation as the surest way of getting rich. Every cent he could save or spare from his trade he put into land at forced sale, or mortgages on land, which were "just as good as the wheat," he was accustomed to say.

Farm after farm fell into his hands, until he was recognized as one of the leading landowners of the county. His mortgages were scattered all over Cedar County, and as they slowly but surely fell in he sought usually to retain the former owner as tenant.

He was not ready to foreclose; indeed, he had the name of being one of the "easiest" men in the town. He let the debtor off again and again, extending the time whenever possible.

"I don't want y'r land," he said. "All I'm after is the int'rest on my money — that's all. Now, if y' want 'o stay on the farm, why, I'll give y' a good chance. I can't have the land layin' vacant." And in many cases the owner remained as tenant.

In the meantime he had sold his store; he couldn't spend time in it; he was mainly occupied now with sitting around town on rainy days smoking and "gassin' with the boys," or in riding to and from his farms. In fishing-time he fished a good deal. Doc Grimes, Ben Ashley, and Cal Cheatham were his cronies on these fishing excursions or hunting trips in the time of chickens or partridges. In winter they went to Northern Wisconsin to shoot deer.

In spite of all these signs of easy life Butler persisted in saying he "hadn't enough money to pay taxes on his land," and was careful to convey the impression that he was poor in spite of his twenty farms. At one time he was said to be worth fifty thousand dollars, but land had been a little slow of sale of late, so that he was not worth so much.

A fine farm, known as the Higley place, had fallen into his hands in the usual way the previous year, and he had not been able to find a tenant for it. Poor Higley, after working himself nearly to death on it in the attempt to lift the mortgage, had gone off to Dakota, leaving the farm and his curse to Butler. This was the farm which Council advised Haskins to apply for; and the next day Council hitched up his team and drove down town to see Butler.

"You jest let *me* do the talkin'," he said. "We'll find him wearin' out his pants on some salt barrel somew'ers; and if he thought you *wanted* a place he'd sock it to you hot and heavy. You jest keep quiet; I'll fix 'im."

Butler was seated in Ben Ashley's store telling fish yarns when Council sauntered in casually.

"Hello, But; lyin' agin, hey!"

"Hello, Steve! how goes it?"

"Oh, so-so. Too dang much rain these days. I thought it was goin' t' freeze up f'r good last night. Tight squeak if I get m' plowin' done. How's farmin' with *you* these days?"

"Bad. Plowin' ain't half done."

"It 'ud be a religious idee f'r you t' go out an' take a hand y'rself."

"I don't haff to," said Butler, with a wink.

"Got anybody on the Higley place?"

"No. Know of anybody?"

"Waal, no; not eggsackly. I've got a relation back t' Michigan who's ben hot an' cold on the idee o' comin' West f'r some time. *Might* come if he could get a good lay-out. What do you talk on the farm?"

"Well, I d'know. I'll rent it on shares or I'll rent it money rent."

"Wall, how much money, say?"

"Well, say ten per cent, on the price — two-fifty."

"Wall, that ain't bad. Wait on 'im till 'e thrashes?"

Haskins listened eagerly to his important question, but Council was coolly eating a dried apple which he had speared out of a barrel with his knife. Butler studied him carefully.

"Well, knocks me out of twenty-five dollars interest."

"My relation'll need all he's got t' git his crops in," said Council, in the safe, indifferent way.

"Well, all right; *say* wait," concluded Butler.

"All right; this is the man. Haskins, this is Mr. Butler — no relation to Ben — the hardest-working man in Cedar County."

On the way home Haskins said: "I ain't much better off. I'd like that farm; it's a good farm, but it's all run down, an' so 'm I. I could make a good farm of it if I had half a show. But I can't stock it n'r seed it."

"Wall, now, don't you worry," roared Council in his ear. "We'll pull y' through somehow till next harvest. He's agreed t' hire it plowed, an' you can earn a hundred dollars plowin' an' y' c'n git the seed o' me, an' pay me back when y' can."

Haskins was silent with emotion, but at last he said, "I ain't got nothin' t' live on."

"Now, don't you worry 'bout that. You jest make your headquarters at ol' Steve Council's. Mother'll take a pile o' comfort in havin' y'r wife an' children 'round. Y' see, Jane's married off lately, an' Ike's away a good 'eal, so we'll be darn glad t' have y' stop with us this winter. Nex' spring we'll see if y' can't git a start agin." And he chirruped to the team, which sprang forward with the rumbling, clattering wagon.

"Say, looky here, Council, you can't do this. I never saw —" shouted Haskins in his neighbor's ear.

Council moved about uneasily in his seat and stopped his stammering gratitude by saying: "Hold on, now: don't make such a fuss over a little thing. When I see a man down, an' things all on top of 'm, I jest like t' kick 'em off an' help 'm up. That's the kind of religion I got, an' it's about the *only* kind."

They rode the rest of the way home in silence. And when the red light of the lamp shone out into the darkness of the cold and windy night, and he thought of this refuge for his children and wife, Haskins could have put his arm around the neck of his burly companion and squeezed him like a lover. But he contented himself with saying, "Steve Council, you'll git y'r pay f'r this some day."

"Don't want any pay. My religion ain't run on such business principles."

The wind was growing colder, and the ground was covered with a white frost, as they turned into the gate of the Council farm, and the children came rushing out, shouting, "Papa's come!" They hardly looked like the same children who had sat at the table the night before. Their torpidity, under the influence of sunshine and Mother Council, had given way to a sort of spasmodic cheerfulness, as insects in winter revive when laid on the hearth.

III

Haskins worked like a fiend, and his wife, like the heroic woman that she was, bore also uncomplainingly the most terrible burdens. They rose early and toiled without intermission till the darkness fell on the plain, then tumbled into bed, every bone and muscle aching with fatigue, to rise with the sun next morning to the same round of the same ferocity of labor.

The eldest boy drove a team all through the spring, plowing and seeding, milked the cows, and did chores innumerable, in most ways taking the place of a man.

An infinitely pathetic but common figure, this boy on the American farm, where there is no law against child labor. To see him in his coarse clothing, his huge boots, and his ragged cap, as he staggered with a pail of water from the well, or trudged in the cold and cheerless dawn out into the frosty field behind his team, gave the city-bred visitor a sharp pang of sympathetic pain. Yet Haskins loved his boy, and would have saved him from this if he could, but he could not.

By June the first year the result of such Herculean toil began to show on the farm. The yard was cleaned up and sown to grass, the garden plowed and planted, and the house mended.

Council had given them four of his cows. "Take 'em an' run 'em on shares. I don't want 'o milk s' many. Ike's away s' much now, Sat'd'ys an' Sund'ys, I can't stand the bother anyhow."

Other men, seeing the confidence of Council in the newcomer, had sold him tools on time; and as he was really an able farmer, he soon had round him many evidences of his care and thrift. At the advice of Council he had taken the farm for three years, with the privilege of re-renting or buying at the end of the term.

"It's a good bargain, an' y' want 'o nail it," said Council. "If you have any kind ov a crop, you c'n pay y'r debts, an' keep seed an' bread."

The new hope which now sprang up in the heart of Haskins and his wife grew great almost as a pain by the time the wide field of wheat began to wave and swirl in the winds of July. Day after day he would snatch a few moments after supper to go and look at it.

"Have ye seen the wheat t'-day, Nettie?" he asked one night as he rose from supper.

"No, Tim, I ain't had time."

"Well, take time now. Le's go look at it."

She threw an old hat on her head — Tommy's hat — and looking almost pretty in her thin, sad way, went out with her husband to the hedge.

"Ain't it grand, Nettie? Just look at it."

It was grand. Level, russet here and there, heavy-headed, wide as a lake, and full of multitudinous whispers and gleams of wealth, it stretched away before the gazers like the fabled field of the cloth of gold.

"Oh, I think — I hope we'll have a good crop, Tim; and oh, how good the people have been to us!"

"Yes; I don't know where we'd be t'-day if it hadn't ben f'r Council and his wife."

"They're the best people in the world," said the little woman, with a great sob of gratitude.

"We'll be in the field on Monday, sure," said Haskins, gripping the rail on the fence as if already at the work of the harvest.

The harvest came, bounteous, glorious, but the winds came and blew it into tangles, and the rain matted it here and there close to the ground, increasing the work of gathering it threefold.

Oh, how they toiled in those glorious days! Clothing dripping with sweat, arms aching, filled with briers, fingers raw and bleeding, backs broken with the weight of heavy bundles, Haskins and his man toiled on. Tommy drove the harvester, while his father and a hired man bound on the machine. In this way they cut ten acres every day, and almost every night after supper, when the hand went to bed, Haskins returned to the field shocking the bound grain in the light of the moon. Many a night he worked till his anxious wife came out at ten o'clock to call him in to rest and lunch.

At the same time she cooked for the men, took care of the children, washed and ironed, milked the cows at night, made the butter, and sometimes fed the horses and watered them while her husband kept at the shocking.

No slave in the Roman galleys could have toiled so frightfully and lived, for this man thought himself a free man, and that he was working for his wife and babes.

When he sank into his bed with a deep groan of relief, too tired to change his grimy, dripping clothing, he felt that he was getting nearer and nearer to a home of his own, and pushing the wolf of want a little farther from his door.

There is no despair so deep as the despair of a homeless man or woman. To roam the roads of the country or the streets of the city, to feel there is no rood of ground on which the feet can rest, to halt weary and hungry outside lighted windows and hear laughter and song within, — these are the hungers and rebellions that drive men to crime and women to shame.

It was the memory of this homelessness, and the fear of its coming again, that spurred Timothy Haskins and Nettie, his wife, to such ferocious labor during that first year.

IV

"'M, yes; 'm, yes; first-rate," said Butler, as his eye took in the neat garden, the pigpen, and the well-filled barnyard. "You're gitt'n' quite a stock around yeh. Done well, eh?"

Haskins was showing Butler around the place. He had not seen it for a year, having spent the year in Washington and Boston with Ashley, his brother-in-law, who had been elected to Congress.

"Yes, I've laid out a good deal of money durin' the last three years. I've paid out three hundred dollars f'r fencin'."

"Um — h'm! I see, I see," said Butler while Haskins went on:

"The kitchen there cost two hundred; the barn ain't cost much in money, but I've put a lot o' time on it. I've dug a new well, and I ——"

"Yes, yes, I see. You've done well. Stock worth a thousand dollars," said Butler, picking his teeth with a straw.

"About that," said Haskins, modestly. "We begin to feel 's if we was gitt'n a home f'r ourselves; but we've worked hard. I tell you we begin to feel it, Mr. Butler, and we're goin' t' begin to ease up purty soon. We've been kind o' plannin' a trip back t' her folks after the fall plowin's done."

"*Eggs*-actly!" said Butler, who was evidently thinking of something else. "I suppose you've kind o' calc'lated on stayin' here three years more?"

"Well, yes. Fact is, I think I c'n buy the farm this fall, if you'll give me a reasonable show."

"Um — m! What do you call a reasonable show?"

"Well, say a quarter down and three years' time."

Butler looked at the huge stacks of wheat, which filled the yard, over which the chickens were fluttering and crawling, catching grasshoppers, and out of which the crickets were singing innumerably. He smiled in a peculiar way as he said, "Oh, I won't be hard on yeh. But what did you expect to pay f'r the place?"

"Why, about what you offered it for before, two thousand five hundred, or *possibly* three thousand dollars," he added quickly as he saw the owner shake his head.

"This farm is worth five thousand and five hundred dollars," said Butler, in a careless and decided voice.

"*What!*" almost shrieked the astounded Haskins. "What's that? Five thousand? Why, that's double what you offered it for three years ago."

"Of course, and it's worth it. It was all run down then; now it's in good shape. You've laid out fifteen hundred dollars in improvements, according to your own story."

"But *you* had nothin' t' do about that. It's my work an' my money."

"You bet it was; but it's my land."

"But what's to pay me for all my ——"

"Ain't you had the use of 'em?" replied Butler, smiling calmly into his face.

Haskins was like a man struck on the head with a sandbag; he couldn't think; he stammered as he tried to say: "But — I never'd git the use — You'd rob me! More'n that: you agreed — you promised that I could buy or rent at the end of three years at ——"

"That's all right. But I didn't say I'd let you carry off the improvements, nor that I'd go on renting the farm at two-fifty. The land is doubled in value, it don't matter how; it don't enter into the question; an' now you can pay me five hundred dollars a year rent, or take it on your own terms at fifty-five hundred, or — git out."

He was turning away when Haskins, the sweat pouring from his face, fronted him, saying again:

"But *you've* done nothing to make it so. You hain't added a cent. I put it all there myself, expectin' to buy. I worked an' sweat to improve it. I was workin' for my self an' babes ——"

"Well, why didn't you buy when I offered to sell? What y' kickin' about?"

"I'm kickin' about payin' you twice f'r my own things, — my own fences, my own kitchen, my own garden."

Butler laughed. "You're too green t'eat, young feller. *Your* improvements! The law will sing another tune."

"But I trusted your word."

"Never trust anybody, my friend. Besides, I didn't promise not to do this thing. Why, man, don't look at me like that. Don't take me for a thief. It's the law. The reg'lar thing. Everybody does it."

"I don't care if they do. It's stealin' jest the same. You take three thousand dollars of my money — the work o' my hands and my wife's." He broke down at this point. He was not a strong man mentally. He could face hardship, ceaseless toil, but he could not face the cold and sneering face of Butler.

"But I don't take it," said Butler, coolly. "All you've got to do is to go on jest as you've been a-doin', or give me a thousand dollars down, and a mortgage at ten per cent on the rest."

Haskins sat down blindly on a bundle of oats near by, and with staring eyes and drooping head went over the situation. He was under the lion's paw. He felt a horrible numbness in his heart and limbs. He was hid in a mist, and there was no path out.

Butler walked about, looking at the huge stacks of grain, and pulling now and again a few handfuls out, shelling the heads in his hands and blowing the chaff away. He hummed a little tune as he did so. He had an accommodating air of waiting.

Haskins was in the midst of the terrible toil of the last year. He was walking again in the rain and the mud behind his plow; he felt the dust and dirt of the threshing. The ferocious husking-time, with its cutting wind and biting, clinging snows, lay hard upon him. Then he thought of his wife, how she had cheerfully cooked and baked, without holiday and without rest.

"Well, what do you think of it?" inquired the cool, mocking, insinuating voice of Butler.

"I think you're a thief and a liar!" shouted Haskins, leaping up. "A blackhearted houn'!" Butler's smile maddened him; with a sudden leap he caught a fork in his hands, and whirled it in the air. "You'll never rob another man, damn ye!" he grated through his teeth, a look of pitiless ferocity in his accusing eyes.

Butler shrank and quivered, expecting the blow; stood, held hypnotized by the eyes of the man he had a moment before despised — a man transformed into an avenging demon. But in the deadly hush between the lift of the weapon and its fall there came a gush of faint, childish laughter and then across the range of his vision, far away and dim, he saw the sun-bright head of his baby girl, as, with the pretty, tottering run of a two-year-old, she moved across the grass of the dooryard. His hands relaxed; the fork fell to the ground; his head lowered.

"Make out y'r deed an' mor'gage, an' git off'n my land, an' don't ye never cross my line again; if y' do, I'll kill ye."

Butler backed away from the man in wild haste, and climbing into his buggy with trembling limbs drove off down the road, leaving Haskins seated dumbly on the sunny piles of sheaves, his head sunk into his hands.

STEPHEN CRANE (1871–1900)

Born in Newark, New Jersey, Crane studied at Lafayette College and Syracuse University, and became a journalist. Gifted with extraordinary creative energy, he published fourteen volumes before he was cut off at the age of twenty-eight. Two of his grim naturalistic novels have distinction: *Maggie, a Girl of the Streets* (1892), and *The Red Badge of Courage* (1895). In the latter, a vivid psychological study of army life in the War of the Secession, he made large use of the conception of war which Tolstoy had impressively set forth in *War and Peace. The Red Badge of Courage* made him his reputation, and he set sail, with $7000 in gold, to report real war for a syndicate. Shipwrecked, he suffered from exposure, further weakened his condition by experiences in the Greek-Turkish war, and died of tuberculosis in Germany.

Crane's powers were also well displayed in his short stories: *The Open Boat and Other Tales of Adventure* (1898), *The Monster and Other Stories* (1899), *Wounds in the Rain* (1900), etc.; and in his two small volumes of verse: *The Black Riders and Other Lines* (1895), and *War Is Kind* (1899). His poems express, in experimental "free verse" of a sort that anticipates the work of later poets, his hatred of sentiment, his passionate irony, his unflinching quest of truth, his naturalistic vision of life. The poems were printed, not inappropriately, on dark gray paper. Had Crane lived on through the first quarter of the new century, he would doubtless have become a foremost figure in the "New Poetry"; as it is, we can only say that he voiced the protest of the nineties and heralded the poetic revival of the early twentieth century. "Modern American literature," Carl Van Doren has declared, "may be said, accurately enough, to have begun with Stephen Crane."

His works were edited in 12 volumes, by Wilson Follett, 1925–26. The same editor issued *Collected Poems*, 1930. For biography, see Thomas Beer, *Stephen Crane*, 1923, to which Joseph Conrad contributed an introduction, and John Berryman, *Stephen Crane*, 1950. Hamlin Garland wrote on "Stephen Crane as I Knew Him," *Yale Review*, April, 1914. Critical comment includes H. G. Wells, "Stephen Crane," *North American Review*, August, 1900; H. Hartwick, *The Foreground of American Fiction*, 1934; A. H. Quinn, *American Fiction*, 1936.

War Is Kind

(1899)

Do not weep, maiden, for war is kind.
Because your lover threw wild hands toward
    the sky
And the affrighted steed ran on alone,

Do not weep.
War is kind.   5

Hoarse, booming drums of the regiment,
Little souls who thirst for fight,
These men were born to drill and die.
The unexplained glory flies above them,

Great is the battle-god, great, and his
    kingdom —   10
A field where a thousand corpses lie.

Do not weep, babe, for war is kind.
Because your father tumbled in the yellow
    trenches,
Raged at his breast, gulped and died,
Do not weep.   15
War is kind.

Swift blazing flag of the regiment,
Eagle with crest of red and gold,
These men were born to drill and die.
Point for them the virtue of slaughter,   20
Make plain to them the excellence of killing
And a field where a thousand corpses lie.

Mother whose heart hung humble as a button
On the bright splendid shroud of your son,
Do not weep.   25
War is kind.

A Little Ink More or Less

(1899)

A little ink more or less!
It surely can't matter?
Even the sky and the opulent sea,
The plains and the hills, aloof,
Hear the uproar of all these books.   5
But it is only a little ink more or less.

The Wayfarer

(1899)

The wayfarer,
Perceiving the pathway to truth,
Was struck with astonishment.
It was thickly grown with weeds.
"Ha," he said,   5
"I see that none has passed here
"In a long time."
Later he saw that each weed
Was a singular knife.
"Well," he mumbled at last,   10
"Doubtless there are other roads."

A Slant of Sun

(1899)

A slant of sun on dull brown walls,
A forgotten sky of bashful blue.

Toward God a mighty hymn,
A song of collisions and cries,
Rumbling wheels, hoof-beats, bells,   5
Welcomes, farewells, love-calls, final moans,
Voices of joy, idiocy, warning, despair,
The unknown appeals of brutes,
The chanting of flowers,
The screams of cut trees,   10
The senseless babble of hens and wise men —
A cluttered incoherency that says at the stars:
"O God, save us!"

The Blue Hotel

In *The Monster and Other Stories*, this story, says Vincent Starrett, "fills a dozen pages of the book; but the social injustice of the whole world is hinted in that space; the upside-downness of creation, right prostrate, wrong triumphant, — a mad, crazy world."

I

The Palace Hotel at Fort Romper was painted a light blue, a shade that is on the legs of a kind of heron, causing the bird to declare its position against any background. The Palace Hotel, then, was always screaming and howling in a way that made the dazzling winter landscape of Nebraska seem only a gray swampish hush. It stood alone on the prairie, and when the snow was falling the town two hundred yards away was not visible. But when the traveler alighted at the railway station he was obliged to pass the Palace Hotel before he could come upon the company of low clapboard houses which composed Fort Romper, and it was not to be thought that any traveler could pass the Palace Hotel without looking at it. Pat Scully, the proprietor, had proved himself a master of strategy when he chose his paints. It is true that on clear days, when the great transcontinental expresses, long lines of swaying Pullmans, swept through Fort Romper, passengers were overcome at the sight, and the cult that knows the brown-reds and the subdivisions of the dark greens of the East expressed shame, pity, horror, in a laugh. But to the citizens of this prairie town and to the people who would naturally stop there, Pat Scully had performed a feat. With this opulence and splendor, these creeds, classes, egotisms, that streamed through Romper on the rails day after day, they had no color in common.

As if the displayed delights of such a blue hotel were not sufficiently enticing, it was Scully's habit to go every morning and evening to meet the leisurely trains that stopped at Romper and work his seductions upon any man that he might see wavering, gripsack in hand.

One morning, when a snow-crusted engine dragged its long string of freight cars and its one passenger coach to the station, Scully performed the marvel of catching three men. One was a shaky and quick-eyed Swede, with a great shining cheap valise; one was a tall bronzed cowboy, who was on his way to a ranch near the Dakota line; one was a little silent man from the East, who didn't look it, and didn't announce it. Scully practically made them prisoners. He was so nimble and merry and kindly that each probably felt it would be the height of brutality to try to escape. They trudged off over the creaking board sidewalks in the wake of the eager little Irishman. He wore a heavy fur cap squeezed tightly down on his head. It caused his two red ears to stick out stiffly, as if they were made of tin.

At last, Scully, elaborately, with boisterous hospitality, conducted them through the portals of the blue hotel. The room which they entered was small. It seemed to be merely a proper temple for an enormous stove, which, in the center, was humming with godlike violence. At various points on its surface the iron had become luminous and glowed yellow from the heat. Beside the stove Scully's son Johnnie was playing High-Five with an old farmer who had whiskers both gray and sandy. They were quarreling. Frequently the old farmer turned his face toward a box of sawdust — colored brown from tobacco juice — that was behind the stove, and spat with an air of great impatience and irritation. With a loud flourish of words Scully destroyed the game of cards, and bustled his son upstairs with part of the baggage of the new guests. He himself conducted them to three basins of the coldest water in the world. The cowboy and the Easterner burnished themselves fiery red with

this water, until it seemed to be some kind of metal-polish. The Swede, however, merely dipped his fingers gingerly and with trepidation. It was notable that throughout this series of small ceremonies the three travelers were made to feel that Scully was very benevolent. He was conferring great favors upon them. He handed the towel from one to another with an air of philanthropic impulse.

Afterward they went to the first room, and, sitting about the stove, listened to Scully's officious clamor at his daughters, who were preparing the midday meal. They reflected in the silence of experienced men who tread carefully amid new people. Nevertheless, the old farmer, stationary, invincible in his chair near the warmest part of the stove, turned his face from the sawdust-box frequently and addressed a glowing commonplace to the strangers. Usually he was answered in short but adequate sentences by either the cowboy or the Easterner. The Swede said nothing. He seemed to be occupied in making furtive estimates of each man in the room. One might have thought that he had the sense of silly suspicion which comes to guilt. He resembled a badly frightened man.

Later, at dinner, he spoke a little, addressing his conversation entirely to Scully. He volunteered that he had come from New York, where for ten years he had worked as a tailor. These facts seemed to strike Scully as fascinating, and afterward he volunteered that he had lived at Romper for fourteen years. The Swede asked about the crops and the price of labor. He seemed barely to listen to Scully's extended replies. His eyes continued to rove from man to man.

Finally, with a laugh and a wink, he said that some of these Western communities were very dangerous; and after this statement he straightened his legs under the table, tilted his head, and laughed again, loudly. It was plain that the demonstration had no meaning to the others. They looked at him wondering and in silence.

II

As the men trooped heavily back into the front room, the two little windows presented views of a turmoiling sea of snow. The huge arms of the wind were making attempts — mighty, circular, futile — to embrace the flakes as they sped. A gate-post like a still man with a blanched face stood aghast amid this profligate fury. In a hearty voice Scully announced the presence of a blizzard. The guests of the blue hotel, lighting their pipes, assented with grunts of lazy masculine contentment. No island of the sea could be exempt in the degree of this little room with its humming stove. Johnnie, son of Scully, in a tone which defined his opinion of his ability as a card-player, challenged the old farmer of both gray and sandy whiskers to a game of High-Five. The farmer agreed with a contemptuous and bitter scoff. They sat close to the stove, and squared their knees under a wide board. The cowboy and the Easterner watched the game with interest. The Swede remained near the window, aloof, but with a countenance that showed signs of an inexplicable excitement.

The play of Johnnie and the gray-beard was suddenly ended by another quarrel. The old man arose while casting a look of heated scorn at his adversary. He slowly buttoned his coat, and then stalked with fabulous dignity from the room. In the discreet silence of all other men the Swede laughed. His laughter rang somehow childish. Men by this time had begun to look at him askance, as if they wished to inquire what ailed him.

A new game was formed jocosely. The cowboy volunteered to become the partner of Johnnie, and they all then turned to ask the Swede to throw in his lot with the little Easterner. He asked some questions about the game, and, learning that it wore many names, and that he had played it when it was under an alias, he accepted the invitation. He strode toward the men nervously, as if he expected to be assaulted. Finally, seated, he gazed from face to face and laughed shrilly. This laugh was so strange that the Easterner looked up quickly, the cowboy sat intent and with his mouth open, and Johnnie paused, holding the cards with still fingers.

Afterward there was a short silence. Then Johnnie said, "Well, let's get at it. Come on now!" They pulled their chairs forward until their knees were bunched under the board. They began to play, and their interest in the game caused the others to forget the manner of the Swede.

The cowboy was a board-whacker. Each time that he held superior cards he whanged them, one by one, with exceeding force, down upon the improvised table, and took the tricks with a glowing air of prowess and pride that sent thrills of indignation into the hearts of his opponents. A game with a board-whacker in it is sure to become intense. The countenances of the Easterner and the Swede were miserable whenever the cowboy thundered down his aces and kings, while Johnnie, his eyes gleaming with joy, chuckled and chuckled.

Because of the absorbing play none considered the strange ways of the Swede. They paid strict heed to the game. Finally, during a lull caused by a new deal, the Swede suddenly addressed Johnnie: "I suppose there have been a good many men killed in this room." The jaws of the others dropped and they looked at him.

"What in hell are you talking about?" said Johnnie.

The Swede laughed again his blatant laugh, full of a kind of false courage and defiance. "Oh, you know what I mean all right," he answered.

"I'm a liar if I do!" Johnnie protested. The card was halted, and the men stared at the Swede. Johnnie evidently felt that as the son of the proprietor he should make a direct inquiry. "Now, what might you be drivin' at, mister?" he asked. The Swede winked at him. It was a wink full of cunning. His fingers shook on the edge of the board. "Oh, maybe you think I have been to nowheres. Maybe you think I'm a tenderfoot?"

"I don't know nothin' about you," answered Johnnie, "and I don't give a damn where you've been. All I got to say is that I don't know what you're driving at. There hain't never been nobody killed in this room."

The cowboy, who had been steadily gazing at the Swede, then spoke: "What's wrong with you, mister?"

Apparently it seemed to the Swede that he was formidably menaced. He shivered and turned white near the corners of his mouth. He sent an appealing glance in the direction of the little Easterner. During these moments he did not forget to wear his air of advanced potvalor. "They say they don't know what I mean," he remarked mockingly to the Easterner.

The latter answered after prolonged and cautious reflection. "I don't understand you," he said, impassively.

The Swede made a movement then which announced that he thought he had encountered treachery from the only quarter where he had expected sympathy, if not help. "Oh, I see you are all against me, I see ——"

The cowboy was in a state of deep stupefaction. "Say," he cried, as he tumbled the deck violently down upon the board, "say, what are you gittin' at, hey?"

The Swede sprang up with the celerity of a man escaping from a snake on the floor. "I don't want to fight!" he shouted. "I don't want to fight!"

The cowboy stretched his long legs indolently and deliberately. His hands were in his pockets. He spat into the sawdust-box. "Well, who the hell thought you did?" he inquired.

The Swede backed rapidly toward a corner of the room. His hands were out protectingly in front of his chest, but he was making an obvious struggle to control his fright. "Gentlemen," he quavered, "I suppose I am going to be killed before I can leave this house! I suppose I am going to be killed before I can leave this house!" In his eyes was the dying-swan look. Through the windows could be seen the snow turning blue in the shadow of dusk. The wind tore at the house, and some loose thing beat regularly against the clapboards like a spirit tapping.

A door opened, and Scully himself entered. He paused in surprise as he noted the tragic attitude of the Swede. Then he said, "What's the matter here?"

The Swede answered him swiftly and eagerly: "These men are going to kill me."

"Kill you!" ejaculated Scully. "Kill you! What are you talkin'?"

The Swede made the gesture of a martyr.

Scully wheeled sternly upon his son. "What is this, Johnnie?"

The lad had grown sullen. "Damned if I know," he answered. "I can't make no sense to it." He began to shuffle the cards, fluttering them together with an angry snap. "He says a good many men have been killed in this room, or something like that. And he says he's goin' to be killed here too. I don't know what ails him. He's crazy, I shouldn't wonder."

Scully then looked for explanation to the cowboy, but the cowboy simply shrugged his shoulders.

"Kill you?" said Scully again to the Swede. "Kill you? Man, you're off your nut."

"Oh, I know," burst out the Swede. "I know what will happen. Yes, I'm crazy — yes. Yes, of course, I'm crazy — yes. But I know one thing ——" There was a sort of sweat of misery and terror upon his face. "I know I won't get out of here alive."

The cowboy drew a deep breath, as if his mind was passing into the last stages of dissolution. "Well, I'm doggoned," he whispered to himself.

Scully wheeled suddenly and faced his son. "You've been troublin' this man!"

Johnnie's voice was loud with its burden of grievance. "Why, good Gawd, I ain't done nothin' to 'im."

The Swede broke in. "Gentlemen, do not disturb yourselves. I will leave this house. I will go away, because" — he accused them dramatically with his glance — "because I do not want to be killed."

Scully was furious with his son. "Will you tell me what is the matter, you young divil? What's the matter, anyhow? Speak out!"

"Blame it!" cried Johnnie in despair, "don't I tell you I don't know? He — he says we want to kill him, and that's all I know. I can't tell what ails him."

The Swede continued to repeat: "Never mind, Mr. Scully; never mind. I will leave this house. I will go away, because I do not wish to be killed. Yes, of course, I am crazy — yes. But I know one thing! I will go away. I will leave this house. Never mind, Mr. Scully; never mind. I will go away."

"You will not go 'way," said Scully. "You will not go 'way until I hear the reason of this business. If anybody has troubled you I will take care of him. This is my house. You are under my roof, and I will not allow any peaceable man to be troubled here." He cast a terrible eye upon Johnnie, the cowboy, and the Easterner.

"Never mind, Mr. Scully; never mind. I will go away. I do not wish to be killed." The Swede moved toward the door which opened upon the stairs. It was evidently his intention to go at once for his baggage.

"No, no," shouted Scully peremptorily; but the whitefaced man slid by him and disappeared. "Now," said Scully severely, "what does this mane?"

Johnnie and the cowboy cried together: "Why, we didn't do nothin' to 'im!"

Scully's eyes were cold. "No," he said, "you didn't?"

Johnnie swore a deep oath. "Why, this is the wildest loon I ever see. We didn't do nothin' at all. We were jest sittin' here playin' cards, and he ——"

The father suddenly spoke to the Easterner, "Mr. Blanc," he asked, "what has these boys been doin'?"

The Easterner reflected again. "I didn't see anything wrong at all," he said at last, slowly.

Scully began to howl. "But what does it mane?" He stared ferociously at his son. "I have a mind to lather you for this, me boy."

Johnnie was frantic. "Well, what have I done?" he bawled at his father.

III

"I think you are tongue-tied," said Scully finally to his son, the cowboy, and the Easterner; and at the end of this scornful sentence he left the room.

Upstairs the Swede was swiftly fastening the straps of his great valise. Once his back happened to be half turned toward the door, and, hearing a noise there, he wheeled and sprang up, uttering a loud cry. Scully's wrinkled visage showed grimly in the light of the small lamp he carried. This yellow effulgence, streaming upward, colored only his prominent features, and left his eyes, for instance, in mysterious shadow. He resembled a murderer.

"Man! man!" he exclaimed, "have you gone daffy?"

"Oh, no! Oh, no!" rejoined the other. "There are people in this world who know pretty nearly as much as you do — understand?"

For a moment they stood gazing at each other. Upon the Swede's deathly pale cheeks were two spots brightly crimson and sharply edged, as if they had been carefully painted. Scully placed the light on the table and sat himself on the edge of the bed. He spoke ruminatively. "By cracky, I never heard of such a thing in my life. It's a complete muddle. I can't, for the soul of me, think how you ever got this idea into your head." Presently he lifted his eyes and asked: "And did you sure think they were going to kill you?"

The Swede scanned the old man as if he wished to see into his mind. "I did," he said at last. He obviously suspected that this answer might precipitate an outbreak. As he pulled on a strap his whole arm shook, the elbow wavering like a bit of paper.

Scully banged his hand impressively on the footboard of the bed. "Why, man, we're goin' to have a line of ilictric street-cars in this town next spring."

" 'A line of electric street-cars,' " repeated the Swede, stupidly.

"And," said Scully, "there's a new railroad goin' to be built down from Broken Arm to here. Not to mintion the four churches and the smashin' big brick school house. Then there's the big factory, too. Why, in two years Romper'll be a metro-pol-is."

Having finished the preparation of his baggage, the Swede straightened himself. "Mr. Scully," he said, with sudden hardihood, "how much do I owe you?"

"You don't owe me anythin'," said the old man, angrily.

"Yes, I do," retorted the Swede. He took seventy-five cents from his pocket and tendered it to Scully; but the latter snapped his fingers in disdainful refusal. However, it happened that they both stood gazing in a strange fashion at three silver pieces on the Swede's open palm.

"I'll not take your money," said Scully

at last. "Not after what's been goin' on here." Then a plan seemed to strike him. "Here," he cried, picking up his lamp and moving toward the door. "Here! Come with me a minute."

"No," said the Swede, in overwhelming alarm.

"Yes," urged the old man. "Come on! I want you to come and see a picter — just across the hall — in my room."

The Swede must have concluded that his hour was come. His jaw dropped and his teeth showed like a dead man's. He ultimately followed Scully across the corridor, but he had the step of one hung in chains.

Scully flashed the light high on the wall of his own chamber. There was revealed a ridiculous photograph of a little girl. She was leaning against a balustrade of gorgeous decoration, and the formidable bang to her hair was prominent. The figure was as graceful as an upright sled-stake, and, withal, it was of the hue of lead. "There," said Scully, tenderly, "that's the picter of my little girl that died. Her name was Carrie. She had the purtiest hair you ever saw! I was that fond of her, she ——"

Turning then, he saw that the Swede was not contemplating the picture at all, but, instead, was keeping keen watch on the gloom in the rear.

"Look, man!" cried Scully, heartily. "That's the picter of my little gal that died. Her name was Carrie. And then here's the picter of my oldest boy, Michael. He's a lawyer in Lincoln, an' doin' well. I gave that boy a grand eddication, and I'm glad for it now. He's a fine boy. Look at 'im now. Ain't he bold as blazes, him there in Lincoln, an honored an' respicted gintleman! An honored and respicted gintleman," concluded Scully with a flourish. And, so saying, he smote the Swede jovially on the back.

The Swede faintly smiled.

"Now," said the old man, "there's only one more thing." He dropped suddenly to the floor and thrust his head beneath the bed. The Swede could hear his muffled voice. "I'd keep it under me piller if it wasn't for that boy Johnnie. Then there's the old woman —— Where is it now? I never put it twice in the same place. Ah, now come out with you!"

Presently he backed clumsily from under the bed, dragging with him an old coat rolled into a bundle. "I've fetched him," he muttered. Kneeling on the floor, he unrolled the coat and extracted from its heart a large yellow-brown whisky-bottle.

His first maneuver was to hold the bottle up to the light. Reassured, apparently, that nobody had been tampering with it, he thrust it with a generous movement toward the Swede.

The weak-kneed Swede was about to eagerly clutch this element of strength, but he suddenly jerked his hand away and cast a look of horror upon Scully.

"Drink," said the old man affectionately. He had risen to his feet, and now stood facing the Swede.

There was a silence. Then again Scully said: "Drink!"

The Swede laughed wildly. He grabbed the bottle, put it to his mouth; and as his lips curled absurdly around the opening and his throat worked, he kept his glance, burning with hatred, upon the old man's face.

IV

After the departure of Scully the three men, with the cardboard still upon their knees, preserved for a long time an astounded silence. Then Johnnie said: "That's the doddangedest Swede I ever see."

"He ain't no Swede," said the cowboy, scornfully.

"Well, what is he then?" cried Johnnie. "What is he then?"

"It's my opinion," replied the cowboy deliberately, "he's some kind of a Dutchman." It was a venerable custom of the country to entitle as Swedes all light-haired men who spoke with a heavy tongue. In consequence the idea of the cowboy was not without its daring. "Yes, sir," he repeated. "It's my opinion this feller is some kind of a Dutchman."

"Well, he says he's a Swede, anyhow," muttered Johnnie, sulkily. He turned to the Easterner: "What do you think, Mr. Blanc?"

"Oh, I don't know," replied the Easterner.

"Well, what do you think makes him act that way?" asked the cowboy.

"Why, he's frightened." The Easterner knocked his pipe against a rim of the stove. "He's clear frightened out of his boots."

"What at?" cried Johnnie and the cowboy together.

The Easterner reflected over his answer.

"What at?" cried the others again.

"Oh, I don't know, but it seems to me this man has been reading dime novels, and he thinks he's right out in the middle of it — the shootin' and stabbin' and all."

"But," said the cowboy, deeply scandalized, "this ain't Wyoming, ner none of them places. This is Nebrasker."

"Yes," added Johnnie, "an' why don't he wait till he gits out West?"

The traveled Easterner laughed. "It isn't different there even — not in these days. But he thinks he's right in the middle of hell."

Johnnie and the cowboy mused long.

"It's awful funny," remarked Johnnie at last.

"Yes," said the cowboy. "This is a queer game. I hope we don't git snowed in, because then we'd have to stand this here man bein' around with us all the time. That wouldn't be no good."

"I wish pop would throw him out," said Johnnie.

Presently they heard a loud stamping on the stairs, accompanied by ringing jokes in the voice of old Scully, and laughter, evidently from the Swede. The men around the stove stared vacantly at each other. "Gosh!" said the cowboy. The door flew open, and old Scully, flushed and anecdotal, came into the room. He was jabbering at the Swede, who followed him, laughing bravely. It was the entry of two roisterers from a banquet hall.

"Come now," said Scully sharply to the three seated men, "move up and give us a chance at the stove." The cowboy and the Easterner obediently sidled their chairs to make room for the new-comers. Johnnie, however, simply arranged himself in a more indolent attitude, and then remained motionless.

"Come! Git over, there," said Scully.

"Plenty of room on the other side of the stove," said Johnnie.

"Do you think we want to sit in the draught?" roared the father.

But the Swede here interposed with a grandeur of confidence. "No, no. Let the boy sit where he likes," he cried in a bullying voice to the father.

"All right! All right!" said Scully, deferentially. The cowboy and the Easterner exchanged glances of wonder.

The five chairs were formed in a crescent about one side of the stove. The Swede began to talk; he talked arrogantly, profanely, angrily. Johnnie, the cowboy, and the Easterner maintained a morose silence, while old Scully appeared to be receptive and eager, breaking in constantly with sympathetic ejaculations.

Finally the Swede announced that he was thirsty. He moved in his chair, and said that he would go for a drink of water.

"I'll git it for you," cried Scully at once.

"No," said the Swede, contemptuously. "I'll get it for myself." He arose and stalked with the air of an owner off into the executive parts of the hotel.

As soon as the Swede was out of hearing, Scully sprang to his feet and whispered intensely to the others: "Upstairs he thought I was trying' to poison 'im."

"Say," said Johnnie, "this makes me sick. Why don't you throw 'im out in the snow?"

"Why, he's all right now," declared Scully. "It was only that he was from the East, and he thought this was a tough place. That's all. He's all right now."

The cowboy looked with admiration upon the Easterner. "You were straight," he said. "You were on to that there Dutchman."

"Well," said Johnnie to his father, "he may be all right now, but I don't see it. Other time he was scared, but now he's too fresh."

Scully's speech was always a combination of Irish brogue and idiom, Western twang and idiom, and scraps of curiously formal diction taken from the story-books and newspapers. He now hurled a strange mass of language at the head of his son. "What do I keep? What do I keep? What do I keep?" he demanded, in a voice of thunder. He slapped his knee impressively, to indicate that he himself was going to make reply, and that all should heed. "I keep a hotel," he shouted. "A hotel, do you mind? A guest under my roof has sacred privileges. He is to be intimidated by none. Not one word shall he hear that would prijudice him in favor of goin' away. I'll not have it. There's no place in this here town where they can say they iver took in a guest of mine because he was afraid to stay here." He wheeled suddenly upon the cowboy and the Easterner. "Am I right?"

"Yes, Mr. Scully," said the cowboy, "I think you're right."

"Yes, Mr. Scully," said the Easterner, "I think you're right."

V

At six-o'clock supper, the Swede fizzed like a firewheel. He sometimes seemed on the point of bursting into riotous song, and in all his madness he was encouraged by old Scully. The Easterner was encased in reserve; the cowboy sat in wide-mouthed amazement, forgetting to eat, while Johnnie wrathily demolished great plates of food. The daughters of the house, when they were obliged to replenish the biscuits, approached as warily as Indians, and, having succeeded in their purpose, fled with ill-concealed trepidation. The Swede domineered the whole feast, and he gave it the appearance of a cruel bacchanal. He seemed to have grown suddenly taller; he gazed, brutally disdainful, into every face. His voice rang through the room. Once when he jabbed out harpoon-fashion with his fork to pinion a biscuit, the weapon nearly impaled the hand of the Easterner, which had been stretched quietly out for the same biscuit.

After supper, as the men filed toward the other room, the Swede smote Scully ruthlessly on the shoulder. "Well, old boy, that was a good, square meal." Johnnie looked hopefully at his father; he knew that shoulder was tender from an old fall; and, indeed, it appeared for a moment as if Scully was going to flame out over the matter, but in the end he smiled a sickly smile and remained silent. The others understood from his manner that he was admitting his responsibility for the Swede's new viewpoint.

Johnnie, however, addressed his parent in an aside. "Why don't you license somebody to kick you downstairs?" Scully scowled darkly by way of reply.

When they were gathered about the stove, the Swede insisted on another game of High-Five. Scully gently deprecated the plan at first, but the Swede turned a wolfish glare upon him. The old man subsided, and the Swede canvassed the others. In his tone there was always a great threat. The cowboy and the Easterner both remarked indifferently that they would play. Scully said that he would presently have to go to meet the 6.58 train, and so the Swede turned menacingly upon Johnnie. For a moment their glances crossed like blades, and then Johnnie smiled and said, "Yes, I'll play."

They formed a square, with the little board on their knees. The Easterner and the Swede were again partners. As the play went on, it was noticeable that the cowboy was not board-whacking as usual. Meanwhile, Scully, near the lamp, had put on his spectacles and, with an appearance curiously like an old priest, was reading a newspaper. In time he went out to meet the 6.58 train, and, despite his precautions, a gust of polar wind whirled into the room as he opened the door. Besides scattering the cards, it chilled the players to the marrow. The Swede cursed frightfully. When Scully returned, his entrance disturbed a cozy and friendly scene. The Swede again cursed. But presently they were once more intent, their heads bent forward and their hands moving swiftly. The Swede had adopted the fashion of board-whacking.

Scully took up his paper and for a long time remained immersed in matters which were extraordinarily remote from him. The lamp burned badly, and once he stopped to adjust the wick. The newspaper, as he turned from page to page, rustled with a slow and comfortable sound. Then suddenly he heard three terrible words: "You are cheatin'!"

Such scenes often prove that there can be little of dramatic import in environment. Any room can present a tragic front; any room can be comic. This little den was now hideous as a torture-chamber. The new faces of the men themselves had changed it upon the instant. The Swede held a huge fist in front of Johnnie's face, while the latter looked steadily over it into the blazing orbs of his accuser. The Easterner had grown pallid; the cowboy's jaw had dropped in that expression of bovine amazement which was one of his important mannerisms. After the three words, the first sound in the room was made by Scully's paper as it floated forgotten to his feet. His spectacles had also fallen from his nose, but by a clutch he had saved them in air. His hand, grasping the spectacles, now remained poised awkwardly and near his shoulder. He stared at the card-players.

Probably the silence was while a second elapsed. Then, if the floor had been suddenly twitched out from under the men they could not have moved quicker. The five had projected themselves headlong toward a common point. It happened that Johnnie, in rising to hurl himself upon the Swede, had stumbled slightly because of his curiously instinctive care for the cards and the board. The loss of the moment allowed time for the arrival of Scully, and also allowed the cowboy time to give the Swede a great push which sent him staggering back. The men found tongue together, and hoarse shouts of rage, appeal, or fear burst from every throat. The cowboy pushed and jostled feverishly at the Swede, and the Easterner and Scully clung wildly to Johnnie; but through the smoky air, above the swaying bodies of the peace-compellers, the eyes of the two warriors ever sought each other in glances of challenge that were at once hot and steely.

Of course the board had been overturned, and now the whole company of cards was scattered over the floor, where the boots of the men trampled the fat and painted kings and queens as they gazed with their silly eyes at the war that was waging above them.

Scully's voice was dominating the yells. "Stop now! Stop, I say! Stop, now ——"

Johnnie, as he struggled to burst through the rank formed by Scully and the Easterner, was crying, "Well, he says I cheated! He says I cheated! I won't allow no man to say I cheated! If he says I cheated, he's a —— ——!"

The cowboy was telling the Swede, "Quit, now! Quit, d'ye hear ——"

The screams of the Swede never ceased: "He did cheat! I saw him! I saw him ——"

As for the Easterner, he was importuning in a voice that was not heeded: "Wait a moment, can't you? Oh, wait a moment. What's the good of a fight over a game of cards? Wait a moment ——"

In this tumult no complete sentences were clear. "Cheat" — "Quit" — "He says" — these fragments pierced the uproar and rang out sharply. It was remarkable that, whereas Scully undoubtedly made the most noise, he was the least heard of any of the riotous band.

Then suddenly there was a great cessation. It was as if each man had paused for breath; and although the room was still lighted with the anger of men, it could be seen that there was no danger of immediate conflict, and at once Johnnie, shouldering his way forward, almost succeeded in confronting the Swede. "What did you say I cheated for? What did you say I cheated for? I don't cheat, and I won't let no man say I do!"

The Swede said, "I saw you! I saw you!"

"Well," cried Johnnie, "I'll fight any man what says I cheat!"

"No, you won't," said the cowboy. "Not here."

"Ah, be still, can't you?" said Scully, coming between them.

The quiet was sufficient to allow the Easterner's voice to be heard. He was repeating, "Oh, wait a moment, can't you? What's the good of a fight over a game of cards? Wait a moment!"

Johnnie, his red face appearing above his father's shoulder, hailed the Swede again. "Did you say I cheated?"

The Swede showed his teeth. "Yes."

"Then," said Johnnie, "we must fight."

"Yes, fight," roared the Swede. He was like a demoniac. "Yes, fight! I'll show you what kind of a man I am! I'll show you who you want to fight! Maybe you think I can't fight! Maybe you think I can't! I'll show you, you skin, you card-sharp! Yes, you cheated! You cheated! You cheated!"

"Well, let's go at it, then, mister," said Johnnie, coolly.

The cowboy's brow was beaded with sweat

from his efforts in intercepting all sorts of raids. He turned in despair to Scully. "What are you goin' to do now?"

A change had come over the Celtic visage of the old man. He now seemed all eagerness; his eyes glowed.

"We'll let them fight," he answered, stalwartly. "I can't put up with it any longer. I've stood this damned Swede till I'm sick. We'll let them fight."

VI

The men prepared to go out of doors. The Easterner was so nervous that he had great difficulty in getting his arms into the sleeves of his new leather coat. As the cowboy drew his fur cap down over his ears his hands trembled. In fact, Johnnie and old Scully were the only ones who displayed no agitation. These preliminaries were conducted without words.

Scully threw open the door. "Well, come on," he said. Instantly a terrific wind caused the flame of the lamp to struggle at its wick, while a puff of black smoke sprang from the chimney-top. The stove was in mid-current of the blast, and its voice swelled to equal the roar of the storm. Some of the scarred and bedabbled cards were caught up from the floor and dashed helplessly against the farther wall. The men lowered their heads and plunged into the tempest as into a sea.

No snow was falling, but great whirls and clouds of flakes, swept up from the ground by the frantic winds, were streaming southward with the speed of bullets. The covered land was blue with the sheen of an unearthly satin, and there was no other hue save where, at the low, black railway station — which seemed incredibly distant — one light gleamed like a tiny jewel. As the men floundered into a thigh-deep drift, it was known that the Swede was bawling out something. Scully went to him, put a hand on his shoulder, and projected an ear. "What's that you say!" he shouted.

"I say," bawled the Swede again, "I won't stand much show against this gang. I know you'll all pitch on me."

Scully smote him reproachfully on the arm. "Tut, man!" he yelled. The wind tore the words from Scully's lips and scattered them far alee.

"You are all a gang of ——" boomed the Swede, but the storm also seized the remainder of this sentence.

Immediately turning their backs upon the wind, the men had swung around a corner to the sheltered side of the hotel. It was the function of the little house to preserve here, amid this great devastation of snow, an irregular V-shape of heavily encrusted grass, which crackled beneath the feet. One could imagine the great drifts piled against the windward side. When the party reached the comparative peace of this spot, it was found that the Swede was still bellowing.

"Oh, I know what kind of a thing this is! I know you'll all pitch on me. I can't lick you all!"

Scully turned upon him panther-fashion. "You'll not have to whip all of us. You'll have to whip my son Johnnie. An' the man what troubles you durin' that time will have me to dale with."

The arrangements were swiftly made. The two men faced each other, obedient to the harsh commands of Scully, whose face, in the subtly luminous gloom, could be seen set in the austere impersonal lines that are pictured on the countenances of the Roman veterans. The Easterner's teeth were chattering, and he was hopping up and down like a mechanical toy. The cowboy stood rock-like.

The contestants had not stripped off any clothing. Each was in his ordinary attire. Their fists were up, and they eyed each other in a calm that had the elements of leonine cruelty in it.

During this pause, the Easterner's mind, like a film, took lasting impressions of three men — the iron-nerved master of the ceremony; the Swede, pale, motionless, terrible; and Johnnie, serene yet ferocious, brutish yet heroic. The entire prelude had in it a tragedy greater than the tragedy of action, and this aspect was accentuated by the long, mellow cry of the blizzard, as it sped the tumbling and wailing flakes into the black abyss of the south.

"Now!" said Scully.

The two combatants leaped forward and

crashed together like bullocks. There was heard the cushioned sound of blows, and of a curse squeezing out from between the tight teeth of one.

As for the spectators, the Easterner's pent-up breath exploded from him with a pop of relief, absolute relief from the tension of the preliminaries. The cowboy bounded into the air with a yowl. Scully was immovable as from supreme amazement and fear at the fury of the fight which he himself had permitted and arranged.

For a time the encounter in the darkness was such a perplexity of flying arms that it presented no more detail than would a swiftly revolving wheel. Occasionally a face, as if illumined by a flash of light, would shine out, ghastly and marked with pink spots. A moment later, the men might have been known as shadows, if it were not for the involuntary utterance of oaths that came from them in whispers.

Suddenly a holocaust of warlike desire caught the cowboy, and he bolted forward with the speed of a broncho. "Go it, Johnnie! go it! Kill him! Kill him!"

Scully confronted him. "Kape back," he said; and by his glance the cowboy could tell that this man was Johnnie's father.

To the Easterner there was a monotony of unchangeable fighting that was an abomination. This confused mingling was eternal to his sense, which was concentrated in a longing for the end, the priceless end. Once the fighters lurched near him, and as he scrambled hastily backward he heard them breathe like men on the rack.

"Kill him, Johnnie! Kill him! Kill him! Kill him!" The cowboy's face was contorted like one of those agony masks in museums.

"Keep still," said Scully, icily.

Then there was a sudden loud grunt, incomplete, cut short, and Johnnie's body swung away from the Swede and fell with sickening heaviness to the grass. The cowboy was barely in time to prevent the mad Swede from flinging himself upon his prone adversary. "No, you don't," said the cowboy, interposing an arm. "Wait a second."

Scully was at his son's side. "Johnnie! Johnnie, me boy!" His voice had a quality of melancholy tenderness. "Johnnie! Can you go on with it?" He looked anxiously down into the bloody, pulpy face of his son.

There was a moment of silence, and then Johnnie answered in his ordinary voice, "Yes, I — it — yes."

Assisted by his father he struggled to his feet. "Wait a bit now till you git your wind," said the old man.

A few paces away the cowboy was lecturing the Swede. "No, you don't! Wait a second!"

The Easterner was plucking at Scully's sleeve. "Oh, this is enough," he pleaded. "This is enough! Let it go as it stands. This is enough!"

"Bill," said Scully, "git out of the road." The cowboy stepped aside. "Now." The combatants were actuated by a new caution as they advanced toward collision. They glared at each other, and then the Swede aimed a lightning blow that carried with it his entire weight. Johnnie was evidently half stupid from weakness, but he miraculously dodged, and his fist sent the over-balanced Swede sprawling.

The cowboy, Scully, and the Easterner burst into a cheer that was like a chorus of triumphant soldiery, but before its conclusion the Swede had scuffled agilely to his feet and come in berserk abandon at his foe. There was another perplexity of flying arms, and Johnnie's body again swung away and fell, even as a bundle might fall from a roof. The Swede instantly staggered to a little wind-waved tree and leaned upon it, breathing like an engine, while his savage and flame-lit eyes roamed from face to face as the men bent over Johnnie. There was a splendor of isolation in his situation at this time which the Easterner felt once when, lifting his eyes from the man on the ground, he beheld that mysterious and lonely figure, waiting.

"Are you any good yet, Johnnie?" asked Scully in a broken voice.

The son gasped and opened his eyes languidly. After a moment he answered, "No— I ain't — any good — any — more." Then, from shame and bodily ill, he began to weep, the tears furrowing down through the bloodstains on his face. "He was too — too — too heavy for me."

Scully straightened and addressed the waiting figure. "Stranger," he said, evenly, "it's all up with our side." Then his voice changed into that vibrant huskiness which is commonly the tone of the most simple and deadly announcements. "Johnnie is whipped."

Without replying, the victor moved off on the route to the front door of the hotel.

The cowboy was formulating new and unspellable blasphemies. The Easterner was startled to find that they were out in a wind that seemed to come direct from the shadowed arctic floes. He heard again the wail of the snow as it was flung to its grave in the south. He knew now that all this time the cold had been sinking into him deeper and deeper, and he wondered that he had not perished. He felt indifferent to the condition of the vanquished man.

"Johnnie, can you walk?" asked Scully.

"Did I hurt — hurt him any?" asked the son.

"Can you walk, boy? Can you walk?"

Johnnie's voice was suddenly strong. There was a robust impatience in it. "I asked you whether I hurt him any!"

"Yes, yes, Johnnie," answered the cowboy, consolingly; "he's hurt a good deal."

They raised him from the ground, and as soon as he was on his feet he went tottering off, rebuffing all attempts at assistance. When the party rounded the corner they were fairly blinded by the pelting of the snow. It burned their faces like fire. The cowboy carried Johnnie through the drift to the door. As they entered, some cards again rose from the floor and beat against the wall.

The Easterner rushed to the stove. He was so profoundly chilled that he almost dared to embrace the glowing iron. The Swede was not in the room. Johnnie sank into a chair and, folding his arms on his knees, buried his face in them. Scully, warming one foot and then the other at a rim of the stove, muttered to himself with Celtic mournfulness. The cowboy had removed his fur cap, and with a dazed and rueful air he was running one hand through his tousled locks. From overhead they could hear the creaking of boards, as the Swede tramped here and there in his room.

The sad quiet was broken by the sudden flinging open of a door that led toward the kitchen. It was instantly followed by an inrush of women. They precipitated themselves upon Johnnie amid a chorus of lamentation. Before they carried their prey off to the kitchen, there to be bathed and harangued with that mixture of sympathy and abuse which is a feat of their sex, the mother straightened herself and fixed old Scully with an eye of stern reproach. "Shame be upon you, Patrick Scully!" she cried. "Your own son, too. Shame be upon you!"

"Shame be upon you, Patrick Scully!" The girls, rallying to this slogan, sniffed disdainfully in the direction of those trembling accomplices, the cowboy and the Easterner. Presently they bore Johnnie away, and left the three men to dismal reflection.

VII

"I'd like to fight this here Dutchman myself," said the cowboy, breaking a long silence.

Scully wagged his head sadly. "No, that wouldn't do. It wouldn't be right. It wouldn't be right."

"Well, why wouldn't it?" argued the cowboy. "I don't see no harm in it."

"No," answered Scully, with mournful heroism. "It wouldn't be right. It was Johnnie's fight, and now we mustn't whip the man just because he whipped Johnnie."

"Yes, that's true enough," said the cowboy; "but — he better not get fresh with me, because I couldn't stand no more of it."

"You'll not say a word to him," commanded Scully, and even then they heard the tread of the Swede on the stairs. His entrance was made theatric. He swept the door back with a bang and swaggered to the middle of the room. No one looked at him. "Well," he cried, insolently, at Scully, "I s'pose you'll tell me now how much I owe you?"

The old man remained stolid. "You don't owe me nothin'."

"Huh!" said the Swede, "huh! Don't owe 'im nothin'."

The cowboy addressed the Swede. "Stranger, I don't see how you come to be so gay around here."

Old Scully was instantly alert. "Stop!"

he shouted, holding his hand forth, fingers upward. "Bill, you shut up!"

The cowboy spat carelessly into the sawdust-box. "I didn't say a word, did I?" he asked.

"Mr. Scully," called the Swede, "how much do I owe you?" It was seen that he was attired for departure, and that he had his valise in his hand.

"You don't owe me nothin'," repeated Scully in the same imperturbable way.

"Huh!" said the Swede. "I guess you're right. I guess if it was any way at all, you'd owe me somethin'. That's what I guess." He turned to the cowboy. " 'Kill him! Kill him! Kill him!' " he mimicked, and then guffawed victoriously. " 'Kill him!' " He was convulsed with ironical humor.

But he might have been jeering the dead. The three men were immovable and silent, staring with glassy eyes at the stove.

The Swede opened the door and passed into the storm, giving one derisive glance backward at the still group.

As soon as the door was closed, Scully and the cowboy leaped to their feet and began to curse. They trampled to and fro, waving their arms and smashing into the air with their fists. "Oh, but that was a hard minute!" wailed Scully. "That was a hard minute! Him there leerin' and scoffin'! One bang at his nose was worth forty dollars to me that minute! How did you stand it, Bill!"

"How did I stand it?" cried the cowboy in a quivering voice. "How did I stand it? Oh!"

The old man burst into sudden brogue. "I'd loike to take that Swade," he wailed, "and hould 'im down on a shtone flure and bate 'im to a jeelly wid a shtick!"

The cowboy groaned in sympathy. "I'd like to git him by the neck and ha-ammer him" — he brought his hand down on a chair with a noise like a pistol-shot — "hammer that there Dutchman until he couldn't tell himself from a dead coyote!"

"I'd bate 'im until he ——"

"I'd show *him* some things ——"

And then together they raised a yearning, fanatic cry — "Oh-o-oh! if we only could ——"

"Yes!"

"Yes!"

"And then I'd ——"

"O-o-oh!"

VIII

The Swede, tightly gripping his valise, tacked across the face of the storm as if he carried sails. He was following a line of little naked, gasping trees which, he knew, must mark the way of the road. His face, fresh from the pounding of Johnnie's fists, felt more pleasure than pain in the wind and the driving snow. A number of square shapes loomed upon him finally, and he knew them as the houses of the main body of the town. He found a street and made travel along it, leaning heavily upon the wind whenever, at a corner, a terrific blast caught him.

He might have been in a deserted village. We picture the world as thick with conquering and elate humanity, but here, with the bugles of the tempest pealing, it was hard to imagine a peopled earth. One viewed the existence of man then as a marvel, and conceded a glamour of wonder to these lice which were caused to cling to a whirling, fire-smitten, ice-locked, disease-stricken, space-lost bulb. The conceit of man was explained by this storm to be the very engine of life. One was a coxcomb not to die in it. However, the Swede found a saloon.

In front of it an indomitable red light was burning, and the snowflakes were made blood-color as they flew through the circumscribed territory of the lamp's shining. The Swede pushed open the door of the saloon and entered. A sanded expanse was before him, and at the end of it four men sat about a table drinking. Down one side of the room extended a radiant bar, and its guardian was leaning upon his elbows listening to the talk of the men at the table. The Swede dropped his valise upon the floor and, smiling fraternally upon the barkeeper, said, "Gimme some whisky, will you?" The man placed a bottle, a whisky-glass, and a glass of ice-thick water upon the bar. The Swede poured himself an abnormal portion of whisky and drank it in three gulps. "Pretty bad night," remarked the bartender, indifferently. He was making the pretension of blindness which is usually a distinction of his class; but it could have been seen that he was furtively studying the half-erased bloodstains on the face of the Swede. "Bad night," he said again.

"Oh, it's good enough for me," replied the Swede, hardily, as he poured himself some more whisky. The barkeeper took his coin and maneuvered it through its reception by the highly nickeled cash-machine. A bell rang; a card labeled "20 cts." had appeared.

"No," continued the Swede, "this isn't too bad weather. It's good enough for me."

"So?" murmured the barkeeper, languidly.

The copious drams made the Swede's eyes swim, and he breathed a trifle heavier. "Yes, I like this weather. I like it. It suits me." It was apparently his design to impart a deep significance to these words.

"So?" murmured the bartender again. He turned to gaze dreamily at the scroll-like birds and bird-like scrolls which had been drawn with soap upon the mirrors in back of the bar.

"Well, I guess I'll take another drink," said the Swede, presently. "Have something?"

"No, thanks; I'm not drinkin'," answered the bartender. Afterward he asked, "How did you hurt your face?"

The Swede immediately began to boast loudly. "Why, in a fight. I thumped the soul out of a man down here at Scully's hotel."

The interest of the four men at the table was at last aroused.

"Who was it?" said one.

"Johnnie Scully," blustered the Swede. "Son of the man what runs it. He will be pretty near dead for some weeks, I can tell you. I made a nice thing of him, I did. He couldn't get up. They carried him in the house. Have a drink?"

Instantly the men in some subtle way encased themselves in reserve. "No, thanks," said one. The group was of curious formation. Two were prominent local business men; one was the district attorney; and one was a professional gambler of the kind known as "square." But a scrutiny of the group would not have enabled an observer to pick the gambler from the men of more reputable pursuits. He was, in fact, a man so delicate in manner, when among people of fair class, and so judicious in his choice of victims, that in the strictly masculine part of the town's life he had come to be explicitly trusted and admired. People called him a thoroughbred. The fear and contempt with which his craft was regarded were undoubtedly the reason why his quiet dignity shone conspicuous above the quiet dignity of men who might be merely hatters, billiard-markers, or grocery clerks. Beyond an occasional unwary traveler who came by rail, this gambler was supposed to prey solely upon reckless and senile farmers, who, when flush with good crops, drove into town in all the pride and confidence of an absolutely invulnerable stupidity. Hearing at times in circuitous fashion of the despoilment of such a farmer, the important men of Romper invariably laughed in contempt of the victim, and if they thought of the wolf at all, it was with a kind of pride at the knowledge that he would never dare think of attacking their wisdom and courage. Besides, it was popular that this gambler had a real wife and two real children in a neat cottage in a suburb, where he led an exemplary home life; and when anyone even suggested a discrepancy in his character, the crowd immediately vociferated descriptions of this virtuous family circle. Then men who led exemplary home lives, and men who did not lead exemplary home lives, all subsided in a bunch, remarking that there was nothing more to be said.

However, when a restriction was placed upon him — as, for instance, when a strong clique of members of the new Pollywog Club refused to permit him, even as a spectator, to appear in the rooms of the organization — the candor and gentleness with which he accepted the judgment disarmed many of his foes and made his friends more desperately partisan. He invariably distinguished between himself and a respectable Romper man so quickly and frankly that his manner actually appeared to be a continual broadcast compliment.

And one must not forget to declare the fundamental fact of his entire position in Romper. It is irrefutable that in all affairs outside his business, in all matters that occur eternally and commonly between man and man, this thieving card-player was so generous, so just, so moral, that, in a contest, he could have put to flight the consciences of nine tenths of the citizens of Romper.

And so it happened that he was seated in this saloon with the two prominent local merchants and the district attorney.

The Swede continued to drink raw whisky, meanwhile babbling at the barkeeper and trying to induce him to indulge in potations. "Come on. Have a drink. Come on. What — no? Well, have a little one, then. By gawd, I've whipped a man tonight, and I want to celebrate. I whipped him good, too. Gentlemen," the Swede cried to the men at the table, "have a drink?"

"Ssh!" said the barkeeper.

The group at the table, although furtively attentive, had been pretending to be deep in talk, but now a man lifted his eyes toward the Swede and said, shortly, "Thanks. We don't want any more."

At this reply the Swede ruffled out his chest like a rooster. "Well," he exploded, "it seems I can't get anybody to drink with me in this town. Seems so, don't it? Well!"

"Ssh!" said the barkeeper.

"Say," snarled the Swede, "don't you try to shut me up. I won't have it. I'm a gentleman, and I want people to drink with me. And I want 'em to drink with me now. *Now* — do you understand?" He rapped the bar with his knuckles.

Years of experience had calloused the bartender. He merely grew sulky. "I hear you," he answered.

"Well," cried the Swede, "listen hard then. See those men over there? Well, they're going to drink with me, and don't you forget it. Now you watch."

"Hi," yelled the barkeeper, "this won't do!"

"Why won't it?" demanded the Swede. He stalked over to the table, and by chance laid his hand upon the shoulder of the gambler. "How about this?" he asked wrathfully. "I asked you to drink with me."

The gambler simply twisted his head and spoke over his shoulder. "My friend, I don't know you."

"Oh, hell!" answered the Swede, "come and have a drink."

"Now, my boy," advised the gambler, kindly, "take your hand off my shoulder and go 'way and mind your own business." He was a little, slim man, and it seemed strange to hear him use this tone of heroic patronage to the burly Swede. The other men at the table said nothing.

"What! You won't drink with me, you little dude? I'll make you, then! I'll make you!" The Swede had grasped the gambler frenziedly at the throat, and was dragging him from his chair. The other men sprang up. The barkeeper dashed around the corner of his bar. There was a great tumult, and then was seen a long blade in the hand of the gambler. It shot forward, and a human body, this citadel of virtue, wisdom, power, was pierced as easily as if it had been a melon. The Swede fell with a cry of supreme astonishment.

The prominent merchants and the district attorney must have at once tumbled out of the place backward. The bartender found himself hanging limply to the arm of a chair and gazing into the eyes of a murderer.

"Henry," said the latter, as he wiped his knife on one of the towels that hung beneath the bar rail, "you tell 'em where to find me. I'll be home, waiting for 'em." Then he vanished. A moment afterward the barkeeper was in the street dinning through the storm for help and, moreover, companionship.

The corpse of the Swede, alone in the saloon, had its eyes fixed upon a dreadful legend that dwelt atop of the cash-machine: "This registers the amount of your purchase."

IX

Months later, the cowboy was frying pork over the stove of a little ranch near the Dakota line, when there was a quick thud of hoofs outside, and presently the Easterner entered with the letters and the papers.

"Well," said the Easterner at once, "the chap that killed the Swede has got three years. Wasn't much, was it?"

"He has? Three years?" The cowboy poised his pan of pork, while he ruminated upon the news. "Three years. That ain't much."

"No. It was a light sentence," replied the Easterner as he unbuckled his spurs. "Seems there was a good deal of sympathy for him in Romper."

"If the bartender had been any good," observed the cowboy, thoughtfully, "he would have gone in and cracked that there Dutchman on the head with a bottle in the beginnin' of it and stopped all this here murderin'."

"Yes, a thousand things might have happened," said the Easterner, tartly.

The cowboy returned his pan of pork to the fire, but his philosophy continued. "It's funny, ain't it? If he hadn't said Johnnie was cheatin' he'd be alive this minute. He was an awful fool. Game played for fun, too. Not for money. I believe he was crazy."

"I feel sorry for that gambler," said the Easterner.

"Oh, so do I," said the cowboy. "He don't deserve none of it for killin' who he did."

"The Swede might not have been killed if everything had been square."

"Might not have been killed?" exclaimed the cowboy. "Everythin' square? Why, when he said that Johnnie was cheatin' and acted like such a jackass? And then in the saloon he fairly walked up to git hurt?" With these arguments the cowboy browbeat the Easterner and reduced him to rage.

"You're a fool!" cried the Easterner, viciously. "You're a bigger jackass than the Swede by a million majority. Now let me tell you one thing. Let me tell you something. Listen! Johnnie *was* cheating!"

"'Johnnie,'" said the cowboy, blankly. There was a minute of silence, and then he said, robustly, "Why, no. The game was only for fun."

"Fun or not," said the Easterner, "Johnnie was cheating. I saw him. I know it. I saw him. And I refused to stand up and be a man. I let the Swede fight it out alone. And you — you were simply puffing around the place and wanting to fight. And then old Scully himself! We are all in it! This poor gambler isn't even a noun. He is kind of an adverb. Every sin is the result of a collaboration. We, five of us, have collaborated in the murder of this Swede. Usually there are from a dozen to forty women really involved in every murder, but in this case it seems to be only five men — you, I, Johnnie, old Scully; and that fool of an unfortunate gambler came merely as a culmination, the apex of a human movement, and gets all the punishment."

The cowboy, injured and rebellious, cried out blindly into this fog of mysterious theory: "Well, I didn't do anythin', did I?"

WILLIAM VAUGHN MOODY (1869–1910)

Moody did all his publishing in the decade after Stephen Crane's premature death and was himself cut short, before his work was fulfilled, within a few years of the poetic revival of 1912–16. Born at Spencer, Indiana, in 1869, he attended Riverside Academy, New York, and Harvard, where he completed the work for the baccalaureate in 1892. He spent a year in Europe, returned to Harvard, took a master's degree, taught English there, and in 1895 joined the faculty of the University of Chicago, where he served as instructor and assistant professor until 1903. *The Masque of Judgment* had been published in 1900, and a volume of *Poems* in 1901. After he had resigned his teaching position to devote his time to writing, there followed *The Fire-Bringer* in 1904, and his most successful drama, *The Great Divide*, in 1907. He collaborated with R. M. Lovett in writing a *History of English Literature*, and found time to edit Milton. Apparently at the height of his powers, he died, at Colorado Springs, in 1910.

Although not an admirer of Whitman's verse form, nor an experimenter in free verse, Moody was plainly a forerunner of the new poets by virtue of his fresh zest for experience and his independent criticism of life.   These he could unite with a vital sense of tradition in life and art.   He was an excellent and devoted Greek scholar, was well acquainted with Dante and mediaeval romances, with modern French and German literature, with the whole range of English literature (his poems show the influence of Shakespeare and Milton, of Keats and Shelley, of Rossetti and Morris, of Browning and Whitman).

The Poems and Plays of William Vaughn Moody were edited by J. M. Manly, 2 volumes, 1912; Selected Poems, by R. M. Lovett, 1931; Some Letters, by D. G. Mason, 1913.   D. D. Henry, William Vaughn Moody, 1934, is a biographical and critical study. Other critical discussion: B. Weirick, From Whitman to Sandburg, 1924; A. H. Quinn, History of the American Drama, second volume, 1927.

Gloucester Moors

(1900)

A mile behind is Gloucester town
Where the fishing fleets put in,
A mile ahead the land dips down
And the woods and farms begin.
Here, where the moors stretch free   5
In the high blue afternoon,
Are the marching sun and talking sea,
And the racing winds that wheel and flee
On the flying heels of June.

Jill-o'er-the-ground is purple blue,   10
Blue is the quaker-maid,
The wild geranium holds its dew
Long in the boulder's shade.
Wax-red hangs the cup
From the huckleberry boughs,   15
In barberry bells the grey moths sup
Or where the choke-cherry lifts high up
Sweet bowls for their carouse.

Over the shelf of the sandy cove
Beach-peas blossom late.   20
By copse and cliff the swallows rove
Each calling to his mate.
Seaward the sea-gulls go,
And the land-birds all are here;
That green-gold flash was a vireo,   25
And yonder flame where the marsh-flags grow
Was a scarlet tanager.

This earth is not the steadfast place
We landsmen build upon;
From deep to deep she varies pace,   30
And while she comes is gone.
Beneath my feet I feel
Her smooth bulk heave and dip;

With velvet plunge and soft upreel
She swings and steadies to her keel   35
Like a gallant, gallant ship.

These summer clouds she sets for sail,
The sun is her masthead light,
She tows the moon like a pinnace frail
Where her phosphor wake churns bright.   40
Now hid, now looming clear,
On the face of the dangerous blue
The star fleets tack and wheel and veer,
But on, but on does the old earth steer
As if her port she knew.   45

God, dear God! Does she know her port,
Though she goes so far about?
Or blind astray, does she make her sport
To brazen and chance it out?
I watched when her captains passed: 50
She were better captainless.
Men in the cabin, before the mast,
But some were reckless and some aghast,
And some sat gorged at mess.

By her battened hatch I leaned and caught
Sounds from the noisome hold, —   56
Cursing and sighing of souls distraught
And cries too sad to be told.
Then I strove to go down and see;
But they said, "Thou art not of us!"   60
I turned to those on the deck with me
And cried, "Give help!"   But they said,
        "Let be:
Our ship sails faster thus."

Jill-o'er'the-ground is purple blue,
Blue is the quaker-maid,   65
The alder-clump where the brook comes
        through

Breeds cresses in its shade.
To be out of the moiling street
With its swelter and its sin!
Who has given to me this sweet,   70
And given my brother dust to eat?
And when will his wage come in?

Scattering wide or blown in ranks,
Yellow and white and brown,
Boats and boats from the fishing banks   75
Come home to Gloucester town.
There is cash to purse and spend,
There are wives to be embraced,
Hearts to borrow and hearts to lend,
And hearts to take and keep to the end, —   80
O little sails, make haste!

But thou, vast outbound ship of souls,
What harbor town for thee?
What shapes, when thy arriving tolls,
Shall crowd the banks to see?   85
Shall all the happy shipmates then
Stand singing brotherly?
Or shall a haggard ruthless few
Warp her over and bring her to,
While the many broken souls of men   90
Fester down in the slayer's pen,
And nothing to say or do?

The Menagerie

(1900)

The idea of evolution permeates the long poems
"The Masque of Judgment" and "The Fire-
Bringer." Indeed, "throughout all Moody's
work is a constant undercurrent of evolutionary
thought." (P. H. Boynton, *History of American
Literature*.)

Thank God my brain is not inclined to cut
Such capers every day! I'm just about
Mellow, but then — There goes the tent-
        flap shut.
Rain's in the wind. I thought so: every snout
Was twitching when the keeper turned me
        out.   5

That screaming parrot makes my blood run
        cold.
Gabriel's trump! the big bull elephant
Squeals "Rain!" to the parched herd. The
        monkeys scold,

And jabber that it's rain water they want.
(It makes me sick to see a monkey pant.)   10

I'll foot it home, to try and make believe
I'm sober. After this I stick to beer,
And drop the circus when the sane folks
        leave.
A man's a fool to look at things too near:
They look back, and begin to cut up queer.   15

Beasts do, at any rate; especially
Wild devils caged. They have the coolest
        way
Of being something else than what you see;
You pass a sleek young zebra nosing hay,
A nylghau looking bored and distingué, —   20

And think you've seen a donkey and a bird.
Not on your life! Just glance back, if you
        dare.
The zebra chews, the nylghau hasn't stirred;
But something's happened, Heaven knows
        what or where,
To freeze your scalp and pompadour your
        hair.   25

I'm not precisely an aeolian lute
Hung in the wandering winds of sentiment,
But drown me if the ugliest, meanest brute
Grunting and fretting in that sultry tent
Didn't just floor me with embarrassment!   30

'Twas like a thunderclap from out the
        clear, —
One minute they were circus beasts, some
        grand,
Some ugly, some amusing, and some queer:
Rival attractions to the hobo band,
The flying jenny, and the peanut stand.   35

Next minute they were old hearth-mates of
        mine!
Lost people, eyeing me with such a stare!
Patient, satiric, devilish, divine;
A gaze of hopeless envy, squalid care,
Hatred, and thwarted love, and dim de-
        spair.   40

And suddenly, as in a flash of light,
I saw great Nature working out her plan;
Through all her shapes from mastodon to
        mite

Forever groping, testing, passing on
To find at last the shape and soul of Man. 45

Till in the fullness of accomplished time,
Comes brother Forepaugh, upon business
    bent,
Tracks her through frozen and through
    torrid clime,
And shows us, neatly labeled in a tent,
The stages of her huge experiment; 50

Blabbing aloud her shy and reticent hours;
Dragging to light her blinking, slothful
    moods;
Publishing fretful seasons when her powers
Worked wild and sullen in her solitudes,
Or when her mordant laughter shook the
    woods. 55

Here, round about me, were her vagrant
    births;
Sick dreams she had, fierce projects she es-
    sayed;
Her qualms, her fiery prides, her crazy
    mirths;
The troublings of her spirit as she strayed,
Cringed, gloated, mocked, was lordly, was
    afraid, 60

On that long road she went to seek mankind;
Here were the darkling coverts that she beat
To find the Hider she was sent to find;
Here the distracted footprints of her feet
Whereby her soul's Desire she came to
    greet. 65

But why should they, her botch-work, turn
    about
And stare disdain at me, her finished job?
Why was the place one vast suspended
    shout
Of laughter? Why did all the daylight
    throb
With soundless guffaw and dumb-stricken
    sob? 70

Helpless I stood among those awful cages;
The beasts were walking loose, and I was
    bagged!
I, I, last product of the toiling ages,
Goal of heroic feet that never lagged, —
A little man in trousers, slightly jagged. 75

Deliver me from such another jury!
The Judgment-day will be a picnic to't.
Their satire was more dreadful than their
    fury,
And worst of all was just a kind of brute
Disgust, and giving up, and sinking mute. 80

Survival of the fittest, adaptation,
And all their other evolution terms,
Seem to omit one small consideration,
To wit, that tumblebugs and angleworms
Have souls: there's soul in everything that
    squirms. 85

And souls are restless, plagued, impatient
    things,
All dream and unaccountable desire;
Crawling, but pestered with the thought of
    wings;
Spreading through every inch of earth's old
    mire
Mystical hanker after something higher. 90

Wishes *are* horses, as I understand.
I guess a wistful polyp that has strokes
Of feeling faint to gallivant on land
Will come to be a scandal to his folks;
Legs he will sprout, in spite of threats and
    jokes. 95

And at the core of every life that crawls
Or runs or flies or swims or vegetates —
Churning the mammoth's heart-blood, in the
    galls
Of shark and tiger planting gorgeous hates,
Lighting the love of eagles for their mates;

Yes, in the dim brain of the jellied fish 101
That is and is not living — moved and
    stirred
From the beginning a mysterious wish,
A vision, a command, a fatal Word:
The name of Man was uttered, and they
    heard. 105

Upward along the aeons of old war
They sought him: wing and shank-bone,
    claw and bill
Were fashioned and rejected; wide and
    far
They roamed the twilight jungles of their
    will:

But still they sought him, and desired him
    still.   110

Man they desired, but mind you, Perfect
    Man,
The radiant and the loving, yet to be!
I hardly wonder, when they came to scan
The upshot of their strenuosity,   114
They gazed with mixed emotions upon *me.*

Well, my advice to you is, Face the creatures,
Or spot them sideways with your weather
    eye,
Just to keep tab on their expansive features;
It isn't pleasant when you're stepping high

To catch a giraffe smiling on the sly.   120

If nature made you graceful, don't get gay
Back-to before the hippopotamus;
If meek and godly, find some place to play
Besides right where three mad hyenas fuss:
You may hear language that we won't dis-
    cuss.   125

If you're a sweet thing in a flower-bed hat,
Or her best fellow with your tie tucked in,
Don't squander love's bright springtime
    girding at
An old chimpanzee with an Irish chin:
There may be hidden meaning in his grin.   130

HENRY ADAMS (1838–1918)

    Henry Adams was born in Boston of distinguished ancestry, studied at Harvard
and in Germany, edited the *North American Review*, taught history at Harvard, wrote
nine volumes of a *History of the United States*, traveled extensively, became interested
in the Middle Ages, wrote a remarkable book on *Mont-Saint-Michel and Chartres*
(1913), and died in 1918.

    In this year, after his death, *The Education of Henry Adams* (first privately printed
in 1907 for circulation among close friends of the author) was published and achieved
an extraordinary success. In this book Adams retraced, with a sturdy honesty, his
quest for the meaning of life in an era of evolutionary science and industrial materialism. Combining both the modern critical temper — exemplified among the
poets by Moody and Robinson — and a yearning for mystical rapture that reminds
one of Jonathan Edwards and Emerson, he wrote an autobiography that reflects
the later nineteenth century as vividly as Franklin's autobiography reflects the
century previous.

    The education of Henry Adams brought this son of the Puritans to his knees be-
fore the Virgin of Chartres. *Mont-Saint-Michel and Chartres* was characterized by
the architect Ralph Adams Cram as "one of the most distinguished contributions to literature and one of the most valuable adjuncts to the study of mediæ-
valism America has thus far produced. . . . Seven centuries dissolve and vanish
away, being as they were not, and the thirteenth century lives less for us than we
live in it and are a part of its gaiety and lightheartedness, its youthful ardor and
abounding action, its childlike simplicity and frankness, its normal and healthy and
all-embracing devotion."

    The sketch in *DAB* is by Allen Johnson. Extended biographies are by J. T.
Adams: *The Adams Family*, 1930, and *Henry Adams*, 1933. A number of volumes
of Adams's letters have been collected. Critical interpretation may be found in
R. Shafer, *Progress and Science*, 1922; V. L. Parrington, *Beginnings of Critical Realism*,
1930; H. S. Commager, *The American Mind*, 1950; V. W. Brooks, *New England: Indian
Summer*, 1940.

From The Education of Henry Adams
1907, 1918
Chaos (1870)

He had been some weeks in London when he received a telegram from his brother-in-law at the Bagni di Lucca telling him that his sister had been thrown from a cab and injured, and that he had better come on. He started that night, and reached the Bagni di Lucca on the second day. Tetanus had already set in.

The last lesson — the sum and term of education — began then. He had passed through thirty years of rather varied experience without having once felt the shell of custom broken. He had never seen Nature — only her surface — the sugar-coating that she shows to youth. Flung suddenly in his face, with the harsh brutality of chance, the terror of the blow stayed by him thenceforth for life, until repetition made it more than the will could struggle with; more than he could call on himself to bear. He found his sister, a woman of forty, as gay and brilliant in the terrors of lockjaw as she had been in the careless fun of 1859, lying in bed in consequence of a miserable cab-accident that had bruised her foot. Hour by hour the muscles grew rigid, while the mind remained bright, until after ten days of fiendish torture she died in convulsions.

One had heard and read a great deal about death, and even seen a little of it, and knew by heart the thousand commonplaces of religion and poetry which seemed to deaden one's senses and veil the horror. Society being immortal, could put on immortality at will. Adams being mortal, felt only the mortality. Death took features altogether new to him, in these rich and sensuous surroundings. Nature enjoyed it, played with it, the horror added to her charm, she liked the torture, and smothered her victim with caresses. Never had one seen her so winning. The hot Italian summer brooded outside, over the market-place and the picturesque peasants, and, in the singular color of the Tuscan atmosphere, the hills and vineyards of the Apennines seemed bursting with mid-summer blood. The sick-room itself glowed with the Italian joy of life; friends filled it; no harsh northern lights pierced the soft shadows; even the dying woman shared the sense of the Italian summer, the soft, velvet air, the humor, the courage, the sensual fulness of Nature and man. She faced death, as women mostly do, bravely and even gaily, racked slowly to unconsciousness, but yielding only to violence, as a soldier sabred in battle. For many thousands of years, on these hills and plains, Nature had gone on sabring men and women with the same air of sensual pleasure.

Impressions like these are not reasoned or catalogued in the mind; they are felt as part of violent emotion; and the mind that feels them is a different one from that which reasons; it is thought of a different power and a different person. The first serious consciousness of Nature's gesture — her attitude towards life — took form then as a phantasm, a nightmare, an insanity of force. For the first time, the stage-scenery of the senses collapsed; the human mind felt itself stripped naked, vibrating in a void of shapeless energies, with resistless mass, colliding, crushing, wasting, and destroying what these same energies had created and labored from eternity to perfect. Society became fantastic, a vision of pantomime with a mechanical motion; and its so-called thought merged in the mere sense of life, and pleasure in the sense. The usual anodynes of social medicine became evident artifice. Stoicism was perhaps the best; religion was the most human; but the idea that any personal deity could find pleasure or profit in torturing a poor woman, by accident, with fiendish cruelty known to man only in perverted and insane temperaments, could not be held for a moment. For pure blasphemy, it made pure atheism a comfort. God might be, as the Church said, a Substance, but He could not be a Person.

With nerves strained for the first time beyond their power of tension, he slowly travelled northwards with his friends, and stopped for a few days at Ouchy to recover his balance in a new world; for the fantastic mystery of coincidences had made the world, which he thought real, mimic and reproduce the distorted nightmare of his personal horror. He did not yet know it, and he was twenty years in finding it out; but he had need of all the beauty of the Lake below and of the Alps above, to restore the finite to its place. For the first time in his life, Mont Blanc for a moment looked to him what it was — a chaos of anarchic and purposeless forces — and he needed days of repose to see it clothe itself again with the illusions of his senses, the white purity of its snows, the splendor of its light, and the infinity of its heavenly peace. Nature was kind; Lake Geneva was beautiful beyond itself, and the Alps put on charms real as terrors; but man became chaotic, and before the illusions of Nature were wholly restored, the illusions of Europe suddenly vanished, leaving a new world to learn.

On July 4, all Europe had been in peace; on July 14, Europe was in full chaos of war. One felt helpless and ignorant, but one might have been king or kaiser without feeling stronger to deal with the chaos. Mr. Gladstone was as astounded as Adams; the Emperor Napoleon was nearly as stupefied as either, and Bismarck himself hardly knew how he did it. As education, the outbreak of the war was wholly lost on a man dealing with death hand-to-hand, who could not throw it aside to look at it across the Rhine. Only when he got up to Paris, he began to feel the approach of catastrophe. Providence set up no *affiches* to announce the tragedy. Under one's eyes France cut herself adrift, and floated off, on an unknown stream, towards a less known ocean. Standing on the curb of the Boulevard, one could see as much as though one stood by the side of the Emperor or in command of an army corps. The effect was lurid. The public seemed to look on the war, as it had looked on the wars of Louis XIV and Francis I, as a branch of decorative art. The French, like true artists, always regarded war as one of the fine arts. Louis XIV practised it; Napoleon I perfected it; and Napoleon III had till then pursued it in the same spirit with singular success. In Paris, in July, 1870, the war was brought out like an opera of Meyerbeer. One felt one's self a supernumerary hired to fill the scene. Every evening at the theater the comedy was interrupted by order, and one stood up by

order, to join in singing the *Marseillaise* to order. For nearly twenty years one had been forbidden to sing the *Marseillaise* under any circumstances, but at last regiment after regiment marched through the streets shouting "Marchons!" while the bystanders cared not enough to join. Patriotism seemed to have been brought out of the Government stores, and distributed by grammes *per capita*. One had seen one's own people dragged unwillingly into a war, and had watched one's own regiments march to the front without sign of enthusiasm; on the contrary, most serious, anxious, and conscious of the whole weight of the crisis; but in Paris every one conspired to ignore the crisis, which every one felt at hand. Here was education for the million, but the lesson was intricate. Superficially Napoleon and his Ministers and marshals were playing a game against Thiers and Gambetta. A bystander knew almost as little as they did about the result. How could Adams prophesy that in another year or two, when he spoke of *his* Paris and its tastes, people would smile at his dotage?

As soon as he could, he fled to England, and once more took refuge in the profound peace of Wenlock Abbey. Only the few remaining monks, undisturbed by the brutalities of Henry VIII — three or four young Englishmen — survived there, with Milnes Gaskell acting as Prior. The August sun was warm; the calm of the Abbey was ten times secular; not a discordant sound — hardly a sound of any sort except the cawing of the ancient rookery at sunset — broke the stillness and, after the excitement of the last month, one felt a palpable haze of peace brooding over the edge and the Welsh Marches. Since the reign of *Pteraspis*, nothing had greatly changed; nothing except the monks. Lying on the turf, the ground littered with newspapers, the monks studied the war correspondence. In one respect Adams had succeeded in educating himself; he had learned to follow a campaign.

While at Wenlock, he received a letter from President Eliot inviting him to take an Assistant Professorship of History, to be created shortly at Harvard College. After waiting ten or a dozen years for some one to show consciousness of his existence, even a

Terebratula would be pleased and grateful for a compliment which implied that the new President of Harvard College wanted his help; but Adams knew nothing about history, and much less about teaching, while he knew more than enough about Harvard College; and wrote at once to thank President Eliot, with much regret that the honor should be above his powers. His mind was full of other matters. The summer, from which he had expected only amusement and social relations with new people, had ended in the most intimate personal tragedy, and the most terrific political convulsion he had ever known or was likely to know. He had failed in every object of his trip. The Quarterlies had refused his best essay. He had made no acquaintances and hardly picked up the old ones. He sailed from Liverpool, on September 1, to begin again where he had started two years before, but with no longer a hope of attaching himself to a President or a party or a press. He was a free lance and no other career stood in sight or mind. To that point education had brought him.

Yet he found, on reaching home, that he had not done quite so badly as he feared. His article on the Session in the July *North American* had made a success. Though he could not quite see what partisan object it served, he heard with flattered astonishment that it had been reprinted by the Democratic National Committee and circulated as a campaign document by the hundred thousand copies. He was henceforth in opposition, do what he might; and a Massachusetts Democrat, say what he pleased; while his only reward or return for this partisan service consisted in being formally answered by Senator Timothy Howe, of Wisconsin, in a Republican campaign document, presumed to be also freely circulated, in which the Senator, besides refuting his opinions, did him the honor — most unusual and picturesque in a Senator's rhetoric — of likening him to a begonia.

The begonia is, or then was, a plant of such senatorial qualities as to make the simile, in intention, most flattering. Far from charming in its refinement, the begonia was remarkable for curious and showy foliage; it was conspicuous; it seemed to have no useful purpose; and it insisted on standing always in the most prominent positions. Adams would have greatly liked to be a begonia in Washington, for this was rather his ideal of the successful statesman, and he thought about it still more when the *Westminster Review* for October brought him his article on the Gold Conspiracy, which was also instantly pirated on a great scale. Piratical he was himself henceforth driven to be, and he asked only to be pirated, for he was sure not to be paid; but the honors of piracy resemble the colors of the begonia; they are showy but not useful. Here was a *tour de force* he had never dreamed himself equal to performing: two long, dry, quarterly, thirty or forty page articles, appearing in quick succession, and pirated for audiences running well into the hundred thousands; and not one person, man or woman, offering him so much as a congratulation, except to call him a begonia.

Had this been all, life might have gone on very happily as before, but the ways of America to a young person of literary and political tastes were such as the so-called evolution of civilized man had not before evolved. No sooner had Adams made at Washington what he modestly hoped was a sufficient success, than his whole family set on him to drag him away. For the first time since 1861 his father interposed; his mother entreated; and his brother Charles argued and urged that he should come to Harvard College. Charles had views of further joint operations in a new field. He said that Henry had done at Washington all he could possibly do; that his position there wanted solidity; that he was, after all, an adventurer; that a few years in Cambridge would give him personal weight; that his chief function was not to be that of teacher, but that of editing the *North American Review* which was to be coupled with the professorship, and would lead to the daily press. In short, that he needed the university more than the university needed him.

Henry knew the university well enough to know that the department of history was controlled by one of the most astute and ideal administrators in the world — Professor Gurney — and that it was Gurney who had established the new professorship, and had cast his net over Adams to carry the double load of mediaeval history and the *Review*. He could see no relation whatever between himself and a professorship. He sought education; he did not sell it. He knew no history; he knew only a few historians; his ignorance was mischievous because it was literary, accidental, indifferent. On the other hand he knew Gurney, and felt much influenced by his advice. One cannot take one's self quite seriously in such matters; it could not much affect the sum of solar energies whether one went on dancing with girls in Washington, or began talking to boys at Cambridge. The good people who thought it did matter had a sort of right to guide. One could not reject their advice; still less disregard their wishes.

The sum of the matter was that Henry went out to Cambridge and had a few words with President Eliot which seemed to him almost as American as the talk about diplomacy with his father ten years before. "But, Mr. President," urged Adams, "I know nothing about Mediaeval History." With the courteous manner and bland smile so familiar for the next generation of Americans, Mr. Eliot mildly but firmly replied, "If you will point out to me any one who knows more, Mr. Adams, I will appoint him." The answer was neither logical nor convincing, but Adams could not meet it without overstepping his privileges. He could not say that, under the circumstances, the appointment of any professor at all seemed to him unnecessary.

So, at twenty-four hours' notice, he broke his life in halves again in order to begin a new education, on lines he had not chosen, in subjects for which he cared less than nothing; in a place he did not love, and before a future which repelled. Thousands of men have to do the same thing, but his case was peculiar because he had no need to do it. He did it because his best and wisest friends urged it, and he never could make up his mind whether they were right or not. To him this kind of education was always false. For himself he had no doubts. He thought it a mistake; but his opinion did not prove that it was one, since, in all probability, whatever he did would be more or less a mis-

take. He had reached cross-roads of education which all led astray. What he could gain at Harvard College he did not know, but in any case it was nothing he wanted. What he lost at Washington he could partly see, but in any case it was not fortune. Grant's administration wrecked men by thousands, but profited few. Perhaps Mr. Fish was the solitary exception. One might search the whole list of Congress, Judiciary, and Executive during the twenty-five years 1870 to 1895, and find little but damaged reputation. The period was poor in purpose and barren in results.

Henry Adams, if not the rose, lived as near it as any politician, and knew, more or less, all the men in any way prominent at Washington, or knew all about them. Among them, in his opinion, the best equipped, the most active-minded, and most industrious was Abram Hewitt, who sat in Congress for a dozen years, between 1874 and 1886, sometimes leading the House and always wielding influence second to none. With nobody did Adams form closer or longer relations than with Mr. Hewitt, whom he regarded as the most useful public man in Washington; and he was the more struck by Hewitt's saying, at the end of his laborious career as legislator, that he left behind him no permanent result except the Act consolidating the Surveys. Adams knew no other man who had done so much, unless Mr. Sherman's legislation is accepted as an instance of success. Hewitt's nearest rival would probably have been Senator Pendleton who stood father to civil service reform in 1882, an attempt to correct a vice that should never have been allowed to be born. These were the men who succeeded.

The press stood in much the same light. No editor, no political writer, and no public administrator achieved enough good reputation to preserve his memory for twenty years. A number of them achieved bad reputations, or damaged good ones that had been gained in the Civil War. On the whole, even for Senators, diplomats, and Cabinet officers, the period was wearisome and stale.

None of Adams's generation profited by public activity unless it were William C. Whitney, and even he could not be induced to return to it. Such ambitions as these were out of one's reach, but supposing one tried for what was feasible, attached one's self closely to the Garfields, Arthurs, Frelinghuysens, Blaines, Bayards, or Whitneys, who happened to hold office; and supposing one asked for the mission to Belgium or Portugal, and obtained it; supposing one served a term as Assistant Secretary or Chief of Bureau; or, finally, supposing one had gone as sub-editor on the *New York Tribune* or *Times* — how much more education would one have gained than by going to Harvard College? These questions seemed better worth an answer than most of the questions on examination papers at college or in the civil service; all the more because one never found an answer to them, then or afterwards, and because, to his mind, the value of American society altogether was mixed up with the value of Washington.

At first, the simple beginner, struggling with principles, wanted to throw off responsibility on the American people, whose bare and toiling shoulders had to carry the load of every social or political stupidity; but the American people had no more to do with it than with the customs of Peking. American character might perhaps account for it, but what accounted for American character? All Boston, all New England, and respectable New York, including Charles Francis Adams the father and Charles Francis Adams the son, agreed that Washington was no place for a respectable young man. All Washington, including Presidents, Cabinet officers, Judiciary, Senators, Congressmen, and clerks, expressed the same opinion, and conspired to drive away every young man who happened to be there, or tried to approach. Not one young man of promise remained in the Government service. All drifted into opposition. The Government did not want them in Washington. Adams's case was perhaps the strongest because he thought he had done well. He was forced to guess it, since he knew no one who would have risked so extravagant a step as that of encouraging a young man in a literary career, or even in a political one; society forbade it, as well as residence in a political capital; but Harvard College must have seen some hope

for him, since it made him professor against his will; even the publishers and editors of the *North American Review* must have felt a certain amount of confidence in him, since they put the *Review* in his hands. After all, the *Review* was the first literary power in America, even though it paid almost as little in gold as the United States Treasury. The degree of Harvard College might bear a value as ephemeral as the commission of a President of the United States; but the government of the college, measured by money alone, and patronage, was a matter of more importance than that of some branches of the national service. In social position, the college was the superior of them all put together. In knowledge, she could assert no superiority, since the Government made no claims, and prided itself on ignorance. The service of Harvard College was distinctly honorable; perhaps the most honorable in America; and if Harvard College thought Henry Adams worth employing at four dollars a day, why should Washington decline his services when he asked nothing? Why should he be dragged from a career he liked in a place he loved, into a career he detested, in a place and climate he shunned? Was it enough to satisfy him that all America should call Washington barren and dangerous? What made Washington more dangerous than New York?

The American character showed singular limitations which sometimes drove the student of civilized man to despair. Crushed by his own ignorance — lost in the darkness of his own gropings — the scholar finds himself jostled of a sudden by a crowd of men who seem to him ignorant that there is a thing called ignorance; who have forgotten how to amuse themselves; who cannot even understand that they are bored. The American thought of himself as a restless, pushing, energetic, ingenious person, always awake and trying to get ahead of his neighbors. Perhaps this idea of the national character might be corrected for New York or Chicago; it was not correct for Washington. There the American showed himself, four times in five, as a quiet, peaceful, shy figure, rather in the mould of Abraham Lincoln, somewhat sad, sometimes pathetic, once tragic; or like

Grant, inarticulate, uncertain, distrustful of himself, still more distrustful of others, and awed by money. That the American, by temperament, worked to excess, was true; work and whiskey were his stimulants; work was a form of vice; but he never cared much for money or power after he earned them. The amusement of the pursuit was all the amusement he got from it; he had no use for wealth. Jim Fisk alone seemed to know what he wanted; Jay Gould never did. At Washington one met mostly such true Americans, but if one wanted to know them better, one went to study them in Europe. Bored, patient, helpless; pathetically dependent on his wife and daughters; indulgent to excess; mostly a modest, decent, excellent, valuable citizen; the American was to be met at every railway station in Europe, carefully explaining to every listener that the happiest day of his life would be the day he should land on the pier at New York. He was ashamed to be amused; his mind no longer answered to the stimulus of variety; he could not face a new thought. All his immense strength, his intense nervous energy, his keen analytic perceptions, were oriented in one direction, and he could not change it. Congress was full of such men; in the Senate, Sumner, was almost the only exception; in the Executive, Grant and Boutwell were varieties of the type — political specimens — pathetic in their helplessness to do anything with power when it came to them. They knew not how to amuse themselves; they could not conceive how other people were amused. Work, whiskey, and cards were life. The atmosphere of political Washington was theirs — or was supposed by the outside world to be in their control — and this was the reason why the outside world judged that Washington was fatal even for a young man of thirty-two, who had passed through the whole variety of temptations, in every capital of Europe, for a dozen years; who never played cards, and who loathed whiskey.

The Dynamo and the Virgin (1900)

Until the Great Exposition of 1900 closed its doors in November, Adams haunted it,

aching to absorb knowledge, and helpless to find it. He would have liked to know how much of it could have been grasped by the best-informed man in the world. While he was thus meditating chaos, Langley came by, and showed it to him. At Langley's behest, the Exhibition dropped its superfluous rags and stripped itself to the skin, for Langley knew what to study, and why, and how; while Adams might as well have stood outside in the night, staring at the Milky Way. Yet Langley said nothing new, and taught nothing that one might not have learned from Lord Bacon, three hundred years before; but though one should have known the *Advancement of Science* as well as one knew the *Comedy of Errors*, the literary knowledge counted for nothing until some teacher should show how to apply it. Bacon took a vast deal of trouble in teaching King James I and his subjects, American or other, towards the year 1620, that true science was the development or economy of forces; yet an elderly American in 1900 knew neither the formula nor the forces; or even so much as to say to himself that his historical business in the Exposition concerned only the economies or developments of force since 1893, when he began the study at Chicago.

Nothing in education is so astonishing as the amount of ignorance it accumulates in the form of inert facts. Adams had looked at most of the accumulations of art in the storehouses called Art Museums; yet he did not know how to look at the art exhibits of 1900. He had studied Karl Marx and his doctrines of history with profound attention, yet he could not apply them at Paris. Langley, with the ease of a great master of experiment, threw out of the field every exhibit that did not reveal a new application of force, and naturally threw out, to begin with, almost the whole art exhibit. Equally, he ignored almost the whole industrial exhibit. He led his pupil directly to the forces. His chief interest was in new motors to make his airship feasible, and he taught Adams the astonishing complexities of the Daimler motor and of the automobile, which, since 1893, had become a nightmare at a hundred kilometres an hour, almost as destructive as the electric tram which was only ten years older; and threatening to become as terrible as the locomotive steam-engine itself, which was almost exactly Adams's own age.

Then he showed his scholar the great hall of dynamos, and explained how little he knew about electricity or force of any kind, even of his own special sun, which spouted heat in inconceivable volume, but which, as far as he knew, might spout less or more, at any time, for all the certainty he felt in it. To him, the dynamo itself was but an ingenious channel for conveying somewhere the heat latent in a few tons of poor coal hidden in a dirty engine-house carefully kept out of sight; but to Adams the dynamo became a symbol of infinity. As he grew accustomed to the great gallery of machines, he began to feel the forty-foot dynamos as a moral force, much as the early Christians felt the Cross. The planet itself seemed less impressive, in its old-fashioned, deliberate, annual or daily revolution, than this huge wheel, revolving within arm's-length at some vertiginous speed, and barely murmuring — scarcely humming an audible warning to stand a hair's-breadth farther for respect of power — while it would not wake the baby lying close against its frame. Before the end, one began to pray to it; inherited instinct taught the natural expression of man before silent and infinite force. Among the thousand symbols of ultimate energy, the dynamo was not so human as some, but it was the most expressive.

Yet the dynamo, next to the steam-engine, was the most familiar of exhibits. For Adams's objects its value lay chiefly in its occult mechanism. Between the dynamo in the gallery of machines and the engine-house outside, the break of continuity amounted to abysmal fracture for a historian's objects. No more relation could he discover between the steam and the electric current than between the Cross and the cathedral. The forces were interchangeable if not reversible, but he could see only an absolute *fiat* in electricity as in faith. Langley could not help him. Indeed, Langley seemed to be worried by the same trouble, for he constantly repeated that the new forces were anarchical, and especially that he was not responsible for the new rays, that were little short of parricidal in their wicked spirit towards science. His own rays, with which he had doubled the solar spectrum, were altogether harmless and beneficent; but Radium denied its God — or, what was to Langley the same thing, denied the truths of his Science. The force was wholly new.

A historian who asked only to learn enough to be as futile as Langley or Kelvin, made rapid progress under this teaching, and mixed himself up in the tangle of ideas until he achieved a sort of Paradise of ignorance vastly consoling to his fatigued senses. He wrapped himself in vibrations and rays which were new, and he would have hugged Marconi and Branly had he met them, as he hugged the dynamo; while he lost his arithmetic in trying to figure out the equation between the discoveries and the economies of force. The economies, like the discoveries, were absolute, super-sensual, occult; incapable of expression in horse-power. What mathematical equivalent could he suggest as the value of a Branly coherer? Frozen air, or the electric furnace, had some scale of measurement, no doubt, if somebody could invent a thermometer adequate to the purpose; but X-rays had played no part whatever in man's consciousness, and the atom itself had figured only as a fiction of thought. In these seven years man had translated himself into a new universe which had no common scale of measurement with the old. He had entered a supersensual world, in which he could measure nothing except by chance collisions of movements imperceptible to his senses, perhaps even imperceptible to his instruments, but perceptible to each other, and so to some known ray at the end of the scale. Langley seemed prepared for anything, even for an indeterminable number of universes interfused — physics stark mad in metaphysics.

Historians undertake to arrange sequences — called stories, or histories — assuming in silence a relation of cause and effect. These assumptions, hidden in the depths of dusty libraries, have been astounding, but commonly unconscious and childlike; so much so, that if any captious critic were to drag them to light, historians would probably reply, with one voice, that they had never supposed themselves required to know what they were talking about. Adams, for one, had toiled in vain to find out what he meant. He had even published a dozen volumes of American history for no other purpose than to satisfy himself whether, by the severest process of stating, with the least possible comment, such facts as seemed sure, in such order as seemed rigorously consequent, he could fix for a familiar moment a necessary sequence of human movement. The result had satisfied him as little as at Harvard College. Where he saw sequence, other men saw something quite different, and no one saw the same unit of measure. He cared little about his experiments and less about his statesmen, who seemed to him quite as ignorant as himself and, as a rule, no more honest; but he insisted on a relation of sequence, and if he could not reach it by one method, he would try as many methods as science knew. Satisfied that the sequence of men led to nothing and that the sequence of their society could lead no further, while the mere sequence of time was artificial, and the sequence of thought was chaos, he turned at last to the sequence of force; and thus it happened that, after ten years' pursuit, he found himself lying in the Gallery of Machines at the Great Exposition of 1900, his historical neck broken by the sudden irruption of forces totally new.

Since no one else showed much concern, an elderly person without other cares had no need to betray alarm. The year 1900 was not the first to upset schoolmasters. Copernicus and Galileo had broken many professorial necks about 1600; Columbus had stood the world on its head towards 1500; but the nearest approach to the revolution of 1900 was that of 310, when Constantine set up the Cross. The rays that Langley disowned, as well as those which he fathered, were occult, supersensual, irrational; they were a revelation of mysterious energy like that of the Cross; they were what, in terms of mediaeval science, were called immediate modes of the divine substance.

The historian was thus reduced to his last resources. Clearly if he was bound to reduce all these forces to a common value, this common value could have no measure but that of their attraction on his own mind. He must treat them as they had been felt; as convertible, reversible, interchangeable attractions on thought. He made up his mind to venture it; he would risk translating rays into faith. Such a reversible process would vastly amuse a chemist, but the chemist could not deny that he, or some of his fellow physicists, could feel the force of both. When Adams was a boy in Boston, the best chemist in the place had probably never heard of Venus except by way of scandal, or of the Virgin except as idolatry; neither had he heard of dynamos or automobiles or radium; yet his mind was ready to feel the force of all, though the rays were unborn and the women were dead.

Here opened another totally new education, which promised to be by far the most hazardous of all. The knife-edge along which he must crawl, like Sir Lancelot in the twelfth century, divided two kingdoms of force which had nothing in common but attraction. They were as different as a magnet is from gravitation, supposing one knew what a magnet was, or gravitation, or love. The force of the Virgin was still felt at Lourdes, and seemed to be as potent as X-rays; but in America neither Venus nor Virgin ever had value as force — at most as sentiment. No American had ever been truly afraid of either.

This problem in dynamics gravely perplexed an American historian. The Woman had once been supreme; in France she still seemed potent, not merely as a sentiment, but as a force. Why was she unknown in America? For evidently America was ashamed of her, and she was ashamed of herself, otherwise they would not have strewn fig-leaves so profusely all over her. When she was a true force, she was ignorant of fig-leaves, but the monthly-magazine-made American female had not a feature that would have been recognized by Adam. The trait was notorious, and often humorous, but any one brought up among Puritans knew that sex was sin. In any previous age, sex was strength. Neither art nor beauty was needed. Every one, even among Puritans, knew that neither Diana of the

Ephesians nor any of the Oriental goddesses was worshipped for her beauty. She was goddess because of her force; she was the animated dynamo; she was reproduction — the greatest and most mysterious of all energies; all she needed was to be fecund. Singularly enough, not one of Adams's many schools of education had ever drawn his attention to the opening lines of Lucretius, though they were perhaps the finest in all Latin literature, where the poet invoked Venus exactly as Dante invoked the Virgin:

"Quae quoniam rerum naturam *sola* gubernas." [Thou who *alone* above all govern the things of nature.]

The Venus of Epicurean philosophy survived in the Virgin of the Schools:

"Donna, sei tanto grande, e tanto vali,
  Che qual vuol grazia, e a te non ricorre,
  Sua disianza vuol volar senz' ali."

[Lady, thou art so great and hast such worth, that if there be he who would have grace yet betaketh not himself to thee, his longing seeketh to fly without wings.]

All this was to American thought as though it had never existed. The true American knew something of the facts, but nothing of the feelings; he read the letter, but he never felt the law. Before this historical chasm, a mind like that of Adams felt itself helpless; he turned from the Virgin to the Dynamo as though he were a Branly coherer. On one side, at the Louvre and at Chartres, as he knew by the record of work actually done and still before his eyes, was the highest energy ever known to man, the creator of four-fifths of his noblest art, exercising vastly more attraction over the human mind than all the steam-engines and dynamos ever dreamed of; and yet this energy was unknown to the American mind. An American Virgin would never dare command; an American Venus would never dare exist.

The question, which to any plain American of the nineteenth century seemed as remote as it did to Adams, drew him almost violently to study, once it was posed; and on this point Langleys were as useless as though they were Herbert Spencers or dynamos. The idea survived only as art. There one turned as naturally as though the artist were himself a woman. Adams began to ponder, asking himself whether he knew of any American artist who had ever insisted on the power of sex, as every classic had always done; but he could think only of Walt Whitman; Bret Harte, as far as the magazines would let him venture; and one or two painters, for the flesh-tones. All the rest had used sex for sentiment, never for force; to them, Eve was a tender flower, and Herodias an unfeminine horror. American art, like the American language and American education, was as far as possible sexless. Society regarded this victory over sex as its greatest triumph, and the historian readily admitted it, since the moral issue, for the moment, did not concern one who was studying the relations of unmoral force. He cared nothing for the sex of the dynamo until he could measure its energy.

Vaguely seeking a clue, he wandered through the art exhibit, and, in his stroll, stopped almost every day before Saint-Gaudens's General Sherman, which had been given the central post of honor. Saint-Gaudens himself was in Paris, putting on the work his usual interminable last touches, and listening to the usual contradictory suggestions of brother sculptors. Of all the American artists who gave to American art whatever life it breathed in the seventies, Saint-Gaudens was perhaps the most sympathetic, but certainly the most inarticulate. General Grant or Don Cameron had scarcely less instinct of rhetoric than he. All the others — the Hunts, Richardson, John La Farge, Stanford White — were exuberant; only Saint-Gaudens could never discuss or dilate on an emotion, or suggest artistic arguments for giving to his work the forms that he felt. He never laid down the law, or affected the despot, or became brutalized like Whistler by the brutalities of his world. He required no incense; he was no egoist; his simplicity of thought was excessive; he could not imitate, or give any form but his own to the creations of his hand. No one felt more strongly than he the strength of other men, but the idea that they could affect him never stirred an image in his mind.

This summer his health was poor and his spirits were low. For such a temper, Adams was not the best companion, since his own gaiety was not *folle*; but he risked going now and then to the studio on Mont Parnasse to draw him out for a stroll in the Bois de Boulogne, or dinner as pleased his moods, and in return Saint-Gaudens sometimes let Adams go about in his company.

Once Saint-Gaudens took him down to Amiens, with a party of Frenchmen, to see the cathedral. Not until they found themselves actually studying the sculpture of the western portal, did it dawn on Adams's mind that, for his purposes, Saint-Gaudens on that spot had more interest to him than the cathedral itself. Great men before great monuments express great truths, provided they are not taken too solemnly. Adams never tired of quoting the supreme phrase of his idol Gibbon, before the Gothic cathedrals: "I darted a contemptuous look on the stately monuments of superstition." Even in the footnotes of his history, Gibbon had never inserted a bit of humor more human than this, and one would have paid largely for a photograph of the fat little historian, on the background of Notre Dame of Amiens, trying to persuade his readers — perhaps himself — that he was darting a contemptuous look on the stately monument, for which he felt in fact the respect which every man of his vast study and active mind always feels before objects worthy of it; but besides the humor, one felt also the relation. Gibbon ignored the Virgin, because in 1789 religious monuments were out of fashion. In 1900 his remark sounded fresh and simple as the green fields to ears that had heard a hundred years of other remarks, mostly no more fresh and certainly less simple. Without malice, one might find it more instructive than a whole lecture of Ruskin. One sees what one brings, and at that moment Gibbon brought the French Revolution. Ruskin brought reaction against the Revolution. Saint-Gaudens had passed beyond all. He liked the stately monuments much more than he liked Gibbon or Ruskin; he loved their dignity; their unity; their scale; their lines; their lights and shadows; their decorative sculpture; but he was even less conscious than they of the force that created it all — the Virgin, the Woman — by whose genius "the stately monuments of superstition" were built, through which she was expressed. He would have seen more meaning in Isis with the cow's horns, at Edfoo, who expressed the same thought. The art remained, but the energy was lost even upon the artist.

Yet in mind and person Saint-Gaudens was a survival of the 1500; he bore the stamp of the Renaissance, and should have carried an image of the Virgin round his neck, or stuck in his hat, like Louis XI. In mere time he was a lost soul that had strayed by chance into the twentieth century, and forgotten where it came from. He writhed and cursed at his ignorance, much as Adams did at his own, but in the opposite sense. Saint-Gaudens was a child of Benvenuto Cellini, smothered in an American cradle. Adams was a quintessence of Boston, devoured by curiosity to think like Benvenuto. Saint-Gaudens's art was starved from birth, and Adams's instinct was blighted from babyhood. Each had but half of a nature, and when they came together before the Virgin of Amiens they ought both to have felt in her the force that made them one; but it was not so. To Adams she became more than ever a channel of force; to Saint-Gaudens she remained as before a channel of taste.

For a symbol of power, Saint-Gaudens instinctively preferred the horse, as was plain in his horse and Victory of the Sherman monument. Doubtless Sherman also felt it so. The attitude was so American that, for at least forty years, Adams had never realized that any other could be in sound taste. How many years had he taken to admit a notion of what Michaelangelo and Rubens were driving at? He could not say; but he knew that only since 1895 had he begun to feel the Virgin or Venus as force, and not everywhere even so. At Chartres — perhaps at Lourdes — possibly at Cnidos if one could still find there the divinely naked Aphrodite of Praxiteles — but otherwise one must look for force to the goddesses of Indian mythology. The idea died out long ago in the German and English stock. Saint-Gaudens at Amiens was hardly less sensitive to the force of the female energy than Matthew Arnold at the Grande Chartreuse. Neither of them felt goddesses as power — only as reflected emotion, human expression, beauty, purity, taste, scarcely even as sympathy. They felt a railway train as power; yet they, and all other artists, constantly complained that the power embodied in a railway train could never be embodied in art. All the steam in the world could not, like the Virgin, build Chartres.

Yet in mechanics, whatever the mechanician might think, both energies acted as interchangeable forces on man, and by action on man all known force may be measured. Indeed, few men of science measured force in any other way. After once admitting that a straight line was the shortest distance between two points, no serious mathematician cared to deny anything that suited his convenience, and rejected no symbol, unprobed or unprovable, that helped him to accomplish work. The symbol was force, as a compass-needle or a triangle was force, as the mechanist might prove by losing it, and nothing could be gained by ignoring their value. Symbol or energy, the Virgin had acted as the greatest force the Western world ever felt, and had drawn man's activities to herself more strongly than any other power, natural or super-natural, had ever done; the historian's business was to follow the track of the energy; to find where it came from and where it went to; its complex source and shifting channels; its values, equivalents, conversions. It could scarcely be more complex than radium; it could hardly be deflected, diverted, polarized, absorbed more perplexingly than other radiant matter. Adams knew nothing about any of them, but as a mathematical problem of influence on human progress, though all were occult, all reacted on his mind, and he rather inclined to think the Virgin easiest to handle.

The pursuit turned out to be long and tortuous, leading at last into the vast forests of scholastic science. From Zeno to Descartes, hand in hand with Thomas Aquinas, Montaigne, and Pascal, one stumbled as stupidly as though one were still a German student of 1860. Only with the instinct of despair could one force one's self into this old thicket of ignorance after having been repulsed at a score of entrances more promising and more popular. Thus far, no path had led anywhere, unless perhaps to an exceedingly modest living. Forty-five years of study had proved to be quite futile for the pursuit of power; one controlled no more force in 1900 than in 1850, although the amount of force controlled by society had enormously increased. The secret of education still hid itself somewhere behind ignorance, and one fumbled over it as feebly as ever. In such labyrinths, the staff is a force almost more necessary than the legs; the pen becomes a sort of blind-man's dog, to keep him from falling into the gutters. The pen works for itself, and acts like a hand, modelling the plastic material over and over again to the form that suits it best. The form is never arbitrary, but is a sort of growth like crystallization, as any artist knows too well; for often the pencil or pen runs into sidepaths and shapelessness, loses its relations, stops or is bogged. Then it has to return on its trail, and recover, if it can, its line of force. The result of a year's work depends more on what is struck out than on what is left in; on the sequence of the main lines of thought than on their play or variety. Compelled once more to lean heavily on this support, Adams covered more thousands of pages with figures as formal as though they were algebra, laboriously striking out, altering, burning, experimenting, until the year had expired, the Exposition had long been closed, and winter drawing to its end, before he sailed from Cherbourg, on January 19, 1901, for home.

The Twentieth Century

The New York Skyline

The Manhattan of today may seem as remote from Main Street as from Irving's little Dutch New York. But the metropolis, through its influence on publishing, entertainment, fashion, and taste, reaches into the life of the small towns, where most of our population lives; and the small towns, as the chief customers for New York's cultural goods, profoundly influence the productions of the metropolis.

Main Street, U. S. A.

"Sixth Avenue and Third Street," by John Sloan

In the twentieth century, artists like Sloan and writers like Dreiser practiced a realism which exposed some of the failures of American city life; but their denunciations were a sign of their belief in the promise of a democratic culture.

"American Gothic," by Grant Wood

The agrarian myth was also candidly explored, and the Puritan basis of Western character was revealed by Grant Wood in painting as it had been earlier by E. W. Howe and others in fiction.

THE Twentieth Century

* *

THE HERITAGE OF THE NINETIES

THE ECONOMIC CRISIS of the nineties passed, but it established a tradition of criticism of democracy, capitalism, and free enterprise which, except for a brief hiatus of complacency in the 1920's, has remained with us ever since. Most of the economic and political reforms demanded by but refused to the Populists have since been adopted. The momentum of their revolt was carried on in the "Muck-Raking" movement of 1902–1906 during which big business and such institutions as the press and education were investigated and exposed by journalists and novelists. This movement was followed by the liberalism which culminated in Woodrow Wilson's "New Freedom." World War I was followed by a prosperity which silenced many radicals but encouraged such critics of American culture as H. L. Mencken and inspired the reaction of the disillusioned writers known as the "Lost Generation." The panic of 1929 ended prosperity and restored the tradition of social criticism.

THE TWENTIES AND THIRTIES

Culturally we had come of age, but in 1914 we were not yet ready to join the world family of nations. When the World War broke out in 1914 America desired only to stay at home. Woodrow Wilson was elected for a second administration with the slogan "He kept us out of war," though we were soon drawn into it — into a war, as the new slogans went, "to end war" and "to make the world safe for democracy." When the war had been won, our high ideals or illusions faded. Refusing to enter the League of Nations, the United States turned inward once more, eager for a restoration of "normalcy," apparently hoping, with a strange myopia, that disarmament conferences and pacts to outlaw war would suffice to keep the outside world on an even keel. Events such as the inauguration of Russia's Five Year Plan in 1928 and Hitler's rise to the place of Chancellor in 1933 did not seem to have the dramatic interest of the Lindbergh flight from New York to Paris.

The America of the 1920's may be seen pleasantly through the vivid picture presented by Frederick Lewis Allen in *Only Yesterday*, under such chapter titles as: Back to Normalcy — The Revolution in Manners and Morals — Harding and the Scandals — Coolidge Prosperity — The Ballyhoo Years — The Revolt of the Highbrows — Alcohol and Al Capone — Home, Sweet Florida — The Big Bull Market — Crash! It was a decade of disillusionment, skepticism, cynicism, a time that lost faith even in democracy. As in the Gilded Age following the Civil War, the American people engaged in a materialistic orgy, using applied science for this purpose in both work and play. The moral tone of the country reached a new low, the stock market a new high. By 1929 many business men and economists were jubilantly proclaiming that the country had learned the secret of perpetual and ever increasing prosperity. At this juncture came the Wall Street panic and the depression.

Between late 1929 and 1931 stock market losses amounting to fifty billions of dollars affected twenty-five million Americans. The phenomena of depression set in with great vigor: the fall of commodity prices and wages, unemployment, foreclosures, business failures, bank failures, apathy, fear, with the added feature of an "act of God" in the form of a series of drought years. Once again the American Dream seemed to be ending in a nightmare — this time a long nightmare with a few false dawns. In 1933 the New Deal of Franklin Roosevelt gallantly undertook to banish fear and restore the functioning of the body politic, the same year when, by ironical coincidence, Chicago was celebrating a Century of Progress. But the depression dragged on and on, and cannot be said to have ended till a second World War proved that the twenty years of pacifism and materialism, of economic inflation and deflation, had constituted only an armistice. Again neutrality was impossible, and with the infamy of Pearl Harbor the country roused its frustrated energies and performed magnificently a task for which it was so well fitted: the organization of industrial production for total war and total victory.

SCIENCE AND THE MODERN MIND

At the beginning of the century, the main organizing principle in thought was the concept of evolution. As Morison and Commager write in *The Growth of the American Republic:*

> By 1900 perhaps three-fourths of the white population believed that man was merely one of the countless organisms that had evolved from the primordial slime, and that this planet was millions instead of thousands of years old. Possibly this belief was no nearer the truth than the other [the belief in special creation]; the important thing is that evolution and science created a new climate of opinion, and one in which we still live. It was not merely the change in man's views as to his origin on this planet that mattered. The implications of evolution were incorporated into every field of thought — law and history, economics and sociology, philosophy, religion, and art. . . .
> Truth could no longer be intuitive, plucked from the inner consciousness of man and beyond

proof or disproof, nor yet what God revealed to man; but a hypothesis that could stand laboratory tests.

More than ever, Protestant Christianity now became secular, preoccupied with the life of this world, till it was with difficulty distinguished from social amelioration, reform, and planning. Supernaturalism gave way to naturalism, the belief that science can account for all phenomena. Free will was ruled out by a materialistic determinism. Moral considerations became social considerations, man being only a bundle of instincts or drives shaped by economic and social forces. Understanding was to be sought, not in the rationalism of armchair philosophy, but in the rising psychological and social sciences based on naturalistic assumptions. There was now only one philosophy that enjoyed wide respect: the new philosophy known as pragmatism or instrumentalism. Employing a naturalistic framework of thought, this philosophy concentrated on the idea of evolution, of endless change, of experiment. We should move forward, as John Dewey asserted, with "faith in the active tendencies of the day" and "the courage of intelligence to follow whither social and scientific changes direct us." Truth is not something already existing and waiting to be found, but something in the making, something that *works* in a given situation, something that is shown to *pay* — a conception that European philosophers often dismissed as an example of American sordidness.

After the first World War the American public — including many writers — turned with rather uncritical hope to the "new psychology." Becoming a laboratory science in the nineteenth century, psychology had attained an impressive body of positive knowledge though little agreement as to fundamental principles. Regarded especially in America as a science to be trusted to reveal without delay the secret of human nature, it enjoyed an extraordinary vogue in the decade of the 1920's, a vogue traced by a trained psychologist, Grace Adams, in an *Atlantic*

Monthly article. As she indicated, a vast number of Americans, literate and illiterate, "renounced the religion of their fathers for redemption by Watson or Freud." For a number of years Freud seemed to be what Darwin had been in the nineteenth century and Newton in the eighteenth. Like Darwin, Freud was soon distorted by the public. In the words of the author of *Only Yesterday:*

The one great intellectual force which had not suffered disrepute as a result of the war was science; the more-or-less educated public was now absorbing a quantity of popularized information about biology and anthropology which gave a general impression that men and women were merely animals of a rather intricate variety, and that moral codes had no universal validity and were often based on curious superstitions. A fertile ground was ready for the seeds of Freudianism, and presently one began to hear even from the lips of flappers that "science taught" new and disturbing things about sex. Sex, it appeared, was the central and pervasive force which moved mankind. . . . The first requirement of mental health was to have an uninhibited sex life.

Since psychoanalysis, in its unraveling of the subconscious, seemed tedious and uncertain, the interest of many shifted to behaviorism. In a world of machines it seemed that man, too, was a machine. His mind, if he could be said to have one, operated simply in terms of "stimulus" and "response." Armed with Watson (*Behaviorism*, 1925, *Ways of Behaviorism*, 1928) one had a simple key, it appeared, to art, to history, to human nature, to happiness and success. But by 1929, according to Dr. Adams, the vogue of psychology was over. Psychology itself, of course, was anything but over. But the public had made a fad of a promising science, and fads do not last. When the economic depression brought mental depression upon the land, the psychologists were "conspicuously silent." As ever new systems of psychology were propounded by a vigorously growing science, the public was not only disappointed but bewildered, and made new fads, briefly of technocracy and even humanism, more persistently of communism.

During the booming years of prosperity the American public and American writers had little interest in the dialectical materialism of Marx. In 1926 the *New Masses* had on its board Michael Gold, Louis Untermeyer, John Dos Passos, Edmund Wilson, and others, but its impact was slight. When the economic crisis arrived a few years later, and the capitalist system was suspected of being outmoded, many persons were inclined to think that Marx held a possible answer to our social problems, or at least that Russian Communism with its recent Five Year Plan was something to be watched with sympathy. The decade of disillusionment and cynicism having ended, the affirmations of communism received a wide hearing. Though few cared to be members of the Communist Party of the United States, and many were communists in any sense only for a brief time, left-wing thought revolved on the axis of Marx and Lenin. But with the development of the Stalin regime and the alliance of Russia and Germany, deep confusion beset the movement in America — a confusion by no means resolved by the subsequent alliance of Russia and America in the war. At no time did communism become a great political force, nor did any of the "proletarian literature" written to promote the cause attain distinction. But at the least the Marxists gave strong impetus to the humanitarian habit of sentimentalizing the common man and of thinking in terms of environment — of the economic and social system — in the manner of the social sciences.

Another phenomenon of the depression years was the waning of faith in science and progress. The horrors of the first World War, the disillusionment following the peace, the materialistic orgy followed by a long depression, cast much doubt upon the notion that human society is forever spiraling upward. When an American edition of Bury's book on *The Idea of Progress* was published in 1922, Charles A. Beard supplied a cautious introduction. "The idea of progress," he said, "cannot be regarded as 'a law of social evolution' or an inevitable interpretation of historical development. . . . At the end the idea of progress remains a reasoned conviction, a hope that may be realized, is indeed in process of realization."

As for science, the public was hearing of a "new physics," and gave to Einstein the acclaim it had given before to Freud. The work of Einstein, Heisenberg, and others was apparently destined to destroy the nineteenth century conception of a mechanically determined universe. "The universe begins to look," said Sir James Jeans, "more like a great thought than like a great machine." Both for the man in the street and for the intellectual, the new conception was hard to grasp and to use, nor was it helpful to learn that the physicists themselves were uncertain as to the nature of knowledge. Plain and fancy Americans alike were puzzled when they read in *Harper's* a statement by Harvard's eminent physicist, Bridgman:

> We have reached the point when knowledge must stop because of the nature of knowledge itself. . . . A bound is thus forever set to the curiosity of the physicist. What is more, the mere existence of this bound means that he must give up his most cherished convictions and faith. The world is not a world of reason, understandable by the intellect of man, but as we penetrate ever deeper, the very law of cause and effect, which we had thought to be a formula to which we could force God himself to subscribe, ceases to have meaning.

Three years later, in 1932, the above passage was quoted in a literary textbook by Lovett and Hughes with this comment:

> Professor Bridgman regards this so-called bankruptcy of science as more serious than the loss of faith in the supernatural which marked the nineteenth century. While such abstruse considerations hardly enter into the mental processes of people in general, their presence creates an atmosphere of doubt; and even the simplest mind can discern the discrepancy between the results of science and the problems of man in society, the fact that the conquest of nature has put into his hands unlimited powers of destruction, and as yet no adequate means of social control to turn that power to constructive uses.

It was not long before even newspaper columnists were accusing the scientists, including the economists, of taking society on "the road to nowhere." As for the new

physics, since it was not understandable, one might as well go on believing in the old mechanistic determinism, especially when the psychologists still seemed to find it good. Since then, however, atomic research has created a new and wholesome respect for physics.

LITERATURE

If it is possible to fix a time for the beginning of modern American poetry, the date is October 1912, when the first issue of Harriet Monroe's *Poetry: A Magazine of Verse* appeared. This Chicago monthly opened its pages freely to poets known and unknown, and encouraged whatever bore the stamp of novel power. Within the next few years appeared — often in the new monthly — a brilliant galaxy of writers. Robinson, to be sure, had started earlier, had published significant volumes in 1897, 1902, and 1910, which were followed by *The Man Against the Sky* in 1916 and by many later books. In 1913 came Lindsay's *General William Booth Enters into Heaven, and Other Poems*, the next year his *Congo and Other Poems*. In 1914 also came Amy Lowell's first successful book, *Sword Blades and Poppy Seeds*, the first imagist anthology, *Des Imagistes*, and Frost's first notable work, *North of Boston*. In 1915 appeared the one widely read book by Masters, *Spoon River Anthology*. The year 1916 added Sandburg, author of *Chicago Poems*, and 1917 added Miss Millay's *Renascence and Other Poems*. All these poets were popular. Two other important poets were not — Ezra Pound, whose many experiments in verse, beginning as early as 1908, had much influence on Eliot and many later poets, and Eliot himself, whose reputation dates from *Prufrock and Other Observations*, 1917. With this remarkable array of talents, the age of realism proved that poetry was still possible. It did more: it proved that a realistic poetry was possible.

The new poetry was determined to get away from romanticism, from the typical romantic moods, the vague flowing eloquence, the diction, allusions, imagery, versification that had become drearily conventional in the whole century following Wordsworth, Coleridge, Byron, Shelley, in England, and following Bryant in America. Instead, it sought a new selection of subject matter and a new technique in keeping with contemporary life. While rejecting the romantic tradition, the new poets nevertheless retained certain elements in the romantic outlook — the emphasis on self, the humanitarianism, the love of nature. But they added scientific observation and scientific standards of thought, a realistic tendency which is apparent in nearly all the representative poets of the period. In Robinson it was the positive and critical spirit of scientific thought. In Miss Lowell it was mainly scientific exactness of sense impressions carried so far that it produced a hard angular objectivity. In Lindsay and Sandburg, again, it was the realistic impulse to reproduce accurately, through a kind of jazz music in the one case and a raucous recitative in the other, certain aspects of social or regional character. In general it was scientific descriptiveness — the detailed record of one's emotion, the analysis of others' mental states, the keen observation of externals in nature and human life. In general it was the conviction (which Whitman had held long before) that nothing, rightly seen, is trivial, or immodest, or ugly. For their new technique the poets went to the language and rhythms of everyday speech, more than to the great tradition of English verse.

If the years following 1912 belonged mainly to poetry, the years following 1920 belonged mainly to prose. The decade of the 1920's saw a new movement in fiction, a group of realists and naturalists coming especially from the Middle West.

Indeed, this was the time when the Middle West flowered in literature. There were such poets as Lindsay, Masters, and Sandburg, the last of whom, in his life of Lincoln, also wrote an imposing prose work. But fiction dominated. One of the finest artists of the novel was Willa Cather. Continuing the faithful realism of Sarah Orne Jewett, Miss Cather first showed her strongest talent in *My Antonia*, 1918, a story of Bohemian immigrants in Nebraska. A series of five novels followed in the 1920's, the outstanding being perhaps *A Lost Lady* and *Death Comes for the Archbishop*. Among her later novels the most distinguished is *Shadows on the Rock*, where she turned from the Midwest and Southwest to Quebec.

In contrast to her quiet selectiveness, Theodore Dreiser stormed upon the scene with vast energy, from *Jennie Gerhardt* in 1911 to *An American Tragedy* in 1925, when his place in the movement became secure. On him, says Parrington, "the impact of the Industrial Revolution and the scientific revolution struck with devastating effect, sweeping away the old faith in a free individualism in a benevolent universe, and substituting a bleak mechanistic philosophy" for which he was much indebted to Huxley, Tyndall, and Spencer. Heir to the naturalism of Crane, he regarded "that animal called man" with warm pity.

Then there was Sherwood Anderson, whose *Winesburg, Ohio*, a collection of short stories published on the eve of the 1920's, announced an original talent for psychological naturalism. While Dreiser's psychology was behavioristic, Anderson's was Freudian, and it dominated his imagination, which brooded over the maladjustments and repressions of obscure people whom their fellows merely found more or less "queer." In his short stories and the novels that followed, beginning with *Poor White* in 1920, he treated the emotional frustrations of such characters with tenderness and a mystical feeling for the supposed identification of man and nature. Another voice of the West, this time satirically realistic rather than naturalistic, was Sinclair Lewis. More than any other one writer, Lewis dominated the twenties. In *Main Street*, 1920, he shocked or delighted an immense audience inhabiting Main Streets from coast to coast. America had mushroomed, his novels declared, to a standardized civilization notable for its ugliness, its dullness, its meanness, its smug self-satisfaction. In *Babbitt*, Lewis focused on the business man, in *Arrowsmith* on the scientist, in *Elmer Gantry*, greatly inferior to the other two, on the evangelical Protestant minister. Lewis had much in common with the satiric critic H. L. Mencken, whose rowdy humor, exhibited in his magazine *American Mercury* and his books of *Prejudices*, irritated or gratified a disillusioned public after World War I.

The sophisticated and the cynical also found satisfaction in still another important creator of fiction — Ernest Hemingway. Though born in the Middle West, Hemingway left it, in every sense, when he enlisted in an ambulance unit in France. Influenced by Ezra Pound and Gertrude Stein, he published in Paris, 1924, a collection of short stories, *In Our Time*. Hard-boiled spokesman for the "lost generation" after the war, he expressed their disillusionment, their spiritual exhaustion, their sense of the futility of all ideals, together with a stoical acceptance of primitive emotions and satisfactions. Among his novels that gained wide recognition in the twenties are *The Sun Also Rises* and *A Farewell to Arms*. In 1940 *For Whom the Bell Tolls* introduced a new note, a return, however tentative, to affirmation. By virtue of his imaginative power and stylistic craftsmanship, as well as his ability to share in the changing temper of the times, Hemingway was clearly one of the dominant figures in the entire period between the two wars.

In the drama, the dominant figure was beyond any question Eugene O'Neill. Where his predecessors had relatively failed (Fitch, Thomas, MacKaye, Moody, before the first war) O'Neill succeeded in giving the American theater its long-awaited *éclat*. Resounding applause greeted his *Beyond the Horizon* in 1920. This naturalistic tragedy of frustration was followed by a long series of plays including *The Emperor Jones*, *Desire Under the Elms*, *The Great God Brown*, *Strange Interlude*, *Mourning Becomes Electra*. The Freudian psychology bulks large in his work, but his interests have been varied, his experimental

devices novel and arresting. In *Ah, Wilderness!* he showed an unexpected humor, in *Days Without End* the hero's cynicism is resolved by the Catholic faith. It was plain, early and late, that in O'Neill America had a richly endowed personality whose development could not be predicted. With O'Neill's plays may be mentioned *What Price Glory?*, 1924, a play of the war, by Laurence Stallings and Maxwell Anderson, the latter of whom rose to further prominence in the 1930's when *Winterset* and *High Tor* were presented. In 1938 came a distinguished play by Robert Sherwood, *Abe Lincoln in Illinois*.

Several poets became important in the 1920's. Robinson Jeffers united a keen sense of natural beauty (of which there was abundance in his California) with a devastating naturalism. Man he conceived as not merely a part of nature but as a sort of impertinence in nature, which will not be clean till the human animal has destroyed itself and left the world to "the primal and the latter silences." Quite different in spirit was Stephen Vincent Benét, whose poetry from *John Brown's Body* in 1928 to *Western Star* in 1943, and much of his prose, as in "The Devil and Daniel Webster," not only genially accepted life but reaffirmed the democratic tradition of America. No less concerned for the democratic tradition but with a more forward-looking spirit is Archibald MacLeish, who was apprenticed in the apparently aloof school of Pound and Eliot but developed a social sense of responsibility.

Meanwhile, one of the commanding poets and critics of the period between the wars was the expatriate T. S. Eliot, who lived in London and described himself as a royalist, an Anglo-Catholic, and a classicist. His poetry, however, drew its main inspiration not from classical sources but from the English Metaphysical poets of the seventeenth century, the French Symbolist poets of the nineteenth century, and the brilliant experimentalist Ezra Pound. Accompanied with an acute critical movement (inaugurated by Eliot's *Sacred Wood*, 1920), a school of "modernist" poetry arose which sought a fit vehicle for the complex modern sensibility. It minimized direct statement, cultivated the allusion and the symbol. In the opinion of John Crowe Ransom, a poet-critic of this school, an excellent characterization of modernist poetry has been made by Randall Jarrell:

Very interesting language, a great emphasis on connotation, "texture"; extreme intensity, forced emotion — violence; a good deal of obscurity; emphasis on sensation, perceptual nuances; emphasis on details, on the part rather than on the whole; experimental or novel qualities of some sort; a tendency toward external formlessness and internal disorganization — these are justified, generally, as the disorganization required to express a disorganized age, or alternatively, as newly-discovered and more complex types of organization; . . . there is a good deal of emphasis on the unconscious, dream-structure, the thoroughly subjective; the poet's attitudes are usually anti-scientific, anti-commonsense, anti-public — he is, essentially, removed.

Poetry of this sort, whatever its virtuosity, was bound to be difficult if not obscure, and its audience limited.

During the decade of the 1930's, a number of writers of prose fiction emerged with established status: Thomas Wolfe after *Look Homeward, Angel*, 1929; Katherine Anne Porter after *Flowering Judas*, 1930; John Dos Passos, after the first novel of his *U. S. A.* trilogy, 1930; William Faulkner after *Sanctuary*, 1931; Erskine Caldwell after *Tobacco Road*, 1932; James T. Farrell after the first novel of his *Studs Lonigan* trilogy, 1934; John Steinbeck after *Tortilla Flat*, 1935, and especially *The Grapes of Wrath*, 1939. More than half of these writers were from the South. At least half of them, whether Southern, Middle Western, or Far Western, reflected the economic and social preoccupations of the depression decade. In many writers of the decade there was a marked regional emphasis. It was illustrated by writers with earlier reputations, such as Ellen Glasgow and Ruth Suckow, who were now joined by Faulkner, Caldwell, and many others. Regionalism also became a self-conscious critical creed, as in the Southern Agrarian group (Ransom, Tate, Davidson, etc.), a creed suited to the mood of an America turned in upon herself by political isolation and economic sickness. In general, it may be said that during the 1930's the newer writers were no longer content with the spirit of negation so prominent in the twenties, but were seeking, if not always finding, positive affirmations.

After the second war broke upon America, many persons felt that our nation could defend civilized values effectively, in the long run, only if it could make these values clear to itself. In unexpected quarters, as, for example, among scientists, much was said of the need of belief in "permanent values," "eternal values." But as a rule these values were left vague. They received no memorable expression in imaginative literature. Yet at least the desire for values brought greater awareness of the fact that, for more than a century, American writers with few exceptions have been increasingly concerned with the changing and relative, rather than the permanent and constant elements in life. As a result they have given primary attention to particulars, instead of universals. Romanticists made much of their own subjective individuality, and also began close observation of concrete particulars in nature and human life. Realists carried observation to a more expert plane, in an exact fidelity to the particular, the local, the special. Naturalists went still further, studying their characters as if each were a unique case, to be understood only through a scientific case history. Symbolic poets, returning to the subjective, placed the emphasis on their own peculiar sensibility in its relations with experience of the outer world. We have thus traveled far from the universal truths of the Puritan mind, which to us are incredible. We have traveled far likewise from the universal truths of the Age of Reason, which had a static context invalidated by our philosophies of evolution or change. Yet we are still aware that the very foundations of our civilization are classical and Christian, and are not prepared to make a complete break with our past.

EDITH WHARTON (1862–1937)

Edith Wharton was a member of the patrician leisure class of her time. That she was no ordinary member of it is indicated by two of her statements: "A frivolous society can acquire significance only through what its frivolity destroys"; and "Leisure, itself the creation of wealth, is incessantly engaged in transmuting wealth into beauty by secreting the surplus energy which flowers in great architecture, great painting, and great literature. Only in the atmosphere thus engendered floats that impalpable dust of ideas which is the real culture. A colony of bees or ants will never create a parthenon." The frivolity of her class and their indifference to "the real culture" is evident in her novels: the main purpose of their life seems to be to dress, eat, and make and meet engagements. What its frivolity destroys is the character and the potentialities of individuals who are in it but not of it. The justification for the existence of the class, apparently, lies in its opportunity to use its leisure for the creation of ideas and art. In most of her novels she skillfully evokes the significance of destruction, but it is her own life rather than that of her characters which illustrates the "secreting of surplus energy."

Her life was spent in New York, Newport, the Berkshires, Italy, and Paris. Her education was that of the intelligent well-to-do of her time — casual but first-hand, episodic but stimulating, achieved through governesses, travel, conversation, and early exposure to good books. Some of the surplus of energy which was to flow into her great novels was channeled into poetry (printed in the *Atlantic Monthly*) when she was only eighteen, but marriage to a wealthy banker when she was twenty-three insured her commitment to the society which was to provide the materials of most of her fiction. She escaped the frustrations of both the society and the marriage (which ended in divorce) by establishing residence in Paris in 1907. There she was able to schedule her time both for writing and for social activity, and to indulge her need for amusing and interesting people without getting involved in routine social obligations.

Meanwhile (1899) she had begun to publish fiction under the tutelage of E. L. Burlingame and W. C. Brownell of *Scribner's*, who encouraged her talent but discouraged her early interest in "depressing" subjects. From the short story (collections include *The Greater Inclination*, 1899, *Crucial Instances*, 1901, *Xingu*, 1916), she moved to the novel, where she ranged in subject matter from historical romance to New England back-country life to social satire and tragedy. Her greatest novels are *The House of Mirth*, 1905 (a best seller), *Ethan Frome*, 1911, and *The Age of Innocence*, 1920.

Mrs. Wharton's career coincided in time with the shift from realism to naturalism, and with the careers of Stephen Crane, Frank Norris, and Theodore Dreiser, whose influence she combatted. Rejecting both "the slice of life" and the "stream of consciousness" theories of fiction, she declared that the latter differs from the former in "noting mental as well as visual reactions, but resembles it in setting them down just as they come, with a deliberate disregard of their relevance in the particular case."

Important for the study of her work is her autobiography, *A Backward Glance*, 1934, her critical essays, *The Writing of Fiction*, 1925, Percy Lubbock's *A Portrait of Edith Wharton*, 1947, and studies by K. F. Gerould, 1922, R. M. Lovett, 1925, and E. K. Brown, 1935. A. H. Quinn has edited *An Edith Wharton Treasury*, 1950.

The Choice

(1916)

I

Stilling, that night after dinner, had surpassed himself. He always did, Wrayford reflected, when the small fry from Highfield came to dine. He, Cobham Stilling, who had to find his bearings, keep to his level, in the big, heedless, oppressive world of New York, dilated and grew vast in the congenial medium of Highfield. The Red House was the biggest house of the Highfield summer colony, as Cobham Stilling was its biggest man. No one else within a radius of a hundred miles (on a conservative estimate) had as many horses, as many greenhouses, as many servants, and assuredly no one else had two motors, or a motor-boat for the lake.

The motor-boat was Stilling's latest hobby, and he rode — or sailed — it in and out of the conversation all the evening, to the obvious edification of every one present save his wife and his visitor, Austin Wrayford. The interest of the latter two, who, from opposite ends of the drawing-room, exchanged a fleeting glance when Stilling again launched his craft on the thin current of the talk — the interest of Mrs. Stilling and Wrayford, had already lost its edge by protracted conversational contact with the subject.

But the dinner-guests — the Rector, Mr. Swordsley, and Mrs. Swordsley, Lucy and Agnes Granger and their brother Addison, and young Jack Emmerton from Harvard — were all, for divers reasons, stirred to the proper pitch of feeling. Mr. Swordsley, no doubt, was saying to himself: "If my good parishioner here can afford to buy a motor-boat, in addition to all the other expenditures which an establishment like this must entail, I certainly need not scruple to appeal to him again for a contribution toward our Galahad Club." The Granger girls, meanwhile, were evoking visions of lakeside picnics, not unadorned with the presence of young Mr. Emmerton; while that youth himself speculated as to whether his affable host would let him, when he came back on his next vacation, "learn to run the thing himself"; and

Mr. Addison Granger, the elderly bachelor brother of the volatile Lucy and Agnes, mentally formulated the precise phrase in which, in his next letter to his cousin Professor Spildyke of the University of East Latmos, he should allude to "our last delightful trip in my old friend Cobham Stilling's ten-thousand-dollar motor-launch" — for East Latmos was still in that primitive stage of social culture on which such figures impinge.

Isabel Stilling, sitting beside Mrs. Swordsley, her head slightly bent above the needlework with which, on such occasions, it was her old-fashioned habit to be engaged — Isabel also had doubtless her reflections to make. As Wrayford leaned back in his corner, and looked at her across the bright, flower-filled drawing-room, he noted first of all — for the hundredth time — the flexible play of her hands above the embroidery-frame, the shadow of the dusky, wavy hair on her forehead, the tired droop of the lids over her somewhat full gray eyes. He noted this, taking in unconsciously, at the same time, the indescribable quality in her attitude, in the fall of her dress and the turn of her head, that set her, for him, in a separate world; then he said to himself: "She's certainly thinking 'Where on earth will he get the money to pay for it?' "

But at the same moment, from his inevitable position on the hearth-rug, cigar in mouth, his hands in his waistcoat pockets, Stilling was impressively perorating.

"I said, 'If I have the thing at all, I want the best that can be got.' That's my way, you know, Swordsley; I suppose I'm what you'd call fastidious. Always was, about everything, from cigars to wom-" — his eye met the apprehensive glance of Mrs. Swordsley, who looked, in evening dress, like her husband with his clerical coat cut slightly lower — "So I said, 'If I have the thing at all, I want the best that can be got.' Nothing makeshift for me, no second-best. I never cared for the cheap and showy. I always say frankly to a man, 'If you can't give me a first-rate cigar, for the Lord's sake, let me smoke my own.' Well, if you have my standards, you can't buy a thing in a minute. You must look round, compare, select. I found there were lots of motor-boats on the market, just as there's lots of stuff called champagne. But I said to myself, 'Ten to one there's only one fit to buy, just as there's only one champagne fit for a gentleman to drink.' Argued like a lawyer, eh, Austin?" He tossed this jovially toward Wrayford. "Take me for one of your own trade, wouldn't you? Well, I'm not such a fool as I look. I suppose you fellows who are tied to the treadmill, — oh, excuse me, Swordsley, but work's work, isn't it? — I suppose you think a man like me has nothing to do but take it easy — loll through life like a woman. By George, sir, I'd like either of you to see the time it takes — I won't say the brains — but just the *time* it takes to pick out a good motor-boat. Why, I went —"

Mrs. Stilling set her embroidery-frame noiselessly on the low table at her side, and turned her head toward Wrayford. "Would you mind ringing for the tray?"

The interruption helped Mrs. Swordsley to waver to her feet. "I think we really ought to be going; my husband has an early service to-morrow."

Her host sounded an immediate protest. "Going already? Nothing of the sort! Why, the night's still young, as the poet says. Long way from here to the rectory? Nonsense! In our little twenty-horse motor we do it in five minutes — don't we, Belle? Ah, you're walking, to be sure —" Stilling's indulgent gesture seemed to concede that, in such a case, allowances must be made, and that he was the last man not to make them. "Well, then, Swordsley —" He held out a thick, red hand that seemed to exude beneficence, and the clergyman, pressing it, ventured to murmur a suggestion.

"What, that Galahad Club again? Why, I thought my wife — Isabel, didn't we — No? Well, it must have been my mother, then. And of course, you know, anything my good mother gives is — well — virtually — You haven't asked her? Sure? I could have sworn; I get so many of these appeals. And in these times, you know, we have to go cautiously. I'm sure you recognize that yourself, Swordsley. With my obligations — here now, to show you don't bear

malice, have a brandy and soda before you go. Nonsense, man! This brandy isn't liquor; it's *liqueur*. I picked it up last year in London — last of a famous lot from Lord St. Oswyn's cellar. Laid down here, it stood me at — Eh?" he broke off as his wife moved toward him. "Ah, yes, of course. Miss Lucy, Miss Agnes — a drop of soda-water? Look here, Addison, *you* won't refuse my tipple, I know. Well, take a cigar, at any rate, Swordsley. And, by the way, I'm afraid you'll have to go round the long way by the avenue to-night. Sorry, Mrs. Swordsley, but I forgot to tell them to leave the gate on the lane unlocked. Well, it's a jolly night, and I daresay you won't mind the extra turn along the lake. And, by Jove! if the moon's out, you can get a glimpse of the motor-boat as you turn the point. She's moored just out beyond our boat-house; and it's a privilege to look at her, I can tell you!"

The dispersal of the remaining guests carried Stilling out into the hall, where his pleasantries echoed genially under the oak rafters while the Granger girls were being muffled for the drive and the carriages summoned from the stables.

By a common impulse Mrs. Stilling and Wrayford had moved together toward the hearth, which was masked from the door into the hall by a tall screen of lacquer. Wrayford leaned his elbow against the chimney-piece, and Mrs. Stilling stood motionless beside him, her clasped hands hanging down before her. The rose on her breast stirred slightly.

"Have you any more work to do with him to-night?" she asked below her breath.

Wrayford shook his head. "We wound it all up before dinner. He doesn't want to talk about it any more than he can help."

"It's so bad?"

"No; but he's got to pull up."

She paused, looking down at her clasped hands. He listened a moment, catching Stilling's farewell shout; then he changed his position slightly, and laid his hand on her arm.

"In an hour?"

She made a faint motion of assent.

"I'll tell you all about it then. The key's in the usual place?"

She nodded again, and walked away with her long, drifting motion as her husband came in from the hall. He went up to the tray, and poured himself a tall glass of brandy and soda.

"The weather's turning queer — black as pitch out now. I hope the Swordsleys won't walk into the lake — involuntary immersion, eh? He'd come out a Baptist, I suppose. What'd the Bishop do in such a case? There's a problem for a lawyer, my boy!"

He clapped Wrayford resoundingly on the thin shoulder and then walked over to his wife, who was gathering up her embroidery silks and dropping them into an old-fashioned work-bag. Stilling took her by the arms and swung her playfully about so that she faced the lamplight.

"What's the matter with you to-night?"

"The matter?" she echoed, blushing a little, and standing very erect in her desire not to appear to shrink from his touch.

"You never opened your lips. Left me the whole job of entertaining those blessed people. Didn't she, Austin?"

Wrayford laughed and lighted a cigarette. "She wasn't quite up to the mark."

"There! You see even Austin noticed it. What's the matter? Aren't they good enough for you? I don't pretend they're particularly exciting; but, hang it! I like to ask them here — I like to give pleasure."

"I didn't mean to be dull," said Isabel, appealingly.

"Well, you must learn to make an effort. Don't treat people as if they weren't in the room just because they don't happen to amuse you. Do you know what they'll think? They'll think it's because you've got a bigger house and more cash. Shall I tell you something? My mother said she'd noticed the same thing in you lately. She said she sometimes felt you looked down on her for living in a small house. Oh, she was half joking, of course; but you see you do give people that impression. I can't understand treating any one in that way. The more I have myself, the more I want to make other people happy."

Isabel gently freed herself and laid the work-bag on her embroidery-frame. "I have a headache; perhaps that made me stupid. I'm going to bed." She turned toward Wrayford and held out her hand. "Good night."

"Good night," he answered, opening the door for her.

When he turned back into the room, his host was pouring himself a third glass of brandy and soda.

"Here, have a nip? Gad, I need it badly, after the shaking up you gave me this afternoon." Stilling gave a short laugh, and carried his glass to the hearth, where he took up his usual commanding position. "Why the deuce don't you drink something, Austin? You look as glum as Isabel. One would think *you* were the chap that had been hit."

Wrayford threw himself into the chair from which Mrs. Stilling had lately risen. It was the one she habitually sat in, and to his fancy a faint scent of her always clung to it. He leaned back and looked up at Stilling.

"Want a cigar?" the latter continued. "Shall we go into the den and smoke?"

Wrayford hesitated. "If there's anything more you want to ask me about —"

"Gad, no! I had full measure and running over this afternoon. The deuce of it is, I don't see where the money's all gone to. Luckily I've got plenty of nerve; I'm not the kind of man to sit down and snivel because he's been touched in Wall Street."

Wrayford rose again. "Then, if you don't want me, I think I'll go up to my room and put some finishing touches to a brief before I turn in. I must get back to town to-morrow afternoon."

"All right, then." Stilling set down his empty glass, and held out his hand with a tinge of alacrity. "Good night, old man."

They shook hands, and Wrayford moved toward the door.

"I say, Austin — stop a minute!" his host called after him.

Wrayford turned, and the two men faced each other across the hearth-rug. Stilling's eyes shifted uneasily in his flushed face.

"There's one thing more you *can* do for me, like a good chap, before you go. Tell Isabel about that loan; explain to her she's got to sign a note for it."

Wrayford, in his turn, flushed slightly.

"You want *me* to tell her?"

"Hang it! I'm soft-hearted — that's the worst of me." Stilling moved toward the tray, and lifted the brandy decanter. "And she'll take it better from you; she'll *have* to take it from you. She's proud. You can take her out for a row to-morrow morning — you can take her out in the motor-launch, if you like. I meant to have a spin in it myself in the morning; but if you'll tell her ——"

Wrayford hesitated. "All right. I'll tell her."

"Thanks a lot, my dear fellow. And you'll make her see it wasn't my fault, eh? Women are awfully vague about money, and if you appear to back me up, you know ——"

Wrayford nodded. "As you please. Good night."

"Good night. Here, Austin — there's just one more thing. You needn't say anything to Isabel about the other business — I mean my mother's securities."

"Ah?" said Wrayford.

Stilling shifted from one foot to the other. "I'd rather put that to the old lady myself. I can make it clear to her. She idolizes me, you know — and, hang it! I've got a good record. Up to now, I mean. My mother's been in clover since I married; I may say she's been my first thought. And I don't want her to hear of this from Isabel. Isabel's a little harsh at times — and of course this isn't going to make her any easier to live with."

"Very well," Wrayford assented.

Stilling, with a look of relief, walked toward the window which opened on the terrace. "Gad! what a queer night! Hot as the kitchen-range. Shouldn't wonder if we had a squall before morning. I wonder if that infernal skipper took in the launch's awnings before he went home."

Wrayford paused a moment in the doorway. "Yes, I saw him do it. She's shipshape for the night."

"Good! That saves me a run down to the shore." Stilling strolled back into the room, whistling cheerfully.

"Good night then," said Wrayford.

"Good night, old man. You'll tell her?"

"I'll tell her," Wrayford answered from the threshold.

"And mum about my mother!" his host called after him.

II

The darkness had thinned a little when Wrayford scrambled down the steep path to the shore. Though the air was heavy, the threat of a storm seemed to have vanished, and now and then the moon's edge showed above a torn slope of cloud.

But in the densely massed shrubbery about the boat-house the night was still black, and Wrayford had to strike a match before he could find the lock and insert his key. He left the door unlatched, and groped his way in. How often he had crept into this warm pine-scented obscurity, guiding himself cautiously by the edge of the bench along the side wall, and hearing the stealthy lap of water through the gaps in the flooring! He knew just where one had to duck one's head to avoid the two canoes swung from the rafters, and just where to put his hand on the latch of the door that led to the balcony above the lake.

The boat-house represented one of Stilling's abandoned whims. He had built it some seven years before, and for a time it had been the scene of incessant nautical exploits. Stilling had rowed, sailed, paddled indefatigably, and all Highfield had been impressed to bear him company and admire his versatility. Then motors had come in, and he had forsaken aquatic sports for the guidance of the flying chariot. The canoes of birch-bark and canvas had been hoisted to the roof, the little sail-boat had rotted at her moorings, and the movable floor of the boat-house, ingeniously contrived to slide back on noiseless runners, had lain undisturbed through several seasons. Even the key of the boat-house had been mislaid, — by Isabel's fault, her husband asserted — and the locksmith had to be called in to make a new one when the purchase of the motor-boat made the lake once more the center of Stilling's activity.

As Wrayford entered he noticed that a strange oily odor overpowered the usual scent of dry pine-wood; and at the next step his foot struck an object that rolled noisily across the boards. He lighted a match, and found he had overturned a can of grease which the boatman had no doubt been using to oil the runners of the sliding-floor.

Wrayford felt his way down the length of the boat-house, and softly opening the balcony door, looked out on the lake. A few yards off the launch lay motionless in the veiled moonlight; and just below him, on the black water, he saw the dim outline of the skiff which Stilling used to paddle out to her. The silence was so intense that Wrayford fancied he heard a faint rustling in the shrubbery on the high bank behind the boat-house, and the crackle of gravel on the path descending to it.

He closed the door again and turned back; and as he did so the other door, on the land-side, swung inward, and a figure darkened the dim opening. Just enough light entered through the round holes above the respective doors to reveal it as Mrs. Stilling's cloaked outline, and to guide her to him as he advanced. But before they met she stumbled and gave a little cry.

"What is it?" he exclaimed, springing toward her.

"My foot caught; the floor seemed to give way under me. Ah, of course —" She bent down in the darkness — "I saw the men oiling it this morning."

Wrayford caught her to him. "Be careful, darling! It might be dangerous if it slid too easily. The water's deep under here."

"Yes; the water's very deep. I sometimes wish —" She leaned against him without finishing her sentence, and he tightened his arms about her.

"Hush!" he whispered, his lips on her hair.

Suddenly she threw back her head and seemed to listen.

"What's the matter?" he asked, listening also. "What did you hear?"

"I don't know." He felt her trembling. "I'm not sure this place is as safe as it used to be —"

Wrayford held her to him reassuringly. "But the boatman sleeps down at the village: and who else should come here at this hour?"

"My husband might. He thinks of nothing but the launch."

"He won't to-night, for I told him I'd seen the skipper roll up the awning, and put the launch shipshape, and that satisfied him."

"Ah, he *did* think of coming, then?"

"Only for a minute, when the sky looked so black half an hour ago, and he was afraid of a squall. It's clearing now, and there's no danger."

He drew her down on the bench, and they sat a moment or two in silence, her hands in his. Then she said wearily: "You'd better tell me."

Wrayford gave a faint laugh. "Yes, I suppose I had. In fact, he asked me to."

"He asked you to?"

"Yes."

She sounded a sharp note of contempt. "The coward! he's afraid!"

Wrayford made no reply, and she went on: "*I'm* not. Tell me everything, please."

"Well, he's chucked away a pretty big sum again —"

"How has he done it?"

"He says he doesn't know. He's been speculating, I suppose. The madness of making him your trustee!"

She drew her hands away quickly. "You know why I did it. When we married I didn't want to put him in the false position of the man who accepts everything; I wanted people to think the money was partly his."

"I don't know what you've made *people* think; but you've been eminently successful in one respect. *He* thinks it's his — and he loses it as if it were."

She shivered a little, drawing her cloak closer. "There are worse things. Go on."

"Isabel!" He bent over her. "Give me your hand again." He lifted it and laid a long kiss on it.

"What was it — exactly — that he wished you to tell me?" she asked.

"That you've got to sign another promissory note — for fifty thousand this time."

She drew a deep breath. "Is that all?"

Wrayford hesitated; then he said: "Yes — for the present."

She sat motionless, her head bent, her hand resting passively in his.

He leaned nearer. "What did you mean, just now, by worse things?"

She paused a moment. "Haven't you noticed that he's been drinking a great deal lately?"

"Yes; I've noticed."

They were both silent again; then Wrayford said with sudden vehemence: "And *yet* you won't —"

"Won't?"

"Put an end to it. Good God! Save what's left of your life."

She made no answer, and in the deep stillness the *throb-throb* of the water underneath them was like the anxious beat of a heart.

"Isabel —" Wrayford murmured. He bent over to kiss her, and felt the tears on her face. "Isabel! I can't stand it! Listen to me —"

She interrupted him. "No; no. I've thought of everything. There's the boy — the boy's fond of him. He's not a bad father."

"Except in the trifling matter of ruining his son."

"And there's his poor old mother. He's a good son, at any rate; he's never hurt *her*. And I know her. If I left him she'd never touch a penny. What she has of her own is not enough to live on; and how could *he* provide for her? If I put him out of doors, I should be putting his mother out, too — out of the little house she's so happy in."

"But surely you could arrange — there are always ways."

"Not for her! She's proud. And then she believes in him. Lots of people believe in him, you know. It would kill her if she ever found out."

Wrayford made an impatient movement: "It will kill you, if you stay with him to prevent her finding out."

She turned toward him and laid her other hand on his. "Not while I have you."

"Have me? In this way?" he echoed with an exasperated laugh.

"In any way."

"My poor girl — poor child!"

She drew back from him suddenly, with a quick movement of fear. "You mean that *you'll* grow tired — your patience will give out soon?"

He answered her only by saying: "My poor Isabel!"

But she went on insistently: "Don't you suppose I've thought of that — foreseen it?"

"Well — and then?" he exclaimed with sudden passion.

"I've accepted that, too," she said.

He dropped her hands with a despairing gesture. "Then, indeed, I waste my breath!"

She made no answer, and for a time they sat silent, side by side, but with a space between. At length he asked in a contrite voice: "You're not crying, Isabel?"

"No."

"I can't see your face, it's grown so dark again."

"Yes. I hadn't noticed. The storm must be coming, after all." She made a motion as if to rise.

He drew close, and put his arm about her again. "Don't leave me yet, dear! You know I must go to-morrow." He broke off with a laugh. "I'm to break the news to you to-morrow morning, by the way; I'm to take you out in the motor-launch and break it to you." He dropped her hands and stood up. "Good God! How can I go away and leave you here alone with him?"

"You've done it often before."

"Yes; but each time it's more damnable. And then I've always had a hope —"

"A hope?" She rose also. "Give it up! Give it up!" she moaned.

"You've none, then, yourself?"

She was silent, drawing the folds of her cloak about her.

"None — none?" he insisted.

"Only one," she broke out passionately.

He bent over and sought for her in the darkness. "What is it, my dearest? What is it?"

"Don't touch me! That he may die!" she shuddered back.

He dropped his hands, and they drew apart instinctively, hearing each other's quick breathing through the obscurity.

"*You* wish that sometimes, too?" he said at length in a low voice.

"Sometimes? I wish it always — every day, every hour, every moment!" She paused, and then let the quivering words break out. "You'd better know it; you'd better know the worst of me. I'm not the saint you suppose; the duty I do is poisoned by the thoughts I think. Day by day, hour by hour, I wish him dead. When he goes out I pray for something to happen; when he comes back I say to myself: 'Are you here again?' When I hear of people being killed in accidents I think: 'Why wasn't he there?' When I read the death-notices in the paper I say: 'So-and-so was just his age.' When I see him taking such care of his health and his diet — as he does, you know, except when he gets reckless and begins to drink too much — when I see him exercising and resting, and eating only certain things, and weighing himself, and feeling his muscles, and boasting that he hasn't gained a pound, I think of the men who die from overwork, who throw their lives away for some big object, and I say to myself: 'What can kill a man who thinks only of himself?' And night after night I keep myself from going to sleep for fear I may dream that he's dead. When I dream that, and wake and find him there, it's worse than ever — and my thoughts are worse than ever, too!"

She broke off on a stifled sob, and the *thump-thump* of the water under the floor was like the beat of a loud, rebellious heart.

"There, you know the truth! Is it too bad for you?"

He answered in a low voice, as if unconscious of her question: "Such things do sometimes happen, you know."

"Do they?" She laughed. "Yes, I've seen it happen — in happy marriages!"

They were silent again, not approaching each other. Abruptly Isabel turned, feeling her way toward the door. As she did so, the profound stillness of the night was broken by the sound of a man's voice, caroling out somewhat unsteadily the refrain of a music-hall song.

The two in the boat-house darted toward each other with a simultaneous movement clutching hands as they met.

"He's coming!" Isabel breathed.

Wrayford detached himself hastily from her hold.

"He may only be out for a turn before he goes to bed. Wait a minute. I'll see if I can make out." He felt his way to the bench, scrambled up on it, and stretching his body forward, managed to bring his eyes in line with the opening above the door. "It's as black as pitch. I can't see anything."

The refrain rang out nearer.

"Wait! I saw something twinkle. There it is again. It's coming this way — down the path. It's his cigar."

There was a long rattle of thunder through the stillness.

"It's the storm!" Isabel gasped. "He's coming to see about the launch."

Wrayford dropped noiselessly from the bench to her side.

"He's coming — yes."

She caught him by the arm.

"Isn't there time to get up the path and slip under the shrubbery?" she whispered.

"No, no; he's in the path now. He'll be here in two minutes. He'll find us."

He felt her hand tighten on his arm.

"You must go in the skiff, then. It's the only way."

"And let him find you here? And hear my oars? Isabel, listen — there's something I must say."

She flung herself against him, shaken with dry sobs.

"Isabel, just now I didn't tell you everything. He's ruined his mother — taken everything of hers, too. And he's got to tell her; it can't be kept from her."

She uttered a startled sound and drew away.

"Is this the truth? Why didn't you tell me before?"

"He forbade me. You were not to know."

Close above them, in the shrubbery, Stilling rolled out:

"Nita, Juanita,
Ask thy soul if we must part!"

Wrayford caught her wrist in a hard grasp. "Understand this — if he comes in, he'll find us. And if there's a scandal you'll lose your boy."

She seemed not to hear him. "You — you — you — he'll kill you!" she cried out.

Wrayford laughed and released her. She drew away and stood shrinking close against the wall, her hands pressed to her breast. Wrayford straightened himself and listened intently. Then he dropped to his knees and laid his hands against the boards of the sliding-floor. It yielded at once with a kind of evil alacrity; and at their feet they saw, in the night, another night that moved and shimmered. Wrayford sprang up, and threw himself back against the wall, behind the door.

A key rattled, and after a moment's fumbling the door swung open noisily. Wrayford and Isabel saw a black bulk against the obscurity. It moved a step, lurched forward, and vanished from them. In the depths there was a long cry and a splash.

"Go! go!" Wrayford cried out, feeling blindly for Isabel in the blackness.

"*Go?*" she shuddered back, wrenching herself away from him with horror.

He stood still a moment, as if dazed; then she saw him suddenly plunge from her side, and heard another splash far down, and a tumult in the beaten water.

In the darkness she cowered close to the opening, pressing her face over the edge, and frantically crying out the name of each in turn. Suddenly she began to see; the obscurity was less opaque, a faint moon-pallor diluted it. Isabel vaguely discerned the two shapes struggling in the black pit below her; once she saw the gleam of a face. Then she glanced up desperately for some means of rescue, and caught sight of the oars ranged on brackets against the wall. She snatched down the nearest, bent over the opening, and pushed the oar down into the blackness, calling her husband's name.

The clouds had swallowed up the moon again, and she could see nothing below her, but she still heard a tumult in the beaten water.

"Cobham! Cobham!" she screamed.

As if in answer, she felt a mighty clutch on the oar, a clutch that strained her arms to the breaking-point as she tried to brace her knees against the runners of the sliding-floor.

"Hold on! hold on! hold *on!*" a voice gasped out from below; and she held on, with racked muscles, with bleeding palms, with eyes straining from their sockets, and a heart that tugged at her like the weight on the oar.

Suddenly the weight relaxed, and the oar slipped up through her lacerated hands. She felt a wet bulk scrambling over the edge of the opening, and Stilling's voice, raucous and strange, groaned out, close to her: "God! I thought I was done for."

He staggered to his knees, coughing and sputtering, and the water dripped on her from his clothes.

She flung herself down, straining over the pit. Not a sound came up from it.

"Austin! Austin! Quick! Another oar!" she shrieked.

Stilling gave a cry. "My God! Was it Austin? What in hell — Another oar? No, no; untie the skiff, I tell you. But it's no use. Nothing's any use. I felt him lose hold as I came up."

After that she remembered nothing more till, hours later, as it appeared to her, she became dimly aware of her husband's voice, high, hysterical and important, haranguing a group of scared lantern-struck faces that seemed to have sprung up mysteriously about them in the night.

"Poor Austin! Poor fellow . . . terrible loss to me . . . mysterious dispensation. Yes, I *do* feel gratitude — miraculous escape — but I wish he could have known that I was saved!"

Edwin Arlington Robinson (1869–1935)

Robinson wrote reflective poetry that seems likely to endure as that of Emerson and Matthew Arnold has endured. Heedless of literary fashions, he quietly composed his own kind of verse — intellectual, realistic in attitude, simple in diction, close to the rhythms of actual speech — through a long term of years, and was eventually regarded as the foremost American poet of the first three decades of the present century.

His detachment, together with his austerity, reticence, and hardness of fiber, may be partly explained by his New England ancestry and his early environment. He was born at Head Tide, Maine, but his family removed to Gardiner when he was one year old. After two years at Harvard he was obliged to terminate his formal education upon the death of his father. During a decade of intense discouragement, Robinson tried to publish his poems and maintain himself in the business world. In neither did he succeed, and by 1905 he was reduced to working as a checker of loads of shale during the building of the New York Subway. He had all but abandoned his poetry when President Theodore Roosevelt became interested in him and gave him a position in the New York Custom House.

Once established as a successful poet, Robinson lived quietly in New York in the winters, and spent the summers at the MacDowell colony in New Hampshire. He was never married.

Robinson's first volume was privately printed in 1896. The next year came *The Children of the Night*, including "Richard Cory"; in 1902 the first of his long monographs, *Captain Craig;* in 1910 *The Town Down the River*, which contained "Miniver Cheevy." But Robinson's high distinction was not clearly recognized till *The Man Against the Sky*, 1916. Responding to the lure of the Arthurian legend, he then wrote *Merlin,* and *Lancelot,* and his greatest popular success, *Tristram*. During the last fourteen years of his life he devoted himself to long blank verse narratives, each with only three or four characters, such as *Avon's Harvest, Dionysus in Doubt*, and *Cavender's House.*

The turn of mind most prominent in the poetry of Robinson is evident also in some of his literary admirations, which included Hardy and Zola. Robinson himself had the cool integrity of the realist, not the warm or facile emotionality of the romanticist. With an inquiring spirit, he analyzed people and the forces that move them to success or failure. In his gray world happiness is won hardly, or at a price, or not at all. But Robinson recoiled from the abyss of sheer naturalism. He would not subscribe to the new dogmas that were displacing the old. He found "gleams" of high meaning in life which he would have regarded it blindness to ignore.

Robinson's *Collected Poems* were issued in 1937. Studies of value include C. Cestre, *An Introduction to Edwin Arlington Robinson*, 1930; H. Hagedorn, *Edwin Arlington Robinson* (a biography), 1938; E. Kaplan, *Philosophy in the Poetry of Edwin Arlington Robinson*, 1940. Newer works are Yvor Winters, *Edwin Arlington Robinson*, 1947 (criticism), and Emery Neff, *Edwin Arlington Robinson*, 1949 (biography).

Cliff Klingenhagen

(1893–96)

Cliff Klingenhagen had me in to dine
With him one day; and after soup and meat,
And all the other things there were to eat,
Cliff took two glasses and filled one with wine
And one with wormwood. Then, without a
    sign   5
For me to choose at all, he took the draught
Of bitterness himself, and lightly quaffed
It off, and said the other one was mine.

And when I asked him what the deuce he
    meant
By doing that, he only looked at me   10
And smiled, and said it was a way of his.
And though I know the fellow, I have spent
Long time a-wondering when I shall be
As happy as Cliff Klingenhagen is.

Richard Cory

(1893—96)

Whenever Richard Cory went down town,
We people on the pavement looked at him:
He was a gentleman from sole to crown,
Clean favored, and imperially slim.

And he was always quietly arrayed,   5
And he was always human when he talked;
But still he fluttered pulses when he said,
"Good-morning," and he glittered when he
    walked.

And he was rich — yes, richer than a king —
And admirably schooled in every grace: 10
In fine, we thought that he was every thing
To make us wish that we were in his place.

So on we worked, and waited for the light,
And went without the meat, and cursed the
    bread;
And Richard Cory, one calm summer night,
Went home and put a bullet through his
    head.   16

Luke Havergal

(ca. 1894)

Go to the western gate, Luke Havergal,
There where the vines cling crimson on the
    wall,
And in the twilight wait for what will come.
The leaves will whisper there of her, and some,
Like flying words, will strike you as they fall;
But go, and if you listen she will call.   6
Go to the western gate, Luke Havergal —
Luke Havergal.

No, there is not a dawn in eastern skies
To rift the fiery night that's in your eyes;   10
But there, where western glooms are gather-
    ing,
The dark will end the dark, if anything:
God slays Himself with every leaf that flies,
And hell is more than half of paradise.
No, there is not a dawn in eastern skies —
In eastern skies.   16

Out of a grave I come to tell you this,
Out of a grave I come to quench the kiss
That flames upon your forehead with a glow

That blinds you to the way that you must go.
Yes, there is yet one way to where she is,   21
Bitter, but one that faith may never miss.
Out of a grave I come to tell you this —
To tell you this.

There is the western gate, Luke Havergal,   25
There are the crimson leaves upon the wall.
Go, for the winds are tearing them away, —
Nor think to riddle the dead words they say,
Nor any more to feel them as they fall;
But go, and if you trust her she will call.   30
There is the western gate, Luke Havergal —
Luke Havergal.

Credo

(ca. 1894)

I cannot find my way: there is no star
In all the shrouded heavens anywhere;
And there is not a whisper in the air
Of any living voice but one so far
That I can hear it only as a bar   5
Of lost, imperial music, played when fair
And angel fingers wove, and unaware,
Dead leaves to garlands where no roses are.

No, there is not a glimmer, nor a call,
For one that welcomes, welcomes when he
    fears,   10
The black and awful chaos of the night;
For through it all — above, beyond it all —
I know the far-sent message of the years,
I feel the coming glory of the Light.

Isaac and Archibald

(1899)

Isaac and Archibald were two old men.
I knew them, and I may have laughed at
    them
A little; but I must have honored them,
For they were old, and they were good to me.

I do not think of either of them now,   5
Without remembering, infallibly,
A journey that I made one afternoon
With Isaac to find out what Archibald
Was doing with his oats. It was high time
Those oats were cut, said Isaac; and he
    feared   10

That Archibald — well, he could never feel
Quite sure of Archibald. Accordingly
The good old man invited me — that is,
Permitted me — to go along with him;
And I, with a small boy's adhesiveness   15
To competent old age, got up and went.
I do not know that I cared overmuch
For Archibald's or anybody's oats,
But Archibald was quite another thing,
And Isaac yet another; and the world   20
Was wide, and there was gladness every-
        where.
We walked together down the River Road
With all the warmth and wonder of the land
Around us, and the wayside flash of leaves, —
And Isaac said the day was glorious;   25
But somewhere at the end of the first mile
I found that I was figuring to find
How long those ancient legs of his would
        keep
The pace that he had set for them. The
        sun
Was hot, and I was ready to sweat blood;   30
But Isaac, for aught I could make of him,
Was cool to his hat-band. So I said then,
With a dry gasp of affable despair,
Something about the scorching days we have
In August without knowing it sometimes;   35
But Isaac said the day was like a dream,
And praised the Lord, and talked about
        the breeze.
I made a fair confession of the breeze,
And crowded casually on his thought
The nearness of a profitable nook   40
That I could see. First I was half inclined
To caution him that he was growing old,
But something that was not compassion soon
Made plain the folly of all subterfuge.
Isaac was old, but not so old as that.   45

So I proposed, without an overture,
That we be seated in the shade a while,
And Isaac made no murmur. Soon the talk
Was turned on Archibald, and I began
To feel some premonitions of a kind   50
That only childhood knows; for the old man
Had looked at me and clutched me with
        his eye,
And asked if I had ever noticed things.
I told him that I could not think of them,
And I knew then, by the frown that left
        his face   55

Unsatisfied, that I had injured him.
"My good young friend," he said, "you
        cannot feel
What I have seen so long. You have the
        eyes —
Oh, yes — but you have not the other
        things:
The sight within that never will deceive,   60
You do not know — you have no right to
        know;
The twilight warning of experience,
The singular idea of loneliness, —
These are not yours. But they have long
        been mine,
And they have shown me now for seven
        years   65
That Archibald is changing. It is not
So much that he should come to his last hand,
And leave the game, and go the old way
        down;
But I have known him in and out so long,
And I have seen so much of good in him   70
That other men have shared and have not
        seen,
And I have gone so far through thick and
        thin,
Through cold and fire with him, that now
        it brings
To this old heart of mine an ache that you
Have not yet lived enough to know about.   75
But even unto you, and your boy's faith,
Your freedom, and your untried confidence,
A time will come to find out what it means
To know that you are losing what was yours,
To know that you are being left behind;   80
And then the long contempt of innocence —
God bless you, boy! — don't think the worse
        of it
Because an old man chatters in the shade —
Will all be like a story you have read
In childhood and remembered for the
        pictures.   85
And when the best friend of your life goes
        down,
When first you know in him the slackening
That comes, and coming always tells the
        end,
Now in a common word that would have
        passed
Uncaught from any other lips than his,   90
Now in some trivial act of every day,
Done as he might have done it all along

But for a twinging little difference
That nips you like a squirrel's teeth —
    oh, yes,
Then you will understand it well enough. 95
But oftener it comes in other ways;
It comes without your knowing when it
    comes;
You know that he is changing, and you
    know
That he is going — just as I know now
That Archibald is going, and that I   100
Am staying. . . . Look at me, my boy,
And when the time shall come for you to see
That I must follow after him, try then
To think of me, to bring me back again,
Just as I was to-day. Think of the place 105
Where we are sitting now, and think of me —
Think of old Isaac as you knew him then,
When you set out with him in August once
To see old Archibald." — The words come
    back
Almost as Isaac must have uttered them, 110
And there comes with them a dry memory
Of something in my throat that would not
    move.

If you had asked me then to tell just why
I made so much of Isaac and the things
He said, I should have gone far for an
    answer;   115
For I knew it was not sorrow that I felt,
Whatever I may have wished it, or tried then
To make myself believe. My mouth was full
Of words, and they would have been com-
    forting
To Isaac, spite of my twelve years, I think; 120
But there was not in me the willingness
To speak them out. Therefore I watched
    the ground;
And I was wondering what made the Lord
Create a thing so nervous as an ant,
When Isaac, with commendable unrest, 125
Ordained that we should take the road
    again —
For it was yet three miles to Archibald's,
And one to the first pump. I felt relieved
All over when the old man told me that;
I felt that he had stilled a fear of mine 130
That those extremities of heat and cold
Which he had long gone through with
    Archibald
Had made the man impervious to both;

But Isaac had a desert somewhere in him,
And at the pump he thanked God for all
    things   135
That He had put on earth for men to drink,
And he drank well, — so well that I proposed
That we go slowly lest I learn too soon
The bitterness of being left behind,
And all those other things. That was a
    joke   140
To Isaac, and it pleased him very much;
And that pleased me — for I was twelve
    years old.

At the end of an hour's walking after that
The cottage of old Archibald appeared.
Little and white and high on a smooth
    round hill   145
It stood, with hackmatacks and apple-
    trees
Before it, and a big barn-roof beyond;
And over the place — trees, house, fields
    and all —
Hovered an air of still simplicity
And a fragrance of old summers — the old
    style   150
That lives the while it passes. I dare say
That I was lightly conscious of all this
When Isaac, of a sudden, stopped himself,
And for the long first quarter of a minute
Gazed with incredulous eyes, forgetful
    quite   155
Of breezes and of me and of all else
Under the scorching sun but a smooth-
    cut field,
Faint yellow in the distance. I was young,
But there were a few things that I could see,
And this was one of them. — "Well, well!"
    said he;   160
And "Archibald will be surprised, I think,"
Said I. But all my childhood subtlety
Was lost on Isaac, for he strode along
Like something out of Homer — powerful
And awful on the wayside, so I thought. 165
Also I thought how good it was to be
So near the end of my short-legged en-
    deavor
To keep the pace with Isaac for five miles.

Hardly had we turned in from the main
    road
When Archibald, with one hand on his
    back   170

And the other clutching his huge-headed
cane,
Came limping down to meet us. — "Well!
well! well!"
Said he; and then he looked at my red face,
All streaked with dust and sweat, and
shook my hand,
And said it must have been a right smart
walk   175
That we had had that day from Tilbury
Town. —
"Magnificent," said Isaac; and he told
About the beautiful west wind there was
Which cooled and clarified the atmosphere.
"You must have made it with your legs, I
guess,"   180
Said Archibald; and Isaac humored him
With one of those infrequent smiles of his
Which he kept in reserve, apparently,
For Archibald alone. "But why," said he,
"Should Providence have cider in the
world   185
If not for such an afternoon as this?"
And Archibald, with a soft light in his eyes,
Replied that if he chose to go down cellar,
There he would find eight barrels — one
of which
Was newly tapped, he said, and to his
taste   190
An honor to the fruit. Isaac approved
Most heartily of that, and guided us
Forthwith, as if his venerable feet
Were measuring the turf in his own door-
yard,
Straight to the open rollway. Down we
went,   195
Out of the fiery sunshine to the gloom,
Grateful and half sepulchral, where we found
The barrels, like eight potent sentinels,
Close ranged along the wall. From one of
them
A bright pine spile stuck out alluringly, 200
And on the black flat stone, just under it,
Glimmered a late-spilled proof that Archi-
bald
Had spoken from unfeigned experience.
There was a fluted antique water-glass
Close by, and in it, prisoned, or at rest, 205
There was a cricket, of the brown soft sort
That feeds on darkness. Isaac turned him out,
And touched him with his thumb to make
him jump,

And then composedly pulled out the plug
With such a practised hand that scarce a
drop   210
Did even touch his fingers. Then he drank
And smacked his lips with a slow patronage
And looked along the line of barrels there
With a pride that may have been forgetful-
ness
That they were Archibald's and not his
own.   215
"I never twist a spigot nowadays,"
He said, and raised the glass up to the light,
"But I thank God for orchards." And
that glass
Was filled repeatedly for the same hand
Before I thought it worth while to discern 220
Again that I was young, and that old age,
With all his woes, had some advantages.
"Now, Archibald," said Isaac, when we
stood
Outside again, "I have it in my mind
That I shall take a sort of little walk —   225
To stretch my legs and see what you are
doing.
You stay and rest your back and tell the boy
A story: Tell him all about the time
In Stafford's cabin forty years ago,
When four of us were snowed up for ten
days   230
With only one dried haddock. Tell him all
About it, and be wary of your back.
Now I will go along." — I looked up then
At Archibald, and as I looked I saw
Just how his nostrils widened once or twice 235
And then grew narrow. I can hear to-day
The way the old man chuckled to himself —
Not wholesomely, not wholly to convince
Another of his mirth, — as I can hear
The lonely sigh that followed. — But at
length   240
He said: "The orchard now's the place
for us;
We may find something like an apple there,
And we shall have the shade, at any rate."
So there we went and there we laid ourselves
Where the sun could not reach us; and I
champed   245
A dozen of worm-blighted astrakhans
While Archibald said nothing — merely told
The tale of Stafford's cabin, which was good,
Though "master chilly" — after his own
phrase —

Even for a day like that. But other
    thoughts   250
Were moving in his mind, imperative,
And writhing to be spoken: I could see
The glimmer of them in a glance or two,
Cautious, or else unconscious, that he gave
Over his shoulder: . . . "Stafford and the
    rest —   255
But that's an old song now, and Archibald
And Isaac are old men. Remember, boy,
That we are old. Whatever we have gained,
Or lost, or thrown away, we are old men.
You look before you and we look behind, 260
And we are playing life out in the shadow —
But that's not all of it. The sunshine lights
A good road yet before us if we look,
And we are doing that when least we know
    it;
For both of us are children of the sun, 265
Like you, and like the weed there at your feet.
The shadow calls us, and it frightens us —
We think; but there's a light behind the stars
And we old fellows who have dared to
    live,
We see it — and we see the other things, 270
The other things. . . . Yes, I have seen it
    come
These eight years, and these ten years, and
    I know
Now that it cannot be for very long
That Isaac will be Isaac. You have seen —
Young as you are, you must have seen the
    strange   275
Uncomfortable habit of the man?
He'll take my nerves and tie them in a knot
Sometimes, and that's not Isaac. I know
    that —
And I know what it is: I get it here
A little, in my knees, and Isaac — here." 280
The old man shook his head regretfully
And laid his knuckles three times on his
    forehead.
"That's what it is: Isaac is not quite right.
You see it, but you don't know what it means:
The thousand little differences — no, 285
You do not know them, and it's well you
    don't;
You'll know them soon enough — God bless
    you, boy! —
You'll know them, but not all of them — not
    all.
So think of them as little as you can:

There's nothing in them for you, or for
    me —   290
But I am old and I must think of them;
I'm in the shadow, but I don't forget
The light, my boy, — the light behind the
    stars.
Remember that: remember that I said it;
And when the time that you think far away 295
Shall come for you to say it — say it, boy;
Let there be no confusion or distrust
In you, no snarling of a life half lived,
Nor any cursing over broken things
That your complaint has been the ruin of. 300
Live to see clearly and the light will come
To you, and as you need it. — But there,
    there,
I'm going it again, as Isaac says,
And I'll stop now before you go to sleep. —
Only be sure that you growl cautiously, 305
And always where the shadow may not
    reach you."

Never shall I forget, long as I live,
The quaint thin crack in Archibald's voice,
The lonely twinkle in his little eyes,
Or the way it made me feel to be with him. 310
I know I lay and looked for a long time
Down through the orchard and across the
    road,
Across the river and the sun-scorched hills
That ceased in a blue forest, where the world
Ceased with it. Now and then my fancy
    caught   315
A flying glimpse of a good life beyond —
Something of ships and sunlight, streets
    and singing,
Troy falling, and the ages coming back,
And ages coming forward: Archibald
And Isaac were good fellows in old clothes, 320
And Agamemnon was a friend of mine;
Ulysses coming home again to shoot
With bows and feathered arrows made
    another,
And all was as it should be. I was young.

So I lay dreaming of what things I would, 325
Calm and incorrigibly satisfied
With apples and romance and ignorance,
And the still smoke from Archibald's clay
    pipe.
There was a stillness over everything,
As if the spirit of heat had laid its hand 330

Upon the world and hushed it; and I felt
Within the mightiness of the white sun
That smote the land around us and wrought
    out
A fragrance from the trees, a vital warmth
And fullness for the time that was to come, 335
And a glory for the world beyond the forest.
The present and the future and the past,
Isaac and Archibald, the burning bush,
The Trojans and the walls of Jericho,
Were beautifully fused; and all went well 340
Till Archibald began to fret for Isaac
And said it was a master day for sun-
    stroke.
That was enough to make a mummy smile,
I thought; and I remained hilarious,
In face of all precedence and respect, 345
Till Isaac (who had come to us unheard)
Found he had no tobacco, looked at me
Peculiarly, and asked of Archibald
What ailed the boy to make him chirrup so.
From that he told us what a blessed world 350
The Lord had given us. — "But, Archibald,"
He added, with a sweet severity
That made me think of peach-skins and
    goose-flesh,
"I'm half afraid you cut those oats of yours
A day or two before they were well set." 355
"They were set well enough," said Archi-
    bald, —
And I remarked the process of his nose
Before the words came out. "But never mind
Your neighbor's oats: you stay here in the
    shade
And rest yourself while I go find the cards. 360
We'll have a little game of seven-up
And let the boy keep count." — "We'll
    have the game,
Assuredly," said Isaac; "and I think
That I will have a drop of cider, also."

They marched away together towards the
    house 365
And left me to my childish ruminations
Upon the ways of men. I followed them
Down cellar with my fancy, and then left
    them
For a fairer vision of all things at once
That was anon to be destroyed again 370
By the sound of voices and of heavy feet —
One of the sounds of life that I remember,
Though I forget so many that rang first

As if they were thrown down to me from
    Sinai.

So I remember, even to this day, 375
Just how they sounded, how they placed
    themselves,
And how the game went on while I made
    marks
And crossed them out, and meanwhile made
    some Trojans.
Likewise I made Ulysses, after Isaac,
And a little after Flaxman. Archibald 380
Was injured when he found himself left
    out,
But he had no heroics, and I said so:
I told him that his white beard was too long
And too straight down to be like things in
    Homer.
"Quite so," said Isaac. — "Low," said
    Archibald; 385
And he threw down a deuce with a deep grin
That showed his yellow teeth and made me
    happy.
So they played on till a bell rang from the
    door,
And Archibald said, "Supper." — After that
The old men smoked while I sat watching
    them 390
And wondered with all comfort what might
    come
To me, and what might never come to me;
And when the time came for the long walk
    home
With Isaac in the twilight, I could see
The forest and the sunset and the sky-line, 395
No matter where it was that I was looking:
The flame beyond the boundary, the music,
The foam and the white ships, and two old
    men
Were things that would not leave me.—And
    that night
There came to me a dream — a shining
    one, 400
With two old angels in it. They had wings,
And they were sitting where a silver light
Suffused them, face to face. The wings of
    one
Began to palpitate as I approached,
But I was yet unseen when a dry voice 405
Cried thinly, with unpatronizing triumph,
"I've got you, Isaac; high, low, jack, and
    the game."

Isaac and Archibald have gone their way
To the silence of the loved and well-forgotten.
I knew them, and I may have laughed at
    them;   410
But there's a laughing that has honor in it,
And I have no regret for light words now.
Rather I think sometimes they may have
    made
Their sport of me; — but they would not
    do that,
They were too old for that. They were old
    men,   415
And I may laugh at them because I knew
    them.

Miniver Cheevy

(1908?)

Miniver Cheevy, child of scorn,
    Grew lean while he assailed the seasons;
He wept that he was ever born,
    And he had reasons.

Miniver loved the days of old   5
    When swords were bright and steeds were
        prancing;
The vision of a warrior bold
    Would set him dancing.

Miniver sighed for what was not,
    And dreamed, and rested from his labors;   10
He dreamed of Thebes and Camelot,
    And Priam's neighbors.

Miniver mourned the ripe renown
    That made so many a name so fragrant;
He mourned Romance, now on the town,   15
    And Art, a vagrant.

Miniver loved the Medici,
    Albeit he had never seen one;
He would have sinned incessantly
    Could he have been one.   20

Miniver cursed the commonplace
    And eyed a khaki suit with loathing:
He missed the mediaeval grace
    Of iron clothing.

Miniver scorned the gold he sought,   25
    But sore annoyed was he without it;

Miniver thought, and thought, and thought
    And thought about it.

Miniver Cheevy, born too late,
    Scratched his head and kept on think-
        ing;   30
Miniver coughed, and called it fate,
    And kept on drinking.

The Man Against the Sky

(ca. 1914)

Between me and the sunset, like a dome
Against the glory of a world on fire,
Now burned a sudden hill,
Bleak, round, and high, by flame-lit height
    made higher,
With nothing on it for the flame to kill   5
Save one who moved and was alone up
    there
To loom before the chaos and the glare
As if he were the last god going home
Unto his last desire.

Dark, marvelous, and inscrutable he moved
    on   10
Till down the fiery distance he was gone,
Like one of those eternal, remote things
That range across a man's imaginings
When a sure music fills him and he knows
What he may say thereafter to few men, —
The touch of ages having wrought   16
An echo and a glimpse of what he thought
A phantom or a legend until then;
For whether lighted over ways that save,
Or lured from all repose,   20
If he go on too far to find a grave,
Mostly alone he goes.

Even he, who stood where I had found him,
On high with fire all round him,
Who moved along the molten west,   25
And over the round hill's crest
That seemed half ready with him to go down,
Flame-bitten and flame-cleft,
As if there were to be no last thing left
Of a nameless unimaginable town, —   30

Even he who climbed and vanished may
    have taken
Down to the perils of a depth not known,

From death defended though by men for-
    saken,
The bread that every man must eat alone;
He may have walked while others hardly
    dared   35
Look on to see him stand where many fell;
And upward out of that, as out of hell,
He may have sung and striven
To mount where more of him shall yet be
    given,
Bereft of all retreat,   40
To sevenfold heat, —
As on a day when three in Dura shared
The furnace, and were spared
For glory by that king of Babylon
Who made himself so great that God, who
    heard,   45
Covered him with long feathers, like a bird.

Again, he may have gone down easily,
By comfortable altitudes, and found,
As always, underneath him solid ground
Whereon to be sufficient and to stand   50
Possessed already of the promised land,
Far stretched and fair to see:
A good sight, verily,
And one to make the eyes of her who bore him
Shine glad with hidden tears.   55
Why question of his ease of who before him,
In one place or another where they left
Their names as far behind them as their bones,
And yet by dint of slaughter toil and theft,
And shrewdly sharpened stones,   60
Carved hard the way for his ascendency
Through deserts of lost years?
Why trouble him now who sees and hears
No more than what his innocence requires,
And therefore to no other height aspires   65
Than one at which he neither quails nor
    tires? —
He may do more by seeing what he sees
Than others eager for iniquities;
He may, by seeing all things for the best,
Incite futurity to do the rest.   70

Or with an even likelihood,
He may have met with atrabilious eyes
The fires of time on equal terms and passed
Indifferently down, until at last
His only kind of grandeur would have been,
Apparently, in being seen.   76
He may have had for evil or for good

No argument; he may have had no care
For what without himself went anywhere
To failure or to glory, and least of all   80
For such a stale, flamboyant miracle;
He may have been the prophet of an art
Immovable to old idolatries;
He may have been a player without a part,
Annoyed that even the sun should have the
    skies   85
For such a flaming way to advertise;
He may have been a painter sick at heart
With Nature's toiling for a new surprise;
He may have been a cynic, who now, for
    all
Of anything divine that his effete   90
Negation may have tasted,
Saw truth in his own image, rather small,
Forbore to fever the ephemeral,
Found any barren height a good retreat
From any swarming street,   95
And in the sun saw power superbly wasted;
And when the primitive old-fashioned stars
Came out again to shine on joys and wars
More primitive, and all arrayed for doom,
He may have proved a world a sorry thing
In his imagining,   101
And life a lighted highway to the tomb.

Or, mounting with infirm unsearching tread,
His hopes to chaos led,
He may have stumbled up there from the
    past,   105
And with an aching strangeness viewed the
    last
Abysmal conflagration of his dreams, —
A flame where nothing seems
To burn but flame itself, by nothing fed;
And while it all went out,   110
Not even the faint anodyne of doubt
May then have eased a painful going down
From pictured heights of power and lost
    renown,
Revealed at length to his outlived endeavor
Remote and unapproachable forever;   115
And at his heart there may have gnawed
Sick memories of a dead faith foiled and
    flawed
And long dishonored by the living death
Assigned alike by chance
To brutes and hierophants;   120
And anguish fallen on those he loved around
    him

May once have dealt the last blow to con-
    found him,
And so have left him as death leaves a child,
Who sees it all too near;
And he who knows no young way to forget
May struggle to the tomb unreconciled.   126
Whatever suns may rise or set
There may be nothing kinder for him here
Than shafts and agonies;
And under these   130
He may cry out and stay on horribly;
Or, seeing in death too small a thing to fear,
He may go forward like a stoic Roman
Where pangs and terrors in his pathway
    lie, —
Or, seizing the swift logic of a woman,   135
Curse God and die.

Or maybe there, like many another one
Who might have stood aloft and looked
    ahead,
Black-drawn against wild red,
He may have built, unawed by fiery gules   140
That in him no commotion stirred,
A living reason out of molecules
Why molecules occurred,
And one for smiling when he might have
    sighed
Had he seen far enough,   145
And in the same inevitable stuff
Discovered an odd reason too for pride
In being what he must have been by laws
Infrangible and for no kind of cause.
Deterred by no confusion or surprise   150
He may have seen with his mechanic eyes
A world without a meaning, and had room,
Alone amid magnificence and doom,
To build himself an airy monument
That should, or fail him in his vague intent,
Outlast an accidental universe —   156
To call it nothing worse —
Or, by the burrowing guile
Of Time disintegrated and effaced,
Like once-remembered mighty trees go
    down   160
To ruin, of which by man may now be traced
No part sufficient even to be rotten,
And in the book of things that are forgotten
Is entered as a thing not quite worth while.
He may have been so great   165
That satraps would have shivered at his
    frown,

And all he prized alive may rule a state
No larger than a grave that holds a clown;
He may have been a master of his fate,
And of his atoms, — ready as another   170
In his emergence to exonerate
His father and his mother;
He may have been a captain of a host,
Self-eloquent and ripe for prodigies,
Doomed here to swell by dangerous degrees,
And then give up the ghost.   176
Nahum's great grasshoppers were such as
    these,
Sun-scattered and soon lost.

Whatever the dark road he may have taken,
This man who stood on high   180
And faced alone the sky,
Whatever drove or lured or guided him, —
A vision answering a faith unshaken,
An easy trust assumed of easy trials,
A sick negation born of weak denials,   185
A crazed abhorrence of an old condition,
A blind attendance on a brief ambition, —
Whatever stayed him or derided him,
His way was even as ours;
And we, with all our wounds and all our
    powers,   190
Must each await alone at his own height
Another darkness or another light;
And there, of our poor self dominion reft,
If inference and reason shun
Hell, Heaven, and Oblivion,   195
May thwarted will (perforce precarious,
But for our conservation better thus)
Have no misgiving left
Of doing yet what here we leave undone?
Or if unto the last of these we cleave,   200
Believing or protesting we believe
In such an idle and ephemeral
Florescence of the diabolical, —
If, robbed of two fond old enormities,
Our being had no onward auguries,   205
What then were this great love of ours to
    say
For launching other lives to voyage again
A little farther into time and pain,
A little faster in a futile chase
For a kingdom and a power and a Race   210
That would have still in sight
A manifest end of ashes and eternal night?
Is this the music of the toys we shake
So loud, — as if there might be no mistake

Somewhere in our indomitable will? 215
Are we no greater than the noise we make
Along one blind atomic pilgrimage
Whereon by crass chance billeted we go
Because our brains and bones and cartilage
Will have it so? 220
If this we say, then let us all be still
About our share in it, and live and die
More quietly thereby.

Where was he going, this man against the
     sky?
You know not, nor do I. 225
But this we know, if we know anything:
That we may laugh and fight and sing
And of our transience here make offering
To an orient Word that will not be erased,
Or, save in incommunicable gleams 230
Too permanent for dreams,
Be found or known.
No tonic and ambitious irritant
Of increase or of want
Has made an otherwise insensate waste 235
Of ages overthrown
A ruthless, veiled, implacable foretaste
Of other ages that are still to be
Depleted and rewarded variously
Because a few, by fate's economy, 240
Shall seem to move the world the way it goes;
No soft evangel of equality,
Safe-cradled in a communal repose
That huddles into death and may at last
Be covered well with equatorial snows — 245
And all for what, the devil only knows —
Will aggregate an inkling to confirm
The credit of a sage or of a worm,
Or tell us why one man in five
Should have a care to stay alive 250
While in his heart he feels no violence
Laid on his humor and intelligence
When infant Science makes a pleasant face
And waves again that hollow toy, the Race;
No planetary trap where souls are wrought
For nothing but the sake of being caught 256
And sent again to nothing will attune
Itself to any key of any reason
Why man should hunger through another
     season
To find out why 'twere better late than
     soon 260
To go away and let the sun and moon
And all the silly stars illuminate

A place for creeping things,
And those that root and trumpet and have
     wings,
And herd and ruminate, 265
Or dive and flash and poise in rivers and seas,
Or by their loyal tails in lofty trees
Hang screeching lewd victorious derision
Of man's immortal vision.
Shall we, because Eternity records 270
Too vast an answer for the time-born words
We spell, whereof so many are dead that once
In our capricious lexicons
Were so alive and final, hear no more
The Word itself, the living word 275
That none alive has ever heard
Or ever spelt,
And few have ever felt
Without the fears and old surrenderings
And terrors that began 280
When Death let fall a feather from his wings
And humbled the first man?
Because the weight of our humility,
Wherefrom we gain
A little wisdom and much pain, 285
Falls here too sore and there too tedious,
Are we in anguish or complacency,
Not looking far enough ahead
To see by what mad couriers we are led
Along the roads of the ridiculous, 290
To pity ourselves and laugh at faith
And while we curse life bear it?
And if we see the soul's dead end in death,
Are we to fear it?
What folly is here that has not yet a name
Unless we say outright that we are liars? 296
What have we seen beyond our sunset fires
That lights again the way by which we came?
Why pay we such a price, and one we give
So clamoringly, for each racked empty
     day 300
That leads one more last human hope away,
As quiet fiends would lead past our crazed
     eyes
Our children to an unseen sacrifice?
If after all that we have lived and thought,
All comes to Nought, — 305
If there be nothing after Now,
And we be nothing anyhow,
And we know that, — why live?
'Twere sure but weaklings' vain distress
To suffer dungeons where so many doors 310
Will open on the cold eternal shores

That look sheer down
To the dark tideless floods of Nothingness
Where all who know may drown.

Flammonde

(1915–16)

The man Flammonde, from God knows
    where,
With firm address and foreign air,
With news of nations in his talk
And something royal in his walk,
With glint of iron in his eyes,
But never doubt, nor yet surprise,
Appeared, and stayed, and held his head
As one by kings accredited.

Erect, with his alert repose
About him, and about his clothes,   10
He pictured all tradition hears
Of what we owe to fifty years.
His cleansing heritage of taste
Paraded neither want nor waste;
And what he needed for his fee   15
To live, he borrowed graciously.

He never told us what he was,
Or what mischance, or other cause,
Had banished him from better days
To play the Prince of Castaways.   20
Meanwhile he played surpassing well
A part, for most, unplayable;
In fine, one pauses, half afraid
To say for certain that he played.

For that, one may as well forego   25
Conviction as to yes or no;
Nor can I say just how intense
Would then have been the difference
To several, who, having striven
In vain to get what he was given,   30
Would see the stranger taken on
By friends not easy to be won.

Moreover, many a malcontent
He soothed and found munificent;
His courtesy beguiled and foiled   35
Suspicion that his years were soiled;
His mien distinguished any crowd,
His credit strengthened when he bowed;
And women, young and old, were fond
Of looking at the man Flammonde.   40

There was a woman in our town
On whom the fashion was to frown;
But while our talk renewed the tinge
Of a long-faded scarlet fringe,
The man Flammonde saw none of that,   45
And what he saw we wondered at —
That none of us, in her distress,
Could hide or find our littleness.

There was a boy that all agreed
Had shut within him the rare seed   50
Of learning. We could understand,
But none of us could lift a hand.
The man Flammonde appraised the youth,
And told a few of us the truth;
And thereby, for a little gold,   55
A flowered future was unrolled.

There were two citizens who fought
For years and years, and over nought;
They made life awkward for their friends,
And shortened their own dividends.   60
The man Flammonde said what was wrong
Should be made right; nor was it long
Before they were again in line,
And had each other in to dine.

And these I mention are but four   65
Of many out of many more.
So much for them. But what of him —
So firm in every look and limb?
What small satanic sort of kink
Was in his brain? What broken link   70
Withheld him from the destinies
That came so near to being his?

What was he, when we came to sift
His meaning, and to note the drift
Of incommunicable ways   75
That make us ponder while we praise?
Why was it that his charm revealed
Somehow the surface of a shield?
What was it that we never caught?
What was he, and what was he not?   80

How much it was of him we met
We cannot ever know; nor yet
Shall all he gave us quite atone
For what was his, and his alone;
Nor need we now, since he knew best,   85
Nourish an ethical unrest:

Rarely at once will nature give
The power to be Flammonde and live.

We cannot know how much we learn
From those who never will return, 90
Until a flash of unforeseen
Remembrance falls on what has been.
We've each a darkening hill to climb;
And this is why, from time to time
In Tilbury Town, we look beyond 95
Horizons for the man Flammonde.

Mr. Flood's Party

(ca. 1919)

Old Eben Flood, climbing alone one night
Over the hill between the town below
And the forsaken upland hermitage
That held as much as he should ever know
On earth again of home, paused warily. 5
The road was his with not a native near;
And Eben, having leisure, said aloud,
For no man else in Tilbury Town to hear:

"Well, Mr. Flood, we have the harvest moon
Again, and we may not have many more; 10
The bird is on the wing, the poet says,
And you and I have said it here before.
Drink to the bird." He raised up to the light
The jug that he had gone so far to fill,
And answered huskily: "Well, Mr. Flood, 15
Since you propose it, I believe I will."

Alone, as if enduring to the end
A valiant armor of scarred hopes outworn,
He stood there in the middle of the road
Like Roland's ghost winding a silent horn. 20
Below him, in the town among the trees,
Where friends of other days had honored him,
A phantom salutation of the dead
Rang thinly till old Eben's eyes were dim.

Then, as a mother lays her sleeping child 25
Down tenderly, fearing it may awake,
He set the jug down slowly at his feet
With trembling care, knowing that most
       things break.
And only when assured that on firm earth
It stood, as the uncertain lives of men 30
Assuredly did not, he paced away,
And with his hand extended paused again:

"Well, Mr. Flood, we have not met like this
In a long time; and many a change has come
To both of us, I fear, since last it was 35
We had a drop together. Welcome home!"
Convivially returning with himself,
Again he raised the jug up to the light;
And with an acquiescent quaver said:
"Well, Mr. Flood, if you insist, I might. 40

"Only a very little, Mr. Flood —
For auld lang syne. No more, sir; that will
       do."
So, for the time, apparently it did,
And Eben evidently thought so too;
For soon amid the silver loneliness 45
Of night he lifted up his voice and sang,
Secure, with only two moons listening,
Until the whole harmonious landscape rang—

"For auld lang syne." The weary throat
       gave out,
The last word wavered; and the song being
       done, 50
He raised again the jug regretfully
And shook his head, and was again alone.
There was not much that was ahead of him,
And there was nothing in the town below —
Where strangers would have shut the many
       doors 55
That many friends had opened long ago.

Karma

(1923)

Christmas was in the air and all was well
With him, but for a few confusing flaws
In divers of God's images. Because
A friend of his would neither buy nor sell,
Was he to answer for the axe that fell? 5
He pondered; and the reason for it was,
Partly, a slowly freezing Santa Claus
Upon the corner, with his beard and bell.

Acknowledging an improvident surprise,
He magnified a fancy that he wished 10
The friend whom he had wrecked were here
       again.
Not sure of that, he found a compromise;
And from the fulness of his heart he fished
A dime for Jesus who had died for men.

ROBERT FROST (1875–   )

Like Robinson, Frost is one of the major American poets of the twentieth century. He was born in San Francisco, but his ancestors for generations had lived in New England, to which he was taken when a boy of ten. He graduated from the high school at Lawrence, Mass., studied for a few months at Dartmouth, married, and spent two years at Harvard. Then he took up teaching, shoemaking, journalism, and farming. He wrote poetry that met no response. Unaware of the sudden revival of poetry that lay just ahead, he sold his New Hampshire farm in 1912 — the very year when Harriet Monroe founded *Poetry* — and settled with his family in a village in England. He published in London in 1913 a slender volume of poems, *A Boy's Will*, and soon received recognition, a recognition firmly established by his second volume, *North of Boston* (1914). America now heeded her new singer. His two books were republished in New York in 1915 and the second one was reprinted four times within the year. "In *North of Boston*, Frost found his own full utterance and himself," says Louis Untermeyer. "It is, as he calls it, a 'book of people.' And it is more than that. It is a book of a people, of the folk of New England, of New England itself with its hard hills and harder certainties, its repressions, its cold humor and inverted tenderness."

Frost returned to America in 1915, published *Mountain Interval* the next year, and has since divided his time between farming and flexible connections as a "tame poet" with Amherst College, the University of Michigan, Harvard (where he became Emerson Professor of Poetry), and Breadloaf, the summer camp for writers in Vermont. He has been three times a Pulitzer Prize winner and the recipient of various distinguished awards and honorary degrees. *New Hampshire* appeared in 1923, *West-Running Brook* in 1928, *A Further Range* in 1936, *The Witness Tree* in 1942, *A Masque of Reason* in 1945.

Growing out of his intimate feeling for rural New England, the poetry of Frost has a regional aspect that links it with the short stories of Sarah Orne Jewett and other New England writers before him. Yet locality seems an accident in his poetry, the real subject of which is human life and human destiny, the universal meanings of experiences that only seem to be slight and random. "The thing that art does for life," he himself says, "is to clip it, to strip it to form." "A poem begins in delight and ends in wisdom." He has put this another way: "A poem begins with a lump in the throat; a homesickness or a love-sickness. It is a reaching out toward expression; an effort to find fulfillment. A complete poem is one where an emotion has found its thought, and the thought has found the words."

Frost's work has been republished in a single volume: *Collected Poems*. Biographies are by G. B. Munson, 1927, and Sidney Cox, 1929. Critical comment may be found in T. K. Whipple's *Spokesmen*, 1928; G. R. Elliott's *The Cycle of Modern Poetry*, 1929; Richard Thornton (ed.), *Recognition of Robert Frost*, 1937; R. P. T. Coffin, *New Poetry of New England: Frost and Robinson*, 1938; L. Thompson, *Fire and Ice*, 1942.

The Death of the Hired Man
(1905)

Mary sat musing on the lamp-flame at the
    table
Waiting for Warren. When she heard his
    step,
She ran on tip-toe down the darkened
    passage
To meet him in the doorway with the news
And put him on his guard. "Silas is back." 5
She pushed him outward with her through
    the door
And shut it after her. "Be kind," she said.
She took the market things from Warren's
    arms
And set them on the porch, then drew him
    down
To sit beside her on the wooden steps.   10

"When was I ever anything but kind to him?
But I'll not have the fellow back," he said.
"I told him so last haying, didn't I?
'If he left then,' I said, 'that ended it.'
What good is he? Who else will harbour him 15
At his age for the little he can do?
What help he is there's no depending on.
Off he goes always when I need him most.
'He thinks he ought to earn a little pay,
Enough at least to buy tobacco with,   20
So he won't have to beg and be beholden.'
'All right,' I say, 'I can't afford to pay
Any fixed wages, though I wish I could.'
'Someone else can.' 'Then someone else
    will have to.'
I shouldn't mind his bettering himself   25
If that was what it was. You can be certain,
When he begins like that, there's someone at
    him
Trying to coax him off with pocket-money, —
In haying time, when any help is scarce.
In winter he comes back to us. I'm done." 30
"Sh! not so loud: he'll hear you," Mary
    said.

"I want him to: he'll have to soon or late."

"He's worn out. He's asleep beside the
    stove.
When I came up from Rowe's I found him
    here,
Huddled against the barn-door fast asleep, 35

A miserable sight, and frightening, too —
You needn't smile — I didn't recognise
    him —
I wasn't looking for him — and he's changed.
Wait till you see."

        "Where did you say he'd been?"

"He didn't say. I dragged him to the
    house,
And gave him tea and tried to make him
    smoke.
I tried to make him talk about his travels.
Nothing would do: he just kept nodding
    off."

"What did he say? Did he say anything?"

"But little."

        "Anything? Mary, confess   45

He said he'd come to ditch the meadow for
    me."

"Warren!"

        "But did he? I just want to know."

"Of course he did. What would you have
    him say?
Surely you wouldn't grudge the poor old
    man
Some humble way to save his self-respect.   50
He added, if you really care to know,
He meant to clear the upper pasture, too.
That sounds like something you have heard
    before?
Warren, I wish you could have heard the way
He jumbled everything. I stopped to look
Two or three times — he made me feel so
    queer —   56
To see if he was talking in his sleep.
He ran on Harold Wilson — you remember—
The boy you had in haying four years since.
He's finished school, and teaching in his
    college.   60

"Silas declares you'll have to get him back.
He says they two will make a team for work:
Between them they will lay this farm as
    smooth!

The way he mixed that in with other things.
He thinks young Wilson a likely lad, though
    daft   65
On education — you know how they fought
All through July under the blazing sun,
Silas up on the cart to build the load,
Harold along beside to pitch it on."

"Yes, I took care to keep well out of ear-
    shot."   70

"Well, those days trouble Silas like a dream.
You wouldn't think they would. How some
    things linger!
Harold's young college boy's assurance
    piqued him.
After so many years he still keeps finding
Good arguments he sees he might have used.
I sympathise. I know just how it feels   76
To think of the right thing to say too late.
Harold's associated in his mind with Latin.
He asked me what I thought of Harold's
    saying
He studied Latin like the violin   80
Because he liked it — that an argument!
He said he couldn't make the boy believe
He could find water with a hazel prong —
Which showed how much good school had
    ever done him.   84
He wanted to go over that. But most of all
He thinks if he could have another chance
To teach him how to build a load of hay — "

"I know, that's Silas' one accomplishment.
He bundles every forkful in its place,
And tags and numbers it for future reference,
So he can find and easily dislodge it   91
In the unloading. Silas does that well.
He takes it out in bunches like birds' nests.
You never see him standing on the hay
He's trying to lift, straining to lift himself."
"He thinks if he could teach him that, he'd
    be   96
Some good perhaps to someone in the world.
He hates to see a boy the fool of books.
Poor Silas, so concerned for other folk,
And nothing to look backward to with pride,
And nothing to look forward to with hope, 101
So now and never any different."

Part of a moon was falling down the west,
Dragging the whole sky with it to the hills.

Its light poured softly in her lap. She saw
And spread her apron to it. She put out her
    hand   106
Among the harp-like morning-glory strings,
Taut with the dew from garden bed to eaves,
As if she played unheard the tenderness
That wrought on him beside her in the night.
"Warren," she said, "he has come home to
    die: 111
You needn't be afraid he'll leave you this
    time."

"Home," he mocked gently.

        "Yes, what else but home?
It all depends on what you mean by home.
Of course he's nothing to us, any more   116
Than was the hound that came a stranger to
    us
Out of the woods, worn out upon the trail."

"Home is the place where, when you have to
    go there,
They have to take you in."   120

        "I should have called it
Something you somehow haven't to deserve."

Warren leaned out and took a step or two,
Picked up a little stick, and brought it back
And broke it in his hand and tossed it by.
"Silas has better claim on us you think 126
Than on his brother? Thirteen little miles
As the road winds would bring him to his
    door.
Silas has walked that far no doubt to-day.
Why didn't he go there? His brother's
    rich,   130
A somebody — director in the bank."

"He never told us that."

           "We know it though."

"I think his brother ought to help, of course.
I'll see to that if there is need. He ought of
    right   135
To take him in, and might be willing to —
He may be better than appearances.
But have some pity on Silas. Do you think
If he'd had any pride in claiming kin   139

Or anything he looked for from his brother,
He'd keep so still about him all this time?"

"I wonder what's between them."

                              "I can tell you.
Silas is what he is — we wouldn't mind
    him —   144
But just the kind that kinsfolk can't abide.
He never did a thing so very bad.
He don't know why he isn't quite as good
As anyone. He won't be made ashamed
To please his brother, worthless though he
    is."

"*I* can't think Si ever hurt anyone."   150

"No, but he hurt my heart the way he lay
And rolled his old head on that sharp-edged
    chair-back.
He wouldn't let me put him on the lounge.
You must go in and see what you can do.   154
I made the bed up for him there to-night.
You'll be surprised at him — how much he's
    broken.
His working days are done; I'm sure of it."

"I'd not be in a hurry to say that."

"I haven't been. Go, look, see for your-
    self.
But, Warren, please remember how it is: 160
He's come to help you ditch the meadow.
He has a plan. You mustn't laugh at him.
He may not speak of it, and then he may.
I'll sit and see if that small sailing cloud
Will hit or miss the moon."   165

                              It hit the moon.
Then there were three there, making a dim
    row,
The moon, the little silver cloud, and she.

Warren returned — too soon, it seemed to
    her,
Slipped to her side, caught up her hand and
    waited.   170

"Warren?" she questioned.

                    "Dead," was all he answered.

Dust of Snow
(*ca. 1906*)

The way a crow
Shook down on me
The dust of snow
From a hemlock tree

Has given my heart   5
A change of mood
And saved some part
Of a day I had rued.

The Mountain
(*1913*)

The mountain held the town as in a
    shadow,
I saw so much before I slept there once:
I noticed that I missed stars in the west,
Where its black body cut into the sky.
Near me it seemed: I felt it like a wall   5
Behind which I was sheltered from a wind.
And yet between the town and it I found,
When I walked forth at dawn to see new
    things,
Were fields, a river, and beyond, more fields.
The river at the time was fallen away,   10
And made a widespread brawl on cobble-
    stones;
But the signs showed what it had done in
    spring;
Good grass-land gullied out, and in the grass
Ridges of sand, and driftwood stripped of
    bark.
I crossed the river and swung round the
    mountain.   15
And there I met a man who moved so
    slow
With white-faced oxen in a heavy cart,
It seemed no harm to stop him altogether.

"What town is this?" I asked.

                    "This? Lunenburg."   20

Then I was wrong: the town of my sojourn,
Beyond the bridge, was not that of the
    mountain,
But only felt at night its shadowy presence.

"Where is your village? Very far from
    here?"

"There is no village — only scattered farms.
We were but sixty voters last election.   26
We can't in nature grow to many more:
That thing takes all the room!" He moved
    his goad.
The mountain stood there to be pointed at.
Pasture ran up the side a little way,   30
And then there was a wall of trees with
    trunks:
After that only tops of trees, and cliffs
Imperfectly concealed among the leaves.
A dry ravine emerged from under boughs
Into the pasture.   35

    "That looks like a path.
Is that the way to reach the top from here? —
Not for this morning, but some other time:
I must be getting back to breakfast now."
"I don't advise your trying from this side. 40
There is no proper path, but those that *have*
Been up, I understand, have climbed from
    Ladd's.
That's five miles back. You can't mistake
    the place:
They logged it there last winter some way
    up.   44
I'd take you, but I'm bound the other way."

"You've never climbed it?"

          "I've been on the sides
Deer-hunting and trout-fishing. There's a
    brook
That starts up on it somewhere — I've
    heard say   49
Right on the top, tip-top — a curious thing.
But what would interest you about the
    brook,
It's always cold in summer, warm in winter.
One of the great sights going is to see
It steam in winter like an ox's breath.
Until the bushes all along its banks   55
Are inch-deep with the frosty spines and
    bristles —
You know the kind. Then let the sun shine
    on it!"

"There ought to be a view around the world
From such a mountain — if it isn't wooded

Clear to the top." I saw through leafy
    screens   60
Great granite terraces in sun and shadow,
Shelves one could rest a knee on getting up —
With depths behind him sheer a hundred
    feet;
Or turn and sit on and look out and
    down,
With little ferns in crevices at his elbow. 65

"As to that I can't say. But there's the
    spring,
Right on the summit, almost like a fountain.
That ought to be worth seeing."

            "If it's there.
You never saw it?"   0
          "I guess there's no doubt
About its being there. I never saw it.
It may not be right on the very top:
It wouldn't have to be a long way down
To have some head of water from above, 75
And a *good distance* down might not be
    noticed
By anyone who'd come a long way up.
One time I asked a fellow climbing it
To look and tell me later how it was."

"What did he say?"   80

          "He said there was a lake
Somewhere in Ireland on a mountain top."

"But a lake's different. What about the
    spring?"

"He never got up high enough to see.
That's why I don't advise your trying this
    side.   85
He tried this side. I've always meant to go
And look myself, but you know how it is:
It doesn't seem so much to climb a mountain
You've worked around the foot of all your
    life.
What would I do? Go in my overalls, 90
With a big stick, the same as when the
    cows
Haven't come down to the bars at milking
    time?
Or with a shotgun for a stray black bear?
'Twouldn't seem real to climb for climbing
    it."

"I shouldn't climb it if I didn't want to —
Not for the sake of climbing. What's its
    name?"   96

"We call it Hor: I don't know if that's
    right."

"Can one walk around it? Would it be too
    far?"

"You can drive round and keep in Lunen-
    burg,
But it's as much as ever you can do,   100
The boundary lines keep in so close to it.
Hor is the township, and the township's
    Hor —
And a few houses sprinkled round the foot,
Like boulders broken off the upper cliff,
Rolled out a little farther than the rest." 105
"Warm in December, cold in June, you
    say?"

"I don't suppose the water's changed at all.
You and I know enough to know it's warm
Compared with cold, and cold compared
    with warm.
But all the fun's in how you say a thing."

"You've lived here all your life?"   111

                          "Ever since Hor
Was no bigger than a — " What, I did not
    hear.

He drew the oxen toward him with light
    touches
Of his slim goad on nose and offside flank,
Gave them their marching orders and was
    moving.   116

Mending Wall
(1913)

Something there is that doesn't love a wall,
That sends the frozen-ground-swell under it,
And spills the upper boulders in the sun;
And makes gaps even two can pass abreast.
The work of hunters is another thing: 5
I have come after them and made repair

Where they have left not one stone on a
    stone,
But they would have the rabbit out of hiding,
To please the yelping dogs. The gaps I
    mean,
No one has seen them made or heard them
    made,   10
But at spring mending-time we find them
    there.
I let my neighbor know beyond the hill;
And on a day we meet to walk the line
And set the wall between us once again.
We keep the wall between us as we go.   15
To each the boulders that have fallen to each.
And some are loaves and some so nearly balls
We have to use a spell to make them balance:
"Stay where you are until our backs are
    turned!"
We wear our fingers rough with handling
    them.   20
Oh, just another kind of outdoor game,
One on a side. It comes to little more:
There where it is we do not need the wall:
He is all pine and I am apple-orchard.
My apple trees will never get across   25
And eat the cones under his pines, I tell
    him.
He only says, "Good fences make good
    neighbours."
Spring is the mischief in me, and I wonder
If I could put a notion in his head:
"Why do they make good neighbours? Isn't
    it   30
Where there are cows? But here there are
    no cows.
Before I built a wall I'd ask to know
What I was walling in or walling out,
And to whom I was like to give offence.
Something there is that doesn't love a wall,
That wants it down." I could say "Elves"
    to him,   36
But it's not elves exactly, and I'd rather
He said it for himself. I see him there,
Bringing a stone grasped firmly by the top
In each hand, like an old-stone savage
    armed.   40
He moves in darkness as it seems to me,
Not of woods only and the shade of trees.
He will not go behind his father's saying,
And he likes having thought of it so well
He says again, "Good fences make good
    neighbours."   45

The Pasture

(ca. 1912)

I'm going out to clean the pasture spring;
I'll only stop to rake the leaves away
(And wait to watch the water clear, I may):
I sha'n't be gone long. — You come too.

I'm going out to fetch the little calf   5
That's standing by the mother. It's so
    young,
It totters when she licks it with her tongue.
I sha'n't be gone long. — You come too.

Home Burial

(1913)

He saw her from the bottom of the stairs
Before she saw him. She was starting down,
Looking back over her shoulder at some
    fear.
She took a doubtful step and then undid it
To raise herself and look again. He spoke   5
Advancing toward her: "What is it you see
From up there always — for I want to know."
She turned and sank upon her skirts at that,
And her face changed from terrified to dull.
He said to gain time: "What is it you see,"   10
Mounting until she cowered under him.
"I will find out now — you must tell me,
    dear."
She, in her place, refused him any help
With the least stiffening of her neck and
    silence.
She let him look, sure that he wouldn't see,   15
Blind creature; and a while he didn't see.
But at last he murmured, "Oh," and again,
    "Oh."

"What is it — what?" she said.

              "Just that I see."

"You don't," she challenged. "Tell me what
    it is."   20

"The wonder is I didn't see at once.
I never noticed it from here before.
I must be wonted to it — that's the reason.

The little graveyard where my people are!
So small the window frames the whole of it.
Not so much larger than a bedroom, is it?   26
There are three stones of slate and one of
    marble,
Broad-shouldered little slabs there in the
    sunlight
On the sidehill. We haven't to mind *those*.
But I understand: it is not the stones,   30
But the child's mound — "

    "Don't, don't, don't, don't," she cried.

She withdrew shrinking from beneath his
    arm
That rested on the banister, and slid down-
    stairs;
And turned on him with such a daunting
    look,   35
He said twice over before he knew himself:
"Can't a man speak of his own child he's
    lost?"

"Not you! Oh, where's my hat? Oh, I don't
    need it!
I must get out of here. I must get air.
I don't know rightly whether any man can."

"Amy! Don't go to someone else this time.   41
Listen to me. I won't come down the stair."
He sat and fixed his chin between his fists.
"There's something I should like to ask you,
    dear."

"You don't know how to ask it."   45

              "Help me, then."

Her fingers moved the latch for all reply.

"My words are nearly always an offence.
I don't know how to speak of anything
So as to please you. But I might be taught
I should suppose. I can't say I see how.   51
A man must partly give up being a man
With women-folk. We could have some
    arrangement
By which I'd bind myself to keep hands off
Anything special you're a-mind to name.
Though I don't like such things 'twixt those
    that love.   56
Two that don't love can't live together
    without them.

But two that do can't live together with
    them."
She moved the latch a little. "Don't — don't
    go
Don't carry it to someone else this time. 60
Tell me about it if it's something human.
Let me into your grief. I'm not so much
Unlike other folks as your standing there
Apart would make me out. Give me my
    chance.
I do think, though, you overdo it a little. 65
What was it brought you up to think it the
    thing
To take your mother-loss of a first child
So inconsolably — in the face of love.
You'd think his memory might be
    satisfied — "

"There you go sneering now!"   70

            "I'm not, I'm not!
You make me angry. I'll come down to you.
God, what a woman! And it's come to this,
A man can't speak of his own child that's
    dead."

"You can't because you don't know how to
    speak.   75
If you had any feelings, you that dug
With your own hand — how could you? —
    his little grave;
I saw you from that very window there,
Making the gravel leap and leap in air,
Leap up, like that, like that, and land so
    lightly   80
And roll back down the mound beside the
    hole.
I thought, Who is that man? I didn't know
    you.
And I crept down the stairs and up the
    stairs
To look again, and still your spade kept
    lifting.
Then you came in. I heard your rumbling
    voice   85
Out in the kitchen, and I don't know why,
But I went near to see with my own eyes.
You could sit there with the stains on your
    shoes
Of the fresh earth from your own baby's
    grave
And talk about your everyday concerns. 90

You had stood the spade up against the wall
Outside there in the entry, for I saw it."

"I shall laugh the worst laugh I ever
    laughed.
I'm cursed. God, if I don't believe I'm
    cursed."   94
"I can repeat the very words you were saying.
"Three foggy mornings and one rainy day
Will rot the best birch fence a man can
    build."
Think of it, talk like that at such a time!
What had how long it takes a birch to rot
To do with what was in the darkened parlor.
You *couldn't* care! The nearest friends can
    go   101
With any one to death, comes so far short
They might as well not try to go at all.
No, from the time when one is sick to
    death,
One is alone, and he dies more alone.   105
Friends make pretence of following to the
    grave,
But before one is in it, their minds are
    turned
And making the best of their way back to
    life
And living people, and things they under-
    stand.   109
But the world's evil. I won't have grief so
If I can change it. Oh, I won't, I won't!"

"There, you have said it all and you feel
    better.
You won't go now. You're crying. Close the
    door.
The heart's gone out of it: why keep it
    up.
Amy! There's someone coming down the
    road!"   115

"*You* — oh, you think the talk is all. I must
    go —
Somewhere out of this house. How can I
    make you — "

"If — you — do!" She was opening the door
    wider.
"Where do you mean to go? First tell me
    that.
I'll follow and bring you back by force. I
    will! — "   120

The Black Cottage

(1914)

We chanced in passing by that afternoon
To catch it in a sort of special picture
Among tar-banded ancient cherry trees,
Set well back from the road in rank lodged
    grass,
The little cottage we were speaking of,   5
A front with just a door between two win-
    dows,
Fresh painted by the shower a velvet black.
We paused, the minister and I, to look.
He made as if to hold it at arm's length
Or put the leaves aside that framed it in.   10
"Pretty," he said. "Come in. No one will
    care."
The path was a vague parting in the grass
That led us to a weathered window-sill.
We pressed our faces to the pane. "You see,"
    he said,
"Everything's as she left it when she died.   15
Her sons won't sell the house or the things
    in it.
They say they mean to come and summer here
Where they were boys. They haven't come
    this year.
They live so far away — one is out West —
It will be hard for them to keep their word.   20
Anyway they won't have the place disturbed."
A buttoned hair-cloth lounge spread scrolling
    arms
Under a crayon portrait on the wall
Done sadly from an old daguerreotype.
"That was the father as he went to war.   25
She always, when she talked about war,
Sooner or later came and leaned, half knelt,
Against the lounge beside it, though I doubt
If such unlifelike lines kept power to stir
Anything in her after all the years.   30
He fell at Gettysburg or Fredericksburg,
I ought to know — it makes a difference
    which:
Fredericksburg wasn't Gettysburg, of course.
But what I'm getting to is how forsaken
A little cottage this has always seemed;   35
Since she went more than ever, but before —
I don't mean altogether by the lives
That had gone out of it, the father first,
Then the two sons, till she was left alone.
(Nothing could draw her after those two
    sons.   40

She valued the considerate neglect
She had at some cost taught them after years.)
I mean by the world's having passed it by —
As we almost got by this afternoon.
It always seems to me a sort of mark   45
To measure how far fifty years have brought
    us.
Why not sit down if you are in no haste?
These doorsteps seldom have a visitor.
The warping boards pull out their own old
    nails
With none to tread and put them in their
    place.   50
She had her own idea of things, the old lady.
And she liked talk. She had seen Garrison
And Whittier, and had her story of them.
One wasn't long in learning that she thought
Whatever else the Civil War was for   55
It wasn't just to keep the States together,
Nor just to free the slaves, though it did both.
She wouldn't have believed those ends enough
To have given outright for them all she gave.
Her giving somehow touched the principle   60
That all men are created free and equal.
And to hear her quaint phrases — so removed
From the world's view today of all those
    things.
That's a hard mystery of Jefferson's.
What did he mean? Of course the easy way   65
Is to decide it simply isn't true.
It may not be. I heard a fellow say so.
But never mind, the Welshman got it planted
Where it will trouble us a thousand years.
Each age will have to reconsider it.   70
You couldn't tell her what the West was
    saying,
And what the South to her serene belief.
She had some art of hearing and yet not
Hearing the latter wisdom of the world.
White was the only race she ever knew.   75
Black she had scarcely seen, and yellow never.
But how could they be made so very unlike
By the same hand working in the same stuff?
She had supposed the war decided that.
What are you going to do with such a person?
Strange how such innocence gets its own
    way.   81
I shouldn't be surprised if in this world
It were the force that would at last prevail.
Do you know but for her there was a time
When to please younger members of the
    church,   85

Or rather say non-members in the church,
Whom we all have to think of nowadays,
I would have changed the Creed a very
    little?
Not that she ever had to ask me not to;
It never got so far as that; but the bare
    thought   90
Of her old tremulous bonnet in the pew,
And of her half asleep was too much for me.
Why, I might wake her up and startle her.
It was the words "descended into Hades"
That seemed too pagan to our liberal youth. 95
You know they suffered from a general on-
    slaught.
And well, if they weren't true, why keep right
    on
Saying them like the heathen? We could drop
    them.
Only — there was the bonnet in the pew.
Such a phrase couldn't have meant much to
    her.   100
But suppose she had missed it from the Creed
As a child misses the unsaid Good-night,
And falls asleep with heartache—how should
    I feel?
I'm just as glad she made me keep hands off,
For, dear me, why abandon a belief   105
Merely because it ceases to be true.
Cling to it long enough, and not a doubt
It will turn true again, for so it goes.
Most of the change we think we see in life
Is due to truths being in and out of favor. 110
As I sit here, and oftentimes, I wish
I could be monarch of a desert land
I could devote and dedicate forever
To the truths we keep coming back and back
    to.
So desert it would have to be, so walled   115
By mountain ranges half in summer snow,
No one would covet it or think it worth
The pains of conquering to force change on.
Scattered oases where men dwelt, but mostly
Sand dunes held closely in tamarisk   120
Blown over and over themselves in idleness.
Sand grains should sugar in the natal dew
The babe born to the desert, the sand storm
Retard mid-waste my cowering caravans ——

"There are bees in this wall." He struck the
    clapboards,   125
Fierce heads looked out; small bodies pivoted.
We rose to go. Sunset blazed on the windows.

Birches
(*1915*)

When I see birches bend to left and right
Across the line of straighter darker trees,
I like to think some boy's been swinging
    them.
But swinging doesn't bend them down to
    stay.
Ice-storms do that. Often you must have
    seen them   5
Loaded with ice a sunny winter morning
After a rain. They click upon themselves
As the breeze rises, and turn many-colored
As the stir cracks and crazes their enamel.
Soon the sun's warmth makes them shed
    crystal shells   10
Shattering and avalanching on the snow-
    crust —
Such heaps of broken glass to sweep away
You'd think the inner dome of heaven had
    fallen.
They are dragged to the withered bracken by
    the load,
And they seem not to break; though once
    they are bowed   15
So low for long, they never right themselves:
You may see their trunks arching in the
    woods
Years afterwards, trailing their leaves on
    the ground
Like girls on hands and knees that throw
    their hair
Before them over their heads to dry in the
    sun.   20
But I was going to say when Truth broke in
With all her matter-of-fact about the ice-
    storm
(Now am I free to be poetical?)
I should prefer to have some boy bend them
As he went out and in to fetch the cows — 25
Some boy too far from town to learn baseball,
Whose only play was what he found himself,
Summer or winter, and could play alone.
One by one he subdued his father's trees
By riding them down over and over again   30
Until he took the stiffness out of them,
And not one but hung limp, not one was
    left
For him to conquer. He learned all there
    was
To learn about not launching out too soon

And so not carrying the tree away   35
Clear to the ground. He always kept his
          poise
To the top branches, climbing carefully
With the same pains you use to fill a
          cup
Up to the brim, and even above the brim.
Then he flung outward, feet first, with a
          swish,   40
Kicking his way down through the air to the
          ground.
So was I once myself a swinger of birches.
And so I dream of going back to be.
It's when I'm weary of considerations,
And life is too much like a pathless wood   45
Where your face burns and tickles with the
          cobwebs
Broken across it, and one eye is weeping
From a twig's having lashed across it open.
I'd like to get away from earth awhile
And then come back to it and begin over.   50
May no fate wilfully misunderstand me
And half grant what I wish and snatch me
          away
Not to return. Earth's the right place for
          love:
I don't know where it's likely to go better.
I'd like to go by climbing a birch tree,   55
And climb black branches up a snow-white
          trunk
Toward heaven, till the tree could bear no
          more,
But dipped its top and set me down again.
That would be good both going and coming
          back.
One could do worse than be a swinger of
          birches.   60

The Road Not Taken

(1915)

Two roads diverged in a yellow wood,
And sorry I could not travel both
And be one traveler, long I stood
And looked down one as far as I could
To where it bent in the undergrowth;   5

Then took the other, as just as fair,
And having perhaps the better claim,
Because it was grassy and wanted wear;

Though as for that the passing there
Had worn them really about the same,   10

And both that morning equally lay
In leaves no step had trodden black.
Oh, I kept the first for another day!
Yet knowing how way leads on to way,
I doubted if I should ever come back.   15

I shall be telling this with a sigh
Somewhere ages and ages hence:
Two roads diverged in a wood, and I —
I took the one less traveled by,
And that has made all the difference.   20

An Old Man's Winter Night

(1915)

All out-of-doors looked darkly in at him
Through the thin frost, almost in separate
          stars,
That gathers on the pane in empty rooms.
What kept his eyes from giving back the gaze
Was the lamp tilted near them in his hand.   5
What kept him from remembering the need
That brought him to that creaking room was
          age.
He stood with barrels round him — at a loss.
And having scared the cellar under him
In clomping there, he scared it once again   10
In clomping off: — and scared the outer
          night,
Which has its sounds, familiar, like the roar
Of trees and crack of branches, common
          things,
But nothing so like beating on a box.
A light he was to no one but himself   15
Where now he sat, concerned with he knew
          what,
A quiet light, and then not even that.
He consigned to the moon, such as she was,
So late-arising, to the broken moon
As better than the sun in any case   20
For such a charge, his snow upon the roof,
His icicles along the wall to keep;
And slept. The log that shifted with a jolt
Once in the stove, disturbed him and he
          shifted,
And eased his heavy breathing, but still
          slept.   25

One aged man — one man — can't fill a
　　house,
A farm, a countryside, or if he can,
It's thus he does it of a winter night

Not to Keep

(*1915*)

They sent him back to her. The letter came
Saying . . . And she could have him. And
　　before
She could be sure there was no hidden ill
Under the formal writing, he was in her
　　sight,
Living. They gave him back to her alive —
How else? They are not known to send the
　　dead —　　　　　　　　　　　　　　　　6
And not disfigured visibly. His face?
His hands? She has to look, to ask,
"What is it, dear?" And she has given all
And still she had all — *they* had — they the
　　lucky!　　　　　　　　　　　　　　　10
Wasn't she glad now? Everything seemed
　　won,
And all the rest for them permissible ease.
She had to ask, "What was it, dear?"
　　　　　　　　　　　　　　　　　"Enough,
Yet not enough. A bullet through and
　　through,
High in the breast. Nothing but what good
　　care　　　　　　　　　　　　　　　15
And medicine and rest, and you a week,
Can cure me of to go again." The same
Grim giving to do over for them both.
She dared no more than ask him with her
　　eyes
How was it with him for a second trial.　20
And with his eyes he asked her not to ask.
They had given him back to her, but not to
　　keep.

Fire and Ice

(*ca. 1919*)

Some say the world will end in fire,
Some say in ice.
From what I've tasted of desire
I hold with those who favor fire.

But if it had to perish twice,
I think I know enough of hate
To say that for destruction ice
Is also great
And would suffice.

Stopping by Woods on a Snowy Evening

(*1923*)

Whose woods these are I think I know.
His house is in the village though;
He will not see me stopping here
To watch his woods fill up with snow.

My little horse must think it queer　　　5
To stop without a farmhouse near
Between the woods and frozen lake
The darkest evening of the year.

He gives his harness bells a shake
To ask if there is some mistake.　　　　10
The only other sound's the sweep
Of easy wind and downy flake.

The woods are lovely, dark and deep.
But I have promises to keep,
And miles to go before I sleep,　　　　15
And miles to go before I sleep.

Once by the Pacific

(1926)

The shattered water made a misty din.
Great waves looked over others coming in,
And thought of doing something to the shore
That water never did to land before.
The clouds were low and hairy in the skies,　5
Like locks blown forward in the gleam of
　　eyes.
You could not tell, and yet it looked as if
The shore was lucky in being backed by cliff,
The cliff in being backed by continent;
It looked as if a night of dark intent　　10
Was coming, and not only a night, an age.
Someone had better be prepared for rage.
There would be more than ocean-water
　　broken
Before God's last *Put out the Light* was spoken.

Come In
(1942)

As I came to the edge of the woods,
Thrush music — hark!
Now if it was dusk outside,
Inside it was dark.

Too dark in the woods for a bird   5
By sleight of wing
To better its perch for the night,
Though it still could sing.

The last of the light of the sun
That had died in the west   10
Still lived for one song more
In a thrush's breast.

Far in the pillared dark
Thrush music went —
Almost like a call to come in   15
To the dark and lament.

But no, I was out for stars:
I would not come in.
I meant not even if asked;
And I hadn't been.   20

EZRA POUND (1885–   )

Of New England stock (distantly related to Longfellow), Pound was born in Idaho and brought up in the East. He studied at the University of Pennsylvania and Hamilton College, taught Romance languages at Pennsylvania, went abroad to get material for a thesis on Lope de Vega. For a few months, in 1907, he taught at Wabash College, Indiana, then returned to Europe, where he lived subsequently — in England, France, Italy. He associated himself with Fascism in Italy. In consequence of his radio broadcasts during the war, he was captured in May, 1945, indicted for treason, flown to the United States, but pronounced "insane and mentally unfit for trial."

In 1908 he published in Venice his first book of poems, *A Lume Spento*, and in 1909 he published in London his *Personae*. In the same year he was foregathering with a group led by T. E. Hulme, who, reacting against the enfeebled romantic tradition of poetry, felt the need of a severe discipline in "accurate, precise, and definite description" and a mode of poetic speech reflecting the complicated modern mind. Pound proceeded to make himself champion of the school of "Imagists" (he is said to have invented the name), and from this time on was active in ever changing poetic speculation, experiment, and propaganda.

He edited a volume, *Des Imagistes*, 1914, of the writing of this school of poets, and the same year became editor of *Blast*, a magazine of the still newer school of "Vorticists." From 1912 to 1919 he served as foreign correspondent of *Poetry: a Magazine of Verse*, which Harriet Monroe was starting at Chicago at this time. To her he sent some of his own work and verse by other American poets not yet recognized, such as Frost, "H. D.," Eliot, as well as non-American writers who had a great reputation ahead, such as Lawrence, Tagore, Yeats, Joyce. Himself the author of *Cathay*, 1915, he stimulated the popularity of Chinese and Japanese poetry.

In short, the value of Pound's poetic achievement seems overshadowed by his remarkable service in discovering fresh talent, winning recognition for it, and impregnating other writers with his successive theories of verse. Among Americans who felt his influence strongly were T. S. Eliot, Archibald MacLeish, and Hart Crane. His winning of the Bollingen poetry award in 1949 was both attacked and defended. The whole episode, which is a significant commentary on the relation between art and politics, is reviewed in *The Case Against the Saturday Review*, 1950, and Archibald MacLeish (a member of the Bollingen award committee), *Poetry and Opinion*, 1950.

T. S. Eliot edited Pound's *Selected Poems*, 1928, and wrote *Ezra Pound: His Metric and Poetry*, 1917. Pound's *Letters*, 1950, have been edited by D. D. Paige. Other interpretive comments may be found in G. Hughes, *Imagism and the Imagists*, 1931; F. R. Leavis, *New Bearings in English Poetry*, 1932; R. P. Blackmur, *The Double Agent*, 1935; Peter Russell, ed., *An Examination of Ezra Pound*, 1950.

A Virginal

(1912)

No, no! Go from me. I have left her lately.
I will not spoil my sheath with lesser bright-
    ness,
For my surrounding air has a new lightness;
Slight are her arms, yet they have bound me
    straitly
And left me cloaked as with a gauze of ether; 5
As with sweet leaves; as with a subtle clear-
    ness.
Oh, I have picked up magic in her nearness
To sheathe me half in half the things that
    sheathe her.

No, no! Go from me. I have still the flavor,
Soft as spring wind that's come from birchen
    bowers.   10
Green come the shoots, aye April in the
    branches,
As winter's wound with her sleight hand she
    staunches,
Hath of the trees a likeness of the savor:
As white their bark, so white this lady's
    hours.

The River Merchant's Wife

A LETTER

(1916)

A translation from Li Po (701–762). With him, Pound says, "the visual art in poetry reached its zenith."

While my hair was still cut straight across my
    forehead
I played about the front gate, pulling flowers.

You came by on bamboo stilts, playing horse,
You walked about my seat, playing with
    blue plums.
And we went on living in the village of
    Chokan: 5
Two small people, without dislike or sus-
    picion.

At fourteen I married My Lord you.
I never laughed, being bashful.
Lowering my head, I looked at the wall.
Called to, a thousand times, I never looked
    back.   10

At fifteen I stopped scowling,
I desired my dust to be mingled with yours
For ever and for ever and for ever.
Why should I climb the look out?

At sixteen you departed,   15
You went into far Ku-to-yen, by the river
    of swirling eddies,
And you have been gone five months.
The monkeys make sorrowful noise overhead.
You dragged your feet when you went out.
By the gate now, the moss is grown, the
    different mosses,   20
Too deep to clear them away!

The leaves fall early this autumn, in wind.
The paired butterflies are already yellow
    with August
Over the grass in the West garden;
They hurt me. I grow older.   25
If you are coming down through the narrows
    of the river Kiang,
Please let me know beforehand,
And I will come out to meet you
                As far as Cho-fu-Sa.
                                    By Rihaku.

From Hugh Selwyn Mauberley

LIFE AND CONTACTS

(1920)

"Pound's major work," says F. B. Millett, "lies in a series of such poems as *Hugh Selwyn Mauberly* (1920), and the *Cantos* which began appearing in 1925. In the Mauberley series, Pound reveals those characteristic devices which have been most widely imitated. Here he sets himself the task of turning into poetry the modern personality and its situation in the contemporary world. Here there is no easy exoticism, no romantic suppression of elements that complicate or denigrate the mood of poetic elevation. Here he adopts the relaxed conversational manner, the tendency toward free association, the rich literary and cultural allusiveness, the conscious utilization of dissonance as an aesthetic principle — devices which were to have a tremendous influence on T. S. Eliot and his followers. These devices are carried much further in the *Cantos*, a formidable series of poetic fragments which constitute as amazing a poetic autobiography as any ever written."

Vocat Aestus in Umbram

Nemesianus Ec. IV.

1

E. P. Ode pour l' Election de son Sepulchre

For three years, out of key with his time,
He strove to resuscitate the dead art
Of poetry; to maintain "the sublime"
In the old sense. Wrong from the start —

No, hardly, but seeing he had been born   5
In a half-savage country, out of date;
Bent resolutely on wringing lilies from the
　　acorn;
Capaneus; trout for factitious bait;
Ἴδμεν γάρ τοι πάνθ᾽, ὅσ᾽ ἐνὶ Τροίῃ[1]
Caught in the unstopped ear;   10
Giving the rocks small lee-way
The chopped seas held him, therefore, that
　　year.

His true Penelope was Flaubert,
He fished by obstinate isles;
Observed the elegance of Circe's hair   15
Rather than the mottoes on sun-dials.

[1] "For we know all the things that are in Troy."

Unaffected by "the march of events,"
He passed from men's memory in *l'an
　　trentiesme
De son eage*; the case presents
No adjunct to the Muses' diadem.   20

2

The age demanded an image
Of its accelerated grimace,
Something for the modern stage,
Not, at any rate, an Attic grace;

Not, not certainly, the obscure reveries   25
Of the inward gaze;
Better mendacities
Than the classics in paraphrase!

The "age demanded" chiefly a mould in
　　plaster,
Made with no loss of time,   30
A prose kinema, not, not assuredly, alabaster
Or the "sculpture" of rhyme.

3

The tea-rose tea-gown, etc.
Supplants the mousseline of Cos,
The pianola "replaces"   35
Sappho's barbitos.

Christ follows Dionysus,
Phallic and ambrosial
Made way for macerations;
Caliban casts out Ariel.   40

All things are a flowing,
Sage Heracleitus says;
But a tawdry cheapness
Shall outlast our days.

Even the Christian beauty   45
Defects — after Samothrace;
We see τὸ καλὸν
Decreed in the market-place.

Faun's flesh is not to us,
Nor the saint's vision.   50
We have the Press for wafer;
Franchise for circumcision.

All men, in law, are equals.
Free of Pisistratus,

We choose a knave or an eunuch   55
To rule over us.

O bright Apollo,

τίν' ἄνδρα, τίν' ἤρωα, τίνα θεόν[1]
What god, man, or hero
Shall I place a tin wreath upon!   60

4

These fought in any case,
and some believing,
        pro domo, in any case . . .

Some quick to arm,
some for adventure,   65
some from fear of weakness,
some from fear of censure,
some for love of slaughter, in imagination,
learning later . . .
some in fear, learning love of slaughter;   70

Died some, pro patria,
        non "dulce" non "et decor" . . .
walked eye-deep in hell
believing in old men's lies, then unbelieving
came home, home to a lie,   75
home to many deceits,
home to old lies and new infamy;
usury age-old and age-thick
and liars in public places.
Daring as never before, wastage as never
        before.   80
Young blood and high blood,
fair cheeks, and fine bodies;

fortitude as never before,

frankness as never before,
disillusions as never told in the old days,   85
hysterias, trench confessions,
laughter out of dead bellies.

5

There died a myriad,
And of the best, among them,
For an old bitch gone in the teeth,   90
For a botched civilization,

' "What man, what hero, what god."

Charm, smiling at the good mouth,
Quick eyes gone under earth's lid,

For two gross of broken statues,
For a few thousand battered books.   95

Canto I
(1924)

1

And then went down to the ship,
Set keel to breakers, forth on the godly sea, and
We set up mast and sail on that swart ship,
Bore sheep aboard her, and our bodies also
Heavy with weeping, and winds from stern-
        ward   5
Bore us out onward with bellying canvas,
Circe's this craft, the trim-coifed goddess.
Then sat we amidships, wind jamming the
        tiller,
Thus with stretched sail, we went over sea
        till day's end.
Sun to his slumber, shadows o'er all the
        ocean,   10
Came we then to the bounds of deepest water,
To the Kimmerian lands, and peopled cities
Covered with close-webbed mist, unpierced
        ever
With glitter of sun-rays
Nor with stars stretched, nor looking back
        from heaven   15
Swartest night stretched over wretched men
        there.
The ocean flowing backward, came we then
        to the place
Aforesaid by Circe.
Here did they rites, Perimedes and Eurylochus,
And drawing sword from my hip   20
I dug the ell-square pitkin;
Poured we libations unto each the dead,
First mead and then sweet wine, water mixed
        with white flour.
Then prayed I many a prayer to the sickly
        death's-heads;
As set in Ithaca, sterile bulls of the best   25
For sacrifice, heaping the pyre with goods,
A sheep to Tiresias only, black and a bell-
        sheep.
Dark blood flowed in the fosse,
Souls out of Erebus, cadaverous dead, of
        brides

Of youths and of the old who had borne
    much;   30
Souls stained with recent tears, girls tender,
Men many, mauled with bronze lance heads,
Battle spoil, bearing yet dreary arms,
These many crowded about me; with shouting,
Pallor upon me, cried to my men for more
    beasts;   35
Slaughtered the herds, sheep slain of bronze;
Poured ointment, cried to the gods,

To Pluto the strong, and praised Proserpine;
Unsheathed the narrow sword,
I sat to keep off the impetuous impotent
    dead,   40
Till I should hear Tiresias.
But first Elpenor came, our friend Elpenor,
Unburied, cast on the wide earth,
Limbs that we left in the house of Circe,
Unwept, unwrapped in sepulchre, since toils
    urged other.   45
Pitiful spirit. And I cried in hurried speech:
"Elpenor, how art thou come to this dark
    coast?
"Cam'st thou afoot, outstripping seamen?"
    And he in heavy speech:
"Ill fate and abundant wine. I slept in Circe's
    ingle.   50
"Going down the long ladder unguarded,
"I fell against the buttress,
"Shattered the nape-nerve, the soul sought
    Avernus.
"But thou, O King, I bid remember me,
    unwept, unburied,
"Heap up mine arms, be tomb by sea-bord,
    and inscribed: 55
"*A man of no fortune, and with a name to come.*
"And set my oar up, that I swung mid fellows."

And Anticlea came, whom I beat off, and then
    Tiresias Theban,
Holding his golden wand, knew me, and
    spoke first:
"A second time? why? man of ill star,   60
"Facing the sunless dead and this joyless
    region?
"Stand from the fosse, leave me my bloody
    bever
"For soothsay."
    And I stepped back,
And he strong with the blood, said then:
    "Odysseus   65

"Shalt return through spiteful Neptune, over
    dark seas,
"Lose all companions." And then Anticlea
    came.
Lie quiet Divus. I mean, that is Andreas
    Divus,
In officina Wecheli, 1538, out of Homer.
And he sailed, by Sirens and thence outward
    and away   70
And unto Circe.
    Venerandam,
In the Cretan's phrase, with the golden crown,
    Aphrodite,
Cypri munimenta sortita est, mirthful, ori-
    calchi, with golden
Girdles and breast bands, thou with dark eye-
    lids   75
Bearing the golden bough of Argicida. So that:

2

Hang it all, Robert Browning,
    there can be but the one "Sordello."
But Sordello, and my Sordello?
    Lo Sordels si fo di Mantovana.   5
So-shu churned in the sea.
Seal sports in the spray-whited circles of
    cliff-wash,
Sleek head, daughter of Lir,
    eyes of Picasso
Under black fur-hood, lithe daughter of
    Ocean;
And the wave runs in the beach-groove: 10
"Eleanor, ἑλέναυς and ἑλέπτολις"[1]
    And poor old Homer blind, blind, as a bat,
Ear, ear for the sea-surge, murmur of old
    men's voices:
"Let her go back to the ships,
Back among Grecian faces, lest evil come on
    our own,   15
Evil and further evil, and a curse cursed on
    our children,
Moves, yes she moves like a goddess
And has the face of a god
    and the voice of Schoeney's daughters,
And doom goes with her in walking,   20
Let her go back to the ships,
    back among Grecian voices."
And by the beach-run, Tyro,
    Twisted arms of the sea-god,

[1] "A hell to ships, a hell to cities," Æschylus, *Agamemnon.* The epithet was applied, with a pun, to
Helen.

Lithe sinews of water, gripping her,
    cross-hold,   25
And the blue-gray glass of the wave tents
    them,
Glare azure of water, cold-welter, close
    cover.

Quiet sun-tawny sand-stretch,
The gulls broad out their wings,
    nipping between the splay feathers;   30
Snipe come for their bath,
    bend out their wing-joints,
Spread wet wings to the sun-film,
And by Scios,
    to left of the Naxos passage,   35
Naviform rock overgrown,
    algæ cling to its edge,
There is a wine-red glow in the shallows,
    a tin flash in the sun-dazzle.

The ship landed in Scios,   40
    men wanting spring-water,
And by the rock-pool a young boy loggy
    with vine-must,
"To Naxos? Yes, we'll take you to Naxos,
Com' along lad." "Not that way!"
"Aye, that way is Naxos."   45
    And I said: "It's a straight ship."
And an ex-convict out of Italy
    knocked me into the fore-stays,
(He was wanted for manslaughter in Tuscany)
    And the whole twenty against me,   50
Mad for a little slave money.
    And they took her out of Scios
And off her course . . .
    And the boy came to, again, with the
    racket,
And looked out over the bows,   55
    and to eastward, and to the Naxos
    passage.
    God-sleight then, god-sleight:
    Ship stock fast in sea-swirl,
Ivy upon the oars, King Pentheus,
    grapes with no seed but sea-foam,   60
Ivy in scupper-hole.
Aye, I, Accetes, stood there,
    and the god stood by me,
Water cutting under the keel,
Sea-break from stern forrards,   65
    wake running off from the bow,
And where was gunwale, there now was
    vine-trunk,

And tenthril where cordage had been,
    grape-leaves on the rowlocks,
Heavy vine on the oarshafts,   70
And, out of nothing, a breathing,
    hot breath on my ankles,
Beasts like shadows in glass,
    a furred tail upon nothingness.
Lynx-purr, and heathery smell of beasts,   75
    where tar smell had been,
Sniff and pad-foot of beasts,
    eye-glitter out of black air.
The sky overshot, dry, with no tempest,
Sniff and pad-foot of beasts,   80
    fur brushing my knee-skin,
Rustle of airy sheaths,
    dry forms in the *aether*.
And the ship like a keel in ship-yard,
    slung like an ox in smith's sling,   85
Ribs stuck fast in the ways,
    grape-cluster over pin-rack,
    void air taking pelt.
Lifeless air become sinewed,
    feline leisure of panthers,   90
Leopards sniffing the grape shoots by
    scupper-hole,
Crouched panthers by fore-hatch,
And the sea blue-deep about us,
    green-ruddy in shadows,
And Lyæus: "From now, Accetes, my
    altars,   95
Fearing no bondage,
    fearing no cat of the wood,
Safe with my lynxes,
    feeding grapes to my leopards,
Olibanum is my incense,   100
    the vines grow in my homage."

The back-swell now smooth in the rudder-
    chains,
Black snout of a porpoise
    where Lycabs had been,
Fish-scales on the oarsmen.   105
    And I worship.
I have seen what I have seen.
    When they brought the boy I said:
"He has a god in him,
    though I do not know which god."   110
And they kicked me into the fore-stays.
I have seen what I have seen:
    Medon's face like the face of a dory,
Arms shrunk into fins. And you, Pen-
    theus,

Had as well listen to Tiresias, and to Cad-
    mus,   115
    or your luck will go out of you.
Fish-scales over groin muscles,
    lynx-purr amid sea . . .
And of a later year,
    pale in the wine-red algæ,   120
If you will lean over the rock,
    the coral face under wave-tinge,
Rose-paleness under water-shift,
    Ileuthyeria, fair Dafne of sea-bords,
The swimmer's arms turned to branches,   125
Who will say in what year,
    fleeing what band of tritons,
The smooth brows, seen, and half seen,
    now ivory stillness.

And So-shu churned in the sea, So-shu also,130
    using the long moon for a churn-stick . . .
Lithe turning of water,
    sinews of Poseidon,
Black azure and hyaline,
    glass wave over Tyro,   135
Close cover, unstillness,
    bright welter of wave-cords,

Then quiet water,
    quiet in the buff sands,
Sea-fowl stretching wing-joints,   140
    splashing in rock-hollows and sand-
    hollows
In the wave-runs by the half-dune;
Glass-glint of wave in the tide-rips against
    sunlight,
    pallor of Hesperus,
Gray peak of the wave,   145
    wave, colour of grape's pulp.

Olive gray in the near,
    far, smoke gray of the rock-slide,
Salmon-pink wings of the fish-hawk
    cast gray shadows in water,   150
The tower like a one-eyed great goose
    cranes up out of the olive-grove,

And we have heard the fauns chiding Proteus
    in the smell of hay under the olive-trees,
And the frogs singing against the fauns in
    the half-light.   155
And . . .

VACHEL LINDSAY (1879–1931)

Born in Springfield, Illinois, in a house where parties had been given to Abraham Lincoln, Nicholas Vachel Lindsay read voraciously in Rawlinson's *History of Egypt* and the "complete works, criticism and all," of Poe while he was being educated in the public schools of the town. Destined by his mother to be an artist, he went from Hiram College to the Chicago Art Institute and the New York School of Art. Five years of this directed his æsthetic passions. In 1905 he indulged another passion, an ardor for reform; for four years he lectured for the Y. M. C. A. and one more for the Anti-Saloon League. Meanwhile, he was expressing a third kind of passion, a novel kind of vagabondage that involved the other two passions — long tramps in which he preached Ruskin's and Morris's gospel of beauty through the country, distributing, in his dual capacity of missionary and minstrel, a little pamphlet of *Rhymes to be Traded for Bread*. The Western preaching tour took place in 1912. In the autumn of that year the magazine *Poetry* began publication in Chicago and Vachel Lindsay was, as Miss Monroe said, "one of its first discoveries." "General William Booth Enters into Heaven" was the first poem in the issue of January, 1913. The poem was republished this same year in a volume entitled *General William Booth Enters into Heaven, and Other Poems*, but failed of wide popularity. When *The Congo and Other Poems* appeared in 1914, Lindsay found himself a poet of national reputation.

He read much of his work aloud, or rather spoke-and-sang it, with great effect, in the course of several "national reciting tours." He believed that poetry, instead of being merely read by the eye, should be spoken-and-sung after a fashion suggested by ancient Greek lyric recitation and modern American vaudeville. Still better, he declared, is a whispered reading, for "All poetry is first and last for the inner ear, and its final pleasures are for the soul, whispering in solitude."

The Chinese Nightingale and Other Poems (1917) was another popular volume. Other publications before his sudden death in 1931 were: The Daniel Jazz and Other Poems (1920), The Golden Whales of California (1920), The Candle and the Cabin (1926), Johnny Appleseed (1928), and Every Soul is a Circus (1929), all in verse; and Adventures while Preaching the Gospel of Beauty (1914), A Handy Guide for Beggars (1916), The Golden Book of Springfield (1920), and The Litany of Washington Street (1929), all in prose.

A volume of Selected Poems appeared in 1929, and his work has several times been collected. On his life there is an Autobiographical Foreword in his Collected Poems, 1923, and a book by E. L. Masters, Vachel Lindsay: a Poet in America, 1935. Critical studies have been written by C. Aiken, Skepticisms, 1919; T. K. Whipple, Spokesmen, 1928; L. Untermeyer, American Poetry since 1900, 1923. Other references are given in F. B. Millett, Contemporary American Authors, 1940.

General William Booth Enters into Heaven

(1912)

[To be sung to the tune of The Blood of the Lamb with indicated instrument]

I

[Bass drum beaten loudly.]
Booth led boldly with his big bass drum —
(Are you washed in the blood of the Lamb?)
The Saints smiled gravely and they said:
    "He's come."
(Are you washed in the blood of the Lamb?)

Walking lepers followed, rank on rank,   5
Lurching bravoes from the ditches dank,
Drabs from the alleyways and drug fiends
    pale —
Minds still passion-ridden, soul-powers
    frail: —
Vermin-eaten saints with mouldy breath,   9
Unwashed legions with the ways of Death —
(Are you washed in the blood of the Lamb?)

[Banjos.]
Every slum had sent its half-a-score
The round world over. (Booth had groaned
    for more.)
Every banner that the wide world flies

Bloomed with glory and transcendent dyes.   15
Big-voiced lassies made their banjos bang,
Tranced, fanatical they shrieked and sang: —
"Are you washed in the blood of the Lamb?"

Hallelujah! It was queer to see
Bull-necked convicts with that land make
    free.   20
Loons with trumpets blowed a blare, blare,
    blare
On, on upward thro' the golden air!
(Are you washed in the blood of the
    Lamb?)

II

[Bass drum slower and softer.]
Booth died blind and still by Faith he trod,
Eyes still dazzled by the ways of God.   25
Booth led boldly, and he looked the chief,
Eagle countenance in sharp relief,
Beard a-flying, air of high command
Unabated in that holy land.

[Sweet flute music.]
Jesus came from out the court-house door, 30
Stretched his hands above the passing poor.
Booth saw not, but led his queer ones there
Round and round the mighty court-house
    square.

Yet in an instant all that blear review
Marched on spotless, clad in raiment new. 35
The lame were straightened, withered limbs
    uncurled
And blind eyes opened on a new, sweet
    world.

[Bass drum louder.]

Drabs and vixens in a flash made whole!
Gone was the weasel-head, the snout, the
    jowl!
Sages and sibyls now, and athletes clean, 40
Rulers of empires, and of forests green!

[Grand chorus of all instruments. Tam-
bourines to the foreground.]

The hosts were sandalled, and their wings
    were fire!
(Are you washed in the blood of the Lamb?)

But their noise played havoc with the angel-
    choir.
(Are you washed in the blood of the Lamb?) 45
O, shout Salvation! It was good to see
Kings and Princes by the Lamb set free.
The banjos rattled and the tambourines
Jing-jing-jingled in the hands of Queens.

[Reverently sung, no instruments.]

And when Booth halted by the curb for
    prayer   50
He saw his Master thro' the flag-filled air.
Christ came gently with a robe and crown
For Booth the soldier, while the throng
    knelt down.
He saw King Jesus. They were face to face,
And he knelt a-weeping in that holy place. 55
Are you washed in the blood of the Lamb?

The Congo

A STUDY OF THE NEGRO RACE

(1913–14)

I.   THEIR BASIC SAVAGERY

Fat black bucks in a wine-barrel room,
Barrel-house kings, with feet unstable,
Sagged and reeled and pounded on the table,
Pounded on the table,
Beat an empty barrel with the handle of a broom,   5
Hard as they were able,
Boom, boom, BOOM,
With a silk umbrella and the handle of a broom.
Boomlay, boomlay, boomlay, BOOM.
THEN I had religion, THEN I had a vision.   10
I could not turn from their revel in derision.
THEN I SAW THE CONGO, CREEPING THROUGH THE BLACK,   *More deliberate.*
CUTTING THROUGH THE FOREST WITH A GOLDEN TRACK.   *Solemnly*
Then along that riverbank   *chanted.*
A thousand miles   15
Tattooed cannibals danced in files;
Then I heard the boom of the blood-lust song
And a thigh-bone beating on a tin-pan gong.
And "BLOOD" screamed the whistles and the fifes of the warriors,   *A rapidly*
"BLOOD" screamed the skull-faced, lean witch-doctors,   20   *piling climax*
"Whirl ye the deadly voo-doo rattle,   *of speed and*
Harry the uplands,   *racket.*
Steal all the cattle,
Rattle-rattle, rattle-rattle,

A deep rolling bass

Bing!   25
Boomlay, boomlay, boomlay, Boom,"
A roaring, epic, rag-time tune   *With a philo-*
From the mouth of the Congo   *sophic pause.*
To the Mountains of the Moon.
Death is an Elephant,   30
Torch-eyed and horrible,
Foam-flanked and terrible.   *Shrilly and with*
                                                         a heavily ac-
Boom, steal the pygmies,   *cented meter.*
Boom, kill the Arabs,
Boom, kill the white men,   35
Hoo, Hoo, Hoo.   *Like the wind*
Listen to the yell of Leopold's ghost   *in the chimney.*
Burning in Hell for his hand-maimed host.
Hear how the demons chuckle and yell
Cutting his hands off, down in Hell.   40
Listen to the creepy proclamation,
Blown through the lairs of the forest-nation,
Blown past the white-ants' hill of clay,
Blown past the marsh where the butterflies play: —
"Be careful what you do,   45
Or Mumbo-Jumbo, God of the Congo,   *All the o sounds*
And all of the other   *very golden.*
Gods of the Congo   *Heavy accents*
Mumbo-Jumbo will hoo-doo you,   *very heavy.*
Mumbo-Jumbo will hoo-doo you,   50   *Light accents*
Mumbo-Jumbo will hoo-doo you."   *very light. Last*
                                                         line whispered.

II.   THEIR IRREPRESSIBLE HIGH SPIRITS

Wild crap-shooters with a whoop and a call   *Rather shrill*
Danced the juba in their gambling hall   *and high.*
And laughed fit to kill, and shook the town,
And guyed the policemen and laughed them down   55
With a boomlay, boomlay, boomlay, Boom.
THEN I SAW THE CONGO, CREEPING THROUGH THE BLACK,   *Read exactly as*
CUTTING THROUGH THE FOREST WITH A GOLDEN TRACK.   *in first section.*
A Negro fairyland swung into view,   *Lay   emphasis*
A minstrel river   60 *on the delicate*
Where dreams come true.   *ideas. Keep as*
The ebony palace soared on high   *light-footed   as*
Through the blossoming trees to the evening sky.   *possible.*
The inlaid porches and casements shone
With gold and ivory and elephant-bone.   65
And the black crowd laughed till their sides were sore
At the baboon butler in the agate door,
And the well-known tunes of the parrot band
That trilled on the bushes of that magic-land.

A troupe of skull-faced witch-men came   70
Through the agate doorway in suits of flame,   *With pomposity.*
Yea, long-tailed coats with a gold-leaf crust

And hats that were covered with diamond-dust.
And the crowd in the court gave a whoop and a call
And danced the juba from wall to wall.   75
But the witch-men suddenly stilled the throng
With a stern cold glare, and a stern old song: —
"Mumbo-Jumbo will hoo-doo you." . . .
Just then from the doorway, as fat as shotes,
Came the cake-walk princes in their long red coats,   80
Canes with a brilliant lacquer shine,
And tall silk hats that were red as wine.
And they pranced with their butterfly partners there,
Coal-black maidens with pearls in their hair,
Knee-skirts trimmed with the jessamine sweet,   85
And bells on their ankles and little black feet.
And the couples railed at the chant and the frown
Of the witch-men lean, and laughed them down.
(Oh, rare was the revel, and well worth while
That made those glowering witch-men smile.)   90

The cake-walk royalty then began
To walk for a cake that was tall as a man
To the tune of "Boomlay, boomlay, BOOM,"
While the witch-men laughed, with a sinister air,
And sang with the scalawags prancing there: —   95
"Walk with care, walk with care,
Or Mumbo-Jumbo, God of the Congo,
And all the other
Gods of the Congo,
Mumbo-Jumbo will hoo-doo you.   100
Beware, beware, walk with care,
Boomlay, boomlay, boomlay, boom.
Boomlay, boomlay, boomlay, boom,
Boomlay, boomlay, boomlay, boom,
Boomlay, boomlay, boomlay,   105
BOOM."
Oh, rare was the revel, and well worth while
That made those glowering witch-men smile.

With a great deliberation and ghostliness.

With overwhelming assurance, good cheer, and pomp.

With growing speed and sharply marked dance-rhythm.

With a touch of Negro dialect and as rapidly as possible toward the end

Slow philosophic calm.

III.   THE HOPE OF THEIR RELIGION

A good old Negro in the slums of the town
Preached at a sister for her velvet gown.   110
Howled at a brother for his low-down ways,
His prowling, guzzling, sneak-thief days.
Beat on the Bible till he wore it out,
Starting the jubilee revival shout.
And some had visions, as they stood on chairs,   115
And sang of Jacob, and the golden stairs.
And they all repented, a thousand strong,
From their stupor and savagery and sin and wrong
And slammed with their hymn books till they shook the room
With "Glory, glory, glory,"   120

Heavy bass. With a literal imitation of camp-meeting racket, and trance.

And "Boom, boom, Boom."
THEN I SAW THE CONGO, CREEPING THROUGH THE BLACK,

Exactly as in the first section.

CUTTING THROUGH THE JUNGLE WITH A GOLDEN TRACK.
And the gray sky opened like a new-rent veil
And showed the apostles with their coats of mail.   125
In bright white steel they were seated round
And their fire-eyes watched where the Congo wound.
And the twelve apostles, from their thrones on high,
Thrilled all the forest with their heavenly cry: —
"Mumbo-Jumbo will die in the jungle;   130
Never again will he hoo-doo you,
Never again will he hoo-doo you."

Sung to the tune of "Hark, ten thousand harps and voices."

Then along that river, a thousand miles,
The vine-snared trees fell down in files.

With growing deliberation and joy.

Pioneer angels cleared the way   135
For a Congo paradise, for babes at play,
For sacred capitals, for temples clean.
Gone were the skull-faced witch-men lean.
There, where the wild ghost-gods had wailed
A million boats of the angels sailed   140
With oars of silver, and prows of blue

In a rather high key — as delicately as possible.

And silken pennants that the sun shone through.
'Twas a land transfigured, 'twas a new creation.
Oh, a singing wind swept the Negro nation;
And on through the backwoods clearing flew: —   145
"Mumbo-Jumbo is dead in the jungle.
Never again will he hoo-doo you.
Never again will he hoo-doo you."

To the tune of "Hark, ten thousand harps and voices."

Redeemed were the forests, the beasts and the men,
And only the vulture dared again   150
By the far, lone mountains of the moon
To cry, in the silence, the Congo tune: —
"Mumbo-Jumbo will hoo-doo you,
Mumbo-Jumbo will hoo-doo you.
Mumbo . . . Jumbo . . . will . . . hoo-doo . . . you."   155

Dying down into a penetrating, terrified whisper.

CARL SANDBURG (1878–   )

Of the many recent poets who sounded their "barbaric yawp over the roofs of the world" (the phrase is Whitman's), none secured a larger audience of admirers and detractors than Carl Sandburg, "laureate of industrial America." Born in Galesburg, Illinois, son of an uneducated Swedish immigrant, he was trained chiefly in the school of experience. Beginning at the age of thirteen, he was driver of a milk wagon, porter in a barber shop, scene-shifter in a theatre, truck-handler in a brick-yard, turner apprentice in a pottery, dish-washer in hotels, harvest hand in Kansas, soldier in Puerto Rico in the Spanish War, "self-help" student at Lombard College, advertising manager for a department store, "Safety First" expert for a business magazine, district organizer for the Social-Democratic Party of Wisconsin, secretary to Mayor Seidel of Milwaukee, etc. Poetic expression of this experience came late. In a pamphlet of twenty-two poems privately printed in 1904, Sandburg was feeling his way, and it was not until 1914, when he was thirty-six, that he found the way — in "Chicago" and other poems printed in the new magazine *Poetry*. Two years later his *Chicago Poems* provoked widespread discussion, and Sandburg had "arrived."

In these, as in much of his later work, there are "two Sandburgs," says Louis Untermeyer: "the muscular, heavy-fisted, hard-hitting son of the streets, and his almost unrecognizable twin, the shadow-painter, the haunter of mists, the lover of implications and overtones." The latter Sandburg — cf. "Fog" — is a relative of the Imagists; the first Sandburg — who wrote "Chicago" — is the more typically Whitmanesque, and the one that has elicited more warm praise and dispraise.

He followed his initial success of 1916 with *Cornhuskers* (1918), *Smoke and Steel* (1920), *Slabs of the Sunburnt West* (1922), *Good Morning, America* (1928), *The People, Yes* (1936). He has written both tales and lyrics for children, and has edited a collection of American ballads, *The American Songbag* (1927).

A major achievement is his voluminous work on the life of Lincoln: *Abraham Lincoln, The Prairie Years*, 2 volumes, 1926, *Abraham Lincoln, The War Years*, 4 volumes, 1939. In the opinion of some critics this work in prose seems more likely to endure than his poetry.

For interpretation and criticism see S. P. Sherman, *Americans*, 1922; L. Untermeyer, *American Poetry since 1900*, 1923; H. Hansen, *Carl Sandburg and His Poetry*, Girard, Kansas, 1925; T. K. Whipple, *Spokesmen*, 1928; and other references given in F. B. Millett, *Contemporary American Authors*, 1940.

Letters to Dead Imagists
(1916)

EMILY DICKINSON:

You gave us the bumble bee who has a
    soul,
The everlasting traveler among the holly-
    hocks,
And how God plays around a back yard
    garden.

STEVIE CRANE:

War is kind and we never knew the kind-
    ness of war till you came;
Nor the black riders and clashes of spear and
    shield out of the sea,   5
Nor the mumblings and shots that rise from
    dreams on call.

Nocturne in a Deserted Brickyard
(1916)

Stuff of the moon
Runs on the lapping sand
Out to the longest shadows.
Under the curving willows,
And round the creep of the wave line,   5
Fluxions of yellow and dusk on the waters
Make a wide dreaming pansy of an old pond
    in the night.

Fog
(1916)

The fog comes
on little cat feet.
It sits looking
over harbor and city
on silent haunches   5
and then moves on.

Chicago

(1914, 1916)

Hog Butcher for the World,
Tool Maker, Stacker of Wheat,
Player with Railroads and the Nations' Freight Handler;
Stormy, husky, brawling,
City of the Big Shoulders: 5
They tell me you are wicked and I believe them, for I have seen your painted women
    under the gas lamps luring the farm boys.
And they tell me you are crooked and I answer: Yes, it is true I have seen the gun-
    man kill and go free to kill again.
And they tell me you are brutal and my reply is: On the faces of women and children
    I have seen the marks of wanton hunger.
And having answered so I turn once more to those who sneer at this my city, and I
    give them back the sneer and say to them:
Come and show me another city with lifted head singing so proud to be alive and
    coarse and strong and cunning.   10
Flinging magnetic curses amid the toil of piling job on job, here is a tall bold slugger
    set vivid against the little soft cities;
Fierce as a dog with tongue lapping for action, cunning as a savage pitted against the
    wilderness,
        Bareheaded,
        Shoveling,
        Wrecking,   15
        Planning,
        Building, breaking, rebuilding,
Under the smoke, dust all over his mouth, laughing with white teeth,
Under the terrible burden of destiny laughing as a young man laughs,
Laughing even as an ignorant fighter laughs who has never lost a battle,   20
Bragging and laughing that under his wrist is the pulse, and under his ribs the heart
    of the people,
        Laughing!
Laughing the stormy, husky, brawling laughter of Youth, half-naked, sweating, proud
    to be Hog Butcher, Tool Maker, Stacker of Wheat, Player with Railroads
    and Freight Handler to the Nation.

I Am the People, the Mob

(1916)

I am the people — the mob — the crowd — the mass.
Do you know that all the great work of the world is done through me?
I am the workingman, the inventor, the maker of the world's food and clothes.
I am the audience that witnesses history. The Napoleons come from me and the
    Lincolns. They die. And then I send forth more Napoleons and Lincolns.   5
I am the seed ground. I am a prairie that will stand for much plowing. Terrible
    storms pass over me. I forget. The best of me is sucked out and wasted. I
    forget. Everything but Death comes to me and makes me work and give up
    what I have. And I forget.
Sometimes I growl, shake myself and spatter a few red drops for history to remember.   10
    Then — I forget.

When I, the People, learn to remember, when I, the People, use the lessons of yester-
    day and no longer forget who robbed me last year, who played me for a
    fool, — then there will be no speaker in all the world say the name: "The
    People," with any fleck of a sneer in his voice or any far-off smile of derision.   15
The mob — the crowd — the mass — will arrive then.

Cool Tombs

(1916)

When Abraham Lincoln was shoveled into the tombs, he forgot the copperheads
    and the assassin . . . in the dust, in the cool tombs.

And Ulysses Grant lost all thought of con men and Wall Street, cash and collateral
    turned ashes . . . in the dust, in the cool tombs.

Pocahontas' body, lovely as a poplar, sweet as a red haw in November or a pawpaw
    in May, did she wonder? does she remember? . . . in the dust, in the cool
    tombs?

Take any streetful of people buying clothes and groceries, cheering a hero or throw-
    ing confetti and blowing tin horns . . . tell me if the lovers are losers . . . tell
    me if any get more than the lovers . . . in the dust . . . in the cool tombs.

From The People, Yes

THE PEOPLE WILL LIVE ON

(1935)

The people will live on.
The learning and blundering people will
    live on.
They will be tricked and sold and again
    sold
And go back to the nourishing earth for
    rootholds,
The people so peculiar in renewal and
    comeback,   5
You can't laugh off their capacity to take
    it.
The mammoth rests between his cyclonic
    dramas.

The people so often sleepy, weary, enigmatic,
is a vast huddle with many units saying: 10
"I earn my living.
I make enough to get by
and it takes all my time.
If I had more time
I could do more for myself   15
and maybe for others.
I could read and study
and talk things over
and find out about things.

It takes time.   20
I wish I had the time."

The people is a tragic and comic two-face:
hero and hoodlum: phantom and gorilla
twisting to moan with a gargoyle mouth:
"They buy me and sell me . . . it's a
game . . . sometime I'll break loose . . ."

Once having marched
Over the margins of animal necessity,
Over the grim line of sheer subsistence,
Then man came   30
To the deeper rituals of his bones,
To the lights lighter than any bones,
To the time for thinking things over,
To the dance, the song, the story,
Or the hours given over to dreaming,   35
Once having so marched.

Between the finite limitations of the five
senses and the endless yearnings of man for
the beyond the people hold to the humdrum bidding of work and food while reaching out when it comes their way for lights
beyond the prison of the five senses, for keepsakes lasting beyond any hunger or death.
    This reaching is alive.
The panderers and liars have violated and
smutted it.   45

Yet this reaching is alive yet
for lights and keepsakes.

The people know the salt of the sea
and the strength of the winds
lashing the corners of the earth.   50
The people take the earth
as a tomb of rest and a cradle of hope.
Who else speaks for the Family of Man?
They are in tune and step
with constellations of universal law.   55
The people is a polychrome,
a spectrum and a prism
held in a moving monolith,
a console organ of changing themes,
a clavilux of color poems   60
wherein the sea offers fog
and the fog moves off in rain
and the labrador sunset shortens
to a nocturne of clear stars
serene over the shot spray   65
of northern lights.

The steel mill sky is alive.
The fire breaks white and zigzag
shot on a gun-metal gloaming.
Man is a long time coming.   70
Man will yet win.
Brother may yet line up with brother:

This old anvil laughs at many broken ham-
    mers.
There are men who can't be bought.
The fireborn are at home in fire.
The stars make no noise.   75
You can't hinder the wind from blowing.
Time is a great teacher.
Who can live without hope?

In the darkness with a great bundle of grief
    the people march.
In the night, and overhead a shovel of stars
    for keeps, the people march: 80
        "Where to? what next?"

WILLA CATHER (1876–1947)

Born near Winchester, Virginia, Willa Cather was taken to a Nebraska ranch when eight years old. Because no school was near, she learned reading and writing at home, read English classics to her grandmothers in evenings, studied Latin with a neighbor. Later she went to the high school in Red Cloud and to the University of Nebraska, from which she graduated at the age of nineteen. In order to hear the music she loved, she went to Pittsburgh, Pennsylvania, served as telegraph editor and dramatic critic for the *Daily Leader*, and taught English in the high schools. She began to contribute to magazines and published a book of verse, *April Twilights*, 1903. Two years later she brought out her first collection of short stories, and in 1906 went to New York to join the staff of *McClure's Magazine*, of which she was managing editor from 1908 to 1912. Then, casting aside all distractions, she devoted herself henceforth to her writing. Making her home in New York, often returning for vacations to the prairies of her girlhood, she wrote quiet books that attained startling successes. Warmly accepted by the public and by discriminating critics, Miss Cather is clearly one of America's leading writers of fiction in the first half of the twentieth century.

Her first novel, *Alexander's Bridge*, appeared in 1912 when she was thirty-six. It was followed by *O Pioneers!*, *The Song of the Lark*, and *My Ántonia*, the last of which, published in 1918 and often regarded as her best novel, tells of a Bohemian family who settled on the Nebraska prairie, bringing with them old memories and habits but facing a new way of life. Then came three more novels, of which *A Lost Lady*, 1923, also Western in setting, is perhaps the best. After this she found a new vein in the sensitive depiction of historical civilizations, the Spanish Southwest in

Death Comes for the Archbishop (1927), old French Quebec in *Shadows on the Rock* (1931), two of her most admired books. In 1935 and 1940 she added *Lucy Gayheart* and *Sapphira and the Slave Girl*.

Highly selective in her art, Miss Cather deplored the detailism of realism, its obsession with facts and material things, as in Balzac, pointing by way of contrast to the economy of Hawthorne's *Scarlet Letter*. In a volume of essays (*Not Under Forty*, 1936) she said: "If the novel is a form of imaginative art, it cannot be at the same time a vivid and brilliant form of journalism. Out of the teeming, gleaming stream of the present it must select the eternal material of art." Novelists should aim "to interpret imaginatively the material and social investiture of their characters; to present their scene by suggestion rather than by enumeration. The higher processes of art are all processes of simplification." In structure, in prose style as well, her own fiction is characterized by economy, suggestion, overtones.

These qualities, along with her balanced concern with human evil and human excellence, appear also in her short stories. Beginning in 1896 with "On the Divide," Miss Cather wrote thirty-four stories and published three collections: *The Troll Garden*, 1905; *Youth and the Bright Medusa*, 1920; *Obscure Destinies*, 1932. She also edited *The Best Stories of Sarah Orne Jewett*, whose work she much admired. Ten of her essays have been collected in Stephen Tennant, ed., *Willa Cather on Writing*, 1950. "Neighbour Rosicky" was printed in *Obscure Destinies* and translated into Czech (Prague, 1933).

Biographical material appears in Mildred R. Bennett, *The World of Willa Cather*, 1951. Criticism includes R. Rapin, *Willa Cather*, 1930; Michael Williams, *Catholicism and the Modern Mind*, 1928; H. Hartwick, *The Foreground of American Fiction*, 1934; H. Hatcher, *Creating the Modern American Novel*, 1935; A. H. Quinn, *American Fiction*, 1936; Carl Van Doren, *The American Novel, 1789–1939*, 1940; David Daiches, *Willa Cather*, 1951.

Neighbour Rosicky

(1932)

I

When Doctor Burleigh told neighbour Rosicky he had a bad heart, Rosicky protested.

"So? No, I guess my heart was always pretty good. I got a little asthma, maybe. Just a awful short breath when I was pitchin' hay last summer, dat's all."

"Well now, Rosicky, if you know more about it than I do, what did you come to me for? It's your heart that makes you short of breath, I tell you. You're sixty-five years old, and you've always worked hard, and your heart's tired. You've got to be careful from now on, and you can't do heavy work any more. You've got five boys at home to do it for you."

The old farmer looked up at the Doctor with a gleam of amusement in his queer triangular-shaped eyes. His eyes were large and lively, but the lids were caught up in the middle in a curious way, so that they formed a triangle. He did not look like a sick man. His brown face was creased but not wrinkled, he had a ruddy colour in his smooth-shaven cheeks and in his lips, under his long brown moustache. His hair was thin and ragged around his ears, but very little grey. His forehead, naturally high and crossed by deep parallel lines, now ran all the way up to his pointed crown. Rosicky's face had the habit of looking interested — suggested a contented disposition and a reflective quality that was gay rather than grave. This gave him a certain detachment, the easy manner of an onlooker and observer.

"Well, I guess you ain't got no pills fur a bad heart, Doctor Ed. I guess the only thing is fur me to git me a new one."

Doctor Burleigh swung round in his desk-chair and frowned at the old farmer. "I think if I were you I'd take a little care of the old one, Rosicky."

Rosicky shrugged. "Maybe I don't know how. I expect you mean fur me not to drink my coffee no more."

"I wouldn't, in your place. But you'll do as you choose about that. I've never yet been able to separate a Bohemian from his coffee or his pipe. I've quit trying. But the sure thing is you've got to cut out farm work. You can feed the stock and do chores about the barn, but you can't do anything in the fields that makes you short of breath."

"How about shelling corn?"

"Of course not!"

Rosicky considered with puckered brows.

"I can't make my heart go no longer'n it wants to, can I, Doctor Ed?"

"I think it's good for five or six years yet, maybe more, if you'll take the strain off it. Sit around the house and help Mary. If I had a good wife like yours, I'd want to stay around the house."

His patient chuckled. "It ain't no place fur a man. I don't like no old man hanging round the kitchen too much. An' my wife, she's a awful hard worker her own self."

"That's it; you can help her a little. My Lord, Rosicky, you are one of the few men I know who has a family he can get some comfort out of; happy dispositions, never quarrel among themselves, and they treat you right. I want to see you live a few years and enjoy them."

"Oh, they're good kids, all right," Rosicky assented.

The Doctor wrote him a prescription and asked him how his oldest son, Rudolph, who had married in the spring, was getting on. Rudolph had struck out for himself, on rented land. "And how's Polly? I was afraid Mary mightn't like an American daughter-in-law, but it seems to be working out all right."

"Yes, she's a fine girl. Dat widder woman bring her daughters up very nice. Polly got lots of spunk, an' she got some style, too. Da's nice, for young folks to have some style." Rosicky inclined his head gallantly. His voice and his twinkly smile were an affectionate compliment to his daughter-in-law.

"It looks like a storm, and you'd better be getting home before it comes. In town in the car?" Doctor Burleigh rose.

"No, I'm in de wagon. When you got five boys, you ain't got much chance to ride round in de Ford. I ain't much for cars, noway."

"Well, it's a good road out to your place; but I don't want you bumping around in a wagon much. And never again on a hay-rake, remember!"

Rosicky placed the Doctor's fee delicately behind the desk-telephone, looking the other way, as if this were an absent-minded gesture. He put on his plush cap and his corduroy jacket with a sheepskin collar, and went out.

The Doctor picked up his stethoscope and frowned at it as if he were seriously annoyed with the instrument. He wished it had been telling tales about some other man's heart, some old man who didn't look the Doctor in the eye so knowingly, or hold out such a warm brown hand when he said good-bye. Doctor Burleigh had been a poor boy in the country before he went away to medical school; he had known Rosicky almost ever since he could remember, and he had a deep affection for Mrs. Rosicky.

Only last winter he had had such a good breakfast at Rosicky's, and that when he needed it. He had been out all night on a long, hard confinement case at Tom Marshall's — a big rich farm where there was plenty of stock and plenty of feed and a great deal of expensive farm machinery of the newest model, and no comfort whatever. The woman had too many children and too much work, and she was no manager. When the baby was born at last, and handed over to the assisting neighbour woman, and the mother was properly attended to, Burleigh refused any breakfast in that slovenly house, and drove his buggy — the snow was too deep for a car — eight miles to Anton Rosicky's place. He didn't know another farm-house where a man could get such a warm welcome, and such good strong coffee with rich cream. No wonder the old chap didn't want to give up his coffee!

He had driven in just when the boys had come back from the barn and were washing up for breakfast. The long table, covered with a bright oilcloth, was set out with dishes waiting for them, and the warm kitchen was full of the smell of coffee and hot biscuit and sausage. Five big handsome boys, running from twenty to twelve, all with what Burleigh called natural good manners — they hadn't a bit of the painful self-consciousness he himself had to struggle with when he was a lad. One ran to put his horse away, another helped him off with his fur coat and hung it up, and Josephine, the youngest child and the only daughter, quickly set another place under her mother's direction.

With Mary, to feed creatures was the natural expression of affection — her chickens, the calves, her big hungry boys. It was a rare pleasure to feed a young man whom she seldom saw and of whom she was as proud as if he belonged to her. Some country housekeepers would have stopped to spread a white cloth over the oilcloth, to change the thick cups and plates for their best china, and the wooden-handled knives for plated ones. But not Mary.

"You must take us as you find us, Doctor Ed. I'd be glad to put out my good things for you if you was expected, but I'm glad to get you any way at all."

He knew she was glad — she threw back her head and spoke out as if she were announcing him to the whole prairie. Rosicky hadn't said anything at all; he merely smiled his twinkling smile, put some more coal on the fire, and went into his own room to pour the Doctor a little drink in a medicine glass. When they were all seated, he watched his wife's face from his end of the table and spoke to her in Czech. Then, with the instinct of politeness which seldom failed him, he turned to the Doctor and said slyly: "I was just tellin' her not to ask you no questions about Mrs. Marshall till you eat some breakfast. My wife, she's terrible fur to ask questions."

The boys laughed, and so did Mary. She watched the Doctor devour her biscuit and sausage, too much excited to eat anything herself. She drank her coffee and sat taking in everything about her visitor. She had known him when he was a poor country boy, and was boastfully proud of his success, always saying: "What do people go to Omaha for, to see a doctor, when we got the best one in the State right here?" If Mary liked people at all, she felt physical pleasure in the sight of them, personal exultation in any good fortune that came to them. Burleigh didn't know many women like that, but he knew she was like that.

When his hunger was satisfied, he did, of course, have to tell them about Mrs. Marshall, and he noticed what a friendly interest the boys took in the matter.

Rudolph, the oldest one (he was still living at home then), said: "The last time I was over there, she was lifting them big heavy milkcans, and I knew she oughtn't to be doing it."

"Yes, Rudolph told me about that when he come home, and I said it wasn't right," Mary put in warmly. "It was all right for me to do them things up to the last, for I was terrible strong, but that woman's weakly. And do you think she'll be able to nurse it, Ed?" She sometimes forgot to give him the title she was so proud of. "And to think of your being up all night and then not able to get a decent breakfast! I don't know what's the matter with such people."

"Why, Mother," said one of the boys, "if Doctor Ed had got breakfast there, we wouldn't have him here. So you ought to be glad."

"He knows I'm glad to have him, John, any time. But I'm sorry for that poor woman, how bad she'll feel the Doctor had to go away in the cold without his breakfast."

"I wish I'd been in practice when these were getting born." The Doctor looked down the row of close-clipped heads. "I missed some good breakfasts by not being."

The boys began to laugh at their mother because she flushed so red, but she stood her ground and threw up her head. "I don't care, you wouldn't have got away from this house without breakfast. No doctor ever did. I'd have had something ready fixed that Anton could warm up for you."

The boys laughed harder than ever, and exclaimed at her: "I'll bet you would!" "She would, that!"

"Father, did you get breakfast for the Doctor when we were born?"

"Yes, and he used to bring me my breakfast, too, mighty nice. I was always awful 'hungry!" Mary admitted with a guilty laugh.

While the boys were getting the Doctor's horse, he went to the window to examine the house plants. "What do you do to your geraniums to keep them blooming all winter, Mary? I never pass this house that from the road I don't see your windows full of flowers."

She snapped off a dark red one, and a ruffled new green leaf, and put them in his buttonhole. "There, that looks better. You look too solemn for a young man, Ed. Why don't you git married? I'm worried about you. Settin' at breakfast, I looked at you real hard, and I seen you've got some grey hairs already."

"Oh, yes! They're coming. Maybe they'd come faster if I married."

"Don't talk so. You'll ruin your health eating at the hotel. I could send your wife a nice loaf of nut bread, if you only had one. I don't like to see a young man getting grey. I'll tell you something, Ed; you make some strong black tea and keep it handy in a bowl, and every morning just brush it into your hair, an' it'll keep the grey from showin' much. That's the way I do!"

Sometimes the Doctor heard the gossipers in the drug-store wondering why Rosicky didn't get on faster. He was industrious, and so were his boys, but they were rather free and easy, weren't pushers, and they didn't always show good judgment. They were comfortable, they were out of debt, but they didn't get much ahead. Maybe, Doctor Burleigh reflected, people as generous and warm-hearted and affectionate as the Rosickys never got ahead much; maybe you couldn't enjoy your life and put it into the bank, too.

II

When Rosicky left Doctor Burleigh's office he went into the farm-implement store to light his pipe and put on his glasses and read over the list Mary had given him. Then he went into the general merchandise place next door and stood about until the pretty girl with the plucked eyebrows, who always waited on him, was free. Those eyebrows, two thin India-ink strokes, amused him, because he remembered how they used to be.

Rosicky always prolonged his shopping by a little joking; the girl knew the old fellow admired her, and she liked to chaff with him.

"Seems to me about every other week you 5 buy ticking, Mr. Rosicky, and always the best quality," she remarked as she measured off the heavy bolt with red stripes.

"You see, my wife is always makin' goose-fedder pillows, an' de thin stuff don't hold in 10 dem little down-fedders."

"You must have lots of pillows at your house."

"Sure. She makes quilts of dem, too. We sleeps easy. Now she's makin' a fedder quilt 15 for my son's wife. You know Polly, that married my Rudolph. How much my bill, Miss Pearl?"

"Eight eighty-five."

"Chust make it nine, and put in some 20 candy fur de woman."

"As usual. I never did see a man buy so much candy for his wife. First thing you know, she'll be getting too fat."

"I'd like dat. I ain't much for all dem slim 25 women like what de style is now."

"That's one for me, I suppose, Mr. Bohunk!" Pearl sniffed and elevated her India-ink strokes.

When Rosicky went out to his wagon, it 30 was beginning to snow — the first snow of the season, and he was glad to see it. He rattled out of town and along the highway through a wonderfully rich stretch of country, the finest farms in the county. He admired this 35 High Prairie, as it was called, and always liked to drive through it. His own place lay in a rougher territory, where there was some clay in the soil and it was not so productive. When he bought his land, he hadn't the 40 money to buy on High Prairie; so he told his boys, when they grumbled, that if their land hadn't some clay in it, they wouldn't own it at all. All the same, he enjoyed looking at these fine farms, as he enjoyed looking at 45 a prize bull.

After he had gone eight miles, he came to the graveyard, which lay just at the edge of his own hay-land. There he stopped his horses and sat still on his wagon seat, looking 50 about at the snowfall. Over yonder on the hill he could see his own house, crouching low, with the clump of orchard behind and the windmill before, and all down the gentle hill-slope the rows of pale gold cornstalks stood out against the white field. The snow was falling over the cornfield and the pasture and the hay-land, steadily, with very little wind — a nice dry snow. The graveyard had only a light wire fence about it and was all overgrown with long red grass. The fine snow, settling into this red grass and upon the few little evergreens and the headstones, looked very pretty.

It was a nice graveyard, Rosicky reflected, sort of snug and homelike, not cramped or mournful — a big sweep all round it. A man could lie down in the long grass and see the complete arch of the sky over him, hear the wagons go by; in summer the mowing-machine rattled right up to the wire fence. And it was so near home. Over there across the cornstalks his own roof and windmill looked so good to him that he promised himself to mind the Doctor and take care of himself. He was awful fond of his place, he admitted. He wasn't anxious to leave it. And it was a comfort to think that he would never have to go farther than the edge of his own hayfield. The snow, falling over his barnyard and the graveyard, seemed to draw things together like. And they were all old neighbours in the graveyard, most of them friends; there was nothing to feel awkward or embarrassed about. Embarrassment was the most disagreeable feeling Rosicky knew. He didn't often have it — only with certain people whom he didn't understand at all.

Well, it was a nice snowstorm; a fine sight to see the snow falling so quietly and graciously over so much open country. On his cap and shoulders, on the horses' backs and manes, light, delicate, mysterious it fell; and with it a dry cool fragrance was released into the air. It meant rest for vegetation and men and beasts, for the ground itself; a season of long nights for sleep, leisurely breakfasts, peace by the fire. This and much more went through Rosicky's mind, but he merely told himself that winter was coming, clucked to his horses, and drove on.

When he reached home, John, the youngest boy, ran out to put away his team for him, and he met Mary coming up from the outside cellar with her apron full of carrots. They went into the house together. On the table, covered with oilcloth figured with clusters of blue grapes, a place was set, and he smelled hot coffee-cake of some kind. Anton never lunched in town; he thought that extravagant, and anyhow he didn't like the food. So Mary always had something ready for him when he got home.

After he was settled in his chair, stirring his coffee in a big cup, Mary took out of the oven a pan of *kolache* stuffed with apricots, examined them anxiously to see whether they had got too dry, put them beside his plate, and then sat down opposite him.

Rosicky asked her in Czech if she wasn't going to have any coffee.

She replied in English, as being somehow the right language for transacting business: "Now what did Doctor Ed say, Anton? You tell me just what."

"He said I was to tell you some compliments, but I forgot 'em." Rosicky's eyes twinkled.

"About you, I mean. What did he say about your asthma?"

"He says I ain't got no asthma." Rosicky took one of the little rolls in his broad brown fingers. The thickened nail of his right thumb told the story of his past.

"Well, what is the matter? And don't try to put me off."

"He don't say nothing much, only I'm a little older, and my heart ain't so good like it used to be."

Mary started and brushed her hair back from her temples with both hands as if she were a little out of her mind. From the way she glared, she might have been in a rage with him.

"He says there's something the matter with your heart? Doctor Ed says so?"

"Now don't yell at me like I was a hog in de garden, Mary. You know I always did like to hear a woman talk soft. He didn't say anything de matter wid my heart, only it ain't so young like it used to be, an' he tell me not to pitch hay or run de corn-sheller."

Mary wanted to jump up, but she sat still. She admired the way he never under any circumstances raised his voice or spoke roughly. He was city-bred, and she was country-bred; she often said she wanted her boys to have their papa's nice ways.

"You never have no pain there, do you? It's your breathing and your stomach that's been wrong. I wouldn't believe nobody but Doctor Ed about it. I guess I'll go see him myself. Didn't he give you no advice?"

"Chust to take it easy like, an' stay round de house dis winter. I guess you got some carpenter work for me to do. I kin make some new shelves for you, and I want dis long time to build a closet in de boys' room and make dem two little fellers keep dere clo'es hung up."

Rosicky drank his coffee from time to time, while he considered. His moustache was of the soft long variety and came down over his mouth like the teeth of a buggy-rake over a bundle of hay. Each time he put down his cup, he ran his blue handkerchief over his lips. When he took a drink of water, he managed very neatly with the back of his hand.

Mary sat watching him intently, trying to find any change in his face. It is hard to see anyone who has become like your own body to you. Yes, his hair had got thin, and his high forehead had deep lines running from left to right. But his neck, always clean-shaved except in the busiest seasons, was not loose or baggy. It was burned a dark reddish brown, and there were deep creases in it, but it looked firm and full of blood. His cheeks had a good colour. On either side of his mouth there was a half-moon down the length of his cheek, not wrinkles, but two lines that had come there from his habitual expression. He was shorter and broader than when she married him; his back had grown broad and curved, a good deal like the shell of an old turtle, and his arms and legs were short.

He was fifteen years older than Mary, but she had hardly ever thought about it before. He was her man, and the kind of man she liked. She was rough, and he was gentle — city-bred, as she always said. They had been shipmates on a rough voyage and had stood by each other in trying times. Life had gone well with them because, at bottom, they had the same ideas about life. They agreed, without discussion, as to what was most important and what was secondary. They

didn't often exchange opinions, even in Czech — it was as if they had thought the same thought together. A good deal had to be sacrificed and thrown overboard in a hard life like theirs, and they had never disagreed as to the things that could go. It had been a hard life, and a soft life, too. There wasn't anything brutal in the short, broad-backed man with the three-cornered eyes and the forehead that went on to the top of his skull. He was a city man, a gentle man, and though he had married a rough farm girl, he had never touched her without gentleness.

They had been at one accord not to hurry through life, not to be always skimping and saving. They saw their neighbours buy more land and feed more stock than they did, without discontent. Once when the creamery agent came to the Rosickys to persuade them to sell him their cream, he told them how much money the Fasslers, their nearest neighbours, had made on their cream last year.

"Yes," said Mary, "and look at them Fassler children! Pale, pinched little things, they look like skimmed milk. I'd rather put some colour into my children's faces than put money into the bank."

The agent shrugged and turned to Anton. "I guess we'll do like she says," said Rosicky.

III

Mary very soon got into town to see Doctor Ed, and then she had a talk with her boys and set a guard over Rosicky. Even John, the youngest, had his father on his mind. If Rosicky went to throw hay down from the loft, one of the boys ran up the ladder and took the fork from him. He sometimes complained that though he was getting to be an old man, he wasn't an old woman yet.

That winter he stayed in the house in the afternoons and carpentered, or sat in the chair between the window full of plants and the wooden bench where the two pails of drinking-water stood. This spot was called "Father's corner," though it was not a corner at all. He had a shelf there, where he kept his Bohemian papers and his pipes and tobacco, and his shears and needles and thread and tailor's thimble. Having been a tailor in his youth, he couldn't bear to see a woman patching at his clothes, or at the boys'. He liked tailoring, and always patched all the overalls and jackets and work shirts. Occasionally he made over a pair of pants one of the older boys had outgrown, for the little fellow.

While he sewed, he let his mind run back over his life. He had a good deal to remember, really; life in three countries. The only part of his youth he didn't like to remember was the two years he had spent in London, in Cheapside, working for a German tailor who was wretchedly poor. Those days, when he was nearly always hungry, when his clothes were dropping off him for dirt, and the sound of a strange language kept him in continual bewilderment, had left a sore spot in his mind that wouldn't bear touching.

He was twenty when he landed at Castle Garden in New York, and he had a protector who got him work in a tailor shop in Vesey Street, down near the Washington Market. He looked upon that part of his life as very happy. He became a good workman, he was industrious, and his wages were increased from time to time. He minded his own business and envied nobody's good fortune. He went to night school and learned to read English. He often did overtime work and was well paid for it, but somehow he never saved anything. He couldn't refuse a loan to a friend, and he was self-indulgent. He liked a good dinner, and a little went for beer, a little for tobacco; a good deal went to the girls. He often stood through an opera on Saturday nights; he could get standing-room for a dollar. Those were the great days of opera in New York, and it gave a fellow something to think about for the rest of the week. Rosicky had a quick ear, and a childish love of all the stage splendour; the scenery, the costumes, the ballet. He usually went with a chum, and after the performance they had beer and maybe some oysters somewhere. It was a fine life; for the first five years or so it satisfied him completely. He was never hungry or cold or dirty, and everything amused him: a fire, a dog fight, a parade, a storm, a ferry ride. He thought New York the finest, richest, friendliest city in the world.

Moreover, he had what he called a happy home life. Very near the tailor shop was a small furniture factory, where an old Austrian, Loeffler, employed a few skilled men and made unusual furniture, most of it to order, for the rich German housewives uptown. The top floor of Loeffler's five-storey factory was a loft, where he kept his choice lumber and stored the odd pieces of furniture left on his hands. One of the young workmen he employed was a Czech, and he and Rosicky became fast friends. They persuaded Loeffler to let them have a sleeping-room in one corner of the loft. They bought good beds and bedding and had their pick of the furniture kept up there. The loft was low-pitched, but light and airy, full of windows, and good-smelling by reason of the fine lumber put up there to season. Old Loeffler used to go down to the docks and buy wood from South America and the East from the sea captains. The young men were as foolish about their house as a bridal pair. Zichec, the young cabinet-maker, devised every sort of convenience, and Rosicky kept their clothes in order. At night and on Sundays, when the quiver of machinery underneath was still, it was the quietest place in the world, and on summer nights all the sea winds blew in. Zichec often practised on his flute in the evening. They were both fond of music and went to the opera together. Rosicky thought he wanted to live like that forever.

But as the years passed, all alike, he began to get a little restless. When spring came round, he would begin to feel fretted, and he got to drinking. He was likely to drink too much of a Saturday night. On Sunday he was languid and heavy, getting over his spree. On Monday he plunged into work again. So he never had time to figure out what ailed him, though he knew something did. When the grass turned green in Park Place, and the lilac hedge at the back of Trinity churchyard put out its blossoms, he was tormented by a longing to run away. That was why he drank too much; to get a temporary illusion of freedom and wide horizons.

Rosicky, the old Rosicky, could remember as if it were yesterday the day when the young Rosicky found out what was the matter with him. It was on a Fourth of July afternoon, and he was sitting in Park Place in the sun. The lower part of New York was empty. Wall Street, Liberty Street, Broadway, all empty. So much stone and asphalt with nothing going on, so many empty windows. The emptiness was intense, like the stillness in a great factory when the machinery stops and the belts and bands cease running. It was too great a change, it took all the strength out of one. Those blank buildings, without the stream of life pouring through them, were like empty jails. It struck young Rosicky that this was the trouble with big cities; they built you in from the earth itself, cemented you away from any contact with the ground. You lived in an unnatural world, like the fish in an aquarium, who were probably much more comfortable than they ever were in the sea.

On that very day he began to think seriously about the articles he had read in the Bohemian papers, describing prosperous Czech farming communities in the West. He believed he would like to go out there as a farmhand; it was hardly possible that he could ever have land of his own. His people had always been workmen; his father and grandfather had worked in shops. His mother's parents had lived in the country, but they rented their farm and had a hard time to get along. Nobody in his family had ever owned any land — that belonged to a different station of life altogether. Anton's mother died when he was little, and he was sent into the country to her parents. He stayed with them until he was twelve, and formed those ties with the earth and the farm animals and growing things which are never made at all unless they are made early. After his grandfather died, he went back to live with his father and stepmother, but she was very hard on him, and his father helped him to get passage to London.

After that Fourth of July day in Park Place, the desire to return to the country never left him. To work on another man's farm would be all he asked; to see the sun rise and set and to plant things and watch them grow. He was a very simple man. He was like a tree that has not many roots, but one taproot that goes down deep. He subscribed for a Bohemian paper printed in Chicago, then for one printed in Omaha. His mind got farther and farther west. He began to save a little money to buy his liberty. When he was thirty-five, there was a great meeting in New York of Bohemian athletic societies, and Rosicky left the tailor shop and went home with the Omaha delegates to try his fortune in another part of the world.

IV

Perhaps the fact that his own youth was well over before he began to have a family was one reason why Rosicky was so fond of his boys. He had almost a grandfather's indulgence for them. He had never had to worry about any of them — except, just now, a little about Rudolph.

On Saturday night the boys always piled into the Ford, took little Josephine, and went to town to the moving-picture show. One Saturday morning they were talking at the breakfast table about starting early that evening, so that they would have an hour or so to see the Christmas things in the stores before the show began. Rosicky looked down the table.

"I hope you boys ain't disappointed, but I want you to let me have de car tonight. Maybe some of you can go in with de neighbours."

Their faces fell. They worked hard all week, and they were still like children. A new jackknife or a box of candy pleased the older ones as much as the little fellow.

"If you and Mother are going to town," Frank said, "maybe you could take a couple of us along with you, anyway."

"No, I want to take de car down to Rudolph's, and let him an' Polly go in to de show. She don't git into town enough, an' I'm afraid she's gettin' lonesome, an' he can't afford no car yet."

That settled it. The boys were a good deal dashed. Their father took another piece of apple-cake and went on: "Maybe next Saturday night de two little fellers can go along wid dem."

"Oh, is Rudolph going to have the car every Saturday night?"

Rosicky did not reply at once; then he began to speak seriously: "Listen, boys; Polly ain't lookin' so good. I don't like to see nobody lookin' sad. It comes hard fur a town girl to be a farmer's wife. I don't want no trouble to start in Rudolph's family. When it starts, it ain't so easy to stop. An American girl don't git used to our ways all at once. I like to tell Polly she and Rudolph can have the car every Saturday night till after New Year's, if it's all right with you boys."

"Sure it's all right, Papa," Mary cut in. "And it's good you thought about that. Town girls is used to more than country girls. I lay awake nights, scared she'll make Rudolph discontented with the farm."

The boys put as good a face on it as they could. They surely looked forward to their Saturday nights in town. That evening Rosicky drove the car the half-mile down to Rudolph's new, bare little house.

Polly was in a short-sleeved gingham dress, clearing away the supper dishes. She was a trim, slim little thing, with blue eyes and shingled yellow hair, and her eyebrows were reduced to a mere brush-stroke, like Miss Pearl's.

"Good evening, Mr. Rosicky. Rudolph's at the barn, I guess." She never called him father, or Mary mother. She was sensitive about having married a foreigner. She never in the world would have done it if Rudolph hadn't been such a handsome, persuasive fellow and such a gallant lover. He had graduated in her class in the high school in town, and their friendship began in the ninth grade.

Rosicky went in, though he wasn't exactly asked. "My boys ain't goin' to town tonight, an' I brought de car over fur you two to go in to de picture show."

Polly, carrying dishes to the sink, looked over her shoulder at him. "Thank you. But I'm late with my work tonight, and pretty tired. Maybe Rudolph would like to go in with you."

"Oh, I don't go to de shows! I'm too old-fashioned. You won't feel so tired after you ride in de air a ways. It's a nice clear night, an' it ain't cold. You go an' fix yourself up, Polly, an' I'll wash de dishes an' leave everything nice fur you."

Polly blushed and tossed her bob. "I couldn't let you do that, Mr. Rosicky. I wouldn't think of it."

Rosicky said nothing. He found a bib apron on a nail behind the kitchen door. He slipped it over his head and then took Polly by her two elbows and pushed her gently toward the door of her own room. "I washed up de kitchen many times for my wife, when de babies was sick or somethin'. You go an' make yourself look nice. I like you to look prettier'n any of dem town girls when you go in. De young folks must have some fun, an' I'm goin' to look out fur you, Polly."

That kind, reassuring grip on her elbows, the old man's funny bright eyes, made Polly want to drop her head on his shoulder for a second. She restrained herself, but she lingered in his grasp at the door of her room, murmuring tearfully: "You always lived in the city when you were young, didn't you? Don't you ever get lonesome out here?"

As she turned round to him, her hand fell naturally into his, and he stood holding it and smiling into her face with his peculiar, knowing, indulgent smile without a shadow of reproach in it. "Dem big cities is all right fur de rich, but dey is terrible hard fur de poor."

"I don't know. Sometimes I think I'd like to take a chance. You lived in New York, didn't you?"

"An' London. Da's bigger still. I learned my trade dere. Here's Rudolph comin', you better hurry."

"Will you tell me about London sometime?"

"Maybe. Only I ain't no talker, Polly. Run an' dress yourself up."

The bedroom door closed behind her, and Rudolph came in from the outside, looking anxious. He had seen the car and was sorry any of his family should come just then. Supper hadn't been a very pleasant occasion. Halting in the doorway, he saw his father in a kitchen apron, carrying dishes to the sink. He flushed crimson and something flashed in his eye. Rosicky held up a warning finger.

"I brought de car over fur you an' Polly to go to de picture show, an' I made her let me finish here so you won't be late. You go put on a clean shirt, quick!"

"But don't the boys want the car, Father?"

"Not tonight dey don't." Rosicky fumbled under his apron and found his pants pocket. He took out a silver dollar and said in a hurried whisper: "You go an' buy dat girl some ice cream an' candy tonight, like you was courtin'. She's awful good friends wid me."

Rudolph was very short of cash, but he took the money as if it hurt him. There had been a crop failure all over the county. He had more than once been sorry he'd married this year.

In a few minutes the young people came out, looking clean and a little stiff. Rosicky hurried them off, and then he took his own time with the dishes. He scoured the pots and pans and put away the milk and swept the kitchen. He put some coal in the stove and shut off the draughts, so the place would be warm for them when they got home late at night. Then he sat down and had a pipe and listened to the clock tick.

Generally speaking, marrying an American girl was certainly a risk. A Czech should marry a Czech. It was lucky that Polly was the daughter of a poor widow woman; Rudolph was proud, and if she had a prosperous family to throw up at him, they could never make it go. Polly was one of four sisters, and they all worked; one was book-keeper in the bank, one taught music, and Polly and her younger sister had been clerks, like Miss Pearl. All four of them were musical, had pretty voices, and sang in the Methodist choir, which the eldest sister directed.

Polly missed the sociability of a store position. She missed the choir, and the company of her sisters. She didn't dislike housework, but she disliked so much of it. Rosicky was a little anxious about this pair. He was afraid Polly would grow so discontented that Rudy would quit the farm and take a factory job in Omaha. He had worked for a winter up there, two years ago, to get money to marry on. He had done very well, and they would always take him back at the stockyards. But to Rosicky that meant the end of everything for his son. To be a landless man was to be a wage-earner, a slave, all your life; to have nothing, to be nothing.

Rosicky thought he would come over and do a little carpentering for Polly after the New Year. He guessed she needed jollying. Rudolph was a serious sort of chap, serious in love and serious about his work.

Rosicky shook out his pipe and walked home across the fields. Ahead of him the lamplight shone from his kitchen windows. Suppose he were still in a tailor shop on Vesey Street, with a bunch of pale, narrow-chested sons working on machines, all coming home tired and sullen to eat supper in a kitchen that was a parlour also; with another crowded, angry family quarrelling just across the dumb-waiter shaft, and squeaking pulleys at the windows where dirty washings hung on dirty lines above a court full of old brooms and mops and ashcans . . .

He stopped by the windmill to look up at the frosty winter stars and draw a long breath before he went inside. That kitchen with the shining windows was dear to him; but the sleeping fields and bright stars and the noble darkness were dearer still.

V

On the day before Christmas the weather set in very cold; no snow, but a bitter, biting wind that whistled and sang over the flat land and lashed one's face like fine wires. There was baking going on in the Rosicky kitchen all day and Rosicky sat inside, making over a coat that Albert had outgrown into an overcoat for John. Mary had a big red geranium in bloom for Christmas, and a row of Jerusalem cherry trees, full of berries. It was the first year she had ever grown these; Doctor Ed brought her the seed from Omaha when he went to some medical convention. They reminded Rosicky of plants he had seen in England; and all afternoon, as he stitched, he sat thinking about those two years in London, which his mind usually shrank from even after all this while.

He was a lad of eighteen when he dropped down into London, with no money and no connections except the address of a cousin who was supposed to be working at a confectioner's. When he went to the pastry shop, however, he found that the cousin had gone to America. Anton tramped the streets for several days, sleeping in doorways and on the Embankment, until he was in utter despair. He knew no English, and the sound of the strange language all about him confused him. By chance he met a poor German tailor who had learned his trade in Vienna, and could speak a little Czech. This tailor, Lifschnitz, kept a repair shop in a Cheapside basement, underneath a cobbler. He didn't much need an apprentice, but he was sorry for the boy and took him in for no wages but his keep and what he could pick up. The pickings were supposed to be coppers given you when you took work home to a customer. But most of the customers called for their clothes themselves, and the coppers that came Anton's way were very few. He had, however, a place to sleep. The tailor's family lived upstairs in three rooms; a kitchen, a bedroom, where Lifschnitz and his wife and five children slept, and a living-room. Two corners of this living-room were curtained off for lodgers; in one Rosicky slept on an old horsehair sofa, with a feather quilt to wrap himself in. The other corner was rented to a wretched, dirty boy, who was studying the violin. He actually practised there. Rosicky was dirty, too. There was no way to be anything else. Mrs. Lifschnitz got the water she cooked and washed with from a pump in a brick court, four flights down. There were bugs in the place, and multitudes of fleas, though the poor woman did the best she could. Rosicky knew she often went empty to give another potato or a spoonful of dripping to the two hungry, sad-eyed boys who lodged with her. He used to think he would never get out of there, never get a clean shirt to his back again. What would he do, he wondered, when his clothes actually dropped to pieces and the worn cloth wouldn't hold patches any longer?

It was still early when the old farmer put aside his sewing and his recollections. The sky had been a dark grey all day, with not a gleam of sun, and the light failed at four o'clock. He went to shave and change his shirt while the turkey was roasting. Rudolph and Polly were coming over for supper.

After supper they sat round in the kitchen, and the younger boys were saying how sorry they were it hadn't snowed. Everybody was sorry. They wanted a deep snow that would lie long and keep the wheat warm, and leave the ground soaked when it melted.

"Yes, sir!" Rudolph broke out fiercely; "if we have another dry year like last year, there's going to be hard times in this country."

Rosicky filled his pipe. "You boys don't know what hard times is. You don't owe nobody, you got plenty to eat an' keep warm, an' plenty water to keep clean. When you got them, you can't have it very hard."

Rudolph frowned, opened and shut his big right hand, and dropped it clenched upon his knee. "I've got to have a good deal more than that, Father, or I'll quit this farming gamble. I can always make good wages railroading, or at the packing house, and be sure of my money."

"Maybe so," his father answered dryly.

Mary, who had just come in from the pantry and was wiping her hands on the roller towel, thought Rudy and his father were getting too serious. She brought her darning-basket and sat down in the middle of the group.

"I ain't much afraid of hard times, Rudy," she said heartily. "We've had a plenty, but we've always come through. Your father wouldn't never take nothing very hard, not even hard times. I got a mind to tell you a story on him. Maybe you boys can't hardly remember the year we had that terrible hot wind, that burned everything up on the Fourth of July? All the corn an' the gardens. An' that was in the days when we didn't have alfalfa yet — I guess it wasn't invented.

"Well, that very day your father was out cultivatin' corn, and I was here in the kitchen makin' plum preserves. We had bushels of plums that year. I noticed it was terrible hot, but it's always hot in the kitchen when you're preservin', an' I was too busy with my plums to mind. Anton come in from the field about three o'clock, an' I asked him what was the matter.

"'Nothin',' he says, 'but it's pretty hot, an' I think I won't work no more today.' He stood round for a few minutes, an' then he says: 'Ain't you near through? I want you should git up a nice supper for us tonight. It's Fourth of July.'

"I told him to git along, that I was right in the middle of preservin', but the plums would taste good on hot biscuit. 'I'm goin' to have fried chicken, too,' he says, and he went off an' killed a couple. You three oldest boys was little fellers, playin' round outside, real hot an' sweaty, an' your father took you to the horse tank down by the windmill an' took off your clothes an' put you in. Them two box-elder trees was little then, but they made shade over the tank. Then he took off all his own clothes, an' got in with you. While he was playin' in the water with you, the Methodist preacher drove into our place to say how all the neighbours was goin' to meet at the school-house that night, to pray for rain. He drove right to the windmill, of course, and there was your father and you three with no clothes on. I was in the kitchen door, an' I had to laugh, for the preacher acted like he ain't never seen a naked man before. He surely was embarrassed, an' your father couldn't git to his clothes; they was all hangin' up on the windmill to let the sweat dry out of 'em. So he laid in the tank where he was, an' put one of you boys on top of him to cover him up a little, an' talked to the preacher.

"When you got through playin' in the water, he put clean clothes on you and a clean shirt on himself, an' by that time I'd begun to get supper. He says: 'It's too hot in here to eat comfortable. Let's have a picnic in the orchard. We'll eat our supper behind the mulberry hedge, under them linden trees.'

"So he carried our supper down, an' a bottle of my wild-grape wine, an' everything tasted good, I can tell you. The wind got cooler as the sun was goin' down, and it turned out pleasant, only I noticed how the leaves was curled up on the linden trees. That made me think, an' I asked your father if that hot wind all day hadn't been terrible hard on the gardens an' the corn.

" 'Corn,' he says, 'there ain't no corn.'

" 'What you talkin' about?' I said. 'Ain't we got forty acres?'

" 'We ain't got an ear,' he says, 'nor nobody else ain't got none. All the corn in this country was cooked by three o'clock today, like you'd roasted it in an oven.'

" 'You mean you won't get no crop at all?' I asked him. I couldn't believe it, after he'd worked so hard.

" 'No crop this year,' he says. 'That's why we're havin' a picnic. We might as well enjoy what we got.'

"An' that's how your father behaved, when all the neighbours was so discouraged they couldn't look you in the face. An' we enjoyed ourselves that year, poor as we was, an' our neighbours wasn't a bit better off for bein' miserable. Some of 'em grieved till they got poor digestions and couldn't relish what they did have."

The younger boys said they thought their father had the best of it. But Rudolph was thinking that, all the same, the neighbours had managed to get ahead more, in the fifteen years since that time. There must be something wrong about his father's way of doing things. He wished he knew what was going on in the back of Polly's mind. He knew she liked his father, but he knew, too, that she was afraid of something. When his mother sent over coffee-cake or prune tarts or a loaf of fresh bread, Polly seemed to regard them with a certain suspicion. When she observed to him that his brothers had nice manners, her tone implied that it was remarkable they should have. With his mother she was stiff and on her guard. Mary's hearty frankness and gusts of good humour irritated her. Polly was afraid of being unusual or conspicuous in any way, of being "ordinary," as she said!

When Mary had finished her story, Rosicky laid aside his pipe.

"You boys like me to tell you about some of dem hard times I been through in London?" Warmly encouraged, he sat rubbing his forehead along the deep creases. It was bothersome to tell a long story in English (he nearly always talked to the boys in Czech), but he wanted Polly to hear this one.

"Well, you know about dat tailor shop I worked in 'n London? I had one Christmas dere I ain't never forgot. Times was awful bad before Christmas; de boss ain't got much work, an' have it awful hard to pay his rent. It ain't so much fun, bein' poor in a big city like London, I'll say! All de windows is full of good t'ings to eat, an' all de pushcarts in de streets is full, an' you smell 'em all de time, an' you ain't got no money — not a damn bit. I didn't mind de cold so much, though I didn't have no overcoat, chust a short jacket I'd outgrowed so it wouldn't meet on me, an' my hands was chapped raw. But I always had a good appetite, like you all know, an' de sight of dem pork pies in de windows was awful fur me!

"Day before Christmas was terrible foggy dat year, an' dat fog gits into your bones and makes you all damp like. Mrs. Lifschnitz didn't give us nothin' but a little bread an' drippin' for supper, because she was savin' to try for to give us a good dinner on Christmas Day. After supper de boss say I can go an' enjoy myself, so I went into de streets to listen to de Christmas singers. Dey sing old songs an' make very nice music, an' I run round after dem a good ways, till I got awful hungry. I t'ink maybe if I go home, I can sleep till morning an' forgit my belly.

"I went into my corner real quiet, and roll up in my fedder quilt. But I ain't got my head down, till I smell somet'ing good. Seem like it git stronger an' stronger, an' I can't git to sleep noway. I can't understand dat smell. Dere was a gas light in a hall across de court, dat always shine in at my window a little. I got up an' look round. I got a little wooden box in my corner fur a stool, 'cause I ain't got no chair. I picks up dat box, and under it dere is a roast goose on a platter! I can't believe my eyes. I carry it to de window where de light comes in, an' touch it and smell it to find out, an' den I taste it to be sure. I say, I will eat chust one little bite of dat goose, so I can go to sleep, and tomorrow I won't eat none at all. But I tell you, boys, when I stop, one half of dat goose was gone!"

The narrator bowed his head, and the boys shouted. But little Josephine slipped behind his chair and kissed him on the neck beneath his ear.

"Poor little Papa, I don't want him to be hungry!"

"Da's long ago, child. I ain't never been hungry since I had your mudder to cook fur me."

"Go on and tell us the rest, please," said Polly.

"Well, when I come to realize what I done, of course, I felt terrible. I felt better in de stomach, but very bad in de heart. I set on my bed wid dat platter on my knees, an' it all come to me; how hard dat poor woman save to buy dat goose, and how she get some neighbor to cook it dat got more fire, an' how she put it in my corner to keep it away from dem hungry children. Dey was a old carpet hung up to shut my corner off, an' de children wasn't allowed to go in dere. An' I know she put it in my corner because she trust me more'n she did de violin boy. I can't stand it to face her after I spoil de Christmas. So I put on my shoes and go out into de city. I tell myself I better throw myself in de river; but I guess I ain't dat kind of a boy.

"It was after twelve o'clock, an' terrible cold, an' I start out to walk about London all night. I walk along de river awhile, but dey was lots of drunks all along; men, and women too. I chust move along to keep away from de police. I git onto de Strand, an' den over to New Oxford Street, where dere was a big German restaurant on de ground floor, wid big windows all fixed up fine, an' I could see de people having parties inside. While I was lookin' in, two men and two ladies come out, laughin' and talkin' and feelin' happy about all dey been eatin' an' drinkin', and dey was speakin' Czech — not like de Austrians, but like de home folks talk it.

"I guess I went crazy, an' I done what I ain't never done before nor since. I went right up to dem gay people an' begun to beg dem: 'Fellow-countrymen, for God's sake give me money enough to buy a goose!'

"Dey laugh, of course, but de ladies speak awful kind to me, an' dey take me back into de restaurant and give me hot coffee and cakes, an' make me tell all about how I happened to come to London, an' what I was doin' dere. Dey take my name and where I work down on paper, an' both of dem ladies give me ten shillings.

"De big market at Covent Garden ain't very far away, an' by dat time it was open. I go dere an' buy a big goose an' some pork pies, an' potatoes and onions, an' cakes an' oranges fur de children — all I could carry!

When I git home, everybody is still asleep. I pile all I bought on de kitchen table, an' go in an' lay down on my bed, an' I ain't waken up till I hear dat woman scream when she come out into her kitchen. My goodness, but she was surprise! She laugh an' cry at de same time, an' hug me and waken all de children. She ain't stop fur no breakfast; she git de Christmas dinner ready dat morning, and we all sit down an' eat all we can hold. I ain't never seen dat violin boy have all he can hold before.

"Two three days after dat, de two men come to hunt me up, an' dey ask my boss, and he give me a good report an' tell dem I was steady boy all right. One of dem Bohemians was very smart an' run a Bohemian newspaper in New York, an' de odder was a rich man, in de importing business, an' dey been travelling togedder. Dey told me how t'ings was easier in New York, an' offered to pay my passage when dey was goin' home soon on a boat. My boss say to me: 'You go. You ain't got no chance here, an' I like to see you git ahead, fur you always been a good boy to my woman, and fur dat fine Christmas dinner you give us all.' An' da's how I got to New York.'

That night when Rudolph and Polly, arm in arm, were running home across the fields with the bitter wind at their backs, his heart leaped for joy when she said she thought they might have his family come over for supper on New Year's Eve. "Let's get up a nice supper, and not let your mother help at all; make her be company for once."

"That would be lovely of you, Polly," he said humbly. He was a very simple, modest boy, and he, too, felt vaguely that Polly and her sisters were more experienced and worldly than his people.

VI

The winter turned out badly for farmers. It was bitterly cold, and after the first light snows before Christmas there was no snow at all — and no rain. March was as bitter as February. On those days when the wind fairly punished the country, Rosicky sat by his window. In the fall he and the boys had put in a big wheat planting, and now the seed had frozen in the ground. All that land would have to be ploughed up and planted over again, planted in corn. It had happened before, but he was younger then, and he never worried about what had to be. He was sure of himself and of Mary; he knew they could bear what they had to bear, that they would always pull through somehow. But he was not so sure about the young ones, and he felt troubled because Rudolph and Polly were having such a hard start.

Sitting beside his flowering window while the panes rattled and the wind blew in under the door, Rosicky gave himself to reflection as he had not done since those Sundays in the loft of the furniture factory in New York, long ago. Then he was trying to find what he wanted in life for himself; now he was trying to find what he wanted for his boys, and why it was he so hungered to feel sure they would be here, working this very land, after he was gone.

They would have to work hard on the farm, and probably they would never do much more than make a living. But if he could think of them as staying here on the land, he wouldn't have to fear any great unkindness for them. Hardships, certainly; it was a hardship to have the wheat freeze in the ground when seed was so high; and to have to sell your stock because you had no feed. But there would be other years when everything came along right, and you caught up. And what you had was your own. You didn't have to choose between bosses and strikers, and go wrong either way. You didn't have to do with dishonest and cruel people. They were the only things in his experience he had found terrifying and horrible; the look in the eyes of a dishonest and crafty man, of a scheming and rapacious woman.

In the country, if you had a mean neighbour, you could keep off his land and make him keep off yours. But in the city, all the foulness and misery and brutality of your neighbours was part of your life. The worst things he had come upon in his journey through the world were human — depraved and poisonous specimens of man. To this day he could recall certain terrible faces in the London streets. There were mean people everywhere, to be sure, even in their own country town here. But they weren't tempered, hardened, sharpened, like the treacherous people in cities who live by grinding or cheating or poisoning their fellow-men. He had helped to bury two of his fellow-workmen in the tailoring trade, and he was distrustful of the organized industries that see one out of the world in big cities. Here, if you were sick, you had Doctor Ed to look after you; and if you died, fat Mr. Haycock, the kindest man in the world, buried you.

It seemed to Rosicky that for good, honest boys like his, the worst they could do on the farm was better than the best they would be likely to do in the city. If he'd had a mean boy, now, one who was crooked and sharp and tried to put anything over on his brothers, then town would be the place for him. But he had no such boy. As for Rudolph, the discontented one, he would give the shirt off his back to anyone who touched his heart. What Rosicky really hoped for his boys was that they could get through the world without ever knowing much about the cruelty of human beings. "Their mother and me ain't prepared them for that," he sometimes said to himself.

These thoughts brought him back to a grateful consideration of his own case. What an escape he had had, to be sure! He, too, in his time, had had to take money for repair work from the hand of a hungry child who let it go so wistfully; because it was money due his boss. And now, in all these years, he had never had to take a cent from anyone in bitter need — never had to look at the face of a woman become like a wolf's from struggle and famine. When he thought of these things, Rosicky would put on his cap and jacket and slip down to the barn and give his work-horses a little extra oats, letting them eat it out of his hand in their slobbery fashion. It was his way of expressing what he felt, and made him chuckle with pleasure.

The spring came warm, with blue skies — but dry, dry as a bone. The boys began ploughing up the wheat-fields to plant them over in corn. Rosicky would stand at the fence corner and watch them, and the earth was so dry it blew up in clouds of brown dust that hid the horses and the sulky plough and the driver. It was a bad outlook.

The big alfalfa field that lay between the home place and Rudolph's came up green, but Rosicky was worried because during that open windy winter a great many Russian thistle plants had blown in there and lodged. He kept asking the boys to rake them out; he was afraid their seed would root and "take the alfalfa." Rudolph said that was nonsense. The boys were working so hard planting corn, their father felt he couldn't insist about the thistles, but he set great store by that big alfalfa field. It was a feed you could depend on — and there was some deeper reason, vague, but strong. The peculiar green of that clover woke early memories in old Rosicky, went back to something in his childhood in the old world. When he was a little boy, he had played in fields of that strong blue-green colour.

One morning, when Rudolph had gone to town in the car, leaving a work-team idle in his barn, Rosicky went over to his son's place, put the horses to the buggy-rake, and set about quietly raking up those thistles. He behaved with guilty caution, and rather enjoyed stealing a march on Doctor Ed, who was just then taking his first vacation in seven years of practice and was attending a clinic in Chicago. Rosicky got the thistles raked up, but did not stop to burn them. That would take some time, and his breath was pretty short, so he thought he had better get the horses back to the barn.

He got them into the barn and to their stalls, but the pain had come on so sharp in his chest that he didn't try to take the harness off. He started for the house, bending lower with every step. The cramp in his chest was shutting him up like a jack-knife. When he reached the windmill, he swayed and caught at the ladder. He saw Polly coming down the hill, running with the swiftness of a slim greyhound. In a flash she had her shoulder under his armpit.

"Lean on me, Father, hard! Don't be afraid. We can get to the house all right."

Somehow they did, though Rosicky became blind with pain; he could keep on his legs, but he couldn't steer his course. The next thing he was conscious of was lying on Polly's bed, and Polly bending over him wringing out bathtowels in hot water and putting them on his chest. She stopped only to throw coal into the stove, and she kept the tea-kettle and the black pot going. She put these hot applications on him for nearly an hour, she told him afterwards, and all that time he was drawn up stiff and blue, with the sweat pouring off him.

As the pain gradually loosed its grip, the stiffness went out of his jaws, the black circles round his eyes disappeared, and a little of his natural colour came back. When his daughter-in-law buttoned his shirt over his chest at last, he sighed.

"Da's fine, de way I feel now, Polly. It was a awful bad spell, an' I was so sorry it all come on you like it did."

Polly was flushed and excited. "Is the pain really gone? Can I leave you long enough to telephone over to your place?"

Rosicky's eyelids fluttered. "Don't telephone, Polly. It ain't no use to scare my wife. It's nice and quiet here, an' if I ain't too much trouble to you, just let me lay still till I feel like myself. I ain't got no pain now. It's nice here."

Polly bent over him and wiped the moisture from his face. "Oh, I'm so glad it's over!" she broke out impulsively. "It just broke my heart to see you suffer so, Father."

Rosicky motioned her to sit down on the chair where the tea-kettle had been, and looked up at her with that lively affectionate gleam in his eyes. "You was awful good to me, I won't never forgit dat. I hate it to be sick on you like dis. Down at de barn I say to myself, dat young girl ain't had much experience in sickness, I don't want to scare her, an' maybe she's got a baby comin' or somet'ing."

Polly took his hand. He was looking at her so intently and affectionately and confidingly; his eyes seemed to caress her face, to regard it with pleasure. She frowned with her funny streaks of eyebrows, and then smiled back at him.

"I guess maybe there is something of that kind going to happen. But I haven't told anyone yet, not my mother or Rudolph. You'll be the first to know."

His hand pressed hers. She noticed that it was warm again. The twinkle in his yellow-brown eyes seemed to come nearer.

"I like mighty well to see dat little child, Polly," was all he said. Then he closed his eyes and lay half-smiling. But Polly sat still, thinking hard. She had a sudden feeling that nobody in the world, not her mother, not Rudolph, or anyone, really loved her as much as old Rosicky did. It perplexed her. She sat frowning and trying to puzzle it out. It was as if Rosicky had a special gift for loving people, something that was like an ear for music or an eye for colour. It was quiet, unobtrusive; it was merely there. You saw it in his eyes — perhaps that was why they were merry. You felt it in his hands, too. After he dropped off to sleep, she sat holding his warm, broad, flexible brown hand. She had never seen another in the least like it. She wondered if it wasn't a kind of gypsy hand, it was so alive and quick and light in its communications — very strange in a farmer. Nearly all the farmers she knew had huge lumps of fists, like mauls, or they were knotty and bony and uncomfortable-looking, with stiff fingers. But Rosicky's was like quicksilver, flexible, muscular, about the colour of a pale cigar, with deep, deep creases across the palm. It wasn't nervous, it wasn't a stupid lump; it was a warm brown human hand, with some cleverness in it, a great deal of generosity, and something else which Polly could only call "gypsy-like" — something nimble and lively and sure, in the way that animals are.

Polly remembered that hour long afterwards; it had been like an awakening to her. It seemed to her that she had never learned so much about life from anything as from old Rosicky's hand. It brought her to herself; it communicated some direct and untranslatable message.

When she heard Rudolph coming in the car, she ran out to meet him.

"Oh, Rudy, your father's been awful sick! He raked up those thistles he's been worrying about, and afterwards he could hardly get to the house. He suffered so I was afraid he was going to die."

Rudolph jumped to the ground. "Where is he now?"

"On the bed. He's asleep. I was terribly scared, because, you know, I'm so fond of your father." She slipped her arm through his and they went into the house. That afternoon they took Rosicky home and put him to bed, though he protested that he was quite well again.

The next morning he got up and dressed and sat down to breakfast with his family. He told Mary that his coffee tasted better than usual to him, and he warned the boys not to bear any tales to Doctor Ed when he got home. After breakfast he sat down by his window to do some patching and asked Mary to thread several needles for him before she went to feed her chickens — her eyes were better than his, and her hands steadier. He lit his pipe and took up John's overalls. Mary had been watching him anxiously all morning, and as she went out of the door with her bucket of scraps, she saw that he was smiling. He was thinking, indeed, about Polly, and how he might never have known what a tender heart she had if he hadn't got sick over there. Girls nowadays didn't wear their heart on their sleeve. But now he knew Polly would make a fine woman after the foolishness wore off. Either a woman had that sweetness at her heart or she hadn't. You couldn't always tell by the look of them; but if they had that, everything came out right in the end.

After he had taken a few stitches, the cramp began in his chest, like yesterday. He put his pipe cautiously down on the window-sill and bent over to ease the pull. No use — he had better try to get to his bed if he could. He rose and groped his way across the familiar floor, which was rising and falling like the deck of a ship. At the door he fell. When Mary came in, she found him lying there, and the moment she touched him she knew that he was gone.

Doctor Ed was away when Rosicky died, and for the first few weeks after he got home he was hard driven. Every day he said to himself that he must get out to see that family that had lost their father. One soft, warm moonlight night in early summer he started for the farm. His mind was on other things, and not until his road ran by the graveyard did he realize that Rosicky wasn't over there on the hill where the red lamplight shone, but here, in the moonlight. He stopped his car, shut off the engine, and sat there for a while.

A sudden hush had fallen on his soul. Everything here seemed strangely moving and significant, though signifying what, he did not know. Close by the wire fence stood Rosicky's mowing-machine, where one of the boys had been cutting hay that afternoon; his own work-horses had been going up and down there. The new-cut hay perfumed all the night air. The moonlight silvered the long, billowy grass that grew over the graves and hid the fence; the few little evergreens stood out black in it, like shadows in a pool. The sky was very blue and soft, the stars rather faint because the moon was full.

For the first time it struck Doctor Ed that this was really a beautiful graveyard. He thought of city cemeteries; acres of shrubbery and heavy stone, so arranged and lonely and unlike anything in the living world. Cities of the dead, indeed; cities of the forgotten, of the "put away." But this was open and free, this little square of long grass which the wind forever stirred. Nothing but the sky overhead, and the many-coloured fields running on until they met that sky. The horses worked here in summer; the neighbours passed on their way to town; and over yonder, in the cornfield, Rosicky's own cattle would be eating fodder as winter came on. Nothing could be more undeathlike than this place; nothing could be more right for a man who had helped to do the work of great cities and had always longed for the open country and had got to it at last. Rosicky's life seemed to him complete and beautiful.

THEODORE DREISER (1871–1945)

Born of poor and strongly religious parents, Dreiser early rebelled against repression and (like some of his fictional characters) yearned for wealth and social success. He attended Catholic and public schools, and, through the help of a kindly woman, spent one year at Indiana University. He worked, in Chicago, in a real estate office and for a furniture company, and in 1892 began a newspaper and magazine career in Chicago, St. Louis, Pittsburgh, and New York, culminating in the editorship of the *Delineator* and all the other Butterick publications. After 1911 he held no editorial position except for his connection with the *American Spectator* in 1932–34. He was twice married and divorced.

From his experience of life and his reading of Balzac and nineteenth century scientists and philosophers (Huxley, Tyndall, Spencer) he developed a naturalistic outlook which dominates his writings. His first novel, *Sister Carrie*, 1900, the publication of which was arranged by Frank Norris, was withdrawn almost immediately because of reaction against its extreme frankness. A whole decade passed, and then came *Jennie Gerhardt*, quickly followed by *The Financier*, *The Titan*, and *The "Genius,"* the last of which was also banned. Then another decade passed, before the publication of *An American Tragedy* (1925), which was banned in Boston but became a popular success and eventually was both dramatized and filmed. Having fought for a quarter of a century for the right of the serious novelist to image life as he sees it, Dreiser now enjoyed secure fame. A strong, relatively short novel, *The Bulwark*, which appeared the year after his death, was well received.

Meanwhile, he had published books of short stories and character studies, *Free and Other Stories*, 1918, and *Twelve Men*, 1919, which were followed years later by *Chains* and *A Gallery of Women*. His voluminous and diverse output included also poems, plays, autobiography, essays, descriptive and travel books, and social and political studies (*Dreiser Looks at Russia*, 1928, *Tragic America*, 1931). He had made a trip to Russia in 1927, and come to believe in socialistic control of the economic system.

Dreiser's grim, depressing naturalism may best be seen in *An American Tragedy*, a heavily documented novel reminiscent of Zola, though he tried to state it directly in the bewildered essays of *Hey Rub-a-Dub-Dub*, 1920. Change, as he conceived, is the only constant factor in life. Men are not responsible for what they do, being determined by environment and physico-chemical compulsions. Parrington, in a lecture on "Theodore Dreiser: Chief of American Naturalists" (*Main Currents in American Thought*, III), has summed up Dreiser's working philosophy as follows: "1. The world is without reason or meaning to us. Why we are here and to what end is unknowable. 2. Men are chemical compounds, existing in a world where they play about like water-flies, skipping restlessly and unintelligently as their legs drive them, whom the universe in its vast indifference suffers for a time. 3. Men divide into the strong and the weak; not the good and the bad. The will to power, the desire for pleasure, drive men on their courses. What restrains? Moral codes and social conventions, often useful, often harmful. 4. Hence the profound need of sympathy and mercy." On the whole, it seems to Dreiser (to use his own words): "Life is a god-damned stinking game."

As a literary craftsman, Dreiser is about as different as possible from an artist like Willa Cather. He could scarcely write a workmanlike sentence, his language is dull or jarring, and he piles up detail as if to match the detail of actual life. Yet he could write with intense power, a power which takes hold of the reader's emotions and draws him to the end, an energy of creation which some critics have found inadequate in Miss Cather. At the same time he contrived to convey his compassion for men, a compassion no doubt murky, but wholly sincere. "I was filled," he says, "with an intense sympathy for the woes of others, life in all its helpless degradation and poverty. . . . I have sobbed dry sobs looking into what I deemed to be broken faces and the eyes of human failures."

Dreiser's work was vigorously attacked by Stuart P. Sherman, "The Barbaric Naturalism of Theodore Dreiser," *On Contemporary Literature*, 1917, and as vigorously defended by H. L. Mencken, *A Book of Prefaces*, 1917. Other criticism: C. Van Doren, *Contemporary American Novelists*, 1922; B. Rascoe, *Theodore Dreiser*, 1925; T. K. Whipple, *Spokesmen*, 1928; R. Shafer, "An American Tragedy" in N. Foerster, ed., *Humanism and America*, 1930; D. Dudley, *Forgotten Frontiers: Dreiser and the Land of the Free*, 1932. Two important recent books about Dreiser are by R. H. Elias, 1949, and F. O. Matthiessen, 1950.

The Lost Phoebe

(*1912*)

They lived together in a part of the country which was not so prosperous as it had once been, about three miles from one of those small towns that, instead of increasing in population, is steadily decreasing. The territory was not very thickly settled; perhaps a house every other mile or so, with large areas of corn- and wheat-land and fallow fields that at odd seasons had been sown to timothy and clover. Their particular house was part log and part frame, the log portion being the old original home of Henry's grandfather. The new portion, of now rain-beaten, time-worn slabs, through which the wind squeaked in the chinks at times, and which several overshadowing elms and a butternut-tree made picturesque and reminiscently pathetic, but a little damp, was erected by Henry when he was twenty-one and just married.

That was forty-eight years before. The furniture inside, like the house outside, was old and mildewy and reminiscent of an earlier day. You have seen the what-not of cherry wood, perhaps, with spiral legs and fluted top. It was there. The old-fashioned four poster bed, with its ball-like protuberances and deep curving incisions, was there also, a sadly alienated descendant of an early Jacobean ancestor. The bureau of cherry was also high and wide and solidly built, but faded-looking, and with a musty odor. The rag carpet that underlay all these sturdy examples of enduring furniture was a weak, faded, lead-and-pink-colored affair woven by Phoebe Ann's own hands, when she was fifteen years younger than she was when she died. The creaky wooden loom on which it had been done now stood like a dusty, bony skeleton, along with a broken rocking-chair, a worm-eaten clothes-press — Heaven knows how old — a lime-stained bench that had once been used to keep flowers on outside the door, and other decrepit factors of household utility, in an east room that was a lean-to against this so-called main portion. All sorts of other broken-down furniture were about this place; an antiquated clothes-horse, cracked in two of its ribs; a broken mirror in an old cherry frame, which had fallen from a nail and cracked itself three days before their youngest son, Jerry, died; an extension hat-rack, which once had had porcelain knobs on the ends of its pegs; and a sewing-machine, long since outdone in its clumsy mechanism by rivals of a newer generation.

The orchard to the east of the house was full of gnarled old apple trees, worm-eaten as to trunks and branches, and fully ornamented with green and white lichens, so that it had a sad, greenish-white, silvery effect in moonlight. The low outhouses, which had once housed chickens, a horse or two, a cow, and several pigs, were covered with patches of moss as to their roof, and the sides had been free of paint for so long that they were blackish gray as to color, and a little spongy. The picket-fence in front, with its gate squeaky and askew, and the side fences of the stake-and-rider type were in an equally run-down condition. As a matter of fact, they had aged synchronously with the persons who lived here, old Henry Reifsneider and his wife Phoebe Ann.

They had lived here, these two, ever since their marriage, forty-eight years before, and Henry had lived here before that from his childhood up. His father and mother, well along in years when he was a boy, had invited him to bring his wife here when he had first fallen in love and decided to marry; and he had done so. His father and mother were the companions of himself and his wife for ten years after they were married, when both died; and then Henry and Phoebe were left with their five children growing lustily apace. But all sorts of things had happened since then. Of the seven children, all told, that had been born to them, three had died; one girl had gone to Kansas; one boy had gone to Sioux Falls, never even to be heard of after; another boy had gone to Washington; and the last girl lived five counties away in the same State, but was so burdened with cares of her own that she rarely gave them a thought. Time and a commonplace home life that had never been attractive had weaned them thoroughly, so that, wherever they were, they gave little thought as to how it might be with their father and mother.

Old Henry Reifsneider and his wife Phoebe were a loving couple. You perhaps know how it is with simple natures that fasten themselves like lichens on the stones of circumstance and weather their days to a crumbling conclusion. The great world sounds widely, but it has no call for them. They have no soaring intellect. The orchard, the meadow, the cornfield, the pig-pen, and the chicken-lot measure the range of their human activities. When the wheat is headed it is reaped and threshed; when the corn is browned and frosted it is cut and shocked; when the timothy is in full head it is cut, and the haycock erected. After that comes winter, with the hauling of grain to market, the sawing and splitting of wood, the simple chores of fire-building, meal-getting, occasional repairing and visiting. Beyond these and the changes of weather — the snows, the rains, and the fair days — there are no immediate, significant things. All the rest of life is a far-off, clamorous phantasmagoria, flickering like Northern lights in the night, and sounding as faintly as cow-bells tinkling in the distance.

Old Henry and his wife Phoebe were as fond of each other as it is possible for two old people to be who have nothing else in this life to be fond of. He was a thin old man, seventy when she died, a queer, crotchety person with coarse gray-black hair and beard, quite straggly and unkempt. He looked at you out of dull, fishy, watery eyes that had deep-brown crow's-feet at the sides. His clothes, like the clothes of many farmers, were aged and angular and baggy, standing out at the pockets, not fitting about the neck, protuberant and worn at elbow and knee. Phoebe Ann was thin and shapeless, a very umbrella of a woman, clad in shabby black, and with a black bonnet for her best wear. As time had passed, and they had only themselves to look after, their movements had become slower and slower, their activities fewer and fewer. The annual keep of pigs had been reduced from five to one grunting porker, and the single horse which Henry now retained was a sleepy animal, not over-nourished and not very clean. The chickens, of which formerly there was a large flock, had almost disappeared, owing to ferrets, foxes, and the lack of proper care, which produces disease. The former healthy garden was now a straggling memory of itself, and the vines and flower-beds that formerly ornamented the windows and dooryard had now become choking thickets. A will had been made which divided the small tax-eaten property equally among the remaining four, so that it was really of no interest to any of them. Yet these two lived together in peace and sympathy, only that now and then old Henry would become unduly cranky, complaining almost invariably that something had been neglected or mislaid which was of no importance at all.

"Phoebe, where's my corn-knife? You ain't never minded to let my things alone no more."

"Now you hush, Henry," his wife would caution him in a cracked and squeaky voice. "If you don't, I'll leave yuh. I'll git up and walk out of here some day, and then where would y' be? Y' ain't got anybody but me to look after yuh, so yuh just behave yourself. Your corn knife's on the mantel where it's allus been unless you've gone an' put it summers else."

Old Henry, who knew his wife would never leave him in any circumstances, used to speculate at times as to what he would do if she were to die. That was the one leaving that he really feared. As he climbed on the chair at night to wind the old, long-pendulumed, double-weighted clock, or went finally to the front and the back door to see that they were safely shut in, it was a comfort to know that Phoebe was there, properly ensconced on her side of the bed, and that if he stirred restlessly in the night, she would be there to ask what he wanted.

"Now, Henry, do lie still! You're as restless as a chicken."

"Well, I can't sleep, Phoebe."

"Well, yuh needn't roll so, anyhow. Yuh kin let me sleep."

This usually reduced him to a state of somnolent ease. If she wanted a pail of water, it was a grumbling pleasure for him to get it; and if she did rise first to build the fires, he saw that the wood was cut and placed within easy reach. They divided this simple world nicely between them.

As the years had gone on, however, fewer and fewer people had called. They were well-known for a distance of as much as ten square miles as old Mr. and Mrs. Reifsneider, honest, moderately Christian, but too old to be really interesting any longer. The writing of letters had become an almost impossible burden too difficult to continue or even negotiate via others, although an occasional letter still did arrive from the daughter in Pemberton County. Now and then some old friend stopped with a pie or cake or a roasted chicken or duck, or merely to see that they were well; but even these kindly minded visits were no longer frequent.

One day in the early spring of her sixty-fourth year Mrs. Reifsneider took sick, and from a low fever passed into some indefinable ailment which, because of her age, was no longer curable. Old Henry drove to Swinnerton, the neighboring town, and procured a doctor. Some friends called, and the immediate care of her was taken off his hands. Then one chill spring night she died, and old Henry, in a fog of sorrow and uncertainty, followed her body to the nearest graveyard, an unattractive space with a few pines growing in it. Although he might have gone to the daughter in Pemberton or sent for her, it was really too much trouble and he was too weary and fixed. It was suggested to him at once by one friend and another that he come to stay with them awhile, but he did not see fit. He was so old and so fixed in his notions and so accustomed to the exact surroundings he had known all his days, that he could not think of leaving. He wanted to remain near where they had put his Phoebe; and the fact that he would have to live alone did not trouble him in the least. The living children were notified and the care of him offered if he would leave, but he would not.

"I kin make a shift for myself," he continually announced to old Dr. Morrow, who had attended his wife in this case. "I kin cook a little, and besides, it don't take much more'n coffee an' bread in the mornin's to satisfy me. I'll get along now well enough. Yuh just let me be." And after many pleadings and proffers of advice, with supplies of coffee and bacon and baked bread duly offered and accepted, he was left to himself. For a while he sat idly outside his door brooding in the spring sun. He tried to revive his interest in farming, and to keep himself busy and free from thought by looking after the fields, which of late had been much neglected. It was a gloomy thing to come in of an evening, however, or in the afternoon and find no shadow of Phoebe where everything suggested her. By degrees he put a few of her things away. At night he sat beside his lamp and read in the papers that were left him occasionally or in a Bible that he had neglected for years, but he could get little solace from these things. Mostly he held his hand over his mouth and looked at the floor as he sat and thought of what had become of her, and how soon he himself would die. He made a great business of making his coffee in the morning and frying himself a little bacon at night; but his appetite was gone. The shell in which he had been housed so long seemed vacant, and its shadows were suggestive of immedicable griefs. So he lived quite dolefully for five long months, and then a change began.

It was one night, after he had looked after the front and the back door, wound the clock, blown out the light, and gone through all the selfsame motions that he had indulged in for years, that he went to bed not so much to sleep as to think. It was a moonlight night. The green-lichen-covered orchard just outside and to be seen from his bed where he now lay was a silvery affair sweetly spectral. The moon shone through the east windows, throwing the pattern of the panes on the wooden floor, and making the old furniture, to which he was accustomed, stand out dimly in the room. As usual he had been thinking of Phoebe and the years when they had been young together, and of the children who had gone, and the poor shift he was making of his present days. The house was coming to be in a very bad state indeed. The bed-clothes were in disorder, and not clean, for he made a wretched shift of washing. It was a terror to him. The roof leaked, causing things, some of them, to remain damp for weeks at a time, but he was getting into that brooding state where he would accept anything rather than exert himself. He preferred to pace slowly to and fro or to sit and think.

By twelve o'clock of this particular night he was asleep, however, and by two had waked again. The moon by this time had shifted to a position on the western side of the house, and it now shone in through the windows of the living-room and those of the kitchen beyond. A certain combination of furniture — a chair near a table, with his coat on it, the half-open kitchen door casting a shadow, and the position of a lamp near a paper — gave him an exact representation of Phoebe leaning over the table as he had often seen her do in life. It gave him a great start. Could it be she — or her ghost? He had scarcely ever believed in spirits; and still —— He looked at her fixedly in the feeble half-light, his old hair tingling oddly at the roots, and then sat up. The figure did not move. He put his thin legs out of the bed and sat looking at her, wondering if this could really be Phoebe. They had talked of ghosts often in their lifetime, of apparitions and omens; but they had never agreed that such things could be. It had never been a part of his wife's creed that she could have a spirit that could return to walk the earth. Her after-world was quite a different affair, a vague heaven, no less, from which the righteous did not trouble to return. Yet here she was now, bending over the table in her black skirt and gray shawl, her pale profile outlined against the moonlight.

"Phoebe," he called, thrilling from head to toe and putting out one bony hand, "have yuh come back?"

The figure did not stir, and he arose and walked uncertainly to the door, looking at it fixedly the while. As he drew near, however, the apparition resolved itself into its primal content — his old coat over the high-backed chair, the lamp by the paper, the half-open door.

"Well," he said to himself, his mouth open, "I thought shore I saw her." And he ran his hand strangely and vaguely through his hair, the while his nervous tension relaxed. Vanished as it had, it gave him the idea that she might return.

Another night, because of this first illusion, and because his mind was now constantly on her and he was old, he looked out of the window that was nearest his bed and commanded a hen-coop and pig-pen and a part of the wagon-shed, and there, a faint mist exuding from the damp of the ground, he thought he saw her again. It was one of those little wisps of mist, one of those faint exhalations of the earth that rise in a cool night after a warm day, and flicker like small white cypresses of fog before they disappear.

In life it had been a custom of hers to cross this lot from her kitchen door to the pig-pen to throw in any scrap that was left from her cooking, and here she was again. He sat up and watched it strangely, doubtfully, because of his previous experience, but inclined, because of the nervous titillation that passed over his body, to believe that spirits really were, and that Phoebe, who would be concerned because of his lonely state, must be thinking about him, and hence returning. What other way would she have? How otherwise could she express herself? It would be within the province of her charity so to do, and like her loving interest in him. He quivered and watched it eagerly; but, a faint breath of air stirring, it wound away toward the fence and disappeared.

A third night, as he was actually dreaming, some ten days later, she came to his bedside and put her hand on his head.

"Poor Henry!" she said. "It's too bad."

He roused out of his sleep, actually to see her, he thought, moving from his bed-room into the one living-room, her figure a shadowy mass of black. The weak straining of his eyes caused little points of light to flicker about the outlines of her form. He arose, greatly astonished, walked the floor in the cool room, convinced that Phoebe was coming back to him. If he only thought sufficiently, if he made it perfectly clear by his feeling that he needed her greatly, she would come back, this kindly wife, and tell him what to do. She would perhaps be with him much of the time, in the night, anyhow; and that would make him less lonely, this state more endurable.

In age and with the feeble it is not such a far cry from the subtleties of illusion to actual hallucination, and in due time this transition was made for Henry. Night after night he waited, expecting her return. Once in his weird mood he thought he saw a pale light moving about the room, and another time he thought he saw her walking in the orchard after dark. It was one morning when the details of his lonely state were virtually unendurable that he woke with the thought that she was not dead. How he had arrived at this conclusion it is hard to say. His mind had gone. In its place was a fixed

illusion. He and Phoebe had had a senseless quarrel. He had reproached her for not leaving his pipe where he was accustomed to find it, and she had left. It was an aberrated fulfillment of her old jesting threat that if he did not behave himself she would leave him.

"I guess I could find yuh ag'in," he had always said. But her cackling threat had always been:

"Yuh'll not find me if I ever leave yuh. I guess I kin git some place where yuh can't find me."

This morning when he arose he did not think to build the fire in the customary way or to grind his coffee and cut his bread, as was his wont, but solely to meditate as to where he should search for her and how he should induce her to come back. Recently the one horse had been dispensed with because he found it cumbersome and beyond his needs. He took down his soft crush hat after he had dressed himself, a new glint of interest and determination in his eye, and taking his black crook cane from behind the door, where he had always placed it, started out briskly to look for her among the nearest neighbors. His old shoes clumped soundly in the dust as he walked, and his gray-black locks, now grown rather long, straggled out in a dramatic fringe or halo from under his hat. His short coat stirred busily as he walked, and his hands and face were peaked and pale.

"Why, hello, Henry! Where're yuh goin' this mornin'?" inquired Farmer Dodge, who, hauling a load of wheat to market, encountered him on the public road. He had not seen the aged farmer in months, not since his wife's death, and he wondered now, seeing him looking so spry.

"Yuh ain't seen Phoebe, have yuh?" inquired the old man, looking up quizzically.

"Phoebe who?" inquired Farmer Dodge, not for the moment connecting the name with Henry's dead wife.

"Why, my wife Phoebe, o'course. Who do yuh s'pose I mean?" He stared up with a pathetic sharpness of glance from under his shaggy, gray eyebrows.

"Wall, I'll swan, Henry, yuh ain't jokin', are yuh?" said the solid Dodge, a pursy man, with a smooth, hard red face. "It can't be your wife yuh're talkin' about. She's dead."

'Dead! Shucks!" retorted the demented Reifsneider. "She left me early this mornin', while I was sleepin'. She allus got up to build the fire, but she's gone now. We had a little spat last night, an' I guess that's the reason. But I guess I kin find her. She's gone over to Matilda Race's; that's where she's gone."

He started briskly up the road, leaving the amazed Dodge to stare in wonder after him.

"Well, I'll be switched!" he said aloud to himself. "He's clean out'n his head. That poor old feller's been livin' down there till he's gone outen his mind. I'll have to notify the authorities." And he flicked his whip with great enthusiasm. "Geddap!" he said, and was off.

Reifsneider met no one else in this poorly populated region until he reached the white-washed fence of Matilda Race and her husband three miles away. He had passed several other houses en route, but these not being within the range of his illusion were not considered. His wife, who had known Matilda well, must be here. He opened the picket-gate which guarded the walk, and stamped briskly up to the door.

"Why, Mr. Reifsneider," exclaimed old Matilda herself, a stout woman, looking out of the door in answer to his knock, "what brings yuh here this mornin'?"

"Is Phoebe here?" he demanded eagerly.

"Phoebe who? What Phoebe?" replied Mrs. Race, curious as to this sudden development of energy on his part.

"Why, my Phoebe, o'course. My wife Phoebe. Who do yuh s'pose? Ain't she here now?"

"Lawsy me!" exclaimed Mrs. Race, opening her mouth. "Yuh pore man! So you're clean out'n your mind now. Yuh come right in and sit down. I'll git yuh a cup o' coffee. O' course your wife ain't here; but yuh come in an' sit down. I'll find her fer yuh after a while. I know where she is."

The old farmer's eyes softened, and he entered. He was so thin and pale a specimen, pantalooned and patriarchal, that he aroused Mrs. Race's extremest sympathy as he took off his hat and laid it on his knees quite softly and mildly.

"We had a quarrel last night, an' she left me," he volunteered.

"Laws! laws!" sighed Mrs. Race, there being no one present with whom to share her astonishment as she went to her kitchen. "The pore man! Now somebody's just got to look after him. He can't be allowed to run around the country this way lookin' for his dead wife. It's turrible."

She boiled him a pot of coffee and brought in some of her new-baked bread and fresh butter. She set out some of her best jam and put a couple of eggs to boil, lying wholeheartedly the while.

"Now yuh stay right there, Uncle Henry, till Jake comes in, an' I'll send him to look for Phoebe. I think it's more'n likely she's over to Swinnerton with some o' her friends. Anyhow, we'll find out. Now yuh just drink this coffee an' eat this bread. Yuh must be tired. Yuh've had a long walk this mornin'." Her idea was to take counsel with Jake, "her man," and perhaps have him notify the authorities.

She bustled about, meditating on the uncertainties of life, while old Reifsneider thrummed on the rim of his hat with his pale fingers and later ate abstractedly of what she offered. His mind was on his wife, however, and since she was not here, or did not appear, it wandered vaguely away to a family by the name of Murray, miles away in another direction. He decided after a time that he would not wait for Jake Race to hunt his wife but would seek her for himself. He must be on, and urge her to come back.

"Well, I'll be goin'," he said, getting up and looking strangely about him. "I guess she didn't come here after all. She went over to the Murrays', I guess. I'll not wait any longer, Mis' Race. There's a lot to do over to the house to-day." And out he marched in the face of her protests, taking to the dusty road again in the warm spring sun, his cane striking the earth as he went.

It was two hours later that this pale figure of a man appeared in the Murrays' doorway, dusty, perspiring, eager. He had tramped all of five miles, and it was noon. An amazed husband and wife of sixty heard his strange query, and realized also that he was mad. They begged him to stay to dinner, intending to notify the authorities later and see what could be done; but though he stayed to partake of a little something, he did not stay long, and was off again to another distant farmhouse, his idea of many things to do and his need of Phoebe impelling him. So it went for that day and the next and the next, the circle of his inquiry ever widening.

The process by which a character assumes the significance of being peculiar, his antics weird, yet harmless, in such a community is often involute and pathetic. This day, as has been said, saw Reifsneider at other doors, eagerly asking his unnatural question, and leaving a trail of amazement, sympathy, and pity in his wake. Although the authorities were informed — the county sheriff, no less — it was not deemed advisable to take him into custody; for when those who knew old Henry, and had for so long, reflected on the condition of the county insane asylum, a place which, because of the poverty of the district, was of staggering aberration and sickening environment, it was decided to let him remain at large; for, strange to relate, it was found on investigation that at night he returned peaceably enough to his lonesome domicile there to discover whether his wife had returned, and to brood in loneliness until the morning. Who would lock up a thin, eager, seeking old man with iron-gray hair and an attitude of kindly, innocent inquiry, particularly when he was well-known for a past of only kindly servitude and reliability? Those who had known him best rather agreed that he should be allowed to roam at large. He could do no harm. There were many who were willing to help him as to food, old clothes, the odds and ends of his daily life — at least at first. His figure after a time became not so much a commonplace as an accepted curiosity, and the replies, "Why, no, Henry; I ain't see her," or "No, Henry; she ain't been here to-day," more customary.

For several years thereafter then he was an odd figure in the sun and rain, on dusty roads and muddy ones, encountered occasionally in strange and unexpected places, pursuing his endless search. Undernourishment, after a time, although the neighbors and those who knew his history gladly contributed from their store, affected his body; for he walked much and ate little. The longer he roamed the public highway in this manner, the deeper became his strange hallucination; and finding it harder and harder to return from his more and more distant pilgrimages, he finally began taking a few utensils with him from his home, making a small package of them, in order that he might not be compelled to return. In an old tin coffee-pot of large size he placed a small tin cup, a knife, fork, and spoon, some salt and pepper, and to the outside of it, by a string forced through a pierced hole, he fastened a plate, which could be released, and which was his woodland table. It was no trouble for him to secure the little food that he needed, and with a strange, almost religious dignity, he had no hesitation in asking for that much. By degrees his hair became longer and longer, his once black hat became an earthen brown, and his clothes threadbare and dusty.

For all of three years he walked, and none knew how wide were his perambulations, nor how he survived the storms and cold. They could not see him, with homely rural understanding and forethought, sheltering himself in haycocks, or by the sides of cattle, whose warm bodies protected him from the cold, and whose dull understandings were not opposed to his harmless presence. Overhanging rocks and trees kept him at times from the rain, and a friendly hay-loft or corn-crib was not above his humble consideration.

The involute progression of hallucination is strange. From asking at doors and being constantly rebuffed or denied, he finally came to the conclusion that although his Phoebe might not be in any of the houses at the doors of which he inquired, she might nevertheless be within the sound of his voice. And so, from patient inquiry, he began to call sad, occasional cries, that ever and anon waked the quiet landscapes and ragged hill regions, and set to echoing his thin "O-o-o Phoebe! O-o-o Phoebe!" It had a pathetic, albeit insane, ring, and many a farmer or plowboy came to know it even from afar and say, "There goes old Reifsneider."

Another thing that puzzled him greatly after a time and after many hundreds of inquiries was, when he no longer had any particular dooryard in view and no special inquiry to make, which way to go. These crossroads, which occasionally led in four or even six directions, came after a time to puzzle him. But to solve this knotty problem, which became more and more of a puzzle, there came to his aid another hallucination. Phoebe's spirit or some power of the air or wind or nature would tell him. If he stood at the center of the parting of the ways, closed his eyes, turned thrice about, and called "O-o-o Phoebe!" twice, and then threw his cane straight before him, that would surely indicate which way to go for Phoebe, or one of these mystic powers would surely govern its direction and fall! In whichever direction it went, even though, as was not infrequently the case, it took him back along the path he had already come, or across fields, he was not so far gone in his mind but that he gave himself ample time to search before he called again. Also the hallucination seemed to persist that at some time he would surely find her. There were hours when his feet were sore, and his limbs weary, when he would stop in the heat to wipe his seamed brow, or in the cold to beat his arms. Sometimes, after throwing away his cane, and finding it indicating the direction from which he had just come, he would shake his head wearily and philosophically, as if contemplating the unbelievable or an untoward fate, and then start briskly off. His strange figure came finally to be known in the farthest reaches of three or four counties. Old Reifsneider was a pathetic character. His fame was wide.

Near a little town called Watersville, in Green County, perhaps four miles from that minor center of human activity, there was a place or precipice locally known as the Red Cliff, a sheer wall of red sandstone, perhaps a hundred feet high, which raised its sharp face for half a mile or more above the fruitful cornfields and orchards that lay beneath and which was surmounted by a thick grove of trees. The slope that slowly led up to it from the opposite side was covered by a rank growth of beech, hickory, and ash, through which threaded a number of wagon-tracks crossing at various angles. In fair weather it had become old Reifsneider's habit, so inured was he by now to the open, to make his bed in some such patch of trees as this to fry his bacon or boil his eggs at the foot of some tree before laying himself down for the night. Occasionally, so light and inconsequential was his sleep, he would walk at night. More often, the moonlight or some sudden wind stirring in the trees or a reconnoitering animal arousing him, he would sit up and think, or pursue his quest in the moonlight or the dark, a strange, unnatural, half wild, half savage-looking but utterly harmless creature, calling at lonely road crossings, staring at dark and shuttered houses, and wondering where, where Phoebe could really be.

That particular lull that comes in the systole-diastole of this earthly ball at two o'clock in the morning invariably aroused him, and though he might not go any farther he would sit up and contemplate the darkness or the stars, wondering. Sometimes in the strange processes of his mind he would fancy that he saw moving among the trees the figure of his lost wife, and then he would get up to follow, taking his utensils, always on a string, and his cane. If she seemed to evade him too easily he would run, or plead, or, suddenly losing track of the fancied figure, stand awed or disappointed, grieving for the moment over the almost insurmountable difficulties of his search.

It was in the seventh year of these hopeless peregrinations, in the dawn of a similar springtime to that in which his wife had died, that he came at last one night to the vicinity of this selfsame patch that crowned the rise to the Red Cliff. His far-flung cane, used as a divining-rod at the last crossroads, had brought him hither. He had walked many, many miles. It was after ten o'clock at night, and he was very weary. Long wandering and little eating had left him but a shadow of his former self. It was a question now not so much of physical strength but of spiritual endurance which kept him up. He had scarcely eaten this day, and now, exhausted, he set himself down in the dark to rest and possibly to sleep.

Curiously on this occasion a strange suggestion of the presence of his wife surrounded him. It would not be long now, he counseled with himself, although the long months had brought him nothing, until he should see her, talk to her. He fell asleep after a time, his head on his knees. At midnight the moon began to rise, and at two in the morning, his wakeful hour, was a large silver disk shining through the trees to the east. He opened his eyes when the radiance became strong, making a silver pattern at his feet and lighting the woods with strange lusters and silvery, shadowy forms. As usual, his old notion that his wife must be near occurred to him on this occasion, and he looked about him with a speculative, anticipatory eye. What was it that moved in the distant shadows along the path by which he had entered — a pale, flickering will-o'-the-wisp that bobbed gracefully among the trees and riveted his expectant gaze? Moonlight and shadows combined to give it a strange form and a stranger reality, this fluttering of bog-fire or dancing of wandering fireflies. Was it truly his lost Phoebe? By a circuitous route it passed about him, and in his fevered state he fancied that he could see the very eyes of her, not as she was when he last saw her in the black dress and shawl but now a strangely younger Phoebe, gayer, sweeter, the one whom he had known years before as a girl. Old Reifsneider got up. He had been expecting and dreaming of this hour all these years, and now as he saw the feeble light dancing lightly before him he peered at it questioningly, one thin hand in his gray hair.

Of a sudden there came to him now for the first time in many years the full charm of her girlish figure as he had known it in boyhood, the pleasing, sympathetic smile, the brown hair, the blue sash she had once worn about her waist at a picnic, her gay, graceful movements. He walked around the base of the tree, straining with his eyes, forgetting for once his cane and utensils, and following eagerly after. On she moved before him, a will-o'-the-wisp of the spring, a little flame above her head, and it seemed as though among the small saplings of ash and beech and the thick trunks of hickory and elm that she signaled with a young, a lightsome hand.

"O Phoebe! Phoebe!" he called. "Have yuh really come? Have yuh really answered me?" And hurrying faster, he fell once, scrambling lamely to his feet, only to see the light in the distance dancing illusively on. On and on he hurried until he was fairly running, brushing his ragged arms against the trees, striking his hands and face against impending twigs. His hat was gone, his lungs were breathless, his reason quite astray, when coming to the edge of the cliff he saw her below among a silvery bed of apple-trees now blooming in the spring.

"O Phoebe!" he called. "O Phoebe! Oh, no, don't leave me!" And feeling the lure of a world where love was young and Phoebe as this vision presented her, a delightful epitome of their quondam youth, he gave a gay cry of "Oh, wait, Phoebe!" and leaped.

Some farmer-boys, reconnoitering this region of bounty and prospect some few days afterward, found first the tin utensils tied together under the tree where he had left them, and then later at the foot of the cliff, pale, broken, but elate, a molded smile of peace and delight upon his lips, his body. His old hat was discovered lying under some low-growing saplings the twigs of which had held it back. No one of all the simple population knew how eagerly and joyously he had found his lost mate.

SHERWOOD ANDERSON (1876–1941)

Like Dreiser, Sandburg, and O'Neill, Sherwood Anderson wrote books that owe almost everything to personal experience of life, little to formal education in "the best that has been thought and said."

He was born in Camden, Ohio, of a family which was "a wandering, gypsy sort of tribe" often moving from place to place just ahead of the collector — each of the seven children was born in a different town. He went to work when he was twelve, and his formal schooling ceased when he was fourteen. He served in Cuba during the Spanish-American war, returned to Ohio, married, and was manager of a paint factory in Elyria. One day he suddenly walked out of the factory, deliberately giving the impression he had lost his mind; left his family, and made his way to Chicago. In the view of Clifton Fadiman, "The dramatization of this moment is his major contribution to the interpretation of American life." Writing for an advertising agency, he met the "Chicago group" — Dreiser, Sandburg, Floyd Dell, Ben Hecht, and others. After many rejections his first novel, *Windy McPherson's Son*, was published in 1916. Then came *Marching Men, Mid-American Chants*, and his most famous book, *Winesburg, Ohio*, 1919, a collection of his short stories. His later novels included *Poor White*, 1920, and *Dark Laughter*, 1925, and his later short story collections *The Triumph of the Egg*, 1921, and *Horses and Men*, 1923. Moving to New York, he took part in the movements associated with *The Masses*, the *Little Review*, the *Seven Arts*, the *Nation*, and the *New Republic*. Finally he moved to Marion, Virginia, editing the town's two newspapers, one Democratic and one Republican. He was married four times.

In the novels and stories of Anderson, the chief characters were all "slip-off sections of himself." They were small-town people, whose inner life was, as he conceived, a fascinating play of emotion, of impulse, of forces only dimly realized. It was his purpose to uncover and suggestively present this hidden life. His understanding of it, however, was not like that of nineteenth-century writers such as Hawthorne, but rather reflected in a general way the naturalistic psychologies popular after the first World War. "Adopting a naturalistic interpretation of American life, he believed that the primal forces of human behavior are instinctive and not to be denied, as he supposed they are, by the standardization of a machine age. His characters are puzzled, groping, baffled, and possess no vision of order or channel for directing their energies against the frustrations of contemporary existence. Primarily through sex, which he endowed with a mystical significance, Anderson conceived man as having an opportunity to escape from the confinement of this regulated life" (Hart, *Oxford Companion to American Literature*).

In structure, his novels have obvious faults; the short stories are better works of art. He devised a style to suit his purpose, a plain, low-pitched, colloquial style, subtle in its rhythms and repetitions, which owed something to Gertrude Stein and in turn influenced such young authors as Ernest Hemingway and James T. Farrell.

Anderson wrote his autobiography in *A Story Teller's Story*, 1924. Some books dealing with him and his work are H. Hansen, *Midwest Portraits*, 1923; C. B. Chase, *Sherwood Anderson*, 1927; T. K. Whipple, *Spokesmen*, 1928; H. Wickham, *The Impuritans*, 1929; H. Hartwick, *The Foreground of American Fiction*, 1934; A. H. Quinn, *American Fiction*, 1936. See also F. B. Millett, *Contemporary American Authors*, 1940.

"Queer"

(1918)

From his seat on a box in the rough board shed that stuck like a burr on the rear of Cowley & Son's store in Winesburg, Elmer Cowley, the junior member of the firm, could see through a dirty window into the printshop of the *Winesburg Eagle*. Elmer was putting new shoelaces in his shoes. They did not go in readily and he had to take the shoes off. With the shoes in his hand he sat looking at a large hole in the heel of one of his stockings. Then looking quickly up he saw George Willard, the only newspaper reporter in Winesburg, standing at the back door of the *Eagle* printshop and staring absent-mindedly about.

"Well, well, what next!" exclaimed the young man with the shoes in his hand, jumping to his feet and creeping away from the window.

A flush crept into Elmer Cowley's face and his hands began to tremble. In Cowley & Son's store a Jewish traveling salesman stood by the counter talking to his father. He imagined the reporter could hear what was being said and the thought made him furious. With one of the shoes still held in his hand he stood in a corner of the shed and stamped with a stockinged foot upon the board floor.

Cowley & Son's store did not face the main street of Winesburg. The front was on Maumee Street and beyond it was Voight's wagon shop and a shed for the sheltering of farmers' horses. Beside the store an alley-way ran behind the main street stores and all day drays and delivery wagons, intent on bringing in and taking out goods, passed up and down. The store itself was indescribable. Will Henderson once said of it that it sold everything and nothing. In the window facing Maumee Street stood a chunk of coal as large as an apple barrel, to indicate that orders for coal were taken, and beside the black mass of the coal stood three combs of honey grown brown and dirty in their wooden frames.

The honey had stood in the store window for six months. It was for sale as were also the coat hangers, patent suspender buttons, cans of roof paint, bottles of rheumatism cure and a substitute for coffee that companioned the honey in its patient willingness to serve the public.

Ebenezer Cowley, the man who stood in the store listening to the eager patter of words that fell from the lips of the traveling man, was tall and lean and looked unwashed. On his scrawny neck was a large wen partially covered by a grey beard. He wore a long Prince Albert coat. The coat had been purchased to serve as a wedding garment. Before he became a merchant Ebenezer was a farmer and after his marriage he wore the Prince Albert coat to church on Sundays and on Saturday afternoons when he came into town to trade. When he sold the farm to become a merchant he wore the coat constantly. It had become brown with age and was covered with grease spots, but in it Ebenezer always felt dressed up and ready for the day in town.

As a merchant Ebenezer was not happily placed in life and he had not been happily placed as a farmer. Still he existed. His family, consisting of a daughter named Mabel and the son, lived with him in rooms above the store and it did not cost them much to live. His troubles were not financial. His unhappiness as a merchant lay in the fact that when a traveling man with wares to be sold came in at the front door he was afraid. Behind the counter he stood shaking his head. He was afraid, first that he would stubbornly refuse to buy and thus lose the opportunity to sell again; second that he would not be stubborn enough and would in a moment of weakness buy what could not be sold.

In the store on the morning when Elmer Cowley saw George Willard standing and apparently listening at the back door of the *Eagle* printshop, a situation had arisen that always stirred the son's wrath. The traveling man talked and Ebenezer listened, his whole figure expressing uncertainty. "You see how quickly it is done," said the traveling man who had for sale a small flat metal substitute for collar buttons. With one hand he quickly unfastened a collar from his shirt and then fastened it on again. He assumed a flattering wheedling tone. "I tell you what, men have come to the end of all this fooling with collar buttons and you are the man to make money out of the change that is coming. I am offering you the exclusive agency for this town. Take twenty dozen of these fasteners and I'll not visit any other store. I'll leave the field to you."

The traveling man leaned over the counter and tapped with his finger on Ebenezer's breast.

"It's an opportunity and I want you to take it," he urged. "A friend of mine told me about you. 'See that man Cowley,' he said. 'He's a live one.'"

The traveling man paused and waited. Taking a book from his pocket he began writing out the order. Still holding the shoe in his hand Elmer Cowley went through the store, past the two absorbed men, to a glass showcase near the front door. He took a cheap revolver from the case and began to wave it about.

"You get out of here!" he shrieked. "We don't want any collar fasteners here." An idea came to him. "Mind, I'm not making any threat," he added. "I don't say I'll shoot. Maybe I just took this gun out of the case to look at it. But you better get out. Yes sir, I'll say that. You better grab up your things and get out."

The young storekeeper's voice rose to a scream and going behind the counter he began to advance upon the two men. "We're through being fools here!" he cried. "We ain't going to buy any more stuff until we begin to sell. We ain't going to keep on being queer and have folks staring and listening. You get out of here!"

The traveling man left. Raking the samples of collar fasteners off the counter into a black leather bag, he ran. He was a small man and very bow-legged and he ran awkwardly. The black bag caught against the door and he stumbled and fell. "Crazy, that's what he is — crazy!" he sputtered as he arose from the sidewalk and hurried away.

In the store Elmer Cowley and his father stared at each other. Now that the immediate object of his wrath had fled, the younger man was embarrassed. "Well, I meant it. I think we've been queer long enough," he declared, going to the showcase and replacing the revolver. Sitting on a barrel he pulled on and fastened the shoe he had been holding in his hand. He was waiting for some word of understanding from his father, but when Ebenezer spoke his words only served to reawaken the wrath in the son and the young man ran out of the store without replying.

Scratching his grey beard with his long dirty fingers, the merchant looked at his son with the same wavering uncertain stare with which he had confronted the traveling man. "I'll be starched," he said softly. "Well, well, I'll be washed and ironed and starched!"

Elmer Cowley went out of Winesburg and along a country road that paralleled the railroad track. He did not know where he was going or what he was going to do. In the shelter of a deep cut where the road, after turning sharply to the right, dipped under the tracks he stopped and the passion that had been the cause of his outburst in the store began to again find expression.

"I will not be queer — one to be looked at and listened to," he declared aloud. "I'll be like other people. I'll show that George Willard. He'll find out. I'll show him!"

The distraught young man stood in the middle of the road and glared back at the town. He did not know the reporter George Willard and had no special feeling concerning the tall boy who ran about town gathering the town news. The reporter had merely come, by his presence in the office and in the printshop of the *Winesburg Eagle*, to stand for something in the young merchant's mind. He thought the boy who passed and repassed Cowley & Son's store and who stopped to talk to people in the street must be thinking of him and perhaps laughing at him. George Willard, he felt, belonged to the town, typified the town, represented in his person the spirit of the town.

Elmer Cowley could not have believed that George Willard had also his days of unhappiness, that vague hungers and secret unnamable desires visited also his mind. Did he not represent public opinion and had not the public opinion of Winesburg condemned the Cowleys to queerness? Did he not walk whistling and laughing through Main Street? Might not one by striking his person strike also the greater enemy — the thing that smiled and went its own way — the judgment of Winesburg?

Elmer Cowley was extraordinarily tall and his arms were long and powerful. His hair, his eyebrows, and the downy beard that had begun to grow upon his chin, were pale almost to whiteness. His teeth protruded from between his lips and his eyes were blue with the colorless blueness of the marbles called "aggies" that the boys of Winesburg carried in their pockets. Elmer had lived in Winesburg for a year and had made no friends. He was, he felt, one condemned to go through life without friends and he hated the thought.

Sullenly the tall young man tramped along the road with his hands stuffed into his trouser pockets. The day was cold with a raw wind, but presently the sun began to shine and the road became soft and muddy. The tops of the ridges of frozen mud that formed the road began to melt and the mud clung to Elmer's shoes. His feet became cold. When he had gone several miles he turned off the road, crossed a field and entered a wood. In the wood he gathered sticks to build a fire by which he sat trying to warm himself, miserable in body and in mind.

For two hours he sat on the log by the fire and then, arising and creeping cautiously through a mass of underbrush, he went to a fence and looked across fields to a small farmhouse surrounded by low sheds. A smile came to his lips and he began making motions with his long arms to a man who was husking corn in one of the fields.

In his hour of misery the young merchant had returned to the farm where he had lived through boyhood and where there was another human being to whom he felt he could explain himself. The man on the farm was a half-witted old fellow named Mook. He had once been employed by Ebenezer Cowley and had stayed on the farm when it was sold. The old man lived in one of the unpainted sheds back of the farmhouse and puttered about all day in the fields.

Mook the half-wit lived happily. With child-like faith he believed in the intelligence of the animals that lived in the sheds with him, and when he was lonely held long conversations with the cows, the pigs, and even with the chickens that ran about the barnyard. He it was who had put the expression regarding being "laundered" into the mouth of his former employer. When excited or surprised by anything he smiled vaguely and muttered: "I'll be washed and ironed. Well, well, I'll be washed and ironed and starched."

When the half-witted old man left his husking of corn and came into the wood to meet Elmer Cowley, he was neither surprised nor especially interested in the sudden appearance of the young man. His feet also were cold and he sat on the log by the fire, grateful for the warmth and apparently indifferent to what Elmer had to say.

Elmer talked earnestly and with great freedom, walking up and down and waving his arms about. "You don't understand what's the matter with me so of course you don't care," he declared. "With me it's different. Look how it has always been with me. Father is queer and mother was queer, too. Even the clothes mother used to wear were not like other people's clothes, and look at that coat in which father goes about there in town, thinking he's dressed up, too. Why don't he get a new one? It wouldn't cost much. I'll tell you why. Father doesn't know and when mother was alive she didn't know either. Mabel is different. She knows but she won't say anything. I will, though. I'm not going to be stared at any longer. Why look here, Mook, father doesn't know that his store there in town is just a queer jumble, that he'll never sell the stuff he buys. He knows nothing about it. Sometimes he's a little worried that trade doesn't come and then he goes and buys something else. In the evenings he sits by the fire upstairs and says trade will come after a while. He isn't worried. He's queer. He doesn't know enough to be worried."

The excited young man became more excited. "He don't know but I know," he shouted, stopping to gaze down into the dumb, unresponsive face of the half-wit. "I know too well. I can't stand it. When we lived out here it was different. I worked and at night I went to bed and slept. I wasn't always seeing people and thinking as I am now. In the evening, there in town, I go to the post office or to the depot to see the train come in, and no one says anything to me. Everyone stands around and laughs and they talk but they say nothing to me. Then I feel so queer that I can't talk either. I go away. I don't say anything. I can't."

The fury of the young man became uncontrollable.

"I won't stand it," he yelled, looking up at the bare branches of the trees. "I'm not made to stand it."

Maddened by the dull face of the man on the log by the fire, Elmer turned and glared at him as he had glared back along the road at the town of Winesburg. "Go on back to work," he screamed. "What good does it do me to talk to you?" A thought came to him and his voice dropped. "I'm a coward too, eh?" he muttered. "Do you know why I came clear out here afoot? I had to tell someone and you were the only one I could tell. I hunted out another queer one, you see. I ran away, that's what I did. I couldn't stand up to someone like that George Willard. I had to come to you. I ought to tell him and I will."

Again his voice arose to a shout and his arms flew about. "I will tell him. I won't be queer. I don't care what they think. I won't stand it."

Elmer Cowley ran out of the woods leaving the half-wit sitting on the log before the fire. Presently the old man arose and climbing over the fence went back to his work in the corn. "I'll be washed and ironed and starched," he declared. "Well, well, I'll be washed and ironed." Mook was interested. He went along a lane to a field where two cows stood nibbling at a straw stack. "Elmer was here," he said to the cows. "Elmer is crazy. You better get behind the stack where he don't see you. He'll hurt someone yet, Elmer will."

At eight o'clock that evening Elmer Cowley put his head in at the front door of the office of the *Winesburg Eagle* where George Willard sat writing. His cap was pulled down over his eyes and a sullen determined look was on his face. "You come on outside with me," he said, stepping in and closing the door. He kept his hand on the knob as though prepared to resist anyone else coming in. "You just come along outside. I want to see you."

George Willard and Elmer Cowley walked through the main street of Winesburg. The night was cold and George Willard had on a new overcoat and looked very spruce and dressed up. He thrust his hands into the overcoat pockets and looked inquiringly at his companion. He had long been wanting to make friends with the young merchant and find out what was in his mind. Now he thought he saw a chance and was delighted. "I wonder what he's up to? Perhaps he thinks he has a piece of news for the paper. It can't be a fire because I haven't heard the fire bell and there isn't anyone running," he thought.

In the main street of Winesburg, on the cold November evening, but few citizens appeared and these hurried along bent on getting to the stove at the back of some store. The windows of the stores were frosted and the wind rattled the tin sign that hung over the entrance to the stairway leading to Doctor Welling's office. Before Hearn's Grocery a basket of apples and a rack filled with new brooms stood on the sidewalk. Elmer Cowley stopped and stood facing George Willard. He tried to talk and his arms began to pump up and down. His face worked spasmodically. He seemed about to shout. "Oh, you go on back," he cried. "Don't stay out here with me. I ain't got anything to tell you. I don't want to see you at all."

For three hours the distracted young merchant wandered through the resident streets of Winesburg blind with anger, brought on by his failure to declare his determination not to be queer. Bitterly the sense of defeat settled upon him and he wanted to weep. After the hours of futile sputtering at nothingness that had occupied the afternoon and his failure in the presence of the young reporter, he thought he could see no hope of a future for himself.

And then a new idea dawned for him. In the darkness that surrounded him he began to see a light. Going to the now darkened store, where Cowley & Son had for over a year waited vainly for trade to come, he crept stealthily in and felt about in a barrel that stood by the stove at the rear. In the barrel beneath shavings lay a tin box containing Cowley & Son's cash. Every evening Ebenezer Cowley put the box in the barrel when he closed the store and went upstairs to bed. "They wouldn't never think of a careless place like that," he told himself, thinking of robbers.

Elmer took twenty dollars, two ten dollar bills, from the little roll containing perhaps four hundred dollars, the cash left from the sale of the farm. Then replacing the box beneath the shavings he went quietly out at the front door and walked again in the streets.

The idea that he thought might put an end to all of his unhappiness was very simple.

"I will get out of here, run away from home," he told himself. He knew that a local freight train passed through Winesburg at midnight and went on to Cleveland where it arrived at dawn. He would steal a ride on the local and when he got to Cleveland would lose himself in the crowds there. He would get work in some shop and become friends with other workmen. Gradually he would become like other men and would be indistinguishable. Then he could talk and laugh. He would no longer be queer and would make friends. Life would begin to have warmth and meaning for him as it had for others.

The tall awkward young man, striding through the streets, laughed at himself because he had been angry and had been half afraid of George Willard. He decided he would have his talk with the young reporter before he left town, that he would tell him about things, perhaps challenge him, challenge all of Winesburg through him.

Aglow with new confidence Elmer went to the office of the New Willard House and pounded on the door. A sleepy-eyed boy slept on a cot in the office. He received no salary but was fed at the hotel table and bore with pride the title of "night clerk." Before the boy Elmer was bold, insistent. "You wake him up," he commanded. "You tell him to come down by the depot. I got to see him and I'm going away on the local. Tell him to dress and come on down. I ain't got much time."

The midnight local had finished its work in Winesburg and the trainsmen were coupling cars, swinging lanterns and preparing to resume their flight east. George Willard, rubbing his eyes and again wearing the new overcoat, ran down to the station platform afire with curiosity. "Well, here I am. What do you want? You've got something to tell me, eh?" he said.

Elmer tried to explain. He wet his lips with his tongue and looked at the train that had begun to groan and get under way. "Well, you see," he began, and then lost control of his tongue. "I'll be washed and ironed. I'll be washed and ironed and starched," he muttered half incoherently.

Elmer Cowley danced with fury beside the groaning train in the darkness on the station platform. Lights leaped into the air and bobbed up and down before his eyes. Taking the two ten dollar bills from his pocket he thrust them into George Willard's hand. "Take them," he cried. "I don't want them. Give them to father. I stole them." With a snarl of rage he turned and his long arms began to flay the air. Like one struggling for release from hands that held him he struck out, hitting George Willard blow after blow on the breast, the neck, the mouth. The young reporter rolled over on the platform half unconscious, stunned by the terrific force of the blows. Springing aboard the passing train and running over the tops of cars, Elmer sprang down to a flat car and lying on his face looked back, trying to see the fallen man in the darkness. Pride surged up in him. "I showed him," he cried. "I guess I showed him. I ain't so queer. I guess I showed him I ain't so queer."

F. Scott Fitzgerald (1896–1940)

This recorder of the effete East was born and brought up in St. Paul, Minnesota, a fact which has not yet been effectively explored. The Triangle Club at Princeton University provided him with his education, which was interrupted by a session in the army in 1917 — where again he had his mind on something else: the writing of fiction. The customary rejection slips greeted his "The Romantic Egoist," but with the help of the great editor, Maxwell Perkins of Scribner's, he rewrote it and published it as *This Side of Paradise* (1920). This proved so popular that it created a fad for college novels, and throughout the twenties college students were identified in the public mind with "gilded youth." His success led to marriage, slick commercial writing for the magazines, and a commitment to literature as a profession.

He now came to be recognized as the most important spokesman for post-war youth and for a decade which, as he himself put it, "bore him up, flattered him and gave him more money than he had dreamed of, simply for telling people that he felt as they did, that something had to be done with all the nervous energy stored up and unexpended in the War." But his novels and short stories of the twenties, particularly *The Great Gatsby* (1925), show that he was above as well as of the slice of American life which he was recording. Youth's shallow wit and cynicism, its bewilderment and rootlessness, its fake suavity and sophistication, its unemotional delight in irresponsible diversion, its parties at which (in Edmund Wilson's phrase) people went off like rockets, were of the age and were Fitzgerald's specialty, but *The Great Gatsby* is a profoundly serious story of illusion and death which is likely to stand up as his finest work.

His autobiographical notes show that financial and reputational success did not bring him happiness. In the thirties he wandered in Europe, and caught the tone of American expatriate life in *Tender is the Night*, 1935. The predictable end of the road for Fitzgerald was Hollywood (where he explored a new unreality in his unfinished novel, *The Last Tycoon*), and a collapse of vital energy which he described in his autobiography "The Crack-Up."

Whether Fitzgerald will eventually be known primarily as an artist or an historian of the twenties it is too soon to say. He died too young to show his full stature, but if we may judge by letters, autobiographical sketches, notebooks, and fragments published in *The Crack-Up* (ed. Edmund Wilson, 1945) after his death, he had attained enough objectivity to declare his world sterile, and enough maturity to wish to dedicate himself to the craft of fiction as a resource as well as a profession. The "revival" of his work beginning in the 1940's has been based in part on the perception that throughout his stories run, in varying degrees, a sense of death and "visions of horror."

In addition to the titles listed above, Fitzgerald's works include *Flappers and Philosophers*, 1920, *Tales of the Jazz Age*, 1922, *The Beautiful and Damned*, 1922, *All the Sad Young Men*, 1926, and *Taps at Reveille*, 1935 (from which "Babylon Revisited" is here reprinted). The Viking Portable *Fitzgerald*, 1945, reprints *The Great Gatsby*, *Tender is the Night*, and some short stories. Of many critical studies, see Maxwell Geismar, *The Last of the Provincials*, 1947, William Troy in *Forms of Fiction*, ed. W. Van O'Connor, 1948, and Arthur Mizener, *The Far Side of Paradise*, 1951.

Babylon Revisited

(1935)

I

"And where's Mr. Campbell?" Charlie asked.

"Gone to Switzerland. Mr. Campbell's a pretty sick man, Mr. Wales."

"I'm sorry to hear that. And George Hardt?" Charlie inquired.

"Back in America, gone to work."

"And where is the Snow Bird?"

"He was in here last week. Anyway, his friend, Mr. Schaeffer, is in Paris."

Two familiar names from the long list of a year and a half ago. Charlie scribbled an address in his notebook and tore out the page.

"If you see Mr. Schaeffer, give him this," he said. "It's my brother-in-law's address. I haven't settled on a hotel yet."

He was not really disappointed to find Paris was so empty. But the stillness in the Ritz bar was strange and portentous. It was not an American bar any more — he felt polite in it, and not as if he owned it. It had gone back into France. He felt the stillness from the moment he got out of the taxi and saw the doorman, usually in a frenzy of activity at this hour, gossiping with a *chasseur* by the servants' entrance.

Passing through the corridor, he heard only a single, bored voice in the once-clamorous women's room. When he turned into the bar he travelled the twenty feet of green carpet with his eyes fixed straight ahead by old habit; and then, with his foot firmly on the rail, he turned and surveyed the room, encountering only a single pair of eyes that fluttered up from a newspaper in the corner. Charlie asked for the head barman, Paul, who in the latter days of the bull market had come to work in his own custom-built car — disembarking, however, with due nicety at the nearest corner. But Paul was at his country house today and Alix giving him information.

"No, no more," Charlie said, "I'm going slow these days."

Alix congratulated him: "You were going pretty strong a couple of years ago."

"I'll stick to it all right," Charlie assured him. "I've stuck to it for over a year and a half now."

"How do you find conditions in America?"

"I haven't been to America for months. I'm in business in Prague, representing a couple of concerns there. They don't know about me down there."

Alix smiled.

"Remember the night of George Hardt's bachelor dinner here?" said Charlie. "By the way, what's become of Claude Fessenden?"

Alix lowered his voice confidentially: "He's in Paris, but he doesn't come here any more. Paul doesn't allow it. He ran up a bill of thirty thousand francs, charging all his drinks and his lunches, and usually his dinner, for more than a year. And when Paul finally told him he had to pay, he gave him a bad check."

Alix shook his head sadly.

"I don't understand it, such a dandy fellow. Now he's all bloated up ——" He made a plump apple of his hands.

Charlie watched a group of strident queens installing themselves in a corner.

"Nothing affects them," he thought. "Stocks rise and fall, people loaf or work, but they go on forever." The place oppressed him. He called for the dice and shook with Alix for the drink.

"Here for long, Mr. Wales?"

"I'm here for four or five days to see my little girl."

"Oh-h! You have a little girl?"

Outside, the fire-red, gas-blue, ghost-green signs shone smokily through the tranquil rain. It was late afternoon and the streets were in movement; the *bistros* gleamed. At the corner of the Boulevard des Capucines he took a taxi. The Place de la Concorde moved by in pink majesty; they crossed the logical Seine, and Charlie felt the sudden provincial quality of the left bank.

Charlie directed his taxi to the Avenue de l'Opera, which was out of his way. But he wanted to see the blue hour spread over the magnificent façade, and imagine that the cab horns, playing endlessly the first few bars of *Le Plus que Lent*, were the trumpets of the Second Empire. They were closing the iron grill in front of Brentano's Book-store, and people were already at dinner behind the trim little bourgeois hedge of Duval's. He had never eaten at a really cheap restaurant in Paris. Five-course dinner, four francs fifty, eighteen cents, wine included. For some odd reason he wished that he had.

As they rolled on to the Left Bank and he felt its sudden provincialism, he thought, "I spoiled this city for myself. I didn't realize it, but the days came along one after another, and then two years were gone, and everything was gone, and I was gone."

He was thirty-five, and good to look at. The Irish mobility of his face was sobered by a deep wrinkle between his eyes. As he rang his brother-in-law's bell in the Rue Palatine, the wrinkle deepened till it pulled down his brows; he felt a cramping sensation in his belly. From behind the maid who opened the door darted a lovely little girl of nine who shrieked "Daddy!" and flew up, struggling like a fish, into his arms. She pulled his head around by one ear and set her cheek against his.

"My old pie," he said.

"Oh, daddy, daddy, daddy, daddy, dads, dads, dads!"

She drew him into the salon, where the family waited, a boy and girl his daughter's age, his sister-in-law and her husband. He greeted Marion with his voice pitched carefully to avoid either feigned enthusiasm or dislike, but her response was more frankly tepid, though she minimized her expression of unalterable distrust by directing her regard toward his child. The two men clasped hands in a friendly way and Lincoln Peters rested his for a moment on Charlie's shoulder.

The room was warm and comfortably American. The three children moved intimately about, playing through the yellow oblongs that led to other rooms; the cheer of six o'clock spoke in the eager smacks of the fire and the sounds of French activity in the kitchen. But Charlie did not relax; his heart sat up rigidly in his body and he drew confidence from his daughter, who from time to time came close to him, holding in her arms the doll he had brought.

"Really extremely well," he declared in answer to Lincoln's question. "There's a lot of business there that isn't moving at all, but we're doing even better than ever. In fact, damn well. I'm bringing my sister over from America next month to keep house for me. My income last year was bigger than it was when I had money. You see, the Czechs ———"

His boasting was for a specific purpose; but after a moment, seeing a faint restiveness in Lincoln's eye, he changed the subject:

"Those are fine children of yours, well brought up, good manners."

"We think Honoria's a great little girl too."

Marion Peters came back from the kitchen. She was a tall woman with worried eyes, who had once possessed a fresh American loveliness. Charlie had never been sensitive to it and was always surprised when people spoke of how pretty she had been. From the first there had been an instinctive antipathy between them.

"Well, how do you find Honoria?" she asked.

"Wonderful. I was astonished how much she's grown in ten months. All the children are looking well."

"We haven't had a doctor for a year. How do you like being back in Paris?"

"It seems very funny to see so few Americans around."

"I'm delighted," Marion said vehemently. "Now at least you can go into a store without their assuming you're a millionaire. We've suffered like everybody, but on the whole it's a good deal pleasanter."

"But it was nice while it lasted," Charlie said. "We were a sort of royalty, almost infallible, with a sort of magic around us. In the bar this afternoon" — he stumbled, seeing his mistake — "there wasn't a man I knew."

She looked at him keenly. "I should think you'd have had enough of bars."

"I only stayed a minute. I take one drink every afternoon, and no more."

"Don't you want a cocktail before dinner?" Lincoln asked.

"I take only one drink every afternoon, and I've had that."

"I hope you keep to it," said Marion.

Her dislike was evident in the coldness with which she spoke, but Charlie only smiled; he had larger plans. Her very aggressiveness gave him an advantage, and he knew enough to wait. He wanted them to initiate the discussion of what they knew had brought him to Paris.

At dinner he couldn't decide whether Honoria was most like him or her mother. Fortunate if she didn't combine the traits of both that had brought them to disaster. A great wave of protectiveness went over him. He thought he knew what to do for her. He believed in character; he wanted to jump back a whole generation and trust in character again as the eternally valuable element. Everything else wore out.

He left soon after dinner, but not to go home. He was curious to see Paris by night with clearer and more judicious eyes than those of other days. He bought a *strapontin* for the Casino and watched Josephine Baker go through her chocolate arabesques.

After an hour he left and strolled toward Montmartre, up the Rue Pigalle into the Place Blanche. The rain had stopped and there were a few people in evening clothes disembarking from taxis in front of cabarets, and *cocottes* prowling singly or in pairs, and many Negroes. He passed a lighted door from which issued music, and stopped with the sense of familiarity; it was Bricktop's, where he had parted with so many hours and so much money. A few doors farther on he found another ancient rendezvous and incautiously put his head inside. Immediately an eager orchestra burst into sound, a pair of professional dancers leaped to their feet and a maitre d'hôtel swooped toward him, crying, "Crowd just arriving, sir!" But he withdrew quickly.

"You have to be damn drunk," he thought.

Zelli's was closed, the bleak and sinister cheap hotels surrounding it were dark; up in the Rue Blanche there was more light and a local, colloquial French crowd. The Poet's Cave had disappeared, but the two great mouths of the Café of Heaven and the Café of Hell still yawned — even devoured, as he watched, the meagre contents of a tourist bus — a German, a Japanese, and an American couple who glanced at him with frightened eyes.

So much for the effort and ingenuity of Montmartre. All the catering to vice and waste was on an utterly childish scale, and he suddenly realized the meaning of the word "dissipate" — to dissipate into thin air; to make nothing out of something. In the little hours of the night every move from place to place was an enormous human jump, an increase of paying for the privilege of slower and slower motion.

He remembered thousand-franc notes given to an orchestra for playing a single number, hundred-franc notes tossed to a doorman for calling a cab.

But it hadn't been given for nothing.

It had been given, even the most wildly squandered sum, as an offering to destiny that he might not remember the things most worth remembering, the things that now he would always remember — his child taken from his control, his wife escaped to a grave in Vermont.

In the glare of a *brasserie* a woman spoke to him. He bought her some eggs and coffee, and then, eluding her encouraging stare, gave her a twenty-franc note and took a taxi to his hotel.

II

He woke upon a fine fall day — football weather. The depression of yesterday was gone and he liked the people on the streets. At noon he sat opposite Honoria at Le Grand Vatel, the only restaurant he could think of not reminiscent of champagne dinners and long luncheons that began at two and ended in a blurred and vague twilight.

"Now, how about vegetables? Oughtn't you to have some vegetables?"

"Well, yes."

"Here's *épinards* and *chou-fleur* and carrots and *haricots*."

"I'd like *chou-fleur*."

"Wouldn't you like to have two vegetables?"

"I usually only have one at lunch."

The waiter was pretending to be inordinately fond of children. "*Qu'elle est mignonne la petite? Elle parle exactement comme une française.*"

"How about dessert? Shall we wait and see?"

The waiter disappeared. Honoria looked at her father expectantly.

"What are we going to do?"

"First, we're going to that toy store in the Rue Saint-Honoré and buy you anything you like. And then we're going to the vaudeville at the Empire."

She hesitated. "I like it about the vaudeville, but not the toy store."

"Why not?"

"Well, you brought me this doll." She had it with her. "And I've got lots of things. And we're not rich any more, are we?"

"We never were. But today you are to have anything you want."

"All right," she agreed resignedly.

When there had been her mother and a French nurse he had been inclined to be strict; now he extended himself, reached out for a new tolerance; he must be both parents to her and not shut any of her out of communication.

"I want to get to know you," he said gravely. "First let me introduce myself. My name is Charles J. Wales, of Prague."

"Oh, daddy!" her voice cracked with laughter.

"And who are you, please?" he persisted, and she accepted a rôle immediately: "Honoria Wales, Rue Palatine, Paris."

"Married or single?"

"No, not married. Single."

He indicated the doll. "But I see you have a child, madame."

Unwilling to disinherit it, she took it to her heart and thought quickly: "Yes, I've been married, but I'm not married now. My husband is dead."

He went on quickly, "And the child's name?"

"Simone. That's after my best friend at school."

"I'm very pleased that you're doing so well at school."

"I'm third this month," she boasted. "Elsie" — that was her cousin — "is only about eighteenth, and Richard is about at the bottom."

"You like Richard and Elsie, don't you?"

"Oh, yes. I like Richard quite well and I like her all right."

Cautiously and casually he asked: "And Aunt Marion and Uncle Lincoln — which do you like best?"

"Oh, Uncle Lincoln, I guess."

He was increasingly aware of her presence. As they came in, a murmur of ". . . adorable"

followed them, and now the people at the next table bent all their silences upon her, staring as if she were something no more conscious than a flower.

"Why don't I live with you?" she asked suddenly. "Because mamma's dead?"

"You must stay here and learn more French. It would have been hard for daddy to take care of you so well."

"I don't really need much taking care of any more. I do everything for myself."

Going out of the restaurant, a man and a woman unexpectedly hailed him.

"Well, the old Wales!"

"Hello there, Lorraine. . . . Dunc."

Sudden ghosts out of the past: Duncan Schaeffer, a friend from college. Lorraine Quarrles, a lovely, pale blonde of thirty; one of a crowd who had helped them make months into days in the lavish times of three years ago.

"My husband couldn't come this year," she said, in answer to his question. "We're poor as hell. So he gave me two hundred a month and told me I could do my worst on that. . . . This your little girl?"

"What about coming back and sitting down?" Duncan asked.

"Can't do it." He was glad for an excuse. As always he felt Lorraine's passionate, provocative attraction, but his own rhythm was different now.

"Well, how about dinner?" she asked.

"I'm not free. Give me your address and let me call you."

"Charlie, I believe you're sober," she said judicially. "I honestly believe he's sober, Dunc. Pinch him and see if he's sober."

Charlie indicated Honoria with his head. They both laughed.

"What's your address?" said Duncan sceptically.

He hesitated, unwilling to give the name of his hotel.

"I'm not settled yet. I'd better call you. We're going to see the vaudeville at the Empire."

"There! That's what I want to do," Lorraine said. "I want to see some clowns and acrobats and jugglers. That's just what we'll do, Dunc."

"We've got to do an errand first," said

Charlie. "Perhaps we'll see you there."

"All right, you snob. . . . Good-bye, beautiful little girl."

"Good-bye."

Honoria bobbed politely.

Somehow, an unwelcome encounter. They liked him because he was functioning, because he was serious; they wanted to see him, because he was stronger than they were now, because they wanted to draw a certain sustenance from his strength.

At the Empire, Honoria proudly refused to sit upon her father's folded coat. She was already an individual with a code of her own, and Charlie was more and more absorbed by the desire of putting a little of himself into her before she crystallized utterly. It was hopeless to try to know her in so short a time.

Between the acts they came upon Duncan and Lorraine in the lobby where the band was playing.

"Have a drink?"

"All right, but not up at the bar. We'll take a table."

"The perfect father."

Listening abstractedly to Lorraine, Charlie watched Honoria's eyes leave their table, and he followed them wistfully about the room, wondering what they saw. He met her glance and she smiled.

"I liked that lemonade," she said.

What had she said? What had he expected? Going home in a taxi afterward, he pulled her over until her head rested against his chest.

"Darling, do you ever think about your mother?"

"Yes, sometimes," she answered vaguely.

"I don't want you to forget her. Have you got a picture of her?"

"Yes, I think so. Anyhow, Aunt Marion has. Why don't you want me to forget her?"

"She loved you very much."

"I loved her too."

They were silent for a moment.

"Daddy, I want to come and live with you," she said suddenly.

His heart leaped; he had wanted it to come like this.

"Aren't you perfectly happy?"

"Yes, but I love you better than anybody.

And you love me better than anybody, don't you, now that mummy's dead?"

"Of course I do. But you won't always like me best, honey. You'll grow up and meet somebody your own age and go marry him and forget you ever had a daddy."

"Yes, that's true," she agreed tranquilly.

He didn't go in. He was coming back at nine o'clock and he wanted to keep himself fresh and new for the thing he must say then.

"When you're safe inside, just show yourself in that window."

"All right. Good-bye, dads, dads, dads, dads."

He waited in the dark street until she appeared, all warm and glowing, in the window above and kissed her fingers out into the night.

III

They were waiting. Marion sat behind the coffee service in a dignified black dinner dress that just faintly suggested mourning. Lincoln was walking up and down with the animation of one who had already been talking. They were as anxious as he was to get into the question. He opened it almost immediately:

"I suppose you know what I want to see you about — why I really came to Paris."

Marion played with the black stars on her necklace and frowned.

"I'm awfully anxious to have a home," he continued. "And I'm awfully anxious to have Honoria in it. I appreciate your taking in Honoria for her mother's sake, but things have changed now" — he hesitated and then continued more forcibly — "changed radically with me, and I want to ask you to reconsider the matter. It would be silly for me to deny that about three years ago I was acting badly——"

Marion looked up at him with hard eyes.

"—— but all that's over. As I told you, I haven't had more than a drink a day for over a year, and I take that drink deliberately, so that the idea of alcohol won't get too big in my imagination. You see the idea?"

"No," said Marion succinctly.

"It's a sort of stunt I set myself. It keeps the matter in proportion."

"I get you," said Lincoln. "You don't want to admit it's got any attraction for you."

"Something like that. Sometimes I forget and don't take it. But I try to take it. Anyhow, I couldn't afford to drink in my position. The people I represent are more than satisfied with what I've done, and I'm bringing my sister over from Burlington to keep house for me, and I want awfully to have Honoria too. You know that even when her mother and I weren't getting along well we never let anything that happened touch Honoria. I know she's fond of me and I know I'm able to take care of her and — well, there you are. How do you feel about it?"

He knew that now he would have to take a beating. It would last an hour or two hours, and it would be difficult, but if he modulated his inevitable resentment to the chastened attitude of the reformed sinner, he might win his point in the end.

Keep your temper, he told himself. You don't want to be justified. You want Honoria.

Lincoln spoke first: "We've been talking it over ever since we got your letter last month. We're happy to have Honoria here. She's a dear little thing, and we're glad to be able to help her, but of course that isn't the question ——"

Marion interrupted suddenly. "How long are you going to stay sober, Charlie?" she asked.

"Permanently, I hope."

"How can anybody count on that?"

"You know I never did drink heavily until I gave up business and came over here with nothing to do. Then Helen and I began to run around with ——"

"Please leave Helen out of it. I can't bear to hear you talk about her like that."

He stared at her grimly; he had never been certain how fond of each other the sisters were in life.

"My drinking only lasted about a year and a half — from the time we came over until I — collapsed."

"It was time enough."

"It was time enough," he agreed.

"My duty is entirely to Helen," she said. "I try to think what she would have wanted me to do. Frankly, from the night you did that terrible thing you haven't really existed for me. I can't help that. She was my sister."

"Yes."

"When she was dying she asked me to look out for Honoria. If you hadn't been in a sanitarium then, it might have helped matters."

He had no answer.

"I'll never in my life be able to forget the morning when Helen knocked at my door, soaked to the skin and shivering, and said you'd locked her out."

Charlie gripped the sides of the chair. This was more difficult than he expected; he wanted to launch out into a long expostulation and explanation, but he only said: "The night I locked her out ——" and she interrupted, "I don't feel up to going over that again."

After a moment's silence Lincoln said: "We're getting off the subject. You want Marion to set aside her legal guardianship and give you Honoria. I think the main point for her is whether she has confidence in you or not."

"I don't blame Marion," Charlie said slowly, "but I think she can have entire confidence in me. I had a good record up to three years ago. Of course, it's within human possibilities I might go wrong any time. But if we wait much longer I'll lose Honoria's childhood and my chance for a home." He shook his head, "I'll simply lose her, don't you see?"

"Yes, I see," said Lincoln.

"Why didn't you think of all this before?" Marion asked.

"I suppose I did, from time to time, but Helen and I were getting along badly. When I consented to the guardianship, I was flat on my back in a sanitarium and the market had cleaned me out. I knew I'd acted badly, and I thought if it would bring any peace to Helen, I'd agree to anything. But now it's different. I'm functioning, I'm behaving damn well, so far as ——"

"Please don't swear at me," Marion said.

He looked at her, startled. With each remark the force of her dislike became more and more apparent. She had built up all her fear of life into one wall and faced it toward him. This trivial reproof was possibly the result of some trouble with the cook several hours before. Charlie became increasingly alarmed at leaving Honoria in this atmosphere of hostility against himself; sooner or later it would come out, in a word here, a shake of the head there, and some of that distrust would be irrevocably implanted in Honoria. But he pulled his temper down out of his face and shut it up inside him; he had won a point, for Lincoln realized the absurdity of Marion's remark and asked her lightly since when she had objected to the word "damn."

"Another thing," Charlie said: "I'm able to give her certain advantages now. I'm going to take a French governess to Prague with me. I've got a lease on a new apartment ——"

He stopped, realizing that he was blundering. They couldn't be expected to accept with equanimity the fact that his income was again twice as large as their own.

"I suppose you can give her more luxuries than we can," said Marion. "When you were throwing away money we were living along watching every ten francs.... I suppose you'll start doing it again."

"Oh, no," he said. "I've learned. I worked hard for ten years, you know — until I got lucky in the market, like so many people. Terribly lucky. It didn't seem any use working any more, so I quit. It won't happen again."

There was a long silence. All of them felt their nerves straining, and for the first time in a year Charlie wanted a drink. He was sure now that Lincoln Peters wanted him to have his child.

Marion shuddered suddenly; part of her saw that Charlie's feet were planted on the earth now, and her own maternal feeling recognized the naturalness of his desire; but she had lived for a long time with a prejudice — a prejudice founded on a curious disbelief in her sister's happiness, and which, in the shock of one terrible night, had turned to hatred for him. It had all happened at a point in her life where the discouragement of ill health and adverse circumstances made it necessary for her to believe in tangible villainy and a tangible villain.

"I can't help what I think!" she cried out suddenly. "How much you were responsible for Helen's death, I don't know. It's something you'll have to square with your own conscience."

An electric current of agony surged through him; for a moment he was almost on his feet, an unuttered sound echoing in his throat. He hung on to himself for a moment, another moment.

"Hold on there," said Lincoln uncomfortably. "I never thought you were responsible for that."

"Helen died of heart trouble," Charlie said dully.

"Yes, heart trouble." Marion spoke as if the phrase had another meaning for her.

Then, in the flatness that followed her outburst, she saw him plainly and she knew he had somehow arrived at control over the situation. Glancing at her husband, she found no help from him, and as abruptly as if it were a matter of no importance, she threw up the sponge.

"Do what you like!" she cried, springing up from her chair. "She's your child. I'm not the person to stand in your way. I think if it were my child I'd rather see her ——" She managed to check herself. "You two decide it. I can't stand this. I'm sick. I'm going to bed."

She hurried from the room; after a moment Lincoln said:

"This has been a hard day for her. You know how strongly she feels ——" His voice was almost apologetic: "When a woman gets an idea in her head."

"Of course."

"It's going to be all right. I think she sees now that you — can provide for the child, and so we can't very well stand in your way or Honoria's way."

"Thank you, Lincoln."

"I'd better go along and see how she is."

"I'm going."

He was still trembling when he reached the street, but a walk down the Rue Bonaparte to the quais set him up, and as he crossed the Seine, fresh and new by the quai lamps, he felt exultant. But back in his room he couldn't sleep. The image of Helen haunted him. Helen whom he had loved so until they had senselessly begun to abuse each other's love, tear it into shreds. On that terrible February night that Marion remembered so vividly, a slow quarrel had gone on for hours. There was a scene at the Florida, and then he attempted to take her home, and then she kissed young Webb at a table; after that there was what she had hysterically said. When he arrived home alone he turned the key in the lock in wild anger. How could he know she would arrive an hour later alone, that there would be a snowstorm in which she wandered about in slippers, too confused to find a taxi? Then the aftermath, her escaping pneumonia by a miracle, and all the attendant horror. They were "reconciled," but that was the beginning of the end, and Marion, who had seen with her own eyes and who imagined it to be one of many scenes from her sister's martyrdom, never forgot.

Going over it again brought Helen nearer, and in the white, soft light that steals upon half sleep near morning he found himself talking to her again. She said that he was perfectly right about Honoria and that she wanted Honoria to be with him. She said she was glad he was being good and doing better. She said a lot of other things — very friendly things — but she was in a swing in a white dress, and swinging faster and faster all the time, so that at the end he could not hear clearly all that she said.

IV

He woke up feeling happy. The door of the world was open again. He made plans, vistas, futures for Honoria and himself, but suddenly he grew sad, remembering all the plans he and Helen had made. She had not planned to die. The present was the thing — work to do and someone to love. But not to love too much, for he knew the injury that a father can do to a daughter or a mother to a son by attaching them too closely: afterward, out in the world, the child would seek in the marriage partner the same blind tenderness and, failing probably to find it, turn against love and life.

It was another bright, crisp day. He called Lincoln Peters at the bank where he worked and asked if he could count on taking Honoria when he left for Prague. Lincoln agreed that there was no reason for delay. One thing — the legal guardianship. Marion wanted to retain that a while longer. She was upset by the whole matter, and it would oil things if she felt that the situation was still in her control for another year. Charlie agreed, wanting only the tangible, visible child.

Then the question of a governess. Charlie sat in a gloomy agency and talked to a cross Bernaise and to a buxom Breton peasant, neither of whom he could have endured. There were others whom he would see tomorrow.

He lunched with Lincoln Peters at Griffons, trying to keep down his exultation.

"There's nothing quite like your own child," Lincoln said. "But you understand how Marion feels too."

"She's forgotten how hard I worked for seven years there," Charlie said. "She just remembers one night."

"There's another thing." Lincoln hesitated. "While you and Helen were tearing around Europe throwing money away, we were just getting along. I didn't touch any of the prosperity because I never got ahead enough to carry anything but my insurance. I think Marion felt there was some kind of injustice in it — you not even working toward the end, and getting richer and richer."

"It went just as quick as it came," said Charlie.

"Yes, a lot of it stayed in the hands of *chasseurs* and saxophone players and maîtres d'hôtel — well, the big party's over now. I just said that to explain Marion's feeling about those crazy years. If you drop in about six o'clock tonight before Marion's too tired, we'll settle the details on the spot."

Back at his hotel, Charlie found a *pneumatique* that had been redirected from the Ritz bar where Charlie had left his address for the purpose of finding a certain man.

DEAR CHARLIE: You were so strange when we saw you the other day that I wondered if I did something to offend you. If so, I'm not conscious of it. In fact, I have thought about you too much for the last year, and it's always been in the back of my mind that I might see you if I came over here. We *did* have such good times that crazy spring, like the night you and I stole the butcher's tricycle, and the time we tried to call on the president and you had the old derby rim and the wire cane. Everybody seems so old lately, but I don't feel old a bit. Couldn't we get together some time today for old time's sake? I've got a vile hang-over for the moment, but will be feeling better this afternoon and will look for you about five in the sweet-shop at the Ritz.

Always devotedly
LORRAINE

His first feeling was one of awe that he had actually, in his mature years, stolen a tricycle and pedalled Lorraine all over the Étoile between the small hours and dawn. In retro-spect it was a nightmare. Locking out Helen didn't fit in with any other act of his life, but the tricycle incident did — it was one of many. How many weeks or months of dissi-pation to arrive at that condition of utter irresponsibility?

He tried to picture how Lorraine had ap-peared to him then — very attractive; Helen was unhappy about it, though she said nothing. Yesterday, in the restaurant, Lor-raine had seemed trite, blurred, worn away. He emphatically did not want to see her, and he was glad Alix had not given away his hotel address. It was a relief to think, in-stead, of Honoria, to think of Sundays spent with her and of saying good morning to her and of knowing she was there in his house at night, drawing her breath in the dark-ness.

At five he took a taxi and bought presents for all the Peters — a piquant cloth doll, a box of Roman soldiers, flowers for Marion, big linen handkerchiefs for Lincoln.

He saw, when he arrived in the apartment, that Marion had accepted the inevitable. She greeted him now as though he were a recalcitrant member of the family, rather than a menacing outsider. Honoria had been told she was going; Charlie was glad to see that her tact made her conceal her exces-sive happiness. Only on his lap did she whisper her delight and the question "When?" before she slipped away with the other chil-dren.

He and Marion were alone for a minute in the room, and on an impulse he spoke out boldly:

"Family quarrels are bitter things. They don't go according to any rules. They're not like aches or wounds; they're more like splits in the skin that won't heal because there's not enough material. I wish you and I could be on better terms."

"Some things are hard to forget," she answered. "It's a question of confidence." There was no answer to this and presently she asked, "When do you propose to take her?"

"As soon as I can get a governess. I hoped the day after tomorrow."

"That's impossible. I've got to get her things in shape. Not before Saturday."

He yielded. Coming back into the room, Lincoln offered him a drink.

"I'll take my daily whisky," he said.

It was warm here, it was a home, people together by a fire. The children felt very safe and important; the mother and father were serious, watchful. They had things to do for the children more important than his visit here. A spoonful of medicine was, after all, more important than the strained relations between Marion and himself. They were not dull people, but they were very much in the grip of life and circumstances. He won-dered if he couldn't do something to get Lincoln out of his rut at the bank.

A long peal at the door-bell; the *bonne de toute faire* passed through and went down the corridor. The door opened upon another long ring, and then voices, and the three in the salon looked up expectantly; Richard moved to bring the corridor within his range of vision, and Marion rose. Then the maid came back along the corridor, closely fol-lowed by the voices, which developed under the light into Duncan Schaeffer and Lorraine Quarrles.

They were gay, they were hilarious, they were roaring with laughter. For a moment Charlie was astounded; unable to understand how they ferreted out the Peters' address.

"Ah-h-h!" Duncan wagged his finger roguishly at Charlie. "Ah-h-h!"

They both slid down another cascade of laughter. Anxious and at a loss, Charlie shook hands with them quickly and presented them to Lincoln and Marion. Marion nodded, scarcely speaking. She had drawn back a step toward the fire; her little girl stood beside her, and Marion put an arm about her shoulder.

With growing annoyance at the intrusion,

Charlie waited for them to explain themselves. After some concentration Duncan said:

"We came to invite you out to dinner. Lorraine and I insist that all this shishi, cagy business 'bout your address got to stop."

Charlie came closer to them, as if to force them backward down the corridor.

"Sorry, but I can't. Tell me where you'll be and I'll phone you in half an hour."

This made no impression. Lorraine sat down suddenly on the side of a chair, and focussing her eyes on Richard, cried, "Oh what a nice little boy! Come here, little boy." Richard glanced at his mother, but did not move. With a perceptible shrug of her shoulders, Lorraine turned back to Charlie:

"Come and dine. Sure your cousins won' mine. See you so sel'om. Or solemn."

"I can't," said Charlie sharply. "You two have dinner and I'll phone you."

Her voice became suddenly unpleasant. "All right, we'll go. But I remember once when you hammered on my door at four A.M. I was enough of a good sport to give you a drink. Come on, Dunc."

Still in slow motion, with blurred, angry faces, with uncertain feet, they retired along the corridor.

"Good night," Charlie said.

"Good night!" responded Lorraine emphatically.

When he went back into the salon Marion had not moved, only now her son was standing in the circle of her other arm. Lincoln was still swinging Honoria back and forth like a pendulum from side to side.

"What an outrage!" Charlie broke out. "What an absolute outrage!"

Neither of them answered. Charlie dropped into an armchair, picked up his drink, set it down again and said:

"People I haven't seen for two years having the colossal nerve ——"

He broke off. Marion had made the sound "Oh!" in one swift, furious breath, turned her body from him with a jerk and left the room.

Lincoln set down Honoria carefully.

"You children go in and start your soup," he said, and when they obeyed, he said to Charlie:

"Marion's not well and she can't stand shocks. That kind of people make her really physically sick."

"I didn't tell them to come here. They wormed your name out of somebody. They deliberately ——"

"Well, it's too bad. It doesn't help matters. Excuse me a minute."

Left alone, Charlie sat tense in his chair. In the next room he could hear the children eating, talking in monosyllables, already oblivious to the scene between their elders. He heard a murmur of conversation from a farther room and then the ticking bell of a telephone receiver picked up, and in a panic he moved to the other side of the room and out of earshot.

In a minute Lincoln came back. "Look here, Charlie. I think we'd better call off dinner for tonight. Marion's in bad shape."

"Is she angry with me?"

"Sort of," he said, almost roughly. "She's not strong and ——"

"You mean she's changed her mind about Honoria?"

"She's pretty bitter right now. I don't know. You phone me at the bank tomorrow."

"I wish you'd explain to her I never dreamed these people would come here. I'm just as sore as you are."

"I couldn't explain anything to her now."

Charlie got up. He took his coat and hat and started down the corridor. Then he opened the door of the dining room and said in a strange voice, "Good night, children."

Honoria rose and ran around the table to hug him.

"Good night, sweetheart," he said vaguely, and then trying to make his voice more tender, trying to conciliate something, "Good night, dear children."

V

Charlie went directly to the Ritz bar with the furious idea of finding Lorraine and Duncan, but they were not there, and he realized that in any case there was nothing he could do. He had not touched his drink at the Peters', and now he ordered a whisky-and-soda. Paul came over to say hello.

"It's a great change," he said sadly. "We do about half the business we did. So many fellows I hear about back in the States lost everything, maybe not in the first crash, but then in the second. Your friend George Hardt lost every cent, I hear. Are you back in the States?"

"No, I'm in business in Prague."

"I heard that you lost a lot in the crash."

"I did," and he added grimly, "but I lost everything I wanted in the boom."

"Selling short."

"Something like that."

Again the memory of those days swept over him like a nightmare — the people they had met travelling; the people who couldn't add a row of figures or speak a coherent sentence. The little man Helen had consented to dance with at the ship's party, who had insulted her ten feet from the table; the women and girls carried screaming with drink or drugs out of public places ——

— The men who locked their wives out in the snow, because the snow of twenty-nine wasn't real snow. If you didn't want it to be snow, you just paid some money.

He went to the phone and called the Peters' apartment; Lincoln answered.

"I called up because this thing is on my mind. Has Marion said anything definite?"

"Marion's sick," Lincoln answered shortly. "I know this thing isn't altogether your fault, but I can't have her go to pieces about it. I'm afraid we'll have to let it slide for six months; I can't take the chance of working her up to this state again."

"I see."

"I'm sorry, Charlie."

He went back to his table. His whisky glass was empty, but he shook his head when Alix looked at it questioningly. There wasn't much he could do now except send Honoria some things; he would send her a lot of things tomorrow. He thought rather angrily that this was just money — he had given so many people money. . . .

"No, no more," he said to another waiter. "What do I owe you?"

He would come back some day; they couldn't make him pay forever. But he wanted his child, and nothing was much good now, beside that fact. He wasn't young any more, with a lot of nice thoughts and dreams to have by himself. He was absolutely sure Helen wouldn't have wanted him to be so alone.

Ernest Hemingway (1898–   )

When the first World War ended, Hemingway was only twenty. A member of the disillusioned "Lost Generation," he became a master of naturalistic fiction.

Son of a physician, Ernest Hemingway was born in Oak Park, Illinois, ran away from home at fifteen but returned, and graduated from high school when America entered the war in 1917. He volunteered as an ambulance driver, then joined the Italian infantry, was twice decorated, was severely wounded and invalided home. In 1920 the Toronto *Star* sent him to the Near East, and the next year he settled in Paris.

In Paris he met Ezra Pound and Gertrude Stein, who strongly influenced his career, and other expatriates who were to become characters in his best-selling novel, *The Sun Also Rises*, 1926. Next year he returned to America, bought a house in Florida, and in 1929 published *A Farewell to Arms*, which carried his reputation to a high point. In 1932 he brought out *Death in the Afternoon*, on bullfighting. In 1936 he went as a writer to Spain, then in civil war, the background of his play *The Fifth Column* and of his vivid novel *For Whom the Bell Tolls*, 1940. While in Spain he met the journalist Martha Gellhorn, who became his third wife.

The first World War and its aftermath produced in Hemingway and his fiction a prevailing mood of disillusionment and cynicism, offset by a grim stoical attitude and a masculine type of epicureanism. His name came to connote not only a distaste for all shams but also a taste for physical prowess, toughness, obscenity, sex, and drinking, the whole colored by an obsession with death. In *For Whom the Bell Tolls*, though "the smell of death" persists, higher values are suggested if not quite affirmed.

His power as a literary artist was displayed at least as brilliantly in his short stories, which were collected in successive volumes: *In Our Time*, 1925; *Men Without Women*, 1927; *Winner Take Nothing*, 1933; *The Fifth Column and the First Forty-nine Stories*, 1938.

Hemingway developed a fresh, attractive style for prose narrative, for which he was largely indebted to Gertrude Stein and Sherwood Anderson, a highly coordinated, colloquial style with subtle rhythms, which becomes bare and clipped in his masterly dialogue.

Biographical and critical studies appear in Gertrude Stein, *The Autobiography of Alice B. Toklas*, 1933; W. H. Frohock, *The Novel of Violence in America*, 1950; C. J. Mc-Cole, *Lucifer at Large*, 1937; J. W. Beach, *American Fiction 1920–1940*, 1941. J. K. McCaffery has collected critical essays in *Ernest Hemingway: The Man and His Work*, 1950. *The Portable Hemingway*, 1944, includes *In Our Time*, many other short stories, and parts of novels.

The Killers
(1927)

A discerning essay on this story may be found is Cleanth Brooks and Robert Penn Warren, *Understanding Fiction*, 1943, pages 316–324.

The door of Henry's lunch-room opened and two men came in. They sat down at the counter.

"What's yours?" George asked them.

"I don't know," one of the men said. "What do you want to eat, Al?"

"I don't know," said Al. "I don't know what I want to eat."

Outside it was getting dark. The streetlight came on outside the window. The two men at the counter read the menu. From the other end of the counter Nick Adams watched them. He had been talking to George when they came in.

"I'll have a roast pork tenderloin with apple sauce and mashed potatoes," the first man said.

"It isn't ready yet."

"What the hell do you put it on the card for?"

"That's the dinner," George explained. "You can get that at six o'clock."

George looked at the clock on the wall behind the counter.

"It's five o'clock."

"The clock says twenty minutes past five," the second man said.

"It's twenty minutes fast."

"Oh, to hell with the clock," the first man said. "What have you got to eat?"

"I can give you any kind of sandwiches," George said. "You can have ham and eggs, bacon and eggs, liver and bacon, or a steak."

"Give me chicken croquettes with green peas and cream sauce and mashed potatoes."

"That's the dinner."

"Everything we want's the dinner, eh? That's the way you work it."

"I can give you ham and eggs, bacon and eggs, liver —— "

"I'll take ham and eggs," the man called Al said. He wore a derby hat and a black overcoat buttoned across the chest. His face was small and white and he had tight lips. He wore a silk muffler and gloves.

"Give me bacon and eggs," said the other man. He was about the same size as Al. Their faces were different, but they were dressed like twins. Both wore overcoats too tight for them. They sat leaning forward, their elbows on the counter.

"Got anything to drink?" Al asked.

"Silver beer, bevo, ginger-ale," George said.

"I mean you got anything to *drink*?"

"Just those I said."

"This is a hot town," said the other. "What do they call it?"

"Summit."

"Ever hear of it?" Al asked his friend.

"No," said the friend.

"What do you do here nights?" Al asked.

"They eat the dinner," his friend said. "They all come here and eat the big dinner."

"That's right," George said.

"So you think that's right?" Al asked George.

"Sure."

"You're a pretty bright boy, aren't you?"

"Sure," said George.

"Well, you're not," said the other little man. "Is he, Al?"

"He's dumb," said Al. He turned to Nick. "What's your name?"

"Adams."

"Another bright boy," Al said. "Ain't he a bright boy, Max?"

"The town's full of bright boys," Max said.

George put the two platters, one of ham and eggs, the other of bacon and eggs, on the counter. He set down two side-dishes of fried potatoes and closed the wicket into the kitchen.

"Which is yours?" he asked Al.

"Don't you remember?"

"Ham and eggs."

"Just a bright boy," Max said. He leaned forward and took the ham and eggs. Both men ate with their gloves on. George watched them eat.

"What are *you* looking at?" Max looked at George.

"Nothing."

"The hell you were. You were looking at me."

"Maybe the boy meant it for a joke, Max," Al said.

George laughed.

"*You* don't have to laugh," Max said to him. "*You* don't have to laugh at all, see?"

"All right," said George.

"So he thinks it's all right." Max turned to Al. "He thinks it's all right. That's a good one."

"Oh, he's a thinker," Al said. They went on eating.

"What's the bright boy's name down the counter?" Al asked Max.

"Hey, bright boy," Max said to Nick. "You go around on the other side of the counter with your boy friend."

"What's the idea?" Nick asked.

"There isn't any idea."

"You better go around, bright boy," Al said. Nick went around behind the counter.

"What's the idea?" George asked.

"None of your damn business," Al said. "Who's out in the kitchen?"

"The nigger."

"What do you mean the nigger?"

"The nigger that cooks."

"Tell him to come in."

"What's the idea?"

"Tell him to come in."

"Where do you think you are?"

"We know damn well where we are," the man called Max said. "Do we look silly?"

"You talk silly," Al said to him. "What the hell do you argue with this kid for? Listen," he said to George, "tell the nigger to come out here."

"What are you going to do to him?"

"Nothing. Use your head, bright boy. What would we do to a nigger?"

George opened the slit that opened back into the kitchen. "Sam," he called. "Come in here a minute."

The door to the kitchen opened and the nigger came in. "What was it?" he asked. The two men at the counter took a look at him.

"All right, nigger. You stand right there," Al said.

Sam, the nigger, standing in his apron, looked at the two men sitting at the counter. "Yes, sir," he said. Al got down from his stool.

"I'm going back to the kitchen with the nigger and bright boy," he said. "Go on back to the kitchen, nigger. You go with him, bright boy." The little man walked after Nick and Sam, the cook, back into the kitchen. The door shut after them. The man called Max sat at the counter opposite George. He didn't look at George but looked in the mirror that ran along back of the counter. Henry's had been made over from a saloon into a lunch-counter.

"Well, bright boy," Max said, looking into the mirror, "why don't you say something?"

"What's it all about?"

"Hey, Al," Max called, "bright boy wants to know what it's all about."

"Why don't you tell him?" Al's voice came from the kitchen.

"What do you think it's all about?"

"I don't know."

"What do you think?"

Max looked into the mirror all the time he was talking.

"I wouldn't say."

"Hey, Al, bright boy says he wouldn't say what he thinks it's all about."

"I can hear you, all right," Al said from the kitchen. He had propped open the slit that dishes passed through into the kitchen with a catsup bottle. "Listen, bright boy," he said from the kitchen to George. "Stand a little further along the bar. You move a little to the left, Max." He was like a photographer arranging for a group picture.

"Talk to me, bright boy," Max said. "What do you think's going to happen?"

George did not say anything.

"I'll tell you," Max said. "We're going to kill a Swede. Do you know a big Swede named Ole Andreson?"

"Yes."

"He comes here to eat every night, don't he?"

"Sometimes he comes here."

"He comes here at six o'clock, don't he?"

"If he comes."

"We know all that, bright boy," Max said. "Talk about something else. Ever go to the movies?"

"Once in a while."

"You ought to go to the movies more. The movies are fine for a bright boy like you."

"What are you going to kill Ole Andreson for? What did he ever do to you?"

"He never had a chance to do anything to us. He never even seen us."

"And he's only going to see us once," Al said from the kitchen.

"What are you going to kill him for, then?" George asked.

"We're killing him for a friend. Just to oblige a friend, bright boy."

"Shut up," said Al from the kitchen. "You talk too goddam much."

"Well, I got to keep bright boy amused. Don't I, bright boy?"

"You talk too damn much," Al said. "The nigger and my bright boy are amused by themselves. I got them tied up like a couple of girl friends in the convent."

"I suppose you were in a convent."

"You never know."

"You were in a kosher convent. That's where you were."

George looked up at the clock.

"If anybody comes in you tell them the cook is off, and if they keep after it, you tell them you'll go back and cook yourself. Do you get that, bright boy?"

"All right," George said. "What you going to do with us afterward?"

"That'll depend," Max said. "That's one of those things you never know at the time."

George looked up at the clock. It was a quarter past six. The door from the street opened. A street-car motorman came in.

"Hello, George," he said. "Can I get supper?"

"Sam's gone out," George said. "He'll be back in about half an hour."

"I'd better go up the street," the motorman said. George looked at the clock. It was twenty minutes past six.

"That was nice, bright boy," Max said. "You're a regular little gentleman."

"He knew I'd blow his head off," Al said from the kitchen.

"No," said Max. "It ain't that. Bright boy is nice. He's a nice boy. I like him."

At six-fifty-five George said: "He's not coming."

Two other people had been in the lunch-room. Once George had gone out to the kitchen and made a ham-and-egg sandwich "to go" that a man wanted to take with him. Inside the kitchen he saw Al, his derby hat tipped back, sitting on a stool beside the wicket with the muzzle of a sawed-off shot-gun resting on the ledge. Nick and the cook were back to back in the corner, a towel tied in each of their mouths. George had cooked the sandwich, wrapped it up in oiled paper, put it in a bag, brought it in, and the man had paid for it and gone out.

"Bright boy can do everything," Max said.

"He can cook and everything. You'd make some girl a nice wife, bright boy."

"Yes?" George said. "Your friend, Ole Andreson, isn't going to come."

"We'll give him ten minutes," Max said.

Max watched the mirror and the clock. The hands of the clock marked seven o'clock, and then five minutes past seven.

"Come on, Al," said Max. "We better go. He's not coming."

"Better give him five minutes," Al said from the kitchen.

In the five minutes a man came in, and George explained that the cook was sick.

"Why the hell don't you get another cook?" the man asked. "Aren't you running a lunch-counter?" He went out.

"Come on, Al," Max said.

"What about the two bright boys and the nigger?"

"They're all right."

"You think so?"

"Sure. We're through with it."

"I don't like it," said Al. "It's sloppy. You talk too much."

"Oh, what the hell," said Max. "We got to keep amused, haven't we?"

"You talk too much, all the same," Al said. He came out from the kitchen. The cut-off barrels of the shotgun made a slight bulge under the waist of his too tight-fitting overcoat. He straightened his coat with his gloved hands.

"So long, bright boy," he said to George. "You got a lot of luck."

"That's the truth," Max said. "You ought to play the races, bright boy."

The two of them went out the door. George watched them, through the window, pass under the arc-light and cross the street. In their tight overcoats and derby hats they looked like a vaudeville team. George went back through the swinging-door into the kitchen and untied Nick and the cook.

"I don't want any more of that," said Sam, the cook. "I don't want any more of that."

Nick stood up. He had never had a towel in his mouth before.

"Say," he said. "What the hell?" He was trying to swagger it off.

"They were going to kill Ole Andreson," George said. "They were going to shoot him when he came in to eat."

"Ole Andreson?"

"Sure."

The cook felt the corners of his mouth with his thumbs.

"They all gone?" he asked.

"Yeah," said George. "They're gone now."

"I don't like it," said the cook. "I don't like any of it at all."

"Listen," George said to Nick. "You better go see Ole Andreson."

"All right."

"You better not have anything to do with it at all," Sam, the cook, said. "You better stay way out of it."

"Don't go if you don't want to," George said.

"Mixing up in this ain't going to get you anywhere," the cook said. "You stay out of it."

"I'll go see him," Nick said to George. "Where does he live?"

The cook turned away.

"Little boys always know what they want to do," he said.

"He lives up at Hirsch's rooming-house," George said to Nick.

"I'll go up there."

Outside the arc-light shone through the bare branches of a tree. Nick walked up the street beside the car-tracks and turned at the next arc-light down a side-street. Three houses up the street was Hirsch's rooming-house. Nick walked up the two steps and pushed the bell. A woman came to the door.

"Is Ole Andreson here?"

"Do you want to see him?"

"Yes, if he's in."

Nick followed the woman up a flight of stairs and back to the end of a corridor. She knocked on the door.

"Who is it?"

"It's somebody to see you, Mr. Andreson," the woman said.

"It's Nick Adams."

"Come in."

Nick opened the door and went into the room. Ole Andreson was lying on the bed with all his clothes on. He had been a heavyweight prizefighter and he was too long for the bed. He lay with his head on two pillows. He did not look at Nick.

"What was it?" he asked.

"I was up at Henry's," Nick said, "and two fellows came in and tied up me and the cook, and they said they were going to kill you."

It sounded silly when he said it. Ole Andreson said nothing.

"They put us out in the kitchen," Nick went on. "They were going to shoot you when you came in to supper."

Ole Andreson looked at the wall and did not say anything.

"George thought I better come and tell you about it."

"There isn't anything I can do about it," Ole Andreson said.

"I'll tell you what they were like."

"I don't want to know what they were like," Ole Andreson said. He looked at the wall. "Thanks for coming to tell me about it."

"That's all right."

Nick looked at the big man lying on the bed.

"Don't you want me to go and see the police?"

"No," Ole Andreson said. "That wouldn't do any good."

"Isn't there something I could do?"

"No. There ain't anything to do."

"Maybe it was just a bluff."

"No. It ain't just a bluff."

Ole Andreson rolled over toward the wall.

"The only thing is," he said, talking toward the wall, "I just can't make up my mind to go out. I been in here all day."

"Couldn't you get out of town?"

"No," Ole Andreson said. "I'm through with all that running around."

He looked at the wall.

"There ain't anything to do now."

"Couldn't you fix it up some way?"

"No. I got in wrong." He talked in the same flat voice. "There ain't anything to do. After a while I'll make up my mind to go out."

"I better go back and see George," Nick said.

"So long," said Ole Andreson. He did not look toward Nick. "Thanks for coming around."

Nick went out. As he shut the door he saw Ole Andreson with all his clothes on, lying on the bed looking at the wall.

"He's been in his room all day," the landlady said downstairs. "I guess he don't feel well. I said to him: 'Mr. Andreson, you ought to go out and take a walk on a nice fall day like this,' but he didn't feel like it."

"He doesn't want to go out."

"I'm sorry he don't feel well," the woman said. "He's an awfully nice man. He was in the ring, you know."

"I know it."

"You'd never know it except from the way his face is," the woman said. They stood talking just inside the street door. "He's just as gentle."

"Well, good night, Mrs. Hirsch," Nick said.

"I'm not Mrs. Hirsch," the woman said. "She owns the place. I just look after it for her. I'm Mrs. Bell."

"Well, good night, Mrs. Bell," Nick said.

"Good night," the woman said.

Nick walked up the dark street to the corner under the arc-light, and then along the car-tracks to Henry's eating-house. George was inside, back of the counter.

"Did you see Ole?"

"Yes," said Nick. "He's in his room and he won't go out."

The cook opened the door from the kitchen when he heard Nick's voice.

"I don't even listen to it," he said and shut the door.

"Did you tell him about it?" George asked.

"Sure. I told him but he knows what it's all about."

"What's he going to do?"

"Nothing."

"They'll kill him."

"I guess they will."

"He must have got mixed up in something in Chicago."

"I guess so," said Nick.

"It's a hell of a thing."

"It's an awful thing," Nick said.

They did not say anything. George reached down for a towel and wiped the counter.

"I wonder what he did?" Nick said.

"Double-crossed somebody. That's what they kill them for."

"I'm going to get out of this town," Nick said.

"Yes," said George. "That's a good thing to do."

"I can't stand to think about him waiting in the room and knowing he's going to get it. It's too damned awful."

"Well," said George, "you better not think about it."

The Snows of Kilimanjaro

(1936)

Kilimanjaro is a snow-covered mountain 19,710 feet high, and is said to be the highest mountain in Africa. Its western summit is called the Masai "Ngàje Ngài," the House of God. Close to the western summit there is the dried and frozen carcass of a leopard. No one has explained what the leopard was seeking at that altitude.

"The marvellous thing is that it's painless," he said. "That's how you know when it starts."

"Is it really?"

"Absolutely. I'm awfully sorry about the odor, though. That must bother you."

"Don't! Please don't."

"Look at them," he said. "Now is it sight or is it scent that brings them like that?"

The cot the man lay on was in the wide shade of a mimosa tree and as he looked out past the shade onto the glare of the plain there were three of the big birds squatted obscenely, while in the sky a dozen more sailed, making quiet moving shadows as they passed.

"They've been there since the day the truck broke down," he said. "Today's the first time any have lit on the ground. I watched the way they sailed very carefully at first in case I ever wanted to use them in a story. That's funny now."

"I wish you wouldn't," she said.

"I'm only talking," he said. "It's much easier if I talk. But I don't want to bother you."

"You know it doesn't bother me," she said. "It's that I've gotten so very nervous not being able to do anything. I think we might make it as easy as we can until the plane comes."

"Or until the plane doesn't come."

"Please tell me what I can do. There must be something I can do."

"You can take the leg off and that might stop it, though I doubt it. Or you can shoot me. You're a good shot now. I taught you to shoot, didn't I?"

"Please don't talk that way. Couldn't I read to you?"

"Read what?"

"Anything in the book bag that we haven't read."

"I can't listen to it," he said. "Talking is the easiest. We quarrel and that makes the time pass."

"I don't quarrel. I never want to quarrel. Let's not quarrel any more. No matter how nervous we get. Maybe they will be back with another truck today. Maybe the plane will come."

"I don't want to move," the man said. "There is no sense in moving now except to make it easier for you."

"That's cowardly."

"Can't you let a man die as comfortably as he can without calling him names? What's the use of slanging me?"

"You're not going to die."

"Don't be silly. I'm dying now. Ask those bastards." He looked over to where the huge, filthy birds sat, their naked heads sunk in the hunched feathers. A fourth planed down, to run quick-legged and then waddle slowly toward the others.

"They are around every camp. You never notice them. You can't die if you don't give up."

"Where did you read that? You're such a bloody fool."

"You might think about someone else."

"For Christ's sake," he said, "that's been my trade."

He lay then and was quiet for a while and looked across the heat shimmer of the plain to the edge of the bush. There were a few Tommies that showed minute and white against the yellow and, far off, he saw a herd of zebra, white against the green of the bush. This was a pleasant camp under big trees against a hill, with good water, and close by, a nearly dry waterhole where sand grouse flighted in the mornings.

"Wouldn't you like me to read?" she asked.

She was sitting on a canvas chair beside his cot. "There's a breeze coming up."

"No, thanks."

"Maybe the truck will come."

"I don't give a damn about the truck." 5

"I do."

"You give a damn about so many things that I don't."

"Not so many, Harry."

"What about a drink?" 10

"It's supposed to be bad for you. It said in Black's to avoid all alcohol. You shouldn't drink."

"Molo!" he shouted.

"Yes, Bwana."

"Bring whiskey-soda."

"Yes, Bwana."

"You shouldn't," she said. "That's what I mean by giving up. It says it's bad for you. I know it's bad for you." 20

"No," he said. "It's good for me."

So now it was all over, he thought. So now he would never have a chance to finish it. So this was the way it ended in a bickering over a drink. Since the gangrene started in 25 his right leg, he had no pain and with the pain the horror had gone, and all he felt now was a great tiredness and anger that this was the end of it. For this, that now was coming, he had very little curiosity. For years it 30 had obsessed him; but now it meant nothing in itself. It was strange how easy being tired enough made it.

Now he would never write the things that he had saved to write until he knew enough 35 to write them well. Well, he would not have to fail at trying to write them either. Maybe you could never write them, and that was why you put them off and delayed the starting. Well, he would never know, now. 40

"I wish we'd never come," the woman said. She was looking at him holding the glass and biting her lip. "You never would have gotten anything like this in Paris. You always said you loved Paris. We could have 45 stayed in Paris or gone anywhere. I'd have gone anywhere. I said I'd go anywhere you wanted. If you wanted to shoot, we could have gone shooting in Hungary and been comfortable." 50

"Your bloody money," he said.

"That's not fair," she said. "It was always yours as much as mine. I left everything and I went wherever you wanted to go and I've done what you wanted to do. But I wish we'd never come here."

"You said you loved it."

"I did when you were all right. But now I hate it. I don't see why that had to happen to your leg. What have we done to have that happen to us?"

"I suppose what I did was to forget to put iodine on it when I first scratched it. Then I didn't pay any attention to it because I never infect. Then, later, when it got bad, it was probably using that weak carbolic 15 solution when the other antiseptics ran out that paralyzed the minute blood vessels and started the gangrene." He looked at her, "What else?"

"I don't mean that."

"If we would have hired a good mechanic 20 instead of a half-baked kikuyu driver, he would have checked the oil and never burned out that bearing in the truck."

"I don't mean that."

"If you hadn't left your own people, your goddamned Old Westbury, Saratoga, Palm Beach people to take me on ——"

"Why, I loved you. That's not fair. I love you now. I'll always love you. Don't you love me?"

"No," said the man. "I don't think so. 30 I never have."

"Harry, what are you saying? You're out of your head."

"No. I haven't any head to go out of."

"Don't drink that," she said. "Darling, please don't drink that. We have to do everything we can."

"You do it," he said. "I'm tired."

Now in his mind he saw a railway station at Karagatch and he was standing with his pack and that was the headlight of the Simplon-Orient cutting the dark now and he was leaving Thrace then after the retreat. That was one of the things he had saved to write, with, in the morning at breakfast, looking out the window and seeing snow on the mountains in Bulgaria and Nansen's Secretary asking the old man if it were snow and the old man looking at it and saying, No, that's not snow. It's too early for snow. And the Secretary repeating to the other girls, No, you

see. It's not snow and them all saying, It's not
snow we were mistaken. But it was the snow all
right and he sent them on into it when he evolved
exchange of populations. And it was snow they
tramped along in until they died that winter.

It was snow too that fell all Christmas week
that year up in the Gauertal, that year they lived
in the wood-cutter's house with the big square
porcelain stove that filled half the room, and they
slept on mattresses filled with beech leaves, the
time the deserter came with his feet bloody in the
snow. He said the police were right behind him
and they gave him woolen socks and held the
gendarmes talking until the tracks had drifted over.

In Schrunz, on Christmas day, the snow was
so bright it hurt your eyes when you looked out
from the Weinstube and saw every one coming
home from church. That was where they walked
up the sleigh-smoothed urine-yellowed road along
the river with the steep pine hills, skis heavy on
the shoulder, and where they ran that great run
down the glacier above the Madlener-Haus, the
snow as smooth to see as cake frosting and as light
as powder and he remembered the noiseless rush
the speed made as you dropped down like a bird.

They were snow-bound a week in the Madlener-
Haus that time in the blizzard playing cards in
the smoke by the lantern light and the stakes were
higher all the time as Herr Lent lost more. Finally
he lost it all. Everything, the skischule money and
all the season's profit and then his capital. He
could see him with his long nose, picking up the
cards and then opening, "Sans Voir." There was
always gambling then. When there was no snow
you gambled and when there was too much you
gambled. He thought of all the time in his life
he had spent gambling.

But he had never written a line of that, nor of
that cold, bright Christmas day with the mountains
showing across the plain that Barker had flown
across the lines to bomb the Austrian officers' leave
train, machine-gunning them as they scattered and
ran. He remembered Barker afterwards coming
into the mess and starting to tell about it. And
how quiet it got and then somebody saying, "You
bloody murderous bastard."

Those were the same Austrians they killed then
that he skied with later. No not the same. Hans,
that he skied with all that year, had been in the
Kaiser-Jägers and when they went hunting hares
together up the little valley above the saw-mill they
had talked of the fighting on Pasubio and of the
attack on Pertica and Asalone and he had never
written a word of that. Nor of Monte Corno, nor
the Siete Commum, nor of Arsiedo.

How many winters had he lived in the Voralberg
and the Arlberg? It was four and then he remembered the man who had the fox to sell when they
had walked into Bludenz, that time to buy presents,
and the cherry-pit taste of good kirsch, the fast-
slipping rush of running powder-snow on crust,
singing "Hi! Ho! said Rolly!" as you ran down
the last stretch to the steep drop, taking it straight,
then running the orchard in three turns and out
across the ditch and onto the icy road behind the
inn. Knocking your bindings loose, kicking the
skis free and leaning them up against the wooden
wall of the inn, the lamplight coming from the
window, where inside, in the smoky, new-wine
smelling warmth, they were playing the accordion.

"Where did we stay in Paris?" he asked
the woman who was sitting by him in a
canvas chair, now, in Africa.

"At the Crillon. You know that."

"Why do I know that?"

"That's where we always stayed."

"No. Not always."

"There and at the Pavillon Henri-Quatre
in St. Germain. You said you loved it there."

"Love is a dunghill," said Harry. "And
I'm the cock that gets on it to crow."

"If you have to go away," she said, "is it
absolutely necessary to kill off everything you
leave behind? I mean do you have to take
away everything? Do you have to kill your
horse, and your wife, and burn your saddle
and your armour?"

"Yes," he said. "Your damned money
was my armour. My Swift and my Armour."

"Don't."

"All right. I'll stop that. I don't want to
hurt you."

"It's a little bit late now."

"All right, then. I'll go on hurting you.
It's more amusing. The only thing I ever
really liked to do with you I can't do now."

"No, that's not true. You liked to do many
things and everything you wanted to do I
did."

"Oh, for Christ sake stop bragging, will
you?"

He looked at her and saw her crying.

"Listen," he said. "Do you think that it is

fun to do this? I don't know why I'm doing it. It's trying to kill to keep yourself alive, I imagine. I was all right when we started talking. I didn't mean to start this, and now I'm crazy as a coot and being as cruel to you as I can be. Don't pay any attention, darling, to what I say. I love you, really. You know I love you. I've never loved any one else the way I love you."

He slipped into the familiar lie he made his bread and butter by.

"You're sweet to me."

"You bitch," he said. "You rich bitch. That's poetry. I'm full of poetry now. Rot and poetry. Rotten poetry."

"Stop it. Harry, why do you have to turn into a devil now?"

"I don't like to leave anything," the man said. "I don't like to leave things behind."

It was evening now and he had been asleep. The sun was gone behind the hill and there was a shadow all across the plain and the small animals were feeding close to camp; quick-dropping heads and switching tails, he watched them keeping well out away from the bush now. The birds no longer waited on the ground. They were all perched heavily in a tree. There were many more of them. His personal boy was sitting by the bed.

"Memsahib's gone to shoot," the boy said. "Does Bwana want?"

"Nothing."

She had gone to kill a piece of meat and, knowing how he liked to watch the game, she had gone well away so she would not disturb this little pocket of the plain that he could see. She was always thoughtful, he thought. On anything she knew about, or had read, or that she had ever heard.

It was not her fault that when he went to her he was already over. How could a woman know that you meant nothing that you said; that you spoke only from habit and to be comfortable? After he no longer meant what he said, his lies were more successful with women than when he had told them the truth.

It was not so much that he lied as that there was no truth to tell. He had had his life and it was over and then he went on living it again with different people and more money, with the best of the same places, and some new ones.

You kept from thinking and it was all marvelous. You were equipped with good insides so that you did not go to pieces that way, the way most of them had, and you made an attitude that you cared nothing for the work you used to do, now that you could no longer do it. But, in yourself, you said that you would write about these people; about the very rich; that you were really not of them but a spy in their country; that you would leave it and write of it and for once it would be written by someone who knew what he was writing of. But he would never do it, because each day of not writing, of comfort, of being that which he despised, dulled his ability and softened his will to work so that, finally, he did no work at all. The people he knew now were all much more comfortable when he did not work. Africa was where he had been happiest in the good time of his life, so he had come out here to start again. They had made this safari with the minimum of comfort. There was no hardship; but there was no luxury and he had thought that he could get back into training that way. That in some way he could work the fat off his soul the way a fighter went into the mountains to work and train in order to burn it out of his body.

She had liked it. She said she loved it. She loved anything that was exciting, that involved a change of scene, where there were new people and where things were pleasant. And he had felt the illusion of returning strength of will to work. Now if this was how it ended, and he knew it was, he must not turn like some snake biting itself because its back was broken. It wasn't this woman's fault. If it had not been she, it would have been another. If he lived by a lie, he should try to die by it. He heard a shot beyond the hill.

She shot very well, this good, this rich bitch, this kindly caretaker and destroyer of his talent. Nonsense. He had destroyed his talent himself. Why should he blame this woman because she kept him well? He had destroyed his talent by not using it, by betrayals of himself and what he believed in, by drinking so much that he blunted the edge of his perceptions, by laziness, by sloth, and by snobbery, by pride and by prejudice, by hook and by crook. What was this? A catalogue of old books? What was his talent anyway? It was a talent all right, but instead of using it, he had traded on it. It was never what he had done, but always what he could do. And he had chosen to make his living with something else instead of a pen or a pencil. It was strange, too, wasn't it, that when he fell in love with another woman, that woman should always have more money than the last one? But when he no longer was in love, when he was only lying, as to this woman, now, who had the most money of all, who had all the money there was, who had had a husband and children, who had taken lovers and been dissatisfied with them, and who loved him dearly as a writer, as a man, as a companion, and as a proud possession; it was strange that, when he did not love her at all and was lying, he should be able to give her more for her money than when he had really loved.

We must all be cut out for what we do, he thought. However you make your living is where your talent lies. He had sold vitality, in one form or another, all his life, and when your affections are not too involved you give much better value for the money. He had found that out, but he would never write that, now, either. No, he would not write that, although it was well worth writing.

Now she came in sight, walking across the open toward the camp. She was wearing jodhpurs and carrying her rifle. The two boys had a Tommie slung and they were coming along behind her. She was still a good-looking woman, he thought, and she had a pleasant body. She had a great talent and appreciation for the bed, she was not pretty, but he liked her face, she read enormously, liked to ride and shoot and, certainly, she drank too much. Her husband had died when she was still a comparatively young woman and for a while she had devoted herself to her two just-grown children, who did not need her and were embarrassed at having her about, to her stable of horses, to books, and to bottles. She liked to read in the evening before dinner and she drank Scotch-and-soda while she read. By dinner

she was fairly drunk and after a bottle of wine at dinner she was usually drunk enough to sleep.

That was before the lovers. After she had the lovers, she did not drink so much because she did not have to be drunk to sleep. But the lovers bored her. She had been married to a man who had never bored her and these people bored her very much.

Then one of her two children was killed in a plane crash and after that was over she did not want the lovers, and drink being no anaesthetic she had to make another life. Suddenly, she had been acutely frightened of being alone. But she wanted someone that she respected with her.

It had begun very simply. She liked what he wrote and she had always envied the life he led. She thought he did exactly what he wanted to. The steps by which she had acquired him and the way in which she had finally fallen in love with him were all part of a regular progression in which she had built herself a new life and he had traded away what remained of his old life.

He had traded it for security, for comfort, too, there was no denying that, and for what else? He did not know. She would have bought him anything he wanted. He knew that. She was a damned nice woman too. He would as soon be in bed with her as anyone; rather with her, because she was richer, because she was very pleasant and appreciative, and because she never made scenes. And now this life that she had built again was coming to a term because he had not used iodine two weeks ago when a thorn had scratched his knee as they moved forward trying to photograph a herd of waterbuck standing, their heads up, peering while their nostrils searched the air, their ears spread wide to hear the first noise that would send them rushing into the bush. They had bolted, too, before he got the picture.

Here she came now.

He turned his head on the cot to look toward her. "Hello," he said.

"I shot a Tommy ram," she told him. "He'll make you good broth and I'll have them mash some potatoes with the Klim. How do you feel?"

"Much better."

"Isn't that lovely? You know I thought perhaps you would. You were sleeping when I left."

"I had a good sleep. Did you walk far?"

"No. Just around behind the hill. I made quite a good shot on the Tommy."

"You shoot marvelously, you know."

"I love it. I've loved Africa. Really. If *you're* all right it's the most fun that I've ever had. You don't know the fun it's been to shoot with you. I've loved the country."

"I love it too."

"Darling, you don't know how marvelous it is to see you feeling better. I couldn't stand it when you felt that way. You won't talk to me like that again, will you? Promise me?"

"No," he said. "I don't remember what I said."

"You don't have to destroy me. Do you? I'm only a middle-aged woman who loves you and wants to do what you want to do. I've been destroyed two or three times already. You wouldn't want to destroy me again, would you?"

"I'd like to destroy you a few times in bed," he said.

"Yes. That's the good destruction. That's the way we're made to be destroyed. The plane will be here tomorrow."

"How do you know?"

"I'm sure. It's bound to come. The boys have the wood all ready and the grass to make the smudge. I went down and looked at it again today. There's plenty of room to land and we have the smudges ready at both ends."

"What makes you think it will come tomorrow?"

"I'm sure it will. It's overdue now. Then, in town, they will fix up your leg and then we will have some good destruction. Not that dreadful talking kind."

"Should we have a drink? The sun is down."

"Do you think you should?"

"I'm having one."

"We'll have one together. *Molo, letti dui whiskey-soda*"! she called.

"You'd better put on your mosquito boots," he told her.

"I'll wait till I bathe . . . "

While it grew dark they drank and just before it was dark and there was no longer enough light to shoot, a hyena crossed the open on his way around the hill.

"That bastard crosses there every night," the man said. "Every night for two weeks."

"He's the one makes the noise at night. I don't mind it. They're a filthy animal, though."

Drinking together, with no pain now except the discomfort of lying in the one position, the boys lighting a fire, its shadow jumping on the tents, he could feel the return of acquiescence in this life of pleasant surrender. She *was* very good to him. He had been cruel and unjust in the afternoon. She was a fine woman, marvelous really. And just then it occurred to him that he was going to die.

It came with a rush; not as a rush of water nor of wind; but of a sudden evil-smelling emptiness and the odd thing was that the hyena slipped lightly along the edge of it.

"What is it, Harry?" she asked him.

"Nothing," he said. "You had better move over to the other side. To windward."

"Did Molo change the dressing?"

"Yes. I'm just using the boric now."

"How do you feel?"

"A little wobbly."

"I'm going in to bathe," she said. "I'll be right out. I'll eat with you and then we'll put the cot in."

So, he said to himself, we did well to stop the quarreling. He had never quarreled much with this woman, while with the women that he loved he had quarreled so much they had finally, always, with the corrosion of the quarreling, killed what they had together. He had loved too much, demanded too much, and he wore it all out.

He thought about alone in Constantinople that time, having quarreled in Paris before he had gone out. He had whored the whole time and then, when that was over, and he had failed to kill his loneliness, but only made it worse, he had written her, the first one, the one who left him, a letter telling her how he had never been able to kill it. . . . How when he thought he saw her outside the Régence one time it made him go all faint and sick inside, and that he would follow a woman who looked like her in some way, along the Boulevard, afraid to see it was not she, afraid to lose the feeling it gave him. How everyone he had slept with had only made him miss her more. How what she had done could never matter since he knew he could not cure himself of loving her. He wrote this letter at the Club, cold sober, and mailed it to New York asking her to write him at the office in Paris. That seemed safe. And that night, missing her so much it made him feel hollow sick inside, he wandered up past Taxim's, picked a girl up and took her out to supper. He had gone to a place to dance with her afterward, she danced badly, and left her for a hot Armenian slut, that swung her belly against him so it almost scalded. He took her away from a British gunner subaltern after a row. The gunner asked him outside and they fought in the street on the cobbles in the dark. He'd hit him twice, hard, on the side of the jaw and when he didn't go down he knew he was in for a fight. The gunner hit him in the body, then beside his eye. He swung with his left again and landed and the gunner fell on him and grabbed his coat and tore the sleeve off and he clubbed him twice behind the ear and then smashed him with his right as he pushed him away. When the gunner went down his head hit first and he ran with the girl because they heard the M.P.'s coming. They got into a taxi and drove out to Rimmily Hissa along the Bosphorus, and around, and back in the cool night and went to bed and she felt as overripe as she looked but smooth, rose-petal, syrupy, smooth-bellied, big-breasted, and needed no pillow under her buttocks, and he left her before she was awake looking blowzy enough in the first daylight and turned up at the Pera Palace with a black eye, carrying his coat because one sleeve was missing.

That same night he left for Anatolia and he remembered, later on that trip, riding all day through fields of the poppies that they raised for opium and how strange it made you feel, finally, and all the distances seemed wrong, to where they had made the attack with the newly arrived Constantine officers, that did not know a god-damned thing, and the artillery had fired into the troops and the British observer had cried like a child.

That was the day he'd first seen dead men wearing white ballet skirts and upturned shoes with pompons on them. The Turks had come steadily and lumpily and he had seen the skirted men running and the officers shooting into them and running then themselves, and he and the British observer had run, too, until his lungs ached and his mouth was full of the taste of pennies, and they stopped behind some rocks and there were the Turks coming as lumpily as ever. Later he had seen the things that he could never think of and later still he had seen much worse. So when he got back to Paris that time he could not talk about it or stand to have it mentioned. And there in the café as he passed was that American poet with a pile of saucers in front of him and a stupid look on his potato face talking about the Dada movement with a Roumanian who said his name was Tristan Tzara, who always wore a monocle and had a headache, and, back at the apartment with his wife that now he loved again, the quarrel all over, the madness all over, glad to be home, the office sent his mail up to the flat. So then the letter in answer to the one he'd written came in on a platter one morning and when he saw the handwriting he went cold all over and tried to slip the letter underneath another. But his wife said, "Who is that letter from, dear?" and that was the end of the beginning of that.

He remembered the good times with them all, and the quarrels. They always picked the finest places to have the quarrels. And why had they always quarreled when he was feeling best? He had never written any of that because, at first, he never wanted to hurt anyone and then it seemed as though there was enough to write without it. But he had always thought that he would write it finally. There was so much to write. He had seen the world change; not just the events; although he had seen many of them and had watched the people, but he had seen the subtler change and he could remember how the people were at different times. He had been in it and he had watched it and it was his duty to write of it; but now he never would.

"How do you feel?" she said. She had come out from the tent now after her bath.

"All right."

"Could you eat now?" He saw Molo behind her with the folding table and the other boy with the dishes.

"I want to write," he said.

"You ought to take some broth to keep your strength up."

"I'm going to die tonight," he said. "I don't need my strength up."

"Don't be melodramatic, Harry, please," she said.

"Why don't you use your nose? I'm rotted halfway up my thigh now. What the hell should I fool with broth for? Molo bring whiskey-soda."

"Please take the broth," she said gently.

"All right."

The broth was too hot. He had to hold it in the cup until it cooled enough to take it and then he just got it down without gagging.

"You're a fine woman," he said. "Don't pay any attention to me."

She looked at him with her well-known, well-loved face from *Spur* and *Town and Country,* only a little the worse for drink, only a little the worse for bed, but *Town and Country* never showed those good breasts and those useful thighs and those lightly small-of-back-caressing hands, and as he looked and saw her well-known pleasant smile, he felt death come again. This time there was no rush. It was a puff, as of a wind that makes a candle flicker and the flame go tall.

"They can bring my net out later and hang it from the tree and build the fire up. I'm not going in the tent tonight. It's not worth moving. It's a clear night. There won't be any rain."

So this was how you died, in whispers that you did not hear. Well, there would be no more quarreling. He could promise that. The one experience that he had never had he was not going to spoil now. He probably would. You spoiled everything. But perhaps he wouldn't.

"You can't take dictation, can you?"

"I never learned," she told him.

"That's all right."

There wasn't time, of course, although it seemed as though it telescoped so that you might put it all into one paragraph if you could get it right.

There was a log house, chinked white with mortar, on a hill above the lake. There was a bell on a pole by the door to call the people in to meals. Behind the house were fields and behind the fields was the timber. A line of Lombardy poplars ran from the house to the dock. Other poplars ran along the point. A road went up to the hills along the edge of the timber and along that road he picked blackberries. Then that log house was burned down and all the guns that had been on deer foot racks above the open fire place were burned and afterwards their barrels, with the lead melted in the magazines, and the stocks burned away, lay out on the heap of ashes that were used to make lye for the big iron soap kettles, and you asked Grandfather if you could have them to play with, and he said, no. You see they were his guns still and he never bought any others. Nor did he hunt any more. The house was rebuilt in the same place out of lumber now and painted white and from its porch you saw the poplars and the lake beyond; but there were never any more guns. The barrels of the guns that had hung on the deer feet on the wall of the log house lay out there on the heap of ashes and no one ever touched them.

In the Black Forest, after the war, we rented a trout stream and there were two ways to walk to it. One was down the valley from Triberg and around the valley road in the shade of the trees that bordered the white road, and then up a side road that went up through the hills past many small farms, with the big Schwarzwald houses, until that road crossed the stream. That was where our fishing began.

The other way was to climb steeply up to the edge of the woods and then go across the top of the hills through the pine woods, and then out to the edge of a meadow and down across this meadow to the bridge. There were birches along the stream and it was not big, but narrow, clear and fast, with pools where it had cut under the roots of the birches. At the hotel in Triberg the proprietor had a fine season. It was very pleasant and we were all great friends. The next year came the inflation and the money he had made the year before was not enough to buy supplies to open the hotel and he hanged himself.

You could dictate that, but you could not dictate the Place Contrescarpe where the flower sellers dyed their flowers in the street and the dye ran over the paving where the autobus started and the old men and the women, always drunk on wine and bad marc; and the children with their noses running in the cold; the smell of dirty sweat and poverty and drunkenness at the Café des Amateurs and the whores at the Bal Musette they lived above. The Concierge who entertained the trooper of the Garde Republicaine in her loge, his horsehair plumed helmet on a chair. The locataire across the hall whose husband was a bicycle racer and her joy that morning at the Cremerie when she had opened L'Auto and seen where he placed third in Paris-Tours, his first big race. She had blushed and laughed and then gone upstairs crying with the yellow sporting paper in her hand. The husband of the woman who ran the Bal Musette drove a taxi, and when he, Harry, had to take an early plane the husband knocked upon the door to wake him and they each drank a glass of white wine at the zinc of the bar before they started. He knew his neighbors in that quarter then because they all were poor.

Around that Place there were two kinds; the drunkards and the sportifs. The drunkards killed their poverty that way; the sportifs took it out in exercise. They were the descendants of the Communards and it was no struggle for them to know their politics. They knew who had shot their fathers, their relatives, their brothers, and their friends when the Versailles troops came in and took the town after the Commune and executed anyone they could catch with calloused hands, or who wore a cap, or carried any other sign he was a working-man. And in that poverty, and in that quarter across the street from a Boucherie Chevaline and a wine co-operative, he had written the start of all he was to do. There never was another part of Paris that he loved like that, the sprawling trees, the old white plastered houses painted brown below, the long green of the autobus in that round square, the purple flower dye upon the paving, the sudden drop down the hill of the rue Cardinal Lemoine to the river, and the other way the narrow crowded world of the rue Mouffetard. The street that ran up toward the Pantheon and the other that he always took with the bicycle, the only asphalted street in all that quarter, smooth under the tires, with the high narrow houses and the cheap tall hotel where Paul Verlaine had died. There were only two rooms in the apartments where they lived and he had a room on the top floor of that hotel that cost him sixty francs a month where he did his writing, and from it he could see the roofs and chimney pots and all the hills of Paris.

From the apartment you could only see the wood and coal man's place. He sold wine too, bad wine. The golden horse's head outside the Boucherie Chevaline where the carcasses hung yellow gold and red in the open window, and the green painted co-operative where they bought their wine; good wine and cheap. The rest was plaster walls and the windows of the neighbors. The neighbors who, at night, when some one lay drunk in the street, moaning and groaning in that typical French ivresse that you were propaganded to believe did not exist, would open their windows and then the murmur of talk.

"Where is the policeman? When you don't want him the bugger is always there. He's sleeping with some concierge. Get the Agent." Till someone threw a bucket of water from a window and the moaning stopped. "What's that? Water. Ah, that's intelligent." And the windows shutting. Marie, his femme de ménage, protesting against the eight-hour day saying, "If a husband works until six he gets only a little drunk on the way home and does not waste too much. If he works only until five he is drunk every night and one has no money. It is the wife of the working-man who suffers from this shortening of hours."

"Wouldn't you like some more broth?" the woman asked him now.

"No, thank you very much. It is awfully good."

"Try just a little."

"I would like a whiskey-soda."

"It's not good for you."

"No. It's bad for me. Cole Porter wrote the words and the music. This knowledge that you're going mad for me."

"You know I like you to drink."

"Oh, yes. Only it's bad for me."

When she goes, he thought, I'll have all I want. Not all I want, but all there is. Ayee, he was tired. Too tired. He was going to sleep a little while. He lay still and death was not there. It must have gone around another street. It went in pairs, on bicycles, and moved absolutely silently on the pavements.

No, he had never written about Paris. Not the Paris that he cared about. But what about the rest that he had never written?

What about the ranch and the silvered gray of the sage brush, the quick, clear water in the irrigation ditches, and the heavy green of the alfalfa? The trail went up into the hills and the cattle in the summer were shy as deer. The bawling and the steady noise and slow moving *mass raising a dust as you brought them down in the fall. And behind the mountains, the clear sharpness of the peak in the evening light and, riding down along the trail in the moonlight, bright across the valley. Now he remembered coming down through the timber in the dark holding the horse's tail when you could not see and all the stories that he meant to write.*

About the half-wit chore boy who was left at the ranch that time and told not to let any one get any hay, and that old bastard from the Forks who had beaten the boy when he had worked for him stopping to get some feed. The boy refusing and the old man saying he would beat him again. The boy got the rifle from the kitchen and shot him when he tried to come into the barn and when they came back to the ranch he'd been dead a week, frozen in the corral, and the dogs had eaten part of him. But what was left you packed on a sled wrapped in a blanket and roped on and you got the boy to help you haul it, and the two of you took it out over the road on skis, and sixty miles down to town to turn the boy over. He having no idea that he would be arrested. Thinking he had done his duty and that you were his friend and he would be rewarded. He'd helped to haul the old man in so everybody could know how bad the old man had been and how he'd tried to steal some feed that didn't belong to him, and when the sheriff put the handcuffs on the boy he couldn't believe it. Then he started to cry. That was one story he had saved to write. He knew at least twenty good stories from out there and he had never written one. Why?

"You tell them why," he said.

"Why what, dear?"

"Why nothing."

She didn't drink so much, now, since she had him. But if he lived he would never write about her, he knew that now. Nor about any of them. The rich were dull and they drank too much, or they played too much backgammon. They were dull and they were repetitious. He remembered poor Julian and his romantic awe of them and how he had started a story once that began, "The very rich are different from you and me." And how someone had said to Julian, Yes, they have more money. But that was not humorous to Julian. He thought they were a special glamorous race and when he

found they weren't it wrecked him just as much as any other thing that wrecked him.

He had been contemptuous of those who wrecked. You did not have to like it because you understood it. He could bear anything, he thought, because nothing could hurt him if he did not care.

All right. Now he would not care for death. One thing he had always dreaded was the pain. He could stand pain as well as any man, until it went on too long, and wore him out, but here he had something that had hurt frightfully and just when he had felt it breaking him, the pain had stopped.

He remembered long ago when Williamson, the bombing officer, had been hit by a stick bomb someone in a German patrol had thrown as he was coming in through the wire that night and, screaming, had begged everyone to kill him. He was a fat man, very brave, and a good officer, although addicted to fantastic shows. But that night he was caught in the wire, with a flare lighting him up and his bowels spilled out into the wire, so when they brought him in, alive, they had to cut him loose. Shoot me, Harry. For Christ sake, shoot me. They had had an argument one time about our Lord never sending you anything you could not bear and someone's theory had been that meant that at a certain time the pain passed you out automatically. But he had always remembered Williamson, that night. Nothing passed out Williamson until he gave him all his morphine tablets that he had always saved to use himself and then they did not work right away.

Still this now, that he had, was very easy; and if it was no worse as it went on there was nothing to worry about. Except that he would rather be in better company.

He thought a little about the company that he would like to have.

No, he thought, when everything you do, you do too long, and do too late, you can't expect to find the people still there. The people all are gone. The party's over and you are with your hostess now.

I'm getting as bored with dying as with everything else, he thought.

"It's a bore," he said out loud.

"What is, my dear?"

"Anything you do too bloody long."

He looked at her face between him and the fire. She was leaning back in the chair and the firelight shone on her pleasantly lined face and he could see that she was sleepy. He heard the hyena make a noise just outside the range of the fire.

"I've been writing," he said. "But I got tired."

"Do you think you will be able to sleep?"

"Pretty sure. Why don't you turn in?"

"I like to sit here with you."

"Do you feel anything strange?" he asked her.

"No. Just a little sleepy."

"I do," he said.

He had just felt death come by again.

"You know the only thing I've never lost is curiosity," he said to her.

"You've never lost anything. You're the most complete man I've ever known."

"Christ," he said. "How little a woman knows. What is that? Your intuition?"

Because, just then, death had come and rested its head on the foot of the cot and he could smell its breath.

"Never believe any of that about a scythe and a skull," he told her. "It can be two bicycle policemen as easily or be a bird. Or it can have a wide snout like a hyena."

It had moved up on him now, but it had no shape any more. It simply occupied space.

"Tell it to go away."

It did not go away, but moved a little closer.

"You've got a hell of a breath," he told it. "You stinking bastard."

It moved up closer to him still, and now he could not speak to it, and when it saw he could not speak, it came a little closer, and now he tried to send it away without speaking, but it moved in on him so its weight was all upon his chest, and while it crouched there and he could not move, or speak, he heard the woman say, "Bwana is asleep now. Take the cot up very gently and carry it into the tent."

He could not speak to tell her to make it go away and it crouched now, heavier, so he could not breathe. And then, while they lifted the cot, suddenly it was all right and the weight went from his chest.

It was morning and had been morning for some time and he heard the plane. It showed very tiny and then made a wide circle and the boys ran out and lit the fires, using kerosene, and piled on grass so there were two big smudges at each end of the level place and the morning breeze blew them toward the camp and the plane circled twice more, low this time, and then glided down and leveled off and landed smoothly and, coming walking toward him, was old Compton in slacks, a tweed jacket, and a brown felt hat.

"What's the matter, old cock?" Compton said.

"Bad leg," he told him. "Will you have some breakfast?"

"Thanks. I'll just have some tea. It's the Puss Moth, you know. I won't be able to take the Memsahib. There's only room for one. Your lorry is on the way."

Helen had taken Compton aside and was speaking to him. Compton came back more cheery than ever.

"We'll get you right in," he said. "I'll be back for the Mem. Now I'm afraid I'll have to stop at Arusha to refuel. We'd better get going."

"What about the tea?"

"I don't really care about it, you know."

The boys had picked up the cot and carried it around the green tents and down along the rock and out onto the plain and along past the smudges that were burning brightly now, the grass all consumed, and the wind fanning the fire, to the little plane. It was difficult getting him in, but once in he lay back in the leather seat, and the leg was stuck straight out to one side of the seat where Compton sat. Compton started the motor and got in. He waved to Helen and to the boys and, as the clatter moved into the old familiar roar, they swung around with Compie watching for wart-hog holes and roared, bumping, along the stretch between the fires and with the last bump rose and he saw them all standing below, waving, and the camp beside the hill, flattening now, and the plain spreading, clumps of trees, and the bush flattening, while the game trails ran now smoothly to the dry waterholes, and there was a new water that he had never known of. The zebra, small rounded backs now, and the wildebeeste, big headed dots seeming to climb as they moved in long fingers across the plain, now scattering as the shadow came toward them, they were tiny now, and the movement had no gallop, and the plain as far as you could see, gray-yellow now and ahead old Compie's tweed back and the brown felt hat. Then they were over the first hills and the wildebeeste were trailing up them, and then they were over mountains with sudden depths of green-rising forest and the solid bamboo slopes, and then the heavy forest again, sculptured into peaks and hollows until they crossed, and hills sloped down and then another plain, hot now, and purple brown, bumpy with heat and Compie looking back to see how he was riding. Then there were other mountains dark ahead.

And then instead of going on to Arusha they turned left, he evidently figured that they had the gas, and looking down he saw a pink sifting cloud, moving over the ground, and in the air, like the first snow in a blizzard, that comes from nowhere, and he knew the locusts were coming up from the south. Then they began to climb and they were going to the east it seemed, and then it darkened and they were in a storm, the rain so thick it seemed like flying through a waterfall, and then they were out and Compie turned his head and grinned and pointed and there, ahead, all he could see, as wide as all

the world, great, high, and unbelievably white in the sun, was the square top of Kilimanjaro. And then he knew that there was where he was going.

Just then the hyena stopped whimpering in the night and started to make a strange, human, almost crying sound. The woman heard it and stirred uneasily. She did not wake. In her dream she was at the house on Long Island and it was the night before her daughter's début. Somehow her father was there and he had been very rude. Then the noise the hyena made was so loud she woke and for a moment she did not know where she was and she was very afraid. Then she took the flashlight and shone it on the other cot that they had carried in after Harry had gone to sleep. She could see his bulk under the mosquito bar, but somehow he had gotten his leg out and it hung down alongside the cot. The dressings had all come down and she could not look at it.

"Molo," she called, "Molo! Molo!"

Then she said, "Harry, Harry!" Then her voice rising, "Harry! Please! Oh Harry!"

There was no answer and she could not hear him breathing.

Outside the tent the hyena made the same strange noise that had awakened her. But she did not hear him for the beating of her heart.

ROBINSON JEFFERS (1887–)

California has long been the home of one of America's most powerful poets. Jeffers was born, however, in Pittsburgh, and lived much in Europe before his family settled in California when he was sixteen. After graduating from Occidental College when only eighteen, he studied at the University of Southern California (three years of medicine) and the University of Washington (a year of forestry). But actually, he says, "I wasn't deeply interested in anything but poetry." "I married Una Call Kuster in 1913. We were going to England in the autumn of 1914. But the August news turned us to this village of Carmel instead; and when the stagecoach topped the hill from Monterey, and we looked down through pines and sea-fog on Carmel Bay, it was evident that we had come without knowing it to our inevitable place." Here, on Point Sur, he built with his own hands a stone house and near it a high tower in which he works — his secluded home ever since.

In 1924 *Tamar and Other Poems*, his third book of verse, created a sensation. *Roan Stallion, Tamar and Other Poems* (1925), *The Women at Point Sur* (1927), *Cawdor and Other Poems* (1928), *Dear Judas and Other Poems* (1929), *Thurso's Landing and Other Poems* (1932), *Give Your Heart to the Hawks and Other Poems* (1933) and later volumes including *Selected Poetry of Robinson Jeffers* (1939) deepened the sensation of *Tamar* into a substantial reputation.

These volumes have maintained the characteristics of Jeffers' verse — a loose but strong musical line, daring choice of subjects (in the long poems), and a stark elemental imagination akin to the strength of his own California rock cliffs. The magnificence of his landscape, the beauty of its detail, give some measure of relief to him in his dark reading of human destiny. This contrast is carried out by two favorite symbols: the stone, or enduring, immemorial earth, and the hawk, the wild, undirected spirit of man, marked for destruction. His attachment is to the granite rocks, the clean beating surf, the redwoods towering in their strength. His philosophy is that of a naturalism based on nineteenth-century science, in which man is of trifling importance, a species here today, gone tomorrow. Man's mistaken self-regard he symbolizes under the guise of incest, which leads man to his doom. Jeffers has expressed his aversion from man and society by such statements as "Cut humanity out of my being, that is the wound that festers." Contemptuous of "the animals Christ was rumored to have died for," he looks forward to a time when the earth will have got rid of man and have reached a "white and most clean, colorless quietness." For "civilization is a transient sickness." Not without satisfaction did he view the destruction of 1914–18, the ensuing international chaos, the economic disorder, the resumption of world conflict. The disillusioned mood of the period between the wars could not go much farther. In this outlook on life Jeffers is more resolutely naturalistic than any other American poet.

Biography and criticism may be found in G. Sterling, *Robinson Jeffers: the Man and the Artist*, 1926; L. Adamic, *Robinson Jeffers: a Portrait*, 1929; S. S. Alberts, *A Bibliography of the Works of Robinson Jeffers* (with commentary by Jeffers on his poetry), 1933; L. C. Powell, *Robinson Jeffers: the Man and His Work*, 1934; H. H. Waggoner, "Science and the Poetry of Robinson Jeffers," *American Literature*, November, 1938. See also F. B. Millett, *Contemporary American Authors*, 1940.

Gale in April
(*ca. 1921*)

Intense and terrible beauty, how has our race with the frail naked nerves,
So little a craft swum down from its far launching?
Why now, only because the northwest blows and the headed grass billows,
Great seas jagging the west and on the granite
Blanching, the vessel is brimmed, this dancing play of the world is too much passion. 5
A gale in April so overfilling the spirit,
Though his ribs were thick as the earth's, arches of mountain, how shall one dare
    to live,
Though his blood were like the earth's rivers and his flesh iron,
How shall one dare to live? One is born strong, how do the weak endure it?
The strong lean upon death as on a rock, 10
After eighty years there is shelter and the naked nerves shall be covered with deep
    quietness,

O beauty of things go on, go on, O torture
Of intense joy I have lasted out my time, I have thanked God and finished,
Roots of millennial trees fold me in the darkness,
Northwest wind shake their tops, not to the root, not to the root, I have passed   15
From beauty to the other beauty, peace, the night splendor.

To the Stone-Cutters

(ca. 1922)

Stone-cutters fighting time with marble, you foredefeated
Challengers of oblivion
Eat cynical earnings, knowing rock splits, records fall down,
The square-limbed Roman letters
Scale in the thaws, wear in the rain.   5
    The poet as well
Builds his monument mockingly;
For man will be blotted out, the blithe earth die, the brave sun
Die blind, his heart blackening:
Yet stones have stood for a thousand years, and pained thoughts found   10
The honey peace in old poems.

Night

(1924)

The ebb slips from the rock, the sunken
Tide-rocks lift streaming shoulders
Out of the slack, the slow west
Sombering its torch; a ship's light
Shows faintly, far out,   5
Over the weight of the prone ocean
On the low cloud.

Over the dark mountain, over the dark pinewood,
Down the long dark valley along the shrunken river,
Returns the splendor without rays, the shining of shadow,   10
Peace-bringer, the matrix of all shining and quieter of shining.
Where the shore widens on the bay she opens dark wings
And the ocean accepts her glory.   O soul worshipful of her
You like the ocean have grave depths where she dwells always,
And the film of waves above that takes the sun takes also   15
Her, with more love.   The sun-lovers have a blond favorite,
A father of lights and noises, wars, weeping and laughter,
Hot labor, lust and delight and the other blemishes.   Quietness
Flows from her deeper fountain; and he will die; and she is immortal.

Far off from here the slender   20
Flocks of the mountain forest
Move among stems like towers
Of the old redwoods to the stream,
No twig crackling; dip shy
Wild muzzles into the mountain water   25
Among the dark ferns.

O beauty of things go on, go on, O
The blasphemies of glowworms, the lamp in my tower, the fretfulness
Of cities, the crescents of the planets, the pride of the stars.
This August night in a rift of cloud Antares reddens,   30
The great one, the ancient torch, a lord among lost children,
The earth's orbit doubled would not girdle his greatness, one fire
Globed, out of grasp of the mind enormous; but to you O Night
What?   Not a spark?   What flicker of a spark in the faint far glimmer
Of a lost fire dying in the desert, dim coals of a sand-pit the Bedouins   35
Wandered from at dawn . . . Ah singing prayer to what gulfs tempted
Suddenly are you more lost?   To us the near-hand mountain
Be a measure of height, the tide-worn cliff at the sea-gate a measure of continuance.

The tide, moving the night's
Vastness with lonely voices,
Turns, the deep dark-shining   40
Pacific leans on the land,
Feeling his cold strength
To the outmost margins: you Night will resume
The stars in your time.   45

O passionately at peace when will that tide draw shoreward?
Truly the spouting fountains of light, Antares, Arcturus,
Tire of their flow, they sing one song but they think silence.
The striding winter giant Orion shines, and dreams darkness.
And life, the flicker of men and moths and the wolf on the hill,   50
Though furious for continuance, passionately feeding, passionately
Remaking itself upon its mates, remembers deep inward
The calm mother, the quietness of the womb and the egg,
The primal and the latter silences: dear Night it is memory
Prophesies, prophecy that remembers, the charm of the dark.   55
And I and my people, we are willing to love the four-score years
Heartily; but as a sailor loves the sea, when the helm is for harbor.

Have men's minds changed,
Or the rock hidden in the deep of the waters of the soul
Broken the surface?   A few centuries   60
Gone by, was none dared not to people
The darkness beyond the stars with harps and habitations.
But now, dear is the truth.   Life is grown sweeter and lonelier,
And death is no evil.

Science

(1925)

Man, introverted man, having crossed
In passage and but a little with the nature of things this latter century
Has begot giants; but being taken up
Like a maniac with self-love and inward conflicts cannot manage his hybrids.
Being used to deal with edgeless dreams,   5

Now he's bred knives on nature turns them also inward: they have thirsty points
    though.
His mind forebodes his own destruction;
Actaeon who saw the goddess naked among leaves and his hounds tore him.
A little knowledge, a pebble from the shingle,
A drop from the oceans: who would have dreamed this infinitely little too much?   10

Apology for Bad Dreams

(1926)

I

In the purple light, heavy with redwood, the slopes drop seaward,
Headlong convexities of forest, drawn in together to the steep ravine. Below, on
    the seacliff,
A lonely clearing; a little field of corn by the streamside; a roof under spared trees.
    Then the ocean
Like a great stone some one has cut to a sharp edge and polished to shining. Be-
    yond it, the fountain   5
And furnace of incredible light flowing up from the sunk sun. In the little clearing
    a woman
Was punishing a horse; she had tied the halter to a sapling at the edge of the wood;
    but when the great whip
Clung to the flanks the creature kicked so hard she feared he would snap the halter;
    she called from the house
The young man her son; who fetched a chain tie-rope, they working together
Noosed the small rusty links round the horse's tongue   10
And tied him by the swollen tongue to the tree.
Seen from this height they are shrunk to insect size,
Out of all human relation. You cannot distinguish
The blood dripping from where the chain is fastened,
The beast shuddering; but the thrust neck and the legs   15
Far apart. You can see the whip fall on the flanks. . . .
The gesture of the arm. You cannot see the face of the woman.
The enormous light beats up out of the west across the cloud-bars of the trade-wind.
    The ocean
Darkens, the high clouds brighten, the hills darken together. Unbridled and un-
    believable beauty   20
Covers the evening world . . . not covers, grows apparent out of it, as Venus down
    there grows out
From the lit sky. What said the prophet? "I create good: and I create evil: I
    am the Lord."

II

This coast crying out for tragedy like all beautiful places,
(The quiet ones ask for quieter suffering; but here the granite cliff the gaunt cy-
    presses' crown
Demands what victim? The dykes of red lava and black what Titan? The hills
    like pointed flames   25

Beyond Soberanes, the terrible peaks of the bare hills under the sun, what im-
     molation?)
This coast crying out for tragedy like all beautiful places: and like the passionate
     spirit of humanity
Pain for its bread: God's, many victims', the painful deaths, the horrible trans-
     figurements: I said in my heart,
"Better invent than suffer: imagine victims
Lest your own flesh be chosen the agonist, or you   30
Martyr some creature to the beauty of the place."   And I said,
"Burn sacrifices once a year to magic
Horror away from the house, this little house here
You have built over the ocean with your own hands
Beside the standing bowlders: for what are we,   35
The beast that walks upright, with speaking lips
And little hair, to think we should always be fed,
Sheltered, intact, and self-controlled?   We sooner more liable
Than the other animals.   Pain and terror, the insanities of desire; not accidents,
     but essential,
And crowd up from the core."   I imagined victims for those wolves, I made the
     phantoms to follow.   40
They have haunted the phantoms and missed the house.   It is not good to forget
     over what gulfs the spirit
Of the beauty of humanity, the petal of a lost flower blown seaward by the night-
     wind, floats to its quietness.

                                        III
Boulders blunted like an old bear's teeth break up from the headland; below them
All the soil is thick with shells, the tide-rock feasts of a dead people.
Here the granite flanks are scarred with ancient fire, the ghosts of the tribe   45
Crouch in the nights beside the ghost of a fire, they try to remember the sunlight,
Light has died out of their skies.   These have paid something for the future
Luck of the country, while we living keep old griefs in memory: though God's
Envy is not a likely fountain of ruin, to forget evil calls down
Sudden reminders from the cloud: remembered deaths be our redeemers;   50
Imagined victims our salvation: white as the half moon at midnight
Some one flamelike passed me, saying, "I am Tamar Cauldwell, I have my desire,"
Then the voice of the sea returned, when she had gone by, the stars to their towers.
. . . Beautiful country, burn again, Point Pinos down to the Sur Rivers
Burn as before with bitter wonders, land and ocean and the Carmel water.   55

                                        IV
He brays humanity in a mortar to bring the savor
From the bruised root: a man having bad dreams, who invents victims, is only the
     ape of that God.
He washes it out with tears and many waters, calcines it with fire in the red crucible,
Deforms it, makes it horrible to itself: the spirit flies out and stands naked, he sees
     the spirit,
He takes it in the naked ecstasy; it breaks in his hand, the atom is broken, the power
     that massed it   60

Cries to the power that moves the stars, "I have come home to myself, behold me.
I bruised myself in the flint mortar and burnt me
In the red shell, I tortured myself, I flew forth,
Stood naked of myself and broke me in fragments,
And here am I moving the stars that are me."   65
I have seen these ways of God: I know of no reason
For fire and change and torture and the old returnings.
He being sufficient might be still. I think they admit no reason; they are the ways
    of my love.
Unmeasured power, incredible passion, enormous craft: no thought apparent but
    burns darkly
Smothered with its own smoke in the human brain-vault: no thought outside: a
    certain measure in phenomena: 70
The fountains of the boiling stars, the flowers on the foreland, the ever-returning
    roses of dawn.

Hurt Hawks

(1927)

I

The broken pillar of the wing jags from the clotted shoulder,
The wing trails like a banner in defeat,
No more to use the sky forever but live with famine
And pain a few days: cat nor coyote
Will shorten the week of waiting for death, there is game without talons.   5
He stands under the oak-bush and waits
The lame feet of salvation; at night he remembers freedom
And flies in a dream, the dawns ruin it.
He is strong and pain is worse to the strong, incapacity is worse.
The curs of the day come and torment him   10
At distance, no one but death the redeemer will humble that head,
The intrepid readiness, the terrible eyes.
The wild God of the world is sometimes merciful to those
That ask mercy, not often to the arrogant.
You do not know him, you communal people, or you have forgotten him;   15
Intemperate and savage, the hawk remembers him;
Beautiful and wild, the hawks, and men that are dying, remember him.

II

I'd sooner, except the penalties, kill a man than a hawk; but the great redtail
Had nothing left but unable misery
From the bone too shattered for mending, the wing that trailed under his talons when
    he moved.   20
We had fed him six weeks, I gave him freedom,
He wandered over the foreland hill and returned in the evening, asking for death,
Not like a beggar, still eyed with the old
Implacable arrogance. I gave him the lead gift in the twilight.
What fell was relaxed,   25
Owl-downy, soft feminine feathers; but what
Soared: the fierce rush: the night-herons by the flooded river cried fear at its rising
Before it was quite unsheathed from reality.

Shine, Perishing Republic

(1925)

While this America settles in the mold of its vulgarity, heavily thickening to empire,
And protest, only a bubble in the molten mass, pops and sighs out, and the mass
    hardens,

I sadly smiling remember that the flower fades to make fruit, the fruit rots to make
    earth.
Out of the mother; and through the spring exultances, ripeness and decadence; and
    home to the mother.

You make haste on decay: not blameworthy; life is good, be it stubbornly long
    or suddenly 5
A mortal splendor: meteors are not needed less than mountains: shine, perishing
    republic.

But for my children, I would have them keep their distance from the thickening
    center; corruption
Never has been compulsory, when the cities lie at the monster's feet there are left
    the mountains.

And boys, be in nothing so moderate as in love of man, a clever servant, insufferable
    master.
There is the trap that catches noblest spirits, that caught — they say — God, when
    he walked on earth. 10

T. S. ELIOT (1888–   )

Thomas Stearns Eliot was born in St. Louis of a New England family. "It was not until years of maturity," he has said, "that I perceived that I myself had always been a New Englander in the South West, and a South Westerner in New England." After graduating from Harvard, A.B. 1909, A.M. 1910, he became a candidate for Ph.D. in philosophy at Harvard, studied philosophy at the Sorbonne, worked on Aristotle at Oxford. Remaining in England from 1914 on, he tried teaching, then took a position in Lloyd's Bank, at the same time doing editorial work on *The Egoist*. He was a frequent reviewer for *The Athenaeum* and the *Times Literary Supplement*, and in 1922 undertook a quarterly review, *The Criterion*. Three years later, he joined the board of the publishing house of Faber and Gwyer, Ltd. He married an English-woman and in 1927 became a British subject. He has lectured at Trinity College, Cambridge, and, in America, at Harvard and the University of Virginia.

Meanwhile, beginning with *Prufrock* in 1917, he published from time to time slight volumes of verse which made a strong impact on the literary intellectuals of his age. They included *Poems*, 1919; *The Waste Land*, 1922; *Ash Wednesday*, 1930; *The Rock* (verse drama), 1934; *Murder in the Cathedral* (verse drama), 1935; *Collected Poems 1909–1935*, 1936; *The Family Reunion* (verse drama), 1939; *Four Quartets*, 1943. While strikingly original, his poetry bore the marks of Dante, the lesser Elizabethans,

Donne and other "Metaphysicals," the French Symbolists, and Ezra Pound. (He dedicated *The Waste Land* to Pound and ventured to call him "probably the most important living poet in our language.") Much of his poetry, as characterized by Untermeyer, "employs a complex verse, combining trivial and tawdry pictures with traditionally poetic subject-matter, linking the banalities of conversation to rich rhetoric, and interrupting the present with flash-backs of the past. This method, not unfamiliar to students of the films, makes for a nervous disintegration, the rapid and, seemingly, unrelated images, the discordant metaphors achieve an emotional response at the expense of a logical progression." To the unaccustomed, poetry of this sort is difficult reading. Taken in chronological order, the poems of Eliot develop from the disillusioned, confused Prufrock to the sterility of Gerontion and *The Waste Land*, which voiced the modern temper of despair in a naturalistic world devoid of meaning, and then to the Christian faith of *Ash Wednesday* and the later poems.

Eliot is also a master of prose, commanding a style cool, precise, almost prim, often (to use his own word) pontifical. Among his writings in prose are *The Sacred Wood*, 1920; *For Lancelot Andrewes*, 1928; *Dante*, 1929; *Selected Essays: 1917–1932*, 1932; *The Use of Poetry*, 1933; *After Strange Gods*, 1934; *The Idea of a Christian Society*, 1940. His literary essays are almost wholly composed of æsthetic criticism, focused upon the technical problems of the artist. The limited meaning which he assigns to "art" may be indicated by his opinion of *Hamlet*: "So far from being Shakespeare's masterpiece, the play is most certainly an artistic failure" (*Selected Essays*, 123).

Through the example of his own poetry and through his prose discussions of technique, Eliot did much to win wide acceptance of "difficult" contemporary poetry and to awaken interest in the older difficult poetry of the English Metaphysicals and the French Symbolists and their successors. His influence was strong on such English poets as Spender, Auden, and Lewis, and on such Americans as MacLeish, Gregory, Aiken, and the Nashville group. As a rule such poets have not followed him, however, in his spiritual development. Repelled by the chaos of modern life and the modern mind, attracted to and then dissatisfied with the humanistic discipline expounded by Irving Babbitt, Eliot proceeded far to the spiritual "Right" by embracing revealed religion — Anglo-Catholicism.

Perhaps the most useful interpretations and criticisms of Eliot are in T. McGreevy, *Thomas Stearns Eliot*, 1931; Edmund Wilson, *Axel's Castle*, 1931; F. R. Leavis, *New Bearings in English Poetry*, 1932; H. R. Williamson, *The Poetry of T. S. Eliot*, 1932; F. O. Matthiessen, *The Achievement of T. S. Eliot*, 1935; D. Daiches, *Poetry and the Modern World*, 1940; J. C. Ransom, *The New Criticism*, 1941; B. Rajan, ed., *T. S. Eliot, A Study of His Writing by Several Hands*, 1949.

Prelude

(1917)

The winter evening settles down
With smell of steaks in passageways.
Six o'clock.
The burnt-out ends of smoky days.
And now a gusty shower wraps   5

The grimy scraps
Of withered leaves about your feet
And newspapers from vacant lots;
The showers beat
On broken blinds and chimney-pots,   10
And at the corner of the street
A lonely cab-horse steams and stamps.
And then the lighting of the lamps.

The Love Song of J. Alfred Prufrock
(1917)

Written while Eliot was still at Harvard, this poem, with its blending of irony and symbolism, long served as a model for many young poets, English and American. "The prematurely old Prufrock is a dilettante, culture-ridden and world-weary, aloof and disillusioned. He is inhibited by his own distorted memory and his confused desires; he recognizes passion, but he cannot rise to it. His isolation is emphasized by the strange opening simile . . . with its mood of sick helplessness, and by the introductory lines from Dante's *Inferno*: 'If I thought my answer were to one who ever could return to the world, this flame should shake no more; but since, if what I hear be true, none ever did return alive from this depth, without fear of infamy I answer thee.' " (Untermeyer.)

A detailed analysis of the theme of the poem is given in C. Brooks and R. P. Warren, *Understanding Poetry*, pages 589–596.

> *S'io credesse che mia risposta fosse*
> *A persona che mai tornasse al mondo,*
> *Questa fiamma staria semza piu scosse.*
> *Ma perciocche giammai di questo fondo*
> *Non torno vivo alcun, s'i'odo il vero,*
> *Senza tema d'infamia ti rispondo.*

Let us go then, you and I,
When the evening is spread out against the sky
Like a patient etherised upon a table;
Let us go, through certain half-deserted streets,
The muttering retreats   5
Of restless nights in one-night cheap hotels
And sawdust restaurants with oyster-shells:
Streets that follow like a tedious argument
Of insidious intent
To lead you to an overwhelming question . . .
Oh, do not ask, "What is it?"   11
Let us go and make our visit.

In the room the women come and go
Talking of Michelangelo.
The yellow fog that rubs its back upon the
    window-panes,   15
The yellow smoke that rubs its muzzle on
    the window-panes
Licked its tongue into the corners of the eve-
    ning,
Lingered upon the pools that stand in drains,
Let fall upon its back the soot that falls from
    chimneys,
Slipped by the terrace, made a sudden leap, 20

And seeing that it was a soft October night,
Curled once about the house, and fell asleep.

And indeed there will be time
For the yellow smoke that slides along the
    street,
Rubbing its back upon the window-panes; 25
There will be time, there will be time
To prepare a face to meet the faces that you
    meet;
There will be time to murder and create,
And time for all the works and days of hands
That lift and drop a question on your plate;
Time for you and time for me,   31
And time yet for a hundred indecisions,
And for a hundred visions and revisions,
Before the taking of a toast and tea.

In the room the women come and go   35
Talking of Michelangelo.

And indeed there will be time
To wonder, "Do I dare?" and, "Do I dare?"
Time to turn back and descend the stair,
With a bald spot in the middle of my hair —
(They will say: "How his hair is growing
    thin!")   41
My morning coat, my collar mounting firmly
    to the chin,
My necktie rich and modest, but asserted by
    a simple pin —
(They will say: "But how his arms and legs
    are thin!")
Do I dare   45
Disturb the universe?
In a minute there is time
For decisions and revisions which a minute
    will reverse.

For I have known them all already, known
    them all:
Have known the evenings, mornings, after-
    noons,   50
I have measured out my life with coffee
    spoons;
I know the voices dying with a dying fall
Beneath the music from a farther room.
    So how should I presume?

And I have known the eyes already, known
    them all —   55
The eyes that fix you in a formulated phrase,

And when I am formulated, sprawling on a pin,
When I am pinned and wriggling on the wall,
Then how should I begin
To spit out all the butt-ends of my days and ways?   60
    And how should I presume?

And I have known the arms already, known them all —
Arms that are braceleted and white and bare
(But in the lamplight, downed with light brown hair!)
Is it perfume from a dress   65
That makes me so digress?
Arms that lie along a table, or wrap about a shawl.
    And should I then presume?
    And how should I begin?

  . . . .

Shall I say, I have gone at dusk through narrow streets   70
And watched the smoke that rises from the pipes
Of lonely men in shirt-sleeves, leaning out of windows? . . .

I should have been a pair of ragged claws
Scuttling across the floors of silent seas.

  . . . .

And the afternoon, the evening, sleeps so peacefully!   75
Smoothed by long fingers,
Asleep . . . tired . . . or it malingers,
Stretched on the floor, here beside you and me.
Should I, after tea and cakes and ices,
Have the strength to force the moment to its crisis?   80
But though I have wept and fasted, wept and prayed,
Though I have seen my head (grown slightly bald) brought in upon a platter,
I am no prophet — and here's no great matter;
I have seen the moment of my greatness flicker,
And I have seen the eternal Footman hold my coat, and snicker,   85
And in short, I was afraid.

And would it have been worth it, after all,
After the cups, the marmalade, the tea,
Among the porcelain, among some talk of you and me,
Would it have been worth while,   90
To have bitten off the matter with a smile,
To have squeezed the universe into a ball,
To roll it toward some overwhelming question,
To say: "I am Lazarus, come from the dead,
Come back to tell you all, I shall tell you all" —   95
If one, settling a pillow by her head,
    Should say: "That is not what I meant at all;
    That is not it, at all."

And would it have been worth it, after all,
Would it have been worth while,   100
After the sunsets and the dooryards and the sprinkled streets,
After the novels, after the teacups, after the skirts that trail along the floor —
And this, and so much more? —
It is impossible to say just what I mean!
But as if a magic lantern threw the nerves in patterns on a screen: 105
Would it have been worth while
If one, settling a pillow or throwing off a shawl,
And turning toward the window, should say:
    "That is not it at all,
    That is not what I meant, at all."   110

  . . . .

No! I am not Prince Hamlet, nor was meant to be;
Am an attendant lord, one that will do
To swell a progress, start a scene or two,
Advise the prince; no doubt, an easy tool,
Deferential, glad to be of use,   115
Politic, cautious, and meticulous;
Full of high sentence, but a bit obtuse;
At times, indeed, almost ridiculous —
Almost, at times, the Fool.

I grow old . . . I grow old . . .   120
I shall wear the bottoms of my trousers rolled.

Shall I part my hair behind? Do I dare to eat a peach?
I shall wear white flannel trousers, and walk upon the beach.

I have heard the mermaids singing, each to
    each.

I do not think that they will sing to me.   125

I have seen them riding seaward on the
    waves
Combing the white hair of the waves blown
    back
When the wind blows the water white and
    black.

We have lingered in the chambers of the
    sea
By sea-girls wreathed with seaweed red and
    brown   130
Till human voices wake us, and we drown.

Morning at the Window
(1917)

They are rattling breakfast plates in base-
    ment kitchens,
And along the trampled edges of the street
I am aware of the damp souls of housemaids
Sprouting despondently at area gates.

The brown waves of fog toss up to me   5
Twisted faces from the bottom of the street,
And tear from a passer-by with muddy skirts
An aimless smile that hovers in the air
And vanishes along the level of the roofs.

The Hippopotamus
(1920)

*Similiter et omnes revereantur Diaconos, ut mandatum
Jesu Christi; et Episcopum, ut Jesum Christum existen-
tem filium Patris; Presbyteros autem, ut concilium Dei et
conjunctionem Apostolorum. Sine his Ecclesia non vocat-
ur; de quibus suadeo vos sic habeo.*
        S. Ignatii ad Trallianos

And when this epistle is read among you, cause
that it be read also in the church of the Laodiceans.

The broad-backed hippopotamus
Rests on his belly in the mud;
Although he seems so firm to us
He is merely flesh and blood.

Flesh and blood is weak and frail,   5
Susceptible to nervous shock;
While the True Church can never fail
For it is based upon a rock.

The hippo's feeble steps may err
In compassing material ends,   10
While the True Church needs never stir
To gather in its dividends.

The 'potamus can never reach
The mango on the mango-tree;
But fruits of pomegranate and peach   15
Refresh the Church from over sea.

At mating time the hippo's voice
Betrays inflexions hoarse and odd;
But every week we hear rejoice
The Church at being one with God.   20

The hippopotamus's day
Is passed in sleep; at night he hunts;
God works in a mysterious way —
The Church can sleep and feed at once.

I saw the 'potamus take wing   25
Ascending from the damp savannas,
And quiring angels round him sing
The praise of God, in loud hosannas.

Blood of the Lamb shall wash him clean
And him shall heavenly arms enfold,   30
Among the saints he shall be seen
Performing on a harp of gold.

He shall be washed as white as snow,
By all the martyr'd virgins kist,
While the True Church remains below   35
Wrapt in the old miasmal mist.

Gerontion
(1920?)

The quotation at the head is from Shakespeare's
Measure for Measure. Leavis remarks, in *New
Bearings in English Poetry*, page 84: "The poem
opens with what is to be a recurrent theme of Mr.
Eliot's: the mixing of 'memory and desire' in
present barrenness. The old man in his 'dry
month,' waiting for the life-giving 'rain' that he
knows will never come, is stirred to envy, then to
poignant recollection by the story of hot-blooded

vitality, which contrasts with the squalor of his actual surrounding. Youthful desire mingles in memory with the most exalted emotions, those associated with the mysteries of religion."

> Thou hast nor youth nor age
> But as it were an after dinner sleep
> Dreaming of both.

Here I am, an old man in a dry month,
Being read to by a boy, waiting for rain.
I was neither at the hot gates
Nor fought in the warm rain,
Nor knee deep in the salt marsh, heaving a
    cutlass,   5
Bitten by flies, fought.
My house is a decayed house,
And the jew squats on the window sill, the
    owner,
Spawned in some estaminet of Antwerp,
Blistered in Brussels, patched and peeled in
    London.   10
The goat coughs at night in the field over-
    head;
Rocks, moss, stonecrop, iron, merds.
The woman keeps the kitchen, makes tea,
Sneezes at evening, poking the peevish gutter.

             I an old man,   15
A dull head among windy spaces.

Signs are taken for wonders. "We would
    see a sign"!
The word within a word, unable to speak a
    word,
Swaddled with darkness. In the juvescence
    of the year
Came Christ the tiger   20
In depraved May, dogwood and chestnut,
    flowering judas,
To be eaten, to be divided, to be drunk
Among whispers; by Mr. Silvero
With caressing hands, at Limoges
Who walked all night in the next room;   25

By Hakagawa, bowing among the Titians;
By Madame de Tornquist, in the dark room
Shifting the candles; Fräulein von Kulp
Who turned in the hall, one hand on the
    door.

       Vacant shuttles   30
Weave the wind. I have no ghosts,
An old man in a draughty house
Under a windy knob.

After such knowledge, what forgiveness?
    Think now
History has many cunning passages, con-
    trived corridors   35
And issues, deceives with whispering ambi-
    tions,
Guides us by vanities. Think now
She gives when our attention is distracted
And what she gives, gives with such supple
    confusions
That the giving famishes the craving. Gives
    too late   40
What's not believed in, or if still believed,
In memory only, reconsidered passion. Gives
    too soon
Into weak hands, what's thought can be
    dispensed with
Till the refusal propagates a fear. Think
Neither fear nor courage saves us. Un-
    natural vices   45
Are fathered by our heroism. Virtues
Are forced upon us by our impudent crimes.
These tears are shaken from the wrath-
    bearing tree.

The tiger springs in the new year. Us he
    devours. Think at last
We have not reached conclusion, when I   50
Stiffen in a rented house. Think at last
I have not made this show purposelessly
And it is not by any concitation
Of the backward devils.
I would meet you upon this honestly.   55
I that was near your heart was removed
    therefrom
To lose beauty in terror, terror in inquisition.
I have lost my passion: why should I need
    to keep it
Since what is kept must be adulterated?
I have lost my sight, smell, hearing, taste
    and touch: 60
How should I use it for your closer con-
    tact?

These with a thousand small deliberations
Protract the profit of their chilled delirium,
Excite the membrane, when the sense has
    cooled,
With pungent sauces, multiply variety   65
In a wilderness of mirrors. What will the
    spider do,
Suspend its operations, will the weevil

Delay? De Bailhache, Fresca, Mrs. Cam-
mel, whirled
Beyond the circuit of the shuddering Bear
In fractured atoms. Gull against the wind,
    in the windy straits   70
Of Belle Isle, or running on the Horn,
White feathers in the snow, the Gulf claims,
And an old man driven by the Trades
To a sleepy corner.

                    Tenants of the house,
Thoughts of a dry brain in a dry season.   75

The Waste Land

(1922)

"In many ways this is the pivotal poem of the
twentieth century. It is at once the most discussed, the most criticized and the most admired
poem of our times; but in spite of the endless controversy which surrounds it, there is no doubt that
the ability to read it marks full maturity in the
art of reading poems" (Wright Thomas and S. G.
Brown, *Reading Poems*, 1941).

Readers may avail themselves of the eight pages
of "Notes on 'The Waste Land' " which Eliot
himself supplied at the end of the text in *Collected
Poems*, pages 91–98. These notes have been
greatly amplified by Messrs. Thomas and Brown
in the book named in the preceding paragraph,
pages 716–731. More general commentary may
be found in Edmund Wilson, *Axel's Castle*, 1931,
ch. IV, and in Cleanth Brooks, *Modern Poetry and
the Tradition*, 1939, ch. VII.

As Robert Penn Warren has said in the *Kenyon
Review*, Autumn, 1939, Eliot's "later poems,
especially *Ash Wednesday* and *Murder in the Cathedral*, have provided, retroactively, a reinterpretation of *The Waste Land*. Much of Eliot's great
importance for contemporary poetry seems to lie
in the fact that his poetry springs from the contemplation of a question which is central in
modern life: can man live on the purely naturalistic
level?"

"Nam Sibyllam quidem Cumis ego ipse oculis
meis vidi in ampulla pendere, et cum illi pueri
dicerent: Σίβυλλα τί θέλεις; respondebat illa: ἀπο-
θανεῖν θέλω."

I. THE BURIAL OF THE DEAD

April is the cruelest month, breeding
Lilacs out of the dead land, mixing
Memory and desire, stirring
Dull roots with spring rain.

Winter kept us warm, covering   5
Earth in forgetful snow, feeding
A little life with dried tubers.
Summer surprised us, coming over the Starn-
bergersee
With a shower of rain; we stopped in the
colonnade,
And went on in sunlight, into the Hof-
garten,   10
And drank coffee, and talked for an hour.
Bin gar keine Russin, stamm' aus Litauen,
echt deutsch.
And when we were children, staying at the
archduke's,
My cousin's, he took me out on a sled,
And I was frightened. He said, Marie,   15
Marie, hold on tight. And down we went.
In the mountains, there you feel free.
I read, much of the night, and go south in
the winter.
What are the roots that clutch, what branches
grow
Out of this stony rubbish? Son of man,   20
You cannot say, or guess, for you know only
A heap of broken images, where the sun beats,
And the dead tree gives no shelter, the cricket
no relief,
And the dry stone no sound of water. Only
There is shadow under this red rock,   25
(Come in under the shadow of this red rock),
And I will show you something different from
either
Your shadow at morning striding behind
you
Or your shadow at evening rising to meet
you;
I will show you fear in a handful of dust.   30

            *Frisch weht der Wind
            Der Heimat zu
            Mein Irisch Kind,
            Wo weilest du?*

'You gave me hyacinths first a year ago;   35
'They called me the hyacinth girl.'
— Yet when we came back, late, from the
hyacinth garden,
Your arms full, and your hair wet, I could
not
Speak, and my eyes failed, I was neither
Living nor dead, and I knew nothing,   40
Looking into the heart of light, the silence.
Oed' und leer das Meer.

Madame Sosostris, famous clairvoyante,
Had a bad cold, nevertheless
Is known to be the wisest woman in Europe, 45
With a wicked pack of cards.   Here, said she,
Is your card, the drowned Phoenician Sailor,
(Those are pearls that were his eyes.   Look!)
Here is Belladonna, the Lady of the Rocks,
The lady of situations.   50
Here is the man with three staves, and here
      the Wheel,
And here is the one-eyed merchant, and this
      card,
Which is blank, is something he carries on
      his back,
Which I am forbidden to see.   I do not find
The Hanged Man.   Fear death by water. 55
I see crowds of people, walking round in a
      ring.
Thank you.   If you see dear Mrs. Equitone,
Tell her I bring the horoscope myself:
One must be so careful these days.

Unreal City,   60
Under the brown fog of a winter dawn,
A crowd flowed over London Bridge, so many,
I had not thought death had undone so many.
Sighs, short and infrequent, were exhaled,
And each man fixed his eyes before his feet. 65
Flowed up the hill and down King William
      Street
To where Saint Mary Woolnoth kept the
      hours
With a dead sound on the final stroke of nine.
There I saw one I knew, and stopped him
      crying: 'Stetson!
'You who were with me in the ships at
      Mylae!   70
'That corpse you planted last year in your
      garden,
'Has it begun to sprout?   Will it bloom this
      year?
'Or has the sudden frost disturbed its bed?
'Oh keep the Dog far hence, that's friend to
      men,
'Or with his nails he'll dig it up again!   75
'You! hypocrite lecteur! — mon semblable,
      — mon frère!'

II. A GAME OF CHESS

The Chair she sat in, like a burnished throne,
Glowed on the marble, where the glass

Held up by standards wrought with fruited
      vines
From which a golden Cupidon peeped out 80
(Another hid his eyes behind his wing)
Doubled the flames of seven branched
      candelabra
Reflecting light upon the table as
The glitter of her jewels rose to meet it,
From satin cases poured in rich profusion; 85
In vials of ivory and colored glass
Unstoppered, lurked her strange synthetic
      perfumes,
Unguent, powdered, or liquid — troubled,
      confused
And drowned the sense in odors; stirred by the
      air
That freshened from the window, these
      ascended   90
In fattening the prolonged candle-flames,
Flung their smoke into the laquearia,
Stirring the pattern on the coffered ceiling.
Huge sea-wood fed with copper
Burned green and orange, framed by the
      colored stone,   95
In which sad light a carvèd dolphin swam.
Above the antique mantel was displayed
As though a window gave upon the sylvan
      scene
The change of Philomel, by the barbarous king
So rudely forced; yet there the nightingale
Filled all the desert with inviolable voice 100
And still she cried, and still the world
      pursues,
'Jug Jug' to dirty ears.
And other withered stumps of time
Were told upon the walls; staring forms 105
Leaned out, leaning, hushing the room en-
      closed.
Footsteps shuffled on the stair.
Under the firelight, under the brush, her
      hair
Spread out in fiery points
Glowed into words, then would be savagely
      still.   110

'My nerves are bad tonight.   Yes, bad.
      Stay with me.
'Speak to me.   Why do you never speak.
'What are you thinking of?   What thinking?
      What?
'I never know what you are thinking.
      Think.'

I think we are in rats' alley 115
Where the dead men lost their bones.

'What is that noise?'
        The wind under the door.
'What is that noise now? What is the wind
    doing?'
        Nothing again nothing. 120
               'Do
'You know nothing? Do you see nothing?
    Do you remember
'Nothing?'

    I remember
Those are pearls that were his eyes. 125
'Are you alive or not? Is there nothing in
    your head?'
               But
O O O O that Shakespeherian Rag —
It's so elegant
So intelligent 130
'What shall I do now? What shall I do?
'I shall rush out as I am, and walk the street
'With my hair down, so. What shall we do
    tomorrow?
'What shall we ever do?'
           The hot water at ten. 135
And if it rains, a closed car at four.
And we shall play a game of chess,
Pressing lidless eyes and waiting for a knock
    upon the door.

When Lil's husband got demobbed, I said —
I didn't mince my words, I said to her
    myself, 140
HURRY UP PLEASE ITS TIME
Now Albert's coming back, make yourself a
    bit smart.
He'll want to know what you done with that
    money he gave you
To get yourself some teeth. He did, I was
    there.
You have them all out, Lil, and get a nice
    set, 145
He said, I swear, I can't bear to look at you.
And no more can't I, I said, and think of poor
    Albert,
He's been in the army four years, he wants a
    good time,
And if you don't give it him, there's others
    will, I said.

Oh is there, she said. Something o'that, I
    said. 150
Then I'll know who to thank, she said, and
    give me a straight look.
HURRY UP PLEASE ITS TIME
If you don't like it you can get on with it,
    I said.
Others can pick and choose if you can't.
But if Albert makes off, it won't be for lack of
    telling. 155
You ought to be ashamed, I said, to look so
    antique.
(And her only thirty-one.)
I can't help it, she said, pulling a long face,
It's them pills I took, to bring it off, she said.
(She's had five already, and nearly died of
    young George.) 160
The chemist said it would be all right, but
    I've never been the same.
You *are* a proper fool, I said.
Well, if Albert won't leave you alone, there it
    is, I said,
What you get married for if you don't want
    children?
HURRY UP PLEASE ITS TIME 165
Well, that Sunday Albert was home, they
    had a hot gammon,
And they asked me in to dinner, to get the
    beauty of it hot —
HURRY UP PLEASE ITS TIME
HURRY UP PLEASE ITS TIME
Goonight Bill. Goonight Lou. Goonight
    May. Goonight. 170
Ta ta. Goonight. Goonight.
Good night, ladies, good night, sweet ladies,
    good night, good night.

III. THE FIRE SERMON

The river's tent is broken: the last fingers of
    leaf
Clutch and sink into the wet bank. The
    wind
Crosses the brown land, unheard. The
    nymphs are departed. 175
Sweet Thames, run softly, till I end my song.
The river bears no empty bottles, sandwich
    papers,
Silk handkerchiefs, cardboard boxes, cigarette
    ends
Or other testimony of summer nights. The
    nymphs are departed.

And their friends, the loitering heirs of city
directors; 180
Departed, have left no addresses.
By the waters of Leman I sat down and
wept . . .
Sweet Thames, run softly till I end my song,
Sweet Thames, run softly, for I speak not
loud or long.
But at my back in a cold blast I hear 185
The rattle of the bones, and chuckle spread
from ear to ear.
A rat crept softly through the vegetation
Dragging its slimy belly on the bank
While I was fishing in the dull canal
On a winter evening round behind the
gashouse 190
Musing upon the king my brother's wreck
And on the king my father's death before him.
White bodies naked on the low damp ground
And bones cast in a little low dry garret,
Rattled by the rat's foot only, year to year. 195
But at my back from time to time I hear
The sound of horns and motors, which shall
bring
Sweeney to Mrs. Porter in the spring.
O the moon shone bright on Mrs. Porter
And on her daughter 200
They wash their feet in soda water
Et O ces voix d'enfants, chantant dans la coupole!

Twit twit twit
Jug jug jug jug jug jug
So rudely forc'd. 205
Tereu

Unreal City
Under the brown fog of a winter noon
Mr. Eugenides, the Smyrna merchant
Unshaven, with a pocket full of currants 210
C. i. f. London: documents at sight,
Asked me in demotic French
To luncheon at the Cannon Street Hotel
Followed by a weekend at the Metropole.
At the violet hour, when the eyes and back 215
Turn upward from the desk, when the human
engine waits
Like a taxi throbbing waiting,
I Tiresias, though blind, throbbing between
two lives,
Old man with wrinkled female breasts, can see
At the violet hour, the evening hour that
strives 220

Homeward, and brings the sailor home from
the sea,
The typist home at teatime, clears her break-
fast, lights
Her stove, and lays out food in tins.
Out of the window perilously spread
Her drying combinations touched by the
sun's last rays, 225
On the divan are piled (at night her bed)
Stockings, slippers, camisoles, and stays.
I Tiresias, old man with wrinkled dugs
Perceived the scene, and foretold the rest —
I too awaited the expected guest. 230
He, the young man carbuncular, arrives,
A small house agent's clerk, with one bold
stare,
One of the low on whom assurance sits
As a silk hat on a Bradford millionaire.
The time is now propitious, as he guesses, 235
The meal is ended, she is bored and tired,
Endeavors to engage her in caresses
Which still are unreproved, if undesired.
Flushed and decided, he assaults at once;
Exploring hands encounter no defense; 240
His vanity requires no response,
And makes a welcome of indifference.
(And I Tiresias have foresuffered all
Enacted on this same divan or bed;
I who have sat by Thebes below the wall 245
And walked among the lowest of the dead.)
Bestows one final patronizing kiss,
And gropes his way, finding the stairs
unlit . . .

She turns and looks a moment in the glass,
Hardly aware of her departed lover; 250
Her brain allows one half-formed thought
to pass:
'Well now that's done: and I'm glad it's
over.'
When lovely woman stoops to folly and
Paces about her room again, alone,
She smooths her hair with automatic hand, 255
And puts a record on the gramophone.

'This music crept by me upon the waters'
And along the Strand, up Queen Victoria
Street.
O City city, I can sometimes hear
Beside a public bar in Lower Thames
Street, 260
The pleasant whining of a mandolin

And a clatter and a chatter from within
Where fishmen lounge at noon: where the
    walls
Of Magnus Martyr hold
Inexplicable splendor of Ionian white and
    gold.   265

The river sweats
Oil and tar
The barges drift
With the turning tide
Red sails   270
Wide
To leeward, swing on the heavy spar.
The barges wash
Drifting logs
Down Greenwich reach   275
Past the Isle of Dogs.
    Weialala leia
    Wallala leialala

Elizabeth and Leicester
Beating oars   280
The stern was formed
A gilded shell
Red and gold
The brisk swell
Rippled both shores   285
Southwest wind
Carried down stream
The peal of bells
White towers
    Weialala leia   290
    Wallala leialala

"Trams and dusty trees.
Highbury bore me.   Richmond and Kew
Undid me.   By Richmond I raised my knees
Supine on the floor of a narrow canoe."   295

'My feet are at Moorgate, and my heart
Under my feet.   After the event
He wept.   He promised "a new start."
I made no comment.   What should I resent?'

'On Margate Sands.   300
I can connect
Nothing with nothing
The broken fingernails of dirty hands.
My people humble people who expect
Nothing.'   305
    la la

To Carthage then I came
Burning burning burning burning
O Lord Thou pluckest me out
O Lord Thou pluckest   310

burning

IV. DEATH BY WATER

Phlebas the Phoenician, a fortnight dead,
Forgot the cry of gulls, and the deep sea swell
And the profit and loss.
    A current under sea   315
Picked his bones in whispers.   As he rose and
    fell
He passed the stages of his age and youth
Entering the whirlpool.
    Gentile or Jew
O you who turn the wheel and look to
    windward,   320
Consider Phlebas, who was once handsome
    and tall as you.

V. WHAT THE THUNDER SAID

After the torchlight red on sweaty faces
After the frosty silence in the gardens
After the agony in stony places
The shouting and the crying   325
Prison and palace and reverberation
Of thunder of spring over distant mountains
He who was living is now dead
We who were living are now dying
With a little patience   330

Here is no water but only rock
Rock and no water and the sandy road
The road winding above among the moun-
    tains
Which are mountains of rock without water
If there were water we should stop and
    drink   335
Amongst the rock one cannot stop or think
Sweat is dry and feet are in the sand
If there were only water amongst the rock
Dead mountain mouth of carious teeth that
    cannot spit
Here one can neither stand nor lie nor sit 340
There is not even silence in the mountains
But dry sterile thunder without rain
There is not even solitude in the mountains
But red sullen faces sneer and snarl
From doors of mudcracked houses   345

If there were water
And no rock
If there were rock
And also water
And water   350
A spring
A pool among the rock
If there were the sound of water only
Not the cicada
And dry grass singing   355
But sound of water over a rock
Where the hermit-thrush sings in the pine
     trees
Drip drop drip drop drop drop drop
But there is no water

Who is the third who walks always beside
     you?   360
When I count, there are only you and I
     together
But when I look ahead up the white road
There is always another one walking beside
     you
Gliding wrapped in a brown mantle, hooded
I do not know whether a man or woman 365
— But who is that on the other side of you?

What is that sound high in the air
Murmur of maternal lamentation
Who are those hooded hordes swarming
Over endless plains, stumbling in cracked
     earth   370
Ringed by the flat horizon only
What is the city over the mountains
Cracks and reforms and bursts in the violet
     air
Falling towers
Jerusalem Athens Alexandria   375
Vienna London
Unreal

A woman drew her long black hair out
     tight
And fiddled whisper music on those strings
And bats with baby faces in the violet light 380
Whistled, and beat their wings
And crawled head downward down a
     blackened wall
And upside down in air were towers
Tolling reminiscent bells, that kept the hours
And voices singing out of empty cisterns and
     exhausted wells.   385

In this decayed hole among the mountains
In the faint moonlight, the grass is singing
Over the tumbled graves, about the chapel
There is the empty chapel, only the wind's
     home.
It has no windows, and the door swings, 390
Dry bones can harm no one.
Only a cock stood on the rooftree
Co co rico co co rico
In a flash of lightning.   Then a damp gust
Bringing rain   395

Ganga was sunken, and the limp leaves
Waited for rain, while the black clouds
Gathered far distant, over Himavant
The jungle crouched, humped in silence.
Then spoke the thunder   400

DA
Datta: what have we given?
My friend, blood shaking my heart
The awful daring of a moment's surrender
Which an age of prudence can never re-
     tract   405
By this, and this only, we have existed
Which is not to be found in our obituaries
Or in memories draped by the beneficent
     spider
Or under seals broken by the lean solicitor
In our empty rooms   410
DA
Dayadhvam: I have heard the key
Turn in the door once and turn once only
We think of the key, each in his prison
Thinking of the key, each confirms a prison 415
Only at nightfall, ethereal rumors
Revive for a moment a broken Coriolanus
DA
Damyata: The boat responded
Gaily, to the hand expert with sail and oar
The sea was calm, your heart would have
     responded   420
Gaily, when invited, beating obedient
To controlling hands

          I sat upon the shore
Fishing, with the arid plain behind me
Shall I at least set my lands in order?   425
London Bridge is falling down falling down
     falling down
Poi s'ascose nel fico che gli affina
Quando fiam uti chelidon — O swallow swallow
Le Prince d' Aquitaine à la tour abolie

These fragments I have shored against my
    ruins   430
Why then Ile fit you. Hieronymo's mad
    againe.
Datta. Dayadhvam. Damyata.
    Shantih shantih shantih

Animula

(1929)

"Issues from the hand of God, the simple
    soul"
To a flat world of changing lights and noise,
To light, dark, dry or damp, chilly or warm;
Moving between the legs of tables and of
    chairs,
Rising or falling, grasping at kisses and toys, 5
Advancing boldly, sudden to take alarm,
Retreating to the corner of arm and knee,
Eager to be reassured, taking pleasure
In the fragrant brilliance of the Christmas
    tree,
Pleasure in the wind, the sunlight and the
    sea;   10
Studies the sunlit pattern on the floor
And running stags around a silver tray;
Confounds the actual and the fanciful,
Content with playing-cards and kings and
    queens,
What the fairies do and what the servants
    say.   15
The heavy burden of the growing soul
Perplexes and offends more, day by day;
Week by week, offends and perplexes more
With the imperatives of "is and seems"
And may and may not, desire and control.   20

The pain of living and the drug of dreams
Curl up the small soul in the window seat
Behind the *Encyclopaedia Britannica.*
Issues from the hand of time the simple
    soul
Irresolute and selfish, misshapen, lame,   25
Unable to fare forward or retreat,
Fearing the warm reality, the offered good,
Denying the importunity of the blood,
Shadow of its own shadows, spectre in its
    own gloom,
Leaving disordered papers in a dusty
    room;   30
Living first in the silence after the viaticum.

Pray for Guiterriez, avid of speed and power,
For Boudin, blown to pieces,
For this one who made a great fortune,
And that one who went his own way.   35
Pray for Floret, by the boarhound slain
    between the yew trees,
Pray for us now and at the hour of our birth.

Ash Wednesday

(1930)

"The balance that is sustained in 'Ash Wednesday' between knowledge of the desert and perception of the garden gives a full tone of authority to
both, and thus to the range of experience which
they encompass. This poem is not an escape from
the problem of life into an easy dream world. The
most urgent notes are suggested by the connotations of its title. On Ash-Wednesday is performed
the ritual of the anointing of the forehead with
ashes, while the priest recites: 'Remember, man,
that thou art dust, and unto dust thou shalt return.'
. . . By the time we reach the last poem of the series,
we have a full sense of the wavering of an individual spirit, its desire to lose itself in the universal
Will, and yet its continual distraction back to the
world of desire and loss." (Matthiessen, *The Achievement of T. S. Eliot.*)

1

Because I do not hope to turn again
Because I do not hope
Because I do not hope to turn
Desiring this man's gift and that man's
    scope
I no longer strive to strive towards such
    things   5
(Why should the agèd eagle stretch its
    wings?)
Why should I mourn
The vanished power of the usual reign?

Because I do not hope to know again
The infirm glory of the positive hour   10
Because I do not think
Because I know I shall not know
The one veritable transitory power
Because I cannot drink
There, where trees flower, and springs flow,
    for there is nothing again   15
Because I know that time is always time
And place is always and only place

And what is actual is actual only for one
    time
And only for one place
I rejoice that things are as they are and   20
I renounce the blessèd face
And renounce the voice
Because I cannot hope to turn again
Consequently I rejoice, having to construct
    something
Upon which to rejoice   25

And pray to God to have mercy upon us
And I pray that I may forget
These matters that with myself I too much
    discuss
Too much explain
Because I do not hope to turn again   30
Let these words answer
For what is done, not to be done again
May the judgment not be too heavy upon us

Because these wings are no longer wings to fly
But merely vans to beat the air   35
The air which is now thoroughly small and
    dry
Smaller and dryer than the will
Teach us to care and not to care
Teach us to sit still.

Pray for us sinners now and at the hour of
    our death   40
Pray for us now and at the hour of our death.

2

Lady, three white leopards sat under a
    juniper-tree
In the cool of the day, having fed to satiety
On my legs my heart my liver and that which
    had been contained
In the hollow round of my skull.   And God
    said   45
Shall these bones live?   shall these
Bones live?   And that which had been
    contained
In the bones (which were already dry) said
    chirping:
Because of the goodness of this Lady
And because of her loveliness, and because 50
She honors the Virgin in meditation,
We shine with brightness.   And I who am
    here dissembled

Proffer my deeds to oblivion, and my love
To the posterity of the desert and the fruit
    of the gourd.
It is this which recovers   55
My guts the strings of my eyes and the in-
    digestible portions
Which the leopards reject.   The Lady is
    withdrawn
In a white gown, to contemplation, in a
    white gown.
Let the whiteness of bones atone to forget-
    fulness.   59
There is no life in them.   As I am forgotten
And would be forgotten, so I would forget
Thus devoted, concentrated in purpose.
    And God said
Prophesy to the wind, to the wind only for
    only
The wind will listen.   And the bones sang
    chirping   64
With the burden of the grasshopper, saying

        Lady of silences
        Calm and distressed
        Torn and most whole
        Rose of memory
        Rose of forgetfulness   70
        Exhausted and life-giving
        Worried reposeful
        The single Rose
        Is now the Garden
        Where all loves end   75
        Terminate torment
        Of love unsatisfied
        The greater torment
        Of love satisfied
        End of the endless   80
        Journey to no end
        Conclusion of all that
        Is inconclusible
        Speech without word and
        Word of no speech   85
        Grace to the Mother
        For the Garden
        Where all love ends.

Under a juniper-tree the bones sang, scattered
    and shining
We were glad to be scattered, we did little
    good to each other,   90
Under a tree in the cool of the day, with the
    blessing of sand,

Forgetting themselves and each other, united
In the quiet of the desert. This is the land
  which ye
Shall divide by lot. And neither division
  nor unity
Matters. This is the land. We have our
  inheritance.   95

3

At the first turning of the second stair
I turned and saw below
The same shape twisted on the banister
Under the vapor in the fetid air
Struggling with the devil of the stairs who
  wears   100
The deceitful face of hope and of despair.

At the second turning of the second stair
I left them twisting, turning below;
There were no more faces and the stair was
  dark,
Damp, jagged, like an old man's mouth
  drivelling, beyond repair,   105
Or the toothed gullet of an agèd shark.

At the first turning of the third stair
Was a slotted window bellied like the fig's
  fruit
And beyond the hawthorn blossom and a
  pasture scene
The broadbacked figure drest in blue and
  green   110
Enchanted the maytime with an antique
  flute.
Blown hair is sweet, brown hair over the
  mouth blown,
Lilac and brown hair;
Distraction, music of the flute, stops and
  steps of the mind over the third stair,
Fading, fading; strength beyond hope and
  despair   115
Climbing the third stair.

Lord, I am not worthy
Lord, I am not worthy

    but speak the word only.

4

Who walked between the violet and the
  violet   120

Who walked between
The various ranks of varied green
Going in white and blue, in Mary's color,
Talking of trivial things
In ignorance and in knowledge of eternal
  dolor   125
Who moved among the others as they walked,
Who then made strong the fountains and
  made fresh the springs

Made cool the dry rock and made firm the
  sand
In blue of larkspur, blue of Mary's color,
Sovegna vos[1]   130

Here are the years that walk between,
  bearing
Away the fiddles and the flutes, restoring
One who moves in the time between sleep
  and waking, wearing

White light folded, sheathed about her,
  folded.
The new years walk, restoring   135
Through a bright cloud of tears, the years,
  restoring
With a new verse the ancient rhyme. Redeem
The time. Redeem
The unread vision in the higher dream
While jewelled unicorns draw by the gilded
  hearse.   140
The silent sister veiled in white and blue
Between the yews, behind the garden god,
Whose flute is breathless, bent her head and
  signed but spoke no word

But the fountain sprang up and the bird
  sang down
Redeem the time, redeem the dream   145
The token of the word unheard, unspoken

Till the wind shake a thousand whispers
  from the yew

And after this our exile

5

If the lost word is lost, if the spent word is
  spent
If the unheard, unspoken   150

[1] "Remember."

Word is unspoken, unheard;
Still is the unspoken word, the Word unheard,
The Word without a word, the Word within
The world and for the world;
And the light shone in darkness and   155
Against the Word the unstilled world still
      whirled
About the center of the silent Word.

O my people, what have I done unto thee.

Where shall the word be found, where will
      the word
Resound? Not here, there is not enough
      silence   160
Not on the sea or on the islands, not
On the mainland, in the desert or the rain
      land,
For those who walk in darkness
Both in the day time and in the night
      time
The right time and the right place are not
      here   165
No place of grace for those who avoid the
      face
No time to rejoice for those who walk among
      noise and deny the voice

Will the veiled sister pray for
Those who walk in darkness, who chose
      thee and oppose thee,
Those who are torn on the horn between sea-
      son and season, time and time, be-
      tween   170
Hour and hour, word and word, power and
      power, those who wait
In darkness?   Will the veiled sister pray
For children at the gate
Who will not go away and cannot pray:
Pray for those who chose and oppose   175

O my people, what have I done unto thee.

Will the veiled sister between the slender
Yew trees pray for those who offend her
And are terrified and cannot surrender
And affirm before the world and deny be-
      tween the rocks   180
In the last desert between the last blue
      rocks
The desert in the garden the garden in the
      desert

Of drouth, spitting from the mouth the
      withered apple-seed.

O my people.

6

Although I do not hope to turn again   185
Although I do not hope
Although I do not hope to turn

Wavering between the profit and the loss
In this brief transit where the dreams cross
The dreamcrossed twilight between birth
      and dying   190
(Bless me father) though I do not wish to
      wish these things
From the wide window towards the granite
      shore
The white sails still fly seaward, seaward
      flying
Unbroken wings

And the lost heart stiffens and rejoices   195
In the lost lilac and the lost sea voices
And the weak spirit quickens to rebel
For the bent golden-rod and the lost sea
      smell
Quickens to recover
The cry of quail and the whirling plover   200
And the blind eye creates
The empty forms between the ivory gates
And smell renews the salt savor of the sandy
      earth

This is the time of tension between dying
      and birth
The place of solitude where three dreams
      cross   205
Between blue rocks
But when the voices shaken from the yew
      tree drift away
Let the other yew be shaken and reply.

Blessèd sister, holy mother, spirit of the
      fountain, spirit of the garden,
Suffer us not to mock ourselves with false-
      hood   210
Teach us to care and not to care
Teach us to sit still
Even among these rocks,
Our peace in His will

And even among these rocks   215
Sister, mother
And spirit of the river, spirit of the sea,

Suffer me not to be separated

And let my cry come unto Thee.

ARCHIBALD MACLEISH (1892–   )

In the course of his development, MacLeish came to have a profound concern for the meaning and destiny of America. Disciplined, in his expatriate years, in the verse modes of Pound and Eliot, preoccupied with the poetic registration of his own sensibility, MacLeish eventually turned outward to his land and people and to the great crises of his time — the depression, the rise of fascism, the peril of America in a second World War, the need of a lasting peace.

Born in Glencoe, Illinois, MacLeish spent his boyhood on the lake shore, was educated in the local schools and in Connecticut, attended Yale College (where the literary group included Benét and Wilder) and the Harvard Law School. In the first World War he served in France in the field artillery, rising to the rank of captain. For three years he tried the practice of law in Boston, but boldly gave it up in favor of a career as poet. Setting forth with his family, he established himself in Paris, 1923–28, to write steadily and read Laforgue, Rimbaud, Valéry, Ezra Pound, T. S. Eliot. Back in America, he lived on a farm, made a trip to Mexico (in preparation for his poem *Conquistador*), became one of the editors of *Fortune*, was appointed Librarian of Congress by President Roosevelt in 1939. During the war he served as director of the Office of Facts and Figures, then as assistant Secretary of State. During the Spanish Civil War he supported the Loyalists, and with Ernest Hemingway and others helped prepare the film "The Spanish Earth."

All along, he had been publishing freely. His first significant poetry, showing the influence of Robinson and Eliot, and revealing him as one of the "Lost Generation" after the first World War, appeared in three books in 1924–25, and the next year he emerged fully in *Streets in the Moon*, a volume containing his well-known "Ars Poetica." *The Hamlet of A. MacLeish*, 1928, strongly colored by T. S. Eliot, was a long, subjective poem of spiritual disintegration.

A new attitude began with *New Found Land*, 1930, and *Frescoes for Mr. Rockefeller's City*, 1933, more independent in poetic style, more responsive to his national and cultural tradition. Between the two books came *Conquistador*, a long account of the conquest of Mexico by Cortez, which received the Pulitzer award. Directing his new social consciousness to the contemporary world, he wrote the verse drama *Panic*, the poems of *Public Speech*, the poetic commentary of a book of photographs *Land of the Free*, the radio verse plays *The Fall of the City* and *Air Raid*. In 1940 came *America Was Promises*, and the same year a public address (quickly published as a book) *The Irresponsibles*, denouncing the writers of the 1920's for having "done more to disarm democracy in the face of Fascism than any other single influence." Four more books came in 1941, including *A Time to Speak*, which contains selections from his prose;

and in 1944 *The American Story*, composed of ten radio scripts based on historical narratives of the discovery and settlement of America.

For interpretation and criticism of MacLeish see the references given by F. B. Millett in *Contemporary American Authors*, 1940.

Ars Poetica

(1924)

A poem should be palpable and mute
As a globed fruit

Dumb
As old medallions to the thumb

Silent as the sleeve-worn stone   5
Of casement ledges where the moss has
        grown —

A poem should be wordless
As the flight of birds

. . . . . .

A poem should be motionless in time
As the moon climbs   10

Leaving, as the moon releases
Twig by twig the night-entangled trees,

Leaving, as the moon behind the winter
        leaves,
Memory by memory the mind —

A poem should be motionless in time   15
As the moon climbs

. . . . . .

A poem should be equal to:
Not true

For all the history of grief
An empty doorway and a maple leaf   20

For love
The leaning grasses and two lights above
        the sea —

A poem should not mean
But be

You, Andrew Marvell

(1926)

And here face down beneath the sun
And here upon earth's noonward height
To feel the always coming on
The always rising of the night

To feel creep up the curving east   5
The earthy chill of dusk and slow
Upon those under lands the vast
And ever climbing shadow grow

And strange at Ecbatan the trees
Take leaf by leaf the evening strange   10
The flooding dark about their knees
The mountains over Persia change

And now at Kermanshah the gate
Dark empty and the withered grass
And through the twilight now the late   15
Few travelers in the westward pass

And Baghdad darken and the bridge
Across the silent river gone
And through Arabia the edge
Of evening widen and steal on   20

And deepen on Palmyra's street
The wheel rut in the ruined stone
And Lebanon fade out and Crete
High through the clouds and overblown

And over Sicily the air   25
Still flashing with the landward gulls
And loom and slowly disappear
The sails above the shadowy hulls

And Spain go under and the shore
Of Africa the gilded sand   30
And evening vanish and no more
The low pale light across that land

Nor now the long light on the sea

And here face downward in the sun
To feel how swift how secretly   35
The shadow of the night comes on . . .

"Not Marble Nor the Gilded Monuments"

(ca. 1926)

The praisers of women in their proud and
        beautiful poems
Naming the grave mouth and the hair and
        the eyes

Boasted those they loved should be forever
    remembered
These were lies

The words sound but the face in the Istrian
    sun is forgotten   5
The poet speaks but to her dead ears no
    more
The sleek throat is gone — and the breast
    that was troubled to listen
Shadow from door

Therefore I will not praise your knees nor
    your fine walking
Telling you men shall remember your name
    as long   10
As lips move or breath is spent or the iron
    of English
Rings from a tongue
I shall say you were young and your arms
    straight and your mouth scarlet
I shall say you will die and none will
    remember you
Your arms change and none remember the
    swish of your garments   15
Nor the click of your shoe

Not with my hand's strength not with
    difficult labor
Springing the obstinate words to the bones
    of your breast
And the stubborn line to your young stride
    and the breath to your breathing
And the beat to your haste   20
Shall I prevail on the hearts of unborn men
    to remember

(What is a dead girl but a shadowy ghost
Or a dead man's voice but a distant and
    vain affirmation
Like dream words most)

Therefore I will not speak of the undying
    glory of women   25
I will say you were young and straight and
    your skin fair
And you stood in the door and the sun was
    a shadow of leaves on your shoulders
And a leaf on your hair

I will not speak of the famous beauty of
    dead women

I will say the shape of a leaf lay once on
    your hair   30
Till the world ends and the eyes are out
    and the mouths broken
Look! It is there!

From Conquistador

(1929–30)

"Richness of color, extension of musical devices, and a mastery of the long breath combine to produce the most accomplished saga-poem of the generation. Founded on Bernál Díaz's *True History of the Conquest of New Spain* and influenced by the accent of Pound's *Cantos*, especially Canto I, the narrative proceeds from one vivid detail to another. . . . *Conquistador*, in spite of being cast in the key of reminiscence, is a record of life in action; and this parade of fighting and feasting, of blood, song, and quick surrenders is tuned to words that live and leap no less actively." (Untermeyer.)

Bernál Díaz, a Spanish warrior, is represented as telling his own story of the conquest of Mexico under Cortes, in a narrative style quite at variance from that of the official history referred to in his "Preface" below.

Bernál Díaz's Preface to His Book

"That which I have myself seen and the
    fighting". . . .

And I am an ignorant man: and this priest
    this
Gómara with the school-taught skip to his
    writing

The pompous Latin the appropriate feasts
The big names the imperial decorations   5
The beautiful battles and the brave deceased

The onward marches the wild Indian nations
The conquests sieges sorties wars campaigns
(And one eye always on the live relations) —

He with his famous history of New Spain —   10
This priest is a learned man: is not ignorant:
And I am poor: without gold: gainless:

My lands deserts in Guatemala: my fig-tree
    the
Spiked bush: my grapes thorns: my children
Half-grown: sons with beards: the big one   15

Breaking the small of his back in the brothel
thills
And a girl to be married and all of them
snarling at home
With the Indian look in their eyes like a cat
killing:

And this Professor Francisco López de
Gómara
Childless; not poor: and I am old: over
eighty: 20
Stupid with sleepless nights: unused to the
combing of

Words clean of the wool while the tale waits:
And he is a youthful man: a sound one:
lightened with
Good sleep: skilled in the pen's plaiting — 24
I am an ignorant old sick man: blind with the
Shadow of death on my face and my hands
to lead me:
And he not ignorant: not sick —

                                        but I

Fought in those battles!   These were my own
deeds!
These names he writes of mouthing them out
as a man would
Names in Herodotus — dead and their wars to
read —   30

These were my friends: these dead my com-
panions:
I: Bernál Díaz: called del Castíllo:
Called in the time of my first fights El Gálan:

I here in the turn of the day in the feel of
Darkness to come now: moving my chair with
the change: 35
Thinking too much these times how the doves
would wheel at

Evening over my youth and the air's strangeness:
Thinking too much of my old town of Medina
And the Spanish dust and the smell of the
true rain:

I: poor: blind in the sun: I have seen   40
With these eyes those battles: I saw Montezúma:
I saw the armies of Mexico marching the
leaning

Wind in their garments: the painted faces:
the plumes
Blown on the light air: I saw that city:
I walked at night on those stones: in the
shadowy rooms   45

I have heard the chink of my heel and the
bats twittering:
I: poor as I am: I was young in that country:
These words were my life: these letters written

Cold on the page with the spilt ink and the
shunt of the
Stubborn thumb: these marks at my fingers: 50
These are the shape of my own life. . . .

                            and I hunted the

Unknown birds in the west with their beautiful wings!

Old men should die with their time's span:
The sad thing is not death: the sad thing

Is the life's loss out of earth when the living
vanish: 55
All that was good in the throat: the hard
going:
The marching singing in sunshine: the show-
ery land:

The quick loves: the sleep: the waking: the
blowing of
Winds over us: all this that we knew:
All this goes out at the end as the flowing of 60

Water carries the leaves down: and the few —
Three or four there are of us still that remem-
ber it —
Perish: and that time's stopt like a stale tune:

And the bright young masters with their bitter
treble
Understanding it all like an old game!   65
And the pucker of art on their lips like the
pip of a lemon! —

"The tedious veteran jealous of his fame!"
What is my fame or the fame of these my
companions?
Their tombs are the bellies of Indians: theirs
are the shameful

Graves in the wild earth: in the Godless
sand: 70

None know the place of their bones: as for
mine
Strangers will dig my grave in a stony land:

Even my sons have the strangeness of dark
kind in them:
Indian dogs will bark at dusk by my sepulchre:
What is my fame! But those days: the shine
of the   75

Sun in that time: the wind then: the step
Of the moon over those leaf-fallen nights: the
sleet in the
Dry grass: the smell of the dust where we
slept —

These things were real: these suns had heat
in them:
This was brine in the mouth: bitterest
foam: 80
Earth: water to drink: bread to be eaten —

Not the sound of a word like the writing of
Gómara:
Not a past time: a year: the name of a
Battle lost — "and the Emperor Charles came
home

"That year: and that was the year the
same   85
"They fought in Flanders and the Duke was
hung —"
The dates of empire: the dry skull of fame!

No but our lives: the days of our lives: we
were young then:
The strong sun was standing in deep trees:
We drank at the springs: the thongs of our
swords unslung to it: 90

We saw the city on the inland sea:
Towers between: and the green-crowned
Montezúma
Walking the gardens of shade: and the stag-
gering bees:

And the girls bearing the woven baskets of
bloom on their
Black hair: their breasts alive: and the
hunters   95
Shouldering dangling herons with their ruffled plumes:

We were the first that found that famous
country:
We marched by a king's name: we crossed
the sierras:
Unknown hardships we suffered: hunger:

Death by the stone knife: thirst: we fared by
the   100
Bitter streams: we came at last to that water:
Towers were steep upon the fluttering air:

We were the lords of it all. . . .
                        Now time has taught us:
Death has mastered us most: sorrow and pain
Sickness and evil days are our lives' lot: 105
Now even the time of our youth has been
taken:
Now are our deeds words: our lives chron-
icles:
Afterwards none will think of the night
rain. . . .

How shall a man endure the will of God and
the
Days and the silence!
                        In the world before us   110
Neither in Cuba nor the isles beyond —

Not Fonséca himself the sagging whore —
Not the Council the Audience even the
Indians —
Knew of a land to the west: they skirted the
Floridas:

They ran the islands on the bare-pole
winds: 115
They touched the Old Main and the midland
shores:
They saw the sun go down at the gulf's beginning:

None had sailed to the west and returned till
Córdova:
I went in that ship: Alvarez handled her:
Trusting to luck: keeping the evening before
him: 120

Sighting after the third week land
And no report of a land there in that ocean:
The Indians clean: wearing the delicate
bands:

Cape Catoche we called it: "conës catoche"—
So they cried to us over the sea flood: 125
Many idols they had for their devotion

Some of women: some coupled in sodomy
So we sailed on: we came to Campéchë:
There by the sweet pool they kindled the
wood-fire:

Words they were saying like "Castilán" in
their speech: 130
They warned us by signs to be gone when
the logs charred:
So we turned from them down to the smooth
beaches:

The boats followed us close in: we departed:
Afterwards there was a *norte* with fine haze:
We stood for Potonchán through the boil of
the narrows: 135

There they attacked us crossing the green of
the maize fields:
Me they struck thrice and they killed fifty
And all were hurt and two taken crazy with

Much pain and it blew and the dust lifted
And the thirst cracked the tongues in our
mouths and before us the 140
Sea-corrupted pools where the river drifts:

And we turned back and the wind drove us
to Florida:
There in the scooped sand in the withered
bed—
There by the sea they encountered us threatening war:

So we returned to the islands half dead: 145
And Córdova did die: and we wrote to
Velásquez—
Diégo the Governor—writing it out: and we
said—
"Excellence: there are lands in the west: the
pass is
"Clean sailing: the scuts of the men are cov-
ered:
"The houses are masonry: gold they have:
baskets 150
"Painted with herbs: the women are chaste
in love"—

Much else of the kind I cannot remember:
And Velásquez took the credit for this discovery:

And all we had was our wounds: and enough
of them:
And Fonséca Bishop of Burgos (for so he was
called) 155
President of the Council: he wrote to the
Emperor

Telling the wonderful news in a mule's volley
And not a word of our deeds or our pains or
our battles:
And Charles gone: and Joanna the poor
queen stalled

In Tordesíllas shaking the peas in a rattle: 160
And Barbarossa licking his chin in Algiers:
And trouble enough in Spain with all that

And the Cardinal dying and Sicily over the
ears—
Trouble enough without new lands to be conquered and
Naked Indians taken and wild sheep
sheared: 165

But as for us that returned from that westward country—
We could not lie in our towns for the sound
of the sea:
We could not rest at all in our thoughts: we
were young then:

We looked to the west: we remembered the
foreign trees
Borne out on the tide from the unknown
rivers 170
And the clouds like hills in the air our eyes
had seen:

And Grijálva sailed next and we that were
living
We that had gear to our flesh and the gold to
find
And an old pike in the stall with the haft to
it silvered—

We signed on and we sailed by the first
tide: 175

And we fought at Potonchán that voyage:
I remember

The locusts covered the earth like a false
shine to it:

They flew with a shrill sound like the arrow
stem:

Often we took the whir of the darts for the
locusts:

Often we left our shields from our mouths as
they came:　180

I remember our fighting was much marred
by the locusts:

And that voyage we came to the river
Tabasco:

We saw the nets as we came in and the smoke
of the

Sea over the bar: and we filled the casks
there:

There first we heard of the farther land —　185
"Colúa" they said "Méjico" — we that were
asking the

Gold there on that shore on the evening
sand —

"Colúa" they said: pointing on toward the
sunset:

They made a sign on the air with their
solemn hands:

Afterward: north: on the sea: and the ships
running　190

We saw the steep snow mountain on the sky:

We stared as dream-awakened men in wonder:

And that voyage it was we came to the Island:

Well I remember the shore and the sound of
that place

And the smoke smell on the dunes and the
wind dying:　195

Well I remember the walls and the rusty
taste of the

New-spilled blood in the air: many among us

Seeing the priests with their small and arrogant faces:

Seeing the dead boys' breasts and the idols
hung with the

Dried shells of the hearts like the husks of
cicadas　200

And their human eyeballs and their painted
tongues

Cried out to the Holy Mother of God for it:

And some that stood there bore themselves
the stone:

And some were eaten of wild beasts of their
bodies:

And none of us all but had his heart fore-
known the　205

Evil to come would have turned from the land
then:

But the lives of men are covered and not
shown —

Only late to the old at their time's ending

The land shows backward and the way is
there:

And the next day we sailed and the sea was
against us　210

And our bread was dirty with weevils and
grown scarce and the

Rains began and the beans stank in the ovens

And we soldiers were thoroughly tired of sea-
faring:

So we returned from that voyage with God's
love:

And they talked about nothing else in the
whole of Cuba:　215

And gentlemen sold their farms to go on discoveries:

And we that had fought in the marches with
no food —

We sat by the palms in the square in the
green gloaming

With the delicate girls on our knees and the
night to lose:

We that had fought in those lands. . . .
and the eloquent Gómara:　220

The quilled professors: the taught tongues of
fame:

What have they written of us: the poor soldiers:

We that were wounded often for no pay:

We that died and were dumped cold in the
bread sacks:

Bellies up: the birds at us: floating for days　225

And none remembering which it was that was
    dead there
Whether of Búrgos or Yúste or Villalár:
Where have they written our names? What
    have they said of us?

They call the towns for the kings that bear
    no scars:
They keep the names of the great for time to
    stare at —   230
The bishops rich-men generals cocks-at-arms:

Those with the glaze in their eyes and the
    fine bearing:
The born leaders of men: the resonant
    voices:
They give them the lands for their tombs:
    they call it *America!*

(And who has heard of Vespucci in this
    soil   235

Or down by the lee of the coast or toward the
    Havana?)
And we that fought here: that with heavy toil

Earthed up the powerful cities of this land —
What are we? When will our fame come?
An old man in a hill town
                 a handful of   240
Dust under the dry grass at Otúmba

Unknown names
              hands vanished
                    faces
Many gone from the day
             unspeakable numbers
Lives forgotten
          deeds honored in strangers
"That which I have myself seen and the
    fighting" . . .   245

WALLACE STEVENS (1879–   )

    Stevens is one of the most rewarding as well as one of the most difficult of the moderns. That his life has been different from that of most poets, and that he has been independent of poetic fashions and schools is evident from his career. He was educated at Harvard and the New York University Law School; has long been a vice-president of a large insurance company in Hartford; published no poetry until he was twenty-five, and no book until he was forty-four; has lived through at least four successive schools of poetic doctrine without subscribing fully to any; and at seventy-two is more productive than he was fifty years ago.

    Stevens has always been centrally concerned with the poet's central problem: how the imagination may be made to serve as man's chief resource in the struggle with the chaos and illusoriness of reality. Ironic criticism of the society in which he lives is often implicit or explicit in his verse, but on the whole he is intent on imposing order on reality through the sense of beauty. His poems are rich in color, and reflect his deep familiarity with music. Much of his recent verse, however, is closer to criticism than to poetry, and should be avoided by the uninitiated.

    His most important volumes of poetry are *Harmonium* (1931 ed.), *Ideas of Order*, 1935, *The Man with the Blue Guitar*, 1937, and *Transport to Summer*, 1947. He states some of his principles in "The Noble Rider and the Sound of Words," published by Allen Tate in *The Language of Poetry*, 1942. The latest long study is W. V. O'Connor's *The Shaping Spirit: A Study of Wallace Stevens*, 1950. A list of criticisms of his work is in G. Arms and J. Kuntz, *Poetry Explication*, 1950.

Peter Quince at the Clavier
(1923, 1931)

I

Just as my fingers on these keys
Make music, so the selfsame sounds
On my spirit make a music, too.

Music is feeling, then, not sound;
And thus it is that what I feel,   5
Here in this room, desiring you,

Thinking of your blue-shadowed silk,
Is music.   It is like the strain
Waked in the elders by Susanna.

Of a green evening, clear and warm,   10
She bathed in her still garden, while
The red-eyed elders, watching, felt

The basses of their beings throb
In witching chords, and their thin blood
Pulse pizzicati of Hosanna.   15

II

In the green water, clear and warm,
Susanna lay.

She searched
The touch of springs,
And found   20
Concealed imaginings.
She sighed,
For so much melody.

Upon the bank, she stood
In the cool   25
Of spent emotions.
She felt, among the leaves,
The dew
Of old devotions.

She walked upon the grass,   30
Still quavering.
The winds were like her maids,
On timid feet,
Fetching her woven scarves,
Yet wavering.   35

A breath upon her hand
Muted the night.
She turned —

A cymbal crashed,
And roaring horns.   40

III

Soon, with a noise like tambourines,
Came her attendant Byzantines.

They wondered why Susanna cried
Against the elders by her side;

And as they whispered, the refrain   45
Was like a willow swept by rain.

Anon, their lamps' uplifted flame
Revealed Susanna and her shame.

And then, the simpering Byzantines
Fled, with a noise like tambourines.   50

IV

Beauty is momentary in the mind —
The fitful tracing of a portal;
But in the flesh it is immortal.

The body dies; the body's beauty lives.
So evenings die, in their green going,   55
A wave, interminably flowing.
So gardens die, their meek breath scenting
The cowl of winter, done repenting.
So maidens die, to the auroral
Celebration of a maiden's choral.   60

Susanna's music touched the bawdy strings
Of those white elders; but, escaping,
Left only Death's ironic scraping.
Now, in its immortality, it plays
On the clear viol of her memory,   65
And makes a constant sacrament of praise.

The Idea of Order at Key West
(1935)

She sang beyond the genius of the sea.
The water never formed to mind or voice,
Like a body wholly body, fluttering
Its empty sleeves; and yet its mimic motion
Made constant cry, caused constantly a cry, 5
That was not ours although we understood,
Inhuman, of the veritable ocean.

The sea was not a mask. No more was she.
The song and water were not medleyed sound
Even if what she sang was what she heard,   10
Since what she sang was uttered word by
      word.

It may be that in all her phrases stirred
The grinding water and the gasping wind;
But it was she and not the sea we heard.

For she was the maker of the song she sang. 15
The ever-hooded, tragic-gestured sea
Was merely a place by which she walked to
    sing.
Whose spirit is this? we said, because we knew
It was the spirit that we sought and knew
That we should ask this often as she sang. 20

If it was only the dark voice of the sea
That rose, or even colored by many waves;
If it was only that outer voice of sky
And cloud, of the sunken coral water-walled,
However clear, it would have been deep
    air, 25
The heaving speech of air, a summer sound
Repeated in a summer without end
And sound alone.   But it was more than that,
More even than her voice, and ours, among
The meaningless plungings of water and the
    wind, 30
Theatrical distances, bronze shadows heaped
On high horizons, mountainous atmospheres
Of sky and sea.

                    It was her voice that made
The sky acutest at its vanishing.
She measured to the hour its solitude. 35
She was the single artificer of the world
In which she sang.   And when she sang, the
    sea,
Whatever self it had, became the self
That was her song, for she was the maker.
    Then we,
As we beheld her striding there alone, 40
Knew that there never was a world for her
Except the one she sang and, singing, made.

Ramon Fernandez, tell me, if you know,
Why, when the singing ended and we turned
Toward the town, tell why the glassy lights, 45
The lights in the fishing boats at anchor there,
As the night descended, tilting in the air,

Mastered the night and portioned out the sea,
Fixing emblazoned zones and fiery poles,
Arranging, deepening, enchanting night. 50

Oh! Blessed rage for order, pale Ramon,
The maker's rage to order words of the sea,
Words of the fragrant portals, dimly-starred,
And of ourselves and of our origins,
In ghostlier demarcations, keener sounds. 55

A Postcard from the Volcano
(1935)

Children picking up our bones
Will never know that these were once
As quick as foxes on the hill;

And that in autumn, when the grapes
Made sharp air sharper by their smell 5
These had a being, breathing frost;

And least will guess that with our bones
We left much more, left what still is
The look of things, left what we felt

At what we saw.   The spring clouds blow 10
Above the shuttered mansion-house,
Beyond our gate and the windy sky

Cries out a literate despair.
We knew for long the mansion's look
And what we said of it became 15

A part of what it is . . . Children,
Still weaving budded aureoles,
Will speak our speech and never know,

Will say of the mansion that it seems
As if he that lived there left behind 20
A spirit storming in blank walls,

A dirty house in a gutted world,
A tatter of shadows peaked to white,
Smeared with the gold of the opulent sun.

HART CRANE (1899–1932)

The short and hectic life of Harold Hart Crane is, as F. O. Matthiessen has said, "a record of the disintegration that can result from modern rootlessness." A high-strung nervous system, incompatible parents, and the boredom of small-town life in Ohio were factors in the discontent that took him to New York at the age of seventeen, where he wrote poetry in Greenwich Village and worshiped Pound, Yeats, and Whitman. Otto Kahn gave him financial help while he was writing his *magnum opus*, *The Bridge*, which he published in 1930. A Guggenheim fellowship took him to Mexico; on the voyage home, during a bout of dissipation, he committed suicide by jumping overboard.

The Bridge, according to Matthiessen, was "designed to be [a] refutation of *The Waste Land*. Convinced of the necessity for poets to repossess the amplitude of myth, his was to be 'the myth of America,' from our earliest history. The content was to be an 'organic panorama, showing the continuous and living evidence of the past in the inmost vital substance of the present,' and its title was meant to suggest an equally vivid span into the future. His declared master was Whitman, since Crane wanted an expansive identification with our life in order to be able to make his 'mystical synthesis.' " His plan, however, was inadequately executed, and the poem runs from extremes of pure poetry to mere absurdity.

His poems were collected in 1933 by Waldo Frank. Biographical and critical studies by Philip Horton (1937) and Brom Weber (1948) are supplemented by articles listed in G. Arms and J. Kuntz, *Poetry Explication*, 1950.

Chaplinesque

(1926)

We make our meek adjustments,
Contented with such random consolations
As the wind deposits
In slithered and too ample pockets.

For we can still love the world, who find   5
A famished kitten on the step, and know
Recesses for it from the fury of the street,
Or warm torn elbow coverts.

We will sidestep, and to the final smirk
Dally the doom of that inevitable thumb   10
That slowly chafes its puckered index toward
      us,
Facing the dull squint with what innocence
And what surprise!

And yet these fine collapses are not lies
More than the pirouettes of any pliant cane;
Our obsequies are, in a way, no enterprise.   16
We can evade you, and all else but the heart:
What blame to us if the heart live on.

The game enforces smirks; but we have seen
The moon in lonely alleys make   20
A grail of laughter of an empty ash can,
And through all sound of gaiety and quest
Have heard a kitten in the wilderness.

From The Bridge

To Brooklyn Bridge

(1926)

How many dawns, chill from his rippling rest
The seagull's wings shall dip and pivot him,
Shedding white rings of tumult, building high
Over the chained bay waters Liberty —

Then, with inviolate curve, forsake our eyes 5
As apparitional as sails that cross
Some page of figures to be filed away;
—Till elevators drop us from our day . . .

I think of cinemas, panoramic sleights
With multitudes bent toward some flashing
        scene   10
Never disclosed, but hastened to again,
Foretold to other eyes on the same screen;

And Thee, across the harbor, silver-paced
As though the sun took step of thee, yet left
Some motion ever unspent in thy stride, — 15
Implicitly thy freedom staying thee!

Out of some subway scuttle, cell or loft
A bedlamite speeds to thy parapets,
Tilting there momently, shrill shirt balloon-
        ing,
A jest falls from the speechless caravan. 20

Down Wall, from girder into street noon leaks,
A rip-tooth of the sky's acetylene;
All afternoon the cloud-flown derricks
        turn . . .
Thy cables breathe the North Atlantic still.

And obscure as that heaven of the Jews, 25
Thy guerdon . . . Accolade thou dost be-
        stow
Of anonymity time cannot raise:
Vibrant reprieve and pardon thou dost show.

O harp and altar, of the fury fused,
(How could mere toil align thy choiring
        strings!)   30
Terrific threshold of the prophet's pledge,
Prayer of pariah, and the lover's cry, —

Again the traffic lights that skim thy swift
Unfractioned idiom, immaculate sigh of stars,
Beading thy path — condense eternity: 35
And we have seen night lifted in thine arms.

Under thy shadow by the piers I waited;
Only in darkness is thy shadow clear.
The City's fiery parcels all undone,
Already snow submerges an iron year . . . 40

O Sleepless as the river under thee,
Vaulting the sea, the prairies' dreaming sod,

Unto us lowliest sometime sweep, descend
And of the curveship lend a myth to God.

Van Winkle

Macadam, gun-gray as the tunny's belt,
Leaps from Far Rockaway to Golden Gate:
Listen! the miles a hurdy-gurdy grinds —
Down gold arpeggios mile on mile unwinds.

Times earlier, when you hurried off to school, 5
— It is the same hour though a later day —
You walked with Pizarro in a copybook,
And Cortes rode up, reining tautly in —
Firmly as coffee grips the taste, — and away!

There was Priscilla's cheek close in the wind, 10
And Captain Smith, all beard and certainty,
And Rip Van Winkle, bowing by the way, —
"Is this Sleepy Hollow, friend — ?"   And
        he —

And Rip forgot the office hours,
                and he forgot the pay; 15
Van Winkle sweeps a tenement
                down town on Avenue A, —

The grind-organ says . . . Remember, re
        member
The cinder pile at the end of the backyard
Where we stoned the family of young 20
Garter snakes under . . . And the monoplanes
We launched — with paper wings and twisted
Rubber bands. . . . Recall —
                the rapid tongues
That flittered from under the ash heap day 25
After day whenever your stick discovered
Some sunning inch of unsuspecting fiber —
It flashed back at your thrust, as clean as fire.

And Rip was slowly made aware
                that he, Van Winkle, was not here 30
Nor there.   He woke and swore he'd seen Broadway
                a Catskill daisy chain in May —

So memory, that strikes a rhyme out of a box,
Or splits a random smell of flowers through
        glass —
Is it the whip stripped from the lilac tree 35
One day in spring my father took to me,
Or is it the Sabbatical, unconscious smile

My mother almost brought me once from
    church
And once only, as I recall — ?

It flickered through the snow screen, blindly 40
It forsook her at the doorway; it was gone
Before I had left the window. It
Did not return with the kiss in the hall.

Macadam, gun-gray as the tunny's belt,
Leaps from Far Rockaway to Golden
    Gate . . .   45
Keep hold of that nickel for car-change,
    Rip, —
Have you got your paper — ?
And hurry along, Van Winkle — it's getting
    late!

The River

Stick your patent name on a signboard
brother — all over — going west — young
    man
Tintex — Japalac — Certain-teed   Overalls
    ads
and lands sakes! under the new playbill
    ripped
in the guaranteed corner — see Bert Williams
    what?   5
Minstrels when you steal a chicken just
save me the wing, for if it isn't
Erie it ain't for miles around a
Mazda — and the telegraphic night coming
    on Thomas

a Ediford — and whistling down the tracks 10
a headlight rushing with the sound — can you
imagine — while an EXPRESS makes time like
SCIENCE — COMMERCE and the HOLYGHOST
RADIO ROARS IN EVERY HOME WE HAVE THE
    NORTHPOLE
WALLSTREET   AND   VIRGINBIRTH   WITHOUT
    STONES OR   15
WIRES OR EVEN RUNning brooks connecting
    ears
and no more sermons windows flashing roar
Breathtaking — as you like it . . . eh?

               So the 20th Century — so
whizzed the Limited — roared by and left 20
three men, still hungry on the tracks, plod-
    dingly
watching the tail lights wizen and converge,

slipping gimleted and neatly out of sight.
The last bear, shot drinking in the Dakotas,
Loped under wires that span the mountain
    stream.   25
Keen instruments, strung to a vast precision
Bind town to town and dream to ticking
    dream.
But some men take their liquor slow — and
    count —
Though they'll confess no rosary nor clue —
The river's minute by the far brook's year. 30
Under a world of whistles, wires and steam
Caboose-like they go ruminating through
Ohio, Indiana — blind baggage —
To Cheyenne tagging . . . Maybe Kalamazoo.

Time's renderings, time's blendings they
    construe   35
As final reckonings of fire and snow;
Strange bird-wit, like the elemental gist
Of unwalled winds they offer, singing low
My Old Kentucky Home and Casey Jones,
Some Sunny Day.   I heard a road-gang chant-
    ing so.   40
And afterwards, who had a colt's eyes — one
    said,
"Jesus! Oh I remember watermelon days!"
    And sped
High in a cloud of merriment, recalled
"— And when my Aunt Sally Simpson
    smiled," he drawled —
"It was almost Louisiana, long ago."   45

"There's no place like Booneville though,
    Buddy,"
One said, excising a last burr from his vest,
"— For early trouting." Then peering in
    the can,
"— But I kept on the tracks." Possessed,
    resigned,
He trod the fire down pensively and
    grinned,   50
Spreading dry shingles of a beard. . . .

                       Behind
My father's cannery works I used to see
Rail-squatters ranged in nomad raillery,
The ancient men — wifeless or runaway   55
Hobo-trekkers that forever search
An empire wilderness of freight and rails.
Each seemed a child, like me, on a loose
    perch.

Holding to childhood like some termless play.
John, Jake, or Charley, hopping the slow
    freight   60
— Memphis to Tallahassee — riding the rods,
Blind fists of nothing, humpty-dumpty clods.

Yet they touch something like a key perhaps.
From pole to pole across the hills, the states
— They know a body under the wide rain;   65
Youngsters with eyes like fjords, old repro-
    bates
With racetrack jargon, — dotting immensity
They lurk across her, knowing her yonder
    breast
Snow-silvered, sumac-stained or smoky blue,
Is past the valley-sleepers, south or west.   70
— As I have trod the rumorous midnights,
    too.

And past the circuit of the lamp's thin flame
(O Nights that brought me to her body
    bare!)
Have dreamed beyond the print that bound
    her name.
Trains sounding the long blizzards out — I
    heard   75
Wail into distances I knew were hers.
Papooses crying on the wind's long mane
Screamed redskin dynasties that fled the
    brain,
— Dead echoes! But I knew her body there,
Time like a serpent down her shoulder,
    dark,   80
And space, an eaglet's wing, laid on her hair.

Under the Ozarks, domed by Iron Mountain,
The old gods of the rain lie wrapped in pools
Where eyeless fish curvet a sunken fountain
And re-descend with corn from querulous
    crows.   85
Such pilferings make up their timeless eatage,
Propitiate them for their timber torn
By iron, iron — always the iron dealt
    cleavage!
They doze now, below axe and powder horn.

And Pullman breakfasters glide glistening
    steel   90
From tunnel into field — iron strides the
    dew —
Straddles the hill, a dance of wheel on wheel.
You have a half-hour's wait at Siskiyou,

Or stay the night and take the next train
    through.
Southward, near Cairo passing, you can see 95
The Ohio merging, — borne down Tennessee;
And if it's summer and the sun's in dusk
Maybe the breeze will lift the River's musk
— As though the waters breathed that you
    might know
Memphis Johnny, Steamboat Bill, Missouri Joe. 100
Oh, lean from the window, if the train slows
    down,
As though you touched hands with some
    ancient clown,
— A little while gaze absently below
And hum *Deep River* with them while they go.

Yes, turn again and sniff once more — look
    see,   105
O Sheriff, Brakeman and Authority —
Hitch up your pants and crunch another
    quid,
For you, too, feed the River timelessly.
And few evade full measure of their fate;
Always they smile out eerily what they
    seem.   110
I could believe he joked at heaven's gate —
Dan Midland — jolted from the cold brake-
    beam.

Down, down — born pioneers in time's
    despite,
Grimed tributaries to an ancient flow —
They win no frontier by their wayward
    plight,   115
But drift in stillness, as from Jordan's brow.

You will not hear it as the sea; even stone
Is not more hushed by gravity . . . But slow,
As loth to take more tribute — sliding prone
Like one whose eyes were buried long ago 120

The River, spreading, flows — and spends
    your dream.
What are you, lost within this tideless spell?
You are your father's father, and the stream —
A liquid theme that floating niggers swell.

Damp tonnage and alluvial march of
    days —   125
Nights turbid, vascular with silted shale
And roots surrendered down of moraine clays:
The Mississippi drinks the farthest dale.

O quarrying passion, undertowed sunlight!
The basalt surface drags a jungle grace   130
Ochreous and lynx-barred in lengthening
      might;
Patience! and you shall reach the biding
      place!

Over De Soto's bones the freighted floors
Throb past the City storied of three
      thrones.
Down two more turns the Mississippi pours
(Anon tall ironsides up from salt lagoons)

And flows within itself, heaps itself free.
All fades but one thin skyline 'round . . .
      Ahead
No embrace opens but the stinging sea;
The River lifts itself from its long bed,   140

Poised wholly on its dream, a mustard
      glow,
Tortured with history, its one will — flow!
— The Passion spreads in wide tongues,
      chocked and slow,
Meeting the Gulf, hosannas silently below.

Cutty Sark
(1926)

O, the navies old and oaken,
      O, the Temeraire no more!
                        — MELVILLE.

I met a man in South Street, tall —
a nervous shark tooth swung on his chain.
His eyes pressed through green grass
— green glasses, or bar lights made them
      so —   5
      shine —
                        GREEN —
                                    eyes —
stepped out — forgot to look at you
or left you several blocks away –   10

in the nickel-in-the-slot piano jogged
'Stamboul Nights' — weaving somebody's
      nickel — sang —

O Stamboul Rose — dreams weave the rose!

Murmurs of Leviathan he spoke,
      and rum was Plato in our heads . . .   15

'It's S.S.*Ala* — Antwerp — now remember
      kid
to put me out at three she sails on time.
I'm not much good at time any more keep
weakeyed watches sometimes snooze — ' his
      bony hands
got to beating time . . . 'A whaler once —   20
I ought to keep time and get over it — I'm a
Democrat — I know what time it is — No
I don't want to know what time it is — that
damned white Arctic killed my time . . .'

O Stamboul Rose — drums weave —   25

'I ran a donkey engine down there on the
      Canal
in Panama — got tired of that —
then Yucatan selling kitchenware — beads —
have you seen Popocatepetl — birdless mouth
with ashes sifting down — ?   30
                  and then the coast again . . .'

Rose of Stamboul O coral Queen —
teased remnants of the skeletons of cities —
and galleries, galleries of watergutted lava
snarling stone — green — drums — drown   35
Sing!
'— that spiracle!' he shot a finger out the
      door . . .
'O life's a geyser — beautiful — my lungs —
No — I can't live on land —!'

I saw the frontiers gleaming of his mind;   40
or are there frontiers — running sands some-
      times
running sands — somewhere — sands
      running . . .
Or they may start some white machine that
      sings.
Then you may laugh and dance the
      axletree —
steel — silver — kick the traces — and
      know —   45

ATLANTIS ROSE drums wreathe the rose,
the star floats burning in a gulf of tears
and sleep another thousand —

                        interminably
long since somebody's nickel — stopped — 50
playing —

A wind worried those wicker-neat lapels, the
swinging summer entrances to cooler hells . . .
Outside a wharf truck nearly ran him down
— he lunged up Bowery way while the
    dawn   55
was putting the Statue of Liberty out — that
torch of hers you know —

I started walking home across the Bridge . . .
    . . . . . .

Blithe Yankee vanities, turreted sprites,
    winged
        British repartees, skil-   60
ful savage sea-girls
that bloomed in the spring — Heave, weave
those bright designs the trade winds drive . . .

   Sweet opium and tea, Yo-ho!
   Pennies for porpoises that bank the keel!   65
   Fins whip the breeze around Japan!

Bright skysails ticketing the line, wink round
    the Horn
to Frisco, Melbourne . . .

Pennants, parabolas —
clipper dreams indelible and ranging,   70
baronial white on lucky blue!
Perennial-*Cutty*-trophied-*Sark!*

Thermopylæ, Black Prince, Flying Cloud through
    Sunda
— scarfed of foam, their bellies veered green
    esplanades,
locked in wind-humors, ran their eastings
    down;   75

   at Java Head freshened the nip
   (sweet opium and tea!)
   and turned and left us on the lee . . .

Buntlines tusseling (91 days, 20 hours and
    anchored!)
            Rainbow, Leander
(last trip a tragedy)   where can you be
Nimbus? and you rivals two —

    a long tack keeping —

                Taeping?
                Ariel?

KATHERINE ANNE PORTER (1894–   )

Great-great-great-granddaughter of Daniel Boone, Katherine Anne Porter was
born at Indian Creek, Texas, and educated in small convent schools in Texas and
Louisiana. "As soon as I learned," she says, "to form letters on paper . . . I began
to write stories, and this has been the basic and absorbing occupation, the intact line
of my life which . . . profoundly affects my character and personality, my social beliefs and economic status. . . ." Miss Porter grew up in literary isolation, having no
contact with literary centers or with writers. Up to her twenty-fifth year, she read
"a grand sweep of all English and translated classics from the beginning up to about
1800"; after that she went on to the moderns. Till she was thirty she did not attempt to publish. Earning a difficult living, she has done much literary "hack work
of all kinds," editing and rewriting other people's manuscripts, writing book reviews,
writing political articles ("my bias is to the left"). In 1931 she received a Guggenheim fellowship. She was in Mexico during the revolution, and has lived in Europe.
She married in 1933, was divorced, and in 1938 married Albert Erskine, Jr., professor of English at Louisiana State University.

Miss Porter built a surprisingly solid reputation on a small published output.
Flowering Judas, 1930, when it reappeared in 1935 as *Flowering Judas and Other
Stories*, firmly established her as one of America's finest short-story writers. Through

hard discipline her art had become pure and strong, subtle and delicate, a fit vehicle for her penetrating understanding of human values. Other collections of stories followed: *Hacienda*, 1934; *Pale Horse, Pale Rider* (three long stories), 1939; *The Leaning Tower and Other Stories*, 1944. There is also a novel, *No Safe Harbor*, 1942, and since 1927 she has worked, off and on, on a study of Cotton Mather.

References to some critical comments are given in Kunitz and Haycraft, *Twentieth Century Authors*, 1942.

María Concepción

(1930)

María Concepción walked carefully, keeping to the middle of the white dusty road, where the maguey thorns and the treacherous curved spines of organ cactus had not gathered so profusely. She would have enjoyed resting for a moment in the dark shade by the roadside, but she had no time to waste drawing cactus needles from her feet. Juan and his chief would be waiting for their food in the damp trenches of the buried city.

She carried about a dozen living fowls slung over her right shoulder, their feet fastened together. Half of them fell upon the flat of her back, the balance dangled uneasily over her breast. They wriggled their benumbed and swollen legs against her neck, they twisted their stupefied eyes and peered into her face inquiringly. She did not see them or think of them. Her left arm was tired with the weight of the food basket, and she was hungry after her long morning's work.

Her straight back outlined itself strongly under her clean bright blue cotton rebozo. Instinctive serenity softened her black eyes, shaped like almonds, set far apart, and tilted a bit endwise. She walked with the free, natural, guarded ease of the primitive woman carrying an unborn child. The shape of her body was easy, the swelling life was not a distortion, but the right inevitable proportions of a woman. She was entirely contented. Her husband was at work and she was on her way to market to sell her fowls.

Her small house sat half-way up a shallow hill, under a clump of pepper-trees, a wall of organ cactus enclosing it on the side nearest to the road. Now she came down into the valley, divided by the narrow spring, and crossed a bridge of loose stones near the hut where María Rosa the beekeeper lived with her old godmother, Lupe the medicine woman. María Concepción had no faith in the charred owl bones, the singed rabbit fur, the cat entrails, the messes and ointments sold by Lupe to the ailing of the village. She was a good Christian, and drank simple herb teas for headache and stomachache, or bought her remedies bottled, with printed directions that she could not read, at the drugstore near the city market, where she went almost daily. But she often bought a jar of honey from young María Rosa, a pretty, shy child only fifteen years old.

María Concepción and her husband, Juan Villegas, were each a little past their eighteenth year. She had a good reputation with the neighbors as an energetic religious woman who could drive a bargain to the end. It was commonly known that if she wished to buy a new rebozo for herself or a shirt for Juan, she could bring out a sack of hard silver coins for the purpose.

She had paid for the license, nearly a year ago, the potent bit of stamped paper which permits people to be married in the church. She had given money to the priest before she and Juan walked together up to the altar the Monday after Holy Week. It had been the adventure of the villagers to go, three Sundays one after another, to hear the banns called by the priest for Juan de Dios Villegas and María Concepción Manriquez, who were actually getting married in the church, instead of behind it, which was the usual custom, less expensive, and as binding as any other ceremony. But María Concepción was always as proud as if she owned a hacienda.

She paused on the bridge and dabbled her feet in the water, her eyes resting themselves from the sun-rays in a fixed gaze to the far-off mountains, deeply blue under their hanging drift of clouds. It came to her that she would like a fresh crust of honey. The delicious aroma of bees, their slow thrilling hum, awakened a pleasant desire for a flake of sweetness in her mouth.

"If I do not eat it now, I shall mark my child," she thought, peering through the crevices in the thick hedge of cactus that sheered up nakedly, like bared knife blades set protectingly around the small clearing. The place was so silent she doubted if María Rosa and Lupe were at home.

The leaning jacal of dried rush-withes and corn sheaves, bound to tall saplings thrust into the earth, roofed with yellow maguey leaves flattened and overlapping like shingles, hunched drowsy and fragrant in the warmth of noonday. The hives, similarly made, were scattered towards the back of the clearing, like small mounds of clean vegetable refuse. Over each mound there hung a dusty golden shimmer of bees.

A light gay scream of laughter rose from behind the hut; a man's short laugh joined in. "Ah, hahahaha!" went the voices together high and low, like a song.

"So María Rosa has a man!" María Concepción stopped short, smiling, shifted her burden slightly, and bent forward shading her eyes to see more clearly through the spaces of the hedge.

María Rosa ran, dodging between bee-hives, parting two stunted jasmine bushes as she came, lifting her knees in swift leaps, looking over her shoulder and laughing in a quivering, excited way. A heavy jar, swung to her wrist by the handle, knocked against her thighs as she ran. Her toes pushed up sudden spurts of dust, her half-raveled braids showered around her shoulders in long crinkled wisps.

Juan Villegas ran after her, also laughing strangely, his teeth set, both rows gleaming behind the small soft black beard growing sparsely on his lips, his chin, leaving his brown cheeks girl-smooth. When he seized her, he clenched so hard her chemise gave way and ripped from her shoulder. She stopped laughing at this, pushed him away and stood silent, trying to pull up the torn sleeve with one hand. Her pointed chin and dark red mouth moved in an uncertain way, as if she wished to laugh again; her long black lashes flickered with the quick-moving lights in her hidden eyes.

María Concepción did not stir nor breathe for some seconds. Her forehead was cold, and yet boiling water seemed to be pouring slowly along her spine. An unaccountable pain was in her knees, as if they were broken. She was afraid Juan and María Rosa would feel her eyes fixed upon them and would find her there, unable to move, spying upon them. But they did not pass beyond the enclosure, nor even glance towards the gap in the wall opening upon the road.

Juan lifted one of María Rosa's loosened braids and slapped her neck with it playfully. She smiled softly, consentingly. Together they moved back through the hives of honey-comb. María Rosa balanced her jar on one hip and swung her long full petti-coats with every step. Juan flourished his wide hat back and forth, walking proudly as a game-cock.

María Concepción came out of the heavy cloud which enwrapped her head and bound her throat, and found herself walking on-ward, keeping the road without knowing it, feeling her way delicately, her ears strumming as if all María Rosa's bees had hived in them. Her careful sense of duty kept her moving toward the buried city where Juan's chief, the American archeologist, was taking his midday rest, waiting for his food.

Juan and María Rosa! She burned all over now, as if a layer of tiny fig-cactus bristles, as cruel as spun glass, had crawled under her skin. She wished to sit down quietly and wait for her death, but not until she had cut the throats of her man and that girl who were laughing and kissing under the cornstalks. Once when she was a young girl she had come back from market to find her jacal burned to a pile of ash and her few silver coins gone. A dark empty feeling had filled her; she kept moving about the place, not believing her eyes, expecting it all to take shape again before her. But it was gone, and though she knew an enemy had done it, she could not find out who it was, and could only curse and threaten the air. Now here was a worse thing, but she knew her enemy. María Rosa, that sinful girl, shameless! She heard herself saying a harsh, true word about María Rosa, saying it aloud as if she expected someone to agree with her: "Yes, she is a whore! She has no right to live."

At this moment the gray untidy head of Givens appeared over the edges of the newest trench he had caused to be dug in his field of excavations. The long deep crevasses, in which a man might stand without being seen, lay crisscrossed like orderly gashes of a giant scalpel. Nearly all of the men of the community worked for Givens, helping him to uncover the lost city of their ancestors. They worked all the year through and prospered, digging every day for those small clay heads and bits of pottery and fragments of painted walls for which there was no good use on earth, being all broken and encrusted with clay. They themselves could make better ones, perfectly stout and new, which they took to town and peddled to foreigners for real money. But the unearthly delight of the chief in finding these worn-out things was an endless puzzle. He would fairly roar for joy at times, waving a shattered pot or a human skull above his head, shouting for his photographer to come and make a picture of this!

Now he emerged, and his young enthusiast's eyes welcomed María Concepción from his old-man face, covered with hard wrinkles and burned to the color of red earth. "I hope you've brought me a nice fat one." He selected a fowl from the bunch dangling nearest him as María Concepción, wordless, leaned over the trench. "Dress it for me, there's a good girl. I'll broil it."

María Concepción took the fowl by the head, and silently, swiftly drew her knife across its throat, twisting the head off with the casual firmness she might use with the top of a beet.

"Good God, woman, you do have nerve," said Givens, watching her. "I can't do that. It gives me the creeps."

"My home country is Guadalajara," exclaimed María Concepción, without bravado as she picked and gutted the fowl.

She stood and regarded Givens condescendingly, that diverting white man who had no woman of his own to cook for him, and moreover appeared not to feel any loss of dignity in preparing his own food. He squatted now, eyes squinted, nose wrinkled to avoid the smoke, turning the roasting fowl busily on a stick. A mysterious man, undoubtedly rich, and Juan's chief, therefore to be respected, to be placated.

"The tortillas are fresh and hot, señor," she murmured gently. "With your permission I will now go to market."

"Yes, yes, run along; bring me another of these tomorrow." Givens turned his head to look at her again. Her grand manner sometimes reminded him of royalty in exile. He noticed her unnatural paleness. "The sun is too hot, eh?" he asked.

"Yes, sir. Pardon me, but Juan will be here soon?"

"He ought to be here now. Leave his food. The others will eat it."

She moved away; the blue of her rebozo became a dancing spot in the heat waves that rose from the gray-red soil. Givens liked his Indians best when he could feel a fatherly indulgence for their primitive childish ways. He told comic stories of Juan's escapades, of how often he had saved him, in the past five years, from going to jail, and even from being shot, for his varied and always unexpected misdeeds.

"I am never a minute too soon to get him out of one pickle or another," he would say. "Well, he's a good worker, and I know how to manage him."

After Juan was married, he used to twit him, with exactly the right shade of condescension, on his many infidelities to María Concepción. "She'll catch you yet, and God help you!" he was fond of saying, and Juan would laugh with immense pleasure.

It did not occur to María Concepción to tell Juan she had found him out. During the day her anger against him died, and her anger against María Rosa grew. She kept saying to herself, "When I was a young girl like María Rosa, if a man had caught hold of me so, I would have broken my jar over his head." She forgot completely that she had not resisted even so much as María Rosa, on the day that Juan had first taken hold of her. Besides she had married him afterwards in the church, and that was a very different thing.

Juan did not come home that night, but went away to war and María Rosa went with him. Juan had a rifle at his shoulder and two pistols at his belt. María Rosa wore a rifle also, slung on her back along with the blankets and the cooking pots. They joined the nearest detachment of troops in the field, and María Rosa marched ahead with the battalion of experienced women of war, which went over the crops like locusts, gathering provisions for the army. She cooked with them, and ate with them what was left after the men had eaten. After battles she went out on the field with the others to salvage clothing and ammunition and guns from the slain before they should begin to swell in the heat. Sometimes they would encounter the women from the other army, and a second battle as grim as the first would take place.

There was no particular scandal in the village. People shrugged, grinned. It was far better that they were gone. The neighbors went around saying that María Rosa was safer in the army than she would be in the same village with María Concepción.

María Concepción did not weep when Juan left her; and when the baby was born, and died within four days, she did not weep. "She is mere stone," said old Lupe, who went over and offered charms to preserve the baby.

"May you rot in hell with your charms," said María Concepción.

If she had not gone so regularly to church, lighting candles before the saints, kneeling with her arms spread in the form of a cross for hours at a time, and receiving holy communion every month, there might have been talk of her being devil-possessed, her face was so changed and blind-looking. But this was impossible when, after all, she had been married by the priest. It must be, they reasoned, that she was being punished for her pride. They decided that this was the true cause for everything: she was altogether too proud. So they pitied her.

During the year that Juan and María Rosa were gone, María Concepción sold her fowls and looked after her garden and her sack of hard coins grew. Lupe had no talent for bees, and the hives did not prosper. She began to blame María Rosa for running away, and to praise María Concepción for her behavior. She used to see María Concepción at the market or at church, and she always said that no one could tell by looking at her now that she was a woman who had such a heavy grief.

"I pray God everything goes well with María Concepción from this out," she would say, "for she has had her share of trouble."

When some idle person repeated this to the deserted woman, she went down to Lupe's house and stood within the clearing and called to the medicine woman, who sat in her doorway stirring a mess of her infallible cure for sores: "Keep your prayers to yourself, Lupe, or offer them for others who need them. I will ask God for what I want in this world."

"And will you get it, you think, María Concepción?" asked Lupe, tittering cruelly and smelling the wooden mixing spoon. "Did you pray for what you have now?"

Afterward everyone noticed that María Concepción went oftener to church, and ever seldomer to the village to talk with the other women as they sat along the curb, nursing their babies and eating fruit, at the end of the market-day.

"She is wrong to take us for enemies," said old Soledad, who was a thinker and a peace-maker. "All women have these troubles. Well, we should suffer together."

But María Concepción lived alone. She was gaunt, as if something were gnawing her away inside, her eyes were sunken, and she would not speak a word if she could help it. She worked harder than ever, and her butchering knife was scarcely ever out of her hand.

Juan and María Rosa, disgusted with military life, came home one day without asking permission of anyone. The field of war had unrolled itself, a long scroll of vexations, until the end had frayed out within twenty miles of Juan's village. So he and María Rosa, now lean as a wolf, burdened with a child daily expected, set out with no farewells to the regiment and walked home.

They arrived one morning about day-break. Juan was picked up on sight by a group of military police from the small barracks on the edge of town, and taken to prison, where the officer in charge told him with impersonal cheerfulness that he would add one to a catch of ten waiting to be shot as deserters the next morning.

María Rosa, screaming and falling on her face in the road, was taken under the arm-pits by two guards and helped briskly to her jacal, now sadly run down. She was re-ceived with professional importance by Lupe, who helped the baby to be born at once.

Limping with foot soreness, a layer of dust concealing his fine new clothes got mysteriously from somewhere, Juan appeared before the captain at the barracks. The captain recognized him as head digger for his good friend Givens, and dispatched a note to Givens saying: "I am holding the person of Juan Villegas awaiting your further dis-position."

When Givens showed up, Juan was de-livered to him with the urgent request that nothing be made public about so humane and sensible an operation on the part of military authority.

Juan walked out of the rather stifling atmosphere of the drumhead court, a definite air of swagger about him. His hat, of un-reasonable dimensions and embroidered with silver thread, hung over one eyebrow, secured at the back by a cord of silver dripping with bright blue tassels. His shirt was of a checker-board pattern in green and black, his white cotton trousers were bound by a belt of yellow leather tooled in red. His feet were bare, full of stone bruises, and sadly ragged as to toenails. He removed his cigarette from the corner of his full-lipped wide mouth. He removed the splendid hat. His black dusty hair, pressed moistly to his forehead, sprang up suddenly in a cloudy thatch on his crown. He bowed to the officer, who appeared to be gazing at a vacuum. He swung his arm wide in a free circle upsoaring towards the prison window, where forlorn heads poked over the window sill, hot eyes following after the lucky departing one. Two or three of the heads nodded, and a half dozen hands were flipped at him in an effort to imitate his own casual and heady manner.

Juan kept up this insufferable pantomime until they rounded the first clump of fig-cactus. Then he seized Givens' hand and burst into oratory. "Blessed be the day your servant Juan Villegas first came under your eyes. From this day my life is yours without condition, ten thousand thanks with all my heart!"

"For God's sake stop playing the fool," said Givens irritably. "Some day I'm going to be five minutes too late."

"Well, it is nothing much to be shot, my chief — certainly you know I was not afraid — but to be shot in a drove of deserters, against a cold wall, just in the moment of my home-coming, by order of that . . ."

Glittering epithets tumbled over one another like explosions of a rocket. All the scandalous analogies from the animal and vegetable worlds were applied in a vivid, unique and personal way to the life, loves, and family history of the officer who had just set him free. When he had quite cursed himself dry, and his nerves were soothed, he added: "With your permission, my chief!"

"What will María Concepción say to all this?" asked Givens. "You are very in-formal, Juan, for a man who was married in the church."

Juan put on his hat.

"Oh, María Concepción! That's nothing. Look, my chief, to be married in the church is a great misfortune for a man. After that he is not himself any more. How can that woman complain when I do not drink even at fiestas enough to be really drunk? I do not beat her; never, never. We were always at peace. I say to her, Come here, and she comes straight. I say, Go there, and she goes quickly. Yet sometimes I looked at her and thought, Now I am married to that woman in the church, and I felt a sinking inside, as if something were lying heavy on my stomach. With María Rosa it is all different. She is not silent; she talks. When she talks too much, I slap her and say, Silence, thou simpleton! and she weeps. She is just a girl with whom I do as I please. You know how she used to keep those clean little bees in their hives? She is like their honey to me. I swear it. I would not harm María Concepción because I am married to her in the church; but also, my chief, I will not leave María Rosa, because she pleases me more than any other woman."

"Let me tell you, Juan, things haven't been going as well as you think. You be careful. Some day María Concepción will just take your head off with that carving knife of hers. You keep that in mind."

Juan's expression was the proper blend of masculine triumph and sentimental melancholy. It was pleasant to see himself in the role of hero to two such desirable women. He had just escaped from the threat of a disagreeable end. His clothes were new and handsome, and they had cost him just nothing. María Rosa had collected them for him here and there after battles. He was walking in the early sunshine, smelling the good smells of ripening cactus-figs, peaches, and melons, of pungent berries dangling from the pepper-trees, and the smoke of his cigarette under his nose. He was on his way to civilian life with his patient chief. His situation was ineffably perfect, and he swallowed it whole.

"My chief," he addressed Givens handsomely, as one man of the world to another, "women are good things, but not at this moment. With your permission, I will now go to the village and eat. My God, *how* I shall eat! Tomorrow morning very early I will come to the buried city and work like seven men. Let us forget María Concepción and María Rosa. Each one in her place. I will manage them when the time comes."

News of Juan's adventure soon got abroad, and Juan found many friends about him during the morning. They frankly commended his way of leaving the army. It was in itself the act of a hero. The new hero ate a great deal and drank somewhat, the occasion being better than a feast-day. It was almost noon before he returned to visit María Rosa.

He found her sitting on a clean straw mat, rubbing fat on her three-hour-old son. Before this felicitous vision Juan's emotions so twisted him that he returned to the village and invited every man in the "Death and Resurrection" pulque shop to drink with him.

Having thus taken leave of his balance, he started back to María Rosa, and found himself unaccountably in his own house, attempting to beat María Concepción by way of re-establishing himself in his legal household.

María Concepción, knowing all the events of that unhappy day, was not in a yielding mood, and refused to be beaten. She did not scream nor implore; she stood her ground and resisted; she even struck at him. Juan, amazed, hardly knowing what he did, stepped back and gazed at her inquiringly through a leisurely whirling film which seemed to have lodged behind his eyes. Certainly he had not even thought of touching her. Oh, well, no harm done. He gave up, turned away, half-asleep on his feet. He dropped amiably in a shadowed corner and began to snore.

María Concepción, seeing that he was quiet, began to bind the legs of her fowls. It was market-day and she was late. She fumbled and tangled the bits of cord in her haste, and set off across the plowed fields instead of taking the accustomed road. She ran with a crazy panic in her head, her stumbling legs. Now and then she would stop and look about her, trying to place herself, then go on a few steps, until she realized that she was not going towards the market.

At once she came to her senses completely, recognized the thing that troubled her so terribly, was certain of what she wanted. She sat down quietly under a sheltering thorny bush and gave herself over to her long devouring sorrow. The thing which had for so long squeezed her whole body into a tight dumb knot of suffering suddenly broke with shocking violence. She jerked with the involuntary recoil of one who receives a blow, and the sweat poured from her skin as if the wounds of her whole life were shedding their salt ichor. Drawing her rebozo over her head, she bowed her forehead on her updrawn knees, and sat there in deadly silence and immobility. From time to time she lifted her head where the sweat formed steadily and poured down her face, drenching the front of her chemise, and her mouth had the shape of crying, but there were no tears and no sound. All her being was a dark confused memory of grief burning in her at night, of deadly baffled anger eating at her by day, until her very tongue tasted bitter, and her feet were as heavy as if she were mired in the muddy roads during the time of rains.

After a great while she stood up and threw the rebozo off her face, and set out walking again.

Juan awakened slowly, with long yawns and grumblings, alternated with short relapses into sleep full of visions and clamors. A blur of orange light seared his eyeballs when he tried to unseal his lids. There came from somewhere a low voice weeping without tears, saying meaningless phrases over and over. He began to listen. He tugged at the leash of his stupor, he strained to grasp those words which terrified him even though he could not quite hear them. Then he came awake with frightening suddenness, sitting up and staring at the long sharpened streak of light piercing the corn-husk walls from the level disappearing sun.

María Concepción stood in the doorway, looming colossally tall to his betrayed eyes. She was talking quickly, and calling his name. Then he saw her clearly.

"God's name!" said Juan, frozen to the marrow, "here I am facing my death!" for the long knife she wore habitually at her belt was in her hand. But instead, she threw it away, clear from her, and got down on her knees, crawling toward him as he had seen her crawl many times toward the shrine at Guadalupe Villa. He watched her approach with such horror that the hair of his head seemed to be lifting itself away from him. Falling forward upon her face, she huddled over him, lips moving in a ghostly whisper. Her words became clear, and Juan understood them all.

For a second he could not move nor speak. Then he took her head between both his hands, and supported her in this way, saying swiftly, anxiously reassuring, almost in a babble:

"Oh, thou poor creature! Oh, madwoman! Oh, my María Concepción, unfortunate! Listen. . . . Don't be afraid. Listen to me! I will hide thee away. I thy own man will protect thee! Quiet! Not a sound!"

Trying to collect himself, he held her and cursed under his breath for a few moments in the gathering darkness. María Concepción bent over, face almost on the ground, her feet folded under her, as if she would hide behind him. For the first time in his life Juan was aware of danger. This was danger. María Concepción would be dragged away between two gendarmes, with him following helpless and unarmed, to spend the rest of her days in Belén Prison, maybe. Danger! The night swarmed with threats. He stood up and dragged her up with him. She was silent and perfectly rigid, holding to him with resistless strength, her hands stiffened on his arms.

"Get me the knife," he told her in a whisper. She obeyed, her feet slipping along the hard earth floor, her shoulders straight, her arms close to her side. He lighted a candle. María Concepción held the knife out to him. It was stained and dark even to the handle with drying blood.

He frowned at her harshly, noting the same stains on her chemise and hands.

"Take off thy clothes and wash thy hands," he ordered. He washed the knife carefully, and threw the water wide of the doorway. She watched him and did likewise with the bowl in which she had bathed.

"Light the brasero and cook food for me," he told her in the same peremptory tone. He took her garments and went out. When he returned, she was wearing an old soiled dress, and was fanning the fire in the charcoal burner. Seating himself cross-legged near her, he stared at her as at a creature unknown to him, who bewildered him utterly, for whom there was no possible explanation. She did not turn her head, but kept silent and still, except for the movements of her strong hands fanning the blaze which cast sparks and small jets of white smoke, flaring and dying rhythmically with the motion of the fan lighting her face and darkening it by turns.

Juan's voice barely disturbed the silence: "Listen to me carefully, and tell me the truth, and when the gendarmes come here for us, thou shalt have nothing to fear. But there will be something for us to settle between us afterward."

The light from the charcoal burner shone in her eyes; a yellow phosphorescence glimmered behind the dark iris.

"For me everything is settled now," she answered, in a tone so tender, so grave, so heavy with suffering, that Juan felt his vitals contract. He wished to repent openly, not as a man, but as a very small child. He could not fathom her, nor himself, nor the mysterious fortunes of life grown so instantly confused where all had seemed so gay and simple. He felt too that she had become invaluable, a woman without equal among a million women, and he could not tell why. He drew an enormous sigh that rattled in his chest.

"Yes, yes, it is all settled. I shall not go away again. We must stay here together."

Whispering, he questioned her and she answered whispering, and he instructed her over and over until she had her lesson by heart. The hostile darkness of the night encroached upon them, flowing over the narrow threshold, invading their hearts. It brought with it sighs and murmurs, the pad of secretive feet in the near-by road, the sharp staccato whimper of wind through the cactus leaves. All these familiar, once friendly cadences were now invested with sinister terrors; a dread, formless, and uncontrollable, took hold of them both.

"Light another candle," said Juan, loudly, in too resolute, too sharp a tone. "Let us eat now."

They sat facing each other and ate from the same dish, after their old habit. Neither tasted what they ate. With food half-way to his mouth, Juan listened. The sound of voices rose, spread, widened at the turn of the road along the cactus wall. A spray of lantern light shot through the hedge, a single voice slashed the blackness, ripped the fragile layer of silence suspended above the hut.

"Juan Villegas!"

"Pass, friends!" Juan roared back cheerfully.

They stood in the doorway, simple cautious gendarmes from the village, mixed-bloods themselves with Indian sympathies, well known to all the community. They flashed their lanterns almost apologetically upon the pleasant, harmless scene of a man eating supper with his wife.

"Pardon, brother," said the leader. "Someone has killed the woman María Rosa, and we must question her neighbors and friends." He paused, and added with an attempt at severity, "Naturally!"

"Naturally," agreed Juan. "You know that I was a good friend of María Rosa. This is bad news."

They all went away together, the men walking in a group, María Concepción following a few steps in the rear, near Juan. No one spoke.

The two points of candlelight at María Rosa's head fluttered uneasily; the shadows shifted and dodged on the stained darkened walls. To María Concepción everything in the smothering enclosing room shared an evil restlessness. The watchful faces of those called as witnesses, the faces of old friends, were made alien by the look of speculation in their eyes. The ridges of the rose-colored rebozo thrown over the body varied continually, as though the thing it covered was not perfectly in repose. Her eyes swerved over the body in the open painted coffin, from the candle tips at the head to the feet, jutting up thinly, the small scarred soles protruding, freshly washed, a mass of crooked, half-healed wounds, thorn-pricks and cuts of sharp stones. Her gaze went back to the candle flame, to Juan's eyes warning her, to the gendarmes talking among themselves. Her eyes would not be controlled.

With a leap that shook her, her gaze settled upon the face of María Rosa. Instantly her blood ran smoothly again: there was nothing to fear. Even the restless light could not give a look of life to that fixed countenance. She was dead. María Concepción felt her muscles give way softly; her heart began beating steadily without effort. She knew no more rancor against that pitiable thing, lying indifferently in its blue coffin under the fine silk rebozo. The mouth drooped sharply at the corners in a grimace of weeping arrested half-way. The brows were distressed; the dead flesh could not cast off the shape of its last terror. It was all finished. María Rosa had eaten too much honey and had had too much love. Now she must sit in hell, crying over her sins and her hard death forever and ever.

Old Lupe's cackling voice arose. She had spent the morning helping María Rosa, and it had been hard work. The child had spat blood the moment it was born, a bad sign. She thought then that bad luck would come to the house. Well, about sunset she was in the yard at the back of the house grinding tomatoes and peppers. She had left mother and babe asleep. She heard a strange noise in the house, a choking and smothered calling, like someone wailing in sleep. Well, such a thing is only natural. But there followed a light, quick, thudding sound —

"Like the blows of a fist?" interrupted an officer.

"No, not at all like such a thing."

"How do you know?"

"I am well acquainted with that sound, friends," retorted Lupe. "This was something else."

She was at a loss to describe it exactly. A moment later, there came the sound of pebbles rolling and slipping under feet; then she knew someone had been there and was running away.

"Why did you wait so long before going to see?"

"I am old and hard in the joints," said Lupe. "I cannot run after people. I walked as fast as I could to the cactus hedge, for it is only by this way that anyone can enter. There was no one in the road, sir, no one. Three cows, with a dog driving them; nothing else. When I got to María Rosa, she was lying all tangled up, and from her neck to her middle she was full of knife-holes. It was a sight to move the Blessed Image Himself! Her eyes were —"

"Never mind. Who came oftenest to her house before she went away? Did you know her enemies?"

Lupe's face congealed, closed. Her spongy skin drew into a network of secretive wrinkles.

She turned withdrawn and expressionless eyes upon the gendarmes.

"I am an old woman. I do not see well. I cannot hurry on my feet. I know no enemy of María Rosa. I did not see anyone leave the clearing."

"You did not hear splashing in the spring near the bridge?"

"No, sir."

"Why, then, do our dogs follow a scent there and lose it?"

"God only knows, my friend. I am an old wo —"

"Yes. How did the footfalls sound?"

"Like the tread of an evil spirit!" Lupe broke forth in a swelling oracular tone that startled them. The Indians stirred uneasily, glanced at the dead, then at Lupe. They half expected her to produce the evil spirit among them at once.

The gendarme began to lose his temper.

"No, poor unfortunate; I mean, were they heavy or light? The footsteps of a man or of a woman? Was the person shod or barefoot?"

A glance at the listening circle assured Lupe of their thrilled attention. She enjoyed the dangerous importance of her situation. She could have ruined that María Concepción with a word, but it was even sweeter to make fools of these gendarmes who went about spying on honest people. She raised her voice again. What she had not seen she could not describe, thank God! No one could harm her because her knees were stiff and she could not run even to seize a murderer. As for knowing the difference between footfalls, shod or bare, man or woman, nay, between devil and human, who ever heard of such madness?

"My eyes are not ears, gentlemen," she ended grandly, "but upon my heart I swear those footsteps fell as the tread of the spirit of evil!"

"Imbecile!" yapped the leader in a shrill voice. "Take her away, one of you! Now, Juan Villegas, tell me —"

Juan told his story patiently, several times over. He had returned to his wife that day. She had gone to market as usual. He had helped her prepare her fowls. She had returned about mid-afternoon, they had talked, she had cooked, they had eaten, nothing was amiss. Then the gendarmes came with the news about María Rosa. That was all. Yes, María Rosa had run away with him, but there had been no bad blood between him and his wife on this account, nor between his wife and María Rosa. Everybody knew that his wife was a quiet woman.

María Concepción heard her own voice answering without a break. It was true at first she was troubled when her husband went away, but after that she had not worried about him. It was the way of men, she believed. She was a church-married woman and knew her place. Well, he had come home at last. She had gone to market, but had come back early, because now she had her man to cook for. That was all.

Other voices broke in. A toothless old man said: "She is a woman of good reputation among us, and María Rosa was not." A smiling young mother, Anita, baby at breast, said: "If no one thinks so, how can you accuse her? It was the loss of her child and not of her husband that changed her so." Another: "María Rosa had a strange life, apart from us. How do we know who might have come from another place to do her evil?" And old Soledad spoke up boldly: "When I saw María Concepción in the market today, I said, 'Good luck to you, María Concepción, this is a happy day for you!'" and she gave María Concepción a long easy stare, and the smile of a born wise-woman.

María Concepción suddenly felt herself guarded, surrounded, upborne by her faithful friends. They were around her, speaking for her, defending her, the forces of life were ranged invincibly with her against the beaten dead. María Rosa had thrown away her share of strength in them, she lay forfeited among them. María Concepción looked from one to the other of the circling, intent faces. Their eyes gave back reassurance, understanding, a secret and mighty sympathy.

The gendarmes were at a loss. They, too, felt that sheltering wall cast impenetrably around her. They were certain she had done it, and yet they could not accuse her. Nobody could be accused; there was not a shred of true evidence. They shrugged their shoulders and snapped their fingers and shuffled their feet. Well, then, good night to everybody. Many pardons for having intruded. Good health!

A small bundle lying against the wall at the head of the coffin squirmed like an eel. A wail, a mere sliver of sound, issued. María Concepción took the son of María Rosa in her arms.

"He is mine," she said clearly, "I will take him with me."

No one assented in words, but an approving nod, a bare breath of complete agreement, stirred among them as they made way for her.

María Concepción, carrying the child, followed Juan from the clearing. The hut was left with its lighted candles and a crowd of old women who would sit up all night, drinking coffee and smoking and telling ghost stories.

Juan's exaltation had burned out. There was not an ember of excitement left in him. He was tired. The perilous adventure was over. María Rosa had vanished, to come no more forever. Their days of marching, of eating, of quarreling and making love between battles, were all over. Tomorrow he would go back to dull and endless labor, he must descend into the trenches of the buried city as María Rosa must go into her grave. He felt his veins fill up with bitterness, with black unendurable melancholy. Oh, Jesus! what bad luck overtakes a man!

Well, there was no way out of it now. For the moment he craved only to sleep. He was so drowsy he could scarcely guide his feet. The occasional light touch of the woman at his elbow was as unreal, as ghostly as the brushing of a leaf against his face. He did not know why he had fought to save her, and now he forgot her. There was nothing in him except a vast blind hurt like a covered wound.

He entered the jacal, and without waiting to light a candle, threw off his clothing, sitting just within the door. He moved with lagging, half-awake hands, to strip his body of its heavy finery. With a long groaning sigh of relief he fell straight back on the floor, almost instantly asleep, his arms flung up and outward.

María Concepción, a small clay jar in her hand, approached the gentle little mother goat tethered to a sapling, which gave and yielded as she pulled at the rope's end after the farthest reaches of grass about her. The kid, tied up a few feet away, rose bleating, its feathery fleece shivering in the fresh wind. Sitting on her heels, holding his tether, she allowed him to suckle a few moments. Afterward — all her movements very deliberate and even — she drew a supply of milk for the child.

She sat against the wall of her house, near the doorway. The child, fed and asleep, was cradled in the hollow of her crossed legs. The silence overfilled the world, the skies flowed down evenly to the rim of the valley, the stealthy moon crept slantwise to the shelter of the mountains. She felt soft and warm all over; she dreamed that the newly born child was her own, and she was resting deliciously.

María Concepción could hear Juan's breathing. The sound vapored from the low doorway, calmly; the house seemed to be resting after a burdensome day. She breathed, too, very slowly and quietly, each inspiration saturating her with repose. The child's light, faint breath was a mere shadowy moth of sound in the silver air. The night, the earth under her, seemed to swell and recede together with a limitless, unhurried, benign breathing. She drooped and closed her eyes, feeling the slow rise and fall within her own body. She did not know what it was, but it eased her all through. Even as she was falling asleep, head bowed over the child, she was still aware of a strange, wakeful happiness.

WILLIAM FAULKNER (1897–   )

Born in an old Mississippi family, Faulkner has since childhood had his home in Oxford, seat of the University of Mississippi. After the fifth grade he went to school only off and on — lived, read, and wrote much as he pleased. In 1918, refusing to enlist with the "Yankees," he joined the Canadian Air Force, and was transferred to the British Royal Air Force. After the war he studied a little at the University, did house painting, went to New Orleans and became a friend of Sherwood Anderson, then to Europe and back home to Oxford. By this time he had written two novels; by 1929 another, *The Sound and the Fury*, employing the stream-of-consciousness method. Financial success came with *Sanctuary*, 1931, which he assisted in filming. His later and generally better books include *These Thirteen* (short stories), 1931; *Light in August*, 1932; *Pylon*, 1933; *Absalom, Absalom!* 1936; *Go Down Moses and Other Stories*, 1942.

Faulkner's reputation for being preoccupied with cruelty and perversion is the result of superficial reading of his work. His fiction is an embodiment of the faith he uttered in his Nobel Prize acceptance speech in 1950: "[Man] is immortal . . . because he has a soul, a spirit capable of compassion and sacrifice and endurance."

The Portable Faulkner was edited by Malcolm Cowley, 1946. Faulkner is the subject of two chapters in J. W. Beach, *American Fiction 1920–1940*, 1941, and of an article by Delmore Schwartz in the *Southern Review*, Summer, 1941. Other references may be found in F. B. Millett, *Contemporary American Authors*, 1940.

A Rose for Emily
(1930)

I

When Miss Emily Grierson died, our whole town went to her funeral: the men through a sort of respectful affection for a fallen monument, the women mostly out of curiosity to see the inside of her house, which no one save an old manservant — a combined gardener and cook — had seen in at least ten years.

It was a big, squarish frame house that had once been white, decorated with cupolas and spires and scrolled balconies in the heavily lightsome style of the seventies, set on what had once been our most select street. But garages and cotton gins had encroached and obliterated even the august names of that neighborhood; only Miss Emily's house was left, lifting its stubborn and coquettish decay above the cotton wagons and the gasoline pumps — an eyesore among eyesores. And now Miss Emily had gone to join the representatives of those august names where they lay in the cedar-bemused cemetery among the ranked and anonymous graves of Union and Confederate soldiers who fell at the battle of Jefferson.

Alive, Miss Emily had been a tradition, a duty, and a care; a sort of hereditary obligation upon the town, dating from that day in 1894 when Colonel Sartoris, the mayor — he who fathered the edict that no Negro woman should appear on the streets without an apron — remitted her taxes, the dispensation dating from the death of her father on into perpetuity. Not that Miss Emily would have accepted charity. Colonel Sartoris invented an involved tale to the effect that Miss Emily's father had loaned money to the town, which the town, as a matter of business, preferred this way of repaying. Only a man of Colonel Sartoris' generation and thought could have invented it, and only a woman could have believed it.

When the next generation, with its more modern ideas, became mayors and aldermen, this arrangement created some little dissatisfaction. On the first of the year they mailed her a tax notice. February came, and there was no reply. They wrote her a formal letter, asking her to call at the sheriff's office at her convenience. A week later the mayor wrote her himself, offering to call or to send his car for her, and received in reply a note on paper of an archaic shape, in a thin flowing calligraphy in faded ink, to the effect that she no longer went out at all. The tax notice was also enclosed, without comment.

They called a special meeting of the Board of Aldermen. A deputation waited upon her, knocked at the door through which no visitor had passed since she ceased giving china-painting lessons eight or ten years earlier. They were admitted by the old Negro into a dim hall from which a stairway mounted into still more shadow. It smelled of dust and disuse — a close, dank smell. The Negro led them into the parlor. It was furnished in heavy, leather-covered furniture. When the Negro opened the blinds of one window, they could see that the leather was cracked; and when they sat down, a faint dust rose sluggishly about their thighs, spinning with slow motes in the single sun-ray. On a tarnished gilt easel before the fireplace stood a crayon portrait of Miss Emily's father.

They rose when she entered — a small, fat woman in black, with a thin gold chain descending to her waist and vanishing into her belt, leaning on an ebony cane with a tarnished gold head. Her skeleton was small and spare; perhaps that was why what would have been merely plumpness in another was obesity in her. She looked bloated, like a body long submerged in motionless water, and of that pallid hue. Her eyes, lost in the fatty ridges of her face, looked like two small pieces of coal pressed into a lump of dough as they moved from one face to another while the visitors stated their errand.

She did not ask them to sit. She just stood in the door and listened quietly until the spokesman came to a stumbling halt. Then they could hear the invisible watch ticking at the end of the gold chain.

Her voice was dry and cold. "I have no taxes in Jefferson. Colonel Sartoris explained it to me. Perhaps one of you can gain access to the city records and satisfy yourselves."

"But we have. We are the city authorities, Miss Emily. Didn't you get a notice from the sheriff, signed by him?"

"I received a paper, yes," Miss Emily said. "Perhaps he considers himself the sheriff . . . I have no taxes in Jefferson."

"But there is nothing on the books to show that, you see. We must go by the — "

"See Colonel Sartoris. I have no taxes in Jefferson."

"But, Miss Emily — "

"See Colonel Sartoris." (Colonel Sartoris had been dead almost ten years.) "I have no taxes in Jefferson. Tobe!" The Negro appeared. "Show these gentlemen out."

II

So she vanquished them, horse and foot, just as she had vanquished their fathers thirty years before about the smell. That was two years after her father's death and a short time after her sweetheart — the one we believed would marry her — had deserted her. After her father's death she went out very little; after her sweetheart went away, people hardly saw her at all. A few of the ladies had the temerity to call, but were not received, and the only sign of life about the place was the Negro man — a young man then — going in and out with a market basket.

"Just as if a man — any man — could keep a kitchen properly," the ladies said; so they were not surprised when the smell developed. It was another link between the gross, teeming world and the high and mighty Griersons.

A neighbor, a woman, complained to the mayor, Judge Stevens, eighty years old.

"But what will you have me do about it, madam?" he said.

"Why, send her word to stop it," the woman said. "Isn't there a law?"

"I'm sure that won't be necessary," Judge Stevens said. "It's probably just a snake or a rat that nigger of hers killed in the yard. I'll speak to him about it."

The next day he received two more complaints, one from a man who came in diffident deprecation. "We really must do something about it, Judge. I'd be the last one in the world to bother Miss Emily, but we've got to do something." That night the Board of Aldermen met — three graybeards and one younger man, a member of the rising generation.

"It's simple enough," he said. "Send her word to have her place cleaned up. Give her a certain time to do it in, and if she don't . . ."

"Dammit, sir," Judge Stevens said, "will you accuse a lady to her face of smelling bad?"

So the next night, after midnight, four men crossed Miss Emily's lawn and slunk about the house like burglars, sniffing along the base of the brickwork and at the cellar openings while one of them performed a regular sowing motion with his hand out of a sack slung from his shoulder. They broke open the cellar door and sprinkled lime there, and in all the outbuildings. As they recrossed the lawn, a window that had been dark was lighted and Miss Emily sat in it, the light behind her, and her upright torso motionless as that of an idol. They crept quietly across the lawn and into the shadow of the locusts that lined the street. After a week or two the smell went away.

That was when people had begun to feel really sorry for her. People in our town, remembering how old lady Wyatt, her great-aunt, had gone completely crazy at last, believed that the Griersons held themselves a little too high for what they really were. None of the young men were quite good enough to Miss Emily and such. We had long thought of them as a tableau; Miss Emily a slender figure in white in the background, her father a spraddled silhouette in the foreground, his back to her and clutching a horse-whip, the two of them framed by the back-flung front door. So when she got to be thirty and was still single, we were not pleased exactly, but vindicated; even with insanity in the family she wouldn't have turned down all of her chances if they had really materialized.

When her father died, it got about that the house was all that was left to her; and in a way, people were glad. At last they could pity Miss Emily. Being left alone, and a pauper, she had become humanized.

Now she too would know the old thrill and the old despair of a penny more or less.

The day after his death all the ladies prepared to call at the house and offer condolence and aid, as is our custom. Miss Emily met them at the door, dressed as usual and with no trace of grief on her face. She told them that her father was not dead. She did that for three days, with the ministers calling on her, and the doctors, trying to persuade her to let them dispose of the body. Just as they were about to resort to law and force, she broke down, and they buried her father quickly.

We did not say she was crazy then. We believed she had to do that. We remembered all the young men her father had driven away, and we knew that with nothing left, she would have to cling to that which had robbed her, as people will.

III

She was sick for a long time. When we saw her again, her hair was cut short, making her look like a girl, with a vague resemblance to those angels in colored church windows — sort of tragic and serene.

The town had just let the contracts for paving the sidewalks, and in the summer after her father's death they began the work. The construction company came with niggers and mules and machinery, and a foreman named Homer Barron, a Yankee — a big, dark, ready man, with a big voice and eyes lighter than his face. The little boys would follow in groups to hear him cuss the niggers, and the niggers singing in time to the rise and fall of picks. Pretty soon he knew everybody in town. Whenever you heard a lot of laughing anywhere about the square, Homer Barron would be in the center of the group. Presently we began to see him and Miss Emily on Sunday afternoons driving in the yellow-wheeled buggy and the matched team of bays from the livery stable.

At first we were glad that Miss Emily would have an interest, because the ladies all said, "Of course a Grierson would not think seriously of a Northerner, a day laborer." But there were still others, older people, who said that even grief could not cause a real lady to forget *noblesse oblige* — without calling it *noblesse oblige*. They just said, "Poor Emily. Her kinsfolk should come to her." She had some kin in Alabama; but years ago her father had fallen out with them over the estate of old lady Wyatt, the crazy woman, and there was no communication between the two families. They had not even been represented at the funeral.

And as soon as the old people said, "Poor Emily," the whispering began. "Do you suppose it's really so?" they said to one another. "Of course it is. What else could . . ." This behind their hands; rustling of craned silk and satin behind jalousies closed upon the sun of Sunday afternoon as the thin, swift clop-clop-clop of the matched team passed: "Poor Emily."

She carried her head high enough — even when we believed that she was fallen. It was as if she demanded more than ever the recognition of her dignity as the last Grierson; as if it had wanted that touch of earthiness to reaffirm her imperviousness. Like when she bought the rat poison, the arsenic. That was over a year after they had begun to say "Poor Emily," and while the two female cousins were visiting her.

"I want some poison," she said to the druggist. She was over thirty then, still a slight woman, though thinner than usual, with cold, haughty black eyes in a face the flesh of which was strained across the temples and about the eye-sockets as you imagine a lighthouse-keeper's face ought to look. "I want some poison," she said.

"Yes, Miss Emily. What kind? For rats and such? I'd recom —"

"I want the best you have. I don't care what kind."

The druggist named several. "They'll kill anything up to an elephant. But what you want is —"

"Arsenic," Miss Emily said. "Is that a good one?"

"Is . . . arsenic? Yes, ma'am. But what you want —"

"I want arsenic."

The druggist looked down at her. She looked back at him, erect, her face like a strained flag. "Why, of course," the druggist said. "If that's what you want. But the law requires you to tell what you are going to use it for."

Miss Emily just stared at him, her head tilted back in order to look him eye for eye, until he looked away and went and got the arsenic and wrapped it up. The Negro delivery boy brought her the package; the druggist didn't come back. When she opened the package at home there was written on the box, under the skull and bones: "For rats."

IV

So the next day we all said, "She will kill herself"; and we said it would be the best thing. When she had first begun to be seen with Homer Barron, we had said, "She will marry him." Then we said, "She will persuade him yet," because Homer himself had remarked — he liked men, and it was known that he drank with the younger men in the Elks' Club — that he was not a marrying man. Later we said, "Poor Emily," behind the jalousies as they passed on Sunday afternoon in the glittering buggy, Miss Emily with her head high and Homer Barron with his hat cocked and a cigar in his teeth, reins and whip in a yellow glove.

Then some of the ladies began to say that it was a disgrace to the town and a bad example to the young people. The men did not want to interfere, but at last the ladies forced the Baptist minister — Miss Emily's people were Episcopal — to call upon her. He would never divulge what happened during that interview, but he refused to go back again. The next Sunday they again drove about the streets, and the following day the minister's wife wrote to Miss Emily's relations in Alabama.

So she had blood-kin under her roof again and we sat back to watch developments. At first nothing happened. Then we were sure that they were to be married. We learned that Miss Emily had been to the jeweler's and ordered a man's toilet set in silver, with the letters H. B. on each piece. Two days later we learned that she had bought a complete outfit of men's clothing, including a nightshirt, and we said, "They are married." We were really glad. We were glad because

the two female cousins were even more Grierson than Miss Emily had ever been.

So we were not surprised when Homer Barron — the streets had been finished some time since — was gone. We were a little disappointed that there was not a public blowing-off, but we believed that he had gone on to prepare for Miss Emily's coming, or to give her a chance to get rid of the cousins. (By that time it was a cabal, and we were all Miss Emily's allies to help circumvent the cousins.) Sure enough, after another week they departed. And, as we had expected all along, within three days Homer Barron was back in town. A neighbor saw the Negro man admit him at the kitchen door at dusk one evening.

And that was the last we saw of Homer Barron. And of Miss Emily for some time. The Negro man went in and out with the market basket, but the front door remained closed. Now and then we would see her at a window for a moment, as the men did that night when they sprinkled the lime, but for almost six months she did not appear on the streets. Then we knew that this was to be expected too; as if that quality of her father which had thwarted her woman's life so many times had been too virulent and too furious to die.

When we next saw Miss Emily, she had grown fat and her hair was turning gray. During the next few years it grew grayer and grayer until it attained an even pepper-and-salt iron-gray, when it ceased turning. Up to the day of her death at seventy-four it was still that vigorous iron-gray, like the hair of an active man.

From that time on her front door remained closed, save for a period of six or seven years, when she was about forty, during which she gave lessons in china-painting. She fitted up a studio in one of the downstairs rooms, where the daughters and granddaughters of Colonel Sartoris' contemporaries were sent to her with the same regularity and in the same spirit that they were sent to church on Sundays with a twenty-five-cent piece for the collection plate. Meanwhile her taxes had been remitted.

Then the newer generation became the backbone and the spirit of the town, and the painting pupils grew up and fell away and did not send their children to her with boxes of color and tedious brushes and pictures cut from the ladies' magazines. The front door closed upon the last one and remained closed for good. When the town got free postal delivery, Miss Emily alone refused to let them fasten the metal numbers above her door and attach a mailbox to it. She would not listen to them.

Daily, monthly, yearly we watched the Negro grow grayer and more stooped, going in and out with the market basket. Each December we sent her a tax notice, which would be returned by the post office a week later, unclaimed. Now and then we would see her in one of the downstairs windows — she had evidently shut up the top floor of the house — like the carven torso of an idol in a niche, looking or not looking at us, we could never tell which. Thus she passed from generation to generation — dear, inescapable, impervious, tranquil, and perverse.

And so she died. Fell ill in the house filled with dust and shadows, with only a doddering Negro man to wait on her. We did not even know she was sick; we had long since given up trying to get any information from the Negro. He talked to no one, probably not even to her, for his voice had grown harsh and rusty, as if from disuse.

She died in one of the downstairs rooms, in a heavy walnut bed with a curtain, her gray head propped on a pillow yellow and moldy with age and lack of sunlight.

V

The Negro met the first of the ladies at the front door and let them in, with their hushed, sibilant voices and their quick, curious glances, and then he disappeared. He walked right through the house and out the back and was not seen again.

The two female cousins came at once. They held the funeral on the second day, with the town coming to look at Miss Emily beneath a mass of bought flowers, with the crayon face of her father musing profoundly above the bier and the ladies sibilant and macabre; and the very old men — some in their brushed Confederate uniforms — on the porch and the lawn, talking of Miss Emily as if she had been a contemporary of theirs, believing that they had danced with her and courted her perhaps, confusing time with its mathematical progression, as the old do, to whom all the past is not a diminishing road but, instead, a huge meadow which no winter ever quite touches, divided from them now by the narrow bottle-neck of the most recent decade of years.

Already we knew that there was one room in that region above stairs which no one had seen in forty years, and which would have to be forced. They waited until Miss Emily was decently in the ground before they opened it.

The violence of breaking down the door seemed to fill this room with pervading dust. A thin, acrid pall as of the tomb seemed to lie everywhere upon this room decked and furnished as for a bridal: upon the valence curtains of faded rose color, upon the rose-shaded lights, upon the dressing table, upon the delicate array of crystal and the man's toilet things backed with tarnished silver, silver so tarnished that the monogram was obscured. Among them lay a collar and tie, as if they had just been removed, which, lifted, left upon the surface a pale crescent in the dust. Upon a chair hung the suit, carefully folded; beneath it the two mute shoes and the discarded socks.

The man himself lay in the bed.

For a long while we just stood there, looking down at the profound and fleshless grin. The body had apparently once lain in the attitude of an embrace, but now the long sleep that outlasts love, that conquers even the grimace of love, had cuckolded him. What was left of him, rotted beneath what was left of the nightshirt, had become inextricable from the bed in which he lay; and upon him and upon the pillow beside him lay that even coating of the patient and biding dust.

Then we noticed that in the second pillow was the indentation of a head. One of us lifted something from it, and leaning forward, that faint and invisible dust dry and acrid in the nostrils, we saw a long strand of iron-gray hair.

JOHN STEINBECK (1902–   )

Salinas, California, was the birthplace of John Steinbeck. After graduating from high school he attended Stanford University for four years as a special student, interested mainly in science. Then, with writing in view as his profession, he did such work as he could find, in New York and in California, reporting, brick-laying, surveying, fruit-picking, etc. Financially, his first three books were failures. But with *Tortilla Flat*, 1935, Steinbeck was launched. Next year *In Dubious Battle* won a medal, and in 1937 *Of Mice and Men* was a best-seller. *The Grapes of Wrath*, 1939, a novel of the migration of the Joad family from the dust bowl to California, provoked vociferous controversy. A social document as well as a work of literary art, it was called "the twentieth-century *Uncle Tom's Cabin*." It was "burned and banned, borrowed, smuggled, but above all, bought." Subsequent novels were *The Moon Is Down*, 1942, and *Cannery Row*, 1945. Meanwhile, in two other books, *The Pastures of Heaven*, 1932, and *The Long Valley*, 1938, the author showed his ability in the short story.

Steinbeck's social leanings are plainly to the left. His favorite characters are common people — especially California rural folk of various types — in whom adversity and oppression do not extinguish a keen love of life. He possesses an unusual tenderness of feeling, which however often slips into sentimentalism, and a desire to face the facts without reticence, which sometimes becomes a melodramatic relish for the striking symbol or violent action. Like many writers of fiction since Balzac, he seems both a romantic and a realist, leaving the two sides of his nature unadjusted.

The Portable Steinbeck contains *Of Mice and Men*, *The Red Pony*, and twenty-eight stories. Steinbeck is the subject of two chapters in J. W. Beach, *American Fiction 1920–1940*, 1941. Other references may be found in Kunitz and Haycraft, *Twentieth Century Authors*, 1942.

The Chrysanthemums

(1938)

This is the opening story in *The Long Valley*. An analysis of the story is given by Joseph Warren Beach in *American Fiction 1920–1940*, pages 311–314.

The high gray-flannel fog of winter closed the Salinas Valley from the sky and from all the rest of the world. On every side it sat like a lid on the mountains and made of the great valley a closed pot. On the broad, level land floor the gang plows bit deep and left the black earth shining like metal where the shares had cut. On the foothill ranches across the Salinas River the yellow stubble fields seemed to be bathed in pale cold sunshine; but there was no sunshine in the valley now in December. The thick willow scrub along the river flamed with sharp and positive yellow leaves.

It was a time of quiet and of waiting. The air was cold and tender. A light wind blew up from the southwest so that the farmers were mildly hopeful of a good rain before long; but fog and rain do not go together.

Across the river, on Henry Allen's foothill ranch there was little work to be done, for the hay was cut and stored and the orchards were plowed up to receive the rain deeply when it should come. The cattle on the higher slopes were becoming shaggy and rough-coated.

Elisa Allen, working in her flower garden, looked down across the yard and saw Henry, her husband, talking to two men in business suits. The three of them stood by the tractor shed, each man with one foot on the side of the Little Fordson. They smoked cigarettes and studied the machine as they talked.

Elisa watched them for a moment and then went back to her work. She was thirty-five. Her face was lean and strong and her eyes were as clear as water. Her figure looked blocked and heavy in her gardening costume, a man's black hat pulled low down over her eyes, clodhopper shoes, a figured print dress almost completely covered by a big corduroy apron with four big pockets to hold the snips, the trowel and scratcher, the seeds and the knife she worked with. She wore heavy leather gloves to protect her hands while she worked.

She was cutting down the old year's chrysanthemum stalks with a pair of short and powerful scissors. She looked down toward the men by the tractor shed now and then. Her face was eager and mature and handsome; even her work with the scissors was overeager, overpowerful. The chrysanthemum stems seemed too small and easy for her energy.

She brushed a cloud of hair out of her eyes with the back of her glove, and left a smudge of earth on her cheek in doing it. Behind her stood the neat white farmhouse with red geraniums close-banked round it as high as the windows. It was a hard-swept-looking little house, with hard-polished windows, and a clean mat on the front steps.

Elisa cast another glance toward the tractor shed. The stranger men were getting into their Ford coupé. She took off a glove and put her strong fingers down into the forest of new green chrysanthemum sprouts that were growing round the old roots. She spread the leaves and looked down among the close-growing stems. No aphids were there, no sow bugs nor snails nor cutworms. Her terrier fingers destroyed such pests before they could get started.

Elisa started at the sound of her husband's voice. He had come near quietly and he leaned over the wire fence that protected her flower garden from cattle and dogs and chickens.

"At it again," he said. "You've got a strong new crop coming."

Elisa straightened her back and pulled on the gardening glove again. "Yes. They'll be strong this coming year." In her tone and on her face there was a little smugness.

"You've got a gift with things," Henry observed. "Some of those yellow chrysanthemums you had last year were ten inches across. I wish you'd work out in the orchard and raise some apples that big."

Her eyes sharpened. "Maybe I could do it too. I've a gift with things all right. My mother had it. She could stick anything in the ground and make it grow. She said it was having planter's hands that knew how to do it."

"Well, it sure works with flowers," he said.

"Henry, who were those men you were talking to?"

"Why, sure, that's what I came to tell you. They were from the Western Meat Company. I sold those thirty head of three-year-old steers. Got nearly my own price too."

"Good," she said. "Good for you."

"And I thought," he continued, "I thought how it's Saturday afternoon, and we might go into Salinas for dinner at a restaurant and then to a picture show — to celebrate, you see."

"Good," she repeated. "Oh, yes. That will be good."

Henry put on his joking tone. "There's fights to-night. How'd you like to go to the fights?"

"Oh, no," she said breathlessly. "No, I wouldn't like fights."

"Just fooling, Elisa. We'll go to a movie. Let's see. It's two now. I'm going to take Scotty and bring down those steers from the hill. It'll take us maybe two hours. We'll go in town about five and have dinner at the Cominos Hotel. Like that?"

"Of course I'll like it. It's good to eat away from home."

"All right, then. I'll go get up a couple of horses."

She said, "I'll have plenty of time to transplant some of these sets, I guess."

She heard her husband calling Scotty down by the barn. And a little later she saw the two men ride up the pale-yellow hillside in search of the steers.

There was a little square sandy bed kept

for rooting the chrysanthemums. With her trowel she turned the soil over and over and smoothed it and patted it firm. Then she dug ten parallel trenches to receive the sets. Back at the chrysanthemum bed she pulled out the little crisp shoots, trimmed off the leaves of each one with her scissors, and laid it on a small orderly pile.

A squeak of wheels and plod of hoofs came from the road. Elisa looked up. The country road ran along the dense bank of willows and cottonwoods that bordered the river, and up this road came a curious vehicle, curiously drawn. It was an old spring-wagon, with a round canvas top on it like the cover of a prairie schooner. It was drawn by an old bay horse and a little gray-and-white burro. A big stubble-bearded man sat between the cover flaps and drove the crawling team. Underneath the wagon, between the hind wheels, a lean and rangy mongrel dog walked sedately. Words were painted on the canvas in clumsy, crooked letters. "Pots, pans, knives, scissors, lawn mowers, Fixed." Two rows of articles, and the triumphantly definitive "Fixed" below. The black paint had run down in little sharp points beneath each letter.

Elisa, squatting on the ground, watched to see the crazy loose-jointed wagon pass by. But it didn't pass. It turned into the farm road in front of her house, crooked old wheels skirling and squeaking. The rangy dog darted from beneath the wheels and ran ahead. Instantly the two ranch shepherds flew out at him. Then all three stopped, and with stiff and quivering tails, with taut straight legs, with ambassadorial dignity, they slowly circled, sniffing daintily. The caravan pulled up to Elisa's wire fence and stopped. Now the newcomer dog, feeling outnumbered, lowered his tail and retired under the wagon with raised hackles and bared teeth.

That man on the wagon seat called out, "That's a bad dog in a fight when he gets started."

Elisa laughed. "I see he is. How soon does he generally get started?"

The man caught up her laughter and echoed it heartily. "Sometimes not for weeks," he said. He climbed stiffly down over the wheel. The horse and the donkey drooped like unwatered flowers.

Elisa saw that he was a very big man. Although his hair and beard were graying, he did not look old. His worn black suit was wrinkled and spotted with grease. The laughter had disappeared from his face and eyes the moment his laughing voice ceased. His eyes were dark and they were full of the brooding that gets in the eyes of teamsters and of sailors. The calloused hands he rested on the fence were cracked, and every crack was a black line. He took off his battered hat.

"I'm off my general road, ma'am," he said. "Does this dirt road cut over across the river to the Los Angeles highway?"

Elisa stood up and shoved the thick scissors in her apron pocket. "Well, yes, it does, but it winds around and then fords the river. I don't think your team could pull through the sand."

He replied with some asperity, "It might surprise you what them beasts can pull through."

"When they get started?" she asked.

He smiled for a second. "Yes. When they get started."

"Well," said Elisa, "I think you'll save time if you go back to the Salinas road and pick up the highway there."

He drew a big finger down the chicken wire and made it sing. "I ain't in any hurry, ma'am. I go from Seattle to San Diego and back every year. Takes all my time. About six months each way. I aim to follow nice weather."

Elisa took off her gloves and stuffed them in the apron pocket with the scissors. She touched the under edge of her man's hat, searching for fugitive hairs. "That sounds like a nice kind of a way to live," she said.

He leaned confidentially over the fence. "Maybe you noticed the writing on my wagon. I mend pots and sharpen knives and scissors. You got any of them things to do?"

"Oh, no," she said quickly. "Nothing like that." Her eyes hardened with resistance.

"Scissors is the worst thing," he explained. "Most people just ruin scissors trying to sharpen 'em, but I know how. I got a special tool. It's a little bobbit kind of thing and patented. But it sure does the trick."

"No. My scissors are all sharp."

"All right, then. Take a pot," he continued earnestly, "a bent pot or a pot with a hole. I can make it like new so you don't have to buy no new ones. That's a saving for you."

"No," she said shortly. "I tell you I have nothing like that for you to do."

His face fell to an exaggerated sadness. His voice took on a whining undertone. "I ain't had a thing to do to-day. Maybe I won't have no supper to-night. You see I'm off my regular road. I know folks on the highway clear from Seattle to San Diego. They save their things for me to sharpen up because they know I do it so good and save them money."

"I'm sorry," Elisa said irritably. "I haven't anything for you to do."

His eyes left her face and fell to searching the ground. They roamed about until they came to the chrysanthemum bed where she had been working. "What's them plants, ma'am?"

The irritation and resistance melted from Elisa's face. "Oh, those are chrysanthemums, giant whites and yellows. I raise them every year, bigger than anybody around here."

"Kind of a long-stemmed flower? Looks like a quick puff of colored smoke?" he asked.

"That's it. What a nice way to describe them."

"They smell kind of nasty till you get used to them," he said.

"It's a good bitter smell," she retorted, "not nasty at all."

He changed his tone quickly. "I like the smell myself."

"I had ten-inch blooms this year," she said.

The man leaned farther over the fence. "Look. I know a lady down the road a piece has got the nicest garden you ever seen. Got nearly every kind of flower but no chrysanthemums. Last time I was mending a copper-bottom washtub for her (that's a hard job but I do it good), she said to me, 'If you ever run acrost some nice chrysanthemums I wish you'd try to get me a few seeds.' That's what she told me."

Elisa's eyes grew alert and eager. "She couldn't have known much about chrysanthemums. You *can* raise them from seed, but it's much easier to root the little sprouts you see there."

"Oh," he said. "I s'pose I can't take none to her, then."

"Why, yes, you can," Elisa cried. "I can put some in damp sand, and you can carry them right along with you. They'll take root in the pot if you keep them damp. And then she can transplant them."

"She'd sure like to have some, ma'am. You say they're nice ones?"

"Beautiful," she said. "Oh, beautiful." Her eyes shone. She tore off the battered hat and shook out her dark pretty hair. "I'll put them in a flower pot, and you can take them right with you. Come into the yard."

While the man came through the picket gate Elisa ran excitedly along the geranium-bordered path to the back of the house. And she returned carrying a big red flower pot. The gloves were forgotten now. She kneeled on the ground by the starting bed and dug up the sandy soil with her fingers and scooped it into the bright new flower pot. Then she picked up the little pile of shoots she had prepared. With her strong fingers she pressed them into the sand and tamped round them with her knuckles. The man stood over her. "I'll tell you what to do," she said. "You remember so you can tell the lady."

"Yes, I'll try to remember."

"Well, look. These will take root in about a month. Then she must set them out, about a foot apart in good rich earth like this, see?" She lifted a handful of dark soil for him to look at. "They'll grow fast and tall. Now remember this. In July tell her to cut them down, about eight inches from the ground."

"Before they bloom?" he asked.

"Yes, before they bloom." Her face was tight with eagerness. "They'll grow right up again. And about the last of September the buds will start."

She stopped and seemed perplexed. "It's the budding that takes the most care," she said hesitantly. "I don't know how to tell you." She looked deep into his eyes searchingly. Her mouth opened a little, and she seemed to be listening. "I'll try to tell you," she said. "Did you ever hear of planting hands?"

"Can't say I have, ma'am."

"Well, I can only tell you what it feels like. It's when you're picking off the buds you don't want. Everything goes right down into your fingertips. You watch your fingers work. They do it themselves. You can feel how it is. They pick and pick the buds. They never make a mistake. They're with the plant. Do you see? Your fingers and the plant. You can feel that, right up your arm. They know. They never make a mistake. You can feel it. When you're like that, you can't do anything wrong. Do you see that? Can you understand that?"

She was kneeling on the ground looking up at him. Her breast swelled passionately.

The man's eyes narrowed. He looked away self-consciously. "Maybe I know," he said. "Sometimes in the night in the wagon there——"

Elisa's voice grew husky. She broke in on him. "I've never lived as you do, but I know what you mean. When the night is dark — the stars are sharp-pointed, and there's quiet. Why, you rise up and up!"

Kneeling there, her hand went out toward his legs in the greasy black trousers. Her hesitant fingers almost touched the cloth. Then her hand dropped to the ground.

He said, "It's nice, just like you say. Only when you don't have no dinner it ain't."

She stood up, then, very straight, and her face was ashamed. She held the flower pot out to him and placed it gently in his arms. "Here. Put it in your wagon, on the seat, where you can watch it. Maybe I can find something for you to do."

At the back of the house she dug in the can pile and found two old and battered aluminum saucepans. She carried them back and gave them to him. "Here, maybe you can fix these."

His manner changed. He became professional. "Good as new I can fix them." At the back of his wagon he set a little anvil, and out of an oily tool box dug a small machine hammer. Elisa came through the gate to watch him while he pounded out the dents in the kettles. His mouth grew sure and knowing. At a difficult part of the work he sucked his under-lip.

"You sleep right in the wagon?" Elisa asked.

"Right in the wagon, ma'am. Rain or shine I'm dry as a cow in there."

"It must be nice," she said. "It must be very nice. I wish women could do such things."

"It ain't the right kind of a life for a woman."

Her upper lip raised a little, showing her teeth. "How do you know? How can you tell?" she said.

"I don't know, ma'am," he protested. "Of course I don't know. Now here's your kettles, done. You don't have to buy no new ones."

"How much?"

"Oh, fifty cents'll do. I keep my prices down and my work good. That's why I have all them satisfied customers up and down the highway."

Elisa brought him a fifty-cent piece from the house and dropped it in his hand. "You might be surprised to have a rival sometime. I can sharpen scissors too. And I can beat the dents out of little pots. I could show you what a woman might do."

He put his hammer back in the oily box and shoved the little anvil out of sight. "It would be a lonely life for a woman, ma'am, and a scary life, too, with animals creeping under the wagon all night." He climbed over the singletree, steadying himself with a hand on the burro's white rump. He settled himself in the seat, picked up the lines. "Thank you kindly, ma'am," he said. "I'll do like you told me; I'll go back and catch the Salinas road."

"Mind," she called, "if you're long in getting there, keep the sand damp."

"Sand, ma'am — sand? Oh, sure. You mean around the chrysanthemums. Sure I will." He clucked his tongue. The beasts leaned luxuriously into their collars. The mongrel dog took his place between the back wheels. The wagon turned and crawled out the entrance road and back the way it had come, along the river.

Elisa stood in front of her wire fence watching the slow progress of the caravan.

Her shoulders were straight, her head thrown back, her eyes half-closed, so that the scene came vaguely into them. Her lips moved silently, forming the words "Good-by — good-by." Then she whispered, "That's a bright direction. There's a glowing there." The sound of her whisper startled her. She shook herself free and looked about to see whether anyone had been listening. Only the dogs had heard. They lifted their heads toward her from their sleeping in the dust, and then stretched out their chins and settled asleep again. Elisa turned and ran hurriedly into the house.

In the kitchen she reached behind the stove and felt the water tank. It was full of hot water from the noonday cooking. In the bathroom she tore off her soiled clothes and flung them into the corner. And then she scrubbed herself with a little block of pumice, legs and thighs, loins and chest and arms, until her skin was scratched and red. When she had dried herself she stood in front of a mirror in her bedroom and looked at her body. She tightened her stomach and threw out her chest. She turned and looked over her shoulder at her back.

After a while she began to dress slowly She put on her newest underclothing and her nicest stockings and the dress which was the symbol of her prettiness. She worked carefully on her hair, pencilled her eyebrows, and rouged her lips.

Before she was finished, she heard the little thunder of hoofs and the shouts of Henry and his helper as they drove the red steers into the corral. She heard the gate bang shut and set herself for Henry's arrival.

His step sounded on the porch. He entered the house, calling, "Elisa, where are you?"

"In my room, dressing. I'm not ready. There's hot water for your bath. Hurry up. It's getting late."

When she heard him splashing in the tub, Elisa laid his dark suit on the bed, and shirt and socks and tie beside it. She stood his polished shoes on the floor beside the bed. Then she went to the porch and sat primly and stiffly down. She looked toward the river road where the willow-line was still yellow with frosted leaves so that under the high gray fog they seemed a thin band of sunshine. This was the only color in the gray afternoon. She sat unmoving for a long time.

Henry came banging out of the door, shoving his tie inside his vest as he came. Elisa stiffened and her face grew tight. Henry stopped short and looked at her. "Why — why, Elisa. You look so nice!"

"Nice? You think I look nice? What do you mean by 'nice'?"

Henry blundered on. "I don't know. I mean you look different, strong and happy."

"I am strong? Yes, strong. What do you mean 'strong'?"

He looked bewildered. "You're playing some kind of a game," he said helplessly. "It's a kind of a play. You look strong enough to break a calf over your knee, happy enough to eat it like a watermelon."

For a second she lost her rigidity. "Henry! Don't talk like that. You didn't know what you said." She grew complete again. "I am strong," she boasted. "I never knew before how strong."

Henry looked down toward the tractor shed, and when he brought his eyes back to her, they were his own again. "I'll get out the car. You can put on your coat while I'm starting."

Elisa went into the house. She heard him drive to the gate and idle down his motor, and then she took a long time to put on her hat. She pulled it here and pressed it there. When Henry turned the motor off she slipped into her coat and went out.

The little roadster bounced along on the dirt road by the river, raising the birds and driving the rabbits into the brush. Two cranes flapped heavily over the willow-line and dropped into the river-bed.

Far ahead on the road Elisa saw a dark speck in the dust. She suddenly felt empty. She did not hear Henry's talk. She tried not to look; she did not want to see the little heap of sand and green shoots, but she could not help herself. The chrysanthemums lay in the road close to the wagon tracks. But not the pot; he had kept that. As the car passed them, she remembered the good bitter smell, and a little shudder went through her.

She felt ashamed of her strong planter's hands, that were no use, lying palms up in her lap.

The roadster turned a bend and she saw the caravan ahead. She swung full round toward her husband so that she could not see the little covered wagon and the mismatched team as the car passed.

In a moment they had left behind them the man who had not known or needed to know what she said, the bargainer. She did not look back.

To Henry she said loudly, to be heard above the motor, "It will be good, to-night, a good dinner."

"Now you're changed again," Henry complained. He took one hand from the wheel and patted her knee. "I ought to take you in to dinner oftener. It would be good for both of us. We get so heavy out on the ranch."

"Henry," she asked, "could we have wine at dinner?"

"Sure. Say! That will be fine."

She was silent for a while; then she said,

"Henry, at those prize-fights do the men hurt each other very much?"

"Sometimes a little, not often. Why?"

"Well, I've read how they break noses, and blood runs down their chests. I've read how the fighting gloves get heavy and soggy with blood."

He looked round at her. "What's the matter, Elisa? I didn't know you read things like that." He brought the car to a stop, then turned to the right over the Salinas River bridge.

"Do any women ever go to the fights?" she asked.

"Oh, sure, some. What's the matter, Elisa? Do you want to go? I don't think you'd like it, but I'll take you if you really want to go."

She relaxed limply in the seat. "Oh, no. No. I don't want to go. I'm sure I don't." Her face was turned away from him. "It will be enough if we can have wine. It will be plenty." She turned up her coat collar so he could not see that she was crying weakly — like an old woman.

SUPPLEMENTARY NOTES

BY WILLIAM CHARVAT

* *

The notes here offered to supplement the period essays, the biographical introductions, and the headnotes in the text are intended to serve two purposes: (1) To explain words and names which are essential to the meaning of the selections, which are not sufficiently clear in their context, and which cannot readily be found in a good desk dictionary such as *Webster's New Collegiate Dictionary* or *The American College Dictionary*. Such works carry many of the obsolete, archaic, and technical terms which were and are used in American literature; proper names such as appear in classical allusions; and biographical and geographical information. (2) To supply commentary on the more difficult authors and selections and on those less difficult pieces which critics often neglect because they seem so simple. The editor's object has been not to utter final critical pronouncements but to provide guides for study and suggest subjects for profitable discussion.

MICHAEL WIGGLESWORTH

The Day of Doom

Pages 12–16. At the beginning of the poem the sleeping world is waked at midnight, the dead rise from their graves, and all are brought before the tribunal of Christ the Judge. The sheep are separated from the goats, the latter including the "civil honest men" who are the subject of stanzas XLII–CVI. The inspiration for this section comes from the parable of the Pharisee and the publican (Luke 18:11). Wigglesworth develops fully (from the Puritan point of view) the implication of the Pharisee's defense that he is not as other men and that he adheres to the laws of the church. Among the "goats" also are the heathen and the infants (stanzas CLVII–CLXXII).

The poem as a whole illustrates the point made in the introductory essay for this section: that the Puritan considered the Bible a complete and infallible guide to the relations of God and man. As a reminder to Puritans that they had this guide, the poem functioned superbly. Because the stanza and meter resemble hymn forms which were familiar to everyone, passages were easily memorized. In the contemporary text of the poem the margins contained references to the Bible which documented almost every stanza. The student can learn much about how the Puritan mind worked by comparing the stanzas with the Biblical texts cited. (Readily available editions which retain the citations are those of K. B. Murdock, 1929, and R. H. Pearce, ed., *Colonial American Writing*, 1950.)

EDWARD TAYLOR

A comparison of the work of Wigglesworth and Taylor reveals strikingly the difference between public and private poetry. Wigglesworth's verse was as utilitarian as a catechism or a textbook; therefore its substance, form, language, and imagery had to be completely clear and familiar. Taylor had no concern with utility except to the extent that poetry served his private purpose of expressing, for his private benefit, his perceptions of the meaning of God's universe.

Taylor's lyrics are almost wholly devoted to the revelation of analogies between the order of God's world and the external realities of man's world. He does not argue the matter of God's order: he assumes it as absolute truth; and his analogies are not fanciful: to him they represent demonstrated truth. In such assumptions he was supported by the then generally accepted anti-Aristotelian logic of Peter Ramus, which asserted that the function of thinking was not investigation but discernment. (For a good brief discussion of Ramist logic, see Perry Miller and T. H. Johnson, eds., *The Puritans*, pp. 28 ff.) In the words of an English Puritan, the duty of man is to "seek out and find this wisdom of God in the world . . . for the world [is] like a book wherein God's wisdom is written. . . ."

To Taylor as a Puritan, poetry, like all man's arts, was infinitely inferior to the works of God, and as a Puritan he did not believe that poetry could or should allow free play to the poet's imagination or be an expression of his whole experience and personality. But within the limits imposed on his poetry by his culture, his imagination worked more powerfully than that of any other colonial poet. That his syntax is often confused, that his rhymes and rhythms are often forced, and that his images are often developed incoherently, is less the result of indifference to the art of poetry than of the fact that he did not intend his poems to be read by his own or any later generation. The distinctive qualities of his verse account at once for its appeal to our own generation and his unwillingness to publish in his own. For as Murdock writes, his verse was "not quite orthodox. ... It is more sensuous, richer in luxurious imagery, and more [mystical] than that of most Puritans." Taylor refers to censers, golden altars, jewels, perfumes; he sometimes describes religious love in carnal terms. All this was authorized, perhaps, by the stylistic qualities of certain portions of the Bible, but not by the use that most Puritans made of the Bible. Thus Taylor's verse is "redolent of the ritualism against which the Puritans rebelled."

Useful discussions of Taylor's verse in addition to those cited in the headnote are K. B. Murdock's Chapter V of the *Literary History of the United States;* R. H. Pearce, "Edward Taylor: the Poet as Puritan," *New England Quarterly,* March, 1950; W. T. Weathers, "Edward Taylor, Hellenistic Puritan," *American Literature,* March, 1946.

The Preface

Page 17. This poem is introductory to Taylor's "God's Determinations," a series of dialogues or debates over the contest of Christ and Satan for man. The central theme of the preface is suggested by the word "nothing": the sense of God's power is evoked by the grandeur of the universe which He created out of nothing. But the idea becomes poetry by being developed through homely analogies between God's creativeness and man's craftsmanship. Most of the images refer to the arts and industries of Taylor's time: *lathe, furnace, bellows, mould, cast; lace, selvedge, quilt, canopy, curtains, curtain rods, tapestry.* Is it true, as Austin Warren says, that these images are without order or arrangement, and that lacking a logical frame they could be added to indefinitely, like Whitman's catalogues?

1.3   lath — lathe.
1.4   riggaled — probably an obsolete term in carpentry which described a groove or channel running around an object.
1.10   smaragdine — emerald-like.
1.30   squitchen — probably "switch."
1.35   fet — an archaic form of "fetched."

The Soul's Admiration

Pages 17–18. The theme is man's utter unworthiness and God's utter glory and power. The thought is characteristically objectified through a series of metaphors related to music — voice, string and wind instruments.

1.15   consents — harmony.
1.18   quavers — eighth notes.
1.30   falls — musical embellishments.
1.33   heft — raise.
1.37   poor snake — an appositive of "me," suggesting both lowliness and wickedness.

The Joy of Church Fellowship

Page 18. The last lyric in "God's Determinations." This poem points up the difference between Taylor and his grimmer contemporaries, who were rarely capable of such ecstasy as is here communicated. Taylor was more interested in the joys of the elect, who ride and sing, than in the sufferings of the damned, and it is characteristic that he should have concluded his "morality play" on this affirmative note. But man's imperfection is never quite lost sight of; even saints get out of harmony ("strings do slip"), and some walk rather than ride happily. Note how the metaphor of song combines with that of fire in stanza 2.

Housewifery

Pages 18–19. This is one of the neatest and most consistently developed of Taylor's lyrics. As Austin Warren says, this precise conceit "tidily analogizes the Christian life to all the instruments and processes of cloth-making — the spinning wheel, the distaff, the reel, the loom, the web, the fulling mills, until the robes of salvation are ready for pious wearing." (*Rage for Order,* p. 14) Such imagery occurred readily enough to a poet born in the weaving district of Warwickshire.

1.3   flyers — arms in a spinning wheel.
1.8   quills — spindles.
1.10   fulling mills — mills for processing cloth.

The Ebb and Flow

Page 19. Communion with God is here explored in terms of fire: tinder, sparks, censer, flint, ignis fatuus (will-o-the-wisp), ashes, bellows. It is typical of Taylor that the title of such a poem should be in terms of water, but the behavior of both fire and water is obviously equivalent to the fluctuations of faith.

JONATHAN EDWARDS

Personal Narrative

Pages 22–29. This famous document tells us much about Edwards, but its usefulness as external autobiography is limited because it is too fragmentary and imprecise as to time and place. Historically it has value as a revelation of the kind of close clinical analysis an intellectual Puritan was capable of performing on himself. Its timeless value resides in its lucid revelation of an individual's struggles with religious experience. One does not have to be a Puritan to understand the process of adolescent emotional discovery of God, backsliding toward sin, remorseful seeking after faith, the mind's rejection and subsequent acceptance of divinity's absolute power, and the final equilibrium in which coordinated emotion and mind arrive at a workable religious reality.

Though the latter half is tiresomely repetitious and somewhat shapeless, the literary quality of the piece as a whole is worth analysis. The dominant word — excessively recurrent, perhaps — is *sweet* — a notable fact, considering the Puritans' reputation for sternness. The course of the argument through many successive paragraphs may be traced through similar repetitions. Thus, in paragraph 1, *duties, secret, delight, affections* (emotions) connote the qualities of religious experience in childhood; paragraph 2 emphasizes words of violence and struggle; paragraph 3 is dominated by the word *mind*. But the essay as a whole makes it clear that neither emotion, struggle, nor rationality is adequate alone for the achievement of grace, and that no one of these constitutes proof of grace.

Sinners in the Hands of an Angry God

Pages 30–39. Much has been written about this most famous of all Puritan sermons, but nothing can mitigate the truth that it is a brutal and bullying document. Literary analysis only confirms the fact that in it Edwards brought all his skills to bear upon a resistant audience (see headnote) which needed to be terrified into repentance. One historian of ideas has attempted to show that it is a peculiarly "modern" sermon; that the physics of Newton and the philosophy of Locke had a profound influence on Edwards's attempts to "get across in the simplest language the meaning of the religious life, of the life of the consciousness." The student who is interested in this proposition should read Perry Miller's *Jonathan Edwards*, especially p. 148, where the idea is brilliantly presented; but the empirical test is the reader's own response to Edwards's oratory.

It is possible, however, to appreciate the literary and strategical devices of the sermon without getting involved in the emotional complex which Edwards built up for his audience. The external structure is simple: four "implications," ten "observations," and four "applications"; yet this orderliness conceals a good deal of repetition, overlapping, and circular motion. The repetitions seem awkward to the modern reader, but can be understood as functional in such oral discourse, for even in the eighteenth century good preachers followed the formula — "Tell them what you are going to say, say it, then tell them that you have said it." The repetitions are also evidence of what Miller calls Edwards's "fascination with language

as a species of incantation" — a fascination shared by Walt Whitman.

Particularly worth noting are Edwards's images (concrete objects used to provoke emotional responses in the reader). Some of these are strictly conventional and often Biblical — *sword, serpent, arrows, whirlwind*. Others derive from the conditions of New England life: the chaff on the threshing floor, the "walks in slippery places," walking on a "rotten covering," which suggests old boards over abandoned wells. The central allusions to fire and to insects shriveling in it must have been familiar to a people who spent long months at the hearth. But perhaps the dominating sense is that of weight dangling on thin thread over threatening fire. (These and other effects are well analyzed by E. L. Cady in "The Artistry of Jonathan Edwards," *New England Quarterly*, March, 1949.)

32.2.9* don't — The use of *don't* for *does not* was common even among cultivated New Englanders, and still survives.

34.1.22 covenant — The promises of God as revealed in the Bible. The meaning of the covenant for Edwards is discussed by Miller, pp. 75–78.

The Freedom of the Will

Pages 39–40. Because the answers to the questions raised in this famous essay are rarely as engrossing or valuable to the modern reader as the arguments by which the answers are reached, the interested student should read the whole essay, which is easily available. He will need the help of such discussions of the problem of free will as can be found in C. H. Faust and T. H. Johnson, *Edwards* (American Writers Series), and Perry Miller's study. For the historical and philosophical background of the idea of free will the student should turn to Crane Brinton's lucid history of Western thought, *Ideas and Men*, pp. 12 ff., 186 ff., 316 ff.

BENJAMIN FRANKLIN

Though Franklin, like Mark Twain, wrote some works of permanent literary worth, the chief value of both men lies in their representativeness as American personalities and their ability to communicate in words their personal quality. But the eighteenth-century character was very different from that of the nineteenth. Franklin's deistic world was one of laws and certainties — in science, philosophy, morals, aesthetics. The individual could find himself — know himself — not by exploring his private ego but by finding his place in the order of the universe and society, an order that was confidently perceived and declared by the thinkers of the day. The individual's personality grew and became integrated in so far as he accepted and understood the assumptions of the culture in which he found himself.

Franklin's personality must be seen in the light of this love of order and certainty. His project to arrive at "moral perfection" was "bold and arduous," as he said, but not impossible — because his age was certain that it knew what moral perfection was, as later ages were not. Similarly, he could with confidence set about achieving a perfect prose style because literary perfection was something prescribed by the rules of rhetoric, these in turn reflecting the order of the universe. (His contemporary, Lord Kames, had declared that "fine arts, like morals, [are] a rational science.")

Franklin's theory of literary expression was, as one might expect, thoroughly social. Good writing, he thought, "should proceed regularly from things known to things unknown, distinctly and clearly without confusion. The words used should be [those] most generally understood . . . no synonyms should be used, or very rarely . . .; the words should be so placed as to be agreeable to the ear in reading," and the words of written discourse should be "as near as possible to the spoken." "In writings intended for persuasion and for general information, one cannot be too clear; and every expression in the least obscure is a fault."

Because, like most Americans of his day, he thought of himself as a product and part of British culture and the inheritor of a set and static language, he was opposed to colloquialisms, provincialisms, and innovations, and his own prose was remarkably free of "Americanisms." Needless to say, his theory of expression has almost no relevance to the romantic literature of individualism which came to prevail by the 1840's.

Autobiography

Pages 41–50. The definitive text of the *Autobiography* was edited by Max Farrand in 1949, and the same editor printed the four basic texts in parallel form as *Memoirs*. These works should be consulted whenever the text here printed seems unsatisfactory.

The first part of the work (represented here by selections to the middle of col. 2, p. 46) was written in 1771 for his son, when Franklin was sixty-five, and the tone is that of a man explaining his success to his family. The rest of our selections are from the second part, written in France when he was seventy-eight, and are addressed to the public in the manner of a man consciously preaching virtue to youth.

The whole constitutes the greatest of American success stories and probably the greatest of our autobiographies. Its special quality lies not in any depth or subtlety of self-revelation but in Franklin's view of himself as a man belonging to the culture of a particular place and time. It is the first of a long line of American autobiographies (including Thoreau's *Walden*, Henry Adams's *Education*, and Lincoln Steffens's *Autobiography*) which present either the individual in terms of the social forces of the day, or the social forces in terms of the individual.

On Liberty and Necessity

Pages 50–51. Franklin here takes part in the great debate over free will and man's relation to the Deity which absorbed minds as unlike as his own and Jonathan Edwards's. Note, however, that in a sense Franklin repudiated this pamphlet in his *Autobiography* (46.1.32 ff.), and that elsewhere he calls his printing of it "another Erratum." The AWS *Franklin* contains the full text, and a discussion in the introduction, pp. cxxiii ff.

A Proposal for Promoting Useful Knowledge

Pages 51–53. This circular records the birth of the first (and still existent) American scientific society, known as the American Philosophical Society. Note that, throughout, "philosophical" is used in the old sense of "scientific."

The Way to Wealth

Pages 53–57. One of the most popular of all Franklin's essays, this work has properly been translated into many of the languages from which he got his aphorisms, a debt which he acknowledges in his last paragraph. He made the aphorisms his own by re-wording and compressing them. The result is an expression of the "American spirit" before that spirit was identifiable. Note his anticipation (53.2.45) of a line from another thoroughly American and equally synthetic piece, Longfellow's "Psalm of Life."

ST. JOHN DE CRÈVECOEUR

Letters from an American Farmer

Pages 59–66. Most of the eighteenth-century writings selected for this volume contain evidence that American culture of the time was international — that we were part of what has been called the "Atlantic Civilization," within which there was a free flow and exchange of ideas and modes of expression.

Crèvecoeur's *Letters*, which were intended primarily for European readers, emphasize the difference between American and European personality and psychology. They were published at a time when American society and its future were the subjects of international debate, and they presented the point of view of those French thinkers who saw America as "the asylum of freedom, . . . the cradle of future nations, and refuge of distressed Europeans." Needless to say, there were groups in Europe whose opinion of America was as hostile as Crèvecoeur's was favorable. The *Letters* did much to establish the ideal of an agrarian republic where the small independent farmer would be the mainstay of society.

THOMAS PAINE
The Age of Reason

Pages 69–79. In the nineteenth century many American towns harbored a character known as the "village atheist." Usually he was not at all an atheist but rather a deist. Rejecting revelation, miracles, and dogma, he believed in a just and benign God and in a morality patterned after what he thought were God's attributes. His bible was Paine's *Age of Reason.* But like Paine he lived in a community which believed in some kind of historical theology and supported some religious institution. Therefore he was on the defensive, and his discourse consisted more frequently of attack than affirmation. Therefore, too, the community counterattacked by calling him an atheist. In the twentieth century he has become respectable (and hence invisible) by joining a "community" church. Such churches "affirm" a deity and a code of morality, as did the deists; but they do not attack the historical religious institutions from which they draw their membership.

The literary student will recognize the religious affirmation in *The Age of Reason* at the same time that he feels the rhetorical power of Paine's offensive against sects. He will perceive many common denominators in the basic beliefs of Paine, Jefferson, Emerson, and Mark Twain. And he will see that Paine's art of persuasion resembles Emerson's in one respect: the use of shock. Paine, like Emerson, overstates because, as he said, "Some people can be reasoned into sense, and others must be shocked into it."

Our selections are made up of the whole of Chapters I–III, IX–XII.

THE FEDERALIST

Pages 80–86. In these historic papers the authors brought to bear all the skills of rhetoric and all the worship of reason, moderation, and balance which we have come to identify with the Enlightenment. The modern reader recognizes that many of the issues considered (for example, that of the relative merits of a democracy and a republic, discussed by Madison in No. X) are still alive. He will also recognize, however, that the terms of the debate were very different from ours. Underlying it was a belief in such absolutes as "justice" and "reason," but at the same time a tough-minded awareness that most human beings are influenced by "passion," "factionalism," and "prejudice." To the eighteenth-century rationalist, conflicting physical forces of nature had their counterpart in conflicts within society. The Constitution which these writers were advocating was designed (like God's universe, as Newton saw it) to take full account of such conflicting forces and to achieve a balance among them.

THOMAS JEFFERSON
The Declaration of Independence

Pages 88–90. Although the Declaration is thought of as having been a revolutionary document in its time, Jefferson did not think that it was. His object, he said, was "not to find out new principles, or new arguments, never before thought of . . . but to place before mankind the common sense of the subject in terms so plain and firm as to command their assent."

For Jefferson's account of the composition of the document, and his indication of changes in the text, see his autobiography as printed in the AWS *Hamilton and Jefferson,* 196 ff., and notes on p. 414.

Notes on Virginia

Pages 90–96. This work was not at first intended for reading by the general public, but constituted a private answer to a series of questions put to Jefferson by the Secretary of the French Legation in Philadelphia. Jefferson published it privately in Paris in 1784. These circumstances explain, perhaps, the appearance of such epithets as "rubbish," applied to common people of no scholastic ability (92.2.20).

Pages 92–94. [*Education for Democracy*] This proposal became the basis for Jefferson's "Plan for Elementary Schools," 1817, a historic document in education because of its attitudes toward the place of history and the classics in the curriculum. Jefferson's own commentary on this section is in his letter to Adams, p. 102.

Pages 94–95. [*Religious Freedom*] This passage is typical of the rationalist's attitude of historical objectivity toward religious institutions.

Page 96. [*Negro Slavery*] As early as 1769 Jefferson had proposed Negro emancipation to the Virginia legislature. In his *Autobiography* he declared that "the public mind would not yet bear the proposition, nor will it bear it even at this day. Yet . . . nothing is more certainly written in the book of fate, than that these people are to be free."

Letters

Pages 99–100. [*Scientific Concerns*] Nothing better illustrates the unity of all knowledge and speculation in the eighteenth century than the scientific curiosity and competence of men like Jefferson and Franklin, who were also "experts" in religion, morals, government, and economics.

Pages 101–104. [*Natural Aristocracy*] Some of the most interesting of all commentary on the important problem of the place of an aristocracy in a democracy is to be found in the correspondence between Jefferson and John Adams. See the year

1813 in the collected correspondence of each of these men.

PHILIP FRENEAU

Freneau deserves the title of "Father of American Poetry" less for what he achieved than for what he attempted. He was both native in outlook and responsive to European thought, but most of his verse was propaganda and would lose little interest if it were paraphrased in prose. The poems on war, emigration, democracy, and religion are here reprinted, like the prose of Franklin and Jefferson, primarily for their historical interest.

The more personal lyrics — "The Wild Honeysuckle," "The Indian Burying Ground," and "To an Author" — deserve closer inspection as poems. They reveal the deep and unresolved contradictions in Freneau's mind. Whereas the propaganda verse is optimistic, affirmative, and vital, the lyrics are almost all concerned with transiency and death. In these latter he retreated from his "official" position that "reason" can solve all of man's problems. For mankind's difficulties he had all the answers; but when he considered himself, as an individual struggling in the imperfect present, his mood was melancholy.

To the Memory of the Brave Americans

Page 107. Though this kind of "public" verse has largely gone out of favor among modern readers of poetry, and is denied by some critics the rank of poetry at all, it has its place in the literature of nations. Emerson recognized this fact in writing the "Concord Hymn," with which this poem should be compared. Scott thought Freneau's poem the finest of its kind in the English language, and adapted line 20 to his own purposes in *Marmion.* Close inspection reveals a platitudinous phrase in almost every line, but originality of diction is not to be expected in a poem which is an expression of feeling that the poet shares with a large public.

On the Emigration to America

Page 108. Any reader may discover defects in the thought, form, and syntax of this poem. Why the word *when* in line 23? In view of his concern for the Negro slave in stanza 9, why the indifference to the fate of the Indian in stanza 4? The poem is valuable, however, as a reminder of the way in which much of the Western world thought about America in the eighteenth and nineteenth centuries.

The Wild Honeysuckle

Pages 108–109. Now the best known of Freneau's lyrics, this poem waited many years for recognition. The theme of the ephemerality of natural beauty was one of Freneau's chief preoccupations as a private poet.

Can the apparent confusion of time sequence in stanza 3 ("to see your future" — "they died" — "shall leave") be justified or explained?

See the note on Bryant's "The Yellow Violet," p. 884.

The Indian Burying Ground

Page 109. The poem is justly famous, but it may well be asked if, after establishing his provocative image of Indians buried in sitting position, Freneau knew quite what to do with it. The contrast stated in lines 1–5 is not clearly resolved in lines 15–16. In stanza 5 there is a shift to elegiac convention, and an implied desertion of Reason for a momentary flirtation with Fancy. Note that the Indian is sentimentalized here but disposed of summarily in "On the Emigration to America."

To an Author

Page 109. This is a realistic and pathetic statement of the plight of the poet in America in Freneau's time — his lack of literary companions or even of respectable competition; the paucity of literary subject matter in American life, bemoaned also by Cooper (see p. 150), Hawthorne, James, and others; the necessity to write satire (here called one of the nine muses). This poem is one of several bitter comments by Freneau about authorship in early America.

Ode

Page 110. The presence in America of Citizen Genêt, representing the new French Republic, raised the question whether our treaties with the old monarchy still held. While our statesmen deliberated, Genêt charmed the public, and this ode, written at the height of his popularity, was for six months a kind of anthem of Republican America. But Genêt overplayed his hand by going over the heads of the government to the people; a reaction set in and his recall was requested.

Note that lines 1–49 can be sung to the tune of "America" ("God Save the King"), but that in the last twelve lines Freneau breaks out of the pattern.

The internationalism of this and the next two poems may well be considered in the light of our twentieth-century foreign problems.

On a Honey Bee

Pages 111–112. Freneau is here drawing on a conventional eighteenth-century humorous theme, evidently using Thomas Gray's "On the Death of a Favorite Cat" as his model.

On the Uniformity and Perfection of Nature *and* On the Religion of Nature

Pages 112–113. These two poems represent, as N. F. Adkins says, the extreme of contemporary French materialism, to the exclusion of all historical and institutional religion. But in the first poem, nature clearly derives her perfection from the "first cause"; in the second, the Absolute is "Creatress Nature," and no separate deity is implied. Stanza 3 of "On the Religion of Nature" contains some of the kind of thinking that went into the Federalist papers (*q.v.*).

WASHINGTON IRVING

Rip Van Winkle

Pages 124–132. When it was originally published the story was preceded and followed by some coy paragraphs about Diedrich Knickerbocker (one of Irving's pen names) and about the "truth" of the legend. Irving's need to prepare his readers for this kind of fiction is evidence that his use of legend in "polite" literature was fairly new in its time.

The plot and the external characterization are so well known that readers tend to overlook Irving's technical mastery in the telling of the tale. The broad focus with which it opens (the view of the mountains) gradually narrows until one inhabitant of the mountains — Rip — fills the picture. At the same time, the atmosphere is set by the use of time-words (*antiquity, time-worn*) and allusions to the supernatural (*magical, ghosts*). Pictorial effects throughout reflect the contemporary taste for "romantic" scenery (first paragraph), "picturesque" views (126.2), and antique costumes (127.2). Even the characterization of Vedder (126.1) is done in terms of picture through two details — the sun-dial and the pipe-smoke.

The tone of the whole, like that of "The Legend of Sleepy Hollow," is pastoral. Implicit in both stories is Irving's love of the old and the rustic, and his recognition that the comfortable, static, agrarian qualities of American life in the pre-industrial age were passing. Of the essence in Rip's character is his aversion to "profitable labor"; in his wife's, noisiness and aversion to idleness. Idleness is the keynote of life in the pleasant village, but loud bustling energy was the new tone of the era in which Irving was writing. The story will probably always feed industrial America's desire for peace and retreat.

(For Irving's commentary on the short story form, see the note on Poe's "Hawthorne's Twice-Told Tales," p. 889.)

The Legend of Sleepy Hollow

Pages 132–147. The leisurely, meandering pace of this classic is deceptive. Within the discursive first twelve pages the student can find, casually strewn about, all the background and the details needed to motivate and sustain the rapid action of the last three pages, where the "plot" is concentrated. The plot is memorable (as Walt Disney's remarkable revival proves), but the sheer bulk of the preliminary material is not the result of loose or careless writing: it shows that that is where Irving's central interest lay. His loving descriptions of the snug, quiet, prosperous rural life; his feeling for the myth and legend associated with the region; his hostile reference to the wilderness and the westward movement; his caricature of Ichabod, a native of Connecticut which "sends forth yearly its legions" not only of schoolmasters but of "frontier woodsmen" (note that Ichabod dreams of selling Van Tassel's lovely lands and moving west to become a speculator) — all these reveal Irving's attachment to the rural past and his distaste for the threatening forces of the future. In 1818, the year this story was written, Tarrytown overlooked a stream of traffic going up the Hudson to supply materials for the digging of the Erie Canal. River and canal were to become the great highway to the frontier, and the highway was the symbol of the new America — restless, expansive, materialistic, progressive. Irving's recognition of the meaning of these phenomena in relation to the "fixed" life of the farming valley is explicit in paragraph 7.

The pastoral tone is enforced by Irving's manipulation of time. The tale, which takes place about 1790, is pulled back by the reminiscences of the villagers to the era of the Revolution; and allusions to seventeenth-century Dutch New York, and frequent use of chivalric terminology, give still greater time-depth to the way of life which is evoked. To Irving the past was "good," the present was to be tolerated. His story is perennially readable because it ministers to the universal nostalgia for the "good old days."

JAMES FENIMORE COOPER

Notions of the Americans

Pages 148–151. Cooper's reputation as a novelist has suffered in the twentieth century, but his social writings continue to grow in importance and significance. The *Notions* purports to be the observations of a foreigner traveling in the United States (a literary device common in eighteenth-century English literature of social criticism). Actually, it is the work of a patriotic American who has acquired breadth and perspective by residence abroad. Read today, it is to be seen as part of the "Paper War" between England and America, a battle of books in which the brunt of criticism and abuse was borne by the Americans. A year after the *Notions* appeared, its popularity was increased by Captain Basil Hall's attack on the United States, *Travels in North America*. In 1832 Frances Trollope's *Domestic Manners of the Americans* prolonged the controversy.

148.2.9 ff.   Though American education was still under strong classical influence, there had long been a reaction against excessive classicism of the kind that prevailed in England.   Cooper's attitude here was anticipated by Jefferson and Freneau.

149.1.24 ff.   What follows is one of the most penetrating of all contemporary comments on American literary conditions and authorship.

149.2.46 ff.   This is commentary on the lack of international copyright.   Cooper, who was one of the two really successful professional authors in America at this time (Irving being the other), suffered less than most from the competition of English and American books.

150.2.3 ff.   This complaint about "poverty of materials" was voiced also by Freneau, Hawthorne, and James, and as often refuted by other critics. It is perhaps evidence that American writers continued to think in terms of British literary forms, ideas, and modes.

England

Pages 151–156.   Though Cooper probably took notes for this book as early as 1828, the point of view is that of 1837 after he had suffered from brutal attacks in the American press.   His insistence on the right of the gentleman to preserve his point of view and way of life in a democracy is reflected in his praise of the Englishman's individualism.

Cooper's commentaries on England deserve comparison with Emerson's great work, *English Traits,* Lowell's "On a Certain Condescension in Foreigners," and the passages on England in *The Education of Henry Adams.*

The American Democrat

Pages 156–157.   This book, published obscurely in Cooperstown, had little hearing in its time, but today it stands as one of the great protests against what Cooper calls (in the preceding selection) "the moral cowardice by which men are led to truckle to what is called public opinion."   We no longer admit the superiority of the "gentleman," discussed so frankly by Cooper, and by Jefferson and Adams (see pp. 101–104), but the rights of the gentleman may easily be identified with those of the independent thinker in the twentieth century.

WILLIAM CULLEN BRYANT

Most of Bryant's best poetry was written between 1811 and 1832 — that is, before the major American romantics had become dominant.   It was a period in which the ideas of two ages (the eighteenth and nineteenth centuries) and two continents (Europe and America) were struggling toward some sort of adjustment.   In Bryant's verse the struggle is apparent in the number of potentially conflicting ideas he held in suspension — deism and Christianity, pantheism and an-

thropomorphism, social progress and unchangeable moral law.   If Bryant's position can be defined, it may be summed up in his belief in the beauty, gladness, and order of God's creation, and his recognition of the mixed good-and-evil of man's world.

As a craftsman he mastered many forms and measures, but he worked usually within established traditions of rhetoric and prosody.   No poet of his time succeeded better in naturalizing British thought and literary idiom, and adapting it to the American environment.

Thanatopsis

Pages 159–160.   Inasmuch as the parts of this poem were composed over a period of ten years (1811–21), a decade during which the poet came to maturity, it is not surprising that it contains disparate, even conflicting, points of view.   The Wordsworthian introduction (lines 1–16), which was written last, is very different in doctrine from the Stoic middle section (lines 16–66), which is the oldest part of the poem, and from the moralistic conclusion.   Though all three sections have their attractions, the "healing sympathy" of nature in the first section has no relation to the nature-as-tomb theme of the second, and the "moral" of the last section has nothing to do with either of the other themes, since we have not been given a basis for an "unfaltering trust" in anything — except the inevitability of death.

The magnificent middle section, with its sustained metaphor of the world as tomb, is the heart of the poem and could stand alone as a coherent lyric.   Yet the work as a whole achieves a certain unity through the solemn and steady tread of Bryant's fine blank verse (in which the line-rhythm is preserved by a final heavily accented syllable), and through the dignified rhetoric, which makes use of standardized phrases and images from British and classical tradition without ever giving the effect of triteness or platitude.

Though this poem seems to have little in common with such a deistic piece as Freneau's "On the Religion of Nature" (p. 113), the two are alike in their imputation to nature of a dynamic force which seems to be self-generated; at least there is no reference to Deity as the generator.

The Yellow Violet

Pages 160–161.   This is one of the many poems Americans have written about the commoner and humbler objects in nature, and Bryant's piece may well be compared with Freneau's "The Wild Honeysuckle" (1786) and Emerson's "The Rhodora" (1834).   All three emphasize the fact that a common flower of great beauty is seen by few. In each case the poet, after contemplating a particular flower, arrives at a general "truth" or meaning.   Although only Bryant's poem offers a specific social analogy (stanza 7), it may well be that the American Poet's perennial interest in the meaning that is latent in the commonest forms of nature is a reflection of democratic ways of thinking. (Further examples may be found in Whitman — e.g., Section 6 of "Song of Myself"; and Emily Dickinson — e.g., "How happy is the little stone.")

Yet it is easy to make too much of this implication, and one might point out that these poems have an anti-democratic implication also, in that the poet perceives that it is *he* who sees the hidden beauty, not the mob — who recognize beauty only in its more spectacular and conspicuous or conventional forms. On the other hand, it is a curious fact that all these poets also had an interest in the more sublime, picturesque, and panoramic aspects of natural beauty. (Note Freneau's vision of the West in "On the Emigration to America," the vastness in Bryant's "Thanatopsis" and "The Prairie," and the broad sweep of Emerson's "The Snow-Storm.") Indeed, if one may judge by the painting of the time, panoramic beauty was preferred by the American artist, for few paintings of the period do for single objects in nature what these three poets attempted in verse.

When one considers these poems as poems rather than as clues to cultural history, one must ask whether the thought evoked by the object seems to derive naturally and inevitably from the object itself, or whether it is a "moral" arbitrarily tacked on to a description in order to justify it. Freneau's "The Wild Honeysuckle" breaks in half when he shifts from the theme of beauty in solitude to that of the brief duration of beauty, and Bryant's seventh stanza is logical but poetically unconvincing.

Inscription for the Entrance to a Wood

Page 161. The bulk of this poem is a clear and firm treatment of a then popular but perhaps timeless theme — the need of guilty and miserable man to escape to the comforts of a joyous and responsive world of nature. The only real difficulty is in lines 10–14, which state that the primal curse fell upon nature as well as upon man, but that since nature was "unsinning" it was spared the misery inflicted upon man. For this concept, go back to the source — Genesis 2: especially 5–9, 15–16; and 3:17–19.

To a Waterfowl

Pages 161–162. Like "Thanatopsis" this poem succeeds partly because of, rather than in spite of, the formal rhetorical tone through which Bryant drew upon the British tradition of thought and expression. Is the "moral" in the final stanza extraneous, or is it, as Yvor Winters says, an explicit statement of the idea governing the poem, inherent but insufficiently obvious in what has gone before? Note that short lines are rhymed with long ones,

and that the final short line in each stanza slows his thought to the pace of brooding contemplation.

A Forest Hymn

Pages 164–165. The impulse to worship without ritual is here magnificently invoked in a poem which reveals itself most fully when read aloud. The first section asks the same question put by Whittier in "The Meeting," p. 440: why should we worship only among the crowd and under roofs? Consider Whittier's answer, lines 66–76, in relation to Bryant's whole argument — and argument it is, though Bryant calls it a hymn.

The first section sets up a proposition about the relation between forest forms and church architecture which finds some support in art history, but it also offers an assumption about the nature of primitive religious worship which is typical of eighteenth-century rationalistic thinking.

The hymn itself, beginning at line 23, is in three parts, each of which celebrates an aspect of deity. The last seven lines attempt to reconcile the humility of religious man and the rationalistic faith of the deist.

The Prairies

Pages 165–167. One fact about America that impressed the Old World was the extent and magnificence of its wildernesses. But many Europeans wished to believe that the New World was in an early stage of geological development, and that accordingly vegetation, animal life, and man were degraded and backward in America. (See R. N. Miller, "Nationalism in Bryant's 'The Prairies,'" *American Literature*, May, 1949.) Americans, in reply, sought not only to defend the beauty of Western nature but to prove that the land had nourished civilizations as old and "romantic," if not as advanced, as Europe's. It is in this context of international debate that "The Prairies" must be understood. Bryant's treatment is at times sentimental, but he is detached enough to imply that the civilization established by the incoming white settlers will be no more immune to decay than that of the mound builders or the Athenians.

1.21 Sonora — a state in Mexico, bordering on Arizona.

1.42 mounds — supposed to have been made by the now extinct mound builders.

1.48 Pentelicus — marble from the quarries of Pentelicus, used in building the Parthenon.

1.96 Oregon — the Columbia River.

EDGAR ALLAN POE

Unlike Bryant, whose verse implies an acceptance of or adjustment to the ideals of his time and culture, Poe was moved to poetic utterance chiefly by his rejection of or conflict with those ideals. In the midst of a materially prosperous and vigorous society, Poe was poor, unpopular, and chronically insecure. Finding no solid values in contemporary social aspirations, little comfort or inspiration in past or present philosophy or religion, no beauty in natural objects except to the extent that he could idealize them, he declared his allegiance to "supernal beauty." Much of his verse consists simply of yearning after this undescribed objective. Occasionally, however, his imagination carries him into unexplored regions of supernatural gloom or madness or loneliness; in such poems he powerfully effects a willing suspension of disbelief, and we are spared the "I-me-my" self-centeredness that pervades so much romantic verse. In his worst as well as in his best poetry there are lines and phrases that are unforgettable — and unequaled in his time. When his verse seems to be obscure, the student should remember that Poe frequently sacrificed sense and meaning in order to achieve sound-effects.

Romance

Page 169. The importance of this poem to Poe may be judged by the fact that he labeled it as the "Preface" to one section of verse in his 1829 edition, and as the "Introduction" to the whole of his collection of 1831. But to the latter edition of the poem he added forty-five lines of some of the worst poetry he ever wrote, which, fortunately, he deleted from the final text. The reader can learn something about Poe's intention, and about the poetic process, by looking at the deleted lines and other alterations in Killis Campbell's edition of the *Poems.*

Note the rhyme pattern of the poem as printed here; line 5 should rhyme with line 7. The last six lines should be considered in relation to Wordsworth's theory of poetry as "emotion recollected in tranquillity."

Sonnet — To Science

Page 169. This sonnet serves as a vestibule to Poe's "Al Aaraaf," a long poem about a region of unearthly beauty, and as a statement of the poet's right to ignore the dissections of science and metaphysics the while he gives full play to the constructive urge of imagination. It is not, of course, to be taken as an attack on science (in which he was deeply interested), but rather as a protest against the intrusion of the scientific point of view into poetry. His symbols for poetry (Diana, the Hamadryad, etc.) are taken from myth and legend. His intention is enlightened by an early form of line 11: "Hast thou not spoilt a story in each star?"

Of "tamarind" (line 14) one needs only to know that it is a gaudy oriental tree; any other exotic growth would have served the purpose as well. Here it is worth noting that Poe did not share the interest of most other poets in the common growths of nature. (See the note on Bryant's "The Yellow Violet," page 884.) His characteristic allusions are to the rarer or more spectacular natural objects — the hyacinth, lily, and asphodel, the eagle and the condor — provided always that the name is euphonious enough for his purposes.

A Dream within a Dream

Page 169. Is the address to another person (lines 1–2) meaningful, or is it a formal rhetorical device that has no relation to the core of the poem? If "grains of sand" equals time, and time equals reality, what is the water into which the grains disappear?

To Helen

Page 169. Poe is trying to evoke a sense of "Helen's" beauty by associating it with ships that bear wanderers home. "Home," the central word of the poem, has two seemingly disparate meanings — the sense of place, of belonging; and antiquity, which to many writers of Poe's generation was the "home" of glory and grandeur. If one needs to go to biography for evidence of the significance of both meanings to Poe, the evidence is there.

For the connotation of "hyacinth," see "Ligeia," 182.1.20–23. Stanza 2 begins with a dangling construction which the reader must straighten out before the statement becomes clear. Note that the rhyme scheme of each stanza is different.

Israfel

Page 170. This poem contains both magnificent images (see especially stanza 2) and flat lines (especially stanza 3). The beginning of stanza 4 makes better syntactical sense if one understands it to mean, "But that angel trod the skies." Line 42 is a clue to Poe's total attitude toward art.

The City in the Sea

Pages 170–171. Before he settled on this final title Poe called the poem in various editions "The Doomed City," "The City of Sin," and "The City in the Sea: a Prophecy." Although he exploits the traditional Biblical symbols of sin, his intent is not moral but aesthetic: gorgeous wickedness simply enforces his central theme of horror and death. It is worth noting that water in Poe's imagery ordinarily connotes gloom or horror, whereas in Whitman it is associated with life and fertility.

Lenore

Pages 171–172. A rather ambiguous statement by Poe in a review of 1844 seems to say that in this "elegiac" poem his intention was to "utter the note of triumph," a purpose which the last stanza fulfills.

1.13 *Peccavimus* — "We have sinned."

The Valley of Unrest

Page 172. This poem has been variously interpreted, and the implied contrast between *Once* and *Now* has been questioned because *Once* describes a condition hardly more joyful than that of *Now*.

Poe here creates another of his ghostly, unhappy regions. The causeless and therefore supernatural unrest in this poem is in contrast with the "hideous" serenity in "The City in the Sea."

The Coliseum

Pages 172–173. This poem, like "To Helen," asserts the continued power and vitality of a physically dead civilization. That the "grandeur" of Rome stirred the "giant minds" of America from Franklin to Emerson and Poe has been demonstrated by many studies of classical influence in our literature.

The action implied in stanza 1 (the kneeling pilgrim), and the use of dramatic blank verse are to be explained by the fact that this poem was once a scene in Poe's unfinished play *Politian*.

1.13   Judean king — Christ.
1.15   rapt Chaldee — a general reference to the Chaldeans who were known as astrologers.
1.19   *bat* is the subject of the clause.
1.36   Memnon — the reference is to a legend that a statue of Memnon in Thebes gave off a note when struck by the rays of the morning sun.

To One in Paradise

Page 173. This poem originally appeared as part of Poe's story "The Assignation," where it is presented as the work of the "hero." A fifth stanza, omitted here and usually in separate printings, links it with the plot of the story. The key to the hero's character in the story is his propensity for dreaming and brooding (the story was originally entitled "The Visionary").

The isle and shrine of the first stanza are recurrent symbols in Poe's work, as is the sand-shore image of stanza 3.

Dream-Land

Pages 173–174. The concept of a land somewhere between life and death is common in Poe's work. Though terror is expressed in descriptions which, as A. H. Quinn says, deny limitations (e.g., *bottomless*, *boundless*, *seas without a shore*, etc.), and in such words as *aghast* and *ill angels*, the situation is conceived of as offering comfort to the traveler whose private woes are "legion" (see lines 39–42).

The Raven

Page 174–176. Explication of this poem cannot go much further than Poe himself carried it in "The Philosophy of Composition." See the note on the latter, p. 889.
1.80   footfalls tinkled — Poe's answer to protests against footfalls "tinkling" on a "tufted floor" was that he intended a supernatural effect.
1.93   Aidenn — the Mohammedan paradise.
1.106   To protest against this line, Poe answered that lighting fixtures placed high above a door were common.

Ulalume

Pages 176–177. To Campbell's commentary (see headnote to the poem in the text) may be added later ones by T. O. Mabbott, *Explicator*, February, 1943, and R. P. Basler, *ibid.*, May, 1944. When a lady asked Poe what the poem meant he quoted Dr. Johnson about the "folly of explaining what, if worth explanation, should explain itself." Conjectures on the meanings of the proper names are numerous but not very useful: Poe chose the names for mood and tone values.

Nevertheless, interpretation of the poem as a whole is needed. The concept of the double-self was a commonplace in Romantic literature. After the loss of his loved one, the speaker wanders in one of Poe's nightmarish but comfortingly responsive regions, the physical man of senses and passions talking with his other self, the soul. He is attracted by the planet Venus, which he sees as Astarte. To Astarte he ascribes warmth and (in the stanza given below) sinfulness; and the reader recognizes the name as that of the Phoenician goddess of fertility. The soul warns against this lure, and prevails against it only when the light of Astarte fades before the doorway of the tomb of the loved one: that is, the light of physical love is extinguished by the fact of death, which the physical man has attempted to evade. (Note a similar renunciation of "Passion accurst" in stanza 6 of "For Annie.") Having faced the reality of death, the divided man becomes one, and in the following stanza, usually omitted, body and soul speak as one rather than alternately:

Said we, then — the two, then: "Ah, can it
    Have been that the woodlandish ghouls —
    The pitiful, the merciful ghouls —
To bar up our way and to ban it
    From the secret that lies in these wolds —
    From the thing that lies hidden in these wolds —
Have drawn up the spectre of a planet
    From the limbo of lunary souls —
This sinfully scintillant planet
    From the Hell of the planetary souls?

The Bells

Pages 177–179. Compared to Poe's more consequential poems this piece is a finger-exercise. Technically it is superior only in so far as he succeeds in imitating verbally the sounds of bells. The reader may derive a simple pleasure from discerning the parallel structures in the four sections (e.g., lines 5, 18, 37, 73). Note that the sections grow longer as they advance from the theme of merriment to that of death.

In such sound-poems as this one must not expect every line to make sense. Phrases like "the people . . . in the steeple . . . [who] are ghouls" should not be examined too closely.

For Annie

Pages 179–180. This poem is a mixture of superb and inept phrasing, but on the whole is one of Poe's more convincing performances. The general conception is a recurrent one in his work: a state resembling death, in that passion, desire, and action are absent, and resembling life, in that consciousness persists. The symbolic function of the two sets of flowers (lines 53–66) is easily discerned if one uses the dictionary to discover their connotations, although "Puritan pansies" is an image that eludes most readers.

1.35   napthaline — the connotation is "inflammable."

Eldorado

Pages 180–181. Inasmuch as "Eldorado" was an epithet commonly applied to the California of the 1849 gold rush, it may be assumed that Poe was here translating the terms of current materialism into his own values. That those values are tied up with the oblivion of death is apparent in lines 15 and 21.

Ligeia

Pages 181–189. In a letter of September 21, 1839, Poe wrote a friend that this story would have been better had he effected a *gradual* perception of Ligeia's reincarnation at the end, but that he had already made use of this device in a similar situation in "Morella." "One point I have not fully carried out — I should have intimated that the *will* did not perfect its intention — there should have been a relapse — a final one — and Ligeia (who had only succeeded in so much as to convey an idea of the truth to the narrator) should be at length entombed as Rowena — the bodily alterations having gradually faded away."

181.1.44   Glanvill — A Joseph Glanvill lived from 1636 to 1680, but Poe seems to have invented this "quotation."

181.2.32   Ashtophet — It is useless to try to equate this allusion with anything specific in mythology. It is probable that Poe here, characteristically, simply invented a name in harmony with the overtones of other words in the clause — "wan," "misty-winged," "idolatrous Egypt."

181.2.36   *person* of Ligeia — Much of the physical description that follows can be keyed to contemporary knowledge of phrenology. See E. L. Hungerford, "Poe and Phrenology," *American Literature*, November, 1930.

182.2.32 ff.   "There is no point . . ." If we may judge by the repetition, in the climax of this paragraph, of the quotation from Glanvill, the "expression" of Ligeia's eyes has to do with her knowledge of the beyond, of immortality. There is no clear relation between this meaning and the "circle of analogies," but one sees in the objects described a possible common denominator consisting of a kind of vitality ("growing" vine, "running" water, "double and changeable" star) which may be related to deathlessness. But perhaps the only demonstrable common denominator is the supernal "Beauty" which Poe so often alludes to but never defines.

183.2.52   Azrael — In Jewish and Mohammedan mythology, the angel of death who takes the soul from the dying body.

184.2.1 ff.   This poem, "The Conqueror Worm," was first published separately and later used in the story.

The Fall of the House of Usher

Pages 189–198. In this story an enfeebled woman surpasses Houdini in getting out of a sealed coffin which is in a locked, copper-lined vault. That such a miracle seems not at all ridiculous when we encounter it in the story itself is proof of Poe's power of creating a mood, an atmosphere, and a state of mind so compelling that our imaginations willingly dispense with physical law.

The theme is one of Poe's favorites — identity: identity of atmosphere and house, house and family, brother and sister, events and works of art, and, to a certain extent, the narrator and Usher. The concepts which bind all these together are morbid sensitivity and abnormal decay. These concepts we apprehend only negatively, by comparing the situation at every point with our own healthy and humdrum normality. In a sense, we as readers are like Madeline's perplexed medical men who make "obtrusive and eager inquiries," but Poe's art requires of us an emotional participation which is in contrast to the mere scientific curiosity of the doctors.

Many of the effects of the story arise from Poe's principle of physical focus, or "close circumscription of space," as he defines it in "The Philosophy of Composition" (220.1.25 ff). Every scene is closely delimited, even out-of-doors in the storm when dense clouds press down upon the house. Such circumscription not only provides a frame, as Poe says, but inasmuch as it suggests agoraphobia, or fear of open space, it is in accord with the general theme of abnormality and insulation.

194.1.2   Porphyrogene — born to the purple.

194.2.18   Our books — It is highly unlikely that Poe expected his magazine public to recognize many of these authors and titles or to look them up. Rather, he probably hoped that his citations would *suggest* the antique, the foreign, the pseudo-scientific, the exotic, and the gloomy, and thus contribute to the mood he was establishing and to the characterization of Usher. His readers probably knew enough Latin to relate the *Directorium Inquisitorum* to the Spanish Inquisition, and the *Vigilae* to "watches of the dead." "Chiromancy" is palmistry.

The Cask of Amontillado

Pages 198–202. The motivation for revenge is revealed at the beginning in the pointed contrast between the words *injury* and *insult.* The reader should study the synonyms for these words. *Insult* in such a society at such a time would have been sufficient cause for murder. The insults implied in "I forget your arms" (200.1.30) and "You? Impossible! A mason?" (200.2.14) should be noted.

The story is full of irony (contrast between appearance, or seeming intention, and actuality), e.g., the gay costume of the condemned, the cough that will not kill.

To whom is the narrator talking? Consider the *you* in the second sentence, the "half a century" in the next to the last sentence, the final Latin phrase, and the country in which the story is set.

199.1.5 gemmary — knowledge of precious gems.

200.1.3 a huge human foot — The coat of arms described is a golden foot on a blue field, crushing a serpent.

The Purloined Letter

Pages 202–211. For a good account of Poe's achievement in the detective story and of his invention of devices which have been used by other writers ever since, see Howard Haycraft's *Murder for Pleasure*, 1941.

202.1.22 *au troisième* — third floor.
203.2.50 hotel — mansion.
204.1.5 *au fait* — familiar with the facts.
206.2.8 *escritoire* — writing desk.
206.2.43 Procrustean bed — Look up "Procrustes" in a dictionary.
209.2.25 *vis inertiae* — force of inertia.

Hawthorne's Twice-Told Tales

Pages 212–215. For the most part, American theories of fiction in the nineteenth century must be deduced from the fiction itself, for only a few of the major writers (notably James and Howells) wrote extensively about their art. This has been particularly true of short fiction; considering America's pre-eminence in the short story form, we have had surprisingly little speculation about it. Before Poe, Irving had perceived that the tale

had qualities which differentiated it from the novel: "There is a constant activity of thought and a nicety of execution required in writings of the kind, more than the world appears to imagine. It is comparatively easy to swell a story to any size when you have once the scheme and the characters in your mind; there mere interest of the story, too, carries the reader on through pages and pages of careless writing, and the author may often be dull for half a volume at a time, if he has some striking scene at the end of it; but in these shorter writings, every page must have its merit. The author must be continually piquant; woe to him if he makes an awkward sentence or writes a stupid page. . . . Yet if he succeed, the very variety and piquancy of his writings — nay, their very brevity, make them frequently recurred to, and when the mere interest of the story is exhausted, he begins to get credit for his touches of pathos or humor; his points of wit or turns of language."

Poe also believed that the short story required finer craftsmanship than the novel, but the opinion of both men was based on the kind of novel that was being published in their time. Neither could have foreseen what Hawthorne and James were to accomplish in the craft of longer fiction.

Poe's celebrated pronouncement (213.1.51 ff.) about how a short story is created is, of course, only a description of his own practice. His belief that the *effect* of a short story is *conceived* and everything else in it *invented* should be compared with Henry James's statements in "The Art of Fiction" (p. 644), though James does not here distinguish between long and short fiction.

215.1.23 plagiarism — Poe did not realize that "Howe's masquerade" had appeared in magazine form one and a half years before "William Wilson."

The Philosophy of Composition

Pages 215–221. This essay should be enjoyed as an exhibition of expert literary logic. It need not be taken seriously as a precise account of Poe's methods of composition, for, as A. H. Quinn has said, he did not have these ideas "all at once, in the preparation of *one poem*, or in the logical order" here given. Nor need his "rules" be accepted as applicable to any poetry but his own, though he presents them as absolute and universal. The purpose of the essay is "journalistic" in the best sense of the word. He tells us (216.1.29) "how interesting" a magazine article might be which would detail the processes by which a particular poem was created, and this essay is the interesting magazine article. As a good journalist, he had to dramatize and oversimplify the creative process in order to make this "peep behind the scenes" meaningful to "the public." The result is a piece of cerebration as interesting and as relentlessly logical as his detective stories — and just about as close to actuality.

RALPH WALDO EMERSON

The Rhodora

Page 223. Lest line 12 be misinterpreted as a belief in art-for-art's-sake, this poem must be read in the light of Emerson's total doctrine. The essays make it clear that to Emerson all earthly and physical beauty is symbolic of the abstract Good, which is the ultimate and sole reality. All beauty in the universe, not merely the beauty which man recognizes as such and cultivates (e.g., the rose), is an expression of this Good. (See the note on Bryant's "The Yellow Violet," p. 884.)

The rhyme scheme should be studied in relation to the content. What is the syntax of the word *there* in the last line?

Each and All

Pages 223–224. The objective of this poem is stated in lines 11 and 12, but the passage leading up to this statement is cryptic because it is presented in terms of four negative assertions. Elucidation begins at line 13 by means of example: three parables (the sparrow, the shells, and the lover) show how the truth is achieved through disillusionment, which is summed up in the statement that beauty seems to be a cheat. This is followed at once by a perception of the totality of beauty, which leads to a positive re-statement of the proposition the poem begins with. The first ten lines should be compared with "The Rhodora," which is a denial that beauty is "wasted" if it is not perceived.

Concord Hymn

Pages 224–225. This poem has become, through familiarity, such a platitude that it is easy to take for granted its perfection as "public" poetry. In most of his poems Emerson makes private statements and struggles to express them in a vocabulary which is necessarily somewhat obscure. In this hymn, however, he is expressing a sentiment which was the property of all his fellow citizens, and his vocabulary is properly the one they associated with poetry. Almost every phrase is a commonplace of eighteenth and early nineteenth century rhetoric, yet the total effect is a tone of authority rather than of triteness.

The Humble-Bee

Page 225. This coastal poet (like Melville) slips naturally into sea imagery when he speaks of land (sail, steerer, waves, etc.). Though Emerson's imagery usually derives from the senses of sight and sound, in this poem the sense of touch (heat) predominates. The senses of taste and smell are alluded to but never fully evoked. "Green silence" is an example of synaesthesia — the description of one sense in terms of another.

The Problem

Pages 225–226. The poet's "problem" may be re-stated thus: he is drawn to those ritualized historic religions, both pagan and Christian, which created, or were the expression of, cultures which motivated the energies of whole nations or societies; but he is unwilling to be assimilated into any system of belief which so dominates the individual. Both the attraction and the repulsion can be explained in terms of W. B. Yeats's celebration of Byzantine art in *A Vision*: ". . . in early Byzantium . . . religious, aesthetic, and practical life were one, and . . . architects and artificers spoke to the multitude and the few alike. The painter and the mosaic worker in gold and silver, the illuminator of Sacred Books were almost impersonal, almost perhaps without the consciousness of individual design, absorbed in their subject matter and that the vision of a whole people." To Emerson, this impersonality, this absorption of the artist and the priest in the faith of a whole people, was a magnificent phenomenon but at the same time a violation of individuality.

ll.25–32   An expression of the organic theory of art — the theory that the form of a work of art is organically related to its content.

l.32   love and terror — i.e., love and fear (of whatever deity prevailed) inspired the artist.

l.65   Chrysostom — (literally "Golden Lips") — John of Antioch, known for his eloquence.

l.68   Taylor — Jeremy Taylor, English divine of the seventeenth century.

The Sphinx

Pages 226–228. This poem, which is given the lead position in the *Poems* of 1847, is a summation of much of Emerson's doctrine, and is difficult to understand without a preliminary reading of the essays. In lines 5–56 the Sphinx propounds the problem: nature's sanity and unity contrasted with man's discord in the universal harmony. The problem is summed up in lines 57–64, where the Sphinx cites the "great Mother's" (nature's) question. Emerson's poet, always a seer, answers the riddle in lines 67–108. Man's soul searches for the truth which is denied to his senses — the truth that the perception of identity unifies all.

l.12   Daedalian — Daedalus ("cunning craftsman"), builder of the Cretan labyrinths.

ll.41–48   The Romantic theory of infancy is implied here. See also "Self-Reliance," p. 273.

ll.49–56   Compare T. S. Eliot's "Animula," p. 834.

l.70   Emerson often equates unreality with "picture." See line 51 of "The Humble-Bee."

l.73   man harries — i.e., harries man.

l.107   curative herbs.

Ode, Inscribed to W. H. Channing

Pages 229–230. The difficulties of this poem arise from the fact that it consists of assertion on two levels. One level is that of public argument. The poem is a reply to an Abolitionist friend who had urged Emerson to join the cause. The friend is refused with reasons which were understandable in terms of the public debate: (*a*) the reformers are deluded in their belief that social progress is real or possible (stanza 3); (*b*) union is a more important issue than slavery (stanza 7); (*c*) pro-slavery sentiment, in both the North and the South, is merely a symptom of the prevailing materialism of the time, which is the real evil to be contended with (stanzas 8–11). These statements were arguable, even refutable — and still are.

Emerson is on poetically safe ground only when he asserts himself on the second level — that of private belief. This belief is irrefutable because it is based on an absolute: the principle that the individual may confidently rely on the moral law which decrees that evils (such as slavery) contain the seed of their own destruction — that only the good is real and permanent (stanza 12).

Thus, though the poem is part of an old controversy — and is "dated" to that extent — it is timeless in so far as it deals with the perennial problem of thoughtful men — the problem of social action. It does not matter that Emerson had already participated in the Abolition movement or that he was later to become an anti-slavery lecturer. As he said in "Experience," "the world I converse with . . . is not the world I think." As a citizen he conversed with the world and recognized the subordinate value of action (see Section III of "The American Scholar"); as poet and philosopher, he questioned the value of political action.

l.1 "grieve" is a transitive verb.

ll.20–23 i.e., freedom-loving New England harbors proponents of slavery. It was believed that the jackal hunted game for the lion. Equate the jackal with New England officers who captured escaped slaves, and the lion with the Southern slave power.

ll.24–27 Compare Emerson's earlier idealism in *Nature*, 238.1.11 ff.

ll.36–43 What boots thy zeal . . . — One section of the Abolitionist Party was advocating that the North secede from the South in order to dissociate itself from the evil of slavery. Emerson (who inherited the Federalists' belief in a strong central union) does not think that the evil would thereby be mitigated. The ideal of freedom, for which the Revolution (Boston Bay and Bunker Hill) was fought, could still "serve," for it is a *truth* which is indestructible. But according to the law of compensation (which is implied in lines 78–97), slavery, being an evil, cannot endure, for it contains the conditions of its own destruction.

This interpretation is not tenable if "things" is taken as an equivalent of materialism (as in lines 50 and 54), and if "snake" carries the usual connotation of evil. The present editor believes that "things" here is to be taken in the very general sense of "phenomena," and that "snake" may perhaps be the Oriental symbol of the snake with its tail in its mouth. The circle thus formed signifies the concept of unity on which the theory of compensation is based.

l.64 granted — assigned or sold to settlers by the government.

ll.86–87 honey . . . lion — See Judges, 14:8.

ll.90 ff. After the failure of the Polish rebellion of 1830–1832, the Czar instituted harsh military rule in Russian Poland.

Bacchus

Pages 230–231. Few Romantic poets were able to resist the temptation to write poems about poetry, for poetry was an outcast of the materialistic world of their day and needed defense. Not all the lines in this defense by Emerson are clear to everyone, but the design of the whole is apparent.

His basic image for poetic inspiration — wine — was a traditional one and inevitable for a poet steeped in the classics as Emerson was. The Platonic theory of poetry as divine madness is implied throughout. The idea of poetry as essence (as wine is the essence of the grape) dominates stanza 3. From line 38 the theme is the function of the wine of poetry in transcending time. Time future ("kings unborn," "grass . . . when it is man") is to be unlocked; but, more important, time past ("far Chaos," "ancient being") is to be recaptured. The past meant here is not the historical past. It is the past Plato discusses in his dialogue "Phaedo, or the Immortality of the Soul" — the timeless past of our souls from which we derive all essential knowledge. "Nature's lotus" (physical existence) makes us forget this knowledge. Hence the "remembering wine": poetry recaptures this forgotten knowledge ("my old adventures") through its immediate communion with the soul.

EMERSON'S PROSE

Modern education, which infuses all branches of learning with the spirit and methods of science and journalism, tends to unfit us for the reading of prose like Emerson's. We are taught to expect logic, order, concreteness, and simple, denotative diction in all expository prose. Emerson's essays look like exposition, and are, in fact, expository up to a point; but they are based on poetic perceptions which are not subject to "proof." The essays have their own logic, their own order, their own concreteness, but these qualities operate in the interest of poetry rather than of the scientifically provable.

I. *The Essay as Unit.* Do not expect to be able to outline an Emerson essay as you would a piece of modern prose. Emerson himself said, "If

Minerva were to offer me a gift I would say, Give me continuity." His thinking is not linear but circular; it does not move along in a straight line from proposition to conclusion, but revolves about one central point, which is fixed and static and not subject to argument. This central point is Emerson's belief in the unique reality, finality, and immutability of *spirit*. This belief is the heart of all of Emerson's writings and of each individual essay. Imagine his total work as a circle. Each essay is an arc on the circumference of that circle. Each arc represents some aspect of experience ("self-reliance," "friendship," "politics," "education," "the poet"). But each arc is also the surface of a sector which has the center of the circle as its terminal point. That center is *spirit*, of which all surface reality is an embodiment.

Since the purpose of each essay would seem to be to arrive at another assertion of spirit, one might expect such assertion to be the climax of each essay. But it almost never is. Explicit assertion, if any is offered, appears unpredictably at any point in the essay. In "Self-Reliance," for example, it appears at about the middle. In some essays it occurs several times; in others, not at all. But always it is *implicit* throughout the whole of the work.

Do not, therefore, expect to progress logically toward a final meaning in any essay: you are in the midst of Emerson's final meaning in every paragraph.

In his earlier essays and addresses Emerson broke his material up into numbered sections (in *Nature*, sub-sections as well). The device looks more helpful to the reader than it really is, and Emerson rightly discarded it as he grew older. It was probably a habit-pattern carried over from his preaching days when ministers guided their congregations with "firstlies," "secondlies," and "thirdlies." It serves to remind us, however, that almost all of his essays were first delivered orally; that all his life he made his living primarily as a speaker; and that all his work has an essentially oral tone.

II. *The Paragraph as Unit.* The structure of Emerson's paragraphs is as elusive as that of his essays, and for the same reasons. You may think you have spotted *the* topic sentence at the beginning of a paragraph, but before you reach the end you will find three or four more. Again, the paragraph is not linear: it consists of a series of re-statements and concrete illustrations. The sentences do not *add up*; they are like the sides of a prism each of which reflects the same light in different color. The only organization his paragraphs have, therefore, is unity of subject matter. Emerson himself was always sure that the sentences of his paragraphs belonged to the same subject; but he was not always sure of the connection between them, and he was too honest to fake continuity where there was none. "Each sentence," he said, "is an infinitely repellent particle."

III. *The Sentence as Unit.* The real formal unit in Emerson's prose is the sentence, which is one reason, perhaps, why he is one of the most quotable of all writers. This primacy of the sentence was appropriate for a writer who believed that truth is a matter of spontaneous perception rather than of logical or laboratory procedure. It is also to be expected that his sentences should consist of confident assertions undiluted with *maybe's* and *perhaps's*. Here again we revert to the forensic quality of Emerson's writings. His object was to persuade his generation; his method of persuasion was bold, epigrammatic, often overstated assertion. Each sentence was intended to make its own impact, independent of its immediate context, but not independent of the spirit of the whole discourse. We read, "I shun father and mother and wife and brother when my genius calls me," and after the shock which makes us read the sentence twice, we realize we are not being incited to brutal egotism, but encouraged to relax emotional attachments whenever these threaten to become crippling bonds. Taken completely out of context many of these sentences can seem absurd; worse, they can be made to serve such alien purposes as business materialism. Emerson is not read to best advantage in Bartlett's Quotations.

IV. *Words.* Emerson's prose gives the impression of abstractness because its purpose is to communicate abstractions; yet his expression is amazingly concrete. It is difficult to find two successive sentences which lack a palpable image or words which name things or actions. The images are, however, limited in sensory appeal: sight and sound predominate; touch, smell, and taste are relatively rare.

The vocabulary is of great range and precision. Some of the explanatory notes below show that one of the chief difficulties of Emerson's diction is its remarkable etymological purity. He often, in effect, uses English words to talk Latin. The wary student soon realizes that by "speculate" Emerson may mean "see" or "observe," and that "virtue" means not only "moral excellence," but "strength" or "power" as well.

Other difficulties for the reader arise from the mode of thinking rather than from the words. The statement "We lie in the lap of immense intelligence" sends no one to the dictionary, but it throws us back on all the resources of religion, philosophy, and imagination we have at our command.

Emerson's theory of words in relation to his whole philosophy is fully and plainly set forth in *Nature*, Section IV — "Language."

Nature

Pages 233–253. Though Emerson desired to create a "religion" which would satisfy both the intellectuals and "the many," this first presentation of his thought has never been popular. He himself was surprised that a work "purely literary and philosophical" should have had an early sale of 500 copies. It was written for a little coterie of like-minded thinkers in eastern Massachusetts, though he probably hoped that Thomas Carlyle was his especially alert and sympathetic listener at the back of the room. Even with this audience he felt the need to organize his thought carefully and plainly, to the extent of labeling and subdividing the several sections. When a bluestocking complained that it "wanted connexion," he replied, "I thought it resembled the multiplication table." And so it did — and does — to those who are attuned to transcendental thinking.

As a literary unit it is too long to be digested in a single session (it is twice as long as his characteristic essays), too short and too dense to offer the advantages of a full-length book in which new ideas might have been given the extended demonstration and discussion they deserved. In a sense, all the later essays are such an extension.

Nevertheless, *Nature* remains a source-book to which one returns again and again for basic presentations of doctrines alluded to or taken for granted in the essays and addresses. With this in mind, the reader should pay special attention to the following sections:

Essential, in the "Introduction," is the definition of "Nature" and "Soul." It is deceptively simple, but the reader of Emerson should never lose sight of it.

Section III, "Beauty," presents Emerson's aesthetics, and is particularly useful in the study of his poetry.

Section IV, "Language," is a guide to his whole theory of symbolism. Though his theory differs from those of Hawthorne and Melville, the section is an indispensable introduction to this all-important aspect of Romantic art.

Section V, "Discipline," points up the crucial distinction between the Understanding (Part 1) and Reason (Part 2). In a letter of 1834 Emerson explained the distinction, as he derived it from "Milton, Coleridge and the Germans": "Reason is the highest faculty of the soul — what we mean often by the soul itself; it never *reasons*, never proves, it simply perceives; it is vision. The Understanding toils all the time, compares, contrives, adds, argues, near-sighted but strong-sighted, swelling in the present, the expedient, the customary. Beasts have some Understanding but no Reason. Reason is potentially perfect in every man — Understanding, in very different degrees of strength. The thoughts of youth, and 'first thoughts,' are the revelations of Reason. The love of the beautiful and of Goodness as the highest beauty, the belief in the absolute and the universal superiority of the Right and the True [are Reason]."

Section VI, "Idealism." Philosophical idealism is an important aspect of transcendental thought. Emerson's definition does not satisfy the systematic philosopher, but his illustrations from nature, poetry, philosophy, metaphysics, and religion bring the concept to life.

Sections VII and VIII were probably intended to be a separate essay. To the beginner they are less intelligible — and less important — than the other sections. In Section VIII the "traditions of man and nature" sung to him by a poet (probably Bronson Alcott) lack the technical merits of both prose and poetry. Even the beginner will find Emerson's own poetry more nourishing.

The American Scholar

Pages 253–263. The emphasis in this oration is not characteristic of Emerson's early work. Almost two-thirds of the space (the sections on action, duties, and the spirit of the age) is devoted to the individual's need for action and to his proper relation to society. Emerson's shift away from his more customary emphasis on privacy is to be explained partly by the social climate of the year 1837 and the status of the audience he was addressing.

In March of that year Martin Van Buren, heir to Jackson's principles and policies, was inaugurated — at just about the time that the worst financial panic to date was developing. The panic merely confirmed Emerson's contempt for materialism. "The present generation," he wrote in his journal that May, "is bankrupt of principles and hope, as of property. . . . This is the causal bankruptcy, . . . that the ideal should serve the actual, that the head should serve the feet. . . . Behold the boasted world has come to nothing. Prudence itself is at her wits' end. Pride, Thrift, and Expediency, who jeered and chirped and were so well pleased with themselves, and made merry with the dream, as they termed it, of Philosophy and Love, — behold they are all flat, and here is the soul erect and unconquered still."

Van Buren's triumph seemed as disastrous as the panic to Massachusetts Whigs of Emerson's class, for they foresaw that the "decline of aristocracy" in politics would continue under Van Buren as it had under Jackson, whose "spoils system" had eliminated many of New England's governing elite. Emerson himself had no reason to fear such a trend, and he was soon to align himself with the "party of the future," as he called the Democrats. Yet he was keenly aware of the fear and despondency among upper-class New Englanders. His speech that August was addressed to the best-educated sons of the class which for decades had sent members of its "natural aristocracy" to Washington and to our foreign embassies. Of the new generation he was demanding a new type of leadership which would resist alike the mob and the complaisant, protected, sterile "scholars."

255.1.24 influences — This word, throughout the essay, must be understood to mean "a flowing into."

255.2.38 seal . . . print — This metaphor is a summation of Emerson's doctrine of the relation of soul to nature. Note that the order implied in the preceding sentence is reversed: seal is soul, and nature is print.

256.2.13   Third   Estate — Historically,   the three "estates" vested with political power were the Clergy, Nobles, and Commons.

257.1.11   idle — Only a careful reading of the entire paragraph prevents misinterpretation of this word.

257.2.37   wit — wisdom.

258.2.1   affections — emotions.

258.2.12–13   antedating — anticipating,   or bringing about before its true time. The sentence is crucial in the paragraph.

259.2.1.   unhandselled — Historical definitions of this archaic word seem not to apply to Emerson's usage or that of Thoreau (329.2.27). The best clue to its meaning is its context.

Divinity School Address

Pages 264–273. In the row that followed the delivery of this address Emerson was abused by the conservative clergy; but with typical quiet courage, and with full knowledge that he might alienate the lecture audiences from whom he made his living, he published the speech at his own expense.

Its significance in theological and church history, particularly in the warfare between Trinitarianism, Unitarianism, and Transcendentalism, is competently explained by C. H. Faust in "The Background of the Unitarian Opposition to Transcendentalism," *Modern Philology*, February, 1938. But the finest values of the address are independent of its historical context. It stands today as the classic statement of one kind of religious thought which has flourished uninterruptedly since the eighteenth century. It is a companion-piece to *The American Scholar* in so far as it calls for the same kind of revitalized leadership from the Protestant clergy as the earlier address asked of "scholars," and it offers, in its opening pages, the same philosophical basis for a renaissance.

265.2.39   myrrh . . . rosemary — The meaning of this series is suggested in the preceding sentence in the word "embalmer" — "that which sweetly preserves from decay." Chlorine is a cleansing and purifying agent; the other three words refer to fragrant, aromatic herbs.

267.1.20–22   Miracle . . . Monster — Essential to the whole passage is the basic meaning of "monster" — i.e., an unfortunate departure from the normal or natural.

Self-Reliance

Pages 273–285. This is a three-part essay, the first extolling self-reliance and attacking dependence; the second giving the grounds of self-reliance;

the third predicting the private and social results of self-reliance. The structural center of the essay is also the philosophical center: the paragraph on the mystical state in which the individual's soul experiences union with the Over-Soul (279.2.34 ff.). Unless one understands this experience as the basis of Emerson's doctrine of self-reliance, he may grossly misinterpret the famous epigrams with which the essay is studded.

274.1.22   pretty oracles — In this paragraph there is a hint of the Romantic theory of infancy which asserted that when we are born we have souls uncontaminated by the corruptions of social experience.

275.1.32   we cannot spend the day in explanation — This is a statement that the reader should supply after each of Emerson's overstatements.

275.1.43   spiritual affinity — Since this paragraph is often cited to show that Emerson was callous in social relationships, it is worth noting that the records of his private life reveal that he was almost literally "bought and sold" by persons for whom he felt this affinity.

277.1.2   Andes and Himmaleh — This simile is essential to the understanding of the oft-quoted passage on consistency.

279.2.34 ff.   An excellent analysis of this and types of religious experience is in William James's *Varieties of Religious Experience*, 1902.

280.1.22   not confident but agent — The comparison is puzzling because though "agent" is a philosophical term, "confident" is not. "Confident," literally, means trusting or reliant, and therefore passive; "agent," literally and philosophically, means a power that acts, a moving force.

280.1.36 ff.   Ultimate power ("virtue") resides only in spirit (the ONE). Any kind of action or force in society (commerce, husbandry) or nature (the tree in the wind) is symbolic of the power of spirit — but it is *only* symbolic. Hence the importance in this passage of the words "examples," "impure," and "demonstration." See "Nature," IV, 3, "Nature is the Symbol of Spirit."

281.1.41 ff.   This dense and difficult passage is set in a framework of ecclesiastical terms ("confessional," "shriven," "absolve"), but the key words are "direct" and "reflex." Note that though Emerson's way is the direct, he accepts the reflex (literally, "bent" or roundabout) also as a way of "clearing yourself." Is there irony in the diminuendo from "father" to "dog"?

283.2.23 ff.   Doric or . . . Gothic — An early statement of the theory of functionalism in architecture. Frank Lloyd Wright, leading modern American architect, often quotes Emerson, Thoreau, and Whitman.

284.1.17   Society never advances — This and 284.2.49 ff. are characteristic Emersonian denials of the theory of social progress.

HENRY THOREAU

Smoke

Pages 286–287. The poem is based on the act of lighting the morning fire. The act is a ritual: the "pure flame" is aspiration, and fresh dedication to purpose with which, for Thoreau, the dawn is always associated. (See 312.1.51 ff.) The prayer for pardon is related to the reference to Icarus, whose waxen wings melted when he flew too near the sun. The significance of the theme of soaring aspiration is realized most fully when the poem is read in its context in Chapter XIII of *Walden*, where Thoreau's fire is in contrast with those of the villagers, who are without wings, waxen or otherwise.

Inspiration

Page 287. This is a short version of a longer poem, parts of which are scattered throughout *A Week on the Concord and Merrimac Rivers.* It is a statement of the transcendental theory of intuition as the source of truth. In the moment of perception of absolute truth, the senses ("ears," "eyes") and traditional fact and belief ("learning's lore") are negated, and the soul becomes "accomplice" in the creative act of the poet.

Civil Disobedience

Pages 287–299. To what extent should the individual allow the state to coerce him in matters of conscience? At its extremes the dilemma has two alternatives — anarchy or totalitarianism, the right of the individual to defy the state whenever he pleases, or the right of the state to destroy the individual's integrity. In this classic defense of the individual against erring political society, Thoreau's solution seems to rest in his faith that the individual will resist the superior force of the state only when his integrity is endangered. His position is a safe one. He knew that most people all too readily sacrifice their rights for security of person and property, and that they must discover their integrity before they can protect it.

It matters little that "times have changed" since Thoreau wrote. His essay is timeless because it is concerned with principle. It has had an immense influence (particularly in Gandhi's India) because to the individual at odds with the state it counsels not violence or rebellion — (means which corrupt ends), but passive resistance, a method which puts the state on the defensive and therefore weakens its power. That is the meaning of Thoreau's crucial statement (292.2.29) about the "*one* HONEST man" who can abolish slavery alone.

287.2.22 The Mexican War (1846–48) was regarded by many Northern liberals as an unjust attack by the United States for the purpose of increasing slave territory.

282.2.42 posse comitatus — sheriff's posse, or group of citizens given legal authority to preserve the peace.

289.2.8 Paley — William Paley, whose *Principles of Moral and Political Philosophy*, 1785, was a standard text in American colleges in Thoreau's time.

290.2.40 Odd Fellow — The Independent Order of Odd Fellows.

290.2.47 virile garb — The Roman boy put on the *toga virilis* when he came of age at the end of his fourteenth year.

292.2.40 My esteemed neighbor — Samuel Hoare of Concord, sent by the Massachusetts governor to protest the imprisonment by South Carolina of colored Massachusetts seamen, was driven out of Charleston.

294.2.16 jail — According to H. S. Canby, this famous episode occurred in July, 1846. Compare Thoreau's account of it with Canby's examination of the facts in *Thoreau*, pp. 231 ff.

298.1.24 men of '87 — The framers of the Constitution, 1787.

Walden

Pages 299–329. Thoreau went to Walden "not to live cheaply . . . but to transact some private business with the fewest obstacles." He did not address his book about his experiences there to those who are content with their lot, nor did he wish to persuade the discontented to move to the woods. He was concerned about "the mass of men" who idly complain of the "hardness of their lot or of the times, when they might improve them," and with those who "lead lives of quiet desperation." If he had specific advice to give, it was that each of us should "be very careful to find out and pursue *his own* way [of life], and not his father's or his mother's or his neighbor's instead."

His book is and always has been disturbing, even annoying, to those who are on the defensive about their way of life. In the twentieth century, amid conditions far worse than those which Thoreau attacked a century ago, the book has greater value than ever for those who realize that their individuality is threatened by mechanization, standardization, and authoritarianism.

But though *Walden* inspires, it is a work of art, not a tract. Thoreau draws upon the experiences of twenty-six months at Walden and upon entries in his journals from 1839 to 1854, but he gives the material a shape corresponding to the four seasons of the year. The book is thus an epitome not only of calendar time, but of the *cycle* of time which promises physical and spiritual rebirth. And though Walden Pond serves as a unifying center, our minds are carried to neighboring farms, to Concord village, to ancient Greece, and to India, as if, in his seclusion, Thoreau were testing not only the simple life but the life of the world he abjured.

As an individualist who rejected the values of

the materialistic world but who wished to communicate to that world, Thoreau found his appropriate stylistic medium in irony and paradox. He discourses about his own values in the language of business, real estate, farming, and railroads. When he says, "I have always endeavored to acquire strict business habits," or "I have travelled much in Concord," the reader must translate. But when the reader meets such a paradox as "I found thus that I had been a rich man without any damage to my poverty," he must cope with thought that is untranslatable. The best practice for the beginner is to study carefully such passages as that on the "purchase" of a farm (309.1.47 ff.) or the discourse on railroads (314.1.2 ff). After that he will be on the alert for Thoreau's numerous and unannounced shifts from literal to figurative or ironic statement.

Finally, Thoreau's work has a quality that has almost disappeared from modern prose. He is a master of the art of reflection, of contemplation, of giving an idea free play and following it to see where it goes. If Emerson's prose consists of restatement, of circular motion, Thoreau's by contrast meanders like a river following its natural course. This kind of thought is often more tentative than it appears, and it tends toward overstatement. But it is not irresponsible, for it all springs from basic principles to which the author is committed.

(For many of the notes below the editor is indebted to Francis H. Allen's edition of *Walden*, Boston, Houghton Mifflin Company, 1910.)

300.1.23 Iolas (a misprint from the first edition for *Iolaus*) — Hercules' charioteer, who helped in the fight with the nine-headed snake, hydra.

330.1.36 peck of dirt — From the old saying, "Everyone must eat a peck of dirt before he dies."

300.1.44 Augean stables — One of Hercules' twelve labors was the cleansing in one day of the stables of Augeas, who had neglected them for thirty years.

302.1.24 raisers — These included Emerson, Bronson Alcott, W. E. Channing the younger, and G. W. Curtis.

304.2.52 Salt — The inclusion of salt within the brace is an ancient typographical error reproduced in most editions after the first.

305.1.28 ff. The fractions are satirical. Thoreau added them at the last moment before printing.

305.2.29 trivial — A technical term for the second or "specific" part of a scientific name, the first part being the "generic" name. "Oleracea" means "partaking of the nature of herbs or vegetables."

307.1.3 Robin Goodfellow — The mischievous elf also known as Puck.

307.1.47 Howards — The eighteenth-century philanthropist, John Howard.

308.1.26 Fry — Elizabeth Fry, nineteenth-century English reformer.

308.2.52 cursing of God — A paraphrase of words from the Westminster Catechism: "to glorify God and to enjoy him forever." See 313.2.12.

309.1.21 Sadi — Persian poet of the thirteenth century.

311.1.34 Harivansa — Sanskrit epic poem, a sacred book of the Hindus.

312.1.21 Damodara — Krishna, of Hindu mythology.

312.2.20 till forbidden — the abbreviation *t.f.* was a printer's sign for a standing advertisement.

312.2.49 Vedas — Early sacred books of India.

313.2.17 clout — patch.

314.1.9 sleepers — railroad ties.

314.1.46 setting the bell — A technical term in bell-ringing; it means, roughly, turning the bell upside down.

315.2.38 Mill-dam — The center of Concord village where people gathered to gossip.

316.1.28 Ulysses — Ulysses had himself tied to the mast when his ship passed the Sirens.

318.2.4 In truth . . . — From "Walden Spring," a poem by W. E. Channing the younger.

319.1.4 cloud-compeller — A name for Zeus or Jupiter.

319.2.38 *Atropos* — The Fate who cut the thread of man's life.

319.2.46 Tell — William Tell, who shot the apple from his son's head.

320.1.36 Long Wharf — In Boston.

323.1.20 aldermanic — Stout, from good living.

323.1.38 under the pond — i.e., under the table, drunk.

324.1.33 great-circle sailing — A nautical term. As used here it means that we sail straight ahead indifferent to the wonders that lie off our course.

325.2.33–34 *hush* and *whoa* — words of command to oxen. *Bright* was a common name for oxen.

325.2.37 *extra-vagant*. See the dictionary for the derivation of *extravagant*.

326.1.9 *translated* — See the dictionary for the derivation.

326.2.18 There was an artist — The story is probably an invention of Thoreau's, told in the manner of Hindu fable.

328.1.12 God is only the president — i.e., God is only the master of ceremonies who introduces important speakers like Webster.

328.1.22 Kittly-benders — Thin ice of such texture that it bends without breaking when walked on.

NATHANIEL HAWTHORNE

Young Goodman Brown

Pages 330–337. The inspiration for this tale probably came from Cotton Mather's *Wonders of the Invisible World*, the relevant passages of which Austin Warren cites as follows:

"The *Devil*, exhibiting himself ordinarily as a small *Black Man*, has decoy'd a fearful knot of proud, froward, ignorant, envious and malicious Creatures, to list themselves in his horrid Service, by entring their Names in a Book by him tendred unto them. These Witches . . . have met in Hellish *Randezvouzes*, wherein the Confessors do say, they have had their Diabolical Sacraments, imitating the *Baptism* and the Supper (the communion or mass) of our Lord. . . . But that which makes this Descent [of the Devil] the more formidable, is the *multitude* and *quality* [i.e., social rank] of Persons accused of an Interest in this *Witchcraft*, by the Efficacy of the *Spectres* which take their Name and Shape upon them. . . . That the Devils have obtain'd the power, to take on them the likeness of harmless people . . ."

It is useless for the student to speculate whether Brown's adventure was dream or reality: either way, the experience was, for Brown, the transformation of a doctrine (the depravity of man) into a literal truth, which he was incapable of absorbing without losing faith in himself and others.

In form, the tale is perfectly self-contained. The action takes place between sunset and sunrise, beginning and ending in the village, but reaching its climax in the forest, which, to the Puritan, was the abode of devils.

331.1.7   pink ribbons — The use of this symbol, recurrent throughout the story, is to be watched carefully.

331.2.21–24   Note that Salem is 17 miles from Boston.

332.1.12   reasoning — The use of reason by the devil is amusingly and cogently explored by C. S. Lewis in *The Screwtape Letters*, 1943.

The Minister's Black Veil

Page 337–344. It is typical of Hawthorne's fictional method that he asks in this story not *why* Mr. Hooper wore the veil, but how his wearing of it affected other people and his own fate. Once again, Hawthorne dramatizes a moral concept by demonstrating, through a series of episodes (wedding, funeral, deputation of parishioners, etc.) that men cannot endure to be reminded of a dread fact which they know in their hearts to be true. As in "Young Goodman Brown," a character's literal and morbid acceptance of a moral doctrine results in isolation. Mr. Hooper's morbidity is plainly stated in 341.1.5–9.

Some critics object that the hint of a specific explanation of Hooper's act (340.1.2–44) spoils the story because it either suggests too much or tells too little.

The Maypole of Merrymount

Pages 344–350. There is no better proof than this tale (once subtitled "A Parable") that though

Hawthorne frequently found his materials in the past he was no mere "historical novelist"; for he criticized the past, and saw it in relation to the present. In this story he recognizes the necessity of the American Puritan victory over the alien culture represented by the Merrymounters, but regrets that the sense of joy in life should have been driven out of New England with them. Hawthorne does not "take sides" in the ordinary sense. If the "iron" Puritans proclaim bounties on the heads of wolves and the scalps of Indians as if there were no difference between beasts and people, the "silken" Merrymounters play with their eyes bandaged, and gaily follow a "flower-decked corpse . . . to his grave." Yet the Puritans must prevail, just as "the moral gloom of the world" must overpower "all systematic gaiety." (See Q. D. Leavis in the *Sewanee Review*, Spring, 1951, for a fresh and interesting interpretation of this story.)

345.2.31   Comus — See Milton's *Comus*, lines 92 ff., for an interesting analogue to this story.

346.2.1–31   The mood of this passage is a foreboding of the climax of the tale. Lines 27–31 are the most significant in the story and perhaps in all Hawthorne's work.

347.1.12   ales — festivals.

349.1.5   Ancient — a corruption of "ensign"; therefore, "ensign-bearer" or "standard-bearer."

Endicott and the Red Cross

Pages 350–353. The student who compares this story with a good historical account of the early settlement of New England will find discrepancies in detail, but he should also discern that Hawthorne's essential purpose was to reveal the kind of colonial character that made the Revolution possible. The "emblem" of that character is the scene mirrored in Endicott's breast-plate: the bloody head of a wolf nailed to a church porch, the whipping post, pillory and stocks — or force, faith, and single-mindedness. One notes as an aspect of the colonial character that the "sinners" are as bold and defiant as their judges; and that the minister, Roger Williams, was banished to Rhode Island in 1636, two years after the events related here, because his beliefs failed to conform with those of the town's rulers. As J. S. Bassett said, "Massachusetts was not established as a home for toleration, but as a fortress for one kind of Puritan faith." Hawthorne's detachment is evident throughout the story.

David Swan

Pages 353–356. This is the kind of story that appealed to Hawthorne's own generation — sentimental, picturesque, slightly melodramatic, weakly moralistic. The form is mechanical: the length of the piece is limited only by the number of types of fate (Fortune, Love, Death) which the author chooses to bring to the scene.

Rappaccini's Daughter

Pages 356–372. Though the beauty of this story is generally recognized, it has often been objected that the symbolism of Beatrice's situation is imperfect because there is an illogical contrast between her body and soul. It may well have been Hawthorne's point, however, that a power-mad scientist could corrupt nature (Beatrice's body) without touching her soul or affecting her innocence, and that (as the dying Beatrice implies) the worst poisons are not the artificially contrived ones of science but those natural to the spirit of depraved man. Note, as a contrast to Beatrice's purity of spirit, the depravity of the three men — Giovanni's shallow selfishness, Rappaccini's lust for power, Baglioni's envy and spite.

More questionable is the disparity between Beatrice's willingness to toss Giovanni a blossom from the poison shrub (361.2.45–49) and her later urgency to save him from it (366.1.10–11).

358.1.3 Vertumnus — Roman god of the seasons or changing year.

358.1.46 Eden — Hawthorne was fond of analogies between the Garden of Eden and the condition of modern man. The analogy here is perverse but recognizable: Rappaccini as the "God" who creates the garden; Beatrice as his first human "creation"; Giovanni "created" afterward because Beatrice alone was incomplete; Baglioni as a kind of serpent whose destroying "Knowledge" brings death to the garden.

Ethan Brand

Pages 372–380. To understand this story fully we must accept the implication of one of Hawthorne's subtitles for it: "A Chapter from an Abortive Romance." N. F. Adkins, who has studied it as an unfinished work, says that it was "the last and crowning chapter of a novel," but that Hawthorne "found it impossible to finish what he had started" (or, from another point of view, to begin what he had finished). The novel "would . . . have developed in detail the eighteen years of Ethan's life, from the time he left his native village." On p. 379 Hawthorne "outlines what would . . . have been the thematic and narrative substance of the novel." ("The Early Projected Works of Nathaniel Hawthorne," *Papers of the Bibliographical Society of America*, Second Quarter, 1945).

Since the "unpardonability" of a sin is a theological problem, there is special interest in the idea advanced by Father L. J. Fick (in an unpublished study of Hawthorne) that Hawthorne's treatment of the problem is in accord with basic Catholic doctrine; i.e., the unpardonability of Ethan's sin lies in his final and willful impenitence in spite of his full recognition of the evil of what he has done. Hence, the "marble heart" of the climax.

372.2.47 "Delectable Mountains" In *Pil-*

grim's Progress, the mountains from which Christian sees the Celestial City.

HERMAN MELVILLE

Benito Cereno

Pages 382–423. Of the three major figures in this story, two — Delano and Babo — are men of action, and their action provides the plot. The third, Cereno, is passive, sensitive, and perceptive; he is acted upon.

On the first page we learn the determinant fact about Delano's character: he is to see all and understand nothing. Yet he serves as the medium through whom four-fifths of the story is told. Like Mark Twain, who told his greatest story through a fourteen-year-old semi-literate boy, Huck Finn — like William Faulkner, who employs children, illiterates, and even idiots as narrators — Melville is using a strategic device to bring his readers' imagination into play. Delano's limitations are so obvious that we look through and beyond his facts and his simple responses to get at the significance of the tale.

The meaning beyond Delano's facts is perceived — is experienced — by Benito Cereno, which is why the story carries his name. The meaning may be stated plainly: malignity in human nature is real, complex, and inscrutable — as real as the slaves' brutality, as complex as their motivation, as inscrutable as the expression on the face of their leader's severed head. But this is as far as explanation can go, for "malignity," "reality," "complexity," and "inscrutability" are words which come alive only to the extent that we respond to the action, imagery, color, and atmosphere of the story. For example, the word "malignity" may be defined as badness arising from man's nature rather than from particular circumstances that provoke him to behave badly. Babo, as a man held in slavery, has abundant reason to behave badly toward his captors. Yet we are made to understand by indirection that something in Babo's conduct goes beyond provocation — that he is malign. But the malignity is suggested rather than argued or stated, and we feel the ambiguity of all good and evil. We wonder if Babo's malignity would have been realized had he not been enslaved; and we reflect that since we are all potentially slaves, we are all potentially malign.

The story is full of suggestions which the reader should not push too far toward explicit statement. One is struck by the many allusions to monks, monasteries, and cowls, and by the descriptions of Cereno's aristocratic character and dress. The temptation to read the story as an allegory of the decline of Spanish imperialism, political and religious, is strong, but should be resisted. Again, Melville in 1855 could hardly have been ignorant of or indifferent to the slave problem in the United States, but it is literal-minded to see the slave-ship as a microcosm of ante-bellum America complete with black rebel, landed aristocrat, and northern businessman. The reader's recognition of these historic parallels enriches the story, but the parallels do not constitute meaning.

Delano's part of the narration is superb, but the story as a whole is imperfect. Melville's use of the long legal depositions is a confession of failure to absorb all the facts into a fictional framework, and the last section, presenting Delano's and Cereno's final talk, represents still another shift in point of view.

384.1.1   San Dominick — Suggesting as it does the Dominican order of mendicant friars, the name of the ship is one of many ecclesiastical allusions.

386.1.50   Charles V retired to a monastery.

387.2.30   mata — probably *maté*, the Paraguay tea referred to in line 19.

389.2.1–2   hawse-hole . . . cabin-window — He got his command through influence, not by earning it.

393.1.43   Rothschild — a famous European banking family.

402.1.18   Guy-Fawkish — Guy Fawkes conspired to blow up the House of Parliament with gunpowder.

408.1.6   Chesterfieldian — Lord Chesterfield was a spokesman for polite and worldly conduct.

412.2.6   the Jew — Judas.

JOHN GREENLEAF WHITTIER

It is appropriate to judge gently a poet so diffident and unassuming that he was able to sum up his own defects more accurately than any modern reader can do for him. Among these he included an "untaught ear," lack of grace, of "rounded art," and of subtlety, and inability to penetrate below the surface of common life. He thought of himself as a man of action, whose chief merits as poet were an "earnest sense of human right," hatred of tyranny, and feeling for his fellow men. He was in every respect a public rather than a private poet, a spokesman who used in his versified tales, pictures, and arguments the long-accredited idioms and rhythms of English poetry. The interest of his verse lies in its always clearly presented subject matter, not in its form or in any originality of expression. Yet, as Van Wyck Brooks has said, "Literature abounds in special sanctions, those that govern national anthems and other expressions of faith — hymns, folk-poems and ballads — where the only point that essentially matters is whether the feeling, being true, is also sufficiently large and important. Whittier possesses this immunity. . . ." (*New England: Indian Summer*, p. 52)

Skipper Ireson's Ride

Pages 426–427. Though Whittier versified many legends and historical episodes, he seldom took pains to verify his facts. A literary historian says of this poem, "In 1808 occurred the regrettable incident of Skipper Benjamin (not Floyd) Ireson, for his crew's cowardice and lying (not for Ireson's hard heart), tarred and feathered and carried in a dory (not cart) by the fishermen (not women) of Marblehead" (G. F. Whicher, in *LHUS*, I, 578). Yet the story had only a local circulation until Whittier breathed life into it, and so demonstrated that the facts of a legend are not as important as what a writer does with them. It is curious that this admirer of Burns had little interest in the literary use of dialect, and that the touches of dialect in this poem are the work of James Russell Lowell — a member of the New England upper-class who specialized in the speech of the folk.

Snow-Bound

Pages 431–439. Just as, for many modern readers, Irving's "Legend of Sleepy Hollow" commemorates the last days of the old, static agrarian life, *Moby Dick* those of the whaling industry, and *Life on the Mississippi* those of steam-boating, "Snow-Bound" celebrates the ancestral farm home which has ceased to be a fact in the lives of Americans. Historians now recognize 1866, the year the poem was published, as approximately the time when the triumph of industrialism and urbanization over the agrarian economy was finally assured. Much of the poem's contemporary popularity was due to the fact that, even this early, many town and city dwellers found that it took them back to their farm childhoods.

The poem is as uncomplicated and artless as most of Whittier's pieces. Its values — mood, vivid and homely detail, honest feeling — are all on the surface. Yet in spite of digressions — sentimental and propagandistic — it is not without a plan that accords with its central purpose. In the first 115 lines there is a gradual closing in — a contraction of scene, from the description of sky and weather, to the more restricted world of house and barn, until the attention is focused on the hearth-fire, the physical center of both poem and homestead. By its light we discern the personalities of the snowbound group as we hear their tales and reminiscences. But the thoughts and memories of the speakers carry them and the reader in imagination out into the past of an earlier New England, and into Canada, Europe, and antiquity. After the family has been presented, the focus is once more narrowed to the fire, which is readied for the night. When morning comes we are let out into the world again by the road-breakers, the doctor, and the village newspaper.

Though the mood of the poem is that of reminiscence, no sentimental "escapism" can be imputed to it. Whittier's vigorous concern with the present is explicit in lines 735–739.

Henry Wadsworth Longfellow

Hymn to the Night

Pages 444–445. This poem was immensely satisfying to nineteenth-century readers, and it still has some admirers. To those who like it, the mood it creates is the important thing — that state of mind in which night brings not an increase of loneliness, trouble, or terror, but a pleasantly sad repose after anxiety. If the poem succeeds with the reader in this respect, the fact that "night" is successively a woman, a house, a drink of water, and a bird will not disturb him, for each image may be taken separately and each contributes to the mood.

l.21   Orestes — Orestes murdered his mother to avenge his father. The expiation and peace which ensued are the subject of Aeschylus' *Eumenides.*

The Skeleton in Armor

Pages 445–447.   l.5   wrapt — embalmed.
l.110   Skaw — the northern point of Jutland.

Mezzo Cammin

Page 447. The title means "midway upon the journey," and is taken from the first line of Dante's *Divine Comedy.*

The Jewish Cemetery at Newport

Pages 448–449. In this poem Longfellow's historical imagination is at its best, and the past of the Jews becomes alive under his sympathetic touch. The last stanza, however, reveals his typically nineteenth-century attitude toward the "progress of civilizations," and may well be studied in the light of recent history.

l.2   seaport town — Newport, Rhode Island, where there was a settlement of Portuguese Jews.
l.52   Ishmaels, Hagars — See the story in Genesis 16:21.
l.34   Ghetto and Judenstrasse — sections in which the Jews were segregated in European towns and cities.
l.41   Anathema maranatha — a curse. See I Corinthians 16:22.
l.43   Mordecai — See the Book of Esther.

Sandalphon

Page 451. According to Longfellow's sources, Sandalphon, of Talmudic legend, is one of the permanent angels (there are others who are created to chant only one hymn before they expire, l.14) who make garlands of the prayers of the Israelites. He stands on earth and his head reaches to the door of heaven.

Divina Commedia

II (*page 452*)

The basis of this magnificent commentary on medieval church architecture is a truth perceived also by Emerson and Yeats (see the note on Emerson's "The Problem," p. 890). Longfellow understands the cathedral as the creation of a whole people, a whole civilization. The beauty described in the first five lines, and the ugliness and treachery in the next three, are visible signs of life as it was experienced by that civilization and expressed in its art. Longfellow's insight is summed up in the phrase, "Poem of the earth and air."

III (*page 452*)

l.30   poet — Dante.
l.35   Ravenna — where Dante was buried.
l.38   tragedies — such as those re-told in *The Divine Comedy.*

IV (*page 452*)

l.44   She — Beatrice.
l.47   rebuke — Cantos 30 and 31 of the Purgatory tell of Beatrice's rebuke to Dante.
l.54   Lethe and Eunoë — In the Purgatory Dante drinks first of Lethe, the river of forgetfulness, and then of Eunoë, the river of memory of the good.

V (*pages 452–453*)

l.60   Rose — a circular window depicting the Trinity and the Blessed arranged like the petals of a rose.
l.70   elevation of the Host — that moment in the mass when the consecrated elements are lifted up before the congregation.

VI (*page 453*)

l.71   star — Dante, as prophet of Italian freedom.

Milton

Page 453.   l.5   ninth wave — In wave motion the ninth billow is said to be the largest. The ninth muse is that of epic poetry, the form of *Paradise Lost.*
l.11   Maeonides — Homer.

The Three Silences of Molinos

Page 454.   l.3.   Spanish monk — Michael de Molinos, whose *Spiritual Guide* was Longfellow's source.

James Russell Lowell

The Biglow Papers

Page 456–466. The Biglow Papers are part of a tradition of "crackerbox philosophy" which began about 1825 and has continued down to our own time. The most notable contributors to the tradition have been "Major Downing" (Seba Smith), Lowell, Artemus Ward (C. F. Browne), Mr. Dooley (F. P. Dunne), and Will Rogers. The common characteristic of the writings of these men is the use of a regional or racial dialect, in prose or rhyme, for purposes of political and social commentary, satire, and propaganda. The advantages of this mode of appeal are obvious. By pretending to be down on the ground with the common man, the commentator escapes the resentment incurred by intellectuals and pundits, and by using the humor which seems to be inseparable from dialect he holds attention and forestalls boredom. "Common sense" is his substitute for sustained and logical argument. Such discourse can be the medium for a wisdom more compelling than logic; it can also be misused as one of the most insidious of all devices for indoctrination.

In these "papers" Lowell is frankly a propagandist for Northern liberalism, but Hosea's opinions are not to be taken as completely identical with the author's. Lowell himself did not believe in disunion, as Hosea seems to; and he did believe that "it is the manifest destiny of the English race to occupy the whole continent and to display there that practical understanding in matters of government and colonization which no other race has given proof of possessing since the Romans," a statement which contrasts oddly with Hosea's attack on the "manifest destiny" slogan (lines 45–46 of "What Mr. Robinson Thinks"). What Lowell said of another of his propaganda poems probably applies to the early *Biglow Papers*: "Had I entirely approved either the spirit or the execution of these verses I had put my name to them. But they were written in great haste, and for a particular object, and I used therefore such arguments as I thought would influence the mass of my readers, viz., a swinging ballad metre, some sectional prejudice and vanity, some denunciations, some scriptural allusions and no cant." (Quoted by Arthur Voss in "Backgrounds of Lowell's Satire in 'The Biglow Papers,'" *New England Quarterly*, March, 1950.)

When read as historical documents these poems must be understood in relation to the politics of their time. Mr. Voss's article is helpful in providing background for this kind of understanding. But Lowell's wit and humor, and his concern with principle, endow the *Biglow Papers* with values which can be appreciated by the modern reader, quite apart from historical context.

456.col.2   cruetin Sarjunt — recruiting sergeant.

eenamost — almost.

chollery — cholera.

Da & martin — Day & Martin, shoeblacking manufacturers, who advertised in rhyme.

457.col.1   Simplex Mundishes — *simplex munditiis*, unsophisticated.

l.11   cotton — an allusion to the Democratic party's motives for war with Mexico.

l.53   pooty — pretty.

l.57   airy — eyrie (eagle's nest).

l.61   Californy — a reference to the proposed "deal" to admit California as a free state if parts of Mexico were taken in as slave territory.

l.88   pus — purse.

l.111   yellers — a disease of peach trees.

ll.121–122   Massachusetts . . . akneelin' — cf. Emerson's "Ode to W. H. Channing," stanzas 3–5.

l.129   colored seamen — See p. 895 for the note on Thoreau's "Civil Disobedience," 292.2.40.

l.130   env'ys w'z — envoys whizz. Apparently a reference to disrespectful treatment of American envoys.

l.154   part — that is, break up the Union — an extreme Abolitionist position.

458.col.2   first recruiting sergeant — Satan.

459.col.1   the Greek phrase means "especially."

Exemplo . . . — "We live more by example than by reason."

What Mr. Robinson Thinks

l.39   *per contry* — *per contra*, on the other side.

l.45   destinies — "manifest destiny," the nineteenth-century slogan used to justify conquest of backward countries.

460.col.2   *Patriae* . . . — "The smoke of one's own country is brighter than the fire of a strange land."

Ubi . . . — "Where liberty is, there is my country."

quasi noverca — "as a stepmother."

The Courtin'

l.17   crook-necks — powder flasks made of horn or wood or gourds.

l.19   queen's arm — musket.

l.31   ton — of hay.

l.43   Ole Hunderd — The tune ("Praise God from whom all blessings flow") traditionally associated with a metrical version of the 100th Psalm.

l.95   cried — announcement in church of intention to marry.

Sunthin' in the Pastoral Line

Lowell's facility was such that he found it almost as easy to write in meter and rhyme as in prose. This piece is really a metered and rhymed essay, a familiar essay, like Holmes's *Autocrat* essays. It is to be enjoyed not as a unified and organized poem, but as a monologue which shifts from subject to subject by a process of loose association. The center of interest at every moment is the *detail* — the turn of a phrase, the flavor of a dialect term, the statement of a homely fact which one does not expect to see in print. The piece ends on a serious note of merely historical interest — the question whether the war should be fought chiefly to crush rebellion or to emancipate slaves. The modern reader finds this "climax" less interesting than the passages on home and nature.

OLIVER WENDELL HOLMES

Like Lowell, Holmes was a facile rhymer who could write on demand a poem for any occasion, and who sometimes wrote speeches and essays in verse. Like many wits he was also a sentimentalist. With a few exceptions his best poems are those in which wit and humor are combined with sentiment, as in "My Aunt," "The Last Leaf," and "At the Saturday Club." In these we come to realize the essential gentleness of Holmes's character.

The Chambered Nautilus

Pages 469–470. Myth, science, and philosophy had prepared the way for Holmes's reflections in this poem, and though the subject had attracted other poets, his treatment of it seems to have been final.

Early myth furnished the nautilus with oars and sail, and early science (up to at least 1832) believed the myth sufficiently to agree that the nautilus had miraculous sailing powers. Meanwhile, eighteenth-century Deism had taught that all things in nature are revelations of divine plan, and Transcendentalism made a system of this belief. (See Emerson's "Nature," 251.1.22 ff.) Thus in the nautilus Holmes had a ready-made symbol. It was an almost unbelievably apt illustration of an idea that the nineteenth century had to believe: that in both physical and spiritual life there is an irresistible progressive force. But whether, in the last stanza, the logic of the analogy between creature and shell, and soul and mansion is satisfactory, the reader must judge for himself.

(The editor is indebted to N. F. Adkins's article on this poem in *American Literature*, January, 1938.)

The Living Temple

Pages 470–471. Like "The Chambered Nautilus," this poem celebrates God's wisdom as revealed in nature, and brings scientific knowledge to the support of religion. The title which Holmes contemplated giving the poem — "The Anatomist's Hymn" — would have been more accurate than the present one, for "caves," "currents," "fountains," "tides," "chains," "threads," and the like, have no relation to the architectural terms imposed upon the subject in the final stanza.

The Autocrat of the Breakfast Table

Pages 475–490. The plan of these essays gives the writer certain privileges and immunities. As "autocrat" he assumes the power to limit the discussion to congenial subjects, digress, deal summarily with criticisms and objections, and be serious or whimsical as the spirit moves him. The breakfasters at the boarding house (an old American institution now almost extinct) constitute a mixed audience whom he can endow with any sort of prejudice or ignorance he wishes to combat. These boarders represent his *Atlantic* readers, of course (Holmes turned down opportunities to reach bigger audiences through more popular magazines), and their attitudes can be taken, with some reservations, as a cross-section of Eastern opinion in the fifties on such subjects as theology, science, aristocracy, love, and poetry.

Yet the interest of the essays is not merely historical. Quite aside from Holmes's wit, humor, wisdom, and charm, his speculations and reflections are of the kind that opens the doors of discussion rather than closes them, and though some of his subjects are "dated," most of them are sufficiently basic to survive as live issues. That he desired to educate the public on serious matters, as well as to amuse it, is evident from his rather bitter remarks (p. 481) that some people would rather enjoy his puns than listen to his ideas about free will, and see him "stand on his head" rather than have him "use it for any purpose of thought."

His ideas about poetry and poets (476.2.13 ff.; 482.1.45 ff.; 486.2.35 ff.) are worth comparing with Poe's in "The Philosophy of Composition." Both writers popularize the subject by giving the reader an "inside view" of the poetic process. But note that it is Holmes, almost exclusively a public poet whose most private perceptions were intelligible to the general reader, who talks about the "dreaming faculty" in poets, and Poe, the dreamer, who discusses the poem as mechanism.

475.2.1　*pons asinorum* — asses' bridge, meaning something difficult for beginners, or a hazard for fools.

476.1.52　— Aet. — aged.

476.2.4　Tupper, Cobb — Writers of best-sellers of the time.

476.2.13　*C'est le . . . coûte* — It's the last step that's the hardest.

477.2.45　*medius lectus* — the middle couch (seat of honor) at a Roman banquet.

478.1.14　*melas oinos* — dark wine.

478.2.48　Day and Martin — manufacturers of shoe polish.

478.2.50　Dr. Wigan — eighteenth-century English physician.

479.2.2　"Marriage à la Mode" — A series of satirical engravings by the eighteenth-century English artist, William Hogarth.

480.1.14　DESIDERII . . . Discourses of Desiderius Erasmus. Amsterdam. Printed by Ludovicus Elzivirius. Translated by William Cookeson of All Souls College, Oxford.

480.2.30　Paternoster — The prayer beginning "Our Father."

480.2.48　Agur — See Proverbs 30:8.

481.1.11　Concilium . . . — Council of Trent, 1545–1563, at which the Roman Catholic creed now held was formulated.

481.1.47　*Jesse Rural* — A simple-hearted clergyman in Dion Boucicault's comedy, *Old Heads and Young Hearts*, 1848.

481.2.20 Sydney Smith — One of the founders of the *Edinburgh Review*, 1802.

481.2.24 "Quarterly" — The *Quarterly Review*, a rival of the *Edinburgh*.

481.2.38 *Bob Logic* — A character in a popular English play, *Tom and Jerry*.

481.2.39 Liston — John Liston, English comedian, whose favorite part was Paul Pry in John Poole's farce of the same name.

483.2.40 Historian — probably John Lathrop Motley.

483.2.45 wittiest of men — probably Thomas G. Appleton.

485.2.42 Ithuriel — See Milton's *Paradise Lost*, IV, 788 ff.

489–490 *The Deacon's Masterpiece*. This is not an attack on Calvinistic theology, specifically, but simply another shot in Holmes's campaign against the tyranny of logic. His poem is a parable on the limitations of all logical systems which operate in an intellectual vacuum and lack "primary relations with truth."

Abraham Lincoln

The best commentary on these famous letters and speeches is the chapter by Carl Sandburg in *Literary History of the United States*.

Walt Whitman

Whitman's poetry is essentially oral in quality. Early in his career he thought of delivering his messages to America from the lyceum platform, but being a poor speaker he turned to poetry for his medium. Through it all, the voice of the public speaker is audible; indeed, its best values emerge not when it is closely analyzed but when it is read aloud. It is like that kind of impressionistic painting which looks merely slovenly when one stands too close to it.

Broad, loose brushwork was appropriate to the purposes of a poet whose subject was nothing less than the whole universe — physical and spiritual, past, present, and future; who set out blithely to settle once and for all the ancient conflicting claims of matter and spirit, of the individual and the mass; and who saw in America the highest, though by no means the final, result of the train of events which was set in motion when life was first generated amidst primal chaos. To a poet of such vision the old and established forms of expression were simply irrelevant: he set out to invent a prosody which would give him the freedom he needed.

That prosody is now described as "organic." The form of organic art is determined solely by its content and purpose — by those natural laws of growth, as Whitman put it, that determine the shape of a leaf or a pear. There is a certain amount of cant in such a concept because a poem cannot "grow" any more than a house can grow; both are artifacts, products of human workmanship. But just as an architect can make a bank look like a bank instead of a Greek temple, a poet can refuse to work from borrowed or predetermined forms, or to force his words into iambic pentameter or fourteen-line packages. Whitman's lines are free of most traditional artificialities; that is, they are not linked by end rhymes which might distort a meaning; their length is determined only by the cadence and content of the thought; and they cannot be scanned into a regular pattern of accents. Similarly, his "stanzas" are uneven packages made up of any number of lines, depending upon what he considers to be a unit of thought within a poem.

This does not mean that all his poems are externally shapeless, though many of them are. Sometimes they contain discoverable stanza patterns. A poem may begin and end with three-line stanzas which have comparable functions, and all the lines in between may be grouped in pairs. Most common is his "wave" or "pyramid" pattern — a gradual lengthening of lines, and then a shortening, with a corresponding expansion and contraction of rhetorical effect. Usually, however, one must be satisfied with such internal unity as the poem achieves through mood and image.

For the values of Whitman's verse other than aesthetic much can be said. The warmth of his love for human beings — in fact, for all *being*; his response to science, technology, and industrialism, whose symbols had generally been excluded from romantic poetry; his nonchauvinistic nationalism, which refused the restrictions of regional cultures while it opened the door to internationalism; his frank and joyous sensuality at a time when literature either sublimated animality or toyed with it pruriently — these were potential correctives for an age which badly needed them. And the relevance of some of them to our own problems is obvious. To the modern reader his urgency on many subjects seems naïve and humorless, but his best poems reveal his vitality without exposing his limitations as a thinker and craftsman.

In the reading of Whitman's poetry one must accept literally his confession that he was attempting to communicate the incommunicable; that he was baffled by the problem of articulation; and that "you [the reader] must do the work." The reader does the work not by trying to make continuous, rational sense of every line and stanza, but by responding to the "hints," "faint clews and indirections," through which Whitman's poetry functions. One necessity is to read *enough* of his verse so that the sheer mass and weight of its detail, reiteration, and restatement can do what other poets achieve through concision and crystallization.

Song of Myself

Pages 495–514. Attempts have been made to discern an over-all pattern in the fifty-two stanzas of this poem, but they are unconvincing. Like Emerson, Whitman circles endlessly around a central concept. Whitman's center is not so easy to define as Emerson's, but in general it may be described as the simultaneous identity and separateness of the *me* and the *not me*, the soul and the body, the self and all other selves, man and nature.

ll.14–16 "Perfumes" here is roughly equivalent to other "selves."

ll.82 ff. This important section records a typical mystical experience in which a truth is revealed in a moment of vision. It is untypical, however, in that it is reported in sexual terms. The items listed in the last three lines are representatives of the lowest, commonest forms of being, and are intended to suggest the range of Whitman's sympathy.

l.109 Kanuck — French Canadian; Tuckahoe — tidewater Virginian; Cuff — Negro.
l.412 level — carpenter's spirit-level.
l.460 amies — friends or lovers.
l.589 base — bass.
l.608 fakes — coils of rope.
l.1129 koboo — savage of the Ladrone Islands.

There Was a Child Went Forth

Pages 514–515. This is an example of Whitman's catalogue method at its best. Simply by naming enough people, things, and sensations he communicates to us the multiplicity and variety of the impressions which constitute childhood experience. The list is full of contrasts — blossoms and weeds, drunkard and school-mistress, mild mother and mean father. But it is characteristic of Whitman's poor organizing ability that the child's perplexity about the nature of reality (lines 26–30) should appear as just another item in the series of the realities he experiences. The poem should be compared with Eliot's "Animula" in which the experience of childhood is recreated through selection rather than accumulation of detail.

Out of the Cradle Endlessly Rocking

Pages 516–521. This and "When Lilacs Last in the Dooryard Bloom'd" are Whitman's two greatest poems — partly because they are free of his sometimes tiresome "official" optimism and affirmation. Both are records of profound emotional experiences which are objectified through strikingly similar symbols. The bird figure is central to both; the drooping moon of the one is parallel with the drooping star of the other; and both are given a place in time by the smell of lilacs.

In "Out of the Cradle" the symbols are not managed as systematically as in "Lilacs," but the imagery is richer and of greater variety. There is constant recurrence of sound-words (*husky, hissing, moaning*); of reciprocal movement (*rocking, shuttling, rising* and *falling*); of natural opposites (*light

and *dark, moon* and *sun, land* and *sea, he* and *she*); of the sense of wetness (*breakers, lapping, laving, tears*); and of roundish forms (*halo, swollen, liquid rims*). The predominating softness of this imagery is in accord with the central female symbols — the mother bird and the mother sea.

But these effects are, after all, only vehicles for the truth the poet discovers and communicates — the identity of love and death.

l.23 Paumanok — Indian name for Long Island.

Come Up From the Fields Father

Pages 521–522. A simultaneous harmony and contrast are achieved by setting the event in autumn — the farmer's time of prosperity and nature's time of death.

Though the title focuses on the father, the tenderness of the poem derives in part from our experiencing the death from the mother's point of view. In most of Whitman's poetry identification is with the mother rather than with the father.

When Lilacs Last in the Dooryard Bloom'd

Pages 525–530. Many of Whitman's failures in verse are the result of unresolved conflict between his impulses to teach and to express himself as a private person. In this poem the conflict is resolved. Lincoln was for Whitman a symbol of the potentialities of democratic culture, but his death stirred the poet to deep personal expression rather than to propagandistic eulogy. The twelve-day journey of the President's body from Washington to Springfield in the spring of the year, and the mourning of the nation are the common ground for the feeling of Whitman and his readers. But the images through which he crystallizes his emotion on this public occasion had always had for Whitman private associations: the April lilacs are like his leaves of grass — "every leaf a miracle" — but they also fix the event in point of time; stars were for him symbols of aspiration and mystery, but here the star is both "western" and "fallen"; in his youth the bird-song had acquired associations with both love and death. The three images recur in different contexts throughout the poem. Emotional climax is reached in the italicized "aria" in Section XIV — a celebration of "lovely and soothing death" which, far from being a stock response to the death of a beloved leader, comes from the depths of the poet's most personal experience.

To a Locomotive in Winter

Page 531. During much of the nineteenth century most poets implicitly denied that the symbols of industrialism had potentialities for poetry. Whitman affirmed not only the significance but the beauty of machinery.

The description of the locomotive in *winter* suggests an intended emphasis on the contrast of black engine and white snow, but most of the impressions are given in terms of sound — the sense which dominates some of Whitman's finest poems.

Compare his method of creating an image of the locomotive with that of Emily Dickinson in "I Like to See It Lap the Miles" (p. 610).

Democratic Vistas

Pages 532–534. This essay is one of the finest examples of the kind of American self-criticism which is based on belief in our potentialities and disappointment in our performance as a democracy. Whitman, of course, had reason to be critical in 1871, for postwar corruption in business and politics was then both conspicuous and shameless. In general, prose was his medium for criticism, and poetry for prophecy and affirmation.

532.1.26   verteber — vertebrae.

William Dean Howells

Howells's critical pronouncements, like Poe's, were inspired quite as much by opposition to objectional literary practices in his time as by a commitment to a new outlook. No one can quite appreciate Howells's animus against contrived plots, fake denouements, pious idealization, excessive moralization, and unconvincing "heroes" without having read some of the mass of nineteenth-century fictional rubbish which he as reviewer was sickened by, as well as some of the better writers — Dickens, Thackeray, George Eliot — whose weaknesses were adopted by the hack novelists. Because Howells won his battle for realism, we are in a position to be critical of *his* realism without being on the defensive about what he called romanticism. Today he would probably be the first to resist any "petrification of taste" (544.2.32) based on standards which he supported in the nineties.

But these are historical considerations. What survives for us in his criticism is his insistence on accurate observation, on the necessity to interpret the facts observed, on the potential beauty and significance of the common life, and on the belief that art must become democratic in America. Keeping in mind this contribution, we can understand without condoning his truckling to an immature female audience, his complacency about American morality, his instinctive recoil from the sordid and the tragic, and his failure to cope effectively with the problems of form in the realistic novel.

(Note: the essays collected in *Criticism and Fiction*, 1891, were first published in *Harper's Monthly Magazine*, 1887–90.)

543.2.3   communistic — in the sense of "community."

543.2.32   amuse — the old meaning was, "to divert the attention in order to deceive."

546.2.16   Matthew Arnold — in *Discourses in America*, 1885.

Mark Twain

The Celebrated Jumping Frog

Pages 550–553. This yarn was well-known in the South and West, and versions of it had appeared in print before Twain made a classic of it. His version has the oral quality of frontier story-telling and preserves the "dead-pan" technique which pretends that the narrator is solemn and the audience bored. It also contains the homely but vivid metaphor and simile which, as Lowell asserted at about this time (preface to the *Biglow Papers*, Second Series, 1867), were characteristic of the common country speech. Twain's peculiar contribution is hard to define, but his imputation of human qualities to the dog and the frog is a touch of art.

Roughing It

Pages 553–559. *Roughing It* records experiences of 1861–66, including a trip across the plains from St. Louis to Nevada, a visit to the Mormons, and life in Virginia City, San Francisco, and the Sandwich Islands.

About half of Mark Twain's work consists of travel books and reminiscences, but, like Melville, Twain was an artist in reporting his experiences. He knew what parts of his past were significant for American history; he knew how and what to select from the multiplicity of impressions and events; and he knew how to dramatize himself and other people. Such works as *Roughing It* can be trusted as history because they preserve the spirit of events and scenes recorded, but Twain manipulated, magnified, and modified details as he pleased.

Life on the Mississippi

Pages 559–570. These chapters from the first and better half of *Life on the Mississippi* are as much a work of the imagination as of reminiscence, for Twain was here reconstructing the river life of his youth as he wished to remember it. He ignored the more unpleasant aspects of piloting and the more sordid side of the life of the region (some of which is recorded in *Huckleberry Finn*) because his object was to present the river as a boy had experienced it and as the boys of his day had invested it with romance.

The Man That Corrupted Hadleyburg

Pages 570–594. Mark Twain's fiction is often poorest when he emphasizes plot, but his plot contrivances in this story are appropriate to his central purpose. The story is an example of complex *casuistry* (in the basic sense of the word: "the doctrine of dealing with cases of conscience and of resolving questions of right or wrong in conduct"). Starting off with an imaginary environment in which the honesty of the inhabitants of a community has been "shielded from the very cradle against every possible temptation," he proceeds to build up a set of circumstances in which the leading citizens all prove to be corrupt. The fact that the Huck-Finn-like Jack Halliday seems to be exempt from environmental influence, and that the Richards's hold themselves morally responsible for their acts suggests that Twain's logic is defective, and that in the deterministic thinking which he tended toward in his old age he got beyond his depth. Yet his assumption of universal depravity and hypocrisy is not very different from Hawthorne's. (Compare "Young Goodman Brown.")

Bret Harte
The Outcasts of Poker Flat

Pages 595–600. Harte did not discover the fictional type known as the "diamond in the rough," but he established for it a popularity which lasted through the whole of that phase of local color fiction which was dominant until the nineties. The assumption in fiction which exploits this type is that though environment or accident may produce social outcasts and underprivileged persons, such individuals may rise above their environment when they are placed in situations which force them to make crucial moral decisions. This assumption results in dramatic contrasts between low social status and high moral conduct. Such is the contrast in this story of "outcasts" who sacrifice their lives for others.

The plot of the story is sentimental, but Harte's method and style are sophisticated. By the use of irony he exposes the "respectable" morality of the town, plays up sympathetically the naïveté of the innocents, and reveals the gem-like hearts of the gambler and the prostitutes.

Sidney Lanier
The Symphony

Pages 601–605. As a thinker, Lanier belongs with the agrarian liberals who opposed industrialism and urbanism and supported those human rights and values which were threatened by commercialism. As a poetic craftsman, he belongs in the Poe tradition of musicality in verse. Liberalism and musicality come together in this poem, which is a poem both of ideas and of sound-effects. Whether the tones and rhythms of the poem have any essential connection with the ideas or the musical instruments which constitute the symphony is a question for the reader to decide.

Emily Dickinson

The two most original poets of the years 1855 to 1890 had little hearing from their contemporaries. The public rejected Whitman, and only a few of Emily Dickinson's poems got into print before her death. In these decades the public arts of theater and architecture sank to their lowest level in American history; the semiprivate arts of fiction and painting (with some notable exceptions) suffered to the extent that they were addressed to a large public; and the private art of poetry flourished most when it was least exposed to readers.

Almost unknown to the frantically energetic America in which she lived, Emily Dickinson humbly and correctly assumed that her tiny poems contained nothing which the verse readers of her time wished to hear. As she wryly reported of her efforts to make herself understood, "All men say 'What?' to me." When some of her verse was published in the nineties after her death, this was the question asked by many critics. Their hearing was poor, but to a certain extent the question was justified by the misreading of her poems by her editors, by the unfinished state of many of her pieces, and by her almost eccentric passion for condensation.

Nothing in romantic or Victorian poetry (except possibly that of Emerson) could have prepared readers for her work. Her perceptions were the product of a life abnormally secluded once she reached maturity, and she used only the images and the idiom that inhered in the facts of her immediate environment. The experiences were with love, nature, religion, and death. The images derived from observation of life in her home, garden, and village. The idiom was a distillation of New England speech, the terminology of law (her father's profession), and the symbols and images of Protestantism. All this implies a restriction of range and a concentration of effect which are in startling contrast to the expansiveness and diffuseness of her contemporary, Whitman. If Whitman may be said to have spread himself over the whole universe, Emily Dickinson tried to bore a hole into the middle of it from the town of Amherst.

A Route of Evanescence

Page 606. Every line of this poem, which is almost a *tour de force* of concision, contributes to the theme of motion so swift as to make the hummingbird almost invisible except for blurs of color. Like the bird itself, the poem is gone before it is fully comprehended, but a second reading resolves most of the difficulties.

The Day Came Slow

Page 607. Much of the pleasure in the reading of Emily Dickinson comes from the surprises in her images — "hindered" rubies, light "spilled" from a gun, birds in "docile" rows. The poem as a whole is a daring mixture of magnificence (lush colors, jewels, "prince," "stupendous") and domesticity ("breadths" of cloth unpacked by a lady, "orchard," "parlor"). The sparkling "Jew" of line 13 suggests the old symbol of the bejeweled Oriental.

Apparently with No Surprise

Page 607. One of the delights of E. D.'s poetry is the variety of her attitudes toward nature. She was sometimes arch or sentimental on the subject, but she did not, like some nature-lovers, close her eyes to the indifferent, resistless forces that operate through natural law.

The Last Night

Pages 607–608. This is one of the many poems in which E. D. closely observes the psychology of the dying or of the witnesses of death.

Examples in this poem of her characteristically oblique use of common words, are "narrow," "consented," and "regulated."

He Preached upon "Breadth"

Page 608. Although, like most major American writers of the nineteenth century, E. D. was profoundly religious, she was also impatient of the limitations of theology, of religious institutions, and of some of the church's official representatives. "Pyrites" (line 6) is "fool's gold."

I Like to See It Lap the Miles

Page 610. This poem should be compared with another about a railroad train, Whitman's "To a Locomotive in Winter." Whitman achieves his effects through accretion of detail; Emily Dickinson, by reducing the complexity of machinery to a single image.

Because I Could Not Stop

Page 610. This exploration of the experience of death is deceptively simple. The terms of the experience are time and motion. Motion is implied in the central image of the carriage, and in the words "horses," "drove," and "passed." Time words are "stop," "slowly," "haste," "leisure," and "paused." In the crucial third stanza, the implication is that we have "passed" motion ("wrestling," "gazing") and time ("the setting sun"). Yet all this is subordinate to the affirmation of immortality, an idea which is not only explicit in the first stanza but implicit in the rest of the poem.

Henry James
The Real Thing

Pages 612–625. James explains in his preface and in his *Notebooks* how this story came to be. George Du Maurier, the illustrator, had told him of a lady and gentleman, in need of money, who had asked him for employment as models. They were well-dressed, well-bred — such perfect specimens of their class that they could assume they would not have to "make believe" when posing for pictures of upper-class characters. The artist rejected them because he already had a pair of professional models — one of them a common, clever London girl, the other an Italian who was small, ill-dressed, and smelled of garlic. But because they were imaginative and had the "pictorial sense" they knew how to pose as upper-class types more successfully than the couple who actually lived the life of the gentry. "What I wish to present," said James, "is the baffled, ineffectual, incompetent character of their attempt, and how it illustrates once again the everlasting English amateurishness — the way superficial, untrained, unprofessional effort goes to the wall when confronted with trained, competitive, intelligent, *qualified* art." He also wished to illustrate his belief that realism is not a literal record, nor a photograph of fixed types, but penetration to the essence of character.

The Death of the Lion

Pages 625–644. This is one of a number of James's stories about the embarrassments or predicaments of the artist "enamoured of perfection, ridden by his idea, or paying for his sincerity." When James was asked where he found his incorruptible artists — his Neil Paradays and other such "supersubtle fry" — his answer was, in effect, that he had to assume their existence; that "in the name of the general self-respect we must take for granted" the reality of artistic integrity.

The existence of the enemy to such integrity was a fact that James was keenly aware of. He had long endured the publicity exploiters, the autograph-hunters and the interviewers, the country-house parties and the lion-hunting hostesses. Such as these never thought of reading the works of the authors they pursued; yet they killed the artist "with the very fury of their selfish exploitation" without really having "an idea of what they killed him *for*." (James's *Notebooks*)

The essence of such situations is irony — a grimly comic contrast between surface appearance and underlying truth. This story is full of such irony, of cutting satire, of anger, and of compassion for the artist-victim.

The Art of Fiction

Pages 644–656. This is the first strong demand in American criticism that the art of fiction be taken seriously. Irving had insisted on the need for close workmanship in the short story; Poe had promulgated doctrines governing the same form; Hawthorne had in his prefaces made statements from which a theory of romantic fiction might be inferred; Howeils was fighting a battle for realism. It remained for James to insist that fiction, like other arts, "lives upon experiment, upon curiosity, upon variety of attempt, upon the exchange of views and the comparison of standpoints. . . ." The essay is a general one, but all its implications are brought out in explicit detail in James's remarkable prefaces to the New York Edition of his novels.

HAMLIN GARLAND
Under the Lion's Paw

Pages 657–664. This story from *Main-Travelled Roads* is important chiefly as a social and historical document. Reading it, one understands something of the force of that rebellion of western farmers known as the Populist Revolt; realizes what the settling of the agricultural west cost the American people in terms of suffering, overwork, and frustration; and perceives that disillusionment was overtaking the old American dream of an agrarian utopia.

Artistically considered, the story is little more than an impassioned Populist speech translated into conventional melodramatic formula. The hero is The Farmer — good-hearted, industrious, creative; the villain is The Rural Capitalist — lazy, contemptuous, predatory, and merciless; the sentimental denouement turns on The Farmer's saving glimpse of a child in a moment of murderous anger. The characters are not fully realized as people but are symbols of Garland's economic convictions.

For Garland's place in American thought about the west, see H. N. Smith's *Virgin Land*, Chapter XXI: The Agricultural West in Literature.

STEPHEN CRANE
The Blue Hotel

Pages 665–680. In this story Crane sets up a situation leading to an action from which a moral judgment emerges: "Every sin is the result of a collaboration." The murderer is released from responsibility in the statement that he "isn't even a noun. He is a kind of adverb." (Adverbs usually qualify verbs, telling how, when, or where an action occurred.) The responsibility is placed on five men who brought about the murder either by concealing facts or by taking sides against the pathological Swede and thus aggravating first his abnormal timidity, and later his abnormal arrogance.

Characteristically, Crane was here attacking and exposing conventional moral patterns and attitudes. If he had a theory of moral causation

it is implied in his statement that "usually there are from a dozen to forty women really involved in every murder." This does not mean *cherchez la femme*, but rather that women are responsible for the public opinion which persecutes, coerces, and intimidates individuals. (Crane once announced a "theory" that the world is governed by middle-aged women who sit in rockers on porches and grunt lethally as "suspicious" persons pass before them.) In this story the five men represent the same unthinking and unsympathetic judgments as Crane imputes to the women.

Incidental to the main theme is Crane's hostility to the conception of the West as a region wild and woolly and so pictured in the popular paintings and dime novels of the late nineteenth century. Note that Crane's gambler (in contrast to Bret Harte's) has "a real wife and two real children in a neat cottage in a suburb."

Crane's impressionism is more than a stylistic device; it is his way of declaring his violent individualism in a world ruled by stuffy conformity. Yet he indulges too often in startling and exaggerated comparisons (two red ears stick out stiffly "as if they were made of tin"; a stove "humming with godlike violence"). His symbolism, too, is sometimes rather raucous, as in the cash register figure at the end of section VIII.

WILLIAM VAUGHN MOODY
Gloucester Moors

Pages 681–682. Moody is, like Lanier, at once a poet of ideas and a craftsman who experiments with forms but is basically conservative and tradiional in his conception of the function and method of poetry.

The central idea of this poem is suggested by the emphasis on the beauties of nature in the first three stanzas. Such delights are the rightful heritage of all human beings, but they are denied to the majority who are exploited by the selfish economic individualism of the "captains" (of industry) who control the ship of state. Moody's point of view is representative of the economic liberalism of the eighties and nineties which was shared by Howells, Bellamy, Henry George, and the Populists, and which culminated in the muck-raking movement and Woodrow Wilson's "New Freedom" after the turn of the century.

HENRY ADAMS
The Education of Henry Adams

Pages 685–695. In the *Education*, Henry Adams dramatizes himself in terms of history, and history in terms of himself. As a guide to the history of Adams's period, the drama is of questionable value. As a revelation of a man in terms of the meaning he finds in historical forces and intellectual movements, it is a moving story. His book has been called a novel, a suggestion which is useful if it leads the reader to focus on the chief character. The role he plays is that of the ignorant and confused but inquiring student, whose ignorance, confusion, and inquiry expose the hollowness and futility of nineteenth-century civilization. His rejection of current values is in the spirit of the intellectually depressed nineties, and springs from the same causes as Mark Twain's pessimism, Howells's socialism, James's aestheticism, and Stephen Crane's iconoclasm. At the end of the century most American writers had to take stock of themselves to find out where they stood as individuals in a culture with which they were out of sympathy.

For Adams, the stock-taking led to a retreat to medievalism, which may be interpreted as a defeat as well as an affirmation. See "The Dynamo and the Virgin" and *Mont-Saint-Michel and Chartres*.

686.1.33 *affiches* — posters.
686.2.40 *Pteraspis* — a hard-scaled ganoid fish of the Silurian period. Adams uses it as a symbol throughout the book, declaring that there has been no evolution since the *pteraspis* — just change. "Whether one traced descent from the shark or the wolf was immaterial even in morals."
690.2.5 Langley — Samuel P. Langley, 1834–1906, physicist and astronomer.
691.2.10 Kelvin — William T. Kelvin, 1824–1907, British mathematician and physicist.
691.2.25 Branley coherer — device for detecting electric waves.

EDITH WHARTON

The Choice

Pages 705–712. Mrs. Wharton was explicit about her philosophy of fiction: "The art of rendering life in fiction can never, in the last analysis, be anything, or need to be anything, but the disengaging of crucial moments from the welter of existence." A "crucial moment" meant to her the point of conflict between an individual and a basic social or moral standard. Stated in another way, drama in the novel consisted for her in the conflict between the social and moral order on the one hand, and the individual's appetite on the other.

In this story (from *Xingu*) the two extremes of Edith Wharton's leisure-class world — the patrician and the plutocrat — come together in a marriage the very existence of which is the only incredible aspect of the situation presented. Conduct is examined in two areas of morals. In one of them — that of decency and refinement in human relations — our sympathies are clearly (occasionally, too obviously) conscripted against the plutocrat. In the other — that which is concerned with the sacredness of marriage and of human life — the plutocrat is not even tested. As usual, Mrs. Wharton reserves her heroic test — her "crucial moment" — for those worthy of meeting it.

EDWIN ARLINGTON ROBINSON

Luke Havergal

Page 714. The voice that speaks from the grave to Luke Havergal, the bereaved lover, is the voice that through much of Robinson's poetry requires that men have both faith and self-knowledge. A whole group of words ("western," "twilight," "dark," the "crimson" leaves of autumn) insists that the fact of death be faced. Concomitantly, the denial of a "dawn in eastern skies" forbids the hope of a reversion to the happy past. The only hope lies in faith in a life beyond the grave ("she will call").

"The dark will end the dark" (l. 12) is in harmony with Robinson's belief that if self-knowledge may mean only knowing the darkness, such knowledge is better than illusion.

Credo

Page 714. The assertion of utter darkness, mitigated only by a "bar of . . . music" and by faith in coming light, is equivalent to the darkness and the "call" in "Luke Havergal."

Isaac and Archibald

Pages 714–720. The quality of this gently ironic but sympathetic portrait of two old men is pointed up by the analogy of the Homeric heroes. The friends' disguised jealousy of each other's vigor is cause for laughter, but their courage, durability, and dignity connote, in the boy's imagination, the foam and the white ships of Homer.

The Man Against the Sky

Pages 720–724. The "dark, marvellous, inscrutable" figure against a blazing sunset sky stirs "a man's imaginings," and we are given glimpses of five possible destinies that await the traveler. These are summed up succinctly in five lines (183–187). We do not know where this man, or any man, is going. But though it is impossible to give reasons why "one man in five should have a care to stay alive" (ll. 249–250); and though even that one man's vision of a "faith unshaken" (l. 183) may be illusion, we may believe in an "orient Word that will not be erased" (l. 229). We can get only "incommunicable gleams" of this Word, but its meaning is probably implicit in our will to survive.

ll.41 ff. sevenfold heat — An allusion to the story of Nebuchadnezzar; Daniel, 3, 4.
l.136 Curse God and die — The advice given Job by his wife.
l.177 Nahum — See Nahum 3:18.

Mr. Flood's Party

Page 725. This tender portrait, like that of "Isaac and Archibald," is enriched by the partly ironical, partly sympathetic, analogy of Eben and Roland (ll. 27 ff.). Eben's armor is made of "scarred hopes," his lifted jug is the equivalent of Roland's lifted horn, and he stands on a hill as Roland stood on a mountain pass. Just as Roland sounds his horn to summon Charlemagne in the valley below, so Eben, through the medium of alcohol, calls his dead friends.

ROBERT FROST

The Death of the Hired Man

Pages 727–729. One must imagine this dialogue as taking place in whispers. Through the talk, Frost communicates a story, a portrait of a person, and two attitudes toward life — the sympathetic, essentially lyric attitude of the wife, and the more objective though not unkind attitude of the husband. How close together and yet how far apart the two are is suggested by their two definitions of "home" in lines 119–122. Note that the moon symbolism is attached to the wife.

Mending Wall

Page 731. A poet of Bryant's time would have made explicit the implications of walls as artificial barriers between human beings and of the neighbor as an "old-stone savage." Frost, for the most part, just talks about walls, and lets the moral evolve naturally from the two "sayings" with which the poem begins and ends.

The Pasture

Page 732. Frost accords this poem special significance by printing it as the prefatory piece in his *Collected Poems.*

The Black Cottage

Pages 734–735. If one focuses too narrowly on the minister's monologue in the latter part of the poem, this piece seems to be little more than a clever and rather glib defense of conservatism. But Frost's conservatism is complex, and if he is here talking through the minister, the minister represents only one side of his conservatism.

Birches

Pages 735–736. Could it justifiably be argued that Frost has finished his job at about line 41, and that the rest of the poem consists of rather forced generalizations?

An Old Man's Winter Night

Pages 736–737. On first reading, this seems to be a poem about the menace of nature, but on closer inspection one notes that it is the old man who scares the house and the night with his clomping that is "so like beating on a box." The point is made explicit in the last three lines.

EZRA POUND

There are two ways to read Pound: (*a*) in a reference library equipped with a full set of dictionaries — English, foreign, and classical; dictionaries of classical mythology; a concordance Bible; and several encyclopedias; (*b*) with no reference equipment at all, but in the receptive mood in which one responds to overtones, discords, and rhythms and accepts them without attempting to find continuity or harmony in the flow of verse.

The first two selections, however, show that Pound was able to communicate in simple, musical verse.

WILLA CATHER

Neighbour Rosicky

Pages 754–770. This story is an evaluation of life in terms of personality: the values become apparent through old Rosicky's acceptances and rejections. Pejorative references to machinery, wealth, "getting on," hurrying, cities, etc., constitute opposition to the forces which dominate twentieth-century American life. Approval of rural life, of handicraft as opposed to mass production (note the emphasis on the joy of "making things"), of family life, of "natural good manners," of the preservation of the sense of leisure in spite of hard work, constitutes acceptance of values which we increasingly associate with the past. Above all, the story emphasizes Rosicky's harmony with nature (his delight in snow, his uncomplaining acceptance of drought, his love of "the noble darkness") and with man (his "gift for loving people"). This harmony is summed up in two symbols: Rosicky's hands, and his attitude toward the graveyard.

His being a Czech has wider implications than the mere fact of the immigrant population in Nebraska. The ideals he serves are those affirmed (though not necessarily realized) by both rural America, particularly the South, and the Old World: the sense of leisure, of manners, and of family; close relation to the land; and respect for personality. We are most like Europe when we are seen through the eyes of a William Faulkner or a Willa Cather.

As to form, the story seems uncontrived but it is skillfully presented. We learn about Rosicky through his relations with other people, and through excursions into his past. The story begins and ends with "the country doctor" (who has long served as a symbol in American literature), and with the fact of death. But Rosicky's sense of death becomes the medium for our realization of his sense of life.

Theodore Dreiser
The Lost Phoebe

Pages 772–786. In both this story and Willa Cather's "Neighbour Rosicky" the central figure is an old man in a western farming community and the central theme is love. But in the latter, love is a principle and a value; in the former, it is a mere dependence. Pursuing the comparison further, one finds that in Dreiser's story, family life is unhappy, home and farm are squalid, the cycle of the seasons is mere monotony, and death is an overdue release rather than a natural end (compare the graveyard in the two stories). Rosicky, at every crucial point in his life, makes a crucial decision, but the Reifsneiders are inert — "fasten themselves like lichens on the stones of circumstance."

Many of the difficulties of the question "What is realism?" may be defined through an analysis and a comparison of the two stories.

F. Scott Fitzgerald
Babylon Revisited

Pages 788–798. Concerning this story the older teacher must turn to the student for instruction, for no one who experienced the 1920's has the detachment to judge Fitzgerald's fiction as all of us can judge, say, Hawthorne's tales of seventeenth-century Salem. The student can and should, of course, read some such historical work as F. L. Allen's *Only Yesterday* to get perspective on Charles Wales's disaster in the incredible twenties. Fitzgerald achieves his own perspective in this story by setting his wasters in relation to a child and to the Peterses, who, like most Americans, witnessed the extravagance without sharing it. Note that the author compresses a whole era and its aftermath into a space of three years, and that Wales's disinheritance is aptly suggested by our meeting and leaving him in a foreign bar.

795.2.41 *pneumatique* — Compressed-air tubes through which communications are sent.

796.1.1 "derby rim . . . and wire cane" — trade-marks of Charles Chaplin.

Ernest Hemingway
The Killers

Pages 799–804. It is easy enough to guess the situation which lies behind the attempted assassination, but it is more important to grasp the significance of the impersonal violence of "the killers." Much of this significance may be seen in the carefully differentiated reactions of four characters: Nick — Can't something be done?; the cook — "You better stay way out of it"; George — "You better not think about it"; the Swede — "There ain't anything to do." These statements pretty well sum up man's responses to the fact of uncontrollable, impersonal force.

The Snows of Kilimanjaro

Pages 804–815. The symbol of the frozen leopard found on the summit of a mountain leads the reader to contemplate the dying man's preoccupation with high altitudes and snow. Height and cold purity stand in contrast to the spiritual abasement which has almost destroyed Harry's creativity, and to the stench of the gangrene which is killing his body. That he is as "bored with dying" as with love is more terrifying than death itself, but there is a kind of wry triumph, which E. A. Robinson would have appreciated, in the self-realization which he achieves in his dying hours, and in the fact that even in his last delirium his impulse to create persists.

804.2.45 Tommies — Thompson's gazelles; antelope.

806.1.33 Sans Voir — without looking.

806.1.50 Kaiser-Jägers — a regiment of sharpshooters.

809.1.49 *letti dui* — bring two.

810.2.14 Dada movement — an art movement (flourishing about 1920) which reflected utter disillusionment. Tzara (l.16) was one of its leaders.

812.1.2 *locataire* — tenant, lodger.

812.2.6 *ivresse* — drunkenness.

812.2.15 *femme de ménage* — charwoman.

813.1.46 Julian — possibly F. Scott Fitzgerald.

T. S. Eliot
The Hippopotamus

Page 826. Jane Worthington (in *American Literature*, March, 1949) translates the first epigraph (the epistle of St. Ignatius to the Trallians) thus: "And likewise let all the deacons be reverenced, as commanded by Jesus Christ; and let the bishop be reverenced, as Jesus Christ, the living son of the Father; also let the presbyters be reverenced, as the council of God and the assembly of the apostles. Without these there can be no church; of these things I persuade you as I can." The second epigraph is from St. Paul, Colossians 4:16. Miss Worthington's commentary is as follows: Both quotations "come from that period, historically known as the Apostolic Age, when the foundations of the church were still to be laid." Both reflect the threat of heresy, the Laodiceans and the Trallians being "unstable in their practice of Christianity." The point, of course, is that the church was once, like the hippopotamus, "weak and frail" and "susceptible to nervous shock." But in becoming strong the church has also become a dead weight and "remains below/Wrapt in the old miasmal mist."

Gerontion

Pages 826–828. The word "dreaming" in the epigraph describes the tone and structure of the poem. As Miss Worthington says, "The mind of Gerontion moves over history with just that broken, sudden kind of movement that the mind follows in a half-waking dream. Sustained passages of reasoning are broken by peculiar, fragmentary glimpses of personal history."

l.12 merds — dung.
l.23 Silvero — these and other proper names are dreamlike memories of the speaker and need not be identified.
l.72 Trades — trade winds.

The Waste Land

Pages 828–834. The epigraph from the *Satyricon* of Petronius has been translated as follows: "Yes, and I myself with my own eyes saw the Sibyl hanging in a cage; and when the boys cried at her: 'Sibyl, Sibyl, what do you want?' 'I would that I were dead,' she used to answer." Miss Worthington writes that at the famous dinner party near the beginning of the *Satyricon* the host says that he has seen the Cumaean Sibyl (prophetess, of Cumae, in Italy) hanging in a cage and heard the boys taunting her. The story is cut short by the arrival of an enormous pig stuffed with sausages and puddings. "The societies of the *Satyricon* and *The Waste Land* are similarly characterized by vulgarity, lust, and greed. In such societies knowledge of good and evil is lost, and the words of the gods are no longer understood. Seers and prophets speak a gibberish. They waste away, and, finally, are regarded as fit only to be hung in cages, and jibed at by boys. Between the Cumaean Sibyl and Tiresias of *The Waste Land* there exists an understandable affinity. Both have been granted immortality without youth, and both have 'foresuffered all.' The Sibyl expresses their natural desire: 'I would that I were dead.'"

The poem is compounded of many themes, and its "meaning" is largely non-verbal, like the "meaning" of a highly complex piece of music. One must feel his way into the poem gradually, by a number of readings, but a necessary first step is to visualize as clearly as possible the many episodes, scenes, and situations which flash by the imagination with almost kaleidoscopic swiftness. Some of these are: a poignant monologue by an aristocratic lady, a warning by a fortune teller of death by drowning, a glimpse of London streets, a game of chess with an enervated lady tragic with world-weariness, a conversation between two women in a London pub, three tawdry sex affairs in a montage with bits of London and the Thames, the predicted death by drowning (Part IV), and finally a series of dream-like images based on desert, rock, and rain. After several readings it will be noticed that the antitheses between water and drought, desert (or rock) and fertile ground appear repeatedly in the poem; rats also are frequently coupled with dryness. Eliot has said of

the poem that "Not only the title, but the plan and a good deal of the incidental symbolism of the poem was suggested by Miss Jessie L. Weston's book on the Grail legend *From Ritual to Romance*." That legend, as Miss Weston saw it, basically concerned the rejuvenation of a desert (waste) land by water, and traced back to the ancient cult of the god Adonis worshiped in Asia Minor, a god who died each autumn and was reborn with the rains of the ensuing spring. To Eliot, drought was a symbol of barrenness, water of fertility and life. And this symbolism he tied up with the refrain in Part V, "Datta, dayadhvam, damyata," which in one of his notes to the poem he translated as "Give, sympathize, control." Thus while the "waste land" is the modern world, it is also a state of mind, and the coming of thunder implies a strong religious longing not yet released by rain.

Ash Wednesday

Pages 834–838. If *The Waste Land* is the voice of the poet crying in the wilderness, *Ash Wednesday* is the same voice as he wins his way toward salvation. Here too it is extremely difficult if not impossible to pin down the thought of the poem to a clear-cut verbal meaning, but again the broad outline of it is reasonably clear. The man who in *The Waste Land* reached the depth of despair is now struggling to renounce the world and to seek union with God. He will not "turn again" to the world, to seek "this man's gift and that man's scope." Through living in the world, his worldly part has been devoured by three mysterious leopards, and he seeks peace and solace, first through the intercession of "the goodness of this Lady" and later through climbing a stair (the medieval mystics spoke frequently of a ladder) away from the evil and even from the good in worldly things (the flute-player — "distraction") toward union with God. Note again the symbols of dryness and water. Another symbol, the garden, seems allied to the life-giving quality, but the life sought here is not the life of fertility; rather it is the life which comes with loss of self in the renunciation of worldly strife and worldly interests, through closeness to God: "Teach us to sit still/Even among these rocks,/Our peace in His will." This is the peace of the mystics. The presence of the lady, elusive though she is, is reminiscent of Catholic theology. Some of the best comment on the poem is in F. O. Matthiessen, *The Achievement of T. S. Eliot*, 1935, revised 1947.

ARCHIBALD MACLEISH

Ars Poetica

Page 839. Since this piece is as much a critical statement as it is a poem, one may risk violating the doctrine declared in the last two lines (which have become a kind of slogan in modern criticism and poetry) by interpreting it in part as follows:

Poetry is a unique form of expression. When it is paraphrased, or reduced to a single or a specific meaning, it becomes something other than itself. But MacLeish is also declaring by implication that much that has been accepted as poetry is not poetry at all ("A poem should be equal to: Not true").

You, Andrew Marvell

Page 839. In Marvell's "To His Coy Mistress," these lines appear:

> But at my back I always hear
> Time's wingèd chariot hurrying near;
> And yonder all before us lie
> Deserts of vast eternity.

Marvell's image is here developed in geographical terms, the shadow, or coming night, moving westward from Persia on to Africa — in MacLeish's own words (in notes he jotted down before he wrote the poem), the "always westward coming on of night."

WALLACE STEVENS

Peter Quince at the Clavier

Page 846. The story of Susanna and the Elders, in the Biblical apocrypha, is the basis for this poem. Susanna, wife of Joakim, a rich man of Babylon, repelled the advances of two elders, who then accused her of adultery. Daniel exposed the plot and the elders were put to death ("Death's ironic scraping"). Stevens tells the story in terms of music, which is "feeling . . . not sound." There is seeming dissonance in Peter Quince's implicit equation of his own love with the lust of the bawdy elders, but his emphasis is on the immortality of that beauty which stirs all kinds of instruments, bawdy strings as well as clear viols.

The Idea of Order at Key West

Pages 846–847. The woman singing on the shore at Key West may be thought of as a symbol of the poet. The poetic imagination imposes order on nature, on all phenomena; the world has meaning only in so far as the singer shapes a meaning for it. Just as lights on dark water "master" it, "arrange" it, so the singer or poet masters or arranges the world: there is no world except the world she makes by singing.

A Postcard from the Volcano

Page 847. The theme of the preceding poem is developed again here. The imagination makes phenomena meaningful, and what we say of anything "becomes a part of what it is."

HART CRANE

Much commentary on Crane's poetry is available. See especially Philip Horton, *Hart Crane*, 1937; Brom Weber, *Hart Crane*, 1948; Yvor Winters, *In Defense of Reason*, 1930; Allen Tate, *Reactionary Essays*, 1936. See also Crane's own explanation of his work in *Poetry*, Vol. XXIX, pp. 34–41.

KATHERINE ANNE PORTER

María Concepción

Pages 854–864. This story deals with direct and primal relationships in the lives of primitive people — relations between mind and body, person and person, person and group, person and nature, and instinct and action. In María Concepción, for example, there is direct relation between perception and physical response (note that her reaction to the discovery of infidelity is given in terms of forehead, spine, knees, throat, ears, and skin), and between her body and the earth (in the last paragraph her breathing is synchronized with that of night and earth). The same kind of unity is exhibited in the villagers' understanding of the situation and their concerted but unplanned protection of María in her crisis. The moral center of the story is in the paragraph beginning 863.1.37.

WILLIAM FAULKNER

A Rose for Emily

Pages 865–869. Only of recent years, largely through the pioneering criticism of Malcolm Cowley, has the full social and moral scope of Faulkner's work come to be appreciated. Because his characters move in a nightmare world of horror, cruelty, and perversion, it seemed to many of his earlier readers that sensationalism in his writing was an end in itself. As time has gone on, however, and as later Faulkner novels have blocked out in more detail the mythical Mississippi region of which he writes, it has become evident that these violent and macabre elements are not simply means of shocking the reader but are the terms in which Faulkner is presenting the drama of man's capacity to endure through the confusions of a changing cultural and moral order.

Like much of Faulkner's work, "A Rose for Emily" appears at first glance to be a "shocker" in the Poe tradition. On one level, it is; but it is also something more — an allegory of the decay of the legendary South, or, by broader extension, an allegory of a confused world in which traditional values no longer have meaning. The old order, symbolized by Miss Emily, is neither able nor willing to come to terms with invading alien cultures or with its own younger generation; it has lost touch with present reality and become a bloated perversion of itself, "like a body long submerged in motionless water."

JOHN STEINBECK
The Chrysanthemums

Pages 870–876. This is a study of a woman whose pride in her power leads to her betrayal. Elisa, like many of Steinbeck's characters, is elemental — in her sympathy with growing things, in her physi-cal and emotional strength, in her wish to be fully attuned to nature. But her strength is not that of economic man, and she is easily exploited by a tinker who discovers that her strength can be used as a weakness. The central symbol that illumi-nates the relation between the two is the young chrysanthemum plants.

CD54

AMERICAN CIVILIZATION

★ A READING LIST ★

★ ★

GENERAL

Literature and the Arts

Blankenship, R. *American Literature as an Expression of the National Mind.* 1931.

Born, W. *American Landscape Painting.* 1948.

Burroughs, A. *Limners and Likenesses: Three Centuries of American Painting.* 1936.

Cahill, H., and A. H. Barr. *Art in America.* 1935.

Canby, H. S. *Classic Americans.* 1931.

CHAL: *Cambridge History of American Literature.* Ed. by W. P. Trent, John Erskine, S. P. Sherman, Carl Van Doren. 4 vols., 1917–21.

Coan, O. W., and R. G. Lillard. *America in Fiction: An Annotated List of Novels.* Revised, 1949.

Cowie, A. *The Rise of the American Novel.* 1948.

Crawford, B. V., and others. *An Outline-History of American Literature.* 1945.

DAB: *Dictionary of American Biography.* Ed. by Allen Johnson and Dumas Malone. 20 vols., 1928–37.

Gloster, H. M. *Negro Voices in American Fiction.* 1948.

Hart, J. D. *The Oxford Companion to American Literature.* Revised, 1948.

Hartmann, S. *A History of American Art.* 1937.

Hastings, W. T., *Syllabus of American Literature.* Revised, 1941.

Howard, J. T. *Our American Music: Three Hundred Years of It.* Revised, 1946.

Jones, H. M. *Ideas in America.* 1944.

—— *The Theory of American Literature.* 1948.

Keppel, F. P., and R. L. Duffus. *The Arts in American Life.* 1933.

Kimball, F. *American Architecture.* 1928.

Krapp, G. P. *The English Language in America.* 2 vols., 1925.

Kunitz, S. J., and H. Haycraft. *American Authors, 1600–1900.* 1944.

Larkin, O. W. *Art and Life in America.* 1949.

Leisy, E. E. *The American Historical Novel.* 1950.

LHUS: *Literary History of the United States.* Ed. by R. E. Spiller, Willard Thorp, T. H. Johnson, H. S. Canby. 3 vols., 1946–48.

Locke, A. *Negro Art, Past and Present.* 1936.

Mencken, H. L. *The American Language.* Revised, 1936. Supplements, 1945, 1948.

Mott, F. L. *Golden Multitudes: The Story of Best Sellers in the United States.* 1947.

Mumford, L. *Sticks and Stones: A Study of American Architecture and Civilization.* 1926.

Parrington, V. L. *Main Currents in American Thought.* 3 vols., 1927–30.

Pattee, F. L. *The Development of the American Short Story.* 1923.

Quinn, A. H. *A History of American Drama.* 3 vols. 1923–27. Revised, 1943.

—— *American Fiction.* 1936.

——, ed. *The Literature of the American People,* 1951.

The Reinterpretation of American Literature. Ed. by N. Foerster. 1928.

Smith, Bernard. *Forces in American Criticism.* 1939.

Taft, L. *The History of American Sculpture.* Revised, 1930.

Tallmadge, T. E. *The Story of Architecture in America.* Revised, 1936.

Taylor, W. F. *A History of American Letters.* 1936.

Van Doren, C. *The American Novel.* Revised, 1940.

Religion, Philosophy, Science

American Church History Series. 13 vols., 1894–1908.

Cole, S. C. *The History of Fundamentalism.* 1931.

Cook, G. W. *Unitarianism in America.* 1902.

Curti, M. *The Growth of American Thought.* 1943.

Dana, E. S. *A Century of Science in America.* 1918.

Draper, J. W. *History of Conflict between Religion and Science.* 1874.

Fiske, J. *A Century of Science.* 1899.

Foerster, N. *Nature in American Literature.* 1923.

[Various authors] "The Early History of Science and Learning in America," *Proceedings of the American Philosophical Society,* 1942.

Gabriel, R. H. *The Course of American Democratic Thought.* 1940.

Gettell, R. G.   *History of American Political Thought.* 1928.

Hall, T. C.   *The Religious Background of American Culture.* 1930.

Haney, L. H.   *History of Economic Thought.* Revised, 1949.

Hofstadter, R.   *Social Darwinism in American Thought, 1860–1915.* 1945.

Hornberger, T.   "Science and the New World," *Catalogue of Huntington Library,* 1937.

Loewenberg, B. J.   "Darwinism Comes to America," *Mississippi Valley Historical Review,* 1941.

Merriam, C. E.   *American Political Theories.* 1903.

Merrill, G. P.   *The First Hundred Years of American Geology.* 1924.

Parrington, V. L.   *Main Currents in American Thought.* 3 vols., 1927–30.

Riley, I. W.   *American Thought from Puritanism to Pragmatism and Beyond.* 1923.

Rowe, H. K.   *The History of Religion in the United States.* 1924.

Schneider, H. W.   *History of American Philosophy,* 1946.

Shea, J. G.   *The Catholic Church in the United States.* 4 vols., 1886–92.

Simms, P. M.   *The Bible in America.* 1936.

Smith, E. F.   *Chemistry in America.* 1914.

Sperry, W. L.   *Religion in America.* 1946.

Sweet, W. W.   *The Story of Religions in America.* 1930.

Townsend, H. G.   *Philosophical Ideas in the United States.* 1934.

White, M. G.   *Social Thought in America.* 1949.

Wiernik, P.   *History of the Jews in America.* 1931.

Geography, Immigration, Economics, Politics, etc.

Aaron, D.   *Men of Good Hope: A Story of American Progressives.* 1951.

Adams, W. F.   *Ireland and Irish Emigration to the New World.* 1932.

Agar, H.   *The People's Choice, from Washington to Harding.* 1933.

Babcock, K. C.   *The Scandinavian Element in the United States.* 1914.

Beard, C. A. and M. R.   *The Rise of American Civilization.* Revised, 1933.

Bemis, S. F.   *A Diplomatic History of the United States.* 1936.

Blair, W.   *Native American Humor.* 1937.

Bowers, D. F., ed.   *Foreign Influences in American Life.* 1944.

Brigham, A. P.   *Geographical Influences in American History.* 1903.

Branch, E. D.   *The Cowboy and His Interpreters.* 1926.

Brogan, D. W.   *The American Character.* 1944.

Cady, E. H.   *The Gentleman in America.* 1949.

Capek, T.   *The Czechs in America.* 1920.

Carrothers, W. A.   *Emigration from the British Isles.* 1929.

Clark, H. H.   "Nationalism in American Literature," *University of Toronto Quarterly,* 1933.

Commons, J. R.   *Races and Immigrants in the United States.* 1920.

Cubberley, E. P.   *Public Education in the United States.* Revised, 1934.

Cunningham, W.   *English Influence on the United States.* 1916.

Dick, E.   *Vanguards of the Frontier.* 1940.

Faust, A. B.   *The German Element in the United States.* 2 vols., 1909.

Foerster, R. F.   *The Italian Emigration of Our Times.* 1919.

Ford, H. J.   *The Scotch Irish in America.* 1915.

Hacker, L. M.   *The Shaping of the American Tradition.* 1947.

Hansen, M. L.   *The Atlantic Migration, 1607–1860.* 1940.

—— *The Immigrant in American History.* 1940.

Harrington, F.   "The Anti-Imperialist Movement in the United States," *Mississippi Valley Historical Review,* 1935.

Hawgood, J. A.   *The Tragedy of German America.* 1940.

Hesseltine, W. B.   *A History of the South.* Revised, 1943.

Hillquit, M.   *History of Socialism in the United States.* Revised, 1910.

Hockett, H. C., and A. M. Schlesinger.   *Land of the Free.* 1945.

Jones, H. M.   *America and French Culture, 1750–1848.* 1927.

Kirkland, E. C.   *A History of American Economic Life.* Revised, 1951.

Knight, E. W.   *Education in the United States.* Revised, 1951.

Lillard, R. G.   *The Great Forest.* 1947.

Mariano, J. H.   *The Italian Contribution to American Democracy.* 1921.

Morison, S. E., and H. S. Commager.   *The Growth of the American Republic.* 2 vols., revised, 1950.

Mott, F. L.   *A History of American Magazines.* **3** vols., 1938.

—— *American Journalism: A History of Newspapers in the United States.* 1941.

Myers, G.   *History of the Great American Fortunes.* 1936.

Nevins, A., ed.   *American Social History as Recorded by British Travellers.* 1923.

Odum, H. W., and H. E. Moore.   *American Regionalism.* 1938.

Parkes, H. B.   *The American Experience.* 1947.

Paxson, F. L. *The History of the American Frontier, 1763–1893*. 1924.

Perlman, S. *A History of Trade Unionism in the United States*. 1922.

Pierce, B. L. *A History of Chicago*. 1937.

Priestley, H. I. *The Coming of the White Man, 1492–1848*. 1929.

Rourke, C. *American Humor*. 1931.

Schafer, J. *The Social History of American Agriculture*. 1936.

Semple, E. C. *American History and Its Geographic Conditions*. Revised, 1933.

Smith, H. N. *Virgin Land; the American West as Symbol and Myth*. 1950.

Stephenson, G. M. *A History of American Immigration, 1820–1924*. 1926.

Tandy, J. R. *Crackerbox Philosophers in American Humor and Satire*. 1925.

Turner, F. J. *The Frontier in American History*. 1928.

—— *The Significance of Sections in American History*. 1932.

Warren, C. *The Supreme Court in United States History*. Revised, 1937.

Wecter, D. *The Hero in America: A Chronicle of Hero-Worship*. 1941.

—— *The Saga of American Society: A Record of Social Aspiration, 1607–1937*. 1937.

Weinberg, A. K. *Manifest Destiny*. 1935.

Wish, Harvey. *Society and Thought in Early America*. 1949.

Wittke, C. *We Who Built America*. 1939.

Woody, T. *History of Women's Education in the United States*. 2 vols., 1929.

PERIODS

The Colonies and the Early Republic

Adams, J. T. *The Founding of New England*. 1930.

—— *Provincial Society, 1690–1763*. 1927.

—— *New England in the Republic, 1776–1850*. 1926.

Andrews, C. M. *The Colonial Period of American History*. 4 vols., 1934–38.

—— *Colonial Folkways*. 1919.

—— *The Colonial Background of the American Revolution*. Revised, 1931.

Becker, C. L. *Beginnings of the American People*. 1915.

—— *The Declaration of Independence*. 1922.

—— *The Heavenly City of the Eighteenth-Century Philosophers*. 1932.

Bowers, C. G. *Jefferson and Hamilton: the Struggle for Democracy in America*. 1925.

Boyd, J. P. *The Declaration of Independence: The Evolution of the Text*. 1943, 1945.

Brasch, F. E. "The Newtonian Epoch in the American Colonies," *American Antiquarian Society Proceedings*, 1939.

Bridenbaugh, C. *Cities in the Wilderness*. 1939.

Bridenbaugh, C. and J. *Rebels and Gentlemen: Philadelphia in the Age of Franklin*. 1942.

Brown, H. R. *The Sentimental Novel in America, 1789–1860*. 1940.

Bruce, P. A. *Social Life in Virginia in the Seventeenth Century*. Revised, 1927.

Cobb, S. H. *The Rise of Religious Liberty in America*. 1902.

Curti, M. "The Great Mr. Locke, America's Philosopher, 1783–1861," *Huntington Library Bulletin*, 1937.

Jones, H. M. *The Literature of Virginia in the Seventeenth Century*. 1946.

Jones, R. M. *The Quakers in the American Colonies*. 1921.

Jorgenson, C. E. "The New Science in the Almanacs of Ames and Franklin," *New England Quarterly*, December, 1935.

Kimball, F. *Domestic Architecture of the American Colonies and of the Early Republic*. 1927.

Koch, G. A. *Republican Religion: The American Revolution and the Cult of Reason*. 1933.

Kraus, M. *Intercolonial Aspects of American Culture on the Eve of the Revolution*. 1928.

Lecky, W. E. H. *The American Revolution*, ed. Woodburn. 1922.

McLaughlin, A. C. *The Confederation and the Constitution*. 1905.

Miller, P. *The New England Mind: The Seventeenth Century*. 1939.

Miller, P., and T. H. Johnson, eds. *The Puritans*. 1938. (With bibliographies.)

Mitchell, M. H. *The Great Awakening*. 1934.

Morais, H. M. *Deism in Eighteenth-Century America*. 1934.

Morison, S. E. *Builders of the Bay Colony*. 1931.

—— *The Puritan Pronaos: Studies in the Intellectual Life of New England in the Seventeenth Century*. 1936.

Murdock, K. B. *Literature and Theology in Colonial New England*. 1949.

—— "The Puritan Tradition," *The Reinterpretation of American Literature* (ed. N. Foerster). 1928.

Nettels, C. P. *The Roots of American Civilization*. 1938.

Nevins, A. *The American States during and after the Revolution*. 1927.

Osgood, H. L. *The American Colonies in the Seventeenth Century*. 2 vols., 1930.

—— *The American Colonies in the Eighteenth Century*. 4 vols., 1924.

Parrington, V. L. *The Colonial Mind*. 1927.

Riley, I. W. *American Philosophy, the Early Schools*. 1907.

Schneider, H. W. *The Puritan Mind.* 1930.

Sweet, W. W. *Religion in Colonial America.* 1942.

Tyler, M. C. *A History of American Literature during the Colonial Time, 1607–1765.* 2 vols., 1897.

—— *The Literary History of the American Revolution, 1763–1783.* 2 vols., 1880.

Walsh, J. J. *Education of the Founding Fathers: Scholasticism in the Colonial Colleges.* 1935.

Warren, C. *The Making of the Constitution.* 1928.

Wertenbaker, T. J. *The First Americans, 1607–1690.* 1929.

—— *The Golden Age of Colonial Culture.* 1942.

Willison, G. F. *Saints and Strangers: The Saga of the Pilgrims.* 1945.

Wright, L. B. "The Classical Tradition in Colonial Virginia," *Papers of the Bibliographical Society of America,* 1939.

—— *The First Gentlemen of Virginia.* 1940.

—— *The Atlantic Frontier: Colonial American Civilization (1607–1763).* 1947.

Wright, T. G. *Literary Culture in Early New England.* 1920.

The United States in the Early and Middle Nineteenth Century

Barnes, G. H. *The Antislavery Impulse, 1830–1844.* 1933.

Billington, R. A. *The Protestant Crusade, 1800–1860.* 1938.

Boas, G., ed. *Romanticism in America.* 1940.

Branch, E. D. *Westward: The Romance of the American Frontier.* 1930.

Brooks, Van W. *The Flowering of New England, 1815–1865.* 1936.

—— *The World of Washington Irving.* 1944.

Brown, H. R. *The Sentimental Novel in America, 1789–1860.* 1940.

Brownell, W. C. *American Prose Masters.* 1909.

Charvat, W. *The Origins of American Critical Thought, 1810–1835.* 1936.

Christy, A. *The Orient in American Transcendentalism.* 1932.

Cole, A. C. *The Irrepressible Conflict, 1850–1865.* 1934.

Craven, A. O. *The Coming of the Civil War.* 1942.

Curti, M. E. *The American Peace Crusade, 1815–1860.* 1929.

Dodd, W. E. *The Cotton Kingdom.* 1919.

—— *Statesmen of the Old South.* 1911.

Ekirch, A. A., Jr. *The Idea of Progress in America, 1815–1860.* 1944.

Fish, C. R. *The Rise of the Common Man, 1830–1850.* 1927.

Foerster, N. *American Criticism.* 1928.

—— *Nature in American Literature.* 1923.

Frothingham, O. B. *Transcendentalism in New England.* 1876.

Gaines, F. P. *The Southern Plantation.* 1925.

Goddard, H. C. *Studies in New England Transcendentalism.* 1908.

Gohdes, C. *The Periodicals of American Transcendentalism.* 1931.

Hayes, C. B. *The American Lyceum.* 1932.

Jones, H. M. "The Influence of European Ideas in Nineteenth Century America," *American Literature,* November, 1935.

Kaufman, P. "The Romantic Movement," *The Reinterpretation of American Literature,* ed. N. Foerster. 1928.

Keiser, A. *The Indian in American Literature.* 1933.

Krout, J. A., and D. R. Fox. *The Completion of Independence, 1790–1830.* 1944.

Landrum, G. C. "Sir Walter Scott and His Literary Rivals in the Old South," *American Literature,* 1930.

Madison, C. A. *A Century of American Protest.* 1947.

Matthiessen, F. O. *American Renaissance.* 1941.

Mesick, J. L. *The English Traveller in America, 1785–1835.* 1922.

Miller, P., ed. *The Transcendentalists.* 1950.

Minnigerode, M. *The Fabulous Forties, 1840–1850: A Presentation of Private Life.* 1924.

Morison, S. E. *The Maritime History of Massachusetts, 1783–1860.* 1921.

Mumford, L. *The Golden Day.* 1926.

Osterweis, R. G. *Romanticism and Nationalism in the Old South.* 1949.

Parrington, V. L. *The Romantic Revolution in America, 1800–1860.* 1927.

Perkins, D. *The Monroe Doctrine, 1823–1826.* 1927.

Pochmann, H. A. *New England Transcendentalism and St. Louis Hegelianism.* 1948.

Post, A. *Popular Free-Thought in America, 1825–1850.* 1943.

Roosevelt, Theodore. *The Winning of the West.* 4 vols., 1894–1910.

Schlesinger, A. M., Jr. *The Age of Jackson.* 1945.

Spiller, R. E. *The American in England during the First Half Century of Independence.* 1926.

Swift, L. *Brook Farm.* 1900.

Tocqueville, A. de. *Democracy in America.* 2 vols., 1838.

Turner, F. J. *The Rise of the New West, 1819–1829.* 1906.

—— *The United States, 1830–1850: The Nation and its Sections.* 1935.

Wellek, R. "Emerson and German Philosophy" and "The Minor Transcendentalists and German Philosophy," *New England Quarterly,* 1942, 1943.

White, S. E. *The Forty-Niners.* 1920.

The United States from the Civil War to 1890

Bowers, C. G. *The Tragic Era: The Revolution after Lincoln.* 1929.

Bowers, D. F. *Foreign Influences in American Life* (chapter on "Hegel and Darwin"). 1944.

Brooks, Van W. *New England: Indian Summer, 1865–1915.* 1940.

Bryce, J. *The American Commonwealth.* 3 vols., 1888.

Buck, P. H. *The Road to Reunion, 1865–1900.* 1937.

Buck, S. J. *The Agrarian Crusade.* 1920.

Conner, F. W. *Cosmic Optimism: A Study of the Interpretation of Evolution by American Poets from Emerson to Robinson.* 1949.

Coulter, E. M. *The South during Reconstruction.* 1947.

De Voto, B. A. *Mark Twain's America.* 1932.

Dewey, J. *The Influence of Darwin on Philosophy.* 1910.

Foster, F. H. *The Modern Movement in American Theology.* 1939.

Fox, D. R., ed. *Sources of Culture in the Middle West.* 1934.

Hazard, L. L. *The Frontier in American Literature.* 1927.

Hubbell, J. B. "The Frontier," *The Reinterpretation of American Literature,* ed. N. Foerster. 1928.

Josephson, M. *The Robber Barons: the Great Capitalists, 1861–1901.* 1934.

Kaempffert, W. *A Popular History of American Invention.* 1924.

Loggins, V. *The Negro Author, His Development in America.* 1931.

Mumford, L. *The Brown Decades: A Study of the Arts in America, 1865–1895.* 1931.

Murrell, W. *A History of American Graphic Humor, 1865–1938.* 1938.

Nelson, J. H. *The Negro in American Literature.* 1926.

Nevins, A. *The Emergence of Modern America, 1865–1878.* 1927.

Oberholzer, E. P. *A History of the United States since the Civil War.* 5 vols., 1922–37.

Parrington, V. L. *The Beginnings of Critical Realism in America, 1860–1920.* 1930.

—— "The Development of Realism," *The Reinterpretation of American Literature,* ed. N. Foerster. 1928.

Pattee, F. L. *A History of American Literature since 1870.* 1915.

Paxson, F. L. *Recent History of the United States, 1865 to the Present.* Revised, 1937.

Perry, R. B. *Philosophy of the Recent Past: an Outline of European and American Philosophy since 1860.* 1926.

Randall, J. G. *The Civil War and Reconstruction.* 1937.

Schlesinger, A. M. "A Critical Period in American Religion, 1875–1900," *Proceedings of the Massachusetts Historical Society,* 1932.

—— *Political and Social Growth of the American People, 1865–1940.* 1941.

—— *The Rise of the City, 1878–1898.* 1933.

Tarbell, I. M. *The Nationalizing of Business, 1878–1898.* 1936.

Taylor, W. F. *The Economic Novel in America.* 1942.

Webb, W. P. *The Great Plains.* 1931.

Weirick, B. *From Whitman to Sandburg in American Poetry.* 1924.

The United States since 1890

Adams, G. P., and W. P. Montague, eds. *Contemporary American Philosophy.* 1930.

Adams, J. T. *Our Business Civilization.* 1929.

Allen, F. L. *Only Yesterday, an Informal History of the Nineteen-Twenties.* 1933.

—— *Since Yesterday, the Nineteen Thirties in America.* 1940.

Beach, J. W. *The Twentieth-Century Novel.* 1932.

—— *American Fiction, 1920–1940.* 1941.

Beer, T. *The Mauve Decade: American Life at the End of the Nineteenth Century.* 1926.

Brooks, Van W. *New England: Indian Summer, 1865–1915.* 1940.

Cargill, O. *Intellectual America: Ideas on the March.* 1941.

Couch, W. T., ed. *Culture in the South.* 1934.

Faulkner, H. V. *The Quest for Social Justice, 1898–1914.* 1931.

Flexner, A. *Universities: American, English, German.* 1930.

Foerster, N. *The American State University.* 1937.

—— *Toward Standards: A Study of the Present Critical Movement.* 1930.

Frohock, W. M. *The Novel of Violence in America: 1920–1950.* 1950.

Gregory, H., and M. Zaturenska. *A History of American Poetry, 1900–1940.* 1946.

Hartwick, H. *The Foreground of American Fiction.* 1934.

Hatcher, H. *Creating the Modern American Novel.* 1935.

Herring, P. *The Impact of War: Our American Democracy Under Arms.* 1940.

Hicks, J. D. *The Populist Revolt.* 1931.

Hoffman, F. J. *Freudianism and the Literary Mind.* 1945.

Hoffman, F. J., and others. *The Little Magazine.* 1946.

[Twelve Southerners] *I'll Take My Stand.* 1930.

Kazin, A. *On Native Grounds.* 1942.

Kendrick, B. B., and A. M. Arnet. *The South Looks at its Past.* 1935.

Boynton, Percy — Some Contemp. Americans

Manly — Contemp. Amer. Lit.

Kouwenhoven, J. A. *Made in America: The Arts in Modern Civilization.* 1948.

Krutch, J. W. *The Modern Temper.* 1929.

Loggins, V. *The Negro Author, his Development in America.* 1931.

Luccock, H. E. *Contemporary American Literature and Religion.* 1934.

Lynd, R. S. and H. M. *Middletown: A Study in Contemporary American Culture.* 1929.

—— *Middletown in Transition.* 1937.

Lyons, E. *The Red Decade, the Stalinist Penetration of America.* 1941.

Merrill, D. K. *The Development of American Biography.* 1932.

Millett, F. B. *Contemporary American Authors.* 1940.

Mowry, G. E. *Theodore Roosevelt and the Progressive Movement.* 1946.

Murrell, W. *A History of American Graphic Humor, 1865–1938.* 1938.

[Various authors] *Naturalism and the Human Spirit,* ed. Y. H. Krikorian. 1944.

Nelson, J. H. *The Negro in American Literature.* 1926.

O'Connell, G. *Naturalism in American Education.* 1936.

O'Connor, W. V. *Sense and Sensibility in American Poetry.* 1948.

Parrington, V. L. *The Beginnings of Critical Realism in America.* 1930.

—— "The Development of Realism," *The Reinterpretation of American Literature,* ed. N. Foerster. 1928.

Pattee, F. L. *The New American Literature, 1890–1930.* 1930.

Paxson, F. L. *Recent History of the United States.* Revised, 1937.

Recent Social Trends in the United States. 2 vols., 1935.

Regier, C. C. *The Era of the Muckrakers.* 1932.

Schlesinger, A. M. *Political and Social Growth of the American People, 1865–1940.* 1941.

Schuster, G. N. *The Catholic Church and Current Literature.* 1930.

Siegfried, A. *America Comes of Age, a French Analysis.* 1930.

Slosson, P. W. *The Great Crusade and After, 1914–1928.* 1930.

Stallman, R. W. *Critiques and Essays in Criticism, 1920–1948.* 1949.

Stearns, H. E., ed. *America Now, an Inquiry into Civilization in the United States by 36 Americans.* 1938.

Sullivan, M. *Our Times: The United States, 1909–1925.* 6 vols., 1926–35.

Taylor, W. F. *The Economic Novel in America.* 1942.

Untermeyer, L. *American Poetry since 1900.* 1923.

——, ed. *Modern American Poetry.* Revised, 1950.

Van Doren, C. *Contemporary American Novelists, 1900–1920.* 1923.

Ware, C. *Greenwich Village, 1920–1930.* 1935.

Whipple, T. K. *Spokesmen: Modern Writers and American Life.* 1928.

Wright, F. L. *Modern Architecture.* 1931.

Zabel, M. D. *Literary Opinion in America.* Revised, 1951.

FOR FURTHER REFERENCES

Allison, W. H., with others. *A Guide to Historical Literature.* 1931. (Section X, compiled by M. W. Jernegan, deals with writings on American history.)

American Bibliography. Annually since 1922 in *Publications of the Modern Language Association.*

American Writers Series, general ed. H. H. Clark. 1934 — . More than a score of volumes chiefly on major writers, with excellent bibliographies. (Title abbreviated AWS in the commentaries in the present text.)

Annual Bibliography of English Language and Literature. Edited for the Modern Humanities Research Association, Cambridge, England, 1921–. (Despite the title, American Literature is included.)

Arms, G., and J. M. Kunitz. *Poetry Explication. A Checklist of Interpretations since 1925.* 1950.

Articles on American Literature Appearing in Current Periodicals. In *American Literature* (journal) since November, 1929.

Articles on American Literature Appearing in Current Periodicals, 1920–1945. A book edited by Lewis Leary. 1947.

Cambridge History of American Literature. Edited by W. P. Trent, John Erskine, S. P. Sherman, and Carl Van Doren. 4 vols., 1917–21. (Contains rather full bibliographies omitted in a later reissue of the work.)

Literary History of the United States. Edited by R. E. Spiller, Willard Thorp, T. H. Johnson, and H. S. Canby. 3 vols. (Vol. 3, valuable Bibliographical Essays.) 1946–1948.

Millett, F. B. *Contemporary American Authors.* 1940.

Murdock, K. B., and others. *The Harvard Reading List in American History.* 1949.

Taylor, W. F. *A History of American Letters.* 1936. (Excellent bibliographies by Harry Hartwick, pp. 447–664.)

Van Patten, Nathan. *An Index to Bibliographies and Bibliographical Contributions Relating to the Work of American and British Authors, 1923–32.* 1934.

Writings on American History. Beginning in 1908, issued annually for 1902 and subsequent years; since 1911, a supplement to the annual report of the American Historical Association.

INDEX OF AUTHORS AND TITLES

Page numbers in italics refer to the Supplementary Notes

* *